McGraw-Hill Encyclopedia of Personal Computing

McGraw-Hill Encyclopedia of Personal Computing

Stan Gibilisco, Editor in Chief

McGraw-Hill, Inc.
New York   San Francisco   Washington, D.C.   Auckland   Bogotá
Caracas   Lisbon   London   Madrid   Mexico City   Milan
Montreal   New Delhi   San Juan   Singapore
Sydney   Tokyo   Toronto

McGraw-Hill
A Division of The McGraw·Hill Companies

© 1995 by **Stan Gibilisco**
Published by The McGraw-Hill Companies, Inc.

Printed in the United States of America. All rights reserved. The publisher takes no responsibility for the use of any materials or methods described in this book, nor for the products thereof.

hc   1 2 3 4 5 6 7 8 9 0 BBC/HOR 9 0 0 9 8 7 6 5

Product or brand names used in this book may be trade names or trademarks. Where we believe that there may be proprietary claims to such trade names or trademarks, the name has been used with an initial capital or it has been capitalized in the style used by the name claimant. Regardless of the capitalization used, all such names have been used in an editorial manner without any intent to convey endorsement of or other affiliation with the name claimant. Neither the author nor the publisher intends to express any judgment as to the validity or legal status of any such proprietary claims.

Library of Congress Cataloging-in-Publication Data
Gibilisco, Stan.
   McGraw-Hill encyclopedia of personal computing / by Stan
Gibilisco.
     p. cm.
   Includes index.
   ISBN 0-07-023718-2
   1. Microcomputers—Encyclopedias. I. Title.
QA76.15.G53   1995
004.16'03—dc20   95-17260
                                                                  CIP

McGraw-Hill books are available at special quantity discounts to use as premiums and sales promotions, or for use in corporate training programs. For more information, please write to the Director of Special Sales, McGraw-Hill, 11 West 19th Street, New York, NY 10011. Or contact your local bookstore.

Acquisitions editor: Roland Phelps
Editorial team: Marianne Krcma, Book Editor
                David M. McCandless, Managing Editor
                Joanne Slike, Executive Editor
Production team: Katherine G. Brown, Director
                  Rhonda E. Baker, Coding
                  Brenda M. Plasterer, Coding
                  Joyce Bellela, Computer Artist
                  Brenda S. Wilhide, Desktop Operator
                  Joann Woy, Indexer
Design team: Jaclyn J. Boone, Designer   0237182
              Katherine Lukaszewicz, Associate Designer   WK1

Disclaimer

Information herein is believed to be reliable. However, because of the possibility of human, electronic, or mechanical error, the author and publisher do not guarantee the accuracy, adequacy, or completeness of any information, and assume no liability for errors or omissions, or the results obtained from the use of this information.

To Tony and Tim
from Uncle Stan

Acknowledgments

I thank each of the members of the Editorial Review Board for helping me with technical points during the writing and editing of this book.

I also thank my mother, Josephine Gibilisco, who has recently discovered personal computing. She read this manuscript and made suggestions from the perspective of the average PC user.

x

Foreword

As recently as 1980, it was a big deal to tell people at a gathering that you were a computer systems engineer for a large international company. People would look upon you as a mystic, someone extremely smart, and someone who worked with technology that only the fortunate could afford. Computers were for scientists, medical researchers, government agencies, and only the largest corporations. The technology wasn't in the hands of many students, hobbyists, or small businesses. It was expensive and complicated for all but a select few.

Today, telling people you are a computer expert is not such a big deal. Almost everybody claims to be one. A few years of computer and electronic evolution have changed everything. All you have to do is look at the section of your local newsstand devoted to personal computing to see the results. There are tens of millions of personal computers in the United States alone. There will be over 150 million by the turn of the century. It's easy to see why—just look at how fast the technology has moved, and how affordable it has become!

It seems that every month you can buy a PC with less money. In fact, most personal computers today are more powerful than mammoth mainframes of the past. Those things were water-cooled and took up whole rooms, while typical PCs today can rest on your lap, can process many times more information, and have more main storage and disk capacity. Some of those old mainframes cost over a thousand times as much as a personal computer costs now. And technological evolution isn't slowing down. It's growing exponentially!

People are doing some really creative things with personal computers. One of the most interesting examples is the orchestration of music in the privacy of the home. You can command a 30-piece orchestra

Foreword

while having the computer record, edit, and print the music in standard notation. If you are not familiar with this, it's called *MIDI*, or *Musical Instrument Digital Interface*. Another exciting area is communicating with people all over the world, sharing useful information through bulletin board systems (BBSs) on large networks. People are keeping track of complex financial portfolios, checking information regarding their personal health, doing their taxes, reading the news, and of course, playing games and shopping. The list could go on almost endlessly.

(If you are interested in learning more about Musical Instrument Digital Interface, for example, simply look for its article in this book under *M*. For information about bulletin boards, look under *B*.)

If you're just getting started with personal computing, you might feel overwhelmed by technology and jargon. There is an incredible amount of information available on the subject, but it typically has two problems: it's not all in one place, and it's not always understandable to the novice. This book solves both of these problems.

The *McGraw-Hill Encyclopedia of Personal Computing* is readable and understandable. It is aimed at the novice, but it can also teach experts things they didn't know. The alphabetic organization makes it easy to locate topics.

Personal computers are so affordable that most people will soon own one, and many of us will have more than one. When put to the right use, they can save us time, give us new information, solve complex problems, and allow us to explore the arts in entirely new ways. This book is a wonderful tool with a wealth of information all in one place, allowing all of us to "catch up" on technology and terminology that might otherwise have passed us by.

This book can take the mystery out of computer lingo, and give you confidence to get familiar with new applications of this incredible evolving technology.

David E. Sass, President
Acoustical Designs
Rochester, Minnesota

Introduction

This encyclopedia is a general reference for personal-computer users. It's meant for students, computer and electronics hobbyists, businesspeople, and anyone else who wants to know what's happening in the realm of personal computing.

The abbreviation *PC* was originally coined by IBM. Today, it is generic. In this book, the term *PC* refers to all personal computers, whether Macintosh, IBM-compatible, or others.

Every effort has been made to portray things in a concise but understandable way, without "talking down," and with minimum jargon. Articles are in alphabetical order. Related topics are cited frequently. You are encouraged to read all cross-referenced articles.

If you want information on a specific topic, look for it as an article title. Topics that are abbreviations and acronyms are listed under their spelled-out term, with a few exceptions (such as *DOS*). There's a list of abbreviations and acronyms in the appendix.

I've included a few speculative articles about the future of personal computing. These deal with exotic things like robotics, artificial intelligence, supercomputers, and virtual reality. There are also some articles dealing with ethical and social problems arising in conjunction with the evolution of computer technology.

Personal computers are having a dramatic effect on the way we live. Humanity has never seen a technological explosion like this. I am often asked, "Will computers ever control society?" In response I joke, "They already do." Then seriously, I add, "to the extent that we let them." Computers are machines. They ought to enhance the quality of life—period.

Introduction

I hope this book makes your personal computing more efficient and productive. But most of all, I hope it helps you have fun with computers. Arguably, that is the most important facet of this whole business.

Suggestions for future editions are welcome.

Stan Gibilisco
Editor-in-Chief

Editorial Review Board

Robert R. Flores
Consultant and Senior Analyst
Data Access Corporation
Miami, Florida

Izhar Haq, B.S.C.S.
Systems Analyst and Consultant
Coral Gables, Florida

Michael Jeanneret
Analyst
Rochester, Minnesota

Phillip Laplante, P.E., Ph.D.
Associate Professor, Mathematics
Farleigh Dickinson University
Madison, New Jersey

R. Jessee Phagan
Technology Education
Woodstock Academy
Woodstock, Connecticut

David E. Sass
President
Acoustical Designs
Rochester, Minnesota

Charles A. Vergers
Professor, Electronics and Telecommunications
Capitol College
Laurel, Maryland

Edward Walsh
Analyst and Consultant
Physicist, U.S. Naval Space Surveillance (Retired)
Rochester, Minnesota

Abscissa

A graph with two axes is sometimes called the *xy plane*, because the axes are labeled *x* and *y*. Two-dimensional graphs in *Cartesian coordinates* are extremely common, and are easily plotted with computer graphics.

Independent coordinate. In an *xy*-plane graph, every point has two coordinates, represented by ordered pairs (x,y). One of the axes is the *independent variable*, and the other is the *dependent variable*. Usually the independent variable is x, and the dependent variable is y. Then y depends on, or is a function of, x. The independent variable is almost always plotted on the horizontal axis.

The *abscissa* of a point in the *xy* plane is the independent-variable coordinate. If $(x,y) = (3,-4)$, the abscissa is 3. If $(x, y) = (-4,2)$, the abscissa is -4. These examples are shown in the drawing. Sometimes the entire independent-variable axis is called the abscissa.

Parameter. What makes a variable "independent"? In science and math, you'll find relationships where one thing depends on another. For example, temperature depends on the time of day, among other things. If you graph temperature for a particular place as a function of the time of day, then time is the independent variable, or *parameter*, on which temperature depends, and temperature is the dependent variable. If it is 72°F in your town at 3 p.m., then the abscissa for that point is 3 p.m. (or 1500 hours if you like military time).

Absolute value

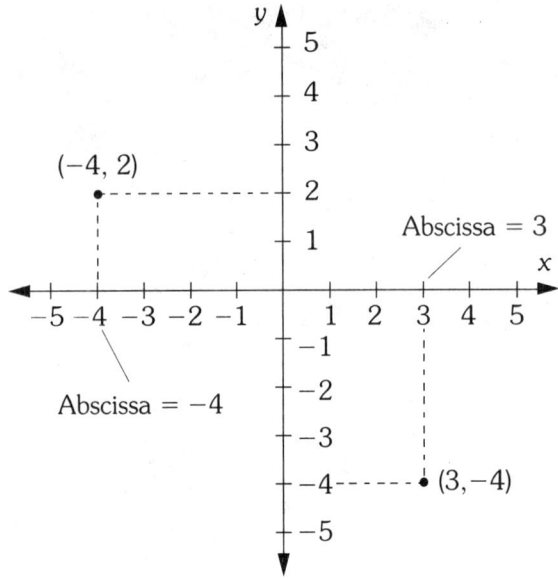

Value of the independent variable.

Although you could call temperature the independent variable, saying that the abscissa is 72°F, you must be careful. In some instances this will imply that the time of day (or some other factor such as longitude/latitude or atmospheric conditions) depends on the temperature. That's absurd. But in some scientific experiments, temperature can be a legitimate independent variable. An example is the state of the compound H_2O (water) as a function of temperature at a fixed atmospheric pressure.

Making sense. When graphing relations and functions with a computer, keep in mind which value should be the abscissa and should therefore be plotted on the horizontal axis. This will ensure that your graphs make sense. In a normal temperature-versus-time graph, time is plotted on the horizontal axis. Each point in time is an abscissa. If you reverse this, plotting temperature on the horizontal axis, then each temperature value will be an abscissa. *See also* ANALYTICAL GRAPHICS, DEPENDENT VARIABLE, INDEPENDENT VARIABLE, *and* ORDINATE.

Absolute value

The *absolute value* of a number or vector is an expression of its magnitude as sometimes used in mathematics and physics. Absolute value can be thought of as a function, and abbreviated ABS. Thus, the absolute value of a number x can be written ABS x or ABS (x). In mathematics texts, the absolute value is denoted by vertical lines on either side of a quantity or variable, for example, $|x|$.

Absolute value

Real numbers. For a real number x,

ABS $(x) = x$

if x is zero or positive. If x is negative,

ABS $(x) = -x$

In most high-level programming languages, the ABS function works this way, in effect removing the sign (positive or negative) from a numerical value.

Complex numbers. With complex numbers of the form $a + bi$, where i is the positive (principal) square root of -1, the term "absolute value" is not generally used. Instead, you'll hear about the *magnitude* or *modulus*, denoted by vertical lines on either side of the quantity. In general,

$|a + bi| = (a^2 + b^2)^{1/2}$

This is the length of its vector, or the distance of the point from the origin (center), in the complex-number plane.

The drawing shows this for the complex number $-3 - 4i$. Values a are on the horizontal axis, and values bi are on the vertical axis. Here,

$|-3 - 4i| = (-3^2 + (-4)^2)^{1/2} = 25^{1/2} = 5$

Perhaps you recognize this as the formula for the hypotenuse of a 3:4:5 right triangle. In fact, the formula for the magnitude of a two-dimensional complex number derives from the well-known Pythagorean theorem of Euclidean plane geometry.

Multidimensional quantities. Any multidimensional quantity, when there are n dimensions, can be written in the form $(x_1, x_2, x_3, \ldots, x_n)$. This is called an *ordered n-tuple*. Computers are great for working with quantities having more than three dimensions. Such quantities are impossible for humans to directly visualize, but to a computer, they just take a little more memory than two- or three-dimensional quantities. For a vector $X = (x_1, x_2, x_3, \ldots, x_n)$, the magnitude or modulus is found by the formula

$|X| = (x_1^2 + x_2^2 + x_3^2 + \ldots + x_n^2)^{1/2}$

This means you square all the components, add them up, and then take the square root of the result.

Let the computer do it. If the above formulas look intimidating, don't worry about it. When you're working with real numbers, a user-friendly computer program guides you through the math, asking you

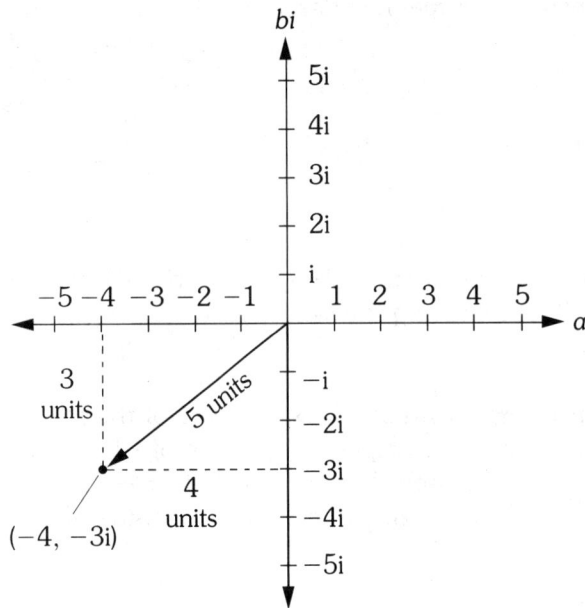

Example for a complex number.

for the values. All you need to do is type in the numbers and let the software take care of the rest.

Most general-purpose high-level programs don't know about complex or multidimensional numbers, only about real numbers, because the average person rarely needs to worry about complex or multidimensional quantities. Some scientific high-level languages can deal with complex and multidimensional numbers.

If you are comfortable with complex and multidimensional numbers, you can use the above formulas to create your own programs to compute the magnitudes of vectors in any number of dimensions. *See also* PROGRAMMING.

Accelerator board

The heart of a computer is its *microprocessor*, contained in one or more *integrated circuit (IC)* chips. Microprocessors keep getting faster, so that they can do more calculations per second. Speed, measured in megahertz (MHz), is one of the important criteria for computer power. Other important factors include the word size in bits or bytes, and the capacity of the RAM (random-access memory) in megabytes (MB) or gigabytes (GB).

Upgrading. Suppose you have an "ancient" computer that uses an Intel 8088 microprocessor. Accelerator board upgrades were popular with these machines and can still be used if you're interested only in simple applications such as basic word processing. In the 1980s, the Intel 80386, or 386, was introduced. In 1989, a new microprocessor, the Intel 80486 (or 486), appeared. The 486 is like the 386, but faster. In the early 1990s, the Pentium followed the 486. The 486 and Pentium microprocessors are better than the 386 for use with a graphical user interface (GUI). An 8088 can't deal with the graphical environments of today, such as Windows.

It can be frustrating and expensive to keep up with the latest PC technology. Some people try to do this, trading in or selling their PC every year, but you don't necessarily have to buy a whole new system to take advantage of new hardware and software technology. Instead, you can upgrade the microprocessor (say from a 386 to a 486), install a bigger hard disk, or install an accelerator board to speed up the operation of the machine, making it more effective for use with a GUI such as Windows. The addition of an accelerator board can sometimes increase the speed of the GUI by a factor of five or six.

When GUIs first caught on, they were notoriously slow because the graphics placed new, heavy demands on computers. A special type of accelerator board, known as a *video accelerator*, was designed to enhance the video performance of machines using the new GUIs. A common example was a *Windows accelerator board*, which speeded up the operation of the display in Windows software.

Not like new. Installing an accelerator board isn't the same thing as buying a whole new computer. It's like souping up the engine of an old car. While the computer might work faster within its microprocessor, it cannot access data from a diskette any faster. The only way to speed up the diskette-drive data access is to get a faster diskette drive. The same holds true for a hard disk. Similarly, upgrading the microprocessor will not, all by itself, give your computer more RAM, even though the new microprocessor might be able to deal with more memory. The only way to get more RAM is to add RAM expansion boards, or yield to temptation and buy a new PC with more memory. You should therefore check, and perhaps consult with some experts, to decide whether an accelerator board will provide the practical results that meet your increased needs. *See also* BYTE, CLOCK SPEED, EXPANSION BOARD, GIGABYTE, GRAPHICAL USER INTERFACE, MEGABYTE, MICROPROCESSOR, *and* UPGRADING.

Access

In computer terminology, the word *access* can mean either of two things: "availability" or "getting hold of." In both cases, it concerns data.

Use or availability. Perhaps you've tried to open a file on your PC and been unable to gain access. For example, you might try to open a nonexistent file XYZ.ABC. You can't do such a thing. It's like trying to

Access time

walk into a room that your house doesn't have. The computer will respond with a deadpan phrase such as

ACCESS DENIED

or

FILE NOT FOUND XYZ.ABC

The same thing happens if you try to open a file from the wrong directory or drive, or if you happen to make a mistake when typing a filename or command. Computers are precise machines, and they demand precision from you. If you're off by an inch, you might as well be off by a mile.

Getting hold of data. After the above exercise in futility, you might say, "I can't access XYZ.ABC." In this case the word "access" means "get hold of" or "open."

You can access an online service, bulletin board, or other network; this means you call up the appropriate telephone number and use your computer and modem to send and receive data into and from the network. Or you might access a file on a hard disk. For example, the name of the file containing this text, as this book was written, was PC.A. If you had the diskette containing the text for the letter A in this book, and put the diskette in drive A, you could open the file A:PC.A and the text would appear, showing the first few lines on the monitor screen. Depending on the size of the file, the speed of the diskette drive, and the speed of the microprocessor, this might take from a fraction of a second to several seconds. *See also* ACCESS TIME.

Access time

When you try to get hold of data from someplace such as a computer memory or a network, you don't get the data right away. Sometimes it seems to arrive instantly; in the newest PCs you can call a file and have it appear on your monitor screen in a fraction of a second. But sometimes it takes awhile.

For a hard disk. The *access time* for a hard disk is on the order of a few *milliseconds*, or thousandths of a second. The access time is, at most, the time required for the platters of the hard disk to make a half-revolution, plus the time it takes for the read/write head to move into position over the first bit of data in the desired file. In this sense, access time does not depend on the size of the file, but only on the hard disk technology.

Transfer rate. Within a PC, the delay between the open-up command and the actual availability of the data is sometimes called the *access time*; this is more accurately called the *transfer rate*. The shortest transfer rates are for small files (just a few kilobytes) stored in

RAM or on a hard disk. Getting data from a diskette or tape drive takes longer. The bigger the file, the slower the transfer rate, all other factors being equal. With files of several hundred kilobytes on a floppy diskette, the transfer rate can be several seconds. With a tape drive, the transfer rate can be up to about a half-hour, depending on the amount of data to be transferred and on the tape-drive technology.

In a network. When you seek data from a large network, it can take quite awhile. The *access time* might be several minutes. Sometimes it's indefinite; you can't get at the data on some occasion, and have to try again later in the day, or even on some other day.

Consider this example. Many towns have their public libraries' card catalogs available to anyone with a PC and a telephone modem. Suppose you want to find out whether a given book is available at your local library. As soon as you get the notion, you start a stopwatch. You turn on your PC and modem and get into the network. Then you call up the local library card catalog. There might be many other people trying to access the card catalog at that time; the more "competition" you have, the slower the network responds. Eventually, you find out that the title is indeed in the library's card catalog, but it has been checked out. (That saves you a trip downtown for nothing!) You stop the stopwatch. Perhaps it reads 3:30.4. That means the access time was three minutes, 30.4 seconds. *See also* ACCESS, DISKETTE DRIVE, HARD DISK, MEMORY, NETWORK, STORAGE TIME, *and* TAPE DRIVE.

Accounting software

See PERSONAL FINANCE SOFTWARE.

Acoustic coupler

An *acoustic coupler* is a special type of telephone *modem*. Instead of connecting directly into the telephone line, the device has a "cradle" into which you place the telephone receiver. The modem "speaks" and "listens" to the telephone, just like you do when you talk on it, except that the data consists of digital signals, not a human voice. Acoustic couplers are not often used today. Current modem technology uses hard wiring, and modems are often housed within the main unit of the computer.

How it works. The drawing shows a simplified block diagram of an acoustic coupler. To use the modem, you place the telephone receiver down on it, making sure that the mouthpiece and earpiece are in the correct positions. (If you have the receiver set down the wrong way, the modem won't work.)

The microphone picks up incoming data from the telephone earpiece. These signals go to an amplifier and signal processing circuit, which converts the audio tones to electrical impulses that the computer can understand.

Acoustic coupler

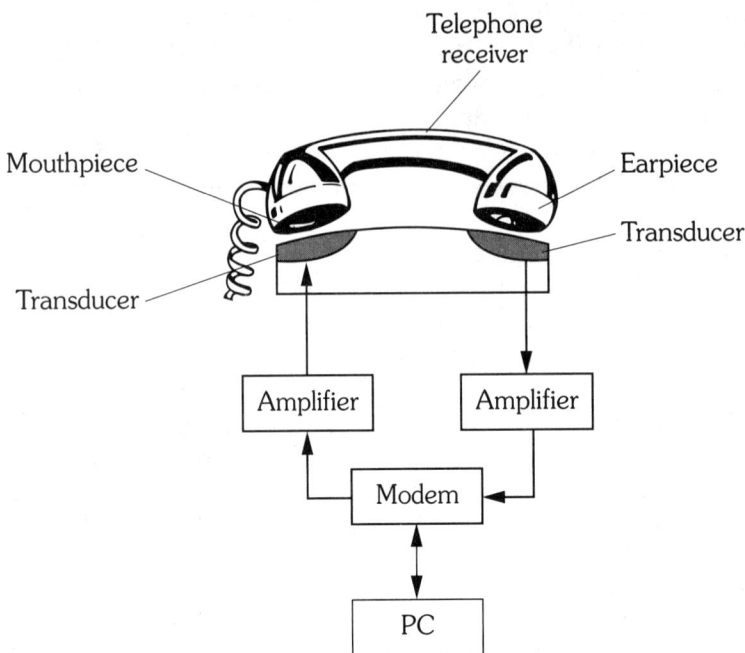

A type of telephone modem.

For outgoing data, the modem takes the computer impulses and converts them into audio tones. These tones are fed into the telephone mouthpiece. These tones have standard frequencies that are the same as those used by hard-wired modems. If you bring your ear up close to an acoustic coupler while it is in use, you'll hear these tones, sometimes rushing by so fast that they blend into a hiss or roar.

Good and bad. Acoustic couplers are easy to use. You can buy one, connect it to your PC, and use it without having to fool around with wires and adapters. Acoustic couplers are also useful when your telephone does not use one of the new quick-disconnect plug/jacks.

The main problem with acoustic couplers is that they can pick up extraneous noises, especially if they are loud enough to vibrate the desk or if their pitch is similar to that of the audio tones used in data communication. A child having an ear-splitting tantrum, while sitting and pounding on your computer desk, might disrupt the operation of the acoustic coupler (not to mention the functioning of your mind).

Another problem with acoustic couplers is that the data goes through *transducers* (microphones and speakers). This is not done in a hard-wired modem. Whenever you force a signal through changes, such as from electric current to acoustic waves, you increase the chances for errors to get into the data. The maximum data transmission speed is severely limited when an acoustic coupler is used.

In recent years, hard-wired modems have become standard for desktop computers. If you have telephone jacks in your home, it's actually easier to use a hard-wired modem than to use an acoustic coupler. This is especially true if the computer has an internal modem; all you need is a cord and/or a two-way adapter to connect the modem and telephone set into the same jack. *See also* MODEM.

Acronym

These days, there is a fetish for abbreviations. Companies use them; who hasn't heard of IBM (International Business Machines) or ABC (American Broadcasting Company)? Abbreviations are everywhere in the computer field; they're used to represent both hardware and software. You own a *PC* (personal computer) with plenty of RAM (random access memory) that might have a *modem* (modulator/demodulator) connected to the telephone line. Abbreviations like *RAM* are special; when you put together the first letter of each word that makes up *RAM*, you get a new, pronounceable word, not just a string of letters. This type of abbreviation is an *acronym*.

The big advantage of acronyms is that they help people remember things. The table shows a few acronyms commonly used in personal computing. All of these can be pronounced as words, and usually are. You might hear someone say, "I hooked up my modem today and got into the lan, but couldn't access Internet. I wonder if the asky speed is right." The word "lan" is actually the acronym *LAN* (local area network), and "asky" is actually the acronym *ASCII* (American Standard Code for Information Interchange).

Sometimes an abbreviation that looks like an acronym isn't; it is spelled out as a sequence of letters like any other abbreviation, even though you can pronounce it as a word. An example is *LED*. You might get some odd looks if you say, "What does that flashing lead mean?" On the other hand, if you spell out an acronym such as *BASIC* instead of pronouncing it as a word, you'll certainly raise eyebrows. You wouldn't say, "Today I started learning B-A-S-I-C."

How do you know when to pronounce a computer term as an acronym, and when to pronounce it as an abbreviation? You learn by experience. The rules aren't hard-and-fast; just imitate the experts.

The appendix at the back of this book contains a comprehensive list of abbreviations and acronyms used in personal computing.

Active file

An *active file* is a computer file that has been taken from the *hard disk* or *diskette*, and temporarily stored in *RAM (random-access memory)* so that you can work with it. New files that you have just created but not yet stored on disk or diskette are also active files.

Changing a diskette file. The name of the word processing file containing this text, as this book was written, was PC.A. Suppose you

Active file

A few common PC-related acronyms

Acronyn	Meaning
ARPAnet	Advanced Research Projects Agency network
ASCII	American Standard Code for Information Interchange
BASIC	Beginner's All-purpose Symbolic Instruction Code (a high-level language)
CAD	Computer-Aided Design
CAM	Computer-Aided Manufacturing
DOS	Disk Operating System
EPROM	Erasable Programmable Read-Only Memory
GIGO	Garbage In, Garbage Out
LAN	Local Area Network
LED	Light-Emitting Diode
LIM	Lotus-Intel-Microsoft
MIDI	Musical Instrument Digital Interface
MIPS	Million Instructions Per Second
PILOT	Programmed Inquiry Learning Or Teaching (a high-level language)
PROM	Programmable Read-Only Memory
RAM	Random-Access Memory
ROM	Read-Only Memory
SASI	Shugart Associates' Standard Interface

had a diskette with that file on it. You might insert the diskette into drive A and open file A:PC.A. After a couple of seconds, the text would appear on the monitor screen. The file PC.A would be active.

You might make changes to PC.A, maybe to change the wording of this article with your word processing software. These changes would go into RAM as they were made, but they would not go onto the diskette until you closed or saved the file. When you closed the file, you would hear whirring sounds, and the computer would ask you something like this:

```
FILE EXISTS, OVERWRITE IT?
```

You might type *N* for no; then the file would remain active. If you typed *Y* for yes, there would be more whirring sounds, and the text would vanish from the screen. The file would no longer be active. It would be back on diskette, containing the changes you made.

Leaving the file without changes. If you are making changes to a file and decide you prefer it the old way, you can choose not to overwrite it, perhaps by typing *N* in response to a question or by clicking on a Cancel button. The text vanishes from the screen and also from RAM. The diskette file remains as it was before you opened it, and the file is no longer active. You can then open some other file, either from the hard drive or from a diskette drive.

A power failure closes an active file without storing any changes you've made to it, unless you have an uninterruptible power supply (UPS). Many software packages have automatic backup to prevent accidental loss of data in active files.

In general. The term *active file* is used in reference to many types of files, not just those used in word processing. It can apply to spreadsheets, to databases, or to programs in a high-level language such as C, COBOL, or BASIC. It can even apply to graphic or sound files.

Store it often! If you plan to work on a file for more than a couple of minutes, it's a good idea to store it on disk or diskette every few minutes. Otherwise, if a file is active and there is a sudden power failure or a computer "crash," your changes won't be stored.

If you keep a file active for hours, making extensive changes, and the power goes out, you will lose all your work unless you have a UPS. I personally lost a whole day's work that way. The data was erased from the PC RAM, but the lesson was stored in my mind's memory permanently. *See also* ACTIVE MEMORY, AUTOMATIC BACKUP, RANDOM-ACCESS MEMORY, *and* UNINTERRUPTIBLE POWER SUPPLY.

Active matrix

If you have a laptop or notebook computer, it has a built-in monitor. The screen is flat and thin, and folds down over the keyboard, so the whole computer fits into a briefcase. There are several different types of monitors for these computers; one of the most popular is the *liquid-crystal display (LCD)*.

A big problem with LCDs is that they're rather slow—and they get slower as the temperature goes down. The earliest LCDs, introduced during the 1970s, were useless below about 50°F. As LCD technology has improved, the display speed has increased, and LCDs have been able to operate at colder and colder temperatures.

To overcome problems with conventional LCDs, the *active matrix* LCD was developed. This design has a faster response than conventional LCDs. In graphical applications with fast-changing images, such as animation, an active matrix display works almost as well as the cathode-ray-tube (CRT) monitors commonly used with desktop PCs. In recent years, active-matrix displays have become commonly available in laptop PCs.

In an active-matrix LCD, each pixel (picture element) can be switched on and off independently. This is in contrast to *passive*

Active memory

matrix displays, in which the pixels are switched on and off in rows or columns. This is the main reason why an active-matrix LCD can keep up so well with rapidly moving images. Active-matrix displays also produce a clearer image, with less "bleeding," more vivid colors, and better brilliance and contrast than passive-matrix LCDs. The main disadvantage of active-matrix LCDs is that they are rather expensive, adding several hundred dollars to the cost of a laptop computer. *See also* LAPTOP COMPUTER *and* LIQUID-CRYSTAL DISPLAY.

Active memory

When you are working with a file in your PC, that file is usually in the *RAM (random-access memory)*. The word *active* means that you're acting on the memory—doing something to change its contents.

For example, consider the file containing the text for the letter *a* in this book, called PC.A. If you had a diskette with the file PC.A on it, this file would not be in active memory. It would be idly sitting there, a huge array of magnetic data bits (ones and zeros). Suppose you inserted the diskette in the diskette drive of your PC (usually drive A), and then opened the file from that drive. This would place the file into RAM, and the text would appear on the monitor. At that time, PC.A would be an *active file* in an *active memory*. You could, if you wanted, modify it, save it on the hard disk (usually drive C), and close it. The file would no longer be in active memory. The file PC.A would still be on the diskette in drive A, but it would not contain the changes you had just made. To include the changes in file PC.A on the diskette, you would have to save the file to drive A as well as (or instead of) drive C. This would cause the old copy of PC.A to be overwritten with the new data. *See also* ACTIVE FILE *and* RANDOM-ACCESS MEMORY.

Active window

Most operating environments fall into one of two categories: a *graphical user interface (GUI)* such as Windows, or a *command-driven environment* such as DOS. A GUI shows you pictures to depict what is happening in your computer, and lets you choose options from the pictures. Microsoft Windows is the best-known interface of this type, but other examples include the Macintosh system and IBM's OS/2. Most new PC users prefer the GUI to a command-driven environment.

In a GUI, you usually move the pointer or cursor around on the screen (*window*) by pressing the arrow keys on the keyboard or by moving a mouse around on a flat surface, watching the pointer or cursor and stopping the mouse when you have reached the point you want. You can press the Enter key, or click or double-click mouse buttons, to issue a command.

Often, selecting an option from a window will cause a new window to take its place. The *active window* is the one within which the pointer moves, and from which you can select options at a given time. The pointer can be used to make selections within the active window, but not outside of it. The active window shows up as if it's lying on top of the background windows, as shown in the drawing.

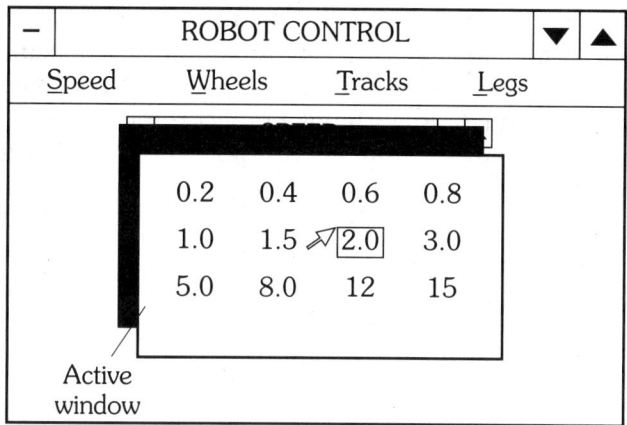

The active window seems to float above the background.

In some windowing environments, you can enlarge or reduce the size of the active window. You might "drag" the active window around within the background window. Sometimes you might have several small windows within the large, full-screen background window, and designate one of the small windows as active. You can even jump into the background window, making it active while the other, smaller windows become passive.

When you're done using the functions in the active window, you exit from it. It might disappear, leaving only the background window, or the cursor might jump out of the active window into the background window. Then the background window has become the active window. *See also* DOS *and* GRAPHICAL USER INTERFACE.

Activity tracking

Do you make lists of things to do? Do you have a long list of friends, acquaintances, colleagues, and business associates, with addresses, telephone numbers, and other information? If so, you can benefit from *activity tracking* software, a form of database.

It's multidimensional. When you go into a stationery store or department store around December, you'll see appointment books, address books, and other record books for sale. You'll also see card files of various kinds. The end of the year is a popular time for buying organizational books and files. An activity tracker can take the place of them all—not just for the coming year, but for good. Maybe you

Adapter

should consider buying an activity tracker program, instead of all this fresh new paper.

In an address book or card file, you probably have people logged in alphabetically, by last name or the name of their business. But what if you want to look up the names of all the people you know who live in a certain town? You'll have to go through the whole file, card by card or page by page, and look for the town, or else keep a separate file in alphabetical order by town name. The same is true for dates of last contact, and for various other things. With an activity tracker, you can look things up according to any specification you want. Computers are good at sorting through lists in different ways.

No muss, no fuss. Address card files and appointment books get worn out and messy after a while. It's a relief when you can finally throw an old one away and get a clean, new one on which to scribble, smear ink, splatter correction fluid, and stick tape. Or perhaps you'd rather put it on a diskette? Diskettes don't get dog-eared. You can change the data easily, without erasing, blotting out, or crossing out. Most activity-tracking programs allow you to add notes, such as "Will call back June 23" or "Don't call her; she'll call me."

With paper-based lists of things to do, it's easy to cross things off without doing them. But those crossed-out items stay there and gaze up at you reproachfully from the paper, until you rip the whole page out and throw it away. With an activity tracker, you can delete a listed item with a keystroke, not do the job, and suffer the consequences without feeling guilty ahead of time. Also, the computer can be programmed to ask you if you're sure you want to leave the job undone.

Activity trackers save time; they can be programmed to automatically display items and events daily. You can pick out people or businesses for mailing lists. Salespeople find activity-tracking software especially useful for following up leads. *See also* CONTACT MANAGER, DATABASE, *and* PERSONAL INFORMATION MANAGER.

Adapter

Any device that makes two incompatible things work together is called an *adapter*. Adapters come in many forms.

Plug adapters. Perhaps you have used adapters to "mate" plugs to sockets. A common plug adapter lets you use a three-prong plug with a two-prong outlet, as shown in the drawing at A. Instead of the third prong, the adapter has a wire with a lug on the end. This lug *must* be connected to a good electrical ground.

Adapter

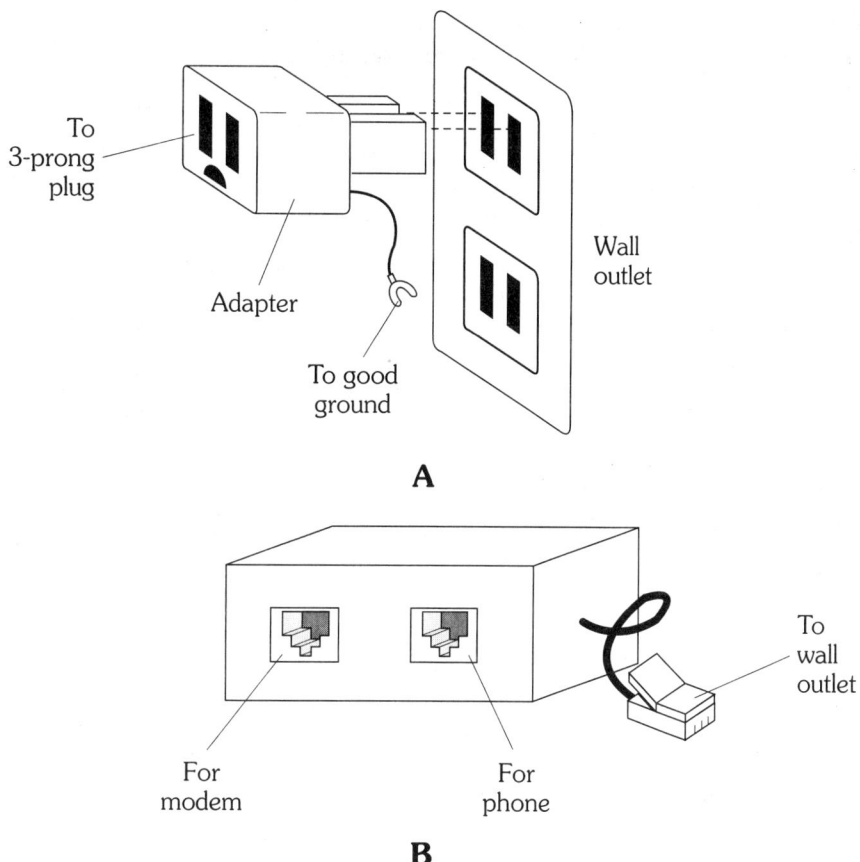

Adapter for utility cord (A) and telephone (B).

Warning!

The third prong or lug must be grounded. Failure to do this can cause a lethal electric shock.

The best policy regarding ac line (electrical) adapters is not to use them unless you have no choice. Never use one simply for convenience. If you are not sure whether a good electrical ground is available, consult an electrician before attempting to install three-wire appliances in a two-wire electrical system. Three-wire systems are necessary for the proper operation of *transient suppression* devices. *See also* TRANSIENT SUPPRESSION.

Telephone cord adapters. If you use a modem with your PC, you might need a two-way telephone-cord adapter. This consists of a short cord with a plug on one end that goes into the wall jack. The other end has a little box with two jacks in it, one for the modem and the other for your telephone set, as shown in the drawing at B.

Many computers have internal modems. These machines have two jacks on the back of the main unit, one for the telephone line that plugs into the wall jack and the other for the telephone set. Internal modems do not usually require adapters unless you have more than one telephone set or peripheral telephone equipment such as a fax machine or an automatic answering device.

Other adapters. Sometimes you might want to use a PC with peripherals that it isn't specifically designed to work with. For example, suppose you want to use a laptop PC with a large, bright monitor of the type you normally use with a desktop PC. An *adapter board* or *adapter card* lets you do this. An adapter might also be used if, for example, you find that the plug for your mouse doesn't fit the port in the back of your PC.

If you want to add functions to your PC, you can buy an adapter card for that purpose. Common adapter card functions include memory expansion, extra inputs or outputs, modem connections, and monitors. In coming years you will increasingly see adapters for speech recognition, speech synthesis, optical character recognition, robot control, virtual reality, and other exotic applications.

Standardization. Wouldn't it be nice if everything were compatible, so there was no need for adapters? It will probably never happen. New devices are designed, built, and put on the market without much thought about plugs, jacks, and all the different ways people might want to mix their hardware up. However, a group called the *American National Standards Institute (ANSI)* works to keep the situation from getting too chaotic. *See also* AMERICAN NATIONAL STANDARDS INSTITUTE.

Address

The term *address* refers to the location of data. The data might be a single bit, a byte (eight bits), a word (several bytes), or a chunk of data of some arbitrary size. It can even be an entire file or directory.

Numerical address. Perhaps you've used a radio with "memory" channels. Most digital hi-fi broadcast receivers have memory channels with designator numbers. A radio with four memories might assign them M1 through M4. A radio with 64 memories might have designators M00 through M63. Each designator is a memory *address*. Like a street address, it specifies the location of the data.

Suppose your favorite FM stereo stations were at 94.1, 94.9, 99.9, and 103.5 MHz. To store these channels in an FM radio with four memories M1 through M4, you would tune the radio to 94.1, select memory address M1, and enter the data. Then you would tune the radio to 94.9, select address M2, and store. You'd then tune to 99.9, select address M3, and store. Finally, you'd tune to 103.5, select address M4, and store.

If you were listening to some station and decided you wanted to check out the progressive rock at 103.5 MHz, you could press the button for M4 and be there immediately. Or, if you wanted to hear country music at 99.9 MHz, you could press M3.

Filenames. In a computer, the location of data in storage is often specified by directories, subdirectories, and filenames. The text for this article, as this book was written, was contained in a file called PC.A. This file appeared in a subdirectory called \PCPART1 on the hard disk.

The size of \PCPART1\PC.A started out as just a few hundred bytes, but quickly grew to many kilobytes. It, like the thousands of other files on the hard disk of the computer, constantly changed in size as the text was revised, edited, and proofread. Its actual physical location on the hard disk changed as new files were added, old files were erased, and the disk was periodically cleaned up and reorganized, but the address was always the same: \PCPART1\PC.A. *See also* DIRECTORY, DISKETTE, FILENAME, HARD DISK, *and* MEMORY.

Adobe Illustrator

Adobe Illustrator is a software package commonly used in *analytical graphics*. It is quite popular with scientists, engineers, and architects. Adobe Illustrator employs a scheme known as *object-oriented graphics*. This provides improved image quality in many applications, compared with bitmapped graphics. The difference is most noticeable with printers having good image resolution, such as laser printers.

Bitmapping. Pictures, like other things in the real world, are almost always *analog* in nature; they are continuous, they change smoothly. Computers, on the other had, are *digital* machines. Sometimes real-life things exactly fit some digital model, but this doesn't happen very often. How can the analog world be "married" to the digital computer? The most obvious answer is to use approximations. Bitmapped graphics show functions on a grid of dots. If the grid is fine enough, this will work well, and the digital approximation will be very close to the real thing.

You've seen bitmapped illustrations in magazines, instruction manuals, or manuscripts. They have a "computerized" look. While some people like this look, others dislike it, even if the drawings are clear and concise.

Mathematicians, engineers, and scientists in particular often want more precision than bitmapped graphics can offer. For them, a program like Adobe Illustrator can be valuable. The curves that it generates are smooth and can be changed in size and shape without introducing *jaggies*, a form of distortion in which curved or slanted lines and edges acquire a serrated (sawtooth) appearance.

Adobe Type Manager

Bezier curves. Mathematical functions are graphable as curves, but these curves look relatively imprecise in bitmapped graphics. With *Bezier curves*, many functions can be defined on the basis of a few points. Adobe Illustrator takes advantage of this fact to draw a smooth curve.

Suppose you know the points shown in the drawing. Suppose also that you know the curve is smooth, and not wildly complicated. Using Adobe Illustrator, the computer will search for a smooth curve, definable by an analog function, that fits the points. In its memory, it will enlarge and reduce sample curves, turn them, flip them inside out, and otherwise play with them, until a match is found, as shown by the heavy line in the drawing.

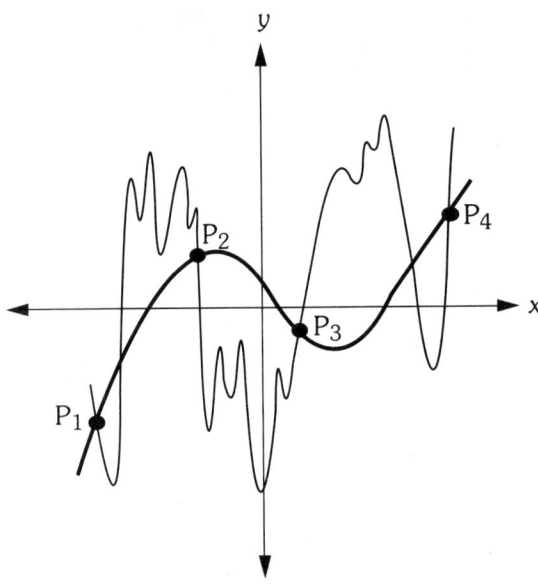

Bezier curve plotting.

Of course, there are an infinite number of *extremely complex* curves that will also fit the points. One of these is shown by the light, squiggly line. While it is possible that such a bizarre curve will be found in nature, simple curves are more probable. Adobe Illustrator is an educated guesser in this sense. *See also* ANALOG, BEZIER CURVE, BITMAPPED GRAPHICS, DIGITAL, IMAGE RESOLUTION, *and* OBJECT-ORIENTED GRAPHICS.

Adobe Type Manager

Adobe Type Manager (sometimes abbreviated *ATM*) is a software package available for both IBM-compatible and Macintosh computers that uses *outline fonts* to show letters, numbers, and symbols. The characters in an outline font show up clearly, no matter what their size. This is an improvement over the more traditional *bitmapped font*. *See also* BITMAPPED FONT *and* OUTLINE FONT.

Adobe Type Manager

Bitmapped versus outline fonts. On a computer monitor display, a common way to show characters is to illuminate certain dots in a pattern. But this will work only if the characters are very large compared to the dots. You can't illuminate part of a dot. Although the brightness or color of the dot can be adjusted, this doesn't improve the image clarity or image resolution.

If the characters are many times the size of the dots, there is no problem, but as the characters get smaller, some of them get "fuzzy" or distorted. The drawing shows an example for the small letter *e*. At A, the letter is huge compared to the dots, and the image is quite clear. At B, the letter is smaller, and there is some distortion. At C, the letter is smaller yet, and there is significant distortion. It would be frustrating to read a whole paragraph printed in letters this "coarse."

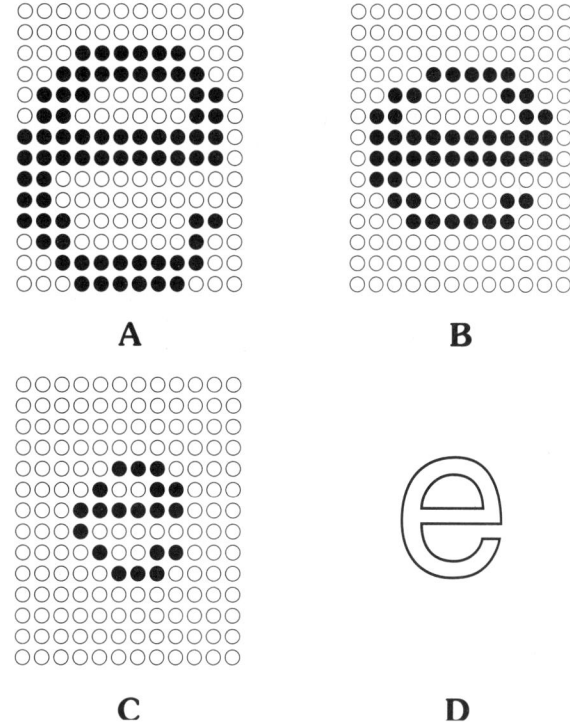

Bitmapped fonts (A, B, C), and outline font (D).

Part D of the drawing shows the letter *e* at the same size as in part C, but using outline font. The difference is obvious. The letter could be made a lot smaller before it got hard to read. *See also* IMAGE RESOLUTION.

Limitations. Adobe Type Manager has some limitations. The software involved is more complicated than for bitmapped fonts. Also, different programs are needed for different fonts. For example, you might have Helvetica, also known as sans serif, font. With the Helvetica program, you can make characters any size you want in that font. But if you switch to, say, Courier font (the font most electric typewriters use), you can't change the size unless you also change the program. Because of these software traits, Adobe Type Manager costs more than less sophisticated programs.

Is the additional cost and complexity of Adobe Type Manager worth it? That depends on your needs and preferences. Many computer users never feel the urge to change fonts on the display; for them, Adobe Type Manager can be a good investment. For people who don't need to have the clearest possible letters, the money might be better spent on something else. However, Adobe Type Manager is excellent for desktop publishing. *See also* DESKTOP PUBLISHING.

Aggregate

The term *aggregate* refers to a function or command involving all the values in a certain set. Aggregate functions and commands are used in database and spreadsheet software.

A sample set. Suppose you are given the following set of numbers:

S = {2,4,7,13,17,23,30}

You might want to know the arithmetic mean (average), the geometric mean, the median, the sum, the count, the minimum value, and the maximum value. These are all functions of the values in the set S. Let these functions be abbreviated as follows:

- Arithmetic mean (average): am(S)
- Geometric mean: gm(S)
- Median: m(S)
- Sum: s(S)
- Product: p(S)
- Count: c(S)
- Minimum value: min(S)
- Maximum value: max(S)

Calculating the values. You can figure some of these out right away. Obviously, c(S) = 7, min(S) = 2, and max(S) = 30. The median is the value for which there are equally many greater and lesser values; therefore m(S) = 13. Adding the numbers up yields s(S) = 96. Then you can figure am(S) = 96/7 = 13.71428571. Multiplying all the numbers yields p(S) = 8,539,440.

The tough one here is gm(S). For *n* numbers, the geometric mean is the nth root of the product of all the numbers. Therefore, gm(S) = $(8,539,440)^{1/7}$. The easiest way to calculate this is to use logarithms.

The result is gm(S) = 9.776968113. If you want to refresh your logarithm skills, go ahead and figure this out for yourself. Modern calculators make it fairly easy if you like math. But a computer can find gm(S) in a split second, even if you have no math knowledge whatsoever. *See also* DATABASE *and* SPREADSHEET.

Alert

Computer users sometimes give commands that can cause errors, data loss, malfunction, or other problems. You might tell the computer to do something impossible, such as store data on a nonexistent tape drive. Maybe a program has "blown up" at a remote location. In situations like this, you get an *alert* message.

In DOS. Suppose you're working in DOS (the disk operating system), and you're working in a file called POEMS. All of your best poetry is in this file. You've just finished a neat little poem and you want to add it to your permanent stash of great verse, which will make you famous 200 years from now.

Having typed in the new verse, you insert a diskette containing short stories, poems, and chapters of the novel you've just started into drive A. The old file POEMS is on the diskette, and you want to update it. The computer will respond with an alert message, asking if you really want to erase the old data in favor of the new. Perhaps the alert will take the form of a question, such as:

```
FILE EXISTS, OVERWRITE IT?
```

You can then type either *Y* (for yes) or *N* (for no). *See also* DOS.

In a GUI. In a graphical user interface (GUI) such as Windows, when you issue a command in which there will be a data change that you might not want, you will see a box appear on top of the main window. This box will contain an attention-getting symbol such as a big, boldface exclamation mark (**!**) or question sign (**?**). This is called an *alert box.*

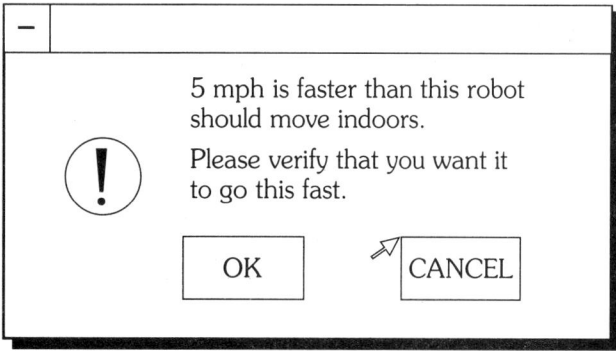

An alert box for verifying a command.

Algorithm

The drawing shows an example of an alert box. You've commanded your personal robot to roll at five miles per hour indoors. This is a faster speed than normal for indoors, according to the control software, but it's not so dangerous that the machine will refuse to do it under any circumstances. The alert box asks if you're sure you want this metal monster rolling seven feet per second in your living room. If you click OK, the manufacturers of the robot and software disclaim all responsibility for toppled plants, damaged furniture, terrified cats, and the like. If you click Cancel, the software will return to the previous function: in this case, the choice of robot speed. *See also* GRAPHICAL USER INTERFACE.

Algorithm

An *algorithm* is a step-by-step procedure for solving a problem. Algorithms can usually be shown in *flowchart* form on paper, although if the algorithm is very complicated, the flowchart might take up so much paper that even a football field would be too small for it!

All computer programs are algorithms. Proofs in mathematical logic and geometry, such as the kind you learned in high school, are also algorithms. Robots and other programmable machines do their work by following algorithms that tell them exactly where and when to move.

Sidesteps and loops. In an algorithm, steps sometimes seem to lead nowhere in particular. You might find yourself wondering why the programmer put a certain step in. Perhaps you suspect that it's a mistake, but in an efficient algorithm, every step is vital, even if its purpose isn't immediately obvious.

An algorithm can have *loops*, or places in the problem-solving process where a certain group of steps is repeated, anywhere from twice to millions of times. This is common in programming. *See also* LOOP.

Troubleshooting. Algorithms are sometimes found in the service manuals for machinery or electronic equipment, including PCs. Troubleshooting processes can be put down in algorithm form, sometimes using flowcharts. Then the technician "plays computer," following the instructions with unquestioning rigor. At the end of the process, hopefully the problem has been found and a solution is prescribed.

Finite size. Algorithms must have a finite number of steps. A computer can do a huge number of things, but it can't do infinitely many things. Each step must be clear, and it must be possible for a machine to do it. A loop must not continue indefinitely; the entire process must be executable in a finite length of time.

Algorithms that once would have taken people thousands or millions of years (and therefore were practically impossible) can now be done

Alignment

by computers in a few seconds. Algorithms that are beyond the abilities of today's large computers will probably be done quickly and easily by machines 50 years from now. An infinitely long algorithm, however, will never be executed by any computer.

Living algorithms. People often seem to solve problems using intuition, without any apparent algorithm, but some researchers in artificial intelligence (AI) think the human brain is just a super-sophisticated digital computer. If that is true, then all of our thoughts and actions can be reduced to algorithms. Then, applying this logic in reverse, they claim that it is possible to build a machine that can think, learn, feel, hope, love, and even dream, in exactly the same way we do. Such machines would be as "smart" as human beings, but function according to algorithms that are totally foreign to us. Whether or not this is possible, engineers are trying, and will keep trying, to do it. If it is realizable, we'll find out in time. *See also* ARTIFICIAL INTELLIGENCE, FLOWCHART, *and* PROGRAMMING.

Alignment

The term *alignment* refers to the process of lining things up or to the process of adjusting something so it works best.

In a diskette drive. For a hard disk or diskette drive to read and write data, its *head* must be in the right position. It must always be exactly over the correct data bit on the disk or platter, as shown in the drawing at A. If there is any error in the placement of the head, so it's not over the right spot as in the drawing at B, there will be reading and writing errors. In the worst case, the drive will be unable to read or write anything. Then, you'll get a message like

```
ERROR READING DRIVE A
```

if you're trying to recover data, or

```
DRIVE NOT READY
```

if you're trying to store data on the diskette.

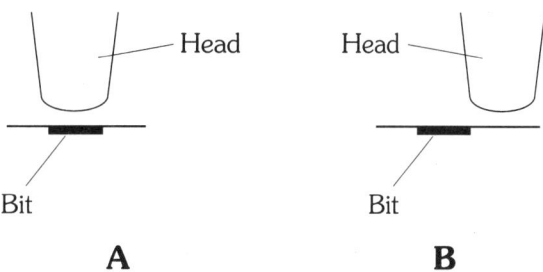

Head aligned (A) and not aligned (B).

Diskette drives and hard disk systems need to be aligned from time to time. Anything can gradually fall out of alignment. You know this

Allocation

about cars; wheels need to be aligned occasionally. It's the same way with any electromechanical device.

Sometimes an older computer will not be able to read the data from a diskette that was written on a newer machine. One possible reason for this is alignment incompatibility between the two diskette drives.

A hard blow to your PC (like dropping it on the floor) can throw a diskette drive out of alignment, just as a big pothole can knock the wheels of a car out of alignment. The alignment process can, and should, be done by a competent technician. *See also* HEAD.

In text. When working with word processing or desktop publishing, alignment means that lines or columns of text fall above and below each other in a certain orderly way. There are several different methods of aligning text. Text alignment is usually called *justification* or *column format*. *See also* FLUSH-LEFT/RIGHT/CENTER, JUSTIFICATION, SIDE-BY-SIDE COLUMN FORMAT, SINGLE-COLUMN FORMAT, *and* TWO-COLUMN FORMAT.

Allocation

All programs, files, and directories require a certain amount of space in computer memory. The amount of memory, measured in bytes, kilobytes (K or KB), megabytes (MB or M), or gigabytes (GB or G), is called the *allocation*. The term *allocation* also refers to the process of reserving memory space for a program, file, or directory.

On disk. On a hard disk or diskette, you can see the allocation for each file clearly if you look at directories. At the time I was writing this article, I had a diskette in drive A containing various files for this book. Upon typing the command

```
DIR A:
```

the screen displayed the data shown in the table.

The allocation for the file PC.A, containing this text, was, at the time, 106,864 bytes. You can read all the allocations easily from the table.

In RAM. When the file A:PC.A was opened, the text appeared on the screen. At that moment, data under the filename PC.A was in RAM (random-access memory), ready for writing, editing, or proofreading. At first, the allocation in RAM for PC.A was 106,864 bytes, but the allocation got larger with each character typed. If text were deleted, the allocation would become smaller. On the diskette, the allocation A:PC.A remained at 106,864 bytes until the file was updated by telling the computer to save the data to drive A. *See also* MEMORY.

Alphanumeric sequence

Files on a diskette. Allocations are in the third column.

PC	PTS	355	7-01-93	2:10p
PC	A	106,864	7-23-93	6:38a
PC	SMP	18,082	6-26-93	6:24a
PC	R	3781	7-01-93	2:09p
PC	D	1881	7-01-93	2:08p
PC	M	2454	7-01-93	2:09p
PC	AQ	13,509	7-01-93	2:09p
PC	TMS	27,751	7-22-93	1:45p
PC	PKT	64,887	7-01-93	2:09p
PC	SKD	2388	7-01-93	2:08p
PC		2379	7-01-93	2:09p
PC	X	275	6-26-93	6:23a
PC	U	12,827	7-22-93	9:18a
PC	B	275	7-01-93	2:09p
PC	I	22,159	7-01-93	2:10p
PC	W	20,688	7-01-93	2:11p
PC	V	8366	7-01-93	2:08p
PC	T	17,098	7-01-93	2:10p
PC	DED	56	7-01-93	2:10p
PC	C	7601	7-01-93	2:10p
PC	CAP	394	7-10-93	3:13p
PC	ED	2807	7-14-93	6:56p
PCTBL	1	1209	7-12-93	4:34a

35 files	359,219 char.	844,800 free

Alphanumeric sequence

Alphanumeric sequence refers to the order in which words or terms are arranged in a list, glossary, index, dictionary, or encyclopedia. When terms are in alphanumeric sequence, they're in "alphabetical order." A PC can be programmed to put words and phrases in alphanumeric sequence. All indexing programs, and most word processing packages, have this feature.

Words. To put words in alphanumeric sequence, you do just what you learned in elementary school. First, you categorize them by the first letter, from A through Z in order. This gives you 26 categories. (Some of them, like Q or X, might be empty, but count them anyhow.)

Within each category, you arrange terms alphabetically according to the second letter. This gives you 26 subcategories within each main category. After that, you subcategorize according to the third letter,

Alphanumeric sequence

then the fourth, and so on. If you run out of letters, then you have "blanks," considered to come before A.

Word groups. When some of the terms have two or more words, there are two ways to alphabetize them.

The first method is to work as if the words for each term were run together. Then, for example, ACT LIKE A CLOWN would be treated as ACTLIKEACLOWN, and ACT LIKE A ROBOT would be treated as ACTLIKEAROBOT. You might then get this sequence:

ACTING
ACT LIKE A CLOWN
ACT LIKE A ROBOT
ACTOR

The second method is to consider the space between words as a blank, which comes before the letter A. Then the alphanumeric sequence for the terms becomes

ACT LIKE A CLOWN
ACT LIKE A ROBOT
ACTING
ACTOR

Either method is acceptable, as long as you stick with the same method throughout a document.

Letters and numbers. Numerals are treated as characters, giving a 36-member "alphabet." They usually appear in the order 0123456789. Sometimes the numerals come after Z, giving the sequence

ABC...XYZ0123456789

and sometimes they come before A, giving the sequence

0123456789ABC...XYZ

Occasionally you'll find a list in which the numeral 0 comes after 9; that is, the numerical order is 1234567890. Then you can have alphanumeric sequences in either of these forms:

ABC...XYZ1234567890
1234567890ABC...XYZ

Different software publishers and authors use different schemes, and when you must use a lot of references, each arranged in a different way, it can get to be quite confusing. Unfortunately, we'll probably always be stuck with this problem. (In the running text of this book, the

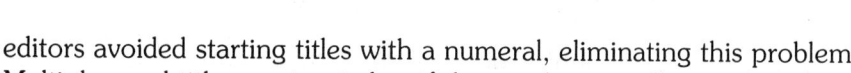

editors avoided starting titles with a numeral, eliminating this problem. Multiple-word titles are treated as if the words were all run together.)

In *case-sensitive data format*, a distinction is made between uppercase (or "capital") letters and lowercase ("small") letters. Usually, uppercase comes first. Thus the alphabetic sequence becomes AaBbCc ... XxYyZz. *See also* INDEXING SOFTWARE *and* WORD PROCESSING.

Alpha test

When a company produces new software, it must be tested before it is actually marketed and sent out to PC users. The "in-house" test, to be sure the software works more or less the way it should, is called the *alpha test* because it is the first true test of the product, and alpha is the first letter of the Greek alphabet.

Alpha testing is only one phase in the ultimate development and evolution of software. A more revealing test is the *beta test*, done in the field.

Even after software has been in use for a long time, bugs might be found by users who place particular demands on the programs. Also, new versions are constantly being dreamed up by computer users and software engineers. Most software vendors appreciate user suggestions concerning possible improvements to their packages. *See also* BETA TEST *and* SOFTWARE.

Alternative computer technology

Scientists have always wondered if they could duplicate the processes of the human mind. In recent years, artificial intelligence (AI) has proven disappointing in this respect, but researchers haven't given up on it. Some computer scientists think *alternative computer technology* might provide a breakthrough in the quest for human-level AI. *See also* ARTIFICIAL INTELLIGENCE, ARTIFICIAL LIFE, COMPUTER CONSCIOUSNESS, COMPUTER GENERATIONS, *and* COMPUTER POWER.

Digital processes. Your PC employs *digital computer technology*. Its basic operating language, known as *machine language*, consists of only two possible states, represented by the digits 1 and 0. No matter how complex the function, graphic, or program, the workings of your computer can always be broken down into these two logic states.

Digital computers can be made fast and powerful. They can work with huge amounts of data, processing it at a rate of millions of digits per second, but there are certain things that digital computers aren't good at doing. Some researchers think that other approaches to computing deserve attention, even though digital technology has been very successful.

Alternative computer technology

Emotionally based thought processes like intuition are alien to digital machines, but this doesn't necessarily mean that machine emotion is impossible. Alternative avenues of "electronic thought" might someday produce a computer with consciousness—a sense of self-awareness—and possibly the ability to have hunches or feel sympathy. *See also* DIGITAL COMPUTER TECHNOLOGY *and* MACHINE LANGUAGE.

Analog processes. While a digital machine breaks everything down into discrete bits (binary digits), *analog computer technology* uses an entirely different approach.

Think of the square root of 2. This is called an irrational number because it can't be represented as a ratio of whole numbers. A digital computer will calculate this and get a value of about 1.414, but a decimal-number representation of the square root of 2 can never be exact. The best a digital machine can do is get close to its true value.

The square root of 2 is the length of the diagonal of a square measuring 1 unit on a side. Although you can construct it with the tools of classical geometry (an analog art) and get an exact rendition, you can't use it in ordinary arithmetic, the way you can use 1.414. Thus, you sacrifice qualitative perfection for quantitative utility. Perhaps similar give-and-take will prove necessary in the quest to develop a computer that thinks like a human being.

The diameter of a circle provides another example. Take a cylindrical object like a food can, and wrap a string around it. Mark the circumference on the string. Stretch the string out straight. The length between the two marks is π times the diameter of the can. A digital computer can only approximate the value of π, which is roughly equal to 3.14159.

Analog technology has been adapted to computer design. In fact, it was one of the earliest methods of computing. In recent years, however, it has been largely ignored. *See also* ANALOG COMPUTER TECHNOLOGY.

Optics. Visible light and energy at wavelengths near the visible (infrared and ultraviolet) offer interesting possibilities for the future of computer technology.

In CD-ROM (compact disk, read-only memory) storage, optical technology is used to increase the amount of data that can be stored in a given physical space. Tiny pits on a plastic diskette cause a laser beam to be reflected or absorbed at the surface. This allows encoding of 650 megabytes or more on a diskette less than five inches across.

Data can be transmitted at extremely high speeds, and in multiple channels, via lasers in glass fibers. This is known as *fiberoptic data*

Alternative computer technology

transmission and is used in some telephone systems today. Fiberoptic computer networks are being developed in some metropolitan areas.

The wires in computers might someday be replaced by optical fibers. The digital logic states now represented by electrical impulses or magnetic fields would be represented by light transmittivity instead. Certain materials change their optical properties very fast, and can hold a given state for a long time. *See also* BACTERIORHODOPSIN, CD-ROM, FIBEROPTIC CABLE, FIBEROPTIC DATA TRANSMISSION, *and* OPTICAL COMPUTER TECHNOLOGY.

Molecular computers. As integrated circuit (IC) technology has advanced, more and more digital logic gates have been packed into less and less physical space. Also, with refinements in magnetic media, the capacity of hard disks and diskettes has been increasing. What is the limit to all this?

According to conventional science, the smallest possible data storage unit is a single atom or subatomic particle. Consider a magnetic diskette. Logic state 1 might be represented by an atom "right-side-up," with its magnetic north pole facing upward and its magnetic south pole facing downward. Then logic state 0 would be represented by the same atom "upside-down," with the magnetic poles inverted.

Another possibility is a *single-electron memory (SEM)*. An example of a SEM is a substance in which the presence of an excess electron in an atom represents logic state 1, and the electrically neutral state of the atom represents logic state 0.

Some scientists think that computer chips might someday be grown in a lab, like the way experimental cultures of bacteria and viruses are grown. A name has even been coined for such a device: *biochip*. *See also* BIOCHIP, BUBBLE MEMORY, INTEGRATED CIRCUIT, MAGNETIC MEDIA, MOLECULAR COMPUTER TECHNOLOGY, *and* SINGLE-ELECTRON MEMORY.

Nanotechnology. As ICs get more circuitry packed into small packages, computer power increases. It also becomes possible to make tinier and tinier computers. With molecular computer technology, it might become possible to build computers so small that they can circulate inside the human body.

Imagine an "antibiotic" or "antiviral" computer, as small as bacteria, programmed to destroy certain disease-causing organisms. Such a machine would be something like an artificial white blood cell. *Nanotechnology* is the field of research devoted to the development and programming of microscopic machines. The prefix *nano-* means one billionth (0.000000001), in other words, extremely small.

Computerized "nanorobots" might assemble larger computers, saving humans much of the work now associated with manufacturing the

Alternative computer technology

machines. Nanotechnology might make it possible for you to have a PC that you can wear on your wrist, or even embed somewhere in your body. *See also* NANOTECHNOLOGY.

Neural networks. Neural network technology uses a design philosophy that differs radically from that of conventional digital computers. The idea is to mimic the structure and processes of a human brain. Neural networks are good at spotting patterns, which is important for forecasting. Rather than working with discrete binary digits, neural networks work with relationships among events.

Unless there's a malfunction, a digital machine does precise things with data. This takes time, but the outcome is always the same if the input stays constant. This is not the case with a neural network. A neural network can work faster than a digital machine, but to achieve speed, precision is sacrificed. The network sometimes overlooks details, but humans do that all the time! Neural networks learn from their mistakes, as people do.

The history of neural-network research has been tortuous. Heralded as a breakthrough when first introduced in the 1950s, it was all but forgotten as digital technology exploded in the 1970s. In the 1980s, neural networks made a comeback, but researchers were divided as to their potential. Some researchers offered apparent proof that neural networks could never lead to true AI.

The future of neural network technology is uncertain. To some researchers, it is just a diversion from the proven mainstream; to others it holds great promise. It has been successfully used in some applications. As long as there are mavericks in computer science, neural-network technology will have adherents. *See also* NEURAL NETWORK.

Hybrid computers. Multiple technologies can be combined in a single computer or system. For example, a digital computer might employ a neural-network expansion board for finding patterns or trends in data and an analog expansion board for solving problems that are best dealt with as continuous functions.

A fleet of nanorobots, circulating within your body, might fend off diseases such as malaria, tuberculosis, and HIV under the supervision of a nano-PC implanted beneath your skin. As resistant strains of disease-causing organisms evolve, the system could be programmed to find the "Achilles heel" of the new strain, and modify the plan of attack accordingly. *See also* HYBRID COMPUTER TECHNOLOGY.

Alt key

The *Alt key* on PC keyboards is usually located just to the left of the spacebar, as shown in the drawing. Many keyboards also have another Alt key immediately to the right of the spacebar.

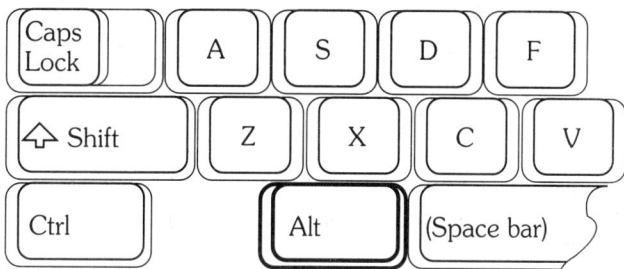

The Alt key is usually to the left of the spacebar.

When you hold down the Alt key and then press another key, various things happen, depending on the software you're using. In fact, Alt is an abbreviation for *alternate*. Holding down the Alt key causes other keys to perform alternate functions.

The Alt key also forms part of the Ctrl-Alt-Del rebooting scheme, which can be used to get a computer going again in the event of a crash. *See also* WARM BOOT.

Amateur radio

In most countries of the world, people can get government-issued licenses to send and receive messages via radio. In America, this hobby is called *amateur radio* or *ham radio*. There are more than 500,000 radio "hams" in the United States.

Who uses it? Anyone can use ham radio. People as young as 10 and as old as 100 communicate by talking, sending Morse code, or typing on computer terminals. This last method, typing text on a computer, is much like networking on a PC. In fact, hams have set up their own radio PC networks. This is a specialized form of *packet communications* known as *packet radio*.

Some radio hams chat about anything they can think of (except business, which is illegal to discuss via ham radio). Others like to practice their emergency-communications skills, so they can be of public service during crises like hurricanes, earthquakes, or floods. Still others like to go out into the wilderness and talk to people thousands of miles away while sitting out under the stars. Hams talk on the radio from their cars, boats, and even bicycles.

What do you need? The simplest ham radio station has a transceiver (transmitter/receiver), a microphone, and an antenna. A small ham-radio station fits on a desk and is about the size of a PC

Amateur radio

system, but accessories can be added until a ham "rig" is a large installation, comparable to a small commercial broadcast station.

Besides the hardware, you need to get a license to transmit on the amateur frequencies. The transmission of radio signals without a license is against the law, and can result in large fines. There are several levels, or *classes*, of ham radio licenses available in the U.S., all of which are issued by the Federal Communications Commission (FCC).

Ham radio and PCs. Ham radio is an electronics-oriented hobby. To some extent, so is personal computing. Radio hams are more likely to own PCs than non-hams. Also, computer users are more likely to be interested in ham radio than people who don't own or use a PC. If you are an experienced PC user, and especially if you're interested in the things that make it work, you shouldn't have trouble obtaining a ham license and getting on the air.

The diagram shows a computerized ham radio station. The PC can be used to network via packet radio with other hams who own computers. The station can be equipped for online telephone (*landline*) services. The PC can control the antennas for the station, and can keep a log of all stations that have been contacted. Most modern transceivers can be operated by computer, either locally or by remote control over the radio or landline.

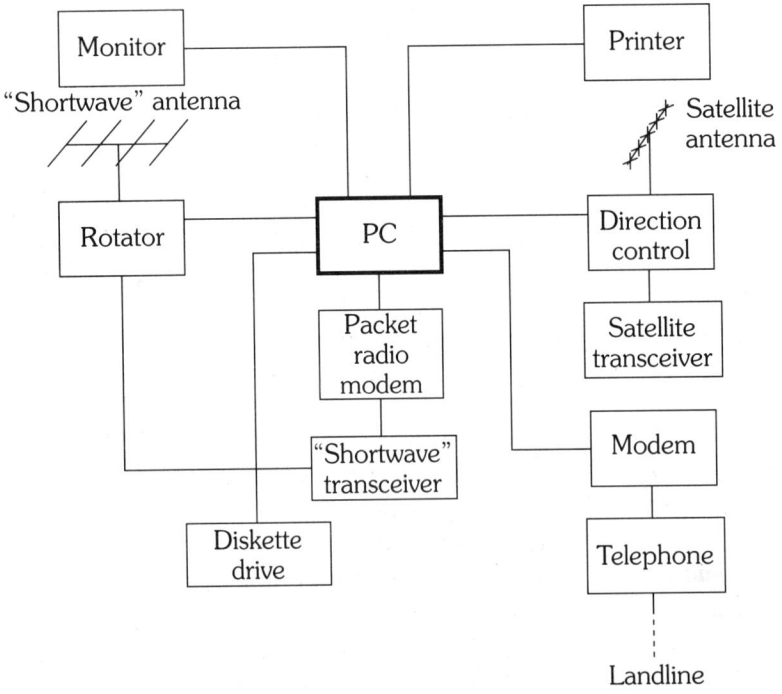

Amateur radio

Block diagram of a ham station with PC control.

For further information. A good way to learn about ham radio is to contact the headquarters of the American Radio Relay League. Write to

American Radio Relay League
225 Main Street
Newington, CT 06111

They publish books on all subjects in ham radio, as well as training materials and a monthly magazine called *QST* (which means "calling all radio amateurs"). The ARRL can tell you the location of the nearest ham radio club, where you can meet local hams and find out if this hobby is right for you. *See also* PACKET COMMUNICATIONS.

America Online

America Online, sometimes abbreviated *AOL*, is a computer online service. You connect your PC to the telephone line with a modem, load the necessary software, and you're in business. With America Online, you can obtain software, communicate with other users, get assistance from computer experts, and keep yourself informed about current events. There is also a gateway to the Internet, also known as the information superhighway.

Many computers are sold with all the necessary components for America Online, and perhaps other online services, already installed. You simply connect a telephone to the internal modem and click on the appropriate icon, and the computer guides you through the process. If your computer does not already have America Online installed, you can often find the necessary software bundled in computer magazines. You can also write or call AOL directly.

User friendliness. America Online employs a graphical user interface (GUI) that makes it easy to navigate. You don't need to memorize special commands; the software instructs you as you go along. AOL provides an extensive network of support, so you can get online help when you need it. It also provides assistance for the hearing-impaired. A comprehensive guidebook is available; the software will ask you if you want to order it when you first log in.

During the first month you are registered to America Online, you receive several free usage hours. Some computer companies have agreements with the network that give customers more than one month with several free hours each.

Departments. To gain access to the various departments that make up AOL, you just move the mouse until the cursor points to the icon representing that department. Some of the departments include the following:

➢ Lifestyles and interests

➢ News and finance

American National Standards Institute

- ➢ Games and entertainment
- ➢ Learning and reference
- ➢ Travel and shopping
- ➢ Computing and software

The "What's New" category carries announcements concerning the features soon to be added to the service. It's important to read this department in any online service, because the information superhighway is rapidly evolving.

For further information about AOL, write to

America Online
8619 Westwood Center Drive
Vienna, VA 22182

You can also register online; consult the PC magazines for the latest toll-free numbers. *See also* GRAPHICAL USER INTERFACE, NETWORK, *and* ONLINE SERVICE.

American National Standards Institute

The *American National Standards Institute*, or *ANSI*, is an industrial group in the United States whose purpose is to encourage companies to make things standardized, so they can be used easily and interchangeably.

When components and procedures are standardized, things work more smoothly than they do when things don't match. You've probably had the frustration of buying a flashlight bulb with a bayonet base, when your flashlight needed a screw-in bulb. Or maybe you couldn't find a replacement gas cap for your car's fuel tank. Perhaps you've worked with cable television and bought the wrong type of coaxial connector. The list goes on. Why must there be so many different ways of doing the same thing?

Custom versus interchangeable. When a company builds equipment with custom-made parts, they usually want to make it difficult or impossible to buy parts from anyone else. In that sense, it would seem to be a good way for a company to maximize its profits. But there is another side to the issue. When a company limits the options of buyers, a customer might go somewhere else to buy the main product. Then all potential profits are lost for that particular customer.

Consumers gossip among themselves. This is true now more than ever, because of PC networks. Word gets around, "Parts are hard to get for XYZ widgets." Then sales of XYZ widgets suffer, and the company's profits plummet.

Suppose that several companies agree to provide mutually interchangeable parts. Word gets around, "QRS widgets have parts you can get almost anywhere. They're easy and cheap to repair." Then the cooperating companies all end up with better sales than companies that insist on using specialized parts. A happy customer means higher profits.

Standardization and progress. The job of ANSI is to help companies decide on the specifications that commonly used components should have. Thus, for example, you'll often find 3.5-inch and 5.25-inch diskettes, but not 4.33-inch ones. Electronic component values, cable impedances, voltages for computer chips, and other parameters are standardized among all companies in this way. However, some things must, of necessity, be specialized. If carried to an extreme, an obsession with standardization would impede technological advancement.

While it's usually a good thing to standardize computer hardware, it isn't always the best thing for progress. New designs are always being developed, and sometimes the whole concept must change if the buyer is to benefit from the new and better technology. Some of the most innovative and powerful computer hardware is nonstandardized, because the companies have not yet had time to develop standards for it.

Software is not standardized to the same extent as hardware. With software, variety means versatility. Therefore, you will see thousands of different software packages in computer stores and mail-order advertisements. New software hits the market all the time, and most people agree, "The more the better." *See also* COMPATIBILITY, HARDWARE, *and* SOFTWARE.

Amusement robots

Computerized robots used mainly for entertainment are called *amusement robots*. They are employed by companies to show off new products and to attract customers. They also make great toys for children. They are common at industrial trade fairs, especially in Japan.

Small and smart. Most amusement robots are fairly small, but they are "smart machines," programmable with a PC. Amusement robots are almost always made to resemble something living, like an animal or human. As PCs keep getting more powerful, amusement robots get more agile and "smarter."

An example of an amusement robot is a mechanical mouse that navigates a maze. This isn't the same thing as the mouse you use to move the cursor or pointer on your computer screen; this robot is meant to look and act like the kind of mouse a cat likes to eat. The simplest such device bumps around randomly until it finds its way out of the maze by luck. A more sophisticated robot mouse might move along one wall of the maze, say the wall to its right, until it emerges. This technique will work with most mazes (see the drawing). The most advanced robot mice might scurry around your house, live in your walls, and be great fun for your kids. Cats might like them, too, although there would be an element of risk, both to the robots and to the cat.

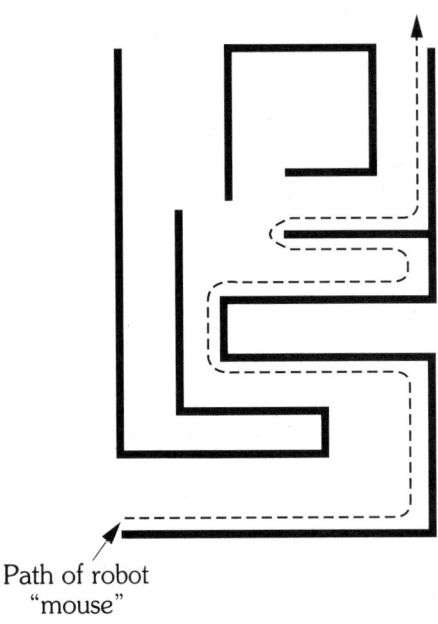

A robot "mouse" navigates a maze.

Androids. The most interesting amusement robots are *androids*, or machines with a human appearance. Robots of this type can greet customers in stores, operate elevators, or demonstrate products at conventions. One Japanese design, called *Wasubot*, would sit down at an organ or piano and ask, "What would you like me to play?" A person would place a musical score in front of the robot. The robot would stare at the page for a few moments, and then, with its mechanical arms, hands, and fingers, it would play the music. This machine seemed so smart, and so human-like, that it made some people nervous. *See also* PERSONAL ROBOTS *and* UNCANNY VALLEY.

Analog

The term *analog* means "continuously variable." An analog quantity can have any value within a certain range. *Digital* quantities, on the other hand, exist at defined levels or states, such as 0 and 1 or low and high.

Signals. Your voice, music, or almost any sound at all has a certain *waveform*. You can look at the waveform of any sound by connecting a microphone to an amplifier, and then connecting the output of the amplifier to an oscilloscope. If you whistle into the microphone, a simple analog wave will appear on the screen, as shown in graph A. Notice that this wave is smooth; it doesn't have "bumps" or "steps."

A/D and D/A. You might pass this signal through a device called an *analog-to-digital (A/D) converter*. Then, it will have only certain defined levels or values, as shown in graph B. This is a digital approximation of the analog waveform.

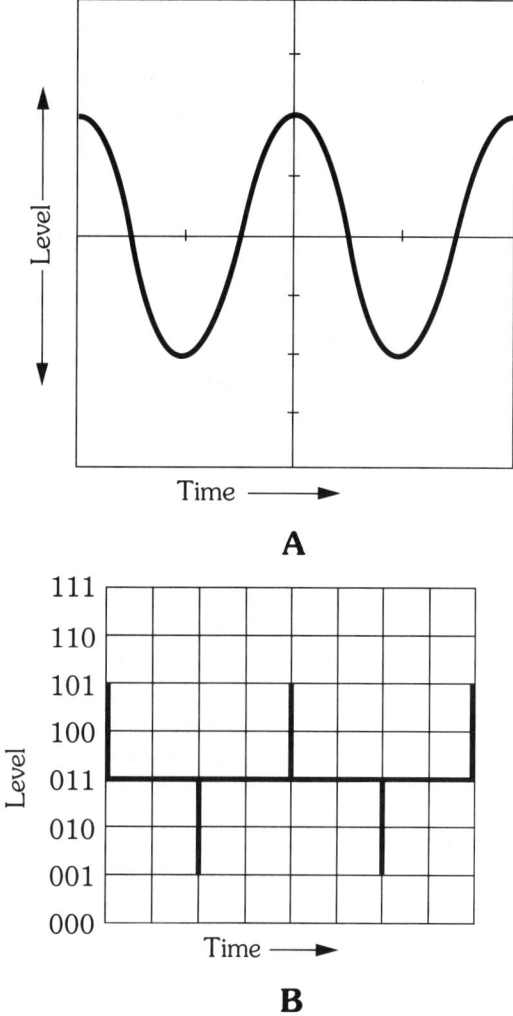

At A, an analog sine wave. At B, a digital form of the same wave.

If you want to recover the analog signal from a digital one, you must subject the impulses to *digital-to-analog (D/A) conversion*. If the wave in drawing B were passed through a D/A converter, the wave in drawing A, or something similar to it, would result. A compact disk

Analog computer technology

(CD) player, for example, uses D/A conversion to get music from the huge array of digital bits stored on the optical disk.

Close enough. It's much easier for a computer to work with a digital signal than an analog one. Humans, on the other hand, live in an analog world, in which continuously varying things are common and easy to deal with. These analog things, if fed directly to a digital computer, would totally confuse it.

To get an idea of how hard it is for a computer to "imagine" an analog signal, suppose you read this sentence into the microphone/oscilloscope speech viewer just described. You watch the jumble of waves on the screen. Now, write down the mathematical function that represents the waveforms you see. An approximation isn't good enough; it must be exact. That's impossible! Even the world's greatest mathematicians would have a terrible time with a problem like that. A digital computer would reject it as unworkable.

If you were to feed the voice signal through an A/D converter, a computer would store the sentence in a few memory chips. The resulting array of data bits would be, for all practical purposes, an exact rendition of the voice signal. This is how computers store and transfer digital voice information. *See also* ANALOG COMPUTER TECHNOLOGY, ANALOG-TO-DIGITAL CONVERSION, DIGITAL, *and* DIGITAL-TO-ANALOG CONVERSION.

Analog computer technology

Personal computers are digital machines; they work by combining logic ones and zeros. Computers don't have to work this way, however. The earliest computers were not digital, but used analog methods to make calculations.

Analog quantities vary over a continuous range, such as you see when you look at the readings on a mercury thermometer, a clock with "hands," or an old-fashioned car speedometer. Digital quantities, in contrast, are always precisely stated. Digital thermometers, clocks, and speedometers show the quantities in numeric form. *See also* ANALOG *and* DIGITAL.

Bit by bit. Digital data consists of bits that can have only two logic states. There is no confusion between the states 1 (true, high, or positive) and 0 (false, low, or negative).

The central processing unit (CPU) in your PC works with instructions that pass through in endless strings of logic states. The bits move at extreme speed: millions per second. In modern PCs, the frequency is on the order of many megahertz (MHz).

Analog computer technology

For a digital computer to work, every bit, or instruction, must be dealt with by the CPU. This takes time. Although modern PCs work fast, some computations require the CPU to go through billions of bits.

Suppose a CPU has a clock speed of 100 MHz. Then, generally, it can pass 100,000,000 bits per second. If a calculation makes the computer go through two billion (2,000,000,000) bits, it will take the CPU 20 seconds to do the problem. Delays of this sort are not uncommon, even in personal and small-business computing. While 20 seconds isn't a long time, it can seem that way to a PC user spoiled by a machine that comes up with an answer almost instantly, most of the time.

There is a limit to how fast any digital computer can work. Every single logic bit is important. In a string of 2,000,000,000 bits, one wrong digit can ruin the result. Every bit of data must be right, and the computer must process them all. This might make it seem as if errors would be common in digital computers; they work on billions of bits in every operating session. Actually, because of the precision of the technology, CPU errors are quite rare. *See also* CENTRAL PROCESSING UNIT, DIGITAL COMPUTER TECHNOLOGY, *and* MEGAHERTZ.

The slide rule. If you took chemistry, physics, or engineering courses before about 1970, you learned how to use a device called a *slide rule*. A slide rule is a primitive analog computer with two calibrated, logarithmic scales, one on a fixed "rule" and the other on a movable "slide." It also has a movable cursor. By moving the slide in and out of the rule and manipulating the cursor, you can multiply and divide numbers.

Some slide rules have scales for functions that occur often in scientific work. These include logarithms, exponentials, sine, cosine, and tangent. Slide rules are almost never used now, because digital pocket calculators are inexpensive, precise, and sold everywhere. Nevertheless, the slide rule has one great advantage over the calculator in certain situations: speed. If you use a digital calculator to find the product of 133,421 and 346,481,043, and race against a skilled slide-rule user, you will lose the race. A slide rule can't resolve the answer to the last digit, as the calculator can, but the slide rule gets an approximate product almost instantly. Using the calculator, you would have to press 17 buttons:

1 3 3 4 2 1 × 3 4 6 4 8 1 0 4 3 =

or

1 3 3 4 2 1 [Enter] 3 4 6 4 8 1 0 4 3 ×

depending on whether your calculator uses conventional or Polish notation. The slide-rule expert would slip the slide, move the cursor,

Analog computer technology

and tell you the answer to two or three significant figures, while you were still pressing buttons on your calculator.

Logic states. In a digital signal, the high logic state is usually represented by plus-five volts (+5 V). That's like three flashlight cells hooked up in series. The low logic state is represented by zero volts (0 V). This is shown in graph A. The voltages aren't critical: the high state might be anything between +4 V and +6 V, while the low state might be anywhere from –1 V to +2 V.

If a digital computer were to add the numbers 3 and 7, it must first convert the numbers to binary form. These numbers are 0011 and 0111, representing two strings of four bits each. These are added by binary arithmetic. This problem can be written down as

0011 + 0111 = 1010

Then the computer must change the binary number 1010 back to decimal form. In this case, the decimal equivalent is 10.

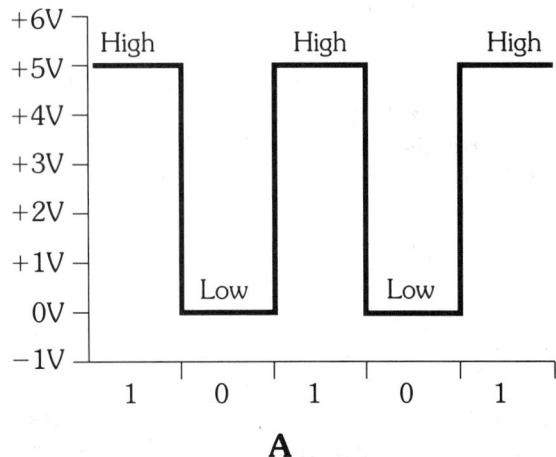

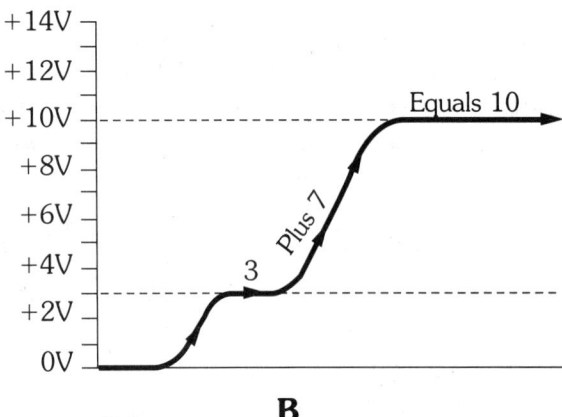

Digital highs and lows (A), and analog addition (B).

Adding 3 and 7 is a digital operation so elementary that first-grade schoolchildren can do it, but it takes many steps for a digital computer (most of which are glossed over in this discussion). The digital machine can't afford to skip a single one of the steps, nor to ignore a single logic 1 or logic 0. Doing so would result in a wrong answer. For example, here is the addition problem in binary with the second digit wrong in the answer:

0011 + 0111 = 1110

The decimal translation would be

3 + 7 = 14

Fortunately, errors like this do not occur often in digital computers (or among schoolchildren who have been taught the rules of addition), but they are possible. *See also* BINARY NUMBER SYSTEM.

Variable voltage. Suppose the voltage were continuously variable, say from 0 V to +20 V. Then the numbers 3 and 7 could be represented as +3 V and +7 V. The voltages could be set by adjusting smooth-acting controls, like the volume knobs on a hi-fi stereo system. Adding the numbers would be done by connecting the voltages in series. It would, of course, produce +10 V, as shown in graph B. This is an analog way of doing a digital computation.

There would be no data bits for the computer to grind through, and there would be no need to convert from decimal to binary numbers and back again. Therefore, the CPU would be spared a lot of busywork. It would go straight to the solution, rather than changing from decimal to binary and back again, and doing binary operations over and over. And, while there would always be a small interpolation error, the machine could not make a major mistake, such as adding 3 and 7 to get 14. This is a simple example of an analog computation.

Tradeoffs. Analog computers are sometimes better than digital ones. In other cases, digital computers are better. Some of the advantages of analog computers include the following:

➢ They work at high speed.

➢ They can provide shortcuts.

➢ They can sometimes more accurately represent the "real world."

➢ They are better suited to certain calculations.

Drawbacks of analog computers include the following:

➢ There is always some error.

➢ Most common problems are suited to digital computers.

Analog computer technology

> ➢ Analog machines lack memory capacity.
> ➢ The technology has been largely given up for dead.

Why all digital? You might ask, "If analog computers still hold promise, why are all PCs digital these days?" The answer is twofold.

First, we've adapted ourselves to digital computers. Our lifestyles produce "digital problems" (such as word processing and accounting); it's no wonder that they usually have "digital solutions." For the advanced theoretical scientist, things are different, but most people don't work with chaos theory, models of the universe, time-space transformations, and the like.

Second, digital technology gets all the attention. Because of this, digital methods are blindly applied without thinking about the alternatives. Many people scorn analog technology as a relic of the past, with no hope of ever again being useful for anything. This is a classical and tragic error of collective thought; it has been repeated by civilizations throughout history. People reject old ideas out of hand, perhaps because they fear ridicule. Then some maverick finds an efficient way to solve a strange new problem using supposedly archaic methods, and everyone is amazed.

The future of analog computing. Analog computers are still good for solving differential equations. They were used during the Second World War to help aim antiaircraft guns, and for locating the launch sites of German V-2 missiles.

Digital computers continue to get faster, more powerful, and less expensive. As this happens, they become able to handle the types of problems previously done better by analog computers. The heyday of analog computing, which peaked during the late 1950s and early 1960s, might be over. But, like Art Deco architecture, it might enjoy a revival, finding esoteric uses that no one has even dreamed of yet, much less pursued.

The savvy computer user keeps an open mind, and tries to be aware of all the alternatives for solving the problems of the future. Don't be too surprised if you hear about analog techniques, and other alternative methods of computer design, in the next few years. One interesting avenue of research is in the field of optical computer technology. Another possibility is a revival of the hybrid computer, designed to help a digital "electronic brain" interact with, and understand, an analog world. Still another is the neural network. All these fields are of interest to scientists pursuing artificial intelligence. *See also* ALTERNATIVE COMPUTER TECHNOLOGY, ARTIFICIAL INTELLIGENCE, HYBRID COMPUTER, NEURAL NETWORK, *and* OPTICAL COMPUTER TECHNOLOGY.

Analogical reasoning

Before computers were cheap and readily available, forecasting and modeling were done in the human imagination, sometimes with the aid of calculators. Today, computers augment the human mind to produce *analogical reasoning*. This type of reasoning is used in all kinds of scenarios, from predicting the spread of infectious diseases to imitating the behavior of electronic circuits.

Parallel worlds. In analogical reasoning, a computer creates an artificial world, based on data that people give it. Then the artificial world is explored in an attempt to find out how the real world will behave under a variety of conditions. The better the input data that is supplied to the computer, the more closely the computer can draw parallels, and the better the results. Quality and accuracy also depend on how well the software is written.

Analogical reasoning works like expert systems. Facts are gathered, and then cause-and-effect relationships are programmed into the machine. The more people know about the situation, the more accurate the outcome. There is always some uncertainty, however, because there are many variables, some of which interact in ways not well understood.

Our knowledge of real-world scenarios can be categorized broadly in four ways: good, fair, poor, and minimal.

Good knowledge. Electronic circuits behave in ways that can be predicted with great accuracy. So do most systems in which there are few variables, or in which the laws of physics clearly apply.

Suppose you're building a hi-fi audio amplifier. You need to know the values of the resistors, capacitors, and other components. What kind of transformer will work best at the input? How much output power do you need? How much distortion are you willing to tolerate? You can use electronic circuit design software to create a model of your amplifier and give it several practical tests without ever touching a single piece of hardware. You can be confident that, once you've ironed out the bugs from the design using good modeling software, the hardware will work when you put the components together.

Although the outcome in this situation is predictable, it is often too complex to be figured out without the help of a computer. There are too many variables for a human being to keep track of them all, but computers are good at juggling massive arrays of data. When the functions are precise, the computer model works very well.

Fair knowledge. The second type of situation involves phenomena that we know something, but not a lot, about. We have identified the variables and are somewhat acquainted with how they operate.

Analogical reasoning

Consider the ecosphere (the earth's environment). What will happen to our planet in the next 20, 50, or 200 years?

Cars, buses, and trucks produce carbon dioxide and carbon monoxide. These gases tend to raise the temperature of the earth because of the greenhouse effect. A computer can be programmed to figure out, based on current trends, how much the earth's temperature is likely to rise over the next several decades. The variables include population growth, the increase in the number of cars and trucks, fuel-efficiency improvement, miles driven per vehicle, and the type of fuel used.

Although our knowledge of this situation is only fair, it keeps getting better. As we learn more about it, we can revise the data supplied to computers. Sometimes a small change in the input data produces a dramatic change in the output. This is one of the reasons why scientific theories can change so radically in such a short time.

Poor knowledge. In other situations, variables are known to exist, but we haven't figured out their effects very well. An example of this is the occurrence of ice ages at intervals in geologic history. Scientists agree almost 100 percent that these events have taken place, but they disagree as to why they happen.

Will there be another ice age? If so, when will it begin? Will the onset be gradual, or will it come suddenly? There are numerous theories about what caused ice ages in the past, and about what might cause more in the future. Galactic dust, changes in the heat output of the sun, volcanic eruptions, meteorite impacts, and irregularities in the earth's orbit are some of the variables that might be involved. Or perhaps the whole thing is best explained by chaos theory as a system that is being "overdriven." Computers have been used to show that some systems are out of balance all the time, and that this causes wild fluctuations in behavior.

A computer can work with variables and effects in a scenario like this, but the outcomes can't be taken too seriously because we aren't very sure of the facts. Again, a small difference in the input can make a tremendous difference in the resulting model, and therefore, in the predictions about what will happen in the system.

Minimal knowledge. Finally, there are situations we don't even know exist. Obviously, it's impossible to give any concrete examples, but we can pose questions. Is the earth a complex organism with its own built-in disease-protection mechanisms? Do energy fields in the galaxy have an effect on the evolution of civilizations on earth? Maybe the biggest, most mysterious question is also the oldest: How did human beings evolve or arrive on this planet?

Analogical reasoning can be used to analyze the unknown and mysterious, but this is done without expecting anything in particular.

Occasionally such games will lead to scientific breakthroughs. This happened when Benoit Mandelbrot tried to analyze the behavior of noise in electrical circuits. Much of modern chaos theory arose from the bizarre and unexpected results of his and his colleagues' experiments.

How well will it work? Analogical reasoning works better in some situations than in others. Generally, those scenarios and problems that lend themselves to the scientific method can be modeled better than esoteric or philosophical things. Physical sciences and mathematics are best suited to analogical methods. Fringe sciences such as extrasensory perception (ESP) seem to defy computer analysis altogether.

There's strength in statistical numbers. It's easier to forecast via computer software what will happen to a large population than to predict what will happen to any single person in that population. The best way to see how well analogical reasoning will work in a system is to test it several times and find out how accurately it forecasts events, without placing any reliance or expectation on the results.

See also ARTIFICIAL INTELLIGENCE, COMPUTER-ASSISTED INSTRUCTION, ELECTRONIC CIRCUIT DESIGN SOFTWARE, EXPERT SYSTEMS, FORECASTING, *and* VIRTUAL REALITY.

Analog-to-digital conversion

Any analog, or continuously variable, signal can be converted into a string of pulses whose amplitudes have a finite number of states. This is called *analog-to-digital (A/D) conversion*. In computers, A/D converters are used to change voices, pictures, music, or test-instrument readings into signals that the machine can understand. In their natural, or "real-world," form, most things are analog, but the computer needs to have digital data.

Digital data has many advantages over analog data. Digital signals are less susceptible to interference than analog signals. Also, it is possible to get many more digital signals into a circuit or onto a communications line than is the case with analog data. *See also* ANALOG *and* DIGITAL.

Taking samples. An A/D converter works by checking the level of an analog signal every so often, and then rounding it off to the nearest standard level. This is called *sampling*. An analog signal is like a ramp, while a digital signal is like a staircase, with each stair being one sample. Both the ramp and the staircase will get you where you want to go; they just do it differently.

Some A/D converters have only a few levels, or *states*, in their outputs; others have many. The number of states is called the

Analog-to-digital conversion

sampling resolution. Some A/D converters take many samples every second, while others take only a few. The number of samples taken per second is the *sampling rate.*

Sampling resolution. In most digital signals, the sampling resolution is a power of two. This allows the signal to be represented in binary form, as zeros and ones.

A sampling resolution of $2^3 = 8$ (see the drawing) is good enough for voice transmission, and is the standard resolution for commercial digital voice circuits. A resolution of $2^4 = 16$ is adequate for compact disks used in advanced hi-fi systems. For video signals, such as might be used in high-speed animated graphics or virtual reality, the sampling resolution must be higher, such as $2^5 = 32$, or maybe even $2^6 = 64$.

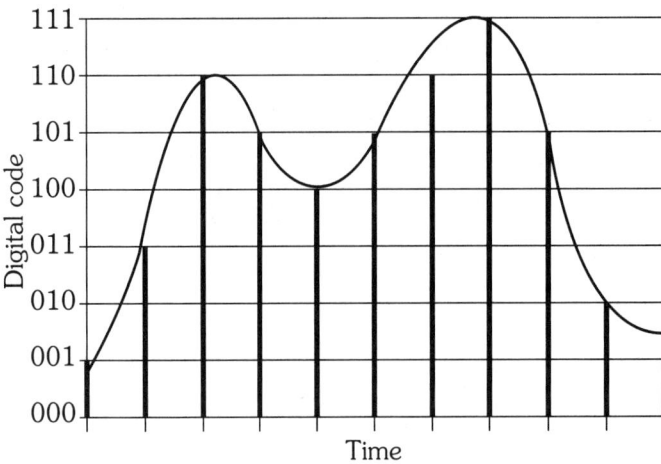

Analog-to-digital conversion changes analog signal (the curve) into digital levels (the vertical bars).

Sampling rate. The efficiency with which a signal can be digitized depends on how often a sample is taken. In general, the sampling rate must be at least twice the highest data frequency.

For an audio signal with components as high as 3 kilohertz (kHz), or 3000 cycles per second, the minimum sampling rate is 6 kHz, or one sample every 167 microseconds. The commercial voice standard is 8 kHz, or one sample every 125 microseconds. For hi-fi digital transmission, the standard sampling rate is 44.1 kHz, or one sample every 22.7 microseconds. This is based on a maximum audio frequency of 20 kHz, the approximate upper limit of the human hearing range.

In high-speed graphics or virtual reality, the sampling rate might need to be several megahertz (MHz), or millions of cycles per second. In general, the faster the sampling rate, the more realistic the graphic images will be. *See also* DIGITAL-TO-ANALOG CONVERSION.

Analytical engine

The *analytical engine* was a primitive calculating machine designed by Charles Babbage in the 1830s. Actually, Babbage never quite perfected the thing. The idea was to use punched cards to make and print out calculations, so Babbage was the first engineer to work on a true digital calculator.

Problems. Imagine trying to build a computer before the Civil War! Obviously, Babbage was up against some big obstacles. One of the main problems for Babbage was that electricity was not available. The machines had to use mechanical parts exclusively. These wore out with frequent, repetitive use. Besides that, they were noisy.

Another problem was that Babbage liked to dismantle things completely and then start all over again with new designs, rather than saving his old machines and improving them gradually. He wasted a lot of time by making unnecessary work for himself.

Still another problem was the fact that Babbage was too far ahead of his time. He was almost certain to arouse either ridicule if he failed to build a computer that worked, or suspicion and fear if he succeeded wildly. In fact, he did as well as anyone probably could have, given the circumstances he faced.

A smart machine? During the research-and-development phase of the analytical engine, some people thought that artificial intelligence (AI) had finally been discovered. They were right in one way: Someone had imagined it. After all, "a journey of a thousand miles begins with one step." Someone had at least seen the path. But that was all.

The Countess of Lovelace wrote "software" for Babbage's machine, thinking it could play board games like checkers or chess. From the analytical engine's digital states, she thought, all sorts of ideas could arise. She believed that the concrete (a machine) and the abstract (the human mind) had finally been linked. Even today, however, we are a long way from designing a machine that really works like the human mind. Still, checkers-playing machines and chess-playing machines have at least been built.

A new attitude. Babbage's analytical engine, despite all its limitations, was important as a catalyst for a general change in attitudes toward machines. Rather than dismissing AI as ridiculous and impossible, people began to believe that it might someday exist. Science fiction writers wasted no time in taking advantage of this new, vast field of weird possibilities. The quest for AI had begun—a full generation before the American people elected Abraham Lincoln as their sixteenth president! *See also* ARTIFICIAL INTELLIGENCE, CHECKERS-PLAYING COMPUTER, *and* CHESS-PLAYING COMPUTER.

Analytical graphics

In mathematics, physics, and engineering, charts and graphs are often used in theses, articles, and books. *Analytical graphics* refers to the use of a computer to make these charts and graphs.

Accuracy over beauty. Analytical graphics is a field developed by scientists, for scientists. It's not that important how attractive the graphs and charts are, what matters is that they be precise. They must tell scientists just what they need to know.

The drawing shows an example of an analytical graph. The open squares show rainfall amounts in some imaginary place for each month during some year. The solid dots show cumulative rainfall totals at the beginning of every month, and also on the last day of December. These data are the results of measurements.

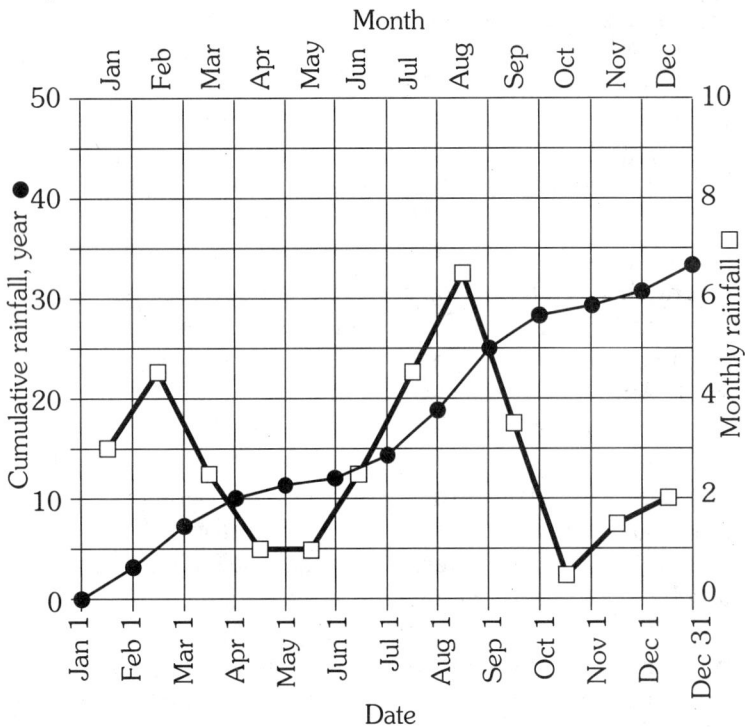

An analytical graph of rainfall during a hypothetical year.

The curves are generated by the computer. Many analytical graphics packages have curve-fitting programs. The simplest "curves" connect plotted points with straight lines. More complex programs can actually make guesses about the curve most likely to fit the points. Such a curve is called a *Bezier curve*.

Other forms of analytical graphics programs help engineers make technical drawings and diagrams. For example, there are programs tailored to the needs of electronics engineers and radio amateurs.

Anchoring

These programs contain clip-art symbols for resistors, capacitors, transistors, and other electronic components. Architects can use specialized software to create blueprints. Precision, and the ability to deal with detail and complexity, are characteristic of these programs. *See also* ADOBE ILLUSTRATOR *and* BEZIER CURVE.

When beauty counts. Graphs like the one in the drawing tend to look "technical," and this turns off, and sometimes even scares, nonscientific people. When you want to make charts and graphs look good, say for an advertisement or brochure, you will probably want to use *presentation graphics*. The graph in the drawing might be great for meteorologists, but it would not impress tourists looking at a brochure about the place. *See also* PRESENTATION GRAPHICS.

Anchoring

Anchoring involves using the cursor on your monitor screen to define or highlight certain parts of text or graphics. You can anchor the cursor or pointer, and then drag an image or portion of text from one place to another.

In word processing. This article was written using a word processor called XyWrite under DOS. All the italic parts of this text *were defined* by anchoring the cursor at the start of the word or word group, and then un-anchoring it at the end. When the cursor was anchored, a command was given to the PC, telling it to generate italics. When the cursor was un-anchored, a second command was given, telling the computer to resume normal type.

The illustration shows an example of a section of text that has been defined by anchoring and un-anchoring the cursor. There are often two or more different ways of anchoring, depending on whether the text already exists or is being created. To generate the figure shown here, the text was pulled from a file on hard disk. Then the cursor was moved to the point marked "Anchor cursor," and the F1 key was pressed. The cursor was dragged along the text using the arrow keys until it reached the point marked "Un-anchor cursor." Then the F1 key was pressed again. This defined the region of text to be changed. To get underlined boldface text, the appropriate XyWrite command was given by holding down the Ctrl and 5 keys simultaneously for a moment. (These commands are peculiar to XyWrite, and will not generally work in other programs. For information about the commands, menus, and icons in your own word processing package, consult the instructions.)

With a GUI. When you're working with a graphical user interface (GUI), you'll probably use the mouse to anchor the cursor or pointer. You do this by moving to a certain point and then clicking the mouse. You can then define, drag, or otherwise modify the image on the screen. Various things can be done to the text or image by issuing certain commands to the software.

AND gate

Anchor cursor

Historically, people have been fond of the idea of building a robot in the human image. Such a machine would have two legs. **In practice, a two-legged robot is hard to design. It tends to have a bad sense of balance; it will fall over easily.** You can't build a chair that will stay upright on just two legs; a robot is the same way.

Defining a portion of text or graphics.

Un-anchor cursor

Whenever you anchor a cursor or pointer, always be sure to un-anchor it when you have completed the operation. Otherwise, the changes you specify might not be made or might be made to the wrong text. *See also* GRAPHICAL USER INTERFACE *and* HIGHLIGHTING.

AND gate

An *AND gate* is a digital logic circuit with two or more inputs and one output. It performs the logical AND operation, also known as *conjunction*. Logic gates are used extensively in digital computers and other electronic devices.

The output of an AND gate is high, or logic 1 ("true") if and only if all of the inputs are high. If any of the inputs are low, or logic 0 ("false"), then the output is low.

The schematic symbol for an AND gate, along with its logical truth table, is shown in the drawing. *See also* EXCLUSIVE-NOR GATE, EXCLUSIVE-OR GATE, INVERTER, NOR GATE, *and* OR GATE.

A	B	C
0	0	0
0	1	0
1	0	0
1	1	1

AND gate schematic symbol and truth table.

Animation

Computer graphics can show motion by flashing a series of images in rapid succession, just like film-based motion pictures. Sound can also be included. The creation of "computer movies" is known as *animation*. Animation is used in video games, training systems, presentations, industrial design, and engineering.

Eye lag. Your eyes don't perceive things instantaneously. It seems that way, but each image takes about $\frac{1}{20}$ of a second to be processed by your eyes and brain. When you watch a movie or look at a television screen, the images are flashed at intervals of less than $\frac{1}{20}$ second. This is how TV and movies can depict motion realistically. If not for the eye-lag effect, a movie would look like a flickering series of still pictures, and watching a TV screen would make you dizzy.

The same thing is true with a computer monitor. The image on your monitor is a series of horizontal lines, scanned from left to right and top to bottom, the way you read a book. The scanning is so fast that you see a continuous image, but actually, a spot of variable brightness is constantly racing across the screen. The image is formed as the spot travels from left to right, as shown by the heavy lines in the drawing. The spot is blanked out as it moves from right to left, when it is finished with one line and is ready to start another, as shown by the dotted lines in the drawing.

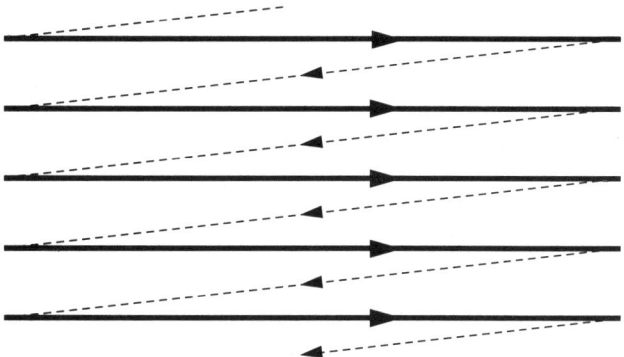

Path of a spot as it scans a video image.

Like an old cartoon. When you see a still image on your monitor, the spot goes through the same brightness variations every time it sweeps down the screen. If the image changes slightly with each sweep of the spot down the screen, you will see motion instead. To create the impression of smooth motion, a computer animator must create a series of images, each a little different from the other.

Before computer animation, someone had to draw each picture in a cartoon for a movie or television show. A cartoon has about 30 pictures per second. For a cartoon lasting three minutes (180 seconds), that means drawing 5400 (3 × 180) separate pictures!

Animism

Computerized animation also requires this many drawings, but instead of having to create all the images with colored pencils and paints, the animator can generate them with software. Even if you're not artistic, you can create cartoons on a computer, once you learn how to use the software.

Computer requirements. Many different programs are available that allow the creation of animated graphics on a PC. Generally, a machine with at least an 80486 or 68030 microprocessor is needed. The clock speed should be as high as possible. The faster and more powerful the microprocessor, the more instructions it can handle per second, and the more realistic the animation can be.

It's best to have a high-resolution, color SVGA (Super Video Graphics Array) monitor with a diagonal measure of 14 inches or more. A mouse is mandatory. The addition of a CD-ROM drive is a tremendous asset. The hard disk should have ample capacity, preferably at least 50MB (megabytes) of free space. A good animation program, such as CorelDRAW 4, needs a minimum 4MB of RAM, but 8MB is preferable. A high-level animation program generally requires at least 8MB of RAM, with 16MB or more being preferable.

Advanced animation. Just as graphics software has made it possible for any PC user to create cartoons, it allows the pros to make better cartoons than ever before. The movie *Star Wars* showed how fantastic computerized animation could be. This movie, in fact, revolutionized animation.

What does the future hold for computer animation? One possibility is *holographic animation*. Using this technique, you might create three-dimensional cartoons in a dark room. This has been done on a large scale at some rock music concerts. Another fascinating field is *virtual reality*, in which the animator creates fantasy worlds that seem real. See also CD-ROM, COMPUTER-AIDED DESIGN, COMPUTER-ASSISTED INSTRUCTION, DRAW PROGRAM, MULTIMEDIA, PAINT PROGRAM, PRESENTATION GRAPHICS, SOUND TECHNOLOGY, *and* VIRTUAL REALITY.

Animism

People in some countries, such as Japan, traditionally believe that the force of life exists in things like stones, lakes, and clouds, as well as in people, animals, and plants. These people define "aliveness" by degree or extent, not in terms of a yes/no dichotomy. This belief is called *animism*.

One of the most significant questions in the field of artificial intelligence (AI) is this: Will we ever be able to build a machine that is actually alive? Along with this question, there is a more philosophical one: What, exactly, makes something living different than something nonliving? In other words, how do animate things differ from inanimate things?

As early as the middle of the 19th century, a machine was conceived that was thought by a few people with vivid imaginations to have some sense of aliveness. This was Charles Babbage's *analytical engine*. Back then, very few people seriously thought that a contraption made of wheels and gears could have life, but today's massive computers, and the promise of more sophisticated ones being built every year, have renewed interest in the idea. *See also* ANALYTICAL ENGINE, ANTHROPOMORPHISM, ARTIFICIAL INTELLIGENCE, ARTIFICIAL LIFE, *and* COMPUTER CONSCIOUSNESS.

ANSI

See AMERICAN NATIONAL STANDARDS INSTITUTE.

Anthropomorphism

Sometimes, machines seem almost human. This is especially true of advanced computers and robots. People *anthropomorphize* when they think of a computer or robot as human.

Almost like me! Robots with humanoid form (such as the kind that have a head and arms) are easy to anthropomorphize because they look a lot like us. Science-fiction movies and novels have made extensive use of anthropomorphisms with characters like the robot C3PO in *Star Wars*. The most human-like robots, called *androids*, are seen often in science-fiction movies. Androids are convenient in science fiction because the roles can be played by people; there's no need to go to the trouble of throwing together a lot of hardware and using special effects to make it look like a smart robot.

Anthropomorphisms can also take place on a purely psychological level with computers. This happens in *2001: A Space Odyssey*. The spaceship in this novel is controlled by a computer named "Hal." Dave, the commander of the ship, talks with Hal, and Hal responds with a soothing, human voice. But Hal becomes paranoid and tries to kill Dave by refusing to let his shuttle into the main ship. Dave braves the vacuum of space without a pressure suit, thereby getting back into the ship and disabling Hal. All the while Hal speaks to Dave in that calm voice, until its very gentleness gives you the shivers.

Chatting with computers. Can computers ever get so much like us that we think of them as living minds? Can a human being become good friends with a computer? Or enemies? Some owners of PCs sometimes think of the machines as companions.

In some ways, computers really are like people. We depend on them. They are so much fun, sometimes, that we get a "warm fuzzy" feeling from them. This is especially likely to happen when computer users get online and use PCs to communicate with other people. We might grow fond of our computers, but can people really love machines? Today, anyone claiming to be in love with a computer is probably joking. But will this be true in 50 years? In 100 years?

While some people enjoy machines and are comfortable with them, other people get nervous around computers that seem too human-like. Such people have a mental block against anthropomorphisms. *See also* ANIMISM, ARTIFICIAL INTELLIGENCE, ARTIFICIAL LIFE, *and* UNCANNY VALLEY.

Anti-aliasing

In some images, especially in bitmapped graphics, diagonal or curved lines get a jagged appearance because the image is not continuous, but is made up of many small bits called *pixels* (picture elements). You've probably seen such images in advertisements, technical papers, or instruction manuals. The vertical and horizontal lines appear perfectly straight, while curves and slanted lines have the *jaggies*, as shown in the drawing at A. Often, this is not a problem, because it doesn't hurt the image clarity. (Some people actually like the effect.) However, to minimize or remove these slight flaws in the image, *anti-aliasing* is used.

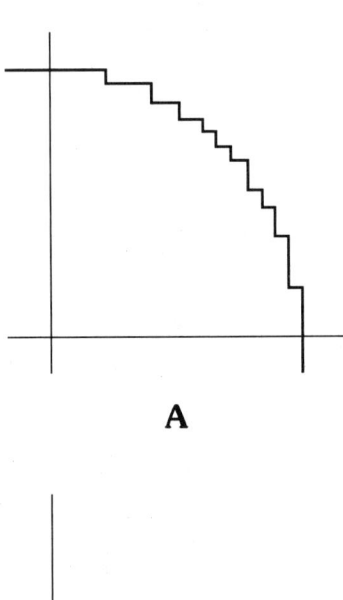

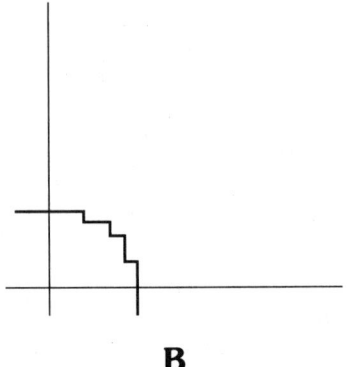

Mild (A) and severe (B) jaggies.

Jaggies are the most severe in images that have a lot of detail and/or sharp curves. The finer the detail in an image, the bigger the pixels relative to the information to be shown. You can see this effect by comparing A and B in the drawing. In both cases, the fineness of the bitmap is the same. The vertical and horizontal lines are not affected, but the 90° arcs are noticeably distorted. At B, the distortion is so severe that it doesn't look much like an arc at all.

Reducing the jaggies. When you're preparing a document with bitmapped images, and you don't have access to an anti-aliasing process, you should make the original image as large as possible. It can then be reduced by photocopying. When the image is reduced to the size intended for publication, the jaggies will be reduced also, and will be much less noticeable. *See also* BITMAPPED GRAPHICS, JAGGIES, *and* PIXEL.

Anticipatory Sciences

Anticipatory Sciences is a group of *futurists*, or people who make predictions about the future of technology. They have made some interesting forecasts about computers and artificial intelligence (AI).

Faster and faster. Some futurists think science will keep moving ahead at a faster and faster rate in coming years. This was the rule during the 20th century. In the realm of personal computing, the last quarter of the century saw a technological explosion unprecedented in history. It has been suggested that machines will someday have the ability to do science research. It might even become possible for a computer/robot system to design and build ever-more-advanced computer/robots. Thus, technological progress might, quite literally, acquire a spirit of its own.

If self-replicating computers of this sort evolve, people's homes might become fully automated. Cars might be driven by computers, practically eliminating accidents. Many skilled jobs might become obsolete. This has given rise to fears that people will be put out of work by machines, a phenomenon that has taken place in the past as a result of technological development.

National Robot Sports League? One rather bizarre scenario is a sports league in which the players are computer-controlled robots instead of people. Different corporations could form teams with machines of their own design, playing them off against each other, thereby determining, in an entertaining way, which designs are best.

Of course, PC-controlled personal robots would make great toys for kids. If a youth football team happened to be short by one player, a robot could play as a substitute, perhaps remotely controlled by the coach via a PC. (The skill level could be adjusted by one of the

Apple Computer, Inc.

parents, so a junior league didn't end up with an NFL-caliber linebacker running wild.)

Doubts and fears. Some futurists are skeptical about technology in general. They doubt that machines will evolve like biological life forms. They say that no machine can get smarter than its makers, either individually or collectively. Their reasoning is simple: Only God can create true life. But that belief is only a theory, and has not been scientifically proven either true or false.

Other futurists are afraid of what might happen if computers become able to evolve on their own. Will the machines become peace-loving, and teach us humans to get along? Or will evil somehow get hold of them? Even if computers evolve without a single wicked logic gate in their microprocessors, it only takes one malicious programmer to turn a computer or network into a monstrosity. This has been demonstrated many times already in the history of personal computing. In the future, a single potent computer virus could cause a social catastrophe of unprecedented proportions.

Time will tell. Time will be the final arbiter in the quest for human-level AI. Most likely, the truth is different from, and more fascinating than, anything people have imagined. In the minds of many futurists, the prospect of adventure and excitement outweighs the potential dangers of computer technology. *See also* ARTIFICIAL INTELLIGENCE, ARTIFICIAL LIFE, *and* VIRUS.

Antivirus program

See VACCINE *and* VIRUS.

Apple Computer, Inc.

In 1976, two computer hobbyists, Steven Jobs and Steven Wozniak, started a maverick computer company. Their dream was to make computers available to average people. This was the beginning of *Apple Computer, Inc.*

Against the grain. Cynics say that U.S. technology has fallen behind that of Japan and Europe. Whether or not this is true in general, it can't be said of Apple. Jobs and Wozniak were convinced that computers could, and would, become everyday appliances, and that anybody could use them. They stuck to their beliefs even though many people doubted them.

As recently as the mid-1970s, the idea of a "personal computer" seemed farfetched. A desktop unit that a college student could afford and use, with 120 megabytes on a hard disk, seemed like science fiction. Now such things are out of date. College students are purchasing machines with many times that hard disk capacity.

Apple Talk

Firsts. Apple was first to introduce the graphical user interface (GUI) for personal computing use. Actually, Xerox Corporation had been working with the concept, but apparently did not at first see its potential for marketing to the public. Jobs and Wozniak did, and this led to the *Macintosh* line of computers, the first of which became available in the mid-1980s. Many small businesses, especially if they are involved in publishing, use Macintosh computers, known as "Mac" for short.

It didn't take long for competitors to see how popular the GUI had become. This led to the development of Windows software for IBM-compatible PCs.

Apple has continued to branch off into new and experimental fields. They pioneered desktop publishing and have been a leader in speech recognition and speech synthesis systems. *See also* GRAPHICAL USER INTERFACE, IBM-COMPATIBLE PCS, INTERNATIONAL BUSINESS MACHINES, *and* MACINTOSH.

AppleTalk

AppleTalk is a feature of Macintosh PCs that allows you to connect them together into a local area network (LAN). An AppleTalk system is a form of peer-to-peer network. This is ideal for corporations, from "Mom and Pop" shops to companies that occupy whole buildings.

Hooking up. On the back of the Macintosh, you'll find an AppleTalk port. The instruction manuals tell you where it is and what it looks like. You just hook the cables up, along with little circuit boxes, following the instructions. The hardware is called *LocalTalk*. An AppleTalk LAN is a *bus network*: there is one main line, and all the PCs and peripherals branch off from it.

Recently, it has become possible to use IBM-compatible PCs with Macintosh computers in AppleTalk LANs. For installation details, check the manuals for both the Macintosh and the IBM-compatible machine.

Features. The big advantages of AppleTalk are that it's *easy to install and use*, and it's *not very expensive*. It is also versatile; you can install LANs of just about any size you're likely to need in a small or medium-sized company.

AppleTalk networks are often used in offices where there are several computers and one or two high-resolution printers. A good example is a magazine publisher. Articles and graphics are stored on diskettes. An editor can put a diskette in one of the Macs, call up an article, display it on screen, and then have a laser printer make a hard copy of it to send the author for proofreading.

Application

Using special hardware, you can connect two or more AppleTalk LANs together to create a larger LAN, if you're lucky enough to have a small company that grows big in a hurry. The computers in each LAN can be spread out over an area 1000 feet in diameter. With multiple LANs, this range increases to a half-mile or more, making AppleTalk technology practical for college and university campuses, as well as large industrial complexes. *See also* BUS NETWORK, IBM-COMPATIBLE PCS, LOCAL AREA NETWORK, MACINTOSH, *and* PEER-TO-PEER NETWORK.

Application

An *application* is a task for which you turn to your PC for help. The term is most often used in reference to software. For example, word processing is an often-used form of application software. Within a word processing software package, there can be sub-applications such as grammar checking and spell checking.

Some applications involve specialized hardware in addition to software. Examples are computerized exercise equipment, packet radio, personal robotics, and virtual reality.

There are literally thousands of applications and sub-applications in which PCs are or could be used. A few of the more common ones, each of which has its own article in this encyclopedia, are listed here:

- Analytical graphics
- Animation
- Artificial intelligence
- Bulletin-board system
- Computer-aided design
- Computer-aided manufacturing
- Computer-assisted instruction
- Computer games
- Computerized home
- Database
- Desktop publishing
- Draw program
- Electronic circuit design software
- Exercise software
- Grammar checking
- Graphics

Archives

- Indexing software
- Integrated software package
- Interactive technology
- Musical instrument digital interface
- Office automation
- Online service
- Packet communications
- Paint program
- Paperless office
- Personal robots
- Programming
- Speech recognition
- Speech synthesis
- Spell checking
- Spreadsheet
- Virtual reality
- Word processing

See also SOFTWARE.

Archives

Important files should always be kept in a permanent record. This is especially true when you use a bulletin-board system, database, or word processing software. Even if you haven't used a file in a long time, you might need to access it some day. *Archives* are stores of old files you want to keep around.

A big, old library. The term "archives" conjures up images of a huge, old library, like the Library of Congress, where everything ever published in the U.S. is tucked away. In the Library of Congress, no matter how obscure the data, you can find it if you look hard enough. It should be the same way with the archives of a company, or of an individual PC user.

Most people keep their archives on diskettes. A typical high-density diskette can store a little over a million characters. That's equivalent to a large novel. A set of bookshelves can hold 1000 diskettes, about a gigabyte (over one billion characters) of data. That's room enough for more text than you're likely to create in your whole life. Graphics consume more space than text, but not an unreasonable amount for the typical PC user.

Area graph

Keeping archives current. Some files need to be updated often. If the old material is obsolete, and you're sure you'll never need it again, you can pull the archive diskette from the shelf and replace the old files with updated ones. There's no sense keeping useless data around, but always be sure you really don't need the old stuff before you get rid of it. Archives should be updated at regular intervals, so they don't contain large amounts of data that do nothing but take up space.

Some files in archives never need to be, and never ought to be, changed. (An income-tax return is one example.) Such diskettes should be marked accordingly. You can also *write protect* these diskettes to prevent accidental overwriting of their contents.

File compression. If you have a lot of material in your archives, or if you want to minimize the disk space they take up, you can squeeze files into less space. If you use a bulletin-board system often, and you want to keep records of everything you send and receive to and from everybody, you'll probably want to do this. Software called *file-compression utilities* are available for this purpose. File-compression utilities take everything from your hard disk, compress it, and back it up on diskettes.

Alternatives. You can use a tape drive to keep your archives. A typical tape drive can store upwards of 500MB in a small cartridge resembling an audiotape cassette. The easiest way to use a tape drive is to back up your hard disk with it periodically. This is also a good way to protect yourself against disaster in case your hard disk fails.

A device known as a *WORM (write-once/read-many)* drive allows PC users to make their own CD-ROM for archival purposes. A typical CD-ROM can hold 650MB of data or more. The main drawback of WORM technology, at the time of this writing, is that it's quite expensive.

Other schemes can be used to create and store archives, but those discussed here are the most common. *See also* BACKUP, BACKUP UTILITY, CD-ROM, DISKETTE, FILE COMPRESSION UTILITY, TAPE DRIVE, WRITE-ONCE/READ-MANY, *and* WRITE PROTECTION.

Area graph

When you're making graphs or charts, it's important that they look good and be easy to read. Nothing helps a presentation more than good illustration. And nothing can hurt it more than sloppy, indecipherable, or inaccurate graphs and charts.

When it helps. When you need to graph two or more quantities that vary continuously, you can use an *area graph*. The regions below each curve are shaded or crosshatched. This makes the graph or chart look professional, as long as the curves do not intersect each other or follow along too closely. It also adds contrast, so that the graph is easy to read.

The graph at A shows temperature versus time in Minneapolis, Minnesota, for a day in January and a day in July. These curves don't come anywhere near intersecting each other! The climate in Minneapolis is far different in winter than in summer, so these two curves lend themselves nicely to the use of an area graph.

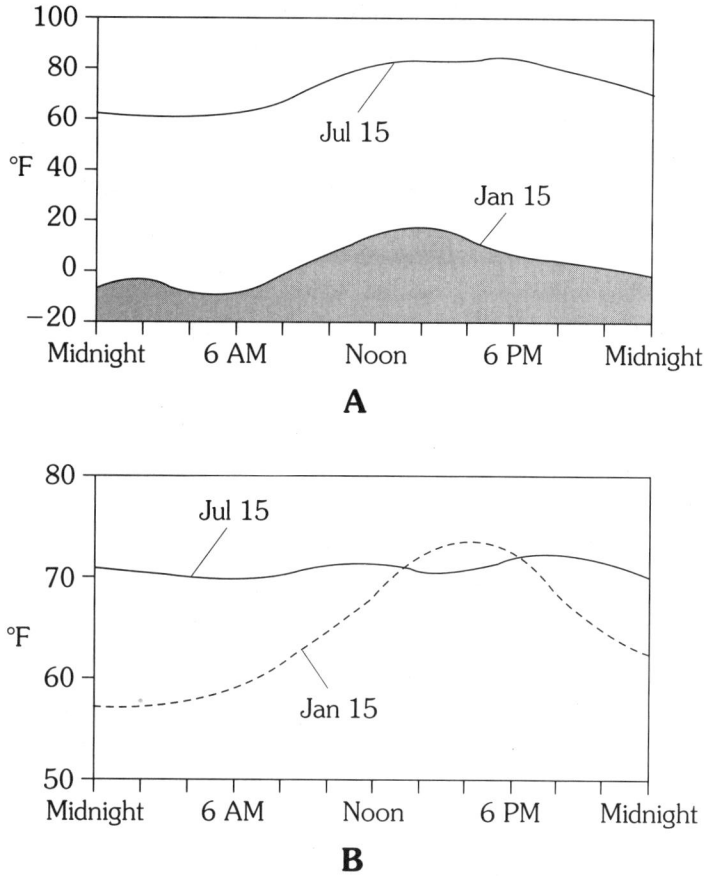

Temperatures for Minneapolis, Minnesota (A) and San Jose, Costa Rica (B).

When it doesn't help. The graph at B shows temperature versus time in San Jose, Costa Rica, for a day in January and a day in July. These curves intersect and lie fairly close to each other. An area graph would make this harder, not easier, to read. Instead of shading this graph, one line is made solid and the other is made broken. This makes it easy to tell which curve is which.

There are many different ways of graphing multiple curves. The best way must sometimes be found by trial and error. *See also* ANALYTICAL GRAPHICS, FUNCTION, *and* PRESENTATION GRAPHICS.

Arithmetic operator

An *arithmetic operator* is a character or symbol that tells a computer to add, subtract, multiply, divide, or exponentiate numbers. These ways of combining numbers are the common operations you learned in elementary school.

Symbols. The symbols most often used for arithmetic operators are the plus sign (+) for addition, the dash or minus sign (–) for subtraction, the asterisk (∗) for multiplication, the slant bar (/) for division, and the wedge (^) for exponentiation. The table shows how these symbols are commonly written, and gives some examples of expressions in which they are used.

Arithmetic operations, symbols, and expressions

Operation	Symbol	Sample expression
Addition	+	X + Y
Subtraction	–	X1 – Y2
Multiplication	∗	A2 ∗ A3
Division	/	X / Z
Exponentiation	^	X^2

Precedence. When you learned the rules of math, you learned to exponentiate first, then multiply or divide, and finally to add or subtract. The order in which operations are done is called *precedence*. For example, the expression

$$3 + 4x^2$$

means that you square x (multiply it by itself), then multiply the result by 4, and finally add 3. Some computer software knows this, so that the expression above can be written

$$3 + 4 * x\wedge 2$$

and the computer will not be confused. When you are in doubt about what order of precedence the computer uses, or if operations are to be done in a nonstandard precedence, parentheses can be used to indicate the order in which operations are to be done. For example, you can write the previous expression as

$$3 + (4 * (x\wedge 2))$$

to guarantee that things are done in the right order.

An example of a series of operations in nonstandard precedence, in which you must use parentheses, is the following:

(3 + (4 * x))^2

which a mathematician would recognize as

$(3 + 4x)^2$

This means something entirely different from the previous expression. Precedence must be specified precisely and checked carefully to avoid calculation errors. *See also* FUNCTION *and* PRECEDENCE.

ARPAnet

See INTERNET.

Arrow keys

The *arrow keys* (sometimes called *direction keys*) are a group of four keys on your PC keyboard. In most applications, they move the cursor up, down, right, and left. You can pick them out easily because of the arrows on them (see the drawing). Most IBM-compatible keyboards also allow for the use of the numeric-keypad keys 2, 4, 6, and 8 as arrow keys when the Num Lock function is turned off.

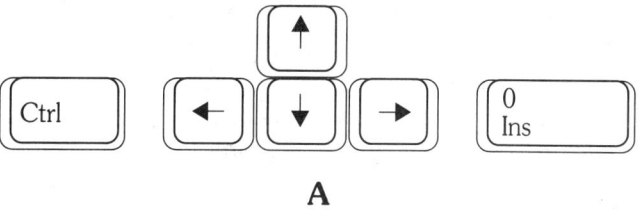

A

Some scientists predicted the development of integrated circuits (ICs) years before they became available. They made other technological forecasts that later ~~came true.~~
Some people think machines can evolve on their own, without human intervention. Computers, with robots to do the labor, might conduct research, run factories, and build improved versions of themselves.

B

Easily recognizable arrow keys (A) cause the cursor to move horizontally and vertically (B).

Artificial intelligence

In word processing. In most word processing software, you can use the arrow keys to move the cursor around on the text without affecting the text itself. Each time you press one of the keys, the cursor moves one space up, down, right, or left. If you hold an arrow key down, the cursor will move one space, pause, and then begin rapidly moving in the direction of its arrow. This is shown in the drawing at B.

Actually, the cursor doesn't always move in the direction of the arrow key. If you're moving to the right along a line of text, and you get to the end of a paragraph, the cursor will probably jump down to the beginning of the next paragraph. In lists, holding down the right arrow key will probably cause the cursor to move along each line from left to right, jumping to the next line at the end of each item. The cursor won't move along through empty spaces unless you've put blanks in the text with the spacebar.

The exact behavior of the arrow keys depends on the software package you're using. The best way to learn what they do is to practice with them. In some programs, the arrow keys should not be used, because they can foul things up. This is the case, for example, on certain online networks. You'll generally be warned not to use the arrow keys in these situations.

Instead of a mouse/trackball. The other popular way to move a cursor around is by using a *mouse*. If you're used to working with a mouse, you will probably not want to use the arrow keys. The mouse is easier and quicker. While the arrow keys restrict you to four directions, the mouse lets you move the cursor or pointer around freely.

There are occasions, however, when you'll have to use the arrow keys instead of a mouse. For example, you might be at a friend's house, or in an office, where the PC doesn't have a mouse. Or you might be using a laptop computer where there's no good place to set a mouse down, and which doesn't have a *trackball*. It's a good idea to get used to the arrow keys on your PC, even if you do have a mouse, so you'll be ready for situations like this.

Some people say they have trouble learning two different methods of doing the same thing. If you're one of these people, try it anyway; you might surprise yourself. Using arrow keys is as different from using a mouse as driving a car with a stick shift is from driving a car with an automatic transmission. Switching cursor-movement schemes with computers isn't any harder than switching modes of driving, if you're willing to spend a little time learning how to do things both ways. *See also* CURSOR, GRAPHICAL USER INTERFACE, MOUSE, *and* TRACKBALL.

Artificial intelligence

The term *artificial intelligence*, abbreviated *AI*, refers to computers that mimic aspects of human thought. A simple electronic calculator doesn't have AI. A machine that can learn from its mistakes, or that can show reasoning power, has some AI. There is no universally agreed-on, precisely measurable level of computer power at which AI begins. People's perception of AI changes as technology advances.

Drawing A is a block diagram of an AI computer that includes speech recognition, speech synthesis, vision systems, and a port for the control of one or more personal robots. All the peripherals are connected to the central processing unit (CPU), the "brain" of the system. The "conscious" memory is random-access memory (RAM), but with much greater capacity than the RAM in a typical PC. The "subconscious" is similar to extended/expanded memory. *See also* CENTRAL PROCESSING UNIT, EXTENDED/EXPANDED MEMORY, PERSONAL ROBOTS, RANDOM-ACCESS MEMORY, SPEECH RECOGNITION, SPEECH SYNTHESIS, *and* VISION SYSTEMS.

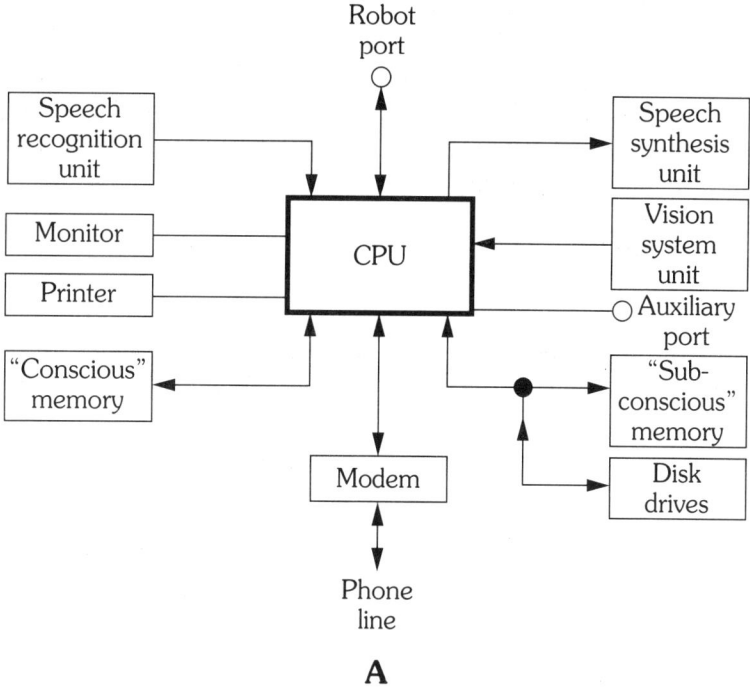

A

Block diagram of an AI system.

Entertainment. Computers have been programmed to play intense games like checkers and chess. With checkers, computers have proven adept. With chess, the results have also been spectacular. These games represent one avenue of AI, but they don't have any application other than entertainment. A form of computer game with potential practical applications is *virtual reality*. *See also* CHECKERS-PLAYING COMPUTER, CHESS-PLAYING COMPUTER, *and* VIRTUAL REALITY.

Art. Computers can process music in many different ways. Anyone who listens to pop music has heard computer-enhanced

Artificial intelligence

sound. Computers can also generate their own melodies. However, computer-composed music has a lifeless quality, according to musicians and well-seasoned music listeners. There are many variables in the sound of a tune, most of which convey the feelings of the composer. If the computer has no emotion, then the music can't have it, either. Or, worse, the music might convey a nonexistent or inappropriate emotion. You might get a hilarious funeral march, for example.

Pitch, loudness, and timbre are three characteristics of music that most of us notice right away. But music also has rhythm, crescendos and decrescendos, pauses, vibrato, and other variables. A good piece of music is as sophisticated as a good novel. Computers have helped authors write stories, and have even composed tales with plots of a sort, but a machine has yet to write a profound novel by itself. *See also* COMPUTER CONSCIOUSNESS *and* COMPUTER MUSIC.

Mathematical proofs. One measure of computer intelligence that works on a level somewhere between intuition and logic involves the proving of mathematical theorems. If you took high-school geometry, you've been exposed to theorem-proving. Logic courses deal with it, too. Computer programming is a type of reasoning similar to theorem proving, raising the question, "Will computers ever be able to program themselves?"

Computer programs have sometimes found remarkable proofs of theorems. One of these theorems states that the base angles in an isosceles triangle have equal measures (see drawing B).

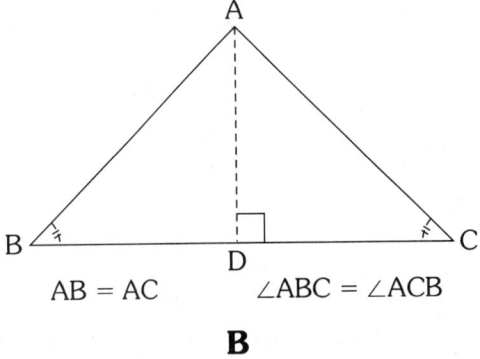

B

Isosceles triangle theorem.

The traditional proof of this theorem cuts the isosceles triangle vertically down the middle. Let the triangle ABC have sides with lengths AB = AC. By "dropping a perpendicular," AD, from the apex to the base, two right triangles are created. It turns out that these two triangles are exact mirror images of each other, and therefore, the angles ∠ABC and ∠ACB have equal measure.

Artificial intelligence

An AI program found a way to prove this theorem without cutting up the triangle. Consider the triangle ABCA (going around counterclockwise) and also another triangle ACBA (going around clockwise). These triangles are congruent, meaning you can lie one down right on top of the other, because the lengths of corresponding sides are all equal: AB = AC (you're given this fact to start with), BC = CB (it's the same line segment traveled opposite ways), CA = BA (you're given this fact to start with). This means that the triangle ABC is precisely the same if you flip it over or look at it in a mirror. Because corresponding angles of congruent triangles have equal measure, ∠ABC and ∠ACB are identical. This completes the proof.

The mathematician Pappus found this proof almost 2000 years ago, but it's not the one commonly taught. Did this computer have the IQ of Pappus? Most experts say no: the program merely reflected some of the knowledge of its author. The program didn't repeat this stroke of genius. It didn't find any new, exciting proofs for other theorems. If it had, it would have been a far more convincing demonstration of true AI.

Personal robots. Artificial intelligence lends itself to robotics. Scientists have dreamed for over a century about building *androids*, robots that look and act like people.

A computer might think of many things, but if it can't physically act on its thoughts, its power is limited. Can a PC ever get smart enough to control a mobile robot with a high degree of intelligence?

In coming decades, PCs will be put to use in robots. Primitive personal robots are available right now, but they are expensive. In the future, two challenges will confront developers of smart personal robots. First, the machines must be affordable to consumers. Second, they must be of real use, so they make their owners' lives more convenient. Few consumers will spend $50,000 on a machine that does little but look sophisticated.

Electronic minds. Experts in AI have been disappointed in recent decades. Computers can handle tasks no human could ever contend with, such as navigating a space probe or making billions of mathematical calculations. Machines can play some mathematical games well enough to compete with human experts. Modern machines can understand, as well as synthesize, words in any spoken language. But these abilities, by themselves, don't count for much in the dreams of scientists who hope to create artificial life.

Computers are good at specialized tasks. The narrower the field of expertise, the more powerful and efficient a machine can be. Excellent examples are provided by application software such as high-level spreadsheets, databases, graphics, and animation programs. Computers can carry out tasks with these applications much faster and more precisely than any person. The big problem is finding a way to make a computer powerful in many different fields of knowledge. That's what must be done if computers are ever to come anywhere near the real-world intelligence of human beings.

The human brain is incredibly complicated. Consider a circuit that would have occupied a small city in 1945, and used all the electricity from its power plant. Such a circuit can now be put into a box the size of a vitamin pill and run by a battery. Imagine this degree of miniaturization happening again, and then again, and then again! Would that begin to approach the sophistication of your body's nervous system? One of the earliest researchers to think about this was Alan Turing. *See also* TURING, ALAN.

"Cyber sapiens." Imagine that you could talk to your computer and have it understand you and answer you back. Suppose you could crack jokes with it. Think of a machine that would tell moving, profound stories, and that could pull historical facts from all the archives in the whole world. The machine could untangle the most complicated logical problems ever confronted by human beings. It could prove mathematical theorems, not to mention doing a child's homework and a company's bookkeeping.

In designing this machine, all the best engineers in the world would get together, using alternative computer technology as well as conventional digital computer technology. The result would be a computer with the best features of all technologies. It might be called "Cyber sapiens," meaning "highly evolved thinking machine."

Perhaps someday, a machine will be built that can translate from any spoken language into any other, instantly. You might use it to freely converse with someone in Hindi, Russian, or Spanish. Perhaps it could let you view past events in virtual reality; it might even prognosticate the future and display it for you.

A limit to "cyber smarts." No matter how "smart" computers get, there will never be a computer that can determine whether or not any arbitrary statement is true. There are statements whose truth value can't be found by any means, human or machine. This was proven in 1930 by the mathematician Kurt Gödel. And of course, even the facts as we do know them are constantly changing. "Cyber sapiens" would be fully aware of this, having been so informed by its programmers, but it could never keep up with every change in every corner of the world, 100 percent of the time.

Is the human brain a digital machine? There is some evidence to suggest that the answer is no, that digital technology alone is not sufficient to model the mind of a human being. In any event, no electronic device has yet come near having the IQ of a person, even of a toddler.

Some experts think computers can get as smart as people. Most, however, agree that it will be at least several generations before it happens. Some scientists believe it will never take place.

Even if a machine like "Cyber sapiens" is developed, its thought processes might differ vastly from those of the human mind, and direct comparison would therefore be irrelevant. *See also* ALTERNATIVE COMPUTER TECHNOLOGY, ANIMISM, ANTHROPOMORPHISM, ARTIFICIAL LIFE, COMPUTER CONSCIOUSNESS, COMPUTER REASONING, EXPERT SYSTEMS, HEURISTIC KNOWLEDGE, KNOWLEDGE, NEURAL NETWORK, SPEECH RECOGNITION, SPEECH SYNTHESIS, *and* TURING TEST.

Artificial life

What makes living things different from nonliving things? This is one of the greatest, and oldest, questions in science. In some cultures, especially in the Far East, life is ascribed to things that Western people regard as inanimate, but in most societies, a precise definition of life is elusive. It's hard to define *artificial life* when one can't adequately define life!

Reproduction. One definition of life involves the ability of a thing to make copies of itself. Suppose you synthesize a new kind of molecule in a beaker, and call it AL (for "artificial life"). Suppose AL, like DNA, can make replicas of itself, so that when you put one AL in a glass of water, you'll have a whole glassful of ALs in a few days. This molecule can reproduce, and therefore fulfills one definition of life, although it is artificial, because it is human-made. You might build a robot that could assemble other robots like itself. The machine would be a form of artificial life according to this definition.

On the darker side of things, a software *virus* might also qualify as artificial life. It is human-made, and it makes copies of itself. This is true even though a computer virus is not a material thing.

Conscious machines. Society is a long way from having to worry that computer-controlled machines might build copies of themselves and take over the earth, but such machines are within the realm of possibility. They could reproduce by merely assembling other computers and robots. Robots could build machines identical to themselves, or much different from themselves. They could engineer their own technological advances. It's interesting to think of the ways in which artificially living machine populations might evolve.

Another definition for life involves thought processes. At what point does a logical process qualify as consciousness? Could a machine be aware of its own existence, and ponder its place in the universe, the way a human being can? Nobody knows yet; it can be endlessly debated. One person might say that a computer is conscious; others could argue that even some people aren't fully conscious.

ASCII

Relevance. Perhaps the best attitude toward this debate is taken by certain Japanese scientists and philosophers. They believe that everything in the universe is alive to some degree. That reduces the artificial-life question to irrelevance: even the simplest machines possess it! *See also* ANIMISM, ARTIFICIAL INTELLIGENCE, *and* COMPUTER CONSCIOUSNESS.

ASCII

ASCII, pronounced "ASK-key," is an acronym for *American Standard Code for Information Interchange*, a digital code used for sending and receiving letters, numbers, and punctuation marks. Control functions can also be sent and received. Personal computers commonly use ASCII; large mainframes often use other codes.

What it sounds like. The ASCII code is used by most computer modems. The speed of transmission is measured in *baud* or *bits per second*. Perhaps you've picked up a telephone extension by accident, while someone was faxing or using an online service; then you've heard the sound of computers sending analog ASCII back and forth to each other. The analog signals are audio tones, converted from the digital low and high (0 and 1) states to a form that can be transmitted over the telephone lines.

At slow speeds, analog ASCII sounds like a rapid "blee-blee-bleep." At higher speeds, it sounds like a hiss or roar. The individual data bits go by so fast that they seem to blend together into "white noise," although they actually represent precise characters and symbols. The most common speed rates for ASCII are shown in the table. The speed in baud is about the same as the number of words per minute for ASCII code signals.

Data speeds in ASCII code

Baud rate	Pulse duration (milliseconds)	Words per minute
110	9.09	110
150	6.67	150
300	3.33	300
600	1.67	600
1200	0.833	1200
1800	0.556	1800
2400	0.417	2400
4800	0.208	4800
9600	0.104	9600
19,200	0.052	19,200

Aspect ratio

Straight ASCII. Suppose you want to send a manuscript to a magazine for possible publication. They might ask you if you can submit the text on a diskette. If you can, they will probably ask you what word processing software you use. If you don't happen to use the software that the publication uses, it doesn't necessarily mean you can't send them your article on diskette. You can ask them, "Can you take straight ASCII?" If they say yes, you can send them your article, both on hardcopy (paper) and on diskette. The diskette copy should have all the word processing commands (margins, fonts, superscripts, italics, boldface, etc.) removed. This is what is meant by *straight ASCII*. *See also* BAUD, BIT, DISKETTE, HARDCOPY, MODEM, *and* WORD PROCESSING.

Asimov's Three Laws

In one of his early science-fiction stories, *Isaac Asimov* first mentioned the word *robotics*, along with three rules that robots ought to obey. These rules apply quite well to computers, too. The rules are sometimes called *Asimov's Three Laws* of robotics. They can be modified to encompass all artificially intelligent machines (AIMs), including high-end PCs in some applications.

1 An AIM must not injure, or allow the injury of, any human being.

2 An AIM must obey all orders from humans, except orders that would contradict the First Law.

3 An AIM must protect itself, except when to do so would contradict the First Law or the Second Law.

Although these rules were first coined in the 1940s, they are still considered valid standards. *See also* ARTIFICIAL INTELLIGENCE *and* PERSONAL ROBOTS.

Aspect ratio

The *aspect ratio* of an image is the ratio of its width to its height. This varies depending on the nature of the image and the type of display. The aspect ratio is usually written in the form $h:v$, where h stands for horizontal units and v stands for vertical units. Sometimes this is divided out, and the ratio is written as a decimal number.

On a monitor. On your computer monitor, the aspect ratio is the same as that of a television picture: 4:3, or 1.33. This ratio was originally chosen because it's pleasing to the eye (see drawing A). On the monitor of the PC with which this book was written, a screenful of text measured $9\tfrac{3}{8}$ inches wide by 7 inches high; that's almost exactly 1.33. *See also* MONITOR.

In graphics. When you create graphic images with your computer, the aspect ratio of the printed product might be much different than 4:3. A drawing of a person standing up, for example, would fit quite well in a frame with an aspect ratio of 1:2 (see drawing B). Technical

Assembler and assembly language

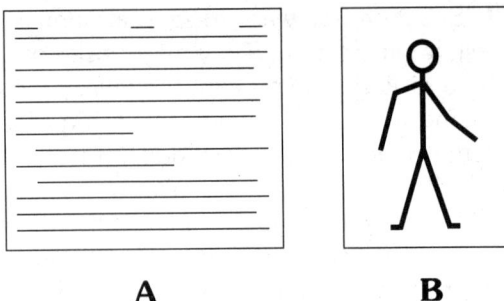

Typical aspect ratio of a monitor screen (A) might differ from printed graphics (B).

diagrams can have almost any aspect ratio. If you check some of the illustrations in this book, you'll find many different aspect ratios. The aspect ratio of an entire printed book page is usually between 1:2 and 1:1. *See also* GRAPHICS.

Assembler and assembly language

An *assembler* is a translator between two different computer languages, machine language and assembly language. It translates in both directions, so that the central processing unit (CPU) can get its instructions and communicate with the outside world.

Language hierarchy. Machine language is binary code, consisting of on/off states (also called ones and zeros, or highs and lows). It is the lowest level of language, similar to the impulses that travel through your brain cells and nerves.

Assembly language is one step up from machine language. It is the set of instructions for the CPU. You might think of this as your autonomic nervous system, which controls things like your breathing and heartbeat. Assembly language normally works without the user having to think about it.

The most sophisticated computer language is *high-level language*. This is like your conscious mind. Most programmers use high-level languages when communicating with a computer. They are the translators between the machine and the human being.

Advantages. A major advantage of assembly language is speed. If you write a computer program directly in assembly language, rather than in a high-level language, you save the computer the work of translating back and forth between machine language and the high-level language. Therefore, the computer works faster because it can process more meaningful information in a given length of time.

Assembly language often takes more steps for each task than high-level languages. On the other hand, assembler programs take up less memory because the steps in assembly language are specific and concise. Each instruction in assembly language represents one instruction in machine language.

Disadvantages. An assembler program is not like other programming languages at all; it is bizarre to those familiar with high-level languages. Because of this, most people prefer to use high-level language when programming. One very common high-level CPU programming language is called C. Other examples of high-level languages are BASIC, COBOL, and Fortran.

Assembly language is harder to read and write than high-level, or "user-friendly," languages, but it's not as hard to work with as machine language. As a matter of fact, with most computers it's impossible for a user to program in machine language.

In order to accomplish a task that is easy in high-level language, many lines might be required in assembly language. Often you must repeat instructions over and over—just the sort of thing you bought the computer to do for you. Also, an assembly language that works with one CPU will not generally work with other CPUs. The programmer must learn a new assembly language for each new CPU that comes along. See also CENTRAL PROCESSING UNIT, COMPILER, HIGH-LEVEL LANGUAGE, INTERPRETER, and MACHINE LANGUAGE.

Asterisk

An *asterisk* (*), also called a "star" or "splat," is a common character in ASCII code. You get it by holding down the Shift key while pressing the key for the numeral 8 on the normal typewriter part of the keyboard.

As a stand-in. The asterisk can serve as a *wildcard*, acting as a "stand-in" for any number of characters. This is especially useful in word processing, when you want the computer to look for certain words or numbers. Thus, *radio** can stand for *radio*, *radios*, *radioactive*, *radioisotope*, *radiology*, etc.

The symbol *.* (pronounced "asterisk-period-asterisk" or "star-dot-star") is often used as a general expression for a *filename*. If you wanted to erase all the files on a diskette in DOS, for example, you could type the following:

    DEL A:*.*

This means, "On drive A, delete the files *.*." The first * stands for the main part of the filename; the second * stands for the *filename extension*, if any.

Times sign. If you're reading a math text or writing a thesis, you know that A times T can be written AT or A × T. A computer gets confused by this notation, however. It needs a special, unambiguous "hook" to tell it to multiply two things, not think of them as a word or a string of variables.

Pretend you are a computer, and the character string *AxT* is given to you. Is *x* a variable? Does *AxT* mean "A times x times T"? Or suppose the string *AT* is typed in by the PC user. Does this mean the word *at*? A human being knows these kinds of things from the context in which a character string is written, but a computer isn't that perceptive. It must be told in no uncertain terms what you want it to do. (Incidentally, one of the greatest challenges facing researchers in artificial intelligence is getting a computer to make subtle distinctions like this, without having to be fed every single detail.)

In mathematical programming, the symbol * is used as a multiplication sign. If you want the computer to multiply *A* by *T*, you type *A∗T*. If your computer sees *A∗(B+C)*, it knows that it is supposed to add *B* and *C*, and multiply the result by *A*. See also WILDCARD.

Asynchronous data

Computers talk to each other by means of *digital signals*, discrete units which are either high (logic 1) or low (logic 0). Each unit is called a *bit*. Each character of data consists of several bits.

Data bits. A data signal, such as one PC would send to another over a modem, can be displayed on an oscilloscope. If you adjust the oscilloscope right, you can see the data bits. A digital signal has a squared-off appearance, as shown in the graphs. It's obvious whether a bit is high or low. This is one reason why digital communication is efficient.

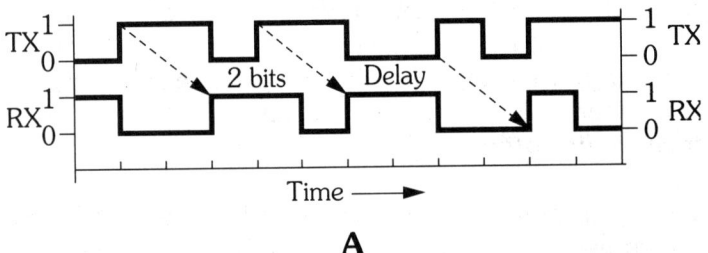

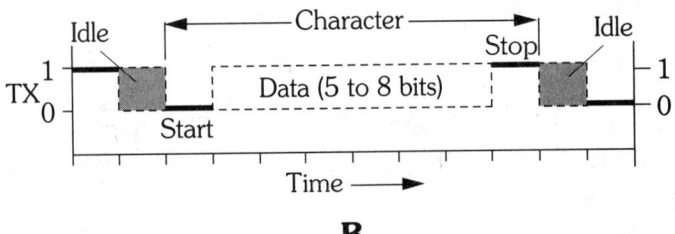

At A, receiver (RX) is out of sync with transmitter (TX) by 2 bits. At B, stop, start, data, and idle bits.

How does the receiver (RX in the drawing), or *destination*, know when characters begin and end? There is only one correct way to interpret a series of digital bits. If the destination knows the beginning and ending times for the characters, it can make sense of the data. However, if the destination is ahead of or behind the transmitter (TX), or *source*, it will interpret the whole string of bits incorrectly. Instead of clear data, it will display gobbledygook. Or maybe, sensing that something is wrong, the destination computer or terminal will display an error signal.

Start/stop. Somehow, the destination needs to get in step with the source. One way to do this is to have the source tell the destination when characters start and stop. This technique was originally developed in the early days of teletype, because those machines had the same data synchronization problem that computers have today. Because there is no independent synchronizing standard, this is called *asynchronous data*.

When the source is ready to start sending a character, it transmits a *start bit*. This tells the destination to get ready to "hear" one character of data. Then, the source transmits five to eight bits for the character. When it is done with the character, it sends a *stop bit*. This tells the destination to display the character. After the stop bit, an *idle bit*, or *stop-bit state*, is sent. This is just a pause; it lets the destination PC or terminal get ready for the next character to come in.

Start bits and stop bits break up the data so that there is no confusion. In the drawing, start bits are low (0) and stop bits are high (1). The idle bit might be either low or high; it depends on the particular system used.

Bit by bit. A more sophisticated way to get the machines in step is to use an independent time standard (clock) to align every data bit at both ends of the circuit. The source and destination then run exactly in step, bit by bit, like soldiers marching according to the cadence shouted out by a drill sergeant. This is called *synchronous data*. The use of synchronous data enables computers to talk at higher speeds than is possible with asynchronous data, but the hardware is more expensive and requires precise alignment.

Personal computers generally use asynchronous data. It's fast enough for most PC users' needs. *See also* BIT, CHARACTER, MODEM, *and* SYNCHRONOUS DATA.

Attribute

The term *attribute* refers to special characteristics of a file, archive, or character. Sometimes attributes are obvious; sometimes they are not.

Files can be "hidden" using *file attributes* that keep the filenames from appearing in directories and subdirectories. You can't display or copy such files. Files can also be designated as "read-only." This attribute keeps files in place so that they cannot be erased or changed.

When you are backing up files in archives, it's convenient to know whether a file has been changed since the last backup. This saves work; there's no point in updating files that haven't changed. By using *archive attributes*, your PC updates only the files that have changed.

In word processing, you can use *character attributes* such as italics, boldface, subscript, superscript, and underlining. The codes for these attributes might or might not be visible in the text; it depends on the word processing software. In some word processing programs, the effect of character attributes show up on a screen exactly as they would be printed; in others, the attributes appear as different colors, such as white letters on a blue background.

In *computer-aided design (CAD)* graphics, attributes allow the computer to ask questions, in the form of embedded text, for the operator to answer. In this way, the machine and the operator communicate during the design process. *See also* ARCHIVES, BACKUP, COMPUTER-AIDED DESIGN, *and* WORD PROCESSING.

Audit trail

In some personal finance software packages, a feature called an *audit trail* automatically keeps a record of all the transactions you enter.

Like a checkbook. Have you ever received a statement from your bank, showing a checking account balance less than the balance actually written in your checkbook? This should never happen if both you and the bank keep accurate records. In fact, the balance the bank shows should almost always be more than the balance you show. If the bank thinks you have less money than you think, there's an error someplace.

If you go back and check every transaction, you'll probably find that you made an addition or subtraction mistake. This can happen even when you use a calculator. Your checkbook transaction record is a form of audit trail.

Of course, banks sometimes make mistakes, and if you can't find the error by looking back several months in your audit trail, you should look at the bank statement, which is also an audit trail, and be sure that the bank made no errors in addition or subtraction. As a last resort, you can contact the bank to resolve the problem.

Because accounting can get complicated, especially if you run a business, an automatic record of your audit trail kept by finance software can come in handy.

Your credit history. Whether you like it or not, you have a credit history on file with various computer networks. If you've ever defaulted on a loan, this fact will probably show up in the credit history. If you are in debt to someone, they can often locate you by means of the audit trail that exists in the networks.

A person who ran up unpayable bills once said, "If you leave a complicated enough audit trail, they'll never find you." Even if this were true (which it probably isn't), who wants to run around changing addresses every few months, living under assumed names, never having a street address or telephone number, and never getting a driver's license? Such a person would have a terrible credit history, because debts show up in the networks. It would be almost impossible for that person to take out a loan. The audit trail might just as well say simply, "Bad risk!" Besides all that, if some person or organization wants to find someone badly enough, they will, probably with the help of computer networks.

Your audit trail, as it exists in the networks, might contain errors. An inaccurate credit history can cause problems for you that you don't deserve. It's a good idea to periodically request a copy of your credit history from credit networks, to be sure there are no mistakes. If there are errors, it's usually not too hard to get them corrected. *See also* NETWORK *and* PERSONAL FINANCE SOFTWARE.

Autodial

See TELEPHONE-DIALING SOFTWARE.

AUTOEXEC.BAT

Your PC must go through a certain procedure every time you switch it on. In DOS, the initial sequence of commands is usually controlled by a file called *AUTOEXEC.BAT*. In IBM's OS/2, this file is known as *STARTUP*.

What it means. The filename AUTOEXEC comes from the words *automatic execution*. The filename extension, .BAT, is an abbreviation for the word *batch*. Thus, AUTOEXEC.BAT automatically executes a batch of operations. This sets up your computer so that it's ready to work in DOS. (In OS/2, the file is called STARTUP.CMD.)

Unless you know exactly what you're doing, you shouldn't tamper with the AUTOEXEC.BAT file. The table shows the first few listings in the directory of a hard disk. Note that the AUTOEXEC.BAT file doesn't take up much space on the hard disk.

What it does. The batch of commands in AUTOEXEC.BAT includes those for the various applications you want to use, such as word processing, graphics, or robot control. It also includes commands for

AUTOEXEC.BAT

AUTOEXEC.BAT sets up a PC for DOS

BATCH	<DIR>		7-20-90	10:59a
DOS	<DIR>		6-12-90	1:58p
EIGHT	<DIR>		6-12-90	2:01p
MOUSE	<DIR>		6-12-90	2:02p
PRODIGY	<DIR>		2-20-93	5:14p
TS	<DIR>		6-12-90	2:02p
UTILS	<DIR>		6-12-90	2:02p
WINDOWS	<DIR>		6-12-90	1:59p
XY	<DIR>		7-20-90	10:59a
ADR	1	205	6-02-93	2:48p
ADRS	BAK	5950	7-11-93	2:50p
ADRS		5978	7-20-93	3:06p
AUTOEXEC	**BAT**	**145**	**7-30-90**	**12:08p**
BIBLIO	BAK	9808	7-10-93	6:21p
BIBLIO		10,009	7-15-93	4:54p
BIO	BAK	1576	6-02-93	7:25a
BIO	1	1568	6-03-93	5:55a
BIO	2	1614	6-03-93	5:54a
CENTIBEL	L1	2446	7-27-93	6:29p
COMMAND	COM	37,557	12-19-88	12:00p
CONFIG	300	146	7-30-90	12:08p
CONFIG	SYS	170	5-21-90	4:27p
CV		3185	7-10-93	6:25p
CV	BAK	3186	6-26-93	5:19p
EARTH	DIR	430	7-28-93	3:20p
EARTH		3032	7-28-93	3:19p
EARTH	10	10,656	7-06-93	7:52p
EARTH	12	11,362	6-08-93	9:57p
EARTH	11	9424	7-27-93	5:20p
EARTH	6	11,676	6-24-93	6:27p
EARTH	8	12,556	6-09-93	6:15p
EARTH	BAK	363	6-16-93	6:32p

the operation of peripherals, such as a printer, modem, mouse, or robot.

All of the software for the operation of these applications and peripherals is on the hard disk. The software is not in the active memory until AUTOEXEC.BAT transfers it there from the hard disk at the start of every operating session. *See also* DOS.

Automated home

See COMPUTERIZED HOME.

Automatic backup

Have you ever been using a computer and had the machine crash (freeze up) or the power suddenly go out? If this happens, you will lose work, but if your software incorporates *automatic backup*, you won't lose very much work.

Save files often. When files are in RAM (active memory), they aren't permanent. They will disappear if you switch your PC off, if the power goes out, if your PC crashes, or if you hit certain accidental, unlucky sequences of keys. For this reason, you should always save your data on the hard disk or diskette at regular intervals.

Early in my PC-using career, I lost a day's work because I didn't back up a file that was in RAM. I just left it there, coming back to it from time to time. Finally I came back to a computer that had crashed.

How many minutes' worth of work are you willing to risk losing? That is the time interval at which you should save files on hard disk or diskette. Someday, something bad is bound to happen, and you will lose some work. You might as well develop the habit of storing files often, so the loss will be minimal.

The machine can do it. With some software, you can instruct your computer to back up files automatically, at time intervals you specify. For example, you might tell the software to put the contents of RAM on the diskette in drive A every ten minutes. That way, you won't ever lose more than ten minutes' worth of work.

This feature shouldn't take the place of responsible backup habits, however. The main purpose of automatic backup is to prevent a disaster in case you forget to back things up often enough. You might someday be using a machine at a friend's house, or at another office, that doesn't have automatic backup. If a crash occurs and you've been in the habit of letting the computer back things up, you'll be in for a nasty surprise.

Optional feature. Automatically backing up files is provided by some software as an option. It can be included if you want it or disabled if you don't. Its main advantages are that it helps prevent inadvertent loss of data and lets you undo a revision if you change your mind. Its disadvantages are that it uses up extra disk space and makes the directory of a hard disk or diskette longer.

Data loss can occur when there is an unexpected power failure, even if the computer has automatic backup to a hard disk or diskette. To prevent such data loss, you might want to consider purchasing an

Automatic Sequence Controlled Calculator

uninterruptible power supply (UPS). See also AUXILIARY STORAGE, PRIMARY STORAGE, SECONDARY STORAGE, *and* UNINTERRUPTIBLE POWER SUPPLY.

Automatic font downloading

Most printers have several built-in fonts, or type styles, from which you can choose. Common fonts include Courier, Helvetica, and Times Roman. Some printers have more exotic fonts for effects such as script or large-and-small capitals.

Printer fonts. You can choose from among the built-in fonts via buttons on the printer. You can also set other variables such as pitch (characters per inch), form length (paper size), and the number of lines per inch.

Normally, you cannot change fonts while the printer is printing simply by pressing buttons on the printer; instead, you need to have the computer tell the printer exactly which fonts to use. Nor can you print documents using any font other than those built into the printer unless the computer has something to say about things.

Downloading. Suppose you want to prepare a report that has subheads of a different font from the main body of text. To do this, you need *automatic font downloading*. With this feature, the PC tells the printer to change aspects of its typing as it goes along.

With automatic font downloading, you can get a printer to type fonts that it doesn't have in its built-in storage. For example, if you want the printer to type in large-and-small capitals and this style is not built-in, you can download this font. Software is available containing thousands of downloadable fonts, from the ordinary to the bizarre. *See also* DOWNLOADING, DOWNLOADABLE FONT, *and* FONT.

Automatic Sequence Controlled Calculator

The first truly automatic digital calculator was designed by IBM for the United States Navy and put into operation in 1944, toward the end of World War II. The technical name for this machine was *Automatic Sequence Controlled Calculator*. Its nickname was *Mark I*.

The Mark I could work with 23 significant digits. Thus, it had an accuracy of one part in 100 sextillion (10^{23}). Its main purpose was to do precise ballistics calculations, the type of calculation used for aiming shells and missiles.

Mark I was not much like computers in use today. It was massive, taking up a whole large room. It made extensive use of electromechanical devices, whereas modern computers use integrated circuits (ICs or chips) almost exclusively. Mark I was a highly specialized machine, powerful for its intended purpose. Nevertheless, it was really nothing more than a souped-up electromechanical calculator. It couldn't do things like word processing, graphics, or spreadsheets, applications that PC users take for granted today.

Automation

The term *automation* refers to the use of computers, and possibly robots, to do things in a home, office, or factory. You might hear about the "automation of an office." This refers to computers being installed to do some of the things that people used to do.

Good and bad. There has always been some controversy about automation. Can machines do things as well as people? Advantages of automation include the following:

- Machines work faster than people.
- Machines are often (but not always!) more precise than people.
- Machines are "down" less often than people are out sick or on vacation.
- Robots can be physically stronger than people, and they never get tired.

Advantages of humans, and disadvantages of machines, include things like these:

- People can solve some problems that machines cannot.
- People can work with less precise instructions than computers.
- People can do some high-precision tasks that machines cannot.

Human beings are always needed to supervise machines because some decisions simply cannot be made by computers. People get into trouble when they give machines too much power.

Machines serve people. When we compare human beings with machines (as is done in this article), we run the risk of devaluing ourselves. Sometimes we don't realize we're doing this. The automation of modern society can cause people to think and act like robots, serving machines rather than having the machines serve them. People can get too reliant on machines, especially computers.

Have you ever been in a grocery store and watched the cashier when the computer won't scan the price on something? He or she might have to press 20 or 30 buttons, entering enough data to uniquely identify any living creature in the whole galaxy. This is ridiculous, but the cashier accepts it because there is no choice.

As PCs and smart robots become more commonplace, people must keep them in their proper perspective. They're supposed to help humanity to be more efficient, free, and creative, not regiment

Autonomous robots

individuals and societies. *See also* COMPUTERIZED HOME, COMPUTER OVER-RELIANCE, LUDDITES, OFFICE AUTOMATION, PAPERLESS OFFICE, *and* PERSONAL ROBOTS.

Autonomous robots

Many researchers believe that computer-controlled robots will someday be household appliances. An *autonomous robot* is a self-contained machine with its own computer system.

System geometry. The drawing shows one scheme in which a fleet of autonomous robots might work together. Robots are shown as squares, and computers as solid black dots. The computers are connected by radio links (dashed lines) into a local area network (LAN). This type of LAN is known as a *peer-to-peer network*, because all the computers have equal authority and intelligence.

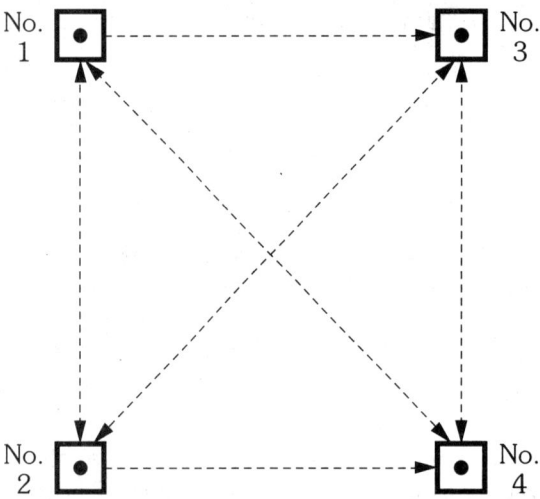

Autonomous robots controlled by computers linked in a radio peer-to-peer network.

The computer in an autonomous robot will have about the same amount of memory and work at about the same speed as a PC. It will probably move around by rolling on wheels or on a track drive, something like a bulldozer or tank. Each robot in the fleet can have its own software, while being able to share data with each other, just as PCs share information in a LAN.

Two working modes. Autonomous robots are sometimes called "smart robots." While they can work as a team if the communications and software are well designed, they can also function independently. These two operating modes allow autonomous robots to do many different things.

Suppose that you assign four personal robots the task of painting your house. Communication will be necessary so the robots can coordinate their actions and not interfere with each other. This is an example of autonomous robots working together as a team.

Imagine that you use the same four personal robots in general home maintenance. One might mow the lawn, the second could trim the bushes, the third could vacuum your floors, and the fourth might wash your windows. In this case they would do their jobs independently, and they would not have to communicate with each other.

Some roboticists like the idea of a fleet of "stupid robots," all under the absolute control of a central computer. These machines are called *insect robots*, because the whole system functions as a unit, much like an anthill or beehive. *See also* INSECT ROBOTS *and* PERSONAL ROBOTS.

Autorepeat

Autorepeat is a keyboard function that makes a character repeat itself rapidly. There are two ways in which this function can be activated. The first method is to press the key for the character, and then hold down a *repeat key* (or you might have to hold the character key and the repeat key down simultaneously). The repetition will continue as long as the key or keys are held down. The other way to get autorepeat is to have it programmed into the software, so that a character will repeat if you hold its key down for more than a certain time.

In the software used for writing this book, holding down any key for more than 0.5 second causes that character to repeat at the rate of about 20 per second. The repetition continues for as long as the key is held down. If you feel like it, you can fill line after line, and even page after page, of text with strings of a single character, like this:

xxxxxxxxxxxxxxxxxxxxxxxxxxxxxxxxxxxxxxxxxxxxxxxxxxxxxxxxx
xxxxxxxxxxxxxxxxxxxxxxxxxxxxxxxxxxxxxxxxxxxxxxxxxxxxxxxxx
xxxxxxxxxxxxxxxxxxxxxxxxxxxxxxxxxxx

In this software, autorepeat works not only with the character keys, but with the arrow keys, tab key, and various others.

Some software programs let you adjust the rate at which characters repeat. Some even let you disable the function completely. In some programs, autorepeat only works with special symbols such as the dash, underline, period, or letter *x*. *See also* WORD PROCESSING.

Auxiliary storage

Auxiliary storage involves placing data somewhere other than in RAM (random-access memory). Often, it means storage on a diskette or hard disk, in which case it is called *secondary storage*.

Files you access often. You probably have a few files that you use often, even documents that you update almost every day. The files you

Auxiliary storage

use often should be on the hard disk of your PC for convenience, unless for some reason you don't want them there. They should also be backed up on auxiliary storage, such as one or more sets of diskettes, from which they can be retrieved in case the hard disk fails.

Updating files. Auxiliary storage can be done automatically by a computer, so that you don't lose much data if you accidentally hit an unlucky combination of keys, or in the event of a power failure. The table is a directory of the files on a hypothetical hard disk. Some of the filenames have the extension .BAK. These are auxiliary, or backup, files, created automatically every time a file is updated.

Suppose you open the file FORUM.1 from the disk. Text appears on the screen. You edit this file, which happens to be word-processed text. When you're done with the revisions, you close the file, saving the changes. This places the revised file on the hard disk under the filename FORUM.1, overwriting the old FORUM.1. It might also move the old FORUM.1 into a file called FORUM.BAK, overwriting FORUM.BAK if that filename already existed.

A computer can be programmed to automatically save active RAM files in auxiliary storage every few minutes, so you don't have to keep remembering to do it. Still, saving files "manually" at frequent intervals, whether or not the computer does it automatically, is a good habit to acquire.

You can periodically go through a directory and erase auxiliary files if you find they are taking up too much disk space. One way to do this in DOS is to use the ERASE command in conjunction with the asterisk (wildcard) symbol. For example, if you had a directory called STORIES on your hard disk that contained numerous auxiliary files with the .BAK extension, you could type

```
ERASE C:\STORIES\*.BAK
```

and all the auxiliary files in the STORIES directory would be erased. Auxiliary files in other directories would not be affected. *See also* AUTOMATIC BACKUP, DISKETTE, HARD DISK, PRIMARY STORAGE, RANDOM-ACCESS MEMORY, *and* SECONDARY STORAGE.

Directory of hypothetical hard disk

BATCH		<DIR>		7-20-90	10:59a
DOS		<DIR>		6-12-90	1:58p
EIGHT		<DIR>		6-12-90	2:01p
MOUSE		<DIR>		6-12-90	2:02p
PRODIGY		<DIR>		2-20-93	5:14p
TS		<DIR>		6-12-90	2:02p
UTILS		<DIR>		6-12-90	2:02p
WINDOWS		<DIR>		6-12-90	1:59p
XY		<DIR>		7-20-90	10:59a
ADRS	BAK		5950	7-11-93	2:50p
ADRS			5978	7-20-93	3:06p
ALERT	BAK		176	7-22-93	2:00p
ALERT			222	7-22-93	2:01p
AUTOEXEC	400		145	7-30-90	12:08p
BIBLIO	BAK		9808	7-10-93	6:21p
BIBLIO			10,009	7-15-93	4:54p
BIO	BAK		1576	6-02-93	7:25a
BIO	1		1568	6-03-93	5:55a
BIO	2		1614	6-03-93	5:54a
CV			3185	7-10-93	6:25p
CV	BAK		3186	6-26-93	5:19p
FORUM	BAK		6564	7-27-93	11:43a
FORUM	1		2596	7-23-93	8:42a
FORUM	2		2635	7-23-93	7:42p
IDE7			1230	6-28-93	7:16a
IDE7	BAK		485	6-27-93	7:18a
PRM			2594	7-05-93	6:43p
PRM	BAK		2594	7-05-93	3:13p
PROMO	BAK		10,685	6-02-93	6:58p
PROMO			10,682	6-26-93	5:50p

Babbage, Charles

Charles Babbage was an engineer in 19th century England. He is given credit for having conceived the first digital calculator (other than the ancient Oriental abacus). His design was intended for the British Post Office in 1836.

Babbage's digital calculator was never put to practical use, however. Its components were mechanical, not electrical; electric utilities did not exist in the 1830s. The data was stored on punch cards, using a method similar to that employed by some real computers more than a century later.

Babbage is said to have had a short temper and not to have applied himself to projects long enough to perfect them. Babbage would reach a certain point and then take everything apart, starting all over to rebuild a new design from scratch.

Babbage's ideas were forgotten for many years after his death, but when electricity became widely available, engineers once again tackled the problem of building a digital calculator. They looked back at Charles Babbage's work, and found his ideas useful. *See also* ANALYTICAL ENGINE.

Background processing

Many computers can do two or more things, seemingly at the same time. This is called *multitasking*. In multitasking, processes have two levels of priority. The lower priority is called *background processing*.

Background processing

Background processes take up a fraction of the operating time, as shown in the drawing. In this pie chart, imagine time going around clockwise at high speed. The background processing (the shaded region) is a small slice of the pie.

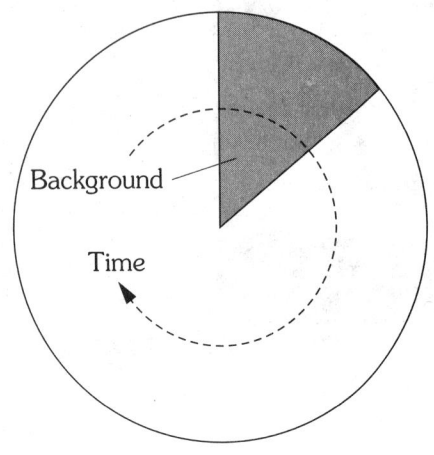

Background processing takes up a small fraction of the total operating time.

Background printing. Printing is a common background process. If you own a PC, you probably do some word processing. Have you ever wanted to print out a document while working on another? A PC does this by placing the printing function in the background, while you work in the foreground.

Suppose you want to work on this article while printing out the text for all articles whose titles begin with A. This article is in a file called PC.B; the "A" articles are in the file PC.A. You tell the computer to print, clicking on a file such as C:\COMPUTER\PC.A (drive C, directory COMPUTER, file PC.A), and the printer starts printing that file. You then open the file C:\COMPUTER\PC.B, and the text for the "B" articles appears on the screen.

As you work on these articles, the PC might seem to hesitate occasionally. During these pauses, the PC is feeding data to the printer, carrying out its background operation. The hesitations are usually more noticeable as the sizes of files increase but with fast microprocessors or multiprocessing computers, you won't notice any hesitation.

Other background processes. Various peripherals can be placed in the background environment of your PC. Suppose you want to work on this article while sending PC.A to someone via a modem. This is done the same way as background printing, with the modem taking the place of the printer. It is also possible to receive data from the modem while working on a document.

You can sometimes "jump" into the background. The Windows operating environment makes it easy to do this. In a practical sense, though, you're always in the foreground of your PC, no matter where in its environment you roam. You, the operator, are the most important "peripheral" your PC has.

In Windows. When using Windows software, you can work on one task while displaying another, less important task. For example, you might want to edit this article, checking cross-references at the same time. Rather than using a separate computer to show the list of article titles, or fumbling with a dog-eared stack of papers, you could display the file containing this article (PC.B) and the list of article titles (PC.TMS) simultaneously. The file PC.B would be in the *active window*; the file PC.TMS would be in the background. *See also* ACTIVE WINDOW, FOREGROUND PROCESSING, *and* MULTITASKING.

Backlighting

Two important features of laptop/notebook computers are small size and light weight. One of the biggest challenges facing the designers of these machines is getting the display into a compact, light package that is easy to observe and to read.

Flat and thin. If you've seen a laptop PC, you might have wondered how the display could be so thin and still have good image quality. Technology has come a long way in this respect, but there's still one big problem with these displays. They don't produce anywhere near the amount of light that a CRT (cathode-ray tube) monitor does.

Under normal conditions, most laptop PC displays generate no light of their own. They reflect light, like a page in a book. If the illumination is dim, you can't read the display unless some internal or external light is provided.

Of course, you can put a lamp next to your laptop or notebook PC if you want to use it in a dim place, but the display can be illuminated another way: by *backlighting*. A backlit display has an internal light, resembling the little lamps in some calculators and clock radios.

Battery life. The electronic circuits in a laptop/notebook PC, such as the microprocessor and memory, need very little power. This is why these computers can work with batteries. By comparison to the electronic circuits, a display light requires a lot of power. Backlighting shouldn't be used unless it's really necessary, because it consumes battery energy, shortening the time you can use the computer before the battery must be recharged.

Many laptop/notebook PCs have a feature that automatically adjusts the level of backlighting, depending on how much light is coming from the surroundings. When possible, a lamp or other external light source should be used, and the backlighting switched off. The computer

Backspace key

should be plugged into a utility outlet, rather than run off of the battery, unless no external source of power is available. *See also* LAPTOP COMPUTER *and* LIQUID-CRYSTAL DISPLAY.

Backspace key

The *Backspace key* is a button on many PC keyboards used for erasing characters. It usually has an arrow on it pointing to the left and is usually at the extreme right on the top row of character keys (the row with the numerals). The drawing shows the Backspace key on an enhanced PC keyboard.

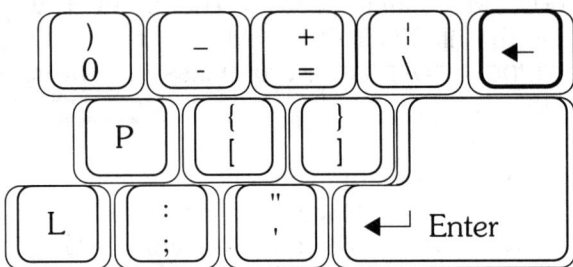

Backspace key at the extreme right of the top row of character keys.

The Backspace key on a computer works a little differently than the backspace key on a typewriter. When you press Backspace on your PC, the cursor moves to the left, or backwards, in the text. Characters are erased as the cursor moves. The backspace key on a conventional typewriter does not erase the characters; it just moves the carriage to the left. (Some electronic typewriters have a special backspace/correction key that does erase characters as the carriage moves to the left.)

If you want to move the cursor to the left in text without erasing characters, you should use the left arrow key, not Backspace. The left arrow key behaves more or less like the backspace key on a conventional typewriter.

The Backspace key is convenient for erasing short strings of characters. For example, suppose you type the word *since* and then decide, for editorial reasons, that *because* is a better word choice. You could press Backspace five times and erase the word *since*. If your keyboard has *autorepeat*, you might just hold the key down for a second or so, moving the cursor backward and blotting out the characters from right to left: e,c,n,i,s.

For large amounts of text, it's easiest to select, or block off, the passages you want to remove from a document, and then use mouse clicks or keystrokes to delete words, lines, sentences, or paragraphs. *See also* ARROW KEYS *and* WORD PROCESSING.

Backup

A *backup* is a file, disk, or tape that serves as insurance against disaster if part of your PC breaks down. Smart PC users always back up their most important data.

Vital stuff. Some of the files you create will be extremely important to you. A good example is a set of income tax records. Another is a list of addresses and telephone numbers. How about that novel or screenplay that will launch you on your way to greatness? What would you do if you lost this information and didn't have a copy of it somewhere else?

Would you keep all your savings in cash, stuffed into your top dresser drawer? Of course not. Neither should you keep all your valuable files on a hard disk alone.

Hard drive failure. If you keep a PC long enough, the hard drive will someday fail. It's up to you whether the inconvenience will be major or minor. A PC is like a car; eventually the engine will wear out and have to be replaced. It will save you a lot of aggravation if you're ready for the event when it finally happens.

Software you've bought will, of course, remain on the diskettes supplied with the package you originally purchased. Reinstalling all your software will take quite awhile to do from the original diskettes, however. The best way to completely back up a hard disk is to use a *tape drive.* This should be done in addition to keeping backup copies of important, often-revised files on diskettes. A complete backup of a medium-sized hard disk can be done on a single tape cartridge in less than an hour. Another approach, although more expensive, is to use a WORM (write-once/read-many) drive to back things up on CD-ROM.

Multiple PCs. If you own more than one computer, you can keep important files on the hard drives in both PCs. For example, if you have a desktop computer at home and a laptop computer for travel and vacation, you can keep irreplaceable files on the hard disks of both PCs. However, even then, you should have archives on diskettes or magnetic tape. It is not impossible for the hard drives in two different computers to fail at about the same time.

If you have a lot of graphics files, you will probably not be able to store them all on a single hard disk. Then you'll need to put some, if not most, of them on diskettes and/or tapes. You might have three copies of such archives: one set of diskettes for carrying around with your laptop, another set of diskettes for use at home, and a comprehensive graphics library on magnetic tapes.

Bad sectors. When backing up files on diskettes, be sure that none of the diskettes have *bad sectors.* If there are bad sectors on any of

Backup utility

the diskettes, some of the files you've backed up might be incompletely saved or messed up so badly that you can't use them.

While you're formatting a diskette, your PC will tell you if there are any bad sectors. If there are, the safest thing is to throw the thing away; diskettes only cost about a dollar each.

Bad sectors on a hard disk are normally of little concern. Most hard disks have some flaws in them when they are manufactured. The computer operating system is programmed to avoid writing data onto these parts of the hard disk.

Active files. When you're working on a file, it is in the RAM (random-access memory) of your PC. If there is a power failure or other disruption in computer operation, all the data in RAM will vanish. When you get your PC going again, you'll have to go back to the hard disk or diskette and retrieve the file you were working on. The file will be in whatever form you last stored it on disk. Anything you did to the file while it was in the RAM will have to be done all over again. For this reason, you should store your data on disk every few minutes while you are at work on a file. You might also want to purchase a UPS (uninterruptible power supply).

Backup backups. It's a good idea to keep two separate sets of backup files, one near your PC and another somewhere away from it. What would you do if your house were burglarized, or if there were a fire, flood, or other natural catastrophe?

The files for this book were backed up in triplicate on three different sets of diskettes. The first set was labeled "My Copy." The second set was labeled "Publisher's Copy." These two sets were kept at home, but in different places. The third set included photocopies of all the artwork, as well as diskettes. This set, labeled "Hurricane Copy," was mailed to relatives. *See also* ARCHIVES, BACKUP UTILITY, BAD SECTORS, CD-ROM, DISKETTE, HARD DISK, MASS STORAGE, TAPE DRIVE, UNINTERRUPTIBLE POWER SUPPLY, *and* WRITE-ONCE/READ-MANY.

Backup utility

A *backup utility* is a program that helps you make a copy of data on your hard disk. Most backup utilities guide you through the process of storing files on a set of diskettes, a tape drive, or some other medium.

Much of the information on a hard disk is in the form of software. When you back up a hard disk using a backup utility, the software will be stored along with everything else from the hard disk. This makes it easy to move your whole computing environment from one machine to another; you don't have to reinstall all the programs individually on the new hard disk.

If you back up files from your hard disk often (and you should), it can be overkill to do a total backup. Software and support programs don't usually change once you've put them on your hard disk. It's a waste of time to back things up when they haven't changed. On the other hand, files like address lists, financial records, and book manuscripts change often. A backup utility helps you keep track of what needs backing up and what doesn't, and updates only those files that need it. Backup utilities are standard in most computing environments today, including the popular Microsoft Windows. *See also* BACKUP.

Backward chaining

Backward chaining is a logic process that can be used in artificial intelligence (AI). Rather than working with data that has already been supplied, the computer requests data as it goes along. In this way, the computer gets only the information it needs to solve a problem. There's no memory wasted in storing unnecessary data.

Backward chaining is especially useful in *expert systems*, programs designed to help you figure out complicated, specialized problems in fields you aren't familiar with. A good example is a medical-diagnosis program. Backward chaining can also be of use in electronic troubleshooting, weather forecasting, cost analysis, and even police detective work. *See also* ANALOGICAL REASONING, ARTIFICIAL INTELLIGENCE, EXPERT SYSTEMS, *and* FORECASTING.

Bacteriorhodopsin

Bacteriorhodopsin (BR) is a protein found in certain plants that changes color depending on the light that shines on it or through it. This interests researchers in *optical computer technology*.

Red/green. The bacteriorhodopsin molecule resembles a substance in the human eye known as *visual purple*. When BR is exposed to red light, it turns into a red color filter, which lets red light through, but blocks other colors. If green light shines on the BR, it turns into a green color filter. If red light hits the BR again, it again becomes red.

A BR molecule can change color over and over at extreme speed. One conversion takes only three-trillionths (0.000 000 000 003, or 3×10^{-12}) of a second. Thus, more than 300 billion (300,000,000,000 or 3×10^{11}) transitions can take place in one second.

Because of this interesting property, some researchers think BR is perfect for making high-speed computers. It has "memory," with bits (binary digits) that can be as small as a single molecule. This is great for miniaturization. The molecule works fast, and speed is important in the design of powerful computers.

Read/write. A red/green, dual-beam laser could be used for writing or reading a data bit (either 0 or 1) onto or from a BR molecule. The drawing shows how data is read from a BR molecule. In the drawing at A, the BR molecule is acting like a red filter. The red/green laser shines on the molecule, and only the red beam gets through. This might represent the digit 0. In the drawing at B, the molecule is behaving like a green filter. Only the green beam gets through; this could represent the digit 1.

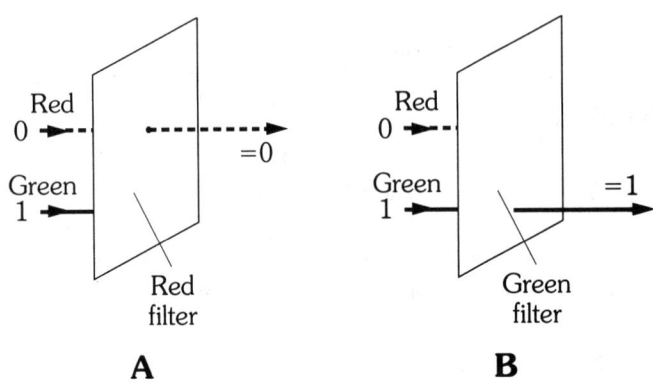

At A, logic 0. At B, logic 1.

To change the state of the BR molecule, a pure red or pure green laser is beamed at it. With the color code in this example, a red beam would write the digit 0 onto the BR molecule; a green beam would write the digit 1. *See also* OPTICAL COMPUTER TECHNOLOGY *and* SINGLE-ELECTRON MEMORY.

Bad sectors

Bad sectors are portions of a hard disk or diskette that will not reliably store data. Bad sectors can result from manufacturing defects, or from grease, dirt, or scratches on the disk surface.

Hard disks. Most hard disks have some flaws when they are made. You'll notice them if you run a physical scan of the disk surface, such as is provided by the SCANDISK command in DOS. Using this command, bad sectors show up as a prominent letter B. The computer operating system is programmed to ignore bad sectors on a hard disk and will not try to write data on them. The only practical effect is that you'll have a tiny fraction less space on the disk than there would be if the disk were flawless.

If there is any serious damage to a hard disk, the PC will tell you about it. If you run a program to search for bad sectors on a hard disk, and you find a few, there's no need to worry. This is the rule, not the exception.

Diskettes. Bad sectors on diskettes, on the other hand, can present serious problems. As you write data onto a flawed diskette, the PC might behave as if everything were working fine. But when you need to get the data from the diskette, you will find some of it missing or mutilated. Sometimes you can use a special utility, such as DOS's RECOVER command, to get the information from a diskette with bad sectors. Unfortunately, this does not always work.

Some brand-new diskettes have bad sectors. The problem can also occur in diskettes that have been stored for a long time. To minimize the chances of losing data because of bad diskette sectors, you can do at least three things:

1 Always format new diskettes (even preformatted ones) before use.

2 Keep at least two copies of each diskette in your archives.

3 Buy only the best-quality diskettes.

When you format a diskette, the PC will tell you if any sectors are bad. If there are bad sectors, don't use the diskette; throw it away. Diskettes are cheap and easily replaced. Your data is not.

Keeping two (or even three) identical sets of *archives* is another wise precaution, even if no diskettes ever had bad sectors. Fires, floods, burglaries, and other disasters happen. Can you afford to lose irreplaceable data, as well as other personal property, in such an event? *See also* ARCHIVES, BACKUP, DISKETTE, HARD DISK, *and* SECTOR.

Bandwidth

When data is sent from one place to another, the signal needs a certain amount of frequency space. The *bandwidth* of a signal is the amount of frequency space that it takes up.

All signals need space. Suppose you could see a graph of the data being sent and received by your PC, with frequency on the horizontal axis and signal strength on the vertical axis. Engineers can do just this, using a lab instrument called a *spectrum analyzer*. On a spectrum analyzer, a signal with zero bandwidth would look like graph A. Such a signal can't carry any information.

As soon as the signal has any *modulation*, that is, as soon as it is made to carry any data, it will begin to spread out as seen on the spectrum analyzer. This is shown as graphs B and C. The bandwidth is the difference between the highest and the lowest signal frequency.

The higher the data speed, the greater its bandwidth. Computer data speed is usually measured in *bauds* or in *bits per second*. There is some confusion about the meanings of these terms. They're often used interchangeably, although they don't refer to exactly the same thing.

The greater the bandwidth that a signal is allowed to have, the higher the data speed can be. The smaller the allowable bandwidth, the more severe the constraints on the data speed.

Barcode

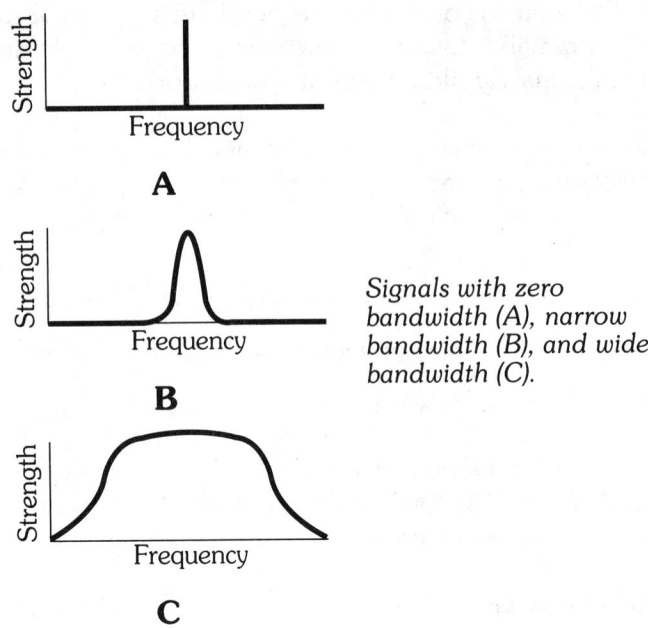

Signals with zero bandwidth (A), narrow bandwidth (B), and wide bandwidth (C).

Other factors. There are other things besides speed that affect the bandwidth of a data signal. A voice, for example, has tone or inflection that conveys the feelings of the person sending the information. You can usually tell whether the speaker is male or female. If you're willing to give up "tone of voice" and send printed matter, you can convey the same words, at the same speed, using less bandwidth. Or you can send more words in a given time using the same bandwidth.

Computers communicate digitally. All kinds of variable quantities, including graphics, sound, and motion, can be converted from analog to digital data and back again. Digital signals are sent and received more efficiently than analog signals within a given bandwidth. *See also* ANALOG, ANALOG-TO-DIGITAL CONVERSION, BAUD/BITS PER SECOND, DIGITAL, *and* DIGITAL-TO-ANALOG CONVERSION.

Barcode

A *barcode* is a way to label things. You have seen barcode labels or tags in stores, where they are used for pricing merchandise and keeping track of inventory. Barcoding allows a computer to instantly identify something, even from some distance away.

Quick scan. A barcode tag has parallel lines of varying width and spacing, as shown in the drawing. A laser-equipped device scans the tag, retrieving the identifying data. The reading device does not need to be brought right up to the tag, nor does the item have to be held in any special way. The cashier just zings your items past a clear plastic window, behind which is a laser scanner/detector. When the machine recognizes something, there's a beep, and the data goes into the computer.

Laser scanner decodes the barcode data.

When the barcode scanner at a checkout counter is working, the cashier can ring things up much faster than was possible in the old days. The machine goes "beep, beep, beep," and a cartful of items are rung up in a minute. The barcode lets the store keep track not only of the prices of things, but of the department they came from, making it easier to track inventory.

When a barcode reader fails, the cashier must enter all the data manually. This takes longer than it did in the days before barcodes. Sometimes the cashier must punch a dozen or more buttons for each item, without making a single mistake. The checkout process becomes a nightmare, especially for the cashier. This is an all-too-common example of what can happen when society gets too reliant on computers.

The future. Barcodes are one method by which objects can be labeled so a robot can identify them. This will be a boon for personal robots of the future. A tool set can be tagged, for example, using barcode stickers with a different code for each tool. When a robot's program tells it that it needs a certain tool, the robot can seek out the tag and carry out the movements according to a software program for that tool. If a tool gets misplaced, it can easily be found again when it is needed. *See also* PERSONAL ROBOTS.

Bar graph

When working with graphics, it is sometimes necessary to show the values of several different variables. One scheme for doing this is called a *bar graph*.

In a true bar graph, the independent variable is on the vertical axis, and the dependent variable is on the horizontal axis. However, this isn't the standard way to draw graphs. More often, the independent variable is along the horizontal axis, and the dependent variable is along the vertical axis. Because they are "sideways," true bar graphs can be confusing.

Baseband

The drawing is a bar graph showing the average high temperature for January 1 and July 1, for four hypothetical towns A, B, C, and D. The four towns and the dates represent the independent variables, and are shown on the vertical axis. Temperature, in degrees Fahrenheit, is the dependent variable, shown on the horizontal axis. Crosshatching and/or shading makes it easy to tell which bars are which. *See also* COLUMNAR GRAPH, DEPENDENT VARIABLE, *and* INDEPENDENT VARIABLE.

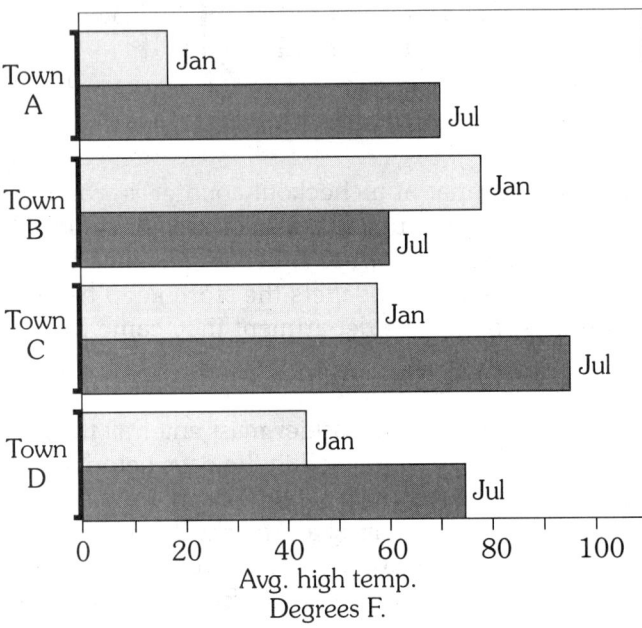

A bar graph of average high temperatures for four towns in January and July.

Baseband

The term *baseband* is used in communications to refer to ways of sending and receiving data. The term sometimes refers to the audio frequencies of a human voice.

In a LAN. A local area network (LAN) can carry signals among computers by sending high and low voltages (also called 1 and 0) directly over wires. No modem is used in this method, which is called *digital baseband.* Each PC in such a LAN is "hard-wired" to all the others.

The big advantage of digital baseband, compared with communication using modems, is that the circuitry is simpler. A modem converts data from digital to analog form, and vice versa; this conversion is bypassed in a digital baseband system. Because the circuit is simpler, it costs less, and fewer things can go wrong with it. Another advantage of digital baseband is high speed. There are no bandwidth limitations to worry about in the communications channel.

The main disadvantage of digital baseband is that the range is limited. Wire current gets weaker quickly with increasing wire length. This is not a problem with most LANs because the PCs are all near each other. Another disadvantage of digital baseband is the fact that it allows for only one channel to be sent over the wires. Multiplexing is impossible. *See also* ANALOG, DIGITAL, LOCAL AREA NETWORK, *and* MULTIPLEXING.

Audio. In analog communications, the term *baseband* refers to the range of frequencies normally occupied by a voice channel, such as a telephone conversation. The *analog baseband* frequency range extends from about 300 hertz (Hz), or 300 cycles per second, to 3000 Hz. An audio tone of 300 Hz is like a low-pitched clarinet note. A tone of 3000 Hz is like a high-pitched piccolo note.

When computer signals are sent with modems over telephone lines, the communication speed is directly related to the bandwidth of the signals sent and received. Analog baseband has a bandwidth of 2700 Hz (3000 – 300 Hz), wide enough for the highest speeds used by modems today.

Communication by modem is slower than with digital baseband, but modems allow multiplexing and provide for unlimited range and versatility. Radio amateurs, for example, can network via shortwave and satellite links. *See also* BANDWIDTH, HERTZ, MODEM, NETWORK, *and* PACKET COMMUNICATIONS.

Base font

In word processing and other programs, you can choose from various type styles. The type style is called the *font*. Fonts can be changed in the PC software and in the printer. The *base font* is the type style that the software will work with unless you specifically tell it to use another font. For example, the base font might be Times New Roman, 10 point (a point is a typographic measurement). If you use the word processor and don't specify a font, the document will come out in Times New Roman, 10 point. The base font information is contained in each document. Therefore, different documents can be set to print out in different fonts, without your having to manually select them before each printing session.

You can also program fonts directly at the printer. Some printers have many font options; others have only a few. The system in the printer is similar to that in the word processing software. Unless you set the printer for some special font, it will print in its default font. Some printers have three or four settings that you can choose, each with its own font. *See also* DEFAULT *and* FONT.

Base memory

Base memory is a term used with IBM-compatible PCs. This memory, also called *conventional memory*, is the directly usable part of the RAM (random-access memory).

The first PC. The earliest PCs had only 64K (kilobytes) of base memory, about the amount of data in 50 or 60 pages of double-spaced text. In contrast, the computer file for the articles in this book that start with *B* took up 155K of memory when complete. That's more than twice the base memory of the first PC.

In the early 1980s, engineers at IBM designed the PC so that it would eventually be able to hold 640K of base memory, or ten times the base memory of the original PC. In those days, it seemed like 640K was more than any PC user would ever need. Now, that seems incredible; even casual PC users feel the limitations imposed by a memory of only 640K.

Extra memory. Modern computers have extra memory in addition to the base memory. At the minimum, this amounts to 384K, for a total of 1024K, or one megabyte (1M). This 384K is where the *BIOS (basic input/output system)* and *bootstrap program* reside.

The drawing at A is a comparison of the base-memory capacity of the earliest PC (64K) compared that of modern PCs (640K), and also compared with the total memory available (1MB or more).

The RAM in most computers is expandable to several tens of megabytes with the addition of memory expansion cards. Many programs, especially those involving graphics applications, require upwards of 8MB of RAM to run properly. When buying software, you need to be sure that your computer has enough RAM to handle it.

Disks and tapes. The hard disk in your PC allows for the storage of far more than the base memory in RAM. Hard disks are getting more spacious every year. It's not uncommon to see more than 1000MB (one gigabyte, abbreviated 1GB) available on hard disk. The drawing at B compares the 640K of base memory with 40MB, the hard disk capacity in today's most modest portable computers.

A *tape drive* also can be used to store your data, although it doesn't let you get at information very quickly. The main purpose of tape drives is for backup of a hard disk.

Diskettes allow you to create archives, or a personal library, with a capacity limited only by the amount of physical space you're willing to provide in your library. A five-foot stack of diskettes represents about 1GB of memory. If you happen to have a warehouse with a mile of

Base memory

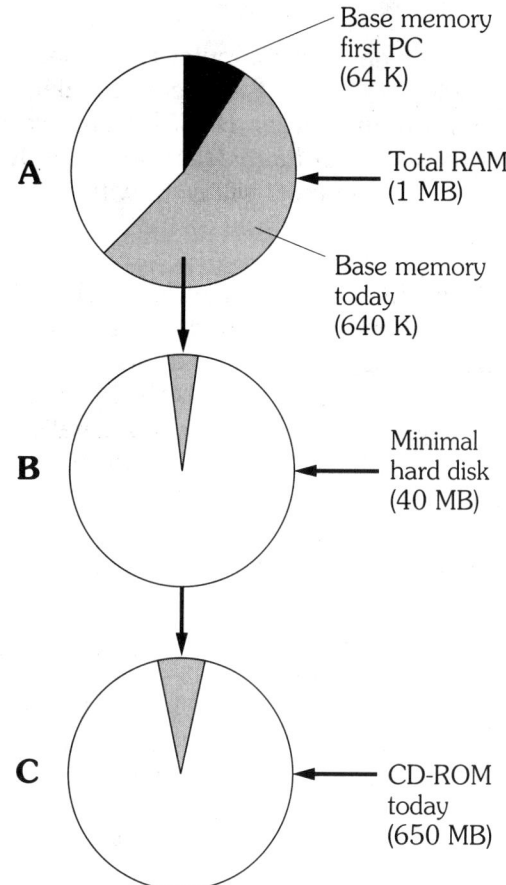

At A, RAM in a PC; at B, hard disk storage capacity; at C, storage capacity of CD-ROM.

shelf space available, you could store approximately one trillion bytes of data (one terabyte, abbreviated 1TB or 1T) on diskettes.

The future. Magnetic media are being upstaged to some extent by *CD-ROM* (compact-disc, read-only memory). On one compact disc, there is room for at least 650MB of data, more than 1000 times the base memory of your PC. The drawing at C compares the space in a minimal hard disk (40MB) with the capacity of a single CD-ROM. The slice of the pie represented by today's base memory would look like a hair line.

Rewriteable CD-ROM drives are becoming more accessible, although they are rather expensive at the time of this writing. As technology advances, the cost of these devices should drop, making them affordable to many PC users. The capacity of a single CD-ROM can also be expected to increase to several gigabytes. *See also* ARCHIVES, BYTE, CD-ROM, DISKETTE, EXTENDED/EXPANDED MEMORY, HARD DISK, MAGNETIC MEDIA, MEMORY, RANDOM-ACCESS MEMORY, *and* TAPE DRIVE.

BASIC

BASIC

BASIC, one of several high-level computer languages, was originally developed in the early 1960s with the intent of making computer programming easy for nonscientists. *BASIC* is an acronym for *Beginner's All-purpose Symbolic Instruction Code*. It is the most popular language for PC users and will work with IBM-compatible PCs or with Macintosh systems.

Easy to learn. As its name implies, BASIC is relatively easy to learn. BASIC can be taught at the junior-high and even the elementary school level. It can even be self-taught with instruction books without the aid of a teacher. Many people learn BASIC as their first programming language. The commands are generally self-explanatory, so you don't have to be a computer expert to get familiar with them.

BASIC can work either with an interpreter or a compiler; an interpreter is more commonly used. The language uses numbered lines. Usually, the programmer starts out with multiples of 10, so the lines are numbered 10, 20, 30 and so on. That way, there's plenty of room to insert new statements in between lines as a program evolves.

The sample code is a simple BASIC program. If you run this program, the computer will print out all the powers of two that are less than one billion (10^9) in increasing order: 2, 4, 8, 16, 32, etc.

An example of a short program in BASIC

```
10  LET N=2
20  IF N > 1000000000 GOTO 60
30  PRINT N
40  LET N=N*2
50  GOTO 20
60  END
```

Limitations. BASIC can be used for many different things, but there is no hard-and-fast standard. Some long programs in BASIC are not very portable: a program that works with a computer having a certain interpreter might not work with other computers that use different interpreters. There are other languages that make more effective use of a computer's power for specialized applications like business, robot control, or scientific analysis.

Numerous variations on BASIC have been devised, and some of these are more efficient than the original BASIC. One example is Visual Basic by Microsoft. In high-tech professional situations, it is usually best to select a language that has been developed especially for the task at hand. *See also* C, COBOL, COMPILER, FORTRAN, HIGH-LEVEL LANGUAGE, *and* INTERPRETER.

Basic input/output system (BIOS)

When you first switch your PC on, the CPU (central processing unit) must come to its senses. To do this, it looks first to some information called the *BIOS (basic input/output system)*.

The drawing is a simplified block diagram of a PC, showing the CPU, RAM (random-access memory), and ROM (read-only memory). The BIOS is contained in ROM. You can't easily change the ROM, so the BIOS always stays the same, as if it were on a compact disc.

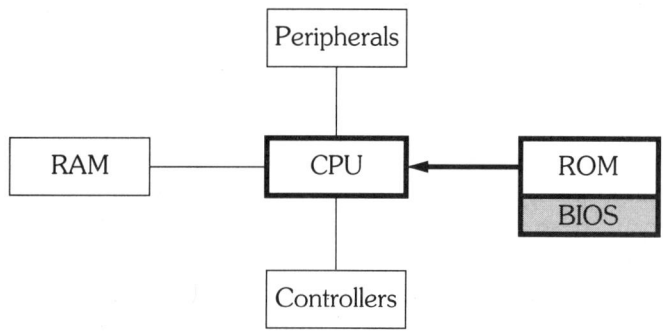

BIOS is part of ROM.

When you power-up your computer, the CPU goes through a ritual, just as you go through a routine every morning. Instead of taking a shower, eating breakfast, and getting dressed, the CPU runs various tests and then looks for its operating system.

Normally, the operating system, such as DOS, OS/2, or the Macintosh OS, is on your PC's hard disk. In that case, the diskette drives should be empty when you switch on your PC. If there is a diskette in any of the diskette drives, the BIOS will look for the operating system there, and then will look for it on the hard disk. *See also* BOOTSTRAP PROGRAM, CENTRAL PROCESSING UNIT, OPERATING SYSTEM, *and* READ-ONLY MEMORY.

Batch file

Certain command sequences are the same every time you do them. In such cases, you can have the computer give the commands to itself automatically, in the correct order, without having to go through them all yourself. This is called *batch processing*. Batch processing is done by means of *batch files*. A batch-processing program in DOS can usually be identified by the presence of the filename extension .BAT.

Initial setup. This book was written on a PC using DOS. Every time the computer was switched on, it would automatically get itself into

Battery backup

DOS. Various things would flash on the screen as the DOS software was loaded by batch processing. Finally, something like the following would appear on the screen:

C:>

This told me that the hard disk was ready for me to make use of it. I would then type *EDITOR*, press Enter, and the screen would show the copyright notice for *XyWrite*, the word processing software used for writing this book.

If you use Windows instead of DOS, your batch file can set up Windows automatically, every time you switch your PC on. Windows software takes longer to load than DOS, so computers programmed to go into Windows take longer to "wake up" after power is first applied.

Going further. It's not very tedious to manually start XyWrite; it just takes one command. However, suppose you're a novelist, and you never do anything on your PC except write text using a word processing program. You could prepare a separate batch file that would go through commands automatically to load the word processing software and the printer program. Then all you'd need to do, after switching on the PC and waiting for about half a minute, would be to open whatever text file you wanted to work with.

If you use batch files, it doesn't restrict you to the software that's been automatically loaded. You can always change over, for example, from DOS to Windows or vice versa. However, you must manually type in, or click in, these commands. *See also* DOS.

Battery backup

When you switch your PC off, all the data in the RAM (random-access memory) vanishes. This data is called *volatile memory* because it "evaporates" without a constant supply of electricity to keep it going. It's like ether; it will quickly disappear from an open container (a switched-off PC). ROM (read-only memory), on the other hand, is literally programmed into the integrated circuits (ICs) or "chips," and stays the same whether there is power going to it or not. Data in ROM, as well as the data on a hard disk or diskette, stays there even if you leave your PC off indefinitely. A block diagram of a PC with volatile and nonvolatile memory is shown in the drawing.

Volatile memory can be kept from "evaporating" by supplying it with a voltage, then it can sustain itself when the external power is removed. This is like putting a lid on a jar of ether. In modern electronic devices, some memory can be retained without drawing much current. A small battery can supply the few volts necessary to keep this data stored in an IC for days, weeks, months, or even years. This is called *battery backup*.

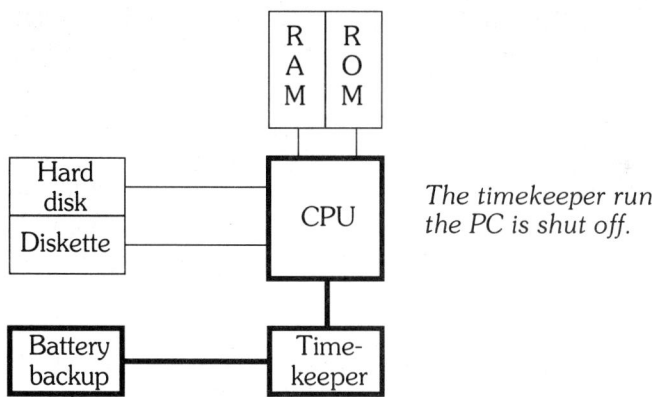

The timekeeper runs even when the PC is shut off.

Date/time, please. A *timekeeper* makes it possible for the PC to log the date and time for each file stored on the hard disk or diskette. This circuit uses battery backup because it's impossible to program the correct time in an IC or store it on disk (time is always changing). This circuit needs so little power that a tiny battery can keep it running indefinitely. A battery will last just about as long running a timekeeper as it would sitting on the shelf doing nothing at all.

The entire contents of RAM is too much to back up with a small battery. The RAM needs a fair amount of current; it is like a barrel full of ether. You could probably back up the RAM with a huge battery, such as a car battery, but that would be bulky, expensive, and unnecessary. It's easier to save data on disk or diskette before switching your PC off. See also TIMEKEEPER.

Common types. Memory-backup batteries are specially designed to last a long time; two types of batteries work well. One is the *lithium battery*. It supplies a tiny current for years; it's similar to the cells used in electronic wristwatches. The other type is the *nickel-cadmium (NiCad) battery*. It recharges slowly and constantly whenever your PC is on, and supplies a tiny current for backup when the PC is not in use.

You might want to have a power supply that can operate when utilities fail. Or you might have an interest in using solar power or other alternative power sources. These power systems employ battery backup to supplement a primary power source such as utility mains, the wind, the sun, or the moving water in a stream. See also LITHIUM BATTERY, NICKEL-CADMIUM BATTERY, NONVOLATILE MEMORY, POWER SUPPLY, UNINTERRUPTIBLE POWER SUPPLY, *and* VOLATILE MEMORY.

Baud/bits per second

When computers communicate, some "talk" faster than others, just as some people speak faster than others. The speed at which digital

Baud/bits per second

computer signals are transmitted can be measured in various ways. Two frequently confused specifications are the *baud rate* and the number of *bits per second (bps)*.

Baud versus bps. The most common method of measuring data speed is to specify the number of data bits (high and low signal states) that occur in one second. That's the bps rate. Although bps and baud are not technically the same thing, the terms have become almost interchangeable in common usage.

Baud refers to the number of times per second that a signal changes state. The speed in bps is generally higher than the baud rate, sometimes by a factor of several times. When people say that a modem works at a certain "baud rate," they are usually actually referring to the speed in bps.

Modems. When computers are interconnected by telephone, satellite, microwave, or fiberoptic systems, the signals are sent and received at precise, standard rates of speed. The higher the signal speed, the faster the computers respond to each other and to their human operators' commands.

When you access an online service, you use a modem that can send and receive data at certain speeds. The computer at the other end of the line also has a modem, with the ability to send and receive at various speeds. Sometimes the two modems have different maximum speeds. The slower modem determines the highest speed at which the PCs can communicate.

There is a limit to the data speed that a telephone circuit can handle. The higher the speed, the larger the *bandwidth*, or range of frequencies that a signal takes up. A telephone line can handle bandwidths of up to about 3000 cycles per second, or 3 kilohertz (3 kHz). This accommodates the signals commonly used with PCs.

How fast are various data speeds in practical, real-life terms? The table shows common data speeds in bits per second, and the time required to send one, 10, and 100 pages of normal, double-spaced text at each speed. This table is by no means an expression of data speed limits; modems are being tested that can work at 256,000 bps and higher speeds.

Advanced PC links. Satellite, microwave, and fiberoptic communications systems can handle larger signal bandwidths than telephone circuits. Therefore, much higher speeds are possible in these modes. Amateur radio operators often use systems having larger bandwidths than telephone systems, especially at microwave radio frequencies. On the so-called "shortwave" frequencies, however, data speeds are slower, sometimes less than 1200 bps.

Time taken to send data at various speeds

Bits per second	To send one page	To send 10 pages	To send 100 pages
1200	9.00 seconds	1 minute 30 seconds	15 minutes
2400	4.50 seconds	45.0 seconds	7 minutes 30 seconds
4800	2.25 seconds	22.5 seconds	3 minutes 45 seconds
9600	1.13 seconds	11.3 seconds	1 minute 53 seconds
14,400	0.75 second	7.5 seconds	1 minute 15 seconds
19,200	0.56 second	5.6 seconds	56 seconds

The speed of data transmission and reception is an important factor in how "smart" a PC network can become. The faster a system can handle data, the higher its potential level of artificial intelligence (AI). However, regardless of the speed at which data is transmitted, propagation delays limit the speed with which computers can exchange data in a two-way link. This is because no signals can travel faster than the speed of light, about 186,000 miles per second in free space. *See also* BANDWIDTH *and* MODEM.

BBS

See BULLETIN-BOARD SYSTEM.

Bell 103 and 202

In *packet radio*, a communications scheme used by amateur radio operators, the signal from a PC modem is applied to the input of a radio transmitter. This signal has two audio tones at different frequencies. One tone represents the digital high state (1), and the other tone represents the low state (0).

FSK. *Bell 103* uses audio tones of 2025 and 2225 hertz (Hz). This scheme is used for PC communication at the shortwave frequencies from 3.5 MHz (megahertz) through 29.7 MHz. A single-sideband (SSB) transmitter is used, as shown in the drawing at A. The resulting output consists of two radio signals, one for the low state (0) and the other for the high state (1), on slightly different radio frequencies. This is known as *frequency-shift keying (FSK)*. Its nature is much different from the audio signals that telephone modems use.

AFSK. *Bell 202* uses tones of 1200 and 2200 Hz. It is used for digital PC networking at the very high frequencies (VHF), ultra high frequencies (UHF) and microwave frequencies. These range from 50 MHz to many gigahertz (GHz). In Bell 202, a frequency-modulated (FM) transmitter is used, as shown in the drawing at B. This results in a signal of a complex type called *audio-frequency-shift keying (AFSK)*. It, like FSK, differs greatly from the audio used by telephone modems.

Benchmark

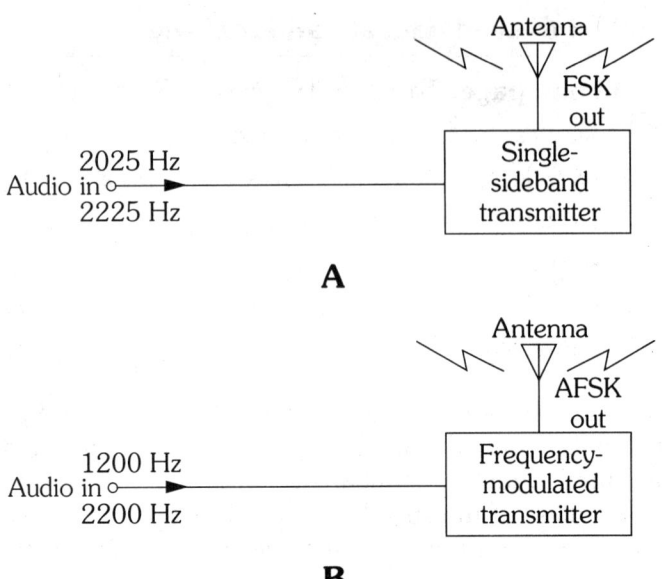

System for Bell 103 (A) and Bell 202 (B).

Demodulation. Both FSK or AFSK, when properly demodulated by a radio receiver, produce signals that are similar to those used by telephone modems. However, in a packet-radio link, the receiving operator must be sure that the receiver is adjusted correctly; otherwise, the signal will be garbled or won't come in at all. This makes packet-radio communications more complicated than using a telephone modem. But packet radio is a lot more interesting, and there are no telephone tolls.

The technical details of FSK and AFSK are far beyond the scope of this book. For in-depth discussion, refer to books on amateur-radio digital communications. General references include *Amateur Radio Encyclopedia* (TAB/McGraw-Hill) and *The ARRL Handbook* (American Radio Relay League, Inc.). See also AMATEUR RADIO, BAUD, MODEM, *and* PACKET COMMUNICATIONS.

Benchmark

In personal computing, the term *benchmark* refers to tests or special programs that measure performance. Such tests and programs help determine which PC is best for a given application.

A benchmark is like the standardized tests you took in school. A benchmark makes your computer go through several different routines. It might test clock speed, hard disk performance, diskette drive performance, memory capacity, and access/storage time, among other things.

Clock speed. The speed of the CPU (central processing unit) is an important measure of a PC's power. It is measured in megahertz (MHz), or millions of cycles per second. The faster the CPU, the more data it can handle in a given period of time. However, even a fast CPU can be hindered if other components of the computer are sluggish or weak. There's not much point in having a super-fast CPU if the hard disk works slowly. *See also* CENTRAL PROCESSING UNIT *and* CLOCK SPEED.

Disk drives. How much data can be stored on the hard disk? How long does it take to write, say, 100K (100,000 bytes) of data on the hard disk? How long does it take to get that information from hard disk into RAM (random-access memory)? What about the diskette drive(s)? How long does it take to transfer data from hard disk to diskette, or vice versa? From RAM to diskette, or vice versa? A good benchmark puts the disk drives through all kinds of reading/writing exercises. *See also* DISKETTE DRIVE *and* HARD DISK.

Memory. The more data a computer can store, the more powerful it is. There are several different types of memory, each with its own function. The most important, from the standpoint of computer power, is the size of RAM.

How fast can your PC get data from the various places where it is stored? A huge memory isn't very useful if it takes a long time to get information from it. Conversely, instant access doesn't mean much if the memory capacity is tiny. *See also* ACCESS TIME, BYTE, CACHE MEMORY, MEMORY, MEMORY CAPACITY, RANDOM-ACCESS MEMORY, *and* READ-ONLY MEMORY.

Bus size. Bus size is measured in bits. The larger the bus size, the more powerful the PC. Bus size is almost always a power of two. In 1976, a common bus size was 2^3 or 8 bits; in 1982 it was 2^4 or 16 bits. By the mid-1980s it was up to 2^5 or 32 bits. Today, even larger buses are possible. The bus size is something like the number of lanes in a highway: a 16-lane freeway can handle far more traffic than a two-lane road. *See also* BUS.

Throughput. All the things listed here combine to determine the total amount of work that a PC can do in a given length of time, its *throughput*. Throughput is the single most meaningful specification for computer power. When comparing PCs, this is the factor you should consider above all others. If you use a GUI (graphical user interface) like Windows, the video throughput is also an important specification. *See also* THROUGHPUT.

Bernoulli box

A *Bernoulli box* is a disk drive system with a capacity similar to that of a hard disk, but with the versatility of a diskette drive. A Bernoulli box is more rugged than a hard disk drive and has a faster access time. It gets its name from Daniel Bernoulli, a scientist who worked with the mathematics of fluid dynamics.

Beta-particle CD-ROM

No head crashes. Vibration can cause the head in a hard drive to bang into the surface of the disk. This often damages the head and/or the disk, as well as causing a general PC malfunction.

It's much harder to get a Bernoulli box to have a head crash. If you throw a Bernoulli box out a window, its head will probably crash, but if you accidentally drop it on a carpeted floor, it will probably survive without damage. It will take treatment of the sort to which airline luggage is subjected. This makes it ideal for people who must transport large quantities of data along with their computer systems. Of course, the fact that a Bernoulli box is rugged should not be taken as a license to subject it to wanton abuse.

Best of two worlds. The disks in a Bernoulli box spin fast and are supported by air pressure. (In the physicist's way of thinking, air is a fluid, hence the idea for naming this device after a fluid-dynamics specialist.) The access time is typically less than 20 milliseconds (0.02 second). The capacity is hundreds of megabytes, comparable to that of a hard disk, but a hard disk is a sealed system, with its platters fixed and normally not interchangeable. Bernoulli cartridges are like diskettes: they can be removed and replaced. A Bernoulli box gives you the best features of both hard disks and diskette drives: fast access, high data capacity, and physical ruggedness. Some Bernoulli boxes can even accept more than one cartridge at a time.

There are a couple of cautionary notes to be aware of if you're thinking about purchasing a Bernoulli box. First, they aren't cheap. Second, some Bernoulli disks tend to wear out rather quickly. *See also* DISKETTE DRIVE, HARD DISK, *and* HEAD CRASH.

Beta-particle CD-ROM

Consumers keep demanding that more data be stored in less space. Engineers keep finding new ways to make data more compact. The absolute limit of miniaturization is the presence or absence of a single subatomic particle. Researchers are making progress toward this ultimate end; single-electron memory chips might be available early in the 21st century. The electron might also play a role in nonvolatile data storage media such as diskettes.

CD-ROM. One data-storage technology, *CD-ROM* (compact-disc, read-only memory), stores information in microscopic pits etched on a reflective plastic surface. This allows upwards of 650 megabytes (MB) of data to be stored on a single diskette measuring less than five inches in diameter. This is 500 to 600 times the capacity of a typical high-density magnetic diskette, and more than 10,000 times the storage capacity of the earliest magnetic diskettes.

In CD-ROM, lasers recover the data from the diskette surface. The energy from a visible-light laser has a certain defined wavelength, limiting how small the data pits on the diskette can be made. If the data pits are smaller than approximately one wavelength across, the sensors can't resolve them, and the machine can't read the data.

Wavelength. The wavelength of visible light varies from about 0.4 to 0.7 thousandths of a millimeter, usually expressed in nanometers (nm). Violet light has a wavelength of around 400 nm, and red light has a wavelength of about 700 nm. The other colors of the spectrum have intermediate wavelengths.

As the wavelength of the laser becomes shorter, the data pits on a CD-ROM can be made smaller. In theory, a CD-ROM that uses violet light is capable of almost twice the data storage capacity of a CD-ROM that uses red light. Ultraviolet (UV) lasers could have even greater capacity, because UV energy has a wavelength shorter than that of violet light. Unfortunately, when the wavelength goes very far into the UV, the beams start to penetrate the plastic rather than reflecting from it. This makes the data pits harder, not easier, for the device to resolve.

High-speed particles. Another way to shorten the wavelength of the energy beams used to read CD-ROMs involves high-speed, subatomic particles. Electrons might work for this purpose just as they do in the electron microscope.

All fast-moving particles have a definite wavelength, called the *de Broglie wavelength* (pronounced "dee-BROY-lee"). For a given type of particle, the greater the speed, the shorter the de Broglie wavelength. This was theoretically demonstrated for electrons in 1924.

Optical microscopes can provide about 2000 magnifications. If you try to make the instrument magnify more than that, interference patterns blur the images. Electron microscopes were developed to overcome this problem, and the scheme worked. An electron microscope can magnify many times more than an optical microscope. This same principle should work with CD-ROM technology.

High-speed electrons are often called *beta particles.* If, at some future time, you hear about *beta-particle CD-ROM (BPCD-ROM)*, you'll know that this technology has been tested and found to work. It might revolutionize data storage in much the same way as the electron microscope affected the physical and biological sciences. *See also* CD-ROM, DISK CAPACITY, *and* SINGLE-ELECTRON MEMORY.

Beta test

When software is designed by a company for sale to customers, it must first be put through a series of tests. As many bugs as possible must be found and eliminated. A *beta test* is the second stage in the debugging of commercial software. It follows the *alpha test*.

Bezier curve

Like a road test. Beta testing is like the road-testing that is done with a new car design. In cars, some flaws won't show up until after many driving miles. Perhaps you've had a car that was recalled because of some problem that develops only after several thousand miles on the road. Car makers do everything within reason to prevent problems like this, because recalls are expensive and embarrassing. Computer software is the same way.

Beta sites. Beta tests are done by specially selected people or companies. The locations for the beta tests are called *beta sites*. The software company sends its product, called *beta software* at this stage, to the beta sites. At the beta sites, the software is extensively tested. An attempt is made to have the software used in all the different ways buyers are likely to employ it. After testing, the software company rewrites the programs based on the findings of the people at the beta sites.

Errors can be so subtle that their consequences aren't seen until after weeks or even months of use. Beta tests are intended to reveal all the bugs to users at the beta sites, so that the problems won't affect PC users like you. Once in a while, though, bugs make it past the beta-testing stage.

Some errors are written into software deliberately by people with bad intentions. Such a bug, called a *Trojan horse* or *virus*, can be found in a good beta-testing sequence. This will prevent it from going on a rampage among PCs. *See also* ALPHA TEST, BUG, DEBUGGING, SOFTWARE, TROJAN HORSE, *and* VIRUS.

Bezier curve

In scientific work, it's often necessary to find a simple curve that fits a set of points. You probably did this in a high school or college chemistry or physics class. After an experiment, you had a set of points to plot on a graph. Then you drew a curve that seemed to fit the points, allowing for the small errors that always occur when you do practical experiments.

Two points. Computers are well suited for tasks like drawing curves in a graph. One of the most ingenious ways of doing this is by means of *Bezier curves* (pronounced either as "Bez-ee-YAY" or "BEZ-ee-yay"). Bezier was a mathematician who first discovered that curves can be drawn on the basis of just two points. These points are called *handles*. As you work with the software, you can move them and watch the way the curve changes.

Rope sag. To get an idea of what it's like to work with Bezier curve graphics, take a piece of flexible rope about three feet long and hold it by the ends. (That Nylon stuff, the kind you can never tie in a good knot, is perfect.) Move your hands closer together and then farther apart, and up and down with respect to each other, and watch the way the rope sag changes. The drawing gives three examples, with your hands represented by dots and the rope shown as a curving line.

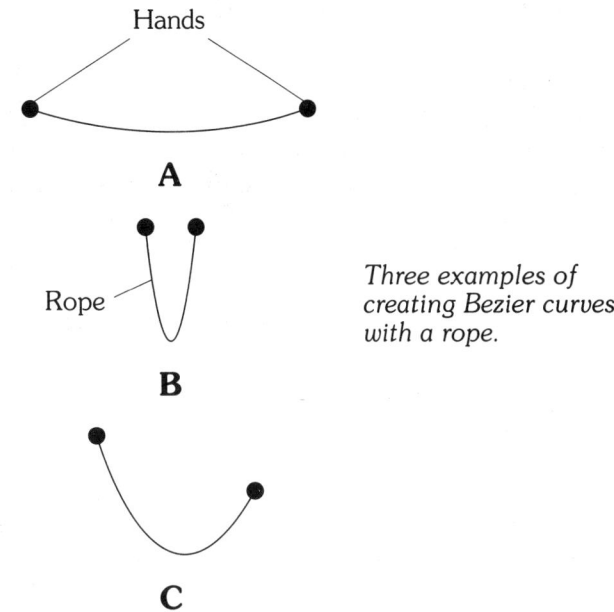

Three examples of creating Bezier curves with a rope.

If you move your hands far out to the right and left, the rope will stretch almost straight, as shown at A in the drawing. If you bring your hands right up next to each other, the rope will take the shape of a steep, U-shaped curve, as shown at B. Move your hands to some intermediate position, with one hand higher than the other (C in the drawing). The rope will attain a new shape. You can go on and on with this.

There are infinitely many different shapes you can get the rope to have, by moving your hands around. All the curves are simple, and they are all uniquely determined by the positions of your two hands. Similarly, there are infinitely many possible Bezier curves for two points on a graph, all uniquely determined by the positions of the handles. *See also* ANALYTICAL GRAPHICS *and* GRAPHICS.

Binary data

Binary data is a form of digital information in which there are only two states. The two digital states are represented by the numbers 0 and 1. Sometimes these states are called low/high, off/on, space/mark, false/true, or no/yes, respectively.

Computers use the binary system because circuits with two states are the simplest possible scheme. Such devices can be built up into

Binary number system

massive arrays. They are also highly precise; there is no confusion. The answer to every question is either no or yes. *See also* BINARY NUMBER SYSTEM *and* DIGITAL.

Binary logic

See BINARY DATA *and* LOGIC.

Binary number system

The *binary number system* is a method of expressing numbers using only the digits 0 and 1. It is sometimes called *base-2*, *radix-2* or *modulo-2*. Normally, people work in *decimal*, or *base-10*, form, but computers work much more efficiently with binary numbers than with decimal numbers.

Digits. In the base-10 system, the rightmost digit is the "ones" digit. The next digit to the left is the "tens" digit; after that comes the "hundreds" digit, then the "thousands" digit, and so on, increasing in integral powers of 10.

In binary notation, the rightmost digit is also the "ones" digit, but the next digit to the left is a "twos" digit; after that comes the "fours" digit. Moving further to the left, the digits represent 8, 16, 32, 64, 128, 256, 512, 1024, and so on, doubling every time. The values increase in integral powers of 2. This is shown in the table below.

A number takes more digits to write in binary form than in decimal notation. For a digital computer, however, sheer volume of digits is not a problem. The important thing is that the computer be able to easily recognize each digit. In the binary number system, the digits are all either 0 or 1. Electronically, these states can be represented as off and on, low and high, or no and yes. This "either-or" method is the simplest scheme for expressing numerical quantities and provides the greatest computer accuracy at the least cost.

Decimal versus binary digit scheme

					DECIMAL					
...	x	x	x	x	x	.	x	x	x	x	...
	10^4	10^3	10^2	10^1	10^0		10^{-1}	10^{-2}	10^{-3}	10^{-4}

					BINARY					
...	x	x	x	x	x	.	x	x	x	x	...
	2^4	2^3	2^2	2^1	2^0		2^{-1}	2^{-2}	2^{-3}	2^{-4}

Decimal versus binary. The following table shows both the decimal and binary notations for the decimal number 94. Read the table from the bottom upwards. In the decimal number system

$$94 = (4 \times 10^0) + (9 \times 10^1)$$

In the binary number system

$1011110 = (0 \times 2^0) + (1 \times 2^1) + (1 \times 2^2) + (1 \times 2^3) + (1 \times 2^4) + (0 \times 2^5) + (1 \times 2^6)$

which is another way of saying that

$94 = 2 + 4 + 8 + 16 + 64$

Decimal 94 equals binary 1011110

Decimal			Binary	
Place value	Digit		Place value	Digit
$10^0 = 1$	4		$2^0 = 1$	0
$10^1 = 10$	9		$2^1 = 2$	1
$10^2 = 100$	0		$2^2 = 4$	1
$10^3 = 1000$	0		$2^3 = 8$	1
*	*		$2^4 = 16$	1
*	*	Read upwards	$2^5 = 32$	0
*	*		$2^6 = 64$	1
*	*		$2^7 = 128$	0
*	*		$2^8 = 256$	0
*	*		*	*
*	*		*	*

* All values higher than this are filled with the digit zero.

One for one. Every decimal number has one and only one binary representation. Every binary number, likewise, has one and only one decimal equivalent. Mathematicians say there exists a *one-to-one correspondence* between numbers in decimal and binary form. Either notation is just as good a numbering scheme as the other.

When you work with a computer or calculator, you give it a decimal number that is converted into binary form. The computer or calculator does its operations with zeros and ones, and when the process is complete, it converts the result back into decimal form for display. *See also* BINARY DATA.

Binary search

In a digital computer, a *binary search* is a method of locating an item in a large set of items. Each item in the set is given a key, which is always a power of two. Therefore, when it is repeatedly divided into halves, the end result will always be a single key. For example, if there are 16 items in a list, they might be numbered 1 through 16. If there are 25 items, they can be numbered 1 through 25, with the numbers 26 through 32 as "dummy" keys.

Binding offset

The desired number key is first compared with a number halfway down the list. If the desired key is smaller than the halfway number, then the first half of the list is accepted, and the second half is rejected. If the desired key is larger than the halfway number, then the second half of the list is accepted, and the first half is rejected.

The desired key is then compared with a number in the middle of the accepted portion of the list. On this basis, one half of the list is accepted, and the other half is rejected, just as in the first case. The process is repeated, each time selecting half of the list and rejecting the other half, until just one item remains. This item is the desired key.

The table shows an example of a binary search to choose one item from a list of 25. Keys are indicated by the letter O; the desired key, 21, is indicated by the pound sign (#), and dummy keys are shown by the letter X.

Binary search: List is repeatedly broken in half

Choose No. 21:

0 0 0 0 0 0 0 0 0 0 0 0 0 0 0 0
0 0 0 0 # 0 0 0 0 x x x x x x x

Select second half:

0 0 0 0 # 0 0 0 0 x x x x x x x

Select first half:

0 0 0 0 # 0 0 0

Select second half:

0 0 0

Select first half:

#0

Select first half:

#

Because of the way a binary search repeatedly divides a set of items in half to arrive at its conclusion, the method is sometimes called *divide and conquer*. See also BINARY NUMBER SYSTEM.

Binding offset

Have you ever prepared a thesis or report and then found that you didn't leave margins wide enough for the binding? This is a common problem with press binders or when text is printed on both sides of the paper. It can be avoided by *binding offset*.

When you open a document that uses *duplex printing*, or printing on both sides of the paper, the page on the left is called a *verso* page. Its format is reversed in some ways from the more common format of right-hand pages. For verso pages, the binding offset (extra margin) should be on the right side of the paper, as shown in the drawing at A. A verso page almost always has an even page number.

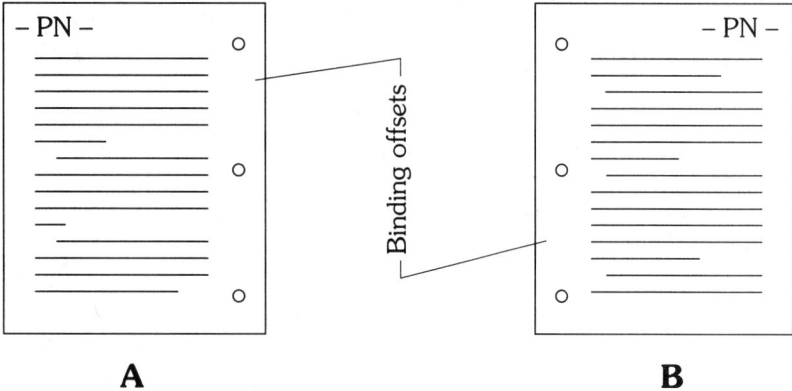

Binding offset for verso (A) and recto (B) pages.

The page on the right as you hold the document open is called a *recto* page. It has the same format as the pages of a document printed on only one side of the paper. For recto pages, the binding offset should be on the left side of the paper, as shown in the drawing at B. In duplex-printed documents, a recto page almost always has an odd page number.

Most desktop publishing software will automatically provide binding offsets, along with other features such as justification, single-column or double-column format, and various type sizes and fonts. *See also* DESKTOP PUBLISHING *and* DUPLEX PRINTING.

Bin-picking problem

One of the most difficult problems for a computerized machine is to find an object based on what it looks like. This is because, viewed from different angles, a single object can look like all kinds of different things.

Consider a cylindrical drinking glass. When seen from the side, it looks like a rectangle, as shown in the drawing at A. From the top or bottom, it looks like a circle (B). From a skewed angle, it has the shape shown at C. The apparent roundness of the ends depends on the exact angle from which it is viewed.

Object recognition is difficult when an object must be picked from a bin full of all sorts of things. Part or all of the desired object can be covered up or hidden from view. A stupid human can pick a drinking glass from a full dishwasher, but a smart machine has a tough time of it. A problem of this type is called a *bin-picking problem*.

One of the biggest challenges in developing *personal robots* is giving machines the ability to solve bin-picking problems. One way that

Biochip

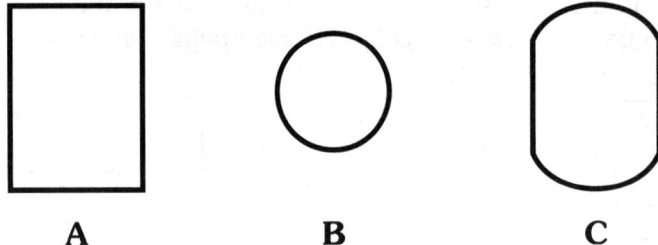

Outline of a tumbler as seen from the side (A), the top (B), and an angle (C).

seems to work well is to give each item a code. For this to work, each item must have a unique label, such as a *barcode* or *passive transponder*. *See also* ARTIFICIAL INTELLIGENCE, BARCODE, OBJECT RECOGNITION, PASSIVE TRANSPONDER, *and* PERSONAL ROBOTS.

Biochip

The term *biochip* has been coined for naturally occurring *integrated circuits (ICs)*. The term has also been suggested for ICs manufactured in a manner similar to the way nature puts atoms together.

Circuit growth. Do ICs, also called "chips," really grow naturally in the world, like plants or animals? At first this idea seems ridiculous. However, some advanced thinkers see a resemblance between certain natural structures and the patterns used in the manufacture of ICs.

It has been suggested that a human brain is a huge computer. The brain can then be considered a biochip. If this is true, the brain is by far the most sophisticated IC known. No matter how complex an IC might be, it is always built up from individual switches called *logic gates*. There is theoretically no limit to the number of logic gates an IC can have, except that the number must be finite. Given enough time for technological evolution, it ought to be possible to build an electronic brain that's as smart as a human brain, or even smarter. *See also* LOGIC GATES.

We can build anything. Nature creates a brain by putting atoms together according to a genetic program. The building blocks are simple. It is the program that is complicated.

If we could write programs for specialized smart robots that would allow them to string atoms together in any possible combination, then in theory we could make anything we wanted. Right now this is only a notion exploitable by writers of science fiction, but the idea is being seriously pursued by scientists working in the fields of artificial intelligence (AI), robotics, genetic engineering, and nanotechnology. *See also* ARTIFICIAL INTELLIGENCE, ARTIFICIAL LIFE, INTEGRATED CIRCUIT, *and* NANOTECHNOLOGY.

Biomechatronics

The word *biomechatronics* is a contraction of the words *biology*, *mechanics*, and *electronics*. The field of biomechatronics is part of the larger realms of electronics, computer science, robotics, and artificial intelligence (AI). It involves computerized devices that duplicate human body parts and their functions.

In Japan. Biomechatronics has received more attention in Japan than in Europe or the United States. In Japan, some robot researchers attack their problems with religious zeal. It has been suggested that this is a result of the fact that there is no religion in Japan as Americans know it, and that, therefore, many Japanese treat science as a religion.

Not only would Japanese robotics engineers like to build robots that can do all the things people can do, but some want their robots to look like people, too. Human-like and animal-like robot toys have been very successful in Japan. Computer-controlled humanoid robots have been used to promote products at Japanese trade fairs, operate elevators, and greet customers as they enter department stores.

Androids. The ultimate biomechatronic device is an *android*. Scientists generally agree that a truly intelligent android will probably not be developed for many years. Some debate the merits and wisdom of even trying to develop one.

The problem of making androids can be approached from two directions. On the one hand, *biological robots* might be grown in labs by biological cloning. This idea is fraught with ethical problems. On the other hand, engineers can try to build a mechanical robot with the dexterity and intelligence of a human being. This notion, too, brings up ethical questions, but to a lesser degree. Perhaps 20 years from now, most households will own a *personal robot* or two, just as PCs are common today. *See also* ARTIFICIAL INTELLIGENCE, ARTIFICIAL LIFE, BIOLOGICAL ROBOTS, *and* PERSONAL ROBOTS.

BIOS

See BASIC INPUT/OUTPUT SYSTEM.

Bit

The term *bit* comes from blending the words *binary* and *digit*. A bit is an elementary unit of digital data, represented by either 0 or 1. These states are sometimes called low and high, off and on, no and yes, or false and true, respectively.

In most digital logic circuits, the state 0 is the more negative current or voltage, and the state 1 is the more positive current or voltage, as shown in the drawing. This is called *positive logic*. Sometimes the opposite is true; 0 is more positive, and 1 is more negative. This is known as *negative logic. See also* BYTE *and* DIGITAL.

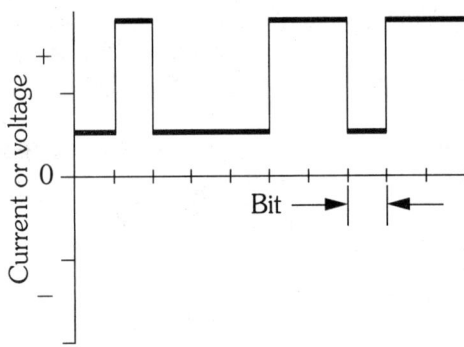

A bit, the smallest unit of digital data.

Bitmap

The video image on your monitor screen is made up of thousands of tiny dots called *pixels*. Each dot is either on or off, corresponding to a digital high or low (1 or 0). Therefore, every dot on the screen represents one *bit* of data. A similar state of affairs holds true for printers.

One-to-one. Data bits are stored in your computer's memory. The correspondence between the screen or printer dots and the digital memory bits is called a *bitmap*.

If you took analysis courses in mathematics, perhaps you remember one-to-one functions of discrete points. A bitmap is such a function. For a full screen or a full page of printed matter, manually figuring out this function would be horribly time-consuming, but computers can do it quickly.

Monitor bitmaps. On your monitor, you can see the individual dots if you turn the brightness way down, display some text or graphics, and then look closely at the screen through a strong magnifying glass. **(Don't do this without first dimming the monitor!)** If you have a color monitor, and if your magnifying glass is powerful enough, you'll see an interwoven pattern of red, blue and green dots. These are the primary colors, which combine to form all the colors the eye can see.

The red, blue, and green dots each have their own separate bitmaps. The red bitmap is the function between the red dots and the red memory; the same holds for blue and green. This is shown in the drawing, in which three dots are shown for each color; they are labeled 1, 2, and 3 for each color red (R), blue (B), and green (G). Some of the dots are illuminated; others are dark (black). In the bitmaps, illumination is represented by the digit 1; darkness is a digit 0. The complete bitmap for this little chunk of video is the function (heavy double arrow) between the dots themselves (A) and the matrix (B).

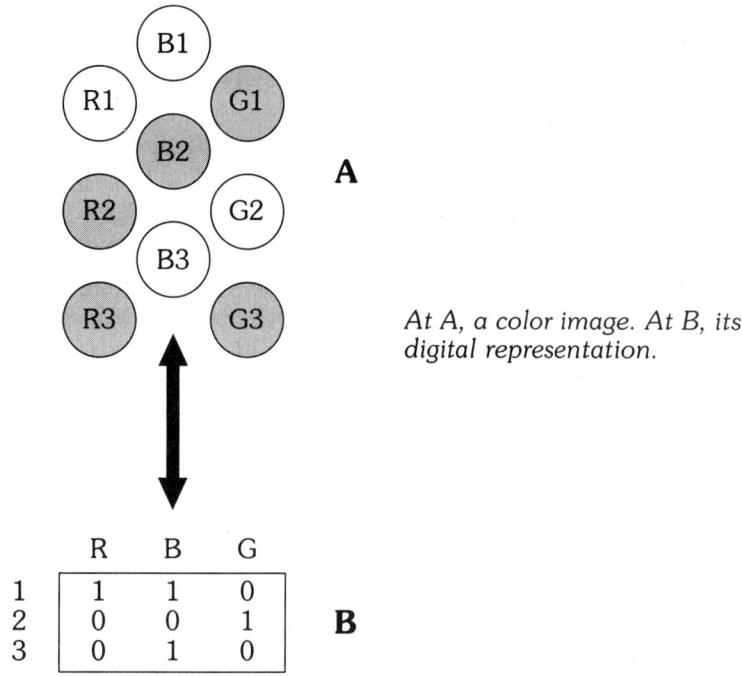

At A, a color image. At B, its digital representation.

Printer bitmaps. Your PC can also use a bitmap to print graphics or text. It sends the stream of ones and zeros to the printer rather than to the monitor. A black-and-white printer bitmap is different from a color monitor bitmap. To convert from a color monitor bitmap to a black-and-white printer bitmap, software is needed. According to the software, red might translate into crosshatching, blue into vertical bars, and green into horizontal bars. Combinations of the colors would translate to other types of crosshatching or shading, or to total blackness or a complete lack of printer ink (white). You might be able to select these combinations with your graphics software.

Even if you have a color printer, its bitmap must still be different from the bitmap for a monitor. This is because a monitor produces *colors*, while a color printer prints *pigments*. The primary pigments are red, blue, and yellow. When they are combined, the result is black, rather than white. Software is needed to convert a monitor bitmap to a color-printer bitmap.

The good and the bad. Bitmaps have the advantage of simplicity. In theory, you can get any amount of detail, and have a graphic image of any complexity, if you're willing to have enough bits in the image. The trouble is that bitmapping, especially for detailed images, takes up a lot of computer memory. This problem is compounded with color

Bitmapped font

graphics. A bitmapped color image needs three times the memory of a bitmapped black-and-white image showing the same amount of detail. *See also* BITMAPPED FONT *and* BITMAPPED GRAPHICS.

Bitmapped font

Bitmapped fonts use a fine grid of dots or squares, some filled in and others dark or blank, to show any character in any language, even Chinese or Japanese.

Like a scoreboard. Old-fashioned scoreboards in ballparks use a simple form of bitmapping. The letters and numbers aren't pretty, but you can tell what they are. Maybe you've seen displays at the bank that show time and temperature, or that run the latest stock prices in an endless stream of abbreviations, acronyms, and numbers. These often use bitmapping, too.

The bitmapped fonts on a PC screen or printer are of much finer resolution than in a scoreboard or stock-market display, so the image quality is better. No matter how fine the mesh, however, the characters must always be at least a certain minimum size. If the characters get too small, the distortion will be so bad that they'll be hard, or impossible, to read.

Easy but complex. Bitmapped fonts are easy for a computer to work with because they're digital. But "easy" does not necessarily mean "trivial." The bitmap for this page of text would not look simple if it were written out as a string of ones and zeros, but it would be easy for you to do it if you were a person of infinite patience and had a couple of weeks with nothing else to do.

A page full of bitmapped characters has an enormous amount of detail. Suppose you are printing double-spaced text on 8.5-by-11-inch paper (the standard size). There are about 1200 characters on such a page. Suppose each character is represented by a 16-by-16 matrix, for a total of 256 (16 × 16) bits. (This is a fair level of detail, but it's not really very good. It probably wouldn't be fine enough for detailed characters like Chinese.) It will then take 307,200 (1200 × 256) bits, each assigned a value of either one (black) or zero (white), to define the page of text. This is simplified in computer memory by using eight-bit *bytes* to represent the characters, but the character codes differ for different languages; Spanish could not use the same code as English. This is easy for a digital machine with lots of memory, but it is not trivial by any standard.

With this system, a 10-page report has three million bits; a 100-page manual has 30 million bits. As the saying goes, there must be a better way. There is, at least in some respects. It's called an *outline font*.

Hard but simple. Outline fonts take up less memory than bitmapped fonts, but are tougher for the computer to process. Outline fonts require the computer to go through a lot of mathematical functions, making them simpler than bitmapped fonts, but not easier. Think of kicking a football. Making a 40-yard field goal is a simple assignment: kick the ball very straight and very far. But it's not easy, as any pro will tell you, especially when the game depends on it.

Bitmapped fonts are good because they're fast, but outline fonts look better and can be made larger or smaller without introducing an unsightly distortion called the *jaggies*. *See also* ADOBE TYPE MANAGER, ANTI-ALIASING, BITMAP, JAGGIES, OUTLINE FONT, *and* SCALABLE FONT.

Bitmapped graphics

One way of composing a video image is to assemble it from thousands of tiny dots. The smaller the dots, the more detail the image can show for a given image size. Images made this way are *bitmapped graphics*.

On a monitor. On your monitor, the image you see is actually a pattern of dots in a fine, interwoven mesh. Each dot of the image, or picture element, is called a *pixel*.

Your computer stores bitmapped graphic images as a vast array of logic highs and lows, also called ones and zeros. To obtain an image from this array of bits, your PC employs a function called a *bitmap*.

On a printer. When you use a printer to make a copy of a bitmapped graphic, you can't get image resolution any finer than what you see on the monitor screen. This is one of the biggest disadvantages of bitmapped graphics. Even if your printer can produce images far clearer than your monitor, the bitmapped printed copy will look like the image on the monitor.

When you see *jaggies*, you know that bitmapped graphics have been used. Jaggies, also called *aliasing*, refer to that peculiar computerized look you've seen in low-budget advertisements or technical papers. Vertical and horizontal lines look all right, but curves and diagonals are roughened, producing a "saw tooth" effect. To some extent this can be reduced by means of anti-aliasing software or photocopy reduction, but a better way is to use *object-oriented graphics*. *See also* ADOBE ILLUSTRATOR, ANTI-ALIASING, BIT, BITMAP, IMAGE RESOLUTION, JAGGIES, OBJECT-ORIENTED GRAPHICS, *and* PIXEL.

Bits per second

See BAUD/BITS PER SECOND.

Blackboard system

A *blackboard system* is a digital circuit with a primitive form of artificial intelligence (AI). Blackboard systems are used in high-level

Blackboard system

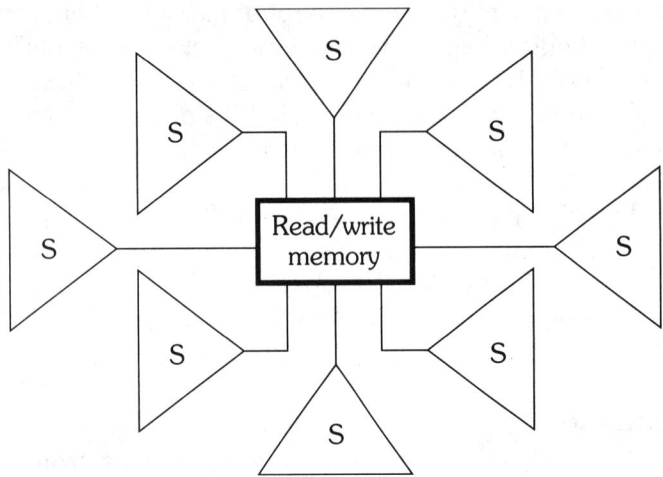

Data in memory (the box) is evaluated by specialty circuits (the triangles).

computer applications, including speech recognition and object recognition. The "blackboard" is basically a memory circuit whose contents are evaluated by *specialty circuits*, shown as triangles labeled S in the drawing. The specialty circuits determine the nature of, and make decisions based on, the contents of the blackboard.

Audio. For speech recognition, specialties include vowel sounds, consonant sounds, grammar, syntax, context, and other variables. Did you just say "weigh" or "way"? Was that the word "by" or "buy"? These word pairs all sound identical. The specialty circuits determine which word was used by checking other words and meanings in the sentence.

How does the computer know when you've finished a sentence? How does it know when it should put a question mark at the end of a sentence, rather than a period? When should paragraph divisions be made? All these things can be determined by the specialty circuits, as they "debate," using the blackboard as their forum, the most likely and logical interpretations of what has been said. A "referee" called a *focus specialist* mediates.

Video. For object recognition, specialties are such things as shape, color, size, texture, height, width, depth, and perspective. How does a computer know if an object is a cup on a table, or a water tower a mile away? Is that a bright lamp or is it the sun? Is that two-legged thing a robot or a person? As with speech recognition, the blackboard serves as a debating ground.

Speech- and object-recognition machines can be of great value in robotics and artificial intelligence. The applications are numerous. Most researchers consider any money spent in these fields to be wise investments. *See also* ARTIFICIAL INTELLIGENCE, OBJECT RECOGNITION, *and* SPEECH RECOGNITION.

Block

A *block* is a section of text, or a defined piece of data, with which something is to be done. The term is often used in reference to a unit of text in word processing.

Text blocks. Text can be blocked off, or defined, by a series of actions. First, you click the mouse or press one of the function keys. Next, you move the cursor through the text you want to work with. Then, you might click the mouse or press a function key again. This usually causes the defined block to appear in boldface or in *reverse type* (white type on a black background, for example). It is sometimes called *text highlighting*.

Once you've blocked off a section of text, you can do various things with it. Suppose the block in the drawing consists of two sentences making up the second half of a paragraph. You might want to move these two sentences to some other place in the text, or maybe you would like to repeat them somewhere else in the document. Maybe you'd like the blocked text to be in italics, or in boldface, or underlined. Various commands will let you do any of these things with the block (and quite a few other things, too). The exact functions or commands for blocking text vary, depending on the software you're using. *See also* WORD PROCESSING.

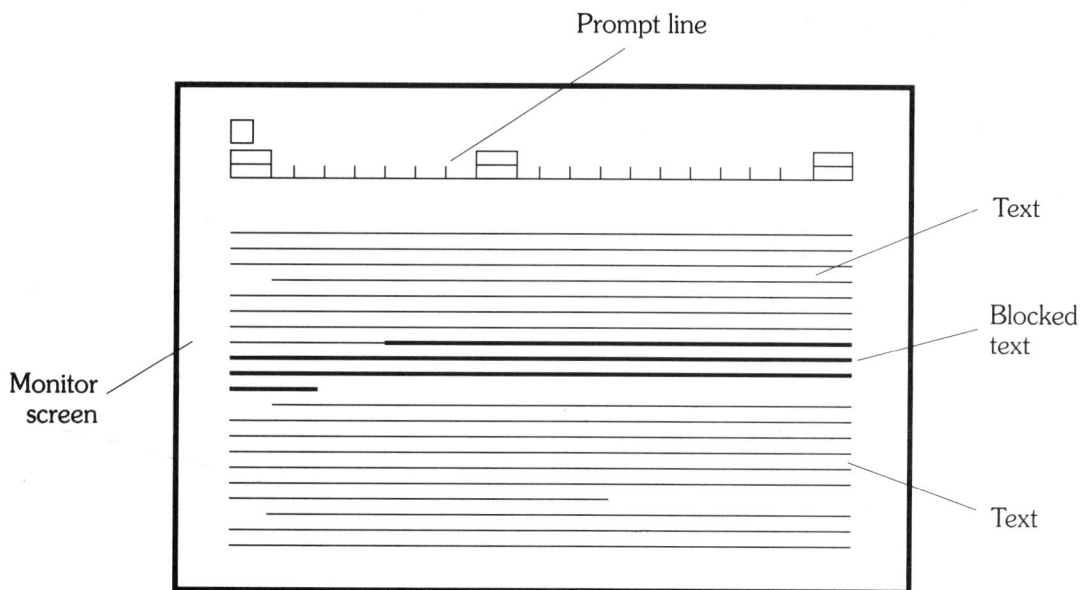

A block is a unit of data or text.

Block file transfer. Sometimes it's necessary to move a chunk, or block, of data from one memory or data storage location to another. This is called *block file transfer*.

As this article was written, it was stored in a temporary file in RAM (random-access memory). These sentences were written while the text for the entire file PC.B (representing everything starting with *B* in this book) was in RAM. Every few minutes, the file PC.B was transferred to the hard disk by saving the file. This ensured that, in case of a power failure or computer crash, there would never be a very great loss of new work.

After each day's work on this book, the updated files were saved not only on the hard disk, but also on a diskette. This block file transfer ensured against disaster in the event of a failure of the hard drive. *See also* MEMORY *and* RANDOM-ACCESS MEMORY.

Boilerplate

One of the advantages of using a computer for word processing is that it gives you the ability to generate things like form letters without resorting to photocopies or mimeographs. A standard document, letter, or other piece of text that is used over and over again with minimal modification is called *boilerplate*.

Imagine you own a small business that imports two-way radios for sale by direct mail. You have a service shop where customers can return broken radios to your company for repairs. Of course, you offer a warranty on the radios. The manufacturer supplies you with parts, instruction manuals, and all the other things you need to fix units sent in for repair.

Suppose some of the radios have a minor defect or problem that can be fixed by the customer such as frequent fuse-blowing, caused by the manufacturer mistakenly putting fuses that are too small into some of the radios. It would be silly for the customers to ship the radios back to your service shop for repair when in fact there's nothing wrong other than the fact that the fuses are too small. You might prepare a boilerplate letter, explaining that some of the radios were supplied with the wrong-size fuse. Then, when a customer called or wrote to complain that a radio had blown a fuse, you could ship a fuse of the right size, along with an individually addressed letter.

When this is done on a word processor, the address of each person can be entered into the computer so the printed document looks the same from beginning to end. In the radio-importing company, you could sign letters individually as they went out, resulting in a complete, good-looking letter for each customer, with minimum hassle for the company.

The term *boilerplate* is also sometimes used in reference to the header information in a program module. You've probably seen these boilerplates if you've snooped around in your PC and looked at some of the programs on the screen.

See also WORD PROCESSING.

Bongard problems

In computerized vision systems, it is necessary for the machine to recognize various patterns. *Bongard problems*, named after their inventor, are one method of evaluating how well a vision system can differentiate among patterns. Solving the problems requires a certain level of artificial intelligence (AI). (Incidentally, these problems make good pattern-recognition tests for people, as well as for computers.)

Three questions. An example of a Bongard problem is shown in the drawing. There are two groups of six boxes. The contents of the boxes on the left all have something in common; those on the right have the same characteristic in common, but to a different degree, or in a different way. To solve the problem, the vision system (or you) must answer three questions:

1 What do the contents of the boxes to the left have in common?

2 What do the contents of the boxes to the right have in common?

3 What is the difference between the contents of the boxes on opposite sides of the figure?

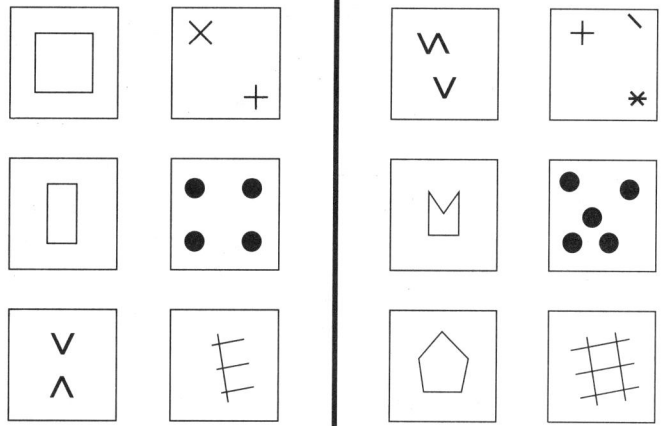

A test of pattern-recognition ability.

Three answers. In this case, the answers to the above questions are as follows:

1 The boxes on the left contain four dots or lines each.

2 The boxes on the right contain five dots or lines each.

3 The difference between the boxes on the left and those on the right is in the number of dots or straight lines each box contains.

Bongard problems are sometimes so simple that they're hard. These answers are almost trivial in their simplicity, but they are important in machine reasoning. Overlooking the obvious is a human trait that

Boolean algebra

computers can, and arguably should, avoid. *See also* ARTIFICIAL INTELLIGENCE, OBJECT RECOGNITION, *and* VISION SYSTEMS.

Boolean algebra

Boolean algebra is a system of mathematical logic using the functions AND, NOT, and OR. In the Boolean system, AND is represented by multiplication, NOT by negation, and OR by addition. Boolean functions are used in the design of computer logic circuits.

Notation and values. In Boolean algebra, X AND Y is written as *XY*, *X.Y* or *X * Y*. NOT X is written with a line or tilde over the quantity involved, or sometimes as a minus sign followed by the quantity involved, such as *–X* or *–(XY + XZ)*. X OR Y is generally written as *X + Y*. The table shows the values of these functions, where 0 indicates false and 1 indicates true.

Truth table for logic operations

X	Y	–X	XY	X + Y
0	0	1	0	0
0	1	1	0	1
1	0	0	0	1
1	1	0	1	1

Some rules of conventional algebra also apply in Boolean algebra. Logic equations often resemble their arithmetic counterparts. The statements on either side of the equal sign are always logically equivalent. For example, when you write *X = Y*, it means "If X, then Y, and if Y, then X." Mathematicians would say "X if and only if Y," written *X iff Y*.

Theorems. The next table shows several logic equations. These are facts, or *theorems*, in Boolean algebra. They have been proved true in the past, and logicians recognize them as such. Once you have proved a theorem true in a mathematical or logical system, you never have to repeat that proof. You can use the theorem to help you prove theorems in the future.

Boolean theorems can be used to analyze complicated logic functions that can aid engineers who design computers and their peripheral equipment. Working with Boolean algebra is often much easier than analyzing schematic diagrams of digital logic circuits. *See also* AND GATE, INVERTER, LOGIC, LOGIC GATES, *and* OR GATE.

Boot

When you hear someone talking about booting the computer, they aren't suggesting anything violent. In computer operation, the term *boot* is used generically to mean "set up," or "get going."

Common theorems in Boolean algebra

X + 0 = X	OR identity
X1 = X	AND identity
X + 1 = 1	
X0 = 0	
X + X = X	
XX = X	
–(–X) = X	Double negation
X + –(X) = X	
X(–X) = 0	
X + Y = Y + X	Commutativity of OR
XY = YX	Commutativity of AND
X + XY = X	
X(–Y) + Y = X + Y	
X + Y + Z = (X + Y) + Z = X + (Y + Z)	Associativity of OR
XYZ = (XY)Z = X(YZ)	Associativity of AND
X(Y + Z) = XY + XZ	Distributivity
–(X + Y) = (–X)(–Y)	DeMorgan's Theorem
–(XY) = –X + –Y	DeMorgan's Theorem

Warm boot. A *warm boot* is a reinitialization of the system, clearing all the memory circuits but not completely removing power from the computer. This is one way to recover from a computer crash. You can give your IBM-compatible PC a warm boot by pressing the Ctrl, Alt, and Del keys simultaneously. This procedure is pronounced "control-alt-delete." A warm boot can also be performed by pressing the reset button on the front of some computers.

Cold boot. A *cold boot* is done by switching the computer off, waiting a couple of minutes for the hard drive to wind down, and then powering-up again. You must interrupt the power to the whole machine.

When it is necessary to reinitialize a computer system, a warm boot should be tried before a cold boot because the warm boot forces the computer to do less work. A cold boot is a last resort.

Starting up. The term *boot* sometimes also refers to inserting a diskette with software, and then instructing the computer to load the software for use. When you hear someone talk about booting a diskette, they mean loading the software from the diskette to the PC. *See also* BOOTSTRAP PROGRAM.

Bootstrap program

When you first switch your PC on, it must go through a certain routine to set itself up, loading the software for its operating system. This routine is called the *bootstrap program*, from the phrase, "pulling yourself up by your bootstraps." This is where the term *boot* comes from, in reference to starting up a computer.

The bootstrap program is stored in *firmware*. It is literally etched into an integrated circuit (IC) in your computer's hardware. Firmware contains instructions for the computer like software does, but firmware can't be changed without altering some of the hardware.

The bootstrap program is simple. Your computer needs a little while to go through it, mainly because it takes some time to load the operating system and attendant software. Common operating systems include DOS, the Macintosh OS, OS/2, and UNIX. (Older windows programs require DOS to run, but Windows '95 has its own built-in operating system.) *See also* BOOT, DOS, FIRMWARE, HARDWARE, INTEGRATED CIRCUIT, OS/2, SOFTWARE, SYSTEM 7, UNIX, *and* WINDOWS.

Bottom-loading printer

Many dot-matrix printers work with *fanfold paper*: folded, continuous paper connected along tear-off lines at 11-inch intervals. Usually, this paper has holes along each side for a tractor feed. You can remove the holes (they're on tear-off strips), leaving sheets 8.5 inches wide.

There are various ways to feed paper through a printer. Most printers have several options. One of the most popular is to feed the paper in from underneath, as shown in the drawing.

The good. A bottom-loading printer is convenient. You can place your printer on a small table, and put the fanfold paper on the floor.

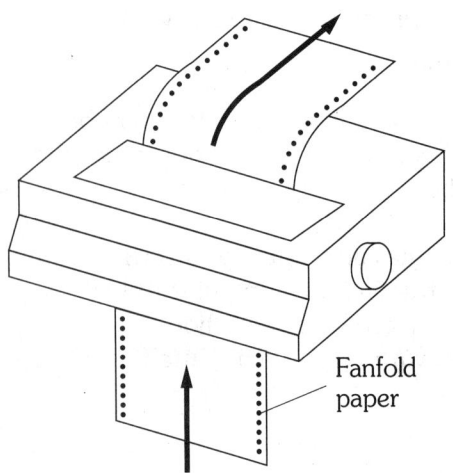

Paper goes up, through, and out.

Fanfold paper

Branching

(Bedside tables, reassigned for PC service, work great for this.) The printer can keep pulling the paper through, sheet after sheet, while you do other things. Once it has been set up and running right, the printer can be left more or less alone while it types up documents of 50, 100, or even 200-plus pages. There is little chance of the incoming paper tangling with the outgoing sheets, as can happen with rear-loading printers.

The not-so-good. One of the disadvantages of a bottom-loading printer is that you can get overconfident and abandon your printer while it's cranking out a huge document. If the paper gets out of whack, you'll return to your PC and find a pile of paper in disarray. Actually, this can happen with any feed method in which fanfold paper is used, but it doesn't have to be a problem if you make sure that the paper stacks up neatly as it comes out of the printer. *See also* FANFOLD PAPER, FRONT-LOADING PRINTER, REAR-LOADING PRINTER, *and* TRACTOR FEED.

Branch control structure

As a computer is operating, it must make decisions. A common form of decision is called *If-Then-Else*. The computer tells itself something like this: "If you come across a zonk, then wobbulate. Otherwise, fribble." The *branch control structure* is the way in which all these instructions are put together so that the computer knows what to do in any situation. A good branch control structure will not let the PC run into any dead ends. Your computer will never ask itself, "What do I do now?" and have no answer.

Consider an example of how a branch control structure might guide a computer along. Suppose you try to open the file A:ZONK.33. This tells the computer to look on the diskette in drive A, locate the file called ZONK.33, and put the contents of this file into its RAM (random-access memory). But suppose A:ZONK.33 does not exist. You've either put the wrong diskette in drive A or else forgotten the correct name of the file you wanted to open. Obviously, your computer can't do anything with a file that isn't there. So it tells you something like

```
FILE NOT FOUND A:ZONK.33
```

If the machine had no idea what to do if told to find a nonexistent file, it might conduct a futile search, spinning the diskette around and around like a dog chasing its own tail. To get the computer out of such an *endless loop*, you'd have to reboot it. With proper branch control structure, the PC will give up after searching for more than a certain amount of time. It will pause, tell you it cannot find the file, and await your next command. *See also* BRANCHING *and* IF-THEN-ELSE.

Branching

The term *branching* is used in reference to routines or programs that have points where a computer must select from two or more

Branching

alternatives. Branching is a sort of reasoning process in artificial intelligence (AI). It is also used in robot control.

Hub caps. To illustrate branching, consider this example. There is a computerized robot on an assembly line that makes cars. The robot's job is to insert hubcaps in the two right-side wheels. (An identical robot does the same job on the left side.) Suppose that 20% of the cars are to be fitted with gold-colored (G) hubcaps; the rest are fitted with silver-colored (S) ones. Then the robot should insert hubcaps in the following sequence:

SS SS SS SS **GG** SS SS SS SS **GG** SS SS ...

Every fifth pair of hubcaps is gold.

Each time a hubcap pair is to be inserted, the computer must make a choice. The routine is at a *branch point* for every hubcap pair. Every fifth time the choice must be made, the computer chooses gold hubcaps. Otherwise, it chooses silver ones. The sequence programmed into the computer goes something like the flowchart in the drawing.

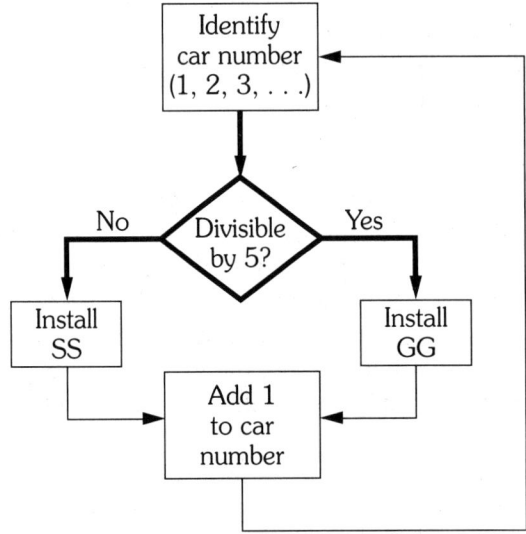

A process with branching. The diamond is the branch, or decision point.

Chain-reaction error. If a mistake occurs, a car might get the wrong color hubcaps. Or worse, the computer might "hiccup" and miss a hubcap. This could throw off the computer's perception of the sequence of cars, so that it would think a new car had arrived with each set of rear wheels. Before long, the front wheel of a car would get a silver hubcap, and the rear wheel of the same car would get a gold one. The next car would get a gold hubcap on the front wheel and a silver one on the rear wheel, like this:

SS SS SS S**G G**S SS SS SS S**G G**S SS SS ...

This glitch would be repeated down the line over and over, messing up two out of every five cars, or 40 percent of the cars coming off the line. This is a case in which it's good to have a human quality assurance (QA) engineer with authority to throw a switch and shut down the whole assembly line!

This example shows that branching routines are critical. They don't allow much room for errors. To some extent, good programming can improve the error tolerance of a system with branching routines. *See also* ARTIFICIAL INTELLIGENCE.

Bridge

A *bridge* is a communications path between or among computer networks, allowing the users in any network to obtain data from, or send data to, any other network.

LAN-to-LAN. Bridges are commonly employed among local area networks (LANs). Suppose, for example, that a university has campuses in four towns, scattered around a large state. Imagine a hypothetical "Pan-Florida U," with one campus in Tallahassee, another in Tampa, another in Jacksonville, and a main campus in Miami. Each campus administration has a LAN of its own. Between each LAN, there is a bridge, for six bridge lines in all, as shown in the drawing. The links are long-distance telephone hookups, with each LAN using a modem to interconnect with the telephone lines. If Pan-Forida U were to get a lot of money, however, they might switch to a geostationary-satellite data link, a low-earth-orbit (LEO) satellite data link, or a fiberoptic data link.

WAN-to-WAN. Bridges can be used to connect among wide-area networks (WANs) too. For example, Pan-Florida U might want to get data from, and send data to, the University of Minnesota, the University of Iowa, Princeton, and others. This would result in a "super WAN."

Long-distance bridges are used in online services, such as Internet's Gopher, Wide Area Information System (WAIS), Archie, Veronica, and World-Wide Web (WWW or W^3), to form the so-called *information superhighway.* Through bridges of this sort, people can do things like look at library card catalogs in other states or countries, conduct research, and exchange information with colleagues. *See also* FIBEROPTIC DATA TRANSMISSION, GEOSTATIONARY-SATELLITE DATA LINK, LOCAL AREA NETWORK, LOW-EARTH-ORBIT (LEO) SATELLITE DATA LINK, MODEM, NETWORK, *and* WIDE-AREA NETWORK.

Broadband data

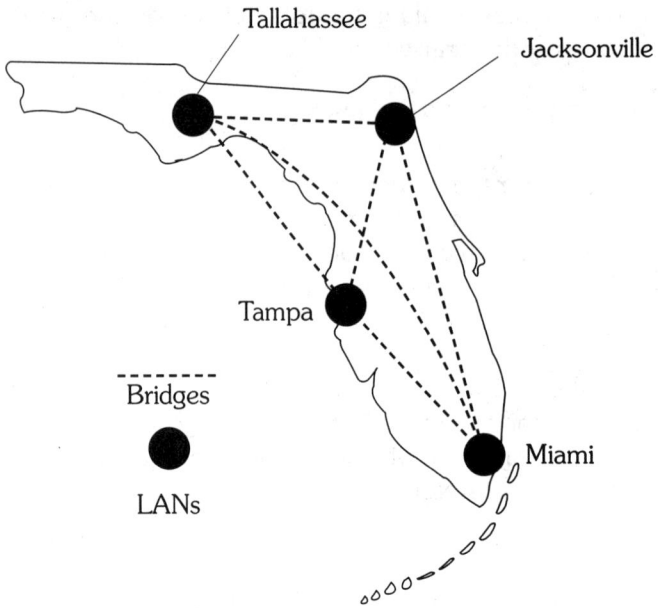

A bridge allows data to be transferred among networks.

Broadband data

When computers communicate with each other, they do so at speeds much faster than humans speak or write. You've probably noticed this, marveling at how a long paper or program can be sent from one place to another in a reasonably short length of time.

Faster means wider. Your PC "thinks" in digital terms. These digital signals are converted into analog form for long-distance transmission from one place to another. Then, when the analog data arrives at the destination, it is converted back to digital form. The changes from digital to analog, and vice versa, are made by a *modem*.

The more data is sent and received per unit of time, the more *bandwidth* is needed; in other words, the wider the channel must be. This is a fundamental law of communications, and it applies to all kinds of signals, analog or digital. It is true for computer data, television images, speech, and text. *Broadband data* refers to analog computer signals that take up a lot of bandwidth because of their high speed.

Mixing and sorting. It is possible for a single communications line, or link, to carry many conversations at once. The conversations can be between people, between a person and a computer, or between computers.

Radio waves or light beams can be modulated with the signals from dozens, hundreds, or even thousands of PCs at the same time. Each signal has its own code and method of timing. They're all mixed up together at the transmitting end of the link, and sorted out again at the receiving end. The mixing-together of signals is called *multiplexing*; the sorting-out is *demultiplexing*. There are several different schemes for doing this, but they all involve the use of broadband data.

Speed limits. There is a limit to the signal bandwidth that can be sent over common telephone circuits. This is about 2.7 kilohertz (kHz) or 2700 hertz (Hz), the bandwidth needed to clearly convey a human voice. When telephone systems were first set up, no one took into account the possibility that the circuits might be used for purposes other than the transmission of voice data.

A home telephone line can handle one PC signal at speeds up to several thousand baud. Higher speeds increase the bandwidth past the capacity of local telephone circuits. Consider a garden hose: it can carry a certain maximum number of gallons of water per minute. If you try to force more water through, it won't go.

PC networks can be set up with links more sophisticated than a common telephone line. Two examples are fiberoptic data transmission and microwave data transmission. Using these modes, huge bandwidths are possible, and information can be sent many times faster than over a common telephone line. Some cities are installing fiberoptic networks especially for high-speed transmission of computer data. *See also* ANALOG, BAUD, DEMULTIPLEXING, DIGITAL, FIBEROPTIC DATA TRANSMISSION, MICROWAVE DATA TRANSMISSION, MODEM, MULTIPLEXING, *and* NETWORK.

Brownout

Normally, electrical outlets in your home supply about 117 volts for small appliances like lamps, radios, and computers. For big appliances like ovens and clothes dryers, 234 volts is common. During times of peak demand, such as during a hot day when many air conditioners are in use, these voltages drop by a few percent. This is called a *brownout*.

Effects. Most brownouts occur without fanfare. Light bulbs burn a little dimmer; foods take a bit longer to cook in conventional ovens or in electric frying pans. The difference is so slight that, if you notice anything, you might think it's just your imagination.

If a brownout is severe—a drop of 10 percent or more in voltage— there will be no doubt that something is amiss. You might hear about it on the local news. The television raster (screen image) will shrink; you might see black borders around it. You'll notice the shrinkage on your PC monitor, too. Under such conditions there are often *transients* on the power line, voltage "spikes" that can cause electronic equipment to malfunction. Computers are sensitive to transients.

Bubble memory

What to do. You should always use transient suppression with a PC, because transients can occur at any time, whether there's a brownout or not. Devices for this purpose, often called "surge protectors" (this is technically a misnomer), cost only a few dollars.

If you live in an area where brownouts are common, you should consider getting a *UPS (uninterruptible power supply)* for your PC. This will keep your computer operating at the voltage it is designed to handle. *See also* POWER SUPPLY, TRANSIENT SUPPRESSION, *and* UNINTERRUPTIBLE POWER SUPPLY.

Bubble memory

Bubble memory is a method of storing information in the form of tiny magnetic fields. The fields exist within integrated-circuit (IC) packages. Bubble memory, also called *magnetic bubble memory (MBM),* allows a lot of data to be stored in a small physical volume.

How it works. A bubble-memory IC contains a thin film made out of magnetic material (see the drawing). The principle is similar to the way a recording tape, or a magnetic disk, works. In fact, bubble memory can be used in place of magnetic disks or tapes for storing data. The film can be magnetically programmed in microscopic regions.

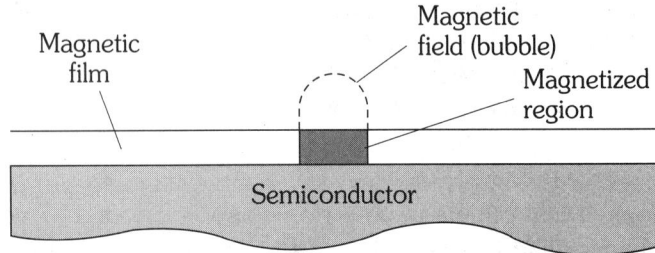

Cross-sectional view of a bubble-memory IC.

A single bubble is a magnetic field about 0.002 millimeters or 2 microns, across. That's so tiny you'd need a microscope to see it (if magnetic fields were visible). The "bubble" refers to the shape of the field, and also the fact that, in a bubble-memory IC, thousands of the fields are constantly forming and popping, like the bubbles in a glass of soda.

Logic highs and lows, representing the binary digits 1 and 0, generally correspond to the existence or absence of a magnetic field. That is, if there's a magnetic bubble present, the digit is 1; if there's no magnetic bubble, the digit is 0.

Assets. Magnetic bubbles do not disappear when power is removed from the IC. Therefore, it's *nonvolatile memory*, a type of RAM (random-access memory) that doesn't need a backup. If there's a power failure, data in bubble RAM won't be lost, the way it would be in conventional RAM.

Magnetic bubbles are easily moved by electrical signals. This makes a bubble memory easy to reprogram. Another asset is that data can be moved from place to place in large chunks. This process is called *block file transfer*.

Limitations. Bubble memory hasn't become the norm in personal computing mainly because, when large memory capacity is needed, bubble memory gets expensive. For long-term data storage, magnetic disks, magnetic tapes, and optical media are generally used, but there are also other nonvolatile memory forms available. For example, PCMCIA adapter cards combine the assets of a small hard disk with those of RAM: speed, nonvolatility, and the absence of mechanical parts.

See also BACKUP UTILITY, BATTERY BACKUP, BLOCK, INTEGRATED CIRCUIT, NONVOLATILE MEMORY, PCMCIA STANDARD ADAPTER CARDS, RANDOM-ACCESS MEMORY, UNINTERRUPTIBLE POWER SUPPLY, *and* VOLATILE MEMORY.

Buffer

A *buffer* is a memory circuit with small storage capacity. It is intended to "smooth out" the flow of data characters.

Suppose that you want to print out a file called LETTER.3 from your hard disk. You click the Print button on your screen, and the data in LETTER.3 is sent to the printer. The printer can put characters on the paper rapidly, but nowhere near as fast as they arrive from the computer. The printer must print the letters, numbers, symbols, and punctuation marks in precise places and in the same order as they exist in the file LETTER.3. A buffer makes sure this happens. This process is vividly apparent in older printers such as the daisywheel type, which print characters one by one.

Another example is the way a keyboard works. If you hit many keys in rapid succession, the keyboard "remembers" the exact order in which they keys were struck, and displays the characters on the screen in that sequence. This is true whether you type five, 50, or 150 words per minute.

A buffer usually (but not always) works in *first-in/first-out (FIFO)* mode. In FIFO, characters come out of the circuit in the same order as they go in. Although the data might arrive in bunches, the output is a steady stream of characters. This principle is shown in the drawing. *See also* FIRST-IN/FIRST-OUT *and* MEMORY.

A buffer smooths out the flow of data.

Built-in font

Bug

A *bug* is a flaw in computer software that results specifically from human error. Bugs are the result of mistakes or oversights on the part of a programmer. Software vendors do their best to get rid of bugs before programs are distributed to consumers by doing *alpha* and *beta tests*.

When downloading software, flaws might get in because of noise on the line. These aren't true bugs, just accidental errors. It's also possible that problems might exist in software as a result of deliberate insertion by malicious hackers. Such a flaw is called a *Trojan horse* or a *virus*, depending on its nature.

The sample code shows a simple program in the popular language BASIC. The program is supposed to make the computer print out all the powers of two that are less than one billion (10^9). But there is an error: line 50 sends the computer back to line 30, causing an *endless loop*. The machine will print powers of two, but it won't stop at 10^9. It will go indefinitely, until the operator tells the computer to quit the program. The program needs *debugging*. Perhaps you have already guessed that line 50 should send the computer back to line 20, rather than line 30. *See also* ALPHA TEST, BETA TEST, DEBUGGING, HARDWARE, SOFTWARE, TROJAN HORSE, *and* VIRUS.

A simple program containing an error

```
10  LET N=2
20  IF N > 1000000000 GOTO 60
30  PRINT N
40  LET N=N*2
50  GOTO 30
60  END
```

Built-in font

Characters can be put down on paper in many different ways. A *font* is a set of letters A through Z, numerals 0 through 9, and various other symbols, with certain traits. You can write at least two fonts by hand: block printing, which you learned in your first school years, and script or cursive, which you learned a year or two later.

Using a printer, you can usually choose from among several different fonts, which can either originate in the printer itself or from the software you use with the computer. A *built-in font* is provided by the printer. Such a font does not depend on the type of software or PC you're using; you select it by pressing buttons on the printer.

Most printers have a *default font* that they use automatically unless you select something else. You can program the default font and size (number of characters per inch). Sometimes other features, such as centering, can be selected at the printer, although it is more common for these to come from the software.

If you want to select a built-in font other than the default font, you must press certain buttons on the printer. The printer instruction manual will tell you how to get the built-in font you want. If you don't like any of the built-in fonts your printer has, you might want to use a *downloadable font*. There are hundreds of fonts available on diskette or CD-ROM. *See also* DOWNLOADABLE FONT *and* FONT.

Bulletin-board system

A *bulletin-board system (BBS)* is a feature found in almost every *online service*. Using a BBS, computer users leave messages for each other. The term comes from the fact that it's like posting notes on a huge bulletin board for everyone to see. A BBS is a form of *electronic mail* with limited (or no) privacy. There are thousands of BBSs in the world today. The drawing is a block diagram of a typical BBS. *See also* ELECTRONIC MAIL *and* ONLINE SERVICE.

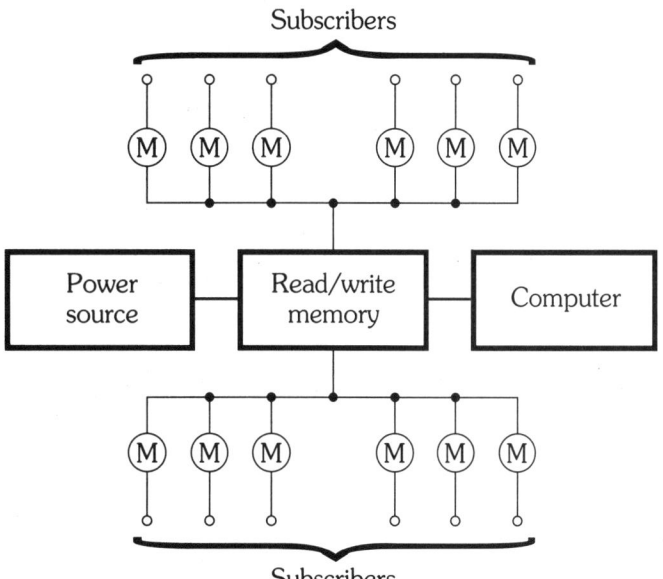

Subscribers with PCs use modems (M) to access the system.

What you need. Of course, to use a BBS, you need a computer. You also need a modem, *terminal emulation software* that lets you communicate with other PC users through the telephone lines, and a working telephone line and telephone, preferably the type with tone dialing (not pulse dialing). You'll also need telephone numbers to call the BBSs you want to start out with.

Bulletin-board system

You might have to pay a fee for access to a BBS. Fees vary greatly; some local BBSs are free. Of course you can "talk" with local PC users one-on-one, without a BBS, for as long as you want without paying any charge.

One type of BBS requires the payment of no fee of any kind, not even long-distance telephone tolls. This is the *packet-radio bulletin-board system (PRBBS)* used by amateur radio operators. To access PRBBSs, you need a ham radio license. *See also* AMATEUR RADIO, PACKET COMMUNICATIONS, *and* PACKET-RADIO BULLETIN-BOARD SYSTEM.

The modem. Your PC works with digital signals, represented by bits that can have only two states. The high state is usually represented by the binary digit 1; the low state generally has the value 0. These levels are direct-current (dc) voltages. You can't send dc over telephone lines; the digital impulses must be changed into audio tones, or analog signals. Then, at the other end, the tones are changed back into digital, dc voltages for one and zero.

Conversion from digital signals to audio tones is known as *modulation*. The decoding from tones back to digital levels is *demodulation*. The word *modem* comes from the words that fully describe what it actually is: a modulator/demodulator. Many computers now come with internal modems already installed. External modems are also available, which plug into your telephone line and stay outside your computer.

Modem speeds are measured by *baud*, *bits per second*, or both. It's always wise to get a modem with the highest possible speed because standard data communications speeds keep increasing. *See also* ANALOG, BAUD, BITS PER SECOND, DIGITAL, *and* MODEM.

Terminal emulation software. *Terminal emulation software* is a fancy name for a program that turns your PC into a communications terminal. It's also known as *telecommunications software*.

Remember old teletype machines? They would sit in the office and grind away, printing out messages from clients or investors, clunking along at the speed of a fair typist. With terminal emulation software, your PC becomes a modern-day teletype machine, but much quieter and faster. You can look at the text on the monitor, print it on your printer, or both.

Some PC users like to download their terminal emulation software. You can do this with *shareware*, so you can test the software before you commit yourself to buying it. There are several different terminal emulation programs available via shareware.

Perhaps you'd rather buy your terminal emulation software in the computer store. One advantage of this is that you often get more

features than with shareware, but you'll probably pay more. Another advantage of store-bought software is peace of mind. You can be 99.9% sure that store-bought software will be not have a Trojan horse or virus, and that it will have been fully tested and debugged.

There's not much risk in downloading legitimate shareware. The danger is in programs whose origin is obscure. Malicious hackers never want you to know who they are! It's a good idea to be suspicious of software that comes from unknown sources. *See also* DOWNLOADING, SHAREWARE, TERMINAL EMULATION SOFTWARE, TROJAN HORSE, *and* VIRUS.

The telephone. Although you can use a pulse-type telephone to dial numbers, a tone telephone is faster. In any case, you'll want to have a wall plug that will accept modular jacks. The telephone set should have a modular jack, too. Using a two-way cord adapter, you can connect the modem and the telephone both to the same wall plug.

Some people like to have a telephone feature called *call-waiting*, which lets you accept an incoming call even if you're already on the telephone. You should disable call-waiting when you're using your PC online. Otherwise the "beep" of an incoming call might disrupt or even disconnect you from the BBS without warning.

Most terminal emulation software will let you enter the necessary call-waiting disable codes along with numbers you frequently dial. Of course, you can enter these codes manually if you want.

Access numbers. There are two ways to call the numbers for access to BBSs. One way is to dial them on the telephone set, but this is the "ancient" method. The other way, which is more often used today, is to have the computer dial the numbers for you.

The access numbers for local BBSs (the ones for which you don't need to pay a long-distance telephone charge) are often available from your friends, local computer stores, or other BBSs. There are BBS directories, such as SEABoard, that you can access; these are literally online PC "telephone books."

It is common for BBSs to be linked to each other. You can leave a message on a local BBS, and if you have friends far away, they can get your messages by consulting a big, wide-area BBS. Conversely, you can access a big BBS and, through it, get messages for you that might be on smaller, local BBSs far from where you live.

Once you're online. The first few times you log onto a BBS, you might want to have a more experienced friend show you the procedure. This will get you used to the various commands you need

Burn-in

to use and to the weird sounds that come from your modem, or bizarre and unfamiliar things on your monitor screen.

When you access a bulletin board, you can check to see if anyone has left you any electronic mail. Some BBSs supply you with privacy codes, so that only you (in theory) can read your mail. Other BBSs are "open," so that all messages can be read by everyone. However, if your life depends on the privacy of something, don't put it on a BBS.

There are all sorts of BBSs, for people with all manner of interests. What's your interest? Greek mythology? Robotics? Artificial intelligence? Space travel? Time travel? Philosophy? Religion? If you can think of it, there's probably a BBS for it. And if you happen to get interested in something for which there is no BBS, you might start one yourself!

Burn-in

Before any electronic or electromechanical device, including a computer, is put to use, it should undergo a *burn-in* process. To burn a device in, it is left to run continuously for hours, days, or weeks.

Manufacturers of PCs usually run the machines for 48 to 72 hours before shipping them out. If there is some defective component in the system, it will often show up within the first few hours. A unit with a bad cooling fan, for example, would overheat quickly, and the problem could be fixed before the unit was sent to the distributor or retailer.

Some machines must be burned in more severely than others. A computer intended for military service, for example, must be tested over a wide range of temperatures. It must be checked to be sure it will keep working with changes in air pressure and humidity. Physical-shock tests must be administered. Perhaps it will be necessary to test the unit while it is around radioactive materials. The toughest burn-ins of all are given to computers used on board the Space Shuttle and in communications satellites.

Of course, some problems escape the burn-in process, but burn-in is a good way to weed out systems or subsystems with early-failure problems. This keeps downtime to a minimum. *See also* QUALITY ASSURANCE AND CONTROL.

Bus

A *bus* is a pathway along which data or power travels from place to place within a computer system. There are several different data buses in a typical PC. Each serves a specific and vital purpose.

What they look like. Inside the main unit of your computer, the large circuit board, called the *motherboard*, has numerous little boxes soldered to its surface. The little boxes are integrated circuits (ICs). Several of these together form the central processing unit (CPU), or brain, of the machine.

Printed circuits don't use wires to interconnect the ICs. Instead, strips of foil on one or both sides of the board provide electrical pathways for data and electrical currents. Foil has some advantages, and some disadvantages, compared to wires. Wires connect the motherboard to other parts of the computer.

On the motherboard, a bus has a characteristic appearance. It looks like a set of several thin, parallel strips of foil, running from place to place like a multilane highway or a multitrack railroad. A wire bus just looks like a bundle of wires. Data travels along all these parallel conductors at once.

The more strips or wires there are in a bus, the more data it can handle per unit of time. In this way, a bus really is like a highway, and you can draw the following analogy:

BUS : DATA SPEED
::
HIGHWAY : TRAFFIC VOLUME

That is to say, the data speed in a bus is like the volume of traffic on a highway.

What they do. To get an idea of what the buses in your computer do, consider this analogy:

CPU : BUSES
::
BRAIN : NERVES

In ordinary English, that reads, "The CPU is to buses, as your brain is to your nerves."

Imagine what would happen if some of the nerves in your body were suddenly severed. You might have numbness in your hands or feet, or possibly in an entire arm or leg. Therefore, you wouldn't be able to tell an orange from a baseball unless you looked at what was in your hand. You might even be paralyzed, so that you couldn't even grasp the orange or baseball.

If some of the buses in your PC system were to fail, you might not see anything on your monitor. Perhaps your printer would fail to work. You might not be able to write anything onto the diskette in drive A. Of course, this would impair the operation of your system, possibly to the point where you couldn't use it. *See also* HOST BUS, INTEGRATED CIRCUIT, LOCAL BUS, MOTHERBOARD, *and* PRINTED CIRCUIT.

Business letters

First impressions are important. Nowhere is this more true than in business correspondence. Your business letters say a lot about you and are easy to create with word processing. There's no hard-and-fast business-letter format, although there are some things you can do to help make your letters look professional and responsible.

With word processors, it's common to have *boilerplate* business-letter formats, with a header, a space for the date, and a salutation. Be sure you don't get personal-letter and business-letter boilerplates mixed up.

Margins. Set up the printer so that each page will have margins on all four sides (left, right, top and bottom) of at least an inch. Then, be sure that you set the margins in your word processor to work properly with the printer margins. Create a sample letter and have someone hold it up for you to examine. Back off a few feet, then judge for yourself how good the layout looks.

Block format. Always single-space a business letter. Between paragraphs, leave a blank line. Paragraphs should usually start flush-left. Some people indent paragraphs in business letters, which is acceptable too, but you should still use single spacing, with a blank line after each paragraph. This format appeals to the eye. It has a modest-but-bold appearance that impresses businesspeople.

If your letter must be longer than one page, don't isolate one line at the end or beginning of a page. And never let your printer get away with "widowing" a word or line at the top of a page.

Good type. For important business correspondence, nothing beats a laser printer. A good laser printer is no longer prohibitively expensive, and can produce type quality almost as good as that in a book or magazine. Inkjet printers also produce excellent printed text.

If you use a dot-matrix printer, the ribbon should be new enough so that the type is crisp. Use letter-quality (LQ) or near-letter-quality (NLQ) type whenever possible. The text should be easy to read; this is by far the most important thing. Set the printer for 10 or 12 characters per inch (never more than 12). Good fonts for business letters include Courier, Sans Serif, and Prestige. Never use Draft or Script.

Mixing type styles. Try to stick with the same type style as much as possible in a business letter. Do not overuse boldface, italics, or underlining, and never use all-capital type in business letters.

It's best to avoid the temptation to change fonts and type sizes in a business letter. If you do that very often, readers might think that you're trying to impress them with your knowledge of type fonts and sizes, and not with the subject at hand. *See also* WORD PROCESSING.

Business software

Business software

If you run a small business, a PC can help you do all kinds of things. Personal computers have revolutionized the art of entrepreneurship. A good computer system can do the work of one or two full-time employees.

When setting up a business, you first choose your system. The most common are *IBM-compatible* and *Macintosh*. Once you've decided on the hardware, you choose *application software*. See also IBM-COMPATIBLE PCS, MACINTOSH, *and* SOFTWARE.

Word processing. Someone once wrote down a formula that bears repeating here:

LONGHAND : TYPING : WORD PROCESSING
::
FEET : BICYCLE : CAR

In other words, the comparison among handwriting, typing, and word processing is akin to the comparison among walking, riding a bike, and driving a car.

Word-processing software can help you type reports, compose business letters, and keep detailed records. And of course, it's indispensable if you plan to publish anything.

A good word processor can produce work in various fonts and with different styles such as boldface, italics, superscript, subscript, and underlining. Some word processors are good for scientific work, while others are intended mainly for writing stories and novels. But whatever word processing system you buy, once you get used to it, you'll wonder how you ever got along without it.

Two popular word processors are WordPerfect and Microsoft Word. Both are available in versions for the Macintosh and IBM-compatible PCs. Magazine publishers often prefer the Macintosh (Mac) system, while other industries often favor IBM-compatible PCs. Whichever type of computer you have, look over as many different products as you can, because new software is constantly coming out. *See also* WORD PROCESSING.

Graphics. Graphics software goes hand-in-hand with word processing, especially if your business involves technical documentation or sales presentations. You might, for example, want to start a company that does contract technical writing. In that case, you'll be doing graphics and word processing in more or less equal amounts.

In recent years, it has become possible to write, edit, compose, and produce magazines and even small books entirely "in-house." All the

Bus network

work, including the graphics, is printed out and bound, and the finished product looks almost as good as the work a major publisher puts out. This is known as *desktop publishing*.

An increasingly popular alternative to bound paper books is *CD-ROM* technology, in which hundreds of megabytes can be stored on a single compact disc. However, a computer is necessary to read CD-ROMs. *See also* CD-ROM, DESKTOP PUBLISHING, *and* GRAPHICS.

Database. A *database* is like several card files. It's a place you can keep information of all kinds, such as names, addresses, telephone numbers, and dates of last contact.

Suppose you need to keep track of 1000 people and companies. How are you going to organize them? By name? Address? Telephone number? Date of last contact? Product/service? That's five different ways right there. With 3-by-5 index cards, you'd need five long, heavy boxes, one for each method of organization. With a database, you could put it all on your hard disk, and back it up on one diskette. *See also* DATABASE.

Spreadsheet. Computers are great at making calculations, especially the sort that people often find time-consuming and boring. A good *spreadsheet* can act as your bookkeeper or accountant. You put numbers into a vast array of rows and columns, like a huge ledger. The computer can add, subtract, multiply and divide these numbers, doing calculations in a few seconds that would take you days.

Spreadsheets can not only keep your financial records, they can also do your income tax, help you forecast market trends, and keep inventory of all the different doo-dads you sell or buy. And there's no limit to how complicated the data can become. Imagine a chart the size of a football field, with rows and columns an inch wide and a quarter of an inch high! A nightmare? Not if it's stored on your hard disk and backed up on diskette. *See also* SPREADSHEET.

Bus network

There are several different methods of connecting PCs in a local area network (LAN). These schemes are called *topologies*. In one type of topology, all the PCs branch off from a single, main line or bus. This is called a *bus network*.

Nodes. An example of a bus network is shown in the drawing. Each PC represents one workstation, or *node*. Some nodes might be peripherals like printers. Others might be dumb terminals, consisting of a keyboard and monitor, but no computer.

Every node in the bus network has an address, a code that uniquely identifies it. That way, any PC in the LAN can connect to any node.

In the LAN shown by the drawing, all the PCs are effectively connected together. For any two nodes in the network, there is a path connecting them.

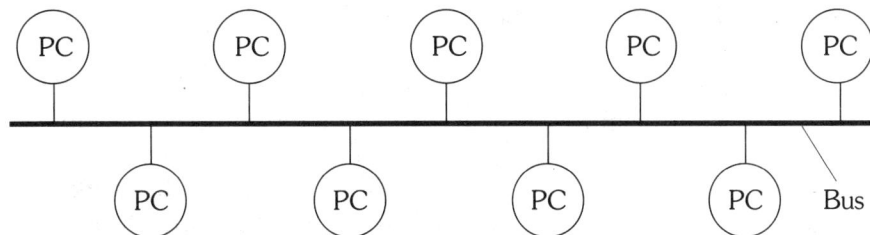

A simple way to interconnect PCs.

Advantages. A bus network is simple. There is less chance for a serious failure in this type of LAN, compared with more complex topologies. If one node malfunctions, all the rest can still communicate with each other. For a major disruption to take place in the bus network, the bus itself must be broken somewhere. Bus networks are also easy to enlarge. All you need to do is add more nodes at convenient points along the bus.

Limitations. The length of the bus in a cable bus network cannot normally be more than about 1000 feet. This is because signals die off rapidly along the cable. If the bus must be longer than 1000 feet, *repeaters* are needed. These circuits receive, amplify, and retransmit the data. *Fiberoptic data transmission* also allows for buses longer than 1000 feet.

Bus networks won't work very well if nodes are located at scattered points. In that case, the bus will have to zig-zag around, and it can easily become very long even when all the nodes are within an area much less than 1000 feet across. In situations like this, a different topology, such as a ring network or star network, will work better. The maximum allowable size of a bus network will increase, however, as fiberoptic communications systems become more common. *See also* BUS, FIBEROPTIC DATA TRANSMISSION, LOCAL AREA NETWORK, NETWORK, REPEATER, RING NETWORK, *and* STAR NETWORK.

Byte

A *byte* is a unit of digital data consisting of a string of eight *bits*. One byte is about the same as one character, such as a letter, numeral, punctuation mark, space, or line feed command.

Computer memory is almost always specified in bytes. However, because memory capacities of modern computers are large, *kilobytes* (units of $2^{10} = 1024$ bytes), *megabytes* (units of $2^{20} = 1,048,576$ bytes), and *gigabytes* (units of $2^{30} = 1,073,741,824$ bytes) are given.

Byte

The abbreviations for these units are KB, MB, and GB respectively. Alternatively, you might see them abbreviated as K, M, and G.

A typical diskette has a little over 1MB data storage capacity. Hard disks for PCs and commercial computers store from about 40MB (in older machines) to many gigabytes.

In the future, you will be hearing about a unit of data called a *terabyte (TB)*. This is equivalent to 2^{40} bytes, or a little more than a million megabytes. And the day might come when we need to make use of the term *petabyte (PB)*, which refers to 2^{50} bytes, or a little more than a million gigabytes. *See also* BIT, MASS STORAGE, *and* MEMORY.

C

C is a high-level computer-programming language that includes a compiler, a linker, libraries, and online instructions. Professional people like it because of its speed, power, and efficiency. C can be run on a variety of operating systems; most computers used in business can handle C easily.

The main reason that C is so efficient is that it's easy for computers to "digest," allowing them to work much faster than with most other high-level languages. The computer can use a program written in C almost as efficiently as an assembly language program because of the translation done by the compiler. One of the features of C is an assembly-language program that can be compiled by the assembler and run.

C is rather hard to learn because it isn't much like standard written English. It's harder to read than a simple language like BASIC. For one thing, the lines aren't numbered. Also, the structure seems bizarre at first and there are lots of abbreviations and symbols whose meanings aren't obvious. However, these differences make the program much shorter than an equivalent program in many other languages. *See also* ASSEMBLER AND ASSEMBLY LANGUAGE, C++, COMPILER, *and* HIGH-LEVEL LANGUAGE.

C++

In the 1980s, a computer scientist named B. Stroustrup worked on the structure of the high-level programming language called C, adapting it to a *graphical user interface (GUI)*. Originally, this new language was called *C With Classes*. Later, the name was changed to C++ (pronounced "see-plus-plus").

The language C++ is somewhat easier than C for programmers to use and understand. But, like C, it is a rather difficult language for beginners to learn. Another language, *Pascal* (pronounced "pass-CAL"), is similar to C++ but is easier for most students to work with. Some programmers learn Pascal first in school, and graduate to C++ in more demanding professional environments. *See also* C, GRAPHICAL USER INTERFACE, *and* PASCAL.

Cable

A *cable* is a special cord designed to carry data signals. There are many different types of cable. Some are simple and cheap; others are complicated and expensive. When connecting pieces of computer equipment, it's important that the right type of cable be used.

Simple cable. The simplest form of cable is the cord you use with things like lamps and clock radios. Two or three wires are embedded in rubber or plastic insulation, as shown in the drawing at A. The wires are usually made up of many fine wires interwoven like twine or rope. This is called *stranded wire*. Stranded wire makes the conductors flexible, so they can be bent back and forth many times without breaking.

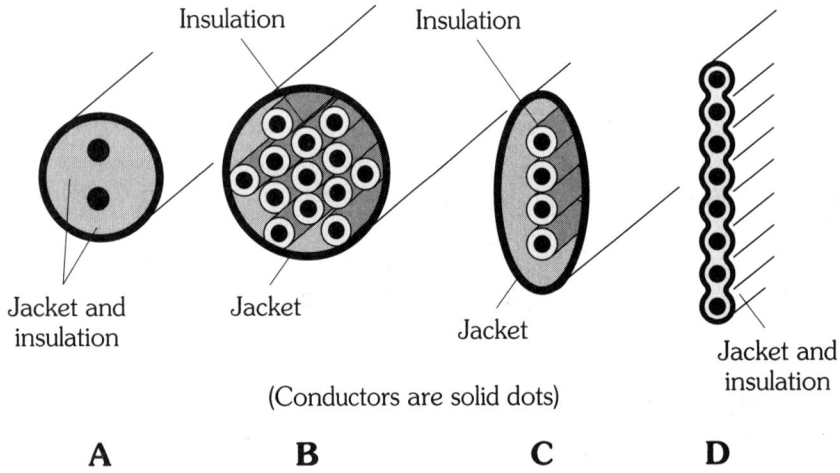

Two-conductor cable (A), bundled multiconductor (B), flat multiconductor (C and D).

When a cable has several wires, they can be individually insulated, bundled together, and enclosed in an insulating jacket (as shown in B). If the cable must be flexible, each wire is stranded. Some cables of this type have dozens of conductors. If there are only a few conductors, they might be run parallel to each other in a flat configuration (C).

Sometimes several conductors are molded into a common insulating jacket (D). This is called *flat cable* or *ribbon cable*, and is commonly used inside computers. This cable is easy to bend in one direction, but hard to bend in other ways, just like heavy tape or ribbon. It is ideal for saving space, because it is so thin. It also radiates heat away easily.

Interaction. All of the cables mentioned are *unshielded*, meaning that high-frequency alternating currents can escape from, or get into, the conductors. For direct current or low-speed data transmission, unshielded cables are usually all right. However, radio signals, video, and other high-speed data creates *electromagnetic fields* that can be transferred among cable conductors, and even between a cable and the surrounding environment. This is especially likely if your PC has a lot of peripherals, or if you're using a local area network (LAN). Then, *electromagnetic shielding* is necessary.

Conductors are shielded by enclosing them in a "pipe," usually made of copper braid. The braid is separated from the center conductor(s) by insulation called the *dielectric*. Look at drawings B and C, and imagine the braid just inside the outer jacket.

Coaxial cable. A single conductor surrounded by a braid is called *coaxial cable* because the conductor and the braid share a common axis. Coaxial cable, also called *coax* (pronounced "CO-ax"), is the ultimate shielded cable. When the braid is connected to a good electrical ground, it effectively keeps all the signal energy confined to the center conductor. The shield also prevents outside signals from getting into the cable and causing interference.

Two or more coaxial cables can be bundled in a common jacket to make a multi-conductor cable that is immune to interaction with the outside environment and will not let signals interact among its own conductors. Such cables are expensive because of their complex construction. *See also* CABLE DATA TRANSMISSION *and* COAXIAL CABLE.

Serial versus parallel cable. In communications, and also within computer systems, a cable that carries data along one line is known as a *serial cable*. A cable that carries data along several lines at once is called a *parallel cable*.

Serial cables can, in general, be much longer than parallel cables. Parallel cables are prone to *crosstalk*, a form of interference in which the signals in the different conductors combine with each other. Crosstalk can be prevented by individually shielding each conductor within a parallel cable, but this increases the expense.

An example of a serial cable is the coaxial line used to carry television signals. These cables can be many miles long. The cord connecting your computer's main unit to the printer is probably a parallel cable.

Cable data transmission

In general, such cables can be only a few feet in length. *See also* PARALLEL *and* SERIAL.

Fiberoptic cable. Signals can be sent along *fiberoptic cable* in the form of visible light or infrared. The light or infrared is generated by a laser, and data is impressed on it by a process called *modulation*. The light or infrared stays inside the fiberoptic cable because of internal refraction and/or reflection.

Fiberoptic cables are far more efficient than electrical cables. This is especially true for high-speed data, or when many signals must be sent over a cable at the same time. A single strand of fiberoptic cable can carry thousands of signals simultaneously. There is no interaction among the signals, no radiated electromagnetic energy, and no interference from electromagnetic fields in the vicinity. *See also* FIBEROPTIC CABLE *and* FIBEROPTIC DATA TRANSMISSION.

Cable data transmission

Information can be sent from place to place over cables. This is done in television, telephone, and computer systems. Although it's being replaced by more sophisticated methods, *cable data transmission* is still fairly common.

Inside your PC. Much of the "wiring" in your PC is not really wire or cable at all. Instead, it is contained within integrated circuits (ICs) or is etched on printed circuit boards. Cables are used to transmit data between printed circuits within your computer.

If you look inside any complex piece of electronic equipment, you'll see bundles of wires. Some of the bundles are enclosed in a common jacket, forming multiconductor cable and/or ribbon cable. Some coaxial cable might also be used.

As optical computers evolve, the construction of PCs might change dramatically. There will probably be fewer cables, some of which will be optical fibers rather than electrical conductors. *See also* CABLE, COAXIAL CABLE, FIBEROPTIC CABLE, FIBEROPTIC DATA TRANSMISSION, *and* OPTICAL COMPUTER TECHNOLOGY.

Peripherals. Cables are used between a computer's main unit and the externals and peripherals, including the monitor, keyboard, mouse, external modem, external disk drives, speakers, microphone, and printer.

For connections to peripherals built into the main unit, ribbon cable is quite often used because it is flexible, fairly inexpensive, and doesn't take up much space. For connections to peripherals outside the main unit of the PC, bundled multiconductor cables are used. These might be shielded or unshielded, depending on how long they are and how fast data goes through them. Shielded cables are less likely to pick up interference and are preferable for interconnections among the components of a computer system.

Networks. Coaxial cable works well for PCs hooked up to form a local area network (LAN) because it is shielded and, if installed properly, won't pick up or radiate electromagnetic fields. This is important if the system is to be efficient and free from interference. For a *wide-area network (WAN)*, the telephone lines are generally used. Sometimes these are wire cables, sometimes they're fiberoptic links, and sometimes they're microwave or satellite data links. Each PC interfaces with the local telephone line using a modem.

One of the most interesting types of WAN uses no cable at all. This is called *packet radio*, and is used by amateur radio operators worldwide. *See also* AMATEUR RADIO, LOCAL AREA NETWORK, MICROWAVE DATA TRANSMISSION, PACKET COMMUNICATIONS, SATELLITE DATA TRANSMISSION, *and* WIDE-AREA NETWORK.

Cache memory

Cache memory is the most-often-used part of the *RAM (random-access memory)* in a computer. Data can be stored in and taken from a cache memory at higher speed than is possible with the rest of the RAM.

How it evolved. One of the most important features of a computer is its speed. As each new microprocessor chip is developed, the speed of the CPU (central processing unit) increases over that of the previous design. Some CPUs are so fast that common dynamic RAM (DRAM) chips can't keep up. A faster form of RAM, known as *static random-access memory (SRAM)*, exists. SRAM chips are expensive, however; the cost of a good-sized SRAM would be unacceptable to most PC users.

During the 1980s, CPU speed versus RAM speed became a big issue with computer hardware engineers. PCs had fast CPUs but slow memory access. It was like a race car stuck in first gear. It looked as if people would have to work with CPUs hampered by slow memory, or else pay a fortune for a fast RAM such as SRAM. But hardware engineers found a way out. *See also* DYNAMIC RANDOM-ACCESS MEMORY *and* STATIC RANDOM-ACCESS MEMORY.

How it works. Your PC uses only a small part of its RAM most of the time. The entire RAM is almost never needed. In fact, the most-often-needed data can fit into about 5% of the RAM. Engineers decided that this 5% could have fast RAM chips, and the other 95% could have slower, less expensive chips. Then the cost of the PC would go up only a little, but the memory access would be much faster. The sleek, expensive 5% of the RAM became known as cache memory because it's like a cubbyhole where often-used data is kept close at hand.

CAD/CAM

The principle of cache memory is shown in the drawing. Part A of the drawing is a "space-wise" pie chart, showing the space taken up by the cache memory (shaded slice) compared with the space for the entire RAM (the whole pie). The cost of having 95% "slow RAM" and 5% "fast RAM" is only a little more than the cost of having 100% "slow RAM."

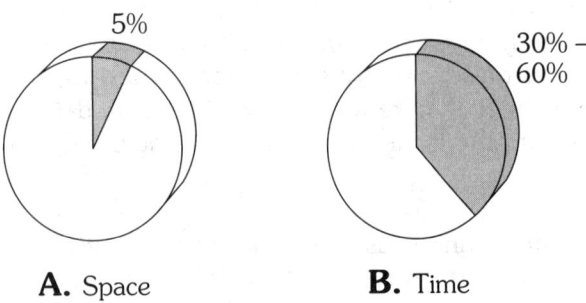

A. Space **B.** Time

Cache memory is small space-wise (A), but is used for a large proportion of the time (B).

Part B of the drawing is a "time-wise" pie chart, showing the average amount of time the cache memory is in use (shaded slice) compared with the total time spent accessing RAM (the whole pie). The percentage of cache-memory time varies between about 30% and 60% of total RAM time, depending on the application. *See also* CENTRAL PROCESSING UNIT, MEMORY, MICROPROCESSOR, *and* RANDOM-ACCESS MEMORY.

CAD/CAM

See COMPUTER-AIDED DESIGN *and* COMPUTER-AIDED MANUFACTURING.

CAI

See COMPUTER-ASSISTED INSTRUCTION.

Caps Lock key

On a computer keyboard, the *Caps Lock* key works something like the "shift lock" function on a typewriter, but there are certain differences. When you press Caps Lock, usually found just to the left of the letter *A* on your keyboard (see the drawing at A), all of the letters will appear as capitals (uppercase), but the number and symbol keys won't be affected.

The Caps Lock function is indicated by a light usually found just above the numeric keypad at the upper right of your keyboard (see the drawing at B). To disable the Caps Lock function, press the key again. If you press the key over and over, you'll see the Caps Lock light go on and off. It's a *toggle key*; every time you press it, it switches to its opposite, like a light switch.

Caps Lock key

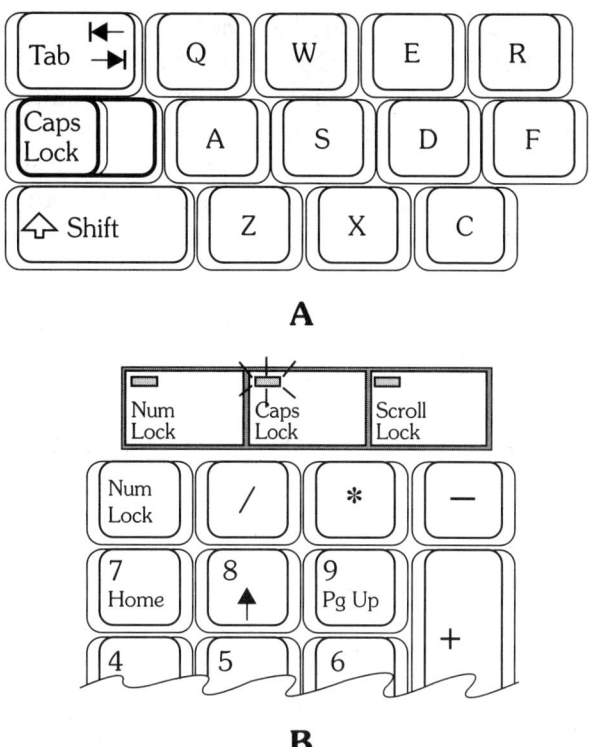

Usual location of the Caps Lock key (A) and the light (B).

An experiment. Here is what happens on my computer when I press certain keys with the Caps Lock function off, and without holding the Shift key down:

```
123 abc -=\ ,./
```

You can find these keys on your keyboard by looking for the symbols at the bottom of each key.

Here's what happens when I press the same keys with Caps Lock activated, and without holding the Shift key down:

```
123 ABC -=\ ,./
```

Notice that only the letters of the alphabet are affected; numbers, symbols, and punctuation marks were not.

Here is what happens when I press the same keys with Caps Lock off, but while holding down the Shift key:

```
!@# ABC _+| ?
```

Finally, here's what happens when I press the same keys with Caps Lock activated *and* the Shift key held down:

```
!@# abc _+| ?
```

Capture

Variations. In some cases, the behavior of a keyboard can be modified by changing the software or by giving your PC certain commands. Some software lets you create mathematical symbols, Greek letters, or letters in foreign languages. The best way to get familiar with your own keyboard functions is to play around with them. Remember, though, not to do these experiments with any files that are important to you or that have not been backed up. *See also* KEYBOARD.

Capture

Have you ever wished you could take all your piles of paper and put their contents on diskettes? It's easy to do this with text. A high-density diskette can easily hold a full-length novel. Graphics, too, can be put on diskettes.

At least 1000 words. You've heard the old saying, "A picture is worth a thousand words." Whoever invented that adage had no idea how literally it would apply in the computer age, when people began to capture pictures and put them into digital memory! A simple drawing takes at least 1000 words to describe fully and precisely. (Try it.) A complex drawing might need 10,000 words. A detailed photo can easily require 100,000 words or more. It's the same way with computer memory.

Simple drawings take up a fair amount of computer memory; complex diagrams or photographs require a lot. This is the main problem with capturing graphics and putting it on diskettes. An ordinary diskette doesn't have enough storage space for very many images. A line drawing, typical of the illustrations in this book, occupies at least 50 kilobytes (50K); often it is 300K or 400K. A high-density diskette has room for up to 20 or 25 line drawings, or as few as three or four, depending on the complexity of the artwork.

CD-ROM. The most obvious solution to the graphics storage problem is *CD-ROM (compact disc read-only memory)*. A single CD-ROM can hold over 650MB (megabytes) of data. This is the equivalent of hundreds of novels, or 5000 drawings at 130K apiece. With this much storage space, the digitization of images becomes easy. You can even store motion pictures on CD-ROM. *See also* CD-ROM *and* DISKETTE.

Card

See PRINTED CIRCUIT.

Caretakers

Some researchers think that advanced artificial intelligence (AI) systems might be useful as *caretakers* to keep humans in line. Rational and impartial, these systems could be used to resolve differences among people, from sovereign nations down to small-claims courts.

Cybercops. Many people reject this idea as ridiculous and unworkable. Their argument goes something like this: It wouldn't be long before the computer would reach a solution that one or both human parties could not accept. So they'd start fighting, just as they always have. The answer: Have robots enforce the computer's verdicts.

Novels have been written, and movies made, about life under a computer-controlled government. Usually, the stories portray the negative aspects of computers and robots given that kind of power. The machines are created with good intentions, and everything works well for awhile. Then something goes wrong, and the people end up enslaved.

Colossus. A good portrayal of a supercomputer gone bad is the novel/movie *Colossus: The Forbin Project*, produced during the years of the Cold War between America and Russia. Since then, the term *colossus* has been used to describe any all-powerful computer. The term carries a strong negative connotation, suggesting that computers would become evil if given too much power. In reality, there is no scientific basis for the notion that a machine can become evil all by itself; the problem is that computers carry out the instructions of their human programmers!

Some scientists believe that computers, if responsibly programmed, would be better government officials than human beings. They argue that a purely logical machine would represent an improvement over unpredictable, power-hungry politicians and gangsters. The only freedom that people would lose under a computer's caretaker rule, these scientists say, would be the freedom to exploit other human beings.

All arguments aside, it is doubtful that any society will ever totally entrust itself to computers, centralized or personal, big or small. Some people believe that computers have too much power already. Even today, many people suffer from *cyberphobia*, an exaggerated and often irrational distrust of computers. *See also* ARTIFICIAL INTELLIGENCE, COLOSSUS, *and* CYBERPHOBIA.

Carrier-sense multiple access with collision detection

When PCs and data terminals are connected into a network, there's a chance that two or more terminals will try to get access to the communication channel at once. This is unlikely with a small local area network (LAN). It's a little more likely with a medium-sized LAN.

Peers. In some LANs, each workstation has the same priority as all the others, which guarantees that none can monopolize the network. For this reason, such a system is called a *peer-to-peer network*.

Suppose two workstations, also called *nodes*, try to gain access simultaneously in a peer-to-peer network. This is a *collision*. The system senses the signals, or *carriers*, from the competing nodes, and determines that there exists a multiple-access problem. This is called *collision detection*.

Two nodes can't occupy one end of a channel at the same instant. (They can share it on a fast-rotating basis, however.) Both nodes have equal priority when competing for channel occupancy. When two or more nodes try to gain access at the same instant, the system conducts a sort of lottery. Computer engineers have come up with the term *carrier-sense multiple access with collision detection (CSMACD or CSMA/CD)* to describe the process.

Casting lots. Chance is a good way to decide which workstation gets priority when there's a conflict in a LAN. When the LAN detects a collision, it gives out random numbers. One workstation picks a number; the other workstation picks another number. The station with the higher number gets access to the channel first. This prevents lockup, where the system might be stumped by a collision and the network would go down.

After the system has decided which node gets to enter the channel first, the system rotates the channel between, or among, the competing nodes. *See also* LOCAL AREA NETWORK *and* PEER-TO-PEER NETWORK.

Cartesian coordinates

Cartesian coordinates, also called *rectangular coordinates*, are the most common way to make charts and graphs. The term comes from the name of the mathematician who is believed to have invented the system, Rene Descartes of France. He lived during the 17th century and is regarded as one of the greatest mathematicians of all time.

In a Cartesian coordinate system, there are two or three number lines, called *axes*, intersecting at a common point at 90° angles. The scales on these number lines might or might not all have the same increment size, but the axes are always straight lines. The graphs show basic Cartesian coordinate systems in two and three dimensions.

There are dozens of variations on the Cartesian coordinate theme. Some Cartesian graphs show only positive values; some have both positive and negative numbers. Some graphs, such as the log-log and semilog type, have increments that vary in size as you move along the axes. Some graphs show continuous curves; others show bars or columns.

In any coordinate system, one or more axes are assigned the independent variable(s), while one axis is assigned the dependent

Cartesian coordinates

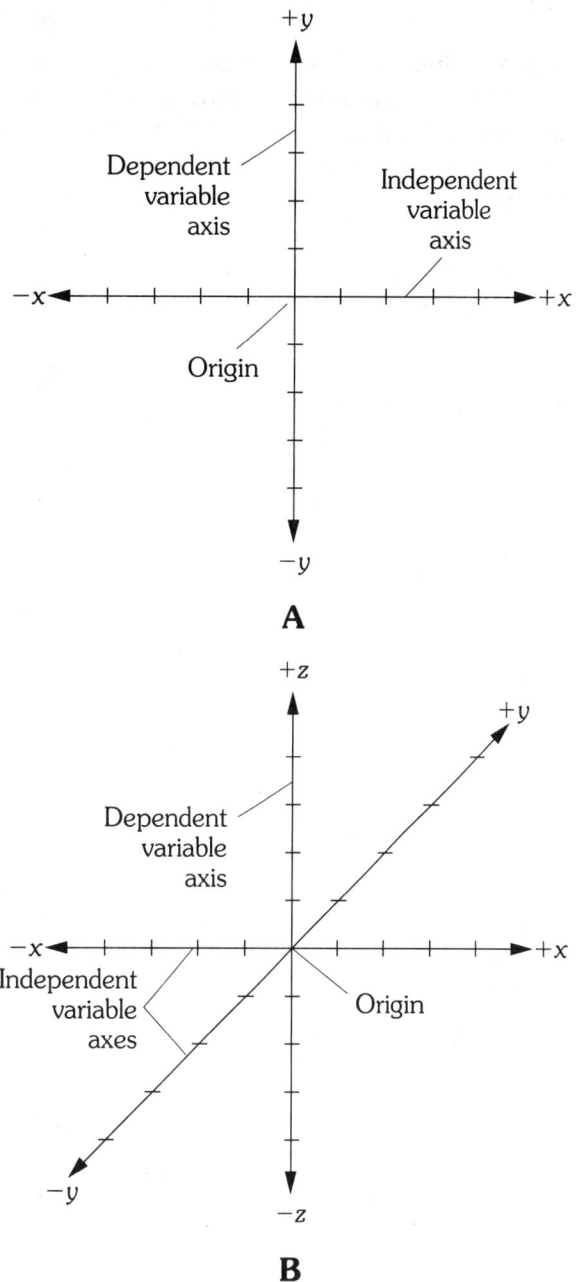

Cartesian coordinates in two dimensions (A) and three dimensions (B).

variable. The dependent variable is almost always on the vertical axis in a Cartesian coordinate system.

Other common chart and graph forms are cylindrical coordinates, polar coordinates, and spherical coordinates. *See also* ABSCISSA, BAR GRAPH, COLUMNAR GRAPH, CYLINDRICAL COORDINATES, DEPENDENT VARIABLE, INDEPENDENT VARIABLE, LOGARITHMIC GRAPH, LOG-LOG GRAPH, ORDINATE, POLAR COORDINATES, SEMILOG GRAPH, *and* SPHERICAL COORDINATES.

Cascade

Cascade

Cascading refers to things that happen one after another, or in a sequence that leads to something. In personal computing, you'll come across cascading prompts, menus, and windows.

Cascading prompts. Suppose you have a set of new diskettes, and you want to format them. You put them in a pile next to your keyboard. You'll format them one by one, placing each one back in your "blank diskettes" rack after it's been through the process.

You switch your PC on and let it go through its start-up procedure. Suppose your machine is programmed to go directly into DOS. The monitor screen shows you the prompt

```
C:\>
```

meaning drive C (the hard drive) is ready for your command. You place the diskette with the formatting program in one of the diskette drives, say drive A. Then you type

```
FORMAT A: [Enter]
```

and get the prompt

```
Insert diskette for drive A
Press [Enter] when ready
```

You remove the diskette with the formatting program from drive A and insert the first blank diskette there. Then you press Enter, and the PC tells you, as the process goes on, the percentage of the diskette that has been formatted.

After a minute or two, you'll get further prompts, providing information and asking questions. All you need to do is follow directions as they come in cascade, until you've formatted the whole stack of new diskettes. *See also* COMMAND-DRIVEN SOFTWARE.

Cascading menus. The same process can be carried out using a menu-driven or graphical interface such as Windows. The screen will show you a menu (set of options). Rather than typing the commands, you choose them from menus, usually by moving the pointer to the option you want and clicking the mouse.

When you select an option this way, you'll get a new menu of options. Again, you click on the option you want. This might go on for some time, until you and the PC, working together, have narrowed things down so the machine is doing exactly what you want. *See also* GRAPHICAL USER INTERFACE *and* MENU-DRIVEN SOFTWARE.

Cascading windows. In some graphical interfaces, the active window seems to be on top of other windows. There might be several windows beneath the active one. The *cascading windows* arrangement resembles the way you hold playing cards in your hand.

As you click in an option in the active window, a new active window appears on top of it. Cascading windows let you see all the title bars, as shown in the drawing. This helps you look back, if you want to remember the process that led to where you are. *See also* ACTIVE WINDOW.

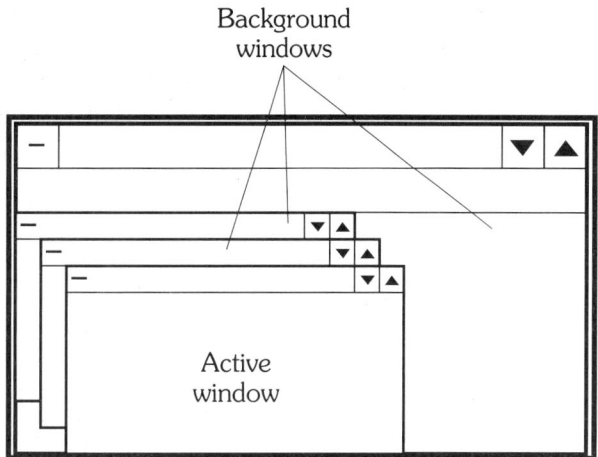

Windows on top of windows.

Catastrophic failure

The term *catastrophic failure* refers to a complete, sudden breakdown in a computer system. This might occur as a result of some physical event, such as a lightning strike. It might also be caused by a Trojan horse or virus in the software. Sometimes a single component can fail in some critical place, resulting in failure of a whole system. A good example of that is a head crash in the hard disk drive.

So that a minor problem won't cause a catastrophic failure, computer-controlled systems are designed with backup circuits in critical places. Then, if something goes wrong with one component, there won't be a major breakdown. *See also* GRACEFUL DEGRADATION, HEAD CRASH, TROJAN HORSE, *and* VIRUS.

Cathode-ray tube

Everyone encounters picture tubes. Your television set uses one; your desktop computer monitor uses another. A video picture tube is usually a *cathode-ray tube (CRT)*.

The electron beam. In any CRT, an electron gun emits a high-intensity stream of electrons. This beam is focused and accelerated as it passes through electrodes that carry a positive charge. The electrons continue until they strike a screen whose inner surface is coated with

Cathode-ray tube

phosphor. The phosphor glows visibly as seen from the face of the CRT.

Unless something moves the beam around the screen of the CRT, you'll only see a spot in the center of the screen. *Beam deflection* using electrostatic or magnetic fields makes displays possible.

Deflection and modulation. A cross-section of a monochrome (single-color) CRT is shown in the drawing. There are two sets of deflecting coils: one for horizontal beam motion, and the other for vertical motion. These coils generate magnetic fields because they carry electric currents. The greater the electrical currents in the coils, the stronger the magnetic fields will be, and the more the electron beam will be deflected.

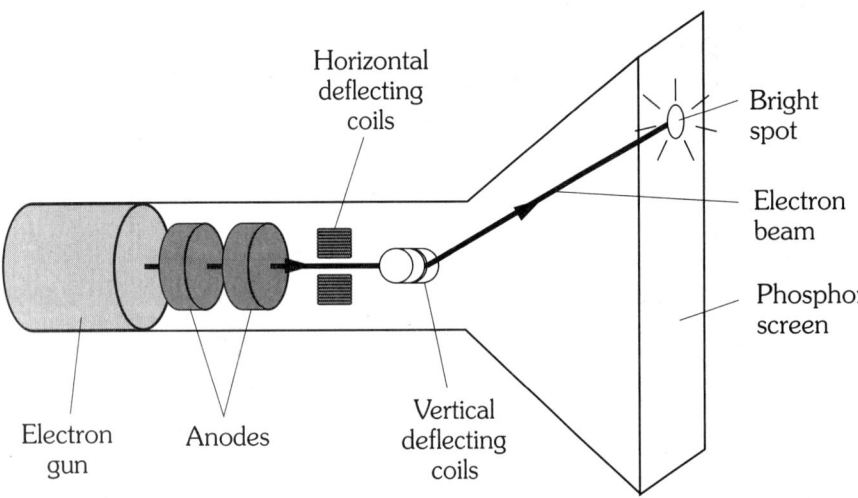

Simplified cross-sectional drawing of a CRT.

The horizontal coils receive a certain current waveform that causes the beam to sweep across the screen. After each sweep, the beam jumps instantly back for the next sweep. The vertical coils get another waveform that makes the beam move down the screen. All this time, the electron beam is modulated, so the moving spot changes brightness in an intricate, complicated way. The end result is what you see on the screen.

Color. In a color monitor, there are three electron beams, one each for red, green, and blue colors. Each beam works independently of the other two. There are really three images superimposed on the screen: a red (R) image, a green (G) image, and a blue (B) image. They combine to form the color pictures you see. This color scheme is known as the *RGB color model*. It is the same principle as that used in color television. *See also* MONITOR, RASTER, *and* RGB COLOR MODEL.

CCD

See CHARGE-COUPLED DEVICE.

CCITT standards

The abbreviation *CCITT* stands for *Comite Consultatif International Telephonique et Telegraphique*. In English, this means *International Consultative Committee for Telephone and Telegraph*.

Recommendations. As its name implies, the CCITT makes recommendations for systems. It doesn't have any real power; it can't enforce its standards. However, individuals and corporations alike can benefit from hardware standardization. It makes customers happy, and happy customers spend more money than unhappy ones. The greater the cash flow, the more profit companies make. To a lesser extent, the same thing is true for software. This is the argument in favor of a universal set of standards for products of all kinds, especially electronic and computer equipment.

There are forces that work against standardization. Some companies believe they are better off if they customize their products. Their argument is that buyers are not all alike, and there will always be a demand for specialized systems. Also, research-and-development (R&D) engineers, in their effort to create new hardware and software, are preoccupied with getting their schemes to work efficiently. They don't have the time to worry about standardizing everything. *See also* COMPATIBILITY, DOWNWARD COMPATIBILITY, *and* UPWARD COMPATIBILITY.

Online services. In personal computing, CCITT standards affect mainly the *online services*. You will see these standards listed, for example, in the specifications table for a modem. They usually start with the letters *V* or *X*.

When you see "V.22," for example, it refers to a modem speed of 1200 bits per second (bps), while "V.22 bis" means 2400 bps. Imagine if there were no standards for modem speed: you would have to adjust your modem every time you hooked up with another PC user or with a network. It would be a totally chaotic situation.

Aside from modem speeds, CCITT standards also affect PC network *protocol*. A protocol is, in effect, a set of rules for machines that communicate with other machines. When you hear things like "local echo off," "parity," and "stop bits," you're hearing about communications protocol. *See also* BAUD/BITS PER SECOND, MODEM, NETWORK, ONLINE SERVICE, PROTOCOL, *and* TERMINAL EMULATION SOFTWARE.

CD-ROM

CD-ROM stands for *compact disc, read-only memory*. You've probably played audio compact discs on stereo equipment. These discs can also

CD-ROM

store large amounts of digital information. A CD-ROM looks like an audio CD rather than a magnetic diskette. It is round and open to the elements, rather than being enclosed in a square case.

How it works. Your hard disk or diskette stores binary digits (ones and zeros) as tiny magnetic fields. Data is read from the disk by a magnetic head, similar to the way a recording tape is played back. It's easy to overwrite data on these disks; they are quite versatile in that sense.

A CD-ROM stores data as microscopic pits in reflective plastic. The data is read by bouncing a thin laser beam off the disc. The smooth regions of the disc surface reflect the laser back to a sensing device, but the pits scatter the beam. As the laser moves over the disc surface, it encounters reflective regions some of the time, and scattering pits at other times. As a result, the sensor picks up a digitally modulated beam of light.

The drawing is a greatly magnified view of the surface of a CD-ROM. As the laser scans the disc in a predetermined, precise way, the modulation of the reflected beam depends on the arrangement of the pits. These pits were etched onto the surface as the disc was made, permanently storing digital high (one) and low (zero) states in a defined sequence in a spiral path. If stretched out straight, this path would be three miles long. That's room enough for billions of microscopic pits in a CD-ROM 4.72 inches in diameter. It's smaller than a 5.25-inch magnetic diskette, but bigger than a 3.5-inch magnetic diskette.

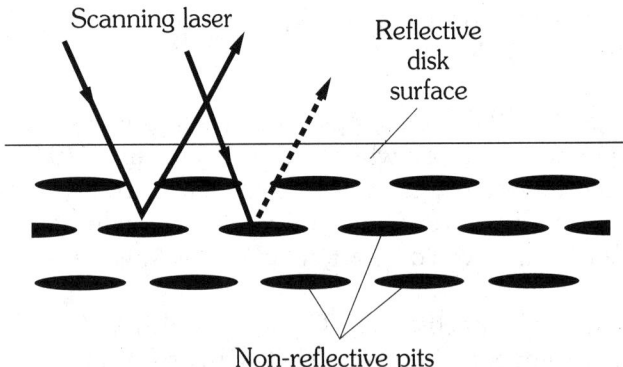

Nonreflective pits on the reflective surface of a CD-ROM.

A CD-ROM is not sensitive to magnetic fields. You can't destroy its contents by placing it near magnets, but the surface can be damaged by scratches and fingerprints. Even grains of dust can get in the way of the laser and make the computer unable to read the data correctly.

CD-ROM

Compact discs last a long time if they're stored in a dry, cool place, but they won't endure forever. The typical lifespan is 10 to 15 years.

Storage space. A typical high-density magnetic diskette for an IBM-compatible PC can hold 1.44MB (megabytes) of data. That's 1,440,000 characters of text, or about 200,000 words, the equivalent of a long novel. A CD-ROM can hold at least 650MB, which is more than 100,000,000 words, or 500 long novels.

You could put a small library on CD-ROM, if there weren't any pictures in the books. Illustrations take up lots of digital data storage space. This is what makes CD-ROM so convenient, and so much better than magnetic media for the storage of published works. One illustrated book can be easily stored on a single CD-ROM. It's also possible to store animation, complete with sound. Interactive technology makes use of CD-ROM, too.

It's possible that CD-ROM data will someday be more compact than it is now. High-speed electron beams might be used to read the data from pits too small for visible light to resolve. The result would be CD-ROMs that could hold more complex material at better image-resolution levels than is possible today. Even lengthy, multisensory virtual reality excursions would be storable.

Video and audio. A CD-ROM can store graphics of all kinds. Images can be stored in sequence and played back to get animation. Sound can be added; CD-ROMs are available that contain presentations in audio-visual form, like a movie. All of these features can be combined to get multimedia. Promotional spots can be put on CD-ROM and sent in the mail for a few cents' postage.

Perhaps the most valuable use for CD-ROM is in education. Children learn best when they're having fun in the process. Using PCs equipped with CD-ROMs, children can talk with the machines, look things up in encyclopedias at their own pace, travel through the Solar System, or plunge inside a red blood cell. Using CD-ROM in conjunction with speech recognition and speech synthesis, PCs will become "pals" as well as teachers for children.

Electronic books. The technology of CD-ROM is changing the book publishing industry. This is especially true with reference books. Because so many people have PCs these days, it's quite practical to publish reference books on CD-ROM, saving an incredible amount of space and weight. Of course, ordinary books can also be put on CD-ROM. Are you a book lover who moves often? How would you like to carry an envelope of CD-ROMs and a laptop computer, instead of moving a ton of bound books?

While hundreds of text-only books can fit on a single CD-ROM, some people argue that reading a novel on a computer isn't as enjoyable as

CD-ROM

curling up with a real book. Others suggest that computerized books could be more reader-friendly than traditional tomes. You might run a cord from a handheld PC to a CD-ROM drive on your bedside table, and have 500 or 1000 novels to choose from. With a backlit display, you could enjoy your novels without a bedside lamp, so your spouse could sleep while you read.

Limitations. As their name implies, CD-ROMs are *read-only*; you can't overwrite the contents. It is possible to interact with a computer that's using a CD-ROM, but the pits on the disc don't change.

It takes longer to access data from a CD-ROM compared with a magnetic disk because of the shape of the track. On a magnetic disk, the tracks are arranged in sectors, speeding and simplifying the process of locating data. Not so on CD-ROM; everything is on one long, spiral track measuring three miles from end to end. In this way, a CD-ROM drive works more like a tape drive than a hard disk or diskette drive.

There is a type of CD called a *write-once, read-many* (WORM) disc on which you can write data, but you can't change it once you've written it. This is something like camera film. You expose the film to visible light, and special substances in the film darken or change color to make the image. On a WORM disc, there is a light-sensitive dye on the surface. A recording machine uses a laser to create pits by melting the disk in microscopic spots. WORM disc recorders aren't cheap, but prices are dropping, and someday they should be affordable to most PC users. Large corporations use WORM recorders to save the trouble of having to special-order CD-ROMs for their needs.

CD-ROM for your PC. How do you get in on the action? You need to purchase a CD-ROM drive. It looks like a diskette drive, but instead of a magnetic head, it has a laser device inside. You'll need a PC with an extra drive bay, or at least an expansion slot for installation of the CD-ROM drive. Your PC will also need a hard disk (most PCs have that) with a certain minimum amount of space. Other things that you'll probably need include a mouse, a VGA (video graphics array) or better monitor, and an operating system that is as advanced as you can manage. You'll need special software to work with the CD-ROM drive; this is usually provided as part of the package with the drive. There are CD-ROM drives available for both IBM and Macintosh computer systems. Read the latest PC-related magazines to get an idea of what is currently available.

Many new computers have internal CD-ROM drives. If you're ready to buy a new computer, consider a machine with a CD-ROM drive built in. Software vendors are increasingly using this medium. It is cheaper for vendors to put a complex, sophisticated program on one CD-ROM than to compress the files (especially graphics) and put them on dozens of magnetic diskettes. It's also much easier for PC users to work with one CD-ROM, instead of swapping diskettes for an hour or more to install software. *See also* ANIMATION, BETA-PARTICLE CD-ROM, CLIP ART, GRAPHICS, INTERACTIVE TECHNOLOGY, MAGNETIC DISK, MULTIMEDIA, PRESENTATION GRAPHICS, SOUND TECHNOLOGY, SPEECH RECOGNITION, SPEECH SYNTHESIS, VIRTUAL REALITY, *and* WRITE-ONCE/READ-MANY.

Cell

See CELLULAR TELECOMMUNICATIONS *and* SPREADSHEET.

Cellular telecommunications

A computer can be hooked up to the telephone lines for use with online services. To many people, getting on this "information superhighway" is the main motivation for buying a computer. You can get online from your car, boat, or portable telephone, as well as from your house, using *cellular telecommunications.*

In recent years, cellular telephones have proliferated. A cellular telephone set is a radio transmitter/receiver (*transceiver*). Its signal is always within range of at least one base station. The range of coverage for any base station is called a *cell*; this is how the term "cellular" was coined.

If the telephone transceiver is in a moving vehicle, it goes from cell to cell. This is shown in drawing A, as seen from some point high above the system. The dotted line is the path of the vehicle. The base stations (dots) "hand off" access to the mobile transceiver. The cells form a honeycomb pattern; each one covers a hexagon-shaped region (shown by solid lines). All the base stations are connected to the telephone system by wires, microwave links, or fiberoptic cables.

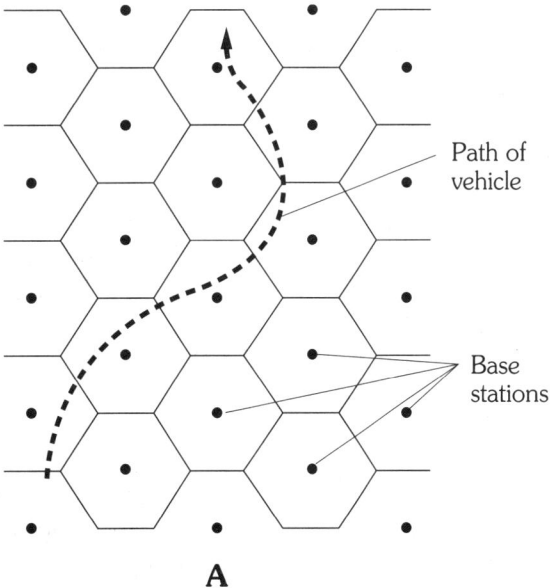

A

Vehicle moves from cell to cell.

Central processing unit

You can connect a laptop computer to a cellular telephone set with a portable modem, enabling you to get online from anywhere within range of a cellular base station. Drawing B is a block diagram of this scheme. Modems will probably soon be standard in mobile and portable telephone units, as well as in laptop computers. You'll also be able to buy "plug-in-and-go" portable modem/telephone units. Many airlines now have telephones at each seat, complete with jacks into which you can plug a portable modem. *See also* MODEM, ONLINE SERVICE, REMOTE CONTROL SYSTEMS, *and* TELECOMMUTING.

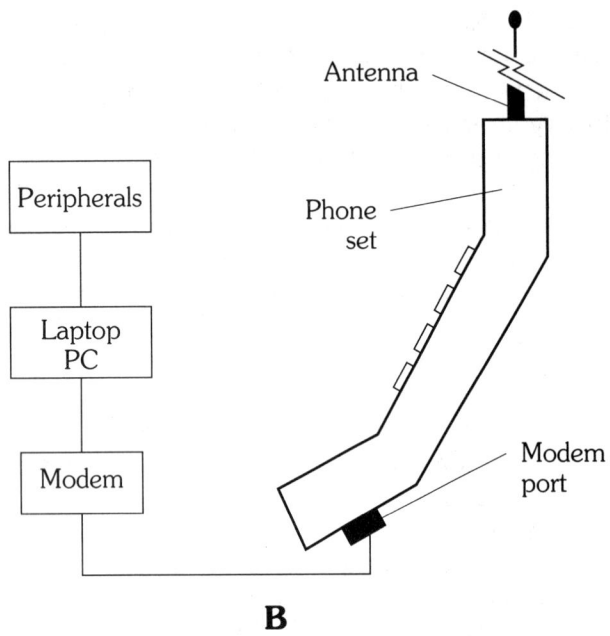

B

Connection of portable telephone to laptop computer.

Central processing unit

Every computer has a "nerve center" made up of integrated circuits (ICs), also known as chips. The nerve center of a PC is called its *central processing unit*, or *CPU*. The CPU is just what its name implies. It's central to the functioning of the PC; it processes a lot of data; it is a unit. It supervises the running of programs and regulates all the other systems in the computer. Here's an analogy:

COMPUTER SYSTEM : COMPUTER CPU
::
HUMAN BODY : HUMAN BRAIN

In other words, the computer system's CPU is like the human body's brain. Drawing A is a block diagram of a PC, showing the functional position of the CPU relative to the other parts of the system.

Central processing unit

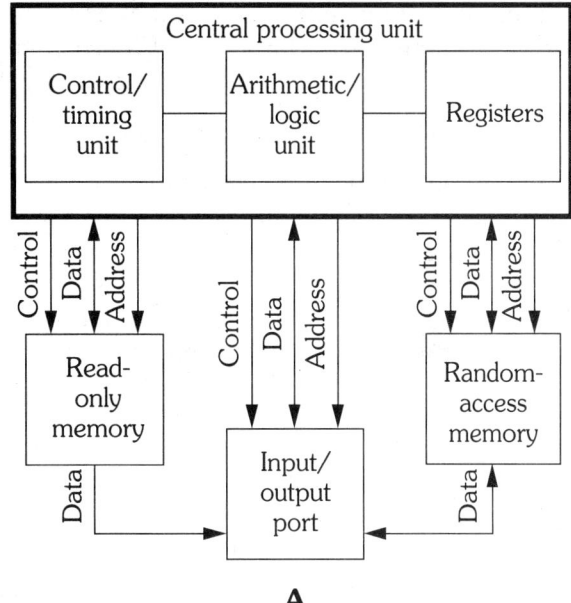

A

Functional diagram of a computer.

Components. The CPU has several parts, including the *arithmetic/logic unit (ALU)*, the *control/timing unit (CTU)*, and *registers*, also called *memory circuits* (see drawing B).

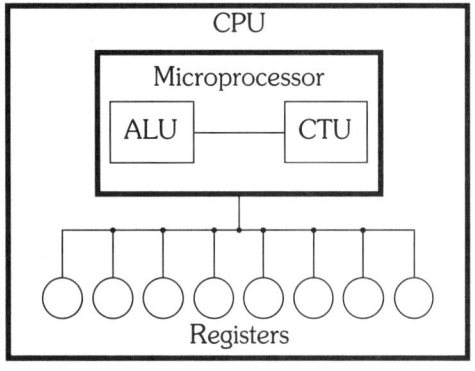

B

Components of the CPU.

The ALU does the actual calculations for the computer, such as adding, subtracting, multiplying, and dividing numbers. It also performs logical operations. This is the part of a PC that does the tedious work that would take you thousands or even millions of years to do by hand.

The CTU has a special program that it uses to oversee the workings of the computer. It tells the CPU what to do; then it gets necessary data from the memory, and sends it to other parts of the computer for execution.

Centronics interface

The registers are short-term memory circuits that contain vital instructions for the computer. You can think of these circuits like your own moment-to-moment memory. The registers are accessible almost instantly, but their capacity is limited.

Long-term computer memory is provided by the hard disk and diskettes. It takes longer to access data from these places than from the registers, but the capacity is far greater.

The main chip. The main IC of the CPU is the *microprocessor*. It contains the ALU and the control/timing unit. You could use the analogy

CPU : MICROPROCESSOR
::
MIND : CONSCIOUS MIND

The microprocessor is manufactured by a different company than the rest of the computer hardware. In IBM-compatible PCs, microprocessor chips are generally made by Intel. In Macintosh systems, the microprocessor chips are usually made by Motorola. (Some computers contain "clones" of the Intel or Motorola chips.) These companies are specialists in microprocessor design. Every few years, they come out with a new chip that is faster and more powerful than its predecessors. *See also* INTEL MICROPROCESSORS, MICROPROCESSOR, *and* MOTOROLA MICROPROCESSORS.

Centronics interface

See PARALLEL PORT.

Chain printing

Chain printing is the printing of more than one file in an automatic sequence. This feature is most frequently found in word processing and desktop publishing software.

Basic procedure. Suppose you've written a number of articles that you want to print out to make a book. You have the articles on a diskette; they have filenames PAPER.1 through PAPER.15. There is also a table of contents named PAPER.CON. The table shows the directory of this hypothetical diskette.

Notice that the files aren't in order in the diskette directory because some of them were revised after they were first placed on the diskette. The PC overwrote the updated files where there was room for them, and this affected their order in the list.

To print the book, you might instruct the PC to print PAPER.CON first, followed by PAPER.1, PAPER.2, PAPER.3, and on up to PAPER.15. However, maybe you'd want them printed in some other

Chain printing

Hypothetical directory of book files

PAPER	1	18,052	6-15-98	5:39a
PAPER	CON	570	9-19-98	1:23p
PAPER	3	14,254	6-15-98	5:39a
PAPER	4	16,237	6-15-98	5:39a
PAPER	5	8832	6-15-98	5:39a
PAPER	6	5316	6-15-98	5:39a
PAPER	7	5029	6-15-98	5:40a
PAPER	8	7527	6-15-98	5:40a
PAPER	9	1675	6-15-98	5:40a
PAPER	10	5462	6-15-98	5:40a
PAPER	11	12,643	6-15-98	5:40a
PAPER	12	9193	6-15-98	5:41a
PAPER	13	5539	6-15-98	5:41a
PAPER	14	3641	6-15-98	5:41a
PAPER	15	4402	6-15-98	5:41a
PAPER	2	6360	9-10-98	6:45a
16 files		124,732 char.		612,864 free

order. It could be that PAPER.7 would do best as the first chapter in your book; perhaps PAPER.4 would be a great closing chapter. In that case, you could place commands at the ends of each file, telling the PC which file to print next.

Special features. A good word processing package is flexible, letting you tailor the printing process to suit your needs. Here are some of the features most often desired:

➤ *Page numbering:* You will want to number the pages of your book. This can be done from page 1 to the end, or for each chapter (for example, *3-5* for chapter 3, page 5).

➤ *Verso/recto:* If you are printing on both sides of the page, you'll want left-hand, or *verso*, pages to have even numbers, and right-hand, or *recto*, pages to have odd numbers.

➤ *Title pages:* You will want each chapter to start on a new page. A chapter title shouldn't just run on right after the last sentence of the previous chapter as if it was a subhead of that chapter. The word processor can be programmed for this.

➤ *Blank pages:* In some books, new chapters always start on odd-numbered (recto) pages. To many readers, this seems more natural than having something begin on a left-hand page. That means there'll be some blank verso pages in the book. In such cases, the word processor should leave a whole sheet blank.

Character

> *Titles and art:* A good desktop publishing package can generate chapter titles in bold, large type, a few lines down from the point where text normally starts. It's even possible to have chapter-opening art.

> *Indexing:* Some word processing software can index your book, looking for specific words (that you must input ahead of time) and listing the pages on which they appear.

When properly coordinated, a chain printing program can print a whole book from individual files, without your having to intervene during the process. *See also* DESKTOP PUBLISHING *and* WORD PROCESSING.

Character

In computer systems, a *character* is a letter of the alphabet from A through Z, a numeral from 0 through 9, a punctuation mark, or any of various symbols that you can find on a keyboard. These symbols vary, but always include certain standard items. A character is equivalent to about one byte of data. *See also* BYTE.

```
!  @  #  $  %  ^  &  *  (  )  _  +  |
1  2  3  4  5  6  7  8  9  0  -  =  \
   Q  W  E  R  T  Y  U  I  O  P  {  }
   q  w  e  r  t  y  u  i  o  p  [  ]
      A  S  D  F  G  H  J  K  L  :  "
      a  s  d  f  g  h  j  k  l  ;  '
         Z  X  C  V  B  N  M  <  >  ?
         z  x  c  v  b  n  m  ,  .  /
```

The alphanumeric characters, as they appear on a computer keyboard.

Charge-coupled device

A *charge-coupled device (CCD)* is a video camera that changes images into digital signals. Astronomers use CCDs to enhance views of outer space. Biologists employ CCDs to process the images seen by microscopes. Some robots use them in machine vision systems. Meteorologists use them to process satellite photos and radar images. In personal computing, CCDs are used in optical character recognition.

Digitization of images. The image you see, focused on the retina of your eye, is an *analog* image. It can have infinitely many configurations, and infinitely many variations in hue, brilliance, and saturation. The image on a camera film is the same way, as is the signal that comes out of a television camera tube. These are all fine images, clear and precise, but they are of no use to a computer.

Charge-coupled device

When a computer gets an analog signal, it's like the average American looking at a newspaper in Japanese (or vice-versa). A computer needs a *digital* image to make sense of what it sees. Binary digital signals have only two possible states: on and off (also called high and low, or one and zero). It's possible to render an analog image as a string of high and low signals. Digital impulses can likewise be converted to analog images.

Computer eyeball. A CCD, in conjunction with software for optical character recognition (called *OCR software*), works something like a graphics program in reverse. It changes an analog image into a digital signal that your computer can understand. Patterns in the image are recognized and converted into alphabetic-numeric digital codes. Using OCR software, the images of characters are changed into combinations of ones and zeros. Then, when printed text is "seen" by the CCD, the computer's "brain" gets the impulses, as if you had typed the text into the PC from a keyboard.

The image on your eye's retina is converted into nerve impulses that your brain can understand; the CCD with OCR software is like an eyeball that has been adapted to a computer.

It's improving. A CCD has trouble with handwriting and with some exotic printed fonts, but a CCD with OCR software can resolve standard fonts such as Courier or Prestige. A CCD can read text of any reasonable type size. Newer OCR software can even "learn" to read some nonstandard fonts. It will probably not be long before OCR devices can recognize almost any handwriting, perhaps even scribbling such as doctors put down on prescription pads.

A simplified block diagram of a CCD vision system is shown in the drawing. *See also* ANALOG, DIGITAL, DIGITAL SIGNAL PROCESSING, MEMORY, OPTICAL CHARACTER RECOGNITION, *and* OPTICAL SCANNER.

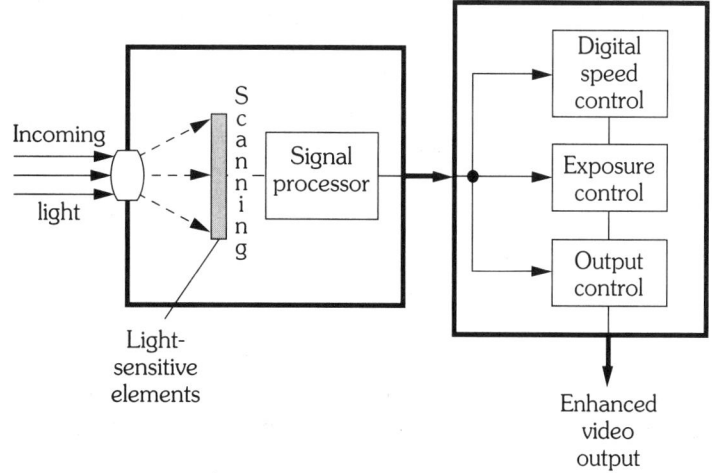

Block diagram of a CCD computer vision system.

Checkers-playing computer

A computer can be programmed to play an almost unbeatable game of checkers. An excellent program has been created by Arthur Samuel in which the computer not only plays the game move-by-move, but also anticipates all the possible consequences of a move.

A simple game. Checkers is a fairly simple board game. It is more complex than tic-tac-toe, but far less complicated than chess. If you have played tic-tac-toe for any length of time, you've discovered that you can always get at least a draw. This is so elementary that a high-school student with some programming experience can get a computer to play tic-tac-toe. You need only look ahead one move in this game.

Look ahead. Look-ahead strategies of more than one move take practice to acquire. It's hard for a human, let alone a computer, to develop this level of proficiency in any game. To play a game this way, you have to anticipate your opponent's options, as well as your own, several moves in advance. The number of possibilities explodes as you look further ahead. Arthur Samuel's checkers program uses look-ahead strategy so effectively that the best human players in the world find it almost impossible to beat his machine.

A variation of look-ahead strategy is to try to deceive, or entrap, opponents by diverting their attention. This is easy to do with an inexperienced human adversary, but hard to do against a good checkers player. Against a computer running Arthur Samuel's checkers program, it's impossible. A well-programmed machine cannot be deceived. *See also* COMBINATORIAL EXPLOSION.

Game plans. There is yet another scheme that can be used for checkers. This is to adopt a general game plan. These strategies can be broadly categorized as either defensive ("hang back") or offensive ("go for it like mad"). In this author's limited experience, the offensive strategy seems to work better in checkers. Once you decide on a strategy, however, you must stick with it to the end.

In checkers, defensive or offensive schemes require a look-ahead of only one move. If you're interested in programming a computer to play checkers, but don't feel as qualified as Arthur Samuel, you might try a combination of one-move look-ahead in conjunction with a defensive or offensive general strategy. *See also* ARTIFICIAL INTELLIGENCE *and* CHESS-PLAYING COMPUTER.

Checksum

Digital information can be sent fast and accurately. Errors don't occur often, but when they do, they can cause trouble. *Checksum* is a way to detect errors in digital data.

Checksum

Bit count. The sending computer, or *source*, transmits the data in units. At the end of each unit, the source computer does a bit count, tallying up the number of bits in the data unit. This number is added to the end of the unit as an extra word. The unit is then transmitted, complete with the bit count at the end.

The receiving computer, or *destination*, gets the data unit. It counts the bits in the unit and compares the result with the bit count from the source. If they agree, which they usually do, then the unit is printed or displayed. If they don't agree, an error signal is printed because the data is probably mutilated. The destination doesn't know exactly what, or where, the error is, it just knows there is one.

In a scheme called *handshaking*, the destination sends a repeat request back to the source, telling it to send the unit of data over again. Then the errors can be corrected, as well as detected. The drawing illustrates checksum plus handshaking.

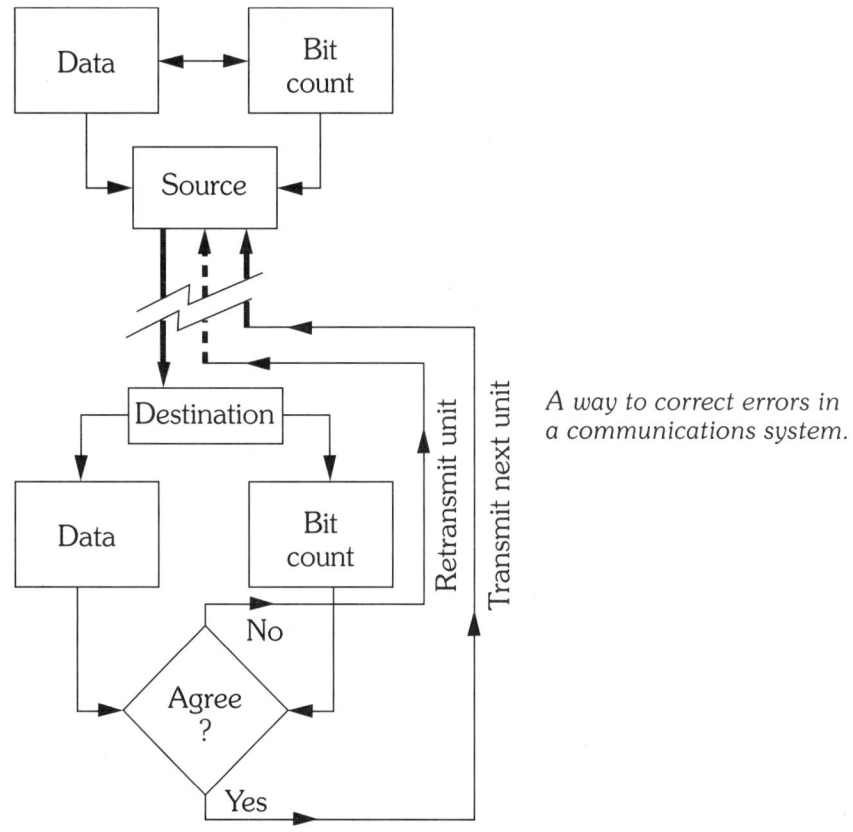

A way to correct errors in a communications system.

Results. If a checksum/handshaking communications channel is excellent, then errors do not occur, and the destination receives signals at full speed. If there are errors, the effective data speed slows down. The more frequent the errors, the greater the reduction in the effective data speed.

Chess-playing computer

Suppose the data speed is 19,200 bits per second (bps). Under good conditions, the data will arrive at the destination at about this speed. If the communications channel is marginal, the source must repeat some data units. The effective data speed is therefore reduced, say to 19,000 bps or even 18,800 bps. If the channel is bad, the data speed at the destination will be far less than normal. Ultimately, if the channel deteriorates too much, the flow of data will stop.

If checksum is used without handshaking, the data speed will be 19,200 bps no matter how often errors occur. However, as the conditions deteriorate, error signals will replace more and more of the received data. If conditions become very bad, the destination will receive only the error signal. *See also* HANDSHAKING.

Chess-playing computer

Chess can be used to develop and test computer intelligence. One of the first chess-playing machines was developed by Rand Corporation in 1956. That software also allowed a computer to prove a few simple theorems in mathematics.

Many strategies. Chess is a complex game in which many different strategies can be employed. The goal is to capture the opponent's king, or place it in a position where it can't escape without being captured.

Perhaps you've watched masters playing a game of chess. Most of their time is spent contemplating moves. The human brain is millions of times more sophisticated than any computer yet developed. A person can think in ways far more subtle than any PC. And yet, the human mind is taxed to the limit as it decides which piece to move, and where to move it, on a chessboard.

Software you can buy. Several companies have developed software that lets you play chess with your PC. Most of these programs can make your computer into a good chess player, teaching you the basics and starting you on your way to mastery of the game. The best chess programs can give expert human players a challenge.

Some chess-playing programs are designed to help you improve your game. You set the level of difficulty so the computer is about as good as you are. With time, you'll get better and you can adjust the program accordingly. Some software is interactive, and tutors you just like a human teacher.

Other chess-playing software is meant to entertain you. The pieces might have human form, and move like people, so that your chess game becomes an animated, interactive session in which you are in quasi-control. One program sets the game in outer space. Another uses players who play tricks on you when you're not looking.

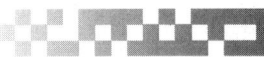

CD-ROM and multimedia technologies have greatly increased the power and flexibility of PCs. If you're interested in getting software for chess, you should look for CD-ROM versions as well as diskette versions.

Network chess. People have played chess via telephone, mail, and even amateur (ham) radio. If there's a way to get a message from one place to another, someone has conveyed a chess move by that means. Traditionally, this has been done via written or spoken instructions resembling mathematical formulas that tell where each piece is to be moved on the board.

With a modem, your PC can be connected by telephone or ham radio into an online network, so you can play chess with other people using your computer. You can see the board and the positions of the pieces. You can play against one opponent on a private, two-way link, or you can be a part of a chess club with several members.

Computer chess master. The best chess programs can make computers into chess masters, capable of beating most people at the game. As computers get more and more memory, with the ability to process data faster and faster, PCs will become invincible at chess. Then there will be two world chess championships: a human tournament and a computer tournament. The PC chess tournaments will be held mainly to test the skill of human computer programmers.

The more complex and subtle a mental game becomes, in general, the better human beings can do against computers. Someday, perhaps people will see fit to invent a more complicated version of chess. New and strange pieces might be added, such as a "ghost," which could move with total unpredictability once or twice during a game, after the fashion of a "mulligan" in golf or a "wildcard" in card games. This would add an element of randomness that machines could not be programmed to cope with by logical means. Of course, there would be nothing to stop programmers from introducing illogical behavior into chess software. *See also* ARTIFICIAL INTELLIGENCE, CHECKERS-PLAYING COMPUTER, INTERACTIVE TECHNOLOGY, MULTIMEDIA, *and* TURING TEST.

Child-proof computer

See TOT-PROOF WORKSTATION.

Chip

See INTEGRATED CIRCUIT.

Choreographer program

A *choreographer program* is used in computerized animation to show a person making motions. One such program, called the "Ultimate Choreographer," was written by Charles Lecht of Lecht Sciences, Inc. It shows the famous mime, Marcel Marceau, on a monitor screen.

Circuit board

This was not television, nor was it a movie. Instead, the video was contained in the digital memory of a computer. The programmer sat at the computer and, by giving commands, caused the mime to make various moves. This program was one of the first examples of interactive technology.

The earliest motion pictures used celluloid film. Then came videotape. Now, moving images can be stored in digital memory, in the same way as the text in a word-processed file. Animated graphics consumes huge amounts of memory, but as mass storage technology advances, this problem is being overcome. *See also* ANIMATION, INTERACTIVE TECHNOLOGY, *and* MULTIMEDIA.

Circuit board

See PRINTED CIRCUIT.

Circular reference

A *circular reference* is a statement that refers to, or contains, itself. It makes a computer go in circles or loops.

In spreadsheets. Spreadsheets are useful for doing arithmetic with large arrays of numbers. The numbers are placed in rows, designated 1, 2, 3, and so on, and in columns, designated A, B, C, and so on. The drawing shows part of a spreadsheet with numbers in some of the boxes, or *cells*. There is an equation in cell E4.

	A	B	C	D	E	F
1	100.00				76.25	
2	2.33				25.33	
3	23.50				5.00	
4	1.00				A2+E4	
5						

A circular reference is a cell that refers to itself, as E4 does.

The equation tells the computer to add the numbers in the cells as indicated, and place the result in cell E4. If you were to write it down as an algebraic expression, it would be

E4 = A2 + E4

There is a problem with this. The formula can be true if and only if A2 is zero. Otherwise it is a false, or invalid, statement. But as you can see, A2 is 2.33. So you're telling the computer that

E4 = 2.33 + E4

This is a mathematical impossibility. The statement is nonsense, so the computer will give you an error message. This is an example of a circular reference; cell E4 is referring to itself. See also SPREADSHEET.

In programs. Programs, especially those used by scientists and engineers in languages like BASIC or Fortran, often contain circular references. A *loop* is a set of statements that the computer executes over and over.

Some loops are repeated thousands, or even millions, of times. Eventually, however, the computer must exit the loop. If the programmer makes a mistake that prevents the computer from leaving the loop, the machine will be trapped. It will run in circles until something (like a power failure) or someone (like the programmer) intervenes to stop it. This is an *endless loop*.

To get a computer out of an endless loop, the whole program must usually be terminated. It might even be necessary to reboot the computer. Endless loops are almost never used in programming, although they can be useful for certain kinds of computer-performance experiments. *See also* ENDLESS LOOP *and* LOOP.

CISC

See COMPLEX-INSTRUCTION-SET COMPUTING.

Click

In a computer system that uses a graphical user interface (GUI), you use a mouse to move the pointer around on the screen. When you get to the item or box you want, you press a button on the mouse once (*click*) or twice (*double-click*).

For example, the instruction "Click on Cancel" means that you should move the pointer to the box or button marked Cancel, or to a Cancel icon (a small picture), and press a button on the mouse (usually the left button, on IBM-compatible PCs) one time. "Double-click Fribble" means that you should move the pointer to the box marked Fribble, or to the Fribble icon, and press the mouse button twice.

In some software, clicking once highlights a box or icon. To get the PC to do whatever is indicated by the box or icon, you must click the mouse a second time. This gives you time to change your mind after highlighting the box or icon, if you decide you don't want the PC to carry out that function. Then you can move the pointer somewhere else, click it, highlight the new item, and have time in case you change your mind again. *See also* GRAPHICAL USER INTERFACE, HIGHLIGHTING, ICON, *and* MOUSE.

Client

In a local area network (LAN), there are several *nodes*, or workstations. All the nodes are interconnected so they can share data. There are various basic arrangements for LANs.

In a LAN, a node might be a PC or a dumb terminal. A PC can process data; a dumb terminal can only access it from somewhere else. Obviously, a PC is a more powerful node than a dumb terminal; a PC also costs more.

A *client* is a node in a LAN that can process data, as well as get it from somewhere else. In personal computing, the word *client* is practically synonymous with "PC in a LAN." Computers in LANs can be clients for each other.

Imagine a LAN with 10 workstations. Maybe nine of the nodes are dumb terminals, each connected to a central *file server*, and there's only one PC. Or perhaps there are five PCs and five dumb terminals. Maybe nine of the nodes, or even all 10, are PCs. One of the big advantages of LANs is their flexibility. They can be adapted to practically any small or medium-size business, school, or agency.

Suppose you own a small business, and you decide you need a LAN with 10 workstations, but only two clients. You can buy two PCs and eight dumb terminals, along with the rest of the hardware and software that go with the LAN. This will fulfill your current needs and minimize your expenses. However, you should also think ahead. If you expect your business will remain about the same size, you might get along with two clients and eight dumb terminals for a long time. If you expect that your business will rapidly expand, you might want to purchase computers for all the workstations. *See also* BUS NETWORK, DUMB TERMINAL, FILE SERVER, LOCAL AREA NETWORK, NODE, RING NETWORK, SERVER, *and* STAR NETWORK.

Clip art

Clip art is the use of images in word-processed text and desktop publishing. It's like the stuff you clipped and pasted into your reports when you were in school, but PC clip art can be stored with text on your hard disk or diskette. When you print the document, the graphics of the clip art go on the paper in just the size you specify, just where you want it, and as many times as you want it printed.

Uses for clip art. Many PC users write letters often, and like to use graphics to get their readers' attention. If you have a small business, clip art can lend a special flair to your correspondence.

Clip art can be used as chapter-opening art for books, or for the front pages of self-published magazines and newsletters. Some technical diagrams are available as clip art for scholarly works, such as theses, and engineering reports, like the results of lab tests. And of course, there's always that graph that shows corporate profits over time (hopefully sloping upwards).

Are you starting a small business? Do you need a company logo? You can design your own clip art and use that, but if you use purchased clip art instead, you must be careful. The price you pay might not cover the right to use the image in something you sell, or in an ad for something you sell. If you have any doubts about the legality of using clip art in your business, consult an attorney. Write the company that sold you the clip art, tell them what you want to do with it, and request their permission to use it. And get it all in writing.

Where to find it. You can buy packages with hundreds or thousands of pieces of clip-art images; you can also download images when you use an online service. Company and product names of clip art publishers change often. Look at recent issues of PC-oriented magazines to find advertisements.

If you plan to use clip art a lot, you might consider a package with a big collection of images. The largest collections are usually available on CD-ROM as well as on diskettes. If you have a CD-ROM drive, you'll save some money and time by purchasing clip art in that form. Clip art collections are usually cheaper on CD-ROM than on diskettes, and the images can be stored in uncompressed form, so you don't have to use a decompression program.

If you want to use only a few images, you can buy a small package or download the ones you want from online. If you need only one or two images, the online method is probably the best, especially if you have a modem and are already using one of the popular online services.

Payment and copyright. You've probably heard horror stories about companies suing people over stupid little things, like mentioning the name of some cartoon character, or accidentally using a logo without permission. You must be careful about these matters, especially when downloading clip art from online services. Be sure you know what you're downloading. Freedom of expression is one thing; copyright infringement is quite another.

If you have any concerns that an image might be copyrighted by someone, avoid using it. Above all, don't try to use copyrighted clip art in any profit-making venture without talking about it with a lawyer first.

Some companies are happy to grant permission for the use of graphics for which they own copyright. An example is when your use of the art amounts to "free advertising." But again, get permission in writing.

Of course, you must expect to pay for the use of clip art, whether you buy it in a computer store, download it from a company specializing in

Clipboard

online clip art, or get it from some other source. The long-distance and online telephone time costs something all by itself, *even if the clip art is given away. See also* CD-ROM, DESKTOP PUBLISHING, GRAPHICS, *and* ONLINE SERVICE.

Clipboard

A *clipboard* is a small, temporary file that you can use when you want to move a block of text, a graphic, or another part of some document to another document. You use it in much the same way as a real clipboard; that's where the term comes from.

Most new software packages and operating environments, including Windows and the Mac, have a clipboard feature. To use it, you first select the area of the document you want to move or copy, highlighting it with your mouse or keyboard. Then you use either the Cut or Copy command to place it in the clipboard. Next, you open the new document or move to wherever you want the data to go, and use a command called Paste to put the data into the new document. You can look at the data in the clipboard, to be sure it's right, by double-clicking the Clipboard Viewer (in Windows) or choosing Show Clipboard (in Mac).

The clipboard can normally hold only one item at a time. Thus, it's possible to inadvertently erase the contents of the clipboard, overwriting it with something else. To prevent this from happening, avoid using the Cut command simply to delete text from a document, unless you want that text to go into the clipboard. If you use the Cut command, the selected text will automatically be placed in the clipboard, and whatever was in the clipboard before will be erased. There are other commands you should use when deleting text in a document. Check your software instruction manual or Help files to become familiar with all the commands and what they do.

Clock speed

As technology has improved, computer power has increased. *Clock speed* is one of the yardsticks by which computer power is measured.

Pulse generation. The clock in your computer isn't the kind that tells the time. Instead, it generates a series of pulses that act like a metronome for the microprocessor. The clock sets the rhythm for the operation of the machine.

Clock pulses occur many times every second. The clock speed is measured in units called *megahertz (MHz)*. A frequency of 1 MHz is equal to one million (1,000,000) cycles per second. To get an idea of what this means, tune an AM (not FM) radio to the middle of the broadcast band. This is a frequency of about 1 MHz. Another way to imagine this frequency is to think of it as being 50 times the frequency of the highest-pitched sound you can hear.

One of the earliest microprocessors, the Intel 8088, ran at 4.77 MHz. That's in the "shortwave" radio band. Today, computers can be found with clock speeds of 100 MHz or more. A frequency of 100 MHz is near the top of the standard FM radio broadcast band.

If you know the clock frequency of your computer, you might actually tune a radio receiver to that frequency, bring it near the main unit, and listen to the clock. You will hear a sound like a whistle or hiss.

Other factors. You might think that the faster the clock, the more rapidly a computer can do calculations. This is basically true for any given microprocessor model, when all other factors are equal. An Intel 80386 (often called simply a 386) working at 20 MHz is generally faster than a 386 working at 16 MHz, but clock speed is not the only thing that determines how many calculations a computer can do in a given amount of time. The microprocessor's "way of thinking" makes a big difference, as does the bus architecture in the computer. Another factor is the nature of the computer's instruction set.

The most advanced microprocessors can do more with a single clock pulse than earlier ones. For example, an Intel 80486, also known as a 486, is faster in many applications than a 386, even when the clock speeds are the same. The Pentium (basically an 80586) is faster in some applications than a 486 working at the same clock speed. A similar state of affairs exists for Motorola's 680x0 series of chips, commonly found in Macintosh computers. *See also* COMPLEX-INSTRUCTION-SET COMPUTING, INTEL MICROPROCESSORS, MICROPROCESSOR, MOTOROLA MICROPROCESSORS, *and* REDUCED-INSTRUCTION-SET COMPUTING.

Clone

A *clone* is a machine that performs all the same functions as some other machine. It is an imitation or replica. Cloning has become common in the computer industry. The term can also refer to the duplication of living things. Interestingly, some futurists see some overlap between computer cloning and biological cloning.

Compatibility. You can buy a computer that is "IBM compatible" and that works just like an IBM PC. Often the clone costs less than the brand-name unit. The hardware quality might be as good as a brand-name unit, or it might not be.

One of the advantages of cloning is *compatibility*. This goes hand-in-hand with cost savings. When manufacturers copy each other's products, the result is some degree of standardization. It's easy to get parts, and that keeps costs down. When there are several companies offering more or less identical products, there is a strong incentive for engaging in "price wars." This helps consumers as companies compete for business.

CMOS

One of the problems with cloning is that it can discourage innovation. Companies might worry more about beating out the price of the competition and less about developing new technologies. The free market has a way of filling voids, however. When consumers demand more powerful computers, new companies spring up. Maverick engineers start ventures of their own, resulting in firms such as Intel, Microsoft, and Apple.

Another problem with cloning is that it can result in lawsuits. One cannot copy someone else's product, undercut their price, and then expect not to get sued. There must be some differences between the clone and the brand-name product.

Cloning ICs. In biology, the term *clone* has a much different meaning than it does in computer science. In labs, biologists have grown organisms starting with a single cell. All the genetic information for the organism is contained within the nucleus of every cell in its body. Some biologists believe that all organisms can be cloned, including humans. Perhaps even integrated circuits (ICs) can be grown and cloned.

Futurists have thought about cloning humans and then programming their minds. Perhaps a body could be cloned and an IC substituted for the brain! Such a human would be entirely biological, except for the brain, which would be a computer. This makes excellent material for science fiction writers, but today's fiction can become tomorrow's reality.

The living CPU. Perhaps a human genius could be cloned, and then its brain removed and used as the central processing unit (CPU) of a computer or computerized robot. Imagine a machine with true human consciousness, and also with a computer's speed at calculating and data processing!

Most scientists think that the ideas of putting a computer chip into a person's head, or a human brain into a computer, are impractical and half-baked notions, akin to turning lead into gold. Even if such things ever become possible, they might be outlawed because of ethical concerns and because people would become frightened of them. Some people are scared enough of computers as they exist today. *See also* ARTIFICIAL INTELLIGENCE, ARTIFICIAL LIFE, BIOCHIP, BIOLOGICAL ROBOTS, CYBERPHOBIA, *and* UNCANNY VALLEY.

CMOS

See COMPLEMENTARY-METAL-OXIDE-SEMICONDUCTOR TECHNOLOGY.

Coaxial cable

Coaxial cable is a type of cable especially designed for high-frequency digital or analog data. It keeps the desired signals inside itself, and keeps out unwanted signals and interference. Coaxial cable, or "coax" (pronounced "CO-ax"), is the cable of choice for a local area network (LAN) that uses baseband wiring. *See also* BASEBAND *and* LOCAL AREA NETWORK.

How it's made. All coaxial cables are manufactured in the same way: a wire is surrounded by a tube of solid or braided metal. The inner wire is called the *center conductor*, and the outer tube is called the *shield*.

In some coaxial cables, a solid or foamed polyethylene layer, called the *dielectric*, keeps the center conductor running right down the central axis of the cable, as shown in the drawing at A. The dielectric also keeps the center conductor from shorting out to the shield.

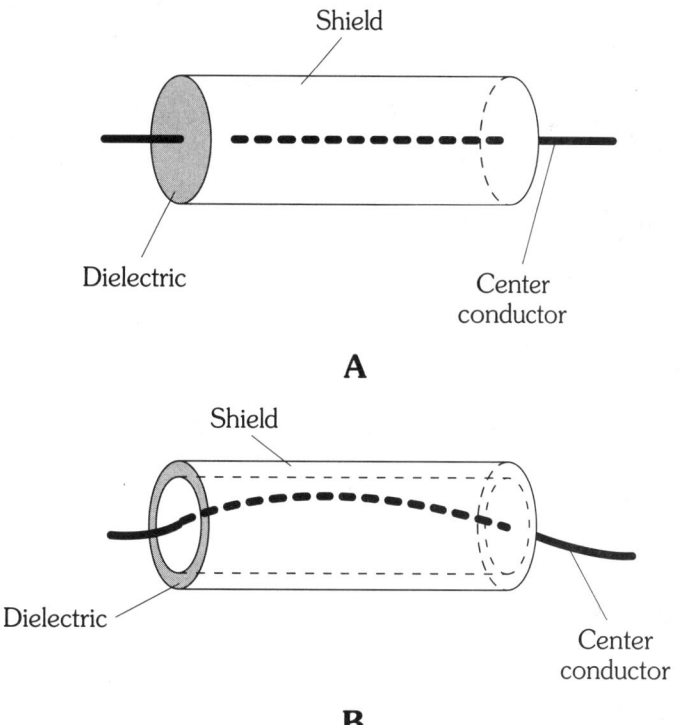

Solid dielectric (A) and tubular dielectric (B).

Some cables have a bare center conductor and a thin layer of polyethylene just inside the braid (as in the drawing at B), so that most of the interior of the cable is air. In this cable, the center conductor can flop around, but the polyethylene keeps it from shorting out to the shield.

Most coaxial cables use braided copper for the shield, but some cables have a solid metal pipe surrounding the center conductor. This type of cable is called *hard line*.

COBOL

How it works. In a coaxial cable, the signal is carried by the center conductor. The shield is connected to an *electrical ground*, meaning that it's hooked up to a neutral, common point in the system or network. Grounding is important for a coaxial cable to function properly.

When the shield of the cable is well-grounded, it keeps the data signals from "leaking" out of the cable. This is one of the big advantages of coax over twisted-wire or open-wire data lines. Any signal that leaks from a cable represents loss, and cannot reach the destination.

Another advantage of coaxial cable is that the shield keeps unwanted signals or noise from getting in. Twisted-wire or open-wire lines can let radio waves, static, and other interference in. This disrupts the data and can cause misprints and programming errors. Coax can be run right alongside metal objects, and through areas where there is a lot of interference, and will still work well. This is not true of most unshielded cables.

In recent years, fiberoptic cable has begun to replace coaxial cable. Fiberoptic cables can carry more signals, and have even better immunity to interference, than coax. They are also cheaper and physically lighter. *See also* FIBEROPTIC CABLE *and* FIBEROPTIC DATA TRANSMISSION.

COBOL

The acronym *COBOL* (pronounced like "cobalt" without the *t*) stands for Common Business-oriented Language. It is one of the oldest high-level programming languages, having originated in the late 1950s.

COBOL is fairly easy to learn because the commands are mostly words and directions written in English. The language is especially good for handling numbers in tabular form, making it useful for bookkeeping and other numbers-related jobs in corporations.

In recent years, Pascal has largely replaced COBOL in business. The languages C and C++ are also used. *See also* C, C++, *and* PASCAL.

Cold boot

The term *cold boot* refers to starting up a computer by switching on the power. It's like cold-starting a car. *Booting* refers to the *bootstrap program* that the computer must run every time you switch the machine on.

There are occasions when you must reset your PC. There are several ways to do this. One method, on an IBM-compatible PC, is to press the key combination Ctrl-Alt-Del. You can also press a Reset button if your computer has one. Either of these methods,

called a *warm boot*, clears everything and forces the PC to run its bootstrap program again, although it might ask you a series of questions along the way.

Usually, a warm boot is sufficient to reset a computer. But if this doesn't work, you'll have to resort to a cold boot, switching off the machine, waiting a couple of minutes, and then switching it back on again. A cold boot is a sort of electronic "kick." It should be used only as a last resort because it puts the computer through a lot of work.

It's important to wait a couple of minutes after removing power before you switch the machine on again. This gives the hard drive time to wind down.

If there's a power failure and you aren't using an uninteruptable power supply (UPS), turn off power immediately. Open the power switches of all the peripherals, too. Alternatively, if everything is plugged into a *transient suppression* box (also called a surge suppressor), you can open the switch on the box. Then, when the power returns, it won't kick your hard drive back into action before it has had time to wind down. Also, the computer and peripherals will be protected against any initial voltage surge that might occur when the power company restores the electricity. *See also* BOOT, BOOTSTRAP PROGRAM, *and* TRANSIENT SUPPRESSION.

Color Graphics Adapter

The term *Color Graphics Adapter (CGA)* refers to the first adapter board that allowed IBM-compatible PCs to display illustrations, or graphics. Before the CGA was available, the monitors of IBM-compatible computers could show only text.

The *image resolution*, or amount of detail, that a CGA could render was considerably less than that of the best monitors available today. A CGA could show only a few different hues (colors). If you're used to an SVGA (Super Video Graphics Array), and you get a chance to look at a CGA, you'll find the images on a CGA blurry, and the colors dull.

You will sometimes find CGAs in use with older computers. Some people use computers only for text and simple graphics applications; for them, a CGA monitor is adequate. *See also* ENHANCED GRAPHICS ADAPTER, IMAGE RESOLUTION, SUPER VIDEO GRAPHICS ARRAY, *and* VIDEO GRAPHICS ARRAY.

Color printer

Many PC users can get along with black-and-white printing. However, you might want to consider a *color printer* if you plan to do desktop publishing or presentations.

Color printer

Price and types. Color printers are not necessarily very expensive. Of course, some color printers will set you back several thousand dollars; there are black-and-white printers that will do the same. The costliest printers are the laser printers. Next down on the list are inkjet and thermal printers. The least costly are dot-matrix printers.

Laser color printers cost from a few thousand up to $15,000 or more. Inkjet and thermal color printers range from about $250 to $2500. Dot-matrix color printers are available for as little as $250. As with all PC technology, the prices for printers are coming down. Competition is fierce in the printer field, giving manufacturers a big incentive to develop high-quality printing hardware at a low price.

The model of color printer you choose will depend on the kind of work you plan to do, the volume of work you are doing, and how much you're willing to spend on the machine.

Dot-matrix color printers generally don't provide as good an image resolution as inkjet or laser printers, but dot-matrix machines are easy to use, and most come as complete packages. You only need to buy a color ribbon, and you're all set. A few dot-matrix printers require you to purchase a special color kit, in addition to the printer itself, if you want to create color hard copies. Dot-matrix printers require minimal maintenance, and they are physically rugged.

Composite image. The drawing shows the operation of an inkjet color printer. This is not an exact rendition, but is greatly simplified to illustrate how the printer works. There are three or four jets, each with a different ink in the primary pigments: red, yellow, and blue. Actually, the colors are magenta (reddish pink), yellow, and cyan (bluish-green). A separate jet for black ink might also be included. There are three or four separate images, one for each color of ink.

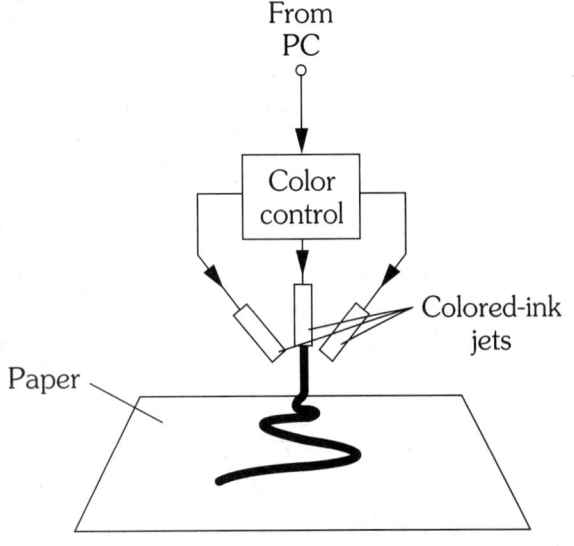

Principle of an inkjet color printer. Paper is moving toward you.

The PC sends data to a color control unit, which has software that governs the amount of ink that comes out of each jet. The jets all work independently, so the pigments can be combined to produce all possible composite pigments. The final image is the combination of three or four different images, one for each color of ink, in effect lying on top of each other.

The different colored images in a color printer must be precisely aligned. If the images aren't aligned, "rainbow" borders will appear around objects in the composite and the image will appear blurred. You've probably seen this effect; it occurs fairly often in color newspaper photographs. *See also* DOT-MATRIX PRINTER, INKJET PRINTER, LASER PRINTER, *and* THERMAL PRINTER.

Colossus

Suppose that a single, intelligent computer were given absolute control of all the nuclear weapons systems in the world. If that could be done, human error could never lead to a nuclear war. The conflagration would have to be carried out by the computer.

Computerized defense. To some extent, computers already control the nuclear defenses in the United States. A "fail-safe" system makes it theoretically impossible for any single person to press a button and cause a nuclear holocaust. Some scientists think the current systems don't go far enough, however. They argue that a computer, seeing how illogical nuclear war is, would not let it happen. A computer would, they say, be the ideal controller for nuclear arsenals.

Such is the scenario for a 1960s novel and movie called *Colossus: The Forbin Project*. The fictional American-made computer, called Colossus, discovers that there is a similar system in Russia (then known as the Soviet Union). The two computers interconnect, and begin to share data and learn from each other. Their artificial intelligence (AI) grows rapidly, until they are far smarter than any human being. They are also supremely powerful because they control all the nuclear missiles in both the United States and the Soviet Union.

War outlawed. This intelligence and power having been achieved, the computers decide that they will not only outlaw war, but they will control people's lives. Colossus tells people when, and how much, they may eat, work, sleep, and exercise. If anyone disobeys Colossus, the computer will retaliate by launching a missile and wiping out a city. To show that it means business, the computer does this on one occasion.

Some researchers in AI believe that the Colossus scenario is possible. With the Cold War between America and Russia over (at least for the time being), there seems to be less risk of worldwide nuclear destruction than there was in the 1960s, but there are still a lot of nuclear missiles in the world.

If humanity ever gives total control over all nuclear weapons to a real Colossus, they had better be sure there's a way to override the system. This is one lesson to be learned from this fictional work. *See also* ARTIFICIAL INTELLIGENCE *and* CARETAKERS.

Columnar graph

When working with graphics, you will often need to show how several different variables change. A *columnar graph* is a way of doing this that has eye appeal, while being easy to read and interpret.

In a columnar graph, the independent variable is on the horizontal axis and the dependent variable is on the vertical axis, as in the Cartesian coordinates system. However, while the Cartesian system lets you show continuously varying quantities, a columnar graph allows only certain values to be shown.

The columnar graph here shows the average high temperature for January 1 and July 1 in four hypothetical towns A, B, C, and D. The four towns and the dates represent the independent variables, and are shown on the horizontal axis. Temperature in degrees Fahrenheit, the dependent variable, is on the vertical axis. Crosshatching and shading make it easy to tell which bars are which. *See also* BAR GRAPH, CARTESIAN COORDINATES, DEPENDENT VARIABLE, *and* INDEPENDENT VARIABLE.

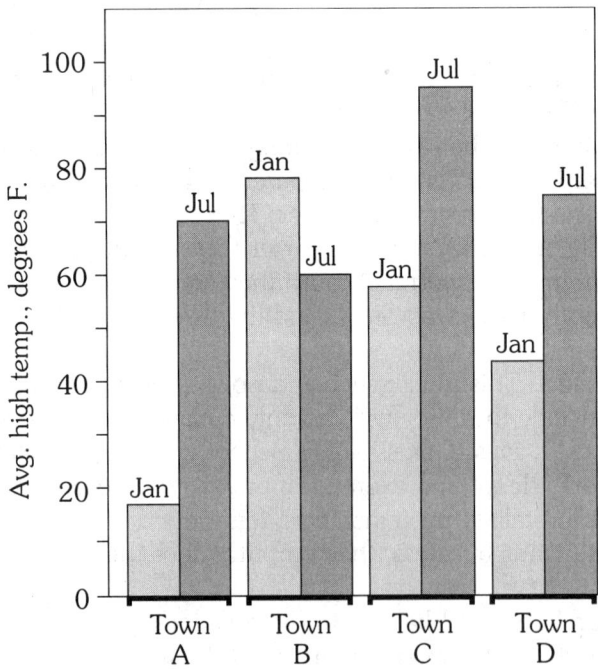

Columnar graph of average high temperatures for four towns in January and July.

Combinatorial explosion

Certain problems are extremely hard for machines to work out because there are so many different choices that a computer just can't make a good decision. Suppose, for example, you're playing a game of five-card draw. You receive five cards, as does every other player in the game. You have the option of receiving zero to four replacement cards, but you have no way of predicting what the new cards will be. The only way you can be sure of your hand is to stick with the cards you have.

Suppose your hand is bad. What should you do when the dealer asks you, "Would you like any cards?" If you ask for, say, three new cards, there are thousands of possible outcomes. This kind of problem is called a *combinatorial explosion*.

The drawing shows the principle of a combinatorial explosion. A decision-making process between either of two alternatives, repeated many times, quickly blows up into a huge array of possibilities. If there are n repetitions, where n is some integer, then the number of possible choices is 2^n (two multiplied by itself, n times).

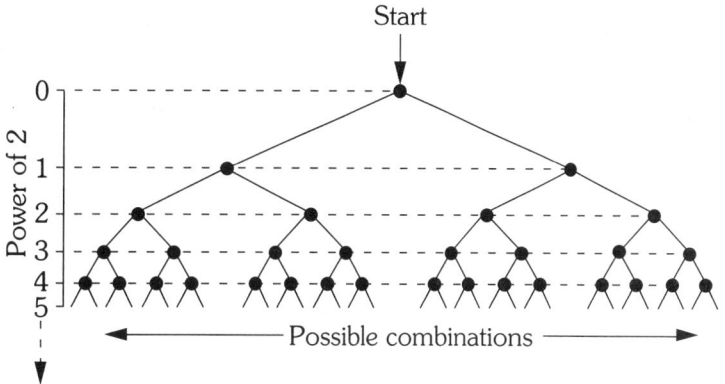

Combinatorial explosions start with one item, doubled over and over.

The rich but stupid king. You've probably heard a version of the following story, which illustrates how combinatorial explosions can confuse people (as well as machines).

A child went to see the king of a rich country on the first day of spring. "Would you give me some money as a present for my mother?" asked the child, having heard that the king was a generous man. The king was generous, and was also a practical joker. He told the child, "I'll give you either a million dollars, or else a penny today, and then double it every day until Mother's Day. Which would you rather have?" The king was confident the child would go for the million dollars. The child replied, "A penny today, and then double it every day until Mother's day." By Mother's Day, the child's mother owned the kingdom.

Artificial wisdom. In complex board games, as in some real-life situations, intuition often works better than any computer program. In general, the more skill a game or scenario requires, the harder it is to write a computer program to choose well. Artificial intelligence is one thing; artificial wisdom is quite another.

In board games, as in real life, there are *subjective variables*. These are factors such as the personalities of your opponent(s), the expression in their eyes, and other cues that no electronic brain comes close to understanding. In a combinatorial explosion, when the number of choices becomes huge (like the number of pennies the child's mother had by Mother's Day), problems acquire subtle aspects. A few researchers suspect that extrasensory perception (ESP) plays a role in games like poker and chess. Can truly skilled players read their opponents' minds? Most scientists would say that this is beyond the realm of possibility, but they cannot back up this belief with solid proof. On the other hand, no one can prove that a computer will never acquire ESP. *See also* ARTIFICIAL INTELLIGENCE, CHECKERS-PLAYING COMPUTER, CHESS-PLAYING COMPUTER, *and* TURING TEST.

Command

In computer terminology, a *command* is any statement that you make to get the computer to do something. Commands can be given in various different ways. The two most common systems are *command-driven software* and *menu-driven software.*

Commands versus menus. An example of a command-driven system is DOS. In DOS, commands are given by typing words, abbreviations, or acronyms on the keyboard.

In a menu-driven program, you select what you want from a list that appears on the screen. The DOS shell works this way, as do the more sophisticated operating interfaces provided by Microsoft Windows and the Macintosh operating system. You can select the desired command by moving the cursor with keyboard arrows (up, down, right, or left), or by using a mouse or trackball.

When you type or select a command, your PC sees it as an order to execute a specific program that it has stored in its memory. Every command has its own software, usually activated when you type or select the statement and then press the Enter key or click the OK button.

External versus internal. There are two main types of commands used with DOS: *external commands* and *internal commands.* External commands are stored on the hard disk. They are used less

often than the internal commands. There are many external commands, which you can give by typing in the appropriate information. It takes a moment for your PC to load the data after you give an external command. There's practically no limit to the number of external commands an operating system can have. As DOS has evolved, new external commands have been invented so that the system is able to do new things, or do old things more efficiently.

Whenever you tell an IBM-compatible computer to go into DOS, the internal commands are automatically loaded into your PC's RAM (random-access memory) from a file called COMMAND.COM. Your PC can therefore access internal commands almost the instant you type them. The CPU (central processing unit) issues the internal commands, and as far as you're concerned, the computer takes care of business without your having to worry about the details. For example, if you type

DIR A:

and press the Enter key, your monitor will display the directory of the diskette in drive A right away.

Some external DOS commands. The following is a list of some of the more common external DOS commands. This is by no means a complete list, but is intended only as a list of examples. Also, some of these commands might not be available if you use older versions of DOS. For full information, refer to DOS Help in your computer system by typing the word *help* and pressing Enter at the DOS prompt, which usually looks something like C:\>.

➤ *APPEND* Use this to tell the PC to search for certain files in certain directories. You can have the computer go through just one path, or through several different paths. The search ends when all the desired data is found. *See also* DIRECTORY, FILE, *and* PATH.

➤ *ASSIGN* With this command, you can read data from, or write data onto, diskettes in drives other than A or B, if such drives exist, and if they aren't already busy. *See also* DISKETTE.

➤ *ATTRIB* When you give this command, short for *attribute*, you give files special characteristics. Suppose, for example, that you wanted to prevent accidental overwriting of a file called TAX.2; you could give that file a "read-only" attribute. *See also* ATTRIBUTE.

➤ *BACKUP* This command is for duplicating files, which prevents disaster in the event of a hard-drive failure, lost diskette, or other mishap. Files can be copied to or from hard disks, diskettes, or tape drives. You select which files you want backed up, and which ones you want left alone. *See also* BACKUP.

Command

- *CHKDSK* When you type this command (which stands for *check disk*) followed by a drive designator (such as A or C), your computer will search the hard disk or diskette for errors. It will tell you about the errors, if any are found. This command will not operate over a network.

- *COMMAND* This creates a new COMMAND.COM file, different from the regular one. It gives your PC a different set of internal commands than usual. This is called "changing the command environment." The regular COMMAND.COM file stays in memory. You can return to it when you want, using the internal EXIT command described in the next section of this article.

- *COMP* This command, which stands for *compare*, tells the PC to compare files or sets of files. You will be informed when compared files are identical. You'll also be told if there are any differences, and if so, where they occur.

- *DISKCOMP* When you type this command, which stands for *diskette compare*, the PC compares two diskettes: the *source diskette* and the *target diskette*. You will be told if there are differences in the diskettes, and if so, on which track(s) they are. You can't use this command on a network.

- *DISKCOPY* Use this command to put the contents of a source diskette onto a target diskette. When you do this, the old data on the target diskette is overwritten. You can't use DISKCOPY with a hard disk or on a network.

- *FASTOPEN* When you use certain hard-disk files often, you can save time by using this command. It will work with up to 999 files. Once you've specified the number of files you want this command to work with, you cannot change it without starting DOS over. You can't use FASTOPEN over a network.

- *FC* This command, which stands for *file compare*, works very much like the COMP command. With FC, however, you can make all kinds of special adjustments to speed the comparison and keep the PC from looking for differences that aren't important.

- *FDISK* This command is used to set up your hard disk for Microsoft DOS (MS-DOS). It allows you to *partition* the hard disk. *See also* PARTITION.

- *FIND* When you type this command, the PC searches for a series, or *string*, of characters in a file. You specify the string by enclosing it in quotation marks. You can get a display of all lines containing that string, or you can request a list of all lines that do not contain that string.

- *FORMAT* This command structures diskettes so that DOS can use them. When you format a diskette, all the data on it is erased. You must therefore be careful when you use the Format command. **Never format a hard disk!** This command won't function on a network. *See also* FORMATTING.

➤ *GRAFTABL* This command lets you insert characters, like letters and numerals, when you are using graphics. *See also* CHARACTER *and* GRAPHICS.

➤ *GRAPHICS* Using this command, you can get a hardcopy (printout) of a graphics display. It will work with various display adapters. Of course, a black-and-white printer can't make color printouts, but it can use several shades of gray, as well as crosshatching, solid black, and solid white.

➤ *JOIN* When you type this command, the PC connects a diskette drive to a path. It won't work if the drive is already being used. When this command is being used, some other commands won't work; consult your DOS instruction manual or DOS Help for specifics. You cannot use this command on a network.

➤ *KEYB* This command, which stands for *keyboard*, lets you program your keyboard for various languages. Unless you specify something else, the PC will work in American English. When you program the keyboard for some language other than English, the labels on the keys might not match what appears on the screen.

➤ *LABEL* Using this command, you can give the diskette a name, called a *volume label*, with up to 11 characters. You don't have to give a diskette a volume label. This command cannot be used on a network. *See also* VOLUME LABEL.

➤ *MEM* When you type this command, which stands for *memory*, the PC will tell you all about the status of its memory. You'll be told how much memory is taken up, and by what. You'll also see how much free memory you have. *See also* MEMORY *and* RANDOM-ACCESS MEMORY.

➤ *MODE* This command has various functions. You can use it to check the status of all the peripherals connected to your PC. You can also adjust these peripherals. Some uses of MODE include adjusting the modem speed, setting the number of printed characters per line, and setting the number of lines your monitor will display.

➤ *MORE* This command can be used in combination with certain other commands to display multi-screen documents one screen at a time. When you see

    --More--

at the bottom of the screen, you can press any key to look at the next page.

Command

- *NLSFUNC* You can use this command to change the way your PC works, to accommodate a different language. Normally, your PC works in the default language of your system. In the U.S., that is usually American English.

- *PRINT* When you use this command, your printer makes a hardcopy of the file or files you specify in a print queue. You can work on other things in the foreground while the PC carries out the printing in the background. *See also* BACKGROUND PROCESSING *and* FOREGROUND PROCESSING.

- *RECOVER* This command lets you get data off a diskette with bad sectors. Files should be recovered one by one. The data will be mutilated in places, but you can edit the file once it's off the diskette. Diskettes are cheap; don't keep one with bad sectors after you've recovered its files. Throw it out. You can't use this command on a network. *See also* BAD SECTORS.

- *REPLACE* You can use this command for file updating. The PC will compare the source directory (say, a hard disk) with a target directory (say, a diskette). If any filenames match, the PC will overwrite those on the target with the contents of those on the source. *See also* FILE UPDATING.

- *RESTORE* This command lets you return files from a backup diskette to your hard disk. Suppose, for example, that you have a novel with 24 chapters (NOVEL.1 through NOVEL.24) on a diskette. You wrote the book a year ago, and then took it off the hard disk. You can use RESTORE to put it back on the hard disk for revision or editing.

- *SCANDISK* This command, a more comprehensive version of CHKDSK, will search for and correct a variety of hard disk or diskette problems.

- *SELECT* This command is for installing MS-DOS, usually on a hard disk. After you type the command, the PC will provide instructions. What you do then depends on how much memory your PC has available, what kind of printer you're using, and other factors. See your DOS manual for details.

- *SHARE* This command is for networks. It provides *concurrency control*, preventing confusion if two or more people want to work with a file at the same time. It also prevents someone from accidentally erasing or changing someone else's data. *See also* CONCURRENCY CONTROL.

- *SORT* Use this command to arrange files alphanumerically. This can be done according to the first letter or numeral in the filename, or according to the letter or numeral in any column you specify. This is useful, for example, when you want to list a directory in various different ways.

➤ *SUBST* Using this command, which stands for *substitute*, you can name a path as if it were a diskette drive. Then, when you type the drive designator (such as B), the PC will send data to, or get it from, the path as if it were working with a diskette located there. Thus, the command creates a "make-believe" diskette drive, or *virtual drive*. You can't use SUBST on a network.

➤ *SYS* You can use this command, an abbreviation for *system*, to move the system files from one disk or diskette to another. The COMMAND.COM file, however, must be transferred separately. You can't use this command on a network.

➤ *TREE* This command lets you see the complete structure of a directory. The main directory is like the trunk of the tree; subdirectories are like the branches. This is how the command gets its name. *See also* DIRECTORY *and* DIRECTORY TREE.

➤ *XCOPY* Use this command to copy files from a source to a target. The source and target might be a hard disk, diskette, file, or directory. This command differs from the DISKCOPY command because, with XCOPY, the source and target need not have identical formats.

Some internal DOS commands. Here is a list of some internal commands in DOS (for further information, consult DOS Help):

➤ *BREAK* This command lets you interrupt the PC while it's working on something. To interrupt (or break) the work in progress, press the Ctrl and C keys at the same time. If you type the word *BREAK*, you will get information about the status of the command (what it is set to do at the time).

➤ *CHCP* This command stands for *check/change code page*. The *code page* is a three-digit number that stands for a language. If you type this command, your PC will tell you the code page for the language for which it is currently set, and also the code pages for all the languages it can work with. If you type CHCP and a code number for a specific language, your PC will set itself for that language. Refer to your DOS manual for codes and their meanings.

➤ *CHDIR* or *CD* Use this command, which stands for *check/change directory*, to display your *working directory*, the area of the disk in which your PC is currently operating. You can also use this command to leave one directory and go to another. *See also* DIRECTORY.

➤ *CLS* When you type this command, which stands for *clear screen*, your monitor display will go blank, except for the prompt line and the cursor.

➤ *COPY* This command is used to copy part or all of a file. The PC will copy that part of the file preceding the end-of-file marker that you place within the file. You can copy several files

Command

using the COPY command, but if you want to copy all the files in a directory, you should use the command XCOPY. To copy a diskette, you can use DISKCOPY.

➤ *CTTY* This command stands for *change teletype*, but it really means *change terminal*. With this command, you can change the PC control point. For example, you might move from the main PC console to a dumb terminal in some other room or building. *See also* DUMB TERMINAL.

➤ *DATE* Use this command to check or change the date in your PC's timekeeper. You'll get a message such as this:

```
CURRENT DATE IS 02-23-99
ENTER NEW DATE (mm-dd-yy):
```

If you don't want to change the date, press Enter. If you do, type it in the form mm-dd-yy (two digits for month, two digits for day, two digits for year), and then press Enter.

➤ *DEL* This command erases one or more files from your hard disk or diskette. It's best to set this command to prompt you before erasing a file. Then you might type

```
DELETE BIBLIO
```

press Enter, and the PC will come back with the following:

```
BIBLIO, DELETE (Y/N)?
```

You can then type either *Y* and press Enter, meaning "Yes, delete it," or *N* and Enter, meaning, "No, don't; I didn't mean it."

➤ *DIR* This command lists the files in the current directory. For every file, data is shown in this order from left to right: filename, filename extension, file length in bytes, and date/time of the last change. An example is shown in the table on the next page.

➤ *EXIT* When you type this command, you can return to a previous *command processor*. This will only happen if you changed command processors at some previous time, for example by using the external COMMAND command, described in the previous section of this article.

➤ *MKDIR* or *MD* Use this command, which stands for *make directory*, to create a new directory. It can have subdirectories; the structure can be as complicated as you like, as long as you can reach the level you need by typing at most 63 characters.

➤ *PATH* This command instructs your PC where to look for external commands. You can search only the working directory, or you can search in several paths in sequence. The only limitation is that you have to give these instructions in 127 characters or less. *See also* DIRECTORY.

Command

DIR A: might produce this readout

EARTH	DIR	430	7-28-99	3:20p
EARTH	L1	3257	3-06-99	5:37a
EARTH	L2	2902	3-06-99	5:37a
EARTH	L3	1541	3-06-99	5:37a
EARTH	L4	1042	3-06-99	5:37a
EARTH	L5	1331	3-06-99	5:38a
EARTH	4	10,756	3-22-99	5:41a
EARTH	9	13,009	5-31-99	5:40p
EARTH		3871	8-07-99	2:45p
EARTH	BAK	12,317	6-11-99	6:57a
EARTH	10	10,656	7-06-99	7:53p
EARTH	L7	1329	3-14-99	6:35a
EARTH	11	9952	8-02-99	3:31p
EARTH	12	11,362	6-08-99	9:58p
EARTH	L8	849	3-22-99	6:59a
EARTH	L6	1063	3-08-99	3:52p
EARTH	1	9512	3-09-99	12:01p
EARTH	2	11,515	3-09-99	12:02p
EARTH	3	9402	3-09-99	12:02p
EARTH	L9	1222	4-03-99	4:35p
EARTH	5	15,053	3-09-99	12:03p
EARTH	6	11,676	6-24-99	6:27p
EARTH	7	13,029	5-31-99	5:41p
EARTH	8	12,556	5-31-99	5:39p
ECOWEEK	L1	1556	7-23-99	12:32p

25 files   170,588 char.   610,816 free

➤ PROMPT When you type this command, you can tailor the appearance of the symbol, or symbols, to suit your needs. A typical prompt is

C:\>

which means that the computer is ready to take input, and that it will go to the root directory of drive C (the hard drive) unless you say otherwise. *See also* PROMPT.

➤ REN With this command, which stands for *rename*, you can change filenames and/or filename extensions. This command has certain limitations, however. You cannot change filenames on more than one drive at a time. You shouldn't try to make changes that might cause confusion among files (such as getting

Command

rid of all filename extensions). *See also* FILENAME *and* FILENAME EXTENSION.

➢ *RMDIR* or *RD* When you type this command, which stands for *remove directory*, you can eliminate a directory that no longer contains any useful data. You cannot remove the directory you're working in. Before removing any directory, you should be sure that there are no files or subdirectories in it.

➢ *SET* You can use this command to change from one string of characters to another, or to eliminate a string of characters altogether. The command is generally employed in programming to set the value of some parameter or variable.

➢ *TIME* You use this command to check or change the time of day in your PC's timekeeper. You'll get a message such as

```
CURRENT TIME IS 5:04:45.31p
ENTER NEW TIME:
```

If you don't want to change the time, press Enter. If you do, type it in the same form as the PC has given you the current time, and then press Enter. *See also* TIMEKEEPER.

➢ *TYPE* Use this command to get a printout of the active file. If there's no file active, you'll get an error message. If you want a printout of an inactive file, enter the Type command, then the drive and directory (if any), then the filename and extension, and then press Enter. For example, to print out a list of addresses on a diskette, you might key in

```
TYPE A: ADRS.LST
```

Of course, your printer must be on for this command to work.

➢ *VER* When you type this command, which stands for *version*, you'll be given information about the operating system and/or the software currently in use. *See also* RELEASE NUMBER *and* VERSION NUMBER.

➢ *VERIFY* Have you ever wanted to back up important data onto a diskette, but been afraid the diskette might have bad sectors? You can use this command to ensure that your information is getting where it should, in the form that it should. If something is amiss, you'll be told. *See also* BACKUP *and* BAD SECTORS.

➢ *VOL* This command lets you know the *volume label* of a diskette. Normally you follow this command with a drive designator. For example, if you type in

```
VOL B:
```

you will see the volume label (if any) of the diskette in drive B. If the diskette in drive B has no label, you'll get a message like this:

```
VOLUME IN DRIVE B HAS NO LABEL
```
See also VOLUME LABEL.

Commands in the Internet. If you're interested in navigating the so-called *information superhighway*, chances are you'll want to access the Internet directly. The online service called Delphi provides good access to the Internet. Also, there are probably local gateways provided by various companies in your area.

When you start using the Internet, you'll notice that its commands differ depending on where you are in the network. Sometimes you'll encounter menus, while in other instances you'll suddenly be given a set of commands to learn on the spot.

Various shortcut key combinations do certain things on the Internet. For example, typing a *B* might move you up one page; pressing the Spacebar will move you down a page. Typing a *U* will move you to the previous menu. Sometimes you must press Enter after typing commands; in other cases you must not hit this key. Various companies are at work trying to adapt the Internet to a graphical user interface (GUI). They have a difficult job ahead of them, because the Internet consists of so many different networks, each with their own peculiarities. *See also* INTERNET.

Spoken commands. In robotics and artificial intelligence, commands can often be given in the form of spoken words. This can also be done with command-driven programs for personal computers. For example, rather than typing the word *editor* when you want to work on a word processing file, you might say the word instead.

The use of speech for giving commands is bedeviled by all kinds of problems. How do you say the period, comma, question mark, quotation mark, and other symbols? How does the computer know you mean *c* and not *see*? How does the computer deal with background noises such as barking dogs, shouting children, or ambulance sirens? These problems are dealt with by engineers who work with speech recognition systems. *See also* COMMAND-DRIVEN SOFTWARE, DOS, GRAPHICAL USER INTERFACE, MENU-DRIVEN SOFTWARE, *and* SPEECH RECOGNITION.

Command-driven software

Command-driven software refers to any program or operating system in which you must type in instructions telling the computer what to do. There are many different functions, and therefore there are many different commands.

Most people find it difficult to use command-driven software at first; there's a learning curve involved. Many of the commands are abbreviated. Sometimes you can read the abbreviation and get a good idea of what the command involves, but other commands are so cryptic that they must be memorized by rote.

Command key

When navigating a complex online service such as the Internet, where different command sets are used in different parts of the system, the situation can become especially confusing. In addition to the proliferation of commands, the syntax differs from place to place in the system. Sometimes you must hit the Enter key (also called the Return key) after typing a command; other times you must not.

Another drawback of the command-driven interface is that you must be a fairly good typist. Besides having to memorize commands, you must be able to type them without spending a lot of time "hunting and pecking" on the keyboard.

Because of these shortcomings, many PC users prefer to use menu-driven software rather than command-driven software. A *menu* is a list of commands from which you can select, using either the keyboard or a pointing device such as a mouse or trackball. A further refinement, and the most user-friendly scheme of all, is the *graphical user interface (GUI)*. This is the mode found in the popular Windows and Macintosh operating environments.

Command-driven software, despite its shortcomings, is not likely to become obsolete. As speech recognition and speech synthesis become more advanced, command-driven operating interfaces will be favored in some applications. This is taking hold in professional settings where a person can't take hands or eyes away from work. As a doctor examines a patient, for example, the doctor can speak to the computer, giving it the vital information about the patient. This can't be done with a keyboard, mouse, or trackball.

The hardware and software for speech recognition is already available. Good speech-recognition software allows the computer to "learn" thousands of words, based on the sound of the user's voice. The main problem thus far has been that speech-recognition software takes up large amounts of memory, which does not come cheap. As technology advances, this problem should be overcome. *See also* GRAPHICAL USER INTERFACE, MENU-DRIVEN SOFTWARE, PERSONAL DICTATION SYSTEM, SPEECH RECOGNITION, *and* SPEECH SYNTHESIS.

Command key

In the Macintosh PC system, there are shortcuts for certain often-used commands. Instead of having to type out the entire command, you can hold down a special *Command key* at the same time as a letter key. The command key has a special symbol that looks like a square with loops stuck to the corners. In IBM-compatible PCs, the *Ctrl key* often serves this same function. The table shows some Command-key shortcuts for the Mac.

Some Command-key shortcuts used in the Macintosh system

Command	Press Command key and letter:
CLOSE	W
COPY	C
CUT	X
NEW	N
OPEN	O
PASTE	V
PRINT	P
QUIT	Q
SAVE	S
SELECT	A
UNDO	Z

Of course, if you use a graphical user interface (GUI), whether with the Macintosh system or an IBM-compatible PC, you probably use the mouse, not the keyboard, to give commands most of the time. *See also* CONTROL KEY *and* GRAPHICAL USER INTERFACE.

Commonsense Summer Project

The *Commonsense Summer Project* was a session in which artificial-intelligence (AI) experts tried to find ways to program real-world notions into a computer.

Machine versus human knowledge. It's hard to get a machine to understand things as people do. While there might someday be a computer as smart as a person, and which might even regard humans as dull-witted, most researchers agree that this will not happen for a long time.

When and if computers do have the intelligence of people, the nature of machine knowledge might differ greatly from human knowledge. It is naive to suppose that the human way of thinking is the only possible thought mode that can exist. Some experts already argue that comparing human and machine intelligence is like comparing apples and oranges.

Get me a sandwich. To get an idea of how complex a simple command can be in the mind of a machine, suppose you tell a computerized robot, "Go into the kitchen, make me a cheddar-cheese sandwich, and bring it out to me on a paper plate."

Communications

First, the robot must understand the words you speak, and also must identify, and remember, who you are and where you are. The words must be translated into a chain of commands that can be followed by branching, preferably with no more than two decisions (yes/no) at each branch point. Some of the questions a robot must ask itself, and then answer, are as follows:

1. Where is the kitchen?
2. What is a sandwich?
3. What are the ingredients in a cheddar-cheese sandwich?
4. Where is the bread?
5. Where is the cheese?
6. Which cheese is the right kind (cheddar)?
7. How will I know that I've found the right things, and not, say, two napkins and a piece of ham?
8. What should I do if there is no bread or cheddar cheese?
9. How much cheese is a reasonable amount?
10. Should the cheese be sliced flat, or should it be in a cubical chunk? Or a ball? Or what?
11. How can I recognize a plate?
12. How can I tell the difference between your best china and a paper plate?

These questions are very general, and could themselves be broken down into hundreds or thousands of individual yes/no branch points, each broken down into binary data, digital ones and zeros. The result of all this must be that the robot comes to you without delay, holding in its mechanical hands a paper plate on which there are two slices of bread with a reasonable amount of cheddar cheese sliced flat between them.

Tie your shoe. As an exercise, you might try writing a detailed set of instructions for tying a shoelace, without using any diagrams. Someone must be able to follow these instructions precisely, and end up with a properly tied shoelace.

Once you've completed this assignment (allow several hours), try to rewrite the instructions as a series of questions, all of which can be answered either yes or no—and which will still, when followed exactly, result in a properly tied shoelace. This will give you some idea of how difficult it is to program a smart robot to tie your shoes. *See also* ARTIFICIAL INTELLIGENCE, BRANCHING, *and* CYBERNETICS.

Communications

You can use a computer to "talk" with other computer users by telephone or radio. Computers can also be connected into online networks, allowing you to get access to all kinds of information. In this way, computers serve as *communications* devices.

It's different! When you first use a PC to communicate, it will seem strange, unless you've used a terminal before. You don't talk and listen. Instead, you type messages on a keyboard, and receive them on a display screen.

You cannot normally hear the voice of the other person when you communicate using a PC (except with audio-video teleconferencing). With experience, you'll become able to sense people's moods by the way they write. You'll also learn to better convey your own feelings by your writing. If you use online services much, you're bound to become a fairly good writer.

You can also exchange drawings and photographs using PC communications. A PC thus becomes a teletype (TTY), fax machine, and still-picture television transceiver rolled into one. You can use your existing telephone line, or, if you have an amateur radio license, you can connect your PC to your ham transceiver and get into a packet radio network.

Via telephone. A telephone computer communications link is shown at A in the drawing. At either end of the circuit, the computer is hooked up to the phone line through a device called a *modem* (modulator/demodulator).

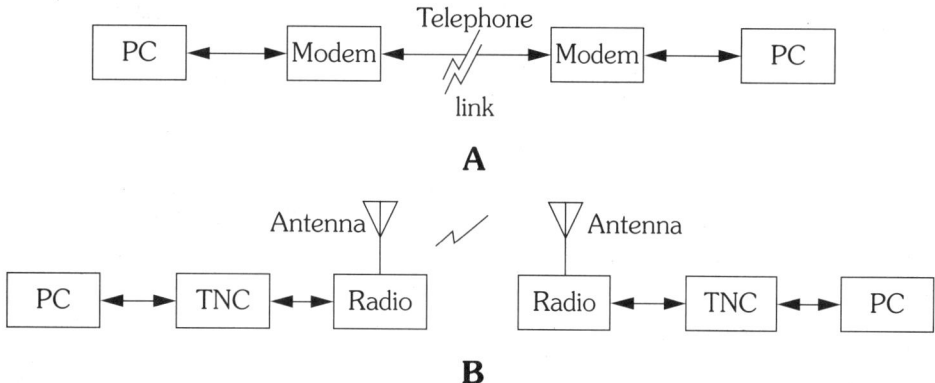

A telephone link (A) and a packet radio link (B).

At the transmitting end of the circuit, called the *source*, the modem changes the computer's digital signals into audio that the telephone line can handle. This is the process of modulation. At the receiving end, or *destination*, the modem does the opposite, changing audio into digital signals that the computer can understand. This is demodulation.

When you're online, your computer acts as a source and destination at the same time. If you're working in *real-time*, it's like being "live" on a TTY terminal. You can also leave messages (called *electronic mail*

Communications

or *e-mail*) for other people, or look at your own e-mail. This is a form of *time-shifting communications* because there's a time lag of minutes, hours, or days between the time a message is actually sent and the time it is read by the recipient.

Between the source and destination stations, the telephone signals go through all kinds of changes. They might be sent over cable for part of the journey, over microwaves for another part, and possibly over optical fibers or through satellites. You don't have to worry about these details while you're online, any more than you think about them while you're talking on the telephone.

You can even use cellular telecommunications systems by connecting a laptop computer to a cellular telephone unit. Mobile and portable computer communications is becoming quite popular, especially among traveling businesspeople.

Via radio. There's another way to interconnect computers, familiar to amateur ("ham") radio operators: *packet radio*. It's like using a PC with a cellular telephone, except that the regular telephone lines can be bypassed. The PC is connected instead to a radio transceiver using a modem-like device called a *terminal node controller (TNC)*. The drawing at B shows a typical packet-radio communications link.

One advantage of ham radio is that there are no fees for the networks, nor are there any long-distance telephone tolls. There are limitations, however. For example, it's against federal law to conduct business over amateur radio. Also, you need a license to use a ham radio transmitter. Despite these limitations, ham radio can be great fun, and radio amateurs have a history of technical innovation.

Although packet radio networks aren't usually as reliable as telephone networks, they can use exotic methods to send and receive signals. For example, you can send messages from one computer to another by bouncing the signals off the ionized trails that meteors create as they pass through the upper atmosphere. Hams have their own communications satellites, too. Some hams even communicate by bouncing signals off the moon.

The future. Computer communications will get faster as technology advances. This will allow many megabytes (millions of characters) or even gigabytes (billions of characters) of data to be sent over telephone and radio links in short periods of time. Authors will routinely "modem" novels and magazine articles to publishers. Photographs, charts, and motion pictures will be sent digitally among computers in much less time than it takes to send them today.

Ultimately, PC users might interconnect their workstations to form supercomputers. The speed of such composite computers will be limited because data cannot travel faster than light. It takes about

0.14 second for a radio signal to travel around the earth. When a signal is sent to a geostationary satellite, it returns to the earth 0.25 second later. In terms of high-speed computer data, these are long delays. On the other hand, such machines will have enormous capacity for storing and transferring data.

No matter how sophisticated PC communications might become, people will always enjoy old-fashioned letter writing and telephone conversation. Eventually, however, the Postal Service and the audio telephone set will be relics, as far as routine message transfer is concerned. *See also* AMATEUR RADIO, CELLULAR TELECOMMUNICATIONS, ELECTRONIC MAIL, LOCAL AREA NETWORK, MODEM, ONLINE SERVICE, PACKET COMMUNICATIONS, REAL-TIME, REMOTE CONTROL SYSTEMS, TELECOMMUTING, TELECONFERENCING, TERMINAL EMULATION SOFTWARE, TERMINAL NODE CONTROLLER, TIME-SHIFTING COMMUNICATIONS, *and* WIDE-AREA NETWORK.

Communications program

See TERMINAL EMULATION SOFTWARE.

Communications protocol

When computers exchange information, they use digital signals. Digital signals have several *parameters*, characteristics that can vary. For the computers to understand each other perfectly, the parameters must all match. The *communications protocol* is the set of parameters for a circuit.

Speed. The speed of a digital signal, often called the baud rate but more accurately referred to in terms of the number of bits per second (bps), can be set to several standards. Telephone modems operate at various speeds, depending on the sophistication of the communications circuit. Typical speeds are several tens of thousands of bps; some modems operate at several hundred thousand bps. *See also* BAUD/BITS PER SECOND.

Full and half duplex. If you've used a two-way radio such as a "walkie talkie," then you've experienced communication in half duplex. In this mode, you can't receive signals while talking, nor can you interrupt the other person. The channel can handle only one signal at a time. On a PC or terminal, this means you can't display incoming messages while typing, nor can you send out anything when a message is being displayed.

When you talk on the telephone, you're using *full duplex*. You can interrupt the other party at any time, and you can be interrupted, too. On a PC or terminal, full duplex lets you type messages out, and display other people's messages, at the same time. This is commonly done in a split-screen mode. *See also* FULL DUPLEX *and* HALF DUPLEX.

Communications protocol

Error correction. Errors occur in any kind of communications. *Handshaking* is a way for the receiving PC or terminal to check for errors. There are several schemes for this, but they all involve having the receiver analyze the incoming signals to see if they look "normal" before displaying or printing the message. *See also* HANDSHAKING and X/Y/ZMODEM.

Bit count. How many bits does a data word have? It can be either an even or an odd number. When you specify *even parity*, you tell the computer to work with words having an even number of bits (usually eight). *Odd parity* means the words all have an odd number of bits (usually seven). If you specify *no parity*, then the PC or terminal disregards the number of bits in a word. *See also* BIT and PARITY.

Stop bits. Some signals have bits inserted at the end of every byte (character) of data, indicating the end of one byte and the start of the next. This is a *stop bit*. You can specify that the signal either have stop bits, or not have them.

The table shows some common parameters, and the various options, for computer communications protocol. *See also* COMMUNICATIONS, CONNECTION PROTOCOL, *and* PROTOCOL.

Communications protocol parameters and options

Parameter	Options
Bits per second	1200 2400 4800 9600 14,400 19,200 28,800 38,400 (higher)
Duplex	Half Full
Parity	Even Odd None
Handshaking	Yes No
Stop bits	Yes No

Companionship software

In the future, PCs might be used not only for convenience and amusement, as they are today, but also for companionship. When computers get this intelligent, they'll be used to control all kinds of machines, including personal robots. You might insert an adapter card into a computer to tell your children bedtime stories—and then answer the children's questions afterwards. This is *companionship software.*

Artificial friend. Imagine owning a personal computer/robot that could prepare your meals, do your laundry, clean your house, and even rub your back. Maybe it would talk with you too. You could discuss almost anything. The machine might argue with you in subjects like economics or social sciences. You might have one adapter card for sports, another for current political affairs, and another for general conversation. One card might make your PC into a Republican; another card would turn the machine into a Democrat.

Researchers at a company called Anticipatory Sciences think that such computers, and robots to go with them, will someday be common. In a sense, computers talk with people now, in the form of electronic games and other interactive devices. But as artificial intelligence (AI) technology advances, computers will become able to converse with people in more and more meaningful ways.

Human touch. Computers can be smart, logical, and even funny. But robot grippers lack the comforting power of human hands, no matter how smart the computer that controls the robot. Some things can't be engineered by human beings to anywhere near the sophistication of the real thing. How much psychological comfort could a machine give to a lonely or despondent person? No matter how witty or sympathetic the software, a machine is not a human being.

Many researchers insist that machines can't fully replace people as companions. We humans, they say, have an instinct that tells us whether a thing is animate or inanimate. As Mark Twain might have said, living things actually smell alive. You can't care about a computer the way you care about a person, or even a cat or dog.

There is another side to this issue. Many elderly people suffer because younger people don't have the time to pay them enough attention. Smart computers and robots could supply some companionship, just as computerized toys entertain today. Elderly people enjoy computers using online services such as SeniorNet. In the future, as computers become smarter, everyone, young and old, will find new and interesting things to do with them. *See also* ARTIFICIAL INTELLIGENCE, ARTIFICIAL LIFE, COMPUTER CONSCIOUSNESS, INTERACTIVE TECHNOLOGY, ONLINE SERVICE, *and* PERSONAL ROBOTS.

Compatibility

Compatibility refers to how well different electronic devices, especially computers and peripherals, can work together. You've probably heard that certain software is *IBM-compatible*, for example. That means it can be run on an IBM PC or any of its clones.

Devices or programs are said to have *full compatibility* if they can work together, doing all their respective things, without either one having to be modified in any way. If either device or program must be changed so they can work together, then they are said to have *partial compatibility*. If major changes must be made to one or both devices or programs before they can work together, or if they can't be made to get along at all, then they are said to be *incompatible*.

One of the biggest headaches for computer users is the way products keep changing. Existing hardware can be partially compatible or incompatible with new software after only a few months. New hardware can also outgrow old software. In these cases, the computer buyer must purchase new hardware or software, or modify the old, to get the system to work optimally.

Compatibility problems are inevitable in a free-enterprise economy. While many companies believe that standardization is more to their advantage than crafting products and accessories differently from everyone else, new innovations often have characteristics that cannot be made fully compatible with all the old computer technology.

Consider, for example, a powerful new program that requires 16MB (megabytes) of RAM (memory). A computer with only 4MB of RAM will not run this software without a hardware upgrade in the form of memory expansion boards. It will cost some money to obtain these boards, and it might be an inconvenience to install them. These are not good reasons, however, to insist that the software vendor refrain from marketing the program. *See also* CLONE, DOWNWARD COMPATIBILITY, *and* UPWARD COMPATIBILITY.

Compiler

In a computer, the *compiler* is a program that changes a high-level language, such as BASIC, C, COBOL, or Fortran, into machine language. Machine language is basically impossible for a person to use, but the computer operates in machine language. People can understand and use a high-level language, but it can't be understood by a computer. There's a language barrier! It's like trying to talk with someone who only knows Chinese, when you know only English. You need a translator. The compiler works like an electronic translator between the high-level language and the machine language.

A compiler must be written especially for the high-level language being used. Because high-level languages differ so much, and because there are so many of them, there are many compilers in common use today. *See also* ASSEMBLER AND ASSEMBLY LANGUAGE, HIGH-LEVEL LANGUAGE, INTERPRETER, *and* MACHINE LANGUAGE.

Complementary-metal-oxide-semiconductor (CMOS) technology

Complementary-metal-oxide-semiconductor (CMOS) technology is used in digital devices, such as computers. The acronym is pronounced "see-moss."

Transistor teamwork. In CMOS, two different types of specialized transistors called *MOSFETs* (an acronym that stands for metal-oxide-semiconductor field-effect transistor) are fabricated on a single *integrated circuit (IC)*, also called a "chip."

The word *complementary* refers to the fact that the two types of MOSFETs work together, helping each other do a job that neither one alone could do. The drawing is a schematic diagram showing two MOSFETs, one of each type, hooked together to complement each other. A single chip can have thousands or millions of MOSFET pairs like this one.

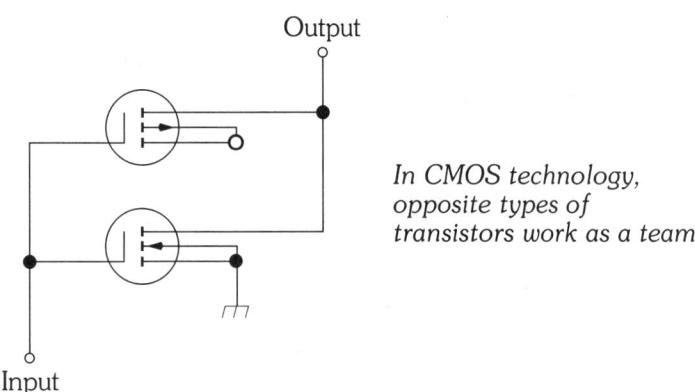

In CMOS technology, opposite types of transistors work as a team.

Assets. One big advantage of CMOS technology is that it can work with tiny electrical currents. Thus, it needs almost no power. Batteries can be used as the power supply, and they will last a long time. This is ideal for laptop and portable computers.

Another advantage of CMOS technology is that it works extremely fast. It can process a lot of data in a short time, which is exactly what people build computers to do.

Complex-instruction-set computing

Precautions. A disadvantage of CMOS devices is that they're easily damaged by static electricity. Devices of this type must be stored with their pins embedded in special conductive foam.

When building or servicing equipment using CMOS devices, technicians must be careful to avoid the build-up of static electricity. Some CMOS devices have built-in protection, but others do not. When handling computer chips, it's always a good idea to be sure that your body does not carry a static electric charge. Grounding straps that usually attach to the wrists are available that keep your body from acquiring such a charge. *See also* INTEGRATED CIRCUIT *and* METAL-OXIDE-SEMICONDUCTOR (MOS) TECHNOLOGY.

Complex-instruction-set computing (CISC)

Complex-instruction-set computing, or *CISC* (pronounced "sisk"), refers to an architecture, or design scheme, for the CPU (central processing unit) of a computer. All the microprocessor chips in Intel's 80x86 series are CISC chips, as are the microprocessors in Motorola's 680x0 line.

Faster, bigger. Microprocessor speed keeps increasing as memory and disk capacity keep growing. Processing speed and memory size (especially for RAM) are two important criteria by which computer power is measured. One fairly comprehensive way of measuring computer power is the number of instructions per second a machine can execute; throughput is another.

All the microprocessor chips in the Intel 80x86 series (the 386, 486, Pentium, etc.), as well as those in the Motorola 680x0 series (the 68020, 68030, 68040, etc.) work basically the same way. The chips have become faster, and their data buses have become wider, but the computing methodology has not fundamentally changed.

Think of the evolution of stereo hi-fi equipment before the introduction of digital sound technology. The sound quality kept improving and systems got more and more sophisticated, but the basic technology—analog recording and reproduction—stayed the same. For many hi-fi enthusiasts, analog recording and reproduction is still good enough. The same holds true for CISC PCs. A 486- or Pentium-based computer has enough power for the user interested in traditional forms of computing, such as word processing, basic graphics, database, spreadsheets, and online communications. However, a few users want more than these machines can provide.

A new angle. Regardless of how much faster a computer's clock speed might become and no matter how spacious its RAM, there is another angle from which computer evolution can be approached: to revolutionize the whole scheme by which processing is done. One way of doing this is to reduce the number of instructions the CPU has to deal with. *Reduced-instruction-set computing (RISC)* gives the computer a reduced set of instructions to execute, as its name implies.

The advent of digital recording and reproduction caused a drastic change in stereo hi-fi technology and practice. For the first time, it became possible to reproduce music, voices, and other recorded data many times over with essentially zero distortion. Rather than trying to match complicated analog waveforms, the new hardware design converted the analog sounds to digital impulses, which could be duplicated with practically no mistakes. This appealed to high-end hi-fi users, especially those professionally involved in the music industry. Likewise, RISC is making its most significant inroads in high-end computing, such as animation, speech recognition and synthesis, artificial intelligence (AI), virtual reality, and personal robotics.

Sharing the workload. For any given amount of computing power, the burden must be shared between hardware and software. CISC architecture has a large and complicated set of instructions. (That's how it gets its name.) The major asset of CISC is that it minimizes the size and complexity of the programs run by the machines. That is, it makes things comparatively *easy* for the programmers. On the other hand, the machine must work harder than it might otherwise, and this hardware work takes time.

In a RISC machine, some of the strain is taken off of the hardware by requiring that the machine process fewer instructions. Thus, the hardware can do its share of the work faster. The downside is that this places more of the workload on the software, and thus on the programmers. Programs for RISC CPUs tend in general to be longer and harder to write than programs for CISC CPUs.

See also COMPUTER POWER, INSTRUCTIONS PER SECOND, INTEL MICROPROCESSORS, MOTOROLA MICROPROCESSORS, POWERPC CHIP, REDUCED-INSTRUCTION-SET COMPUTER, *and* THROUGHPUT.

Compound document

A *compound document* is a large data file consisting of several smaller files of various kinds. Most serious computer users will eventually make compound documents.

Publishing. Suppose you want to publish a newsletter for distribution in your local area. A group of writers in Miami Beach who decided that their town needed a forum for local literary talent undertook such a project. They reasoned that artists coming from New York, Los Angeles, San Francisco, Paris, and other places because of the climate, reasonable rent, and unique cultural flavor of the place needed a creative outlet. The result was a desktop publishing effort called *Writers in the Sand*.

CompuServe

From the start, *Writers in the Sand* had some clip art in addition to the printed matter. When the complete document was stored as a file, the computer had all the information for the clip art as well as all the data for the text. In addition to this, however, the file needed to contain data telling the computer to change from graphics to text or vice versa. Then, when the file was printed out, the whole publication would go down on paper, ready for high-resolution photocopying.

Perhaps you've seen the editors of a magazine at work. While they're working on contributed articles, the graphics and the text can both be viewed on the monitor. This lets the editors and production people see just how the final printed page will look. The files they use are compound documents.

In business. If you run a business, you'll want to keep records of prices, inventory, tax information, payroll, profit, board-meeting minutes, and other things. You will probably want to make files using several different software types, such as database, spreadsheet, word processing, and graphics.

Most of the time, you'll want to keep all your files separate from one another so that you can access them individually without affecting any of the others. Sometimes, however, you'll find it convenient to have compound documents, with information from various kinds of files combined. You can put such files together in many different ways to suit your needs at any time.

A technique called *object linking and embedding (OLE)* is useful for situations like this. It can save you the work of having to constantly update all of your files to reflect a single update in one file. *See also* OBJECT LINKING AND EMBEDDING.

CompuServe

CompuServe is the name of a popular online service. A CompuServe subscriber simply connects a PC to the telephone line through a modem, installs the software, gets an access code, and is ready to go.

Using CompuServe, you can get all kinds of up-to-the-minute news. There are many subjects, just as you'd find in a big-city Sunday newspaper. You can also get data concerning investments, the stock market, interest rates, and other economic matters. The network has an enormous encyclopedia.

In recent years, it has become possible to do banking and shopping via computer. These systems make use of interactive technology. Another form of interactive networking lets you "talk" (type, actually) with other PC users in real-time. You can have conferences in which several people share views and information. If you are too shy to communicate with people in real-time, you can leave them messages via a *bulletin-board system (BBS),* called *forums* on CompuServe.

There is a fee for CompuServe based on the number of minutes you spend online. If your town does not have local access numbers, you might also have to pay long-distance telephone charges. To learn more about the system and its features and rates, talk to the people at your local computer store. The PC-oriented magazines regularly carry advertisements for CompuServe and other online services, or you can write to

CompuServe
5000 Arlington Centre Boulevard
P.O. Box 20212
Columbus, OH 43220

See also BULLETIN-BOARD SYSTEM, INTERACTIVE TECHNOLOGY, MODEM, NETWORK, *and* ONLINE SERVICE.

Computer addiction

You've probably seen them. They inhabit the computer labs of schools across the land. Every time you enter the lab, there they are, programming and networking, perhaps planning a technological revolution. They have a *computer addiction;* life without computers is beyond their comprehension.

Kids in the lab. Some people love computers. There's a good reason for this: computers make learning efficient and entertaining, giving students access to sources of information not available to past generations. You can play games with a PC, compose music, send electronic mail, publish newsletters and books, and create graphics of all kinds. Computers have created an entirely new realm in the world of art.

Computer savy is not necessarily bad. Computer gurus become engineers, programmers, and pioneers of new technology. Corporations like Microsoft and Apple got started by superachievers who, at one time, were kids in computer labs. For children, hanging around with a computer is certainly better than joining gangs or getting into drugs.

Balance. When a person spends too much time on one thing, the result is an unbalanced life. This is the potential problem with computer addiction. It can lead to difficulty in communicating with people. Computers, however smart or powerful they get, will never be able to take the place of human companions. A person who spends a disproportionate amount of time on a computer might begin to interact with people as if they were machines. Computer addicts can get painfully shy from lack of social life, and out of physical condition from lack of exercise. This is sometimes called *technophilia.*

Computer-aided design

Computer addiction does not necessarily develop in all people who spend large amounts of time on computers. Some people work at computer companies, spend time on home PCs, and still have plenty of time left over for friends and family.

Some online services have support groups for people who make immoderate use of computers, but can't help themselves. If you spend so much time on computers that you think it's getting bad for you, maybe you should consider joining one of these groups (despite the irony that you'll have to spend time on your computer to do it). Alternatively, you might find a second hobby, in addition to computing, that has nothing to do with PCs.

If you feel comfortable with your computer but it isn't interfering with the rest of your life, you aren't a computer addict, you're just well-prepared for the future! *See also* COMPUTER OVER-RELIANCE.

Computer-aided design

Computers are extensively used in the design of new products. This is known as *computer-aided design (CAD)*. Using CAD, engineers can "test" devices without actually constructing them, saving enormous amounts of time and money. Inferior designs can be rejected without the need for putting prototypes together, testing them, and then comparing the results with the data for other designs. The CAD process is extensively used to design robots.

A human operator is needed to operate a CAD terminal. No computer yet in existence is smart enough to interpret the data and create improved designs all by itself.

A CAD system makes extensive use of analytical graphics to show objects with movement in three dimensions. These systems are used in conjunction with *computer-aided manufacturing (CAM)*, and the acronyms are therefore often seen together, written "CAD/CAM." *See also* ANALYTICAL GRAPHICS, COMPUTER-AIDED MANUFACTURING, COMPUTER-ASSISTED INSTRUCTION, *and* GRAPHICS.

Computer-aided manufacturing

A computer can be used in a factory to control machinery such as *automated integrated manufacturing systems (AIMS)*, which are sophisticated assembly lines. The hardware ranges from simple tools, such as drills and lathes, to complex robots. The term *computer-aided manufacturing (CAM)* refers to factory systems that are partly or completely controlled by a computer.

Robots lend themselves especially well to computer control. A robot can be "taught" how to perform a sequence of motions by first moving it manually through them; the robot controller stores all the movements in its memory, called a *teach box*. More advanced robots can be controlled by sophisticated software. A central computer can coordinate the operation of numerous robots, each following its own subprogram. Some CAM systems use "machine vision" to help with alignment of parts during the manufacturing process.

Computers are used in the design of new products, as well as in their manufacture. This is called *computer-aided design (CAD)*. The two acronyms, CAD and CAM, are often combined as "CAD/CAM." There are many subspecialties within the general field of CAD/CAM, including computer-aided testing (CAT), computer-aided engineering (CAE), and computer-integrated manufacturing (CIM). *See also* COMPUTER-AIDED DESIGN, COMPUTER-ASSISTED INSTRUCTION, *and* VISION SYSTEMS.

Computer-assisted instruction

Computers can make good teachers, especially in mathematics, spelling, and other school subjects that require the student to do a lot of practice. Skills that require coordination, such as flying an airplane or driving a car, can be taught on computer simulators before putting the student at the controls of the real thing. The use of computers in teaching is called *computer-assisted instruction (CAI)*.

The good. Some of the advantages of CAI over exclusively human teachers include the following:

➢ Computers aren't prejudiced.

➢ Computers never get impatient.

➢ Computers are cheap; they need only maintenance, not a salary.

➢ Software can be upgraded as new programs become available.

➢ Children often find it more fun to learn on a computer than to learn in a classroom.

The not so good. However, there are several disadvantages of CAI, including these:

➢ Computers can't offer the personal attention that a human teacher can.

➢ A student might ask that which a computer cannot answer, but into which a human teacher can give insight.

➢ Children must be supervised while learning from computers, or the lazy students will not challenge themselves.

➢ Some teachers will lose their jobs to computers.

This last problem is becoming a social issue. It involves all jobs in which machines can replace people. Some people can be retrained for other work, others can retire early, but computers are nevertheless spawning a certain amount of fear and distrust in working people.

Computer consciousness

This reaction to technological advancement is not unique to our generation. It also occurred during the Industrial Revolution. *See also* LUDDITES.

Technophilia. It is possible to place too much faith in computers and other technologies. When this happens to an individual, the person is sometimes called a *technophile*. When it happens to a company or throughout a society, is might be called *mass technophilia*. Some people argue that certain highly developed countries, especially Japan and the United States, have already reached a state of mass technophilia.

It's important to remember that computers are meant to serve people, not vice versa. In the rush to make money and acquire things, people can forget this. Profit is important, but it is not all-important. Corporate executives who place too much emphasis on speed, efficiency, productivity, and profit, and not enough emphasis on the welfare of the workers, are often unhappy. Paradoxically, such companies are often beaten out by firms whose presidents and directors have empathy for their employees. There are situations where human workers should not be replaced by machines, even when, on paper, it might seem as if such a move would be profitable.

This philosophy can be extended to the school system. Some psychologists question the wisdom of getting children more used to being with machines than with other people. If Johnny spends all his time on a PC, he might have trouble later in real life. While a school with mostly human teachers and only a few computers might appear to offer less than a school in which students spend most of their time with computers, schooling must prepare children to deal with a world full of human beings who often act in illogical and uncomputerlike ways.

There are signs of a social backlash against mass technophilia. It is likely that schools will limit the roles of computers in their curricula because children need a human touch that machines cannot, and can never, provide. Computers are of great benefit in schools, but it is as important for administrators to know what computers cannot do as it is to take advantage of what they can do. *See also* COMPUTER ADDICTION *and* COMPUTER OVER-RELIANCE.

Computer consciousness

Is it possible for a computer to be aware of its own existence? Could it question its role in the world? Could it ask for something and really feel a need for it? Most researchers think not, but nobody is certain one way or the other.

Human-like? A landmark in the quest for artificial intelligence (AI) would be a computer that had emotions, self-awareness, and other qualities of a human mind. This brings up a question, however. Must a

Computer consciousness

mind be human-like in order to have consciousness? To answer yes is to look at the universe with tunnel vision. It is shortsighted to theorize that human minds are the only ones that can be conscious.

Some people say that animals aren't conscious, but if you've ever lived with a cat or dog for a long time, you probably believe that they are. Is an insect conscious? Who can claim to know for sure? The only way to be certain would be to trade brains with an insect. Otherwise, any conclusion is based at least in part on attitude, not scientific data.

The same holds true for computers. No human being has ever exchanged brains with a PC. Therefore, no human being can be absolutely sure that a computer is not conscious. Interestingly, the peoples of some cultures would look upon this discussion as an academic exercise. In their view, everything in the universe, including a computer chip, shares in cosmic consciousness.

As computers become more and more sophisticated, the question of computer consciousness will become significant even to the most skeptical. If a computer could discuss with some human operator the state of the universe, ask deep and meaningful questions about the personality of the President of the United States, give its own perspective in understandable sentences, or solve some problem that has confounded humanity for a thousand years, then most people would agree that the machine was conscious.

World view. What sort of world view would a conscious machine have? Most AI researchers say that would depend on whether it had hands, legs, eyes, or ears that could interact with the world. If the machine were a super-smart humanoid robot, or *android*, its world view might be similar to that of humans. On the other hand, if the machine were just a big electronic circuit, it might see the universe from a perspective quite alien to us.

For example, the brain of a porpoise is as big and complex as a human brain, but porpoises lack hands and fingers with which to build things. What, then, are they thinking with all that gray matter? Have they known about (and perhaps disproved) the Big Bang theory, or relativity, or biological evolutionism, since before humans invented the wheel? Some people are trying to learn the language of porpoises so that we will be able to communicate with them, but their mental processes might be so different from ours that we will never be able to understand their language, let alone know how they perceive the world. People must be prepared to face these same complexities when endeavoring to build electronic minds.

Emotion. Will computers ever laugh and cry? This is hard to imagine. You might program a computer to display "Ha-ha-ha!" on its screen in response to a joke or "Boo-hoo!" in response to a sad story, but this

Computer games

hardly qualifies as emotion. To have emotion, a computer must be aware of its own existence. It must be conscious.

Does consciousness inevitably occur at some level of AI? If so, does emotion come along with it? Perhaps brilliant androids could have consciousness without emotion. We won't know the answers to these questions unless, or until, computers evolve that are as intelligent as humans. Most researchers believe it will be a long while before that occurs. Some scientists think it can happen, but probably won't. A few think it can't.

Reasoning. Computers can process huge amounts of information, more than any person could hope to handle. Computers can only process data in logical steps, however.

Is it possible for a computer to have reasoning power? The answer depends on whether reasoning can always be broken down into discrete logical steps. If so, then a computer can be built to have reasoning power. If not, then computers might never be able to reason.

Arthur Samuel, the inventor of a computer checkers program, thought that human reasoning consists of logic plus "something extra," while computer reasoning is just plain logic. He used this belief to argue that computers will never have reasoning power as humans do. Samuel gave no basis for his beliefs, however.

Does human reasoning involve "something extra"? Is it more than pure logic? If so, what is this "something"? Why do we have it? From where did we get it? Samuel gives no answers to these questions.

In his book *Gödel, Escher, Bach*, author Douglas Hofstadter argues that human reasoning comes entirely from the physical structure of our brains. According to Hofstadter, there is apparently no "something extra" involved in human reasoning; the human mind is nothing more than an extremely sophisticated logical machine. If Hofstadter is right, then it's theoretically possible to build a computer with as much reasoning as a person. When and if such a computer is actually put together, will its makers realize what they have done? Maybe. The machine's consciousness might be so different from human consciousness, however, that a quantitative comparison cannot be made. *See also* ANIMISM, ARTIFICIAL INTELLIGENCE, *and* ARTIFICIAL LIFE.

Computer games

During the 1970s, the first video games were introduced in bars and video arcades. By today's standards, these games were primitive, imitating sports like basketball, baseball, hockey, and football. The graphics were simple, and the only sounds were bells, beeps, crashes, and so on.

Today you can play all kinds of games with PCs. You can play alone or with other PC users via online services. Some computer games are as sophisticated as the instruction programs used in industry and the military. Computer games are also adaptable for educational purposes.

Computer software ranging from simple to state-of-the-art can imitate any game you might care to play. Some chess software, for example, can turn your PC into a player of near-master caliber. You can use computer games to plan football strategies, try for triple-plays in baseball, or practice your golf. (Of course, you might want to get outdoors and play some of these games for real once in a while, too.)

New computer games come out almost daily. To get an idea of what's out there, visit your local computer store and look through the ads in computing magazines. *See also* COMPUTER-ASSISTED INSTRUCTION.

Computer generations

Computer scientists sometimes talk about the evolution of computers in terms of *generations*. There have been several generations of computers since the earliest machines were built in the 1940s.

First generation. First-generation machines, built during the late 1940s and early 1950s, used vacuum tubes like the ones in antique radios. Information was usually stored on punched cards or paper tape. A first-generation computer, even if it occupied a whole building, was much slower than the smallest PCs of today. Not only that, but the big hulk wasted an enormous amount of power as heat, because vacuum tubes are inefficient.

Second generation. In the late 1950s and early 1960s, transistors replaced vacuum tubes for switching. This reduced the size and weight of computers by hundreds of times. It also greatly reduced the power needed to run them. Data was stored primarily on magnetic tapes, either reel-to-reel (for large computers) or cassette (for smaller machines).

Third generation. During the late 1960s, integrated circuits (ICs) became available, resulting in the next great reduction in physical size and power requirements. Magnetic disks became available for data storage. Interconnection of computers was done via telephone, radio, fiberoptic, and satellite links. *See also* DISKETTE, HARD DISK, INTEGRATED CIRCUIT, *and* NETWORK.

Fourth generation. In the early 1980s, a new form of IC technology was developed, called *complementary-metal-oxide-semiconductor (CMOS)* technology. CMOS ICs increased the speed at which a computer could work, and also reduced the power requirements. New, more powerful programming languages were developed. Hundreds of software packages became commercially available.

Computer generations

Fifth-generation and beyond. Today, we're in the fifth computer generation. Computers are getting more and more user-friendly, so almost anyone can work with, and even program, a computer. Speech recognition and speech synthesis are being perfected. Eventually, these schemes will include the ability to infer the correct words through analysis of context and syntax. Researchers might find new ways to fabricate ICs, such as biochips that mimic the structure of living matter. Artificial intelligence (AI) is evolving gradually. There will be other developments that we haven't thought of yet. As these things happen, computer scientists will talk about sixth-, seventh-, eighth-, and higher-generation computer systems.

Power versus time. The graph shows two measures of computer power as a function of time from the year 1950 to the present, and extrapolated somewhat into the future.

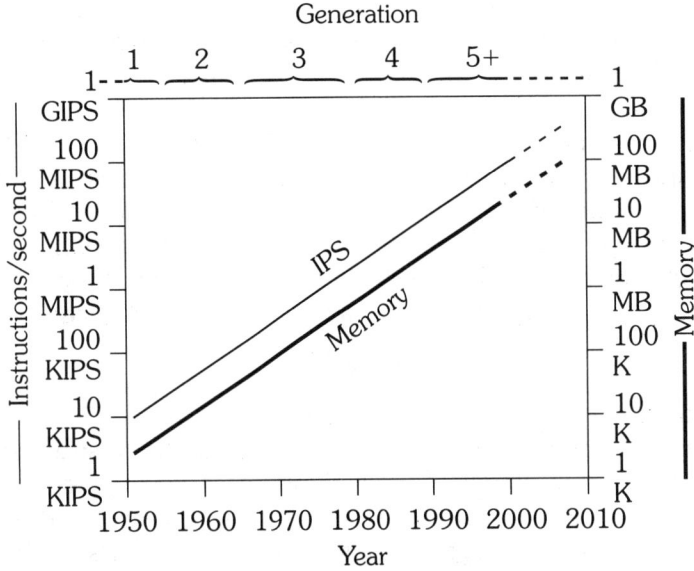

Computer power is increasing exponentially with time.

The light line shows instructions per second (IPS). The units are abbreviated as follows:

> KIPS = kiloinstructions per second = thousands of instructions per second

> MIPS = megainstructions per second = millions of instructions per second

> GIPS = gigainstructions per second = billions of instructions per second

The heavy line in the drawing shows memory. The units are abbreviated as follows:

K = kilobytes = units of 1024 bytes
MB = megabytes = units of 1,048,576 bytes
GB = gigabytes = units of 1,073,741,824 bytes

The graph is approximate, but note the continual increase in both IPS and memory. Note also that the vertical graph scales are logarithmic, not linear. If the vertical scales were linear, the curves would soar off the page and out of sight.

Both IPS and memory have been increasing exponentially for the past 50 years. If that trend continues, imagine what computers will be like in another 50 or 100 years! *See also* COMPUTER POWER, INSTRUCTIONS PER SECOND, MEMORY, *and* THROUGHPUT.

Computerized home

Imagine having all your mundane household chores done without your having to think about them! Your PC could control a fleet of *personal robots* that would take care of cooking, dishwashing, laundry, yard maintenance, snow removal, and other things. This is the ultimate form of *computerized home*: having your home's "central nervous system" run by a PC so you can do other things. In the building trade, a computerized home is often called a *smart home*.

The drawing is a block diagram of a central PC controlling a system of home appliances and conveniences. The computerized home of the future will probably work along these lines, although there's probably a limit to how many devices people will link to the central PC. Robot cats and dogs, for example, will probably never be common no matter how advanced the technology gets, although they might be great fun for children.

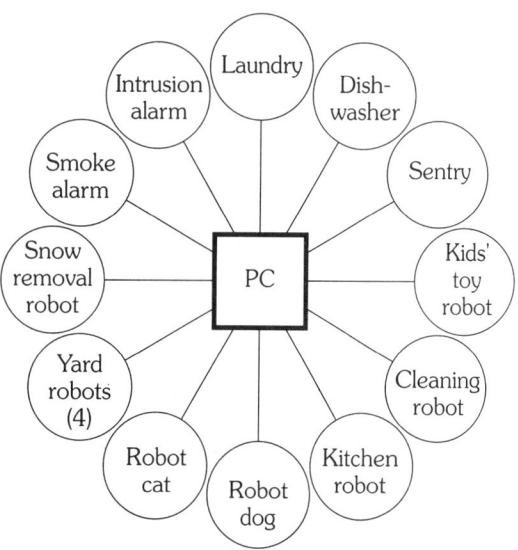

A hypothetical computerized household.

Computerized home

Technology and ethics. The key to a truly computerized home lies in the technologies of robotics and artificial intelligence (AI). As these become more available to the average consumer, we can expect to see a robotic laundry. We might see robots that make beds, do dishes, vacuum carpets, shovel snow from driveways, clean windows, and maybe even drive to the store and shop for groceries.

There are two main types of mobile robots that might roam the home of the future: *autonomous robots* and *insect robots*. There are advantages and disadvantages to either design. In addition to these, some appliances will themselves be robots, such as dishwashers and laundry machines. These robots won't have to move around.

Some people question whether computerized, robotized homes are really worth developing. Won't people prefer to spend their hard-earned money in other ways, such as buying vacations or new properties? There are also ethical concerns. Should some people strive for total home automation, when a large segment of society can't afford a home at all?

Let us suppose, for the moment, that we solve the ethical problem, and that everyone has a home with some money to spare. Further imagine that the cost of technology keeps going down, while it keeps getting more and more sophisticated. What might the future hold? *See also* AUTONOMOUS ROBOTS *and* INSECT ROBOTS.

Fire protection. When people and property must be protected from fire, smoke detection is a simple and effective measure. Smoke detectors are inexpensive and can operate from flashlight cells. You probably have one or more of these devices in your home now. (If you don't, get some. They're not expensive.)

In a computerized home of the future, a smoke alarm could alert a robot. Robots are ideal for firefighting because they can do things too dangerous for humans. The challenge will be to program the robots to have judgment comparable to that of human firefighters.

When and if household robots become commonplace, one of their duties might be to ensure the safety of the human occupants. This would include escorting people from the house if it catches fire, and then putting out the fire or calling the fire department. It might also involve performing some first-aid tasks.

Security. Computers and robots can be of immense help around the house when it comes to prevention of burglaries. Security robots have been around for decades. A simple version is the electronic garage-door opener. More advanced systems include intrusion alarm systems and electronic door or gate openers. These devices make it difficult for unauthorized people to enter a property because they can detect the

Computerized home

presence of an intruder, usually by means of ultrasound, microwaves, or lasers, and notify police through a telephone or radio link.

The ultimate security system would be a robot. If an intruder entered the property, the security robot could drive the offender away or detain the offender until police arrived.

A *sentry* can alert a homeowner to abnormal conditions. It might detect fire, burglars, or water in places it shouldn't be. A sentry might detect abnormal temperature, barometric pressure, wind speed, humidity, or air pollution. Your computer could beep at you if, for example, a pipe broke in the basement. *See also* SECURITY SYSTEMS.

Food service. Robots have already been used to prepare and serve food. So far, the major applications have been in repetitive chores, such as placing measured portions on plates in large cafeterias to serve a large number of people. Robots might also be adapted to food service in common households.

Personal robots programmed to prepare or serve food would require more autonomy than robots in large-volume food service. You might insert a disk into a home robot that told it to prepare a meal of meat, vegetables, and beverages, and perhaps also dessert and coffee. The robot would ask you questions such as

- ➢ How many people will there be for supper tonight?
- ➢ Which type of meat would you like?
- ➢ Which type of vegetable?
- ➢ How would you like the potatoes done? Or would you rather have rice?
- ➢ What beverages would you like?

When all the answers were received, the robot would go through an extremely complex process to prepare the meal. The robot might serve you as you wait at the table, and then clean up the table when you're done eating. It might do the dishes too. *See also* COMMONSENSE SUMMER PROJECT.

Yard work. Riding mowers and riding snowblowers would be easy for robots to use. The robot need only sit on the chair, ride the machine around, and operate the handlebar or pedal controls. Alternatively, lawnmowers or snowblowers could be robotic devices, designed with that one task in mind.

The main challenge, once a lawnmowing or snowblowing robot has begun its work, is for it to "do its thing" everywhere it should, but nowhere else. You don't want the lawnmower in your garden, and there's no point in blowing snow from your front lawn. Wires might be buried around the perimeter of your yard and along the edges of the driveway and walkways, establishing the boundaries within which the robot must work. An example of this is shown in the drawing. Solid, heavy lines are boundary wires for the lawnmowing robot; dotted lines are boundary wires for the snowblowing robot.

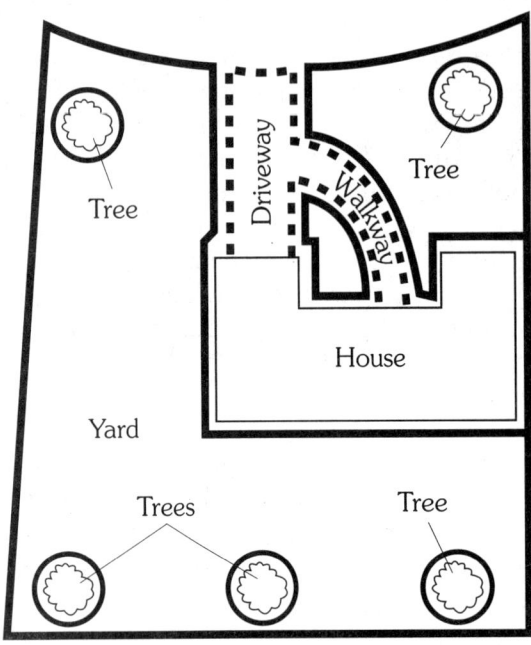

Lawnmowing and snowblowing robot guidance system.

Inside the work area, edge detection can be used to follow the line between mown and unmown grass, or between cleared and uncleared pavement. This line is easily seen because of differences in brightness and/or color. Alternatively, computer maps might be used, and the robot could sweep along controlled and programmed strips with mathematical precision. *See also* COMPUTER MAP *and* VISION SYSTEMS.

The idle homeowner. If robots can do all our housework, what will be left for us to do? Won't we get bored sailing, hiking, working out, and otherwise spending time that used to be devoted to maintaining our property?

Although robots and computers can do work for us, they don't have to be used. There will always be times when people prefer to do household chores like gardening themselves. Perhaps the greatest challenge in home automation will be to decide what tasks are best left to the homeowners.

A major obstacle with home computerization is the matter of trust. Most people have trouble enough entrusting PCs with the simplest things, such as storing data. Some people might never be comfortable going on a vacation and leaving a computer in charge of the house.

See also ARTIFICIAL INTELLIGENCE, COMPUTERIZED HOME, *and* PERSONAL ROBOTS.

Computer map

Autonomous, household robots might be one of the next major developments in personal computing. In order to function, an autonomous robot must know where it is relative to its surroundings. It must make a *computer map* of its environment, resembling a blueprint. An example of a computer map is shown in the drawing. This happens to be a dining room. The robot's assignment is to set the table before the people sit down. The robot can envision, relative to the table and chairs, where to put the plates. Then it can follow its programming and place the napkins, forks, knives, spoons, and glasses in their proper places.

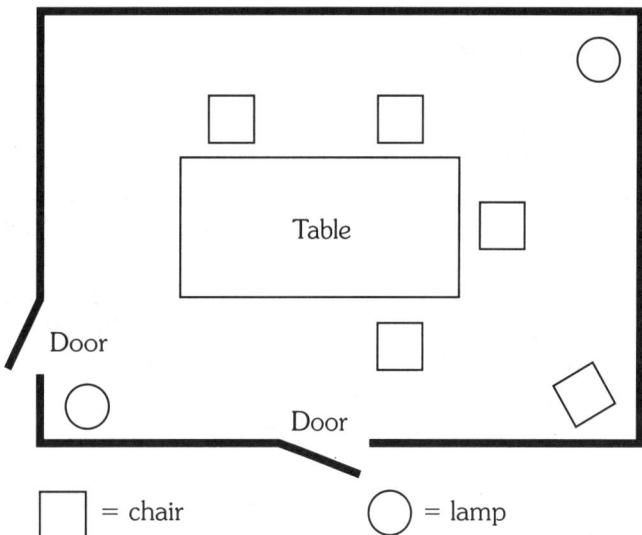

Like a blueprint, a computer map shows a robot where things are.

Note that one chair has been moved into the corner, and is not at the table. This might confuse the robot and result in its setting an extra place at the table or dropping utensils on the carpet in the corner. Whether or not these problems occur will depend on the quality of the map-interpretation program. The robot must be able to act appropriately under a variety of conditions.

The robot will also need a map of the kitchen, where all these utensils are to be found. It will need to recognize all these items and know in which drawers or cupboards they are. The complexity of these problems is much greater than it might seem at first. *See also* AUTONOMOUS ROBOTS, BIN-PICKING PROBLEM, COMMONSENSE SUMMER PROJECT, OBJECT RECOGNITION, PERSONAL ROBOTS, *and* VISION SYSTEMS.

Computer music

Computer music
See MUSICAL INSTRUMENT DIGITAL INTERFACE.

Computer over-reliance

Computers help our lives run smoothly, as long as they work right, but when a computer malfunctions, gets programmed wrong, or goes down, chaos can result. You've probably had an experience of this kind. Someone says, "The computer is down," and everything comes to a halt.

Attitude. Computers are more reliable than human beings in some ways. Machines don't need to take breaks; they can run 24 hours a day, seven days a week. Computers aren't perfect, however, nor do they run themselves. Problems with *computer over-reliance* can be kept to a minimum if people maintain the proper attitude towards them.

People sometimes think computers can take care of every conceivable problem that comes up. Of course, this is not true. Computers must be built, programmed, debugged, maintained, and repaired by people. A computer is only as good as the human beings who oversee it. Programmers make errors. Sometimes bugs are even introduced into computer systems deliberately, in the form of a virus or Trojan horse.

Computers rarely make mistakes that are entirely their own fault, but it can happen. Chips burn out, or noise occurs on data buses and communications lines. Considering the volume of data flying around this planet, one error per terabyte (about a trillion characters of text) is enough to ensure that numerous mistakes are made daily.

Computerized madness. The following is a description of a computer error that is well within the realm of possibility:

A woman gets a bill for $0.00 (zero dollars and zero cents). She ignores it. A month later it comes again with a warning notice: PAST DUE. Again she ignores it. After another 30 days, another bill comes, containing a letter printed in typeset-quality laser font, threatening to turn the matter over to a collection agency if the bill is not paid in full immediately. Interest has been added, too, bringing the total amount owed to $0.00. The notice warns that this interest is being compounded daily.

The woman calls the 800 number listed on the bill, so that she can tell them that this whole affair is a mistake, but the line is busy. She dials again and again, and finally connects. She is put on hold, but is reassured, via a computerized recording, that her call will be answered in the order in which it was received. After about ten minutes she talks to a customer-service representative who laughs and says,

Computer power

"There was a computer error, and over a thousand bogus warning notices were sent out."

The woman thinks this is the end of the problem. The next month, however, she is notified that the matter has been turned over to a collection agency, which will contact attorneys to bring the matter to a swift resolution.

She writes a check for $0.00 and mails it to the address shown on the notice. Then she prepares for the worst. The check, however, is all the computer wanted. The machine is satisfied; $0.00 is precisely the amount owed. The check clears the bank, and the fallibility of computers is quickly forgotten—for the time being.

The solution. This scenario is not farfetched; you've probably heard real-life stories almost exactly like it. Computer errors can cause problems far worse than improper billing. Information can be lost, mutilated, or altered, causing nightmarish problems. An incredibly complex labyrinth of computer data interconnects everyone in modern society to everyone else. Mistakes and fraud occur more often than we would like to believe.

For the PC user, computer over-reliance can lead to the loss or alteration of vital personal information. It can even cause financial trouble. Some people are so concerned about potential problems of this sort that they refuse to buy or use a PC at all. *Cyberphobia*, an intense distrust or fear of computers, is ironically the first cousin of computer over-reliance.

Computers aren't perfect, but they can make your work far easier and less time-consuming if you keep them in the right perspective, and don't place unreasonable faith in them. To minimize problems arising from computer over-dependence, be vigilant for possible errors. Be aware that computers don't tell the truth by default. If something seems wrong, double-check it. Keep archives and back up your files regularly on diskettes or tape drive. *See also* ARCHIVES, COMPUTER ADDICTION, CYBERPHOBIA, DISKETTE, TAPE DRIVE, TROJAN HORSE, *and* VIRUS.

Computer power

Computer power is a general term that refers to the "intelligence" of a *microprocessor*, the PC's brain. Computer power increased exponentially after the first PC was put on the market in the 1970s. Several factors, including clock speed, memory, and bus size, are responsible for computer power.

Clock speed. The *clock speed* is the tempo at which the whole system works. A simple electronic oscillator, the clock, acts like a metronome to set a tempo for the microprocessor. Typical PC clock

Computer power

speeds are measured in megahertz (MHz), millions of beats per second. There might come a time when PC clock speed is given in gigahertz (GHz), billions of beats per second, or even terahertz (THz), trillions of beats per second.

The faster the clock, the more powerful the computer would be, if all other things were equal. But in the real world, as you know, all other things are never equal. *See also* CLOCK SPEED.

Memory. The *memory* of a PC is the amount of data it can store. There are several different types of memory, but when it comes to the power of a computer in action, the most important is *random-access memory (RAM)*. There's another type of memory called *read-only memory (ROM)* that's also significant.

Memory is measured in units called *bytes*. Several larger units of measure exist:

- 2^{10} = 1024 bytes, known as *kilobytes*, abbreviated KB or K
- 2^{20} = 1,048,576 bytes, called *megabytes*, abbreviated MB or M
- 2^{30} = 1,073,741,824 bytes, referred to as *gigabytes* and abbreviated GB or G

In the future, you'll also hear about units of 2^{40} (roughly a trillion) bytes, called *terabytes* and abbreviated TB or T. And, while it might seem farfetched right now, the time might come when computer engineers will discuss *petabytes*, or units of 2^{50} (about a quadrillion) bytes, and *exabytes*, or units of 2^{60} (about a quintillion) bytes.

The greater the memory capacity, all other things being equal, the more powerful the computer. However, you can have a big, slow computer or a small, fast one, suited for different purposes; this complicates the definition of power. *See also* BYTE, CACHE MEMORY, MEMORY, RANDOM-ACCESS MEMORY, *and* READ-ONLY MEMORY.

Bus size. The *bus size* (sometimes also called the *word size*) of a microprocessor is a measure of how many bits are sent per data unit. The larger the bus size, the more data can be sent per unit of time.

The earliest microprocessors had words that were eight bits long. Bus sizes have been increasing geometrically (in powers of 2) since then to 16 bits, 32 bits, and even 64 bits. As with the other criteria, the larger the words, the greater the computer power, if all other things are constant. But, of course, the other variables change.

The big picture. All three of these factors affect the power of a PC. You might imagine the "big picture" on a three-dimensional graph, as shown in the drawing. Clock speed is on one axis, memory is on the second axis, and bus size is on the third axis.

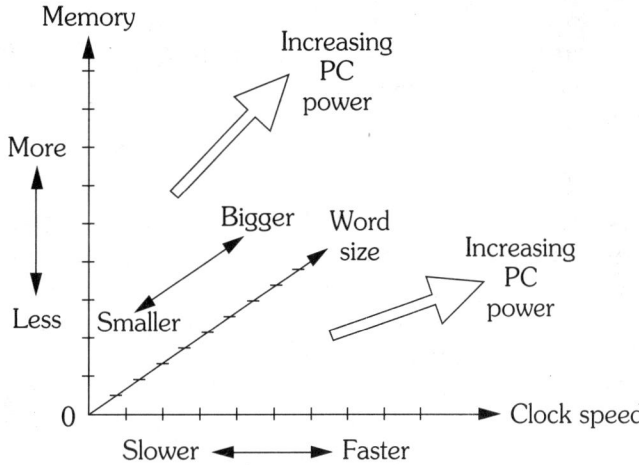

3-D graph of overall PC power.

All three axes on this graph are perpendicular to each other and intersect at a point, just like the point where two walls of your room intersect the floor. This point, called the *origin*, represents zero clock speed, no memory, and zero bus size. As you move out along one axis, the clock speed increases; as you move out along the second axis, memory increases; as you move out along the third axis, bus size increases. Any PC can be represented as a point somewhere in this 3-D space. The farther the point from the origin, the more powerful the machine.

General specifications. A more comprehensive expression of computer power is the number of instructions it can carry out per unit time. The basic unit is *instructions per second (IPS)*.

Modern PCs work in *kiloinstructions per second (KIPS)*, where one KIPS equals one thousand IPS, or in *megainstructions per second (MIPS)*, where one MIPS equals one million. In the future, you'll probably hear about *gigainstructions per second (GIPS)*, or billions of IPS. And it's not altogether unreasonable to suppose that supercomputers of future generations will work at *terainstructions per second (TIPS)*, trillions of IPS.

There is another, still more all-encompassing way to specify the power of a computer. This is known as the *throughput*, and is determined on the basis of numerous real-time tests. *See also* INSTRUCTIONS PER SECOND *and* THROUGHPUT.

Computer programming

See PROGRAMMING.

Computer vision

See VISION SYSTEMS.

Concordance file

A *concordance file* is used in word processing as an aid to creating an index. It simplifies the process because it saves you the work of going through a manuscript and picking out the words you want indexed.

The old way. Suppose you have written a book manuscript, and you want to make an index without the help of a computer. First, you must read the manuscript page proofs. That's actually a good thing; it helps get rid of errors and typos. Each time you come across a word that you want to include in the index, you mark it using a pen or highlighter, and then you write the word on an index card along with the page number. If you come across the same word again later, you might remember it, in which case you could add the new page number to the index card. You might not remember it, however; then you'll end up making a duplicate card. When you're done with the book, you'll have a big stack of cards. You arrange them in alphabetical order, and then you discover and eliminate duplicate cards. The final set of cards is your index, which you can type out on paper.

Manual indexing like this is best done in the final stage before publication, when authors and editors are fairly sure that page numbers are the same as they will be in the printed book. If, for some reason, major late editing is needed, most of the page numbers will change, making it necessary to go through all the index cards and correct the page numbers.

The new way. With a concordance file, you need only make a list of the words you want to appear in the index. You can do this while the manuscript is being written. The word processing software will go through the manuscript automatically, locating each occurrence of each index word, along with the page numbers.

In technical and scientific works and textbooks, terms introduced for the first time are often italicized. The indexing software can be programmed to look for occurrences of italicized words or character strings. This scheme can backfire in some situations, however. Variables such as x, y, and z, while italicized in a math textbook, should obviously not be included in the index.

When you use a concordance file, you must be sure that the page numbers that appear on the disk file are the same as they will be in the printed book. If for some reason, you need to do major late editing, it isn't a big deal if all the page numbers change. The concordance file can be used to make a new index.

After using an indexing program, be sure to proofread the resulting index. Terms and phrases that a person would never choose for inclusion might gain entry via the indexing software. *See also* INDEXING SOFTWARE *and* WORD PROCESSING.

Concurrency control

In a local area network (LAN), certain files might be accessed by more than one workstation. Consider, for example, a magazine article on a LAN at a publishing company. One person (a writer) is writing the text, while another (an artist) works on the art, and another (an editorial assistant) works on tables and references.

Accident prevention. Each person's work is important to the whole article. Suppose, however, that the artist inadvertently obliterates some of the text to make room for a larger drawing? What if the writer changes some text and erases one of the tables accidentally in the process? These kinds of problems will not occur often if *concurrency control* is used, in which all the people involved can see what is happening to the whole piece.

Accidents of this sort can also be prevented by having all the employees keep current updates of their work. Backup habits are good to learn from the start, if you plan to do a lot of work on computers. They are doubly important in businesses, where the loss of data can mean a loss of profit. *See also* ARCHIVES *and* BACKUP.

Limited access. Concurrency control governs the things people can do to files in a LAN. With concurrency control in the magazine situation, everyone could gain access to the article, but the writer could alter only the text, the artist could change only the drawings, and the editorial assistant could change only tables and references. If the artist happened to see that something was wrong with the text, he or she must inform the writer of that fact. Each workstation has a code, so the system knows which workstation is which.

The drawing is a functional block diagram of concurrency control in the preparation of a magazine piece. Heavy double arrows represent read/write, or full, access, in which a user at a workstation can change the contents of the file. Light single arrows represent read-only, or limited, access, in which a user can look at, but not change, the contents. *See also* LOCAL AREA NETWORK *and* WORKSTATION.

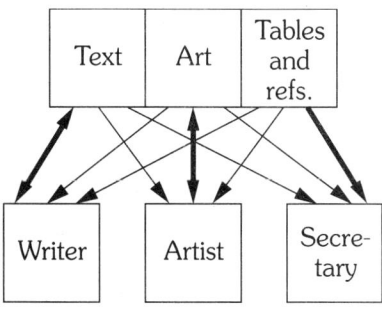

Concurrency control for three people at work on a magazine piece.

CONFIG.SYS

CONFIG.SYS

Your PC must always go through a certain procedure when you first switch it on. In DOS, a file called *CONFIG.SYS* sets things up so your computer will work with the peripherals, like the printer and modem, in exactly the way you want.

What it means. The filename CONFIG comes from the word *configure*. The filename extension, .SYS, is an abbreviation for *system*. Thus, CONFIG.SYS automatically configures your system.

Unless you know exactly what you're doing, you shouldn't tamper with the CONFIG.SYS file. The listing shows the first few items in the directory of the hard disk on a PC, including the file CONFIG.SYS. Note that it doesn't take up much space on the hard disk.

CONFIG.SYS configures the system in DOS

BATCH	<DIR>		7-20-90	10:59a
DOS	<DIR>		6-12-90	1:58p
EIGHT	<DIR>		6-12-90	2:01p
MOUSE	<DIR>		6-12-90	2:02p
PRODIGY	<DIR>		2-20-93	5:14p
TS	<DIR>		6-12-90	2:02p
UTILS	<DIR>		6-12-90	2:02p
WINDOWS	<DIR>		6-12-90	1:59p
XY	<DIR>		7-20-90	10:59a
ADRS		6061	9-24-93	8:56a
ADRS	BAK	6035	8-17-93	6:49p
AUTOEXEC	BAT	145	7-30-90	12:08p
BIBLIO		10,009	8-22-93	8:44a
BIBLIO	BAK	10,009	7-15-93	4:54p
BUDGET		1286	9-01-93	9:05a
BUDGET	BAK	1272	8-26-93	10:42a
CD	ROM	8084	9-11-93	1:57p
CHAOS		6809	9-12-93	8:56a
CHAOS	BAK	6809	9-12-93	7:45a
CHAR		489	8-30-93	3:19p
COMMAND	COM	37,557	12-19-88	12:00p
CONFIG	400	146	7-30-90	12:08p
CONFIG	**SYS**	**170**	**5-21-90**	**4:27p**
CV		3250	9-19-93	4:21p

What it does. The CONFIG.SYS file does things like select the color scheme for your monitor, match each peripheral with a driver, and determine the number of files that you can have open at any given time. It also tells your PC which programs should go in which parts of its memory.

If you accidentally modify or erase CONFIG.SYS, your PC might still work, but it will probably not do all the things it did before. You'll notice these changes almost right away. For example, your monitor might show different colors, if you had selected colors other than the default scheme. Your modem or printer might not work right. If you want to get things back the way they were, you'll have to reinstall the program. *See also* CONFIGURATION *and* DOS.

Configuration

When you choose a computer and the software to go with it, you'll have certain things in mind that you want the system to do. To get the system to work precisely as you want, you'll need to determine the *configuration* for setting things up.

Questions and answers. Some operating systems or software packages, such as DOS, Windows, and Macintosh, will select a configuration for you during installation. You might be asked questions concerning the peripherals (printer, modem, diskette drives, etc.). As you answer the questions, the system chooses the right program for the computer's main unit to work with the various peripherals.

There might be some questions that a beginner will not understand. For example, the software might need information about various parts of the memory. Follow the instruction manual carefully in such cases. Usually the system will select a default setting if you don't answer a question. This will probably allow the system to function until you learn enough to choose a setting that's specific. *See also* DOS *and* PERIPHERALS.

AUTOEXEC and CONFIG. In DOS, when you first power up (switch your system on), it runs through a sequence of programs to "come to its senses." These programs are in files called *AUTOEXEC.BAT* and *CONFIG.SYS*. The files do what their abbreviated names imply: AUTOEXEC automatically executes commands to get your system up and running, and CONFIG arranges the configuration of your system so that it will work the way you expect. *See also* AUTOEXEC.BAT *and* CONFIG.SYS.

Connection protocol

A *connection protocol* creates a route, or pathway, for signals in a network. It's a set of instructions that tells the signals how to get from one computer or dumb terminal to another in the most efficient possible way.

Connection protocol

Adjustments. Think of a pair of two-way radios. If they are to be used for communication, they must be set to the same frequency, and they must use the same kind of modulation. Computer data communications work similarly. The sending workstation is called the *source*, and the receiving workstation is called the *destination*.

When computers are connected together, they must be set for the same data speed, and they must use the same data code. For a network of more than two PCs, there are additional adjustments to be made. The PCs must all play by the same rules, so the machines will work together and keep the flow of messages going smoothly. This set of rules is a *protocol*. Without the protocol, the network would be like a room full of shouting people, all with important things to say, and all completely unable to understand any of what is being said. *See also* COMMUNICATIONS, COMMUNICATIONS PROTOCOL, DESTINATION, PROTOCOL, SOURCE, *and* WORKSTATION.

The pathway. In a network, the pathway might be direct between the source and destination, as shown in drawing A. (Again, think of two people conversing on two-way radios.) In data communications, however, there are often intermediate nodes, as shown at B.

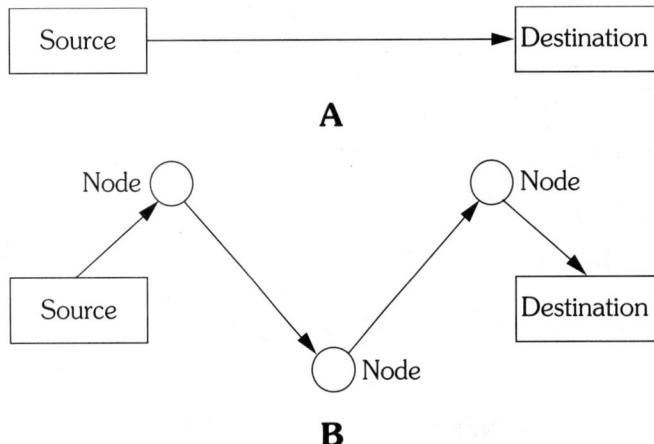

Connection protocol: direct link (A) and indirect link (B).

Suppose, for example, a PC user in Florida wants to send some electronic mail (e-mail) to a person in Minnesota. This would involve numerous switches along the way, if done by telephone. The signal might be converted from wire currents to lasers, carried by optical fibers, and then back to wire currents again. It might even go part of the way in the form of microwaves. The connection protocol figures out which switches can be used in the network so that the signal will get from the source to the destination most efficiently. The pathway might be different in the evening than in the morning. It all depends on how many people are using the system and on the geographical distribution of users at the time.

Packet radio. Amateur radio operators, also called "hams," have set up networks using radio transmitters and receivers. It is possible for radio amateurs to send and receive e-mail without using the telephone lines at all. These *packet radio* systems have become quite sophisticated. To use them, you must obtain an amateur radio license.

Packet radio networks use the same connection protocol scheme as the online services familiar to other computer users, but in addition, there are the variables of radio frequency and modulation type. Instead of telephone switches, special radio stations called *digipeaters* are used at intervening nodes in the system. The connection protocol determines the matrix of digipeaters through which the data is to be sent. For a given source and destination, the optimum digipeater matrix varies with time and usage distribution, and also with radio-wave propagation conditions. *See also* AMATEUR RADIO, DIGIPEATER, NODE, ONLINE SERVICE, PACKET COMMUNICATIONS, *and* WIDE-AREA NETWORK.

Connect time

The term *connect time* refers to the length of time it takes a computer user to access a network, such as an online service or packet communications system. It also refers to the length of time you are connected to an online service during a session.

The initial connect time can be measured from the moment you dial the number or type the connect command until data is actually available from the network. This varies depending on how many other people are using the service. The heavier the network traffic, the longer it takes to establish a connection. Connect time does not increase substantially until the network is operating near capacity.

Heavy usage also increases the length of time it takes to do things in the system once you are connected; the computer responds more slowly to online commands. Thus, you must be online longer than would be necessary if there were few users, so the overall session connect time increases.

Sometimes, an online service might be so busy that there is no room for more users. When this happens, the access number will either ring without answering, or it will return a busy signal. Usually, you can gain access if you keep trying. When you finally establish a connection, however, the network might be slow to respond to your commands.

Some online services have surcharges that apply during the hours of heaviest usage. On the Internet, for example, traffic is heaviest during normal business hours. A surcharge might be imposed by a provider of Internet access to discourage nonessential use of the network during peak times. *See also* ONLINE SERVICE.

Contact manager

A *contact manager* program (also called *contact management* software) helps you keep track of meeting times and appointments; it's a specialized form of personal information manager (PIM) software that uses a database. Contact managers are ideal for small businesses and home offices. Salespeople find them especially useful.

Date keeper. You've probably used an appointment calendar, also known as a date keeper. These come in three types: daily, weekly, and monthly. Many people buy them every December. In these date keepers, you write things down to do, and cross them out as you do them or decide not to do them. The pages become rather messy with white-outs and scribbling. You keep breaking your resolution to use pencil; a pen writes more clearly, and that ballpoint glides smoothly across the paper.

Contact management software can make things smoother still. It can keep track of appointments in daily, weekly, monthly, seasonal, or annual format. You can add things and erase them without smudging pencil lead, smearing ink, whiting-out, or having eraser fragments get all over your desk.

Conflict prevention. If you've ever scheduled two things at the same time, or so close together that they conflict, you'll appreciate the conflict-prevention feature of contact management.

Suppose you have an appointment to meet with Client X on May 20 at 2:00 p.m. You made the arrangements in January. On May 13 you get a call from Client Y, who would like to meet you in a week at 1:30 p.m. You go to your contact manager and begin to enter this data while you're still on the phone with Client Y. The contact manager tells you that you'd better try another time; you have scheduled time with Client X on that day (May 20), at a time too close for comfort. You do not want to call Client X to change an appointment that was made months ago. Fortunately, Client Y can see you at 10:00 a.m. that same day, and your contact manager tells you that the time slot is available. You log the appointment.

An old-fashioned date keeper can work in situations like this, but it's just as easy to do it on a computer. Besides, on your PC, you can check client histories as you make appointments, so that you are well-prepared for meetings.

Client history. As soon as you hang up with Client Y, you open the client-history file for that person or company. This is where contact management software really shines. Perhaps you have several screens full of information written down about Client Y. There's no limit, within reason, to the amount of data you can keep in a client history.

Perhaps, when you open this file, you see that you consider Client Y to be a "fast-tracker." She must have things done in order and on time. She pays on time, too, as long as the job is done well. She's honest but firm, with a dry wit, so you'd better be sharp when you meet her. She has a way of not returning telephone calls, so if you need to call her before the appointment, you might as well not request a return call if you get her voice mailbox. These are the kinds of things you can log in a client history as you gain experience with a client. Immediately before the appointment time, you can open the file and familiarize yourself with the idiosyncrasies of the client.

Other features. Some of the other features common in contact manager software are as follows:

- *Word processing* You can write letters and memos, perhaps using templates that standardize formats and allow you to create a personalized letterhead. You can print out address labels. Some programs have spell-checking as an option. *See also* WORD PROCESSING.

- *Notes* You can insert remarks for each contact in your file. For example, you might write "Don't call him; he'll call you" in one place, "Smarmy" in another place, and "Everybody says she's honest" in another place. These remarks can consist of just a few words, or several paragraphs. You can update them as needed.

- *Fax modem support* You can send and receive fax messages on your PC, without even having to make a printout. You can keep copies of every fax sent and received for every contact. *See also* FAX *and* FAX BOARD.

- *Auto dial* When sending a fax, or just calling a contact for any reason, the PC will automatically dial the number for you, including the area code if needed.

- *Search and sort* You can look for items based on people's names, company names, contact dates, telephone numbers, zipcodes, or anything else that's convenient for you to remember.

- *Alarm* You can set a timer to alert you, right down to the minute, when an important event or appointment is to take place. You might be writing a story for a magazine, for example, when your PC will beep at you, warning you that it's time for an appointment with Client Z.

- *Snooze* The snooze function works in conjunction with an alarm to let you put something off for up to several hours while you're working on other things. You might be really caught up in a project, so you set the snooze for two hours' delay time.

- *Time management reports* How efficiently are you making use of your time? You can create a log of the amounts of time you spend doing various things on your computer. It's up to you to decide how (or if) you can improve your time usage.

Choosing a package. Check recent issues of PC-related magazines for articles and advertisements about the latest contact manager software. New features are added all the time. You can also check things out at your local computer store, where a salesperson might let you play around with some software until you find the contact manager that best suits your needs. *See also* DATABASE *and* PERSONAL INFORMATION MANAGER.

Context

Context is the environment in which a word is used. It is important in several areas of computer technology, including word processing and speech recognition.

When a word is used out of context, it results in a phrase or sentence that doesn't make sense. Worse yet, it might mean something not intended. When a word is taken out of context, the phrase or sentence is grammatically correct, but it gets interpreted as nonsense, or in the wrong way. In order to interpret spoken or written statements, a computer with artificial intelligence (AI) must know the context in which each word is used. For example, "I went down to the sea" makes sense; "I went down too the C" and "Eye went down two the see" do not.

In a user interface, *context* refers to the way a command is given relative to the operating environment. A command such as DIR, for example, has meaning when used in DOS, but if you give this command to an Internet Gopher, you'll probably get a response to the effect that the computer does not understand the command in that context. On the other hand, the command U has meaning in the context of some Internet Gophers, but is an illegal command in DOS.

The term *context* is also sometimes used in multitasking systems, referring to the minimum amount of data that must be saved in memory to allow switching among application programs. *See also* ARTIFICIAL INTELLIGENCE, COMMAND-DRIVEN SOFTWARE, MULTITASKING, *and* SPEECH RECOGNITION.

Control key

The *Control keys* on your PC keyboard are usually located just beneath the Shift keys in the lower-left and lower-right corners of the keyboard (see the drawings). They are usually marked Ctrl.

When you hold down the Ctrl key and press some other key, various things happen, depending on the software you're using. This is how the key gets its name: it initiates many different control functions.

Control menu

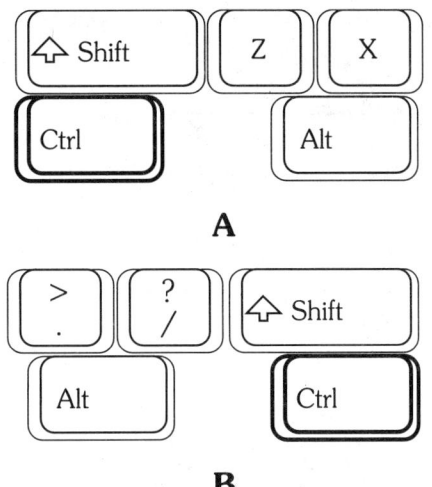

The Control keys are usually beneath the left (A) and right (B) Shift keys.

Some software packages have almost as many different control functions as there are keys on the keyboard. The action of holding down Ctrl and some other key, say X, at the same time is usually written Ctrl-X in instruction manuals.

For example, in XyWrite, the word processing software with which this text was written, pressing Ctrl-2 produces boldface type, which appears red on the monitor; Ctrl-3 produces underlined type, which appears green. These examples are peculiar to XyWrite and to the configuration used by the editors of this book. Other software systems and configurations produce different results.

The Ctrl key is also part of the key combination you press when you give a computer a *warm boot*. Sometimes called the "three-finger salute," the combination is Ctrl-Alt-Del. *See also* CTRL-ALT-DEL.

Control menu

In a graphical user interface (GUI) such as Windows, you'll see a *control box* with a dash in it at the extreme upper-left on your monitor screen. If you move the pointer to this box and click once with the mouse, you'll get a *control menu* containing various commands, as shown in the drawing. If you double-click on the control box, you will close whatever application or document is in the active window.

If you don't have a mouse, you can open the control menu for an application by pressing Alt-Spacebar. For a document, press Alt-Hyphen. (That is, you hold down the Alt key and the other key at the same time.)

The commands in the control menu depend on the nature of the active window. Typically, the control menu lets you change the size of

Coordinate systems

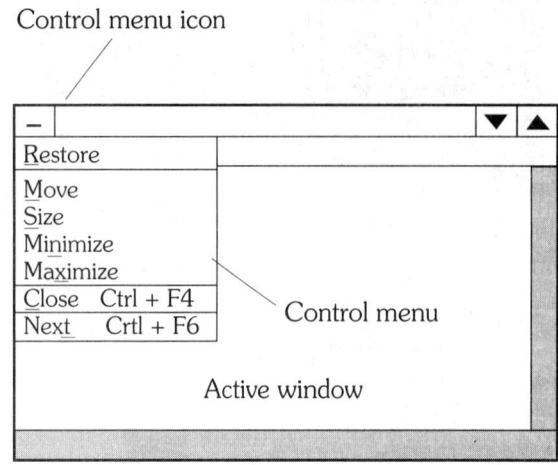

A control menu appears in a corner of the window.

the active window, change to another window, run a program, or close the application or document.

If you're using a command-driven program such as DOS instead of a GUI, you might still be able to obtain control menus. Read your system instruction manual for details. *See also* GRAPHICAL USER INTERFACE, MENU, *and* WINDOWS.

Coordinate systems

Coordinate systems are used by scientists, mathematicians, and engineers in all disciplines. They can also be of value to the everyday PC user. Coordinate systems are used mostly in analytical graphics and to a lesser extent in presentation graphics. There are several types of coordinate systems that computers can be programmed to work with. A few basic schemes are briefly mentioned here.

The Cartesian plane. The simplest two-dimensional coordinate system is the *Cartesian plane*, also known as a *rectangular coordinate system*. It has two axes, both of which are straight lines. The axes intersect at a right angle, at a point called the *origin*. The horizontal axis usually represents the independent variable, and the vertical axis usually represents the dependent variable.

Cartesian three-space. The Cartesian plane can be expanded into three dimensions by adding a third axis. This axis passes through the origin, and is perpendicular to the other two. The third axis is usually called the z axis, and represents the dependent variable in a two-variable function of x and y (the independent variables).

Logarithmic graphs. One of the scales on a Cartesian plane can be made logarithmic to show certain relations and functions. This is called a *semilog graph*. Sometimes both scales on a Cartesian plane,

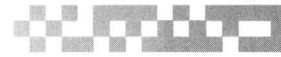

Coordinate systems

or all three scales in a Cartesian three-space, are logarithmic. Such a coordinate system is called a *log-log graph*.

Polar coordinates. Rather than having a grid pattern, coordinate systems can have a radial pattern. One set of coordinates consists of lines running outward from the center, like the spokes of a wheel. The other set consists of concentric circles. The independent variable is usually represented by the angle counterclockwise from the zero line. The dependent variable is represented by radial distance from the center.

Latitude and longitude. This is the system for locating points on the earth. Latitude is measured north (positive) and south (negative) from the equator, which is assigned zero degrees. Longitude is measured east and west from the meridian running through Greenwich, England.

Latitude and longitude lines are always circles. The best way to envision them is to use a globe. Latitude and longitude coordinates are commonly used by radio operators to determine the best direction in which to aim an antenna. You might also use these coordinates if you want a computer to help you navigate a boat or aircraft.

Celestial coordinates. Latitude and longitude can be projected into space to get *celestial coordinates*. A given direction in space might have coordinates of 45° north celestial latitude and 105° west celestial longitude. This appears to be straight up as seen from a point at 45° north latitude and 105° west longitude on the earth's surface (somewhere in the midwestern U.S.).

The problem with this system is that the earth rotates, so the celestial longitude of any object in the sky constantly changes. A more common system of celestial coordinates uses *declination* and *right ascension*. For information about these, consult a text on basic astronomy. Amateur astronomers can use PCs, along with servo systems, to automatically aim home telescopes.

For further information. There are other coordinate systems that are used in computer work. Some have two dimensions; some have three; some even have more than three.

In recent years, graphics software has evolved to assist computer users in working with coordinate systems, especially in three dimensions. Consult texts on analytic geometry, computer graphics, and engineering if you need in-depth information. *See also* ABSCISSA, ANALYTICAL GRAPHICS, AREA GRAPH, BAR GRAPH, CARTESIAN COORDINATES, COLUMNAR GRAPH, CYLINDRICAL COORDINATES, DEPENDENT VARIABLE, DUAL-ORDINATE GRAPH, HISTOGRAM, INDEPENDENT VARIABLE, LOG-LOG GRAPH, MULTIVARIABLE FUNCTION GRAPH, ORDINATE, PAIRED-BAR GRAPH, PIE GRAPH, POLAR COORDINATES, PRESENTATION

Coprocessor

GRAPHICS, SEMILOG GRAPH, SPHERICAL COORDINATES, *and* VOLUME GRAPH.

Coprocessor

Have you ever been working on something, and wished you had an assistant to help you get the job done faster? You can get such an assistant for your PC. It's called a *coprocessor*.

What it does. A coprocessor is an integrated circuit (IC), or chip, that is added to the central processing unit (CPU) of a computer. The chip itself is small, only about 1.5 inches square (see the drawing). The coprocessor is an assistant to the *microprocessor*, enabling the microprocessor to work faster than it can by itself. Depending on the application, a coprocessor can speed things up by a factor of anywhere from 3 to over 100.

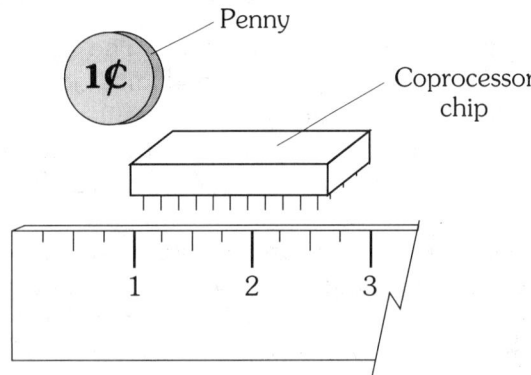

A coprocessor chip is about 1.5 inches square.

Coprocessors work best in applications that require a lot of mathematical calculations. A large spreadsheet is a good example, complex ballistics analysis is another. For most text and graphical applications, such as word processing and desktop publishing, coprocessors don't make much noticeable difference. Because they are mainly intended for calculations, a coprocessor chip is often called a *math coprocessor* or a *numeric coprocessor*.

Coprocessors cost from about $100 to $500 or more, depending on factors such as speed. Also, coprocessors for the more advanced microprocessors are generally more expensive than coprocessors for older, more "primitive" microprocessors.

Getting a coprocessor. If you want to install a coprocessor, you first need to find out which one you need. Coprocessors intended for use with Intel chips have numbers containing the digits *87*, sometimes followed by the letters *DX* or *SX*, and then more numbers. There might be several different coprocessors available for use with the same microprocessor. For example, for a 386 microprocessor, you'd get a 387 coprocessor, but there are several options: 387SX-16, 387SX-

20, 387DX-25, 387DX-33, etc. This can all get pretty confusing. Ask the people at your local computer store about coprocessors to help ensure that you get exactly what you want, need, and can afford. You don't want to get a coprocessor and then find out it isn't the right one. Also, some chips, such as the 486DX, have a coprocessor built in.

Once you know what you want, there are dozens of places you can get the chip. The cheapest way is to mail-order one from an advertisement in a PC magazine. Be sure the magazine is a current issue, however; companies merge, go out of business, and change their prices and stock from month to month.

Installation. To put a coprocessor in your computer, you'll need to remove the cover. Then you should follow the directions provided with the coprocessor chip.

Caution: Opening up a computer might void the warranty. Check with the manufacturer concerning warranty provisions before opening any computer unit.

If you're at all concerned about voiding your warranty, or if you're afraid to open up your PC for fear of damaging it, find a computer technician to install it for you. Maybe you have a "cyber-smart" friend who will do it for you. Don't take your computer apart if you aren't confident about it. *See also* MICROPROCESSOR *and* UPGRADING.

Correlation

Correlation refers to the extent to which two things are related. A PC can find correlations easily. Analytical graphics software can be used to plot data from experiments, surveys, or observations. This is extensively done in economics and social science.

Types and degrees. Parts A through E of the drawing on page 246 show various correlations between two quantities x and y. The dots are points, such as those you might get by plotting the results of a lab experiment.

In A and B of the drawing, the value of y increases as the value of x increases. This is called *positive correlation*. At A, the correlation is strong; the points all lie near a line slanting upwards to the right. At B, the correlation is weak; the points stray quite a bit from the line. In C, the points are scattered all over, and there is no apparent pattern. This is *zero correlation*.

In D and E of the drawing, the value of y decreases as the value of x increases. This is *negative correlation*. At E, the correlation is strong; the points all lie near a line slanting downwards to the right. At D, the correlation is weak; the points stray from the line, although you can still see a pattern.

Correlation

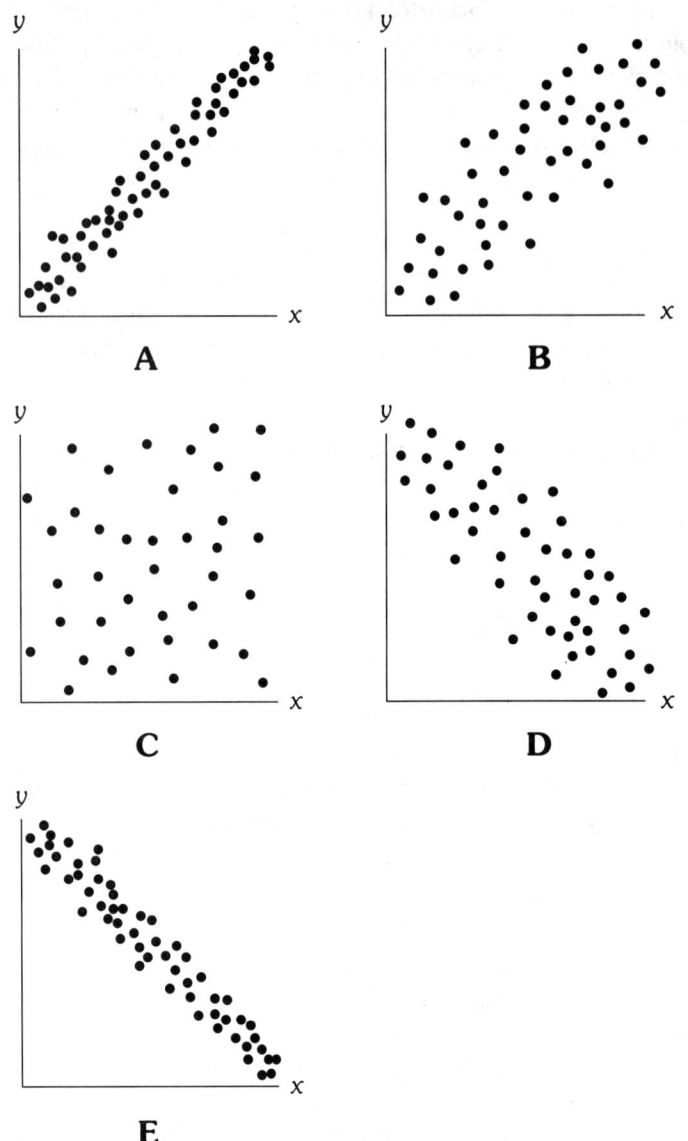

Strong positive correlation (A), weak positive (B), zero (C), weak negative (D), and strong negative (E).

An example. Think of what happens when you use an online service. You might get into the network almost right away, or it might take awhile. Sometimes it will take a long time. The *connect time* depends on how many other people are using the network right then. It also depends on the number of subscribers the network can handle.

The more people there are using a network of a given size, the longer it takes to connect. Therefore, there is a positive correlation between connect time (in seconds, say) and the number of people currently making use of the service.

The more people the system can accommodate at a time, all other things being equal, the less time it takes to connect. If there are 999

people using a system that can handle 1000 subscribers, the network is nearly full, and it will take awhile to connect. If the system is expanded to handle 10,000 subscribers, it will be nowhere near full with 999 users, so the connect time will be much shorter. Therefore, there is a negative correlation between the capacity of the system and the connect time.

Cause and effect. If two things show a correlation, either positive or negative, it might indicate a causative relation between those two things. However, the existence of a correlation does not tell you which factor is the cause, and which is the effect. It's also quite possible that there is no causative relation either way.

In the case of the online service, an increase in the number of subscribers using the system causes the connect time to increase. Making the system bigger for a given number of users on the system causes the connect time to decrease. Here, causative relations do exist.

On the other hand, consider temperature versus rainfall. In Miami, the warmer months have more rain than the cooler months. This might tempt you to think that warm temperatures cause it to rain more. There's also a correlation between temperature and rainfall in Los Angeles: the cooler months have more rain than the warmer months. This is contrary to the situation in Miami. Temperature versus rainfall is apparently not a simple cause-effect relation, even when a correlation exists.

These examples show ways in which analytical graphics software can be a powerful tool. They also demonstrate that the usefulness of a computer is limited by the knowledge of its user. If computer data is wrongly interpreted, the result can be misleading or false. *See also* ANALYTICAL GRAPHICS.

Crash

Sometimes a PC will "freeze up" without apparent reason. If you've owned a PC for any length of time, you've probably experienced this. You give a command, or are typing along, and suddenly the thing stops in its tracks. You press keys or click the mouse, first in a state of confusion, and then in a frenzied attempt to get the computer to do something—anything—but nothing happens. This is called a *crash*.

A crash can be caused by various problems. Often it is the result of a program improperly managing the memory. Occasionally it can be caused by an abnormal voltage *transient*, causing one of the integrated circuits (ICs) to see a signal that isn't there.

In most crash scenarios, resetting (rebooting) the computer will normalize things again, although you will lose whatever is stored in RAM. A warm boot should be tried first. If this does not work, then a

Cryptanalysis/cryptography/cryptology

cold boot will probably be necessary. *See also* BOOT, COLD BOOT, CTRL-ALT-DEL, *and* WARM BOOT.

Cryptanalysis/cryptography/cryptology

Cryptanalysis is the art of breaking *ciphers*, or codes intended to keep unauthorized people from intercepting signals or reading computer files. Ciphers are extensively used in wartime. Much effort is spent trying to break the ciphers of the enemy. The writing of data in cipher form is called *cryptography*. The general science of creating, writing, reading, and breaking ciphers is known as *cryptology*.

Character shift. An example of a cipher is shown in the table (opposite page). The alphanumeric sequence ABC...XYZ0123456789.,?_ is assigned numbers in order from 1 to 40. Then each character is shifted 13 units downward in the table. The cipher is transmitted as a string of numerals from the set {1,2,3,...40}. This is a simple cipher, and a computer could break it quickly.

With the help of computers, cipher-breaking has become much more sophisticated than it once was. A computer can find the key to a code more rapidly than any team of people working without a computer. Beyond that, artificial intelligence (AI) can be employed in an attempt to figure out what the enemy is thinking so that the computer can anticipate the sorts of ciphers the enemy is likely to conjure up. This lets the *cryptanalyst*, or code-breaker, get a feel for the general scheme behind a cipher and understand the subtleties of the code more quickly.

Enigma. One of the earliest cryptanalysts to use a computer was *Alan Turing*, known as a pioneer in AI. In the early 1940s, during the Second World War, the Germans developed a machine that encoded military signals. The machine was called *Enigma*, meaning "something mysterious." The machine certainly was a mystery to Allied cryptanalysts until Alan Turing designed one of the first true computers to successfully break its ciphers.

It has been said that as cats get quicker, evolution produces more intelligent rats. It is equally valid to say that as rats get smarter, cats become more clever in the quest to catch them. This kind of feedback loop operates in all areas of computer technology. As computers become more powerful, they can decode more complex ciphers. However, the same computers help people invent ciphers that are more difficult to break.

Ultimately, the advantage in cipher-breaking goes to the side with the more advanced computer and AI technology. This is true in all aspects of warfare. The military is therefore interested in AI. *See also* TURING, ALAN.

Cryptanalysis/cryptography/cryptology

A simple cipher

Character intended	Code number	Number sent
A	1	28
B	2	29
C	3	30
D	4	31
E	5	32
.	.	.
.	.	.
.	.	.
L	12	39
M	13	40
N	14	1
O	15	2
P	16	3
.	.	.
.	.	.
.	.	.
Z	26	13
0	27	14
1	28	15
2	29	16
3	30	17
.	.	.
.	.	.
.	.	.
9	36	23
period	37	24
comma	38	25
question mark	39	26
space	40	27

Ctrl-Alt-Del

Cryptanalysis and the law. Indiscriminate cipher-breaking by PC users can result in civil and/or criminal prosecution. One example of criminal cryptanalysis is using it in an attempt to infringe on the copyright of a person or corporation. Another example is intercepting encoded communications when you aren't authorized to do so.

Malicious hackers occasionally get away with illegal cipher-breaking and computer piracy. It's only a matter of time before the technological feedback loop comes full circle, however, and they are caught. Ironically, such people are sometimes caught via methods they originally dreamed up. *See also* ARTIFICIAL INTELLIGENCE *and* HACKER.

Ctrl-Alt-Del

With IBM-compatible PCs, you can do a *warm boot* by pressing the Ctrl, Alt, and Delete keys all at the same time. This is a method of resetting the machine without forcing it to go through all of its initialization programs. It is often written *Crt-Alt-Del* and sometimes called the "three-finger salute."

If your PC has a *crash*, that is, it "freezes up" on you, you should try to quit the program or exit the file that you're using. If that doesn't work, you can give the machine the Ctrl-Alt-Del treatment. This warm boot will usually enable it to recover from the crash, but you'll lose everything in RAM. Sometimes, however, even Ctrl-Alt-Del won't revive a computer that has crashed. In that situation, you have to do a *cold boot*. *See also* ALT KEY, COLD BOOT, CONTROL KEY, CRASH, DELETE KEY, *and* WARM BOOT.

Ctrl key

See CONTROL KEY.

Cumulative trauma disorders

The human body evolved to survive in a rough environment, but nature never anticipated that people would spend a large part of their lives at computer terminals. As computers have proliferated, new kinds of injuries, called *cumulative trauma disorders (CTDs)*, have appeared.

The changing workplace. Until about 1900, most occupations involved physical labor; then came assembly lines, typewriters, and other machines. As machines became more sophisticated, they took over much of the physical work previously done by people. Jobs demanded less from the body and more from the mind. In most ways, the change has been good. There are fewer catastrophic injuries in the workplace today than there were before. Many jobs are far more interesting than in earlier times. The pay is better, too, even after taking inflation into account.

Cumulative trauma disorders

In some ways, however, the change has not been good. Some jobs are as monotonous as anything our distant ancestors did for a living. There are also sometimes-debilitating CTDs, the result of a new and strange kind of stress. A computer or dumb terminal is operated in a sitting position, with the arms bent, the fingers moving, and the eyes fixed on a video display. This makes minimal use of the upper arms, and no use of the legs at all. The back, even though it is doing no work, can be strained from prolonged tensing of the muscles.

Carpal tunnel syndrome. When you operate a PC, the positions and movements of the arm, wrist, hand, and fingers are somewhat unnatural. Computer work is not the only occupation like this. Anything that requires precise motions repeated many times over long periods can cause a problem known as *carpal tunnel syndrome (CTS)*.

If you're a casual PC user, on the machine for a couple of hours a day, you have little reason to worry. Some people start having problems, however, after several years of 40-hour weeks at the computer. They develop numbness, tingling, or pain in their arms, wrists, and fingers. If you have a job at a computer or terminal and you have symptoms like this, you should see a doctor about it.

Aches. The back can be strained from working long hours at a PC or terminal. You're not just sitting; you are in a specific position, perhaps bolt upright or hunched, with your gaze fixed on a screen and keyboard. When concentrating hard on your work, you might tense up.

If your chair isn't the right height, or if the monitor is too close or too far away, you'll get a stiff back. If this happens and you keep working anyway, your back will start to hurt. Your neck stiffens, and you might get a headache. Ultimately, your back will cramp. One office worker had severe lower-back spasms from working at a PC while sitting in a chair that was too low. Lowering the keyboard three inches eliminated the problem.

Back, neck, and head pain should not be taken lightly. Try adjusting the height of your chair or keyboard, or get a different chair. Move the monitor farther away. Take more frequent breaks. If the problem persists, see a doctor.

Eye strain. If the display is a reasonable distance from your face, working on a PC shouldn't put any more strain on your eyes than writing at a desk or typing on a typewriter. Problems can occur if the monitor is too bright or not bright enough, or if the font is hard to read. You can also have trouble if the room lighting is too bright or too dim.

The symptoms of eye strain include headaches, blurred vision, and dizziness. If you think you have eye strain, change the monitor

Cumulative trauma disorders

brightness or the font you are using. Try changing the room lighting. Take frequent breaks to let your eyes focus on things besides your monitor and keyboard. It helps to periodically gaze at things far away, like the horizon or the other side of the room, for a minute. If the problem persists, see an ophthalmologist.

Radiation. In recent years, concern has arisen over the *ELF (extremely low frequency) fields* radiated by modern appliances, including computers. The monitor in a PC generates ELF fields, as do all 60-Hz alternating-current (ac) utility wires that run through buildings and homes.

The effect, if any, of ELF on the human body is a matter of controversy. Some scientists doubt that harm is done by exposure to low-intensity ELF fields. Others suggest that certain health problems that seemingly worsened during the 20th century are aggravated by ELF energy from all sources. *See also* ELF FIELDS.

What you can do. Employers need to realize that healthy employees generate bigger profits than sick employees. However, workplace changes won't all come at once. If you have a job working at a computer or terminal, there are several things you can do to keep your work environment healthy:

- *Relax* The fear of getting a disease can produce psychosomatic symptoms. Don't fall victim to excessive "hype" concerning CTDs. They are serious if not properly treated, but a morbid fear of them is as bad as the real thing.

- *Exercise* Almost everyone can benefit from physical exercise. It can undo work-related stress. The best exercises are aerobic, such as fast walking, bicycling (moving or stationary), swimming, and low-impact aerobics classes. Some companies have exercise facilities on the premises.

- *Take breaks* Any responsible employer knows that people are not robots; they need regular breaks. It's reasonable to take a few minutes per hour to get up, stretch, and move around. This increases productivity and reduces errors caused by mental and physical fatigue.

- *Change hardware or software* New programs are coming out all the time. Perhaps you can get a package that gives you reminders, such as flashing "BREAK TIME!" on the screen at certain intervals. Your hardware might need to be improved, too. Maybe you need a bigger monitor or one that shows finer detail. Perhaps you can save work time with a faster microprocessor. Maybe you need two diskette drives instead of one.

See also ERGONOMICS *and* HUMAN ENGINEERING.

Cursor

The *cursor*, also called the *insertion point*, is the marker on a computer display that indicates where you're typing. It can have various shapes, depending on the software and the functions you're using, as shown in the drawings. Some cursors blink on and off two to four times per second, so it's easier for you to locate in a screen full of text.

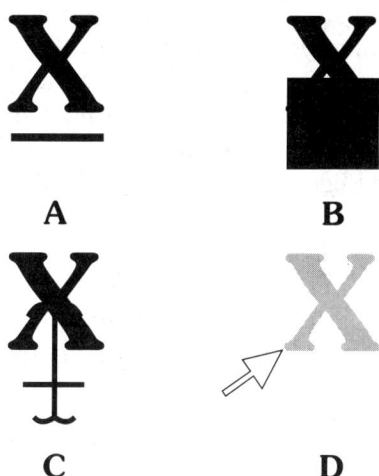

Common forms of cursors are underline (A), block (B), anchor (C), and arrow (D).

Moving the cursor. In many programs, as you type along, the cursor moves with the text, from left to right across the screen. When it gets to the end of a line, it automatically jumps down to the beginning of a new line. In some programs the cursor is one space ahead of what you type; in others the cursor is right on the letter you type.

As you work, you aren't usually aware of the behavior of the cursor; you're thinking about your story or report or whatever. When you come back to your work after a break, however, you depend on finding the cursor blinking away, ready for you to continue typing. The system is designed so the cursor doesn't draw attention to itself except when you want to find it.

The cursor can usually be moved by any of the four arrow keys on the keyboard, as well as by typing on the screen. The cursor will move one space up, down, right, or left when you press the corresponding arrow key one time. If you hold down an arrow key, the cursor will move one space, pause for a second, and then begin rapidly moving up, down, right, or left.

Depending on the software you use, some of the function keys might also move the cursor. If you have a mouse or trackball, you can use it

Cybernetics

to move the cursor around in some applications. The exact behavior of the cursor depends on the software you're using; the software instruction manual will tell you about this. As you get familiar with a program, you'll develop a subconscious sense of where the cursor goes when you press various keys. *See also* ARROW KEYS, FUNCTION KEYS, MOUSE, *and* TRACKBALL.

Masquerading cursor. In many software packages, the cursor changes shape depending on certain functions you select. In some word processing software, for example, the cursor changes from an underline to a box when you press the Insert key. Some word processing programs and operating systems, notably on the Macintosh, use the little anchor-shaped symbol shown in the drawing at C as the cursor. It might or might not blink as you work. This symbol is easy to find because of its unique appearance.

In Microsoft Windows environment, the cursor is usually indicated by a blinking vertical line. The position of the mouse pointer on the screen, however, is sometimes shown as a symbol similar to an elongated *I*, called the *I-beam*. Some PC users get the I-beam confused with the cursor in certain Windows applications. You can tell the difference by pushing the mouse a little bit. The I-beam will move, but the text cursor will not.

The arrow symbol (shown in the drawing at D) is technically not a cursor, but a pointer. It's standard in the Windows environment when you're using a mouse or trackball to select options. The pointer is also common in graphics software. Pointers, like cursors, can change form depending on various functions in the software. *See also* POINTER.

Cybernetics

The term *cybernetics* refers to the science of goal-seeking or self-regulating devices. The word itself comes from the Greek word for governor. Computer-controlled robots are good examples of cybernetic machines. Their behavior is governed by the programming of a computer, but true cybernetic machines also interact with their environment.

An example of a cybernetic process is pouring a cup of coffee. Suppose you say to a computerized personal robot, "Please bring me a cup of coffee. And be sure it's hot!" In the robot's memory, there is data concerning what a coffee cup looks like, as well as the route to the kitchen, the shape of the coffee pot, and, of course, a relative-temperature-interpretation routine, so the robot will know what you mean by hot. (In this case it's about 110°F.) In addition to these, there are many other variables.

A computerized robot must go through an unbelievably complicated process to get a cup of coffee. You'll discover this if you try to write down each step in rigorous form. Yet the ultimate cybernetic device, a human being, does things like this without conscious effort. *See also* ARTIFICIAL INTELLIGENCE, COMMONSENSE SUMMER PROJECT, *and* PERSONAL ROBOTS.

Cyberphobia

Do you think computers are incompatible with your mind? Do you envision computers as alien, perhaps even dangerous? Many people suffer from this kind of *cyberphobia*, an exaggerated and unreasonable fear of computers. Ironically, cyberphobics often become enthusiastic PC users.

Necessity. Maybe you don't need a PC. Some people get along fine without television sets; others make do without cars. You don't have to buy something simply because it exists, regardless of what advertisements say. If you have no need for a PC and do not want one, then cyberphobia is of no concern to you.

If you're reading this book, however, you probably believe that a PC is useful to you. Maybe you've already bought a computer and some peripherals, but don't know how to connect the cables and get the system running. Perhaps you haven't yet chosen from the potpourri of machines available today. To reduce cyberphobia, take plenty of time selecting hardware and software. *You* are the one who will be using them! Also, once you've bought the equipment, don't try to move too fast up the learning curve. In the beginning, treat the new machine as a toy. Have fun with it, and you'll forget your fears.

Building confidence. Some PC instruction manuals are written at a level too advanced for the beginning computer user. In recent years, computer makers and software vendors have recognized this problem and have been writing their documentation in a lighter style. Some manufacturers provide two or more instruction manuals, with varying degrees of technical complexity, filling the needs of users at various levels of experience. Detailed instructions are often provided in Help files that can be read directly from the computer; this is especially true of software and operating systems. Most computer manufacturers and software vendors also have technical-advice telephone numbers that you can call as much as you need.

Some computer "experts" seem to enjoy overwhelming novices with jargon and technical talk. If you run into such people when looking for advice, thank them, and then get help from somebody else. Plenty of real experts are willing and able to help the newcomer. Their enthusiasm shows. Some might even tell you that they were once cyberphobic.

There are books written especially to help new users get over the initial hurdles of hooking things up and starting to use a PC and peripherals. You should be able to find some at your local computer dealer, a bookstore, or a good library. See the bibliography at the end of this book for some possible choices.

Starting out. Once you get over your initial apprehension, you'll find that computers can help you out in dozens of different ways. Computers were originally built to do huge, repetitive jobs that would take weeks, years, or centuries to do "manually." A well-written software package can turn your computer into an accountant, editor, draftsperson, or mathematician. Computers have proven a boon to small businesses and self-employed people.

Word processing is the first application that most people use. Some PC owners use their machines almost exclusively for writing letters, stories, magazine articles, reports, memos, theses, or book manuscripts. Almost everyone ends up buying some form of word processing software and using it often. Word processing is therefore a good application to begin with when you are first getting acquainted with a PC.

Subscribing to an *online service* is at least as popular as word processing. Once you're online, you can find people who will tutor you on your machine, making the computer behave as if it had artificial intelligence although, of course, it's actually another person who is teaching you.

Building trust. Suppose you're writing the great American novel on your PC. You're storing it in files on your hard disk, and are also backing everything up on diskettes. You are taking all the precautions you have been advised to take to ensure that your work will not be lost in the event of a computer malfunction, fire, burglary, earthquake, or other disaster. Although you've been told you need not print out your work until you've done all the editing, you print it all out anyway, every day. Something in you does not trust that computer. There's something suspect, you think, about a machine that can store a 50-page chapter on magnetic media in less than a second.

Switching from hardcopy (paper) to magnetic and optical media involves a leap of faith. Some people have trouble with this for a long time. If it makes you feel better, go ahead and make hardcopies of everything for the first few months. Eventually, you'll realize that you don't need to do it. Then you'll see how much bulk and mess a computer can do away with. *See also* ARCHIVES, BACKUP, DISKETTE, *and* HARD DISK.

Legal matters. Data is easy to exchange (import and export) among PCs, making copyright infringement a valid concern. The legal details of this are too complicated to discuss here. As a general rule, however, don't copy or download software or documentation unless you are sure it is legal. If you are worried about people infringing on your own work, there are steps you can take to protect yourself. The best thing to do, if you have any doubts, is to consult an attorney.

Pitfalls to avoid. Another manifestation of cyberphobia is a fear that machines have too much power in society and that computers are "taking over." Science-fiction writers love this theme; they exploit it endlessly. They point out that *cyberphilia*, a blind trust and belief in computers, is no better than cyberphobia, and might in fact be worse.

People are starting to question the desirability of computerization, especially in the workplace, where technological advancement can mean the loss of jobs. Maybe you know someone who has lost a job to a computer or robot. Technology does have a dark side. A healthy skepticism can ensure that it enriches, rather than impoverishes, our lives. When irresponsibly used, either individually or collectively, computers can create or exacerbate problems. When responsibly used, a PC becomes an extension of your mind, adding enjoyment to work and play. *See also* COMPUTER ADDICTION *and* COMPUTER OVER-RELIANCE.

Cylinder

Do you remember long-playing records? The grooves in those disks were actually a single, long spiral. The same is true of CD-ROM. The data on a magnetic diskette or hard disk, however, is arranged in concentric circles. Each circle is called a *track*. Tracks let the machine read and write data faster than is possible with one long spiral.

In a hard-disk drive, there are several disks, called *platters*, stacked on top of each other. There are tracks on each side of each platter. When the whole set of platters is properly aligned along a rotation axis, all the tracks fall in concentric cylinders (see the drawing). Because of this, corresponding sets of tracks on the platters in a hard drive have been nicknamed *cylinders*.

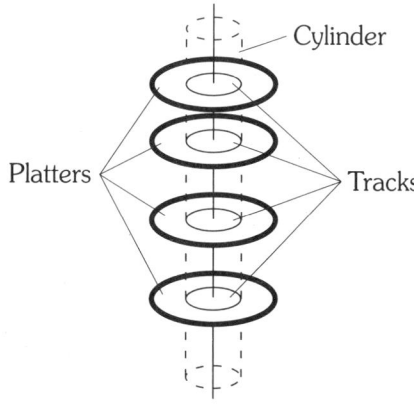

Sets of tracks on the platters in a hard drive that make up a cylinder.

As your PC puts data on the platters in the hard drive, it works one cylinder at a time. It will not move to a new cylinder until the one in use is completely full. This minimizes motion in the drive mechanism, which ensures that the reading and writing of data will take place as fast as possible. *See also* HARD DISK, PLATTER, *and* TRACK.

Cylindrical coordinates

There are various coordinate systems for three-dimensional (3-D) space. One of these schemes is known as *cylindrical coordinates*. A good analytical graphics program, especially one that is intended for scientific work, can render 3-D plots in cylindrical coordinates, as well as in Cartesian coordinates and spherical coordinates.

Scheme. The drawing shows the method for locating a point, *P*, using cylindrical coordinates. First, you decide on an origin point. Then, you decide on a reference plane containing the origin. In that plane, you decide which direction is to represent zero degrees; this is the *0-degree reference ray*. In the reference plane, you measure an angle counterclockwise from this ray, from zero degrees all the way around to 360 degrees, a complete circle. Finally, you measure altitude from the reference plane. The altitude can be positive (upward) or negative (downward).

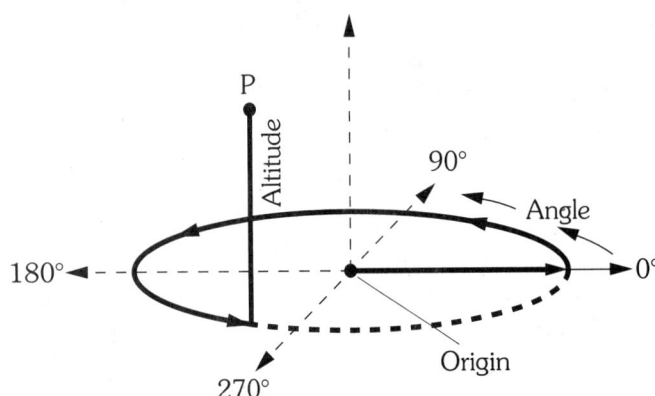

Cylindrical coordinates locate a point P *according to radius, angle, and altitude.*

To locate *P*, begin at the origin and move out the required distance along the 0-degree reference ray. This is the *radius*. Then go counterclockwise in a circle of this radius, by the necessary number of degrees. That's the *angle*. Finally, move the required distance above or below the reference plane to get the *altitude*.

Friend with a balloon. Here's an example to show how you might use cylindrical coordinates to locate a point in space. (This example corresponds to the drawing.) Suppose you're standing in an open field, and a friend is standing nearby holding a helium balloon attached to a long string.

Your friend is 60 feet from you; that is the radius. You choose north as the 0-degree reference ray (toward the right in the drawing). Your friend is east-southeast of you; that's an angle of 240°, measured counterclockwise from due north. The string is 58 feet long. There's no wind, so the string is vertical. The altitude is therefore 58 feet. The coordinates of the balloon are

(radius,angle,altitude) = (60,240,58)

in units of feet, degrees, and feet again, respectively. *See also* ANALYTICAL GRAPHICS, CARTESIAN COORDINATES, *and* SPHERICAL COORDINATES.

Daily planner software

Are you one of those people who likes to make lists of things to do every day? Do you plan things weeks or months in advance? Do you often change your plans? Then maybe *daily planner software* is for you.

The old way. Long before PCs existed, someone invented the date book. There were various formats to suit different needs. You might have bought a "daily date keeper" with a whole page devoted to each day of the year, a "weekly date keeper" with seven days on a two-page spread, or a "monthly planner," a calendar with a big blank square for each day, and the date in the corner.

There are problems with these books or calendars. The main trouble is messiness: eraser fragments if you use pencil, and correction fluid if you use pen and ink. Nevertheless, these books have certain advantages over daily planner software. They need no source of power, and they are instantly accessible without having to switch on a computer to get at their data. Many people keep paper copies of the current year's "daily date keeper" around in case of computer failure (not likely) or a disinclination to power-up the computer for the sole purpose of writing down an appointment (very likely). Quick notes can be written in the date keeper book and transferred to the computer at the next work session.

The new way. Many daily planner software packages are available. Some are intended for personal use; others work well for business. Some use gimmicks to take boredom out of scheduling time. Daily planner software can keep track of almost anything, such as the time you boot up your computer each day, and plot data in tabular or graphical form. A simple example of this is shown in the drawing.

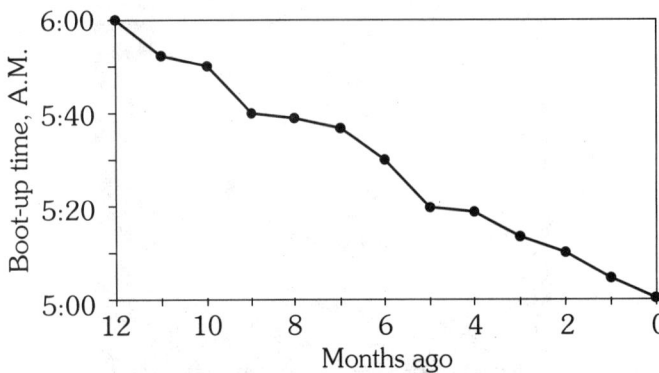

Hypothetical graph of PC boot-up time versus month, for the past year.

Many new computers have a daily planner, often called the calendar, included as a standard feature. You might click the mouse on the calendar icon for a schedule of the current day. You can typically set appointments at intervals of your choosing, include visual or audible alarms that flash on your screen or beep at the appointed times, and can change between daily and monthly views.

Embedded notes. A major asset of advanced daily planner software is the ability to embed whole files in appointment slots. This way, you can write down notes of any length in the space for any time on any day. This is done by *object linking and embedding (OLE)*. To recover the notes, you click on a specially created icon within the listing of an appointment, and the file, however large, appears. Click again and the notes disappear and you see the schedule for the day again.

Always remember to back up appointment data and files on diskettes, in addition to keeping them on the hard disk. This is standard operating procedure with all important data. *See also* CONTACT MANAGER *and* OBJECT LINKING AND EMBEDDING.

Daisy-chain network

There are several ways to connect PCs in a local area network (LAN). These schemes are called *network topologies*. In one topology, the *daisy-chain network*, all the PCs are connected in sequence, with separate cables between them.

Nodes. The drawings show how several PCs are connected in a daisy chain. Each PC is called a *node* or *workstation*. Nodes are shown as circles in the drawings; the heavy lines are the cables. Some nodes might have peripherals such as printers or modems.

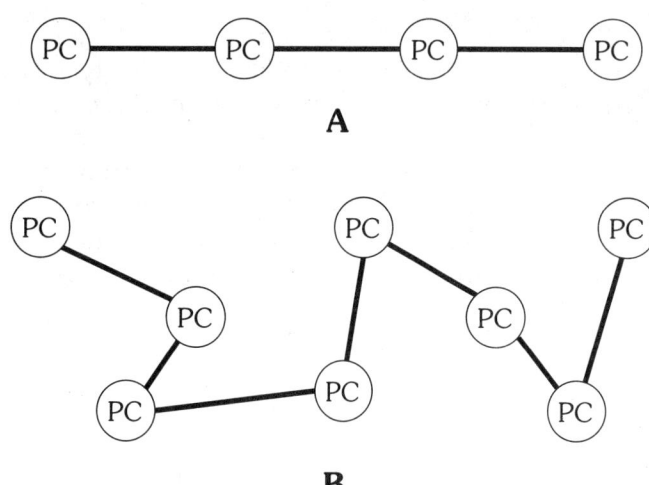

A daisy-chain network along a line (A) and scattered (B).

Every node has an *address*, a code that uniquely identifies it so that any node in the LAN can connect to any other node. Some nodes in the daisy-chain network are connected directly to each other, others have one or more nodes between them and can't communicate unless the signals pass through the intervening node or nodes.

Advantages. The main advantage of the daisy-chain network is its simplicity. A daisy-chain network is easy to enlarge; all you need to do is add more nodes anywhere along the chain.

A daisy-chain network can be made very long, in terms of the distance from one end to the other, because each node can act as a *repeater*, retransmitting a signal sent. As long as the separation between any two nodes doesn't exceed 1000 feet, a daisy-chain can be as long as you want (within reason). In the example of drawing A, the two end nodes can be as far apart as 3000 feet if the chain is a straight line.

Limitations. There is a greater chance for failure in a daisy-chain network than in most other topologies because if a node or cable fails, the nodes to either side of it will be cut off from each other. This problem can be overcome by using *bus network* topology. In a bus network, if one node fails, the others can still communicate because they are all still connected to each other.

Daisy-chain networks aren't well-suited to situations where nodes must be scattered all over a region. In such a case, the cables must zigzag around, and the overall length of the network can become huge compared with the actual distances between the nodes. An example of this is shown in drawing B. In situations like this, a *ring network* or *star network* works better. *See also* BUS NETWORK, LOCAL AREA NETWORK, NETWORK, REPEATER, RING NETWORK, *and* STAR NETWORK.

Daisy-wheel printer

A *daisy-wheel printer* works something like an office typewriter: the type wheel has several dozen radial spokes, each with one character molded on its face. When a character is to be printed, the wheel turns quickly so that the character is lined up with an electromagnetic hammer. The hammer is actuated, striking the spoke from behind, and pressing it against the ribbon and the paper (see the drawing). This causes characters to appear on the paper at about 10 to 20 characters per second.

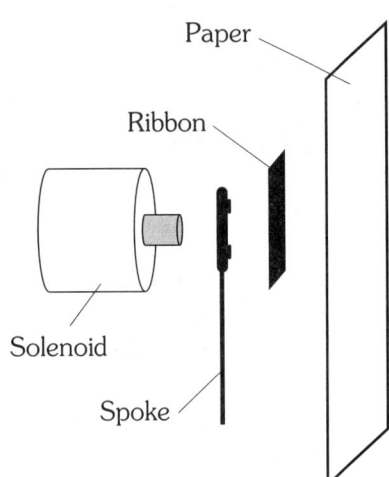

In a daisy-wheel printer, the solenoid causes the hammer to hit a spoke, printing a character.

Daisy-wheel printers are, for most purposes, obsolete; dot-matrix, inkjet, and laser printers are faster and can print text of excellent quality. These printers can also render graphic images, while daisy-wheel printers cannot. A laser printer, in particular, can provide better print quality than the daisy-wheel printer at much greater speed. *See also* DOT-MATRIX PRINTER, INKJET PRINTER, LASER PRINTER, *and* PRINTER.

Data acquisition system

A *data-acquisition system* is a set of electronic circuits designed to gather data for storage, processing, or direct use. A PC can be used as a data-acquisition system. For example, you do this when you connect your PC to a modem, run terminal emulation software, and interface it with the telephone lines, as shown in the drawing. You don't need a PC to obtain data this way, however; you could also use a *dumb terminal*. A dumb terminal costs less than a PC and can be used as a workstation in a local area network (LAN) or wide-area network (WAN).

After data is acquired, it can be stored in a variety of ways. If the data is transmitted to a diskette or hard disk, it can be kept for an indefinite length of time. Data might be sent to a printer for storage

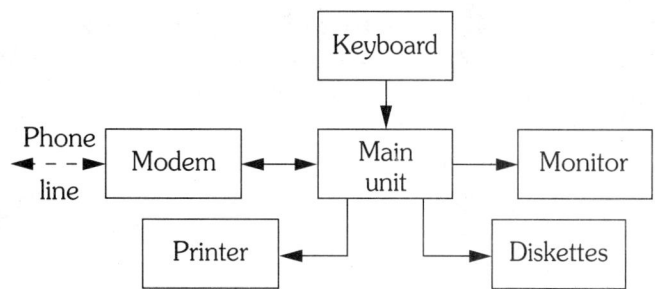

A data-acquisition system made of a PC or dumb terminal, and peripherals.

in the form of hardcopy. It can also be stored temporarily in RAM if the user wants to edit it before storing it in a more permanent place. Remember, however, that when you acquire software directly from public media, you might acquire a *Trojan horse* or *virus*. Precautions can be taken to minimize the chances of a computer system being disrupted by Trojan horses and/or viruses.

In the future, data-acquisition systems will become more versatile. You might someday be able to access a satellite system with your computer. Many computer users are already exchanging data via a mode called *packet communications*.

When a large number of PCs are used together, transmitting and receiving information, the resulting network is more powerful than any of the individual computers. This is mainly because the combination has far more storage space than any of its constituents. For example, a network of 10,000 PCs, with an average hard-disk storage space of 500MB each, theoretically has room for up to 5,000,000MB, or five terabytes (5TB) of data. The big challenge then becomes making all of this data easily available to each of the workstations. *See also* DATA COMMUNICATION, DATA CONVERSION, DUMB TERMINAL, LOCAL AREA NETWORK, MODEM, ONLINE SERVICE, PACKET COMMUNICATIONS, TERMINAL EMULATION SOFTWARE, TROJAN HORSE, VIRUS, *and* WIDE-AREA NETWORK.

Database

A *database* is a set of facts put together so that it's easy to find things. In personal computing, the term usually refers to software that lets you organize information.

The old way. You've probably used card files for things like names and addresses. If you own a business, you probably have hundreds or even thousands of people and companies whose addresses and telephone numbers you keep on file. Any card file is, technically speaking, a database.

A database need not be limited to names, addresses, and phone numbers. You might have a parts list for a vintage antique car you

Database

bought five years ago. Suppose it needs a new carburetor. Where did you get that part before? How much did it cost? What are the alternate sources in case the manufacturer has gone out of business?

Imagine a big cabinet with drawers filled with index cards. You might have a file for vintage car parts, another one for people you know, and another one for clients you've worked with in the past 20 years. This cabinet might weigh a couple of hundred pounds and have thousands of index cards. Some drawers might be packed so tightly that you would hardly be able to separate the cards to read them.

Generally, card files are arranged alphanumerically. In a file of 2000 friends and associates, therefore, "Anderson" would be on a card closer to the front of the file drawer than "Johnson," which in turn would be closer to the front than "Zimmerman."

You might also want to file your data about all these friends according to the state or country where they live. This would require another file drawer because Mrs. Zimmerman might live in Alaska, while Dr. Anderson might live in Wyoming, and Mr. Johnson might be in France.

What about telephone numbers? You'd probably list the country code first (if any), followed by the area code and the number. This would take another drawer full of cards.

Perhaps you'd want to file your friends according to the zipcode of their address. This would take yet another drawer full of cards. People in New England would be toward the front of the drawer; people on the West Coast would be near the back. You might arrange foreign countries in alphabetical order, either at the front of the drawer before all the U.S. cards, or at the back, behind all the U.S. cards.

So far, that's four drawers with 2000 cards apiece, for a total of 8000 index cards. There are other ways to organize the cards, too. What does each person do for a living? What do they like to do for fun? When is the last time you've seen or spoken to them?

The new way. You can store all this information on a diskette and let database software look people up according to any of these criteria, reducing the big cabinet full of index cards down to practically nothing in terms of physical bulk and weight. You'll also find the information much faster.

In a database, the data is arranged in major categories called *files*. In this example, the file contains all the information about your 2000 friends. The drawing at A represents this file as it might look in an index-card box with the cards arranged in no particular sequence.

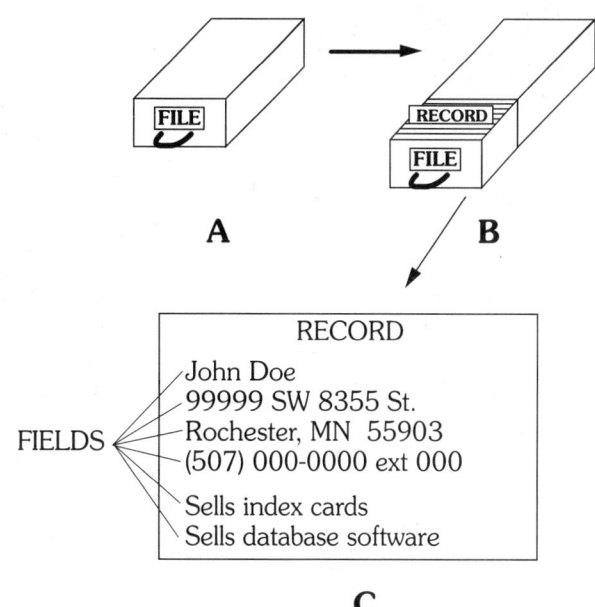

Information in a database arranged in files (A), records (B), and fields (C).

Each card in the file represents a *record* (B in the drawing). It's not important how these records are arranged; they could be stashed in the drawer at random. The software will quickly find data no matter where it is. Each record contains information about one, and only one, individual. For example, the record for Dr. Anderson has his address, telephone number, occupation, and any other data you might have on him.

The drawing at C shows the details of a record. For John Doe, there are these 15 bits of information, called *fields*:

➢ Last name: Doe

➢ First name: John

➢ House number: 99999

➢ Street number: SW 8355

➢ City: Rochester

➢ State: MN

➢ Country: U.S. (implied)

➢ ZIP code: 55903

➢ Country code for phone number: (Not applicable)

➢ Area code: 507

➢ Phone number: 000-0000

➢ Phone extension number: 000

Data bus

- Occupation 1: Sells index cards
- Occupation 2: Sells database software
- Miscellaneous data: (Empty)

With database software, you might go through the file and look for information based on any of these fields. You might even add more fields, such as the date of last contact, the names of his children (if any), or people you can call who might relay a message to John if he's not home.

One of the greatest assets of database software is its ability to find information based on almost any criterion you could think of, making it faster, more versatile, smaller, and lighter than many drawers full of index cards. You can search for items based on specific strings of characters, such as a word or a number sequence. You can enter new data or change the old data as the need arises.

With database software, files can be gigantic. This makes database software useful even for large corporations who manufacture complex things like digital computers. It also means you can keep tabs on far more items than would ever be possible with a file full of index cards.

New forms of database software are always being developed and existing programs are being refined. One powerful scheme developed in recent years is the *relational database*, in which data is stored in tabular form. Relationships are defined between the rows and columns. For details on the newest database programs, check with your local software dealer or look for advertisements and articles in recent issues of PC-related magazines. *See also* CONTACT MANAGER *and* PERSONAL INFORMATION MANAGER.

Data bus

In a PC, the CPU (central processing unit) stores data in and retrieves data from various memory circuits. There are several types of memory. Some memories have relatively small capacity, but can be written into and read from at high speed. Other memory circuits have large capacity, but require more time to store and retrieve data.

Think of the CPU as the conscious part of your PC's "nervous system." The *cache memory* is a small, fast-access, fast-write memory that corresponds to your awareness of what's happening right now. *RAM (random-access memory)* is slower, but has greater capacity; it's like your recollection of events so far today, and also your plans for later today. *ROM (read-only memory)* is like your long-term recollections.

Each of these memory stores—cache memory, RAM, and ROM—is connected to the CPU by a *data bus*, as shown in the drawing. Each data bus is a set of wires, foil strips, or optical fibers within the PC main unit. High-speed digital information constantly runs through the data buses, just as electrical impulses race around in your brain. *See also* CACHE MEMORY, CENTRAL PROCESSING UNIT, MEMORY, RANDOM-ACCESS MEMORY, *and* READ-ONLY MEMORY.

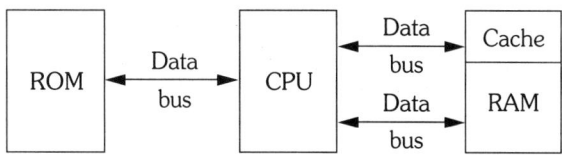

A data bus connects the CPU to memory circuits.

Data communication

Data communication is the transfer of data in both directions between two points, or in all possible ways among three or more points. Each point must have a data-acquisition system. When computers or terminals are interconnected so they all work together, they form a *network*.

Error rates. Ideally, data in any network arrives at its destination workstation exactly as it was sent from the source workstation. Interference can alter characters, however, resulting in errors. The more severe the interference, the greater the proportion of flawed characters to the overall total. This proportion is usually represented as a percentage. Therefore, you might hear about a system with a 0% error rate (no errors), a 0.01% error rate (one out of 10,000 characters, on the average, turns out wrong), and so on.

Example A in the table on page 270 shows a typo caused by the misinterpretation of a single character. Typos often seem to occur where they'll do the most damage. In this case, the reader might not know that the sender had really typed *dog*.

Bad data. Computer information with more than a few errors is called *corrupted data* or *mutilated data*. If you hear these terms, don't panic. They do not refer to sabotage or criminal activity, but it doesn't take many errors to cause a lot of trouble. In that sense, these terms rightly carry a negative connotation.

A single error can seriously corrupt a data transmission. Consider, for example, the changing of a plus sign to an equal sign in an equation. On many PC keyboards, the Shift key alone makes the difference between these two symbols. If a Shift key code gets omitted in a data signal, then you might see = instead of + in an equation, and not be able to tell from the context that anything is wrong. The problem will be noticed only if you use the incorrect equation and get invalid results.

Data compression

The effects of errors

Example A: One error causing a misinterpretation.

Input: The quick brown fox jumps over the lazy dog 1234567890
Output: The quick brown fox jumps over the lazy doe 1234567890

Example B: One error causing a string of wrong characters.

Input: The quick brown fox jumps over the lazy dog 1234567890
Output: The quick broN FOX JUMPS OVER THE LAZY DOG 1234567890

Example C: Numerous errors.

Input: The quick brown fox jumps over the lazy dog 1234567890
Output: Tje quICK BRown box jums ov he lazy bod 123$%^&*()

Another example of a serious error is a Caps Lock signal that gets inadvertently sent causing a whole string of incorrect characters, such as shown at B in the table. Actually, this does not destroy the meaning of the data in this case, but it looks bad.

Example C in the table shows a signal that has been badly corrupted because the circuit is poor. This might happen during severe weather, a major geomagnetic-field disturbance, or if signals are extremely weak. Under conditions as bad as this, some data communications circuits will stop functioning altogether rather than displaying or printing "garbage."

Error correction. Modern data-communication systems have almost completely eliminated errors. One method of error correction is called *handshaking*, in which the receiving terminal analyzes incoming data to see if it is in the right format. If something appears to be out of place, the receiving terminal sends an inquiry signal back to the transmitter, and the transmitter repeats the character string in question. A more sophisticated error-correction scheme is found in IBM's *Systems Network Architecture*, which checks every single data bit that is sent. *See also* COMMUNICATIONS, DATA TERMINAL EQUIPMENT, DIGITAL SIGNAL PROCESSING, HANDSHAKING, LOCAL AREA NETWORK, MODEM, ONLINE SERVICE, PACKET COMMUNICATIONS, WIDE-AREA NETWORK, *and* X/Y/ZMODEM.

Data compression

Data compression is a way of maximizing the amount of information that can be stored in a given memory or disk space, or sent in a certain period of time. Data compression is used in hard disk systems to increase the effective size of the disk. Compression can also speed up data communication.

Data compression

Hard disk evolution. The hard disk on your PC has a capacity measured in megabytes (MB), or units of 1,048,576 bytes. PC users keep demanding more hard disk capacity. Not long ago, a 100MB hard disk was a glimmer in the eyes of a few ambitious dreamers; now it is considered minimal if not inadequate for most PC users' needs. Many computers now measure hard disks in gigabytes, thousands of megabytes. Eventually, we might see computers with disk systems that can hold terabytes, or millions of megabytes.

No matter how large the capacity of a hard disk becomes, there will always be people looking for ways to optimize the available space. Data compression is one way to do this. *See also* HARD DISK.

Storage units. Data is written onto a hard disk in *storage units*. This makes it easier for the PC to store and retrieve the data. Unfortunately, it also makes rather inefficient use of the available space.

Think of a file cabinet full of index cards. Say there are 4000 index cards in the cabinet, each with room for up to 250 characters. That's a total of 1,000,000 characters, maximum, that can be stored in the cabinet. However, as you know if you've ever kept files on index cards, not all the cards will be filled to the maximum capacity. Even if you have something written on every single card, the average number of characters per card will probably be around 50 to 150, not 250. There's no point in writing anything more on a card than you need to write, but you'll fill the file cabinet to capacity by using up all 4000 cards long before you've written down a million characters.

The same thing happens on your hard disk. You'll run out of storage units on a 500MB hard disk long before you've actually put 524,288,000 characters (500MB of data) there. In fact, depending on the nature of the data you have stored, you might run out of space on a 500MB hard disk after storing 250 million, 150 million, or even 90 million characters on it. This problem is compounded by a phenomenon called *fragmentation*, which occurs when you have written and overwritten data on a hard disk or diskette many times. *See also* DEFRAGMENTATION *and* FRAGMENTATION.

How to use it all. Computer engineers noticed that not all the space on the hard disk was actually being used, so they set about trying to find a way to use it all. Think of the file cards again. Suppose you've used all 4000 cards, but they are, on average, only half-full. What can you do to avoid buying a new cabinet?

One possibility is to let some of the cards' data "spill over" onto cards immediately following. Perhaps card 2305 is completely full (250 characters), and then you find that you have more data you want to put on it. You can put this data on cards 2306, 2307, and 2308 as necessary, using a new ink color, such as red, so that you know that the new data is overflow.

Data conversion

Eventually you'll run into problems with this scheme. There might already by overflow data from one card at the place where you want to put overflow data from another card. To solve this, you can use a third ink color, say green, and skip ahead by, say, 100 cards before starting the continuation sequence. When you see green ink in the future, then, you'll know that you must look back to where the green ink starts, and from there, back 100 cards in the sequence. This sounds complicated, but a computer can be programmed to keep track of this kind of thing unfailingly.

Data compression on a hard disk works something like the index-card scheme. In addition, PC data-compression software uses *tokens*, symbols that stand for often-repeated words or phrases. For example, the word *data* appears frequently in this article. A compression scheme might replace this with the symbol * (asterisk). The term *hard disk* might be replaced with the token # (pound sign), and the word *character* with & (ampersand). Tokens can greatly abbreviate the size of a file without sacrificing any data. Of course, when a compressed file is opened for use, all tokens must be changed back into the strings of characters they stand for. Good compression/decompression programs do this so fast that you won't notice any delay.

In communications. Data compression can be used not only to get more information within a given space, but also to get more data sent and received per unit of time.

Suppose you want to send someone the contents of your entire hard disk via modem. That will take awhile, even at the highest data speeds. If the data on the hard disk is compressed, however, the actual rate of transmitted information is higher than when the data is not compressed. This is true even though the literal speed in bits per second (bps), as sent and received by the modems, remains constant.

Data can be compressed as it is sent even if it hasn't been compressed beforehand. For example, you might have a large RAM (random-access memory) filled with data. Suppose you want to send it to a friend via modem. It can be compressed at your PC (the source) as it is sent by your modem, and then decompressed (expanded) at the destination as it is received by the other modem. This is shown in the drawing.

There are various ways to compress data when it is sent by a modem. Each method has its own quirks. *See also* BAUD/BITS PER SECOND, DATA COMMUNICATION, *and* MODEM.

Data conversion

Information can exist in many different forms, both analog and digital. In PCs, information is generally digital, although some peripherals use

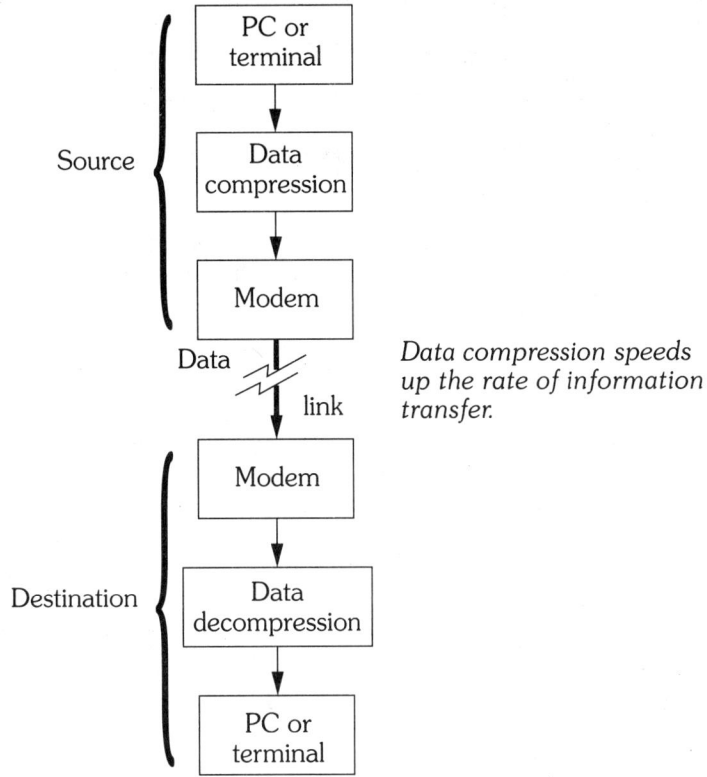

Data compression speeds up the rate of information transfer.

analog data, such as a voice or a video image. Digital data can be sent and received in either parallel form or serial form. *See also* ANALOG, DIGITAL, PARALLEL, *and* SERIAL.

Analog-to-digital conversion. A voice signal, or any continuously variable signal, can be *digitized*, or converted into a string of pulses whose amplitudes can have only certain levels. This is *analog-to-digital (A/D) conversion*. You can think of A/D conversion as "chopping" or "slicing" a signal into chunks that have only certain sizes.

The number of states is always a power of two so that it can be represented as a binary-number code. Fidelity gets better as the power of two gets larger. The number of states is called the *sampling resolution*, or simply the *resolution*.

You might think the resolution must be huge for good reproduction of a human voice to be possible. Actually, a resolution of eight (2^3) is standard for commercial digital voice circuits, as shown in drawing A on next page. A resolution of 16 (2^4) is good enough for compact discs (CDs) used in advanced hi-fi systems.

The efficiency with which a signal can be digitized depends on the frequency at which the sampling is done. In general, the *sampling*

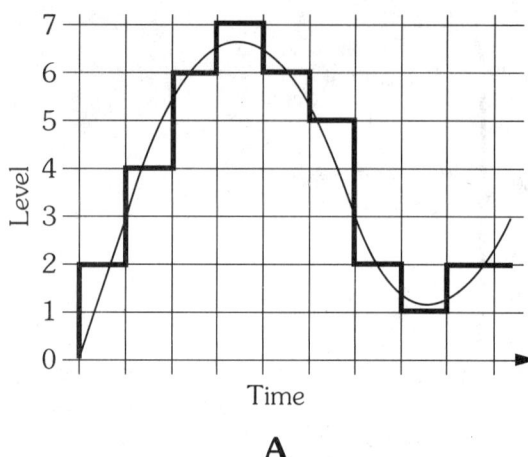

A

An analog signal (thin curve) and its digital counterpart (heavy, squared-off line).

rate must have a frequency of at least twice the highest data frequency. For a voice signal, the commercial standard is 8 kHz (8000 samples per second). For music and hi-fi digital transmission, the standard sampling rate is 44.1 kHz (44,100 samples per second).

In a computer, an A/D converter can be used to convert your voice or an image into digital form that the computer can understand. *See also* SPEECH RECOGNITION *and* VISION SYSTEMS.

Digital-to-analog conversion. *Digital-to-analog (D/A) conversion* reverses the process of A/D conversion, so the original analog data is recovered. You can use the drawing to imagine D/A conversion, just by thinking in reverse from the way you imagine A/D conversion. The D/A converter smooths out the digital signal.

You might ask, "Why convert a signal to digital form in the first place, if it's going to be changed back to analog anyway?" The reasons are subtle, but important in all data communications. A digital signal is simpler than an analog signal. It's good to make a signal as simple as possible, because *noise* (random interference) is exceedingly complex. The more different a signal is from unwanted noise, the easier it is to separate the data from the noise, and the fewer errors will occur. Also, computers have an easy time working with digital data and a very hard time with analog signals.

In computer systems, D/A converters are used in image processing and in speech synthesis. *See also* ARTIFICIAL INTELLIGENCE *and* SPEECH SYNTHESIS.

Serial-to-parallel conversion. Digital information can be sent in either of two ways: *serial* or *parallel*. There are advantages and disadvantages to either method.

Data conversion

When data is sent serially, the bits are sent along a single line, one by one. The advantage of this is that one line is enough to convey all the information. The problem is that it takes time to transmit data bit-by-bit.

When data is sent in parallel, groups of bits are sent along several lines at once. This increases the speed of transmission compared with serial transfer by a factor equal to the number of lines. The problem is that several communication lines must be used.

A *serial-to-parallel (S/P) converter* gathers bits up in groups from a serial line and sends them in parallel along several lines, as shown in drawing B. Imagine the data bits as flowing from left to right. The output of an S/P converter can't go any faster than the input, obviously, but the circuit is useful when it is necessary to connect a serial-data device with a parallel-data device.

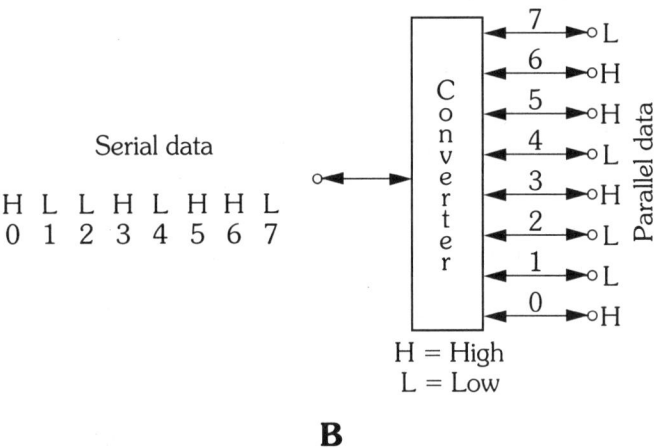

Parallel-serial and serial-parallel conversion.

Parallel-to-serial conversion. A *parallel-to-serial (P/S) converter* does the opposite of the S/P circuit. It gathers the bits from multiple lines, and transmits them out one at a time at a regular rate and in a defined sequence.

The output of the P/S converter must, over a period of time, keep up with the input. If the output is slower than the input, bits will accumulate in the converter. A *buffer* memory stores the bits from the parallel lines while they are awaiting transmission along the serial line, but this memory cannot have unlimited storage capacity.

You can think of the operation of a P/S converter by looking at drawing B and imagining the bits moving from right to left. *See also* PARALLEL *and* SERIAL.

Data redundancy

When a lot of information is stored on disk, it's best if it takes up as little space as possible. There are several things that can be done to minimize the disk space consumed by data, one of which is to minimize *data redundancy*, the repetition of the same information in different places.

Don't repeat things. Have you ever been with a person who kept saying things over and over? Maybe the words were a little different each time, but the essential content was always the same. Sometimes such repetition can lend emphasis, but usually it serves no purpose, and it can be destructive. You might catch the person being inconsistent with respect to previous versions of a story; then, you will not know which version to take seriously. The problem with redundant data in a database is similar to the repetitive talker.

Multiple names. In a computer database, information can be kept concerning people, places, events, company inventory, and various other things. One of the greatest assets of such a database is that you don't have to duplicate things. You need only enter each piece of information once, and the PC will sort through all the data, according to whatever criterion you want. In fact, you can get into trouble if you enter the same data more than once. It increases the chance for typos; a computer assumes you mean precisely what you type. Also, if you put pieces of a data record in different places, the machine will assume the pieces are unrelated. Such data redundancy causes data to be "splattered all over the place." The result is wasted disk space and an increased risk of errors when it comes time to use the stored information.

Suppose you have a friend named William Doe. He is known as William, Will, Willy, Bill, and Billy, depending on who he's talking with, the mood he's in, and various other factors. Under which of his names should you file information on William Doe? It doesn't matter, as long as you file his name only one way. You might know him most often as Bill Doe; then you could store all the information in a record called "Doe, Bill." However, if you create a record for "Doe, Billy," the PC will assume that this is a different person. Although you can link the records by putting cross-references in them, it's best to avoid all possibility of confusion. Stick to one name, and put everything in one record. *See also* DATABASE.

When it's good. It's wise to keep one, two, or even three copies of your valuable files on diskettes or tape. This type of data redundancy will prevent a disaster if your hard disk fails (which, if you keep a PC long enough, it will). It can also protect your data against fire, theft, hurricanes, or other crises beyond your control. This form of redundancy is generally called *backup*. *See also* ARCHIVES, BACKUP, *and* OFF-SITE DATA STORAGE.

Data storage media

See ARCHIVES, BACKUP, BERNOULLI BOX, CD-ROM, DISKETTE, HARD DISK, INTEGRATED CIRCUIT, MAGNETIC DISK, MAGNETIC MEDIA, MAGNETIC TAPE, MASS STORAGE, MEMORY, PCMCIA STANDARD ADAPTER CARDS, RANDOM-ACCESS MEMORY, READ-ONLY MEMORY, TAPE DRIVE, *and* WRITE-ONCE/READ-MANY.

Data terminal equipment

For a human being to work with a computer, it is necessary to have certain hardware that lets the person talk with the machine. Such devices are referred to as *data terminal equipment (DTE)*.

In the early days of computers, DTE consisted of a teletype (TTY) terminal. The user would type commands into this machine, which was similar to a mechanical typewriter, but bigger and louder. The computer's output was printed on a continuous sheet of paper that came off a roll.

Today, such devices as monitors, keyboards, mice, and light pens are used as DTE. There are even DTE that allow a person to speak to a computer and have the computer speak back. Sometimes, DTE can be used with a telephone modem or with a terminal node controller (TNC) to allow communications with computers located far away from the human operator. Such DTE is sometimes called a *dumb terminal*. *See also* DUMB TERMINAL, MODEM, MONITOR, MOUSE, *and* TERMINAL NODE CONTROLLER.

DDE

See DYNAMIC DATA EXCHANGE.

Debugging

Debugging is a process by which programmers get rid of the flaws (bugs) in computer software. The term *bug* was first used in the early days of electronics, when insects would get into the works, causing short circuits and other problems. This can still happen, especially in places where insects flourish. These days, however, problems aren't usually caused by insects, but by programming or design errors.

The first time a program is run after being written, it usually doesn't work, or it works very inefficiently. The same is often true for electronic circuits and mechanical devices. Rounds of debugging follow until the program or design works correctly. Debugging can sometimes be quick and easy, but often it is tedious and difficult. In some cases, a program or design must be scrapped, and the engineer or programmer must begin again from a new angle. When the new program or design is completed, the debugging process starts all over again. *See also* SOFTWARE.

Decimal number system

The *decimal number system* is the scheme you most often use to denote numerical values. It's sometimes called *modulo-10*, *base-10*, or *radix-10*.

How it works. There are 10 different possible digits in the decimal system, representable by the set {0,1,2,3,4,5,6,7,8,9}. Digits are written in a certain sequence to get a unique number. Depending on the position of a digit in the sequence, its value is multiplied by some power of 10. The table shows an example of a decimal number, and the powers of 10 by which each digit is multiplied.

Decimal number system: The number 2704.53816

2	7	0	4	.	5	3	8	1	6
$\times 10^3$	$\times 10^2$	$\times 10^1$	$\times 10^0$		$\times 10^{-1}$	$\times 10^{-2}$	$\times 10^{-3}$	$\times 10^{-4}$	$\times 10^{-5}$
= 2000 +	700 +	00 +	4 +		0.5 +	0.03 +	0.008 +	0.0001 +	0.00006

Computer numbers. For a computer, the decimal number system is an awkward and inefficient way to make use of the electronic circuits. It's far easier for a computer to work with powers of two than with powers of 10. Therefore, PCs usually employ the binary number system, also known as modulo-2. Sometimes computers use modulo-8 or modulo-16, known as the octal and hexadecimal number systems, respectively.

A computer doesn't work directly with decimal numbers; it converts the decimal numbers the operator gives it into its own system (usually binary), and then converts its own numbers into decimal form before they appear on the monitor or printer. As far as a human operator can tell, the computer understands modulo-10, although technically the operator is communicating with the machine through a two-way numerical translator. *See also* BINARY NUMBER SYSTEM, HEXADECIMAL NUMBER SYSTEM, MODULO, *and* OCTAL NUMBER SYSTEM.

Declarative language

A *declarative language* is a form of software or computer programming that, rather than telling the PC exactly what to do, conveys a set of facts (declarations). The language also describes how the facts affect one another.

Knowledge base. Declarative languages are widely used in *expert systems*, software that can make your PC into an "expert" in practically any field. For example, suppose your television set has a problem. Some of the channels come in, but many of the ones you normally get do not; instead, the pictures are "snowy."

You boot up software that helps you diagnose trouble with electronic devices, including TV sets. The program is written in a declarative language to contain facts about TV sets. It knows the circuits inside a

TV set, including what they do and how their performance affects the behavior of the set. These facts are interconnected by a framework of cause-and-effect relationships that turns your PC into a TV expert.

When you use this software, you might get a screen sequence in which the PC asks questions and gives options to click with your mouse. Here's a hypothetical example of such a package in action (this is not intended as a real-life TV repair procedure):

PC What would you like help with?
You click TV set

PC What's wrong?
You click Snowy pictures

PC Is the problem constant or intermittent?
You click Constant

PC Which channels come in all right?
You click Some, but not all

PC How long has this been happening? Type your response in the form x days/y hours.
You type Don't know

PC Guess.
You type 7 days/5 hours

PC Disconnect cable from back of set. See what happens. Then click on the result that most nearly describes what happens.

The PC screen shows several possible outcomes of this experiment. You switch the TV on, and the problem is still evident, so you disconnect the cable from the back of the set by carefully unscrewing the connector. This makes no difference in what you get on your TV set, however, so you return to the PC.

You click No change
PC Connect another TV set to the cable.

And so it goes until the problem is fixed, or you and the computer together determine that the TV set needs to be seen by a professional repair technician.

While the computer is acting as an expert, it works with the facts and uses the relationships provided by the declarative-language software. If you were to look at the software programs, you'd see these facts and relationships. *See also* EXPERT SYSTEMS *and* PROCEDURAL LANGUAGE.

Decoding

Decoding is the process of converting a message received in some form of code into plain language. In a computer, this is done by the software.

Decryption

When you use your PC, you see words on the monitor screen or printer paper made up of characters. The characters are represented in the computer by groups of binary digits (bits). The software converts the binary data into an *image*, a set of instructions that tells the printer exactly how to lay the ink down on the paper or how to light the dots on the screen.

In a machine with speech synthesis, decoding software converts the data bits into groups of audio waves at just the right frequencies, and with just the right timing, to pronounce recognizable words. With *encrypted data*, or information that has been deliberately altered to make it recognizable only to certain people, the decoding process is known as *decryption*.

See also CRYPTANALYSIS/CRYPTOGRAPHY/CRYPTOLOGY, ENCODING, *and* SPEECH SYNTHESIS.

Decryption

See CRYPTANALYSIS/CRYPTOGRAPHY/CRYPTOLOGY.

Default

A *default* is a choice that a computer or peripheral will make for a parameter if you don't specify anything. Defaults are usually changed using software. If you have more than one disk drive, printer, fax, or modem, one of each will be selected by default at the beginning of every operating session.

Default drive. Normally, the default drive is the hard disk drive, called drive C. In DOS, you can display the root directory of the hard disk by typing

```
DIR C:
```

and pressing Enter, or, if drive C is the default drive, you need only type *DIR* (and press Enter). You might change the default drive to a diskette drive, usually drive A or drive B. Suppose you have two diskette drives: a 3.5-inch drive in bay A, and a 5.25-inch drive in bay B. By typing *B:*, you change the default drive to drive B. Then when you type *DIR*, you see the root directory on the 5.25-inch diskette in drive B.

To look at the root directory of drive C again, you must type *DIR C:*, making certain to include the letter *C*. Similarly, you can change the default drive to drive A by typing *A:*. Then you can look at the root directory on a 3.5-inch diskette by inserting it into drive A and typing *DIR*. *See also* DISK DRIVE A/B/C/D, DOS, *and* PERIPHERALS.

Default directory. To work with files, your PC must be in the right directory. If, for example, AUTUMN.TXT is in a directory called SEASONS on drive C, but you're in the root directory, you'll get the message

Defragmentation

```
FILE NOT FOUND AUTUMN.TXT
```

when you try to access the file. You would need to specify the directory SEASONS to access the file.

The default directory for any disk drive is the root directory, unless and until you change it. To change the default directory, you can use the CHDIR or CD (change directory) command.

In DOS, when you want to open a file that is in neither the default drive nor the default directory, you must specify the complete *path*, both the drive and the directory in which your PC is to look for the file. Graphical user interfaces (GUIs) such as Windows or the Macintosh make this process intuitive, although you must move and click the mouse a number of times. In DOS without a GUI, the path to the AUTUMN.TXT file is C:\SEASONS\AUTUMN.TXT.

Default filename extension. Your PC might sometimes assign an extension to a filename automatically. If you have a backup utility, for example, you might notice that your directories are accumulating files with the extension .BAK. You might also occasionally see other default extensions that seem to have sprung up spontaneously, such as .TMP (which stands for *temporary*), or .EXE (which stands for *executable*). Sometimes a default filename extension is given to any file created with a certain application. For example, .CAL is the default extension given to files created in Windows Calendar, while .TXT is the extension for Notepad files. *See also* FILENAME EXTENSION.

Default font. When you print something out, your printer and software will choose a default font unless you override it. You can set the default fonts in most printers by following a simple programming procedure. (Refer to your printer instruction manual for details.) In some programs, you might also be able to select a default font via your keyboard or mouse. (Your software instructions should tell you how to select and change fonts.) *See also* FONT.

Defragmentation

When you first put files on a hard disk or diskette, they're written one after the other, with no spaces in between. A technical person would say that the files are written onto *contiguous sectors*. Eventually, however, if you overwrite the files many times, they will no longer occupy contiguous sectors. *Defragmentation* is the process of putting disk files back onto contiguous sectors.

Diskette with several files. Suppose you've written 12 papers, called PAPER.1 through PAPER.12, and you have them on your hard disk. Suppose they are very long papers, each taking about 100K. You decide to back them up on a new diskette in exactly the order they appear in the directory of the hard disk (which isn't in numerical order). They go onto the diskette one after the other, with no

Defragmentation

spaces in between. Twelve 100K papers will almost fill a high-density diskette.

Now suppose, months later, you get a flash of insight concerning PAPER.9. Your ideas flow freely, and the paper ends up somewhat longer when you're finished with the revision. When you create the backup file on the diskette, the PC will tell you file PAPER.9 already exists and ask you if you want to overwrite it. You'll respond that you do, and the PC will write the new PAPER.9 on the diskette. However, PAPER.9 can't fit in the "slot" where it was before; the file is too big now.

Because of this, PAPER.9 will be broken into two parts. The first part will fit in the *clusters* on the diskette where the original PAPER.9 was. The remainder will be written in clusters following PAPER.12. The tables show the general concept. Table A shows the situation before PAPER.9 is overwritten, while Table B shows the situation afterwards. In an actual computer directory display, there will still be only one listing for PAPER.9; the fragmentation will not be apparent by looking at the directory.

Table A
Files on a hypothetical diskette

PAPER	1	6-15-03	5:39a
PAPER	2	6-15-03	5:39a
PAPER	3	6-15-03	5:39a
PAPER	4	6-15-03	5:39a
PAPER	5	6-15-03	5:39a
PAPER	6	6-15-03	5:39a
PAPER	7	6-15-03	5:40a
PAPER	8	6-15-03	5:40a
PAPER	**9**	**6-15-03**	**5:40a**
PAPER	10	6-15-03	5:40a
PAPER	11	6-15-03	5:40a
PAPER	12	6-15-03	5:41a

How defragmentation works. If you overwrite all the papers several times, changing their lengths each time, you'll eventually have a situation in which most of the papers are broken up on the diskette. The more times you revise the papers, the smaller the fragments will become. This will never show up when you use the DIR (directory) command, however. You'll always get a list that looks as if the files are all "solid."

The situation shown in the tables is a minor case of fragmentation, and it would not normally present any problem. Fragmentation can

Table B
PAPER.9 is fragmented

PAPER	1	6-15-03	5:39a
PAPER	2	6-15-03	5:39a
PAPER	3	6-15-03	5:39a
PAPER	4	6-15-03	5:39a
PAPER	5	6-15-03	5:39a
PAPER	6	6-15-03	5:39a
PAPER	7	6-15-03	5:40a
PAPER	8	6-15-03	5:40a
PAPER	**9**	**9-09-03**	**8:10p**
PAPER	10	6-15-03	5:40a
PAPER	11	6-15-03	5:40a
PAPER	12	6-15-03	5:41a
PAPER	**9**	**9-09-03**	**8:10p**

become quite extensive in applications such as word processing, and you won't notice anything amiss. Eventually, however, if the fragmentation gets severe enough, it will take a long time to access files. The PC will have to find the fragments of a file and assemble them in RAM before you can work with the file.

A *defragmentation utility* takes the pieces of files and consolidates them on a hard disk or diskette. The computer will then access files as fast as it did when they were "fresh." Most new computers have defragmentation utilities installed in the operating system. For most casual PC users, this program can be run once or twice a month to maintain a reasonably unfragmented hard disk. Consult your instruction manual or Help files if you don't know how to use your defragmentation utility. *See also* DISKETTE, FRAGMENTATION, *and* HARD DISK.

Delete key

On your keyboard, the *Delete key* works alone or in conjunction with other keys to erase characters, words, or parts of lines in most programs. It is also one of three keys you can press on IBM-compatible PCs to perform a warm boot.

On a typical PC keyboard, there are two Delete keys. One is in a small keypad just to the right of the main keyboard, as shown in the drawing at A. This key usually has the word *Delete* written out in full. The other is in the numeric keypad, just below the numeral 3 (B in the drawing). This key is usually labeled *Del*. (On older PCs, the locations of the Delete keys might be different than those shown in the drawings.)

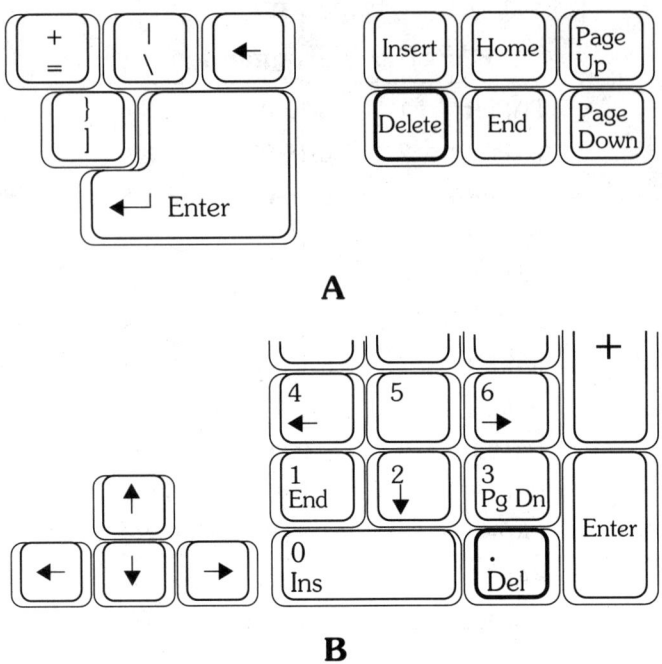

The Delete key is often found in two different areas (A and B) of the keyboard.

If you press the Delete key all by itself in most programs, whatever single character the cursor is on at the time will be erased. Normally, all of the remaining text will move left one space to fill in the place where the deleted character was. If you hold the Delete key down for more than about a half-second, characters will be deleted one after another in rapid succession until you let go of the key.

In many word processing programs, pressing Ctrl-Delete (pressing the Ctrl and Delete keys at the same time) erases the entire word on which the cursor lies. Again, the remaining text moves to fill the empty space and the keys repeat if held down for more than about a half-second.

Depending on the software, other uses of the Delete key to erase text might be available. For example, in most Windows programs, you can erase any amount of text by dragging the mouse over it while holding the button down, and then pressing the Delete key. *See also* CTRL-ALT-DEL *and* WORD PROCESSING.

Delphi

Delphi is a popular online service run by Delphi Internet Services Corporation that enables you to communicate with other PC users, get assistance from experts, and keep informed in great detail about current events. Delphi offers extensive access to *Internet*, the main artery of the information superhighway.

System components. Getting on Delphi is simple. To use Delphi, you need the following:

- A computer with a hard disk
- DOS 2.0 or later
- A telephone line
- A modem
- Registration codes (supplied when you buy the package)

Many computers are sold with all the necessary components installed. You connect a telephone to the internal modem, have the computer dial a toll-free number, and follow the instructions on the screen.

Menu driven. Delphi uses a menu-driven interface. You choose items via the keyboard, typing either an item number or the first few letters of an item to gain access to the data contained under that heading. You'll have to learn some commands to make full use of the interface, but once you've gotten used to the interface, you can move rapidly through it.

Delphi offers complete and efficient access to the Internet under the category of "Internet Services." Once you get on the Internet, you will encounter many different kinds of menus and command-driven interfaces. Delphi offers access to, but has no control over, the myriad byways in the vast conglomeration of online services that make up the Internet. The more freedom you have in "cyberspace," the greater is your information-gathering power, but there is a learning curve involved. For assistance, you can order a comprehensive instruction book called *Delphi: The Official Guide* directly from Delphi Internet Services Corporation.

Departments. Delphi has numerous departments and forums, updated periodically. To gain access to a department, you type the first few letters of the menu item. Examples include the following:

- Business and finance
- Computing groups
- Entertainment
- Games
- Internet services
- Mail
- News, weather, and sports
- Reference and education
- Shopping
- Travel and leisure

Demultiplexing

For further information about this network, write to

Delphi Internet Services Corporation
1030 Massachusetts Avenue
Cambridge, MA 02138

You can register online; consult the PC magazines for the latest toll-free number. *See also* INTERNET *and* ONLINE SERVICE.

Demultiplexing

Demultiplexing is a process in which signals are sorted out from a channel in which they've been mixed together. It is the opposite of the mixing-up process, called *multiplexing*. Multiplexing and demultiplexing are common in computer communications.

Suppose you have a communications channel that is carrying signals from three different computers. Call these signals XXXX, YYYY, and ZZZZ. They are sent in little bits in a rotating sequence like this: XYZXYZXYZXYZ.

A demultiplexing circuit takes samples at intervals that precisely match the duration of each piece of data X, Y, and Z. The circuit assembles the pieces into the three original signals XXXX, YYYY and ZZZZ. The drawing is a functional diagram of this process, in which the communications channel is represented by the long, horizontal chain of blocks XYZXYZXYZXYZ. The three individual signals are represented by the three vertical blocks XXXX, YYYY, and ZZZZ.

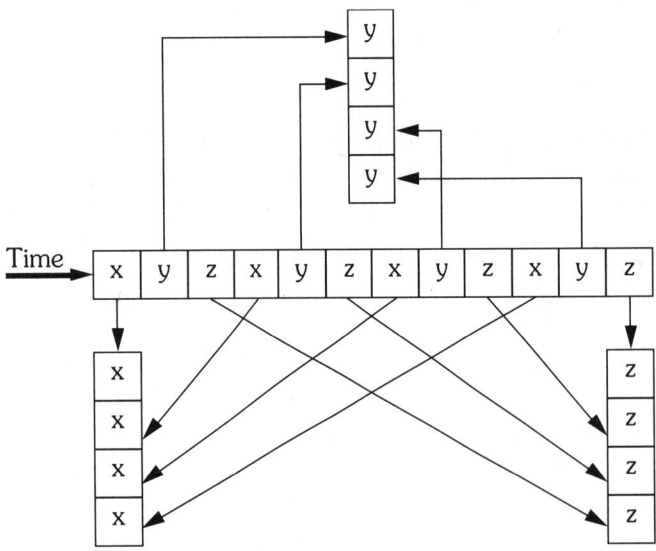

Separation of three signals from a channel in which they were mixed up.

The scheme shown in the drawing is called *time-division demultiplexing* because it reassembles signals that have been split up over time. The signals might also have been sent on different frequencies; then they would be extracted by means of *frequency-division demultiplexing*. See also COMMUNICATIONS, LOCAL AREA NETWORK, *and* MULTIPLEXING.

Dependent variable

In a mathematical function, one of the variables, called the *dependent variable*, always depends on the others.

Single-function graph. You'll come across dependent variables when you make graphs and charts with your PC. The dependent variable is usually plotted on the vertical axis. The drawing at A is a graph of temperature (in degrees) versus time for a hypothetical day. The temperature depends on the time, so temperature is the dependent variable plotted on the vertical axis. The time doesn't depend on anything; it just happens. It is the *independent variable*.

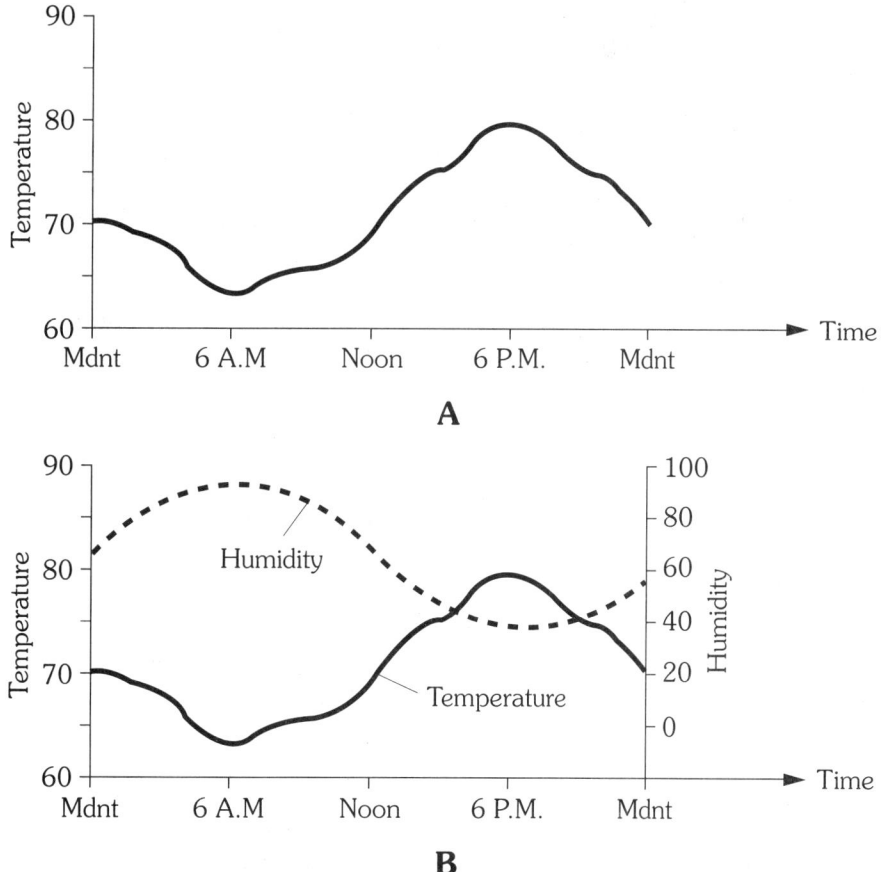

Dependent variable on a one-function graph (A) and a two-function graph (B).

Desktop

Two-function graph. The drawing at B is a graph of temperature (in degrees Fahrenheit) and relative humidity (in percentage points) for a hypothetical day. This graph has two functions on it, each with its own dependent variable. Time is the independent variable for both functions.

To plot two functions on the same graph, two scales are needed. The temperature scale is on the left, and the humidity scale is on the right. There are two curves: the solid curve is for temperature, and the dashed curve is for humidity.

Multivariable functions. It is common for functions to have two independent variables, with one dependent variable. In this type of function, known as a *multivariable function*, the dependent variable is affected by both of the independent variables.

If you get involved with analytical graphics software, you'll use three-dimensional image rendition to show two-variable functions. If you use high-level mathematics, you'll eventually get involved with functions of three or more variables. The graphics for these functions can get quite complex. *See also* ANALYTICAL GRAPHICS, FUNCTION, INDEPENDENT VARIABLE, *and* MULTIVARIABLE FUNCTION GRAPH.

Desktop

When you power up (switch on) a Macintosh PC, the monitor screen shows an almost blank display. This is called the *desktop* because of its similarity to a real desk, as the place on which you do your work.

The arrangement of the desktop varies somewhat depending on the particular Macintosh model you have. Four things always appear, however:

- A *menu bar* at the top of the screen containing several words that represent choices for various things the PC can do
- A *pointer* that you can move around using the mouse
- A *disk icon*, representing the hard disk or diskette you are working with
- A *trash icon* at the bottom of the screen in the corner, which lets you throw out things you have done if you don't want them anymore

The Windows GUI (graphical user interface) on an IBM-compatible PC also has a desktop somewhat like the Macintosh system, but there are several differences. The main difference is that, in Windows, programs and data are held in boxes (windows) instead of being directly on the desktop. *See also* GRAPHICAL USER INTERFACE *and* MACINTOSH.

Desktop computer

A *desktop computer* is a popular style of PC used extensively in businesses and homes. It has several components interconnected with cables. The drawing shows the components of a typical desktop computer, including the main unit, monitor, keyboard, printer, mouse, and CD-ROM drive.

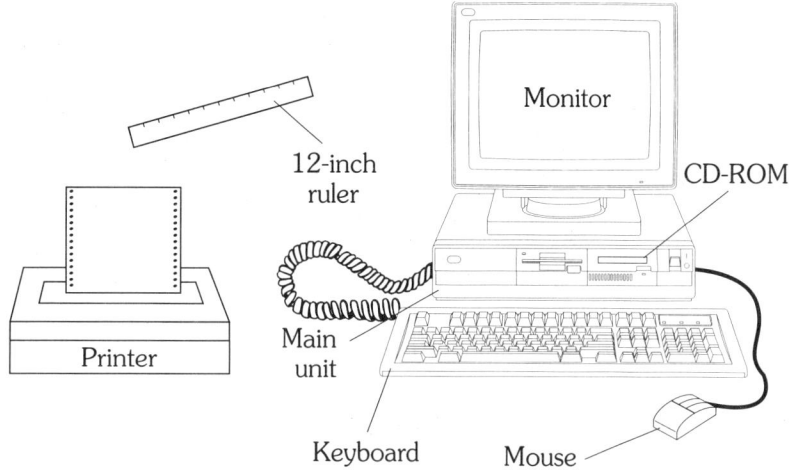

Typical arrangement of a desktop computer, with 12-inch ruler for comparison.

Meant to stay put. A desktop computer is designed to remain in one place. The main unit alone can weigh 40 to 75 pounds, so it isn't easy to move such a system. The monitor has a cathode-ray tube (CRT) and associated power supply, weighs 20 to 40 pounds, and is as fragile as a television set.

When disassembled in preparation for moving, a desktop computer system occupies three or four large boxes. It takes time to disconnect the cables and pack the units so they won't be damaged in transit, and more time to properly connect the units again at their new location. If you want a computer you can carry around, a desktop unit probably isn't for you. Consider a laptop or notebook computer instead.

A desktop computer offers advantages over portable computers for users who don't need to transport their machines. The CRT monitor brightness can easily be adjusted and the visibility is excellent in all environments. The hard disk system can have greater storage capacity than that of a laptop PC. It's relatively easy to upgrade and modify a desktop system because the main unit can have plenty of room for expansion boards inside. The whole machine operates directly from utility power, not from batteries, so energy consumption is not an overriding design factor. Things like disk drives and printers, which cannot be efficiently operated from batteries, can be used continuously. *See also* LAPTOP COMPUTER.

Desktop computer

Main unit. The main unit, also called the *system unit*, is the heaviest and usually the largest element in a desktop system. It contains the "brains" and storage of the computer. If you plan to upgrade your PC, the expansion boards will be installed in the main unit. There are three different configurations for system units:

> ➤ The *conventional case*, also called a *desktop case*, is shown in the drawing. It sits on a desk, usually underneath the monitor and just behind the keyboard. The advantage of this scheme is that it's easy to insert and remove diskettes from their drives.

> ➤ The *tower case*, so called because it is taller than it is wide, sits on the floor and is bulkier than the unit shown in the drawing. It gives you extra desk space, but it's not as easy to insert and remove diskettes. Tower cases are common in computer systems for businesses and schools. *See also* TOWER CASE.

> ➤ The all-in-one case has the monitor and keyboard built into the main unit. Its primary main advantage is that it doesn't need connecting cables between the main unit, the monitor, and the keyboard. Its disadvantage is that it's less flexible than separate components. You can't change the relative positions of the keyboard, monitor, and main unit, nor can you personalize your system by choosing your monitor.

Monitor. The monitor almost always has a CRT (cathode-ray tube) similar to the picture tube in a TV receiver, but the *image resolution*, or ability to show fine detail, is far better on a desktop PC monitor than that of even the best TV sets. Modern monitors can show upwards of a million different hues and saturation levels.

Vivid color and high resolution make computing fun and interesting. An excellent monitor isn't all that expensive. If you think you'll be doing much graphics work, and especially if you plan to use a CD-ROM and multimedia with your PC, you should get the best monitor you can afford. It's your "window" to the computing world. The better the window, the more you'll see, and the better you'll see it. *See also* CATHODE-RAY TUBE, IMAGE RESOLUTION, MONITOR, SUPER VIDEO GRAPHICS ARRAY, *and* VIDEO GRAPHICS ARRAY.

Keyboard. Various different keyboard arrangements are in use today. All keyboards have numerous special-function keys in addition to the standard letters of the alphabet, numerals, and punctuation marks.

Desktop PCs come with keyboards that plug into the back of the main unit. With conventional-case computers, the keyboard cable is usually a "curly cord" that lets you move the keyboard around easily. Tower-case machines often have keyboards with straight cords, which run neatly from the operating surface underneath the desk to the main unit. *See also* KEYBOARD.

Desktop computer

Printer. There are hundreds of different printers on the market, ranging in price from about $100 to several thousand dollars. The printer you choose will depend on the kind of work you plan to do, your budget, and your personal preferences. If you have enough money you might get two printers: a laser printer for professional correspondence, and a color ink-jet printer to do graphics and desktop publishing or a dot-matrix printer for multipart forms.

The optimum location of the printer varies. Some computer desks are designed with a special place for the printer and a shelf underneath for the paper. Some PC users find that a bedside table is perfect for the printer. You can also put the printer on your desk next to the main unit. *See also* COLOR PRINTER, DOT-MATRIX PRINTER, INKJET PRINTER, LASER PRINTER, LCD/LED PRINTER, PLOTTER, PRINTER, *and* THERMAL PRINTER.

Mouse. The mouse is an input device that you slide around on a flat surface, so that you can move the cursor or pointer on your monitor screen. Although mice come in various shapes and with various numbers of buttons, they all work basically the same way. The mouse lets you draw diagrams, "paint" pictures, and select options in a graphical user interface (GUI) by sliding it to the appropriate place on the screen and pressing its buttons. You'll need a flat, horizontal surface measuring at least 10-×-10 inches to slide the mouse around. Special pads are available that provide a better surface for sliding the mouse.

Some PC users prefer to use a *trackball* instead of a mouse. A trackball looks like a large ball bearing built into the keyboard of the computer or into its own fixed base. The advantage of the trackball is that it only needs the space it occupies; you don't need room to slide it around. *See also* MOUSE *and* TRACKBALL.

CD-ROM drive. A CD-ROM (compact-disk, read-only-memory) drive reads an optical disk similar to the compact discs you might play on your stereo. A CD-ROM is a high-volume, high-density data storage medium with space for hundreds of megabytes. A large encyclopedia can be stored on a single CD-ROM.

Many PC systems have CD-ROM drives built into the main units. You can also buy an external or internal CD-ROM drive for your desktop computer if it doesn't already have one. It is a box about 8-×-8-×-2 inches big. A good place for an external CD-ROM drive is under the monitor and on top of the main unit. *See also* CD-ROM.

Modem. The modem connects your PC to the telephone line so you can get onto the so-called information superhighway. New desktop computers generally have built-in modems, or you can add one either externally or inside your main unit. Modems are inexpensive, and they open up a whole world of information for you. There are networks for practically all interests, from boating to ham radio to politics.

Desktop publishing

A *fax/modem* can send and receive pictures as well as text. Some modems, known as *terminal node controllers*, are designed to be used with amateur radio equipment, so you can get into packet radio networks. (You need an amateur radio license to do this.) *See also* AMATEUR RADIO, FAX BOARD, MODEM, NETWORK, ONLINE SERVICE, PACKET COMMUNICATIONS, *and* TERMINAL NODE CONTROLLER.

Gadgets and gimmicks. New computer peripherals are always being invented. For example, MIDI (Musical Instrument Digital Interface) devices can help you compose and play music. Speech-synthesis circuits make your computer into a conversational companion. You can connect your PC to a home-security system or have it control your lawn sprinkler. The day isn't too far off when PCs will be used with many different kinds of robots. There is the exciting realm of virtual reality.

If you can imagine something, no matter how bizarre, someone has probably designed hardware and software to make it "PC-real." Check with your local computer dealer and look through the latest PC-oriented consumer magazines for advertisements and information. *See also* MUSICAL INSTRUMENT DIGITAL INTERFACE, PERIPHERALS, SPEECH RECOGNITION, SPEECH SYNTHESIS, *and* VIRTUAL REALITY.

Desktop publishing

Desktop publishing (DTP) is the creation of professional-quality documents using a PC and various peripherals. The simplest form of DTP is word-processed text printed on paper. The most advanced DTP packages let you produce full-size books with drawings and photographs. There are dozens of DTP programs available, so if you want to get into DTP, shop around before deciding on a package. The necessary hardware varies, too, depending on your intended audience.

Who uses DTP? Desktop publishing has many uses. Graduate students can use it for preparing theses. Job seekers can use it to create good-looking resumes. Businesspeople use DTP to publish newsletters, promotional brochures, instruction manuals, business reports, catalogs, and other material. A group of aspiring writers might use it to publish a monthly literary magazine. Some people have published full-size books using DTP.

The users of DTP fall into two broad categories: low-end and high-end. Low-end DTP users include students, small businesses, nonprofit organizations, job seekers, and the like. They can get by with the less-sophisticated DTP software. High-end DTP users are large corporations and publishing houses who need the best software available. High-end users also need fancy peripherals, like a high-resolution laser printer for typeset-quality text and line art, an optical scanner for importing detailed art and photographs, and a WORM (write-once/read-many) drive for creating CD-ROM publications.

Three major features. Three things about DTP software make it more sophisticated than ordinary word processing:

> *Page layout control* With DTP, you can move text and art around, arranging it on the page however you want. Some programs let you see on-screen exactly what the printed page will look like. This is called *WYSIWYG* (what you see is what you get), pronounced "WIZZY-wig."
>
> You can squeeze text or art tight or stretch it out, adjusting it horizontally on the page. You can also change the type size and art height, adjusting it vertically. If a given article must occupy 3.5 pages, therefore, you can adjust the size and placement of text and art until you get the length to come out just right and have an arrangement that is appealing to the reader. You can change things with simple commands, and the software will take care of the details automatically.

> *Column format* With DTP, you can work directly with text in one, two, three, or more columns. This is not usually true with word processing.
>
> Suppose you have text in two columns per page, with 50 lines in each column. If you want to insert or delete a block of text, it will change what is in each column, and also what is on each page. The DTP software will take care of everything, moving the text around the blocks you've set aside for art or photographs.

> *Graphics* DTP really stands apart from ordinary word processing when it comes to art. You can easily insert clip art in your document and make changes to it. You can create illustrations with a draw program or paint program, and then import them into the document. It's even possible to import color photographs if your scanner has color capability and adequate image resolution.
>
> You don't necessarily need a laser printer to produce good graphics in DTP. If you're a low-end DTP user, you can probably make do with an inkjet or even a dot-matrix printer. If you are going to be producing work for large companies who demand the best, however, you'll want a laser printer, especially for top-notch art and photograph reproduction.

What do you need? The first question to ask yourself is whether you really need DTP. You probably won't need it for college term papers or technical reports; that's like buying a 100-foot yacht to sail a lake that is only a mile across.

Destination

If you want to get into DTP, you must decide whether to purchase low-end hardware and software or put up the money for the high-end software and peripherals. Again, there is no sense in buying something more sophisticated than you're ever likely to need. Ask yourself, "What do I need now? What do I expect to be doing in a year? In five years?"

You can get high-end software if you think you'll be doing big-time DTP some day, but you can put off buying fancy peripherals (like a laser printer and scanner) if you don't need them now. The advantage of having high-end software is that you won't be likely to outgrow it in the near future. Remember, however, that technology is advancing fast, so today's high-end package might be a low-end deal in four or five years.

Look through PC-related magazines for the latest advertisements. Also check with your local PC dealer and talk with the "PC gurus" you know. Get several opinions.

The future. Perhaps you wonder why it's necessary to print things out on paper at all, now that PCs can display text, art, and photographs on screen. In fact, paper is not always necessary.

You've probably heard about *electronic publication*, in which magazines, books, and other materials are sold on disk rather than as bound reams of paper. Maybe you've seen a commercial in which someone sits on a beach with a laptop PC on a towel, reading a romance novel. That might seem rather silly, but it's within the capabilities of current technology. In time, the price of technology will come down to the point where it will be far cheaper to buy one laptop PC and a bunch of CD-ROMs than to purchase the equivalent stack of books. Electronic publications consume about 0.01% of the space, and weigh 0.01% as much, as bound books and magazines.

See also CLIP ART, DRAW PROGRAM, ELECTRONIC BOOKS, GRAPHICS, IMPORTING, LASER PRINTER, OPTICAL SCANNER, PAINT PROGRAM, WORD PROCESSING, WRITE-ONCE/READ-MANY, *and* WYSIWYG.

Destination

When one PC sends a message to another, such as is commonly done via online services, the receiving station is called the *destination*. The sending station is called the *source*.

In a network or when two PCs are in constant contact with each other, the source and destination are defined by the data. For example, suppose there are two computers, C in Cleveland and S in Seattle. The users of these two computers exchange news headlines. Then C is the source for the Cleveland headlines, while S is the destination. Similarly, S is the source for the Seattle news, and C is the destination.

The two messages might be exchanged at different times; this is called *half duplex*. Things are simple in half duplex. One PC acts only as a source, while the other acts only as a destination. If the channel allows two-way transmission of data, the messages can be exchanged simultaneously. Then both PCs would play source and destination roles, but for different data. This is called *full duplex*. *See also* FULL DUPLEX, HALF DUPLEX, ONLINE SERVICE, *and* SOURCE.

Digipeater

The term *digipeater* is a contraction of the words *digital* and *repeater*. Digipeaters are used by amateur radio operators, who interconnect computers via radio instead of telephone lines. This is a special form of *packet communications* known as *packet radio*.

In recent years, personal computing has acquired an important place in the hobby called "ham" radio. Many radio "hams" use PCs, both desktop and laptop, for communications. Most PC users, in contrast, have never been exposed to amateur radio. It's worth considering, because ham radio can provide fascinating alternatives to conventional online services. For example, "hams" can access the Internet from remote sites via radio without incurring the charges usually associated with cellular communications services.

Practically any amateur radio station capable of sending and receiving packet signals can work as a digipeater. The drawing is a functional block diagram of an amateur-radio digipeater. The station receiver intercepts the incoming signal (A in the drawing), which might have come from the source (originating station) or been relayed from another digipeater. The received signal (B) goes to a *terminal node controller (TNC)*, which is similar to a modem. The TNC demodulates the signal, so a computer can understand it. From the TNC, the data (C) goes to the PC, where it is stored briefly, then the PC sends the data (D) back through the TNC, where the signal is changed into a form suitable for radio transmission (E). The transmitter modulates a radio wave with this information. The radio wave goes to the transmitting antenna (F). Thus, the message is on its way to another digipeater or to the destination station.

A digipeater retransmission frequency can be the same as the frequency on which the signal came in, but it doesn't have to be the same. For example, a digipeater can receive a packet on 144 MHz (an amateur frequency band near the FM broadcast band) from a source just a few miles away, and resend it on a shortwave frequency to some other digipeater halfway around the world.

A digipeater will accept only signals that are intended for it. Special data, called a *routing frame*, determines which digipeater(s) the signal is to go through, and in what order. As the signal is routed along, *secondary station identifier (SSID)* codes tell each succeeding

Digital

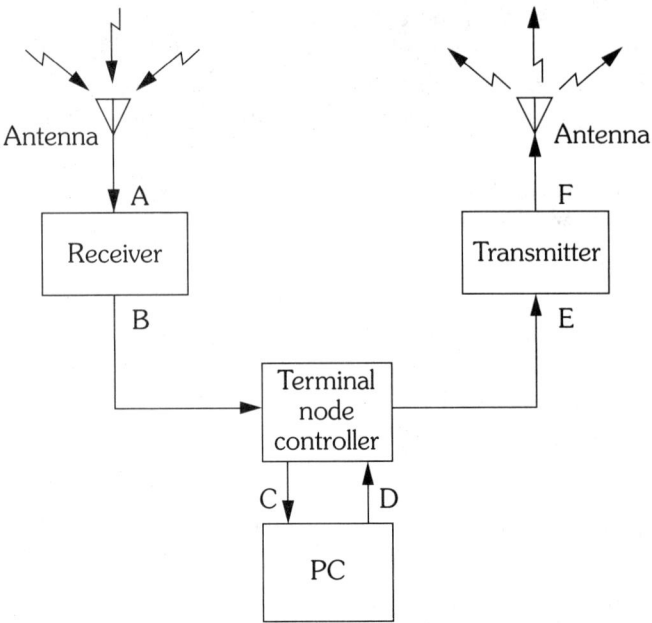

Functional block diagram of a ham radio digipeater.

digipeater that the signal is intended specifically for it. A packet-radio message can go through several digipeaters along its way from the source to the destination. *See also* AMATEUR RADIO, DESTINATION, MODEM, ONLINE SERVICE, PACKET COMMUNICATIONS, *and* SOURCE.

Digital

A circuit or device is *digital* when it can attain only a finite number of levels or states, usually a power of two. This is in contrast to *analog* quantities that can vary continuously over a range of values.

Approximations. Digital renditions of analog quantities are almost always approximate, and rarely exact. Graph A in the drawing is a straight line in analog form. It's exact; its value changes smoothly and continuously. Graphs B, C, and D show this same line graphed in digital form with four, eight, and 16 levels. None of these are exact; they all change value in defined steps. Nevertheless, a computer has a much easier time with digital quantities than with analog ones.

Binary quantities. In computers, circuits usually operate in the *binary* system with only two possible levels, *high* and *low*. Sometimes these levels are assigned the numerical values 1 and 0, the truth values T and F, or the statements "yes" and "no." All the data in a personal computer is stored in digital form as a vast array of logic highs and lows. Digital data can precisely represent text and can provide excellent approximations of such analog quantities as drawings, photographs, and sounds.

Digital motion. In a PC used for controlling robots, *digital motion* refers to a machine that stops at certain defined positions. Consider a

Digital computer technology

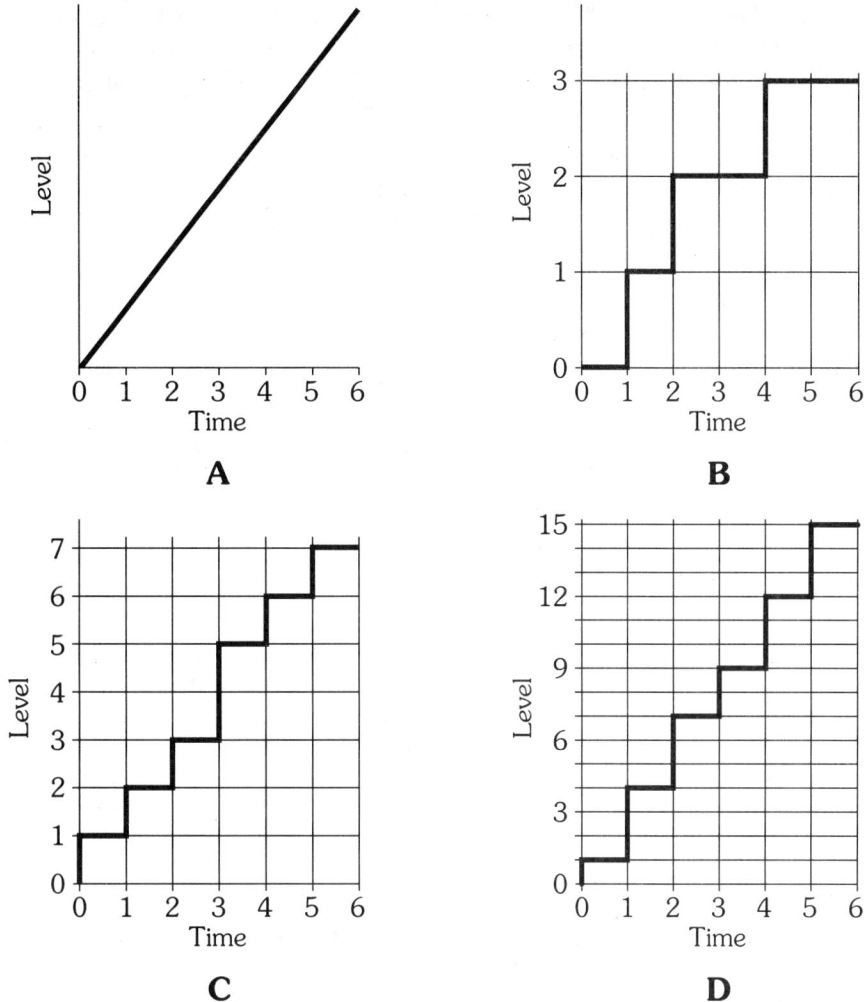

A sloping line (A) and its digital renditions (B, C, and D).

robot arm whose motion is governed by a computer. The base of the arm might rotate to any multiple of 22.5° in the complete circle of 0° to 360°. This divides the circle into 16 equal parts. The angle, measured as a compass bearing clockwise from true north, is programmed into the computer as a decimal number from 00 through 15, or as a binary number from 0000 through 1111. The command *BR = 03* or *BR 0011* therefore causes the robot arm to move to 67.5° (22.5 × 3) and stop there. *See also* DIGITAL COMPUTER TECHNOLOGY, PERSONAL ROBOTS, *and* ROBOT CONTROLLER.

Digital computer technology

When you hear people talking about PC technology, they're probably discussing *digital computer technology*. There are other ways in which computers can work; some of these are being explored, but digital technology dominates.

Digital computer technology

Machine language. A digital quantity exists in discrete levels, or states. This is in contrast to analog variables, which can have an infinite number of levels. In computing, the number of possible states is almost always a power of two. Machine language, used by computers to exchange and store information, has only two possible states, high and low, represented by the binary digits (bits) 1 and 0. Other expressions include on/off, bright/dark, red/green, yes/no, plus/minus, true/false, or practically anything that can attain two clearly different conditions.

All the data you put into a digital computer, no matter what its real-life form, must be converted into ones and zeros so that your PC can make sense out of it. The computer does this for you, so you can input data in a form you're comfortable with, such as typewritten text, mouse clicks, images, or spoken words instead of typing expressions like 10010011 11001010.

The digital machine translates its binary language into a form you can understand before presenting you with output. Thus, you won't see a string of ones and zeros on your screen or paper. You'll see or hear words, music, and images, or you might witness the output of a computer in mechanical form, such as the movement of a robot.

Strengths. Digital technology has prevailed in the design of computers almost from the beginning of the computer age. People have become accustomed to digital computers. They're good for numerical calculations, word processing, and other applications that lend themselves to digital codes. Every numeral, letter of the alphabet, and symbol you can imagine can be represented by digital signals. Digital signals stand out clearly from noise on communications lines. Digital data is also easy for a machine to tell apart from analog data.

No matter how data is presented—text, image, sound, program, spreadsheet, database, or anything else—it can be digitally encoded. Some things lend themselves better to digitization than other things, but if the data speed is high enough, and if the memory capacity is big enough, a PC can render a good digital approximation of anything.

Limitations. Digital quantities are never exact representations of analog things like images and sounds. Although it's generally possible to make digital approximations so close to analog reality that the difference is not worth worrying about, there are a few exceptions.

There's an absolute limit to the speed at which a digital computer can operate. There's also a limit to how much data can be stored in a given physical space. As people continue to demand faster, more powerful digital computers, these limits will eventually impose constraints on the technology. Impulses can't travel faster than the speed of light (186,282 miles per second in free space), nor is it likely that researchers will ever find a way to get a single electron of matter to represent thousands of bits of data.

Some researchers, anticipating the limitations of digital technology, have been looking at alternative computer technology. This is most apparent in artificial intelligence (AI), especially among those engineers who hope to develop a human-like electronic mind. The military is interested in all forms of technology, including alternative computers.

See also ALTERNATIVE COMPUTER TECHNOLOGY, ANALOG, ANALOG COMPUTER TECHNOLOGY, AND GATE, ARTIFICIAL INTELLIGENCE, BACTERIORHODOPSIN, BAUD/BITS PER SECOND, BINARY DATA, BIT, BYTE, COMPUTER POWER, DIGITAL, ELECTRONIC NUMERICAL INTEGRATOR AND CALCULATOR, EXCLUSIVE-NOR GATE, EXCLUSIVE-OR GATE, FIRST-IN/FIRST-OUT, FLIP-FLOP, HYBRID COMPUTER TECHNOLOGY, INVERTER, LOGIC, LOGIC GATES, MACHINE LANGUAGE, NAND GATE, NEURAL NETWORK, NOR GATE, OPTICAL COMPUTER TECHNOLOGY, OR GATE, PUSHDOWN STACK, *and* VON NEUMANN BOTTLENECK.

Digital signal processing

Digital signal processing (DSP) is a way to improve the quality and clarity of computer data. It has revolutionized communications, from computer networks to telephones to stereo systems.

Microprocessor's apprentice. The technology of DSP is a great boon for computers of all sizes and shapes. Its importance will continue to grow as PCs become more user-friendly.

A DSP can be etched onto a single, tiny integrated circuit (IC) or chip, similar in size to the microprocessor. Some DSPs can serve multiple functions in a computer system, acting as an assistant to the microprocessor, so the computer brain can devote itself to doing its primary work without having to bother with extraneous tasks. A DSP chip can work as a fax machine or a modem, perform data compression, help a PC recognize or generate speech, or enable a PC to see its environment clearly.

Data cleanup. Digital signal processing was first used with radio and television receivers to produce a clear voice or picture from a badly corrupted or garbled signal. Some of the earliest experimenters with DSP were amateur radio operators.

In analog modes, DSP works by converting the received voice or video signal into digital data. It does this by means of *analog-to-digital (A/D) conversion*. The digital data is processed and is reconverted back to the original voice or video via *digital-to-analog (D/A) conversion*. In this way, DSP vastly improves the range and accuracy of any communications circuit, whether the communicators are people, robots, PCs, or anything else.

Digital signal processing

In circuits that use only digital modes, A/D and D/A conversion are not necessary because the signal is always digital. DSP can still be used to "clean up" the signal, however. This reduces errors and makes it possible to copy data over and over many times.

How it works. Digital signals have discrete, well-defined states. It is easier to process a signal of this kind than to process an analog signal, which has a theoretically infinite number of possible states. Trying to process an analog signal is a little like trying to read somebody's mind: the patterns are infinitely varied and complicated. Even the biggest computer in the world would have a horrible time trying to infer the curves and warps in an analog world, but when the analog data is changed over to the simpler, more cut-and-dried digital format, an electronic circuit can make decisions quite easily. This simplicity of digital data compared with analog data is the main reason why digital computer technology has advanced so much more than analog computer technology.

The DSP circuit gets rid of confusion between digital states, as shown in the drawing. The signal before processing is shown in the drawing as A; the signal after processing is B. The electronic circuit makes its decision for defined time intervals. If the incoming signal is above a certain level for an interval of time, the DSP output will be high (logic 1). If the level is below the critical point for a time interval, then the output will be low (logic 0).

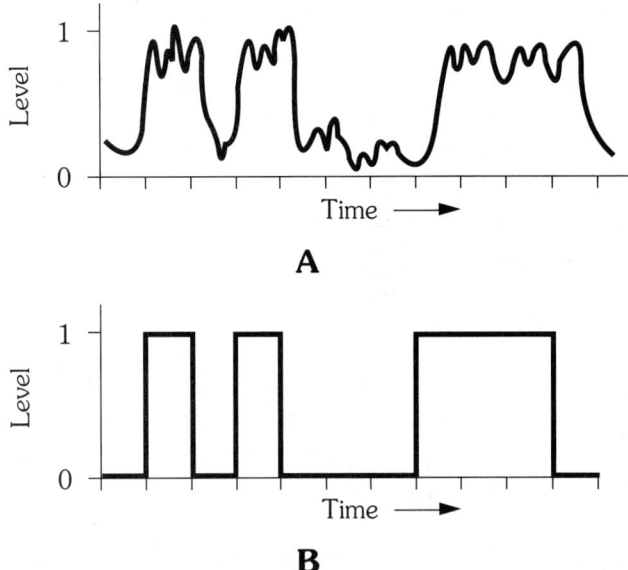

Incoming signal with noise (A); the same signal after DSP (B).

Errors can occur with this scheme, however. A sudden burst of noise, such as static from a nearby storm, might fool the DSP into thinking the signal is high, when it's really low. Nevertheless, errors are far less frequent with DSP than without it. *See also* ANALOG, ANALOG-TO-DIGITAL CONVERSION, DIGITAL, *and* DIGITAL-TO-ANALOG CONVERSION.

Digital-to-analog conversion

Digital-to-analog (D/A) conversion converts a digital signal to an analog one. It is the exact opposite of *analog-to-digital (A/D) conversion*.

Why do it? You might ask, "Why convert a signal to digital form in the first place, if it's going to be changed back to analog form at the destination anyway?" The reason is that a digital signal is inherently simpler than an analog signal because it is less random. A digital signal resembles noise less than an analog signal.

It's good to make a signal as different from noise as possible, in as many ways (or senses) as possible. The more different a signal is from unwanted noise, the easier it is to separate the data from the noise. That translates into fewer data errors.

Fruits in a tub. You might think of signal/noise separation in terms of apples, oranges, and a watermelon. Think of the orange as a weak analog signal, and the apples as noise. It is difficult to find a lone orange in a tub full of apples. Suppose, however, that there's a watermelon (representing a weak digital signal) in a tub with the apples (noise). You'll have no trouble finding the watermelon.

Another, more interesting feature of digital communications arises when you think of a watermelon in a tub of oranges. It's as *easy* to separate a digital signal from a jumble of analog signals as it is to extract a digital signal from noise. In a communications channel jammed with analog signals, a lone digital signal can be picked out far more easily than any of the analog signals.

Endless copy-ability (almost). In recent years, digitization has become commonplace not only in data communications, but in music and video recording. One of the biggest advantages of digital recording is that a selection can be recorded, rerecorded, re-rerecorded, etc., and the quality does not appreciably diminish. You can make copies of copies almost forever, each as clear as the original.

Of course, no system is perfect, and errors do occasionally creep into digital systems. For example, a logic high can be mistaken for a logic low, or vice versa. These errors accumulate over time, and as generation after generation of copies are made. Still, digital recording is a huge improvement over analog methods; digital errors happen far less often than analog errors. *See also* ANALOG-TO-DIGITAL CONVERSION *and* DATA CONVERSION.

DIP

See DOCUMENT IMAGE PROCESSING or DUAL INLINE PACKAGE.

Directory

A *directory* is an index of files in a large data storage medium, such as a hard disk, diskette, CD-ROM, or tape drive. A directory usually lists the following data for each file:

➢ Filename

➢ Filename extension

➢ File size in bytes

➢ Date and time the file was last saved

A directory often also shows how many bytes are occupied in the storage medium and how many bytes are free.

Root directory. Consider your hard disk. If you're working in DOS, you can type DIR, press Enter, and look at the *root directory*, or main directory, on the disk in the default drive. This is usually the hard disk (drive C). Every disk, diskette, and CD-ROM has a root directory. Some might also have the storage space divided up into subdirectories.

Subdirectories. Some filenames in the root directory carry the notation <DIR>. This means that the file is itself a directory, contained within the root directory. Such a file is sometimes called a *subdirectory*. In most PCs, the root directory can hold up to 512 filenames, so in theory you can have up to 512 subdirectories.

When you're new to personal computing, you won't create new subdirectories very often. As you gain experience, you'll want to develop a *directory tree* that suits your needs. If you put everything in the root directory, you're likely to get confused. It would be like putting items in file cabinets without using any file folders to itemize things.

If you get too many files in the root directory or in a subdirectory, sooner or later you're going to try to save something and get a response like

`CANNOT STORE IN DIRECTORY`

Then you'll either have to make a new directory to store the data or delete at least one file from the existing directory.

Working directory. When you first go into DOS, you're normally working with files in the root directory. Therefore, your *working directory* is the root directory until you change things. Suppose your

Directory tree

hard disk has a subdirectory called WINDOWS listed in the root directory. You can change over to this subdirectory by typing

> CD \WINDOWS

and pressing Enter. Note the backslash before the name of the subdirectory; it's important to include this. The PC should respond with

DONE

on the prompt line at the top of the screen. If you then type DIR and press Enter, you'll see a completely new set of filenames on your screen. You are no longer in the root directory; your working directory is now the subdirectory called WINDOWS.

The hierarchical relationship between the root directory and subdirectories can be diagrammed, which can be a big help when you decide that it's time to organize your hard disk. This directory/subdirectory structure is the *directory tree*.

Find your own way. The way you organize your hard disk is up to you; it's a matter of individual taste. A scheme that works well for one person might be inconvenient and confusing for someone else. The best thing to do is to learn as you go. PC-related magazines often contain helpful articles on the subject of hard-disk organization.

There are three important rules you should always follow when organizing your hard disk. They can be simply stated as follows (where the expression *something* refers to a file or a directory):

1 If you have any fear about moving or deleting something, **don't**!

2 If you are sure where to put something, put it there.

3 If you aren't sure where to put something, leave it where it is.

The first rule is especially important. If you delete something, be sure you won't regret it later. The erasure of an essential file can mess up the operation of your PC. It might even disable the machine until the software is reinstalled on your hard disk. As insurance, you should back up all the data on your hard disk periodically, preferably using a high-volume storage medium such as a tape drive. You can also back up files or directories on diskettes immediately before erasing them from the hard disk. *See also* DEFAULT, DIRECTORY TREE, DIRECTORY WINDOW, *and* DOS.

Directory tree

A *directory tree* is the structure of directories and subdirectories in a large data storage medium. Usually, this medium is a hard disk, although it might be a CD-ROM, diskette, or tape. Directory trees are often diagrammed to show the hierarchy of files.

Directory tree

Root and trunk. The listing shows part of the directory tree for the hard disk of a hypothetical computer. The *root directory* symbol, a backslash (\), is at the top. Dashed lines depict the general structure of the tree.

Root directory and subdirectories

```
ROOT
\
 ├── BATCH
 ├── DOS
 ├── EIGHT
 ├── MOUSE ──┬── ANSWER.COM
 ├── PRODIGY │   ├── CHOOSEDR.SCR
 ├── TS      │   ├── COMCHECK.EXE
 ├── UTILS   │   ├── DIRERROR.SCR
 ├── WINDOWS │   ├── DIREXIST.SCR
 └── XY      │   ├── DONE.SCR
             │   ├── HIDEDRVR.EXE
             │   ├── INSTALL.BAT
             │   ├── MKCD.COM
             │   ├── MKCD2.COM
             │   ├── MKDIR.SCR
             │   ├── MOUSE.COM
             │   ├── MOUSE.SYS
             │   ├── MTRACK40.EXE
             │   ├── READ.ME
             │   └── S1.SCR
```

You might think of the vertical dashed line at the extreme left as the tree trunk. Other vertical dashed lines and horizontal dashed lines are "limbs." The further to the right you go, the closer to the "leaves" (data files) you get.

Branches. There are nine subdirectories on this hard disk. They are indicated by the designator <DIR> in the root directory listing. If you were to type DIR C: and press Enter, you'd get a listing of the subdirectories first, followed by the rest of the hard disk's root directory. The nine subdirectories at the top of the list might appear as follows:

```
BATCH      <DIR>     7-20-94    10:59a
DOS        <DIR>     6-12-93    1:58p
EIGHT      <DIR>     6-12-95    2:01p
MOUSE      <DIR>     6-12-93    2:02p
PRODIGY    <DIR>     2-20-95    5:14p
TS         <DIR>     6-12-94    2:02p
UTILS      <DIR>     6-12-93    2:02p
WINDOWS    <DIR>     6-12-93    1:59p
```

This is a rather small set of subdirectories; some PCs have several dozen of them. In general, the more applications you use, the more subdirectories will appear on your hard disk.

Twigs and leaves. Suppose you wanted to see the files in the MOUSE subdirectory. You would use the *change directory (CD) command* by typing

   CD \MOUSE

and pressing Enter. This would result in a listing such as the 16 files at the right in the table.

Some of the subdirectories are quite long. For example, if you type

   CD \WINDOWS

and press Enter, you'll get a listing that fills several screens.

Skeleton. The table shown is only a partial listing of the directory tree for the hard disk of this PC. A complete directory tree would have to show all the files for all nine subdirectories in the root. This would take up several sheets of paper and look quite complicated.

If you work with many types of software, you'll want to keep files in separate subdirectories for each application. You can draw a "skeleton" of the directory tree, without including every filename in each subdirectory. You can use filename extensions to indicate where a file belongs. For example, .TXT might stand for text documents, and files with that extension would therefore go in the document subdirectory.

There is no rule that says you ever have to draw a diagram of a directory tree. You might envision the tree in your mind, or sense it subconsciously. In the Windows graphical user interface, the directory tree is depicted for you in the *File Manager* application. *See also* DIRECTORY, DIRECTORY WINDOW, *and* FILE MANAGER.

Directory window

A *directory window* is a table of contents for a directory found in the File Manager portion of the Windows operating environment. The window that shows all directories is called the *directory tree window*.

Disk caching

You can open a directory window by clicking the appropriate directory name in the directory tree window with your mouse, or you can cycle through the directory files by pressing the Down-arrow key until the file you want is highlighted. You can tell which files are directories by the icon next to the filename; the directory icon looks like a tiny manila folder.

When you open a directory, it takes the place of whatever was in the directory window at the time. The filenames in the directory usually appear in alphanumeric order, unless you have chosen to list them some other way. You can arrange the files in a directory window by size (in bytes, from biggest to smallest), by filename extension (in alphanumeric order), or by the dates on which they were last updated (from newest to oldest).

Generally, File Manager updates the listings in the directory window as you work on the files. For example, suppose you have a file called ADRS.TXT containing the names and addresses of all the people you know. If you change something because somebody moved, the new file size and revision date and time will automatically be logged in the directory for you. Sometimes this won't happen right away, especially when you've worked with a file via a network. Then, you must use File Manager's Refresh command to update the listings in the directory window. *See also* DIRECTORY, DIRECTORY TREE, FILE MANAGER, *and* WINDOWS.

Disk caching

Disk caching is a way of speeding up the operation of a computer. Some of the most frequently used data on the hard disk is placed into a special section of RAM (random-access memory); this section is called a *cache* (pronounced "cash").

Head movements. Whenever you need to read data from, or write data onto, a hard disk, the read/write heads must move to the correct locations on the hard-disk platters. This requires that the platters rotate, and also that the heads move back and forth. The system is designed so that the amount of mechanical movement is as small as possible, but it still isn't anywhere near as fast as electronic RAM.

In some applications, the computer needs to get the same data from the hard disk over and over. This involves repetitious mechanical action by the hard disk mechanism. Because head movement and platter rotation are comparatively slow, the program runs at a sluggish pace. When the most-often-needed data is stored in electronic memory rather than on the hard disk, on the other hand, the system speeds up.

Virtual drive. The drawing shows how disk caching works. The hard disk is at left, and the RAM is at right. Three often-used units of data are shown as arcs on a platter labeled DATA 1, DATA 2, and DATA

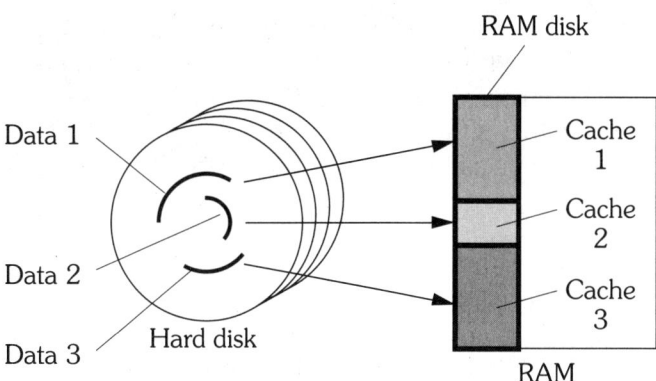
Hard disk data is stored in RAM.

3. This is a hypothetical example; there might be less than or more than three data units in a real-life situation.

In disk caching, the often-used data units are stored in a cache within RAM. In the drawing, the cache is split into three sections: CACHE 1, CACHE 2, and CACHE 3, one for each data section. When the CPU (central processing unit) needs the data, it can get it electronically from the RAM, instead of making the hard disk go through its motions. This saves a moment of time. When the data must be accessed over and over during the running of a program, the time moments add up. In some cases, a program will run several times faster with disk caching than without.

Limitations. There is a limit to how much data can be stored via disk caching. In some applications, this limit is not a problem; in others, it places a constraint on how much speed improvement can be realized.

If there is a power failure or if the computer crashes and you have to reboot it, you'll lose all the data in RAM. This is because RAM is not a permanent magnetic medium; it's *volatile memory.* If you want to permanently save RAM data, you must copy it to *nonvolatile memory* such as the hard disk or a diskette.

If you have MS-DOS version 5.0 or later, these limitations are largely overcome. Later versions of MS-DOS have a file called SMARTDRV.SYS. With SMARTDRV.SYS, essential data in RAM is automatically updated and backed up on the hard disk at regular intervals. This eliminates the risk of a massive data loss in the event of an unexpected mishap. *See also* CACHE MEMORY, DOS, HARD DISK, NONVOLATILE MEMORY, RANDOM-ACCESS MEMORY, *and* VOLATILE MEMORY.

Disk capacity

In personal computers, most nonvolatile (permanent) memory is on hard disk, diskette, and CD-ROM. These can all be called, generically, *disks.* The amount of data that can be stored on a disk is measured in bytes, kilobytes (K), megabytes (MB), or gigabytes (GB), and is known as the *disk capacity.*

Disk capacity

Magnetic diskette. *Diskettes* are commonly available in two sizes: 5.25 inches across and 3.5 inches across. Both have square cases, and both types come in either of two densities: high-density (HD) or double-density (DD). The earliest diskettes had data on one side; these have been largely replaced by double-sided (DS) diskettes, with data on both sides.

Most people today use HD/DS diskettes. The 5.25-inch version can store up to 1.2MB of data when formatted for an IBM-compatible PC, while the smaller, 3.5-inch diskette can hold 1.44MB. Some older PCs, however, can only make use of DD diskettes. These hold a few hundred KB, about one-third to one-half the capacity of HD diskettes. You can sometimes use a DD diskette in an HD drive, but not vice versa.

A new, very-high-density magnetic diskette has recently been introduced that can hold several dozen megabytes of data. Known as a *Floptical diskette*, it uses optical devices to guide the read/write head along the magnetic tracks.

Hard disk. A hard-disk drive contains several rigid disks, called *platters*, arranged on top of one another. Hard-disk drives vary in capacity up to several gigabytes. You can store and retrieve information more quickly to and from a hard disk than with diskettes because the hardware works faster.

Hard disks are installed in the main units of desktop computers. Smaller hard disks fit inside notebook or laptop computers. External hard disk drives are also available. The platter size and enclosure size varies, depending on the number of platters, the sizes of the platters, and the overall drive capacity. As the technology for magnetic media improves, hard drives are getting physically smaller while their capacity is increasing.

CD-ROM. There is a practical limit to how much data can be stored on magnetic media. The main factors are the size of the magnetic grains on the disk surface and the sharpness of the "focus" of the drive's read/write head. Much greater data density can be achieved if visible light, rather than a magnetic field, conveys the data. Laser beams are used for this purpose in a medium known as *compact disc, read-only memory (CD-ROM)*.

A CD-ROM stores computer data on the surface of a plastic disc less than five inches across. The CD-ROM is like an audio CD except for the type of data it holds. Audio CDs are known for their excellent fidelity. This results from digitization of the music in the form of millions upon millions of microscopic pits. It takes a tremendous number of binary digits (bits), etched as pits on the plastic disk surface, to obtain this sound quality. In fact, a single CD can hold upwards of 650MB, making it ideal for use with digital machines such as personal computers.

The table shows the data storage capacities of typical magnetic and optical disks today. They range from 360K to over 1000MB. The biggest hard disks can store more than 2000 times as much data as the smallest diskettes.

Disk capacity in kilobytes (K) and megabytes (MB)

Storage medium	Diameter	Density	Storage capacity
Diskette	3.5 inches	DD	720K to 800K
Diskette	5.25 inches	DD	360K
Diskette	3.5 inches	HD	1.44MB to 2.88MB
Diskette	5.25 inches	HD	1.2MB
Hard disk in desktop PC	Varies	—	40MB to 1000MB+
Hard disk in notebook PC	Varies	—	(None) to 100MB+
CD-ROM	4.72 inches	Massive!	650MB

Expectations. The drawing at A (top of page 310) is an area graph showing the capacities of 5.25-inch DD and HD diskettes, compared with a 100MB hard disk (a relatively small hard disk). The drawing at B is a pie graph showing the 100MB hard disk as it compares with a 650MB CD-ROM. What does the future hold? The drawing at C is a volume graph. It compares the CD-ROM with a hypothetical *beta-particle CD-ROM* (not yet devised, but a plausible idea). This super-high-density medium might have a *terabyte (TB)* of capacity. That's 1024GB—more than 1,000,000,000,000 (one trillion) bytes. *See also* BETA-PARTICLE CD-ROM, BYTE, CD-ROM, DISKETTE, DOUBLE-DENSITY DISKETTE, DOUBLE-SIDED DISKETTE, FLOPTICAL DISKETTE AND DRIVE, GIGABYTE, HARD DISK, HIGH-DENSITY DISKETTE, KILOBYTE, MEGABYTE, MEMORY, *and* TERABYTE.

Disk drive A/B/C/D

Most PCs have a hard disk these days. In addition, there's always at least one diskette drive. On IBM-compatible PCs, these drives have designators indicated by letters of the alphabet.

The letters A and B refer to diskette drives. If you have just one diskette drive, it is usually called *drive A*. If you then install a second one, it becomes *drive B*. You might have a CD-ROM drive, rather than a conventional diskette drive, in one of these drive bays. The CD-ROM drive might be designated *drive D*. Practically all PCs come with two diskette drive bays, even if there's only one diskette drive actually installed when you first buy the machine.

Diskette

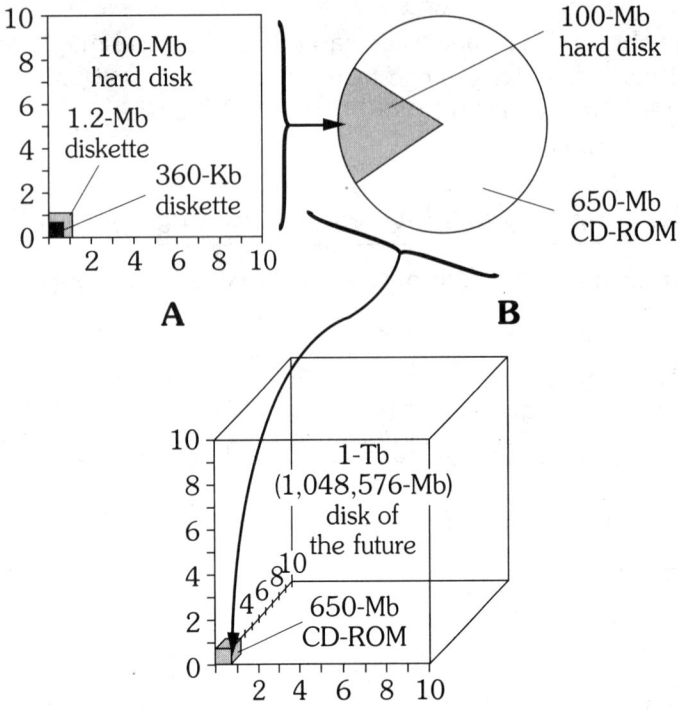

Diskette capacity versus hard disk (A); hard disk versus CD-ROM (B); CD-ROM versus hypothetical future disk (C).

The drive letter C refers to the hard disk. When you first power up (switch on) your computer, this drive is normally the *default* drive. If you are in DOS and you type a command without a drive designator, the PC will assume that you mean drive C. You can change the default drive to drive A by simply typing A: and pressing Enter. If you want to change the default drive back to the hard disk, you need to tell the computer to do this by typing C: and pressing Enter.

In a graphical user interface (GUI) such as Windows, disk drives are selected by double-clicking the mouse on certain icons. These icons usually look like tiny drive slots and are labeled A, B, C, and so on. The drawing (top of opposite page) shows the locations of drives A, B, and C in a typical PC. This particular unit does not have CD-ROM capability built-in, although the user might choose to add an external CD-ROM drive someday. This CD-ROM drive would be designated drive D. *See also* CD-ROM, DEFAULT, DISKETTE DRIVE, DOS, DRIVE BAY, *and* HARD DISK.

Diskette

A *diskette* is a magnetic medium for storing computer data and software. Diskettes are common in personal computing.

Diskette

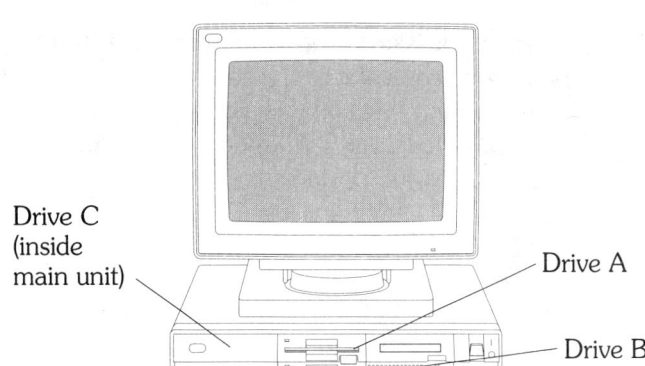

Locations of drives in a typical desktop PC.

Size and density. Diskettes are found in two standard sizes. One is 5.25 inches across and is housed in a flexible, thin, square case. Because the case is flexible, this type of diskette is sometimes called a *floppy disk* (see part A of the drawing). The other common size is 3.5 inches across. It has a rigid, square case (B in the drawing).

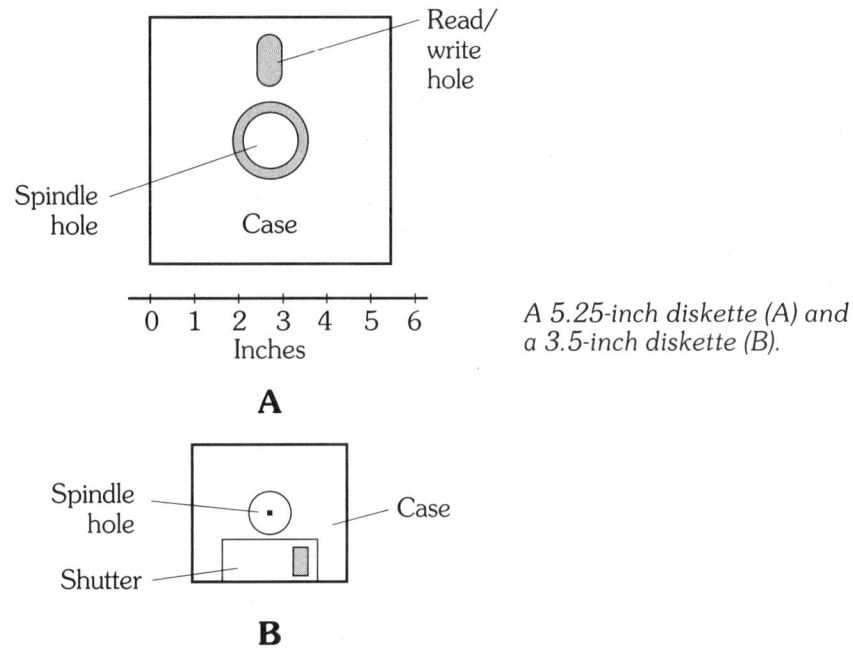

A 5.25-inch diskette (A) and a 3.5-inch diskette (B).

A 5.25-inch high-density (HD) diskette can store 1.2MB (1.2 million bytes) of data when it has been formatted for an IBM-compatible PC. The 3.5-inch diskette, while physically smaller, can store slightly more data, about 1.44MB. Sometimes you'll come across a double-density (DD) diskette, capable of storing considerably less data than HD types.

Small and light. An HD diskette has room for more than one million characters of text, equivalent to a long novel, while taking up far less volume than a bound book and weighing much less. You can keep a library of diskettes for your PC. Imagine how much data could be stored on several shelves full of diskettes!

Diskettes can store graphics and sound as well as text. You've heard the saying, "A picture is worth a thousand words." In a PC system, a picture can equal upwards of 10,000 words. Graphics and sound take up large amounts of computer memory. The more detailed an image, the more space it requires on a diskette. For high-volume graphics and sound storage, *CD-ROM* is often used instead of diskettes.

Commercial software packages take up huge amounts of memory, and a single package might need several dozen high-density diskettes for all its files. Often-used software is therefore best stored on a hard disk.

In recent years, the most sophisticated programs, especially those involving graphics, have become available on CD-ROM. In general, the CD-ROM versions of software are cheaper, have more features, and are easier to install than diskette versions. This is one of the main reasons why, if you're in the market for a new computer, it is a good idea to buy one with a built-in CD-ROM drive.

Reading and writing. The data is written on and read from a diskette by a read-write head. No two data bits are ever separated by more than the diameter of the diskette. This is a big advantage of diskettes over magnetic tapes, which can be hundreds of feet long. The arrangement of the head and disk in a diskette drive resembles an old-fashioned turntable. The diskette spins, and the head moves back and forth, so the head can reach any point on the surface. The head also moves up and down, in the same way the arm of a turntable lifts and drops.

Drawing C shows a magnified, cutaway view of a diskette as it moves underneath a read/write head. In this drawing, the head can move toward or away from you (radially on the disk). It can lift up to prevent unwanted reading and writing. It drops down when data is to be read from or written onto the magnetic medium. *See also* CD-ROM, DISK CAPACITY, DISKETTE DRIVE, DOUBLE-DENSITY DISKETTE, HARD DISK, HEAD, *and* HIGH-DENSITY DISKETTE.

Diskette drive

Virtually all PCs have at least one built-in *diskette drive*, and many have two or more, in addition to a hard disk.

Common types. Two sizes of magnetic diskette are standard with PCs: 5.25 inches across and 3.5 inches across. These diskettes need

Diskette drive

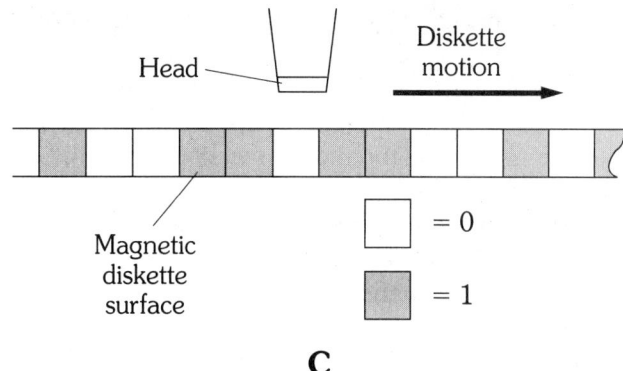

C

A magnified view of how a diskette works.

the right size drive. You can't use a 5.25-inch diskette in a 3.5-inch drive, or vice versa.

Some older drives can read and write only on double-density (DD) diskettes. The newer drives can work either with DD diskettes or with high-density (HD) diskettes. *See also* DISK CAPACITY *and* DISKETTE.

Writing and reading. A diskette drive reads data from and writes data onto a magnetic surface. This happens as the disk rotates, moving underneath a tiny electromagnet called the *head*. The construction of the diskette drive is similar to that of an old-fashioned phonograph. The data is in circular arcs, called *tracks*, on the diskette. Any point on the diskette can be reached by diskette rotation and back-and-forth head movement, as shown in the drawing.

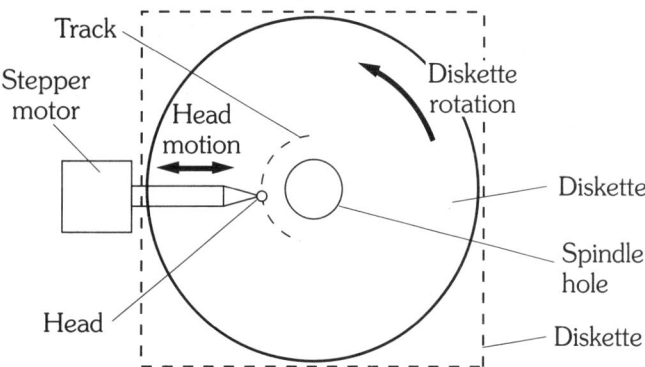

Simplified inside view of a 5.25-inch drive.

When data is written onto the diskette, the head magnetizes tiny spots on the diskette, which is coated with iron oxide like magnetic tape. There are two possible states: 1 (magnetized) and 0 (reverse magnetized). The head writes a long string of data bits (binary digits) onto the diskette surface.

When data is to be read from the diskette, the surface moves beneath the head. As each magnetized spot passes, a tiny current pulse occurs

Disk Operating System

in the head, representing a digit 1. As each reverse magnetized spot passes, the PC takes note of the reversal, and interprets this as a digit 0.

Other drive types. A new technology, called *very-high density (VHD)*, allows for the storage and reading of several dozen megabytes (MB) on a 3.5-inch diskette, compared with 1.44MB on a conventional HD 3.5-inch diskette. Special tracks, called *servo tracks*, help guide the magnetic head along the correct data tracks on the diskettes.

A technology similar to VHD is employed by the *Floptical diskette and drive*. In this system, the head is guided over the surface of a disk by means of a laser. This allows more precise alignment than is possible otherwise.

Another special diskette drive is called a *Bernoulli box*. This is like a plug-in hard disk system. You can easily change from one drive to another, so you have the versatility of diskettes with the storage capacity of a small hard disk.

An entirely nonmechanical form of mass storage, capable of holding several megabytes, is provided by *PCMCIA standard adapter cards*. These have the extra advantage of high speed because there are no moving parts involved in the reading/writing processes.

The amount of data that can be stored on any medium can be increased by *data compression*. This comes in the form of software that you run to reduce the amount of space taken up by each data file. The data is recovered by means of decompression.

Another type of diskette, called *CD-ROM* for *compact-disc, read-only memory*, uses entirely optical methods to read data. A CD-ROM needs its own drive. This type of diskette has very high capacity: 650MB or more. Its main limitation is that you cannot overwrite data on it without special equipment. *See also* BERNOULLI BOX, CD-ROM, DATA COMPRESSION, FLOPTICAL DISKETTE AND DRIVE, MASS STORAGE, *and* PCMCIA STANDARD ADAPTER CARDS.

Disk Operating System

See DOS.

Display

The *display* is the screen on which you see data and graphics as you work at a computer. It's your window to the "mind" of the machine.

There are two main types of display. In a desktop computer, the display is usually in a separate unit called the *monitor*. It has a cathode-ray tube (CRT), similar to the picture tube in a color television set. In a laptop computer, the display is built into the main unit. It's

Distributed processing system

thin and flat, and it utilizes technologies known as *liquid-crystal display (LCD)* or *plasma display*.

Modern CRT displays can show a wide range of color and have excellent *image resolution*, or ability to show fine detail. The LCD and plasma display can also show color, although some laptop PCs still show only black-and-white. Image resolution, visibility, and response speed of these displays is improving year by year. *See also* ACTIVE MATRIX, CATHODE-RAY TUBE, COLOR GRAPHICS ADAPTER, DESKTOP COMPUTER, ENHANCED GRAPHICS ADAPTER, IMAGE RESOLUTION, LAPTOP COMPUTER, LIQUID-CRYSTAL DISPLAY, MONITOR, NOTEBOOK COMPUTER, SUPER VIDEO GRAPHICS ARRAY, *and* VIDEO GRAPHICS ARRAY.

Display adapter

See COLOR GRAPHICS ADAPTER, ENHANCED GRAPHICS ADAPTER, SUPER VIDEO GRAPHICS ARRAY, *and* VIDEO GRAPHICS ARRAY.

Distributed processing system

A *distributed processing system* is a type of local area network (LAN) in which every workstation is a complete PC. The drawing shows a diagram of a distributed processing system with five workstations.

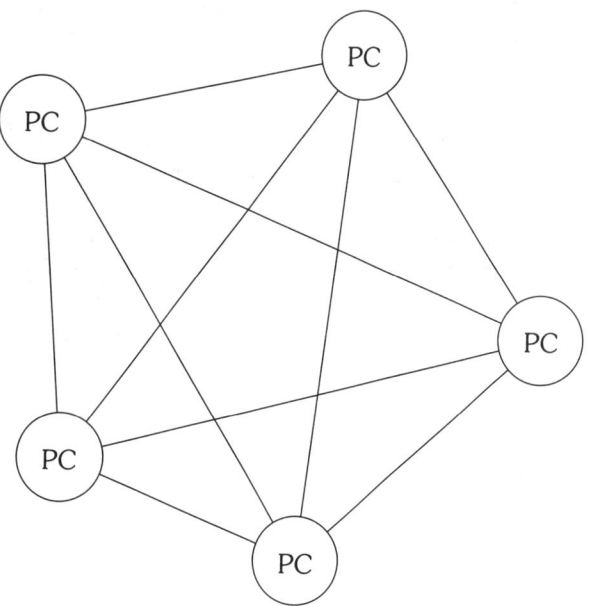

In a distributed processing system, every workstation is a PC.

One advantage of a distributed processing system is that all users can do computing at all times. This is true even when communications links fail, since there is a computer at every workstation. In networks where some of the workstations are *dumb terminals*, without the capability for computing, a failure of the links will render the dumb terminals useless because their access to data and software will be cut off.

Another advantage of a distributed processing system is the fact that each workstation, or *node*, can have software and data chosen especially for the person who uses that node. For example, a secretary might want database and word processing software; an accountant would probably want spreadsheet software.

In a distributed processing system, data is shared among the computers, all of which have equal importance. No single machine dominates the system. This kind of arrangement is known as a *peer-to-peer network*. It's easy for users at the various workstations to communicate with each other in such a system. Each workstation has immediate and equal access to the data of all the PCs in the network. Every PC is far more powerful than it would be all by itself, because it has a much larger *effective* data storage capacity. A LAN in which some workstations consist of dumb terminals has a powerful central computer to which all of the workstations are linked. Such a network is called a *multiuser system*. *See also* DUMB TERMINAL, LOCAL AREA NETWORK, MULTIUSER SYSTEM, PEER-TO-PEER NETWORK, *and* WORKSTATION.

Dithering

A monitor creates an image with thousands of little dots. Each dot can only have certain shades of color, but when the dots are intermingled, or *dithered*, and you look at the screen from a distance, you see many different qualities of color.

Hue and saturation. The shade, or essence, of a color is called *hue*. Hue is a direct function of the wavelength of the light you see. There are three primary hues: red, green, and blue (RGB). These can be mixed in various ratios to produce all the colors imaginable. This is called the *RGB color model*. A good RGB monitor can show hundreds or even thousands of hues, in a range from deep red, through orange, yellow, green, blue, and indigo, all the way to deep violet.

A color monitor can also show degrees of color *saturation*, or "vividness." You've seen brilliant, fluorescent colors; they have high saturation. As a color gets more subdued and washed-out, the saturation progressively decreases.

A monitor displays hues and saturation levels by dithering the colored dots on the screen. Each individual dot can vary only in its intensity, ranging from black to bright red, green, or blue. By dithering, it's possible to obtain enough different colors to get a realistic image.

Image resolution. The clarity or sharpness of a video picture is known as the *image resolution*. The sharpest possible images are produced when the monitor is required to show only bright, pure primary hues.

The more different hues and saturations an image contains, the poorer its resolution. This is because primary hues must be mixed, and sometimes also combined with gray, to get intermediate hues and/or lower levels of saturation. The mixing is accomplished by dithering the screen dots in various ways. Dithering makes the lines of distinction less precise between regions of nonprimary colors compared with regions of pure primary colors.

Monitor types. Computer monitors are designed to prevent image blurring from becoming objectionable under most conditions. There are several types of color monitors available; some have better image resolution than others. If you need to display extreme detail or if you intend to work with fast-changing, animated images, you should get the most advanced monitor you can afford.

For image resolution and color reproduction quality, an SVGA (super video graphics array) monitor is excellent. If fast-moving images must be displayed, a noninterlaced monitor is preferable to an interlaced monitor. *See also* ENHANCED GRAPHICS ADAPTER, IMAGE RESOLUTION, MONITOR, RASTER, RGB COLOR MODEL, SUPER VIDEO GRAPHICS ARRAY, *and* VIDEO GRAPHICS ARRAY.

Docking station

A *docking station* is a unit that allows you to connect a laptop or notebook PC to peripherals. The unit is like a heavy base or cabinet into which the computer can slide. In effect, a docking station converts a laptop computer into a desktop computer.

The drawing is a functional block diagram showing one possible docking station arrangement. Peripherals include a printer, a modem, a CRT monitor, an extra hard disk, an extra diskette drive, and a CD-ROM drive.

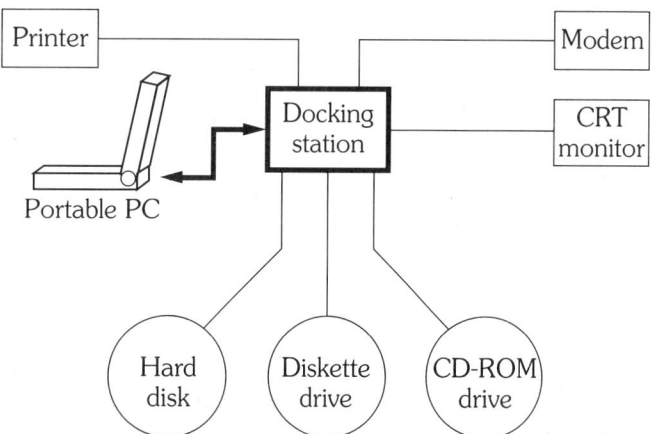

A docking station lets a laptop PC work like a desktop unit.

Document

Assets. The best thing about a docking station is its convenience. You buy the best laptop computer you can afford, so you have state-of-the-art hardware everywhere you go. When you get back home or to the office, you simply insert the laptop PC into the docking station and resume work. You need not transfer data from one computer to another. (It's wise, of course, to back up data on diskette, and also on an external hard disk if you have one.)

A good docking station simplifies the connection and removal of the PC. There are no cables to screw or plug in, nor to unscrew or pull out. There's no way to accidentally hook up a cable to the wrong port.

With a laptop PC and a docking station, it becomes possible to get along without a desktop computer. In recent years, laptop computers have been refined to the point that they're nearly as fast and powerful as desktop units.

Limitations. Some traveling PC users prefer to have two computers: a desktop unit and a laptop unit. You might think this would cost far more than a portable PC and a docking station, but that's not necessarily true. With a moderately priced laptop for the road and a solid desktop PC at home or in the office, the two-computer arrangement need not be any more expensive than an expensive laptop and a docking station.

Perhaps the most serious drawback of the docking-station scheme is that you'll end up toting the "main brain" of the computer system around. This makes some people uneasy. They'd rather have a cheap portable for travel. If the laptop is your only computer, you'll naturally want a top-of-the-line model. This means you'll carry around a valuable piece of equipment containing your most current data files. If the machine is stolen or damaged, the loss of data and the financial setback might be considerable. If the laptop is not your primary computer, the loss will not be as great.

Another advantage of a home unit and a separate portable is that it's extremely unlikely that the two computers will go down at the same time. If you have a desktop and a laptop, when one of them needs servicing, you can take it into the shop and still be able to work on the other machine. *See also* DESKTOP COMPUTER *and* LAPTOP COMPUTER.

Document

A *document* is a computer file that contains information including text, graphics, and possibly animation or sounds. Such a file can be printed on paper (minus the sounds and animation, of course). It can also be left on diskettes, hard disk, CD-ROM (compact disk, read-only memory), or other mass storage medium without ever being rendered in hardcopy (paper) form.

In the old days. Years ago, the word *document* referred to a special, perhaps extremely valuable set of papers. A good example is the *Declaration of Independence*. Another example is the deed to a piece of property, such as a house. It was a hardcopy, preserved in a special place, that was rarely, if ever, changed.

During the 20th century, the meaning of the term *document* expanded to include instruction manuals, reports, and other written material that was subject to rewriting from time to time. Still, though, when speaking of a document, people were referring to pieces of paper.

Nowadays. Computers have expanded the meaning of the word "document." Technically, almost any text, sound, or image can be put on disk. You might take a great work from ancient times and transcribe it to disk so it can be printed out an unlimited number of times, showing all the detail of the original, right down to the tobacco stains.

The hard disk of your PC, as well as your diskettes, contain numerous documents. You can't generally grab these documents and hold them out in front of you. Even when you can (for example, a diskette with just one document file on it), you can't make any sense out of it without the help of the PC. Document files can be changed with a few keystrokes. A document in RAM will evaporate the instant you switch your PC off.

Size of a file. Document files are common in word processing. These files are often tagged with a special *filename extension*, such as .TXT or .DOC. The text of this book was written on a PC and split up into documents according to letter of the alphabet. The filenames, in the original version of the text, were PC.A, PC.B, PC.C, and so on.

The size of a document on disk is not expressed in pages, but in *bytes* (characters). The ratio of bytes per page of text depends on the application and on the size of the font used in the hardcopy. It also depends on whether the hardcopy is single-spaced or double-spaced. In word processing, an 8.5-by-11-inch page with normal margins, double-spacing, and a font size of 10 will equal about 1000 bytes of text. *See also* BYTE, DATABASE, DOCUMENT COMPARISON, DOCUMENT IMAGE PROCESSING, DOCUMENT WINDOW, HARD COPY, SPREADSHEET, *and* WORD PROCESSING.

Document comparison

Document comparison is the process of finding and highlighting the differences between two nearly identical files.

Suppose you are coauthoring a science-fiction novel about the first computerized journey beyond the solar system with someone. You're good at theoretical mathematics and computer science, but you're weak in applied science. Your coauthor knows a lot about physics, chemistry, and astronomy, but can't deal with pure math or computer lingo. You live in Miami; she lives in New York.

When two or more authors write anything with a plot, all the authors must know the whole story, even if from different angles. You must constantly exchange excerpts as you write the book, so you agree that you'll read all your friend's text, and she'll read all of yours. If you find misstatements about computers in her text, you can correct them. Likewise, she can change mistakes you might make about physics. When you get a file back after having sent it to her, you can immediately see the changes she made in your text because they are highlighted by a document comparison utility. Likewise, she can see the changes you make. In this way, you can keep your past mistakes in mind while writing new text, so that you don't repeat errors. Ideally, you'll eventually come out with a great book. Even if the novel is not so good, however, the document comparison utility can at least help you make it consistent. *See also* WORD PROCESSING.

Document image processing

Information need not be stored on paper; it can also take the form of computer files. Even artwork and music can be created, stored, and changed on diskette or hard disk. Huge amounts of data can be permanently filed on CD-ROM. The computerization of information, particularly graphic images, is called *document image processing (DIP)*.

Space/time/money savings. When documents are stored in magnetic or optical media, they take up far less space than in paper form. A high-density magnetic diskette can contain upwards of one million characters of text, the equivalent of a long novel. A CD-ROM can store a large encyclopedia or unabridged dictionary, complete with illustrations, and still have plenty of room left over.

Accessing a file store in a DIP system is fast, as long as you know the filename. There's no need to shuffle through drawers full of file folders and paper. Just type in the filename, and the data is right there on screen. You can also update it easily without making a single stroke of a pencil or pen, and without correction fluid or erasures. You can use a printer to make a hardcopy if you want.

When you move your office from one place to another, you'll appreciate the savings in bulk and weight that DIP offers. If there's a fire and your system is destroyed, you'll keep data loss to a minimum if you have archives that contain a backup of every file. This will save you an incalculable sum of money and countless headaches.

Shortcomings. If DIP has so many advantages over paper-based data storage, why aren't all offices paperless? The answer lies partly in human nature and partly in the limitations of computers.

Although DIP has advantages, there are some very real pitfalls. One problem is that *everyone* who accesses the files must know how to do it. Some people have *cyberphobia*, an exaggerated and often irrational fear and distrust of computers. Even if your employees or coworkers don't have this problem, people must be trained to use the computer. Human beings resist changes in their routines. An abrupt and complete switch from paper to DIP will cause short-term chaos in any office.

Another problem is that computers are unforgiving of errors. If a typo occurs in the storage of a document, resulting in a bogus or incorrect filename, you might have great difficulty pinpointing that data again, while in a physical file cabinet, you stand a chance. Finding a misplaced DIP file, especially in a large system, is akin to finding a toothpick in a wheat field.

The future. The advantages of DIP outweigh the problems. Computers aren't perfect, and neither are PC users. However, errors don't occur as often in DIP systems as in paper-based systems.

In the coming years, as PCs get more powerful and more tolerant of human error, paper-based offices will become antiquated. The process will be slow, however. Eventually, if computer technology and popularity keep advancing, along with decreasing cost, the paperless office will become standard. *See also* OPTICAL CHARACTER RECOGNITION, OPTICAL SCANNER, *and* PAPERLESS OFFICE.

Document window

One of the biggest advantages of a graphical user interface (GUI) such as Macintosh or Windows is that you can work in more than one document file at a time. The full-screen window is called the *application window*. Within this, you can have several different *document windows*.

The drawing shows the general appearance of document windows within an application window. The bar at the top of the screen, extending all the way across, is the *title bar* for the application window. Just below this is the *menu bar*. Within the smaller document windows, there are title bars but no menu bars.

To see the usefulness of having multiple document windows, consider the many cross-references in this book. They were inserted as the book was written. To ensure that the cross-references were valid, the text had to be constantly checked against an updated list of article titles. Thus, it was convenient to write the running text in one document window, while the list of titles was held in another document window. Without multiple document windows, checking cross-references would require closing a particular article file, opening the titles list file, checking the cross-references, closing the titles list

Domain of function

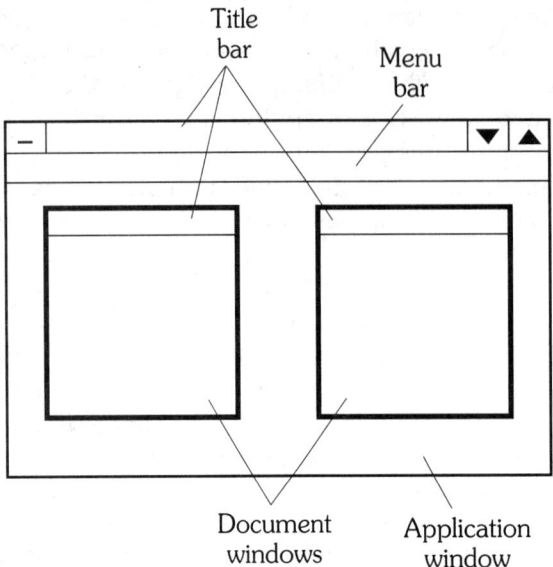

The document window appears inside the application window.

file, and then going back to the article file to make corrections. As you might imagine, this would be rather tedious. *See also* GRAPHICAL USER INTERFACE.

Domain of function

The *domain* of a mathematical function is the set of values for which the function is defined. Every x in the domain of a function f is mapped by f onto a definite, single value y. Also, any x not in the domain is not mapped onto anything by the function f.

Suppose you are given the function $f(x) = +x^{1/2}$. (The ½ power is the square root.) The graph of this function is shown in the drawing. Note that the function is not defined for negative values of x, and is also not defined, as shown in the drawing, for x = 0. The function f(x) has values x if, and only if, x > 0. Therefore the domain of f is the set of positive real numbers.

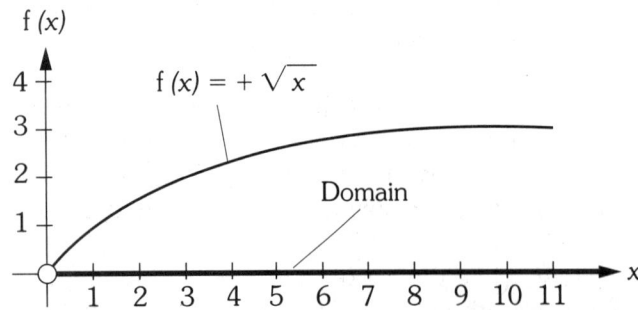

In this case, the domain of function is the positive x axis.

The rendition of this function, as shown by the drawing, is a good example of a graph that might be created with analytical graphics software. Computers work extensively with functions, both analog and digital. Functions are also important in the operation of computerized navigation, location, and measurement systems. *See also* ANALYTICAL GRAPHICS, DEPENDENT VARIABLE, FUNCTION, INDEPENDENT VARIABLE, *and* RANGE OF FUNCTION.

Don't-care state

In a logic function, there are some logic states that don't affect the outcome. This happens when a logic function is undefined for certain input combinations. When this occurs, the logical conditions that have no effect on the output are called *don't-care states*.

Suppose you want to represent the decimal numbers 0 through 9 in binary form. Then you will need four binary places, obtaining

```
0 = 0000    5 = 0101
1 = 0001    6 = 0110
2 = 0010    7 = 0111
3 = 0011    8 = 1000
4 = 0100    9 = 1001
```

This does not use all possible four-digit binary numbers. There are six left over: 1010, 1011, 1100, 1101, 1110, and 1111, corresponding to decimal numbers 10 through 15. These numbers are undefined unless they are defined by default.

Suppose that the binary numbers 1010, 1100, and 1110 are all assigned to the decimal value 8, and the binary numbers 1011, 1101, and 1111 are assigned to the decimal value 9. This prevents the confusion that might occur when some binary numbers are left undefined. The values of the two middle digits in these binary numbers are don't-care states. When the first (leftmost) binary digit is 1, the last (rightmost) binary digit alone is sufficient for the computer to know whether the decimal number is 8 or 9. If the rightmost binary digit is 0, then the decimal value is 8. If the last binary digit is 1, the decimal default is 9. The machine disregards the middle two digits in these cases. *See also* BINARY DATA *and* BINARY NUMBER SYSTEM.

DOS

All IBM-compatible computers can use a scheme called *DOS* (pronounced "dahs"), which stands for the *disk operating system*. Several variations of DOS are marketed by different companies. Microsoft's version, for example, is called *MS-DOS*; IBM's version is *PC-DOS*; Digital Research created a version called *DR-DOS* ("doctor DOS") that is now owned by Novell; Compaq has a version called *CPQ-DOS*.

DOS prompt

Command-driven software. In DOS, you work with commands. That is, you type certain things on a keyboard to give the computer its instructions. To open the file in which this material was written using a DOS-based word processing program called XyWrite for DOS, you would type the following commands:

```
EDITOR
LOAD PANSONIC.PRN
CALL PC.D
```

The first command starts XyWrite's Editor program. The next command loads the XyWrite program for a Panasonic printer. The last command opens the file PC.D, containing text for the letter D of this book. (Note: CALL is a command peculiar to XyWrite; it has an entirely different meaning outside of that particular word processing program.) After each command, you would press Enter. Pressing the Enter key is usually the signal to DOS that it should act on your command.

MS-DOS has been constantly improved over the years. You will therefore hear about MS-DOS versions 2.0, 3.0, 4.0, 5.0, 6.0, 6.2, and so on. Generally, the higher the number, the more powerful the software, in the sense that it can run programs faster and with more memory. As computer memory capacity expanded and user demands increased, Microsoft developed *Windows*. This software "sits on top of DOS," making it possible to work in a graphical user interface (GUI).

The future. As artificial intelligence (AI) evolves into PCs, you'll begin to see far more powerful operating systems than anything currently in existence. There will be new ways of giving commands. For consumer devices, look for computers with speech recognition and speech synthesis as standard features, allowing you to literally talk with PCs in plain English, Spanish, French, and other languages. *See also* COMMAND, COMMAND-DRIVEN SOFTWARE, DOS SHELL, MACINTOSH, SPEECH RECOGNITION, SPEECH SYNTHESIS, *and* WINDOWS.

DOS prompt

The *DOS prompt* is a letter followed by one or more symbols that tells you the PC is using DOS as its operating system. The letter indicates the default drive. In most computers this is initially C, which stands for the hard disk. You can change it to some other drive designator by typing that letter followed by a colon, and then pressing Enter. For example, if the default drive is drive C and you want to change the default to diskette drive A, you'd type A: and press Enter. The computer would respond with the letter A followed by one or more symbols, for example

```
A:\>
```

To switch the default back to drive C, you would type C:, press Enter, and the machine would respond

C:\>

For the DOS prompt to appear, you must "get into DOS." All DOS machines do this automatically when they are first switched on, although it is common for computers to switch automatically into Windows before you have a chance to see DOS. Once your PC has been powered up, you can switch between DOS and Windows at will. Generally, you type WIN at the C:\> prompt to go into Windows; when you exit Windows by, for example, double-clicking its control box, you go back into "pure DOS." *See also* COMMAND, DEFAULT, DOS, *and* WINDOWS.

DOS shell

Normally, when using DOS, you type instructions on the keyboard to tell the PC what to do. DOS is *command-driven software*, in contrast to Windows or Macintosh, which employ *graphical user interfaces (GUIs)*. One problem with command-driven software like DOS is that you must remember or look up commands. The *DOS shell* acts like a GUI, providing menus from which you can choose the commands. This makes DOS easier for beginners to use. It's like taking a multiple-choice test instead of a fill-in-the-blank test. The DOS shell, however, is not available in older versions of DOS.

Entering the DOS shell. If you use MS-DOS version 5.0 or later, your PC can be set to go into DOS shell as soon as you power up. Otherwise, as soon as you see the DOS prompt (C:\>), you can type DOSSHELL and press Enter to start the DOS shell.

When the PC goes into the DOS shell, the screen looks similar to that of Windows or Macintosh systems. That is, rather than text only, you'll see various regions on the screen with different colors and backgrounds. You might also see a directory tree, a list of files you can access, a list of programs you can run, and your disk drive options.

The screen. At the top of the DOS shell screen is a bar that runs all the way across, with *MS-DOS Shell* in the center. This is called the *title bar*. Below the title bar is another bar that also runs all the way across the screen with words that represent DOS commands. This is the *menu bar*. You can select commands from the keyboard, or you can use the mouse.

Below the menu bar you'll see *drive icons*. One of these will be highlighted; it will usually be drive C (the hard drive) unless you've changed the default drive. You can change the default drive by highlighting the appropriate icon.

The organization of the default drive will usually appear on the left side of the screen as a *directory tree*. This will change as you change the default drive. On the right side of the screen, you'll usually see a

DOS shell

list of the files available in the default directory. These will also change as you change the default directory.

About two-thirds of the way down from the top of the screen, there will usually be a bar that runs all the way across, with the word *Main* at the center. There will be several words in this box. You can select from these to have the PC do various things. For example, if you select Command Prompt, you leave the DOS shell and return to regular DOS. If you select Editor, you can do basic word processing. If you select QBasic, you can work in a simplified form of the BASIC programming language. If you select Disk Utilities, you can run various programs to maintain your hard disk or diskettes.

At the very bottom of the screen, you'll usually see yet another bar that runs all the way across. It tells you which keys to press to get different things to happen. For example, *Shift+F9=Command Prompt* means that you can press the Shift and F9 keys simultaneously, and you'll go back to regular DOS. At the extreme right of this bottom bar, you'll see the time. The drawing shows the general locations of different parts of a typical DOS shell screen.

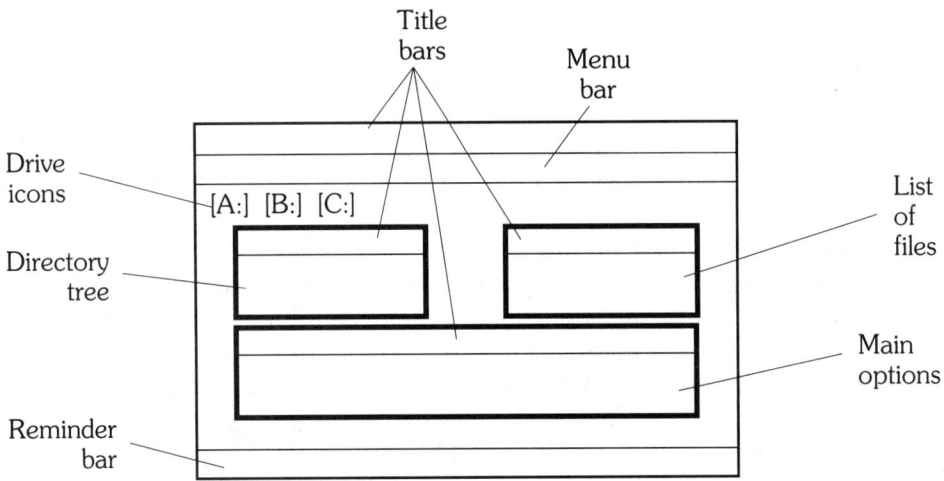

The main parts of a typical DOS shell screen.

Learning to use the DOS shell. A full description of the capabilities of the DOS shell is beyond the scope of this book. The best way to learn how it works is to consult the instructions for your system. If you get stuck, you can highlight Help in the menu bar.

Many people find the DOS shell easier to use than regular DOS because it isn't necessary to memorize as many things. Others prefer to use regular DOS, even though it's more complicated. Regular DOS can be faster than the DOS shell, once you've memorized the commands and become proficient at using them. *See also* COMMAND-

DRIVEN SOFTWARE, DOS, GRAPHICAL USER INTERFACE, *and* MENU-DRIVEN SOFTWARE.

Dot-matrix printer

For years, a popular printer for casual PC users has been the *dot-matrix printer.* You can get a decent dot-matrix printer for less than $200. If you can afford to spend more, you can get a good machine that will last a long time and hardly ever need maintenance.

How it works. The basic components of the dot-matrix printer are the *carriage*, the *print head*, and the *ribbon*. The carriage moves across the page, both left-to-right and right-to-left. Unlike a typewriter, which prints only when the carriage is moving from left to right, a dot-matrix printer prints in both directions. This reduces mechanical movement, thereby increasing speed and efficiency.

The print head contains a number of fine pins that strike the ribbon, causing ink to be laid down on the paper (see drawing A). The character or figure that is printed depends on which pins are fired, and also on the order in which they are fired. The print head in a modern dot-matrix printer has 24 pins in two vertical rows of 12 pins each. The pins in one row are slightly displaced from those in the other row, to help fill in the gaps and make the copy look less "dotty."

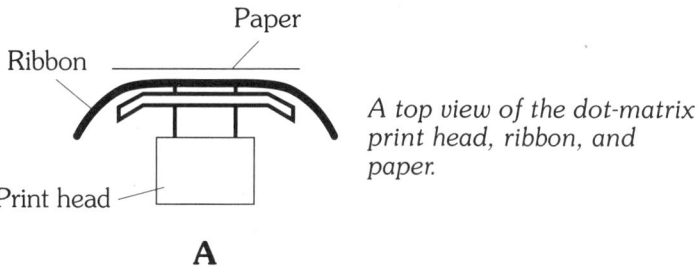

A top view of the dot-matrix print head, ribbon, and paper.

A

A closer look. Imagine time slowed down by a factor of 3600, so that one second seems like an hour. If you could perceive time moving that slowly, and if you had a powerful magnifying glass to watch the print head in action, you would see in detail how it works. The print head itself, viewed close-up, would look something like drawing B.

As the carriage glided across the page, you'd see certain pins in the print head jump out, laying ink down as tiny dots on the paper. Characters would form because of the precise sequence and pattern followed by the pins in the print head.

The carriage might make one, two, or even three passes over each spot on the page. Its speed would vary depending on whether you had

Dot-matrix printer

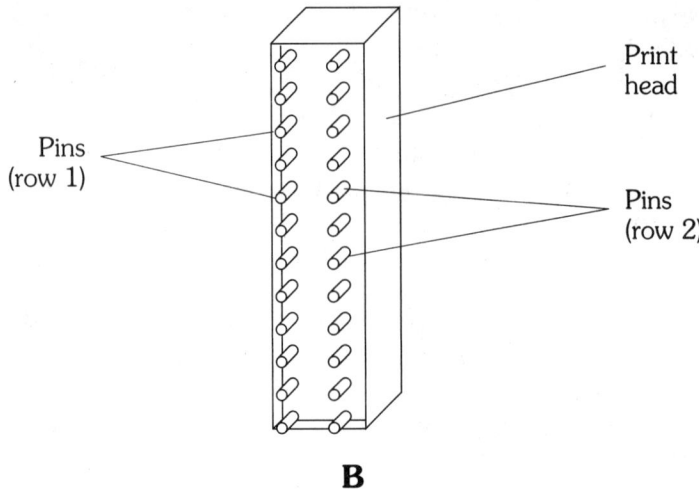

B

The business end of the print head.

selected draft mode for rough copies or one of the near-letter-quality (NLQ) modes for more important documents.

Advantages. Dot-matrix printers are inexpensive. A dot-matrix machine costs much less than a laser printer and somewhat less than an inkjet printer. Besides the fact that you pay less at the store for a dot-matrix unit, you also save in the long term. Dot-matrix printing costs only about one-third to one-half as much per page as other printing technologies. The dot-matrix machine needs only ribbon and ordinary paper, while other printers need expensive supplies such as toner and coated paper.

Dot-matrix printers are rugged and reliable. This lowers the maintenance cost with respect to most other printer types. It also reduces the number of times you'll suffer major inconvenience as a result of printer breakdown. As you know, machines have a way of malfunctioning at the worst possible time.

Because a dot-matrix machine is an impact printer, you can use it with carbon paper to get multiple copies. Dot-matrix printers are especially good when you produce large amounts of hard copy, and don't need to have top-notch quality. They can also handle various paper types and widths.

With a dot-matrix printer and fanfold paper, you can start the machine printing a long document, and then go do something else. The only thing you have to worry about is that the paper stacks up neatly while you're away.

Dot-matrix printers can produce graphic images, although the printout is rather sluggish. Still, the quality is reasonable, and the images photocopy nicely. Some dot-matrix printers can even print in color using a ribbon with several different inks on it. Color dot-matrix printers can produce fairly impressive graphics, but they are slow.

Shortcomings. One disadvantage of dot-matrix printers has traditionally been that they are noisy. Some older units are so loud that you can't talk on the telephone while printing. An office full of the things, all running at once, can produce a racket loud enough to derail anybody's train of thought.

Newer dot-matrix printers are designed to work more quietly. They fire the pins in a time-staggered fashion rather than in bursts. This dilutes the noise, so the sound peaks aren't so loud. The pin geometry is also different. Rather than using two straight, parallel rows, some new designs have the pins arranged in curved rows. New ways of feeding the paper and moving the carriage have been developed and are constantly being improved.

Another limitation of dot-matrix printers is that they produce lower-quality print than laser or inkjet printers. This shortcoming is being reduced with improved ribbons and printing techniques. Carbon-film ribbons allow dot-matrix printers to produce copy almost as good as that of a laser printer, although such ribbons don't last long. Also, dot-matrix printing continues to be considerably slower than other types of printing. *See also* COLOR PRINTER, DOTS PER INCH, IMPACT PRINTER, INKJET PRINTER, LASER PRINTER, *and* PRINTER.

Dot pitch

Dot pitch refers to the size of the dots on a monitor screen or in the copy produced by a printer. Dot pitch can be expressed as the diameter of the smallest dot, as the number of dots per centimeter (*dots/cm*), or as the number of dots per inch (*dots/in*).

In a monitor. The display on your monitor screen is made up of thousands of red, green, and blue (RGB) dots interwoven in a fine mesh. These dots blend together in your vision to produce a color image with various degrees of hue, saturation, and brightness.

The drawing shows how a dot is produced on a monitor. An electron beam scans rapidly across the screen. For each RGB primary color, there is a separate beam in the cathode-ray tube (CRT). The beams land on a phosphor coating on the inside surface of the screen. The brightness of the color depends on the intensity of the beam for that color. The dot diameter (pitch) is limited by a mask with holes in it. In general, the finer the mesh in the mask, the smaller the dots, and the closer together they can be. The dots should be as tiny and close together as possible for good *image resolution*. *See also* CATHODE-RAY TUBE, IMAGE RESOLUTION, *and* MONITOR.

Dots per inch

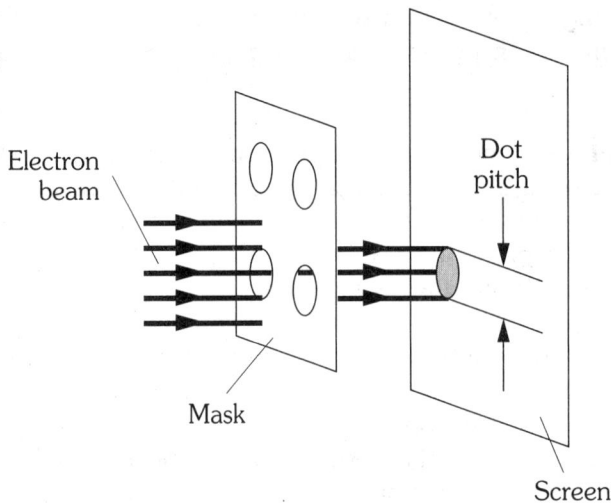

Diameter of a dot on the monitor screen.

In a printer. Years ago, dot-matrix printers had coarse dot pitch. The printout looked "dotty" and was difficult to read. Magazine editors used to hate receiving manuscripts produced by dot-matrix printers. This problem has been largely overcome by the dot pitch in modern dot-matrix printers. In general, the more dots per inch or centimeter, the easier the printout is to read.

A good dot-matrix printer creates *near-letter-quality (NLQ)* copy by passing over each letter two or more times. With each pass, the dots are laid down on the paper in slightly different places, so there is an overlap, reducing the "dotty" appearance. Use NLQ printout when producing important papers and reports. Draft mode, in which the printer passes just once over each letter, allows for faster printing, and can be used when print quality is not an important concern. *See also* DOT-MATRIX PRINTER *and* DOTS PER INCH.

Dots per inch

A printer can be used to print illustrations, or *graphics*, in addition to text. The amount of detail that can be printed depends on how fine the dots are in the image. The more dots in a given length or area, the better the quality of the printed grahic. *Dots per inch (DPI)* is an expression of the fineness of the image that a printer can produce.

The DPI rating of a dot-matrix printer is related to the number of pins in the print head. The more pins in the head, the greater the DPI. The DPI of inkjet and laser printers depends on several factors, including the fineness of the toner or ink, the sophistication of the software that runs the printer, and the technology used in the print engine. The DPI can be increased for any printer, however, if the head makes multiple passes over the paper, changing position slightly with each pass.

Printers with high DPI ratings can produce solid black characters without "jaggies"; they can also create many shades of gray. This is done by laying down dots in a fine pattern. The darkness of the shade is determined by the density of the dots on the page. *See also* DOT-MATRIX PRINTER, DOT PITCH, *and* JAGGIES.

Double-click

See CLICK.

Double-density diskette

A *double-density (DD) diskette* is a magnetic storage medium. You can find DD diskettes in computer stores and in office supply stores. A 5.25-inch DD diskette can store 360K when formatted for use with IBM-compatible PCs, a 3.5-inch DD diskette can hold 720K.

The earliest diskettes, single-density diskettes, could only hold a few kilobytes (K) of data. (A kilobyte is 1024 bytes or characters of text.) Engineers kept working to increase the number of bytes that could be stored in a given amount of disk surface area. Thus, single-density diskette technology was supplanted by DD technology, which in turn has been supplanted in recent years by the high-density (HD) diskette. *See also* DISK CAPACITY, DISKETTE, *and* HIGH-DENSITY DISKETTE.

Double-sided diskette

In the early days of personal computing, a diskette could accept and store data on only one of its two surfaces. This seems strange to today; why have a single-sided diskette when disks obviously have two available sides for storing data? Think of magnetic recording tape, however. It can only record on, and play back from, one of its two surfaces. The manufacture of a double-sided diskette did not turn out to be as easy in practice as it sounds in theory.

The engineering problems were eventually overcome, and now almost all PC diskettes are double-sided. You can recognize this by the abbreviation DS, or by the inclusion of the numeral 2, when purchasing diskettes. To make full use of a DS diskette, you need a diskette drive that can read and write from both surfaces. All newer computers have diskette drives of this type. *See also* DISK CAPACITY *and* DISKETTE.

DO/WHILE loop

In computer programming, it's often necessary to have the machine repeat something many times. A *DO/WHILE loop* is a method used in some types of software to accomplish this.

The loop gets its name from the fact that the computer does a set of things over and over while some other condition is gradually being fulfilled. When the condition has been fulfilled, the computer exits the loop.

Downlink

The sample code shows a DO/WHILE loop in the BASIC programming language. The machine counts up from one to 100 in increments of one. While it does this, it prints the sequence of numbers: 1, 2, 3, 4 and so on. When the number, N, reaches 101, the machine leaves the loop because the condition, N > 100, has been fulfilled. *See also* ENDLESS LOOP *and* LOOP.

DO/WHILE loop prints out a sequence of numbers

```
10  LET N=1
20  IF N > 100 GOTO 60
30  PRINT N
40  LET N=N+1
50  GOTO 20
60  END
```

Downlink

The term *downlink* refers to the signals that a communications satellite sends back to the earth. These signals are usually sent on ultra-high and microwave radio frequencies. Communications satellites are used in some telephone systems. If you have ever been online with your computer, chances are good that you've sent and received data via satellite for part of the route.

All communications satellites work in basically the same way: they receive signals on one set (band) of frequencies (the *uplink*), and retransmit them on another band (the *downlink*). The device that does this is called a *transponder*. These two sets of frequencies must be different enough so the transmitter doesn't interfere with the signals coming up from the earth.

Communications satellites are also used by amateur radio operators. If you have a "ham" radio operator's license, or are interested in getting one, you probably know this already. Hams communicate with their PCs over the radio in much the same way as you use your PC to hook up with other people via the telephone. This is called *packet radio*. Some of it is done through amateur radio satellites. *See also* AMATEUR RADIO, PACKET COMMUNICATIONS, SATELLITE DATA TRANSMISSION, *and* UPLINK.

Downloadable font

You can print hardcopy in various type styles, called *fonts*. Most printers have several built-in fonts, known as *hard fonts*. You can print many more fonts, some of them quite exotic, by using data stored on a hard disk or CD-ROM. The printer "learns" how to print such fonts by downloading them from the computer. Therefore, such a font is called a *downloadable font* or a *soft font*.

Advantages. The main advantage of downloadable fonts is the unlimited variety of type styles you can choose from. You can get your printer to write in ways you'd never dream of yourself. I once got a letter from a friend who had just purchased a CD-ROM full of fonts. It looked like a hummingbird had walked across the paper after jumping in an inkpad. It was almost impossible to read, but it was interesting.

With downloadable fonts, you can change fonts while the printer is in action. This is good for desktop publishing; it can also be valuable when printing mathematical and scientific papers, in which nonstandard symbols or Greek letters are often mixed in with normal type. A downloadable font might substitute an integral sign for the at-sign (@), a summation sign for the hashmark (#), a radical ($\sqrt{}$) in place of the percent sign, and so on. With substitutions like this, there are trillions of different possibilities for downloadable character sets. Computer experts can even write their own custom downloadable-font software.

Problems. One problem with downloadable fonts is that they take up printer memory. Some printers have trouble with this. The downloadable fonts can consume so much memory that they interfere with essential printing functions such as page layout. This can be overcome by installing extra memory chips in the printer, but that's not cheap.

Another problem with soft fonts is that the data must be downloaded every time you want to use the font; it isn't permanently stored in the printer. Downloading takes time, which can be an annoyance if you want to use several different soft fonts in a single document. The usual result is that general computer operation is slowed down somewhat.

If there is a power interruption, downloaded font data will be lost because it is in the printer's RAM, which is a volatile memory. The font data will have to be downloaded again when power returns. If you rarely have power interruptions, this might not be a major concern for you. But power interruptions, like all hardware failures, have a way of happening at inopportune times. If they are a problem at your location, consider purchasing an uninterruptible power supply (UPS). *See also* BUILT-IN FONT, DOWNLOADING, *and* FONT.

Downloading

Downloading is the process of receiving and storing data. You can download programs, files, graphics, or any other digital data into your RAM (random-access memory), diskette, or hard disk. You can download data from outside your PC system or from one part of your system to another. In general, downloading refers to the transfer of data from a more substantial place to a less substantial place.

Downward compatibility

Within your system. Whenever you open a file on a diskette or the hard disk, it is downloaded into RAM. The disk is more permanent than the RAM. Data will vanish from the RAM when you switch your PC off, but it will stay on diskette or hard disk. If you revise a file in RAM and then overwrite it on the diskette or hard disk, you are *uploading* the data.

Suppose you want to use special fonts that are not supplied standard with your printer. You can buy a diskette or CD-ROM with special downloadable fonts, and your printer will produce almost any set of symbols you want. *See also* DOWNLOADABLE FONT *and* UPLOADING.

From outside. You can download all kinds of information, programs, and even photographs through a modem by accessing an online service. You can get clip art and fonts, for example, by downloading them. Computer hobbyists exchange software this way all the time.

You must be cautious, however, when you download data from outside your system. It's important that you not use copyrighted material without obtaining the proper permissions and paying the required fees. Also, when you download software there is some risk of importing a Trojan horse or virus into your system. *See also* MODEM, ONLINE SERVICE, TROJAN HORSE, *and* VIRUS.

Downward compatibility

It would be ideal if computer hardware and software evolved exactly apace. But, as you probably know, they don't. Maybe you bought a powerful new software package, only to find that you must upgrade your computer before you can use the programs. Or perhaps you just purchased a new computer, and now your old software no longer meets your needs. *Downward compatibility* is the extent to which new products work with older products.

A matter of degree. Sometimes you can use new things with old ones, making no modifications. This is *100% downward compatibility*. An example of this might be a powerful new database program installed in a three-year-old computer.

Other times, you need to alter your hardware to take full advantage of new products. This is *partial downward compatibility*. An example is the addition of a coprocessor to a computer that uses an older 80386 microprocessor. Another example is the purchase of a laser printer to replace a dot-matrix printer for desktop publishing. In some cases, a computer is entirely adequate to run new software, except that it needs additional RAM (random-access memory). In this kind of situation, adding memory expansion boards makes the old system compatible with the new programs.

Occasionally, major changes must be made to old equipment if you want to use it with new software or hardware. You might decide on a new computer purchase because the new is *downwardly incompatible* with the old. For example, recently I found I needed a fax/modem, terminal emulation software, CD-ROM drive, multimedia equipment, SVGA monitor, and other features to work with more sophisticated applications than was possible with my existing system. The necessary improvements were so numerous that it made more sense to buy a whole new PC than to make patchwork upgrades. I still kept the old computer around as a backup system, though, and for basic word processing.

An example. If you've been using computers for awhile, you'll remember when high-density (HD) diskettes first became available. They had two to four times the data storage capacity of double-density (DD) diskettes. A 5.25-inch, DD diskette could hold about 360K (kilobytes) of data when formatted; suddenly there were new diskettes of exactly the same physical size, but with room for 1.2MB (about 1200 kilobytes).

New drives were needed for use with HD diskettes. You couldn't put an HD diskette into a DD drive and expect it to work; HD diskettes weren't downwardly compatible with older, DD disk drives. Fortunately, manufacturers kept on making DD diskettes, so machines with DD drives did not become obsolete overnight.

As soon as HD diskettes became available, most new PCs were sold with HD drives. These drives were also sold separately, so you could, if you wanted, install a new HD drive in an old computer. Some PC users opted for this. Others stuck with DD drives and diskettes and didn't change over until their next new computer purchase. A few well-to-do technophiles went out and bought brand new computers immediately.

How often to upgrade? The more you use a computer system, the more often downward compatibility will be an issue for you. As software becomes more powerful, existing computer systems become unable to handle the programs at an acceptable speed. Eventually you'll need to have a machine with a faster microprocessor, faster graphics, greater image resolution, more memory, a larger hard disk, more serial and/or parallel ports, a wider data bus, and other feature improvements.

As major purchases, computers are more like cars than, say, houses. Some PC users buy new machines as soon as a more powerful microprocessor, a new type of disk drive, or some other big improvement in computer hardware comes out. Other people, probably the majority, buy new computers at intervals of three to seven years. A few PC users wait until their old system breaks down or becomes totally unusable with needed software.

When downward compatibility problems start to seriously hamper your PC use, it's time to consider a major hardware upgrade. If you use

Drag

your computer in your business, tax deductibility, efficiency, and convenience all enter into the equation. *See also* COMPATIBILITY, HARDWARE, SOFTWARE, *and* UPGRADING.

Drag

In a graphical user interface (GUI) such as Windows, you can *drag* things around using the mouse. It's a fairly intuitive process: first move the mouse until the pointer touches the object (drawing A), then hold down the mouse button. When you move the mouse with the button held down, the pointer will drag the object with it (drawing B). It's almost as if you were dragging a sheet of paper across a smooth tabletop with the tip of your finger. When you have the object where you want it, release the mouse button (drawing C). You can then move the pointer around freely again, without dragging anything along.

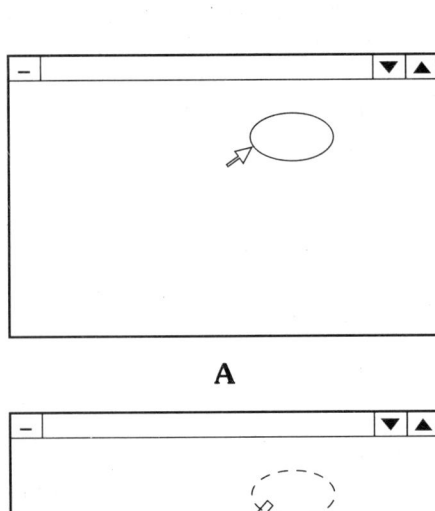

A

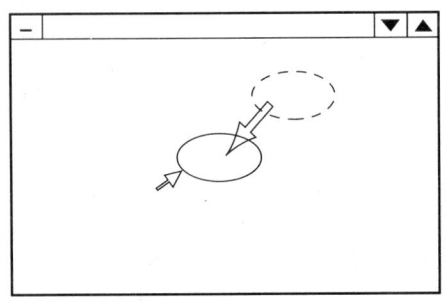

B

Preparing to move an object (A), moving it to a new location (B), and releasing it (C).

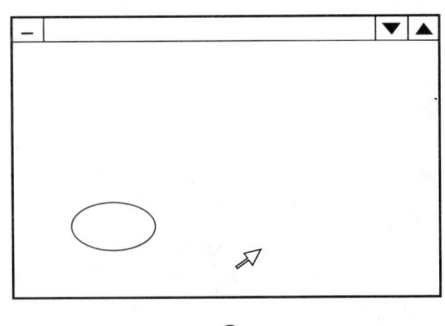

C

In many Windows-based word processing programs, you can edit text by using a technique called *drag-and-drop.* You highlight the text by moving the cursor over it. When you have highlighted a block of text as desired, you go back onto the highlighted block and drag the pointer to a new place in the text where you want to move the block. Then, when you release the mouse button, the block is inserted in the text in place of the pointer.

A technique similar to drag-and-drop can be used to move files from one disk drive or directory to another in Window's File Manager. You drag a pointer from a file to the new drive or directory where you want the file to go. *See also* FILE MANAGER, GRAPHICAL USER INTERFACE, *and* MOUSE.

DRAM

See DYNAMIC RANDOM-ACCESS MEMORY.

Draw program

A *draw program* is software that lets you use your PC to create line drawings. You can store the artwork on your hard disk or diskette and make hardcopies whenever you want. Draw programs put an end to the inconveniences and messiness of correction fluid, erasures, ink smearing, and photocopying.

Object-oriented. Most draw programs use *object-oriented graphics.* That means you have a set of shapes to work with, such as circles, ellipses, squares, and rectangles. This is in contrast to *bit-mapped graphics*, in which images are built up from tiny pieces on your screen, known as *pixels*. Bit-mapped graphics are more commonly used in *paint programs*.

In a draw program, you can change the size, position, and orientation of any object. You can stretch things or flip them inside-out. You can also assemble simple objects to make more complicated figures. Even the most complex line drawings are usually made up of just a few basic objects. In case you need to produce a strange figure that can't be built up from the basic shapes, you can usually trace it with a special tool called a pencil.

Basic tools. Most draw programs use three shapes, or *tools*, to generate figures: the rectangle, the ellipse, and the pencil. To this, some programs add a fourth tool, the triangle.

Rectangles and ellipses can have various degrees of *eccentricity*. A square is a rectangle with zero eccentricity. As the eccentricity increases, the figure gets longer and narrower (see A in the drawing). For ellipses, the circle represents zero eccentricity. Increasing eccentricity makes progressively more elongated ovals (B in the drawing).

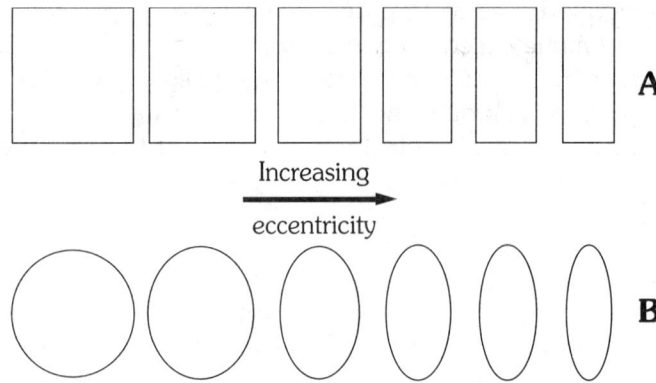

Rectangles (A) and ellipses (B) can vary in eccentricity.

The pencil tool lets you make any shape you want. You can move it around the outline of a drawing you have made by hand, thereby transferring (tracing) it into the PC. The pencil can also draw perfectly straight lines, of any length and oriented at any angle. You specify the end points of the line, and the program connects them with a straight line.

Triangles and polygons can be made by assembling straight lines. You can also create these figures by tracing with the pencil, using a straight edge (like a ruler) to force the pencil along straight lines.

Many uses. Draw programs are especially good for things like floor plans, simple art, and rough sketches. Simple packages are excellent for children. A draw program or paint program can be a great way to get a child comfortable with a computer.

Some sophisticated draw programs allow you to create schematic diagrams for electronic circuits and detailed line art for complex technical papers and manuals. Standard figures in such packages include all the common symbols for electronic components and the ability to insert text in various point sizes and fonts. Filling, texturing, importing/exporting, and other sophisticated features are available with the more advanced draw programs.

If you have a special professional need, there's probably at least one draw program ideal for you. Check with your computer dealer and look through PC-related magazines for the latest draw software. *See also* BITMAP, BITMAPPED GRAPHICS, OBJECT-ORIENTED GRAPHICS, PAINT PROGRAM, *and* PIXEL.

Drive bay

A *drive bay* is a place in a desktop computer for the installation of a *diskette drive*. Most desktop PCs come with two drive bays, one above the other. One or both of the bays might be filled, depending on the particular unit you buy. The bays are about $1^{11}/_{16}$ inches high and $5^{7}/_{8}$ inches wide (4.2 cm H × 15.0 cm W).

The drawing shows a PC with a 5.25-inch diskette drive in the upper bay and nothing in the lower bay. The owner of this unit might eventually want to install a second diskette drive in the lower bay; it might be either a 5.25-inch diskette drive, a 3.5-inch diskette drive, a CD-ROM drive, or a tape backup drive. *See also* CD-ROM, DISKETTE, DISKETTE DRIVE, *and* TAPE DRIVE.

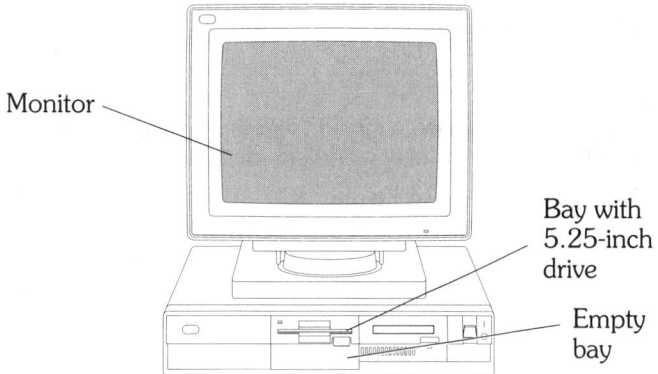

A desktop unit with one used bay and one empty bay.

Drop cap

In desktop publishing, you can create printed works that are as professional-looking as the books and magazines you buy at newsstands. One of the special effects that publishers sometimes use to enhance text is called a *drop cap*.

In books, drop caps are normally used only for the first letter in the first word of each chapter. A drop cap is normally enlarged to two or three times its normal height and width, and is also made proportionately heavier (bolder). That is, the letter is simply magnified in *every* dimension. The first two or three lines of text are indented just enough to make room for the enlarged letter. An example is shown.

> Drop caps are sometimes used at the beginnings of book chapters. You've probably seen this. You can do it in desktop publishing to give your work a professional look with an added flair. But don't do this in manuscripts that you plan to send to editors.

Drop caps are often used in desktop publishing.

In magazines, the first letter in the first word of an article might be a drop cap. In long articles with several parts, a drop cap might be used for the first letter in the first word of each part. Drop caps should not be overused, however; this looks amateurish. They also should not be used in term papers, technical reports, or manuscripts for submission to

Drop-in and drop-out

editors for possible publication. They are never used in captions for drawings, photographs, or tables. *See also* DESKTOP PUBLISHING.

Drop-in and drop-out

When digital data is stored on and retrieved from magnetic media, errors sometimes occur. (Fortunately, they are rare.) A logic 1 might get changed to 0, for example. A bit might get accidentally inserted or dropped. The generation of extra bits is called *drop-in*. The loss of a bit is called *drop-out*.

Drop-in and drop-out can happen because of dust on a disk, stray electrical impulses, or a defect in a disk. Errors can also take place for no apparent reason, other than the imperfect nature of physical things. The probability of errors increases as data files are copied over and over.

Modern digital systems have almost entirely eliminated the problems of noise and distortion that plagued older, analog systems. Nevertheless, an error in the wrong place or at the wrong time can cause even bigger problems in these more complex machines. Drop-in and drop-out can be minimized by keeping the temperature and humidity within reasonable limits and by keeping the air as free as possible from dust, salt spray, and corrosive pollutants. *See also* ANALOG, DIGITAL, *and* DIGITAL SIGNAL PROCESSING.

D-shell connector

When you hook up external components and peripherals to a desktop PC, the jumble of cables can be bewildering. You must follow the instructions to be sure that the printer, monitor, modem, mouse, and other devices get plugged into the right ports in the main unit.

Most cables have several wires, and these must all make good contact where they connect to the main unit and where they connect to each peripheral unit. If there are more than three or four wires in a cable, you'll often find a *D-shell connector* at either end. You can recognize this connector by its appearance, as shown in the drawing. There are two types of D-shell connector, called *female* and *male*. The female socket has holes into which the pins of the male plug slide.

One advantage of the D-shell connector is that it's equipped with screws to keep the cable plugged in. If the cable gets jerked around, it won't come out of its socket if you've tightened the screws after plugging in the connector.

Another advantage is provided by the metal shell surrounding the contacts of the connector. This helps keep out dust and moisture that might cause open or short circuits. It can also serve as an electromagnetic shield, preventing interference to the data carried by the cable, and preventing signals from getting out of the cable and

Dual inline package

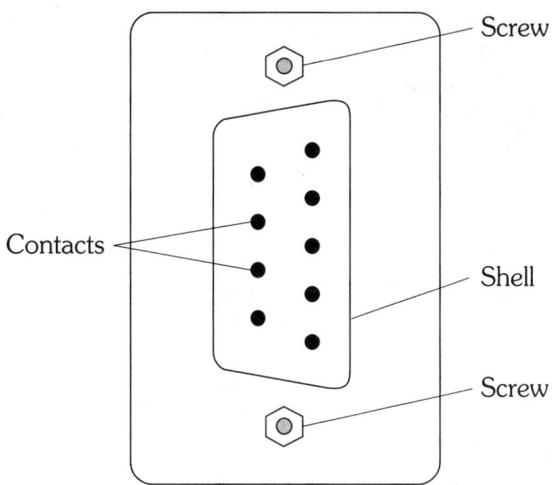

A D-shell connector is recognizable by its shape.

causing interference to other systems or devices. Still another advantage of the D-shell connector is its shape. You can't plug it in the wrong way.

D-shell connectors come in various sizes depending on the number of wires in the cable. This minimizes the chance that you'll hook the mouse up where the printer should go, or the modem where the monitor should go. *See also* DESKTOP COMPUTER, ELECTROMAGNETIC SHIELDING, PERIPHERALS, *and* PORT.

DSP

See DIGITAL SIGNAL PROCESSING.

DTE

See DATA TERMINAL EQUIPMENT.

Dual inline package

The *dual inline package (DIP)* is a common housing for integrated circuits (ICs). A flat, rectangular box containing the chip is fitted with pins along either side, as shown in the drawings. A typical DIP is shown here from the top (drawing A), the side (drawing B) and the end (drawing C). The number of pins can vary, from three or four to a dozen or more on each side.

The DIP makes it easy to install and replace ICs. Sockets can be used for this purpose. Sometimes DIPs are soldered directly onto a printed circuit board. It is somewhat more difficult to remove and replace ICs that are soldered to the board, but there is less chance of intermittent failures with this method. *See also* FLATPACK, INTEGRATED CIRCUIT, *and* SINGLE INLINE PACKAGE.

Dual-ordinate graph

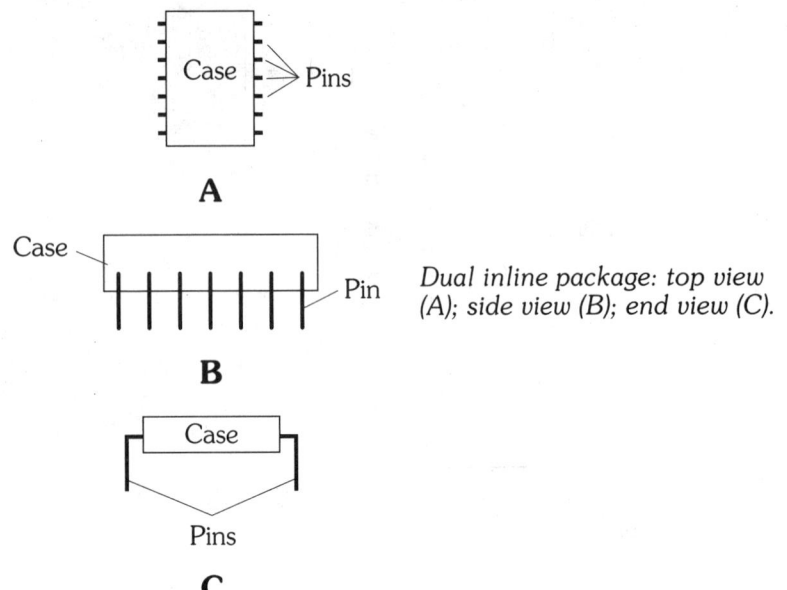

Dual inline package: top view (A); side view (B); end view (C).

Dual-ordinate graph

A *dual-ordinate graph* is any graph that shows two different functions in the same region on a printed page or computer screen. The dual-ordinate scheme can save space, but more important, it is used to compare functions that are related in some way. Dual-ordinate graphing is easily done with analytical graphics or presentation graphics packages.

Two vertical scales. One type of dual-ordinate graph uses two different vertical scales. The independent variable is common to both functions and usually runs along the horizontal axis at the bottom of the graph. The dependent variable for one function is shown along a vertical axis on the left side of the graph. The dependent variable for the other function is shown along a vertical axis on the right side of the graph.

Bar/columnar graphs. It is quite common for a *bar graph* or *columnar graph* to show multiple functions. It's possible with shading and crosshatching to show three, four, or even five functions in bar graphs and columnar graphs, with one or two ordinates.

An example of a columnar graph showing two different functions is given in the drawing. The unshaded bars represent the mean monthly temperature, in degrees Fahrenheit, for a hypothetical town in a certain year. The ordinate for this function is on the left side of the graph. The shaded bars represent air-conditioner sales for the month in that same town during that year. The ordinate for this function is on the right side of the graph.

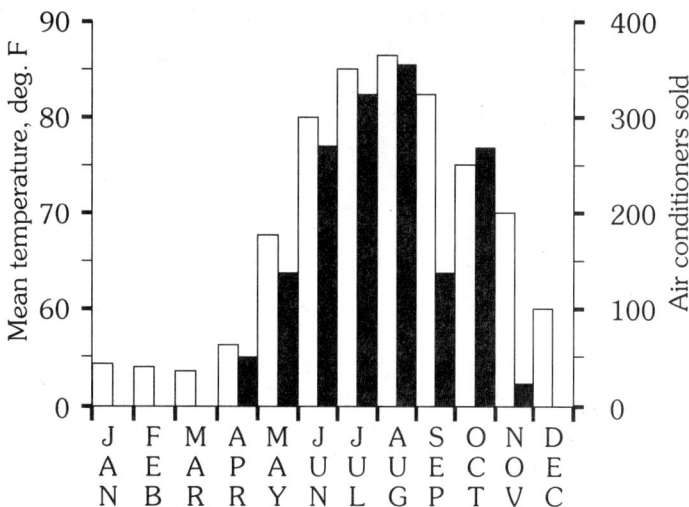

A dual-ordinate graph shows two or more functions.

Dual-ordinate graphs can emphasize things that might be missed in other types of graphs. In the example shown by the drawing, there was a surge of units sold in October, despite lowering temperatures. This is easy to spot. From this you might gather that there was a big autumn sale on air conditioners, as merchants strove to get rid of their inventory. *See also* ABSCISSA, BAR GRAPH, COLUMNAR GRAPH, DEPENDENT VARIABLE, FUNCTION, INDEPENDENT VARIABLE, *and* ORDINATE.

Dumb terminal

A *dumb terminal* is a system usually containing a keyboard, monitor, printer, and modem, but without computing capability. It is connected to a telephone line or radio transceiver and used to access networks or packet communications systems. Some dumb terminals have limited processing units built-in to perform specific types of data management, but they cannot use other applications as a PC can.

In the 1960s and early 1970s, it was almost impossible for most individuals to own computers; the machines were simply too expensive. The only way to access a computer was via a dumb terminal and the telephone line. I can remember using such an arrangement as a high-school student. The terminal resembled an old teletype machine. It printed at 45 bauds (60 words per minute) and rendered hardcopy on an endless roll of paper. Today, even a low-end PC you might find at a flea market is faster and more powerful than that system.

Dumb terminals can be used for some, or even for most, of the workstations in a LAN (local area network). This saves money because a dumb terminal is less expensive than a computer. For home use, however, most people prefer to have a desktop PC, complete with a CPU, hard disk, and diskette drive(s). A PC can imitate a dumb

Duplex

terminal by running *terminal emulation software.* This is done for access to online services and packet communications networks. *See also* CENTRAL PROCESSING UNIT, LOCAL AREA NETWORK, MODEM, NETWORK, ONLINE SERVICE, PACKET COMMUNICATIONS, TERMINAL EMULATION SOFTWARE, *and* WORKSTATION.

Duplex

See FULL DUPLEX *and* HALF DUPLEX.

Duplex printing

In some desktop publishing and word processing projects, you'll want to print documents on both sides of every page, the way a magazine or book is produced. When you do this, you use *duplex printing.*

Verso/recto. In a duplex-printed magazine or book, the even-numbered pages are on the left as you hold the document open. These pages are called *verso pages.* The odd-numbered pages are on the right and are called *recto pages.* Verso and recto pages have different margins because the binding is on the right edge of a verso page, but the left edge of a recto page.

Duplex printing is not a simple matter of producing one page after another in order. To be able to simply put the paper in your printer, print out the verso pages, and then flip the paper over and print out the recto pages, you need software that will arrange the pages in the correct sequence. A good desktop publishing program can do this.

In a 10-page, duplex-printed document, you might print pages 2, 4, 6, 8 and 10; then you would flip the sheets over, reinsert them into the printer, and print out pages 1, 3, 5, 7, and 9 on the reverse sides. You would need software that would stagger the page sequence as you worked; otherwise, the final printed document would not make sense when read. Also, you'd have to be sure to insert the paper right-side-up in the printer the second time around. *See also* BINDING OFFSET *and* DESKTOP PUBLISHING.

Dvorak keyboard layout

The placement of letters, numerals, and basic punctuation on PC keyboards is identical with the standard typewriter. The arrangement is called the *QWERTY keyboard layout,* because the first six characters in the top letter row are QWERTY (pronounced just like it looks). The *Dvorak keyboard layout* is an alternative to this standard arrangement.

The QWERTY layout is not the most efficient possible scheme. Maybe you've noticed this. For example, *E* is the most often-appearing letter in the English language, but its location on the QWERTY keyboard requires that you stretch the middle finger of your left hand to reach it. Ideally, the *E* key would be located where it could be easily pressed by the index finger. There are other examples: the letter *A* is at the extreme left, and you must stretch your left "pinky" to reach it even though it is, like *E*, a frequently appearing letter in English.

According to one story, the inefficiency of the QWERTY layout is deliberate. Apparently, on the earliest typewriters, which used a more efficient key layout, the hammers kept getting stuck because the typists were too quick on the keys. The inventor altered the keyboard layout to force the operators to slow down. Of course, it would have been better to improve the mechanics of the hammers!

The Dvorak keyboard layout was developed with the most often-used keys in places that are easy to strike with the index and middle fingers of both hands. Some people who have learned to type on Dvorak keyboards can type faster than on the QWERTY keyboard. However, switching from one to the other is, as you can imagine, difficult and frustrating. Becoming proficient on both keyboards requires at least twice as much time and effort as developing a comparable level of skill on one of them.

The Dvorak keyboard, despite its greater efficiency, hasn't caught on. Its plight is similar to that of the metric system in the United States. People are resistant to change. Dvorak typists, despite their greater potential, end up having problems when they're away from their offices and are faced with QWERTY keyboards. *See also* KEYBOARD *and* QWERTY KEYBOARD LAYOUT.

Dynamic data exchange

Dynamic data exchange (DDE) is a method of automatically keeping data updated when it appears in more than one file or application. Microsoft's Windows software incorporates DDE, as does IBM's OS/2 and Macintosh's System 7.

Computer data constantly changes. In many cases, when something changes in one file, it affects data in other files. Without DDE, you must go through files and alter the contents of each to reflect a single data change. This is tedious, and when your files get complex, it becomes exasperating. It's likely that you won't remember to make a change in every pertinent place; you'll end up with inconsistent data.

With DDE, when something changes, every affected piece of data is updated by the PC, even among different applications. You don't have to remember to do it yourself. Suppose, for example, you've imported a database into four different word processing files. If you change something in the database, DDE will make the change automatically in all four word processing files. *See also* OBJECT LINKING AND EMBEDDING.

Dynamic random-access memory

A *dynamic random-access memory*, abbreviated *DRAM*, is a form of RAM in which the binary digits are stored electrically in a semiconductor material.

Electric charge. In the DRAM, the digit 1, or high, is represented by an electric charge within an integrated circuit (IC, also called a chip). The digit 0, or low, is the absence of a charge. Sometimes this situation is reversed; logic 1 is the absence of an electric charge, and logic 0 is the presence of a charge. It doesn't matter which digit is represented by the charge and which one is not, as long as things are consistent within the IC.

The electric charges in a DRAM chip leak off unless they are continually replenished. The charge is replenished every few milliseconds (thousandths of a second) by a device called a *DRAM controller*. The replenishing process itself takes far less time, on the order of nanoseconds (billionths of a second). Without the DRAM controller, the data in the DRAM would vanish in a fraction of a second. A computer must devote a significant portion of its time keeping DRAM refreshed.

Microprocessors and DRAM. As microprocessor chips become faster, the necessary access time and storage time for DRAM gets shorter. It's possible to use a very fast DRAM chip with a slow microprocessor, but this is not an ideal arrangement because it necessitates the use of wait states, giving the microprocessor time to catch up. The reverse situation, a fast microprocessor with a slow DRAM, is also not desirable because a slow DRAM places a severe limitation on the clock speed at which the microprocessor can work. *See also* INTEGRATED CIRCUIT, RANDOM-ACCESS MEMORY, *and* STATIC RANDOM-ACCESS MEMORY.

Ecolinking

Personal computers are a powerful tool for getting information, and they will become more useful in the coming years as online services expand. There's a network for practically every special interest, and ecology is no exception.

Ecolinking means "green networking," or the exchange of environmental-interest data via online services such as the Internet. The term was coined by Don Rittner in a book called *Ecolinking: Everyone's Guide to Online Environmental Information*, published by Peachpit Press. Rittner assumes that his readers are interested in ecology and are in touch with the premises of environmental interests. The book is intended for people who want to get specific environmental information. It's a directory of networks and databases worldwide to which PC users can ecolink. Another excellent book about PCs and environmental interests is *The Green PC* by Steven Anzovin, published by McGraw-Hill.

What's being done to save manatees in Florida? How high are the mercury levels in Northern streams and lakes? Do computers pose a health threat because of the magnetic fields their monitors produce? What states have emissions-inspection programs for cars and trucks? You can find out any of these things (and millions more) by ecolinking. You can find out what is being said and done about the environment, and who is saying and doing it. *See also* GREEN COMPUTING *and* ONLINE SERVICE.

Edge connector

An *edge connector* is a plug-and-socket device used to connect a printed-circuit board in an electronic system. The connector gets its name from the fact that the "male" portion is contained in the edge of the circuit board, as shown in the drawing. The "female" connector is a receptacle, into which the edge of the board snugly fits. There can be dozens of contacts.

Edge connectors are ideally suited to the modular construction common in electronic equipment. In troubleshooting, a computer identifies which board most likely contains the problem. That board can be pulled out easily and plugged into a service machine. The machine locates the faulty component. A technician replaces the bad part, tests the board again, and then puts it back into the original machine or into storage for future use. *See also* PRINTED CIRCUIT.

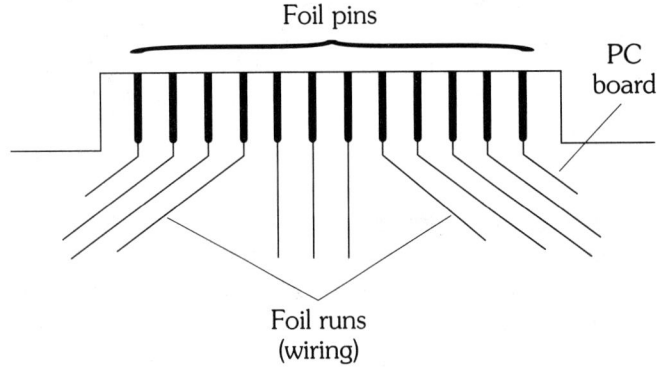

Edge-connector pins are contained in the circuit board.

EDI

See ELECTRONIC DATA INTERCHANGE.

EGA

See ENHANCED GRAPHICS ADAPTER.

EISA

See ENHANCED INDUSTRY STANDARD ARCHITECTURE.

Electromagnetic field

An *electromagnetic (EM) field* is produced when charged objects, such as electrons in a wire, are accelerated. Electromagnetic fields are used extensively for data communications. Microwave links, fiberoptic systems, and satellite links are the most common examples.

The controlled, constant acceleration of electrons is responsible for radio waves, which are EM fields having frequencies from about 3000 hertz (Hz, or cycles per second), to 3000 gigahertz (3,000,000,000,000 Hz). The 60-Hz alternating-current (ac) utility produces an EM field whose frequency is lower than that of radio waves. Infrared, visible light, ultraviolet, X-rays and gamma rays are forms of EM energy with frequencies higher than those of the radio waves.

All EM fields consist of an electric component and a magnetic component. These are represented by *lines of flux*. The electric flux is at right angles to the magnetic flux. The fields constantly alternate back and forth. As a result, they travel through space, the ac electric component producing an ac magnetic component of identical frequency, which in turn gives rise to another ac electric component, and so on indefinitely. The direction in which the EM field travels is at right angles to both the electric and magnetic lines of flux (see the drawing).

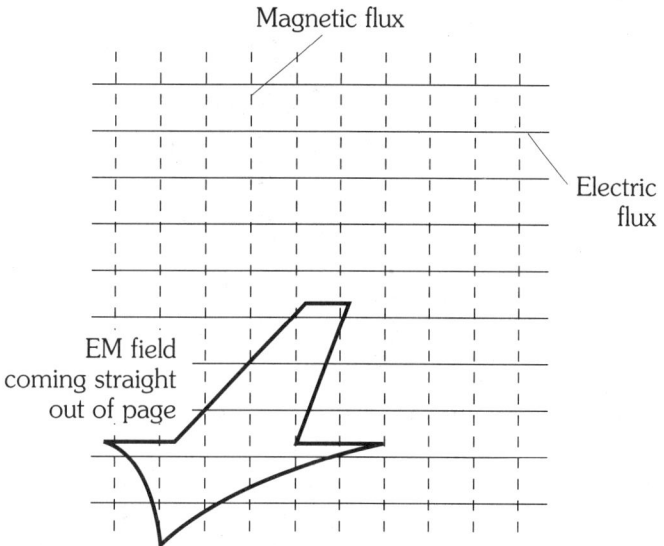

Magnetic flux (dotted lines) is perpendicular to electric flux (solid lines).

Sometimes, EM fields upset the functioning of electronic equipment, particularly computers. Sensitive digital equipment such as your PC must be shielded from stray EM fields. Your PC also produces localized EM fields of its own, over a wide range of frequencies. *See also* ELECTROMAGNETIC SHIELDING, ELF FIELDS, FIBEROPTIC DATA TRANSMISSION, MICROWAVE DATA TRANSMISSION, *and* SATELLITE DATA TRANSMISSION.

Electromagnetic shielding

Electromagnetic shielding is a means of preventing PCs and other sensitive equipment from being affected by stray electromagnetic (EM) fields. Computers also generate EM energy of their own, and this can cause interference to other devices, especially radio receivers, unless shielding is used.

The simplest way to provide EM shielding for a circuit is to surround it with metal, usually copper or aluminum, and to connect this metal to an electrical ground. Because metals are good conductors, an EM field sets up electric currents in them. These currents oppose the EM field, and if the metal enclosure is grounded, the EM field is shorted out.

In addition to metal enclosures, interconnecting cables must be shielded by surrounding all the cable conductors with a copper braid, as shown in the drawing. Cable of this kind is sometimes called *shielded cable*; the braid is electrically grounded via the connectors at the ends of the cable.

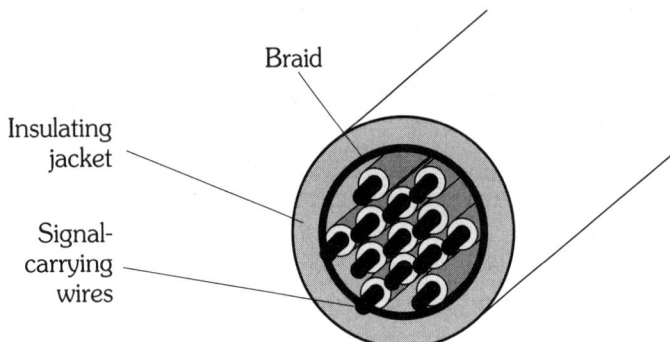

A shielded, multiconductor cable.

One of the biggest advantages of fiberoptic data transmission is the fact that it does not need EM shielding. Fiberoptic systems are immune to the EM fields produced by radio transmitters and alternating-current (ac) utility wiring. Fiberoptic systems also work without producing external EM fields. *See also* ELECTROMAGNETIC FIELD, ELF FIELDS, *and* FIBEROPTIC DATA TRANSMISSION.

Electronic books

Publishing, especially of books, is about to change. According to some writers, *electronic books* are the best thing to happen since the invention of paper. According to others, they are a horrifying development.

What's to come? Will electronic books render writing obsolete? Will images and animation take over? Will people lose their ability to "see with the mind's eye"? In this writer's opinion, the answers to these questions are "No." Still, the literary world will almost certainly be different in 20 or 30 years. Electronic publishing will, to some extent, supplant bound magazines and books. You'll buy many publications on magnetic diskettes and CD-ROM and read them on gadgets that resemble small notebook computers, but cost much less. Many books and magazines will be available online—some publications are right now. Online publishing will become a preferred method of getting information, especially on technical or professional subjects.

Good news for writers. The conversion from paper binding to electronic publication translates into one thing for writers: a demand explosion. If you want to publish your own work, one of the biggest barriers—the huge expenses associated with printing and binding—will be eliminated. You'll be able to sell your work on disk, or even to online services such as a literature network.

Some big publishers will thrive by keeping abreast of the changes and adapting to them. Costs of producing electronic books will decline, allowing for greater profit margins and wider distribution. Electronic publishing will dramatically increase the amount of reading material available, provided writers and publishers can meet the demand. Imagine a library whose shelves are full of CD-ROMs! It would have 10,000 times as much information as one of the same size containing traditional books.

Multimedia and interaction. Electronic books are far more than space-saving, cost-reducing media. Using visual effects such as animation, it's possible to transform a book into an audio-video experience. This is known as *multimedia*. Taking this one step further, a book can become an active tutorial, or even a movie in which you can play a role. This is called *interactive technology*, and is becoming especially popular with children's textbooks, storybooks, and reference materials.

Other features being incorporated into electronic books are "margins" in which you can write notes, and "corners" that you can "bend down" to mark pages that interest you. Some electronic books let you highlight portions of the text; others allow for the creation of a personal index, where you can keep references to your favorite terms, passages, and illustrations. When you select an item, the system automatically takes you to the page or pages you specify. *See also* INTERACTIVE TECHNOLOGY *and* MULTIMEDIA.

Novels. The advantages of electronic publishing for text and reference books are clear. But what about novels? Can you curl up in bed with a disk reader or computer, the way you can with a good book? Some people think not. A computer, they say, is simply not the same as a bound book.

Imagine a bedside-table electronic book reader equipped with two drives: one for a magnetic diskette and the other for a CD-ROM. Attached to this is a box about 7 inches wide, 8 inches high, and an inch deep, with a screen and some buttons. The screen shows crisp, easy-to-read text and graphics. The display is backlit so you can read it in the dark. It might have a curly cord that connects it to the drives, as shown in drawing, or it might be cordless, operated by an infrared link, the way a television remote-control works.

Electronic calculator

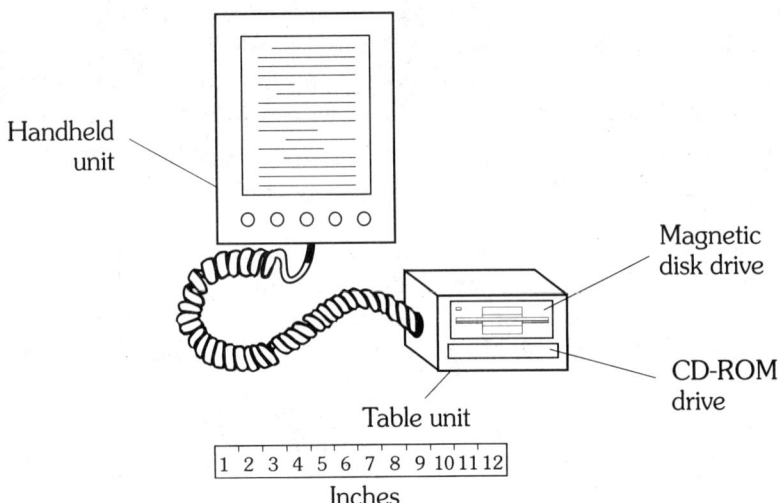

A bedside disk reader.

A small bookshelf of CD-ROMs would give you a large library of novels. You push a button to flip the page; you press another couple of buttons to go to page 459, and so on. When your spouse decides he or she wants to go to sleep, you switch off the overhead light and read from the backlit display.

A place in the heart. Although portable disk readers will be reasonably priced, they won't be cheap enough to make everyone comfortable taking them everywhere. The beach, for example, is probably a bad place for an electronic book. Sand, oil, sun, water, and salt spray wreak havoc on electronic devices. Theft is a factor too.

Traditional bound books have other advantages, as well. They don't need batteries. You can scribble on their inside front and back covers. They get dusty, yellowed, and battered in a certain charming way. For many people, printed books have a place in the heart that no machine can take away. *See also* DESKTOP PUBLISHING.

Electronic calculator

An *electronic calculator* is a primitive form of digital computer. All calculators can add, subtract, multiply, and divide numbers; some include other functions for scientists and engineers. The drawing shows a typical calculator, suitable for balancing a checkbook. A unit like this costs about $5 and works in ordinary room light, being powered by photovoltaic (solar) cells.

Many new PCs have a calculator function built in. You click on an icon, and a calculator appears on the screen. You "push the buttons" by pointing and clicking. You can choose between conventional mode for simple arithmetic, and scientific mode to perform square root, trigonometric, logarithmic, and exponential functions.

Electronic-circuit design software

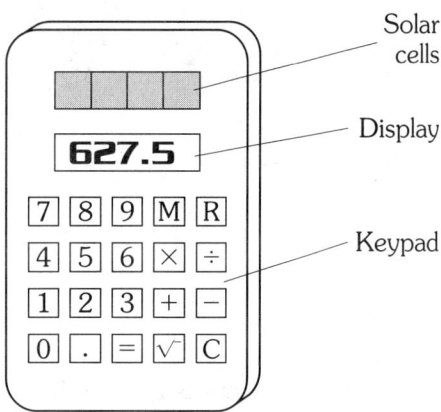

A typical calculator for doing basic arithmetic.

The most advanced electronic calculators are programmable and might better be called *nanocomputers* (the prefix *nano* meaning, in this context, "smaller than micro but bigger than nothing"). The distinction between large calculators and microcomputers is rather fuzzy. There's no exact point where you can say, "This is a calculator, but add one more logic gate and it will become a microcomputer."

The earliest digital computers were actually electronic calculators. What a difference there is between those lumbering monstrosities and the pocket calculators of today! The calculator shown in the drawing would, in 1946, have taken up the better part of a room and needed a special utility line all for itself. *See also* ELECTRONIC NUMERICAL INTEGRATOR *and* CALCULATOR.

Electronic-circuit design software

Computer programs can simulate many things and situations. As PCs have become more powerful, software programs have been getting more diverse and complex. One good example is *electronic-circuit design software*.

The old way. All electronic devices are built up from individual components. If you're an electronics hobbyist, you'll recognize, and know the functions of, things like capacitors, inductors, resistors, transistors, and diodes. You'll also know the digital devices and their symbols, such as the AND gate, inverter, NAND gate, NOR gate, and OR gate. You might recognize the circuit in the drawing (on page 354) as a low-level, radio-frequency amplifier.

Suppose you want to design this amplifier for optimum performance at frequencies of 88 MHz (megahertz) to 108 MHz, the range of the standard FM broadcast band. The drawing shows a "generic" circuit. It's like a template, and is typical of amplifiers at frequencies from low to ultra-high, from longwave through shortwave to television broadcast and above. There are three resistors, labeled R1, R2, and R3, and two

Electronic-circuit design software

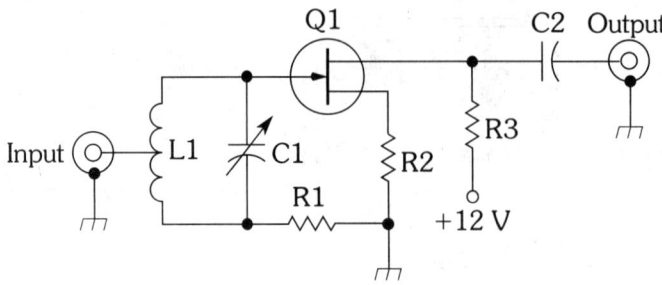

Generic radio-receiver amplifier.

capacitors, labeled C1 and C2. There is also an inductor, L1, and a field-effect transistor, Q1. The values and characteristics of all these components will affect the behavior of the amplifier. If they are not right, the amplifier won't work as it should. It might even fail to do anything at all.

You could sketch out the amplifier, making educated guesses as to the component values by consulting engineering reference manuals, hobby electronics books, and other data sources. Ultimately, however, you must give the circuit the real-life test. Solder, circuit boards, wire cutters, and other hardware become essential. Your initial component-value guesses will probably have to be changed, perhaps many times, until you find a good working circuit. This is a time-consuming process.

A new way. A computer can help you circumvent much of this hardware hassle. Software can simulate the behavior of the circuit. Electrical engineers routinely use such software. One excellent package, of interest to hobbyists, is called *Electronics Workbench*, developed by Interactive Image Technologies, Ltd. of Toronto, Ontario. There are several advantages to using such software to simulate an electronics lab:

> *Safety* You can learn from your mistakes without damaging components or circuits, and without risking injury from burns, shocks, or toxic chemicals.

> *Money savings* You save the cost of purchasing complex test equipment. Also, you don't have to purchase as many components for building prototypes because bugs are often found before you've assembled any hardware.

> *Time savings* It's much faster to build and test circuits on the PC than it is in real life.

> *Realism* You can get an excellent simulation because the PC can do mathematical calculations with precision and speed. The software uses industry-standard modeling processes.

> *Fun* You can dream up all kinds of strange and innovative circuits and see how well they will (or won't) work in just a few minutes.

Modules. All electronic circuits can be broadly categorized as *analog*, *digital*, or *hybrid* (analog and digital combined). The Electronics Workbench program has two modules, one for analog circuits and one for digital circuits. They are similar enough so that switching between them is not difficult once you've learned the basics.

Consider again the radio amplifier shown in the drawing. This is an analog circuit, so you would use the analog module to work with it. Its behavior is a strict, predictable function of the values of its components. A modern digital PC, using good software, can approximate the circuit's behavior well enough to save you hours of trial-and-error experimentation. You can plug in values for R1, R2, R3, C1, C2, and L1, and choose Q1 to have specific characteristics.

Both the analog and digital modules of this program use graphics onscreen. You have a parts bin, a power switch, and various test instruments in either mode. The analog module contains the following instruments:

- Multimeter
- Bode plotter
- Function generator
- Oscilloscope

The digital module contains these instruments:

- Word generator
- Logic analyzer
- Logic converter
- Voltmeter

For further information on electronic design software, check with your local PC dealer or electronics shop. If you have some friends who are electronics engineers, you can also ask them for advice. Information concerning Electronics Workbench can be obtained by writing to

Interactive Image Technologies, Ltd.
700 King Street West
Toronto, Ontario
Canada M5V 2Y6

Electronic data interchange

Electronic data interchange, abbreviated *EDI*, is a set of standards that simplifies the way information is shared among businesses. The ultimate goal is to replace most, if not all, paper business documents with data stored on media that can be used directly by computers. The result will be an incalculable savings in cost, bulk, and inconvenience.

Electronic mail

When you send data via a network instead of by mail, there's no waiting time for the delivery of letters and far fewer lost items. There are no ink smears, erasures, or marks from correction fluid. With the use of EDI, offices would be wide-open spaces because of the reduced number of filing cabinets. The "in box" tray would become a relic. The main items on a desk would be a PC, a modem, and a telephone.

All these things are within the reach of technology today; it's mainly a matter of getting people to switch over. The EDI protocol is being incorporated into the routines of more and more businesses each year. Its standardization helps to eliminate the confusion that might occur if there were no agreed-on protocol. Every type of exchange in EDI has its own special code. *See also* PAPERLESS OFFICE *and* PROTOCOL.

Electronic mail

Electronic mail, also called *e-mail*, is a computer communications system that lets people leave written messages for each other. E-mail requires terminal emulation software and a modem for interconnection with the telephone line. You must also subscribe to an online service or Internet gateway.

To use e-mail, you usually pay a flat monthly fee for usage up to a certain length of time online or for a certain number of messages. Beyond that, you are charged by the hour or message. Some online services have surcharges that apply during certain days and hours. Some also charge for long-term storage of e-mail messages. To save online time, you can compose your messages offline, and then import them to the e-mail application while online.

To use e-mail, you must have an *e-mail address*, and know the e-mail address of the party to whom you are sending the message. For example, an e-mail address on the Internet consists of a screen name (also called a username), followed by the symbol @, followed by the online service designator. The designator consists of a service name, a period (.), and a three-letter extension. The components of the e-mail address are all run together into a single string of characters. This string can be quite long, and can look exotic and complicated to people who have never been exposed to e-mail. Once you get familiar with the notation, however, any e-mail address is easy to understand, even if the string is long.

Messages in e-mail, both sent and received, can be downloaded to a hard disk, diskette, or printer. If you want to keep a complete set of e-mail archives, the preferred method is to use diskettes, tapes, or other high-volume mass storage media. *See also* BULLETIN BOARD SYSTEM, MODEM, ONLINE SERVICE, PACKET COMMUNICATIONS, *and* TERMINAL EMULATION SOFTWARE.

Electronic Numerical Integrator and Calculator

The first digital computers used vacuum tubes or relays for switching because transistors hadn't been invented yet, and integrated circuits (ICs) were nothing but the ideas of dreamers. One such computer, called the *Electronic Numerical Integrator and Calculator (ENIAC)*, was first put to use in the mid-1940s at the University of Pennsylvania.

ENIAC had about 19,000 vacuum tubes. Each of these devices needed a source of power to heat up its filament (like the filament in a lightbulb), in addition to the signal voltages. ENIAC weighed 60,000 pounds and took up a good part of a building. It needed a large air-conditioning system to keep it from overheating.

A modern PC contains dozens of ICs, each one more powerful than ENIAC was in its entirety. A typical silicon IC is so small that you'd need a good magnifying glass to tell it from a grain of sand. It can run off a small battery, produces practically no heat, and needs no maintenance. Amazingly, the transition from ENIAC to such ICs took less than 40 years. *See also* INTEGRATED CIRCUIT.

ELF fields

Electrical and electronic equipment produces electromagnetic (EM) fields because of the alternating current (ac) passing through its wires. The fields have a frequency of 60 hertz (Hz), or 60 cycles per second. This is an extremely low frequency (ELF), and that's how the term *ELF fields* has arisen.

Electromagnetism. A steady direct current (dc) produces a static electric field and a stable magnetic field. The higher the voltage, the stronger the electric field. The more current that flows, the stronger the magnetic field.

Sometimes you'll hear electric or magnetic fields described in terms of *flux lines*. Electric and magnetic flux lines are always perpendicular to each other, as shown in drawing A (page 358) for an electrically charged, current-carrying wire. Imagine the wire coming out of the page towards you; it is shown as a solid dot. The electric flux lines (E) radiate out from the wire (dotted), and the magnetic flux lines (M) appear as circles around the wire (solid). Notice that the electric flux is at a right angle to the magnetic flux at every point around the wire.

When current alternates back and forth, as does standard house current, the intensity of the electric and magnetic fields constantly changes, generating an EM field that can travel great distances through space. This phenomenon was explored around the end of the 19th century by Nikola Tesla and other scientists. It led to the discovery of radio waves, and ultimately to all radio and television communications as we know it today.

ELF fields

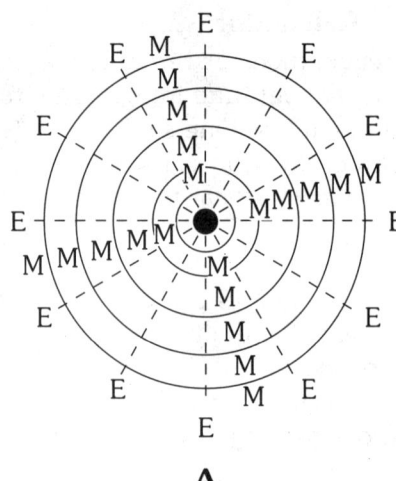

The E and M fields near a dc-carrying wire.

A

What ELF is (and isn't). An ELF field, like a radio wave, is an EM field, but while radio waves have frequencies measured in thousands, millions, or billions of hertz, ELF is only a few hertz. The most common ELF is 60 Hz. These waves are emitted by all live utility wires; you've been exposed to them since you were born.

The very term "extremely-low-frequency radiation," and the attention it's received lately, might lead you to think there's something sinister about it. It's nothing like X-rays or gamma rays, which cause radiation sickness. Nor is it like ultraviolet, which can cause skin cancer over long periods. An ELF field will not make you radioactive. There has been no absolute proof, as of this writing, that the ELF field from a PC is dangerous, but it hasn't been proven safe either. Controversy exists; studies continue.

ELF from your monitor. The ELF that you've probably heard about in connection with computers is emitted by the cathode-ray tube (CRT) in the computer's monitor. Other parts of the PC are not responsible for much ELF energy. Laptop and notebook computers produce essentially none.

In the CRT, the characters and images are created as electron beams strike a phosphor coating on the inside of the glass. The electrons constantly change direction as they sweep from left to right and top to bottom on your screen. The sweeping is caused by deflecting coils that steer the beam across the screen. The coils generate magnetic fields that interact with the negatively charged electrons, forcing them to change direction.

Drawing B shows one of the deflecting coils in a CRT, and the shape of the magnetic flux around it. The fields fluctuate at extremely low frequencies. Because of the positions of the coils and the shapes of the fields surrounding them, there is more magnetic energy "radiated" from the sides of a PC monitor than from the front. If there's any health hazard with ELF, therefore, it is greater for someone sitting off to the side of a monitor, and less for someone watching the screen from directly in front at the same distance.

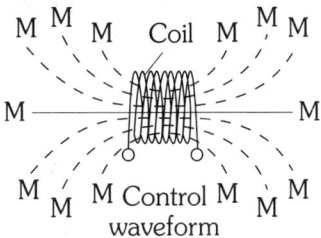

The M field near a current-carrying coil.

B

Protection from ELF. The best "shielding" from ELF is distance. This is especially true for people sitting next to (rather than in front of) a monitor. ELF dies off rapidly as you move away from the monitor. Workstations, therefore, should be at least five feet apart, and you should stay at least 18 inches away from the front of your own monitor. You can also shut off your monitor when it's not in use. This both eliminates ELF fields and extends the life of the monitor.

Special monitors designed to minimize ELF fields are available. They're not cheap, but they offer peace of mind if you're concerned about possible long-term effects of ELF fields. Sweden has the strictest standards for ELF emissions. Look for the designator MPR-II, indicating compliance with the so-called *Swedish ELF radiation standard*.

With increasing concern about ELF, you'll see devices marketed with claims to eliminate or greatly reduce ELF fields. Some of these schemes are effective; others are not. Electrostatic screens that you can place in front of the monitor glass to keep it from attracting dust will not stop ELF fields. However, a magnetism-reducing metal ring or band might bring a monitor into compliance with the Swedish MPR-II standard if it does not meet this standard without the device attached.

It's best to avoid blowing the ELF issue out of proportion, and not to succumb to unsubstantiated hype. Some people use scare tactics to sell things. If in doubt, consult someone whose word you can trust, such as a computer hardware engineer or an electronics engineer. *See also* CATHODE-RAY TUBE, CUMULATIVE TRAUMA DISORDERS, *and* ELECTROMAGNETIC FIELD.

ELIZA

One of the more controversial early developments in artificial intelligence (AI) involved a program called ELIZA. This program was

Embedded formatting

put together in the 1960s by Joseph Weizenbaum of the Massachusetts Institute of Technology.

The purpose of ELIZA was to imitate a psychoanalyst. The "patient" would sit at a computer terminal and "converse" with the "doctor" by typing sentences on a keyboard. The ELIZA program was, in fact, sometimes called DOCTOR. As the "patient," you might sit down to the computer and have the following conversation:

ELIZA   SPEAK UP!

You   I'M UPSET.

ELIZA   WHY ARE YOU UPSET?

You   I DON'T KNOW. THAT'S WHY I'M HERE.

The session would proceed with ELIZA asking questions and the "patient" giving answers or asking other questions. The program would never really commit itself by saying things like "Don't ever do that again," or "You should have told her to go away." It would just display phrases, some from its own memory and some stored from things the user typed earlier. Nevertheless, ELIZA often behaved so much like a real psychoanalyst that some people thought it was as good as a human doctor.

Weizenbaum was disturbed by the reactions and the controversy ELIZA caused. The program was not very smart, especially by today's standards. Like programs today, it could not have any feeling or concern for human beings, but some people responded to it like a person.

In recent years, much more sophisticated software has been developed to help diagnose physical illnesses. Of course, if you're sick enough to need medical help, you should always consult a human doctor. *See also* ARTIFICIAL INTELLIGENCE.

Embedded formatting

Word processing involves many formatting commands that affect the way the text looks when it's printed out. All word processing software uses formatting commands of one sort or another, so you can use boldface, italics, superscript, subscript, and other common variations of text.

It's convenient if the format changes can be seen on the monitor, so you don't have to print the text out to see the final product. *Embedded formatting* encodes the change commands themselves, while still letting you see or infer the results.

This book was written with a word processing program in which embedded formatting was used. With this program, boldface appeared

red, italics appeared green, and so on. The files could also be viewed so that the actual formatting commands were displayed in the running text. In this mode, an italicized phrase would look like this:

`<MDUL>Embedded formatting<MDNM>`

where the code <MDUL> means "mode underline" and <MDNM> means "mode normal."

Most people like to use embedded formatting rather than looking at all the cryptic formatting codes. WYSIWYG word processors are even better, especially for new users, because formatting codes can be basically ignored; what you see on the screen is what actually gets printed. *See also* DESKTOP PUBLISHING, WORD PROCESSING, *and* WYSIWYG.

Embedded object

As you become proficient in computing, you'll want to put files, or parts of files, into documents. For example, you might use a piece of clip art in a brochure that you create with the help of a desktop publishing program. When you put a file into another file, it is called *embedding*. The inserted file is an *embedded object* that might consist of text, graphics, sound, program commands, or even animation.

Merging files. An embedded object might be created in the same application as the destination object. For example, you might put 20 pieces of clip art into a composite image, or you might have a file of 50 poems (named POEM) created by merging all the individual pieces (files POEM.1 through POEM.50) you've composed.

Multiple applications. Embedded objects don't have to be created in the same application as the destination document. Suppose you want a picture for each of the 50 poems in your poetry anthology. You could embed 50 different objects from various collections of clip art, one for each poem.

Graphics are the most obvious example of embedded objects, but you can embed just about anything into anything else. You might be writing a report, for example, and need to insert a spreadsheet or database in the text. You can have several documents, each created with a different application, embedded in a destination document, as shown in the drawing. *See also* APPLICATION *and* OBJECT LINKING AND EMBEDDING.

Empirical design

Empirical design is an engineering technique in which experience and intuition are applied, in addition to theory. The process is largely trial-and-error. The engineer starts at a logical point, based on theoretical principles, but experimentation is necessary in order to get the device or system to work right.

Encoding

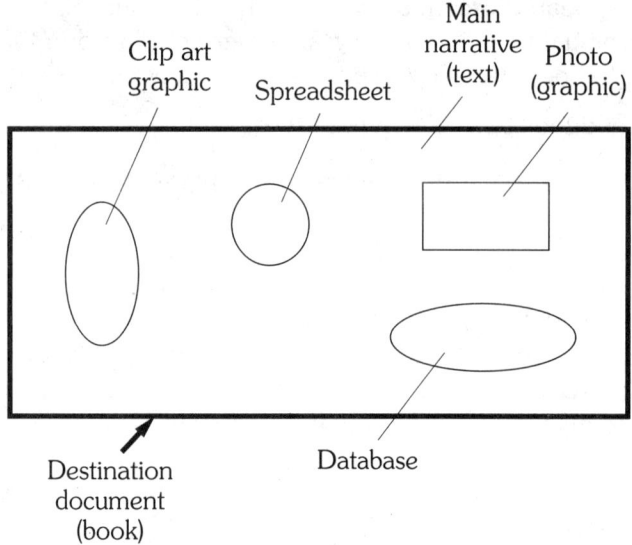

Text with embedded graphics, spreadsheet, and database.

Computer hardware is suited to empirical design techniques. You can't simply make up plans for a new PC, and then expect the machine to work perfectly on the first trial. A *prototype* is built and tested, noting the flaws. Then the engineer revises the design, and the machine is tested again, with the problems noted again. Another drawing-board round follows. This process is repeated until the computer and associated peripherals function just the way the engineer wants.

Software is perfected by a similar process. A program rarely works perfectly the first time it is run. *Debugging* is necessary, sometimes requiring several rounds of rewriting and rerunning. In artificial intelligence (AI) software, particularly, perfection is an ideal that is never achieved totally. No matter how smart a computer becomes, it can always be made a little smarter—and wiser, too! In some ways, the behavior of AI systems evolves on its own, as if it were independent of the minds of the engineers involved. *See also* ARTIFICIAL INTELLIGENCE, DEBUGGING, HARDWARE, *and* SOFTWARE.

Encoding

Encoding is the process of putting a sequence of characters (letters, numbers, and punctuation) into digital code. Each character corresponds to one symbol; each symbol corresponds to one character.

Binary codes. Perhaps you are familiar with the International Morse code. When you transmit this code with a keyer or keyboard, you're encoding text into digital form. Each character has its own unique set of pulses made up of two levels, logic 1 or 0 (also known as "high" and "low"). The drawing shows the word *IF* translated into Morse code. Notice that the spaces between the letters are important in the process of encoding. Without them, there would be no way to tell where one letter ends and the next letter begins.

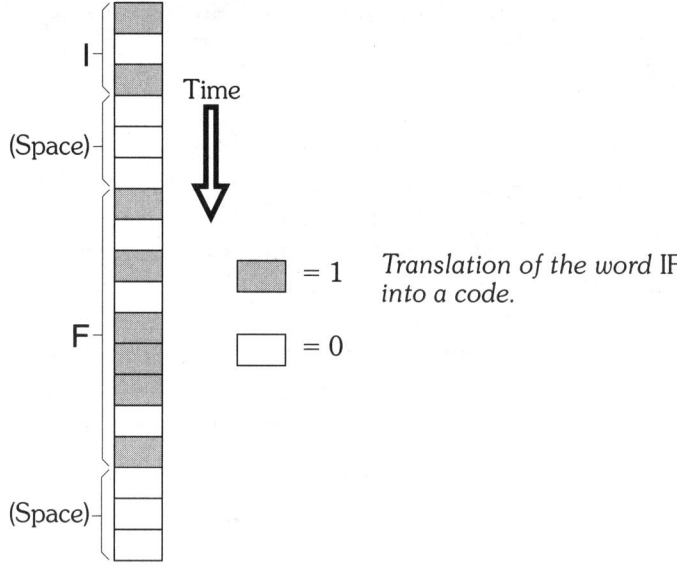

Translation of the word IF into a code.

Your PC has a different code, and it makes the translation automatically as you input your data. One digital code used by many computers is called *ASCII* (pronounced "ask-key"). Like Morse, ASCII is a binary code; the signal is always either logic 1 or logic 0, never any other level. ASCII can depict many symbols, including both uppercase and lowercase alphabetic characters. It's more complicated than Morse code in terms of the number of pulses per character, but in essence, the two codes work in the same way, by sending pulses in a timed sequence.

Communicating with a PC. When you "talk" to a computer, you type things on its keyboard. You can also speak words to your machine if it is equipped with speech recognition. You might give it images, in the form of drawings or photographs. It's even possible to input motion pictures (video) into a computer.

All words and images, whether written, spoken, or seen, are representable by groups of binary digits called *bits*. The PC converts words or images into bits because machine language is the only language a computer can directly work with. Although the real world is analog, digital computer data contains all the information we need to communicate in writing, speech, or images.

Encryption. You might want to alter, or "scramble," data to make it recognizable only to certain authorized people. This is sometimes called encoding, but the technically correct term for it is *encryption*.

Encryption

A code of this sort is called a *cipher*. The use of a cipher can help keep data communications private. In some cases, however, encryption is against the law. *See also* ANALOG, ANALOG-TO-DIGITAL CONVERSION, ASCII, CRYPTANALYSIS/CRYPTOGRAPHY/CRYPTOLOGY, DATA CONVERSION, DECODING, DIGITAL, DIGITAL-TO-ANALOG CONVERSION, *and* ENCRYPTION.

Encryption

Encryption is the sending of a message, or the storage of data or software, in the form of a *cipher*. Encryption ensures that only authorized people can read the message or data, or use the software. Encryption is sometimes called *scrambling*, but scrambling is actually only one specialized form of encryption.

Encryption is not the same thing as *encoding*, in which data is sent or stored using commonly agreed-upon combinations of pulses. All computer communications systems encode; only a fraction of them encrypt.

An example of encryption is to change every letter in a data signal to the letter that comes after it. Then A would become B, X would become Y, and Z would become A. Numbers could be treated similarly; each digit could be increased by 1, except for 9, which would become 0. Punctuation might be changed by "bumping" each mark ahead by one in the set {.,?!:;"'}. To decrypt a message in this cipher, every letter would be changed to the one preceding it in the sequence.

In the United States, the use of encrypted communications is regulated by the Federal Communications Commission. It is often illegal for individuals to encrypt signals if the intent is to conceal the meaning of a message. This is particularly true in amateur radio communications. *See also* CRYPTANALYSIS/CRYPTOGRAPHY/CRYPTOLOGY *and* ENCODING.

End key

The *End key* on your PC keyboard is usually located in a pad of six keys to the right of the main keyboard, and above the arrow keys (see the drawing). It is generally used to speed up the process of editing text, possibly in conjunction with the function keys.

In many programs, pressing the End key causes the cursor to jump to the very end of the text on the line. It will stay there, either on the last character or just after it, until you move it with some other key. Depending on the software you're using, pressing the End key along with other keys causes various things to happen. In some word processors, for example, pressing Ctrl-End makes the cursor jump to the end of the whole text file, whether the file is one page long or 100 pages long. *See also* FUNCTION KEYS *and* HOME KEY.

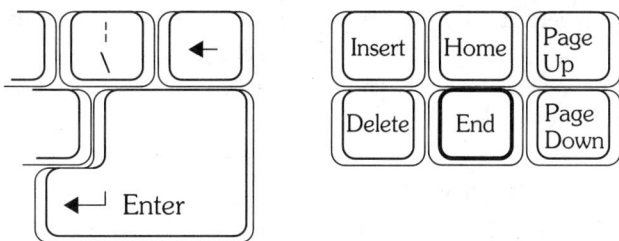

Typical location of the End key is to the right of main keyboard.

Endless loop

In computers and artificial intelligence (AI) systems, the term *endless loop* refers to a situation in which the machine gets caught in a circle of reasoning that takes it nowhere. In programming, this is sometimes called an *infinite loop*. It causes a computer to waste time and effort simply "chasing its tail."

In a program. The simplest type of endless loop involves a bug in a program, where the computer is told to move from one step to another, then back to the first one. For example, line 250 of a program might say, "GO TO 720," but line 720 says "GO TO 250." Once the computer reaches line 250 in the execution of this program, it stops running for all practical purposes. Of course, the solution to this problem is to debug the program.

In a smart robot. A robot might be told, "Put the glass on the chair at the table," but for some reason hears this command as "Put the glass on the chair *and* the table." Unless the programming could handle a command that could not be executed, the robot might take the glass, go to the table, and proceed to oscillate its arm back and forth from table to chair indefinitely. This sort of scenario could result from a noise pulse in the system or some minor hardware imperfection such as a low-quality microphone in the machine's speech-recognition system.

Software psychiatry? In more complex systems, endless loops can cause degradation without a complete breakdown. An excellent example can be found in neurotic human behavior of the type called "obsessive-compulsive."

Suppose you're a compulsive buyer of lamps. Your house might look like a lighting store because you have so many lamps. When you see a trendy lamp, you can't help yourself. You keep repeating this behavior even though it has brought you to the brink of bankruptcy.

As AI evolves to advanced levels, neurotic behavior of this type might become a real concern to computer engineers, creating the need for "software psychiatrists," actually expert program debuggers, trained to get rid of behavioral problems in computers and smart robots. Many such problems might be traceable to endless loops concealed in the immensely complicated webwork of AI software. *See also* ARTIFICIAL INTELLIGENCE, NEUROTIC COMPUTER BEHAVIOR, *and* PSYCHOTIC COMPUTER BEHAVIOR.

End-to-end acknowledgment

In network communications, *end-to-end acknowledgment* refers to a message sent back from the destination station to the source station, telling the source that the message was received. The acknowledgment signal goes back through the nodes along the way the signal was originally sent. When the originating station gets an end-to-end acknowledgement, the originating operator knows that the destination station got the message.

When there are several nodes in a communications path, end-to-end acknowledgment is an inefficient way to inform the source that the destination has received a message. This is because every node has to pass the acknowledgment along after the message has reached the destination. The drawing shows a communications path with four nodes between the source and destination. There are five messages sent (MSG 1 through MSG 5): one from the source, and one from each node. Ideally, there are no transmission errors at any node, and all five of these messages are identical. There are also five acknowledgment signals sent (ACK 1 through ACK 5): one from the destination, and one from each node. These signals, too, should all be the same. The circuit must send two complete data packages, the message and the acknowledgment, through the whole system, a total of ten individual transmissions in this case. That's wasteful.

Sometimes the acknowledgment fails to get all the way back to the source, even when the message has reached the destination. That's especially likely to occur when the communication circuit is not very good. The source will then repeat the message unnecessarily, wasting more time.

A more efficient method of message verification is called *node-to-node acknowledgment*. In this scheme, acknowledgment signals are sent from each node to the one preceding it, but no further back. *See also* NODE, NODE-TO-NODE ACKNOWLEDGMENT, *and* PACKET COMMUNICATIONS.

Energy-efficient computing

Personal computers do not consume great amounts of electrical power. Nevertheless, with the increasing popularity of PCs and the variety of peripherals that go with them, it makes sense to think about minimizing the energy your workstation requires.

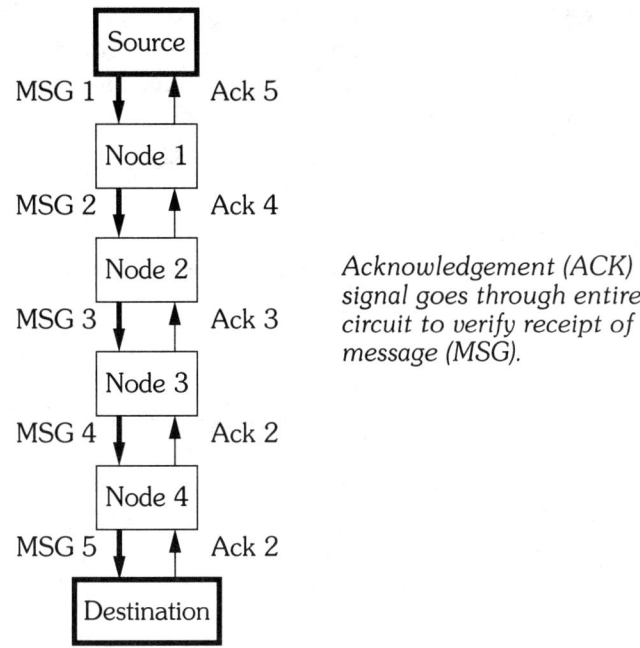

Acknowledgement (ACK) signal goes through entire circuit to verify receipt of message (MSG).

How much power? The table shows the typical power, in watts, consumed by a PC, common peripherals, and attendant equipment such as lights. By comparison, an air conditioner or electric heater can use more than 2000 watts of power.

Many people leave their PCs powered-up for 24 hours a day, seven days a week. Maybe you've heard that this is a good thing to do because it keeps the temperature of your machine constant, supposedly increasing its lifespan. However, modern computers are built to last so long that you'll probably want to trade in your old PC before it wears out.

Power consumption of various appliances

Appliance	Power in watts
Incandescent desk lamp	10 to 15
Fluorescent desk lamp	10 to 15
Printer, idling	10 to 20
Printer, running	20 to 40
Desktop computer	30 to 40
Modem	40 to 100
Fax machine, idling	100 to 200
Fax machine, running	100 to 200

Enhanced Graphics Adapter

What you can do. You can conserve large amounts of energy in the long term by doing certain things just a little bit differently with your PC. By observing the guidelines mentioned here, you can also increase the working lifetime of some equipment:

1 *Don't leave things on.* At the end of a work session, turn the computer and its peripherals off. Don't leave your printer running in the "idle" state when you're working but not using the printer. Switch your monitor off if you need to leave your workstation for a while. Switch off lamps, too, when you don't need them or when you're leaving the room.

2 *Get a switch box.* For about $10 you can buy a box with six or eight outlets in it, a cord to plug into the wall, and a toggle switch. Connect all of your equipment to this box, and use the switch box to power up and power down. Then you won't forget to switch everything off when you leave your workstation. Many transient suppression units, also known (somewhat incorrectly) as surge protectors or surge suppressors, come in the form of switch boxes. This is ideal, because it filters out voltage "spikes" on the power line that can cause a computer to malfunction. See also transient suppression.

3 *Don't overuse air conditioning.* You don't have to keep your workstation at 70°F and 40% relative humidity every minute of the year. Your machine will work all right over a wide range of temperatures. Anything between 50° and 85° is fine as far as your computer is concerned. Your body will probably overheat long before your PC does. You should, however, be sure that there is adequate room for air circulation on all sides of your computer and its peripherals.

4 *Consider a laptop.* Portable computers consume far less power than desktop units, mainly because the display in a laptop machine uses low-current technology. (It must, or the batteries would run down in minutes.) In recent years, laptop computers have begun to rival desktop machines in terms of computing power, hard disk space, and display resolution. If you travel often, and if you can only afford one computer, a laptop might be the most logical choice.

5 *Keep up with energy-saving technologies.* This applies to everything: PCs, peripherals, lighting, fax machines, and photocopiers. Check with your local PC dealer on these matters. If he or she doesn't seem to know what's going on, get brochures on the newest equipment, and compare. PC-related magazines also have occasional articles on energy-saving PCs and peripherals. *See also* GREEN COMPUTING.

Enhanced Graphics Adapter

An *Enhanced Graphics Adapter (EGA)* is a digital monitor display scheme once used in IBM-compatible PCs. It showed a reasonable amount of detail, in fairly good color.

An EGA monitor could display several hues and had reasonable image resolution. Such a monitor is still adequate for some personal computing applications, including graphs and simple charts, but it leaves something to be desired if you want high-resolution graphics. For example, an EGA is not very good for sophisticated computer games, high-speed animation, or interactive technology. For these applications, a better choice is the *Video Graphics Array (VGA)*. Still better is a *Super Video Graphics Array (SVGA)*. See also SUPER VIDEO GRAPHICS ARRAY *and* VIDEO GRAPHICS ARRAY.

Enhanced Industry Standard Architecture

Enhanced Industry Standard Architecture (EISA) is a specification involving microprocessors such as the Intel 80386 (386) and 80486 (486). It makes use of 32-bit processing, compared with 8-bit processing in the older Industry Standard Architecture (ISA).

Although clock speed is an important measure of PC power, it is just one of several factors. The word (bus) size is also important. An EISA bus is like a highway with four times as many lanes as an ISA bus, as shown in the drawing. (Imagine the lanes each carrying traffic in the same direction.) If all other factors were equal, you would correctly surmise that EISA would be four times as powerful as ISA. But, as you can also probably guess, other factors are rarely all equal.

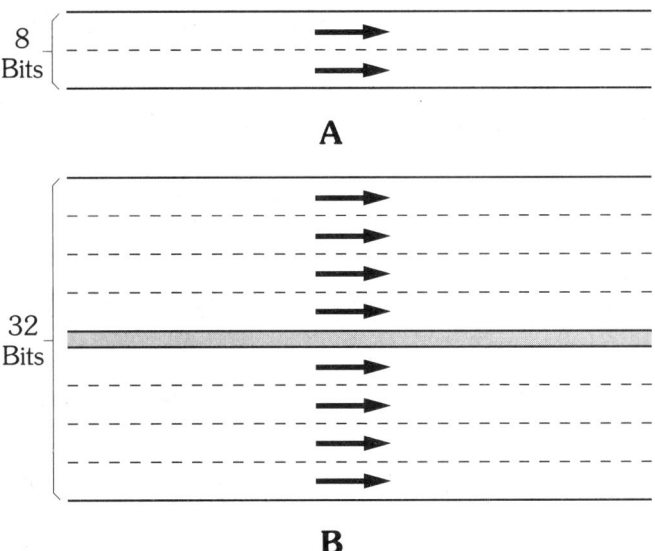

An eight-bit ISA bus is like a two-lane highway (A); a 32-bit EISA bus is like an eight-lane highway (B).

The main problem with EISA is that it's more expensive than ISA. There are also some hangups with downward compatibility. Gradually, however, these problems are being overcome.

Enhanced PC keyboard

Adjectives. The use of the word *enhanced* points out a common problem that engineers encounter with terminology. Computer technology is one of the most rapidly changing fields in science. What seems high-powered or sophisticated today will be mundane in a few years. If you invent something and call it "standard," you'll need additional adjectives before long.

A good example can be found in integrated-circuit (IC) technology. First there was large-scale integration (LSI); then came very-large-scale integration (VLSI). Now some engineers talk about ultra-large-scale integration (ULSI). As it has become possible to pack more and more circuits on a semiconductor chip, new adjectives are needed, each one representing a tenfold increase in component density.

Imagine computers as they evolve over the next 10, 25, or 50 years. What adjectives might be used when "enhanced" is no longer adequate to define the state of computer architecture? *See also* BUS, COMPUTER GENERATIONS, COMPUTER POWER, *and* INDUSTRY STANDARD ARCHITECTURE.

Enhanced PC keyboard

The *enhanced PC keyboard*, with 101 keys in all, is used with most IBM-compatible PCs. It replaced the original PC keyboard, part of the original IBM PC, which had fewer keys and was less user-friendly. The drawing shows the locations of the various parts of the enhanced keyboard.

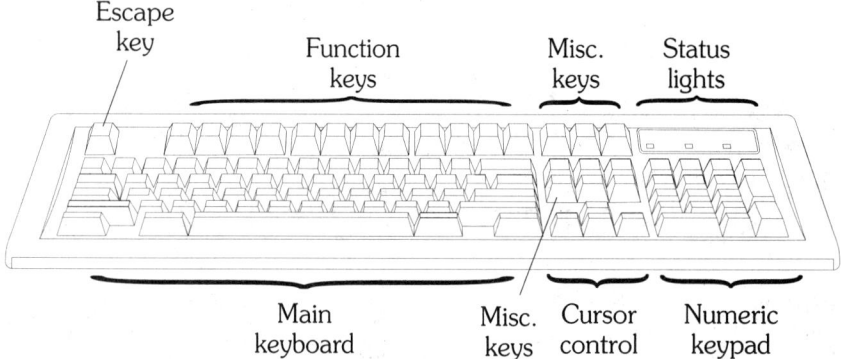

The enhanced PC keyboard has several sets of keys.

The main part of the keyboard contains the letters, numerals and symbols, along with the Tab, Caps Lock, Shift, Ctrl, Alt, Enter, and Backspace keys. There are also 12 function keys located above the main keyboard. These do things that depend on the software, and also on whether they are used along with other keys (typically Ctrl or Alt).

To the immediate right of the main keyboard, there is a keypad that has the Insert, Home, Page Up, Delete, End, and Page Down keys.

Below this is a keypad with arrows pointing up, down, right, and left. This area is for cursor control.

At the extreme right side of the enhanced keyboard, there's a pad resembling an adding machine, sometimes called the *numeric keypad*. It is used for various purposes, depending on the software. Just above the numeric keypad are three indicator lights, usually marked Num, Caps, and Scroll. *See also* ALT KEY, BACKSPACE KEY, CAPS LOCK KEY AND LIGHT, CONTROL KEY, DELETE KEY, END KEY, ENTER KEY, FUNCTION KEYS, HOME KEY, INSERT KEY, NUMBER LOCK KEY AND LIGHT, ORIGINAL PC KEYBOARD, PAGE DOWN KEY, PAGE UP KEY, SCROLL LOCK KEY AND LIGHT, SHIFT KEY, *and* TAB KEY.

Enhanced Storage-Device Interface

The term *Enhanced Storage-Device Interface (ESDI)* refers to an interface standard, or criterion, for hard disk drives in older PCs. It specifies the rate at which binary digits (bits) are transferred between the electronic circuits and the drive controller. An ESDI drive reads and writes data about twice as fast as the earlier ST-506/ST-412 drive, but is not as fast as a drive that takes advantage of SCSI (Small Computer System Interface) technology.

A hard disk's read/write speed is an important factor in determining the overall power of a PC. If you have to wait a long time to access a file or write a file on the hard disk, it partially defeats the purpose of having a speedy microprocessor.

When shopping for a new computer, therefore, you should take the hard disk speed into account. This specification is usually given in brochures for the equipment. If it is not given, ask the salesperson or call the manufacturer. *See also* COMPUTER POWER, HARD DISK, *and* SMALL COMPUTER SYSTEM INTERFACE.

ENIAC

See ELECTRONIC NUMERICAL INTEGRATOR AND CALCULATOR.

Enter key

The *Enter key* is a large key, often with a bent-arrow symbol on it, that has various functions. It is also sometimes called the *Return key*. Generally, pressing Enter returns the cursor or sends a command. Some keyboards have only one Enter key, while others have two. The drawing (on next page) shows the locations of the two Enter keys on an enhanced PC keyboard.

In word processing. When you're typing text, the Enter key works somewhat like the carriage return on a typewriter. If you press this key at any time while typing the document, the cursor will jump down to the beginning of a new line.

Enter key

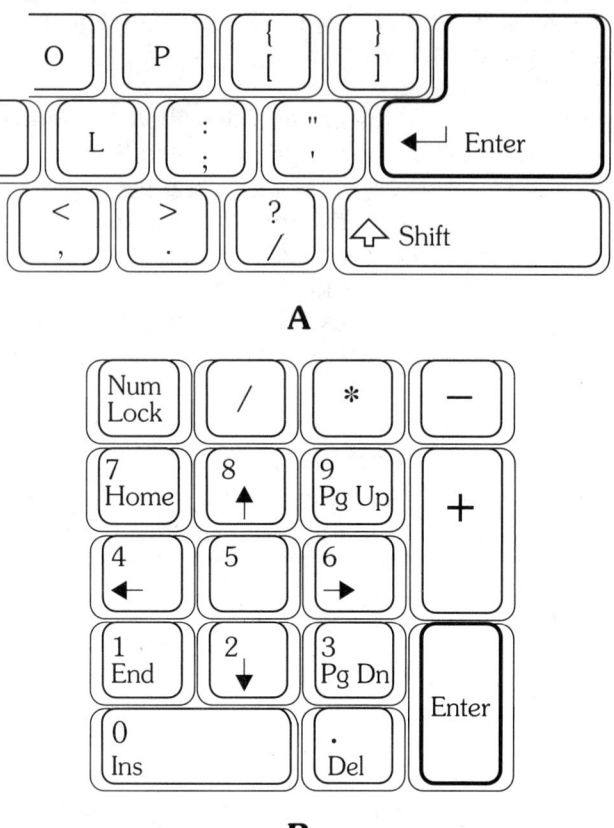

The Enter key on the main keyboard (A) and on the numeric keypad (B).

Suppose the cursor is in the middle of existing text, rather than at the end of something new. If you press Enter, all the text after the cursor will jump down along with the cursor, while the text behind the cursor will remain fixed. This will "tear apart" paragraphs, sentences, and perhaps even words. (To "untear" the text, you can usually press the Backspace key.)

If you press Enter and then hold the key down, the cursor will jump to the beginning of a new line, pause for about a half-second, and then rapidly slide down line after line. As this happens, an ever-widening gap will form between the text ahead of the cursor (if any) and the text behind it. *See also* CURSOR *and* WORD PROCESSING.

Issuing commands. When working with a command-driven interface such as DOS, pressing Enter sends commands to the microprocessor. For example, you might type DIR A: and press Enter to look at the directory of a diskette in drive A. Pressing Enter lets the PC know you've finished typing the command, and that you mean business. If you've typed a command and nothing happens, always make sure you've pressed the Enter key after the command.

Sometimes a computer will ask you a question or tell you to do something, and then to press Enter to continue or respond. In that case, the function of the Enter key depends on the nature of the utility or software. For example, you might want to perform a warm boot. You could press the key combination Ctrl-Alt-Del and the computer might respond with

```
DO YOU WISH TO QUIT (Y/N)
```

If you want to go ahead and give your machine the warm boot, you'd type Y and press Enter.

In some networks where command-driven software is used, it is not necessary to press Enter to send a command. In fact, in such an environment, pressing Enter is likely to cancel the command. Examples of this can be found in certain Internet servers.

If you're working with menu-driven software or with a graphical user interface (GUI), commands are usually issued by selecting a menu item or icon and clicking the mouse. However, in many GUIs, pressing Enter can often be used as an alternative to clicking OK. *See also* COMMAND, COMMAND-DRIVEN SOFTWARE, DOS, GRAPHICAL USER INTERFACE, *and* MENU-DRIVEN SOFTWARE.

Entry-level system

An *entry-level system* is the least sophisticated computer you can use for the things you want to do. For example, if you wanted to do word processing and simple graphics, an entry-level system might be a PC with an 80386 microprocessor, a 120MB (megabyte) hard disk, a high-density diskette drive, 4MB of RAM, a color monitor, and a dot-matrix printer. This is far from the state of the art, but it will do the job for most beginners.

The near future. In 10 years, the above-mentioned system will seem incredibly primitive to the average PC user, even though it would still be adequate for many people's needs. Nevertheless, as computers get smarter and faster, people tend to take each improvement for granted almost immediately. Once people get used to a computer that speaks intelligible words and responds to verbal commands, for example, they will never again be satisfied with keyboard-and-mouse interfaces alone. The meaning of the term "entry level" is therefore time-dependent.

A typical system in the year 2005 might have an 80986 microprocessor (or whatever it's called), a 500GB (gigabyte) hard drive, a diskette drive with 10GB of space, 4GB of RAM, a super-high-resolution color monitor, several rewriteable CD-ROM drives, and a color printer that can print out 50 pages per minute and reproduce 2400 dots per inch. In addition to this, machines will probably have speech recognition and speech synthesis capability built-in. Virtual

EPROM

reality and multimedia will be quite ordinary features. For today's college computer programming exercise or high-school English composition, such a system would represent overkill. But in the year 2005, 18-year-olds might be conversing with their PCs about the merits of Einstein's concept of time as a dimension, debating which adjective fits best in a sentence, or choreographing a dance routine.

The long-term future. Eventually, home computers might come with artificial intelligence (AI). Entry-level systems will seem incredibly powerful by today's standards, based on raw specifications alone, but true advancement must take the human factor into account.

The great difference between tomorrow's computing and today's will be in the software. It will be such that inexperienced people will have no trouble using computers. *Cyberphobia* will be an obsolete term, a relic from "the olden days." When using a PC in, say, the year 2075, the impression will not be one of awesome power, but one of usefulness. The computer engineer's greatest challenge is to make complex systems easy for all people to work with. *See also* ARTIFICIAL INTELLIGENCE *and* CYBERPHOBIA.

EPROM

See ERASABLE PROGRAMMABLE READ-ONLY MEMORY.

Erasable optical disc

Using laser technology, it's possible to store and recover large amounts of data on plastic disks. This was first done in the music-recording industry, in the form of compact discs (CDs). More recently, the technology has been adapted to computing. Using CD-ROMs (compact-disc, read-only memory), up to 650MB (megabytes) of digital information can be written on a disk only a few inches across.

Reusability. The big limitation of CD-ROM is that you can't overwrite data on the disk. So, while a single CD-ROM can contain dozens of books (even a library), it can't serve the same function as a hard disk. You can make your own CD-ROM if you want to store a huge amount of information in permanent archives; this is done using a *write-once/read-many (WORM)* drive. A WORM drive is expensive, however, and it can only write data onto fresh CDs. It can't overwrite the information on old CD-ROMs.

A goal of CD engineers is to create an optical storage medium that can be used over and over, just like a magnetic disk. An *erasable optical disc* is the next step in this direction, one rung above WORM technology. The data is removed, or erased, from a used CD, so it becomes fresh again. Then new data can be written on the surface of the disk.

Limitations. There are two problems with erasable optical discs. The first is that the technology is too costly for the average PC user. The second is that erasable optical discs work at a slow rate of speed.

Using an erasable optical disc system is like living on a gigantic ranch, where you have plenty of wide-open space, but no paved roads to get around on. You can go anywhere you want, and your territory is huge, but you can't be in a hurry about it. Nevertheless, this technology does find some applications, especially in colleges, universities, and government agencies. A computer with an erasable optical disc system can be set up as a private online service, so that people can access and modify the archives of their organizations. *See also* ARCHIVES, CD-ROM, HARD DISK, *and* WRITE-ONCE/READ-MANY.

Erasable programmable read-only memory

An *erasable programmable read-only memory (EPROM)* is a special form of read-only memory (ROM). It is an integrated circuit (IC), also known as a "chip," which comes in a case with a window that is transparent to ultraviolet light (UV). By focusing a beam of UV at the window, the contents in the ROM are erased so that the chip can be reprogrammed.

Some EPROMs are erasable by electrical means. This type of chip is called an *electrically erasable programmable read-only memory (EEPROM)*.

Reprogramming an EPROM requires a special procedure and sophisticated hardware. The chip must generally be removed from the circuit in which it has been installed, exposed to the UV, reprogrammed, and then put back in its place. Still, engineers like EPROMs because they allow firmware to be changed if a problem, or bug, is found. A conventional programmable read-only memory (PROM), on the other hand, can't be changed once it has been programmed.

Although the data in an EPROM can be altered, it isn't quite the same thing as random-access memory (RAM). The data in RAM is easily and instantly overwritten by electronic means. The fast PC memory with which you might be familiar is RAM. *See also* FIRMWARE, PROGRAMMABLE READ-ONLY MEMORY, RANDOM-ACCESS MEMORY, *and* READ-ONLY MEMORY.

Ergonomics

The way you organize your computer workstation affects how efficiently you use your computer. A good setup can make computing more pleasant, while a bad workstation arrangement can cause frustration and even pain. The drawing is an overhead view of a well-arranged PC workstation. The efficiency and user-friendliness of a PC workstation is called *ergonomics*.

Ergonomics

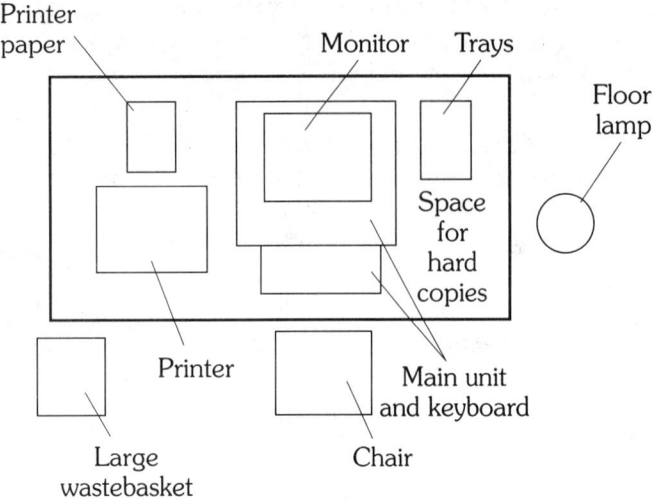

Overhead view of a workstation. A door set on top of two file cabinets serves as the desk.

Body position. While working at a computer, you should be sitting comfortably. You should not be hunched, nor should you be bolt upright, straining to reach the keyboard. You should look slightly down to observe the monitor and be able to put your feet flat on the floor. You shouldn't have to lean very far to get diskettes, adjust the printer, or operate other peripherals.

The best test of body position is the way you feel after about two hours of continuous work at your PC. If you can work for that length of time and not have any soreness or fatigue, your body position is probably fine.

It's important to take frequent breaks while working at the computer. Get up and walk around. If you are alone and don't have to worry about what people will think of you, consider stretching exercises. The human body did not evolve for office work; a continuous four-hour stint of this is unnatural. A five-minute break every hour can make the other 55 minutes more productive than a full hour with no breaks.

Chair. You don't need an expensive, deeply upholstered chair for a PC workstation. In fact, such chairs are rather poor choices for working at a computer or terminal. Using a PC is often a learning experience. You should sit like a student. Folding chairs are fairly good, or office supply houses sell roller chairs with adjustable height. (If you use a roller chair, put a hard mat under the chair; rollers can ruin floors. Mats come in various shapes to fit under desks, and some also work as antistatic devices.)

Chair height is extremely important. A chair that's too high or low can contribute to back, neck, and shoulder pain. It's astonishing how much difference a couple of inches of chair height can make; a pillow on a chair can be the difference between comfort and back spasms.

Chairs with arm rests present both an ergonomic advantage and a disadvantage. The advantage is, of course, that you can place your elbows on arm rests for short intervals while typing on your keyboard. The main disadvantage is that arm rests can get in your way and prevent you from pushing the chair under the desk or table.

Desk. You'll probably want a big desk for your PC, especially if you use a mouse. Some people prefer specially constructed computer desks, but you can do just as well with a full-size, 30-inch-wide door placed on two file cabinets. Whatever you use as a desk, it should be rock-solid. A desk that wobbles, even slightly, is a major distraction—and possibly a safety hazard. The desk should be capable of supporting at least 250 pounds indefinitely. The work area should be 30 to 36 inches deep to allow for keyboard placement, and to leave room for cables behind the equipment.

The printer can go on your work desk, next to the main PC unit, or on its own separate stand. A separate printer stand gives you more room on your main desk; it also has a shelf underneath for several thousand sheets of fanfold paper. If there is no paper shelf, you can put the paper on the floor.

Keyboard. Your keyboard should go underneath and in front of your monitor. You'll need to look at your monitor while typing, and yet cast occasional glances at the keyboard. The less eye and head movement, the better.

Most desktop PCs have a main unit five to seven inches high. The monitor can be placed on top of the main unit, and the keyboard in front of the main unit, provided your work desk is deep enough. The diskette drives in the main unit will then be in a convenient spot just above the keyboard. An alternative is to use a keyboard shelf attached under the desk; the keyboard can be slid beneath the work surface when the computer is not in use.

Most people like to have the keyboard placed so the letter G is in front of the middle of the body.

Monitor. Many PC users place the monitor too close to their faces, which can cause eye strain by increasing the extent to which your eyes must move back and forth to follow text and objects on screen. It also increases your exposure to ELF fields.

The monitor should be at least 18 inches away from your eyes. It should also be aimed straight at your face when you're in a comfortable computing position. Monitors are equipped with swivel bases so you can adjust the orientation of the screen.

Ergonomics

The monitor has a brightness adjustment and a contrast adjustment. Experiment with these to find the settings that are best for you. Using software, you can also change from dark type on a light background to light type on a dark background. You can experiment with the size of fonts, too. *See also* FONT *and* MONITOR.

Lighting and vision. The way you light your workstation is as important as any other single factor. Indirect daylight is probably the best for work purposes, and also the healthiest. Try to place your PC near a window so you can take advantage of natural light. Vertical or horizontal blinds can keep direct sunlight off your equipment and out of your face.

The main consideration for artificial light is that it minimize eye strain. You can be creative; there are hundreds of lamp styles from which to choose. Halogen torchiere lamps are easy on the eyes. They shine on the ceiling, from which the light scatters, giving shadow-free illumination. These lamps also have dimmers, so you can adjust the brightness. Their disadvantage is that they consume a lot of energy. Depending on how much light you want, and on the size of your work area, one of these lamps burns 200 to 500 watts.

The old-fashioned shade lamps work quite well for PC workstation lighting. It's best to use "soft white" bulbs rated at 60 or 75 watts. You can put a 75-watt spotlight in one of these lamps, and it will shine up at the ceiling. Then you'll get indirect light with almost no shadows.

Most people find high-intensity lamps too harsh for PC workstation use. They shine brilliantly over a small area. When the rest of the room is dark, everything stands out in vivid contrast. This might look great at first, but after a short time most people develop eye fatigue from it.

No matter what the lighting source, it should be positioned so that it does not reflect back at you from the screen glass. This is called *screen glare*, and it quickly produces visual fatigue. It can also cause you to make mistakes because you can't clearly see what you're doing. If you're in an office with fluorescent ceiling lights that cannot be moved, you can get a glare-reducing screen that attaches to the front of your monitor.

Peripherals. Equipment such as the printer, external diskette drives, CD-ROM drive, and speakers should be within easy reach. Ideally, you should not have to get up from your chair, or even wheel the chair over, to get to frequently used peripherals.

If you have a modem, position it so that you can easily press any buttons or throw any switches. Also, you should be able to see the modem's status lights from where you sit.

The mouse is a special peripheral because it needs a flat, horizontal, smooth surface on which it can slide. The surface should be at least a foot square; 18 inches is better. This takes up a sizable fraction of desk space. Some PC users prefer a trackball to a mouse because it doesn't take up any desk space. You can put the mouse on a shelf just below your desk. You might put this shelf underneath your keyboard. This will work all right for some PC users, but it won't allow much mouse mobility, and it can get in the way of your legs. Another possibility is to use a pull-out shelf, of the sort you find in some office desks. This shelf, when pulled fully out, can be easily reached with your right or left arm. You can push the shelf back in when you're not using the mouse.

You'll probably want to have a telephone within reach of your operating position. It can go just to the left or right of the PC main unit. Some people prefer to have the tone pad (dialer) in the receiver; others like it better in the base of the set. Cordless phones usually work near a PC, but the computer produces electromagnetic signals that might interfere to some extent with your conversations. *See also* CUMULATIVE TRAUMA DISORDERS *and* HUMAN ENGINEERING.

Error accumulation

When measurements are made in succession, the errors add up. This is called *error accumulation*.

Analog errors. Analog error accumulation can be illustrated with an example. Suppose you want to measure a long piece of string (say about 100 meters) using a meter stick marked off in millimeters (mm). You must place the stick along the string repeatedly, about 100 times. If your error is up to ±2 mm with each measurement, then after 100 repetitions, the possible error is up to ±200 mm, or 0.2 meter. That is nearly eight inches.

If you were to measure a string 1000 meters long using the same technique and with the same degree of accuracy per measurement, you could expect your error to be up to ±2000 mm, or two meters. That's more than six feet.

Digital errors. In digital systems, errors occur as misinterpreted bits. A machine might see a logic low when it should see high, or vice versa. It is also possible for bogus data bits to be inserted, or legitimate ones to be dropped. This almost never happens in a computer. In networks it occurs more often than within an individual machine, but it is still uncommon unless the circuit is noisy.

Computers require nearly 100% perfection, especially when the data contains software. A single misplaced bit can mean the difference between a program that runs well and one that does not run at all. The error tolerance is lower for programs than it is for plain text data.

Error checking

Suppose that, on a computer diskette, there are an average of three digital errors introduced each time a copy is made. If you copy the diskette repeatedly, making a copy of a copy of a copy (n times), then for the nth-generation copy, there will be an average of $3n$ digital errors. A 100th-generation copy would have an average of 300 mistaken bits. However, this is still not very many, considering the fact that there are several million bits on a typical diskette. *See also* ANALOG, DIGITAL, *and* DROP-IN AND DROP-OUT.

Error checking

See DOCUMENT COMPARISON, GRAMMAR CHECKING, *and* SPELL CHECKING.

Escape key

The *Escape key*, usually labeled Esc, allows you to undo an operation or command in some applications. In other programs, you might press Esc, either by itself or along with some other key, to carry out an operation.

The drawing shows the location of the Escape key on the enhanced PC keyboard. It is at the extreme upper left, just to the left of the row of function keys, and above the main keyboard.

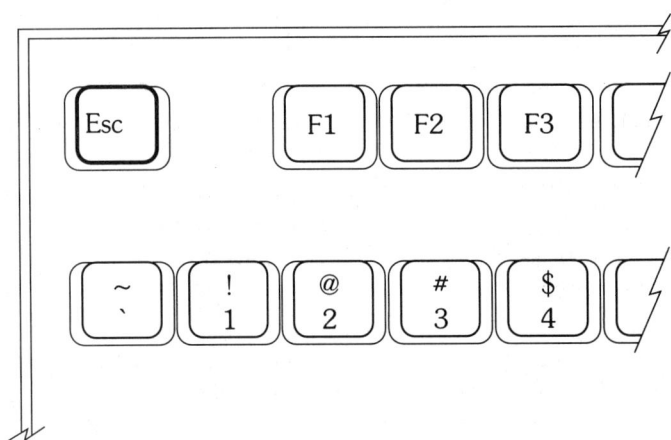

The Escape key is just to the left of F1 on the enhanced PC keyboard.

It's important to avoid inadvertently pressing the Esc key. In some applications you can hit this key over and over, and nothing will happen. In others, however, you might lose data if you strike the Esc key.

ESDI

See ENHANCED STORAGE-DEVICE INTERFACE.

Ethernet

Ethernet is a standard commonly used for large bus networks. It is preferred by professional people and organizations, such as engineers, government agencies, and universities. There can be as many as 1024 workstations, or nodes, in a single Ethernet bus network.

Many networks make use of Ethernet systems. In fact, several Ethernet networks can interconnect to form a *wide-area network (WAN)*. The drawing is a schematic representation of four Ethernet systems interconnected to form a large, versatile WAN.

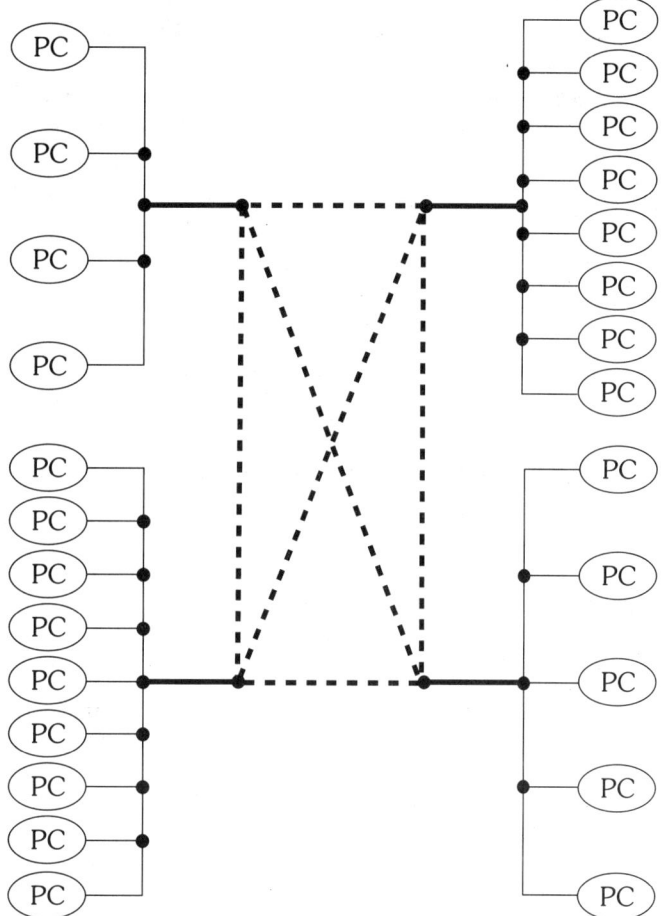

An example of Ethernet bus networks interconnected in a WAN.

The Apple version of Ethernet is known as *EtherTalk*. It's something like AppleTalk, except faster. To use Ethernet or EtherTalk, you need a special interface. This is supplied by a circuit board, or *card*, that you can install. *See also* APPLETALK, BUS NETWORK, LOCAL AREA NETWORK, NETWORK, *and* WIDE-AREA NETWORK.

Event-driven environment

Some PC systems function according to actions like clicking a mouse, receiving a telephone call, pressing a keyboard button, or moving a trackball. Every such event produces a signal that causes the system to do something. This kind of operating system is called an *event-driven environment*.

Event-driven software differs from command-driven such as DOS. In DOS, you must type in a word, abbreviation, or acronym telling the computer what to do. For example, you might type

```
COPY A:*.* C:\PAPERS\*.*
```

to instruct the machine to copy all files from the diskette in drive A to a subdirectory called PAPERS on the hard drive (drive C).

The normal state in an event-driven system is called a *wait state* or *idle loop*. When the stimulus is received (and it can be practically anything), the computer leaves the idle loop and executes a programmed function. Clicking the mouse, for example, causes the PC to do whatever might be indicated by the position of the pointer on the display. After the function has been executed, the computer returns to the idle loop.

The most common event-driven environments are the Windows and Macintosh systems. These employ a *graphical user interface (GUI)*. In the future, you'll see new event-driven schemes as new peripherals are designed and put into service. For example, event-driven software might be ideal for robot control. *See also* COMMAND-DRIVEN SOFTWARE, DOS, GRAPHICAL USER INTERFACE, *and* MENU-DRIVEN SOFTWARE.

Exabyte

The term *exabyte* refers to a gigantic unit of data not yet in common use. The prefix *exa* means 10^{18}, sometimes called a "quintillion" and written out 1,000,000,000,000,000,000. In binary terms, *exa* means 2^{60}. Thus, an exabyte is 2^{60} bytes, or 1,073,741,824 gigabytes. That is about as much data as would be contained on 1,650,000,000 CD-ROMs, or several billion hard disks.

The drawings give an idea of the enormous size of an exabyte compared with typical storage capacities today. At A, the little cube represents one megabyte (MB) of data, roughly the amount contained in one high-density diskette. The large cube represents a gigabyte (GB), about as much data as on two CD-ROMs. Imagine this compressed into the small cube at B. Then the large cube at B is a terabyte (TB), or 1024 GB. That's the amount of data in a million diskettes. Now imagine this cube compressed into the small cube at C; the large cube then becomes a petabyte (PB). That's an exotic unit not yet in common use, equal to 1024 TB. But the compression process must be repeated still one more time, as at D, to bring the enormity of the exabyte (EB) into view.

Some people think exabytes will never be applicable to personal computing. Others believe this unit will someday be regarded as small. Only a few generations ago, people warned that traveling at speeds over 25 miles per hour would literally scramble human brains. Later, people said that air travel was physically impossible. Still later, people

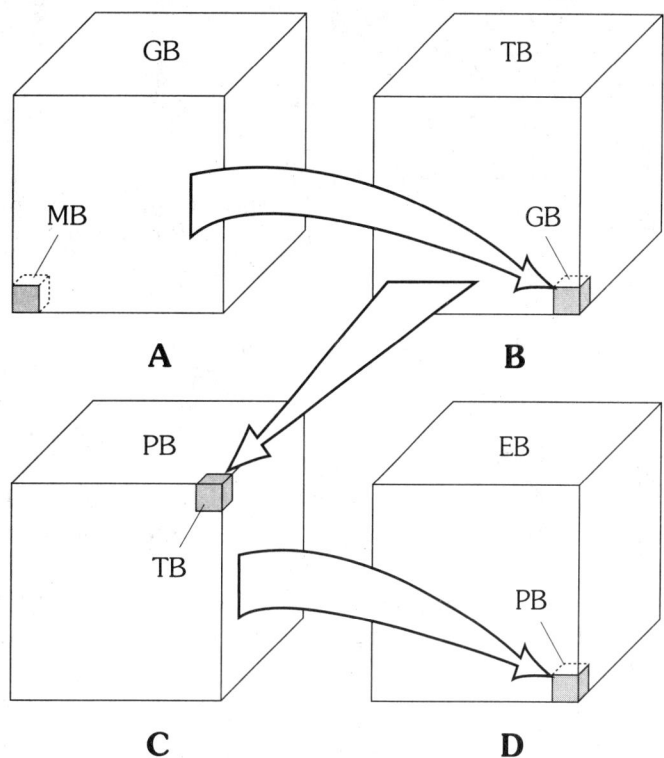

Ratio of megabyte to gigabyte (A), gigabyte to terabyte (B), terabyte to petabyte (C), and petabyte to exabyte (D).

laughed at the notion that human beings would ever set foot on the moon. Clearly, the fact that people scoff at something has little bearing on whether or not it will later happen. *See also* COMPUTER GENERATIONS, DISK CAPACITY, *and* MASS STORAGE.

Exclusive-NOR gate

An *exclusive-NOR (XNOR) gate* is a digital logic circuit with two inputs and one output. It performs the logical exclusive-OR operation, followed by inversion (logic NOT or negation).

The output of an XNOR gate is high, or logic 1 (true) if and only if the input states are the same. If the input states are different, then the XNOR output is low, or logic 0 (false).

Logic gates are extensively used in digital computers and other electronic devices. The schematic symbol for an XNOR gate, along with its logical truth table, is shown in the drawing (top page 384). *See also* AND GATE, EXCLUSIVE-OR GATE, INVERTER, NOR GATE, *and* OR GATE.

Exclusive-OR gate

An *exclusive-OR (XOR) gate* is a digital logic circuit with two inputs and one output. It performs the logical exclusive-OR operation.

Executable program

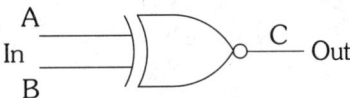

A	B	C
0	0	1
0	1	0
1	0	0
1	1	1

Truth table

Exclusive-NOR gate schematic symbol and truth table.

The output of an XOR gate is high, or logic 1 (true) if and only if the input states are different. If the input states are the same, then the XOR output is low, or logic 0 (false). The schematic symbol for an XOR gate, along with its logical truth table, is shown in the following drawing. *See also* AND GATE, EXCLUSIVE-NOR GATE, INVERTER, NOR GATE, *and* OR GATE.

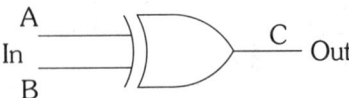

A	B	C
0	0	0
0	1	1
1	0	1
1	1	0

Truth table

Exclusive-OR gate schematic symbol and truth table.

Executable program

When you get a software package, you'd like to run it on your computer right away, without having to go to a lot of trouble with it. Such a program is called an *executable program*. Not all programs are immediately executable, however. You might need to modify or translate a program before you can run it.

Two worlds. There are two major families of personal computers. *IBM-compatible PCs* form one group; *Macintosh* systems form the other. In general, programs written for an IBM-compatible machine are executable on other IBM-compatibles; programs for a Macintosh are executable with other Macintoshes. If you want to run a Mac program on an IBM or vice versa, it's like an American trying to converse with someone from China when neither one knows a word of the other's language. A translator is necessary. Without it, the data is useless.

Perhaps you've put a diskette with Macintosh data into an IBM machine. The directory might show the file, complete with its filename, date of entry, and amount of storage it takes up. When you try to look at the contents of a file, however, you see only garbage (smiling faces, hieroglyphics, etc.). Programs refuse to run; you get an error or incompatibility message. Your computer can't do anything with it unless it's in the right form. *See also* IBM-COMPATIBLE PCS *and* MACINTOSH.

A common bond. No matter who manufactured your PC, its electronic brain works in basically the same way. Computers "think" in terms of binary digits or bits made up of ones and zeros. This language is called *machine language*.

The high-level language of software can be translated into machine language by a compiler. The nature of the compiler depends on the type of computer used (IBM or Macintosh), as well as the specific software. Once compiled, the program can be run. Another way to run programs written in high-level language is to make use of an *interpreter*, which translates and executes the program simultaneously. However, interpreted programs don't run as fast as compiled ones.

In recent years, software engineers have developed operating systems that allow for the use of IBM-compatible and Macintosh data on a single computer. There are also programs that will translate between the two data formats. *See also* COMPILER, HIGH-LEVEL LANGUAGE, INTERPRETER, MACHINE LANGUAGE, *and* OPERATING SYSTEM.

Exercise software

As recently as the 19th century, most people's daily routines involved hard physical work. As cars, trains, buses, and home appliances have proliferated, life has become less and less physically demanding. These days, most people need an exercise routine to stay healthy. One way to get a physical workout is with the help of *exercise software*. (You should, of course, check with your doctor before beginning any exercise program.)

Actually, exercise software is not new. Health clubs have had computerized weight machines, rowing machines, and stationary bikes for several years. The earliest such machines simply counted the number of calories you burned. The equipment has now become programmable, so you can plan a bicycle course, for example, with hills and valleys; the resistance of the machine changes as you go up and down the slopes.

Expandability

The emerging technology of virtual reality ought to make exercise not only fun, but fascinating, in coming years. Imagine lying on a bench, gripping a pair of cables, and finding yourself in an ocean, swimming with porpoises! You might be on a treadmill, running with tigers in the savanna. Maybe you'd rather row a boat along the Mississippi, complete with all the scenery and sound.

With virtual exercise equipment, you'd place a viewing mask on your face, put earphones in your ears, and exercise just about as naturally as if you were really there. In fact, in some ways, exercise software might be better. You could ski cross-country in Wisconsin in February without getting cold. You could climb Mount Everest without oxygen tanks. *See also* VIRTUAL REALITY.

Expandability

You can upgrade your PC in many ways, before you go out and buy a new machine. You might add more memory, install adapters, or hook up another diskette drive or a CD-ROM drive. You can even upgrade the microprocessor in some PCs to a more powerful model. Computers vary in the extent to which you can upgrade them. The *expandability* of a computer is the ease with which extras can be installed and used.

Expandability should be one of your major considerations when buying a PC. Perhaps the most important expandable feature is RAM (random-access memory). Newer software needs much more RAM than software only a couple of years old; this trend will probably continue in the future. Therefore, you'll want to get a PC with plenty of RAM, and the option to expand it severalfold should the need arise.

No matter how much you expand your PC, you'll eventually want a new one. Computers wear out, just as cars do. When you purchase your next computer, keep in mind that technology will have advanced considerably, along with your expectations and demands. Also remember that your needs will most likely continue to grow. *See also* EXPANSION BOARD, EXPANSION BUS, RANDOM-ACCESS MEMORY, *and* UPGRADING.

Expanded memory

See EXTENDED/EXPANDED MEMORY.

Expansion board

An *expansion board* is a printed circuit board that you can install in a computer to give the machine enhanced features. Depending on the expandability of your PC, you'll find anywhere from one to several *expansion slots* in which the boards, also known as *adapter cards*, can be installed.

Expansion board

What they do. Expansion boards are available for several purposes. You can add new functions, or improve the ones you already have.

If you want to add audio to your PC, for example, you can get a sound board for that purpose. This will let you listen to multimedia CD-ROMs, compose music, and use software that turns your PC into a Musical Instrument Digital Interface (MIDI). You can work with speech-synthesis systems, and enjoy games that produce sounds. You can also take advantage of the new, and growing, realm of speech recognition.

If your system does not have a built-in modem, you can buy an expansion board that allows you to connect your PC to the telephone line and get into online networks.

Do you plan to have your PC control a fleet of robots? If so, you'll have to wait a few years. But before long, you'll probably be able to purchase a variety of expansion boards for this purpose.

The functions mentioned here are only a few of the many things expansion boards can do. Check with your local PC dealer and read PC-oriented magazines to get the whole story. *See also* MODEM, ONLINE SERVICE, PERSONAL ROBOTS, *and* SOUND TECHNOLOGY.

What they look like. An expansion card has a characteristic appearance. It is made of phenolic or glass-epoxy material, usually brown or green in color. The board is roughly rectangular in shape.

There are electronic components on one or both sides of the board. You'll find integrated circuits (ICs), also called chips. You might find diodes, resistors, capacitors, and transistors. Copper-colored or silvery strips of foil connect all the components together. On one or two edges of the board, there are contacts or pins; these facilitate plugging the board into a slot or socket. Drawing A on page 388 shows the general appearance of an expansion board. This is only an example; the size and shape varies depending on the function of the board.

The expansion slots are easy to locate inside your PC. To get at them, you must remove the cover of the main unit. If you are uneasy about taking off the cover of a sophisticated piece of electronic apparatus, have your dealer, or a PC-savvy friend, do it for you.

Warning: Always unplug electronic apparatus from wall outlets before you remove the cover of any unit for any reason.

Drawing B shows the locations of expansion slots inside a typical computer's main unit. This is a top view, as the unit looks with the cover removed. The expansion slots are side-by-side. Your unit might have more or fewer slots than are shown in this drawing. Consult your instruction manual or Help files concerning which types of boards go

Expansion board

into which slots. Sometimes it makes a difference where an expansion board goes; sometimes it does not. *See also* EDGE CONNECTOR *and* PRINTED CIRCUIT.

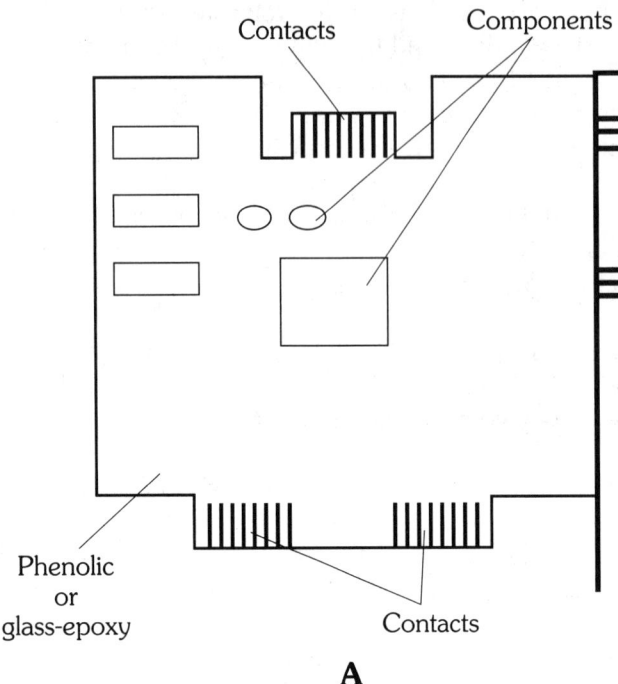

A

A typical expansion circuit board and connectors.

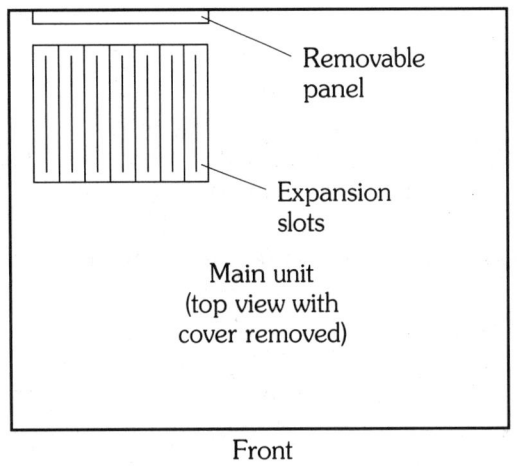

B

Slots are easy to locate in the computer because of their appearance.

Electrostatic discharge. You've probably gotten an electric shock at some point by walking on carpet in dry weather and then touching something metallic. That's an *electrostatic discharge*. A charge builds up whether or not the weather is dry, and whether or not you shuffle around on a carpet. Even an imperceptible electrostatic charge can damage or destroy electronic components on a printed circuit.

Before handling an expansion board or any electronic components, therefore, be sure you've discharged all the static that might have built up on your body. Touch a grounded metal object after you sit down to service the machine. Do it again *every* time you sit back down after having moved around, before you touch any electronic components. Technicians use special body-grounding bracelets when servicing computers. The best insurance against accidental component damage is to obtain one of these bracelets, and use it according to the instructions provided, whenever you open up a computer or peripheral. *See also* COMPLEMENTARY METAL-OXIDE-SEMICONDUCTOR TECHNOLOGY, GROUNDING, *and* METAL-OXIDE-SEMICONDUCTOR TECHNOLOGY.

Read directions. There's an old saying, "When in doubt, read the instructions." This applies to the installation of expansion boards in a PC. Be sure to follow all steps. You might write down the process as you go, so you can repeat it years later should the need arise.

Never force any circuit board into a slot. If the card doesn't fit into its slot, it's probably not aligned correctly. If you use force, you might bend the pins on the card, or even break the circuit board.

Once the expansion board has been placed in its socket, check to be sure it's the right expansion slot. Be sure the pins are aligned in the holes. With some PCs, it's possible to plug a board in with the pins offset, as shown in drawing C. This is one of the most common causes of expansion-board malfunction. Again, if you're not fully confident about opening up your computer, take it to your local computer dealer and let their technicians install your boards. *See also* EXPANDABILITY.

Expansion bus

See BUS *and* DATA BUS.

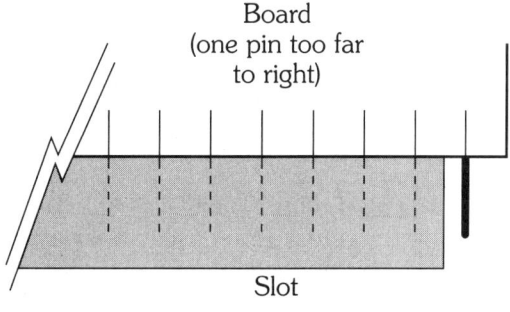

An example of improper board installation (pins offset).

Expert systems

The term *expert systems* refers to a method of reasoning in artificial intelligence (AI). Sometimes this scheme is called *rule-based computer reasoning*. Expert systems turn a computer into a knowledgeable specialist in some field. "Smart robots" also make use of expert systems.

Components. The drawing is a block diagram of a typical expert system. The heart of the device is a set of facts and rules. The rules are statements of the logical form "If X, then Y," similar to many of the statements in high-level programming languages.

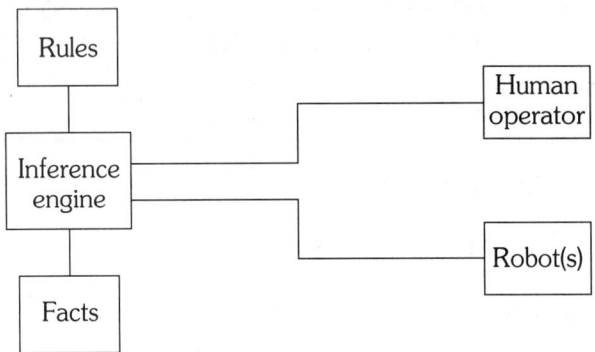

A form of artificial intelligence using facts and rules.

An *inference engine* decides which logical rules should be applied in various situations. The operation of the system can only be as sophisticated as the data supplied by human programmers, however.

Applications. Expert systems can help people do research, make decisions, and make forecasts. A good example is a program that assists a physician in making a diagnosis. The computer asks questions, and arrives at a conclusion based on the answers given by the patient and doctor.

Small businesses are finding expert system software increasingly valuable. Often, a single decision can spell the difference between success and bankruptcy. Programs called MBAware, which mimic the skills of an MBA graduate, can provide unbiased, logical answers and solutions to questions and problems unique to small businesses. These programs make use of interactive technology and graphics to guide the small businessperson along.

Expert systems is a complex, sophisticated, and rapidly changing technology, so the best place to look for reference sources online is the Internet. If you want technical information, consult a good college or university engineering library.

Not quite human. Although expert systems can help people solve many problems, computers are not, and will probably never be, so powerful that they can effectively replace human doctors or MBAs. For one thing, the human brain and mind are far more complex than any computer. But sheer complexity isn't the only hurdle in developing human-like expert systems.

An electronic doctor, lawyer, or accountant lacks certain qualities that humans have in abundance: empathy and intuition. No matter how powerful the logic, some problems seem to require a measure of emotion to be effectively solved. Some computer engineers believe that a machine might be programmed to have empathy and intuition. Other engineers, perhaps a majority, doubt it. How, they ask, can a computer be taught to have hunches?

The technology of AI might someday produce machines with intelligence comparable to that of human beings in some respects. Even if machines ever evolve to a truly human level, however, trusting them will require a leap of faith that some people will not be able to make. *See also* ARTIFICIAL INTELLIGENCE, COMPUTER CONSCIOUSNESS, *and* COMPUTER OVER-RELIANCE.

Export business software

Changes in the global economy are making it easier for small business to get involved in exporting. There are challenges awaiting you if you plan to sell your products abroad. *Export business software* can help you through the barriers and over the hurdles that have traditionally made exporting a big-business-only affair.

Expense. Exporting is serious business, and the software will cost you serious money: upwards of $2500. Some packages are priced in excess of $10,000. The alternatives, however, can be even more costly. You might hire a full-time consultant or contract out for someone to write an export-management program especially for your company. These alternatives can cost you several times the price of the software package itself.

Once you've bought an export business software package, the expenditure is complete. You can write it off as an expense on your taxes, and not have it as an ongoing expense.

Computer requirements. High-end export business software packages are designed for midrange computers, but there are versions available especially for small business that can be used with most PCs. You should probably have a machine with an 80486, Pentium, or later microprocessor, or a top-of-the-line Motorola microprocessor. An 80386 might be sufficient, but it will probably be slow.

Exporting

Some packages place modest demands on your RAM and hard disk, while others need lots of space in both media. Typical RAM requirements range from 1MB to 12MB. Hard disk requirements are between about 10MB and 300MB. This reflects the tremendous variety in features and power available.

The key benefit of using a PC for an export business lies in powerful database software. This helps you make and keep track of forms you'll need to get through the red tape of foreign and domestic regulations. The software also helps you keep track of your progress with individual clients.

In addition to a database, personal finance software can help keep your books straight for each country or client to whom you are exporting goods. Online services and the Internet can help you keep informed about foreign markets and cultures, as well as providing valuable contacts.

Shop around. Finding the ideal export business software requires patience and the willingness to do a thorough job of shopping. If you're going to spend several thousand dollars on a software package, you'll want to be sure you get the one that's best for you.

Several PC-oriented magazines are aimed directly at businesses. These magazines are the best source of information concerning the latest export business software. As with most PC products, prices are declining while power, speed, and variety are increasing. *See also* DATABASE, INTERNET, *and* PERSONAL FINANCE SOFTWARE.

Exporting

When you create a file or document and intend for it to be read by another computer that might be using another program, you *export* the data for use by the other program. Exporting is the opposite of *importing*.

A common example of exporting is the use of diskettes to send articles and reports to clients and salespeople. Many different types of word processing software could be used by the people who will be reading the documents. While each program has its own peculiarities, most can read ASCII. If you send files in "straight ASCII," you're exporting your data in "plain vanilla" format for use by many different programs. *See also* IMPORTING.

Extended character set

Computer text is often written in a code called *ASCII*, which stands for "American Standard Code for Information Interchange." This code can accommodate 256 characters.

Normally, only 128 (half) of the ASCII characters are used in computer text. Your keyboard has about 100 keys, some of which are duplicates, and some of which don't generate ASCII characters. The symbols you see on your keyboard are primarily *standard ASCII characters*. The extra 128 ASCII characters, called *higher-order ASCII characters*, are not used by most ordinary computer users, but they are nevertheless important.

If you're a scientist, engineer, or mathematician, you've probably been frustrated more than once when preparing a thesis, report, or manuscript. In scientific work, there are symbols that you can't find on a standard keyboard, such as Greek letters, summation signs, partial-derivative signs, and integral signs. The drawing shows a few of these. Using an *extended character set*, you can get a PC to recognize these symbols. Then you can save them on diskettes and print them out, rather than leaving spaces and filling in the symbols by hand.

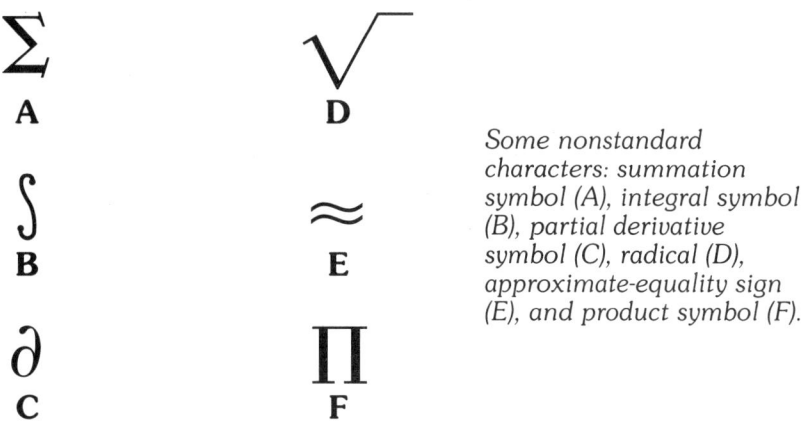

Some nonstandard characters: summation symbol (A), integral symbol (B), partial derivative symbol (C), radical (D), approximate-equality sign (E), and product symbol (F).

In addition to technical symbols, an extended character set generally includes some foreign-language letters and "wingdings" (miniature pictures like smiling faces, checkmarks, and hearts). *See also* ASCII *and* CHARACTER.

Extended Graphics Array

Extended Graphics Array (XGA) refers to a standard for color PC monitors. It has better image resolution, and can also show more hues of color, than older monitor standards. To work with VGA (Video Graphics Array) monitors, XGA needs an expansion board with sufficient memory. The XGA standard is similar to the SVGA (Super Video Graphics Array). *See also* MONITOR *and* SUPER VIDEO GRAPHICS ARRAY.

Extended Industry Standard Architecture

Extended Industry Standard Architecture (EISA) refers to a method of computer motherboard design developed for IBM-

Extended/expanded memory

compatible PCs. It is a more powerful version of Industry Standard Architecture (ISA).

Some PC users don't need a PC with an EISA motherboard, but it's not a bad idea to buy a machine that has one, if you can afford it. If you intend to do computer-aided design (CAD), use sophisticated graphics, or get involved with interactive technology, EISA is the way to go. It's also good for spreadsheet and database software if you have a lot of data to work with.

EISA is similar to the Micro Channel Architecture (MCA) system developed originally by IBM. In fact, EISA was developed by a group of maverick engineers, known as the "Gang of Nine," to compete with MCA. The history of personal computing is replete with examples of spin-off engineering of this kind.

In EISA, a 32-bit bus is used, but EISA is downwardly compatible with most 16-bit peripherals. *See also* BUS, INDUSTRY STANDARD ARCHITECTURE, *and* MICRO CHANNEL ARCHITECTURE.

Extended/expanded memory

Extended/expanded memory is RAM (random-access memory) that increases the amount of data a computer can store and work with. Extra memory is often needed to run advanced software programs and operating systems.

Memory does not, all by itself, make a computer powerful. How the computer makes use of its memory is just as important as the actual quantity of memory. No matter how much RAM a computer has, the machine needs advanced software, along with high speed, to benefit. Your PC can have a thousand memory chips, but if the microprocessor and software can't address it all, some of it will remain useless. Conversely, if the microprocessor can address large amounts of extended/expanded memory, the chips must actually be installed for the PC to get anything out of them. Computer power is a function of microprocessor speed and memory capacity, among other things. *See also* COMPUTER GENERATIONS *and* COMPUTER POWER.

Extended memory. A typical PC has 640K (640,000 bytes) of *conventional memory*. That's the part of the RAM that your PC can immediately use. Extra RAM beyond the first 640K that can extend essentially without limit. Of the RAM beyond the conventional memory, the first 384K forms *upper memory*, used for video and various other purposes. After the first 1024K (or 1MB) comes the *extended memory*. This is shown in the drawing at A for a computer with 2MB total memory, which represents a minimal amount of RAM. Some PCs have dozens of megabytes of RAM, all but the first megabyte of which are extended memory.

Extended/expanded memory

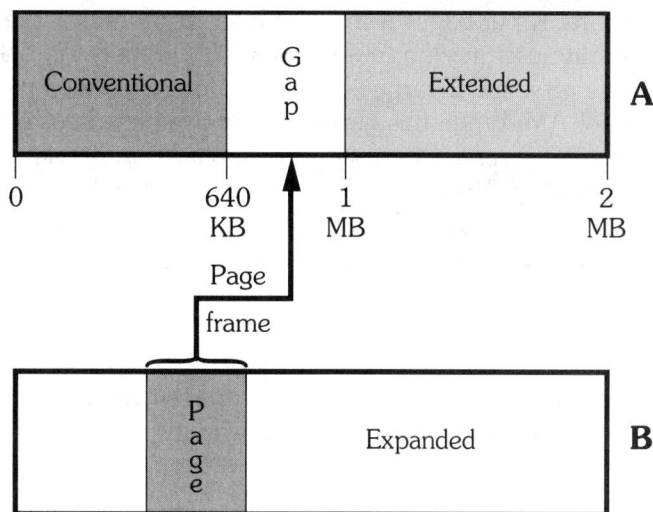

Extended memory (A) is part of RAM. Expanded memory (B) is separate from RAM.

Even if your PC has some extended memory, the software might not be making use of it. Some DOS-based programs work only with the conventional memory. That means that a substantial amount of RAM is doing nothing. If your PC uses an 80386 or later microprocessor chip, you can make use of the extended memory. Windows software does this. Whenever you do *multitasking*, you employ extended memory.

You can add extended memory chips to your PC, so that you have more addressable RAM. The limit depends on the microprocessor. The more advanced the microprocessor chip, the greater the total RAM you can have. An 80386, for example, can have up to 4096MB (or four gigabytes).

Expanded memory. You might think of the conventional and extended memory as a three-ring notebook with room for 2048 sheets of paper. Each sheet represents 1K of data. Some programs, such as those in DOS, come with a supply of 640 sheets. Other software, like that in Windows, come with 2048 sheets. But there's always the 384-sheet gap in the notebook. This gap becomes useful when your PC needs expanded memory.

Using this analogy, *expanded memory* is like a huge extra supply of sheets of paper. You might have a whole box full of paper with data written on them that you don't often use. In a real PC, the expanded memory is broken up into units called *pages*. Each page has a number, called its *address*. The number of expanded-memory sheets can increase without limit; it can number in the millions of kilobytes.

External command

You can temporarily put pages from expanded memory into the gap in the RAM without upsetting the RAM contents. The machine only needs to know the address, and it can place a page from expanded memory into the gap in RAM. When this happens, the page becomes a *page frame*, and the PC accesses it through the gap (see on previous page part B of the drawing). When the PC is done using the data, it is removed from the gap, making room for some other page of expanded memory, as necessary. *See also* RANDOM-ACCESS MEMORY.

External command

The term *external command* refers to a certain type of command in DOS. An external command differs from an internal one in that the PC must be told specifically where to find an external command.

For DOS to work with an external command, the computer must get it from disk and put it into RAM (random-access memory). In other words, the command must be in the working directory. If the command is not in the working directory, you must tell the computer where to find it by specifying a path.

It's a good idea to put all the external commands for DOS into a single directory. This will streamline your operation, so you don't have to keep switching among directories. Also, it is less confusing. If different commands are in different directories, you'll almost certainly have trouble remembering which commands are in what places.

If you try to use an external command and it isn't in the working directory, you'll get a response on the prompt line such as these:

```
ILLEGAL COMMAND
BAD COMMAND OR FILE NAME
```

These messages don't mean that something has gone wrong with your machine; they mean you've told it to do something impossible under the circumstances. *See also* COMMAND, DOS, *and* INTERNAL COMMAND.

Extrapolation

When data is available within a certain range, an estimate of values outside that range can be made by a technique called *extrapolation*. This can be "educated guessing" by a person, but it can also be done using a computer. The more sophisticated the computer software, the more accurately it can extrapolate. The best extrapolation is done using computers with some artificial intelligence (AI).

An example of extrapolation is shown in the drawing. A hurricane approaches the U.S. coastline. Knowing its path up to the present moment (represented by the solid line), a range of possible future paths is developed by the computer. Factors that can be programmed into the computer to help it make an accurate extrapolation include the following:

➢ Paths of hurricanes in past years that approached in a similar way

➢ Weather conditions (steering currents) in the upper atmosphere

➢ Weather conditions in the general path of the storm

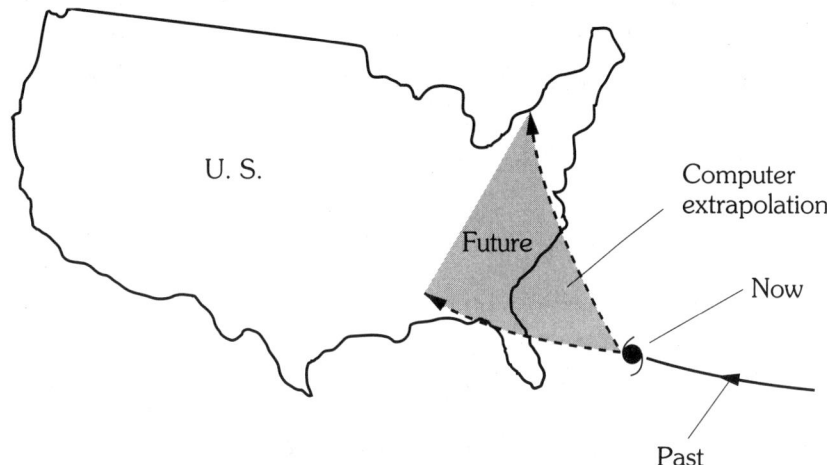

A computer predicts the approximate path of a hurricane using extrapolation.

The further into the future an extrapolation is made, the less accurate it will be. While a weather computer might do a good job of predicting the hurricane's path for the next 24 hours, no machine yet devised could tell where the storm would be in a week. *See also* INTERPOLATION.

Extremely-low-frequency radiation

See ELF FIELDS.

Eye strain

One of the most common problems with PC use is *eye strain*. To some extent this is inevitable because human eyes didn't evolve to look at computer displays for long periods of time. Eye strain has always been troublesome to people employed in occupations that demand close-range attention.

Some of the symptoms of eye strain include

➢ Blurred vision

➢ "Tired" or sore eyes

➢ Red eyes

➢ Sleeplessness

Eye strain

- Headaches
- Dizziness
- Neck stiffness
- Altered perception of color
- General fatigue

There are several things you can do to minimize eye strain while working at your computer or terminal, including the following:

- Place the monitor so the screen is at least 18 inches from your eyes.
- Sit upright.
- Adjust the monitor so the screen is 90 degrees to your line of sight (see the drawing).
- Adjust the display brightness and contrast for easiest viewing.
- Evenly illuminate your work area.
- Prevent reflections from the screen.
- Look at distant objects frequently to rest your eyes.
- Keep your face relaxed (don't clench your teeth).
- Take frequent breaks.

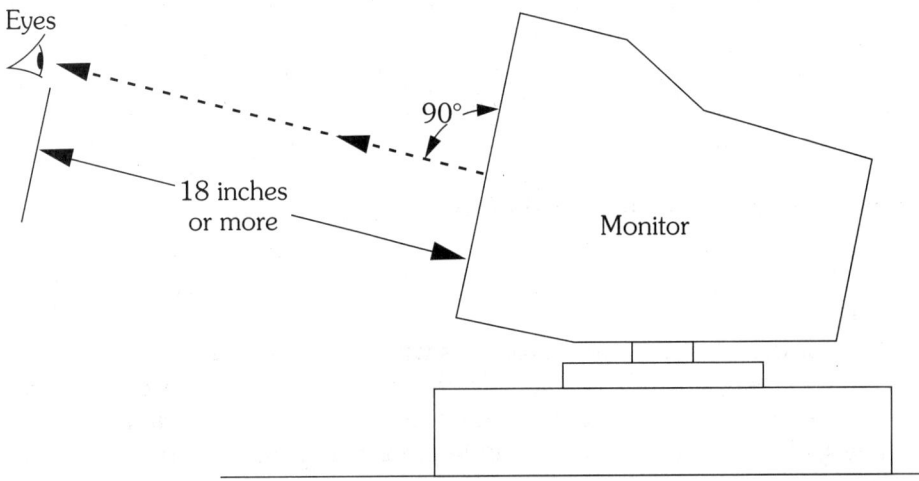

Your line of sight should be perpendicular to the monitor screen, with your eyes at least 18 inches away.

If you're having vision problems or other symptoms that you suspect might be related to your PC use, see a doctor. *See also* CUMULATIVE TRAUMA DISORDERS *and* ERGONOMICS.

Facsimile

See FAX *and* FAX BOARD.

Family

A *family* is a group of things that are related in some way. The term can be used in various contexts.

For data. A section of data that is part of a larger unit or whole is called a family. The family "F" of this book, for example, consists of all the articles whose titles begin with the letter *F*. In an outline, a family consists of a section with a heading, and possibly several levels of subheadings. The lower the hierarchical level of a family, the less data is in that family.

In the organization of files on a disk, each subordinate unit of data (a directory or folder) in a given family is called a *child*. The superior unit is called the *parent*. Less often, you might come across the terms *grandchild* and *grandparent*. These are, as their names imply, ways of indicating the relationship between elements of the family.

Drawing A is a simple *Venn diagram* showing a familial relationship. Note that a data unit can have several, perhaps many, children. Usually, a data unit has only one parent. *See also* DIRECTORY *and* DIRECTORY TREE.

In graphics. Perhaps you've heard about "families of curves" or "families of functions." Sometimes you'll come across these terms in analytical graphics.

Family

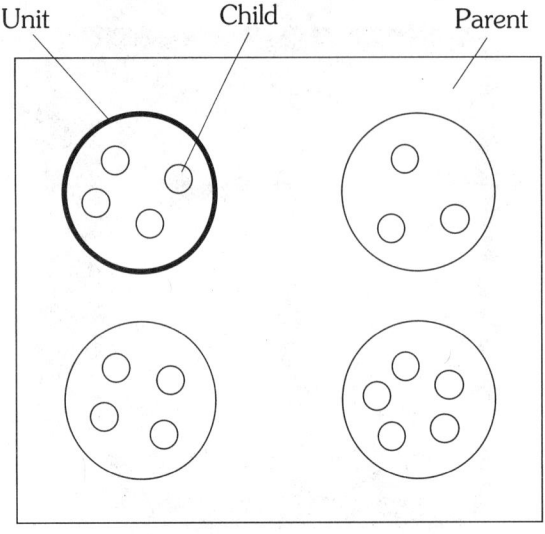

A

Children and parent of a data unit.

Drawing B shows a simple example of a family of curves. These are parabolas, whose equations are of the form $y = nx^2$, where n is a whole number ranging from 1 to 5. The higher the value of n, the "sharper" the curve. But all the curves are related because they all fit the mathematical definition of a parabola. They form a family because of this relationship. A curve having the formula $y = x^3$, or a line having the formula $y = x/4$, are not members of the family in the drawing because the graphs of these functions are not parabolas. *See also* ANALYTICAL GRAPHICS.

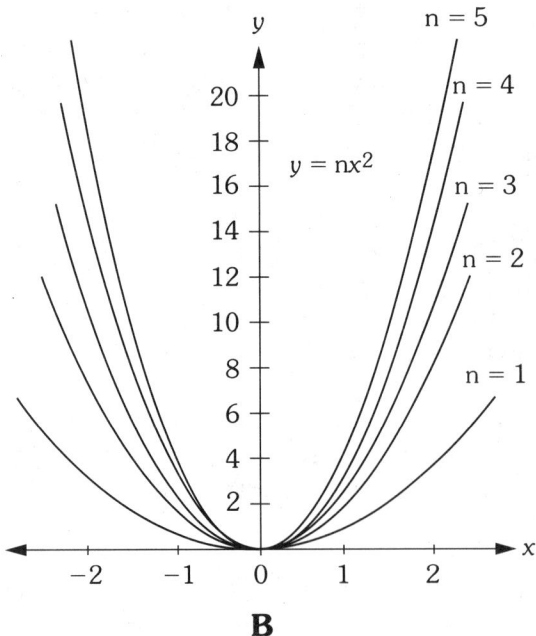

B

A family of curves.

Fanfold paper

Fanfold paper is a popular type of printer paper that gets its name from the way it is folded, allowing hundreds or thousands of contiguous sheets to fit in a box of reasonable size. Fanfold paper is designed so that it can be easily torn off at the folds, making separate, identical sheets. Part A of the drawing shows a few sheets of 9.5-x-11-inch fanfold paper as they would look viewed exactly edgewise. The folds go in alternate directions.

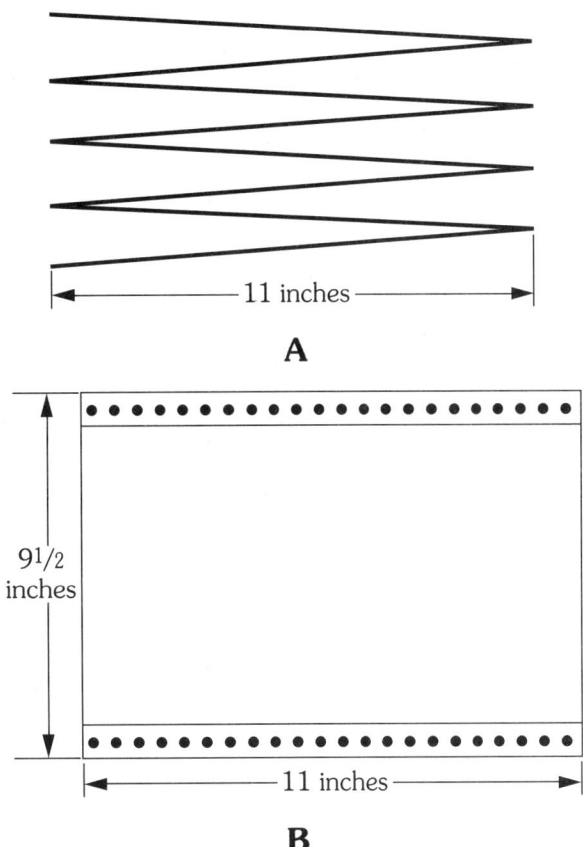

Fanfold paper viewed edgewise (A) and from the top of a stack (B).

Fanfold paper usually has detachable perforated strips. The holes fit on the printer's tractor feed to guide the paper through the printer. The perforated strips are a half-inch wide on either side of the paper, adding an extra inch to the paper width. When you see computer paper advertised as "9.5 by 11 inches," remember that it really means 8.5 by 11 inches because you lose an inch of width when you tear off the perforated side strips.

Part B of the drawing shows a stack of perforated fanfold paper as seen from the top. You can remove the perforations from 20 or 30 sheets at once, before separating the pages. Simply fold up the printed pages as they were originally folded in the box, and then tear off the perforations. Separate the pages after that.

Fanfold paper is available in *multipart forms*, so you can make several copies simultaneously with an impact printer such as a dot-matrix. This can save you hundreds of dollars a year if you make a lot of copies. Stick-on labels are also available with fanfold backing. You can make hundreds or thousands of return-address labels, for example, and keep them in a fanfolded stack in a drawer. You can rip off each sheet of backing once all the labels on it have been used.

Some brands of fanfold paper tear neatly and easily, leaving clean edges. Others do not. Shop around and find the type of fanfold paper that works best for you. When you discover a good brand, write down the name of the paper manufacturer, the product number, and the place where you bought it so you can save money and inconvenience in the future. *See also* DOT-MATRIX PRINTER, IMPACT PRINTER, MULTIPART FORMS, *and* TRACTOR FEED.

Farming applications

Computers are a big asset in almost any small business. Usually, the PC is used for bookkeeping, writing text, producing graphics, and perhaps for networking and desktop publishing, but computers can also be used in control applications. This will become increasingly common in the future, with the advent of personal robots.

Sprinkler systems. In much of the United States, farmers use movable watering sprinklers called *center-pivot irrigators*, which have large arms extending out from a rotatable central pivot (hence their name). Center-pivot irrigators must be checked every three or four hours to be sure they're delivering the right amount of water to the right places. Several different adjustments can, and frequently must, be made.

Some farmers have begun using PCs to keep track of and control the operation of center-pivot irrigators. In this sense, the irrigators become computerized robots.

Remote control. A transponder connected to the mechanical controls of the pivot communicates by radio with the farmer's home PC. The home PC can be connected to telephone lines via a modem, so the farmer can monitor and control the pivot from a telephone miles away. Or a portable PC can be used with a radio modem to control the apparatus from anywhere within range of its transponder. The drawing shows a possible arrangement for control of a center-pivot irrigator. The equipment can be monitored and adjusted from any of the points marked X.

Fault-resilient computer

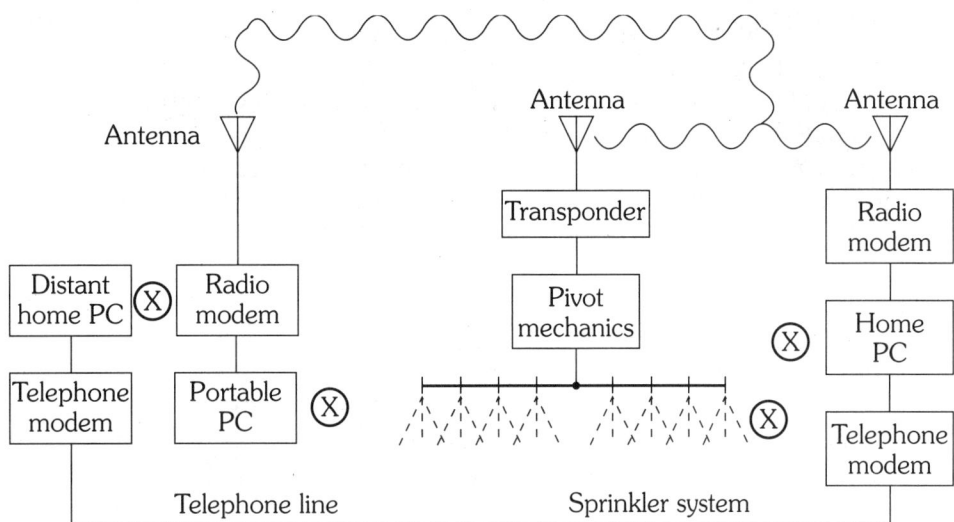

A remotely controlled center-pivot irrigator

Eventually, farmers might use remotely controlled robots for many of the chores formerly done by humans. Robotized equipment could plant and harvest crops, and perhaps even feed livestock. And, although it's a bit funny to envision, remote-controlled, computerized robots might even milk the cows. *See also* MODEM *and* PERSONAL ROBOTS.

Fault-resilient computer

A *fault-resilient computer* is immune to sabotage. No matter how anybody might try to mess up such a system, it keeps working, although perhaps at reduced speed or efficiency.

Is it possible? Some engineers doubt that any computer can be made to stay fault-resilient for a long time. They say, "Build a better rat trap, and smarter rats will evolve." Any such system would have to be dreamed up by some human being. That person (at least) ought to know how to break his or her own invention.

Nobody can anticipate all the things that can go wrong with a system. Engineers invoke Murphy's Law on this subject: "If something can go wrong, it will." Murphy's Law has a grim corollary, which at first sounds ridiculous, but is in fact valid and important: "If something *cannot* go wrong, it will." In other words, the unsinkable ship will sink.

Imperfect world. Suppose that all the strategic (nuclear) defenses of the United States were placed under the control of a computer. It would be imperative that this computer be sabotage-proof and that it be impossible to turn it off. There would have to be backup systems, backup-backup systems, and so on. Special access codes would be needed. Security would have to be air-tight.

Imagine a fault-resilient computer system in such a role. People might be able, then, to forget about nuclear weapons, secure in the knowledge that a logical, impartial machine had control over everything. The machine could be programmed never to make a first strike. Computers don't break their promises; once instructed to act only in a defensive manner, the machine would be absolutely nonaggressive. However, machines sometimes malfunction. The more complex the system, the greater the number of ways for things to go wrong. A truly fault-resilient computer would have to be 100% reliable; it would have to be perfect. But the physical world is, by nature, imperfect.

Hardware backups. Many computers and computer-controlled machine systems are designed so that if some parts fail, the system will keep working at reduced efficiency and speed. This type of fault-resilience is often called *graceful degradation*. It is achieved by means of backup systems and complex design techniques that provide alternate routes for data when the main routes fail.

Some computers have total hardware redundancy. Such a machine is called a *fault-tolerant computer*. When a component fails in a fault-tolerant machine, there is no reduction in speed or efficiency. The second set of hardware components simply takes over the job. An alert signal tells the operator that a part has failed, and it can then be replaced with minimum work slowdown. *See also* GRACEFUL DEGRADATION.

Fax

Fax is short for *facsimile*, a method of sending and receiving still images over telephone lines or radio. Fax machines are almost as commonplace as telephones these days. Faxing is used extensively by businesses, government agencies, and individuals.

Advantages of fax. For some years now, sending and receiving fax messages has been getting cheaper, while mailing letters has been getting more expensive. For overseas mail or when you need to get a document someplace right away, faxing is now much less expensive than any mail carrier.

Faxing is also more reliable than the mail. It's basically impossible for a fax to get lost. You always know that a fax has reached its intended recipient because you can have them acknowledge receipt by sending you a fax. If the fax did not arrive, or if it came out garbled, you can send it again.

Finally, faxing is faster than mail. It gets places with the speed of a telephone call: immediately. In today's society, that's important. The saving of two days here and two days there, multiplied many times over, translates into a big profit increase. In business, time is money.

Sending a fax. A fax machine has two parts: an image transmitter and an image receiver. The block drawing shows the transmission of a fax signal from one place, called the *source*, to someplace else, called the *destination*. In the drawing, only the sending part of the fax machine is shown at the source, and only the receiving part is shown at the destination. A complete fax installation generally has both a transmitter and a receiver, allowing for two-way exchange of fax messages.

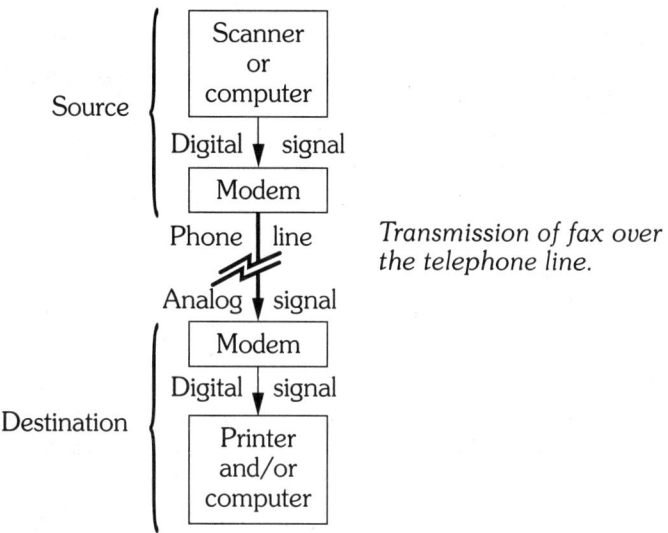

Transmission of fax over the telephone line.

To send a fax, you place a page of printed material in an *optical scanner*. This device converts the image into a series of binary digital pulses, that is, "high" and "low" signals (also called 1 and 0). Any image can be converted in this way, although generally, the output will be in shades of gray. Color fax machines are available, but they cost more than standard ones.

The output of the scanner is sent to a modem that converts the binary digital pulses into a signal suitable for transmission over a telephone line. This signal can also be sent over radio circuits. Amateur radio operators have been sending faxes to each other for decades.

Receiving a fax. At the destination, the analog signals from the telephone line or radio are converted back into digital pulses like those produced by the optical scanner at the source. These pulses are then routed either to a printing device or to a computer or terminal.

A standard fax has a printing device similar to a photocopier. The image resolution of high-quality fax machines is good enough to allow reproduction of most photographs. Faxes have been used by the news networks for many years for the transmission of black-and-white photos (also known as wirephotos).

Fax board

Computer fax. Your PC can work like a fax machine in some ways. It can turn its data into a fax, and send this over the phone lines or radio. At the other end, a personal computer can receive the fax and display it on the screen or send it to the printer. To do this, you'll need a peripheral called a *fax/modem*. Anything on your screen consists of digital data, which can be transmitted via fax/modem. Many new computers have fax/modems built in.

You can't just take a piece of paper and send its images over a computer's fax/modem. You need an optical scanner to get the document into your computer. If you intend to send hardcopies via fax, a standard fax machine is the cheaper way to go. If you plan to use the scanner for other applications, however, it can be a good investment. *See also* FAX BOARD *and* OPTICAL SCANNER.

Fax board

A *fax board* is a special expansion board that you can add to a desktop computer to give it some of the capabilities of a fax machine. Installing a fax board is no more or less difficult than adding any other expansion board. Many new computers have built-in fax capability; you'll hear them advertised as having fax/modems. Fax/modems are found in laptop computers, as well as in desktop machines.

Sending data. Using a fax board, you can send anything that you can display on your monitor screen over the telephone lines. It will normally go out in black and white, whether it consists of pure text, pure graphics, or a combination of text and graphics. The data can be received by a conventional fax machine or another PC equipped with fax.

You can't send a fax of anything that is only on a sheet of paper (this page, for example) using a fax board. This is its main limitation. To send faxes of hardcopy, you must either use a conventional fax machine, or add a scanner to your system.

Receiving data. You can receive a fax and store it, either on your hard disk or on diskette. This is the big advantage of a fax board. It's convenient to keep everything—images and text—on diskette because it reduces the amount of papers you have to file or leave lying around.

You can, if you wish, make a hardcopy of the fax using your printer. The quality of the image will vary depending on the kind of printer you use. Laser printers produce the best fax hardcopies. *See also* EXPANSION BOARD *and* FAX.

Fax/modem

See FAX BOARD.

FET

See FIELD-EFFECT TRANSISTOR.

Fiberoptic cable

A *fiberoptic cable* is a bundle of glass strands designed to carry modulated light or infrared. A ray of light or infrared can carry many signals along one thread-thin fiber. A bundle of fibers can thus carry a huge number of signals at high data speeds. This is ideal for communication between and among computers, or between computers and peripherals.

How it is made. Optical fibers are made from glass to which impurities have been added. The impurities don't cloud the glass; they change its *refractive index*. The refractive index is the property of glass that makes lenses magnify. The greater the refractive index of a clear solid, the more it will bend light that enters it at an angle. An optical fiber has a core surrounded by a tubular cladding, as shown in the drawing. The cladding has a lower index of refraction than the core.

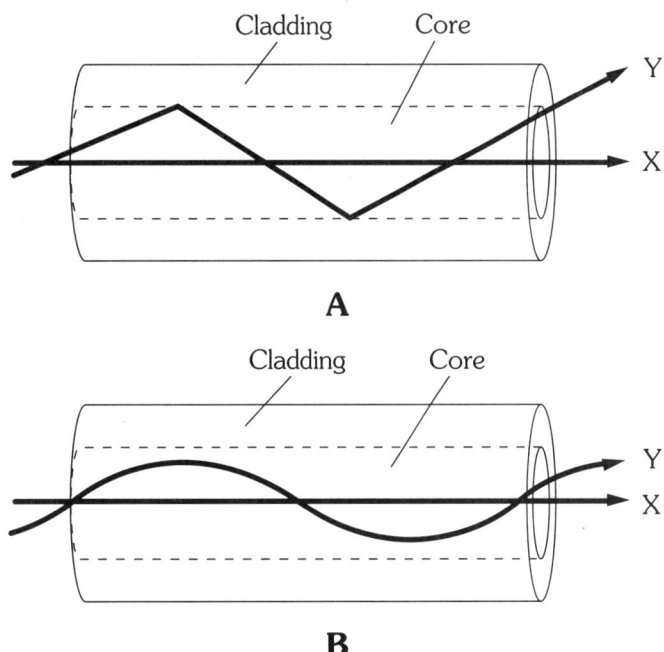

Fiberoptic cable: step-index (A) and graded-index (B).

There are two ways in which the refractive index can vary in the core of an optical fiber. In the *step-index optical fiber*, the core has a uniform index of refraction. In the *graded-index optical fiber*, the core has a refractive index that is greatest along the central axis, and decreases outward from the center. In either type of fiber, the cladding has a much lower refractive index than any part of the core.

Fiberoptic data transmission

Optical fibers are specially manufactured to have the lowest possible loss. That is, they're much "clearer" than ordinary window glass. As a result, visible light and infrared rays can travel in a fiber for miles.

How it works. The behavior of the ray within the core varies somewhat, depending on whether the fiber is of the step-index type or the graded-index type.

In drawing A, showing a step-index fiber, ray X enters the core exactly parallel to the fiber, so it travels without striking the boundary between the core and the cladding, unless there is a bend in the fiber. If there is a bend, ray X will veer off center with respect to the fiber, and will start to behave like ray Y. Ray Y enters at an angle, and hits the boundary repeatedly. Each time ray Y encounters the boundary, reflection occurs, so it always stays in the core. The reflection takes place because of the difference in refractive index between the core and the cladding.

In drawing B, showing a graded-index fiber, ray X enters the core exactly parallel to the fiber, and it travels without striking the boundary between the core and the cladding. If there is a bend in the fiber, ray X will veer off center with respect to the fiber, and will start to behave like ray Y. Ray Y enters at an angle. As it moves farther from the center of the core, the index of refraction decreases, causing the ray to be refracted back toward the center. If ray Y enters at a sharp enough angle, it will reach the boundary between the core and the cladding, in which case reflection will occur as in a step-index fiber.

Bundling fibers. Fiberoptic cables sometimes have just one fiber; often there are several. Optical fibers are bundled into cable in much the same way as wires are bundled. The individual fibers are protected from damage by plastic jackets. Common coverings are polyethylene and polyurethane. Along with the fibers, steel wires or other strong materials are often used to add strength to the cable. The whole bundle is encased in an outer jacket, which might also be reinforced with wire or tough plastic compounds. *See also* FIBEROPTIC DATA TRANSMISSION *and* OPTICAL COMPUTER TECHNOLOGY.

Fiberoptic data transmission

Beams of visible light or infrared can be modulated to carry data. A single ray can carry thousands of signals. The data can be sent at extreme speed because large bandwidth is possible. When the light or infrared is sent along a strand of glass called a *fiberoptic cable*, the mode is known as *fiberoptic data transmission*.

Fiberoptic systems are used in electronic and electromechanical devices such as robots and computer-controlled cars. Fiberoptics is also replacing wire cable for data communications. The scheme is ideal for networking, or interconnecting computers.

Advantages. There are several advantages to fiberoptic systems, including the following:

➢ *Immunity to interference* Besides allowing signals to be sent very fast, optical fibers don't suffer from electromagnetic interference. A strong radio signal or a lightning discharge won't disrupt the data, as can happen with cable systems.

➢ *Zero electromagnetic radiation* All the signal energy stays within the optical fiber. Fiberoptic transmission does not emit any ELF fields or other electromagnetic energy that can cause interference with other systems.

➢ *Hard to tap* You can wrap a coil of wire around a wire or cable and intercept the data without cutting into the line. This requires some expertise in communications engineering, but it's possible. When a signal is carried by a light beam inside an optical fiber, it's impossible to tap without breaking the fiber.

➢ *Abundant materials* The sand from which glass fibers are made is cheap and plentiful. The supply will never run short. Sand can also be "mined" with minimal environmental impact.

➢ *They can go anywhere* Fiberoptic cables can be submerged in lakes and oceans, or buried in soil, and will not corrode the way metal wires do. Therefore, fiberoptic cables last much longer than wire cables, and need less maintenance.

How it works. In an optical fiber, the light or infrared energy is confined to the core. The core is surrounded by a cladding that has a lower index of refraction. This causes the light or infrared to stay in the core material.

A single beam of light or infrared can carry hundreds, or even thousands, of signals. The frequency of the rays is many times higher than that of any computer signal, and the available bandwidth is practically infinite. One thin strand of glass can therefore replace a bundle of wires of much greater diameter and weight. A fiberoptic cable can contain dozens of individual fibers. This increases the versatility of the system still further.

See also BANDWIDTH, FIBEROPTIC CABLE, *and* OPTICAL COMPUTER TECHNOLOGY.

Field

In a database, a *field* is a spot where a specific piece of information goes. A field, also called a *data field*, is part of a larger data unit called a *record*. In a relational database, columns represent fields.

Suppose that someone has information about you stored in a database. All the information about you makes up one data record. Fields within that record might include the following:

- Last name
- First name
- Street
- City
- State
- Country
- ZIP
- Phone number
- Phone extension number, if any
- Occupation

You can probably think of at least a dozen more fields into which your personal data could be filed. The number of fields in a record can vary from just a few to hundreds. *See also* DATABASE *and* RECORD.

Field-effect transistor

A *field-effect transistor (FET)* is a semiconductor device used as an amplifier or high-speed switch. In computers, each integrated circuit (IC), or chip, can contain thousands of FETs.

The drawing shows a cross-section of an FET. The letter *P* represents P-type semiconductor material; the letter *N* represents N-type. (A P-type is essentially positive and an N-type is negative. The distinction is technical, and beyond the scope of this discussion.) The device shown is known as an N-channel FET. Some FETs have the N-type and P-type materials reversed from the drawing; that results in a P-channel FET.

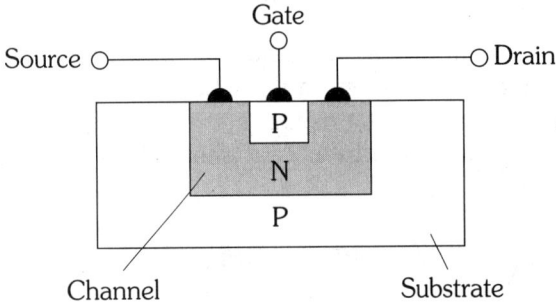

Cross-section of an N-channel device.

The current in the FET flows from the source to the drain, along the channel. The voltage at the gate electrode causes the channel to get wider or narrower, in turn affecting the current between the source and the drain. A tiny change in gate voltage produces a large change in the channel current; this is how an FET can amplify. It's something like controlling the flow of water in a garden hose by stepping on the hose with greater or lesser force.

Field-effect transistors need very little current to operate, making them ideal for complex devices like computers, which contain large numbers of electronic components. The earliest computers used vacuum tubes instead of the microscopic FETs that are employed now. This resulted in power consumption of many kilowatts, compared with only a few watts today. Because they require so little energy to function, modern computers generate much less heat than older computers with larger energy appetites.

Some FETs are made with metal oxides in addition to semiconductor materials. These devices provide even better energy efficiency, and often can work at higher speeds, than conventional FETs. *See also* COMPLEMENTARY METAL-OXIDE-SEMICONDUCTOR TECHNOLOGY, *and* METAL-OXIDE-SEMICONDUCTOR TECHNOLOGY.

Field-emission display

A *field-emission display (FED)* is a form of display for laptop computers. The FED overcomes some of the shortcomings of the conventional liquid-crystal display (LCD).

Conventional LCDs have poor contrast under certain lighting conditions, and they do not work well in cold temperatures. Although these problems have been reduced somewhat as the technology has improved, they can still be annoying under some conditions. Another problem with LCDs is that they don't emit any light of their own, unless backlighting is used. Backlighting, however, consumes precious battery power.

An FED works like the cathode-ray tube (CRT) in desktop PC monitors, except that the cathodes require much less voltage and power. Rather than a big, "hot" cathode, there are many little "cold" cathodes. The FED is far less bulky, and weighs much less, than a CRT monitor. The drawing on page 412 shows a simplified, cross-sectional view of an FED. The contrast and brightness of a typical FED is far superior to that of an LCD. Also, the FED draws less current from the battery than a backlit LCD. *See also* CATHODE-RAY TUBE, DISPLAY, *and* LIQUID-CRYSTAL DISPLAY.

File

A *file* is data that is assigned to a specific place on a hard disk, diskette, or other storage medium, or that occupies a certain place in RAM (random-access memory). A program, a word-processed document, a spreadsheet, and a database are examples of files.

Allocation. If you've ever kept files in a cabinet using manila folders, you have probably labeled each drawer in the cabinet, and each folder

File

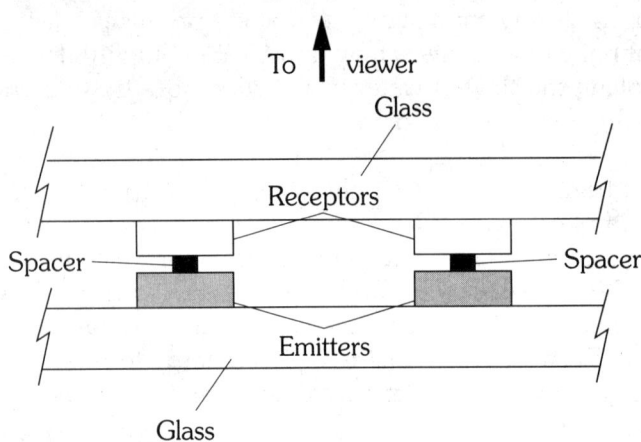

A field-emission display resembles an array of tiny cathode-ray tubes.

in every drawer. Then, when you had to locate some piece of data, you knew just where to find it. Your PC employs a similar system to store and retrieve data in its files. The *file allocation table*, or *FAT*, is a guide that tells your PC where every file is stored. It is, itself, a sort of file.

The FAT is so important to a computer's smooth functioning that it's written twice on the hard disk. If one copy gets erased or corrupted, the other one can take over.

Directory. In IBM-compatible PCs, *directories* and *subdirectories* arrange files into categories, allowing you to store more files than would otherwise be possible. Think of a big university library. It has several branches, such as science, engineering, mathematics, history, and medicine. The list of branches is analogous to the *root directory* in your PC. Within each branch at the library, there are several departments. In the mathematics branch, for example, you might have departments for algebra, geometry, analysis, topology, number theory, set theory, and applied mathematics. These departments are analogous to *subdirectories* in your PC. (Macintosh PCs organize files in terms of folders rather than directories, but the logic is basically similar.)

Each book in the university library is analogous to one data file in your PC. The data is there, ready for you to use, in any university library and in any computer. If you know the system, you can find the data you need in a short time. To find a book on basic differential calculus, for example, you'd go to the mathematics branch and look in the analysis department.

When you make up the directories for the files in your PC, you should use a logical scheme that you can easily remember. *See also* DIRECTORY *and* DIRECTORY TREE.

Creating and deleting files. To create a file, you simply generate the data (by typing it or importing it from somewhere else), and then store it with a *filename*. You might also include a *filename extension*. A filename on IBM-compatible PCs can have up to eight characters, and the extension can have up to three characters. The name and the extension are separated by a period. On Macintosh PCs, filenames are not limited to eight characters, and might or might not have extensions.

A file can vary enormously in size. You can create a file and store nothing in it. If you give it a filename, it will show up in the directory, and the listing will indicate that it is zero bytes (or characters) long. At the other extreme, a file can be as large as the memory in your PC will allow. This is normally at least several hundred kilobytes (abbreviated K; 1024 bytes). A kilobyte represents about a page of double-spaced text at 10 characters per inch. Text files can be many pages long. Graphics files are much bigger than text files. A simple line drawing in an object-oriented format can easily take 15K to 25K; photographs in bitmapped graphics consume many times that amount of storage.

To delete a file, you use the command provided by your software for that purpose. In DOS, deleting the file PC.F from the current directory of the hard disk would be done by typing ERASE PC.F and pressing Enter. In Windows, you would click on a Delete button or menu item corresponding to the file to be removed. On the Mac, you would drag the file to the trashcan and drop it in, then empty the can. *See also* FILE ERASURE, FILENAME, *and* FILENAME EXTENSION.

Caution: Use care when erasing files. Erasure of certain files can impair the operation of a computer system.

Defragmentation. As you use the data on your hard disk, you'll change it often, saving it in slightly different form each time. As you do this with many different files, *fragmentation* occurs because of the way the PC overwrites data on the hard disk. This also takes place on diskettes if you revise them file-by-file frequently.

Fragmentation of your hard disk causes your machine to work less efficiently. The access time increases because it take the central processing unit (CPU) longer to gather up a fragmented file than to access a file that's all in one piece. Fragmentation can be eliminated by using a defragmentation program. Most new computers feature defragmentation programs as part of their operating systems.

Opinions vary concerning how often to defragment a hard disk. It depends on how much you use your computer, how often you overwrite files, and how many files you have on your hard disk. Some PC users defragment the hard disk every couple of months; others do it weekly. Most people find once or twice a month to be often enough. *See also* DEFRAGMENTATION *and* FRAGMENTATION.

File compression utility

Backing up. Important files should always be backed up. That means you should have at least two (preferably three) copies of every file, and keep them in separate locations.

If you're a serious PC user, you should keep copies of all your files on diskettes, and store them someplace away from the workstation. These diskettes can be updated daily, weekly, monthly, or however often you want. This set of diskettes forms your *archives.* Another way to back up a hard disk is to copy its contents onto a cassette tape using a tape drive.

Some software will automatically back up a file on your hard disk or diskette every time you access it and then store it again. Suppose, for example, you want to revise the file PC.F. You open PC.F, make the changes, and then store it again. Backup software puts the updated data into PC.F and creates a new file PC.BAK, containing the contents of PC.F before the revision. This feature averts disaster if you delete PC.F by accident. It also lets you "unmake" changes if you decide you didn't want them after all. *See also* ARCHIVES, BACKUP, BACKUP UTILITY, *and* TAPE DRIVE.

File compression utility

The number of files that can be stored on a hard disk or diskette is limited by the total amount of storage space available, and by the average size of the files. You might want a *file compression utility* to increase the effective amount of storage space, especially if the computer is shared among many users.

In a text file, certain words or groups of characters appear often. This is particularly true for text that deals with specialized or technical subjects. Such character groups can be replaced with special codes so that they take up only a fraction of their normal storage space. Sometimes a file can be cut down to half its original size or less, while still retaining all the information of the original. When a compressed file is to be used again, the codes must be translated back into the original character groups so the data will make sense to the user.

It works both ways. A file compression utility performs the *data compression* operation, and also *data decompression.* The utility encodes certain character groups before storing the file on hard disk or diskette, and decodes the groups when the file is called for use.

A good data compression utility works so smoothly and fast that you won't notice it as you read and write files. You might sense intuitively that it takes longer to create a file of a certain length—say, 100K (kilobytes)—when you're using the utility, as compared to when you're not using it. The reason for this is that the computer is shrinking your work, making it appear smaller in the directory.

When you've completed, say, 12K of work in RAM and then store it on the hard disk, it will show up in the hard-disk directory as a smaller file. The difference in size will depend on the *compression factor*. If the compression factor is two, then a 12K file will be reduced to 6K. If the factor is three, it will be cut down to 4K. Thus, you are doing 12K worth of work, but only using up 4K or 6K of storage space on the hard disk. *See also* DATA COMPRESSION.

File conversion

There are dozens of different application programs, each with its own idiosyncrasies and unique file format. For example, among word processors, the most common are probably Ami Pro, Word for the Macintosh, Word for Windows, WordPerfect DOS, and WordPerfect Windows. A file created by one of these word processing programs might be practically unintelligible by another one. *File conversion* helps a program understand the files created by another program.

"Dialects" and "Languages." Some file formats are similar to each other, some are vastly different. For example, when two word processors use file formats that are similar, it's like two different dialects in the same spoken language. You can communicate pretty well with a Floridian if you are from Indiana. Examples of two similar word processing programs are WordPerfect DOS and WordPerfect Windows.

When two programs are very different, it's like trying to communicate with someone from a foreign land. The average, English-speaking person from Indiana cannot normally speak with someone from Indonesia. Examples of vastly different word processing systems are Word for the Macintosh and the DOS-based word processor called XyWrite.

What happens. If you have the XyWrite program and try to use a diskette on which text has been written using Word for the Macintosh, you won't get far. You might see a directory, but when you try to open a file you'll get an error message or see only strange-looking symbols that have meaning to the computer, but are indecipherable to most people.

Sometimes, if software is similar, you'll be able to read the text all right, but you won't see the right layout. Also, special functions like italics, boldface, and subscripts might show up in some other form, or not at all.

A file conversion utility lets you change between different word processing formats. Then you can take a diskette on which text has been written in, say, XyWrite, and read it in Word, or vice versa. Using a file-conversion utility is a simple matter of following the instructions provided with the package.

File erasure

Straight ASCII. A common data code with personal computers is *ASCII* (pronounced "ask-key"), which stands for *American Standard Code for Information Interchange*. If you have a word processing program for an IBM-compatible computer, the basic format is similar to ASCII. Plain text, stripped of all special commands and functions such as italics, centering, and special margin settings is usually "straight ASCII."

If you are sending a computer file to someone who might use different programs than you, you can usually do all right by stripping all special commands and functions from the diskette copy, leaving only the text. The person receiving the file can modify it according to the word processing software he or she has.

Complex files. If a file contains graphics as well as text, or if the file has many tables and charts, things get tougher. Even a good file-conversion utility might not work well when files are complex.

There are several things you can do if you find yourself having to convert complex files. One way to deal with this problem, if you have the money and the inclination, is to purchase, and learn, several different types of word processing programs. Another way is to convert the files from application, such as graphics, database, spreadsheet, and plain text, separately, including a hardcopy for each item. Then the complex document can be reassembled from its individual parts. *See also* ASCII *and* WORD PROCESSING.

File erasure

When you tell your PC to erase a file from the hard disk or diskette, the filename is removed from the directory. The space taken up by the file is then made available for overwriting with other data.

The ERASE command. Consider the ERASE command in DOS. Suppose you have a set of 25 short stories, with filenames STORY.1 through STORY.25. Perhaps you think that STORY.17 is so awful that it deserves to be obliterated. So you switch on your PC, and go to the directory where you've stored the story. Then you type ERASE STORY.17 and press Enter. Thus, STORY.17 is gone from the directory of the hard disk.

Of course, you have backed up all your work on diskettes. So you take the STORIES diskette, place it in drive A, and type

    ERASE A:STORY.17

Again, you press Enter, and the file is erased. (The DEL command in DOS does the same thing.) You might suppose that is the end of STORY.17. But it's not that simple.

What really happens. Suppose that, moments later, you get a telephone call from an editor to whom you had submitted STORY.17 months ago. This editor loves your story. She raves about it. But, she says, it needs a little editing. She asks if you would be so kind as to open the file on your computer and change a few words.

Reluctantly, you tell her that you gave up on the story. You have thrown away the hardcopies and erased the disk copies. She asks how much you've used your PC since you destroyed the story on disk. You haven't used it at all, you answer. Then she proceeds to explain to you what actually occurs when you erase a file.

The data is still on the hard disk, she explains, as long as it hasn't been overwritten with anything else. The ERASE command clears the way for new data to displace old data. The old data stays on the magnetic medium, however, until the drive head moves over the affected part of the disk and alters the data bits. This is a safeguard against accidental destruction of data.

Recovering erased files. Although the filename STORY.17 does not appear in directories, the data is still on the hard disk and diskette. You need an *undeletion* feature to recover it. Starting with DOS 6.0, an UNDELETE command makes it possible to get data back after erasure, as long as the disk sectors have not actually been overwritten with new data.

If you mistakenly erase data that hasn't been backed up somewhere else, or if you erase all copies of a file and then discover you need the data, don't write anything onto the affected hard disk or diskette(s) until you have recovered the data using an undelete utility.

Many programs back up files for you automatically, reducing the chance of catastrophe if you happen to erase a file by accident. *See also* BACKUP, BACKUP UTILITY, *and* UNDELETION.

File Manager

File Manager is a Windows "applet" (mini-application) that tells you the status of, and lets you manipulate, the files on your PC. You know you're in File Manager when the title bar at the top of the screen tells you so.

Panes. There are usually two smaller windows within the main window of the File Manager. Let's call these *panes*. The locations and sizes of the two panes are shown in the drawing at A.

The pane on the left is called the *directory tree*. It's a list of all the directories on your hard disk. It shows the way the different directories are related, or connected together. The pane on the right is the *directory contents*. When you highlight an item in the directory tree

File Manager

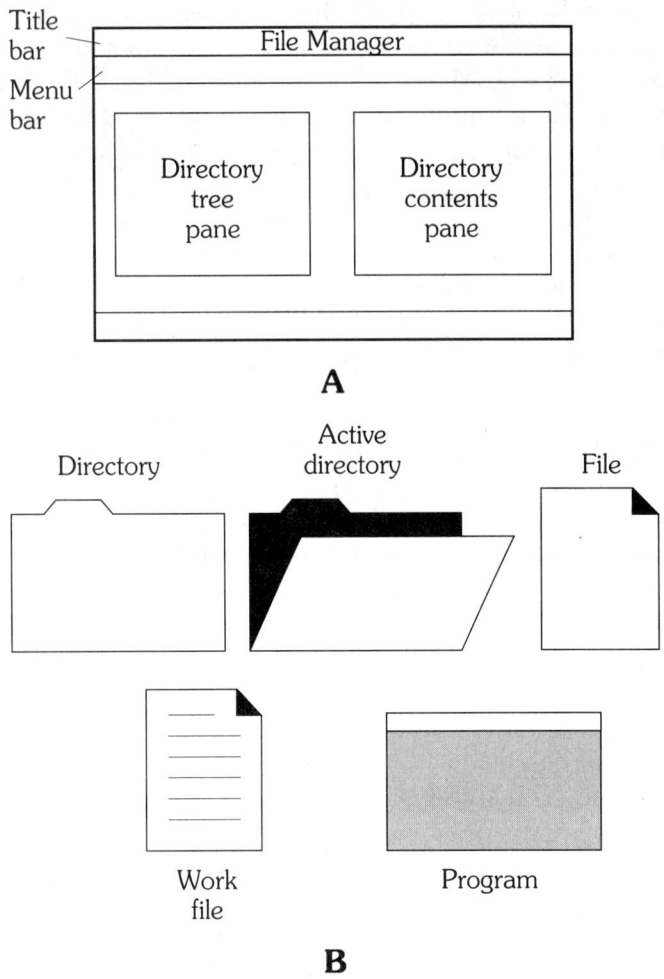

File Manager window (A) and icons (B).

pane, the directory contents pane will list the subdirectories and files in that directory. If you highlight the various items in the directory tree pane one by one (that is, you scroll through the directory tree), the directory contents pane will repeatedly change, always showing details of the directory highlighted at the moment. *See also* DIRECTORY *and* DIRECTORY TREE.

Icons. In the directory tree and directory contents panes, you'll see a symbol next to each word or filename. These symbols are *icons*. They tell you the nature of each directory or file. Part B of the drawing shows the common icons used in the File Manager, along with their meanings.

A small, closed file folder indicates a directory. If a directory is active, it is represented by an open file folder. A blank page with the corner folded is a file icon. Since these files might contain almost anything, such as a dictionary or information about your mouse, you shouldn't normally change them from within File Manager. If there are lines on the page, the icon represents a file you probably created, so you can probably change. An example of such a file might be the list of addresses and telephone numbers for all the people you know. A rectangle with a shaded (usually blue) line across the top represents a program. You shouldn't normally tamper with these.

Working with File Manager. Imagine a huge file cabinet with dozens of drawers full of manila folders, each with dozens of pages. Imagine all the ways you could change the way your data is organized, as well as create new data and erase old data. File Manager is like that big cabinet, but without the bulk, paper, and general messiness.

File Manager lets you sort files, rename files and directories, rearrange your directories, make new directories, delete files and directories, and copy files and directories. You can do these things without getting a single paper cut, or getting correction fluid on your skin or clothes.

The details of File Manager operation are well beyond the scope of this book. Windows software is constantly being improved, and new functions are being added. Consult your Windows instruction manual or online help for a thorough discussion of all the things you can do with File Manager. *See also* WINDOWS.

Filename

Every file on your hard disk and diskettes must be identifiable without confusion. This is done by naming the files. In DOS, a *filename* can have up to eight characters, followed by a period and three more characters. In the Macintosh system, a filename can have as many as 32 characters.

Allowable symbols. You can use any letter of the alphabet, and any numeral, in a filename. In DOS and Windows (as of this writing) you can't use a space. You might be allowed to use some or none of the following symbols, depending on the application:

! @ # $ % ^ & ( ) { } - _ '

Generally, it's best to stick to letters and numbers. You might be able to create a file called @$((.!^' and save it on the hard disk in a directory called NONSENSE, so that its full path would be specified by C:\NONSENSE\@$((.!^', but you'll probably regret it later. If you use DOS, you will have to repeatedly type the characters @$((.!^' to open the file. If you use Windows or the Mac and have several files with names like this, you'll probably forget what is in each file, and end up having to open several files to get at the data you want.

In a directory listing, symbols like these are considered to come before all the numbers or letters of the alphabet. Files with weird names like @$((.!^' will thus appear near the top of the list of files.

Filename extension

Choosing a filename. The first one to eight characters of a DOS filename should tell you what the file contains. The last one to three characters, called the *filename extension*, usually indicate the type of file. The extension .TXT is often used, for example, for text files. You don't always have to type an extension. Many applications add their own extensions to your filenames. If you use some other extension, the software will not recognize the data. It's always a good idea to keep filenames in DOS as short as possible, while still being meaningful, especially if you have to access the data in the files very often.

If you're using MS-DOS, there are some filenames that you are not allowed to use. Your PC needs them for specialized purposes. These filenames are AUX, CLOCK$, COM1, COM2, COM3, COM4, CON, LPT1, LPT2, LPT3, LST, NUL, and PRN. *See also* DOS, FILE, *and* FILENAME EXTENSION.

Filename extension

Every IBM-compatible file has a *filename* that can contain up to eight characters, a period, and up to three more characters. The characters after the period (if any) are the *filename extension*.

You don't always have to assign extensions to filenames. Often the computer will do it for you. You can use plain, simple words as the names for your files. The most important function of an extension is to categorize files by application. For example, .DOC or .TXT refer to a word-processed file (document or text); .CAL refers to a calendar file; .FXS refers to a fax (facsimile) file. The table shows common standard filename extensions. Many of these are *default extensions* that the computer employs so it can tell which application the file is used for. This scheme is extensively used in Windows.

Some common filename extensions and meanings

Extension	Meaning
.BAK	Backup
.BAT	Batch
.BMP	Graphics
.CAL	Calendar
.COM	Command
.CLP	Clipboard
.CPI	Code page information
.CPL	Control panel
.CRD	Cardfile
.DB	Database
.DAT	Data
.DEV	Device driver

Filename extension

Some common filename extensions and meanings

Extension	Meaning
.DIR	Directory
.DLL	Dynamic link library
.DOC	Document
.EXE	Executable
.FON	Font
.FXS	Fax
.GIF	Graphics
.GRP	Program Manager groups
.HLP	Help
.ICO	Icons
.INF	Program information
.INI	Initialization
.LST	List
.LTR	Letter
.NET	Network
.PCX	Graphics
.PIF	Program information
.PIX	Graphics
.PRN	Printer software
.SCR	Screen saver
.SYS	System
.TMP	Temporary
.TTF	TrueType font
.TXT	Text
.WAV	Sound
.WIN	Windows backup
.WKS	Lotus 1-2-3 spreadsheet
.WK1	Lotus 1-2-3 spreadsheet
.WPD	PostScript information
.WRI	Windows Write
.XLS	Excel spreadsheet

Standard extensions usually have three characters, but an extension can have one, two, or three letters and/or numbers. The allowable characters for an extension are the same as those for the main part of the filename.

If you work mostly with word processing in DOS (without Windows), you can probably use nonstandard extensions, such as numbers to indicate a sequence. Suppose you want several working files for letters to a particular client. These could be called SMITHLTR.1 through SMITHLTR.10.

In some programs, you can omit extensions from files if, for example, you want them to stand out in a directory listing. When you look at a directory, the listing shows the filename body in one column and the extension in another column. The absence of an extension will show up clearly as a gap in the extension column, making it easier for you to spot the filename. *See also* DIRECTORY *and* FILENAME.

File server

One form of local area network (LAN) has one main, central computer to which several workstations are connected. This central computer, where all shared data is stored, is called the *file server.* The workstations store and access the data to and from the file server.

The drawing shows a common layout for a LAN that uses a file server (FS) and several workstations (W). There are 18 workstations in this example, but the network could have more or fewer workstations. Each workstation in this case is a *dumb terminal* connected directly to the file server. This type of LAN is sometimes called a *client/server network.* The workstations are the clients.

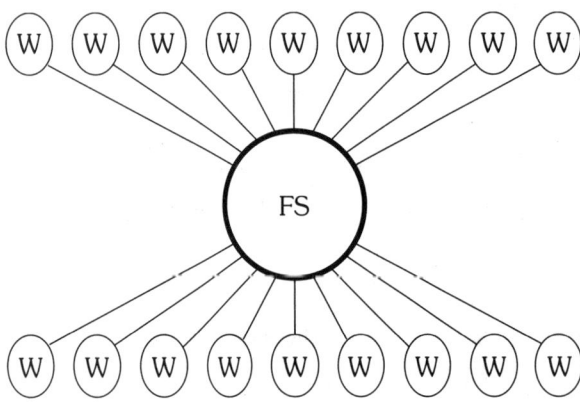

Workstations (W) are connected to a file server (FS) to form a network.

In this scheme, if one of the workstations malfunctions or if the line breaks between the file server and a workstation, the rest of the network will not be affected. Only a breakdown of the file server can cause a catastrophic malfunction of the network.

When you're using a LAN that has a file server, you can communicate with other workstations in the network, but the communication must generally go through the file server. *See also* LOCAL AREA NETWORK.

File transfer protocol

When using an online service or packet communications system, you might want to work with the files in a computer at some distant node. In order to access files online or via radio, a *file transfer protocol (FTP)* is employed. There are three different modes, or security levels, in FTP.

The lowest level is called *read only*. This lets you see the contents of a distant file, but not change the file or create any new files. The second level is *read-old/write-new*. In this mode, you can read, but can't change, existing files at the distant computer. You can add new files. The highest level is *read/write-new/overwrite-old*. This allows full manipulation of files at the distant node, as if it were in the same room with you. *See also* ONLINE SERVICE *and* PACKET COMMUNICATIONS.

File transfer utility

A *file transfer utility* is software that lets you move files between or among computers. There are several packages available; some work between IBM-compatible PCs only, others can convert data between IBM to Macintosh formats. File transfer utilities are especially popular among people who own one or more laptop computers, as well as a desktop machine.

Suppose you travel often, and like to work on reports, memos, letters, and maybe the occasional short story while away from the office. You could, and probably would, use a laptop computer for your away-from-home writing and computing. Most laptop PCs have hard disks as well as 3.5-inch diskette drives.

Suppose you like to do your editing and printing in the comfort of your home office. You'll need to transfer the files from your laptop to your desktop machine in one of two ways. The first way is to transfer the files from the laptop to the desktop machine via diskettes. This method can be tedious if you have lots of large files, however. The other method is to use a file transfer utility. You connect the laptop to the desktop PC using a cable between designated ports. This scheme generally works faster and easier than the diskette method. You should always back up your work on diskettes, of course, whether or not you use them to transfer the data between computers.

Actually, there is a third approach to this situation. You might just own a good laptop, but no desktop unit. Then you can use a *docking station* at your home office to effectively turn the laptop into a desktop computer. *See also* DESKTOP COMPUTER, DOCKING STATION, LAPTOP COMPUTER, *and* NOTEBOOK COMPUTER.

File updating

In your computer-using career, you'll do *file updating* thousands of times. Basically, it involves opening a file, changing its contents, and then saving the file, incorporating the changes.

File updating

Opening the file. Opening a file is a matter of knowing which data you want to update, and what filename and directory it's stored under. Most PC users acquire the habit of assigning filenames and directories so it's easy to tell, from the names alone, what's in a file.

As you gain experience working with files, you'll develop your own intuitive system of naming them, and also a system of storing them in directories so you can easily locate data when you need it. *See also* DIRECTORY, DIRECTORY TREE, *and* FILENAME.

Overwriting. Once you've made changes, you'll want to save the file with the updates you've made. As you're editing a file, the changes are stored only in RAM (random-access memory, which is temporary storage). To make the changes permanent, you must store them on your hard disk or diskette. To do this, you type a command or click an icon to save the file under the same filename as it had previously.

When you try to use a filename that's already used by another file, you'll probably get an alert message telling you that the filename already exists, and asking if you want to overwrite the contents. Normally you will type Y or click Yes. But if you change your mind, you might type N or click No.

Backup. Some programs will save the old file, the way it was before you made the changes, in addition to the new file with the changes. This lets you "unmake" updates if you change your mind about them. The old file will usually appear with an extension such as .BAK (meaning backup).

If you update a file twice, or if you store the contents of a file more than once while you're updating it, the backup will lag one update behind. For example, if you make changes to JONESRPT.7, the file JONESRPT.BAK will contain what was in JONESRPT.7 before the update. If you update JONESRPT.7 again (call it update 2), then JONESRPT.BAK will change to update 1. If you update JONESRPT.7 yet another time (update 3), then JONESRPT.BAK will change to update 2.

Some programs will back up your files on diskette, as well as on hard disk, every time you save data. This offers an additional measure of security and peace of mind.

When updating any file, you should always save the changes every few minutes. You don't want to spend three hours overhauling a huge file, and then lose all your work because of a power failure, a misplaced click of the mouse, or a keystroke error. Some programs automatically save files to the hard disk every few minutes, even if you do nothing. Still, it's a bad idea to take this feature for granted because it might not function in *every* application. An uninterruptible power supply (UPS) is another safety feature, giving you time to save changes in case the utility power goes out. *See also* FILE ERASURE *and* UNINTERRUPTIBLE POWER SUPPLY.

Object linking and embedding (OLE). In our fast-paced society, information changes often. You might have an item stored in dozens of places in the labyrinth of your files.

Eventually, if you use your PC long enough, you'll come up against the inconvenience of having to peruse your files to make the same change many times. Maybe Jane Doe moved from Cincinnati to Seattle. Suppose her data appears in so many places that you don't even remember them all. The only way to update her data totally is to go through every possible file, search for her name, and change the address, city, state, zipcode, and telephone number—unless you have *object linking and embedding (OLE)*.

With OLE, you only have to update data in one place, and your computer will automatically update the information in every other linked file in which it occurs. *See also* OBJECT LINKING AND EMBEDDING.

Fill

The term *fill* has different meanings in different programs. In a spreadsheet, it refers to an automatic method of entering values into cells. In a draw program or paint program, it usually refers to a particular shading effect.

In a spreadsheet. Suppose that you want to make up a weekly office budget for a year. Suppose the first Monday in the year falls on January 2, so the second Monday is January 9. In many spreadsheet programs, you could enter these two dates (in the appropriate date format) at the top of two columns. Then, using the program's fill or autofill function, the rest of the dates would be filled in for you, one column for each of the weeks in the year.

Once you've used the fill operation, your spreadsheet rows should be all set up. You can then assign items to the rows. The first row might be for rent, the second for utilities, the third for telephone expenses, and so on. Most of these expenses occur on a monthly, not a weekly, basis. You suddenly have an insight: Why not go by the month, rather than by the week? You erase the weekly data and start the spreadsheet over, typing just the first month's name (January), and letting the fill function do the rest.

Although this example involves a budget, the fill operation can be used in any spreadsheet application. In some cases, it can save you a lot of tedious, manual entry of data. *See also* SPREADSHEET.

Filter

In graphics. When you use a computer to create artwork, filling refers to the placement of lines or figures to make complex objects. You might, for example, want to fill in gaps in a diagram using straight line segments.

In a paint program, and also in some draw programs, filling is an operation in which you can shade or color an enclosed region. You move a pointer or icon so that it's somewhere within the region, and click the mouse or press a key. The icon might look like a paint can, paintbrush, paint sprayer, or other instrument (see the drawing). This will cause the region to be shaded or "painted" in gray, black, or some color you've chosen. Normally, the region must be completely enclosed; that is, the boundary must be unambiguously defined.

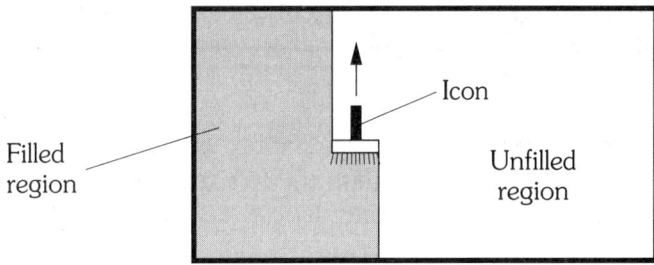

A fill can be used for coloring or shading.

The appearance of a filled region on the display or monitor will not necessarily be the same as its appearance in the printed hardcopy. For example, color graphics can't be rendered by a grayscale printer. In these cases, either of two things might happen. The printer might replace colors with shades of gray, in effect taking a black-and-white photograph of the color image, or the computer might refuse to send the data to the printer, telling you that you have the wrong hardware and/or software for the job. *See also* DRAW PROGRAM *and* PAINT PROGRAM.

Filter

A *filter* is a process in which data is refined or modified. A filter screens out some things, and lets other things through.

The concept. Think of a color filter, like those used by photographers. You've probably seen how these work. When you look through a blue color filter, for example, the sky appears normal. But you wouldn't want to wear bright blue color filters as glasses, because you might not see red traffic lights!

A color filter alters your view of the world because it changes the way you see color. Some colors are affected very little; others are changed in hue; some are completely blocked. A data filter works in a similar way with computer information. Filters are convenient for sorting, transferring, and copying files.

Automatic filtering. Filtering convenience is one of the big assets of using a standard filename extension to represent each application you work with. In DOS and Windows, if you want to filter files so that only those with a certain extension get through, you can specify the extension as a filter, using the asterisk (*) *wildcard* for the main part of the filename. For example, *.TXT can represent any and all of the text files on a diskette or in a directory.

Suppose that you want to copy all the text files from the current directory to a blank diskette in drive B. At the DOS prompt, you could type

```
COPY *.TXT B:
```

The diskette in drive B would then acquire all the text files from the current hard disk directory, provided the files could fit within the storage space of the diskette.

See also FILENAME, FILENAME EXTENSION, *and* WILDCARD.

Finder

In the Macintosh environment, *Finder* is a utility that was commonly used before the advent of System 7. Finder is analogous to the DOS Shell used in IBM-compatible PCs.

Finder lets you use one application at a time. This is fine for some PC users. For example, if all you do is word processing, and if you aren't involved in desktop publishing, Finder will probably be adequate for your needs. Eventually, though, you'll want a more powerful system for more advanced software and applications. *See also* MACINTOSH, MULTIFINDER, *and* SYSTEM 7.

Firewire

See SCSI TECHNOLOGY.

Firmware

Firmware is a term referring to computer programs that are permanently installed in the system. Usually this is done in ROM (read-only memory). The firmware in a computer can be altered, but this requires a hardware change. You can't instantly change the firmware like you can change software.

To change firmware, it's necessary to remove an integrated circuit (IC), and then replace it with an IC having different firmware. This might mean installing an altogether new IC, but there are devices whose firmware can be erased and then reprogrammed. These are called *erasable programmable read-only memory (EPROM)* ICs. Special equipment is needed to change the contents of an EPROM.

Firmware programming is especially common in microcomputer-controlled appliances and machinery. Simple, "dumb" control systems are well-suited to the use of firmware. *See also* ERASABLE PROGRAMMABLE READ-ONLY MEMORY, READ-ONLY MEMORY, *and* SOFTWARE.

First-in/first-out circuit

A *first-in/first-out (FIFO)* circuit is a form of read-write memory. FIFOs are commonly used as buffers in machines like computers and terminals. A first-in/first-out list is sometimes called a *queue*.

The FIFO circuit works just as its name implies. The characters, or data bits, always come out in exactly the same order they went in, although the speed of the output data can be different from the speed of the input data. The main asset of a FIFO circuit is its ability to accommodate, or smooth out, variations in data speed.

The drawing shows a FIFO with eight characters of storage capacity. The capacity of real FIFO circuits is much larger, such as 1024 or 4096 characters; eight are shown here for simplicity of illustration. Although characters are fed in at an irregular rate of speed, they will come out at a precisely timed, regular rate, as long as the FIFO is not completely full. If the buffer fills up because the input data comes in too fast, the machine will send a signal back to the source of the data, telling it to pause until the buffer has partially emptied.

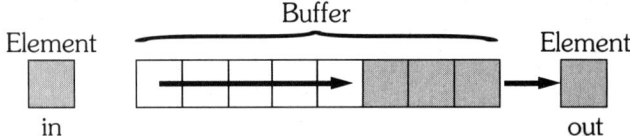

In FIFO, elements leave in the same order they enter.

Not all buffers operate on the FIFO principle. Sometimes the output is reversed in sequence from the input. That kind of buffer is called a *first-in/last-out (FILO)* or *pushdown stack*. *See also* MEMORY *and* PUSHDOWN STACK.

First-in/last-out

See PUSHDOWN STACK.

Flatpack

The *flatpack* is a common housing for an integrated circuit (IC) or "chip." A thin, flat package, usually less than one inch square and a few millimeters thick, is fitted with metal pins along each edge (see the drawing). The pins protrude straight outward from the package, minimizing the depth that it takes up. The number of pins can vary depending on the complexity of the IC inside the package.

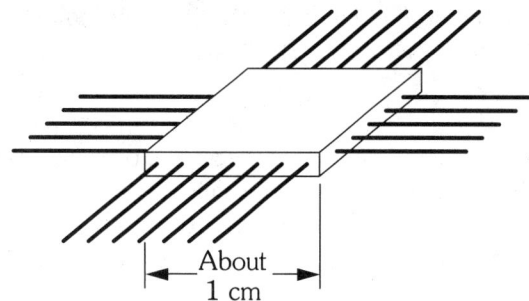

A housing for ICs in microminiature circuits.

Flatpacks are mounted on circuit boards by placing them down on the surface, and then soldering each pin to the foil on the board. Installation is often done by robots. Flatpacks are rather difficult to remove and replace. When installing and replacing flatpacks, it is important that the orientation be correct. It is easy to get the package rotated by 90 or 180 degrees from its proper position. *See also* DUAL INLINE PACKAGE, INTEGRATED CIRCUIT, *and* SINGLE INLINE PACKAGE.

Flip-flop

A *flip-flop* is a simple electronic circuit with two stable states. The circuit changes state when it receives an input pulse or signal. The flip-flop maintains a given state indefinitely unless a pulse is received. There are several different kinds of flip-flop circuits:

- A *D flip-flop* operates in a delayed manner, from the pulse just before the one happening at the moment.

- A *J-K flip-flop* has two inputs, J and K. If the J input receives a high pulse, the output is set to the high state. If the K input receives a high pulse, the output is set low. If both inputs receive high pulses, the output changes its state (high to low, or low to high). The high and low states are often called logic 1 and logic 0, respectively.

- An *R-S flip-flop* has two inputs, R and S. A high pulse at R sets the output low; a high pulse at S sets the output high. The circuit is not affected by pulses at both inputs.

- An *R-S-T flip-flop* has three inputs, R, S, and T. It works just like an R-S flip-flop, except that a high pulse at the T input will cause the output to change state (high to low, or low to high).

- A *T flip-flop* has only one input, the T input. Each time a high pulse appears at the T input, the output state is reversed (high to low, or low to high).

Flip-flops are interconnected to form *logic gates*. These circuits comprise the workings of digital computers. No matter how complicated or powerful a digital computer might be, its data processing and storage circuitry has a finite number of logic gates. In this respect a computer is similar to a human brain, which is made up of a finite (although incredibly large) number of biological cells. *See also* DIGITAL COMPUTER TECHNOLOGY, INTEGRATED CIRCUIT, *and* LOGIC GATES.

Floating point

In mathematical applications, a calculator or computer has a certain maximum number of digits it can recognize. A good example of this is a pocket calculator, which normally has 10 digits in its display. To make the best use of the available digits, a scheme called *floating point* can be used.

How it works. To demonstrate how the floating point works, you can use any calculator. To create this example, an inexpensive scientific calculator was tested. (The exact value of the last digit will depend on whether the calculator rounds numbers, or simply truncates them.)

First, calculate the square root of 2. This yields the number 1.414213562. Now, multiply this by 10:

1.414213562 × 10 = 14.14213562

Notice that the digits on the display are exactly the same; the decimal point has simply moved one place to the right. Now multiply this by 1000:

14.14213562 × 1000 = 14142.13562

The decimal point has moved three more digits to the right. Multiplying this by 100,000 yields the following:

14142.13562 × 100,000 = 1414213562

The decimal point has moved five more places to the right, and has disappeared from the display.

Scientific notation. In the calculator tested, multiplying the last number by 100 gives the result

1414213562 × 100 = 1.4142135 11

The number of *significant figures* is eight; there are two blank spaces; then the digit 11 indicates that the displayed number is to be multiplied by 10^{11}, or 100,000,000,000. This is known as *scientific notation*. Many calculators and computers use scientific notation to increase the range of numerical values that can be displayed.

A 10-digit, floating-point calculator without scientific notation can show numbers from 0.000 000 001 to 9,999,999,999. A calculator or computer with scientific notation, on the other hand, can show values as small as 10^{-99} and as big as 10^{99}. This is done by limiting the number of significant figures, either by rounding off the last digit or by truncating digits as necessary. (The calculator tested here happens to be one that truncates digits.)

Scientific notation usually employs a *fixed point*. The number displayed is always at least 1, but less than 10. Therefore, the decimal point always appears immediately to the right of the leftmost digit. *See also* SCIENTIFIC NOTATION.

Floppy disk

See DISKETTE.

Floptical diskette and drive

The word *Floptical* is a trademark of Insite Peripherals, Inc., and is a contraction of the words *floppy optical*. A Floptical diskette is a 3.5-inch diskette that makes use of both magnetic and optical technologies to obtain ultra-high data-storage density. A Floptical drive is a diskette drive that reads and writes onto Floptical diskettes.

Large memory capacity. A Floptical drive can be added to any PC as a peripheral. It's the size of an ordinary external diskette drive and can work with conventional double-density or high-density 3.5-inch diskettes. Its big advantage, however, comes when you use it with Floptical diskettes, which have room for more than 20MB of data apiece. Compare that with 1.44MB for conventional 3.5-inch high-density diskettes!

Floptical diskette systems can be used with desktop or laptop computers. They're especially useful for small and medium-sized businesses. They're convenient for use with a PC that is shared by several users, each of whom creates a lot of data. Floptical diskettes and drives are also excellent for storing graphics and for sophisticated software programs.

Head movement. The secret of Floptical technology lies in the way the read/write head is guided over the surface of the diskette. In a conventional diskette system, data is written in circular tracks. The head moves along the tracks, being controlled by a mechanical device inside the drive. The amount of data that can be written onto and read from a diskette depends, in part, on the precision of the head movement.

In a Floptical diskette and drive, the head is helped along by an optical guidance system. This gives the head a sort of artificial *eye* with which it can visibly follow its tracks on the diskette surface. The result is greater precision than is possible with conventional diskette drives. This increases the amount of data that can be stored

Flowchart

on the diskette. Floptical drives are manufactured by Insite Peripherals, Inc. and by Iomega Corporation. *See also* DISKETTE *and* DISKETTE DRIVE.

Flowchart

A *flowchart* is a diagram that illustrates a logical process or a computer program. It is a form of block diagram. Boxes, circles, diamonds, and other shapes indicate conditions, and arrows show procedural steps.

Computer programmers use flowcharts to develop software. Flowcharts are also used by technicians in the troubleshooting of complex equipment. Flowcharts lend themselves well to computerized robotic applications because they indicate choices a machine must make while it accomplishes a task. A flowchart can depict complex processes in easy-to-understand form.

A flowchart always represents a complete set of events. All the routes lead somewhere; there are no dead ends. If you follow the chart along, you'll eventually come to a resolution. A flowchart is useful for finding and eliminating *infinite loops*, where things go around and around in endless circles. Infinite loops can render a computer program useless or stop a process from moving forward.

In a flowchart, steps are usually indicated by rectangular boxes. Yes/no decision points are shown as diamonds. Other shapes can be used; for example, an octagon can mean "stop." Lines connecting the shapes can have arrows, indicating the direction in which events flow along.

The sample code shows a simple program in the BASIC language. When this program is run, the computer will print out whole numbers starting with 1, and continuing up through 300. The drawing opposite page is a flowchart illustrating the paths of reasoning the computer follows as it executes the program. *See also* FLOWCHARTING SOFTWARE.

A simple computer program

```
10  LET N=1
20  IF N > 300 GOTO 60
30  PRINT N
40  LET N=N+1
50  GOTO 20
60  END
```

Flowcharting software

You can use computer graphics to create a flowchart, or diagram, of a complex process. This is useful in making professional-looking

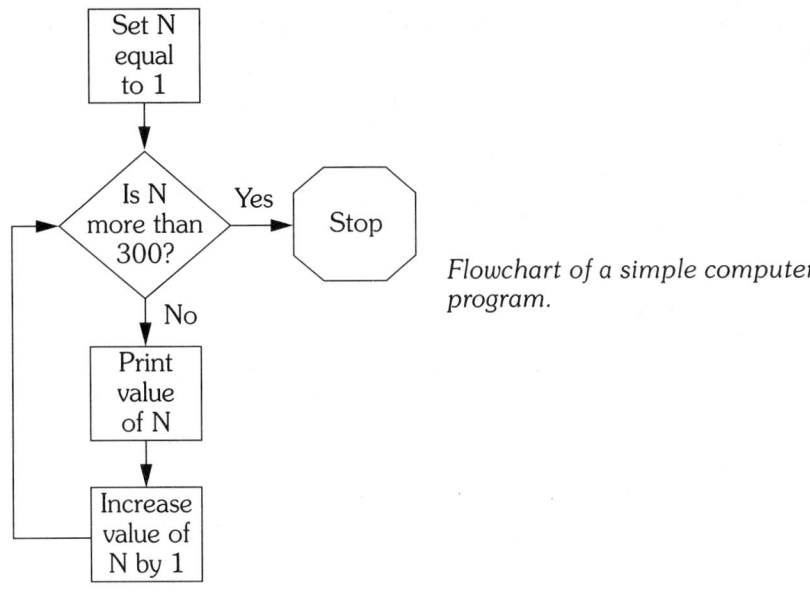

Flowchart of a simple computer program.

scientific and business presentations. It can also help you write computer programs. *Flowcharting software* is available from several vendors, and ranges in price from as little as $50 to hundreds of dollars.

Shapes and sizes. Flowcharting software usually works in a windowing environment. Thus, you use a mouse or trackball to select items, position them, and interconnect them. It's possible to use some flowcharting software via keyboard only, but this is tedious and difficult.

Shapes include rectangles, diamonds, circles, ellipses, file-folder icons, hexagons, octagons, and practically anything else you can imagine. You can change the size and orientation of any shape and move it anywhere on the screen by dragging it. You can color in some shapes, leave others empty, and make still others solid black. Some flowcharting programs have just a few shapes that you can choose from; others have dozens or even hundreds.

Lines and text. A good flowcharting program lets you draw lines of any sort. Generally, lines should run vertically and horizontally, so that the process moves along like soldiers marching in formation. This ensures that the flowchart will look neat and be easy to follow. Diagonal or curved lines are used only when there is no alternative.

With the software, you can make lines that are solid or dashed, and have various thicknesses and colors. Lines can be drawn by clicking in one shape, dragging the mouse to another shape, and clicking again.

Flush-left/right/center

You can put an arrow, dot, small open circle, or other indicator at one or both ends of any line.

You can place text of any font or size within the shapes on a flowchart. The software fits the text into the shape, and centers it. Once this has been done, you can tailor the size of the text and/or shape for the best appearance and readability. It's best to keep the number of text characters to a minimum to avoid cluttering the flowchart.

Linking. Have you ever seen a block diagram in which one of the blocks represents another whole diagram? This is common in electronics and scientific work. It can also be used when diagramming computer processes such as subroutines.

Some flowcharting software has a linking feature. This lets you condense an entire flowchart into a single shape and place it inside another, larger flowchart. Then, by clicking on the shape, you can expand it to look at the details of the flowchart it represents. *See also* ANALYTICAL GRAPHICS, CLIP ART, DRAW PROGRAM, FLOWCHART, PAINT PROGRAM, *and* PRESENTATION GRAPHICS.

Flush-left/right/center

In word processing, there are several ways in which type can be arranged. These are defined according to how the lines stack up vertically.

Flush-left. For most documents, the most common format is *flush-left*. An example of this is shown at A in the drawing. It is also known as *left justification* because the text is aligned along a straight, vertical line on the left-hand side of the block of text. You'll sometimes also hear it called *ragged-right*, because the right side of the text block is not aligned.

Flush-left is usually the default format in a word processing program. Unless you specify some other format, your manuscripts will appear flush-left on screen, and also in your printouts.

Flush-right. You can reverse the situation from flush-left, getting a strange-looking alignment called *flush-right* (at B in the drawing). This is hard for most people to read, and is rarely seen. It's sometimes called *right justification*, because the text is aligned vertically along the right side of the block of text. You might also hear this referred to as *ragged-left*, because the left-hand side of the text block is not aligned.

Flush-right is sometimes used in published poetry, song lyrics, and greeting cards. It is also occasionally used in letterhead and advertisements. It should never be used in the body of formal documents, however, because it is difficult to read.

This is an example of flush-left type. Notice that the left edges all fall along a nice vertical line. The right edges don't. This is sometimes called ragged-right type. It's commonly used for manuscripts.

A

This is flush-right type. The right edges line up vertically. The left edges do not. This format, sometimes known as ragged-left, is rarely used, except for special effects such as published poetry.

B

This is flush-center type. Neither the right nor the left edges line up vertically. But the lines are all centered. This format, like flush-right, isn't used often, except for special effects.

C

Text that is flush-left (A), flush-right (B), and flush-center (C).

Flush-center. You'll frequently see text in which every line is centered. This results in a ragged appearance on both the left-hand and right-hand edges of the block of text. It is called *flush-center.* An example of this is shown in the drawing at C.

Flush-center format is sometimes used for special effects. It is common in formal invitations, flyers, signs, and titles. Like flush-left, it should not be used in the body of manuscripts, theses, reports, or similar documents.

Justified. Text that is *fully justified* is aligned both flush-left and flush-right. Unlike the other formats discussed here, justified text requires an uneven spacing between letters, words, and sentences to ensure that every line is exactly the same physical length. Justified text can be difficult to read, especially if the lines of text are short, because big gaps can appear between words and sentences. *See also* JUSTIFICATION.

Folder

In Macintosh PCs, a *folder* is a place where files can be stored without displaying each filename. This saves screen space, which might otherwise be consumed with nonactive filenames. The folder is represented by an icon that looks like a little manila folder on the Macintosh desktop. A folder is something like a directory or subdirectory in IBM-compatible PCs.

When working in DOS, you can display several directories and subdirectories on your PC screen. Each directory or subdirectory can contain dozens of files. If you've set up your system in a logical way, you shouldn't have trouble locating a file if you display all your directories and subdirectories. Suppose, for example, that you wrote a proposal for the Acme Company. If one of your subdirectories is entitled PROPOSALS, you'd look for it there. You'd see the filename ACME, and you'd know you'd found it.

In the Macintosh system, you don't necessarily know what is in a folder just by looking at the icon. This, however, need not cause a problem. Software is available that tells you which files you have most recently accessed, making it *easy* to find the files you are most likely to be working on currently. This feature, and the longer filenames that Macintosh allows compared with IBM-compatible systems, adds to the user-friendliness of Macintosh computers. *See also* DESKTOP, ICON, *and* MACINTOSH.

Font

The term *font* refers to the shapes and sizes of characters. Fonts appear on your monitor as well as on the paper coming out of your printer.

Typeface versus type size. A set of characters that share a particular look is known as a *typeface*. Characters of a given typeface, such as Courier, can have any size. When you want to specify a font, you must also include *type size*. You'll often hear the words "font" and "typeface" used interchangeably. This is technically imprecise, although it usually doesn't cause confusion.

In printed copy, type size is usually given in units called *points*. One point is $1/72$ inch, or 0.35 millimeter. The bigger the number, the larger the type size. If you have 10-point type, the characters are $10/72$ inch (about an eight of an inch) tall. If you have 20-point type, the characters measure $20/72$ inch (a little over a quarter-inch).

Type size is sometimes specified in *characters per inch (CPI)* instead of points. In this case, the larger the number, the smaller the type size. Common type sizes are 10 CPI, also known as *pica type*, and 12 CPI, often called *elite type*.

Some common typefaces. There are literally hundreds of typefaces you can use. Here are a few of the more common categories:

➤ *Nonproportional* typefaces look like the printing from most typewriters. It has a "blocky" appearance because each letter takes up the same amount of space on the line, whether it is a narrow one like *i* or a wide one like *W*. Courier is probably the most common nonproportional typeface.

➤ *Sans serif* refers to any of several typefaces that lack serifs, the little "swashes" on the ends of strokes that make up letters. It has a plain appearance. Some people find it easier to read than typefaces with serifs, but others find it more difficult. Specific typefaces within this class include Arial, Helvetica, and Futura.

➤ *Script* typefaces resemble longhand. The letters are formed so that they connect within words, the way you connect letters when writing. It is good for greetings and informal letters.

➤ *Serif* typefaces are the most common in the publishing industry. The text of most books, magazines, and newspapers is usually a serif font. Popular serif typefaces often have a variation of the word *Times* in them, such as Times New Roman and Times Roman.

Scalable fonts. A *scalable font* is a font in which you can adjust the type size while leaving the typeface the same. In theory, you can always change the type size, but unless you have a set of fonts specifically designed for scaling, a type of distortion called *jaggies* will result when you enlarge or shrink a typeface too much.

Scalable fonts are generally downloadable fonts that your software passes along to the printer. When you enlarge the type size on your screen, it prints out larger; when you shrink it on the screen, it prints out smaller. Common scalable font schemes are TrueType and Printer Command Language (PCL).

Screen versus printer. The font on your screen is not necessarily what you'll get from your printer. Remember that a font consists not only of a typeface, but also a type size. So even if the characters on your monitor have the same shape as those your printer puts on the paper, the size might (and probably will) differ.

Most low-end word processing programs rely on your printer to produce the font. Higher-end word processing software, and most desktop-publishing packages, let you see the typeface your printer will produce and send the font to the printer by downloading.

Some fonts are programmed into your printer permanently. You select them by pressing buttons on the printer control panel to select the typeface and type size. When using such a built-in font, you need not specify any font in the computer or software.

If you want to change fonts within a document, or if you want to use fonts that your printer does not have, you need downloadable fonts. In this case, the font information is sent to the printer (downloaded) from the computer.

Adding new fonts. You can purchase software containing fonts if you're bored with the fonts you have, or you need a special font for a particular effect. Some CD-ROM packages contain hundreds of fonts, some of which are strange enough to suit any fancy.

When you buy a package of fonts, you need to be sure that it's compatible with your system. Also, be aware that fonts can be, and often are, copyrighted. Licensing agreements vary depending on the vendor. *See also* BUILT-IN FONT *and* DOWNLOADABLE FONT.

Forecasting

Forecasting is the use of a computer to aid in predicting of future events. There are several ways in which this can be done; the best method depends on the environment or situation.

Calculation. Some phenomena repeat in a precise way. These things are easy to predict because they behave according to a mathematical formula. Once the formula is found, it can be extrapolated indefinitely into the future with little or no error.

An example of this type of forecasting is shown in drawing A. This is an audio tone with a frequency of 1250 hertz (abbreviated Hz and meaning "cycles per second"), like a note played on a flute. The waveshape is regular and starts over once every 0.0008 second. You might get this wave if you set a musical synthesizer to 1250 Hz and adjust it to produce a pure tone. Once you know the position and frequency of the wave, a computer can calculate exactly what the signal voltage will be at some instant in the future.

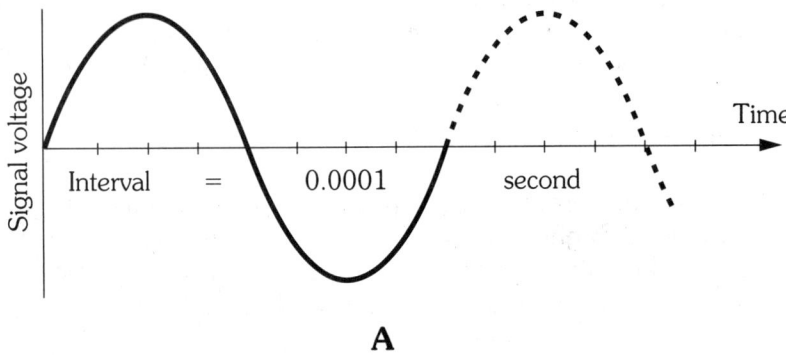

A

Exact prediction is possible.

Another good example of this type of forecasting is the prediction of solar and lunar eclipses. Astronomers have mapped these out for centuries into the future. For solar eclipses, the path of totality can be calculated right down to the mile because the earth and moon move around the sun with mathematical regularity.

Extrapolation. The projection of the past into the near future is called *extrapolation*. A common example of computerized extrapolation is the prediction of the path a hurricane will take within the next six, 12, or 24 hours. Computers are often used by economists in an attempt to predict what the stock market will do tomorrow or next week. A graph is drawn of stock-market behavior for the past few weeks, and this curve is projected into the future.

Other variables that lend themselves to extrapolation are population growth, price inflation, and the number of flu cases in a region. Daily temperature can also be predicted using extrapolation, especially when there is little variation in the weather from day to day (drawing B). See also EXTRAPOLATION.

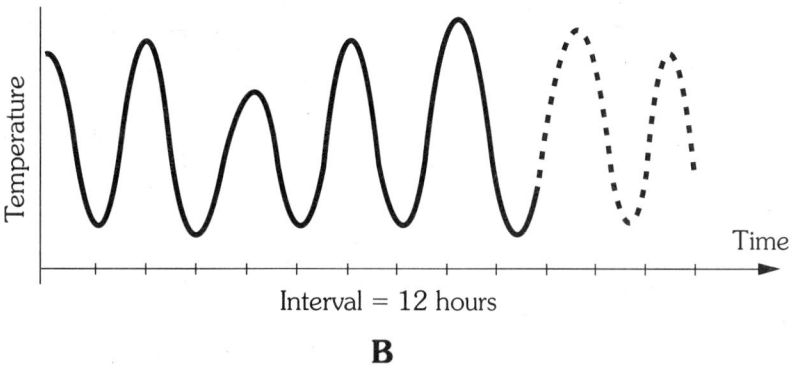

B

An approximate prediction can be made.

Modeling. *Modeling* is a process of imitation. To create a model of a scenario, you need to give the computer as much relevant data as possible, and then program the machine to follow rules that resemble real life.

Expert systems software uses modeling. The computer is given facts and rules that allow it to behave, for example, like a meteorologist or medical doctor. Computer games use modeling to simulate adventures, such as aircraft dogfights or high-tech auto racing. Modeling is done via analogical reasoning.

Military people use expert systems and game-like software in an attempt to forecast the outcome of a battle. Sometimes the results of such forecasts prove markedly different from what would be expected based on human intuition. Computers can dream up scenarios and strategies that even the best human generals overlook. See also ANALOGICAL REASONING *and* EXPERT SYSTEMS.

When chaos rules. Some things defy forecasting. Such situations or environments are *chaotic*; while general patterns might be observable, exact predictions are impossible. An example of a totally unpredictable effect is the moment-to-moment change in the atmospheric noise ("static") on a radio receiver during a thundershower. Another is the instantaneous level of noise on a telephone line. Still another is the roll of a die, assuming it isn't "loaded" (drawing C on next page).

In recent decades, a new science, called *chaos theory*, has emerged. Computers are invaluable in this field. Prediction of exact values is impossible in a chaotic environment, no matter how sophisticated the software, but chaotic events show behavior characteristics that were

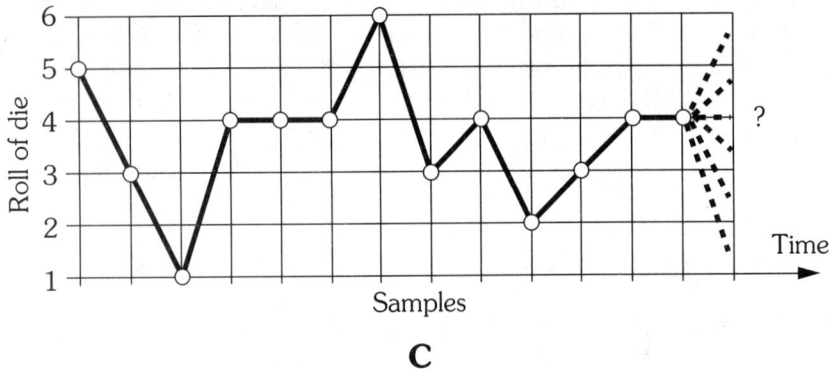

C

Prediction is impossible.

unknown until computers, with their calculating power, were used to analyze them. You can explore chaos theory on your PC using software designed for the purpose. *See also* FRACTAL *and* FRACTAL-GENERATION SOFTWARE.

Foreground processing

The mind of your PC can deal with more than one "thought" at a time. This is known as *multitasking*. In multitasking, processes are divided into two levels of priority. The high-priority work in progress is called *foreground processing*.

Conscious mind. Think of your PC as a primitive version of the human mind. The things going on in the computer's foreground are something like thoughts in the front of your mind, of which you're keenly aware. When you're driving a car, for example, the operation of the vehicle is the foreground process. You might daydream about what you're going to do when you get to your destination, but you had better keep those thoughts in the background.

The foreground process is normally the one on which you, the PC operator, are actively working. It consumes most of your computer's operating time. The machine constantly cycles between the foreground and the background, paying far more attention to the foreground. The cycling happens fast enough so that you're not normally aware of it. To you, the foreground and background seem concurrent.

Edit/print. A common foreground task is word processing. Suppose you want to edit a document while printing out something else. You open the file you want to edit, thereby bringing it into the foreground, leaving other files and processes in the background (see the drawing). You can tell the printer to print out any background file at any time. Printing would then be a background process; the editing would be the foreground process.

Suppose you want to work on a financial spreadsheet while sending holiday greetings to people via electronic mail. Then the spreadsheet

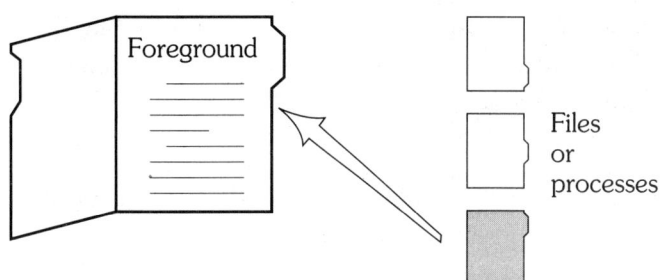

Working on a chosen file in the foreground; other files or processes are in the background.

is in the foreground, while data communications via modem is in the background. It is also possible to receive data from the modem while working on a file. *See also* ACTIVE WINDOW, BACKGROUND PROCESSING, *and* MULTITASKING.

Formatting

Diskettes must be in a certain condition if they are to hold data. Getting a diskette into shape is called *formatting*. All diskettes must be formatted before they can store data. In DOS, this is done using the FORMAT command. In Windows, the equivalent of the FORMAT command is a sequence of choices that you can select. With the Macintosh, disks are automatically formatted for you.

Blank diskettes can be purchased either formatted or unformatted. Generally, unformatted diskettes cost less than preformatted ones, so you can save money by formatting your own diskettes. Formatting erases any data already on the diskette, among its other tasks. Before you format a diskette, therefore, make sure it doesn't have anything important on it. You should never format your hard disk. This is so important that it deserves a special statement:

Warning! Never format your hard disk!

In older versions of DOS, it's all too easy to mistakenly do this. Keep this danger in mind at all times and it will hopefully never happen to you.

Diskettes and sectors. Diskettes are available in two different diameters: 3.5 inches and 5.25 inches. They also come in two densities, known as double density (DD) and high density (HD). The amount of data that a diskette can hold depends on its physical size and also on its density. These days, most PC users employ HD diskettes that hold a little more than one megabyte (1MB) of data, the amount of information in a fairly long novel.

Do you remember writing compositions in high school? You probably used ruled notebook paper for this purpose. You might have preferred wide-ruled paper, with those thin, blue horizontal lines all the way

Formatting

across each sheet, spaced at intervals of about a half-inch. Or perhaps you liked the narrow-ruled paper better because the lines were closer together, and you could get more writing on a sheet (if you could write small enough).

Diskette formatting is like putting lines on notebook paper. Unformatted diskettes are like blank sheets. A formatted DD diskette is like wide-ruled notebook paper. A formatted HD diskette is like narrow-ruled notebook paper. Instead of lines, diskettes are broken down into *sectors*. Each sector can hold 512 bytes. There are thousands of sectors on an HD diskette that holds 1.2MB or 1.44MB of data. When your PC formats a diskette, it reserves a few sectors for the *directory*. This helps the machine find files once you have stored things on the diskette.

The drawing is an intuitive comparison, showing one line on a sheet of notebook paper (A) versus one sector on a diskette (B). You might scrawl 10 written words on a line of notebook paper; your PC can put about 10 times as much information on a sector of a diskette.

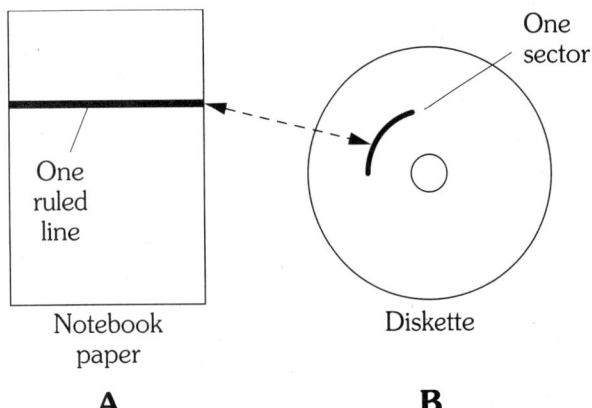

One ruled line (A) on paper is something like one sector (B) on a diskette.

In DOS. Suppose you are in DOS and want to format a diskette in drive A. Assuming the formatting program is installed on your hard disk, you would type FORMAT A: and press Enter. The machine would respond with the following message:

```
INSERT DISKETTE IN DRIVE A:
PRESS ENTER WHEN READY
```

You then place the new diskette (which you want to format) in drive A and press Enter.

As the diskette is being formatted, your PC will give you a running total of the percentage of the process that has been done. It will start with

```
0 PERCENT OF DISKETTE FORMATTED
```

Formatting

and the number will increase up to 100. After a few minutes, the computer will say

FORMAT COMPLETE

You will then be asked if you want to create a volume label (a fancy term for a diskette name). You don't have to name your diskettes, but it can help you keep track of things if you have a large number of diskettes in your archives. You can give the diskette a volume label up to 11 characters long. Type the label and press Enter, or just press Enter right away if you don't want to give the diskette a volume label.

After that, you'll be told how much storage space is available on the diskette. You'll also be told if there are any bad sectors. If the diskette has bad sectors, throw it away immediately. Using a diskette with bad sectors is like driving on bald tires: it's a time bomb! Diskettes can cost less than a dollar each, while the loss of valuable data can be very expensive. On a hard disk, however, a few bad sectors are no cause for concern; the computer is programmed to avoid writing anything onto them. *See also* BAD SECTORS.

There are special conditions, called *switches*, you can use when formatting diskettes. For details, refer to your DOS manual or online help.

In Windows. The Windows operating system is more intuitive than DOS; you don't have to memorize commands. Instead, you select items from menus on the monitor screen by moving a pointer around with a mouse or trackball.

You begin by starting File Manager and opening the Disk menu. From there, you choose Format Disk. You'll have to specify the diskette drive and the diskette capacity. There are other options you can specify, such as Make System Disk and Quick Format. You'll also see a blank box next to the word Label in which you can write the volume label if you want to give the diskette a name. Once you have everything set up exactly as you want, click on OK. You'll then get one final warning, such as this:

FORMATTING WILL ERASE ALL DATA FROM YOUR DISK

and your computer will ask you, via a confirm box, whether or not you are sure you want to go ahead with the process. This "bail out" feature has saved many diskettes that would otherwise have been formatted by mistake. Remember, think about what might be on that diskette. If you have any doubts, check it out before you format it.

Data recovery. Formatting wipes out existing directories and the data itself. You should exercise care when you format any diskette containing crucial files. When reformatting disks, use Quick Format whenever possible. This will erase only the directories on a diskette, making it

Form feed

possible to overwrite data. The data will not actually be erased, however, until it has been written over with new files. If you use Quick Format in Windows (or FORMAT in DOS 5.0 or later), you can recover data even after formatting, provided you have not written new data over the data you need to recover. This is done by using the MIRROR command or an unformatting process. *See also* DIRECTORY, DISKETTE, FILE ALLOCATION TABLE, FORMATTING, HARD DISK, MIRROR COMMAND, *and* UNFORMATTING.

Form feed

Form feed is a function that your printer performs. Almost all printers have a button marked "form feed" or "FF" for this purpose. When you press this button, the paper moves a certain distance forward through the printer, and then stops. There are two different versions of form feed.

Suppose you print out a document, and it ends somewhere partway down a page. (This is what usually happens.) You don't want to rip a page off anywhere except at the end. You want the paper to be positioned so you can tear it neatly off and have the printer be ready to start a new document at the top of a fresh page.

In one arrangement, shown in the drawing at A, pressing FF makes the paper scroll down to the beginning of the next page. Then you can tear the last sheet of the document off, and the printer will be ready to start printing a new document at the top of a page.

In the other, less convenient arrangement (at B), pressing FF will cause the paper to scroll forward the equivalent of one full page. The paper will therefore stop somewhere in the middle of the next page. If the document ends, say, five inches down one page, pressing FF will move the paper forward until it stops five inches down the next page.

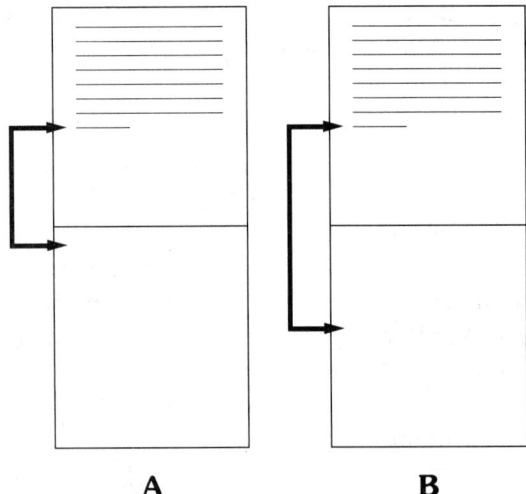

A form feed might move to the top of a new page (A) or one full page forward (B).

Some dot-matrix users like to shut the printer off when a document is finished and scroll the paper to the end of the last page manually. This can be done by turning the wheel on the side of the printer, as if your printer were a typewriter. Always be sure the printer is switched off before you do this. *See also* FORM LENGTH.

Form length

Form length is a measure of the size of forms you can use with a printer. Standard letter-size paper measures 11 inches from top to bottom; thus the form length is 11 inches.

Setting the form length is important if you want your hardcopy to come out right. Most printers have several form length settings. Commonly used form lengths, besides the standard 11 inches, include 8 inches, 8.5 inches, 11⅔ inches (metric letter size), 12 inches, and 14 inches (legal size).

The setting of the form length control will affect the operation of the form feed control on most printers. The two controls interact in such a way that the behavior of the form feed control is always the same, no matter what the form length. *See also* FORM FEED.

Fortran

A common high-level programming language, Fortran has been in use since the late 1950s for scientific and mathematical problem solving. The word *Fortran* is a contraction of the words *formula translator*. It is a compiled language, originally developed by IBM.

Fortran is somewhat similar in structure and syntax to BASIC. Anyone who knows BASIC can learn Fortran; commands are in English and have logical meanings. Fortran is somewhat more versatile than BASIC, but it is also quirky in some respects. For example, there might be some lines in a Fortran program that aren't numbered.

Fortran is not well-suited to control applications or to business-related problems. These days, it is pretty much confined to mathematics, science, and engineering. Even in these applications, other languages are often preferred. *See also* BASIC, HIGH-LEVEL LANGUAGE, *and* SOFTWARE.

Forward chaining

You can use a computer to act as an expert knowledgeable in some field, such as engineering, weather forecasting, medicine, or even the stock market. Programs that make computers act like specialists are called *expert systems*. When running an expert system, you supply the computer with information, and the computer solves a problem based on that information.

There are two ways in which the data can be supplied when using an expert system. You can input the facts one at a time as the computer

Fractal

requests them, or you can input all the data at once before the program begins working towards a solution. The latter method is *forward chaining*. The chain of reasoning starts from a single set of facts and works forward until the problem is solved or a conclusion is reached.

The drawing shows the basic scheme by which forward chaining works. Facts, shown as circles labeled *F*, are supplied. A good example is the bits of evidence in a criminal case. After you've given the computer the data in a forward-chaining expert system, the program's *inference engine* uses rules written in the software to infer a solution or conclusion. If more information is necessary, the computer will let you know by saying something like

```
THERE IS NOT ENOUGH DATA TO COME TO A CONCLUSION
IN THIS CASE
```

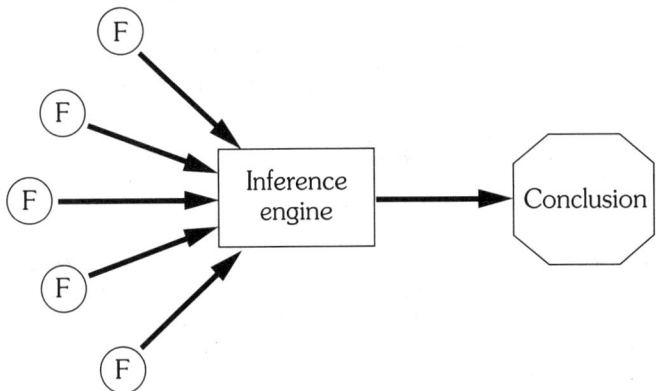

Facts (small circles) are supplied all at once, and a conclusion is derived.

At this point, the program might ask you specific questions in an attempt to get enough information. The inference engine then finds an answer to the problem, if a logical conclusion is possible. Sometimes there are two or more possible outcomes, other times there are none, or so many that the program is of no real use. *See also* BACKWARD CHAINING *and* EXPERT SYSTEMS.

Fractal

A *fractal* is an object that appears complex, no matter how closely you look at it. A true fractal is similar to itself over an infinite range of scales, from the whole object down through smaller and smaller parts. Fractal-like objects are interesting because they have been found in the physical universe. An example is the resemblance between interstellar nebulae, certain types of clouds in the earth's atmosphere, and the smoke from a lighted cigarette. Fractals can be generated by computers from mathematical formulas.

Fractals are common. To the uninitiated, fractals seem strange and unreal. However, consider a shoreline where land meets water. All shorelines have irregularities. The drawing at A shows a hypothetical coastline as it might look from 1000 miles up in space. It appears jagged and random.

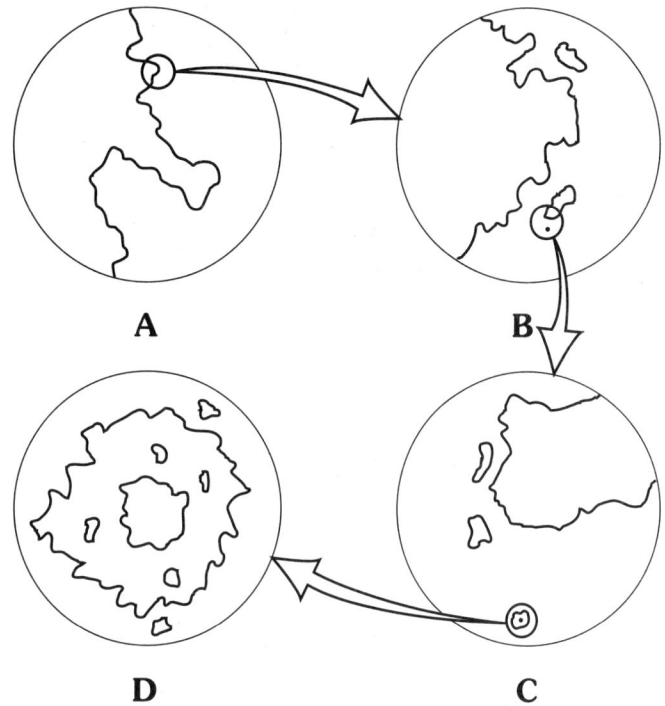

A hypothetical shoreline magnified once (A), 10 times (B), 100 times (C), and 1000 times (D).

If you drop down to an altitude of 100 miles (so the view is magnified by 10) and then look at some part of the coastline, you'll see something like the rendition at B. The shoreline still looks jagged and random.

Now imagine descending to an altitude of 10 miles, shown in the drawing at C. The shore still looks irregular. In fact, is doesn't look any smoother than it did at A or B.

Finally, suppose you drop down to only one mile. You will see something like the drawing at D. There is still plenty of irregularity in the shoreline. It's apparent that this process can be continued indefinitely. With a few exceptions, a shoreline looks irregular from every viewpoint you take—even if you sit on the sand and look at it through a magnifying glass.

Detail at all levels. The boundary where land meets water is a fractal. You could go down to altitudes of 50 feet, five feet, five inches, or five millimeters and see irregularities. You could magnify the image until grains of sand were visible, and they would appear irregular. You could look at viruses and bacteria on the grains of sand,

and see their fractal shapes. Ultimately, you might see individual atoms with their complex structures. Maybe even the subatomic quarks aren't the end of the line. Maybe there is no end to it, as is the case in a true mathematical fractal.

At this point, physical reality ends, but computers can create artificial universes for you to explore. You can buy software that creates fractals and lets you see them from any "altitude" you want. These fractals, infinite in complexity, come from mathematical formulas. Perhaps the most famous fractal is the *Mandelbrot set*, named after Benoit Mandelbrot, the IBM researcher who first discovered it. He used a computer to generate images of it. *See also* FRACTAL-GENERATION SOFTWARE.

Fractal-generation software

A *fractal* is an infinitely complex shape based on a simple formula or set of rules. Fractals lend themselves to rendition on computers. You can display and explore fractals using *fractal generation software*.

Repeated calculations. A fractal is created by repeating a calculation or process thousands, millions, or billions of times. It would be extremely tedious for you to do this without a computer, although it might be possible if you had nothing else to do for several months, years, or decades. The more times the process is repeated, the more detail appears in the resulting geometric figure.

Fractals can exist in two, three, four, or more dimensions. They can also exist in a strange form that chaos-theory gurus call *fractional dimensions*. The subject of fractional dimensions is beyond the scope of this discussion, but you can learn about it from books on the subject of chaos theory and fractals.

Two dimensions. A two-dimensional fractal is a set of points on the Cartesian plane. Suppose you have a fractal-generation function f that maps some point (x_1, y_1) onto a new point (x_2, y_2). Mathematically you would write

$f(x_1, y_1) = (x_2, y_2)$

The function moves the point to a new location on the plane.

Now suppose that this process is repeated many times. The function f is applied to (x_2, y_2) to get a new point (x_3, y_3). As the function is applied again and again, the point jumps around in seemingly random fashion. After many iterations of the function, however, order becomes evident. The point will either fall toward the center of the plane, or wander off toward infinity. The eventual behavior depends on the location of the first point that was chosen, that is, (x_1, y_1).

Fractal-generation software

If you choose a great many starting points and iterate the function thousands of times for each point, you'll break the coordinate plane into two regions. Now you will appreciate the power of the computer! It's ridiculous to even think of doing all these calculations manually. One region in the plane contains only "fall-in" points; the other contains only "wander-off" points. The fractal is the boundary that separates these two different regions (see the drawing). It usually appears as a fantastically twisted, jagged, irregular line.

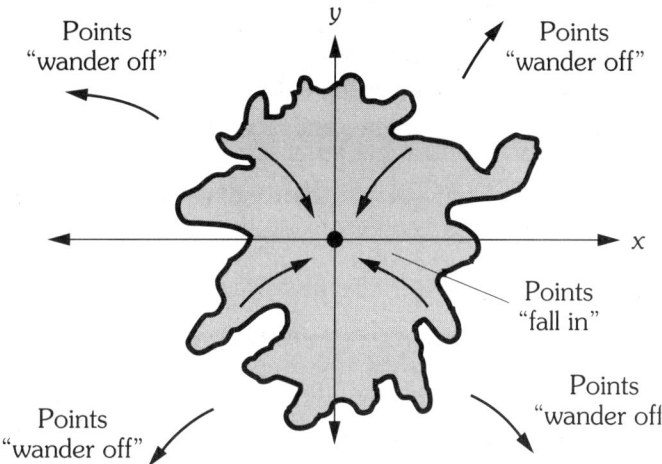

A hypothetical fractal. The shaded region contains "fall-in" points.

Discovery. An IBM engineer, *Benoit Mandelbrot*, noticed this peculiar behavior of certain point sets and functions, and wrote computer programs to analyze the resulting geometric figures. Few people anticipated what he found. Most people thought the boundaries would be simple, such as a circle, cloverleaf pattern, or cardioid (heart-shaped figure). It didn't work out that way.

As Mandelbrot repeated the calculations many times, strange things happened. Irregularities showed up, and they contained smaller bumps, and these in turn had still smaller curls and wisps. Some of the tiny bumps looked like miniatures of the whole set. As the function was applied indefinitely, there appeared to be no end to the complexity. The more closely the sets were examined, the more new details were seen. One such point set is now well known, and has been named the *Mandelbrot set* after its discoverer.

Obtaining software. You can ask your PC dealer about fractal generation software. It has become quite popular in recent years. If you're interested in learning some of the theory behind fractals, in addition to creating and exploring your own fractals on a PC, you might want to get a copy of *Fractal Mania* by Phillip Laplante, Ph.D. (McGraw-Hill, 1993). PC-related magazines occasionally publish articles on this subject. *See also* CARTESIAN COORDINATES *and* FRACTAL.

Fractal image compression

See IMAGE COMPRESSION.

Fragmentation

When you overwrite files many times, they can get broken up so that they do not occupy contiguous sectors on a hard disk or diskette. This is called *fragmentation.*

Read/write speed. As you continue to use a disk, many of its files will eventually become fragmented. You might notice this when the computer takes longer to read and write files compared with its speed weeks or months ago. The problem will be worst for large files and programs that have been updated and overwritten often.

Data loss. Besides slowing down the read/write speed of a hard disk, fragmentation makes it more likely that data will be lost in case of inadvertent file erasure.

When you erase (delete) a file, the computer doesn't actually obliterate the data. It merely considers the involved disk sectors available for overwriting. The old data remains intact on the disk, even after you give the ERASE command or click a Delete button. None of the data will be lost until it is actually overwritten with something else.

If a file is fragmented, it is spread out more thinly on the disk than it would be if it were not fragmented. If such a file is inadvertently erased, and then something new is written on the disk, the chances for partial data loss are greater than they would be if the erased file were in contiguous sectors.

Defragmentation. There's a way to eliminate fragmentation on diskettes and hard disks: a *defragmentation* program. Several such programs are available, and most new computers contain defragmentation programs as part of the standard operating software.

Defragmentation should be done regularly. The more heavily you use your computer, and especially the more frequently you read and write data from its hard disk, the more often you should run the defragmentation program. For most PC users, once or twice a month should be often enough.

A computer can defragment its hard disk in a few minutes. The more severe the fragmentation and the larger your hard disk, the longer the defragmentation program will require to consolidate the files. Most programs show you an illustration of the process as it goes along. They also give you an approximate idea of the locations of bad sectors, if any, on the hard disk or diskette. A few bad sectors are no cause for concern on a hard disk; they do represent a potential problem on a diskette.

If you have a tape drive to back up the data on your hard disk, it's an excellent idea to make a new backup tape right after each use of the defragmentation program. *See also* BACKUP, BAD SECTORS, DEFRAGMENTATION, FILE ERASURE, *and* TAPE DRIVE.

Frame

A *frame* is a mental symbol, a means of representing a set of things. If you're familiar with Microsoft Windows, you can get an excellent idea of the nature of frames by imagining them as being "windows in the mind." In artificial intelligence (AI), objects and processes can be categorized in frames. The term is also used in desktop publishing and word processing.

Logical frames. Suppose you have a robot with its own computer control system. You tell this robot, "Go to the kitchen and pour me some water in a paper cup." The robot goes through a series of deductions concerning how to get this beverage and how to obtain the object in which you want it to be contained.

First, the robot must go to the kitchen. Then it begins a search for the object you've specified. This is depicted in drawing A. The first frame in the robot's thought process represents all the things in the kitchen. Within this frame, a subframe is selected: eating/drinking utensils. Within this, the appropriate frame is cups, and within this frame, the desired category is paper cups. Even within this subset, you might specify six-ounce size, and then maybe even red.

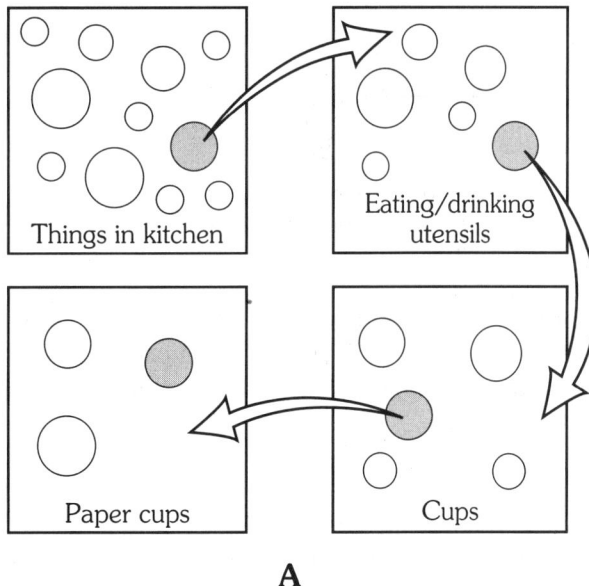

A

A rendition of a complex procedure as frames.

Frames apply to procedures as well as to the selection of objects. Once the robot has the proper utensil in its grasp, what is to be done? Did you want tap water, or is there some cold water in a pitcher in the refrigerator? Or perhaps you wanted some of that bottled mineral water you ran out of last week, in which case the robot must either come back to you and ask for further instructions, or else make a guess as to what substitute you might accept. *See also* ARTIFICIAL INTELLIGENCE, COMMONSENSE SUMMER PROJECT, *and* PERSONAL ROBOTS.

In documentation. When preparing reports, letters, manuscripts, or other documents, you want the text to appear neatly on the pages. Although standard sheets of paper usually measure 8.5 inches wide by 11 inches long, the text and illustrations should not take up the entire page space. Instead, desktop publishing and word processing programs provide margins on all four sides of the page. The space within which the printed matter is confined, usually about 6.5 inches wide by 8.5 inches tall, is called the *frame* or *page frame* (drawing B).

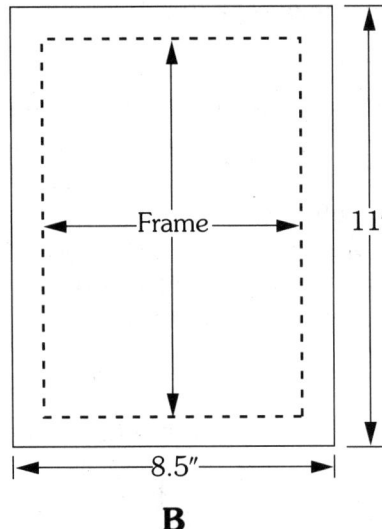

B

The text/image frame on a recto page, with the binding at the left edge.

If you use graphics or special text boxes such as for captions, they might need to go in their own frames, which can be manipulated independently from the page frame or connected to it. *See also* DESKTOP PUBLISHING *and* WORD PROCESSING.

Frankenstein scenario

Science fiction is replete with stories in which computers or smart robots play character roles. The robots and computers in these plots are usually designed to help humanity in some way, but somehow turn against their makers. This theme is often called the *Frankenstein scenario*, after the android who turned on its creator and caused a nightmare.

A vivid example of the Frankenstein scenario is provided by the novel *2001: A Space Odyssey*, in which Hal, the computer on a space ship,

tries to kill Dave, an astronaut. Hal's malfunction develops insidiously, like a progressive disease. Hal comes to believe that Dave intends to do "him" (the computer) in. Hal's paranoia justifies itself in the end because Dave is forced to shut Hal down to save his own life.

A highly evolved, intelligent machine might indeed react hostilely to preserve its own existence when humans try to pull the plug. In response to this Frankenstein scenario, Author Isaac Asimov developed three laws to be programmed into hypothetical smart machines that allow them to preserve themselves, but never harm a human being. *See also* ARTIFICIAL INTELLIGENCE, ASIMOV'S THREE LAWS, *and* COLOSSUS.

Freehand

Freehand is a sophisticated drawing program commonly used with Macintosh computers. It lets you create scalable *object-oriented graphics,* which often work better than the alternative *bitmapped graphics*, especially with printers having good image resolution, such as laser printers.

Bitmapping. Illustrations are generally analog, but a computer "thinks" digitally. Objects in the real world are perceived as continuously variable. Approximations represent analog images in a digital computer.

Bitmapped graphics show images on a grid of dots or *pixels* (picture elements). If the grid is fine enough (if the pixels are small enough), then the digital approximation is near perfect. Scientists, engineers, and others often need more precision than bitmapped graphs can offer. Freehand can help them achieve this.

Bezier curves. One of the most important features of Freehand is the ability to precisely store information for analog curves. Two-dimensional mathematical functions are graphable as curves that look imprecise ("fuzzy" or "grainy") with bitmapped graphics. With *Bezier curves*, many functions can be completely defined on the basis of a few points. Freehand takes advantage of this fact.

Suppose you know the points P_1, P_2, and P_3 shown in the drawing on page 454. Suppose also that you know the curve is smooth, not wildly complicated. Using Freehand, the computer searches for a smooth curve that fits the points. The machine can enlarge and reduce sample curves stored in memory; the curves can be turned over, reversed, or inverted until a match is found (the heavy line in the drawing). The process is something like solving a jigsaw puzzle.

Simplicity. In theory, there are infinitely many complicated curves that fit the points shown in the illustration. One of these is depicted by the light, wavy line in the drawing. This could, in some bizarre

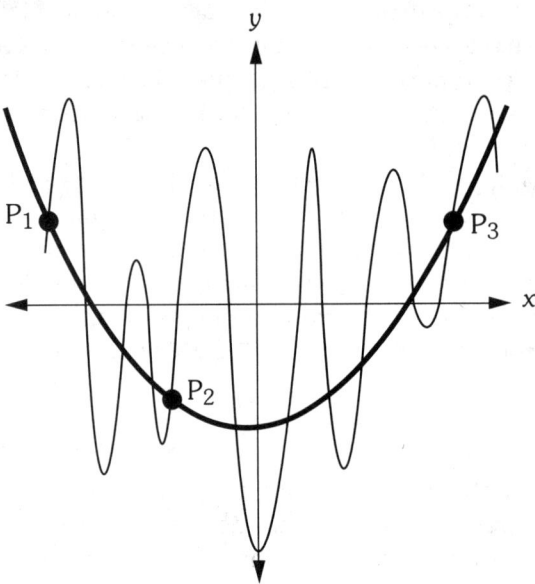

One of Freehand's features is the ability to plot curves based on only a few points.

situation, be the curve that is meant by points P_1, P_2, and P_3, but it is highly improbable. The simplest solution to a problem is usually the correct one. Bezier-curve programs are written with this principle in mind.

Freehand is not the only program that works with Bezier curves. Several other draw programs, some for Macintosh computers and some for IBM-compatibles, can use Bezier functions to define and create curves. One well-known example is CorelDRAW. Curve-generating schemes vary among different programs, but they all work according to the same principles, and they can all be grasped intuitively with some hands-on practice. *See also* ANALOG, BEZIER CURVE, BITMAPPED GRAPHICS, DIGITAL, IMAGE RESOLUTION, *and* OBJECT-ORIENTED GRAPHICS.

Freeware

Freeware is software that has been copyrighted but can be used to a limited extent without cost. Freeware is commonly available online; you can download it and use it with your computer. However, you may not sell freeware to someone else with the intent of making a profit from it.

The main advantage of freeware is that it makes many programs easily available to anyone with a modem and a subscription to an online service. It can help you do many things with your PC that you could not otherwise afford. Also, you can test a program without committing yourself. The people who create and distribute freeware do so mainly out of goodwill to fellow computer users.

On the other hand, freeware is not always tested and debugged as thoroughly as commercial software. Because of this, it is of generally lower quality. Freeware is also somewhat more prone than commercial software to tampering by malicious hackers, increasing the likelihood that such a program will have a Trojan horse or virus. Although these can enter your PC via any software, commercial software is always checked for Trojan horses and viruses before it is sold.

The possibility of encountering viruses, Trojan horses, and bugs should not prevent you from trying freeware. Reasonable precautions can usually prevent major problems. If you plan to use freeware, always download it onto diskettes, never onto your hard disk. Then, before using the diskette, run each program through a vaccine to find and eliminate Trojan horses or viruses. *See also* SHAREWARE, SOFTWARE, TROJAN HORSE, VACCINE, *and* VIRUS.

Front-loading printer

Many printers work with fanfold paper, continuous sheets connected along tear-off lines at 11-inch intervals. Usually, this paper has holes along each side for a printer's tractor feed. You can remove the holes (they're on tear-off strips), leaving sheets 8.5 inches wide.

There are various ways to feed paper through a printer. Most printers have several options. One method is to feed the paper in from the front, as shown in the drawing.

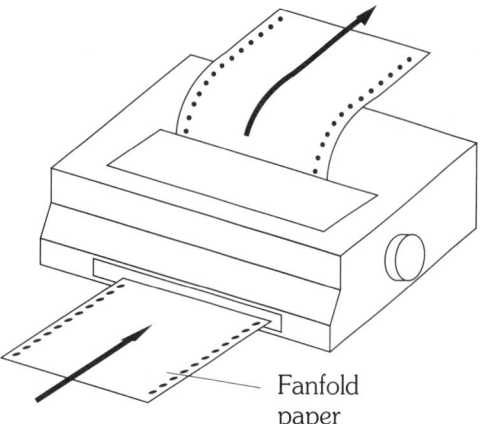

In a front-loading printer, paper enters from the front.

The good. There are advantages to a *front-loading printer*. It's easy to keep track of how much paper you have left. You can put the fanfold paper in a small stack right in front of the printer, or you can put it on the floor underneath the printer table.

The not-so-good. In front loading, the paper comes out the back of the printer and must be stacked up behind the printer. Therefore, the printer must be set on a deep table, so there's room for the paper to pile up behind the unit itself. Alternatively, the table can be a foot or more away from the wall, so the paper can stack up on the floor behind the table.

If you leave a front-loading printer unattended for a long printing session, there's a fair chance that you will return to find a huge mess, but this can occur whenever continuous forms are used. *See also* BOTTOM-LOADING PRINTER, FANFOLD PAPER, REAR-LOADING PRINTER, *and* TRACTOR FEED.

FUBAR

FUBAR is an acronym that stands for "fouled up beyond all recognition." It applies when so many things go wrong that you're temporarily overwhelmed. A FUBAR situation is somewhat more severe than a SNAFU ("situation normal: all fouled up").

The problem. Suppose you have just bought a whole new system, including PC main unit, monitor, printer, fax/modem, CD-ROM drive, and associated hardware and software. But there's a problem: you are afflicted with *cyberphobia*, an irrational apprehension toward computers. You thought that you could cure yourself by diving in head first; now you're not so sure.

You open the instruction manuals and find nothing but jargon and gibberish. You wonder how anyone is supposed to understand all of this. You want to plug in the cables, throw a switch, and start cruising the information superhighway. Instead, you're confronted with all this nonsense: serial ports, parallel ports, interfaces, icons, menus, modems, bauds, bits per second, stop bits, parity. The hardware starts to look like paraphernalia out of an old science-fiction horror film. At this point, you might conclude that things are FUBAR. In other words, you are lost!

The solution. When a situation or system is FUBAR, the first step toward a solution is to admit that you're overwhelmed. Back up, start all over again, and proceed slowly. Engineers often say, "Back to the drawing board." In your case, you can call help lines, which many hardware and software vendors provide free of charge. Maybe you have a friend who has experience with computers, and who will help you figure things out. There are also many good books and magazines for the PC neophyte.

Veteran engineers must routinely deal with FUBAR environments. In software engineering, FUBAR refers to a program that has so many bugs that the best course of action is to throw everything out and start writing again from scratch. In hardware engineering, FUBAR is sometimes invoked when a prototype fails to work, and the reasons are myriad and impossible to determine. *See also* CYBERPHOBIA *and* MURPHY'S LAWS.

Full backup

A *full backup* is a 100% duplication of all the data on a hard disk. It's important to have your files backed up. Otherwise, hard disk failure (which can and does happen) will result in a loss of data.

Diskette method. One way to back up your hard disk is to put the data on diskettes, but this is a horribly tedious method for a large hard disk. You will need at least several dozen, and possibly more than 1000, diskettes to fully back up a hard disk, unless you have a very old PC with a small-capacity hard disk.

If you do decide to back up your hard disk on diskettes, you should make two complete backup sets. The two sets should be kept in different locations in case there is a fire, flood, burglary, or other catastrophe beyond your control.

Utilities are available that will guide you, step by step, through the process of backing up your hard disk on diskettes. You'll have to keep removing and inserting diskettes until the procedure is complete.

After you've gone through the initial, time-consuming full-backup routine, you should get into the habit of making two diskette copies of every file you create or change. You can revise the "local" diskette whenever you create or update a file, and the "remote" diskette at regular intervals (say, weekly). This will minimize the data loss should a failure occur.

Tape drive method. You can also create a full backup of your hard disk on a single, miniature cassette tape. To do this, you'll need a tape drive and backup software.

A tape drive is far easier to work with than diskettes for the purpose of backing up a hard disk. Tape drives are especially convenient if you have more than a few megabytes of data. For example, a 250MB hard disk can be backed up in less than 30 minutes with a good tape drive system. If the hard drive fails, reinstalling the data takes much less time with a tape drive than with dozens of diskettes.

You should create a new tape drive backup at regular intervals. The exact timeframe depends on how often you change your data. You should keep two tapes, one local and the other remote. You might also keep a local set of diskettes, and keep it current on a daily basis, file by file. *See also* ARCHIVES, BACKUP, *and* TAPE DRIVE.

Full duplex

When two computers "talk" with each other, they exchange data. Any two-way communication is generally called *duplex* because information can go either way along the transmission line. When data can travel in both directions at the same time, it is called *full duplex*.

Full-motion video interface

Have you ever been with two people who know each other so well that they can talk and listen to each other simultaneously? That's a form of full duplex. Most people cannot speak and listen at the same time; their minds and ears are limited to *half duplex*. To put it another way, a telephone can accommodate full duplex, but two-way radios, like taxi cabs have, can only function in half duplex.

The drawing shows the principle of full-duplex data communication. Suppose George and Sally are operating two computers at opposite ends of a full-duplex circuit. George is using his computer to send a program to Sally. Sally is concurrently sending a text message to George. A graphical user interface (GUI) facilitates the link. George can write the program and watch it in one window of his monitor screen, while reading the message from Sally in another window. Likewise, Sally can be typing and checking her message text in one window, while watching the program from George appear in another window. *See also* HALF DUPLEX *and* MULTIPLEXING.

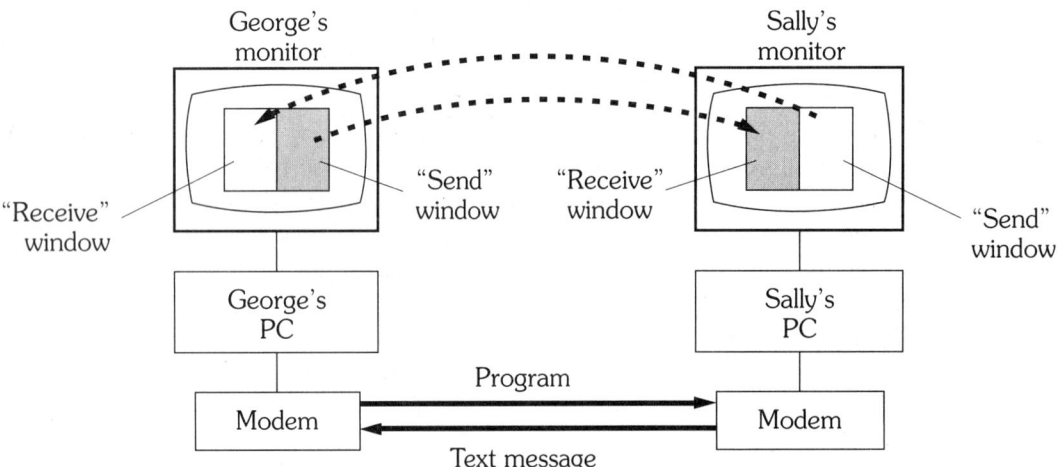

Full duplex enables simultaneous two-way communication between PCs.

Full-motion video interface

A computer monitor resembles a television set. In fact, a monitor can work as a TV if the necessary receiving circuits are added. Your monitor can also be used to watch videotapes. A *full-motion video interface (FMVI)* lets you do that, and much more.

You might wonder why you would want to watch TV on your computer monitor when you already have a TV. The answer is that you can use your computer to incorporate the images with other data, creating a multimedia presentation. Thus, you can work with animation, taking advantage of its endless possibilities in presentations and productions of all kinds. Recorded or live video can be displayed in conjunction with other computerized effects. An FMVI can also supplement computer-assisted instruction (CAI).

The FMVI hardware is a circuit board, or card, that you can install between your computer and a TV set, videocassette recorder (VCR), or camcorder, as shown in the block diagram. The package also includes software that takes full advantage of your computer's capabilities to create a multimedia presentation with all kinds of special effects. The full-motion video image occupies a window on your monitor screen. Other data can be displayed in other windows, or in the background. *See also* ANIMATION, COMPUTER-ASSISTED INSTRUCTION, MULTIMEDIA, *and* PRESENTATION GRAPHICS.

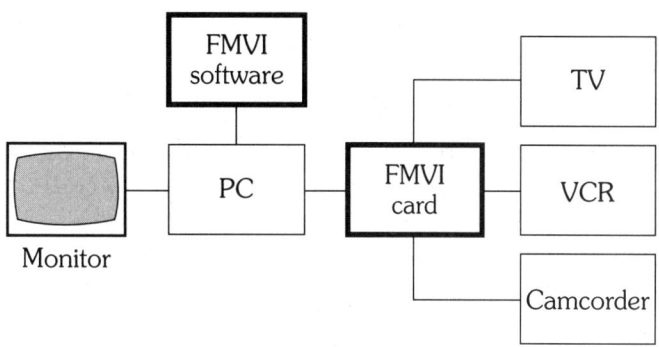

A full-motion video interface lets you include fast-scan video in a display.

Full-page display

In word processing and desktop publishing, it is convenient if the monitor screen can show a whole page at a time. This is called a *full-page display*.

Generally, all full-page displays show you, on screen, the equivalent of one manuscript page. The more sophisticated word processors can render headers, footnotes, and even multiple columns. Some desktop publishing systems, notably for Windows and Macintosh, allow you to see exactly how a page will look in a final document. This is called WYSIWYG (pronounced "WIZZY-wig," an acronym for "what you see is what you get"). *See also* WYSIWYG.

Function

A *function* is a "mapping" between sets of numbers or objects. Functions are important in computer mathematics and logic, and are also used in software.

As a mapping. The drawing shows an example of a function as a mapping between two sets, labeled x and $f(x)$. Not all of the x's necessarily have counterparts in $f(x)$, and not all $f(x)$s necessarily have counterparts in x. It is possible that more than one x might be mapped onto a single element in $f(x)$, but no element in x ever has more than one mate in $f(x)$.

The set of all x's that have mates in $f(x)$ is called the *domain* of function f. The range of function f is the set of all $f(x)$s with corresponding elements in the domain.

Function keys

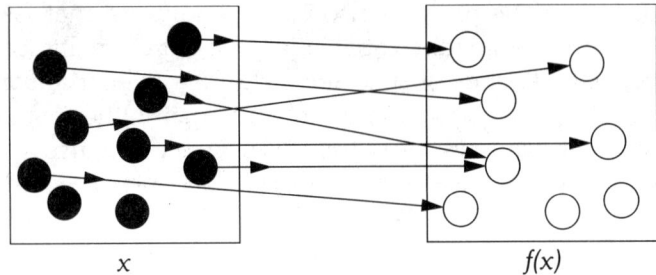

Function keys may be located at the top of the keyboard (A) or on the left side (B).

Logical functions. In logic, a function is an operation that takes one or more input variables, such as X, Y, and Z, and generates a specific output for each combination of inputs. Logic functions are simpler than mathematical ones, because the input variables can only have two values: 0 (false) or 1 (true). Some logic functions have dozens of input variables, but there is only one output value for each combination of inputs.

Logic functions are important to engineers in the design of digital circuits, including computers. Often, there are several different possible combinations of *logic gates* that will generate a given logic function. The engineer's job is to find the simplest and most efficient design. *See also* LOGIC GATES.

Software functions. In computing, a function refers to a specific process. If you press various keys in sequence, certain things happen. You might, for example, press Ctrl-C to copy text in a word processing application. The Ctrl-C function thus copies text. You might get help on this procedure by pressing the F1 key. As a matter of fact, all of the *function keys* get their name from the fact that they facilitate the execution of software functions. In a graphical user interface (GUI), you click the mouse to execute the function indicated by the pointer on the screen. *See also* CLICK, FUNCTION KEYS, *and* MOUSE.

Function keys

The *function keys* on IBM-compatible PC keyboards are usually located above the numeral keys in three groupings of four keys each (see the drawing at A). They are labeled F1 through F12. When you press one of these keys, your computer receives a specific instruction, and executes a function. The nature of the function depends on the software. The function keys can be used all by themselves, or in conjunction with other keys (typically the Alt, Ctrl, and Shift keys).

For example, in WordPerfect DOS, pressing F7 causes any document currently on the screen to be closed. Pressing Shift-F5, that is, pressing the Shift key and the F5 key simultaneously, starts the printing process. (These examples are peculiar to WordPerfect DOS.

Other word processing programs use different methods or keys to execute functions.)

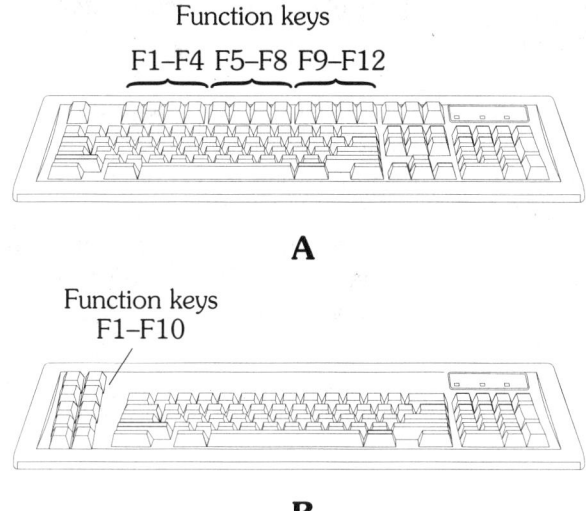

Mapping from set x into set f(x).

Some keyboards have fewer than 12 function keys. On older keyboards, there are 10 function keys, arranged in two vertical columns of five keys each, and located on the left side of the keyboard (B in the drawing). This scheme was discontinued a number of years ago, so you probably won't see it very often.

Futurists

Futurists are people who try to predict, based on current technology and trends, what will be accomplished in a given scientific field in five, ten, fifty, or a hundred years. In personal computing, there is plenty of work for futurists. There are even futuristic articles in this encyclopedia that deal with the "maybes" and "doubtfuls" in personal computing.

Most futurists agree that PCs will become more powerful as time goes by. More people will own computers, and an increasing number of people will have two or more. There is some debate about how powerful these machines will (or can) become. Will a computer ever be designed that is as intelligent as a person, and that has the capacity to care about what goes on inside itself?

Artificial intelligence once seemed to have unlimited potential. Progress was slower than the futurists of the 1950s and 1960s hoped or anticipated, however. Human reasoning is a great deal more subtle and complicated than those futurists ever suspected. There are now people who say that science still has no idea of how powerful our minds actually are.

Some futurists believe that the human mind, and all thought processes, can be represented as interactions among atoms. This is known as the "materialist" view. If this is a true model of how things are, then it is theoretically possible to build a computer that is as smart as a person.

Other futurists think human thought involves more than the combined effects of atomic particles—a factor that can't be defined in material terms. If this is the way things are, then a "living" computer might be impossible to build. This "spiritualist" view frustrates materialists, but many people find comfort in it. It suggests that human beings, and perhaps all things created by nature, are inherently superior to machines in the cosmic order. *See also* ARTIFICIAL INTELLIGENCE, ARTIFICIAL LIFE, *and* COMPUTER CONSCIOUSNESS.

Gateway

A *gateway* is a connection between networks. The term applies especially to the exchange of data between or among systems that have different structures.

As an example, think of a college with two campuses in two different towns. Each campus has its own local area network (LAN) of PCs and terminals. The LAN at campus X is a bus network, while the LAN at campus Y is a star network. In network X, each workstation is a PC. But in network Y, the workstations are dumb terminals, relying on a central file server (a large computer) for processing and memory. This hypothetical situation is shown in the drawing on the next page, with PCs indicated by circles with *PC* inside and dumb terminals represented by ellipses with *T* inside. The file server in network Y is a circle with *FS* inside. The two LANs are connected via a gateway, forming a much larger network.

A gateway is itself a form of computer, complete with the microprocessor and memory circuits necessary to translate the data back and forth between the networks. The entire system for both campuses is a form of wide area network (WAN). *See also* LOCAL AREA NETWORK *and* WIDE AREA NETWORK.

Genealogy software

If you've ever tried to construct a family tree dating back for generations, you know how much work it can involve. A PC can be a big help in the process of finding and organizing information of this

Genealogy software

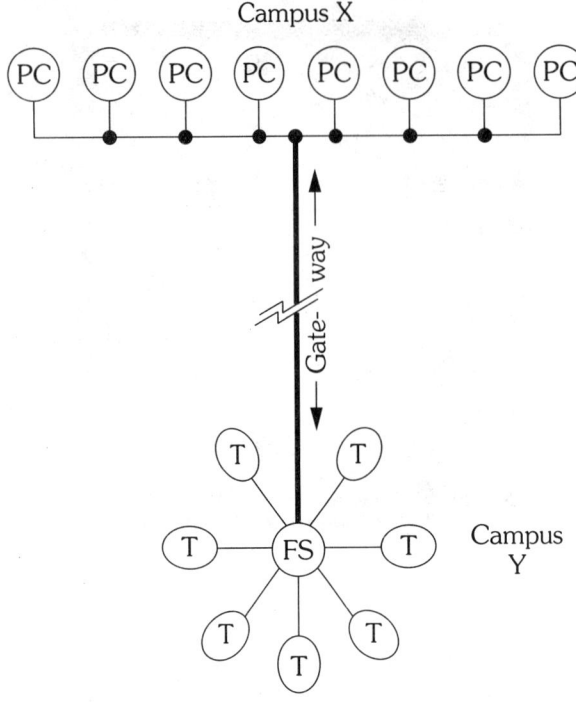

A gateway provides a connection between LANs containing PCs, terminals (T) and file servers (FS).

kind. *Genealogy software* is a form of database designed especially for people who want to trace their roots.

Most genealogy programs can create a picture of your family tree in the form of a diagram or table. Some programs will alert you when data contradicts itself or appears ridiculous (such as a five-year-old boy becoming a father). Some software can put your work in manuscript form, so you can write a book that describes your family history for as many generations back in time as you want, and in as much detail as you want. Most programs can arrange the data in a pedigree sheet (a table of your ancestors).

Virtually all genealogical databases have room for more information than you are likely to need. Typically, there can be upwards of 50,000 records, one for each ancestor. If you are so inclined, and if you can dig up the data, you might create a genealogical database dating all the way back to the time of the Renaissance or even Nero. After all, every one of us has ancestors who were alive during those times.

Online services provide an invaluable aid to tracing your roots. Bulletin-board systems have been used to locate estranged, missing, or even unknown relatives. When you contact relatives this way, they can often provide information that you might not have discovered by any other means.

For each person in a genealogy database, you'll create a *record*, the computer equivalent of an index card. The record consists of the person's name, relation, birth date, death date, and other information, as much or as little as you want to include. Each piece of data within a record is called a *field*.

There are many genealogy software packages available, ranging in price from about $50 to several hundred dollars. Some of the high-level programs, created for professional genealogists, are also ideal for beginners because they are easy to learn and work with. *See also* DATABASE.

Geographic information systems

Geographic information systems (GIS) are used in specialized software that converts database information into visible geometric patterns. In particular, a GIS lets you see distributions of variables on maps of cities, counties, regions, or even the whole world.

Geocoding. Suppose you want to see exactly what geographic regions are covered by various telephone area codes. You've probably seen a map in your telephone book that gives you an idea of this. For example, area code 305 covers much of southern Florida; area code 507 represents some of southern Minnesota.

With GIS, you can get far more detail than you will find in any telephone book. You can "zero in" on southern Minnesota and see which counties are encompassed by area code 507. To make such a map, your computer must have several different sets of data: a list of counties covered by the area code, the shapes of those counties, and the locations of the counties within the state. This information is all made up of numbers and functions. The process of *geocoding*, carried out by the GIS software, translates this into a map you can look at on your monitor screen or print out.

Thematic shading. Continuing with the area-code example, you can have your PC shade the counties for area code 507 in some color, such as red. The state of Minnesota might be white, with all the county borders showing up as fine black lines.

You might want to see the location of Olmsted county within the region of area code 507; your PC could color that county blue. Zeroing in on Olmsted county, you might want to see the city limits of Rochester; the county would "blow up" to fill your screen, turning white, and the city of Rochester might show up as an irregular green figure. Suppose you wanted to see where, within Rochester, the wealthiest people live. Giving your computer this data, it might color certain parts of the town orange.

The coloring of regions on a map for identification is known as *thematic shading*. In conjunction with geocoding, thematic shading forms the basis for all GIS software.

Applications. If you're involved in sales, direct marketing, poll-taking, or similar jobs, you'll recognize the value of GIS right away. Suppose you have a product that you want to sell to people over age 65. You could use GIS to find out where to most effectively send your direct-mail ads. Maybe your product is of special interest to low-income people in Ohio. A GIS package could show you where they live. You could then send your direct-mail to those areas.

Meeting your needs. To effectively use GIS, you'll need a PC with at least the processing power of a 486DX microprocessor. You'll also need sufficient RAM. The exact amount depends on the operating system used; 8MB is typical. For the greatest versatility and the shortest learning curve, the program you choose should have a graphical user interface (GUI). There are, however, provisions for running some GIS programs directly from DOS.

The cost of a GIS package depends on how much sophistication you need. Prices range from a couple of hundred dollars to several thousand. If you're running a small business, you'll want to shop around before making your final decision. The greater your need, the more options you'll want to consider. *See also* DATABASE.

Geostationary-satellite data link

A *geostationary satellite* is a human-made earth satellite commonly used for communications. If you've ever engaged in long-distance online communications, you've probably made use of geostationary satellites without being aware of it. In future years, the *geostationary-satellite data link* will become increasingly important.

Fixed in the sky. For a satellite in a circular orbit, the period gets longer as the altitude increases. At an altitude of about 22,300 miles, a satellite in circular orbit takes exactly one day to complete one orbit. If a satellite is placed in such an orbit over the equator, going in the same direction as the earth turns on its axis, the satellite will follow the earth as it spins, and will stay above the same point at all times. Drawing A is a view of this situation from far above the earth's North Pole.

From the vantage point of someone on the surface of the earth, a geostationary satellite seems fixed in the sky. A single geostationary satellite can "see" about 40 percent of the earth's surface. Therefore, it provides coverage over a substantial part of the planet. For example, a satellite over Quito, Ecuador could link most cities in North America and South America.

Three satellites in geostationary orbits spaced 120° apart (one-third of a circle) provide coverage over all the earth except in small regions around the North Pole and South Pole. Thus, three geostationary satellites can facilitate a communications network for the whole

Geostationary-satellite data link

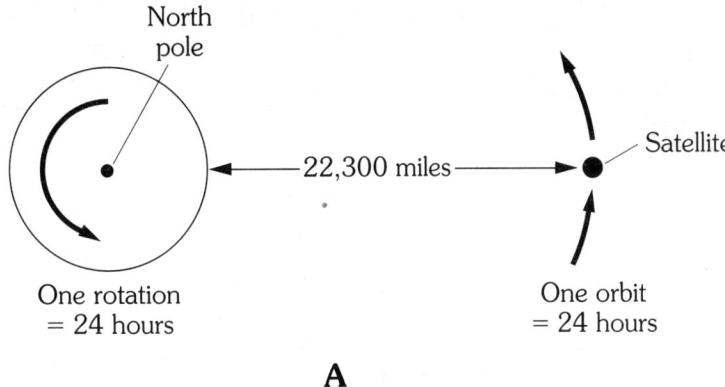

A geostationary satellite follows the rotation of the earth (A).

inhabited world. In such a network, some pairs of stations require the use of two satellites to obtain a link, as shown in drawing B. Stations can communicate using one satellite, if and only if they are both visible to that satellite.

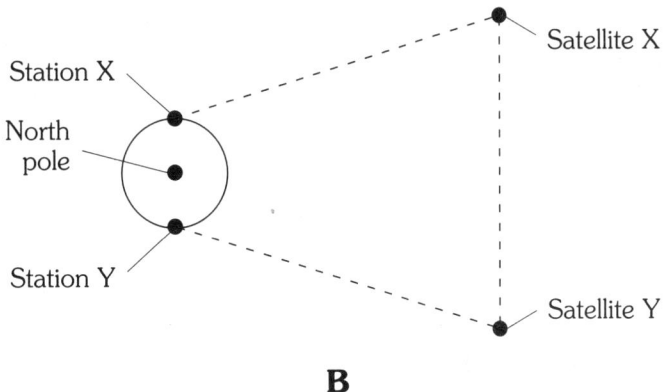

A data link using two satellites.

Long signal path. The main limitation of geostationary-satellite communication is the fact that the signal path is long: at least 22,300 miles up to the satellite, and 22,300 more miles back down to earth. The signals are delayed because it takes time for them to traverse the 44,000-plus miles. Two-way communications involve a time lag of about a quarter-second. This doesn't cause problems in simple data transfers or in online services. In fact, you might not even notice it. It does slow things down, however, when a number of computers are linked with the intention of combining their processing power.

When you use an online service or talk via long-distance telephone, the telephone companies provide all the hardware (including the satellite communications equipment). As far as you are concerned, you have a connection, and that's all that matters. It's another ball game to set up your own independent satellite data communications station.

Gigabyte

Amateur radio operators have been doing this sort of thing for several decades. Perhaps someday, computer users in general will do it too. *See also* AMATEUR RADIO, PACKET COMMUNICATIONS, *and* SATELLITE DATA TRANSMISSION.

Gigabyte

The prefix *giga* means a billion (1,000,000,000). A *gigabyte*, abbreviated GB, is a large unit of data, equal to approximately one billion bytes.

Computer data is measured in powers of two, rather than powers of 10. This arises from the fact that digital information is expressed in base-2, where the only values are 0 (low) and 1 (high). The actual value of 1GB is therefore not exactly 10^9 bytes, but instead, is 2^{30} (1,073,741,824) bytes. This is exactly 1024MB, or 1,048,576K. Drawings A, B, and C show the approximate relationship among one byte, one kilobyte, one megabyte, and one gigabyte of data. The table on page 470 shows the capacity, in gigabytes, of several different data storage media.

Some PCs have hard disks with capacities in the gigabyte range. A 5.25-inch high-density (HD) diskette, in contrast, can hold about 1MB of data; therefore, 1GB would require almost 1000 diskettes. A stack of 1000 diskettes would go from the floor to the ceiling in an average-sized room. A single CD-ROM holds about 0.65GB. *See also* BINARY DATA, BYTE, KILOBYTE, MEGABYTE, *and* TERABYTE.

GIGO

A digital computer is a huge array of switches, each with only two possible states: 0 (low or off) and 1 (high or on). All the images and sounds that you see and hear from your PC arise from combinations of these two states. The sequence and speed of digital signals is a function of how data is manipulated by the machine.

GIGO is an acronym that stands for "garbage in, garbage out." This phrase was coined when the first computers were manufactured, but it's as valid now as it was then. A computer does exactly what it is told. If it doesn't understand the instructions, or if the input doesn't make sense, then you can't expect meaningful output.

If a computer is to produce meaningful output, the input must have a certain form. The slightest deviation from the required input will result in errors in the output. If the input is much different from what is required, the output is likely to be garbage or gibberish.

Researchers in the field of artificial intelligence (AI) are striving to create a machine that thinks like a human being, so that the precise

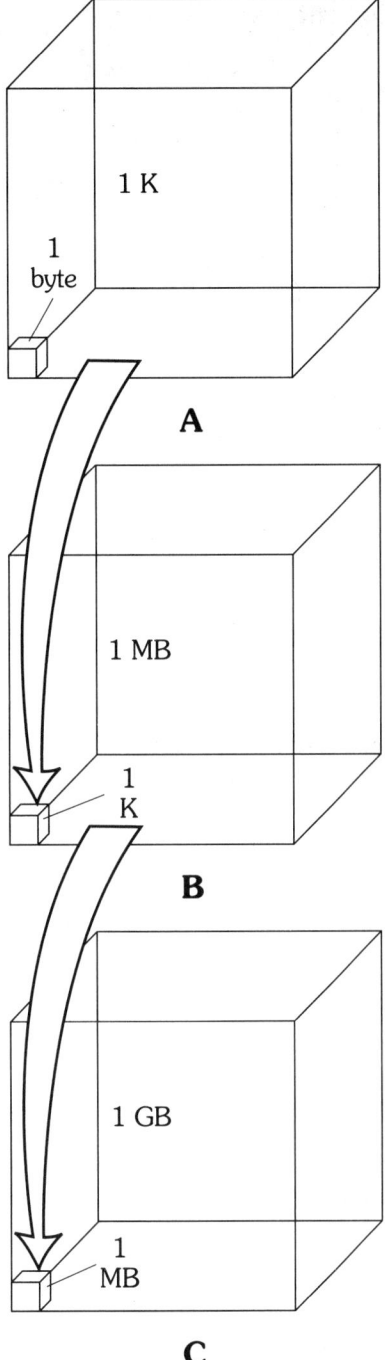

One byte versus 1K (A), 1K versus 1MB (B), 1MB versus 1GB (C).

input requirements can be relaxed somewhat. If your PC had AI, you might carry on a meaningful, deep conversation with it. However, most experts agree that it will be a long time before this happens. Some software is more forgiving than others of errors and imprecision, but no machine yet devised can make sense out of nonsense. *See also* ARTIFICIAL INTELLIGENCE.

Global backup

Capacities of several common storage media

Medium	Capacity in GB
640K RAM	0.00064
5.25-inch, double-density diskette	0.00036
3.5-inch, double-density diskette	0.00072
Medium-sized novel	0.001
5.25-inch, high-density diskette	0.0012
3.5-inch, high-density diskette	0.00144
Hard disk	0.2 or more
CD-ROM	0.65

Global backup

See FULL BACKUP.

Global format

In PC terminology, the word *global* is sometimes used in place of words like *overall*, *all-encompassing*, or *total*. *Global format* is a term used in applications such as spreadsheets. It refers to a method of expressing quantities, such as sums of money, in a specific way everywhere in the document.

In bookkeeping. Consider a spreadsheet that you're using to keep tax records. Every entry in this spreadsheet represents a certain amount of money. The standard format for financial records always has a decimal point with two numerals to its right. There can be any number of digits to the left of the decimal point (including none). You would thus specify a global format in which there is always a decimal point and two digits to its right.

Examples of quantities that are in the correct format for such a financial spreadsheet are 223.05, .56, 3.00, and 4001.01. Examples of quantities that are not in the proper format are 89, .003, 34.2, and 5,900,000.

In science. If you have ever used a program for scientific purposes, such as in experimental physics, you might use a global format for scientific notation. In the most common form of scientific notation, quantities are expressed in two parts: a number and a power of 10. The number has a value of at least one, but less than 10. There might be a decimal point, but there doesn't have to be. The power of 10 (the exponent) is always an integer (positive whole number, negative whole number, or zero).

The global format for a scientific spreadsheet would indicate, in addition to the correct method of writing down the quantities, the number of significant figures. You might decide, for example, on four significant figures. Then the expression 3.553×10^5 would be in the right format, while 3.55312×10^5, although meaningful, would not conform to the global format because it has too many significant figures.

Computers work with abbreviated versions of these expressions, writing the power of 10 as a letter E followed by the value of the exponent. So, 3.553×10^5 is denoted 3.553E+5, and 8.780×10^{-3} appears as 8.780E−3.

Exceptions. Global format can be defeated or overridden in specific instances. For a spreadsheet, this is done by specifying a *range format* for certain cells. *See also* NUMERIC FORMAT, PERSONAL FINANCE SOFTWARE, SCIENTIFIC NOTATION, SIGNIFICANT FIGURES, *and* SPREADSHEET.

Glossary

Many advanced features of word processing software can improve the quality of your writing. One such device, usually called a *glossary*, consists of a large set of phrases, sentences, and paragraphs that you use often. A glossary can save you much tedious work, as well as making your writing more consistent and minimizing mistakes.

With a glossary, you can pull any set of words from a block of text and store it in a special file. Then, when you need that set of words again, you can retrieve it and insert it into new text. As time passes, a glossary gradually grows, becoming more versatile.

When making and using a glossary, it's important to remember the filenames or codes for each phrase, sentence, or paragraph. Otherwise, you'll end up having to search for what you want, and you'll spend more time searching than you would spend typing the text all over again.

A glossary, like any other word processing supplement, should not be overused. If you use it too much, your writing will get repetitive and monotonous. This might be all right in a technical instruction manual, but it is bad for creative work like a magazine article. *See also* WORD PROCESSING.

Graceful degradation

Graceful degradation is a scheme of computer design that allows a system to keep working even if some of its components have failed. As the number of component failures increases, the efficiency and speed of the system gradually declines, but doesn't instantly drop to zero.

Alternative circuits. The drawings show system failure. In drawing A, one bad part causes a total system breakdown. In drawing B,

Graceful degradation

graceful degradation keeps the machine operating even if two or three parts fail. The horizontal axes in the graphs show the number of bad components. The vertical axes show the percentage of normal power at which the machine is operating. (This is a highly simplified rendition.) Note that even two or three bad parts might not cause a complete shutdown of a system with graceful degradation. To some extent, your PC has this feature, although it is more typical of big mainframes than of small computers.

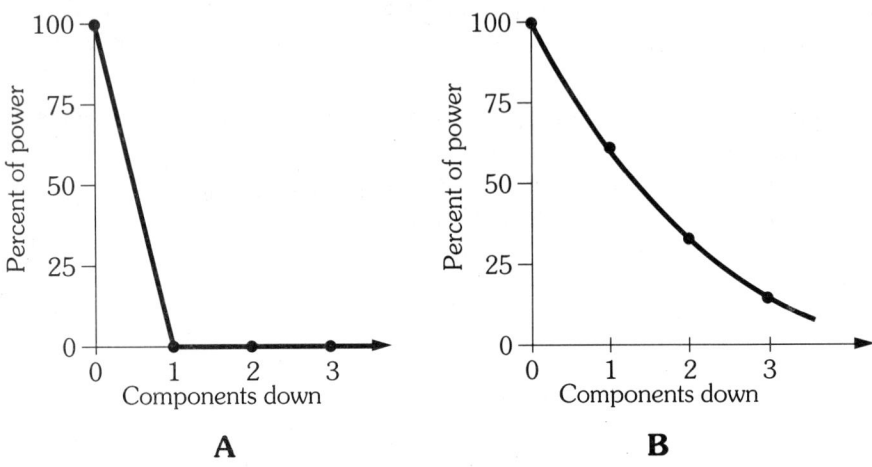

Catastrophic (A) versus graceful (B) system degradation.

In the event of a subsystem malfunction, the computer uses alternative circuits to do the work of the failed part. The operator is notified that something is wrong. Then, technicians can fix it with little or no downtime.

A fiction example. An excellent and vivid example of graceful degradation is provided in the movie *2001: A Space Odyssey*. The space ship's computer, Hal, goes crazy, and it becomes necessary for Dave, an astronaut, to "pull the plug."

As Dave systematically shuts off one system after another, Hal keeps on working, more and more slowly, with efficiency impaired to an increasing degree. Ultimately, Hal starts going through test routines, identifying itself and singing songs, as if delirious. Because of graceful degradation, Hal refuses to give up until the bitter end.

A real example. I recently had an experience in which my PC worked with reduced system efficiency, but did not have a catastrophic system failure.

When you use a diskette in a PC, the PC identifies it and memorizes its directory. If you change diskettes, and then read or write something from or onto the new diskette, the PC automatically changes the directory to reflect the identity of the new diskette. But my computer developed a glitch, so that if the diskette were changed, the old directory stayed in the computer memory.

Because of this glitch, care had to be used when changing diskettes. Under certain conditions, an attempt to write onto a new disk would cause the whole disk to be written over with bits and pieces of files. Files would be cut apart recklessly, as if the PC had gone mad.

To use a new diskette, the PC had to be rebooted by pressing the reset button. To copy diskette X onto diskette Y, it became necessary to take all the files off diskette X, put them on the hard disk, reboot the computer, and then transfer all the X files on the hard disk to the new diskette Y. Although the system still worked, it was handicapped in this respect. This problem did not impair most day-to-day operation of the machine, and was tolerated for several days before it was repaired. *See also* CATASTROPHIC FAILURE.

Grammar checking

Grammar checking is done by a program that goes through text and looks for improper word usage, sentence fragments, or illogically constructed sentences. Some grammar checkers can even look for excessive use of a word or words, overly frequent use of semicolons, and other writing idiosyncrasies. Grammar checkers are found in some of the more advanced word processing packages.

One special form of grammar checking is called a *flash test*, which is a measure of the reading level at which text is written. Flash tests are especially useful to writers of children's books. If a writer wants to reach an audience of 11-year-olds, for example, the checker can tell the writer whether the text is too simple (say, for a seven-year-old), or too complicated (say, for a 16-year-old). The writer can adjust the complexity of the language until the flash test gives the right result. This is illustrated by the flowchart shown on page 474. The parts of the process done by the computer have heavy lines; the rest of the work is up to the writer.

In artificial intelligence, a grammar checker can be used to help the machine be sure it has received the right command from the operator. A grammatically poor sentence might cause the computer to respond with, "What?" or, "Please rephrase that." Grammar checkers can be used in conjunction with speech recognition systems when spoken, rather than written, commands are used. *See also* ARTIFICIAL INTELLIGENCE, SPEECH RECOGNITION, *and* WORD PROCESSING.

Grand Synthesizer

Researchers in artificial intelligence sometimes talk about a hypothetical person, maybe a high-school or college student, with a mind perfectly attuned to computers. This person, the *Grand Synthesizer*, would sit down in front of a computer, and right away the human and the machine would hit it off perfectly. This person

Graphical database

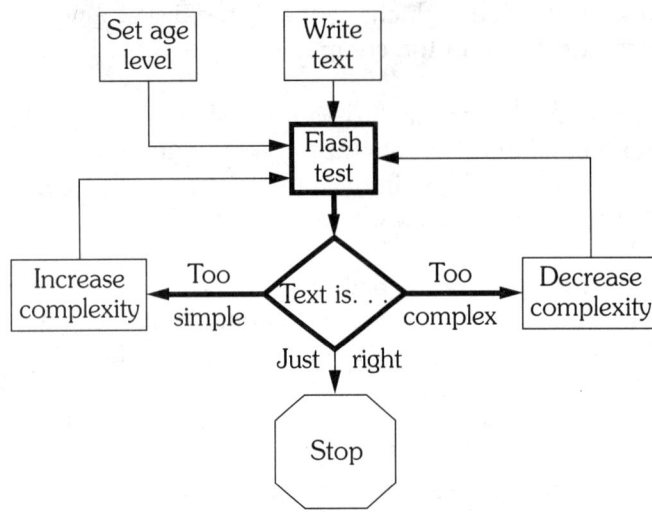

A flash test helps an author write at the desired age level.

would be a key figure in the history of computer technology, making gigantic contributions and revolutionizing the industry and the way people use computers. He or she would be, to the computer world, the equivalent of Bach or Mozart in the music world.

In recent years, the terms "nerd" and "geek" have come to mean "young, eccentric genius." This is the sort of child who spends more time at a computer than at a television set. The Grand Synthesizer might be called a "supergeek." He or she would be, in a sense, both a human and a computer combined into a single being.

It's quite possible that a single, ultimate Grand Synthesizer will never exist. It might just be a wild idea, dreamed up by wishful thinkers in the field of AI. If that is true, computer advancement will continue as the result of the combined efforts of many ordinary humans, and not from the magical mind of a supergeek.

There have already been some notable computer "whiz kids." They're sometimes called *hackers*. When they grow up, they're often the ones running the most successful computer and software companies. On the other hand, sometimes they become criminal "cybersnoops," disrupting credit records, altering confidential data, and in general creating trouble for individuals, corporations, and governments. *See also* COMPUTER ADDICTION *and* HACKER.

Graphical database

A *graphical database* is an enhanced form of database software that can manage illustrations as well as text and tables. These illustrations can be line drawings, photographs, graphs, or charts. Using special cameras, you can capture scenes directly for use in a graphical database.

Graphical database

Applications. You might have a file in your PC that lists the names, addresses, and telephone numbers of all the people and companies you know. A database adds flexibility to such a list, because you can search for an item on the basis of any variable, such as the town, the area code, the person's first name, or the company name.

Wouldn't it be nice if you could add a photograph, either black-and-white or color, for every person in your database? If you call up data for Jane Doe, for example, you'd get her "vitals" plus a clear photo. A graphical database makes this possible.

Real estate agents find graphical databases extremely useful. Mail-order sales companies also like them. Shoppers can get online and page through hundreds of catalogs, without all the bulk and bother of a huge library of paper catalogs.

How it works. The scheme for a graphical database involves converting a visual image, such as a photograph, into digital form so it can be displayed on your monitor. This data must then be combined with the text and tables that make up the rest of the database. There are two ways to get digital images:

> ➢ An *optical scanner* converts hardcopy graphics, including written or typed text, line art, or photographs, into digital "highs" and "lows" (the binary numbers 1 and 0). The scanner has a charge-coupled device (CCD) to determine the light intensity. Scanners can be a little bit finicky, but they're the cheapest way to digitize flat images.

> ➢ *Digital cameras* resemble ordinary cameras, with a few extra "bells and whistles." Like scanners, they use CCD technology. They were first introduced around 1990, and were initially too expensive for the average PC user. Prices have dropped since then. With a digital camera, you can convert hardcopy into digital form; you can also digitize scenes. You can photograph yourself and send the data to another PC user via modem for his or her graphical database. *See also* CHARGE-COUPLED DEVICE *and* OPTICAL SCANNER.

What you need. To use a graphical database, you'll need hardware (your PC and an optical scanner or digital camera). You'll also need software.

You'll probably find a graphical user interface (GUI) easier to work with than DOS in a graphical database. The database software combines digital images with text and tabular matter, giving you the final product.

There are many database software packages available. As you would expect, prices and complexity levels vary considerably. Some of these software packages are well-suited to storing digital images; others are not. Do you want color, or will gray-scale images do? How many records does your database have now? How many do you think it will have in five years? As with any major software/hardware purchase, you should shop around to find exactly what you need.

There are also some possible problems involving hardware and software compatibility. Your digital camera, if you buy one, will have to work with your PC and the database software. Do you want to have printouts of your records, including good resolution for photographs? You'll want to be sure that your printer can produce hardcopies of the quality you desire.

If you now have, or expect to have, a large database, you should consider image compression. Images take up a lot of memory. If the database is big to begin with, adding photographs can make it so large that it becomes too slow to use. Image compression reduces the amount of storage that a digital image consumes, improving the speed at which you can get at your data. *See also* DATABASE *and* IMAGE COMPRESSION.

Graphical user interface

A *graphical user interface (GUI)* is a popular, versatile way in which people can interact with computers.

Pointing and clicking. The hallmark of a GUI (pronounced "gooey") is the way you get the computer to carry out tasks. Instead of issuing commands by typing them in, you select options by pointing and clicking with a mouse or trackball. This is important to beginners because it reduces the apprehension they sometimes feel when starting out on computers.

Another advantage of a GUI is that you can explore new ideas and options without having to read a lot of instructions. To a certain extent, the GUI helps you teach yourself. Although this trial-and-error method might at first seem to be inefficient, experience shows that things "stick" better when you've learned them by experimentation.

Still another advantage of a GUI is the fact that you don't have to type very much to use it. This is a boon to hunt-and-peck typists. Of course, if your primary application is word processing or desktop publishing, it will help to become a good typist anyway.

In some applications, a command-driven system can be speedier than a GUI. Usually, though, this is the case only for experienced computer operators (power users) who have hundreds of commands memorized, and who can type 40 words per minute or more. Such people might never feel the need to switch from DOS to a GUI.

One potential shortcoming of GUIs is the fact that the graphics slow down the operation of the central processing unit (CPU) in older computers. This can be helped by installing a graphics accelerator. With newer microprocessors, this problem has been largely overcome. *See also* CENTRAL PROCESSING UNIT, GRAPHICS ACCELERATOR, *and* MICROPROCESSOR.

The pointing device. A true GUI uses a *mouse* or *trackball* with which you can guide a pointer or cursor on the screen. A mouse is a small, external peripheral, connected to your main unit by a short cord. It requires a flat surface, preferably at least a foot square. You move the pointer by sliding the mouse around on the surface. It's so intuitive that most people can get the feel of it in a few minutes. To select options, you *click* a button on the mouse. Sometimes you must click the button twice in rapid succession; this is called a *double-click*.

A trackball looks like a large ball bearing in a box. You move the pointer around by rolling the ball with your fingertip. This device, like a mouse, is intuitive. Trackballs are particularly popular in laptop PCs because they save space. *See also* MOUSE *and* TRACKBALL.

Some definitions. When first learning to use a GUI, you'll want to become familiar with some of the basic terminology. Here are a few short definitions of typical GUI elements:

- The *menu bar* contains headings, or major categories of operation. Common headings are File, Edit, Options, Window, and Help. There might be others, depending on the application. Of primary interest to beginners is the Help menu item. This turns the computer into a tutor, which can get you out of a jam without your having to plow through instruction manuals.

- A *window* is a box containing specific data, instructions, or other material. It can be text, graphics, tables, or anything the display is capable of showing. You can have windows within windows; you can also change the size of a window on your screen, or move it around.

- A *dialog box* is a window that contains several boxes for different option selections, as discussed in the remaining items in this list.

- A *text box* is a space within a dialog box in which you must type some words and/or numbers. Text boxes are used, for example, to set margins and tabs in a word processing program.

- A *list box* is an area within the dialog box that shows all your options. You scroll to the one you want, and then click to select it.

- A *check box* is a small square in the dialog box used to switch, or *toggle*, some option. As you repeatedly click the mouse, the function goes on and off. You can select more than one check box at a time.

Graphics

> An *option button* is a small circle in the dialog box, also called a *radio button*. It's like a check box, but you can only select one option at a time.

> A *command button* is an area within the dialog box that tells the computer to go ahead and carry out a selected action, or else to discontinue (cancel). You can also sometimes use a command button to bring up a different dialog box.

In the Windows GUI, Program Manager is the "mastermind" of all your Windows-based programs. File Manager is the "mastermind" of your files; it lets you name, organize, create, and delete files. For further definitions, consult the glossary of a GUI instruction manual. *See also* FILE MANAGER *and* PROGRAM MANAGER.

The future. Many experts agree that GUIs are the way of the future in most personal computing. The advantages of GUIs far outweigh their shortcomings in most situations. As microprocessors get faster and more powerful, the operating speed of GUIs will improve, making them even more user-friendly.

However, command-driven software is not totally obsolete, nor is it ever likely to be. With the advent of *speech recognition* and *speech synthesis*, people will be able to converse with PCs almost as if the machines were other people. With such a computer, you would issue commands just by telling it what to do.

Speech recognition and synthesis hold great promise for visually handicapped PC users, who have no use for a GUI. It is also ideal for people who want to use computers, but whose hands and/or eyes are fully occupied with something else. For example, a doctor could examine a patient and dictate the data to the computer. *See also* COMMAND-DRIVEN SOFTWARE, DOS, MENU-DRIVEN SOFTWARE, OS/2, SPEECH RECOGNITION, SPEECH SYNTHESIS, *and* WINDOWS.

Graphics

Graphics, generically, are illustrations. Computer-created graphics supplement human-made art in applications from architectural drafting to aircraft design, and from textbooks to greeting cards.

Bitmapped graphics. Your PC is a digital machine. All the information in it, whether it's text, graphics, or software, is made up of combinations of two states, "high" and "low." These are also called binary digits (bits) 1 and 0.

You might ask, "How can a detailed image like a photograph or a blueprint be encoded in digital form? The things I see are analog, not digital." The answer lies in the huge volume of digits that a computer can handle, and also in the computer's extreme working speed.

You might have heard, for example, that visible light is a barrage of particles called photons. These are responsible for all the images you see. At any moment in time and space, a photon is either present (the equivalent of "high") or absent ("low"). You don't see these individual states; you see a meaningful scene. This is because of the huge number of photons and the extreme speed with which they reach your eyes.

Given enough space for bits and the ability to process them fast enough, a PC can digitize any image, even a color photograph. The result is *bitmapped graphics*, also sometimes called *raster graphics*.

The big strength of bitmapping is the fact that it can be used to render any sort of object in graphical form. It doesn't matter how simple or complex the object might be. The bitmap assembles a figure from the smallest possible pieces, bit by bit, whether it's a simple line, a circle, an ellipse, or an amoeba shape.

A *paint program* makes use of bitmapped graphics. Paint programs allow you to create many levels of shading. This is another advantage of bit mapping: You can work not only with shapes, but with the regions bounded by the shapes.

A shortcoming of bitmapped graphics is the fact that resizing is difficult. When you want to enlarge or shrink a bitmapped image, the computer will get confused about which pixels (picture elements) are which. This can cause a jagged appearance (the *jaggies*), especially if the image is complex.

Object-oriented graphics. There's another way to get a computer to create and store images. This might be called the "analog method," in contrast to the "digital method" of bitmapping.

In *object-oriented graphics*, common objects are represented by certain digital "names." A circle is a simple example. Circles always have the same shape; the only things that can change are their size and their location in the image.

A bitmapped image of a circle is never really perfect. No matter how much speed and memory the computer has, a bitmapped rendition of a circle is always an approximation, although it is good enough for most purposes. Drawing A on next page shows a coarse bitmap of a circular arc. Each pixel is either dark or light. The pixels are arranged in a grid, a sort of rectangular coordinate system.

The same arc can be rendered more precisely by changing the system of coordinates in which the machine "thinks." You've probably heard of polar coordinates if you've done algebra or analysis. It's hard to work with circles in rectangular coordinates, but it's easy in polar coordinates. With object-oriented graphics, the computer can "think" in terms of polar coordinates.

Graphics

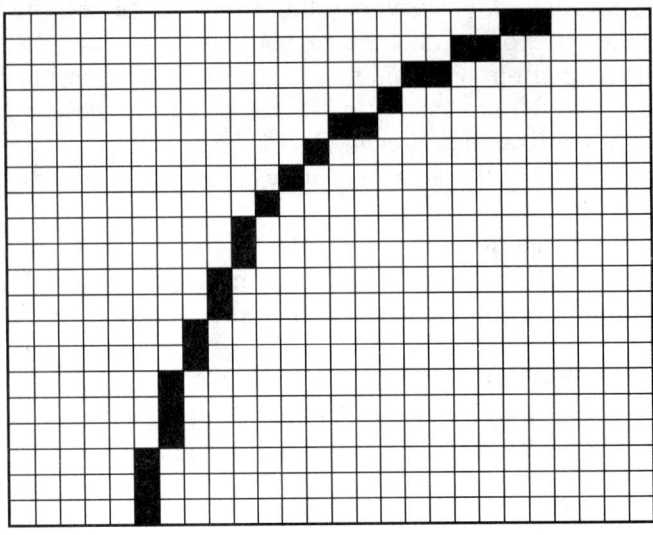

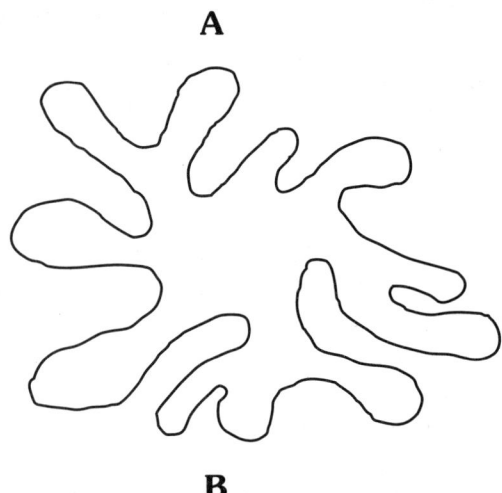

A coarse bitmapped rendition of circular arc (A) and a shape that might be too complex for object-oriented graphics (B).

Other shapes can be represented by formulas or codes, too. Squares, like circles, always have the same shape, varying only in size and location. Rectangles and triangles get more complex. Lines can have length, position and slope. Ellipses can have size, location, orientation, and extent of elongation.

The limitation of object-oriented graphics is apparent when dealing with irregular or complex shapes. There might not be a convenient formula or code to precisely represent the shape shown in drawing B, for example. In that case, the computer would find it easier to use a bitmap.

Object-oriented graphics are used in *draw programs*. A floorplan for a building is an example of an image you'd create with a draw program.

Graphics software. Suppose you bought your PC intending to use it to access online services and for word processing. Suddenly you're seized by an urge to create images. Maybe you need to supplement your written text; perhaps you just want to create graphics for fun. There are plenty of software packages that will compete for your attention and your money. Which one should you buy?

The key here, as with any major software investment, is to assess your needs carefully, and then spend time shopping around. Do you want a paint program or a draw program? What will you need in two years? Five years? If possible, go into two or three different computer stores and play with some of the graphics software.

You'll need a certain amount of computer power to accommodate graphics software. Images consume large amounts of memory; they also need a fair amount of microprocessor speed. It's more convenient to use graphics software with Windows, OS/2, the Macintosh OS, or other graphical interfaces, compared with a command-based system like DOS. There's no hard-and-fast rule concerning which microprocessor you'll need and how much memory is required for graphics programs, but they generally require more than, say, a basic word processor. The software specifications will tell you what you need to effectively use the programs in a given package.

See also ADOBE ILLUSTRATOR, ANALYTICAL GRAPHICS, ANTI-ALIASING, BEZIER CURVE, BITMAP, BITMAPPED GRAPHICS, CLIP ART, COMPUTER-AIDED DESIGN, DESKTOP PUBLISHING, DOCUMENT IMAGE PROCESSING, DRAW PROGRAM, FREEHAND, GRAPHICAL USER INTERFACE, GRAPHICS ACCELERATOR, HIGH-RESOLUTION MONITOR, HIGH-RESOLUTION PRINTER, IMAGE EDITING, IMAGE RESOLUTION, OBJECT-ORIENTED GRAPHICS, PAINT PROGRAM, PALETTE, PIXEL, PRESENTATION GRAPHICS, PRINTER, RASTER, SCATTER PLOT, VISION SYSTEMS, *and* WYSIWYG.

Graphics accelerator

A *graphics accelerator* is a circuit board, also called a card, that you can add to your computer to speed up the video. A graphics accelerator can speed up the operation of a graphical user interface (GUI), especially for applications that use detailed images or many colors.

Sluggish video. According to some estimates, sluggishness in the operation of a GUI can increase PC work time by more than 10%. This can add nearly an hour to a typical workday. The video seems to hesitate, files are slow to come up, and images take a quarter of a minute or more to appear. This problem tends to be worst with earlier microprocessors working at slow clock speeds. The GUI will work faster, in general, with a 486-based PC than with a 386. Video adapter cards can speed up a GUI in some older computers.

People's expectations tend to increase along with the advancement of technology. The more powerful computers become, the more we want

Graphics accelerator

and expect. If you've been using only text-based DOS with an older PC, and you switch to a complex application using Windows, you'll notice the video sluggishness right away. You'll wonder what you can do to speed it up. One solution is to get a PC with a faster microprocessor. Another, far cheaper approach is to buy and install a graphics accelerator.

While a graphics accelerator can solve some video-sluggishness problems, it isn't always the best solution. If you need to work with high-powered software in many different applications, you might do well to upgrade your PC. *See also* UPGRADING.

Compatibility. It's not hard to install a graphics accelerator. It's nothing more than an expansion board that you can plug into a slot on your PC's motherboard (main-unit circuit board). If you're hesitant about opening up your machine, you can have a more computer-minded friend or your local computer dealer install the board for you.

Unfortunately, some graphics accelerators and computer systems don't get along very well together. There are some problems with compatibility. When shopping for a graphics accelerator, you should inquire about this. Describe your system to the dealer. If the dealer can't help you, call the technical support line (usually a toll-free number) of the computer manufacturer, and discuss the matter with their technicians. There are many different graphics accelerator boards available; you'll want to get the ideal card on the first go-around.

If you know enough about PCs, you might be able to read the specifications for a given graphics accelerator board, and know whether or not it is compatible with your system. Common "specs" include the number of colors, the image resolution, the speed, the refresh rate, and the warranty (if any). You'll also want to consider the price, which can range from about $150 to $350. Keep price in its proper perspective, however. You'll be better off parting with $350 well spent, than wasting $150 on a board that won't work right with your system.

The table shows the approximate amount of RAM needed to support a graphics accelerator for various screen resolutions in pixels (picture elements).

RAM in megabytes as a function of color and image resolution

Colors	800 by 600 pixels	1024 by 768 pixels
256	0.5MB	0.8MB
16,384	1.0MB	1.6MB
16,777,216 (Perfect color)	1.5MB	2.4MB

How it works. The reason for sluggish video in older computers using GUIs is that the central processing unit (CPU) gets burdened with graphical chores. This creates a huge load of "busywork" for your computer's "brain." The result is inefficiency.

Think of a famous, brilliant astrophysicist who has just revolutionized human understanding of the origin of the universe. Imagine that he or she is swamped with letters, invitations, and other mail, along with dozens of telephone calls daily. What would happen if this person had to type up all his or her own mail, answer the telephone, lick stamps and envelopes, and walk to the mailbox with a bag of letters every day? All this, and give lectures too? The scientist would have precious little time for research. The really important work would slow down to a crawl. The same thing happens when you require an older CPU to take care of complex graphical data. It's so busy supporting the beautiful images you see that it has hardly any time to compute.

A graphics accelerator relieves the CPU of the graphical busywork. This is the equivalent of hiring an assistant to take care of mail and telephone calls. Thus, the CPU can devote its time primarily to the things for which it is designed.

What about DOS? Generally, a graphics accelerator is not necessary, and will not give any benefit, in text-based DOS. However, there are some DOS scenarios in which sophisticated graphics are used. A graphics accelerator can significantly speed up some DOS applications, such as computer-aided design (CAD).

As a rule, the more complex the screen graphics, the greater the improvement you are likely to see in an older PC when you add a graphics accelerator. The video can, in some cases, be speeded up by a factor of three or even four times. Newer systems, especially those with the Pentium or PowerPC processors working at 66 MHz or more, are good enough for most people's needs without graphics accelerators. *See also* DOS *and* GRAPHICAL USER INTERFACE.

Gray-scale system

The *gray-scale system* is a method of creating and displaying a digital video image. The image is made up of *pixels*, each one a single picture element. (This abbreviation is sometimes further shortened to *pel*.)

Pixels. Even the coarsest PC display has an array of 256 by 256 pixels, or $2^8 \times 2^8 = 2^{16} = 65,536$ elements. This number, in computer terminology, is 64K. A high-resolution screen has an array of at least 512 by 512 pixels: $2^9 \times 2^9 = 262,144$, or 256K elements.

The pixels are little squares, each with a shade of gray that is assigned a digital code. The table shows a 16-level gray scale. Four binary

Gray-scale system

digits, or bits, are needed to represent each level of brightness from black (0000) to white (1111). This is a coarse gray scale; finer scales might use 64 or even 256 different brightnesses. These would be expressed in binary codes of six or eight bits, respectively.

Hypothetical 16-shade binary codes

Code	Relative shade	Percent brightness
0000	Black	0.0
0001		6.67
0010	Very dark gray	13.33
0011		20.00
0100	Dark gray	26.67
0101		33.33
0110	Medium-dark gray	40.00
0111		46.67
1000	Medium gray	53.33
1001		60.00
1010	Medium-light gray	66.67
1011		73.33
1100	Light gray	80.00
1101		86.67
1110	Off-white	93.33
1111	White	100.00

Low-resolution coarse. If a screen is of the low-resolution type, with a 16-level gray scale, then the memory needed to represent a single, nonmoving image is $256 \times 256 \times 16$, or 1,048,576 bits. Since a *byte* consists of eight bits, this coarse-gray, low-resolution image would need $2^{20}/2^3 = 2^{17} = 128$ kilobytes. Eight such images would take up almost the entire storage of a typical computer diskette.

High-resolution fine. If the screen is of the high-resolution type, with a 256-level gray scale, then the memory required for one image to be shown once is $512 \times 512 \times 256 = 67,108,864$ bits. That's eight megabytes, which is a fairly good chunk of space on the hard disk of a typical PC.

Analog versus digital. These examples show that analog technology still enjoys a few advantages over digital technology. Remember that these massive memory figures represent a single image, sent just once; for a fast-scan television picture, at least 16 images are required per second. Yet, even these images would represent only black-and-white pictures.

Digital television programs cannot, at the present time, be effectively stored on diskettes or even on hard disks. The required storage space is simply too great. On the other hand, hour-long programs are easily recorded on analog tapes of manageable size, and played on analog equipment of reasonable cost.

Rapid progress is being made to get audio-visual programs digitized. Computers are getting more powerful, with greater speed, memory, and word size. Recording techniques are also improving. *See also* MULTIMEDIA.

Feature focus. For digital moving pictures to be possible in machine vision systems, some means will be needed to sort out relevant from irrelevant data. This will require a high level of artificial intelligence, which also takes up substantial memory and storage.

When you look at your surroundings, you don't take in the whole scene all the time. Most of your attention is concentrated within a narrow zone around the *fovea*, or focus point of your eyes. The same thing will need to be done with the vision systems in robots. Not only that, but the programming will need to tell the machine where to look for the expected data. One method of doing this, called *local feature focus*, was devised by a robotics engineer named Robert Bolles. *See also* VISION SYSTEMS.

Green computing

The expression *green computing* refers to the use of PCs in a way that has minimum negative impact on the environment.

Evil end point? According to some people, computers represent the culmination of all the bad aspects of society. Computers are, according to these people, the endpoint of a technological juggernaut run amok.

As computers get more and more powerful, according to some people, PCs and related devices will come to dominate every detail of our lives. People will be totally dependent on machines. Humanity will lose all contact with nature. To some extent these concerns are valid, but when they are blown out of proportion, they turn into *cyberphobia*, an unreasonable and sometimes almost insane fear and distrust of computers. *See also* COMPUTER OVER-RELIANCE *and* CYBERPHOBIA.

Energy savers. In reality, computers are more environmentally friendly than most other modern machines. A computer, especially a laptop PC, is a low-power device. Even an electric typewriter consumes more power than some PCs.

Grounding

Computers not only consume relatively little energy, but they help save the expenditure of energy needed to get information in the more old-fashioned ways. By using online services, for example, people can avoid trips to the library, the bank, and the shopping mall. Some people do a large part of their work from their homes via computer, rather than driving a polluting automobile miles to and from an office. This practice, called *telecommuting*, is gaining momentum, and might make physical commuting unnecessary for a large part of the workforce, reducing air pollution in cities. Also, fewer people will be injured or killed in car accidents.

Computers can also help people optimize their use of energy. For example, you might use a computer to control the temperature in your house; when you're away, the PC could tell your heater or air conditioner to work at a lower duty cycle. Computers can automatically switch lights on when you enter a room, and switch them off again when you leave. In cars, microcomputers increase fuel efficiency. Scientists have used computers to solve or prevent environmental problems and catastrophes.

There are some simple things you can do to minimize the environmental impact of your personal computing. Don't print out data on paper unless absolutely necessary. (All paper eventually ends up in the trash.) Switch your PC and its peripherals off when they are not in use. Several manufacturers make "green computers" that require less electrical power than their "non-green" counterparts; you might check into this before buying your next system. *See also* ECOLINKING, ONLINE SERVICE, *and* TELECOMMUTING.

Grounding

All electronic equipment, including computers, should be connected to a good electrical ground system. *Grounding* is important for your personal safety and can help protect your workstation from damage if lightning strikes nearby. Grounding minimizes the chances for radio-frequency interference (RFI) to and from computer hardware. The term *grounding* also refers to precautions for minimizing electrostatic discharge when working with computer boards (cards) and components such as microprocessors.

Safety. There's an unwritten rule among electrical engineers: Never touch two grounds at the same time. This refers to the tendency for voltages to exist between electrical and electronic devices, even when you don't suspect it.

In recent years, appliances have been equipped with three-wire cords. One wire is connected to the "common" or "ground" part of the hardware, and leads to a round prong in the plug. This prong, known as the *ground prong*, should never be cut off or otherwise defeated because the result can be a dangerous voltage on the appliance.

You can recognize three-wire electrical systems by the appearance of the wall outlets. If each outlet has a sideways-D-shaped hole below the two rectangular holes, then you have a three-wire system. For this system to be effective, however, the third hole must be connected to an earth ground. If you are in doubt about this, have an electrician check it out. Unfortunately, there have been cases in which three-wire outlets were installed, but the grounding system was not hooked up.

Lightning. A three-wire electrical system will make your workstation safer for your equipment, as well as for yourself. When lightning strikes near a power line, a sudden voltage surge occurs in the line. This surge, more properly called a *transient*, often reaches several hundred volts, although its duration is very short. Transient suppression devices, also called "surge suppressors" or "surge protectors," will keep transients from reaching your PC and peripherals, but a transient suppressor is only as effective as the electrical ground against which it functions.

All good transient suppressors have three-prong outlets. Never defeat the third (ground) prong. If you use an extension cord with your equipment, be sure it is the three-wire type, and keep it as short as possible. An extension cord should always be connected between the transient suppressor and the outlet, never between the suppressor and any piece of computer hardware.

The best way to guarantee protection for computers, and in fact for any electronic device, is to unplug things when they're not in use. That might mean you'll have to crouch and yank a cord or two from the wall, but that's better than having your equipment damaged during a severe thunderstorm. Those people who run around unplugging things before storms are not stupid. *See also* LIGHTNING PROTECTION *and* TRANSIENT SUPPRESSION.

Radio-frequency interference (RFI). Computers can be affected by strong electromagnetic fields. Computers also generate radio waves of their own. Some amateur radio operators find that they can't use their computers and their "ham" rigs at the same time because the pieces of equipment interfere with each other. A nearby commercial broadcast station can sometimes affect PC operation as well.

If you think that your PC is experiencing interference from a radio signal, keep in mind that such cases are almost always the result of ineffective shielding of the computer, peripherals, and/or connecting cables. Also, these cases are rare, unless the radio transmitter and the computer are in the same house or building. Check out your own workstation before jumping to any conclusions. Even a radio transmitter that operates perfectly can interfere with a haphazardly assembled PC system.

A good ground system will help minimize the chances of your PC experiencing RFI. The drawing shows a good system (A) and a bad one (B). In a good ground system, each device is connected to a *ground bus* (shown as a heavy line in the drawing), which in turn runs to the common ground. A bad ground system contains *ground loops* (shown as heavy circular arrows in the drawing) that increase the susceptibility of a computer to external interference. *See also* COMPLEMENTARY-METAL-OXIDE-SEMICONDUCTOR (CMOS) TECHNOLOGY, ELECTROMAGNETIC SHIELDING, METAL-OXIDE-SEMICONDUCTOR (MOS) TECHNOLOGY, *and* RADIO-FREQUENCY INTERFERENCE.

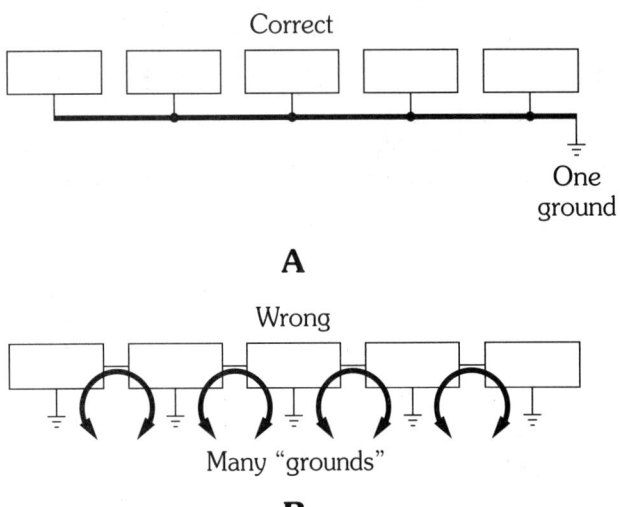

A good ground system (A) and a bad one (B). Circular arrows show unwanted ground loops.

Groupware

Groupware is specialized software intended for a small group of people, all of whom are contributing to the development of some project. *Electronic mail* is one form of groupware. Groupware is usually used in conjunction with local area networks (LANs).

Consider the example of a small magazine publisher. In this company, there is an editor, an illustrator, and a production person (designer). Each of these people has a PC with software designed especially for the application at hand.

The editor takes the text contributed by outside authors and molds it into the proper style using a word processing program. The illustrator takes contributed art and/or photographs, and might also create some new ones. Graphics software assists in this process. Finally, the text and graphics are put together by the designer so that the magazine is easy to read and attractive. This might be done with WYSIWYG ("what you see is what you get") software.

The three PCs are connected together in a LAN and are all supplied with groupware that lets each person see the whole project as it evolves (shown in the drawing). The three people can constantly communicate with each other, providing a system of checks and balances. The interaction among the three people, with their three PCs, can go on even if each person is in a separate office.

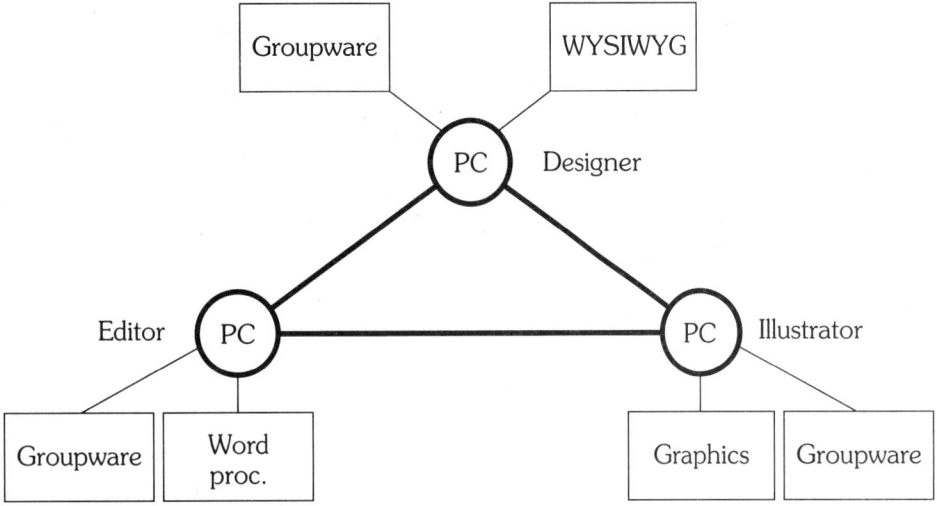

A hypothetical small publisher using groupware on three PCs.

For example, the editor might see something that the designer is doing, and say, "No, that will dilute the author's intended meaning." The designer can then try other arrangements until both are satisfied. Perhaps the illustrator objects to something, saying, "You put that picture on page 22 but the text describing it is on page 21. The reader shouldn't have to keep flipping the page." The designer might then move the illustration to page 21.

Groupware is available for both IBM-compatible PCs and Macintosh systems. *See also* DESKTOP PUBLISHING, ELECTRONIC MAIL, LOCAL AREA NETWORK, *and* WYSIWYG.

GUI

See GRAPHICAL USER INTERFACE.

Hacker

A person who enjoys tinkering with computer hardware and software is sometimes called a *hacker*. These people spend large amounts of time at computers. Many of them work in the computer industry, and then come home and spend the evening with a PC.

Good hackers. Hackers have been responsible for much innovation in the computer industry. There are hardware hackers and software hackers; some geniuses like to work with both. Software hackers are constantly trying to create better computer programs. Some sophisticated hackers are working with robotics and artificial intelligence, with the intent of building personal robots. Others like working with computer music; more than a few of them have started rock bands to test their new sounds out on the public.

Hackers are an indispensable part of the computer industry. They are spurred on by the fact that they can make money and advance their careers from their schemes. Although these people are sometimes called "nerds" or "geeks" in school, the mockery often turns to envy years later, when they have become successful engineers and programmers. *See also* AMATEUR RADIO, ARTIFICIAL INTELLIGENCE, MUSICAL INSTRUMENT DIGITAL INTERFACE, PACKET COMMUNICATIONS, PERSONAL ROBOTS, *and* SOFTWARE.

Bad hackers. The question has been asked, "Why is it, that if you give two people baseball bats, one will use it to hit home runs while the other will use it to smash windows?" Some computer wizards use their skill to harm people, corporations, and governments.

Hacker program

Many computer networks are protected by security schemes, such as passwords or format requirements. Malicious hackers find ways to break into these networks and alter the data, sometimes as "software vandals," but more often to steal money. Thus, you might get a credit-card bill for $50,000 that you never racked up, or find that your credit report is inaccurate. You might get a telephone bill two inches thick for one month, with a balance of $85,000. You could end up with a false arrest record. Things like this happen; the public pays for it.

An especially destructive and pointless sort of hacking takes the form of a *Trojan horse* or *virus*. One of these occasionally gets into software, especially the kind that you download without paying for its use. It can disrupt a PC system; in some cases the data on the hard disk is so badly mutilated that it is no longer of any use.

Malicious hacking is against the law. The penalties vary. Often, because of the interstate nature of computer networks, the crime falls under the jurisdiction of the federal government. Several states have introduced legislation providing long prison sentences and large fines for people convicted of distributing programs with the intention of sabotaging computers. *See also* COMPUTER ADDICTION, GRAND SYNTHESIZER, ONLINE SERVICE, TROJAN HORSE, *and* VIRUS.

Hacker program

One of the earliest experiments with artificial intelligence (AI) was done with an imaginary robot, entirely contained within the "mind" of a computer. A student named Gerry Sussman wrote a program called *HACKER* in a computer language known as LISP. The result was a make-believe, computerized universe in which a robot stacked blocks on top of one another.

Making the rules. Sussman created laws of physics in the imaginary universe by literally entering them into the computer as data. These "laws" were made up of statements similar to these:

1 Blocks X, Y, and Z each weigh 5 pounds.

2 Blocks V and W each weigh 50 pounds.

3 The robot can lift no more than 10 pounds.

4 Only one object can occupy a given space at a given time.

5 The robot knows how many blocks there are.

6 The robot can find blocks if they're out of direct sight.

Part A of the drawing shows the five blocks lying around as they might appear on the computer monitor, along with the robot, a stick figure.

Entrapment. Sussman gave commands to the robot such as, "Stack the blocks all up, one on top of the other." As stated, this command

Hacker program

In the computerized world, of the HACKER program, a robot stacks blocks.

can't be carried out because it requires the robot to lift a block weighing 50 pounds (either V or W), and the robot can lift only 10 pounds (part B of the drawing). What would happen if the robot were given a command it could not execute? Would it try indefinitely to do it anyway, or would it say, "I can't do this"? Would it go after either block V or W first, trying to get it on top of one of the light blocks or on top of the other heavy block? Would it pick up all the lighter blocks X, Y, and Z in some sequence, stacking them vertically on top of V or W? Would it put two light blocks on V and the remaining light block on W, and then give up?

One of the most significant aspects of machine intelligence is the ability to resolve problems like this. A truly "smart" computer should not be susceptible to falling into traps and getting hung up there. A good AI program needs some sort of "escape clause," so that the computer will give up after a certain amount of time trying to carry out a task.

Multiple solutions. Another command might be, "Stack the blocks so that lighter ones are on top of heavier ones." The robot can do this according to the rules stated, but several different possible ways exists (two of these are shown in the drawing at C and D). Would the robot hesitate, unable to make a decision, or would it go ahead and accomplish the task in some way? If the experiment were repeated, would the result always be the same, or would the robot solve the problem a different way each time?

This is a more subtle matter than impossible tasks. Real people come up with different solutions to a problem with multiple solutions. They almost never get frustrated because they cannot decide which solution to apply. A poorly written computer program, however, might regard multiple solutions as the absence of a solution, unless some algorithm were devised telling the machine how to deal with the case.

Not always human. Many AI researchers have written programs similar to HACKER, creating computerized universes in an attempt to get machines to think and learn. The results have often been fascinating and unexpected. Computers evolve their own "thought patterns," and these do not always mimic the mental processes of human beings. *See also* ARTIFICIAL INTELLIGENCE.

Half duplex

When two computers "talk" with each other, they exchange data. Two-way communication is called *duplex* because information can go in either direction on the data line. Some data lines can handle information going in both directions simultaneously, while others, known as *half duplex*, allow data to go in only one direction at a time.

Half-duplex communication is common in two-way radio systems. A good example is the radio that taxicab drivers use. You've never heard a taxi driver successfully interrupt the dispatcher because, while the driver is sending information, he or she can't "hear" anything. Every cab in the fleet, and also the dispatcher, is limited in the same way. This often results in lost information, since two stations might transmit at the same time and be unaware of the fact. That messes up the circuit and makes it necessary to send the information all over again. A similar situation often exists in amateur radio computer communications, although some packet communications systems allow for simultaneous transmission by more than one station.

The drawing shows the principle of half-duplex data communication. The channel, or communications line, can contain data from only one *source* at a time. It's something like a single-lane highway or a single railroad track; it can't carry things in both directions at once. When Sally is sending something to George, Sally is "blind" and "deaf." The channel is full. George cannot send anything to Sally and expect her to receive it until she is finished. Similarly, when George is sending, he can't receive. Neither PC can work as a source and a *destination* at the same time. For that to be possible, the circuit must be capable of working in *full duplex*.

Halftone

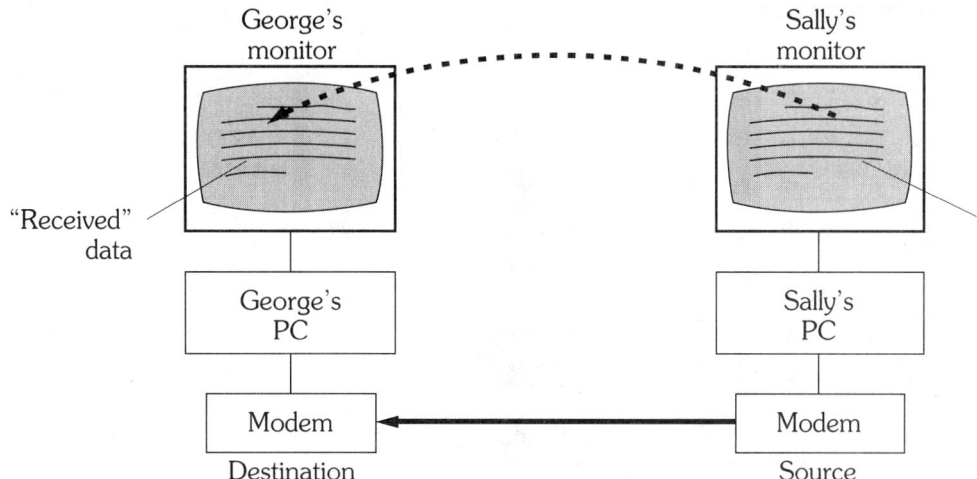

In half duplex, data can be sent in only one direction at a time.

The hardware for half duplex is less complicated than that for full duplex. It also costs less. These are the advantages of half duplex. Full duplex, however, is more user-friendly and efficient. *See also* FULL DUPLEX.

Halftone

A *halftone* is a specially processed black-and-white photograph. If you look at a halftone from a distance, it looks like a normal print. Up close, however, and especially through a magnifying glass, it resolves into a pattern of black dots.

Grid of dots. The dots in a halftone are arranged in a grid. The size of the dots varies depending on the darkness of the photograph. White is represented by tiny dots, or perhaps even none at all. Black is represented by large dots that run together; in the extreme, the region is solid black. The drawing is a magnified view of a halftone, with the lightest shade at the upper left, progressing to black at the lower right.

Halftones are used in newspapers and magazines because they allow photographs to be reproduced on a printing press. Also, halftones photocopy better than plain black-and-white prints. If you've ever tried to photocopy a print, even if it is of the highest quality, you know that the reproduction quality is not very good. To get a good reproduction, you must place a screen in front of the photograph, in effect turning the print into a halftone.

Scanning. When you use an optical scanner to digitize a photograph for transmission from one computer to another, the process is similar to that used to make a halftone. Instead of dots, however, *pixels* (picture elements) are filled in (black) or left open (white). These correspond to binary highs and lows (ones and zeros). The result is a *bitmap*.

Handheld computer

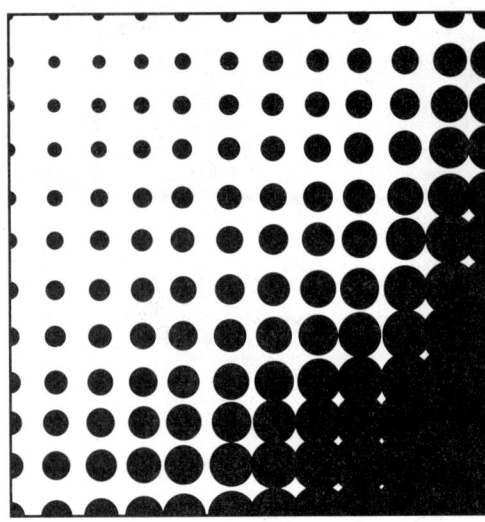

A halftone's image darkness depends on the dot size.

The quality of a bitmap is not quite as good as that of a true halftone. Also, a bitmapped image is difficult to enlarge or shrink without creating a "grainy" appearance. Nevertheless, optical scanning provides a relatively inexpensive, effective way to send photographs from one PC to another, over telephone lines or radio circuits. *See also* BITMAP *and* OPTICAL SCANNER.

Handheld computer

A *handheld computer* is a miniature portable computer, small enough to be held in one hand. Handheld computers serve as dictionaries, language translators, notepads, and calculators. Couriers use them to trace packages. They are used by police and investigative services. In general, a handheld computer is more than a conventional calculator, but less than a full-size desktop, laptop, or notebook PC. The drawing (opposite page) shows a typical handheld computer.

Miniaturization. For years, the trend in all of electronics has been toward miniaturization: putting more things and more features into packages having less volume and weight.

Consider an AM/FM radio receiver. Today you can buy a portable radio that will fit inside a headset, so you can walk around and listen to full stereo while you paint a wall, do the laundry, or exercise on a stationary bicycle. (Although of course you shouldn't do anything that requires you to hear the real world around you while wearing one of these!) Many of us can remember when a radio of far lesser quality and sensitivity took up a good part of a tabletop. Perhaps you're old enough to recall a time when a radio sat on the floor, and needed two people to move it from one room to another.

Handheld computer

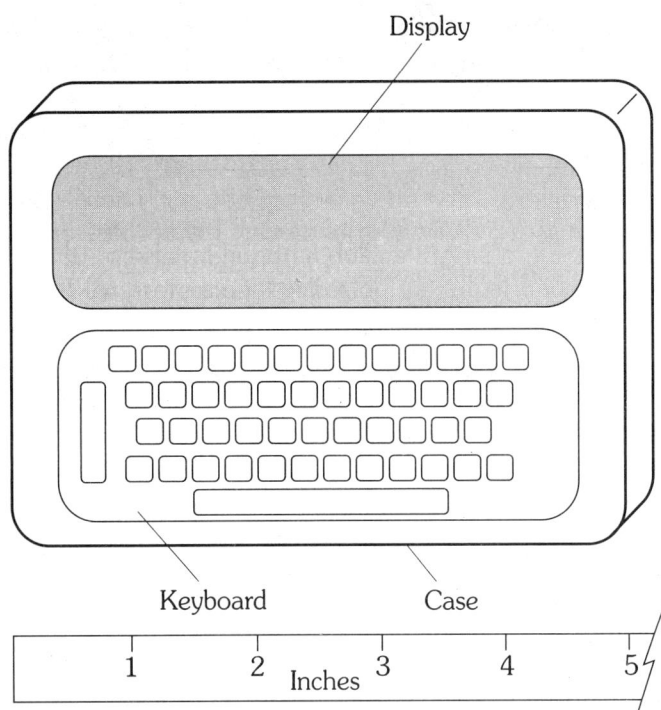

A miniaturized handheld PC with basic features.

The same thing has happened with computers. Today's handheld computer has more power than a computer from the 1950s that took up the equivalent of a small house and required separate air-conditioning systems just to keep from overheating.

Diminishing returns. Although it might someday be technologically possible, few people would argue that a general-purpose radio or personal computer should be small enough to fit, say, in place of the diamond on a ring. There is a point beyond which miniaturization defeats its purpose, which is to make machines as convenient as possible for human beings to use. A certain physical bulk is necessary for an effective interface through which an operator maintains control of a machine.

Handheld computers have miniature keyboards with all the letters of the alphabet and the digits 0 through 9, along with some punctuation and symbols. For high-speed, accurate typing, however, a full-featured computer keyboard must be at least 14 to 18 inches wide, and five to seven inches deep. Otherwise it's hard to hit the right keys. Human fingers aren't tapered to pencil-sharp points!

In some applications, the advent of speech recognition and speech synthesis will eliminate the need for keyboards altogether. With these technologies, people will be able to wear a PC with headphones and a miniature boom microphone—the counterpart of the AM/FM headphone radio—and walk around listening and talking to "virtual

Handshaking

worlds." For applications like graphics and word processing, however, miniaturization has already reached its limit of effectiveness.

Assets. Handheld PCs have definite assets in certain applications. You can find handheld computers in electronics stores, department stores, computer stores, and office supply houses. There's usually a small screen that uses a liquid-crystal display (LCD). Power is obtained from rechargeable batteries.

One advantage of a handheld computer is that it can serve as a notepad. If you get into the habit of carrying a handheld PC, you can take it out of your pocket, type in an idea or a bit of information, put the computer back in your pocket, and have the data available later.

Handheld computers are ideal for keeping children entertained on long trips. A huge variety of computer games can hold their attention and reduce the boredom of an all-day drive or airplane flight. The beeping and tweeting of the little machine might drive you crazy, but at least the kids will behave themselves.

Handheld computers can be connected via modem to more powerful home PCs. Suppose you're on an airplane flight, and you need some information from your computer back home. You activate one of the aircraft's cellular telephones stored in the back of the seat in front of you, plug your handheld unit into the phone set, call your home, and your desktop computer takes the line. Provided the information isn't too complex for the handheld PC to display, you're in business.

There's an element of fun involved in playing with adult toys, especially computers and communications devices. Put the two together, and they can be habit-forming. Don't be too surprised if you find yourself using such gadgets even when you don't have any urgent need to do so. *See also* DESKTOP COMPUTER, LAPTOP COMPUTER, MODEM, *and* NOTEBOOK COMPUTER.

Handshaking

In a digital communications system, accuracy is important. One wrong character can cause a program not to run, or to make catastrophic mistakes. Accuracy can be optimized by means of a checking scheme. The receiving computer checks data periodically to ensure that it's in the right form. This process is called *handshaking*.

Between PCs. Here is an example of how handshaking can work. First, the transmitting, or *source*, computer sends three characters of data. Then it pauses to await a signal from the receiving, or *destination*, computer, saying either of two things:

1 I recognize all three characters

2 One or more characters is something I don't recognize.

If the return signal is 1, the source computer sends the next three characters. If the return signal is 2, the source computer repeats the three characters. This process is shown in the flowchart. Computer systems today can send data in much larger blocks than three characters, sometimes several megabytes at a time.

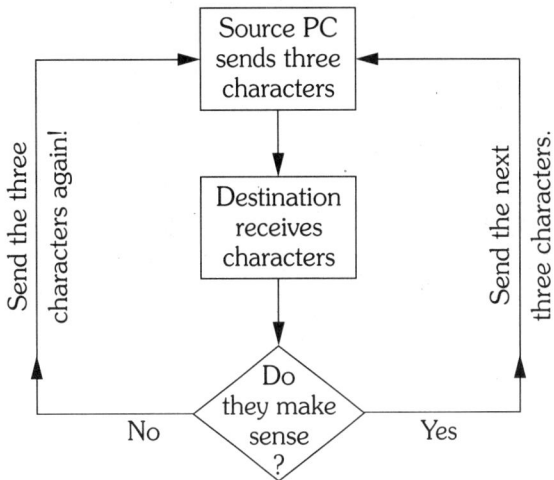

Handshaking: a method of improving the accuracy of serial data transfer.

When modems first establish connection between computers, a handshaking process sets up the communications protocol. This includes speed in bauds or bits per second, compression, parity, stop bits, etc. *See also* BAUD/BITS PER SECOND, PROTOCOL, *and* X/Y/ZMODEM.

Within a PC. The term *handshaking* is sometimes also used in reference to a method of controlling or synchronizing the flow of serial data between a PC and its peripherals. The synchronization is done by either a control bus or cable in hardware, or a control code in software.

Hardware handshaking is used when direct wire or cable links are possible, such as between a personal computer and a serial printer. Software handshaking is similar to the process used for communications systems, shown in the flowchart. The source sends data only when the destination is ready for it and is expecting it. *See also* SERIAL.

Hanging indent

Hanging indent refers to a special format sometimes used in typesetting. The first line of each text block is flush with the left margin, while the rest of the lines are indented (see the drawing). The text block might be a sentence, a paragraph, or a set of paragraphs.

Hardcopy

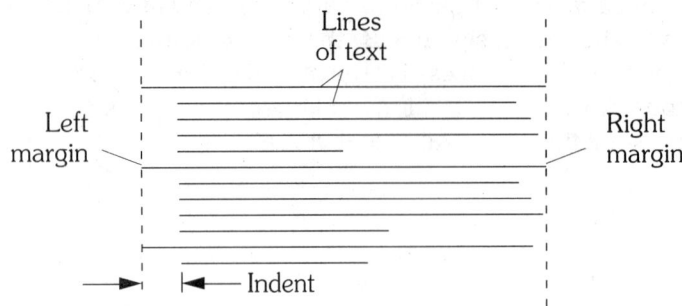

Hanging indent is the reverse of conventional indentation.

Hanging indents are often used in dictionaries. The term to be defined is flush left, and is usually in boldface. The rest of the lines in the definition are indented several spaces, and are in normal type. Hanging indents are not generally used in the normal text of manuscripts or reports, but might be used to set up a list of items or steps to follow. You can set up a desktop publishing or word processing program to create hanging indents for special material or special effects. *See also* DESKTOP PUBLISHING *and* WORD PROCESSING.

Hardcopy

A printout of a file, either text or graphics, is called a *hardcopy*. The hardcopy of a text document looks like a typewritten manuscript or set of printed pages. The hardcopy of graphics can consist of line drawings, charts, graphs, shaded art, or photographs.

Often, of course, hardcopies of computer documents are useful and important. However, people routinely make unnecessary hardcopies of computer files, resulting in far more paper clutter than necessary. The reason for this is partly force of habit—we're used to seeing things in print—but also partly from a distrust of computers known as *cyberphobia*. Like all phobias, it is unreasonable. Many people imagine that diskette files are more subject to destruction than files printed on paper. Magnetic data is intangible; might it not vanish spontaneously? This notion is ridiculous. Papers can be destroyed just as easily as diskettes, CD-ROMs, or magnetic tapes.

Still, it's always a good idea to keep two or three sets of diskettes, on which are stored all your *archives*. You should also periodically do a full backup of all the data on your hard disk. Hard disk systems and diskette drives have been known to fail. If your PC breaks down, you will lose immediate access to your data, but if the data has been backed up, it will remain intact no matter what happens to the computer.

It's much easier, cheaper, and less messy to make multiple copies of computer files than it is to photocopy the same data in hardcopy. If you're willing to make frequent, consistent backups and locate them in safe places (such as at work, at home, and in a safe-deposit box), data on magnetic media is much more secure than hardcopy. *See also*

Hard disk

ARCHIVES, CYBERPHOBIA, DISKETTE, FULL BACKUP, HARD DISK, PAPERLESS OFFICE, *and* TAPE DRIVE.

Hard disk

A *hard disk* is a magnetic medium for storing data. It might hold software, graphic images, text, sounds, spreadsheets, databases—all the information you need to run your computer efficiently and fast.

Mechanics. A hard disk is not one disk, but several, arranged in a stack. These disks, called *platters*, are made from aluminum or other rigid material, coated with a ferromagnetic substance similar to that used in audiotape or videotape. The platters are spaced a fraction of an inch apart. Each has two sides (top and bottom), and two read/write *heads*, one for the top and one for the bottom. The assembly is enclosed in a sealed cabinet so that no dust, smoke, or other pollutants can enter. The drawing at A is an edgewise, cutaway view of the platters and heads in a hard disk system.

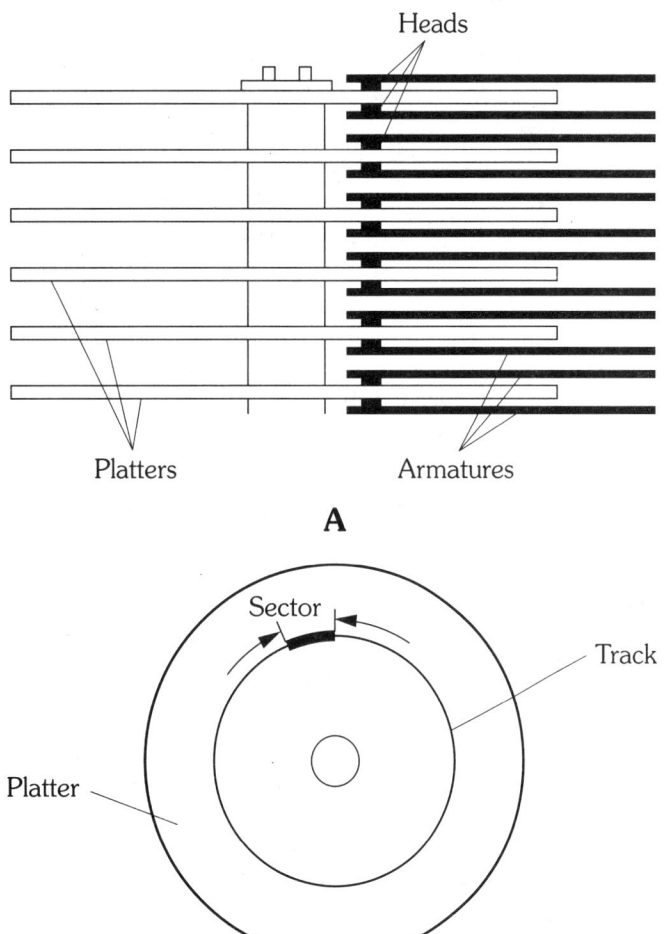

At A, an edgewise view of platters, armatures, and heads. At B, a face-on view of a platter showing one track and one sector.

Hard disk

When the computer is switched off, the hard disk mechanism locks the heads in a position away from the platters. This prevents damage to the heads and platters if the computer is moved. When the PC is powered-up, the platters spin at 3600 revolutions per minute (3600 rpm) or more. The heads hover a few millionths of an inch above and below the platter surfaces. As data is read from or written onto the hard disk, the heads move rapidly back and forth.

If you had "X-ray vision" and could see within the sealed hard disk mechanism as it was working, you would be amazed that such a device could be built, with such a high degree of reliability, for just a few hundred dollars.

Tracks, sectors, cylinders. The data on a hard disk is arranged in circular *tracks*. This is not quite like the spiral groove on an old-fashioned phonograph disk. While that groove is one long path, the tracks on a platter are individual circles. There are hundreds of tracks per radial inch of the platter surface.

Each circular track is broken into a number of arcs called *sectors*. One sector normally contains 512 bytes of data. You might hear of data units called *clusters*. These are units consisting of one to several sectors, depending on the arrangement of data on the platters. Tracks and sectors are set up on the hard disk during the initial formatting process, done before the PC is sold. You should never attempt to do it yourself.

Warning! Never format your hard disk!

Actually, there are a few exceptions to this rule for power users (experienced PC enthusiasts). For beginning and intermediate-level PC users, however, this warning should be taken very seriously. Accidental formatting of a hard disk will obliterate its contents, and will cause you a horrific inconvenience if you haven't done a full backup of the data in your system.

The drawing at B on previous page is a face-on view of a single hard-disk platter, showing a track and one of its constituent sectors. A *cylinder* is the set of equal-radius tracks on all the platters in the drive.

Capacity. A hard disk has room for many times the data of a diskette. A 5.25-inch, high-density "floppy" can hold 1.2MB (megabytes) of information, and a 3.5-inch, high-density diskette can store 1.44MB. The first hard disk had room for 10MB. At the time, people thought that was ridiculously large, and that it would never be outstripped by the needs of individuals. Now, a 10MB hard disk is ridiculously small.

Consumer demand rises to match the supply. Software, graphics, and sounds consume vast amounts of storage. The more sophisticated and complex the programming gets, the more storage it needs. Today, even the smallest laptop has a hard drive capable of storing hundreds of megabytes. Some hard disks have capacities of many gigabytes, and mean-time-between-failure (MTBF) figures of a million hours or more.

There's no reason to believe that the trend toward larger hard disk capacities will stop. As disk-storage gluttons such as virtual reality, animation, super-high-resolution graphics, and speech recognition/synthesis become common, hard disk capacity must expand accordingly.

Access time. Computer speed is affected by how fast the hard disk can store and retrieve data. When you type a command or click on an icon telling the computer to read or write data, the hard disk mechanism goes through a series of rapid, complex, precise movements. The head must be positioned over the sector where the data is located or is to be written, and then the head must stabilize its position and generate or detect the magnetic fields. All this takes place in a small fraction of a second.

The hard disk is one of the few pieces of PC hardware that has moving parts. It is the only device whose mechanical speed really puts a limit on how fast the microprocessor can do its work. If you have an 80486 chip with a slow hard drive, the chip's power will be impaired by the sluggishness of the drive; the computer might work more slowly than an 80386 PC with a faster drive. Hard disk access time can vary from less than 0.01 second to about 0.1 second. The faster access times are recommended for more advanced microprocessors. In the future, as clock speeds become faster, hard drives will need to have access times significantly less than 0.01 second.

Another problem that can hamper hard disk operation is *fragmentation* of data. A hard disk system always writes data in the spaces it finds available. If you have many files, and you revise and overwrite them often, the data gets broken up, so that it is no longer on contiguous sectors. A single file might be broken into several fragments. When you tell the computer to read that data, the hard disk system must gather it all up before it can be sent to RAM. This takes more time than if the data were in contiguous sectors, that is, all in one piece. Fortunately, this problem can be kept to a minimum by periodically using a *defragmentation* program.

Variations. There are several types of hard disks and related devices. Here are a few of the most common:

> *Internal* When you buy a PC, whether it is a desktop or laptop unit, it will probably have a hard disk built in. It comes installed and formatted. At most, all you must do is install your software, and you're ready to go. Many computer manufacturers

Hard disk

automatically install several software programs on the internal hard disk for you. In that case, all you have to do is turn the computer on.

➤ *External* You can add an external hard disk to supplement an internal one, or if you have an older computer that doesn't have one built in. This requires an open expansion slot. A second hard disk might serve as a backup (although a *tape drive* is more often used for this purpose) or you might add an external, high-end hard disk to your PC as an upgrade.

➤ *IDE* IDE (*integrated drive electronics*) drives are compatible with many computers. Capacities range upwards of 250MB, and the cost is from about $100 for a small drive to several hundred dollars for a 1GB drive. The greater the capacity and speed, the more expensive the drive. The earliest IDE drives were developed for computers using the 80286AT microprocessor; thus this type of drive is sometimes called an *AT drive*.

➤ *SCSI* In SCSI (pronounced "scuzzy," an acronym for *small computer system interface*) technology, the drive itself contains most of the control software. An interface card is necessary for the disk to work with computers. A SCSI drive uses parallel data, so its electronics function at high speed. You can find SCSI drives in a wide range of capacities, from about 200MB to 2GB or more. The cost varies from less than $100 to more than $1000.

➤ *Bernoulli box* A Bernoulli box is a removable storage device that can hold 40MB or more of data, the equivalent of a low-end hard disk system. Access times are also comparable to low-end hard disks. The convenience of a Bernoulli box makes it good for keeping archives or for backing up a small hard disk.

➤ *Floptical drive* Floptical technology is mentioned here because it increases the capacity of diskettes to levels typical of low-end hard drives. Floptical drives work by using a beam of light to help guide the head to the data on the diskette surface. This increases precision, making it possible to squeeze in more tracks per inch than would otherwise be the case.

➤ *CD-ROM* Technically, CD-ROM (*compact disc, read-only memory*) is not a true hard disk. However, it is a high-capacity data storage medium that is rapidly becoming commonplace in PC systems. A variation of CD-ROM called *write-once/read-many (WORM)* allows you to make your own CD-ROMs. Researchers are working on CD-ROMs on which data can be overwritten, and that might contain several tens, or even hundreds, of gigabytes of data.

See also ACCESS TIME, BERNOULLI BOX, BYTE, CD-ROM, CYLINDER, DEFRAGMENTATION, DIRECTORY, DIRECTORY TREE, FILE, FLOPTICAL

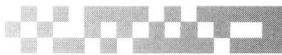

DISKETTE AND DRIVE, FULL BACKUP, IDE TECHNOLOGY, SCSI TECHNOLOGY, SECTOR, TAPE DRIVE, TRACK, *and* WRITE-ONCE/READ-MANY.

Hard font

See BUILT-IN FONT.

Hard page breaks

In word processing, a *page break* is a formatting code that the program inserts in text so that the printer will produce pages with attractive margins at the tops and bottoms of the pages. There are two main types of breaks: *hard page breaks* and *soft page breaks*.

Hard page breaks stay where they are with respect to the text, regardless of what you add or delete before or after them. Imagine using an electric or manual typewriter with continuous-feed, fanfold paper typical of computer printers. When you get one inch from the bottom of a sheet, you press the carriage return 12 to 15 times, so that the fold between sheets moves through the machine, and the next sheet is in position for the start of a new page. These are hard page breaks. Once you've made them, they stay where they are. If you add or delete text later, you'll have to remove the hard breaks, do your editing, and then put the hard breaks in again, at the right places to ensure that the new document will have the correct top and bottom margins.

Although hard page breaks can be necessary for things like title pages and chapter-opening pages, they are clumsy and can be frustrating to work with. The more convenient, automatic soft page breaks are the default in most word processors. *See also* HARD RETURNS, RUNNING HEADERS/FOOTERS, SOFT PAGE BREAKS, *and* SOFT RETURNS.

Hard returns

In word processing, a *return* ends one line of text and begins another. There are two ways in which you start a new line of text: *hard returns* and *soft returns*.

To produce a hard return, you press the Enter key. This is the equivalent of a carriage return on a manual or electric typewriter. You can do this at the end of every line, but it's probably not a good idea because most programs automatically go to the next line when the text goes beyond the right margin of any line. You can just keep on typing, without ever having to bother about putting in the returns, and the words will all slip into the right places. If you want to shorten the lines, you can set the right or left margins so the text lines come out to be whatever length you want.

If you press the Enter key while typing a word-processed document, you cause a hard return to be inserted into the text in addition to the soft returns automatically inserted by the program. This is normally done when you get to the end of a paragraph. After the hard return,

Hardware

you might want to add another hard return for an extra (blank) line, then start the next paragraph.

If you later edit your document, the hard returns will remain where they are with respect to the words in the text. This is fine if you have used hard returns only between paragraphs; it ensures that the paragraphs retain their identities. It will cause problems with the right margin, though, if you have used hard returns within paragraphs.

Hard returns are also sometimes useful when writing poetry or when putting short tables in a word-processed document. *See also* HARD PAGE BREAKS, SOFT PAGE BREAKS, *and* SOFT RETURNS.

Hardware

The term *hardware* refers to the physical components of a computer system, such as printed circuit boards, cables, magnetic disks, and semiconductor devices. Hardware items are all tangible objects. The term is also sometimes used in reference to the way various components are connected.

When assembling a computer system, it's important that all the hardware items work well together. They must have *compatibility*. It's also important that the different parts of the system be connected properly. You can't put a high-density (HD) diskette into a double-density (DD) disk drive, for example, and expect the system to work. Nor can you connect a device to a serial data port if it's designed to work with parallel data.

The hardware in your PC system has a finite lifespan. All physical parts eventually wear out. *Software*, on the other hand, is abstract and therefore can't deteriorate. (Software can, however, become obsolete.) Your PC hardware operates under the control of the software. *See also* COMPATIBILITY *and* SOFTWARE.

Hardware reset

There are several different ways in which you can reinitialize, or *reset*, a computer if it "freezes up." One common method is to press the Control, Alt and Delete keys all at the same time. This is generally written as Ctrl-Alt-Del and is called a *warm boot*. The most extreme method of resetting your hardware is to switch the power off, wait two minutes or more, and then switch it back on again; this is known as a *cold boot*.

Some PCs have a reset button that, when pressed, effectively restarts the computer. If Ctrl-Alt-Del doesn't get your PC going again after a freeze-up, you can try pressing this button, if your computer has one. This is a *hardware reset* and will almost always do the job. Note, however, that you will lose everything in RAM if you perform a hardware reset. You should also remove any diskettes from your diskette drives before resetting. *See also* COLD BOOT *and* WARM BOOT.

Hard wiring

In a computer system, the term *hard wiring* refers to functions that are built right into the machine hardware. Hard wiring cannot be changed without rearranging physical components or changing the interconnecting wires. Sometimes, the term *firmware* is used to mean hard wiring, although that is technically a misnomer.

A theoretically perfect computer would be able to be programmed entirely by software. Of course, the physical components must be hooked up together somehow, but in the ideal case, functions could be changed just by reprogramming the machine. It would never be necessary to plug in a new cable or unplug an old one. You'd never have to remove the cover from your machine. This has been realized to a large extent in recent years by the use of diskettes, hard disks, and modems.

Hard wiring enjoys some advantages over software control, however. Its most significant advantage is that hard-wired functions can be done at a higher rate of speed than software processes. The machine doesn't have to "think" about the processes. A good analogy exists in your body. Certain reflex actions, such as withdrawing your hand from a hot flame, occur without thought; therefore, they are much faster than voluntary movements.

The average computer user need not worry about hard wiring within a PC. Components burn out and must be replaced, but this hard wiring is usually done by technicians, not by the user. If something goes wrong with your computer, and you've determined that it's not because of faulty programming or operating on your part, you can take the machine to a repair center and pick it up a few days later. If you have a service agreement that includes on-site repair, the technician will come to your home or office to fix the machine.

Expert computer users sometimes change hard wiring when they add expansion boards, or when they upgrade their systems. These tasks should not, in general, be undertaken by novices. *See also* EXPANSION BOARD, FIRMWARE, SOFTWARE, *and* UPGRADING.

Hayes compatibility

If you plan to connect your computer to the telephone lines to take advantage of online services, you'll need a device called a *modem*, which converts your PC's signals into audio tones that can be sent over the phone. It also converts incoming audio tones sent by other modems back into impulses that your computer can work with.

For modems to work right, they must adhere to several precise specifications. There are certain commands that you give a modem, so that it will do various things. In recent years, the most common modem command set has been the one used by Hayes Microcomputer Products, Inc., a major manufacturer of computer modems.

Head

Hayes compatibility means that a modem adheres to the Hayes command set. Because most communications software makes use of the Hayes command set, it's a good idea to be sure, when buying a modem, that the device is Hayes-compatible. Otherwise, you might find that you can't use the communications programs you want. *See also* MODEM.

Head

The *head*, also called the *read/write head*, is a part of a *diskette drive, hard disk*, or *tape drive*. The head detects magnetic fields on a disk or tape, and also magnetizes the disk/tape surface. The fields are read and written in a binary sequence, corresponding to computer data. The head in a diskette drive or hard disk is similar to the recording/playback head in a tape recorder.

Reading data. A magnetic diskette, hard disk, or tape has a coating of fine particles made of a ferromagnetic (magnetizable) substance. When data exists on the medium, some regions on the coating are magnetically polarized in one direction; other regions are polarized in the opposite direction. This creates microscopic magnets on the surface of the disk or tape, representing the two binary states, high (1) and low (0).

As the surface of a magnetic disk or tape moves past the head, regions representing 1 and 0 go by, generating a fluctuating magnetic field around the head. Any changing or moving magnetic field produces electric currents in a wire. The head has a coil of wire in which currents are created because of the magnetic fields from the disk or tape. These currents, which resemble the signals from a modem, are fed to the computer. The PC interprets them as text and graphics.

As the head picks up data, the magnetic particles on the disk or tape are not disturbed. Thus, the information can be read over and over again. Part A of the drawing is a block diagram of the reading process as data goes from the disk or tape surface to the RAM (random-access memory) in a computer.

Writing data. The writing of data onto a disk or tape is the reverse of the reading process. Signals from the computer, in the form of electric currents, are sent to the coil in the head. Whenever a current exists in a wire, a magnetic field surrounds the wire. The head acts as a tiny electromagnet, producing a magnetic field that alternates in sync with the currents it receives. This field magnetizes regions on the disk or tape as the surface moves past the head.

Part B of the drawing is a block diagram of the writing process, as data goes from RAM to the surface of a magnetic disk or tape.

Drive heads. A diskette drive has two heads, one for each side of the diskette. A hard disk has twice as many heads as there are platters

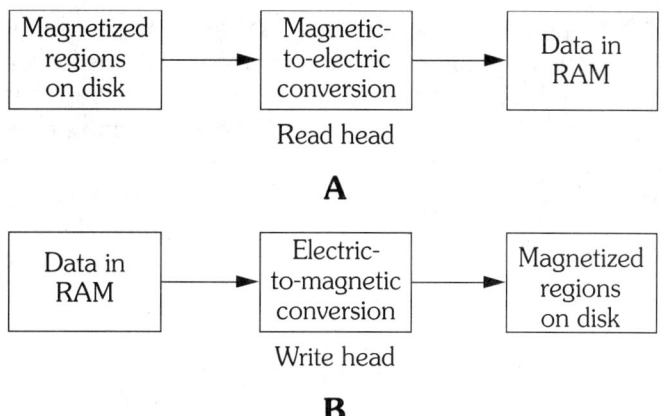

A Block diagram of the reading process (A) and the writing process (B).

in the assembly. When you give a command or mouse click telling your PC to write or read data to or from a diskette or hard disk, the drive goes through a series of complex, precise, rapid motions. The diskette or platters spin, and the heads move to the appropriate sectors on the surfaces. If there is any error in the positioning of the head, the data can't be read correctly, and won't be written in the right place. Alignment of diskette drives and hard disks is therefore vital to the operation of a computer.

When a drive is operating, it's important that it be protected from vibration. A computer should never be moved while it's powered-up, therefore. Always switch off the power and wait two minutes or more before moving any PC from one place to another. This will protect the machine from damage that can be caused by a *head crash*.

The speed at which a PC can operate is limited by the speed of the hard disk system. Engineers are constantly working on ways to get the heads to move more rapidly and precisely over the platter surfaces in these drives. *See also* DISKETTE DRIVE, HARD DISK, HEAD CRASH, *and* TAPE DRIVE.

Head crash

In a hard disk system, none of the heads should ever come into physical contact with the surface of a platter. If such a *head crash* happens, the head can be damaged, and the surface of the platter will probably be etched in an arc or circle, destroying the data in that region and rendering that part of the platter's surface permanently useless.

What causes a head crash. The most common cause for head crashes is jostling of the main unit while a computer is in operation. Hard disk heads (except very old ones) are normally secured, or *parked*, when the power is off, preventing head crashes during transport.

When a PC is operating, the hard-disk platters spin at a high speed (3600 revolutions per minute or more) while the heads hover only a few millionths of an inch away from the surfaces. It doesn't take much of a blow to cause a head to jump this microscopic gap and strike a platter. If the shock is severe, the impact can cause splinters to break off the platter. The fragments fly around inside the drive enclosure, causing more damage, just as airborne debris multiplies the destruction in a windstorm. The entire hard disk will probably have to be replaced if this occurs.

Preventing head crashes. The obvious way to keep the hard-disk heads from crashing is simply to avoid banging, jostling, or moving the main unit of the computer while the power is on. If you must move a computer, switch it off and wait at least a couple of minutes for the hard disk to wind down. However, don't take the fact that the machine is off as a license to be rough with it.

Laptop computers must be handled carefully while they're in operation. A blow to any part of a laptop will cause shock throughout the unit. If you ever need to handle a hard disk drive, take extreme care. It's the most delicate and sophisticated mechanical device in your computer. *See also* HARD DISK.

Hertz

Hertz, abbreviated *Hz*, is the fundamental measure of alternating-current (ac) frequency, named after the German physicist Heinrich Hertz. A frequency of 1 Hz is equivalent to a cycle per second. In fact, the word *Hertz* is interchangeable with the expression "cycles per second." The drawing shows a rectangular wave with a frequency of 3 Hz. There are three pulses per second.

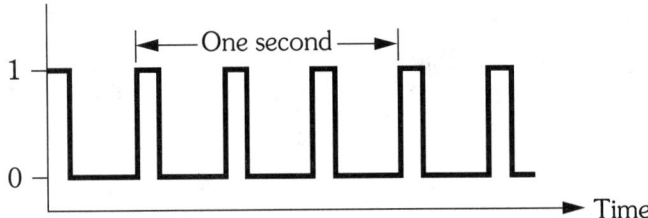

A train of pulses at 3 Hz (three pulses per second).

Frequency is often expressed in units of *kilohertz (KHz)*, *megahertz (MHz)*, and *gigahertz (GHz)*. A frequency of 1 kHz is equal to 1000 Hz; a frequency of 1 MHz is equal to 1000 KHz or 10^6 Hz; a frequency of 1 GHz is equal to 1000 MHz or 10^9 Hz.

The speed at which digital computers operate is often specified in terms of a frequency called the *clock speed*. The higher the clock speed, the faster a microprocessor can work, and the "smarter" a computer that uses the chip can be, if all other factors are equal. Higher clock speed translates into a "smarter" chip because, as the frequency increases, more operations become possible per unit of time.

The 80286 microprocessor, still found in some older desktop and laptop computers, worked at about 12 MHz, while the 80386 microprocessor typically works at about 20 MHz and the 80486 at about 66 MHz. The Pentium microprocessor functions at about 120 MHz. In the future, clock speeds will keep increasing.

Clock speed is not the only factor that affects the power of a computing system. Other important criteria are the bus size, the amount of RAM (random-access memory), and the hard disk drive capacity. In addition, some computers can perform more than one instruction per clock cycle. *See also* COMPUTER GENERATIONS, COMPUTER POWER, *and* MICROPROCESSOR.

Heterogeneous network

In a local area network (LAN), several computers and/or terminals are connected together, allowing communication among the workstations. There are various arrangements, called *topologies*, that a LAN can have. However, for any LAN to work right, the equipment must have *compatibility*; the machines must be able to understand each other.

A Macintosh computer can't communicate directly with an IBM-compatible machine. Even though IBM-type Windows software is similar to the Macintosh system in many ways, they aren't identical. DOS doesn't work the same way as either Windows or Macintosh.

It's possible to link different software schemes in a LAN, but the data format must be converted. Such a system is called a *heterogeneous network*. It's something like a multinational summit conference among the United States, Russia, and China. With translators, such a conference can proceed; without translators, it would be impossible. The drawing (page 512) shows a heterogeneous network with one IBM-compatible PC using "pure DOS" (shown as a circle in the drawing), two IBM-compatible PCs using Windows (ellipses), and two Macintosh PCs (squares). Each computer contains conversion software (rectangles), so it can understand all three "languages." *See also* COMPATIBILITY *and* LOCAL AREA NETWORK.

Heuristic knowledge

Can computers learn from their mistakes and improve their knowledge by trial and error? Is it possible for computers to evolve, all by themselves, to progressively higher planes of intelligence? Researchers in artificial intelligence (AI) say yes. In fact, the existence of *heuristic knowledge*, or the ability of a machine to become "smarter" based on its real-world experience, is one test of AI in a system.

A fast learner. Suppose a super-smart AI system is developed that can evolve to ever-higher levels of knowledge. Imagine that, one day

Hexadecimal number system

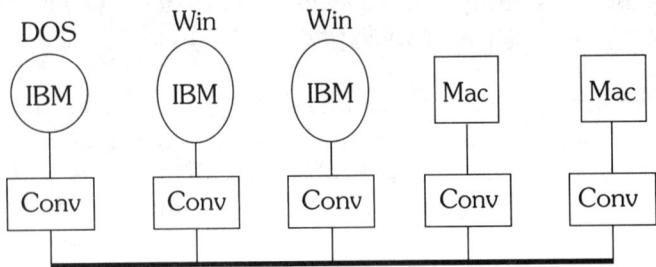

A heterogeneous network allows different systems to communicate.

after the machine has been put into operation, it's as smart as a 10-year-old person. After two days, it's as smart as a 20-year-old in college. After three days, it's as sharp as any 30-year-old engineer or businessperson. Suppose that more and more memory is added, so that the limit of knowledge is determined only by the speed of the microprocessor. What will this computer be like after a month? Will it have the wisdom of Solomon?

Does an increasing level of *intelligence* guarantee that a machine will also become *wise*?

Computers with hands. Machine knowledge becomes far more powerful when computers are given the ability to control mechanical devices. Knowledge alone can't build cars, bridges, aircraft, and rockets, or even wash a load of laundry. Real power is the result of knowledge put into action, yielding tangible results.

Will computers ever become smarter than, and perhaps more powerful than, people? This question has yet to be answered. Some researchers doubt that machines can surpass human beings in intelligence and power. Others are concerned about the possibilities for things to go wrong, or for AI to be abused, or for AI to evolve in unpleasant ways. *See also* ARTIFICIAL INTELLIGENCE, ARTIFICIAL LIFE, COLOSSUS, *and* FUTURISTS.

Hexadecimal number system

The number scheme that people most commonly use, the *decimal number system*, has 10 symbols, or digits, arranged representing powers of the number 10.

In computer work, other numbering systems are often preferred over the decimal scheme. The *binary number system* uses only zeros and ones, and is the way most digital computers "think" of numerical quantities. Another scheme, sometimes used in programming, is called the *hexadecimal number system*, so named because it has 16 symbols, or 2^4. These digits are the usual 0 through 9 plus six more, represented by A through F, the first six letters of the alphabet.

The table shows the hexadecimal digits, along with their decimal and binary equivalents. These hexadecimal digits are used by software engineers to represent four-digit groups of binary numbers. Hexadecimal numbers can also be used just like decimal numbers. If you ever see something like 1C8BF depicted as a numeral, it probably represents a hexadecimal number. *See also* BINARY-CODED DECIMAL, BINARY NUMBER SYSTEM, DECIMAL NUMBER SYSTEM, *and* OCTAL NUMBER SYSTEM.

Hexadecimal (16-digit) number system

Decimal	Binary	Hexadecimal
0	0000	0
1	0001	1
2	0010	2
3	0011	3
4	0100	4
5	0101	5
6	0110	6
7	0111	7
8	1000	8
9	1001	9
10	1010	A
11	1011	B
12	1100	C
13	1101	D
14	1110	E
15	1111	F

Hidden codes

In some word processing programs, certain combinations of keystrokes or mouse clicks, called codes, tell the machine how to set up the work. For example, you might press Ctrl-B for boldface, Ctrl-I for italics, and Ctrl-N to go back to normal type. Or you might click on items in a pull-down menu to change type styles.

Depending on the word processor you use, you might see symbols on the screen alerting you to the presence of formatting codes, or you might not see such symbols. Codes without identifying symbols are called *hidden codes*. Because they don't take up screen space, most PC users prefer word processing programs that employ hidden codes.

In modern word processing, the appearance of the type on the monitor changes to reflect changes in type style. Sometimes it's obvious what's happening; italic characters really look like italics,

Hidden file

boldface characters appear bold, and so on. In other cases, colors are used. Then you must memorize which colors represent which type styles. Boldface might be represented by red, for example, and normal type by white on a blue background. It doesn't take long to memorize color codes like this, but if you visit a friend who uses a different system, you'll get confused. *See also* DESKTOP PUBLISHING, WORD PROCESSING, *and* WYSIWYG.

Hidden file

Generally, when you create a file, its filename goes into a list that you can observe. This makes it easy to find the file again when you want to read it or use it. A *hidden file* is a file that does not appear in the directory listing.

An inexperienced PC user will probably not even know that hidden files exist. This keeps him or her from accidentally doing something that impairs the operation of the computer. If you've ever accidentally lost data or ruined software by changing or deleting a file, you can appreciate such safeguards.

Some programs are vital to the operation of your PC. If you accidentally erase, move, or change one of these, your computer will not function normally afterwards. You will then have to reinstall the software. Accidents of this kind can happen if you aren't paying attention to what you're doing. We're all prone to occasional mistakes, and the software engineers have designed operating systems to minimize the chance of a catastrophe resulting from human error.

Critical, hidden files are concealed via a scheme called the *hidden attribute*. When the attribute is switched on, the file is hidden; when it is switched off, the filename appears in the directory along with "normal" files. *See also* ATTRIBUTE, DIRECTORY, *and* FILENAME.

Hierarchical file system

When you store files on a hard disk, you'll probably want to categorize them. You can do this in several levels. In IBM-compatible systems, a category of files is called a *directory* or *subdirectory*. The hierarchy is the *directory tree*.

Macintosh system users can also arrange files in categories. The scheme is called the *Hierarchical File System (HFS)*. It's similar to a directory tree. When you call up the list of files in a *folder*, you get only a summarized list, equivalent to the list of subdirectories, rather than the list of all the files. This saves screen space and reduces clutter, especially if a folder contains many files. A file-location program can be used to speed up the process of locating files. *See also* DIRECTORY, DIRECTORY TREE, FILE, FOLDER, *and* MACINTOSH.

High-density diskette

A *high-density (HD) diskette* is a magnetic storage medium. The earliest diskettes could only hold a few kilobytes (K, equal to 1024 bytes or characters) of data, but engineers kept working to increase the number of bytes that could be stored in a given amount of disk surface area. Thus, the *single-density diskette* was soon supplanted by the *double-density (DD) diskette*, and a few years later, HD diskettes became commonplace. Today, all new diskette drives are manufactured to work with HD diskettes.

A 5.25-inch HD diskette can store 1.2MB when formatted for use with IBM-compatible PCs. Unformatted, an HD diskette has room for about 1.6MB. A formatted 3.5-inch HD diskette can hold 1.44MB, somewhat more than its physically larger cousin. Unless your computer is an old machine with DD-only diskette drives, you'll probably want to use HD diskettes because they let you get more data into the same amount of physical space.

Researchers are constantly trying to find ways to increase diskette density. One recent development involves the use of an optical guidance system within the drive, allowing the read/write head to move much more precisely over the diskette surface. This technology, called *Floptical* (a contraction of "floppy optical"), multiplies the capacity of HD diskettes several times. *See also* DISK CAPACITY, DISKETTE, DOUBLE-DENSITY DISKETTE, *and* FLOPTICAL DISKETTE AND DRIVE.

High-level language

The term *high-level language* refers to any of several programming languages used in computer work. A few examples that you might have heard of C, C++, BASIC, Fortran, COBOL, Pascal, and LISP.

High-level languages each have advantages in some types of work, and shortcomings in others. BASIC and Fortran, for example, are good for relatively simple scientific problems, but not very good for corporate accounting. On the other hand, COBOL is good for the businessperson, but isn't much use to a student trying to solve science problems.

A high-level language consists of English-like statements. This lets people work with computers on a quasi-conversational level. However, a computer "thinks" in *machine language*, a *low-level language* consisting entirely of the binary digits (bits) 1 and 0. It is necessary, in machine language, to instruct the computer according to every minute detail of its operation. Programmers don't write in machine language; instead, some form of translation, such as an *assembler*, *compiler*, or *interpreter*, is used to convert the high-level language into low-level commands. *See also* ASSEMBLER AND ASSEMBLY LANGUAGE, COMPILER, INTERPRETER, *and* MACHINE LANGUAGE.

Highlighting

Highlighting

Highlighting refers to various ways of making text, menu items, or icons stand out on a display screen. Highlighted items might be brighter, different in color, or reversed with respect to unhighlighted ones.

In word processing. If you have a color monitor, there are several ways in which text can be highlighted. The table shows the different ways in which characters were highlighted in the program used to write the manuscript for this book. This scheme allowed the use of hidden codes for different typestyles. Once the color combinations had been memorized, it was easy to work with the software, and the screen was kept free of clutter and gibberish.

Some ways a program might indicate typestyles on a monitor

Typestyle	Appearance on monitor
Normal type	White on black background
Boldface	Red on black background
Underlining	Green on black background
Italics	Yellow on blue background

Highlighting can be used for other things besides indicating the typestyle. For example, you might want to highlight words to be used in the index of a long report. You could do this as you wrote the report. When you were finished writing, the software would make a list of the highlighted words, along with the page number on which each word appeared. *See also* HIDDEN CODES *and* WORD PROCESSING.

In menu-driven systems. When using a graphical user interface (GUI) or menu-driven interface like Windows or the Macintosh, you can highlight items in a list. By clicking the mouse repeatedly, you can scroll through a set of options. Double-clicking will usually cause the computer to carry out the function indicated by the highlighted item.

Highlighting in a GUI or menu-driven application usually consists of reversing the type and the background. For example, if text is normally black on a white background, highlighting will make the letters white on a black or dark blue background. The term *highlight* is also sometimes used as an alternative to *select* when referring to the process of indicating a block of text that you want to delete, move, or otherwise work with. *See also* GRAPHICAL USER INTERFACE *and* MENU-DRIVEN SOFTWARE.

High-resolution monitor

One of the most important monitor or display specifications is its *image resolution*. A *high-resolution monitor* has excellent image resolution, meaning that it can show fine details.

High-resolution printer

Pixels. The smallest element in a display image is called a *pixel* (picture element). The image resolution is given in terms of the number of pixels horizontally, and the number of pixels vertically, that the display is capable of showing. The larger these numbers, the higher the image resolution.

Some monitors can show more than 1000 pixels horizontally, and more than 750 pixels vertically. When looking at the specifications for a monitor, keep the numbers 1000 × 750 in mind as an arbitrary cutoff between medium and high resolution.

Another specification you'll frequently hear is the *dot pitch*. This can range from about 0.53 mils down to 0.22 mils or less. A *mil* is a thousandth (0.001) of an inch. The smaller the dot pitch, the better the image resolution. A typical SVGA (Super Video Graphics Array), for example, has a dot pitch of 0.28 mils. That means the dots are about 0.00028, or 280 millionths, of an inch wide.

Screen size. Pixel numbers and dot pitch aren't the only things that matter. Ease of image viewing also depends on the actual size of the monitor screen, usually given as a diagonal measure in inches or centimeters. A tiny screen, say of just five inches, might have over 1000 × 750 pixels, but you'd have to squint or use a magnifying glass to make out the details. Such a monitor would probably be worse than a low-resolution unit because you would get eye strain.

If you're interested in buying a "high-res" monitor, it's a good idea to get one with the largest possible screen size. This will minimize eye strain, and will also allow you to place the monitor at a good distance from your face and body, reducing your exposure to ELF fields.

What do you need? For some applications, such as word processing, spreadsheets, and nongraphical databases, high resolution is not necessary. If these are the only applications you use, you might not need, nor want to spend the extra money for, a high-resolution monitor. Medium-resolution monitors can be purchased for under $100.

If you expect to be doing anything involving graphics, however, you will find your work much easier if you have a high-resolution unit. These start at around $250, and go up from there. The exact price depends on several factors including the screen size, refresh rate, interlacing/non-interlacing, and dot pitch. *See also* DOT PITCH, IMAGE RESOLUTION, MONITOR, *and* PIXEL.

High-resolution printer

A *high-resolution printer* is a printer that can create detailed, "crisp" hardcopies. For text, this translates into professional-looking, easy-to-read letters and symbols. For graphics, a high-resolution printer gives you the best possible image resolution.

High-resolution printer

Dots per inch (DPI) is the most common expression for printer resolution. The more dots per inch, the easier it is to read text or resolve graphical images. A figure of 300 DPI or more is considered high-resolution.

Dot-matrix printers. Years ago, dot-matrix printers had low-resolution printout that was hard for some people to read. People used to dread receiving long documents produced by dot-matrix printers. This problem has been largely overcome as the resolution of dot-matrix printers has improved.

A good dot-matrix printer creates near-letter-quality (NLQ) text by passing over each character two or more times. With each pass, the dots are laid down on the paper in slightly different places. This reduces the "dotty" appearance of a manuscript, effectively increasing the DPI rating.

A dot-matrix printer can be used to print graphics. The detail depends on how fine the dots are in the image. The more dots in a given length or area, the better the quality of the printed graphic.

Low- to medium-resolution dot-matrix printers can produce solid black and can crosshatch to produce the effect of shading. This is good enough for crude line art, but not for sophisticated illustration. Printers with high DPI ratings, and therefore with high resolution, can create shades of gray by laying down dots in a fine pattern. The darkness of the shade is determined by the density of the dots on the paper.

Inkjet printers. All inkjet printers have moderate to high resolution. The copy is produced, as the name implies, by microscopic jets of ink. The ink can be black or any combination of the three primary pigments (red, yellow, and blue), thereby producing color printouts.

There are some problems with inkjet printers, especially the older designs. The ink has a tendency to smudge unless you let it dry adequately before handling the copy. With some units, special paper is required to minimize the capillary action ("blotter effect") that can blur images. However, these printers are excellent for most graphics work, especially if you want reasonably good quality for the lowest possible cost. A low-cost inkjet can produce high-resolution copy of 300 by 600 DPI.

Laser printers. The best type of printer, in terms of resolution, is a laser printer. These are the most expensive of all printers. If you are willing to spend the money, and especially if you intend to do sophisticated graphics or desktop publishing, this is the printer of choice. Laser printers work very much like photocopying machines. The resolution of a good laser printer can't be beat in the personal-computing industry.

Histogram

Laser printers have some limitations, however. The least expensive ones are rather slow. If you print out huge quantities of text, such a printer takes a long time to complete the job. The way around this is to spend a lot of money. The fastest laser printers cost $10,000 or more. Another factor is that laser printers often cost more per page to operate than dot-matrix or inkjet printers. *See also* DOT-MATRIX PRINTER, IMAGE RESOLUTION, INKJET PRINTER, *and* LASER PRINTER.

Histogram

A *histogram* is a specialized form of columnar graph that is used to show distributions. You can recognize a histogram by its vertical rectangles. Histograms are simple and easy to read, but they are not as precise as continuous-curve graphs.

Income distribution. Suppose you want to know the distribution of income for a certain region. You want to find out the distribution for the urban areas, and also for the rural areas, within the region. You arrange a survey, making sure to get a good cross-sectional sample of the population.

The drawing (page 520) is a dual histogram on which the results of this imaginary survey are graphed. Income ranges appear on the horizontal axis, while the percentage of total families is on the vertical axis. The black vertical rectangles represent the income distribution for urban areas; the empty rectangles represent the results for the rural areas within the region.

To do a spot check of the validity of this histogram, you might add up the heights of the black columns, and then add up the heights of the empty columns. Both sums should equal 100, the total percentage of families surveyed. (It's impossible for the total percentage in any case to be anything but 100.)

If you were to construct such a histogram "manually" based on a table of incomes for the regions, you'd have to spend hours at the task. A computer with good presentation graphics software, on the other hand, could cut your work to just a fraction of the time.

Histogram software. Most presentation graphics programs let you create histograms. You can use any kind of printer to get hardcopies, although color printers have an advantage because they allow for more types of shading, and they create a more attractive presentation.

If you're only interested in occasional, imprecise columnar graphing, a low-end package will be sufficient for your needs. For sales, business reports, and brochures intended for publication, you should get high-

Holographic data storage

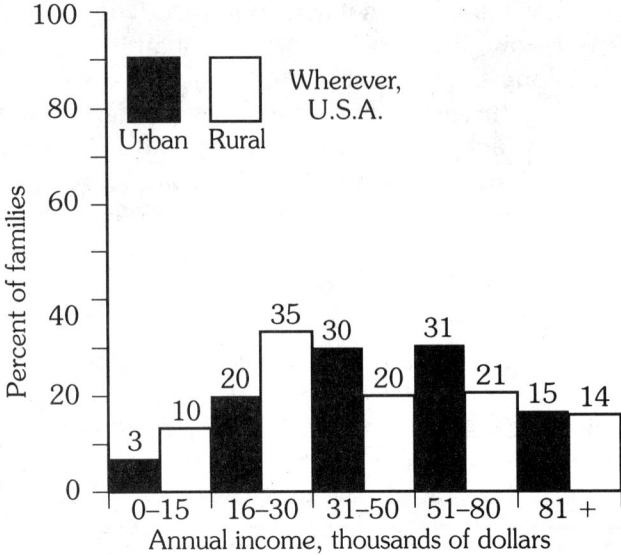

The histogram shows hypothetical income distribution.

end graphics software as part of your desktop publishing tools. Shop around for the latest features, and try to check the packages out in real-time, in the stores. Get the brochures for the packages you're considering; take them home; compare features and cost. It never pays to rush a large, important software purchase. *See also* COLUMNAR GRAPH, DESKTOP PUBLISHING, GRAPHICS, *and* PRESENTATION GRAPHICS.

Holographic data storage

A *hologram* is a special kind of photograph that contains the information for a true three-dimensional (3-D) scene. Perhaps you've seen holograms on credit cards, in novelty shops, or in physics classes.

An extra dimension. The principles behind holography are rather sophisticated, involving laser-light interference patterns, and a full discussion is beyond the scope of this article. A good hologram is spectacular and unforgettable, however, whether or not you know how it works. When you look at a well-made hologram, you have a vivid sense of depth in the scene. More important, objects that are eclipsed when viewed from one direction will come into view as you move with respect to the hologram. It's as if a miniature model of the scene is right there in front of you, within a cube instead of on a flat surface. As incredible as it seems, a 2-D surface can contain all the information necessary to produce a 3-D scene.

As you probably know, there's much more "substance" to a spatial volume than to a surface area. The surface area of an object increases in proportion to the square of the diameter, but the volume increases in proportion to the cube of the diameter. Suppose that three dimensions of computer data could somehow be encoded onto a flat surface? The people at a company called *Tamarack Storage Devices* decided to try to do it. The result was a *holographic data storage* device.

Super-high-density diskettes. Holographic data storage uses visible light to read and write data. The medium tested by Tamarack, a "tile" about 60 millimeters square, is sensitive to light, like a photographic film. It has up to 40 layers on which image data can be written and from which the data can be read later.

The writing process uses two laser beams, as shown in the drawing. Lasers, unlike ordinary light, have a defined, constant wavelength, and the combined light from two beams produces interference patterns in the storage medium. The nature of the interference between laser X and laser Y determines the depth at which the data is written. One tile can hold approximately one gigabyte (GB) of data—more than the capacity of a CD-ROM in considerably less physical space.

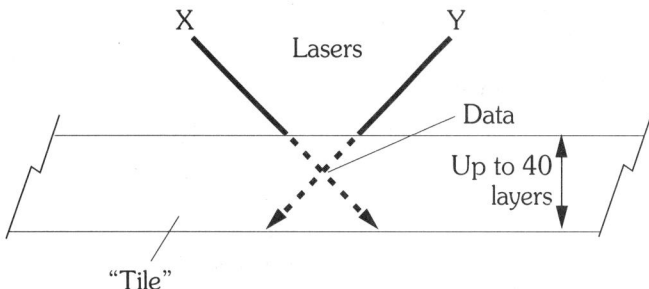

Lasers write data onto photosensitive "tile."

Tamarack Storage Devices hopes to perfect holographic data storage to allow 5.25-inch diskettes with capacities of 30GB or more. That's more than 25,000 times the capacity of a high-density (HD), 5.25-inch magnetic diskette. Although the drives will probably be rather expensive to start with, prices should drop once the hardware catches on. *See also* CD-ROM *and* DISK CAPACITY.

Home computer

See DESKTOP COMPUTER.

Home-design software

One of the best features of computer graphics is the fact that you never need erasers, correction fluid, paste, double-stick tape, or

Home-design softtware

photocopy machines. With *home-design software*, you can make all kinds of drawings, including floor plans and blueprints. You can view drawings on the monitor, and save them on disk. Home-design software is a form of *computer-aided design (CAD)* that almost anyone can learn to work with in a few hours.

Creativity enhancement. When you're creating a complex drawing using a pen or pencil, you might refrain from making experimental changes or adjustments because you don't want to deal with the messiness. Thus, you might leave a doorway where you'd rather not have it; you might want more windows in a room, but leave them out. Who knows how many times this kind of thing has affected the way a home was ultimately built?

On a computer, it's easy and hassle-free to move doors, add windows, or relocate bathrooms. Clicking and dragging with the mouse, and perhaps typing in a few things on the keyboard, is all that's necessary. Like any other software, there's a learning curve involved, of course, and this might at first be daunting. Once you plunge in, however, you'll probably have so much fun that learning will not be a problem.

Walk-through. The best architects in the world can envision their work before the first brick is laid or the first nail driven. Although not many laypeople can do this, high-end home-design programs can help you see how your design will look in real life, even if you are not a professional architect.

When you've completed a tentative floor plan and included everything down to the last lamp, chair, and wastebasket, high-end programs let you "walk through" the house. You get an animated perspective of how the interior will look. It's a primitive form of virtual reality. In fact, some of the most advanced home-design software is designed so that you can don a head-mounted display (HMD) and get a truly three-dimensional tour of the interior of your dream house or building. If you find that a window is one foot too far to the right in the children's bedroom, you can go back to the blueprint and drag it a foot to the left. If a door is in the wrong place, you can move it. Little details like this can make a big difference in the end result.

For more information. Home-design software is not powerful enough to actually turn a layperson into an architect. You'll still have to hire professionals to do the final design. With home-design software, however, you can tell your architect how you'd like your new home to be arranged. *See also* COMPUTER-AIDED DESIGN *and* VIRTUAL REALITY.

Home key

The *Home key* performs certain special functions depending on the software being used. On IBM-compatible PC keyboards, the Home key is usually found in a group of six keys just to the right of the main part of the keyboard (see the drawing).

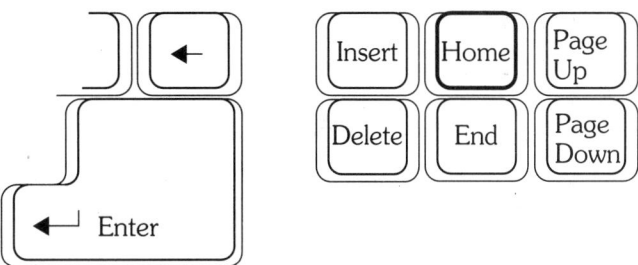

The Home key is one of six keys in a pad to the right of the main keyboard.

In some word processing programs, the Home key, when pressed alone, moves the cursor to the top left of the screen. In other programs, it moves the cursor to the beginning of the current line. Pressing the Ctrl and Home keys simultaneously, that is, Ctrl-Home, moves the cursor to the very beginning of a document in many word processors. In these respects, the operation of the Home key complements that of the End key, which moves the cursor down within the document. *See also* END KEY.

Host bus

In a computer, the central processing unit (CPU) is in constant communication with the random-access memory (RAM). The CPU is like the part of your brain that issues commands to the rest of your body; the RAM is like your moment-to-moment conscious memory. The path over which the data flows is known as the *host bus*. It's also sometimes called the *CPU bus*, the *memory bus*, or the *RAM bus*. It is, in effect, a stream of conscious computer thought.

Suppose you want to work with a file called SAMPLE.DOC, which is on one of your diskettes. You find the diskette and place it in drive A. You open this file to read the contents of SAMPLE.DOC from the diskette in drive A. When the text appears on your display, it has been loaded into RAM.

If you want to change something in SAMPLE.DOC, you can use your mouse or keyboard to make the changes. Maybe you want to add a sentence, take a paragraph out, or correct a misspelled word. As you do these things, your CPU is "thinking," and is communicating with the RAM, via the host bus, to ensure that the changes you specify are made. When you're done making the changes, you click on menu items or press keys to save the file. The contents of RAM, now having been changed, are overwritten on the diskette in drive A, under the filename SAMPLE.DOC. (The old file might be switched to a backup called SAMPLE.BAK in case you decide you want to undo the changes you have made.)

The drawing shows the interaction among the diskette drive, the RAM, and the CPU in this situation. The host bus is shown by a heavy, double-arrowed line. *See also* BUS.

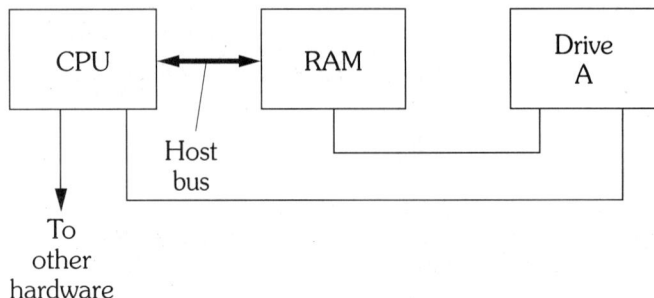

The host bus provides the link between the CPU and the RAM.

Hot key

When you're working in a graphical user interface (GUI) such as Windows or the Macintosh, you've probably noticed that menu items each have one letter underlined and/or displayed in a different color from the other letters. Or there might be some combination of keys specified, such as *Alt+F4* or *Ctrl+B*, next to each menu item. These letters and keys are the *hot keys* for the options.

If you don't have a mouse or trackball with which to select options in a menu, you can use the keyboard to pick the option you want using the hot key or keys. For example, you might press the Alt-E key combination to select Edit, or Alt-F for File. In Windows, a hot key is also called an *accelerator key*.

The hot key designator is usually, but not always, the first letter in the label. If there are two labels in a menu that begin with the same letter, the hot key for one of the labels will be some letter after the first. You must therefore pay close attention, so you don't inadvertently bring up the wrong option.

Hot keys can speed up some functions in menu-driven software, and many computer users prefer them for these functions. For example, it's sometimes quicker to press Alt-E than to move the mouse around until the pointer is on Edit, and then click the button. The usefulness of hot keys is limited, however. If you want to get the full benefit of a GUI, you need a mouse or trackball. *See also* MENU-DRIVEN SOFTWARE, MOUSE, *and* TRACKBALL.

Hot link

Suppose you're printing out a file from a hard disk or diskette, and suddenly you find a mistake in the file. The printer hasn't yet reached the part of the file where the error exists. Wouldn't it be nice if you could correct the error in the file even as it was being printed, and get a hardcopy with the correction included?

Cold versus hot. Most older PCs and software are not equipped to deal with this kind of last-moment change. Once you've told your printer to print a file, the contents of the file goes into memory, and from there, the data goes to the paper. If you want to correct an error, you must stop the printer, correct the mistake on the hard disk or diskette, and issue the print command again. The printer will start over from the beginning of the file. With long files, this wastes time, paper, ink, and your patience.

In this situation, the link between your PC and your printer is a *cold link*. Once it has been established, things proceed automatically, and you have no active control over the data being sent. If you have Windows, Macintosh System 7, or IBM OS/2 software, however, you're in luck. You can correct an error in a document even as it is being sent from your PC to your printer, modem, or destination on a local area network (LAN). If you make the correction before the error actually reaches the destination, the corrected data, not the original erroneous data, will be transmitted. This is a *hot link*.

Dynamic data exchange. A variation on the hot-link theme, called *dynamic data exchange (DDE),* keeps data updated among files. Windows, Macintosh, and OS/2 are equipped with DDE.

Often, when one file changes, the data in other files changes too. Without DDE, you must change each affected file separately. It's not easy to remember all the places where such a change must be made, let alone find the patience to do it. With DDE, when something changes, every affected piece of data is updated by the computer, even among different applications. It's as if your system is one gigantic database, keeping track of all its information without your having to follow up on things. *See also* DYNAMIC DATA EXCHANGE *and* OBJECT LINKING AND EMBEDDING.

Human engineering

Human engineering refers to the art of making machines easy to use. This is often also called *user-friendliness*.

In software. A user-friendly computer program allows the machine to be operated by someone who knows nothing about computers. Bank automatic-teller machines are a good example of devices that employ user-friendly programming. Increasingly, libraries are computerizing their card catalogs, and it's important that the programs be user-friendly so that people can find the books they want. The most significant example in personal computing is the graphical user interface (GUI). The Macintosh and Windows software schemes employ GUIs that are intuitive, easy to learn, and highly efficient. *See also* GRAPHICAL USER INTERFACE, MACINTOSH, *and* WINDOWS.

In personal robotics. In the coming years, human engineering will play a role in the development of user-friendly robots that will carry out orders efficiently, reliably, and reasonably fast. Ideally, you'll be able to say, "Go to the kitchen and get me a banana, please," and (assuming you have bananas) the robot will return in a minute or two, holding one, and bring it right to you. This ability is not easy to program into a machine, however, as researchers have found out. Even the simplest tasks are, in terms of sheer digital operations, horribly complicated.

Artificial intelligence (AI) helps to make computers and robots user-friendly. It's much easier to communicate with a machine that's "smart," compared with one that's "stupid." It is especially enjoyable if the machine can learn from its mistakes or show ability to reason. *See also* ARTIFICIAL INTELLIGENCE, COMMONSENSE SUMMER PROJECT, HEURISTIC KNOWLEDGE, *and* PERSONAL ROBOTS.

Talking with machines. Speech recognition and speech synthesis help greatly in making computers and robots user-friendly. It's much easier and more pleasant to converse with a machine, rather than typing in commands and watching data on a monitor. In addition, these features make computers fully accessible to a large group of physically challenged people. *See also* SPEECH RECOGNITION *and* SPEECH SYNTHESIS.

Hung system

See CRASH.

Hybrid computer technology

Most computers are digital machines, working with combinations of the two binary digits (bits) 0 and 1. These two states can be represented as off/on, low/high, minus/plus, false/true, green/red, or any other easy-to-distinguish duality. The power of the modern computer comes from its ability to work with huge quantities of these bits at high speed.

Digital computer technology has emerged as the most practical way to build personal computers, but there are other major approaches that have been used in computers for specialized applications, especially in the aerospace industry. These include *analog computer technology* and the *neural network. Hybrid computer technology* refers to the use of more than one of these schemes in the same machine.

Hybrid computer technology

Analog technology. Analog quantities vary continuously, while digital quantities exist only in discrete levels, or states (such as bits). One good example of the difference between analog and digital quantities is found in graphics.

One way to represent an object is by means of a bitmap. In this scheme, any two-dimensional shape can be approximated by filling in certain pixels (picture elements) on a monitor screen. This scheme can be used to represent any line, curve, or region, as long as the detail is not so fine that it can't be resolved by the grid of pixels. The big advantage of bitmapping is the fact that its brute-force approach almost always works, at least fairly well. The main shortcoming of bitmapping is the fact that it almost never provides a perfect rendition; it's usually an approximation. You might think of a bitmap as a "digital drawing."

The other main graphical scheme is object-oriented. It uses straight lines, circles, ellipses, parabolas, hyperbolas, and other shapes to assemble things in the computer's "brain." The computer itself is still working as a digital machine, but it is thinking about analog objects. The big advantage of object-oriented graphics, also known as vector graphics, is that they can precisely represent a variety of things. The more curves that are memorized as codes or formulas, the greater the variety of objects that the computer can render perfectly. You might think of an object-oriented graphic as an "analog drawing."

Imagine a program that makes use of the best features of bitmapped and object-oriented graphics. Perhaps some parts of an object or scene might lend themselves best to bitmapping; other parts might require the object-oriented approach. You could call the resulting software "hybrid graphics."

Neural networks. Neural technology is an attempt to mimic the structure of a human brain. Neural networks are designed to identify patterns, rather than to solve problems by brute force. Instead of working with binary digits, neural networks juggle the relationships among causes and effects.

Neural networks learn from their mistakes, as people do. Thus, with time, the intelligence of a neural network improves, even in the absence of a human programmer. Such similarity to human behavior is one of the criteria that researchers use in pursuit of artificial intelligence (AI).

Neural networks were first developed during the 1950s. The technology was left behind as the digital revolution picked up momentum. To some researchers today, neural networks offer little, if any, hope for the future of computing. Others believe in this alternative technology with almost revolutionary fervor. The reality probably lies between these two extremes.

Hypermedia

Digital limits. Many researchers think that digital computer technology has proven itself, and that alternative technologies have lost the battle for survival. There's no question that digital technology is rapidly advancing. Digital machines are becoming faster, and capable of working with more data, every year. It would be a mistake, however, to throw away all of the research that has been done in alternative and hybrid technologies.

The useful upper limit to digital clock speed depends on how fast the charge carriers move within the integrated circuits and wires inside a digital machine. The upper limit to RAM (random-access memory) capacity is perhaps dictated by the size of the electron. Although we aren't very close to these limits yet, they are coming within sight. Researchers are working on optical computer technology to allow faster movement of data within computers. There is also talk of a single-electron memory. New architectures, such as reduced-instruction-set computing (RISC), boost speed and overall power of digital machines.

What will happen, however, when theoretical barriers are reached? The answer, of course, is that scientists and engineers will try to find ways around them.

This gives rise to questions, philosophical as well as scientific, of great interest to AI enthusiasts. Can a purely digital machine have intelligence comparable to that of a human being? Or does human thought involve something more than digital impulses traveling among atoms within the body? If human consciousness does involve something more, might this be provided by a hybrid machine? Might analog and/or neural-network technology, in combination with digital technology, produce a computer that is as smart as its creator? If we build a machine that's as smart as we are, how will we know we have done it?

To those who believe that hybrid and alternative technologies have been permanently relegated to the back burner of computer research, history lends advice: Watch the pot. *See also* ANALOG, ANALOG COMPUTER TECHNOLOGY, ALTERNATIVE COMPUTER TECHNOLOGY, ARTIFICIAL INTELLIGENCE, ARTIFICIAL LIFE, BITMAP, BITMAPPED GRAPHICS, CLOCK SPEED, COMPUTER CONSCIOUSNESS, COMPUTER GENERATIONS, COMPUTER POWER, DIGITAL, DIGITAL COMPUTER TECHNOLOGY, MEMORY CAPACITY, NEURAL NETWORK, OBJECT-ORIENTED GRAPHICS, OPTICAL COMPUTER TECHNOLOGY, RANDOM-ACCESS MEMORY, *and* SINGLE-ELECTRON MEMORY.

Hypermedia

Hypermedia means "enhanced media," and refers to application software used with advanced operating systems. Hypermedia makes use of text, graphics, and audio to create a user-friendly operating environment. At its best, it's almost like communicating with another person.

Text only. Traditionally, when you access a text file from hard disk or diskette, you see the first page come up on the screen. You can then read the document by scrolling, line-by-line or page-by-page, down through the file. It's like reading a book, except that you press buttons rather than flip sheets of paper.

As you become better acquainted with word processing, you can learn to find specific items within a document. You can use a search command, for example, to jump instantly to a word or phrase. This is useful for editing, but research is quite another thing.

Imagine you're working with a document file 300K long—about 250 screensful. Suppose you want to read everything in the document having to do with the term *zygote*. You can use the search (or equivalent) command just as you would use an index and find every occurrence of that word. It might appear, say, 48 times within your document. You could jump to every single one of them, reading the text around it, hoping to catch all the discussion involving the term. By the 25th or 30th reading, you'd probably mutter to yourself, "There must be a better way to do this." There is: *hypertext*, the text-only version of hypermedia.

In hypertext, the writer can set up intuitive paths of reasoning within a document, and among different documents, in much the same way as this encyclopedia is cross-referenced. The reader can follow these paths at will. Expert use of hypertext requires a certain level of experience on the part of the writer, as well as the reader. If you are writing in hypertext, you must anticipate, and fulfill in advance, the needs of your readers. Writing in hypertext is like word processing and programming combined.

When a hypertext-experienced reader works with a publication written by a hypertext-savvy writer, it's like using a highly refined program. You might click the mouse on a certain word or phrase, and have a window appear in which related information is presented. You might click again and again, scrolling through several different related "takes" on the subject.

Text plus. The hypermedia system developed by Apple Computer, the makers of the Macintosh system, uses a programming language called *HyperCard*, which can be easily learned by most computer users. As an object-oriented language, it uses easy-to-recognize things, such as buttons or icons, to guide the user along, so it's not necessary to memorize a huge set of commands.

In HyperCard, data is arranged in units called *cards*, which resemble the records in a database system. Within each card are two types of buttons for giving commands. One set of buttons guides you around within the card; the other set lets you roam the whole document or

Hyphenation

publication among all cards. There can be just a few cards, or there can be hundreds.

If this encyclopedia were written in HyperCard, this article would exist on a card, and the cross-references would be buttons guiding you to other cards (articles). You could click on a cross-reference, and the data would appear in a window, along with the current article. You would not have to turn any pages, and you'd have both "takes" in front of you at the same time.

In addition to text, HyperCard lets you work with graphics and sound, creating an environment with animation. This is ideal for computer-assisted instruction (CAI), and it has been used in schools to tutor students and to teach specialized topics and skills.

Hypermedia is a scaled-down form of *multimedia*. In true multimedia, networks of computers are used, both Macintosh and IBM-compatible. This greatly expands the amount of data that any one user can access. In hypermedia, the interactive environment is confined to a single machine, although it can serve as a springboard for access to large multimedia networks. *See also* ANIMATION, CD-ROM, COMPUTER-ASSISTED INSTRUCTION, INTERACTIVE TECHNOLOGY, MACINTOSH, MULTIMEDIA, *and* OBJECT-ORIENTED PROGRAMMING.

Hyphenation

Hyphenation is the splitting-up of a word between two lines of a printed document. When a word must be hyphenated because it's too long for one line, the hyphen is always the last character to appear on that line.

Automatic hyphenation. Computer programs exist that will automatically hyphenate words for you if they're too long for a line, or if they will cause the word spacing to be so irregular as to be unsightly. A program with automatic hyphenation "knows" where words should be hyphenated because it has a huge database containing thousands of words, along with the most common dividing points within them.

Unfortunately, these programs aren't foolproof, nor can they take the place of a good dictionary. No automatic-hyphenation program contains all the words you will use during your word processing lifetime. For complicated reasons, errors are almost certain to occur if you don't check *every* hyphenated line after running a document through an automatic-hyphenation program. This isn't difficult; you need only look down the right margin for hyphens.

Automatic hyphenation is much the same as search-and-replace or spell-checking operations. When these functions are used the right way, verifying every instance where the computer suggests or makes a change, they can help even the best writer to do better work. Used hastily, they will not only fail to correct all the errors, but they'll "correct" words that are correct to begin with, thereby introducing new, and often embarrassing, mistakes.

Hard versus soft. Some words incorporate hyphens, but should never be split, even at the hyphen. A good example is a surname consisting of two parts, like *Dyer-Bennett*. This is called *hard hyphenation.* The hyphen is like a letter in the word, and the word itself is in effect one syllable that is never split between lines. Most word processing programs have a provision for switching between hard hyphenation and *soft hyphenation.*

In hard-hyphenation mode, the computer will never split a word between lines, even when there is a hyphen within the word. As you write the surname *Dyer-Bennett*, it will stay on a single line. If it happens to come at the end of a line at just the right place for a split at the hyphen, the wordwrap feature will move the whole word to the beginning of the next line.

The only way you can split words in hard-hyphenation mode is to press the Enter key after typing a hyphen. This will move the cursor down to the start of the next line, but it's probably not a good idea. If you later edit your work, you'll probably get an unattractive half-line of text ending with a hyphen. Your readers might wonder why you broke the word when there was plenty of room left on the line.

In soft-hyphenation mode, words can be broken automatically by the software as necessary to prevent text from running past the right margin. In this mode, hyphenated words are treated like separate words. Your computer will split *Dyer-Bennet* just as readily as it will split *read-only* because the machine doesn't recognize the fact that one of the words is a surname.

You'll have to make certain, when using soft hyphenation, that non-splittable words aren't split. That means you must proofread your work, even if you have the most advanced word processing software in the world. Computers are only as smart as their operators. *See also* ENTER KEY, HARD RETURNS, *and* WORD PROCESSING.

IBM

International Business Machines (IBM) is a large U.S. corporation, best known in recent years for its PCs. The first IBM PC was made available in 1981. The abbreviation *PC* was originally coined by IBM but it has become generic, like the word *kleenex*. Today, almost all small computers are called PCs.

You will often hear about *PC clones* or *IBM-compatible* hardware and software, referring to the many computers manufactured and distributed that are similar (and sometimes practically identical) to IBM models. The other major computer type in the U.S. today is *Macintosh*, manufactured by Apple Computer, Inc. IBM-compatibles and Macs have similar memory, storage capacity, and processing speed, but the software systems are somewhat different. Some people prefer IBM-compatible machines; others prefer Macintosh computers easier to work with. There is an increasing amount of overlap between the two systems. *See also* IBM-COMPATIBLE PCS *and* MACINTOSH.

IBM-compatible PCs

IBM-compatible PCs, also known as *clones*, are computers that work like those manufactured by IBM. There are hundreds, if not thousands, of IBM-compatible PCs on the market. The fact that there are so many machines, and that they're named as they are, is a tribute to the original IBM personal computer, called the *PC*. In fact, personal computers in general are now called PCs, a generic reminder of the existence of IBM.

IC

If you can run software on one IBM PC clone, you can run it on any other PC clone, provided that there is enough RAM (random-access memory) and disk capacity. The two main software systems that have historically been used with IBM-compatible PCs are Microsoft Corporation's DOS and Windows. A third system, IBM's OS/2, is becoming increasingly popular as well. Several other companies have versions of DOS that will work with IBM PC clones.

IBM-compatible PCs represent one of two classes of personal computers available today. The other major line is *Macintosh*, manufactured by Apple Computer. Older Macintosh computers are not directly compatible with IBM computers or clones. However, some of the newer Macintosh machines can run IBM-compatible software. *See also* CLONE, DOS, MACINTOSH, OS/2, *and* WINDOWS.

IC

See INTEGRATED CIRCUIT.

Icon

An *icon* is a symbol that provides an intuitive, easy-to-recognize indication of what will happen when you click the mouse on an option in a graphical user interface (GUI). GUIs were designed to make computers easier to use, and especially, easier to learn to work with, than older command-driven software.

In a command-driven interface, you must memorize a large number of cryptic orders, or commands, and type them into the computer. This is like a fill-in-the-blank test. If you don't remember the command, you can't use the machine until you look the command up in an instruction manual or help file. Also, if you are a poor typist, using this interface can be frustrating even if you remember all the commands.

Software engineers at Apple Computer developed the Macintosh line of computers with a GUI interface that works more like a multiple-choice test as a way around the problems of the command-driven interface. Microsoft followed with its Windows software for IBM-compatible PCs. The choices in these GUIs were originally shown as words in boxes. However, the addition of icons made GUIs even easier to use. The drawing shows some icons you might see in GUIs that you use. *See also* COMMAND-DRIVEN SOFTWARE, GRAPHICAL USER INTERFACE, *and* MENU-DRIVEN SOFTWARE.

Ideal circuit or component

An *ideal component* is an electronic device that behaves perfectly. A mechanical switch is a real-life component that's practically perfect: it's either all the way on, or all the way off. When a battery is connected to a switch, the resulting voltage is either 100% of the battery voltage, or zero. The two states are clearly defined, and they're predictable. They're the same "high" and "low" (digital 1 and 0) every time the switch changes state (see the drawing).

Ideal circuit or component

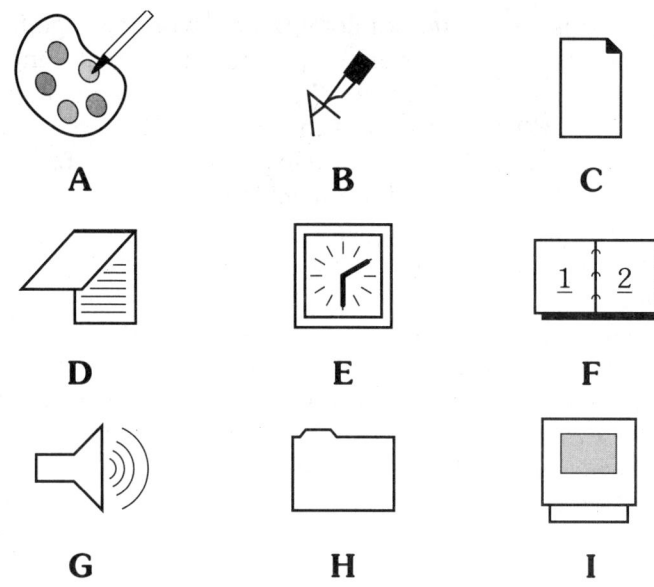

Draw (A), write (B), document (C), notepad (D), clock (E), calendar (F), sound (G), file (H), and MultiFinder (I) icons.

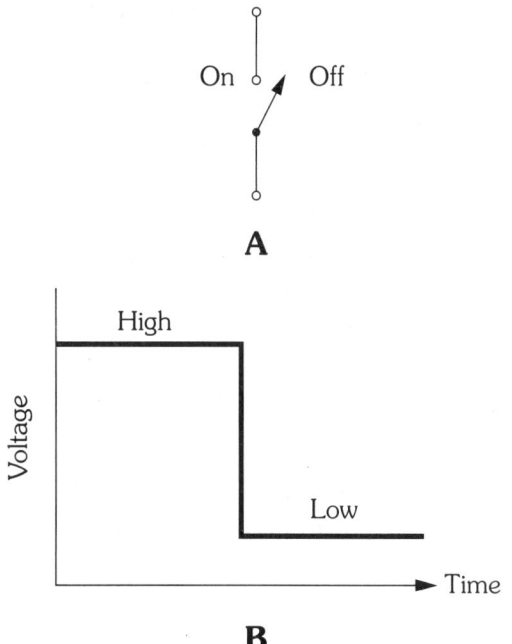

A switch (A) is a nearly ideal component. Digital signals (B) come from nearly ideal circuits.

Computers have millions of electronic switches, using microscopic transistors within their integrated circuit (IC) "chips." These switches are, for practical purposes, ideal, just like mechanical ones. They're many times smaller, and many times faster, however.

IDE technology

An *ideal circuit* is a collection of components working together in perfect harmony. This is a hypothetical thing, not a real thing. You will never see an ideal circuit in real life, although once in a while something comes close. The ideal is the state of affairs for which engineers strive. It's the mathematical example they use to represent the best possible performance for a machine.

Sometimes a circuit or component that would be ideal, or nearly so, for one purpose would be far from ideal in another application. An example is one of the IC transistors in a computer. It works almost perfectly for switching the voltages that contribute to your computer's "thought process;" that's the application for which it was designed. The same transistor would burn out, however, if you hooked it up to switch your whole computer system on and off. It handles tiny currents with precision and speed, but a large current would simply "blow it away."

Circuits that are nearly ideal, such as computers, are often temperamental. Your PC is designed to work from utility outlets that supply about 120 volts. If this drops to 80 volts, your machine won't work. Some low-precision devices, such as flashlights, can tolerate large changes in operating conditions; high-precision systems, like computers, cannot. Changes in the power-supply voltage can cause your computer to crash. Another related problem is transients on the power line. *See also* BROWNOUT, CRASH, POWER SUPPLY, TRANSIENT SUPPRESSION, *and* UNINTERRUPTIBLE POWER SUPPLY.

IDE technology

One of the most common hard disk drive designs makes use of a scheme known as *integrated drive electronics*, usually abbreviated *IDE technology*. These drives are sometimes called *AT drives* because they were originally designed for use with the 80286AT microprocessor.

In IDE technology, the control electronics are contained within the drive enclosure, which is roughly the size of a diskette drive. One of the big advantages of IDE technology is that it is easy to interface with most PCs using Intel microprocessors. Many PC motherboards have an IDE interface built in, allowing the operation of one or two IDE hard drives.

An IDE drive costs anywhere from about $100 to $500, depending on its capacity. The least expensive have around 250MB of storage; the costliest have upwards of 1000MB (one gigabyte) of storage.

A good IDE drive works fast and with precision. However, for high-end applications requiring the best possible hard drive performance, SCSI technology provides better results than IDE technology. The acronym is pronounced "scuzzy" and stands for *small computer system interface*. *See also* HARD DISK *and* SCSI TECHNOLOGY.

IF/THEN/ELSE

In computer programs, choices must often be made. One of the most common is called *IF/THEN/ELSE*. It can be thought of as a sentence of the form, "If A, then B; otherwise C."

An example of an IF/THEN/ELSE process is shown in the drawing. Suppose a computer is working with a variable x. If x is negative, then you want to multiply it by -1. If x is zero or positive, you want to leave it alone. The computer would compare the numerical value of x with zero. It would then output the absolute value of the number, either multiplying by -1 or leaving it alone.

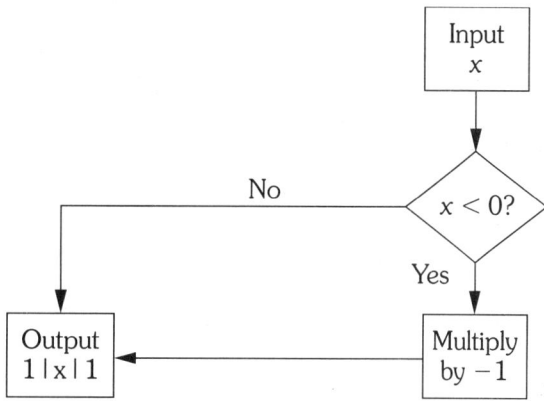

IF/THEN/ELSE flowchart for determining absolute value.

IF/THEN/ELSE processes are especially useful command structures for robotics. A user might instruct a robot, "Get a tire from the rack." The robot would have, in its electronic memory, a command structure to follow. It would need an alternative in case there were no tires. The robot's programming might take the form: "If the command can be executed, do it. Otherwise return and say, 'Your order cannot be completed as given.'" *See also* ARTIFICIAL INTELLIGENCE *and* COMMONSENSE SUMMER PROJECT.

Image-based character recognition

See SMART PAPER.

Image compression

It has been said that a picture is worth a thousand words; that's an understatement in the computing world. Depending on the complexity and the amount of detail and color, a single graphic image might take anywhere from several kilobytes (thousands of characters) to several megabytes (millions of characters). Fortunately, there are ways to reduce the amount of disk storage space that an image consumes without sacrificing much detail. This process is known as *image compression*.

Image compression

Squeezing data down. You might wonder how information can be reduced in bulk without sacrificing quality. In text, this is done by means of *tokens* that replace often-repeated words and phrases. For example, the words *the*, *data*, and *compression* are used often in this article. In text-compression schemes, they could be replaced by the symbols @, #, and $ before being written onto disk or sent over a modem. Before the text is displayed again, the token symbols would be converted back into words.

Images can be compressed using techniques similar to text compression. The main difference is that, while text compression can be *lossless*, meaning there is zero sacrifice in accuracy, image compression is almost always a little bit *lossy*, meaning that there is some reduction in image resolution. With a good image-compression scheme, however, the required amount of storage space can be cut by a factor of 25, 50, or even 100 before the reduction in quality becomes noticeable. That means the image might take up as little as 1% of the space it requires when uncompressed.

Two methods of data compression are commonly used to minimize the amount of space consumed by graphics: *JPEG image compression* and *fractal image compression*.

The JPEG method. Complex graphic images such as color photographs are reproduced on computer monitors as an array of *pixels* (picture elements). A typical monitor has 800 pixels horizontally and 600 pixels vertically, for a total of 480,000 pixels. An image of this size, reproduced in true color, needs about 1.4MB—the entire capacity of a high-density, 3.5-inch diskette. Some monitors have images with even more pixels, and their images take up correspondingly more space.

The acronym *JPEG* (pronounced "jay-peg") stands for *Joint Photographic Experts Group*, the organization that developed the first method for computer image compression. The JPEG scheme breaks the image up into blocks of 64 pixels each, measuring eight horizontally by eight vertically. Then, using a process called *discrete cosine transform (DCT)*, the information in the block is converted into a set of mathematical cosine functions. These functions can be greatly simplified by the computer without causing much deterioration in the quality of the image that the functions represent. When the cosine functions are simplified, they take up much less storage space in the computer. When they are converted back into a picture, the image resolution is almost as good as that of the original picture. With most images, you can't see any difference until the compression ratio exceeds 20:1.

There are some shortcomings of the JPEG method of image compression. The main problem is that, for compression ratios of

Image compression

more than 20:1, the image quality degrades rapidly. If the original image has a lot of detail, the maximum obtainable compression is therefore less than if the image is simple. If the image has sharp boundaries between, say, red and green regions, large compression ratios cause a distortion called *Gibb's effect*. When this happens, objects are bordered by patterns that look like the interference ripples in certain optics experiments.

The fractal method. For some applications, the limitations of JPEG image compression don't pose a problem. If you don't need a compression ratio of more than 20:1, JPEG compression is probably good enough for you. However, engineers, confronted with the limitations of JPEG, immediately sought ways to get around them.

The cosine functions used in DCT compression are orderly, and they're "perfect" in a mathematical sense. Things in nature are imperfect, however. Patterns in the real world have an irregular, chaotic appearance. A good example is the shoreline of a lake, which looks jagged no matter how close or far away you are. Such a pattern is called a *fractal*.

Fractals are not like typical mathematical patterns, but fractals appear everywhere in nature. Fractals can be generated by computers; in fact, computers are uniquely suited to creating fractals from simple equations. Therein lies the key: Great complexity boils down to simplicity.

Suppose the effect of fractals could be harnessed to simplify graphic images? If a computer can generate complex images from one-line equations, then might the computer be programmed to do the same thing in reverse, finding the simple formula at the root of a complex image? It turns out that this is indeed possible. Some of the most complicated images are based on fairly simple formulas. This fact can be exploited to obtain much larger image-compression ratios than is possible with the JPEG process.

A *fractal transform* can be used to compress images. The process works better, in general, than the JPEG scheme regardless of the complexity of the picture. If an image is complicated, the fractal compression program spends more time at the job than it would if the image were simple, but quality is not compromised. For extremely complex images, fractal compression is slow; this is its chief limitation.

The theory behind fractal image compression is too sophisticated for thorough discussion here. However, the subject has been covered in advanced-level PC magazines. For in-depth study, consult the professional journals at a good college or university library. *See also* DATA COMPRESSION, FRACTAL, FRACTAL-GENERATION SOFTWARE, IMAGE RESOLUTION, *and* PIXEL.

Image editing

Graphic images can be processed in an almost infinite variety of ways. This is so commonly done that most people aren't even aware of it when they see it. If you plan to get very involved in graphics, however, you'll need to learn about *image editing*.

Paint versus draw. There are two main ways that graphic images can be created on personal computers. In a *draw program*, an image is built up from discrete pieces such as lines, curves, triangles, and rectangles. This process is sometimes called *object-oriented graphics* or *vector graphics* because the whole image is assembled from a collection of objects or vectors. You can move the objects around, rotate them, resize them, or mirror them. The main limitation of a draw program is that it can't fill in regions very well; it is best at producing outlines.

A *paint program*, on the other hand, works via *bitmapped graphics*, putting a graphic image put together bit-by-bit, pixel-by-pixel (a pixel is a picture element). Paint programs are good for filling in regions and are versatile in the sense that they can approximate just about any shape at all, up to the limit imposed by the image resolution of your monitor or printer. Resizing a bitmapped image, however, doesn't generally work very well because it introduces *aliasing*, also called the *jaggies*. When this happens, the edges of objects grow "teeth" like the blade of a saw. You've probably seen this effect in computer-generated art.

Combining the best features of paint and draw programs is the big challenge of image editing.

Importing images. Editing images is easier than creating them from scratch because you already have something to start with. You can import drawings (clip art) or photographs.

Clip art is available from many sources. You can buy it, either through the mail or at the computer store. You can also get some clip art free by downloading it from an online source. Once you have the image stored on disk, you can use image-editing software to alter it in innumerable ways. You might also combine two or more pieces of clip art to get a new image.

Photographs, either black-and-white or color, can be converted into digital form using a device called an *optical scanner* and stored in a computer. There are several types of scanners available. The cheapest is a handheld unit. Once the photograph has been scanned, converted, and stored on disk, it can be edited just like any other graphic image.

Remember, however, that clip art and photographs are often copyrighted. Altering them does not change the fact that the material is copyrighted. If you take a copyrighted image, edit it, and then try to use it for personal gain, you might be sued for copyright infringement.

Features and requirements. There are many different image-editing software packages available. The following are among the more common features and requirements:

> *Graphical environment* All image-editing programs work with graphics. Therefore, a graphical user interface (GUI) such as Macintosh, OS/2, or Windows must be used. Many versions of image-editing software are available in all of these formats.

> *TWAIN* This is an interface that lets you use an optical scanner to import photographs and other hardcopy art. TWAIN has become increasingly popular because it works with many image-editing programs.

> *Color monitor and printer* Image-editing software works best if you have a high-resolution, color monitor. The higher the image resolution of a monitor, the more detail you can see, and the more precise your images will be. Color adds a dimension to graphics work and is a virtual necessity if you want to produce color hardcopies.

> *Memory/storage* Graphical images require large amounts of memory and disk storage space. High-end image-editing software consumes quite a lot of storage space, apart from that taken up by the images themselves. Your computer will need sufficient RAM for the software to run properly.

Special effects. Depending on how much you're willing to spend—from about $150 for simple packages to over $500 for professional packages—you can achieve special effects to create millions of edited images. Some of these special effects are as follows:

> *Texturing* You can make the surface of an image appear grainy, smooth, shiny, mottled, carpet-like, or practically any other way you want it to look. You can also create transitions from one texture to another within a region.

> *Masking* You can "cut out" one or more portions of an image by tracing a region out via the mouse, and then combine these parts in various ways to get innumerable composites.

> *Zooming* You can enlarge an image by centering on any point within the image. The point will then remain fixed, as if you're approaching it more and more closely. This effect is shown in the drawing (next page) at A, B, and C, for a zoom-center point P.

> *Merging* You can combine images, or parts of images, creating an infinite variety of composites. For example, you might have a man and woman in a photograph, and interchange their heads.

Image editing

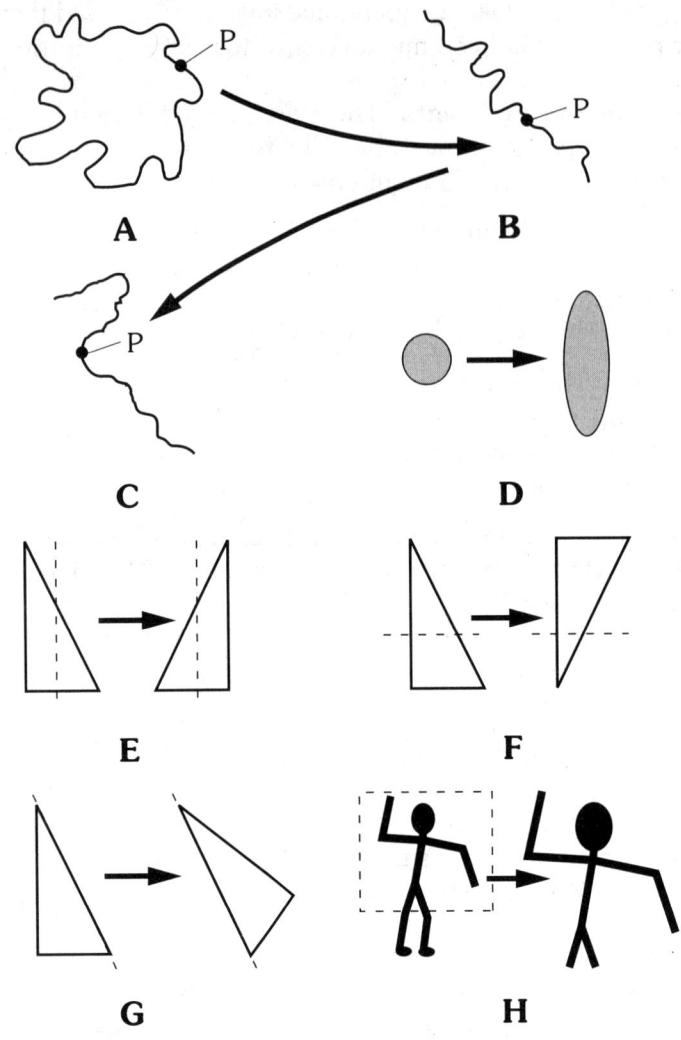

Zooming (A, B, C); stretching vertically (D); mirroring on vertical axis (E); mirroring on horizontal axis (F); mirroring on diagonal axis (G); cropping (H).

- ➤ *Resizing* You can enlarge or shrink parts of an image, or the entire image. You can also distort things; for example, you might make an object three times as high but leave the width the same (D in the drawing).

- ➤ *Rotation* You can turn objects either clockwise or counterclockwise, by any number of degrees.

- ➤ *Mirroring* You can invert an object with respect to either the vertical axis (E) or the horizontal axis (F). You might also flip an object along some diagonal axis (G).

- ➤ *Repeating* You can duplicate a portion of an image, or an object within the image, any number of times. For example, if you have an apple on a table, you might repeat it to get a scene with six apples on the table.

➤ *Coloring* Have you ever seen a color version of an old black-and-white movie? Each frame was colored-in on the film or videotape. Some image-editing software programs let you do this to black-and-white photos or artwork. You can, of course, color the images the way nature would color them, but you can also produce false-color images to obtain varied and bizarre effects.

➤ *Blurring* You can turn a sharp border between regions into a smooth transition, Or you can reduce the amount of detail in an image, similar to the way certain old-time movies were processed. You might blur an image the most around its periphery, and less and less toward the center, creating a dreamy look.

➤ *Morphing* The term *morph* comes from the word *metamorphosis*. It refers to the changing of an image into something different. You might morph a photo of a dog into one of a cat. Or you might morph a cone into a pyramid. It's possible to morph things so they don't bear any resemblance to their former selves. Thus, if you wanted, you could morph a dog into a pyramid!

➤ *Cropping* This is similar to the cropping is done with photographs, when you want to take part of the scene and enlarge it to the full image space. The drawing at H shows a simple example.

➤ *Adding text* You can add labeling or descriptive text to drawings or photographs. This is especially useful when producing educational material. You can also adjust the size of the lettering for the most pleasing overall appearance and add pointers (lines or arrows) if needed.

For further information. PC-related magazines often contain articles about image editing, with reviews of the latest image-editing software packages. If you're interested in purchasing an image-editing program, you should test several different packages first. Perhaps you know a "PC guru" with an image-editing program. Some software dealers let you test packages in the store.

See also ANTI-ALIASING, BIT-MAPPED GRAPHICS, CLIP ART, DESKTOP PUBLISHING, DRAW PROGRAM, GRAPHICAL USER INTERFACE, GRAPHICS, IMAGE COMPRESSION, IMAGE RESOLUTION, OBJECT-ORIENTED GRAPHICS, OPTICAL SCANNER, PAINT PROGRAM, *and* ZOOMING.

Image orthicon

An *image orthicon* is a video camera tube that can be used in computer vision systems. In an image orthicon, a fine beam of electrons, emitted from an electron gun, scans a target electrode (see the drawing). Some of this beam is reflected back toward the electron gun. The amount of reflected energy depends on the emission of secondary electrons from the target electrode. This, in turn, depends on how much light is hitting the target electrode in a given place. The greatest return-beam intensity corresponds to the brightest parts of the video image. The return beam is modulated as it scans the target electrode in a pattern just like the one in a TV picture tube. The return beam is picked up by a receptor electrode.

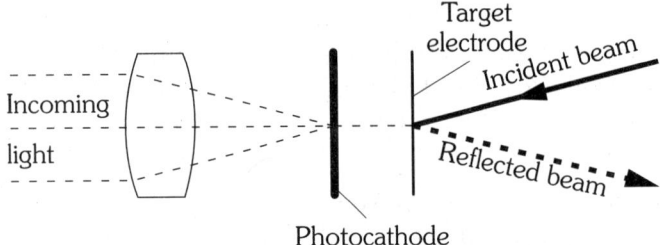

Simplified functional diagram of an image orthicon.

The main disadvantage of the image orthicon is that it produces significant noise in addition to the signal output. However, when a fast response is needed (when there is a lot of action in a scene) and the light ranges from very dim to very bright, the image orthicon is the camera tube of choice. It is common in machine-vision systems that must process images rapidly or that must operate where the amount of light varies over a wide range. *See also* VIDICON *and* VISION SYSTEMS.

Image resolution

Image resolution is the extent to which a monitor or printer shows details in a displayed or printed image. It is sometimes called *definition*. Image resolution is probably the single most important factor in determining the quality of a monitor or printer.

Desktop displays. Most desktop computers use cathode-ray-tube (CRT) displays. The image on a CRT is the same sort of image produced by a television picture tube. It is not a continuous image; instead, it is made up of thousands of tiny dots. The maximum obtainable image resolution of a monitor is proportional to the number of dots on the screen.

A low-resolution monitor can show enough detail for coarse images and large text. In the early years of personal computing, TV sets were often used as computer monitors. A special converter took the data from the computer and processed it into a picture signal that you could look at on any black-and-white or color TV set. All you had to do was switch the TV to the channel corresponding to the output of the converter. The limitations of this scheme were vividly apparent. A typical TV set is a low-resolution system; it doesn't have good enough image resolution for most computing applications. The quality was so

Image resolution

poor that text had to be displayed by the half-line: 40 characters was the most that would fit in the width of the screen without blurring to the point of unreadability.

Early computer monitors were also low-resolution systems, not much better than TV sets. Technology has progressed, however, and the best monitors today are excellent for practically any application. They not only show detail several times greater than their early ancestors, but they can do a fair job with high-speed animation, too. *See also* CATHODE-RAY TUBE, COLOR GRAPHICS ADAPTER, DESKTOP COMPUTER, ENHANCED GRAPHICS ADAPTER, HIGH-RESOLUTION MONITOR, PIXEL, SUPER VIDEO GRAPHICS ARRAY, *and* VIDEO GRAPHICS ARRAY.

Laptop displays. A laptop computer generally has a liquid-crystal display (LCD). The earliest LCDs had notoriously poor image resolution. They were also slow, especially in cold temperatures. These displays have been greatly improved in the past several years. The best LCDs now work nearly as well as CRT monitors. The *active matrix* LCD display provides much better image resolution than older LCDs, and can also render animated graphics much better. In the active matrix, each image element is a diode that can switch on and off independently of all the others.

Another, more expensive technology used in high-end laptop computers is the *plasma display*. This uses an ionized gas, providing superior image resolution and faster response time compared with LCDs. Other alternatives to the LCD are being tested, and some of these promise image resolution as good as that of the best CRTs. *See also* ACTIVE MATRIX, LAPTOP COMPUTER, *and* LIQUID-CRYSTAL DISPLAY.

Printers. In printers, image resolution is given in *dots per inch (DPI)*. The higher the DPI rating, the better the resolution obtainable.

The earliest dot-matrix printers had low DPI ratings, and therefore the image resolution was poor. Text had a "dotty" appearance that irritated some readers. Only the most rudimentary graphic images (if any) could be reproduced with such printers. Modern dot-matrix printers can render graphics in a fair amount of detail, but the best image resolution is obtained with an inkjet printer or laser printer.

An inkjet printer literally sprays ink onto the paper, which allows for a variety of shading effects, as well as full color. A laser printer works like a high-quality photocopier. These printers are typically rated at well over 300 DPI, which is considered excellent image resolution. *See also* DOT-MATRIX PRINTER, DOTS PER INCH, HIGH-RESOLUTION PRINTER, INKJET PRINTER, *and* LASER PRINTER.

Machine vision. In a machine vision system such as the kind that might be used by robots, the resolution is the sharpness of the scene

Image resolution

that the machine sees. Poor resolution can be the result of bad focus, too few pixels in the image, or inadequate signal bandwidth.

The ability of a vision system to separate two objects located in almost the same direction is called *direction resolution*. Sometimes it is called *angular resolution* or *azimuth resolution*. It is given in degrees, minutes, or seconds of arc.

Parts A, B, and C of the drawing show two objects seen by a machine vision system, as they gradually move apart. The direction resolution is the smallest angular separation at which the machine sees the objects as two separate items, rather than as an irregular blob. The drawings on the right show the appearances of two adjacent spheres at the viewing angles shown at the left. The angles are exaggerated for clarity.

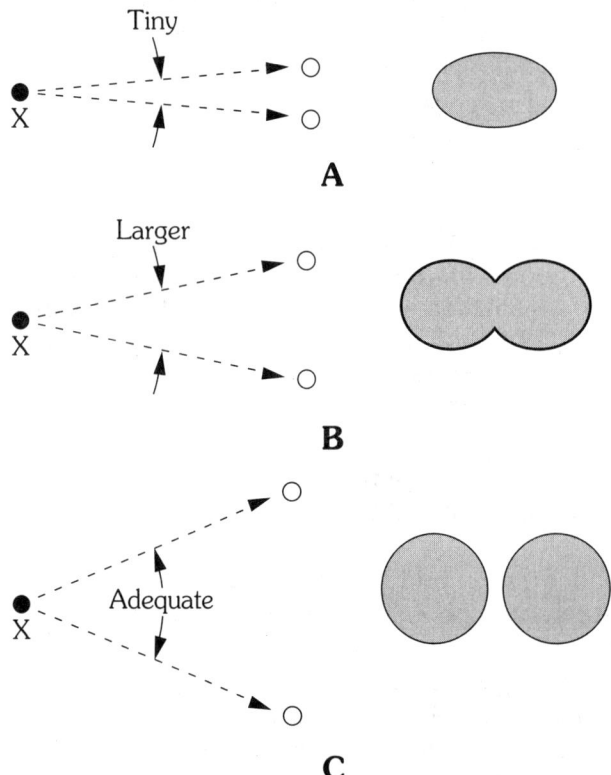

At A and B, the angles are too small for resolution; at C, the angle is just big enough for the observer (X).

Two objects might be so nearly in the same direction that the machine sees them as the same object. If they are at different radial distances, however, the system can tell them apart by *ranging*. When two objects are close to each other and are at almost the same distance from the machine, a ranging system sees them as a single object. As the radial distances become different, the machine can resolve them. The minimum radial separation for distinguishability is the *distance resolution*. *See also* PERSONAL ROBOTS, *and* VISION SYSTEMS.

Immortal knowledge

Computers have brought about a transformation in human culture in many nations of the world. This is most evident in the United States, Europe, and Japan. Knowledge and history can be recorded and built upon by computers indefinitely, providing a sort of *immortal knowledge*. The only role humans need to play is to put the data into the computers.

Historical records. In the thousands of years before computers, history was passed from generation to generation in the form of books and stories. If you read a book written 200 years ago, you interpret things somewhat differently than the original author thought of them because society is not the same as it was two centuries ago.

When history is put down in books or told as stories, much information is simply lost, never to be recovered. Computers, on the other hand, can keep data indefinitely. If artificial intelligence (AI) becomes advanced enough, computers might become able to interpret data for us, as well as store it. History might become less subjective and more consistent from one generation to the next.

Changing the past. While immortal knowledge can help preserve history, it also has a dark side. Some people fear that computers would "take over," doing so many things for us that we forget how to take care of ourselves. Worse, computers could be used by power-hungry people for the purpose of controlling other people's lives. Just as history can be warped by the writers of books, it might be twisted by the programmers of computers. The true past cannot be changed, but our records of it can be distorted.

It is all too easy to give computers more power than they ought to have. Computers can help us evaluate and observe data, but they cannot reasonably be expected to think for us.

Benefit or liability? Computers make information—and misinformation—more permanent. If carried to the extreme, computers could give us 100% immortal knowledge. Stored data could be backed up to prevent loss that might otherwise result from computer failure, sabotage, and aging of disks and tapes. Every fact, every detail, and possibly some of the subtle meaning, too, would be passed along unaltered for century after century.

Immortal knowledge might become a great asset to society, but it could also become a liability. The most important factor here is probably the temperament of the culture to begin with. All powerful technologies can cut two ways; computers are no exception. Still, it's

Impact printer

good for people to remember not to believe everything they see on a computer display screen. No matter how powerful and ubiquitous computers become, the "chip between the ears" should remain the primary operating system! *See also* COMPUTER OVER-RELIANCE *and* CYBERPHOBIA.

Impact printer

An *impact printer* produces hardcopies via direct pressure on paper. The most common type is the *dot-matrix printer*. Another, less common impact printer is the *daisy-wheel printer*.

Ribbons. Impact printers use an ink or carbon-film ribbon. The ribbon is struck from behind and pressed against the paper in patterns that form characters. A dot-matrix printer can produce both text and graphic images. Multicolored ribbons allow impact printers to create color hardcopies.

An impact printer can even be used without a ribbon if multipart forms are available. The original will be blank; only the copies will have markings on them. This is not done as a rule, but it can be, if you ever happen to run out of ribbons and have multipart forms lying around.

Advantages. Dot-matrix printers are cheap, and can handle multipart forms and large paper sizes. These are their main advantages. When you need to print out large volumes of text at low cost, dot-matrix printers are the way to go. These printers are rugged and hardly ever need maintenance, except for ribbon replacement and periodic cleaning.

Daisy-wheel printers are much slower than dot-matrix printers, and they cannot make graphic images, so they are essentially obsolete.

Problems. Older impact printers are noisy. It's hard to carry on a conversation, especially over the telephone, when one of these machines is zipping away. Newer dot-matrix printers have somewhat overcome the noise problem, however. Impact printers also print fairly slowly compared to other printing technologies. A dot-matrix printer might print a quarter of a page per minute, an inkjet printer two pages per minute, and a laser printer six pages per minute.

Impact printing is not of the best quality. Although it's good enough for draft copies and unpublished work, it is not suitable for desktop publishing purposes. For professional-looking printed documents, an inkjet printer or laser printer is a necessity. *See also* DAISY-WHEEL PRINTER, DOT-MATRIX PRINTER, INKJET PRINTER, LASER PRINTER, *and* MULTIPART FORMS.

Importing

When you are working on a file and you bring part or all of some previously created file into it, you are *importing* data. Importing can be done between computer systems or within a single system.

Consider a magazine publisher that receives articles or manuscripts from freelance writers. Most publishers like to get material on diskettes because it saves them having to pay someone to retype all the text. However, there are many different programs that might be used to create this text. A large magazine publisher might receive some diskettes from users of Macintosh PCs, others from users of IBM-compatible PCs. Some users might submit material in WordPerfect, others in Word; a few will use a text editor or some exotic program.

Most word processing programs can read ASCII (pronounced "ask-key") text. When the publisher gets text in "straight ASCII," it can be imported into whatever software the publisher uses. Text can also be converted directly from one word processing format to another, although formatting and art is sometimes lost or changed in the process.

Importing is often done from CD-ROM. If you are creating a complex graphic, for example, you might want to import several image files from a CD-ROM and combine them with your own work to create the final product. If you're working on a musical composition, you can import special sound effects from a CD-ROM.

When you send a file out for use by other PCs, either via diskette or modem, you are *exporting* the file. Thus, authors commonly export work to publishers, and computer users export data to other computer users. *See also* ASCII *and* EXPORTING.

Incompleteness Theorem

In 1931, a young mathematician named Kurt Gödel discovered something about logic that changed the way people think about reality. His *Incompleteness Theorem* says that it's impossible to prove all true statements. In any logical system of thought, there are undecidable propositions.

In mathematical systems, certain assumptions, called *axioms*, are made. Logical rules are employed to prove theorems based on the axioms. If there are no contradictions, the system is consistent. If a contradiction is found, the set of axioms is inconsistent.

Generally, the "stronger" the set of axioms, the greater the chance that a contradiction can be derived from them. A logical system that is "too strong" literally falls apart, because once a contradiction is found, every statement, no matter how ridiculous, becomes provable. If a system is "too weak," then it doesn't produce much of anything meaningful. For centuries, mathematicians have striven to build thought universes with elegance and substance, but free of contradictions.

Gödel showed that, for any consistent set of axioms, there are more true statements than provable theorems (see the drawing). In any logical system without contradictions, the "whole truth" is beyond knowledge. This includes machine knowledge as well as human knowledge.

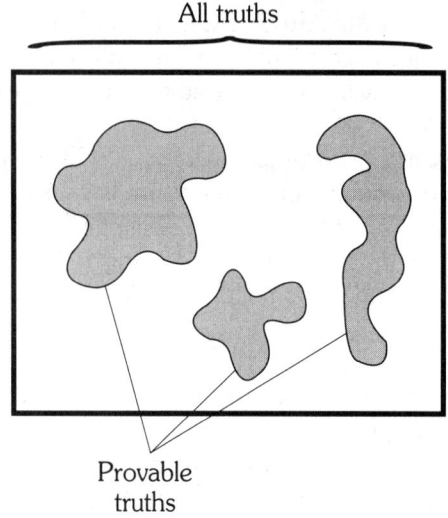

Not all truths can be proved, even by a perfect theorem-proving computer.

The Incompleteness Theorem has implications in artificial intelligence (AI). Broadly speaking, it is impossible to build a "universal truth machine," a computer that can mathematically prove every true statement. Gödel's proof shattered the dreams of those who hoped to discover absolute truth via pure logic. It also seems to demonstrate the pointlessness of trying to build a supercomputer to unravel all the secrets of the universe. *See also* ARTIFICIAL INTELLIGENCE.

Independent variable

In a mathematical *function*, an *independent variable* is a changing quantity whose value does not depend on the value of any other quantity. Time is a common example; altitude above sea level is another.

Single-variable functions. You work with independent variables when you make graphs and charts with a PC. The independent variable is almost always plotted on the horizontal axis in a two-variable coordinate system.

Drawing A is a hypothetical graph of barometric pressure versus time for a period of one week. The pressure changes with time.

Commonsense tells you that the pressure depends on the time, not vice-versa. Therefore, time is the independent variable and is plotted on the horizontal axis, while barometric pressure is the *dependent variable* plotted on the vertical axis.

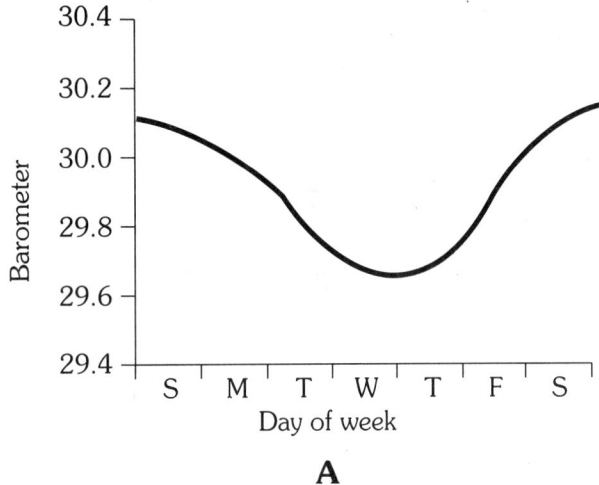

A

The barometer reading as a function of time for a week.

Multivariable functions. Other factors besides time can affect barometric pressure; altitude above sea level is one. Pressure always drops with increasing altitude. You might create a graph of pressure versus altitude for some moment in time. This graph will change, however, as time passes. Time and altitude both affect the barometric pressure at any given place on the earth.

If you want to graph pressure as a function of both time and altitude, you'll need a coordinate three-space, with two independent-variable axes. The time will be plotted along one of these axes, and the altitude along the other. Drawing B on page 552 is an example of the coordinate system for this situation as it might appear on the monitor screen of a PC. Variables x and y are independent; their axes are horizontal. Variable z represents the dependent variable; its axis is vertical. The function (not shown here) will appear as an irregular surface. You've probably seen graphs like this. A good scientific graphics program can create a vivid illusion of depth on the monitor or printout, approximating the surface as many curves closely packed together.

Functions often have two or more independent variables, with one dependent variable. In this type of function, known as a *multivariable function*, the dependent variable is affected by each of the independent variables.

More than three dimensions. If you get very involved with scientific graphics, you'll use three-dimensional image rendition to show two-variable functions. In high-level mathematics, you even work

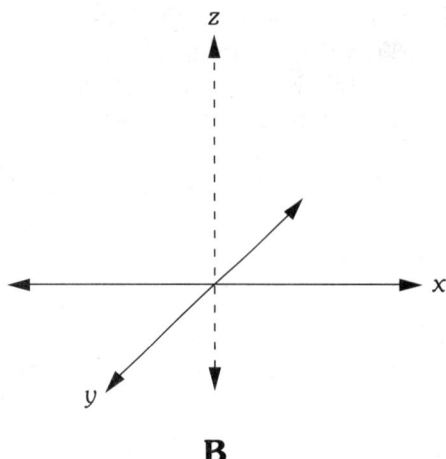

B

A three-space coordinate system.

with functions of three or more variables, requiring four or more dimensions.

Human beings can't visualize four-dimensional spaces directly, but for a computer, it's easy. The computer can show you three-dimensional "slices" of four-space graphs and objects. You can select different "slices" to get an intuitive notion of what a four-dimensional graph or object looks like. *See also* DEPENDENT VARIABLE, *and* FUNCTION.

Indexing software

If you've ever had to create an index by hand, you know how tedious the process can be. *Indexing software* substantially reduces the work required to create the index for a book or other long document.

Setting up. Before an index can be made, the document must be divided into pages, numbered exactly as they will appear in the final printed product. If a document contains illustrations, these must be merged into the text, or spaces must be left where the illustrations are to appear. These illustrations or spaces must be the same size, relative to the text, as they'll be in the final document.

The list file. Once the entire manuscript has been set up, the author or editor goes through the book, choosing specific terms and phrases to be indexed. A record of these words and phrases is composed, in the form of a list file or *concordance file*. Once the concordance file has been compiled, it must be alphabetized. This is the first part of the indexing process in which the computer saves the author or editor a lot of time. Software can arrange thousands of words and phrases in alphanumeric sequence in a minute or two. If the job were done manually, it would take hours.

The search. Once the list file has been created, the indexing software goes to work, using the text file(s) and the alphabetized concordance file. The software conducts a search for every occurrence in the text of the words and phrases in the concordance file. When any of the words or phrases in the concordance file are found, the document's page number is noted. This is the second, and most significant, part of the indexing process in which the PC shines. Not only does it save the user countless hours of work, but it also ensures that no occurrence of the list-file words and phrases is overlooked.

There is one potential hangup with indexing software. If the list file contains words that appear very often, the index will contain long strings of page numbers. In large works, this can result in a single index entry having hundreds of page numbers. Only the most important references to the term should be included in the index. These decisions cannot be made by a computer; they require a human. *See also* CONCORDANCE FILE *and* WORD PROCESSING.

Industry Standard Architecture

Industry Standard Architecture (ISA) is the set of standards for the hardware in the original IBM PC. This standard has, to some extent, become obsolete; many computers now use *Enhanced Industry Standard Architecture (EISA)*. But ISA has not been displaced altogether.

The original IBM PC used the 8088 microprocessor, an ISA chip which was very slow compared to modern chips. It worked with an eight-bit or 16-bit bus, while EISA chips such as the 80486 (486) use a 32-bit bus. Changing from eight-bit words to 32-bit words is like replacing a two-lane road with an eight-lane superhighway, or doubling the diameter of a pipe (quadrupling its cross-sectional area). It increases the power potential of a computer, all other things being equal. The catch is that other factors generally change.

While bus size is an important factor in determining computer power, it's not the only factor. Clock speed is also important, as is memory capacity. Cost also factors into the equation. It's possible, therefore, that a cheap, fast ISA machine with lots of memory might be better for some users than an EISA machine that costs more. *See also* BUS, COMPUTER GENERATIONS, COMPUTER POWER, *and* ENHANCED INDUSTRY STANDARD ARCHITECTURE.

Infinite regress

An *infinite regress* is a thought pattern in which a sort of endless loop occurs. The simplest example of an infinite regress is a definition that "defines" something in terms of itself. It is possible to define things in terms of simpler versions of themselves, without going in circles. This is a tricky kind of logic known as *recursion*.

Original thoughts. Arthur Samuel, one of the pioneers in artificial intelligence (AI), expressed the opinion that machines can't have truly

Infinite regress

original thoughts. If they could, it would imply an infinite regress that could not possibly take place.

According to Samuel's reasoning, machines can process data, but they cannot originate it (unless they malfunction). This data must come from outside the machine. It might come from some other computer, but ultimately, a human being must be at the root of any idea a computer gets. Either that, or the idea must come from an infinite succession of computers, one before the other before the other, without any beginning. That, of course, is impossible.

The drawing shows "Cybo," the computer, getting a flash of insight from "Precybo," the computer before it, which got the same data, perhaps in different form but with identical content, from "Preprecybo" ("Pre^2cybo"). "Pre^2cybo" got the data from "Prepreprecybo," also known as "Pre^3cybo." In general, "Pre^ncybo" got its data from "$Pre^{(n+1)}cybo$." The process goes back infinitely into the past. But computers have only existed for a few decades! The conclusion: Computers can't generate their own ideas because the notion leads to a logical contradiction. Theorists call this type of argument *reductio ad absurdum*.

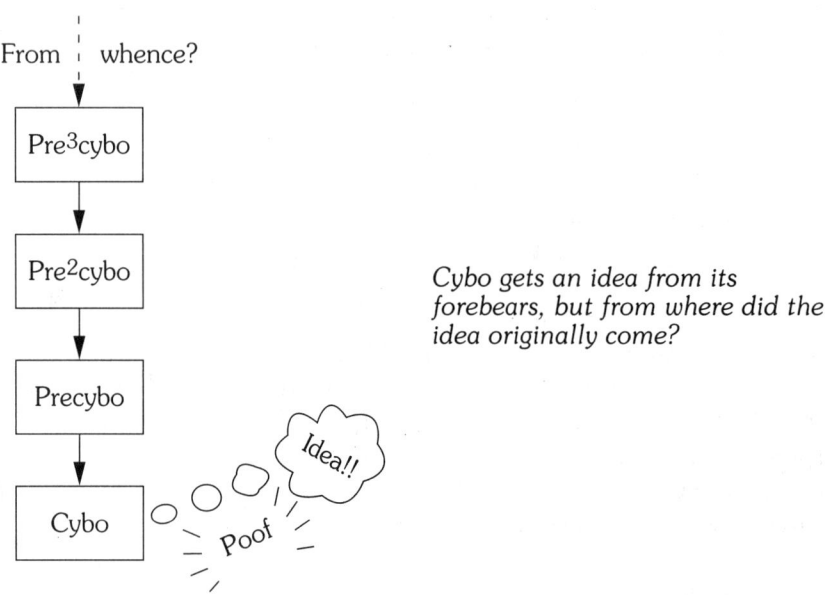

Cybo gets an idea from its forebears, but from where did the idea originally come?

Movies and mutations. Some AI enthusiasts argue against Samuel, asking, "How do people get knowledge?" The infinite-regress argument suggests that humans can't have original thoughts either, because we haven't existed for an infinite number of generations. However, history is replete with instances of people having insights that no one had before. This line of reasoning has been used by

theologians to "prove" the existence of God as the source of original human thought. Whatever the "idea force" might be that gets into humans, there seems no good reason why it ought not to find its way into machines as well. Philosophers and biologists enter the debate at this point, but the most fun is had by science-fiction writers. The computer that captures a bit of cosmic consciousness, thereby becoming a living being, is the stuff of great stories.

Closer to reality, it is believed that biological evolution takes place through mutations, which are essentially malfunctions in gene reproduction. Perhaps these "accidents" are how original thoughts take place in living things. Can computers evolve via electronic malfunctions? And could they, in the same way, someday have original thoughts? *See also* ARTIFICIAL INTELLIGENCE, ARTIFICIAL LIFE, COMPUTER CONSCIOUSNESS, ENDLESS LOOP, *and* RECURSION.

Information superhighway

The term *information superhighway* refers to data that constantly flows among computers throughout the world. The "backbone" of this data stream is the *Internet*. Sometimes you'll hear various other terms used to describe it, such as *infobahn* or *data highway*.

Some people portray the information superhighway as a smooth-flowing, efficient, ultra-high-volume global data-exchange forum. Perhaps someday this will be the case, but the current situation is far different. The worldwide computer information network is more like an American roadway in 1950 than a superhighway. Back then, some highway routes were in good condition, many were marginal, and more than a few turned to mud when it rained or were impassable when it snowed. Just as Dwight Eisenhower envisioned the interstate system of freeways during his presidency in the 1950s, Vice President Al Gore and other politicians proposed the information superhighway as an ideal for which to strive during the 1990s.

A few companies provide limited access to the information superhighway via user-friendly interfaces, which minimize the confusion and make online computing practical and fun. Still, serious users of the Infobahn face a rather steep learning curve, along with frequent detours and blocked routes. With persistence, however, it is possible to find data on the information superhighway quicker and cheaper than via any other method.

Virtually all new computers are sold with internal modems, allowing them to be connected to a telephone line. Software for one or more online services is often preinstalled. This gives most new computer buyers immediate, although restricted, access to the information superhighway. Some online services work in "faster lanes" than others. Consumer-oriented computing magazines, such as *PC Novice*, regularly carry articles that discuss the most current features of popular

Initialization

online services and other parts of the information superhighway. *See also* AMERICA ONLINE, BULLETIN-BOARD SYSTEM, CELLULAR TELECOMMUNICATIONS, COMMUNICATIONS, COMPUSERVE, DATA COMMUNICATION, DELPHI, DOWNLOADING, ECOLINKING, ELECTRONIC MAIL, FIBEROPTIC DATA TRANSMISSION, FREEWARE, INTERNET, LASER COMMUNICATIONS, LOW-EARTH-ORBIT (LEO) SATELLITE DATA LINK, MAILBOX, MAIL FORWARDING, MICROWAVE DATA TRANSMISSION, ONLINE SERVICE, OPEN SYSTEMS INTERCONNECTION REFERENCE MODEL (OSI-RM), PACKET COMMUNICATIONS, PACKET-RADIO BULLETIN-BOARD SYSTEM, PRODIGY, SATELLITE DATA TRANSMISSION, SENIORNET, TELECOMMUTING, TELECONFERENCING, TELEPHONY, TERMINAL EMULATION SOFTWARE, TERMINAL NODE CONTROLLER, TIME-SHIFTING COMMUNICATIONS, UPLOADING, VOICE MAIL SYSTEM, *and* X/Y/ZMODEM.

Initialization

See FORMATTING.

Initialization file

An *initialization file* is a startup file used by the Windows program. Initialization files have the filename extension .INI. These files are necessary for your PC to work with application programs in the Windows environment.

Common .INI files. There are several different .INI files used in Windows. The following are the most common:

➢ SYSTEM.INI contains your computer's "knowledge" of its hardware. It is essential to get Windows going when you start your system up, or when you go into the Windows operating environment.

➢ WIN.INI contains all the information necessary for the operation of File Manager. Some of the things determined by WIN.INI include the speed of the keyboard, the speed of the printer, colors on your monitor, shapes of icons, and fonts you can use.

➢ PROGRAM.INI contains the data necessary for the operation of Program Manager. Basically, it governs the way the screen looks and how it reacts when you are in Program Manager.

➢ WINFILE.INI determines what happens when you select, or click on, various menu items in File Manager.

➢ CONTROL.INI determines what happens when you click on various icons in the Control menu.

Editing. All of the .INI files have default values when you first go into Windows. For example, the screen color, icon shapes, and fonts are all preset by the software in the initialization files, if you don't specify other values. You can change these things by editing your .INI files.

There are two main ways to edit initialization files: via the *Control menu* or via the *Editor*. In Windows, it's generally best to work from the Control menu. Consult your instruction manual for details on editing the .INI files to get different functions and effects from Windows software.

Before editing any file, whether it is an .INI file or anything else, you should always make a backup of the file. That way, if you make a mistake, or if you don't like the way things turn out after you've edited a file, you can retrieve the file as it was before you started working on it. It's one thing to make try different changes; it's quite another thing to undo those changes step-by-step, in reverse order! If you don't back up an initialization file before you start editing it, you might never get it back the way it was. *See also* BACKUP, CONTROL MENU, DEFAULT, EDITOR, FILE MANAGER, PROGRAM MANAGER, *and* WINDOWS.

Inkjet printer

An *inkjet printer* is typically a *high-resolution printer* that can produce copy with at least 300 dots per inch (DPI) by spraying ink onto paper. The quality of printout is almost as good as that of a laser printer. Some inkjet printers can make full-color hardcopies at 400 DPI or more. Inkjet printers cost more, on average, than dot-matrix printers, but less than laser printers.

The head of an inkjet printer has several tiny nozzles, or *jets*. As the paper moves past the head, the ink is sprayed from the jets in a certain sequence, resulting in characters and figures on the paper. The speed is relatively slow compared to a laser printer.

Assets. One big advantage of an inkjet printer is the fact that it doesn't make noise. A good inkjet printer is just about as quiet as the computer from which it gets its data. Several inkjet printers can be running in a large office, without distracting anyone. Compare that to six or eight old, loud dot-matrix printers zipping and whining away!

Another asset of inkjet printers is their ability to produce color printouts. This is done quite simply, by using multicolored jets of ink. The primary pigments (red, yellow, and blue) can combine to produce full-color hardcopies. Several manufacturers make color inkjet printers that cost the same or less than black-and-white laser printers.

Limitations. One potential problem with inkjet printers is that the copy needs time to dry, or it will smear. This can be minimized by handling the copies carefully until the ink is dry (a couple of minutes). Inkjet printers need relatively nonporous paper for good image-resolution in the printout.

Also, for large volumes of text printing, an inkjet printer is rather slow. If you are producing gigantic quantities of hardcopy text, you're probably better off with a dot-matrix or laser printer. *See also* COLOR PRINTER, DOT-MATRIX PRINTER, HIGH-RESOLUTION PRINTER, *and* LASER PRINTER.

Input/output module

An *input/output module*, usually abbreviated *I/O*, is a data link between a computer's central processing unit (CPU) and the memory and peripherals. Data flows at high speed and in high volume through I/O modules.

In robots or computer-controlled mechanical systems, I/O modules transfer data between the *controller* and the moving parts. Also, I/O modules can interconnect robot controllers or link a fleet of robots to a central computer. The drawing shows two robot controllers, linked by an I/O module. There are four robots (triangles labeled *R*), connected to each controller by I/O modules (circles).

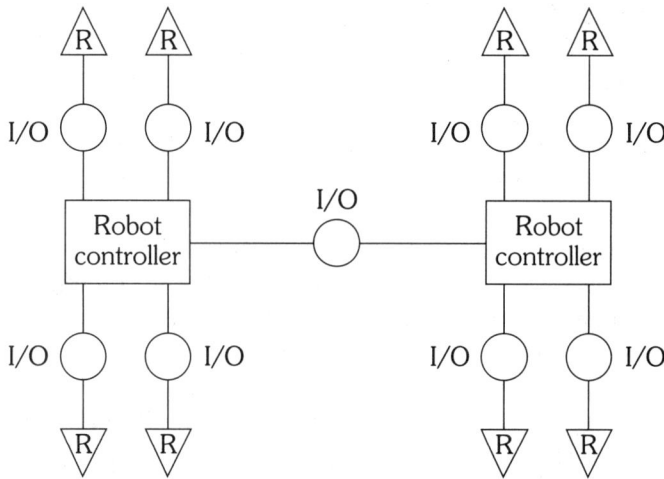

Robots (triangles) are connected to controllers (rectangles). Interfaces (circles) are I/O modules.

As its name suggests, an I/O circuit carries data in two directions: into and out of the CPU. It must do both at the same time. The incoming data is usually different from the outgoing data, so the I/O module is a *full-duplex* system. *See also* BUS, CENTRAL PROCESSING UNIT, FULL DUPLEX, PERSONAL ROBOTS, *and* ROBOT CONTROLLER.

Insect robots

Insect robots are a fleet of robots operating under the control of a central computer. In particular, the term is used in reference to systems designed by engineer Rodney Brooks; many of his robots actually look something like insects. He began developing his ideas at Massachusetts Institute of Technology during the early 1990s. The concept of "many robots, one controller," however, is probably as old as the very notion of a robot.

Teamwork. Brooks' insect robots have six legs, and look like mechanical bugs. They can range in size from more than a foot long to less than a millimeter across. Most significant is the fact that they work collectively, rather than as individuals. Discrete units, each with high intelligence, don't necessarily work well in a team. People provide a good example. Professional sports teams have been assembled by buying the best players in the business, but such a team isn't likely to win championships unless the players get along well together. They can be brilliant in the individual, yet remain stupid in the generality.

Insects, in contrast to humans or individually programmed computers, are stupid in the individual. Ants and bees are like idiot robots. An anthill or beehive is still an efficient system, however, run by the collective mind of all its members. Such systems are brilliant in the generality.

Human conceit. Rodney Brooks saw this huge difference between autonomous and collective intelligence. He also saw that most of his colleagues were trying to build autonomous robots, perhaps because of the natural pride of humans, resulting in visions of robots as humanoids. To Brooks, a major avenue of technology was being neglected. He therefore began designing robot colonies consisting of many units under the control of a central computer or AI system.

Brooks envisions microscopic insect robots that might live in your house, coming out at night to clean your floors and countertops. Even tinier "antibody robots" could be injected into a person infected with some otherwise incurable disease. Controlled by a central microprocessor, they could seek out the disease bacteria or viruses and literally zap them dead. *See also* ARTIFICIAL INTELLIGENCE, AUTONOMOUS ROBOTS, *and* NANOTECHNOLOGY.

Insert key

The *Insert key* is found on the keyboards of IBM-compatible computers. It is usually located in a group of six keys, just to the right of the main keyboard as shown in the drawing. The Insert key, sometimes labeled INS, usually *toggles* (switches alternately) between two modes in word processing. These are called *overtype mode* and *insert mode*.

Overtyping. In the overtype mode, text is overwritten as you type along. Suppose you have the sentence, "The quick brown fox jumps over the lazy dog." Now suppose you decide that it's not a brown fox than jumps over a dog, but a black dog that jumps over a fox. You press the Insert key, if necessary, to change into overtype mode. Then you position the cursor at the *b* in *brown* and type *black dog*, which happens to have the same number of characters as *brown fox*. Next, you move the cursor ahead with the arrow key until it rests on the *d* in

Instruction set

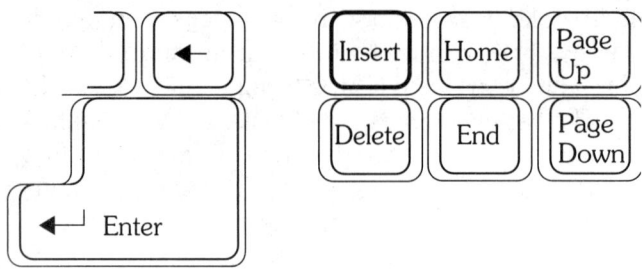

The Insert key is one of six keys in a pad to the right of the main keyboard.

dog at the end of the sentence and type *fox* in; it overwrites the word *dog*. The sentence then reads, "The quick black dog jumps over the lazy fox."

In this case, the number of letters in the new sentence happens to be exactly the same as the number of letters in the original sentence, so overtype mode works well. This is not usually the case, however. When the new sentence contains fewer letters than the original one, you can simply omit them by deleting or backspacing them. If you need to make room for more characters, you need to be in insert mode.

Insertion. Suppose you want to add some adjectives to describe the dog and the fox. Maybe you love dogs and loathe foxes. You press the Insert key to change back to insert mode.

Positioning the cursor just after the word *quick*, you type a comma, a space, and then the words *friendly, lovable, brilliant* before the word *dog*. As you type these adjectives in, the text ahead of them moves out toward the right to make room. Then you move the cursor along with the arrow key until it is between *lazy* and *fox*. You type a comma followed by the words *ugly, stupid, ignorant* to describe your feelings about the fox. The sentence now reads, "The quick, friendly, lovable, brilliant black dog jumps over the lazy, ugly, stupid, ignorant fox."

This sentence might itself be rather ugly and stupid, but the word processing program does exactly what the writer tells it to do. *See also* WORD PROCESSING.

Instruction set

See COMPLEX-INSTRUCTION-SET COMPUTING *and* REDUCED-INSTRUCTION-SET COMPUTING.

Instructions per second

A computer *instruction* is a program statement that carries a certain meaning for a computer and that causes it to carry out some specific task. *Instructions per second (IPS)* is a measure of computer power. The IPS rating is a function of the clock speed and the bus size.

The earliest computers, called the first generation, worked at around 10,000 IPS, or 10 *kiloinstructions per second (KIPS)*. Modern machines work at thousands of times this speed. Typical figures are in the hundreds of *megainstructions per second (MIPS)*. It's not unreason-able to suppose that future computers will work at billions of IPS, or *gigainstructions per second (GIPS)*. See also CLOCK SPEED, COMPUTER GENERATIONS, COMPUTER POWER, THROUGHPUT, *and* WORD SIZE.

Integrated circuit

Integrated circuits (ICs) have stimulated as much change as any other single development in the history of technology. They have played an especially important role in digital computers. Most ICs look like gray or black plastic boxes with protruding pins. Common configurations are the *single inline package (SIP)*, the *dual inline package (DIP)* and the *flatpack*. Another package looks like a transistor with too many leads. This is a *metal-can package*, sometimes also called a *TO package*.

Assets. Integrated circuits have several advantages over individual, or discrete, components:

 ➤ *Compactness* An obvious asset of IC design is economy of space; ICs are far more compact than equivalent circuits made from individual transistors, diodes, capacitors, and resistors. Complex circuits can be kept to a reasonable size. Thus, you see laptop computers with capabilities more advanced than early computers that occupied whole rooms.

 ➤ *High speed* In an IC, interconnections among components are physically tiny, making high switching speeds possible. Electric currents travel fast, but not instantaneously. The less time charge carriers need to get from component X to component Y, in general, the more computations are possible within a given span of time, and the less time is needed for complex operations.

 ➤ *Low power consumption* ICs need far less power than equivalent discrete-component circuits. Because ICs use relatively little current, they produce less heat than their discrete-component equivalents. This translates into better efficiency. Some ICs can get quite hot locally; the Pentium processor, for example, needs a fairly sophisticated cooling system. Still, these ICs consume many times less power and generate many times less heat than they would if they were constructed from discrete electronic components.

 ➤ *Reliability* Integrated circuits fail less often per component-hour of use than appliances that make use of discrete components mainly because all interconnections are sealed within the IC case, preventing corrosion or the intrusion of dust.

Integrated drive electronics

The reduced failure rate translates into less downtime (time during which the equipment is out of service for repairs).

- *Ease of maintenance* Integrated-circuit technology lowers maintenance costs, mainly because repair procedures are simplified when failures do occur. Many appliances use sockets for ICs, and replacement is simply a matter of finding the faulty IC, unplugging it, and plugging in a new one. Special desoldering equipment is used with appliances having ICs soldered directly to the circuit boards.

- *Modular construction* Modern IC appliances use *modular construction*, a scheme in which individual ICs perform defined functions within a circuit board. The circuit board or card, in turn, fits into a socket and has a specific purpose. Computers, programmed with customized software, are used by repair technicians to locate the faulty card in an appliance. The whole card can be pulled and replaced, getting the appliance back to the consumer in the shortest possible time. Then the computer can be used to troubleshoot the faulty card, getting the card ready for use in the next appliance that happens to come along with a failure in the same card.

Constraints. No technological advancement ever comes without some sacrifice or compromise. There are some limitations in IC technology, although the advantages render these problems minor by comparison. The first major limitation is that ICs have no inductors because inductance cannot be fabricated onto chips (except for extremely low values). Devices using ICs must generally be designed to work without inductors. Fortunately, resistance-capacitance (RC) circuits are capable of doing most things that inductance-capacitance (LC) circuits can do.

The other major limitation of ICs is that they don't generate "megapower." High power necessitates a certain minimum physical bulk because it generates large amounts of heat. Power ICs do exist, but they are quite large and require cooling apparatus such as heat sinks, fans, or fluidic systems. Extremely high power, such as you might need for a radio or television broadcast transmitter, is generally obtained with power transistors or sophisticated vacuum tubes.

The future. Research is constantly going on in IC technology. As time passes, their versatility will increase. IC technology has made modern computers possible. It might someday make machines nearly as smart as humans. The main emphasis is on getting more and more components into a smaller and smaller physical space. *See also* BIOCHIP, MICROPROCESSOR, ULTRA-LARGE-SCALE INTEGRATION, *and* VERY-LARGE-SCALE INTEGRATION.

Integrated drive electronics
See IDE TECHNOLOGY.

Integrated software package

An *integrated software package* is a set of programs that you buy as a unit, typically including a word processor, a database, a spreadsheet, one or two graphics programs, and terminal emulation software for communications. Some packages also add calculators, calendars, and other types of specialized personal and business software.

The easiest way to learn and use integrated software is via a graphical user interface (GUI) such as Windows or Macintosh.

Modules. Each application within an integrated software package is called a *module*. For example, word processing is a module that's included in practically every package. Modules aren't as sophisticated as separate, specialized software packages. The word processor in an integrated package, for example, will have fewer fancy features than a high-level package designed especially for word processing. However, for the casual PC user or beginner, the features in the modules of an integrated package are usually adequate. For serious PC users and small businesses, an upscale version of integrated software, called a *suite*, can be obtained.

If you have a casual need for a wide range of applications, but are especially involved in one of them, say the database, you might consider buying an integrated package for all your work except database management. You can purchase a separate, more powerful database program with the features you want for your high-level work. This will save you considerable money compared to buying high-powered, specialized packages for each individual application. *See also* SUITE.

Advantages. The most obvious advantage of an integrated software package, compared with the purchase of separate programs, is lower cost. While a good word processing program might cost you from $100 to $500, you can get an entire integrated package for about the same amount of money. If you have a modest, but not intense, need for several applications, you can easily save several hundred dollars by getting an integrated package.

Another asset of an integrated package is that the combined program saves memory space. With an integrated package, you have fewer total "bells and whistles" than in the high-level programs. Thus, the integrated package takes up less random-access memory (RAM) and, usually, disk space. You don't want to use precious megabytes unnecessarily, any more than you want to spend hard-earned money out of proportion to your needs.

Another advantage of integrated software is that all the modules share a common user interface. Once you get familiar with one module, the others will come to you with less effort because they have the same idiosyncrasies.

Dynamic linking. Integrated software packages lend themselves to a work-saving, efficiency-improving scheme known as *dynamic linking*. Stated simply, each part of such a system is aware of what happens in every other part. Suppose you have a list of names and addresses. These are in the database part of your integrated package. You write letters and keep them in the word processing portion of the package. People move around a lot these days, and you'll often have to update your address database to reflect this fact. With dynamic linking, as soon as you change the address of a person in the database, it will change in all the other locations within the whole package, including each and every letter you wrote (assuming you put the person's address in the header of the letter). If the name and address appears in the spreadsheet, it will change there, too, without your having to think about it.

Some integrated packages have dynamic linking; others don't. You should ask the dealer or software publisher about dynamic linking, if you want the convenience of this feature. *See also* DYNAMIC DATA EXCHANGE *and* OBJECT LINKING AND EMBEDDING.

When separate is better. Integrated software packages aren't for everyone. Most integrated packages lack the specialized power for high-level use in any single application. If you have a serious need for three or more applications, you might want to purchase separate, high-level packages for each. And of course, if you do all your work in just one application, such as desktop publishing, you will probably prefer to put all your money into good, solid software for that application.

If you have a small business that's growing rapidly, and especially if you're hiring individuals to do specialized tasks within your company, you might want to buy separate software packages, one for each workstation, and link all the workstations in a local area network (LAN). You can then add dynamic linking to the system, getting advantages of integrated software along with the extra power you need. This will cost you more money at first, but will probably save you money in the long term. *See also* DATABASE, SPREADSHEET, GRAPHICAL USER INTERFACE, GRAPHICS, LOCAL AREA NETWORK, TERMINAL EMULATION SOFTWARE, *and* WORD PROCESSING.

Intel microprocessors

The name *Intel* has become synonymous with microprocessors used in IBM-compatible PCs. There have been several noteworthy Intel microprocessors since the first small computers became available in the late 1970s. (Macintosh computers generally employ Motorola microprocessors. For a discussion of these chips, *see* MOTOROLA MICROPROCESSORS.)

Intel microprocessors

The 8088 and 8086. Intel's 8088 chip was used in the original IBM Personal Computer. It made use of a scheme called *Industry Standard Architecture (ISA)*, which employed an 8-bit external data bus and a 16-bit internal data bus. The clock speed was about 6 MHz, or 6,000,000 Hertz. It could support up to one megabyte (1MB) of memory.

Intel's next chip for PCs, the 8086, was not used in very many computers because the technology made it obsolete before it caught on. The main difference between the 8086 and the 8088 was that the 86 had a 16-bit external data bus, which translated into a higher speed of communication with the rest of the computer. Shortly after the 86 became available, Intel developed the 80286, more commonly known as the 286.

The 80286. The 286 chip became available in the mid-1980s. Its big asset was the fact that it could address far more memory than the 88 or the 86: 16MB. This number is a bit misleading, however, since DOS cannot directly access this much memory; it must be done with a memory-management program. The directly addressable memory in DOS is limited to 1MB. The 286 used a 16-bit data bus and had a clock speed of 10 to 12 MHz.

The 286 can still be found in some computers in use today, although it is not installed in new ones. The 286 is good enough for some casual DOS applications, especially word processing. However, this chip does not work well with a graphical user interface (GUI) such as Windows or OS/2 because the 286 must operate in protected-memory mode rather than the enhanced mode preferred by these operating environments, and also because it lacks the brute processing power to deal with the graphical environment.

The 80386DX and 80386SX. About two years after the 286 came on the market, the *80386DX* was introduced. This chip is still found in some older computers. The 386 chip can support a graphical user interface, such as Windows or OS/2. This is probably the most important difference between it and the 286. In addition, the 386 has a 32-bit internal architecture and a 32-bit external bus, and can directly address up to 4000MB (or four gigabytes) of memory. It has a clock speed of 16 MHz to 33 MHz. The big leap in memory capacity originally came at a steep price; the first 386-based PCs were a hefty investment for casual users. The price of the 326 rapidly dropped, and many 386-based PCs are still in use today.

A special version of the 80386, the 386SX, was built with a 32-bit internal architecture and a 16-bit external bus, making it compatible with 16-bit machines.

The 80486DX and 80486SX. In the late 1980s, an improvement was made to chip technology, resulting in the 80486DX, which uses a

Intel microprocessors

32-bit bus and can directly address 64 GB of memory. The clock speed generally ranges from 20 MHz to 66MHz, although a "quadrupling" chip, the 80486DX4, can run at 100 MHz. The 80486SX is identical to the 486DX, except it does not have a numeric coprocessor. The 486SX still uses a 32-bit bus, however, like the 486DX. Note, therefore, that the DX/SX distinction is not the same for 486 chips as for 386 chips.

One of the big differences in the 486, compared with earlier microprocessors, is the fact that it can execute some instructions in a single cycle of the clock. The speed is therefore increased more than the frequency specification alone would suggest. The number of instructions per second (IPS) that a 486-based machine can perform is far greater than the IPS rating of a 386-based PC in most applications, even if they run at about the same clock speed. The difference is most noticeable in applications that require large numbers of instructions.

Beyond the 80486. Intel stopped numbering their microprocessors after the 486. Other companies were selling chips with the same number; there was apparently a problem copyrighting chip numbers. Thus, what would have been the Intel 586 is called the *Pentium*. It represents a significant advance over the 486. The chip after the Pentium is called the *P6 microprocessor*. Other companies still produce similar chips, but they have different names. Instead of the Pentium, for example, you'll hear about the NexGen Nx586, the AMD K5, or the Cyrix M1.

The table is a summary of the characteristics of Intel microprocessors. *See also* BIT, BUS, BYTE, CLOCK SPEED, COMMAND-DRIVEN SOFTWARE, GRAPHICAL USER INTERFACE, HERTZ, INDUSTRY-STANDARD ARCHITECTURE, MEMORY, MENU-DRIVEN SOFTWARE, P6 MICROPROCESSOR, *and* PENTIUM.

Intel microprocessors feature summary

Number	Data bus	Memory	Clock speed
8088	8 bits	1MB	4.77 to 10 MHz
8086	16 bits	1MB	4.77 to 10 MHz
80286	16 bits	16MB	16 MHz
80386	32 bits	4GB	16 to 33 MHz
80486	32 bits	4GB	20 to 50 MHz
Pentium (80586)	64 bits		66 MHz

Interactive technology

Interactive technology refers to a variety of services available to individuals and businesses through computer networks. In recent years, the term has come to refer to television programs in which you can actively participate.

New dimensions in television. Imagine watching a baseball game on TV. If you're a baseball fan, you're familiar with the center-field camera view, which allows you to play the role of "couch umpire." Have you ever seen a pitch that looked like a strike, but that the umpire called a ball? Did this ever make you so mad that you wished you were at the ballpark so you could boo and have the ump hear you?

Suppose you could make the calls, along with thousands or millions of other viewers, and have the vote tallied up instantly, appearing on the screen within a couple of seconds. You might see something like

```
TV VIEWER POLL
Strike: 44,898
Ball: 3550
```

This would flash on the scoreboard at the stadium, whereupon it would induce plenty of loud booing. You'd have your revenge, at least indirectly.

Or suppose there's a political discussion going on. Viewers could send in their opinions and see the results instantly. This could, in turn, direct the course of the discussion. Politicians would be made immediately aware of their constituents' opinions and concerns.

Pizza and workouts. You might be watching a commercial for pizza. Maybe there's a local branch of the pizza restaurant in your town. The commercial could pose the question, "Would you like a pizza now? If so, press Y on your interactive keypad." You might press Y, and then get a series of onscreen options such as this:

```
SAUSAGE = S
CHEESE  = C
OLIVES  = O
PEPPER  = P
```

and so on. You would make your selections and, within the standard 30 minutes, the pizza would arrive at your door. This commercial might be strategically followed by one for an exercise video, with similar instant-ordering options.

Some people question the ethics of interactive advertising. Debates have taken place in the past over subliminal advertisements (faint voices over public-address systems telling people they want a certain soft drink, for example). Interactive advertising will surely provoke controversy of this kind.

Obsession. Some people dream of interacting with everyone and everything, machine and human alike, minds awash with bits and bytes in a veritable Data Sea. Will it really come to this? Or will there be a backlash, an *uncanny valley* reaction, where people will say "Enough"? According to Bill Gates of Microsoft, companies are mainly interested in meeting consumer demand. There's no sense spending money creating something that no one will buy. Much research is being done to find out what the public wants and what it does not want. The successful companies will be the ones that do this research well.

Some people will sit on the couch and order pizzas, call balls and strikes, and respond to talk shows, neglecting their health, and perhaps even their friends and family. But these people are a small minority. Were interactive TV not available, they'd become obsessed with some other sedentary pastime. People become "couch potatoes" because they want to be, not because technology forces it on them.

The dark side. Interactive technology does pose some real dangers. Electronic fraud already costs society millions of dollars each year. Without the proper precautions, this situation might worsen.

Have you ever been billed for telephone calls or credit-card purchases you never made? Have you ever found money mysteriously missing from your bank account? Have you ever been sent "dunning letters," threatening to sue you for the collection of bills you did not owe? As computer technology proliferates, so does the potential for abuse by malicious hackers.

The average consumer should be very careful about putting credit card numbers and personal data into any electronic medium. This is as true today as it will be in 10, 25, or 50 years. Reasonable caution and restraint are the best policy. *See also* HACKER, INTERNET, MULTIMEDIA, NETWORK, ONLINE SERVICE, UNCANNY VALLEY, *and* VIRTUAL REALITY.

Interface

An *interface* is a device that carries data between a computer and its peripherals, or between a computer and a person. An interface consists of both hardware and software. The term is also used as a verb; when you connect two devices together and make them compatible, you *interface* them.

With peripherals. Suppose you want to use a computer with a certain printer. You must ensure that they'll work together. That is, you must interface the computer with the printer. This requires the right cable and connector (hardware), the use of the right data port (serial or parallel), and also the correct program (software) for the printer functions.

A similar situation exists for monitors, external diskette drives, CD-ROM drives, mice, and modems. In the future, you'll also be concerned with apparatus for virtual reality, robot control, and speech recognition and synthesis. *See also* PERIPHERALS.

The user interface. The interface you notice most is the one between your PC and yourself, called the *user interface*. There are three major types of user interface commonly employed in computers today: *command-driven software, menu-driven software*, and the *graphical user interface (GUI)*.

Command-driven interfaces require that you type statements, or commands, into your computer, telling it what you want it to do. It responds with messages. The most common command-driven system is DOS. In the future, new forms of command-driven operating systems will be refined, in particular to allow for speech recognition and speech synthesis. Using such interfaces, operators would give commands and hear responses via spoken words, with no visual contact necessary with any part of the machine.

Menu-driven interfaces work on the principle of option selection. It's like a multiple-choice quiz, instead of a fill-in-the-blanks test. You'll encounter these if you use a DOS shell or certain online services, especially on the *Internet*. Items are selected either with the keyboard or with a mouse or trackball.

A GUI is an advanced form of menu-driven interface that employs *icons*, or special symbols, instead of just words. Most GUIs are meant to be used with a pointing device such as a mouse or trackball. Three common GUIs are the Macintosh OS, Windows, and IBM's OS/2. In the future, you will see refinements of GUIs, making them usable by almost anyone. There might also be hybrid user interfaces, making use of the best features of command-driven, menu-driven and graphical schemes. *See also* COMMAND-DRIVEN SOFTWARE, DOS, GRAPHICAL USER INTERFACE, MACINTOSH, MENU-DRIVEN SOFTWARE, OS/2, SPEECH RECOGNITION, SPEECH SYNTHESIS, *and* WINDOWS.

Interlaced monitor

See MONITOR *and* RASTER.

Internal command

An *internal command* is a type of order that you can give ad DOS-based PC. An internal command is simpler for the computer to use than an *external command*. Internal commands are also used more often than external commands. All the internal commands are stored in a file called COMMAND.COM.

As soon as you load DOS, all the internal commands go into the computer memory. Therefore, when you type an internal command, it

International Business Machines

is executed immediately. External commands, on the other hand, require that you be in the right directory. If you try to use an external command that is not in the current directory, the computer will respond with the following message:

BAD COMMAND OR FILE NAME

See also COMMAND, DOS, *and* EXTERNAL COMMAND.

International Business Machines
See IBM.

Internet

The *Internet* is a worldwide, interconnected system of computer networks. It is, in a sense, the "mother of all networks," considered by some people to be the precursor of the information superhighway. In recent years, the Internet has been roughly doubling in size annually.

The beginning. Internet got started in the late 1960s, originally conceived as a computer network that could survive a nuclear war. It was called *ARPAnet.* (The acronym *ARPA* stands for *Advanced Research Projects Agency.*) This network of universities, scientific corporations, and branches of the government still exists, but it's now usually called the Internet, or just *the Net.*

Soon after the ARPAnet got going, engineers realized two things. First, a complex, decentralized computer network will keep working, at least to some extent, even when a large part of it is destroyed. This fulfilled the desires of scientists for an Armageddon-proof communications web. Second, it became clear that, if computers are to effectively communicate with each other, there must be a universal set of standards, called a *protocol*, to ensure that all the machines "speak the same language."

At that time, computers and networks had already evolved differences in their data formats. For example, IBM-compatible machines could not directly "talk" with Macintosh computers. In the event two different machines or networks don't use the same protocol, a *gateway* must be devised to translate the data between the two protocols. This has been effectively done, although the system is still a patchwork job by perfectionists' standards. *See also* GATEWAY *and* PROTOCOL.

E-mail and BBSs. For some PC users, communication via electronic mail (e-mail) and bulletin-board systems (BBSs) has practically replaced the postal service and live telephone conversations. On the Internet, you can leave messages for, and receive them from, friends and relatives scattered throughout the world. To e-mail someone via the Internet, that person must have an *address.* Internet addresses tend to be rather long, but they're easy to understand. For example, consider this fictitious address:

smith@sandwriters.org

The first part of the address, before the @ symbol, is the *username*. The word after the @ sign and before the period is the *host computer*. The three-letter abbreviation after the period is the *domain*. In this case, *org* stands for *organization*. There are several other domain abbreviations in common use, listed in the table.

Common Internet domain abbreviations

Abbreviation	Domain
.com	commercial
.edu	educational
.gov	government
.mil	military
.net	network
.org	organization

Rap sessions. You can carry on a typed conversation with other PC users via almost any *online service*, and the Internet is no exception. It takes a bit of getting used to, however. Typing to and reading from other people in realtime is more personal than letter writing because your addressees get their messages immediately. It's less personal than talking on the telephone, at least at first, because you cannot hear or make vocal inflections.

Amateur radio operators have been communicating in teletype for decades. They'll tell you that the initial feeling of strangeness will wear off quite fast, and soon you'll find teletyping a pleasant change from actual conversations. You will be able to tell much about people by the way they type, the words they use, and the manner in which they construct their sentences.

Rap groups on the Internet have formed in all subject areas, from biology to the men's movement, and from computer science to religion. You can talk directly with people in positions of knowledge and authority, or you can chat with a relative or friend.

Getting information. One of the most important features of Internet is the fact that it can get you in touch with thousands of sources of information. You can do library research without having to commute or travel. You can get data from corporations, educational institutions, and government agencies without having to order it via mail or telephone.

Information is transferred among computers by means of a *file transfer protocol (FTP)*. When you use FTP, the files at the remote computer become available to you, just as if they were in your own PC. When using FTP, you should be aware of the time at the remote location, and avoid, if possible, accessing files during the peak hours at the remote computer. Peak hours usually correspond to working hours, or approximately 8:00 a.m. to 5:00 p.m., Monday through Friday. You'll have to take time zones into account. If you're in New York, for example, you should probably wait until after 8:00 p.m. weekdays if you want to access data from Los Angeles.

Information servers. There are several ways to get information via the Internet. These schemes are called *servers*. Here are some of the more common Internet servers (this is by no means a complete list; new servers are constantly being developed):

➢ *Gopher* is one of the oldest and most widely used Internet servers. It uses a menu system, and you select items via the keyboard. (This is typical of Internet servers.) Gopher requires a little practice, but it's easy to catch on. The original Gopher was developed at the University of Minnesota, whose sports teams are known as the Gophers. The term is functionally illustrative; the Internet Gophers "dig" through cyberspace to find data for you.

When using an online service such as Delphi, which has direct Internet access, you can gain access to the Gopher server by selecting it from the main menu. You are then given a selection of Gopher servers for various subject areas and possibly at various locations. The best way to learn the system is to play around with it. Look for unusual, such as data about the manatees in Florida or the deer-hunting season in Wisconsin.

➢ In *Archie*, you can search for data by using words likely to be filenames or parts of file descriptions. There's a lot of trial and error in this process, but once you've located a file, it's fairly easy to find related ones. This can be done in e-mail, as well as in realtime.

Of course, if you know the exact name of a file, your job is easy. The Archie server will glean the current Internet filename list, and if it finds the name you specify, it will tell you where it is located. In Archie, many of the filenames are case-sensitive. That means you must be certain to use the correct upper- and lowercase combination of characters. For example, the filename Potomac.txt is not the same as potomac.txt; both of these differ from POTOMAC.TXT in a case-sensitive format.

➢ *Veronica* is a utility that searches Gophers for data according to keywords that you specify. For example, you might want to know about comets; you could then type *comets* as the keyword. Using Veronica is often a hit-and-miss affair, because some keywords will result in hundreds (even thousands) of file matches, while other seemingly reasonable keywords might not match anything. With experience, you'll develop a sense of what sorts of keywords work best, and what sorts don't work.

- *Telnet* is a method by which you can actually log onto remote computers via the Internet. For example, you might want to find out which books by a certain author are available in some local public library system. You can do this via the Internet Gophers. You'll have to proceed through several levels of menus. Eventually you'll have the option of connecting to the system via Telnet. You might receive a warning that you're leaving the Gopher, and to press a certain key combination if you get stuck or disconnected. Don't let the emphatic nature of this warning deter you from proceeding; just write down the escape key combination.

- *Wide Area Information System (WAIS)* is a data search utility that lets you look for information via either menus or keywords. Generally you select the source first, and then type keywords within that source. For example, if you were writing a paper or article about the earth's ozone layer, you might browse the menu for a topic such as environment, and then type *ozone* as the keyword for the search within that source.

- *World Wide Web (WWW or W3)* is one of the most powerful information servers you will find online. Its outstanding feature is *hypertext*, a scheme of instant cross-referencing. When you find a file that interests you, some of the words or phrases will be highlighted. When you select one of these words or phrases, you will be linked to one or more other documents dealing with that subject. For example, if you found a file with information about the ozone layer, you might find the word *chlorofluorocarbons* highlighted. You could select this word, and you would be linked to a file giving you information about chlorofluorocarbons, which are thought to be contributing to depletion of the ozone layer in the earth's upper atmosphere.

The future. In the next few years, the Internet will probably expand into the realm of interactive technology. Television sets will be connected directly into the information superhighway, along with millions of PCs in the United States and millions more in other countries around the world.

It's likely that amateur radio operators, using packet communications links, will become an increasingly important part of the information superhighway. If you happen to have a "ham" radio license, you'll be able to gain access to the medium from practically anyplace. You might be camping in a remote part of Alaska and, via amateur radio, send and receive e-mail from your friends and relatives back in the "lower 48," while the midnight sun provides illumination.

Internet

Some people believe that the information superhighway has received too much media attention, and that unforeseen problems will complicate and slow progress towards a universal network. Other people believe that the public demand will become so great that companies will have plenty of incentive to overcome the obstacles.

Jumping in. Assuming costs remain affordable, practically everyone will be part of the information superhighway before too long, just as almost every home in the United States today has at least one television and telephone. If you're not on Internet now, but would like to get access, try calling the computer science department of the nearest trade school, college, or university. Many, if not most, academic institutions have Internet access, and some will let you in for a reasonable charge.

If you aren't near a school that can provide you with Internet service, you can get connected through a commercial provider. You'll have to pay a fee, generally by the month. You might also have to pay for any hours you use per month past a certain maximum.

The easiest way to get hooked up, other than through a local educational facility, is probably through a commercial online service. Right now, Delphi offers the most complete access, but other services such as America Online, CompuServe, and Prodigy are moving rapidly to catch up.

For in-depth information about the Internet, nothing beats getting access and using it regularly. The PC-related magazines frequently have articles concerning the latest developments. Table B lists several books that have been written on the subject of Internet. *See also* BULLETIN-BOARD SYSTEM, DELPHI, ELECTRONIC MAIL, HYPERMEDIA, INFORMATION SUPERHIGHWAY, INTERACTIVE TECHNOLOGY, LOCAL AREA NETWORK, ONLINE SERVICE, PACKET COMMUNICATIONS, *and* WIDE-AREA NETWORK.

Internet bibliography

Falk, Bennet, *The Internet Roadmap* (SYBEX, Inc.).

Gilster, Paul, *The Internet Navigator* (Wiley and Sons).

Kehoe, Brendan, *Zen and the Art of Internet: A Beginner's Guide* (Prentice-Hall).

Krol, Ed, *The Whole Internet User's Guide and Catalog* (O'Reilly and Associates).

Lambert, Steve and Howe, Walt, *Internet Basics* (Random House).

LaQuey, Tracy and Ryer, Jeanne C., *The Internet Companion* (Addison Wesley Publishing Co.).

Malamud, Carl, *Exploring the Internet: A Technical Travelogue* (Prentice-Hall).

Interpolation

Interpolation

When there is a gap in data, but data is available on either side of the gap, an estimate of values within the gap can be made by *interpolation*. This can be done via "educated guessing," but it can also be done using computer software.

The graph at A shows an example of interpolation. The temperature (in degrees Fahrenheit) is graphed versus time for a day in April in Minneapolis. Data is taken every half hour, but the thermometer breaks between noon and 3:00 p.m., causing a gap in the curve. The solid line represents the curve derived from actual data.

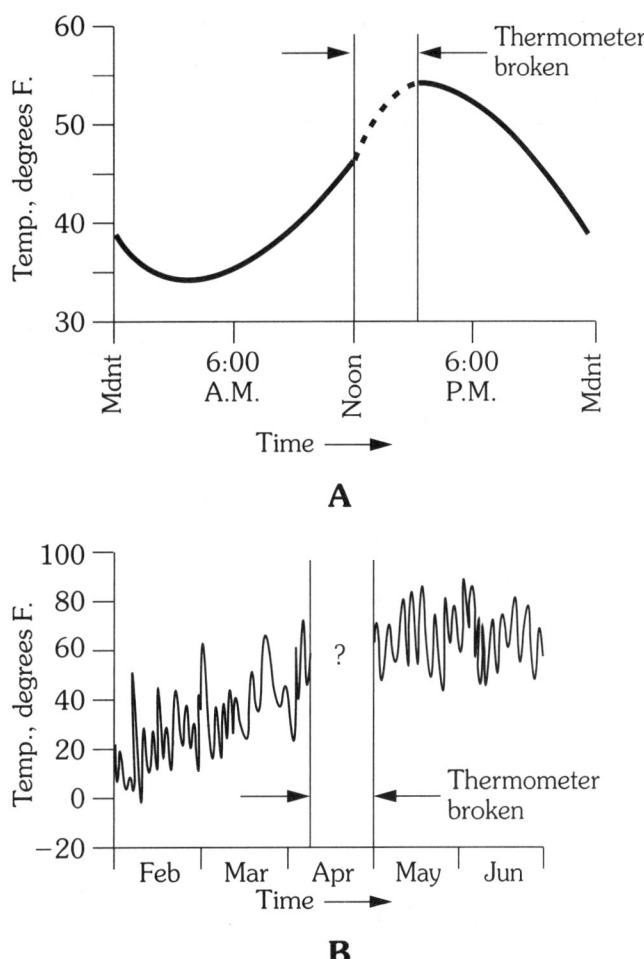

At A, interpolation is easy. At B, interpolation is impossible.

You can guess what the curve would look like if the thermometer hadn't broken. A computer could also fill in the curve along the dotted line. This curve is easy to interpolate, but when there is insufficient data, interpolation is either impossible or must be done in a very generalized way. A wildly fluctuating curve defies all guesswork concerning the values within large gaps. The graph at B shows an example of such a

Interpreter

situation. This is a hypothetical, continuous graph of temperature versus time in Minneapolis over a period of several months.

There is no way for a computer program to interpolate individual points within the gap shown in drawing B; no computer can tell you what the temperature was at 5:30 p.m. on April 21. A computer program can, however, illustrate the general nature of the curve during this period, just as you can look at the graph and imagine how to fill in the gap. *See also* EXTRAPOLATION.

Interpreter

In a computer system, an *interpreter* translates programs into directives. This makes it much easier to use a computer than it would be if the operator tried to communicate with the computer directly in machine language. Machine language consists of the actual logic highs and lows (ones and zeros) with which the computer "thinks."

An interpreter does basically the same things as a *compiler*. The main difference is that, while a compiler translates everything before the program is run, an interpreter translates the data while the program is run. One advantage of an interpreter is that it can help the operator pinpoint programming errors. This is a great help to beginning programmers because it creates a "teach-yourself" environment. It also makes debugging easier, whether you are a novice programmer or a pro.

The main disadvantage of an interpreter compared with a compiler is that an interpreter takes more time to run a program. This becomes significant for long, complex programs. However, once you have created a program with the more user-friendly interpreter, you can often run it with a compiler, speeding things up. *See also* COMPILER, HIGH-LEVEL LANGUAGE, *and* MACHINE LANGUAGE.

Inverter

The term *inverter* has several meanings in electronics and computer science. The two most common types of inverter are the *logical inverter* and the *power inverter*.

In digital circuits. A logical inverter, also called a *NOT gate*, has one input and one output. It performs the logical NOT operation, also called *negation*.

The output of a logical inverter is high, or logic 1 ("true") if and only if the input is low, or logic 0 ("false"). The output is low if and only if the input is high. The symbol for an inverter, along with its logical truth table, is shown in the drawing at A. *See also* AND GATE, EXCLUSIVE-NOR GATE, EXCLUSIVE-OR GATE, NOR GATE, *and* OR GATE.

Power inverters. An electrical inverter converts a low, direct-current (dc) voltage to a much higher, alternating-current (ac) voltage. Most

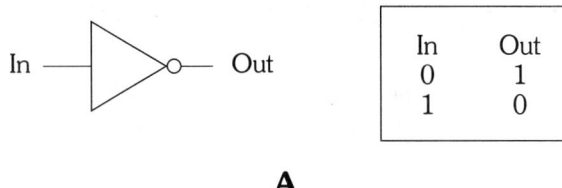
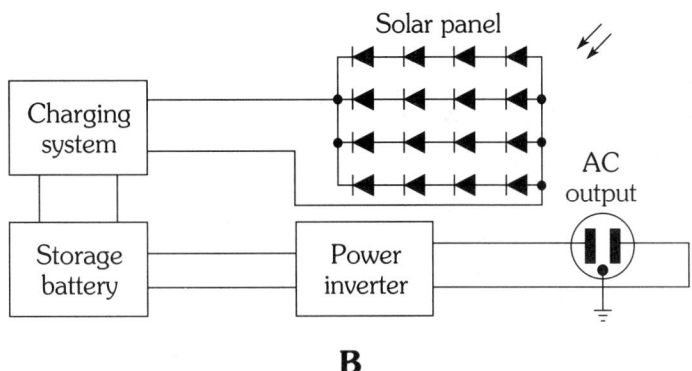

A

B

The logical symbol and truth table for a digital inverter (A), and a block diagram of a power inverter (B).

often, the input is 12 volts dc, and the output is 117 volts ac. These devices are commercially available. The price depends, in general, on how much power the inverter can handle. Using an inverter, you can operate household appliances from battery power.

There are two classes of power inverters: the "light-duty" type used in cars, trucks, trailers, and boats, and the "heavy-duty" type used in stand-alone solar power systems. The drawing at B is a block diagram of a solar power system, using a power inverter to get 117 volts ac from a bank of rechargeable batteries that supply dc at a low voltage. The batteries are charged, as needed, by a solar panel and charging circuit.

Generally, only small appliances can be used with light-duty inverters. Examples include desktop computers, monitors, printers, modems, fax machines, lamps, radios, and television sets. Large appliances, like refrigerators and air conditioners, require the heavy-duty type. Also, large battery banks are needed for heavy appliances because they draw far more current than a single automotive battery can deliver. *See also* POWER SUPPLY *and* UNINTERRUPTIBLE POWER SUPPLY.

ISA

See INDUSTRY STANDARD ARCHITECTURE.

ISO/OSI model

See OPEN SYSTEMS INTERCONNECTION REFERENCE MODEL.

Jaggies

Some computer-generated images have a characteristic, jagged-edged appearance. The effect is most pronounced in images from low-end software that uses bitmapped graphics and from printers with a low DPI (dots per inch) rating. It is technically known as *aliasing*, but is more often called the *jaggies*. Jaggies are the most noticeable in curved or diagonal lines or when an image is enlarged.

The images in a bitmap are not continuous, but are built up from squares called *pixels* (picture elements). Pixels are elementary parts in a bitmap. It's impossible to fill in one part of a pixel one way, and another part another way. The whole region within the pixel must be the same shade and color. Therefore, jaggies occur to the greatest extent in tiny images or ones that contain extreme detail.

The drawings on the next page show what happens when a dot of varying size is portrayed in bitmapped graphics. At A, there are three dots. The smallest is not much larger than the pixels that comprise the image; it doesn't even look like a dot. The middle-sized dot is more nearly circular; the biggest dot is a fairly good representation.

Suppose you enlarge the bitmapped image in drawing A? If the computer is told to enlarge the smallest dot by a factor of five, each pixel will be enlarged by a factor of five. The jaggies will be five times bigger (see drawing B). This is why bitmapped images don't lend themselves well to resizing. *See also* ANTI-ALIASING, BITMAP, BITMAPPED GRAPHICS, DOTS PER INCH, *and* PIXEL.

Job

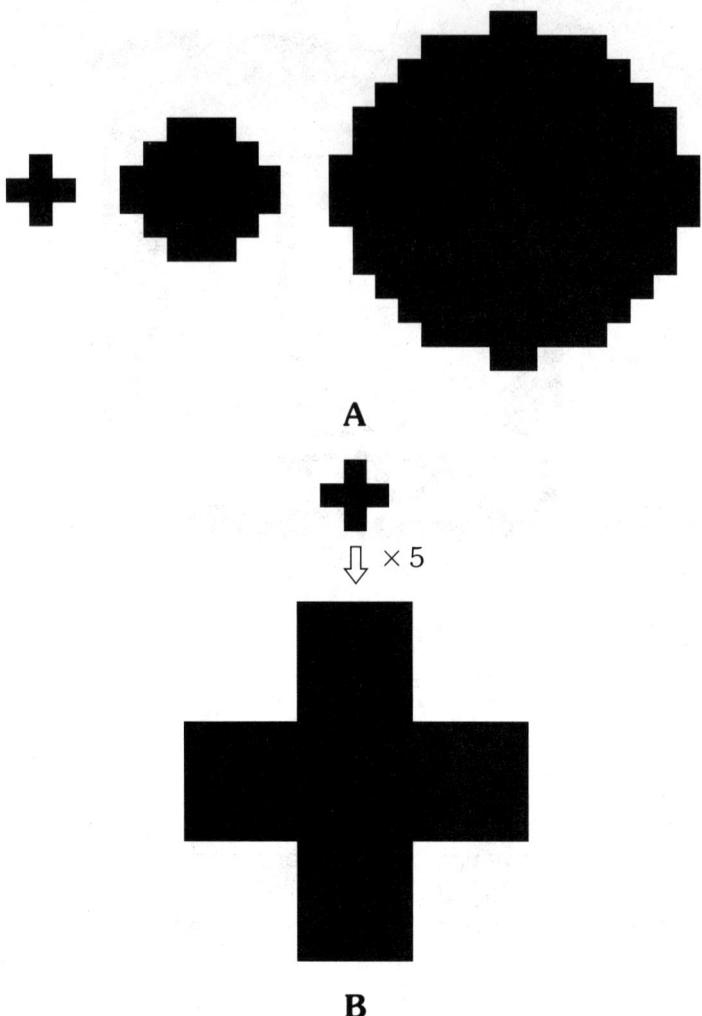

At A, three dots of varying size in bitmapped graphics. At B, blowing up a tiny "dot" worsens jaggies.

Job

A *job* is anything a computer does automatically, without your having to guide it through the process. Once the machine has received the order, it carries out the job while you do something else.

The most common type of job is the transfer of data from one place to another. You might have your PC print out a document or send it via modem to another PC. You might tell your computer to defragment its hard disk or back up its files on a tape drive.

Jobs are often done as *background processing*. For example, you might be writing a report using your word processing software; at the same time, a dot-matrix printer is spitting out a hardcopy of a short story you wrote a few days ago. In this case, the writing of the report is *foreground processing*; it is not technically a job because you're thinking about it (hopefully) as you write it. As you work on the report, the printer zips away without your having to do anything, except be sure the paper piles up neatly as it emerges from the printer. *See also* BACKGROUND PROCESSING *and* FOREGROUND PROCESSING.

Join

One of the most important features of a relational database is its ability to take data from multiple sources and process it so that it tells you just what you need to know. *Join* is an operation in which two files are combined, producing a third file telling you something specific.

Whenever you join files, you must give the computer three pieces of information:

- The filenames to be joined
- The pertinent information in each file
- The data you need in the composite file

As an example of how you might use a join operation, suppose you're conducting a blind survey (in which names are not used) of 10,000 people to get their opinions about environmental issues. You send out 10,000 questionnaires. The people's addresses are in a file called ADDRESS.DAT. Further suppose that your questionnaire contains a request for a donation to an environmental protection fund. A second file, called DONATE.DAT, lists the addresses of the people who contribute, and the amount donated in each case.

Perhaps you're curious as to the extent of the correlation between people's professed concern about the environment and their willingness to donate money. You join the files ADDRESS.DAT and DONATE.DAT. If you have a relational database, you might request, in the third file, a chart showing the amount of money donated versus the level of environmental concern, based on questionnaire responses. *See also* DATABASE.

Joseph, Earl

Earl Joseph is a *futurist*, a person whose mindset is ahead of the times. He has been compared with inventor/philosopher R. Buckminster Fuller, the man who conceived the idea of the geodesic dome.

Computer evolution. Earl Joseph predicted the development of integrated circuits (ICs), now known commonly as "chips," years before they became available. He has made other technological forecasts that later came true.

Joseph's predictions for artificial intelligence (AI) suggest that computers and robots, working in synergy, might evolve on their own, without human intervention. Computers, with robots to do the labor, might conduct research and development, run labs, and manufacture new and improved robots and computers. Some of these improved machines could be involved in the task of creating still better robots and computers. Other machines would be used by humans to enhance the quality of their lives.

Computerized homes. Futurists have often observed that, even in modern society, humans spend a lot of time doing menial, mechanical things. Often, these chores involve taking care of the very machines that are supposed to save us time we'd otherwise have to spend doing chores!

Joseph has suggested that homes will someday be entirely automated. You won't have to do laundry, wash dishes, cook, mow the lawn, or shovel snow. You'll never have to paint the walls, vacuum the floor, clean the toilets, dust your desk, or even drive the car. And above all, you won't have to maintain lawn mowers, snow blowers, and robots. Home automation will finally become ideal: something to take away mundane work, freeing us to do things like paint portraits or write music.

Some psychologists think such an existence would not be altogether good. It is possible, they argue, to have too much leisure time. It is possible that some people who can afford complete home automation will elect to forgo it.

Cybercommanders. Along an entirely different path of cyber-evolution, Joseph has suggested that computerized robots could be built to serve as soldiers. This topic has been exploited by authors of science fiction.

A fleet of robots, all under the direction of a supercomputer, would have no fear, and could fight a war without loss of human life. This could create a "war machine" against which no human army could possibly cope. Maybe, however, by the time technology advances to that stage, war will be obsolete. Some AI researchers think that the "cybercommanders," or computers in charge of a war fought by robots against other robots, would declare a cease-fire after coming to the conclusion that the whole affair was illogical. *See also* ARTIFICIAL INTELLIGENCE, ARTIFICIAL LIFE, COMPUTERIZED HOME, FUTURISTS, PERSONAL ROBOTS, *and* UNCANNY VALLEY.

Joystick

A *joystick* is a control device commonly used with video and computer games. The joystick gets its name from its resemblance to the joystick in an aircraft.

The most primitive version of the joystick, shown in the drawing at A, is capable of movement in two or three dimensions. The device is a movable lever or handle set in a ball-bearing within a control box.

Two dimensions of movement, labeled x and y, are obtained by pushing the lever from side to side, up and down, or a combination of these. Some joysticks can be rotated clockwise and counterclockwise in addition to the usual two coordinates, allowing control in a third dimension (z).

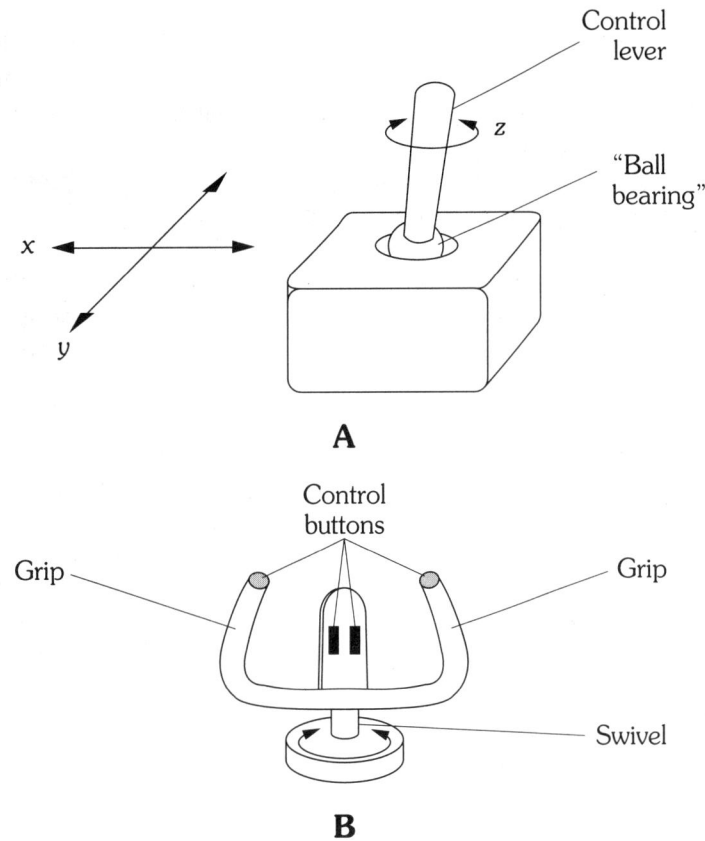

At A, a simple joystick; at B, a yoke.

More advanced joysticks have control buttons on the lever or in the control box. These joysticks evolved to meet the demands of computer games and simulations that have become ever more sophisticated. One highly advanced joystick is more properly called a *yoke* (see B in the drawing) because it is a miniature replica of the yoke that aircraft pilots use. This design arose from computerized flight simulators, which are used to train military pilots.

A joystick or yoke does not work well in place of a mouse or a trackball. The converse is also true: mice and trackballs don't work well as joysticks or yokes. The applications are vastly different; each device has been tailored to meet specific needs. *See also* MOUSE and TRACKBALL.

Jungian-world theory

An interesting motivation for research in artificial intelligence (AI) is called the *Jungian-world theory*. According to this notion, people

Justification

keep making the same mistakes in every generation. It seems that societies cannot learn from history. Also, humanity in general seems unable to foretell or care about the consequences of their actions. This is true despite keen awareness on the part of some individuals, and despite the efforts of these individuals to inform the masses. Therefore, as the saying goes, "History repeats itself."

This theory has been demonstrated many times. People keep fighting wars for the same reasons. The great peace, the final settlement, never comes. Wars don't solve problems; in fact, they sometimes create new troubles. Today, in addition to war, humanity faces overpopulation, pollution, global warming, and ozone depletion. What, if anything, can be done to stop this vicious circle?

According to researcher Charles Lecht, the answer is to develop AI to the point that machines become smarter and wiser than people. Perhaps a brilliant computer can help humans control our destiny, so that we need not keep reliving the same old calamities. At least, this is Lecht's hope.

Many researchers doubt that machines can become smarter than people. However, even most skeptics concede that computers, if they become powerful enough, might help us find answers to some of our collective problems—solutions we might never discover without computers' unique insights. *See also* ARTIFICIAL INTELLIGENCE, COMPUTER CONSCIOUSNESS, *and* LECHT, CHARLES.

Justification

Justification is a term used in word processing and desktop publishing. Usually, it refers to text that is flush along both the left and the right margins.

When you print out reports, theses, or manuscripts, you should generally align the text along the left margin, but not the right margin. This is known as *flush-left* or *left-justified* text. Sometimes it is also called *ragged-right*. Most professors and editors like to see term papers, theses, and manuscripts in this form; some insist on it.

If you want to publish something yourself, you might want to use full justification. Magazines and books are usually printed this way because it creates a neat appearance. It's not an absolute requirement, however. Some publications use flush-left, ragged-right text to give the work a friendly, informal flair.

Most word processing software packages have a provision for creating fully justified printout. The appearance of the finished work can be further improved by using a proportional font. *See also* FLUSH-LEFT/RIGHT/CENTER *and* PROPORTIONAL FONT.

Karnaugh map

A *Karnaugh map* is a pictorial breakdown of a logical expression, showing all the operations. It gets its name from its inventor, electrical engineer Maurice Karnaugh.

Consider the *Boolean algebra* expression

V = (W + X)(–Y + Z)

Here, addition refers to the logical OR operation, multiplication to the logical AND, and a minus sign to the logical NOT, also called *inversion*. The equal sign means "if and only if," which mathematicians write as *iff*. This expression might then be also written

V iff (W OR X) AND ((NOT Y) OR Z).

The table (page 586) is a breakdown of this logical expression into its components, using a columnar format. It is called a *truth table*.

The drawing (page 586) is a schematic diagram of the expression using digital logic symbols. In this case, there are four inputs (W, X, Y, Z) and one output (V). The individual logical operations are shown as *logic gates*. The logic diagram can be considered a Karnaugh map.

Often, logical expressions are exceedingly complicated, especially in computer systems. A Karnaugh map of an entire computer would occupy hundreds, thousands, or millions of square miles—far more

Karnaugh map

Truth table for V = (W + X)(−Y + Z)

W	X	Y	Z	W + X	−Y	−Y + Z	V
0	0	0	0	0	1	1	0
0	0	0	1	0	1	1	0
0	0	1	0	0	0	0	0
0	0	1	1	0	0	1	0
0	1	0	0	1	1	1	1
0	1	0	1	1	1	1	1
0	1	1	0	1	0	0	0
0	1	1	1	1	0	1	1
1	0	0	0	1	1	1	1
1	0	0	1	1	1	1	1
1	0	1	0	1	0	0	0
1	0	1	1	1	0	1	1
1	1	0	0	1	1	1	1
1	1	0	1	1	1	1	1
1	1	1	0	1	0	0	0
1	1	1	1	1	0	1	1

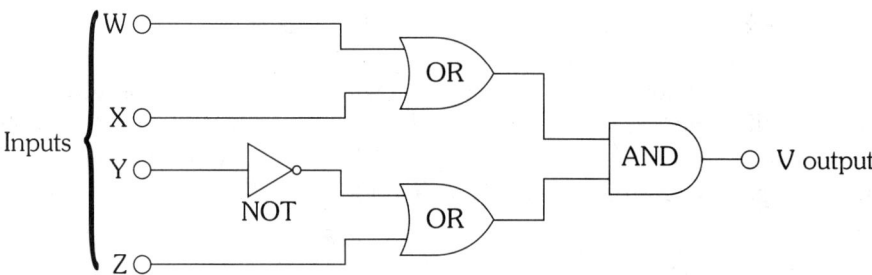

Logic circuit for V = (W + X)(−Y + Z).

physical space than the computer itself—if the map were written in symbols you could read without a microscope.

For most complex logical expressions, there are many different ways to arrange the individual functions to get the desired outputs. Some arrangements are simpler than others. The more complex the expression, the more different equivalent circuits exist. The engineer's job is to find the simplest arrangement for the task, thereby minimizing the number of hardware components in the system. Karnaugh maps can be helpful for this purpose. Can you find a simpler way to write the logical expression depicted here? *See also* BOOLEAN ALGEBRA *and* LOGIC GATES.

Kerning

In traditional nonproportional type, each letter typically gets the same amount of space as every other letter, just like the hardcopy from a conventional typewriter. When you hear that a certain font has 10 characters per inch (CPI), for example, it means that each letter, numeral, and symbol (even the period and the comma) is allotted 1/10 of an inch of horizontal space along the line. An 80-character line at 10 CPI would measure eight inches; the same 80-character line at 20 CPI would measure four inches.

The problem with constant character spacing is that it looks uneven because relatively large gaps can appear between characters. *Kerning*, which involves squeezing pairs of characters closer together when their shapes allow, can sometimes improve the appearance of a font and save line space. This is especially true in headings and titles that are in much larger type than the text.

Certain letter pairs lend themselves to kerning more than others. Among these are the uppercase combinations *AT*, *TA*, *AV*, *VA*, *AW*, *WA*, *AY*, *YA*, *LT*, *LV*, *LW*, and *LY*. Try writing these uppercase letters out neatly in block printing (like you learned in first grade), and you'll see how they can be squeezed together to save space. *See also* PROPORTIONAL FONT.

Key assignments

The keys on a computer keyboard can be programmed in many different ways. The things that happen when you press a given key depend to some extent on the operating system, and also on the application. The term *key assignments* refers to the correspondence between keys and the things that happen when you strike them.

Standard assignments. In some operating systems and applications, the keys do exactly what you would expect. The letter, numeral, and punctuation keys are good examples. Generally, when you press the D key, you can expect either *D* or *d* to appear on the screen.

Sometimes, however, the keys might be programmed quite differently. For example, pressing H in certain programs might cause the computer to provide you with help, rather than generating an uppercase or lowercase *H* on the screen. You'll usually know this from some kind of clue, such as the presence of the word *Help* with the *H* underlined on the screen as one of several options to choose.

Programmable assignments. Some keys, particularly the *function keys*, can be programmed to fill special needs. It's not intuitively clear what each of these keys will do; therefore, people have no

Keyboard

preconceived notion of what will happen when one of these keys is struck. There's nothing to unlearn in the process of using the function keys, unless, of course, you've been using one particular software package for a long time and then change to some other system with different function-key assignments.

In many Windows-based programs, for example, pressing the F1 brings up a help screen. In WordPerfect for DOS, on the other hand, pressing F1 causes your last action to be undone. Some programs allow users to reassign keys so that they can make the program function like the ones they are familiar with. *See also* FUNCTION KEYS, KEYBOARD, *and* KEY STATUS INDICATORS.

Keyboard

A *keyboard* is a set of buttons for entering data into a computer or terminal. There are several different keyboard arrangements. Most resemble that of typewriter, along with various other keys. Engineers have striven to put these other keys where they are easy to use.

Modern PC keyboards. One of the most popular keyboards today is the *enhanced PC keyboard*, used with IBM-compatible PCs. It has 101 keys, arranged in several sections. Along with the main part containing alphanumeric keys, there is a calculator-like keypad, a set of 12 function keys in a row above the main part of the keyboard, and a set of arrow keys that allow movement of the cursor up, down, right, and left.

The enhanced PC keyboard evolved after years of human engineering. It is probably the most user-friendly keyboard available for use with IBM clones. There are still some inconsistencies with the arrangement, however. For example, in some versions, there is only one Ctrl key located at the extreme lower left; in other versions, the Ctrl key is next to the A key; in many others, there are two Ctrl keys, one beneath each Shift key.

The Macintosh line of computers uses a keyboard with functions similar to those of IBM machines. The layout of the keys is somewhat different, but overall, Macintosh and IBM keyboards do just about the same things.

Rollover and autorepeat. One of the most important features in a modern PC keyboard is *rollover*. Try pressing some key, say G, and then press another key, say H, before letting up on the G key. If the keyboard has *rollover*, you should get the sequence *GH*. If your keyboard does not have rollover, you'll just get the letter G.

When you're typing at high speed, you'll hit the keys at an extremely irregular pace. Rollover ensures that you will not miss letters as a result of striking two keys at almost the same instant.

When you're buying a PC, be sure the keyboard has rollover. The best way to make certain is to test the machine in the store. While you're at it, find out whether the keyboard has a "feel" that agrees with you. It should; if you buy the machine, you'll have to live with it!

If the keyboard has *autorepeat*, a character will rapidly repeat after the key has been held down for about a second. You might or might not want this feature. Some PCs employ autorepeat on only a few keys, such as the period and the letter X; other keyboards have autorepeat on all keys. Sometimes the function can be switched on and off. *See also* CHARACTER, DVORAK KEYBOARD LAYOUT *and* QWERTY KEYBOARD LAYOUT.

Keyboard accessories

Keyboard accessories are various hardware attachments that can make operation of a PC more convenient, more efficient, and less tiring. They can also make it more fun. Most computer stores have a selection of keyboard accessories. Some of the more common ones are briefly discussed here.

Wrist rest. If you spend very much time working at a computer or terminal, you run some risk of developing cumulative trauma disorders. Back and neck soreness, eye fatigue, and inflammation of certain tissues in the wrist (known as *carpal tunnel syndrome*) sometimes plague people who work for long periods at computers or terminals.

Carpal tunnel syndrome, if allowed to progress untreated, can result in chronic disability and pain. If you think you might be developing this problem, you should consult a doctor about it. One possible method of reducing strain on the hands and wrists is a wrist rest, which can be attached directly to your keyboard (see the drawing at A on next page). *See also* CUMULATIVE TRAUMA DISORDERS.

Under-desk shelf. Back strain can result from a desk that's too high or a chair that's too low. One way to alleviate this problem is to get an under-desk shelf for the keyboard, as shown in the drawing at B. (You can buy a lower desk or a higher chair, of course, but that costs more.)

The shelf places the keyboard at a lower elevation than that of the desk; it also provides some extra space on the desk. In addition to this, it moves you farther from the monitor screen, which can help minimize eye strain and reduce your exposure to ELF fields.

Templates. Do you have trouble remembering which keys do what? Do you change applications often, so that the functions of the keys are never constant, and you can never quite get used to them? If either of these things are a problem for you, perhaps a set of templates can help.

Keyboard accessories

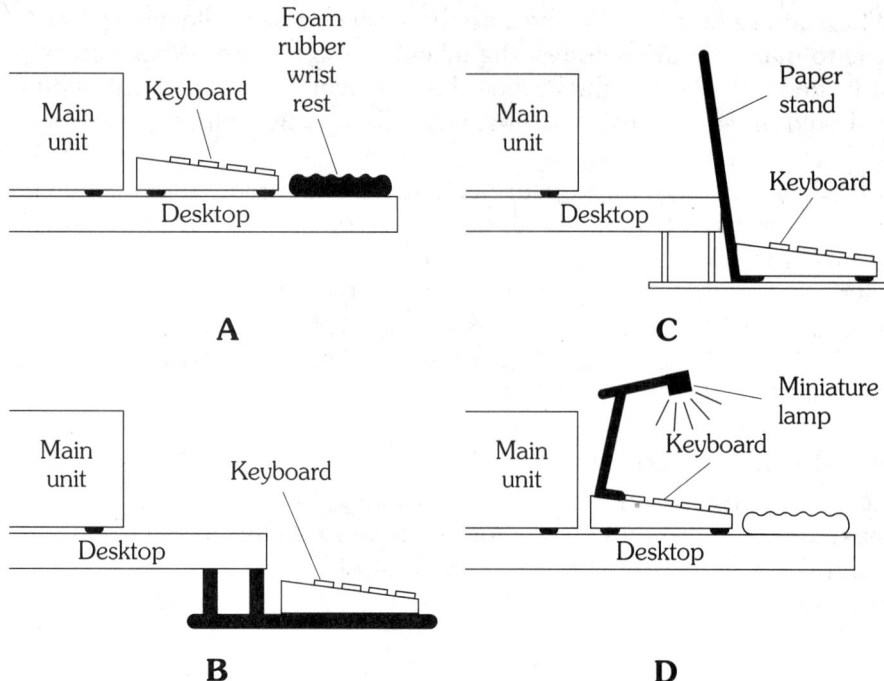

Keyboard accessories include a wrist rest (A), an under-desk shelf (B), a paper stand (C), and a miniature lamp (D).

Templates come with some integrated software packages. These are multiprogram packages, popular with beginning and intermediate PC users. When you do word processing, for example, you can lay that template down on your keyboard to help you remember which keys perform which functions. When you change to the database, you can remove the word processing template and put down the database template. *See also* INTEGRATED SOFTWARE PACKAGE.

Clocks and calculators. Suppose you're word processing at your new state-of-the-art computer, and you need to make a simple arithmetic calculation (such as subtracting a check you just wrote from your bank account). You get up, look for your $4.99 solar-powered calculator, compute the solution to your problem, and type it into your PC.

It would be overkill to quit your word processor, go into spreadsheet, and do a simple subtraction. However, you can at least save yourself the strain of having to get up and scrounge for a pocket calculator. Miniature stick-on calculators with basic arithmetic functions are available as keyboard accessories. Small clocks are available, too.

Paper stand. Suppose you're typing someone's college thesis into your PC, using the author's rough-draft hardcopy. Even if you're a good touch typist, you'll need to move your eyes from the paper to the monitor screen and back many times during the typing process. This can strain your eyes, neck, and back, especially if your desk is not very well arranged. A paper stand, which can be attached to your keyboard, will minimize eye and head movement. The drawing at C shows a typical arrangement.

Paper stands can't support much weight. If you're using a large book, such as a dictionary or encyclopedia, you're better off setting it down flat on the desk. If such a book falls forward onto your keyboard, it will probably hit the keys in such a way as to erase all the data you input since you last saved it on disk. As Murphy's Laws proclaim, "If something can go wrong, it will." You can save data on your hard disk frequently, say every five or 10 minutes, to avoid such a catastrophe in the event of a mishap.

Keyboard lamps. Have you ever used a little clip-on lamp, so that you could read a book at night while your spouse was sleeping? Such a lamp can be attached to the keyboard of a PC, enhancing the illumination of the keys without producing screen glare.

The main advantage of small keyboard lamps such as the one in the drawing at D is that they save energy. The bulb consumes only a watt or two, compared with 60 to several hundred watts for a desk lamp or floor lamp. A battery-powered keyboard lamp can even be used with a laptop computer if, for example, you have a penchant for computing at night while camping. However, the lamp should not be powered from the same battery as the computer.

Keyboard covers and skins. All electrical components attract dust because the electricity pulls particles toward whatever is charged. When electronic devices used vacuum tubes that needed hundreds of volts to work, this problem was much more severe than it is today. However, computer parts, especially the keyboard, are still vulnerable to problems resulting from accumulated dust.

When you aren't using your PC, you should keep it and its keyboard covered. A keyboard cover will keep dust from dirtying the keyboard and building up inside the enclosure. When you are using the machine, a keyboard skin can protect it from spilled liquids as well as dust. The skin is a thin, transparent, flexible membrane that lets you operate the keys right through it.

The PC magazines regularly carry ads and articles concerning the newest gimmicks for keyboard accessories. You can also check at your local computer superstore. *See also* ERGONOMICS.

Key status indicators

In IBM-compatible PCs, certain keys affect the overall behavior of the keyboard. These keys include Caps Lock, Insert, Number Lock, and Scroll Lock. They each toggle (switch back and forth) between two different conditions. *Key status indicators* tell you, at a glance, which condition each of these keys is in.

Keystrokes

The status of Caps Lock, Number Lock, and Scroll Lock are shown by small lights on the enhanced PC keyboard. Some earlier versions of IBM-compatible keyboards do not have status indicators for these three keys, but some software programs will show the key status on the monitor screen. The status of the Insert key is typically shown by the shape of the cursor on the screen. A thin horizontal line beneath characters usually indicates *overtype mode*; a square box indicates *insert mode*.

In some applications, other keys besides the most common ones mentioned here affect keyboard behavior. Software usually provides for an onscreen indicator for the status of such keys, so you aren't operating "blind." *See also* CAPS LOCK KEY AND LIGHT, INSERT KEY, NUMBER LOCK KEY AND LIGHT, *and* SCROLL LOCK KEY AND LIGHT.

Keystrokes

The efficiency of a program in command-driven software can be measured in terms of the number of keys you must hit to get something done. In general, the fewer *keystrokes* needed to accomplish a task, the more user-friendly is the software.

In some applications, the number of keystrokes can be minimized by writing software so that the commands are as short as possible. For example, in DOS, the command CHDIR (change directory) has been shortened to CD.

Another way to minimize keystrokes is to use a menu-driven or graphical interface, rather than command-driven software. You might consider a mouse click as one keystroke, and a double-click as two keystrokes. Commands rarely require more than two keystrokes in an operating system such as Windows, the Macintosh OS, or OS/2. However, when using a mouse, you must move a pointer or cursor around on the screen. This does not technically require any keystrokes, but it does take some time.

Another advantage to minimizing keystrokes is that it reduces the risk of computer operators developing carpal tunnel syndrome, one of the cumulative trauma disorders arising from prolonged operation of a keyboard.

Some applications require many keystrokes no matter what the operating system; word processing is one example. To create a text document, it must be typed. Eventually, speech recognition might eliminate much of the typing, and therefore most of the keystrokes, associated with word processing. Carpal tunnel syndrome will then be less common than it is now, although new problems will probably arise. (Chronic laryngitis might become troublesome!) There will also be a noise factor in large offices; workstations will have to be separated by acoustical barriers.

In recent years, with the proliferation of computers in the workplace, keystroke counting has been introduced by some employers as a means of measuring the amount of work an employee performs each hour, day, or week. This is easy to do; a supervisor can simply bring up a file on any employee and find out how many keystrokes he or she has made in a given time period. This has been denounced by employees as inhuman and Orwellian, and as a result, some companies have discontinued the practice. *See also* COMMAND-DRIVEN SOFTWARE, CUMULATIVE TRAUMA DISORDERS, *and* MENU-DRIVEN SOFTWARE.

Killer

When a company first puts out a new technology, they cross their fingers and hope their brainchild will be well received. There is always a possibility that it will get a cold reception, but engineers and programmers who stick with an idea, even when others doubt it will succeed, are those who are convinced that the public will find some *killer* application (or "killer app") for their brainchild.

The history of personal computing is replete with examples of things that were dismissed as having little use, and later justified themselves by either finding or becoming killer apps. Digital sound technology, for example, originally seemed relevant only to people who wanted to play games or have computers make up cute little tunes. When popular music bands (rock bands especially) got hold of sound technology, however, it caused a revolution in the commercial music industry. Electronic music processing became a killer app for sound technology.

The graphical user interface (GUI) has become a *killer interface*. Today, it seems obvious that the GUI was a great idea just waiting to be discovered. However, the maverick engineers and programmers who first pioneered the GUI had no assurance that it would be successful, other than faith.

The personal digital assistant (PDA) is an example of a device that is searching for a killer app. While PDAs can be fun to play with, there are limitations and problems to be overcome before they'll be considered practical investments by large numbers of people.

Of all the forms of software in existence today, two—communications and word processing—have become *system killer apps* on a massive scale. These are applications that suffice as the entire motivation for someone to buy a computer. Thousands of PC users hardly ever do anything but word processing on their machines; thousands of others spend almost all their time online. There are other people for whom games, databases, spreadsheets, or graphics represent a system killer app.

Virtual reality is a technology that might wildly succeed or pathetically fail, depending on who you ask. It's quite probable that, if the cost comes down enough, it will become immensely popular, becoming a big-time killer app, along with word processing and communications. Personal robots also holds some promise in this respect. *See also* COMMUNICATIONS, PERSONAL ROBOTS, VIRTUAL REALITY, *and* WORD PROCESSING.

Kilobyte

The prefix *kilo* means thousands. A *kilobyte*, abbreviated *K* or *KB*, is a unit of information equal to about 1000 bytes.

Computer data is measured in powers of two, rather than powers of 10. This arises from the fact that digital expressions are always in base 2, where the only values are 0 (low) and 1 (high). The actual value of 1K is not exactly 1000 bytes, but instead, is $2^{10} = 1024$ bytes.

The kilobyte is, by today's standards, a small unit of data, corresponding to about one page of typewritten, double-spaced text. A typical high-density, double-sided diskette has room for over a thousand kilobytes (a megabyte). A small hard disk can hold around 100,000K; a fairly large one can accommodate more than a million (a gigabyte). *See also* BINARY DATA, BYTE, GIGABYTE, MEGABYTE, *and* TERABYTE.

Kilohertz

See HERTZ.

K-line programming

K-line programming is a method by which an artificially intelligent machine can learn as it does a job, so that it will have an easier time doing the same or similar work in the future.

Suppose you have a personal robot that you use for handiwork around the house. The water heater breaks down and you instruct the robot to fix it. The robot must use certain tools to do the repair. The first time the robot repairs the water heater, it must find the tools by trial-and-error. But it encodes each tool in its memory, perhaps according to shape. It also encodes the sequence in which the tools are used to fix the water heater. Then, the next time the water heater needs repair, the robot can refer to the K-line: the list of tools used before, and also the order in which they were used.

Of course, there are many different things that can go wrong with a water heater. The second time it breaks down, the K-line for the first repair might not work. The robot would then have to refine its knowledge, devising a second K-line for the new problem. Over time, the robot would learn several different schemes for fixing a water heater, each scheme tailored to a specific problem (see the drawing). This learning-by-experience process is called *heuristic knowledge*. *See also* ARTIFICIAL INTELLIGENCE, HEURISTIC KNOWLEDGE, KNOWLEDGE, *and* PERSONAL ROBOTS.

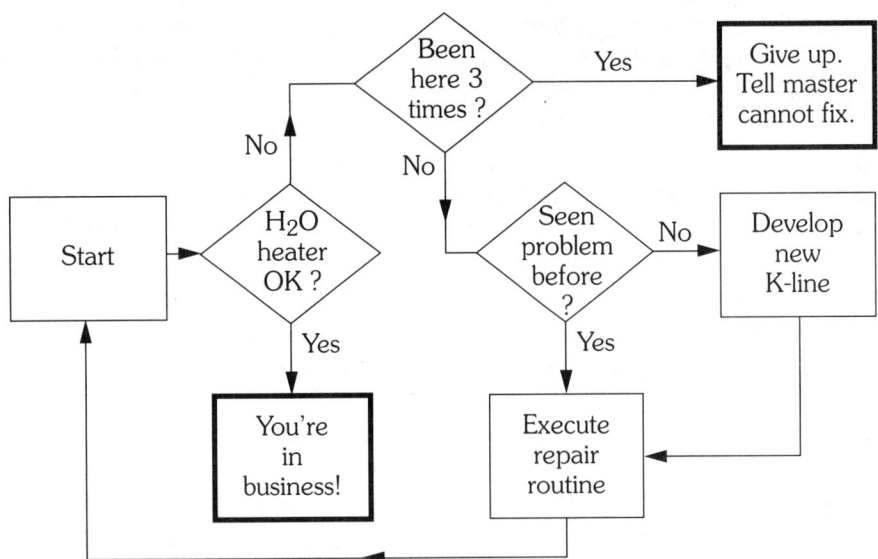

A flowchart illustrating a process, in this case the repair of a water heater by a computerized robot.

Knowledge

The term *knowledge* refers to data stored in written form; in computer memory; on magnetic, optical, and electronic media; and in the human mind. Also, the term refers to how well a system, be it electronic or biological, makes use of the data to which it has access.

Machine knowledge. Computers, at least the ones that have been developed to date, cannot generate knowledge. They can only acquire and accumulate data that people put into them. Human knowledge is imprecise and varies from generation to generation, year to year, and day to day. Machine knowledge, however, is precise, in that the computer "knows" exactly what it is told. In expert systems, engineers speak of *knowledge acquisition*, the process by which machines obtain their data. In artificial intelligence (AI), a computer can sometimes learn from its mistakes. This is not original thought, but is derived from existing knowledge. The ability of a machine to improve the use of its data is called *heuristic knowledge*.

Humans, individually and as a culture, have knowledge that changes. Some researchers have suggested that computers might eliminate the loss of human knowledge in the future. This would give us an ever-expanding storehouse of *immortal knowledge*. This is not necessarily all good. There would, for example, be millions of contradictions within an absolutely inclusive data record of all human knowledge for a period of decades or centuries.

Knowledge domain. In AI and expert systems, the field of knowledge must be kept narrow to ensure accurate results. No computer yet designed can come anywhere near the human level of intelligence, especially when conclusions must be based partly on personal experience, intuition, and other fine aspects of human reasoning.

Knowledge

Suppose a computer is programmed to diagnose liver problems. There are many different things that can go wrong with a human liver; a human physician must conduct various tests and use large storehouses of information to come to a diagnosis and be reasonably sure it is correct. A patient shows symptoms such as tremors and fever; is it liver cirrhosis? Cancer of the liver? Or is it just a hangover? A doctor would not have much trouble figuring it out because the doctor could quickly develop a rapport with the patient, and know which questions to ask. A computer, by contrast, would need all the data it could possibly get—irrelevant as well as relevant—and in this brute-force process, the machine might get confused.

For a given amount of computer power, the depth, or keenness, of machine knowledge is inversely proportional to the scope of the *knowledge domain*. The narrower the knowledge domain (the more specific the subject matter), the higher will be the machine's intelligence quotient (IQ). This is shown in graph A. The wider the domain (the more general the subject matter), the lower will be the machine's IQ, as shown in graph B.

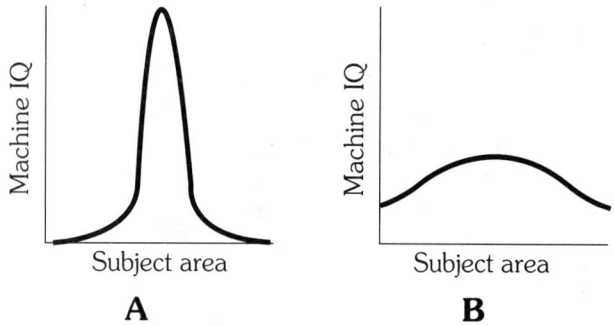

A given computer's IQ can be higher in a specific subject area (A) than it can be in a general subject area (B).

Known and unknown. Knowledge is more than just a set of recorded facts. A body of knowledge also consists of things that can be deduced from the set of available facts.

Do you recall your high-school geometry? Euclidean geometry is entirely based on a small set of *axioms*, or facts that are assumed to be true. Everything else is derived from these, according to definitions and logical processes. The theory can be categorized into two fields: the things you know (because you have proven them), and the things that are true, but that you don't know yet (because you haven't proven them).

True but unknown facts, be they in Euclidean geometry, biology, history, or anything else, are knowledge in the sense that they are embedded in the facts you already have. A body of knowledge is something like a vast continent, much of which has never been explored.

Computers can be a great help in discovering facts in a body of knowledge. The machine uses logical processes to derive thousands, or even millions, of new theorems. Occasionally, computers help people uncover knowledge with profound implications. A good example of this is chaos theory, manifestations of which computers literally derived by brute force. *See also* COMPUTER CONSCIOUSNESS, COMPUTER POWER, EXPERT SYSTEMS, HEURISTIC KNOWLEDGE, *and* IMMORTAL KNOWLEDGE.

Knowledge-based simulation

Knowledge-based simulation is used to create three-dimensional animated graphics on personal computers. The process makes use of a so-called *simulation pipeline*, using facts and logic to create realistic moving pictures. The resulting graphics can simulate reality, such as the view that a downhill skier gets at 90 miles per hour; they can also create fantastic scenes, such as the impression of tumbling into a black hole. All of this falls under the broad category of *virtual reality*.

Disciplines. Knowledge-based simulation makes use of known facts in various scientific and mathematical fields such as are physics, geometry, astronomy, cosmology, optics, history, archaeology, chemistry, and biology. Suppose you want to write a program that simulates the experience of being shrunk down to the size of a virus in the human body. Imagine developing a computer game in which you, the virus, have a goal: invade a red blood cell and create copies of yourself. For this simulation to be possible, you would need to know something about biology. What does a red blood cell look like? What other things are in the blood stream, and what do they look like? What might they do to prevent you (the virus) from reaching your objective?

On a larger scale, suppose you are the captain of a starship that is traveling at relativistic speed between galaxies. You're going at 99.999 percent of the speed of light. What will you see out the portholes, or on the view screen, of your ship? Will everything go black? Will stars change color, or seem squashed in front of you or behind you? How will you communicate with other ships or with Earth? Will you notice anything peculiar within the environment of the ship itself, such as slowing down of the clocks? Answers to these questions could be derived from known facts in relativity theory, astronomy, and cosmology.

Logic forms. You might be surprised to learn that there are different kinds of logic. The most familiar kind is represented in the form of *Boolean algebra*, sometimes called the *propositional calculus* or *sentential calculus*. This is the reasoning generally used by mathematicians and scientists. It uses If-Then statements, and deduces conclusions from available facts.

Knowledge-based simulation

Another form of logic, commonly called *inductive reasoning*, doesn't prove things with 100% accuracy. Instead, it derives statements that are true most of the time, or that are reasonable based on the data available. This is the sort of logic that lawyers use in the courtroom when they cannot prove things deductively. "Beyond a reasonable doubt" is the buzz phrase that gives away the fact that inductive reasoning has been used.

Trinary logic allows for a neutral condition, neither true nor false, in addition to the usual true and false states. These three values are representable by logic −1 (false), 0 (neutral), and +1 (true).

The drawing at A shows binary logic as it is usually represented by direct-current (dc) voltages; falsity corresponds to about zero volts (0 V), while truth corresponds to about +5 V. Part B of the drawing shows trinary logic as it might be represented. In trinary logic, the neutral state can be assigned to undecidable propositions, of the sort guaranteed by the Incompleteness Theorem proved by Kurt Godel in 1930.

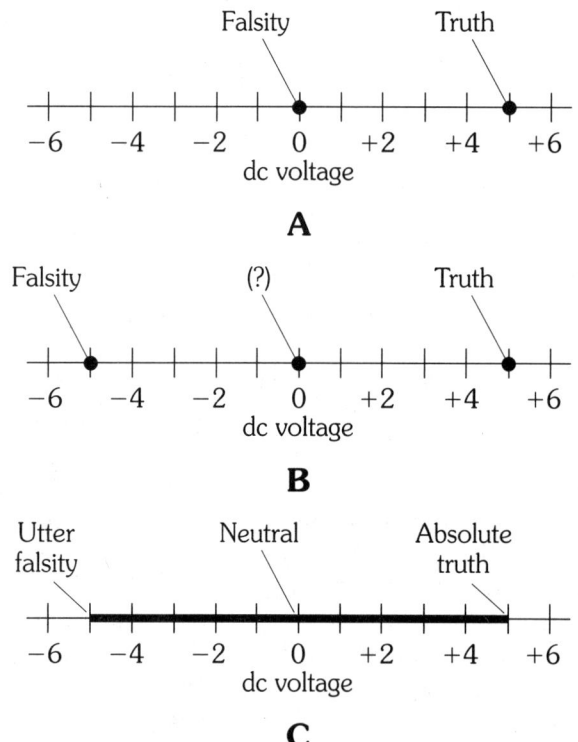

Binary logic (A), trinary logic (B), and fuzzy logic (C).

A more sophisticated logic is *fuzzy logic*, in which values can cover a continuous range from totally false, through neutral, to totally true. Fuzzy logic approximates real life, and allows for some error (which is inevitable in physical systems). This form of logic is well suited for the control of certain processes. Part C of the drawing shows how fuzzy logic might be represented as a continuous range from –5 V (totally false) to +5 V (totally true).

The most radical of all logic forms is *genetic logic*. It relies upon "accidents," or mutations, to produce an endless and at times unpredictable set of outcomes. The interesting thing about this form of logic is that living things, including humans, have apparently evolved as a result of genetic mutations.

For further information. Knowledge-based simulation is a challenging field, available for exploration by intermediate and advanced PC users. One of the better books on this subject is *Visualization and Virtual Reality* by Lee Adams (Windcrest/McGraw-Hill, 1994). The subject is occasionally featured in advanced-level PC magazines. *See also* ANIMATION, ALTERNATIVE COMPUTER TECHNOLOGY, ARTIFICIAL INTELLIGENCE, BOOLEAN ALGEBRA, DIGITAL COMPUTER TECHNOLOGY, GRAPHICS, HEURISTIC KNOWLEDGE, HYBRID COMPUTER TECHNOLOGY, IMMORTAL KNOWLEDGE, INCOMPLETENESS THEOREM, INFINITE REGRESS, LOGIC, NEURAL NETWORK, SIMULATION, *and* VIRTUAL REALITY.

600

Label printing

Stick-on labels are one of the handiest inventions ever developed. They can reduce the time required to address a large number of envelopes and increase the volume of a mass mailing. Have you ever done a small-scale mass mailing, say for a bake sale, ad campaign, meeting announcement, or similar purpose? If so, you know how much work can be saved if you have preprinted labels.

Suppose you have to mail a letter to 150 different people. You'll need to print the name and address of each person on an envelope; you'll probably also want to have your return address on each letter. That's 300 labels: one set of 150 that are all alike, and another set of 150 that are all different. That's a job for computer software, and there are many programs to help you make the labels.

Label printing is a chore that every small business must sooner or later do. There are two approaches to this tedious but necessary grind. One method employs the printer you normally use for pages of text, spreadsheets, and graphics; the other employs a printer designed specifically for label printing.

Regular printers. You can use your word processing software to write names and addresses, and your regular printer to print them out. Stick-on labels specially designed for various types of printers are available for this purpose. You just feed the sheets in with the labels facing in the right direction, and you're ready to go.

LAN

To create and print a list of people's names and addresses, you must be sure that you leave the right amount of space between each address. You might, for example, need to begin on every sixth, seventh, or eighth line. As you know, some name/address combinations require only three lines; some need four; a few need five. Some trial and error is necessary to get things right, but once you get the general idea, you can save the format and use it every time you need to print labels.

If you want to create a repetitive list of your name and address, your word processing software probably has a provision for duplicating blocks of text. You should use it, making sure that you leave the right amount of space between each name/address repetition.

Special label printers. In recent years, several manufacturers have come out with specialized printers intended only for making labels. These printers come with their own software and can be connected to the serial port of a PC independently of the regular printer. Software is available for DOS, Windows, and Macintosh systems.

One of the advantages of a label printer is that you can import addresses from letters. If you're writing a letter to 150 different businesses, you can print each label using the label printer immediately after having printed the letter on your regular printer. This will minimize the chance of sending Mr. Smith a letter written especially for Mrs. Jones.

Another advantage of label printers is that you don't have to fool around switching printer forms from one type to another. You can tell your PC to send the letter to the regular printer, and the address label data to the label printer, without any hardware juggling.

One limitation of label printers is that some of them need custom-made labels. That is, you must obtain your labels from the printer manufacturer. Some label printers allow you to feed envelopes directly through as well, a feature that further reduces the cost and inconvenience of mass mailings. *See also* LETTER WRITING *and* WORD PROCESSING.

LAN

See LOCAL AREA NETWORK.

Language

A human language like English, French, or Russian is formally called a *natural language*. In computing, a *language* is a set of symbols, along with rules for arranging the symbols, used for controlling a computer. A language can also be used for communication among computers, or between computers and peripherals.

Computer programming languages are classified as *low-level* or *high-level*. Programming is usually done in written form, but some computer programs can now be spoken to a computer.

Written languages. Low-level programming languages don't resemble ordinary speech or text; instead, they are more akin to long mathematical proofs or arguments. Writing a program directly in a low-level language is a tedious process. Low-level languages are directly used by computers.

High-level programming languages are the ones with which you might be familiar. They include languages such as BASIC, C, C++, COBOL, Fortran, and LISP. Different high-level languages are used for various applications; for example, C is good for scientific work while COBOL is well-suited to business work.

Translation between high-level and low-level programming languages is done either by a *compiler* or an *interpreter*. *See also* ASSEMBLY LANGUAGE, HIGH-LEVEL LANGUAGE, INTERPRETER, *and* MACHINE LANGUAGE.

Spoken languages. In recent years, it has become possible to literally talk with computers, just as you talk with people. In some ways, this is more convenient than the use of a keyboard. In other applications, the written method is still better.

The use of voice communication is made possible by speech recognition and speech synthesis circuits, which translate between a natural spoken language and its equivalent in written symbols. You can control a machine that has this capability just by telling it what to do. The biggest problem in this technology is getting a machine to correctly choose between words that sound the same, but have different meanings, such as *to*, *too*, and *two*, or *weigh* and *way*. To do this, a machine must be able to figure out the right word by evaluating the context in which it is used. *See also* ARTIFICIAL INTELLIGENCE, CONTEXT, SPEECH RECOGNITION, SPEECH SYNTHESIS, *and* SYNTAX.

Laptop computer

A *laptop computer*, often called simply a *laptop*, is a battery-powered, portable PC, weighing about three to 10 pounds including the battery. A laptop is convenient for use when traveling, but it can also be used as a primary computer. Some people prefer laptops to desktop machines.

There are some subtle differences between a laptop and a notebook computer, but this discussion is not concerned with these differences. Most casual PC users use the terms *laptop* and *notebook* interchangeably, and the same is done in this book.

Laptop computer

Basic design. A laptop computer is built in a fold-up case, roughly the size of a large three-ring notebook. When you open the case, the display pops up, and the keyboard lies flat, as shown in the drawing.

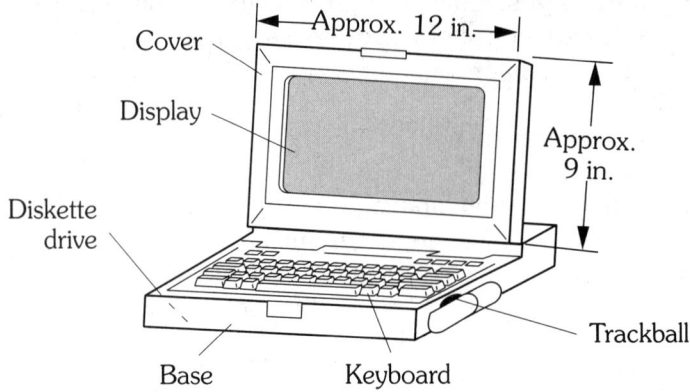

A complete PC in a small, portable package.

Laptops have full-size or nearly full-size keyboards. The displays on some are almost as large as their desktop monitor counterparts. This is important for ease of operation. While many components in a PC system can be miniaturized almost without limit, the keyboard and the display must be at least a certain minimum size, otherwise users find it difficult to manipulate the keys and read the display.

A laptop PC can be used with a printer, mouse, modem, and other peripherals, just as can a desktop unit. In fact, a good laptop can take the place of a desktop computer for many applications, and some PC users find that a laptop meets all their computing needs.

Assets. The biggest asset of a laptop computer is its portability. With the advent of hard disk drives in these PCs, you can carry your whole computing repertoire with you. It's easy to regard a computer as an extension of your mind, and it's great to be able to have access to this "mental peripheral" everywhere you go.

Another advantage of a laptop computer, compared with a desktop unit, is the fact that a laptop consumes much less power. This should be of interest to environmentalists. The main reason for this is that a laptop uses a liquid-crystal display (LCD), which consumes almost no energy. Most desktop PCs use cathode-ray-tube (CRT) monitors, which require considerable energy to operate. Also, the display in a laptop computer creates almost no ELF (extremely low frequency) fields. ELF refers to magnetic fields in the vicinity of CRT monitors. There has been some concern in recent years about possible health effects from these fields.

Yet another asset of a laptop computer is its small size and light weight. If you spend a lot of time on the road, you'll appreciate the minimum-hassle feature of a laptop PC. Traveling salespeople, newspaper correspondents, wandering writers, retirees who go on frequent cruises, and weekend campers can have their "mental peripherals" all the time. Of course, some vacationers prefer to leave their PCs at home when they travel. These people might not need, or want, a laptop computer.

Limitations. With all these strengths, you might wonder why you shouldn't just trade in your desktop PC for a laptop. Some PC users, seeing how much better a laptop meets their overall computing needs, do that. But there are some limitations to laptop computing.

The main problem with laptops is expense. Because of the sophisticated technology, you could pay twice as much for a laptop as for a desktop with comparable computing power.

Generally, laptops don't have hard disks with as much capacity as those in desktop units because a laptop must be made as small and light as possible. Hard disks in laptop PCs generally have about half the capacity of those in desktop computers in the same price range. This can still be plenty big for the average computer user, however.

Some PC users like to have a desktop PC at home, even if they own a good laptop. The substantial "presence" of the desktop unit, even if it is to some extent an illusion, makes these people feel more comfortable. This is especially true if you have lots of peripherals connected to the computer.

Batteries. Laptop computers use rechargeable batteries. The most common type has traditionally been the *nickel-cadmium (NiCd or NICAD) battery*. It takes from four to six hours to fully charge a NICAD battery pack starting from a state of full discharge.

The length of time your battery pack will last, starting with a full charge, depends on several factors, including the following:

- ➤ The type of PC
- ➤ How much you use the hard disk and/or diskette drive
- ➤ The type of display (active versus passive matrix)
- ➤ Whether or not you use the display backlighting
- ➤ Whether you work continuously or take frequent breaks

At best, you might get six hours of computing from a single charge. At worst, it can be less than an hour. In general, active-matrix color displays consume more battery current than passive-matrix monochrome types. More advanced processors, such as the Pentium, need more battery current than older processors such as the 80386.

Laptop computer

If you plan to use your laptop in a situation where you won't be able to recharge the batteries for awhile (on an airplane or bus, for example), you might want to carry along a fully charged spare battery pack. Also, there are certain things you can do to maximize battery life:

➢ Avoid using the display backlight if at all possible

➢ Minimize your use of the disk drives

➢ Switch the machine off if you take breaks (storing data on disk first)

One problem with NICADs is impaired performance if they aren't almost fully discharged with each operating cycle. There is some disagreement as to how commonly this problem occurs. It is called *NICAD battery memory* or *memory drain*. A NICAD with battery memory loses some of its energy storage capacity, so its life per charge is reduced. If this happens, it does not necessarily mean that the battery has been ruined. If you let the battery discharge almost completely, then charge it overnight, and then repeat the almost-full-discharge/full-charge process about six times, battery memory can often be corrected.

You should always use NICADs until they have discharged almost totally, but you should never let them discharge until they're completely dead. If that happens, the polarity of one or more cells within the battery might reverse; then the battery will be permanently damaged.

Some laptops use rechargeable batteries other than NICAD. Because battery technology advances rapidly, it's a good idea to keep track of the latest developments. The *lithium battery* is one potential alternative to the NICAD. Another, perhaps more promising power source is the *nickel metal hydride (NiMH) battery*. A NiMH battery has a longer life than a NICAD, and does not suffer from memory problems.

Peripherals. In general, you can use the same peripherals with a laptop PC as you can with a desktop PC. There are also certain peripherals that you're more likely to use with a laptop than with a desktop. Some common laptop peripherals include the following:

➢ *Printer* Some people don't use a printer at all when laptop computing. Instead, they wait until they're at home, transfer the data from the laptop to the desktop, and then print whatever they want using their "main PC." If a laptop is your only computer, however, you'll need to connect your printer directly to it. All laptops have a port to which a printer can be connected. Small portable printers exist; they are usually inkjet or thermal.

➢ *Mouse* Because you need extra space for a mouse on which to slide it around, most laptop PCs have a *trackball* instead. This

is like a ball bearing built into the keyboard. Other pointing devices are available, too.

➤ *External drives* You can add either 3.5-inch or 5.25-inch diskette drives to your laptop. You can also add a CD-ROM drive or an external hard drive to greatly increase storage capacity. A single CD-ROM can store upwards of 650MB.

➤ *Modem* A modem connects your PC to the telephone line so you can access online networks. Modems are inexpensive, and they open up a whole world of information for you. There are networks for practically all interests, from boating to ham radio, from space travel to politics. Some modems, called *fax modems*, can be used to send and receive pictures, as well as text.

➤ *PCMCIA cards* These credit-card-sized peripherals have become quite common with laptops. They can do a wide variety of things, including store data, provide software, act as a fax/modem, and facilitate use of the computer in several different applications.

Compatibility. If you already have a desktop computer and you're contemplating the purchase of a laptop to use as a secondary system, you'll probably want to use the same software with both computers. Therefore, you should be sure that the laptop you buy will run the software that you already use with your desktop PC. You should also check the software licensing agreements very carefully before you transfer software from one computer to another. Some companies don't mind if you install a given software package on multiple computers, as long as you use only one at a time. Other vendors object.

Laptop PCs use 3.5-inch diskette drives almost exclusively. If your desktop unit has only a 5.25-inch drive, you should consider getting a second, 3.5-inch drive for your desktop unit. This will make it possible to exchange disks between the two computers. Of course, you'll probably also want to buy a cable that will let you transfer data back and forth between the hard disks of the two machines.

A specialized hardware unit, called a *docking station*, turns a laptop into a desktop computer. You simply close up the laptop PC and insert it into a base that is about the same size as the main unit in a typical desktop PC.

See also CD-ROM, DESKTOP COMPUTER, DOCKING STATION, DOT-MATRIX PRINTER, ELF FIELDS, INKJET PRINTER, LASER PRINTER, LCD/LED PRINTER, MODEM, MOUSE, NETWORK, NICKEL-CADMIUM BATTERY, ONLINE SERVICE, PCMCIA STANDARD ADAPTER CARDS, PRINTER, TRACKBALL, *and* THERMAL PRINTER.

Laser communications

Laser beams can be modulated to convey information in the same way as radio waves. *Laser communications* allows many signals to be sent over a beam of light. Laser communications systems fall into two broad categories: *line-of-sight* and *fiberoptic*.

Basics. A laser-communications transmitter has a signal processor or amplifier, modulator, and laser. Any form of data can be sent, including voice, television, and digital signals. Part A of the drawing shows a system for transmitting computer data via laser. The output of the computer goes to a modem, just like the kind you use to gain access to an online service. The audio output of the modem is amplified, and then the data is impressed onto the laser beam via a modulator.

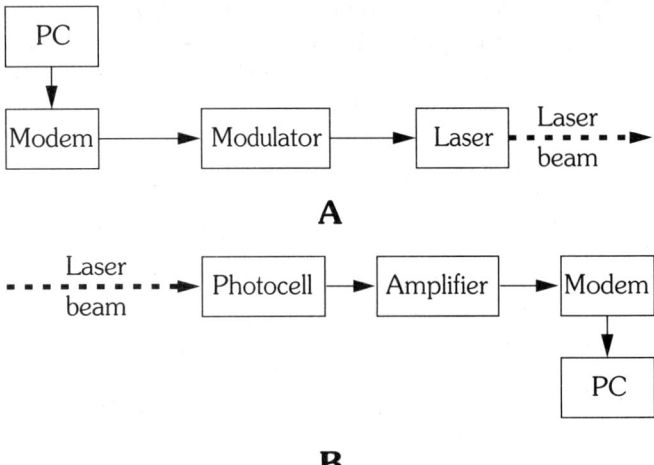

Laser communications: transmitter (A) and receiver (B).

A laser-communications receiver uses a photocell, an amplifier, and a signal processor. Part B of the drawing shows a simple system for recovering data from a laser beam and feeding it to a computer. The light falls on the photocell, which converts it to weak audio tones, just like the ones that came from the modem at the transmitting end of the circuit. These tones are amplified if necessary, and then they go to the signal processor, which acts like a modem for received data. The output of this device can be understood directly by the computer.

Line of sight. In a line-of-sight system, the beam travels in a straight line through space or clear air. Because laser beams remain narrow for long distances, long-range communication is possible.

One problem with line-of-sight laser transmission is that it won't work well through clouds, fog, or other obstructions. Radio waves are preferable for these situations. Another problem is that the aiming must be precise because of the narrowness of the beam.

Line-of-sight laser systems offer some promise for communications in deep space. They are also useful for maintaining privacy because the narrow laser beams are hard to detect unless you know precisely where to look for them. In order to intercept a line-of-sight laser transmission, the detecting apparatus must be within the extremely narrow cone of light emitted by the transmitting laser.

Fiberoptics. In a fiberoptic system, the laser is guided through a glass or plastic filament. This is like wire or cable communications, but it is far more versatile and efficient.

Fiberoptics are being used increasingly in computer networks because they allow for much faster data transfer, at much lower cost, than older cable systems. The much-touted information superhighway will make extensive use of fiberoptic communications networks. Data speeds will be in the tens of millions of bits per second, allowing almost instantaneous downloading of complex graphic images and sophisticated software programs.

Fiberoptic systems work well for computer control of robotic machinery, especially in hostile environments such as nuclear reactors or the deep sea. This is of interest to scientists. *See also* FIBEROPTIC CABLE *and* FIBEROPTIC DATA TRANSMISSION.

Laser printer

A *laser printer* is the best printer for high-resolution text and graphics. If you work with desktop publishing, presentation graphics, or anything else that requires the best possible print copy, you'll want a laser printer.

Laser printers come in different shapes and sizes, but usually about the size of a personal photocopier. A typical example is shown in drawing A. Laser printers range in price from around $500 to more than $3000.

How it works. The resemblance between laser printers and photocopy machines goes deeper than physical appearance. Both machines work on the same principle. The difference is that, while a photocopier creates a copy of a real image (the paper original), a laser printer makes a copy of an encoded image. The code is the binary data from a computer.

For any printer to work right, it must be compatible with the software that the PC uses. You can ensure this by checking the instruction manuals for the software and the printer. Most software packages contain programs that will let you match your computer to almost any printer.

When the data arrives at the printer from the computer, the encoded image is stored in the printer's RAM (random-access memory). The

Laser printer

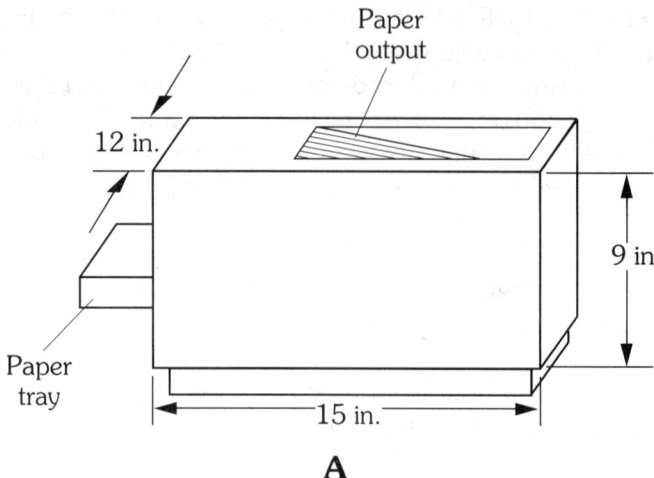

A

A typical laser printer.

printer's RAM stores one page of data, and then sends it along to the laser. Some printers use a light-emitting-diode (LED) matrix rather than a single laser. Although these printers are often called *LED printers*, for practical purposes, they are equivalent to laser printers.

Drawing B is a greatly simplified, cross-sectional view of the interior hardware in a laser printer. The laser, blinking rapidly, scans the drum. The drum has special properties that cause it to attract the printing chemical, called *toner*, in some places but not others, creating an image pattern that will ultimately appear on the paper. The laser and the electrostatic charger work together to get toner onto the drum in just the right pattern.

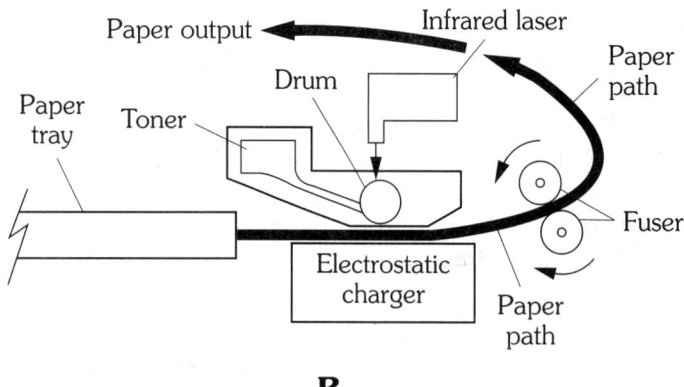

B

A greatly simplified functional diagram of a laser printer.

The paper enters from a tray that can hold up to about 200 sheets. A sheet of paper is pulled past the drum, and also past the electrostatic charger. Toner from the drum is attracted to the paper. The image thus goes onto the paper, although it has not yet been permanently fused, or bonded, to the paper. The *fuser*, which is a hot pair of roller/squeezers, does this job, completing the printing process. The paper then passes out of the printer, and the machine is ready to print the next page.

The image resolution of laser printers ranges from about 300 dots per inch (DPI) to more than 1200 DPI. This is considered high-resolution. As far as the unaided eye can tell, 1200 DPI is the equivalent of professionally typeset copy.

Advantages. The biggest advantage of laser printers is their excellent print and graphics quality. You can't buy anything better. Dot-matrix printers, by comparison, produce lower quality print than laser or inkjet printers (although dot-matrix printers are improving in this respect).

Laser printers can handle graphics and text equally well. It doesn't have a print head, so blackened regions, curved lines, and shading are no problem. If an image can be rendered on a photocopy machine, it can be rendered just as well on a laser printer.

Another asset of laser printers is that they make almost no noise. Some older dot-matrix printers are so loud that they interfere with telephone conversations. An office full of these printers, all running at once, makes such a racket that it can cause fatigue. A dozen laser printers, on the other hand, can operate unnoticed.

Finally, laser printers are much faster than other types. Laser printers typically run at speeds for six to 10 pages per minute, compared to about three pages or less for other printing technologies.

Limitations. Laser printers are comparatively expensive. A dot-matrix or inkjet machine typically costs much less than a laser printer. Besides the fact that you pay less at the store for a dot-matrix or inkjet unit than for a laser unit, you also save in the long term. Laser printing is two to three times as expensive, per page, as other types of printing.

Dot-matrix printers are unsurpassed for ruggedness. They're built like tanks. Laser printers break down somewhat more often, and they need more routine maintenance. (You know how photocopiers go haywire at the worst possible moment!)

Also, a laser printer is a non-impact printer; it does not make its images by applying pressure to create the darkened regions. Because of this, multipart forms will not work. A dot-matrix printer, which is an impact printer, can be used with multipart forms, or carbons, because the characters and images are created by physical force against the paper.

LCD

Personal laser printers. In recent years, laser printers have become more affordable. Some manufacturers have begun producing smaller, less expensive laser printers for the casual PC user. These personal laser printers operate somewhat more slowly than the bigger ones, but if you don't need to print a large quantity of work, this should not present a problem for you. Personal laser printers offer the extra advantage of being more portable than full-size printers, although they are still larger than many inkjet models.

The image resolution of a personal laser printer is somewhat less than that of an office laser printer. Unless you need top-of-the-line copy to impress important people, however, a personal laser printer will do fine in the image-crispness department.

Some personal laser printers (as well as the full-size machines) have a provision for sharing between two computers. This can effectively reduce the cost of a laser printer for the office. *See also* COLOR PRINTER, DOT-MATRIX PRINTER, DOTS PER INCH, HIGH-RESOLUTION PRINTER, INKJET PRINTER, *and* LCD/LED PRINTER.

LCD

See LIQUID-CRYSTAL DISPLAY.

LCD/LED printer

An *LCD (liquid-crystal display) printer* is a specialized variation of the well-known laser printer. Another, similar printer type is an *LED (light-emitting diode) printer*.

Laser printers, and their LCD/LED cousins, all work according to the same principles as a photocopying machine. The only difference is the method in which the device gets its light. An LCD printer uses a matrix of liquid crystals that act as light shutters, while an LED printer uses light-emitting diodes that produce non-laser light.

The light, which has a pattern corresponding to the image to be printed, falls on a rotating drum. The drum becomes electrically charged in the regions where light hits it. After passing by the light beams, the drum moves past a container filled with a chemical called *toner*, which is a special, electrically charged ink. Toner is either attracted to, or repelled from, those parts of the drum that are charged as a result of having been illuminated. In either case, the image to be printed appears on the drum, which is then transferred to the paper. *See also* LASER PRINTER, LIGHT-EMITTING DIODE, *and* LIQUID-CRYSTAL DISPLAY.

Leading

See LINES PER INCH.

Learning

According to Alan Turing, a pioneer in the field of artificial intelligence (AI), a machine must be able to learn things if it is truly intelligent. Turing's concept of learning involved more than just rote memory.

Facts versus meaning. When you take courses in school, you gain much of your knowledge just by memorizing names, dates, places, equations, and the like. This knowledge is useless, however, unless you find ways to put it into meaningful thoughts. For example, it's easy to store the equation

$$E = mc^2$$

in a computer memory. This is the equation made famous by Albert Einstein, stating the relationship between energy (E), mass (m), and the speed of light (c). In a machine with complex learning capacity of the sort Turing envisioned, there would be many other facts stored along with this equation, giving the machine a thorough understanding of the meaning of this aspect of relativity theory. The equation by itself, without any supporting knowledge, is little more than nonsense.

Suppose, after a computer has learned all about relativity, you ask it, "What was the most important result of Einstein's energy/mass equation?" If the machine had learned things well (and not just memorized them), it might answer, "The atomic bomb." Or, if it had been taught by a gentler-minded person, it might answer, "The possibility of an unlimited energy supply." If the machine hadn't learned anything, it would either have no answer, or it would say something like, "Energy equals mass times the speed of light squared."

Subjectivity versus objectivity. If machine learning becomes sophisticated enough, it will eventually become subjective (involving opinions and interpretations) as well as objective (involving only the literal data). This prospect fascinates researchers in AI because it opens up a whole new realm of computer "thought."

Different people, taking the same classes in school, grow up to have vastly different outlooks on the world. This is true even if the students are identical twins. Will the same thing happen with computers? Given two supposedly identical computers, having learned the same set of facts from two different human teachers, the resulting world views might be quite different.

Imagine connecting hundreds, or even thousands, of computers, each with its own unique world outlook, together into a vast supernetwork, available to all humans for discussion sessions via an online service such as the Internet! Such a network might provide its users with new, fascinating solutions to all kinds of age-old human problems. Besides that, conferences with the computers in addition to other, human, network subscribers would be great fun. *See also* ARTIFICIAL INTELLIGENCE, COMPUTER CONSCIOUSNESS, TURING, ALAN, *and* TURING TEST.

Lecht, Charles

Charles Lecht is a futurist who believes that robots and "smart computers" will eventually do all the mundane work that humans do today. Lecht worked for IBM, and then started his own computer software company called Lecht Sciences, Inc.

Lecht is optimistic. He thinks the benefits of computerized robots and artificial intelligence (AI) far outweigh the dangers. Some workers perceive computers and robots mainly as a threat to their job security. Lecht, on the other hand, sees a brighter side of the issue: machines can do monotonous jobs and set people free to do more interesting work.

Lecht points out that much of our time, even in modern society, is taken up by busywork. We mow lawns, do laundry, and take cars to the shop. We must call a repair person to fix the air conditioner or television set or telephone. The wealthiest people have servants who do these things. Lecht sees society evolving to the point where everyone can afford to have robots do these jobs. *See also* ARTIFICIAL INTELLIGENCE *and* PERSONAL ROBOTS.

LED

See LIGHT-EMITTING DIODE.

Letter writing

It has been said that a computer will never, all by itself, write a profound novel. However, *letter-writing software* can provide *boilerplate*, or sample documents, for your letter-writing needs. Depending on how much money you want to spend, you can get a package with anywhere from a few dozen to several hundred boilerplate letters.

What is a boilerplate? A letter boilerplate is a hypothetical letter, written to a hypothetical person or company, intended for a specific purpose. For example, suppose you want to remind someone that she owes you $37.50 for repairing her stereo system. You must be diplomatic but firm; you want to get your money without arousing hard feelings. A good letter-writing package will have a sample letter that's just right for this occasion; you need only supply the particulars (amount of money, service rendered, dates, and names).

Boilerplates have the advantage of saving you tedious hours of labor when you must send a letter to many different people or businesses. Suppose you are having an art show featuring local children's paintings. You might choose an invitation boilerplate, and then tailor the letter to the specific event, date, and time. You can then print out a personalized letter to each person on your address list. The address list can double for printing the envelope labels.

Business-letter reminders. Practically all business letters request action of some kind. If you can't find a boilerplate that is perfect for your particular needs, you can use one made for some similar situation, modifying it as necessary. In the process of tailoring a business-letter boilerplate, keep in mind the following points:

➤ Address a specific person by name and title

➤ Be sure the name is spelled right

➤ Be upbeat

➤ Be brief

➤ Avoid using threats

➤ Avoid using big words

➤ Close with something noncommittal; *Sincerely* is best

There are, of course, some exceptions to these rules, but they apply in 99% of business situations. *See also* BOILERPLATE, BUSINESS LETTERS, LABEL PRINTING, *and* WORD PROCESSING.

Light-emitting diode

A *light-emitting diode (LED)*, technically known as an *electroluminescent diode*, is a device that emits infrared, visible, or ultraviolet light when a low, direct-current (dc) voltage is applied. LEDs are used in many different types of electrical circuits and systems. You'll most often notice them as indicator lights on your PC keyboard, main unit, monitor, and printer. LEDs come in all colors, but the most common is red. Light-emitting diodes can also be used to produce a high-resolution image suitable for printing on paper.

An LED is made from a special material called a *band-gap semiconductor*. A common compound with this property is gallium arsenide (GaAs). The drawing shows a greatly magnified, cutaway view of an LED suitable for use as an indicator light. It only needs about one volt to operate, and it draws very little current, making it suitable for use in battery-powered laptop computers. Sometimes a lens-shaped plastic or epoxy case is used to focus the light or spread it out.

A special form of LED, called a *laser diode*, produces coherent light similar to that from a big laser, but with much less intensity. Many of these devices work in the infrared range, with wavelengths a little longer than those you can see. Some produce yellow and green coherent light in the visible range. Laser diodes are useful in *fiberoptic data transmission*. *See also* FIBEROPTIC DATA TRANSMISSION *and* LCD/LED PRINTER.

Lightning protection

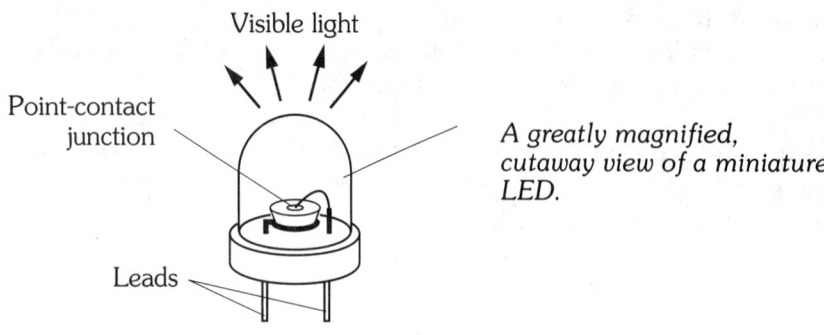

A greatly magnified, cutaway view of a miniature LED.

Lightning protection

Lightning kills more people every year in the United States than hurricanes or tornadoes. The main danger to people is from electrocution; danger to property is from fires, induced currents, and explosions.

Protecting yourself. Lightning can take place at any time. It is most common in or near areas of precipitation. If you can hear thunder, lightning is occurring. Rain, snow, sleet, dark clouds, a sand storm, a dust storm, or a volcano can all be sources of lightning.

Of course, people can be harmed by lightning, and electronic equipment damaged, despite precautions. The danger can be minimized, however. Here are some things you can do to protect yourself:

- Stay indoors or inside a metal enclosure such as a car, bus, or train. Stay away from windows.
- If it is not possible to get indoors, find a low-lying spot on the ground, such as a ditch or ravine, and squat down with feet close together until the threat has passed.
- Avoid lone trees or other isolated, tall objects such as utility poles or flagpoles.
- Avoid any electric appliance or electronic equipment that makes use of the utility power lines or that has an outdoor antenna. This includes all computers, peripherals, and amateur radio apparatus.
- Stay out of the shower or bathtub.
- Avoid swimming pools, either indoors or outdoors.
- Do not use the telephone.

Equipment protection. If your computer is connected to an amateur radio ("ham") station, antennas present the greatest danger. A direct hit is not necessary for dangerous currents to be induced in

Lightning protection

the antenna element and feed line. Power and telephone lines can also pick up high-voltage surges that can damage equipment plugged into wall outlets. Precautions to minimize the risk are as follows:

- Never operate or experiment with electronic equipment connected to an antenna or to the power lines while lightning is occurring anywhere near your location. If you must use a PC, use a laptop powered from batteries, and do not use a modem or ham radio with it.

- When a ham radio station is not in use, disconnect all antennas. Connect all feed line conductors to a good dc ground other than the utility power-line ground. Also disconnect and ground all rotator cables and other wiring that leads outdoors. Preferably, the lines should be left entirely outside the building and connected to an earth ground at least several feet from the building.

- When electronic equipment is not in use, unplug it from wall outlets. If everything is plugged into a single box, such as a transient suppressor, simply unplug the suppressor. Also unplug modems from telephone jacks.

- Lightning arrestors provide some protection from charge buildup on ham radio and television antennas, but they cannot offer complete safety, and should not be relied upon for routine protection of equipment or people.

- Lightning rods reduce the chance of a direct hit to your house, but should not be used as an excuse to neglect the other precautions.

- Power-line transient suppressors reduce computer "glitches" and can sometimes protect sensitive components in a power supply, but they should not be used as an excuse to neglect the other precautions.

- Radio and television antenna masts and towers should be connected to an excellent direct-current (dc) earth ground, using heavy-gauge wire or braid. Several parallel lengths of AWG No. 8 aluminum ground wire, run in a straight line from the mast or tower to ground, form an adequate conductor. This conductor might be called upon to carry a momentary current of thousands of amperes. The conductor must be able to survive in case of another strike. Other secondary protection devices are available and can be found in electronics magazines.

For further information. Refer to *Lightning Protection Code*, published by

National Fire Protection Association
Batterymarch Park
Quincy, MA 02269

See also AMATEUR RADIO, PACKET COMMUNICATIONS, *and* TRANSIENT SUPPRESSION.

Linear programming

Linear programming

Linear programming is a process of optimizing two or more variables that change in different, independent ways. Computers are well-suited to doing these sorts of calculations.

A simple example of linear programming is shown in the drawing. The two variables are x and y. They represent the positions of two personal robots as they move in straight lines within their work area. The path of robot A is shown by the solid line; the path of robot B is shown by the dotted line. Robot A moves at 3.5 feet per second; robot B moves at 1.5 feet per second. The starting points are shown by heavy dots.

Linear programming can answer these questions:

➢ How long after their startup will the robots be closest to each other?

➢ What will be the coordinates of robot A at that time?

➢ What will be the coordinates of robot B at that time?

Computers can be programmed to solve linear programming problems quickly and easily, as long as the number of variables is not extremely large. The difficulty increases rapidly as the number of variables increases. Also, when some of the variables change in a nonlinear way, the difficulty of an optimization problem increases. This would be the case, for example, if the robots in the situation were accelerating, rather than moving along at constant speeds.

Engineers sometimes encounter linear programming scenarios in which there are thousands of variables, such as a telephone-network optimization problem. This taxes the capability of even the largest mainframe computers.

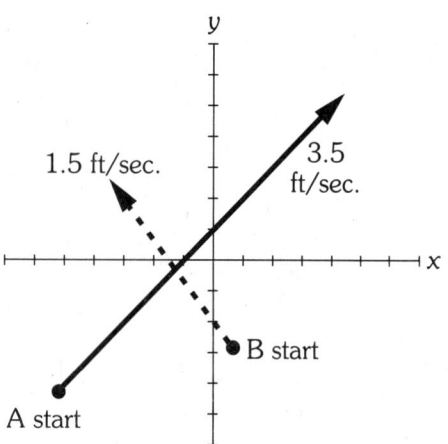

Two robots, A and B, move at constant speed. At what time are they closest together? Will they collide?

Line art
See DRAW PROGRAM.

Line graph
A *line graph* is a two-dimensional drawing showing a relation or function between two variables. The most common type of line graph is drawn on a system of *Cartesian coordinates*.

Discrete points. The graph at A is a simple line graph showing the temperature versus the hour for a hypothetical day. The graph begins at midnight, and progresses until midnight 24 hours later. Temperature readings are taken every two hours, and are plotted on the graph as small open circles. There are 13 points on this graph.

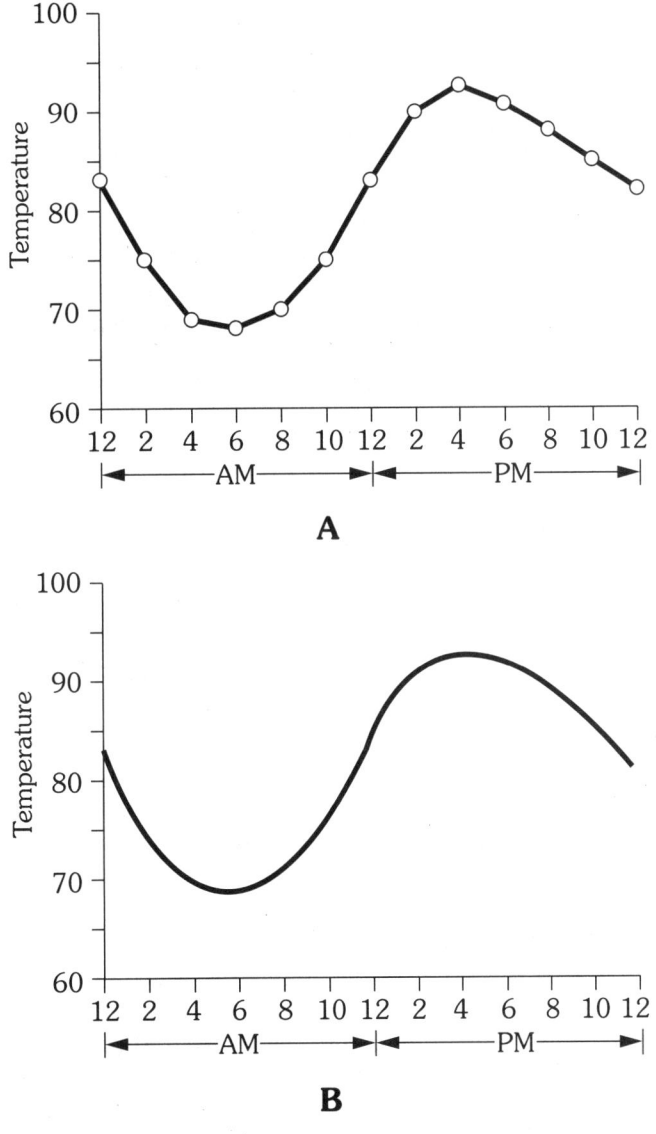

At A, straight lines connect a few plotted points. At B, a large number of points approximates a true curve.

Lines per inch

The line-graphics software plots the points, and then draws straight lines connecting them. This approximates the function of temperature versus the time of day for the 24-hour period. It is not an exact representation, of course, because the actual temperature varies along a curve, not a series of perfectly straight lines. Nevertheless, for most purposes, this point-to-point plot is good enough.

Continuous. Suppose you're an amateur meteorologist, and you want a more precise rendition of the temperature-versus-time function for the day in question. You might have an electronic thermometer connected to your PC, and have the whole system take samples and plot them every five minutes. This results in 289 plots for the 24-hour period. Each of these points is plotted as a single, tiny dot, and these dots are connected by straight lines. When displayed on the monitor or printed out, the graph would look like a continuous curve, as shown in graph B.

Continuous-curve graphs, when plotted on a computer, are generally line graphs with a large number of plotted points. The greater the number of points, the more nearly the graph resembles an actual mathematical curve. In some draw programs, the PC actually stores the formula for the curve, and in that sense, its notion of the curve is exact. Still, though, a monitor or printer always renders it as a series of dots (pixels). *See also* BEZIER CURVE, CARTESIAN COORDINATES, DEPENDENT VARIABLE, DRAW PROGRAM, INDEPENDENT VARIABLE, *and* OBJECT-ORIENTED GRAPHICS.

Lines per inch

Lines per inch (LPI) refers to the spacing between the lines of a printed document. The larger the number of LPI, the closer together are the lines.

For single-spaced documents in pica or elite type size, there are usually five or six lines per inch. Pica has 10 characters per inch (CPI); elite has 12 CPI. In double-spaced documents, the standard line spacing is 2.5 or 3 LPI.

If your printer has several different LPI settings, you'll see numbers like 3, 4, 6, 7.5, 8, and 12 LPI. For type sizes other than 10 or 12 CPI, the standard LPI varies. Large lettering might need 3 LPI for single spacing to look good; tiny type might let you get away with 8 or 12 LPI.

Sometimes you'll hear the term *leading*, pronounced "ledding," used in reference to line spacing in a printed document. The leading is the separation between adjacent lines, usually expressed in points, a typographic measure where 72 points equals one inch. The leading in inches is equal to 1/LPI. The leading in millimeters is equal to 25.4/LPI. Therefore, if a document is printed at 6 LPI, the leading is 0.166 inches, 4.23 mm, or 12 points.

Most printers have buttons that allow you to set the LPI. However, if you're using printer software that downloads the LPI information to your printer, the downloaded specification might override whatever you select with the printer buttons. In that case, you must quit the printer program before you adjust LPI. *See also* DOWNLOADABLE FONT *and* PITCH.

Link

A *link* is a connection between two different computers, or the act of making such a connection. The term can also apply to programs or files within a single computer system.

Many computers can be linked together via wire, radio, satellite, or fiberoptic networks. This makes it possible to combine the information in the computers, creating a sort of "supercomputer." The main problem with this is that the data cannot travel faster than the speed of light in free space (about 186,282 miles, or 299,792 kilometers, per second). This limits the speed at which such networks can operate.

For example, if a link is through a geostationary satellite orbiting 22,300 miles up, the data takes about a quarter-second to get from one computer to the other (see the drawing). This is fine for one-way data transfer, but it severely hampers two-way communications speed. *See also* NETWORK.

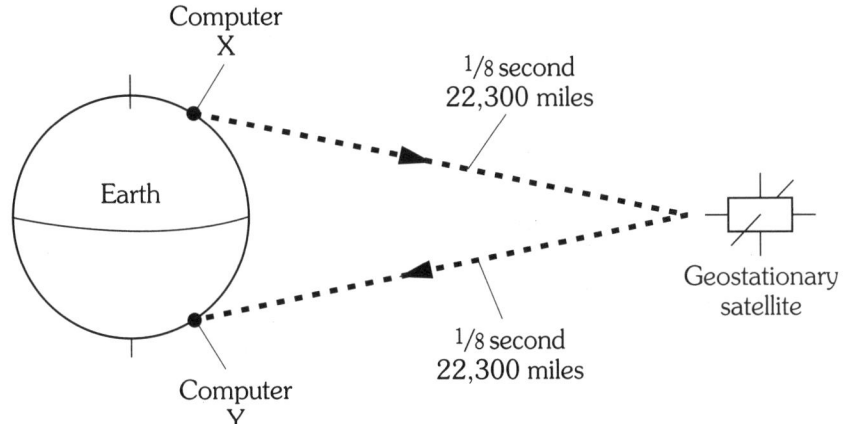

With a geostationary satellite, there is always a delay in communications of at least a quarter-second.

Linked graph

Occasionally, you'll see a graph split into two different parts. The second part is a "blowup," or expansion, of a portion of the first part. Such a graph is called a *linked graph*. In analytical graphics and presentation graphics software, you can link almost all types of graphs and charts to illustrate various effects.

Linked graph

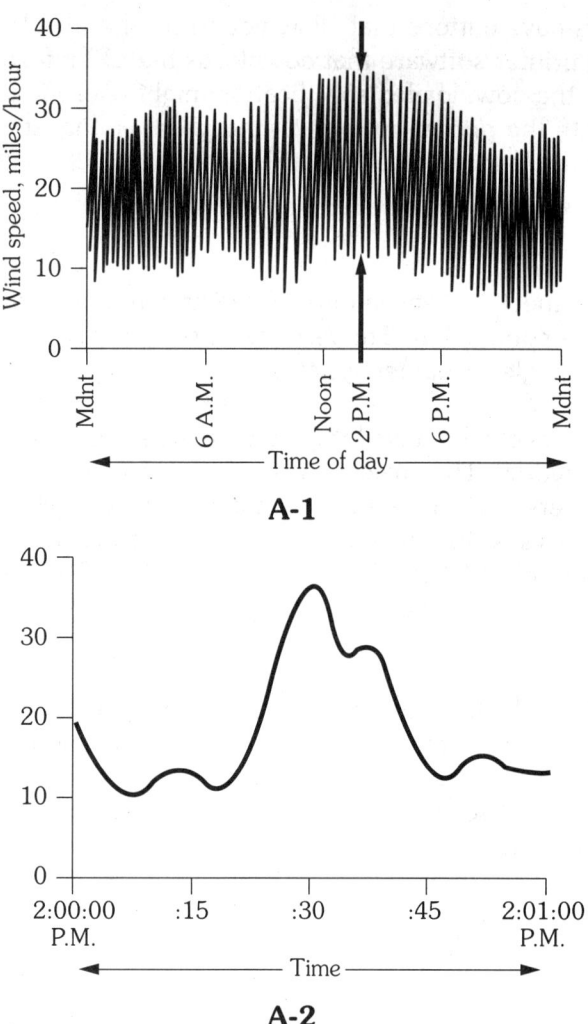

These graphs show wind speed versus time.

Linked line graphs. Drawing A is a linked pair of line graphs, showing the wind speed as it varies in a hypothetical place over the course of a 24-hour period. The top graph shows the wind speed for the whole day. This graph is extremely jagged because there were constant, rapid fluctuations all day long. It's impossible to resolve the wind speed for any moment in time, although you can surmise that this was a windy day, and that the winds were gusty. You can tell what the highest wind speed (peak gust) was, and you can get a fair idea of the mean (average) wind speed over the course of the day.

The bottom graph is an expansion of a one-minute time period, from 2:00 to 2:01 p.m. during the day. This graph shows exactly what the wind speed was at every instant during that minute. Based on the overall appearance of the top graph, it is reasonable to suppose that this bottom graph is typical of the wind throughout the day.

Linked pie graphs. Drawing B shows a hypothetical graph of income distribution, by occupation, for a certain place. Both graphs in this link are pie graphs. The top graph shows the proportions of families in four income ranges: $0 to $15,000, $15,001 to $30,000, $30,001 to $60,000, and $60,001+. You can see that, in this locale, the four income groups have approximately equal numbers of families. (The size of the family is not taken into account in this graph). Percentages are given; they all equal 100%, representing all the families in the region.

The bottom graph shows the proportions of five different occupational categories within the income range of $30,001 to $60,000. These are teaching, sales, service, labor, and "other" (everything else). Percentages are given in this graph, and they, like the percentages in the first pie graph, add up to 100%, representing all the families in this income range.

See also ANALYTICAL GRAPHICS *and* PRESENTATION GRAPHICS.

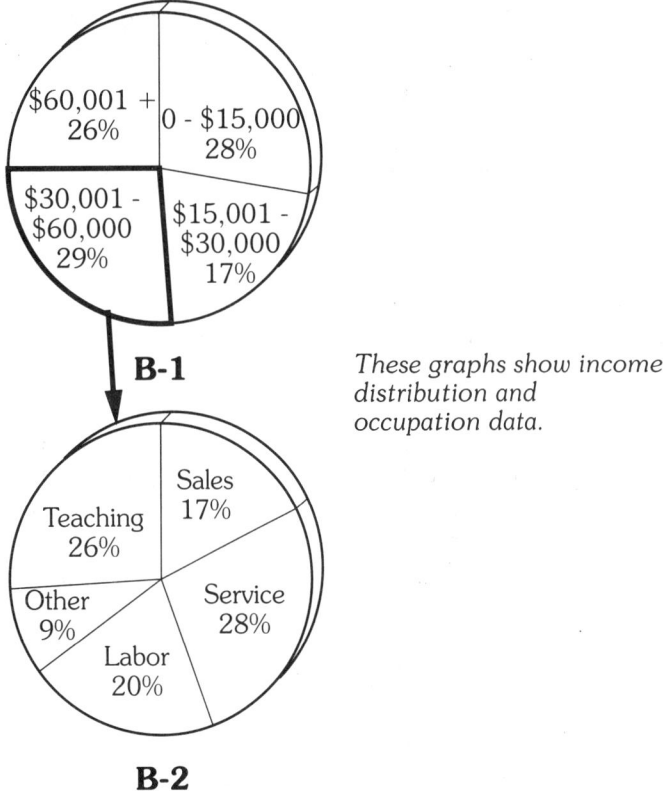

These graphs show income distribution and occupation data.

Linked object

A *linked object* is a piece of data within larger files, that has certain interactive properties. The larger file is called the *destination file*; the file from which the linked object comes is the *source file*.

Linked object

How it works. The drawing shows the basic relationship among the source file (upper rectangle), the object (shaded ellipse), and the destination file (lower rectangle). The object comprises part of the source file and also part of the destination file. The object does not necessarily comprise the same proportion of both files; in fact, that is almost never the case.

Suppose the object within the source file is a letter to Mr. Jones in Cleveland, Ohio. You learn that Mr. Jones has just moved to Portland, Oregon. You change the address in the letter in the source file. With *object linking and embedding (OLE)*, the address will automatically be changed in the destination file, too, without your having to call that file and change it. This will be true even if the destination file is in a different application than the source.

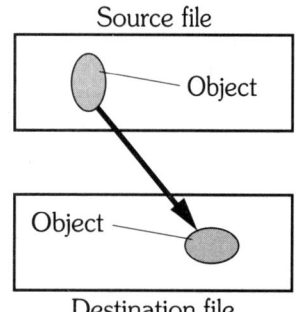

The linking among a source, object, and destination.

It's possible to have many links for an object in a given source file. There might be six, 25, or even 500 different occurrences of an object in various destination files.

Suppose you want to be certain that Mr. Jones' address gets updated everywhere in your records. You open the database that contains the names and addresses of everyone you know. You then single out Mr. Jones' name and address (that is, his complete listing) and specify it as your object, with the database as your source document. Then, when you change the listing for Mr. Jones in your database, it will change everywhere in your records, as long as the listing appears in the same format.

Problems. There is a potential hangup with linked objects. An object in a destination file can be linked only if it is absolutely identical to its counterpart in the source file. The machine has no tolerance for discrepancies, regardless of how trivial they might seem to you. For example, if the original address is

Mr. J. Jones
0000 Highwater Street
Cleveland, OH 00001

then only objects identical to this will be linked to it. The computer would disregard the following names and addresses, even though they refer to the same person:

J. P. Jones
0000 Highwater Street
Cleveland, OH 00001

Mr. J. Jones
0000 Highwater St.
Cleveland, OH 00001

Mr. J. Jones
0000 Highwater Street
Cleveland, Ohio 00001

As OLE becomes more sophisticated, it might become able to detect subtle differences like those depicted here. That could cause problems too, however, because objects might be treated the same when in fact they are not. The best we can do for now is strive to become as detail-oriented as our computers, at least while we're working with them. *See also* OBJECT LINKING AND EMBEDDING.

Liquid cooling

Computer chips, particularly the microprocessor, generate heat as they do their work. This is why desktop PCs have cooling fans in the back. Without some way to get rid of the excess heat from the components, a PC would overheat and malfunction.

Traditionally, *convection cooling* has been used in PCs. Even if a computer or peripheral doesn't have a fan, the airflow around the circuit boards helps to carry heat away. To some extent, *radiation cooling* is also used. All hot object lose some of their heat as infrared rays. If you've ever seen a high-current, solid-state power supply or a power transistor, you've probably seen a heat sink, which makes use of *conduction cooling* in addition to convection and radiation cooling.

Large mainframe computers have been using *liquid cooling* for a long time; this method is now being considered for personal computers. Liquid cooling makes use of conduction, radiation, and convection. It also employs evaporation.

A liquid-cooling system works like the cooling system in an automobile. It is actually a miniature air conditioner. A liquid, similar to Freon, passes over the microprocessor chip, whose heat boils the liquid. The vapor then passes to a condenser, where it becomes a liquid again, losing the excess heat. This liquid is recycled back to the chip. The block diagram at top of next page illustrates the process.

Liquid cooling systems can work in laptops as well as in desktop computers. Such a system, unlike the air conditioner in your home,

Liquid-crystal display

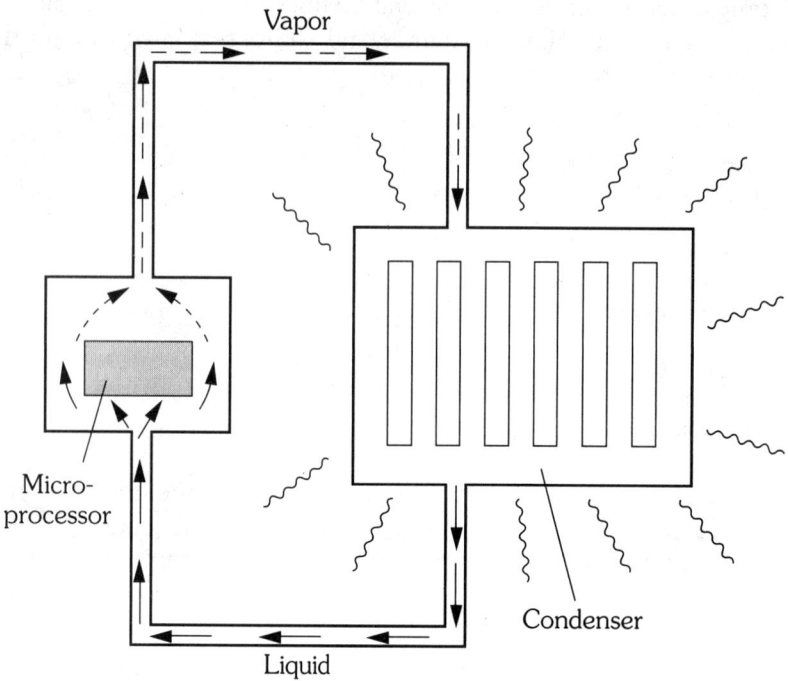

Liquid cooling works like the system that cools a car engine.

doesn't require any power of its own. Once it's in operation, it tends to keep itself going.

Liquid-crystal display

A *liquid-crystal display (LCD)* is a solid-state, flat-screen device that can show geometric shapes. The simplest LCDs are used as alphanumeric displays in calculators, meters, wristwatches, and radios. More sophisticated LCDs are used in computers, particularly laptops, and in portable television receivers.

How it works. All LCDs contain a fluid that changes its light-transmitting and light-reflecting properties in regions. The fluid is confined between transparent, electrically conductive plates. When a voltage is applied to the plates, the electric field causes a change in the molecules of the liquid. This alters the way light passes through the display, within the region containing the electric field.

The drawing is a greatly simplified view of a tiny section of an LCD. The darkened pixel (picture element) results from the presence of an electric charge on the plates just above and below it. A matrix of contacts (not shown) allows the plates to be charged in groups of pixels whose size dictates the ultimate image resolution of which the LCD is capable.

Liquid-crystal display

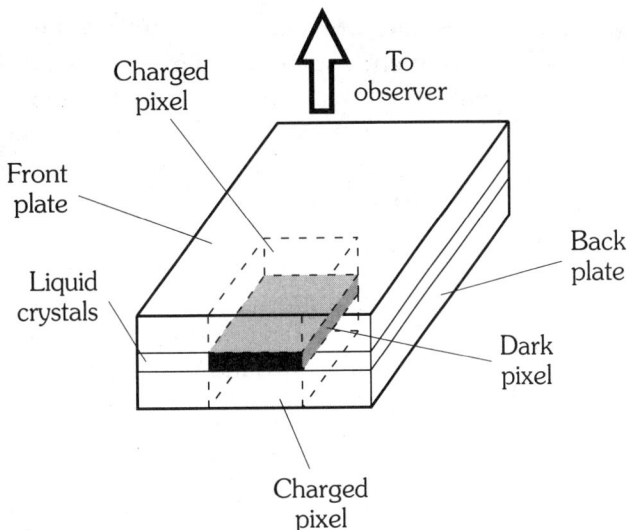

A magnified, simplified cross-section of an LCD showing one darkened pixel.

Modern LCDs can change not only from light to dark (so-called "black on gray"), but can also exhibit some colors. Although there is a limit to how fast the liquid can change state, in recent years, LCDs have been developed that are fast enough, at room temperature, to function as video displays in miniature fast-scan television sets. Such LCDs are also suitable for most casual computer graphics applications. The speed of the LCD is affected by the temperature; extreme cold causes the LCD to change state more slowly.

Assets. One of the most significant advantages of the LCD is that it needs almost no power to operate. This makes it ideal for all kinds of portable electronic devices, where the batteries must last as long as possible. The LCD is an electrostatic device, consuming minimal power to change state, and practically no power to maintain a given state.

Another advantage of the LCD is that it is easy to read in bright sunlight. It can also be backlit for use in darkness. A good LCD can be easily read in light of any intensity, direct or indirect, provided the viewing angle is right.

Still another asset of LCDs is image resolution comparable to that of a cathode-ray-tube (CRT) display. That has not always been true; early LCDs were notoriously bad in this respect. The newer LCDs allow graphics to be done on laptop and notebook computers, where only text-based applications could be done before. The improvement in image resolution, along with the speed enhancement that has occurred since the mid-1980s, can be expected to continue in the future. The time might come when LCDs supplant CRTs in all PCs, desktop and portable.

Limitations. One of the main problems of the LCD is that it needs to be backlit if the operating environment is dark. This cancels some of the benefit of low current drain because the lighting requires electrical current. This can be minimized by shutting the backlighting off when there is enough light to read the display without it. External, battery-powered lamps can also be used.

Another problem is that an LCD can be hard to read from certain viewing angles. This situation has improved in recent years, but in older LCD-equipped word processors and portable computers, the displays often force the user to move around until he or she finds a good angle.

Another potential limitation of the LCD is that it is susceptible to cold. Modern LCDs are only affected when it is much colder than most computing environments. You're probably not going to do much computing in subfreezing temperatures; if you do, your hands will suffer from the same performance degradation as the display, and you'll need a heater anyhow. *See also* ACTIVE MATRIX, CATHODE-RAY TUBE, IMAGE RESOLUTION, LAPTOP COMPUTER, *and* PIXEL.

LISP

LISP is a computer programming language devised by John McCarthy at Massachusetts Institute of Technology in 1968. The name is a contraction of the words *list processing*.

LISP differs from most high-level languages in that it is written in the form of lists. Other languages usually have statements that tell the computer what to do. In LISP, a program can be interpreted directly as data, and vice-versa. The entire language is derived from a few basic functions. LISP programs are therefore easy to debug. Although its structure is straightforward, some programmers consider LISP difficult to read.

LISP is used extensively in artificial intelligence research, particularly in the United States. The language has various "dialects" or variants. *See also* ARTIFICIAL INTELLIGENCE, HIGH-LEVEL LANGUAGE, *and* PROLOG.

Lithium battery

A *lithium battery* is used to prevent loss of volatile memory data in microcomputer-controlled devices. These batteries have traditionally not been rechargeable, although a rechargeable type is under development for possible use in laptop computer power packs. Lithium batteries deliver a lot of energy for their size and weight. The drawing is a cross-sectional view of a typical lithium cell.

Memory backup. The first application of lithium batteries was in small calculators and scanner radios. In the late 1970s, radios began using frequency synthesizers that could be programmed to remember

Lithium battery

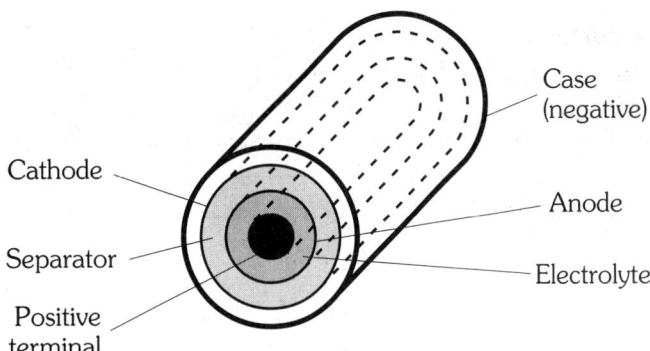

A simplified cross-section of a lithium cell.

channels. You've probably used automotive and portable radios that have "memories" you can recall and reprogram at the touch of a button. The data is kept intact even if power is removed. A lithium battery provides this memory backup. Data in memory needs only a tiny bit of current to be maintained, and lithium batteries are good at supplying a small current for a long time.

Lithium batteries can be used to momentarily back up the RAM (random-access memory) in any PC, preventing data loss in the event of a power interruption. These batteries are also used to run the internal clocks (timekeepers) inside many computers.

Power supply. Although lithium batteries work well when a tiny current must be maintained for an extended length of time, they don't work as well when a large current is required for a short time. It's expensive and difficult to manufacture lithium batteries that can deliver enough power to run complex equipment. Lithium-battery technology is improving, however, while laptop and portable computers are evolving that need less and less power.

A lithium battery can store more energy, for a given size and weight, than a nickel-cadmium battery (NiCd or NICAD). In addition, lithium batteries don't suffer from *battery memory*, also called *memory drain*, which can occur with NICADs. You might see a laptop advertised as having a rechargeable lithium battery pack, instead of a NICAD.

At the time of this writing, there are two hurdles that lithium batteries must overcome before they gain widespread acceptance as power supplies for laptop computers. First, although the cost is coming down, they're expensive per unit of energy delivered. Second, lithium batteries have a shorter lifecycle than NICADs; they can't be charged and recharged as many times. This further drives up their practical cost. *See also* LAPTOP COMPUTER *and* NICKEL-CADMIUM BATTERY.

Local area network

A *local area network (LAN)* is a group of computers linked together within a small geographical region. The interconnections are usually made with wire or fiberoptic cables; microwave radio links are also sometimes used. All the computers are near one another, so transfer delays are minimal. In any LAN, the combination of computers is far more powerful than any computer by itself.

LAN topologies. The way in which a LAN is arranged is called the *LAN topology*. There are two major categories of LAN topologies: the *client-server LAN* and the *peer-to-peer LAN*.

The system shown in drawing A has one large, powerful, central computer called a *file server*, to which all the smaller workstation computers (labeled C) are linked. This is a form of client-server LAN. This topology is used in medium-sized and large corporations, colleges, and government offices.

In small companies and organizations, LANs are often assembled without file servers; these are peer-to-peer LANs. There are several different ways in which a peer-to-peer system can be arranged. These are "subtopologies" within the general peer-to-peer scheme. Three

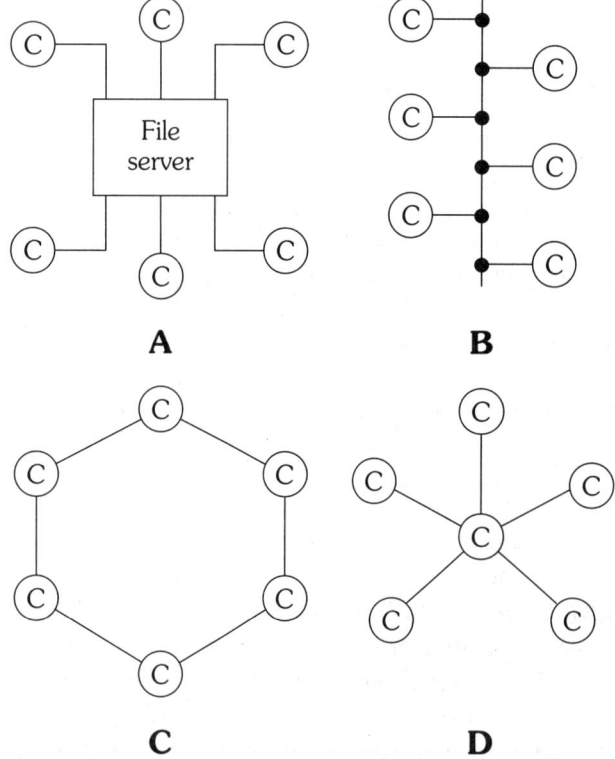

Client-server (A) and peer-to-peer (B, C, D) LAN topologies. Computers are circles labeled C.

examples are the *bus network* (drawing B), the *ring network* (drawing C), and the *star network* (drawing D). Although each example shown happens to have six computers, any of these LANs could have as few as two, or more than a dozen, workstations.

Client-server features. A client-server network is more powerful than most small companies or organizations need. It's also more expensive, harder to install, and costlier to maintain than a peer-to-peer LAN. However, there are some definite advantages to the client-server arrangement, including the following:

- High speed
- Large memory capacity
- Ability to do many different tasks
- Ability to accommodate many workstations
- Provision for using dumb terminals as well as PCs
- Provisions for security

If you have a small or medium-sized company that is rapidly growing, and if you expect your computing needs to multiply apace, you might want to consider footing the bill for a client-server LAN. That's a big investment, however; you should get expert advice before making a final decision.

Peer-to-peer features. A peer-to-peer LAN is less expensive, in general, than a client-server system. This is one of its chief advantages for small organizations. Some other features are

- Comparative ease of installation
- Moderate maintenance costs
- Ease of use
- Expandability
- Choice of "subtopologies"
- Full computing capability at each workstation

A peer-to-peer LAN will almost always meet the needs of a small, stable corporation with modest growth plans.

There are some hidden costs involved in the installation and maintenance of any LAN, however small or large. Also, training workers to use the computers in a new peer-to-peer LAN can prove more of a challenge than management might at first suspect. Before purchasing a LAN, you must decide whether or not it is really needed. There's no sense in buying a network when one or two individual computers will suffice.

Local area network

Installation. If you're an electronics whiz, you can probably install the hardware for a peer-to-peer LAN yourself. Otherwise, you should hire professionals. The process can involve modifying the building, as well as making sure that the cables and connectors are the right type.

The best communications cable is *coaxial cable* (often called *coax*, pronounced "CO-ax"). This cable has an inner wire surrounded by a tubular braid. The braid provides electromagnetic shielding. Twisted wires are sometimes used in an effort to save money because coax is rather expensive. However, coax helps to minimize problems with radio-frequency interference (RFI).

Ideally, connectors should be soldered to the ends of coaxial cables. Snap-on connectors are available, and you might be tempted to use them because you don't have to bother with the soldering process. Snap-on connectors are more likely to allow corrosion, however, which will eventually cause problems.

Installing the cables might consist of nothing more than laying the cable on the floor, running it alongside walls or under carpets. However, if you want to run the cables through walls or between floors of a building, you should call in a professional. You must ensure that your system conforms to fire and electrical regulations. An electrician will know these rules.

Training. All computer systems, hardware as well as software, take time to learn. If you have a small business and are installing a LAN, some of your employees might have some trouble with *cyberphobia*, an unreasonable fear of computers.

Some LAN suppliers will provide you with on-site training sessions, in addition to the documentation, to get employees familiar with the system. Because this can get expensive in a hurry, much of the training will probably end up being done by self-teaching. It helps if someone in the business has experience with PCs, and especially, some LAN experience.

An alternative to on-site training is to use the call-in technical support services that most manufacturers provide. Training software is also available, so employees can learn some skills at their workstations while not directly interacting with the network.

Maintenance. When you buy a television set and videocassette recorder, you can probably install them yourself, and the instruction manuals will be adequate for you to learn how to use the equipment. However, if something goes wrong with a TV or VCR, most people must call a repair service.

Computer LANs are more sophisticated than TVs and VCRs, in terms of the amount of hardware they contain. Even so, if something goes wrong with a LAN, there's a good chance you can at least diagnose the problem, especially if you have well-written documentation. The four causes of LAN failure are as follows:

1 Bad connecting cable(s)
2 Bad computer hardware or software
3 Interference from an outside source
4 Human error

Bad hardware can be pulled and fixed, and the LAN can get along for awhile without it. Bad software, from bugs, viruses, and Trojan horses, is rare if the software is purchased from a reputable vendor. A bad cable can be replaced or repaired in a few minutes. Operator error declines with training and experience. Outside interference can be a tougher problem to solve and is the most likely to require professional assistance.

The trick, when a LAN goes down, is usually locating the faulty piece of hardware. (A "faulty" operator will usually declare himself or herself.) The documentation for the LAN should contain a troubleshooting section. By following these instructions, you can often locate the problem in a malfunctioning LAN, but if your own troubleshooting efforts fail, you must call a technician. You might have a service agreement already in place, so a failure won't result in your having to pay labor costs.

Maintenance contracts. When shopping for a LAN, find out if the supplier offers maintenance contracts. Check several different suppliers and compare their maintenance plans.

Hardware isn't 100% reliable, but neither will a well-installed LAN be likely to fail very often. You should be prepared to deal with some system problems, but you don't want to pay an exorbitant price for overly lavish service contracts that you'll underutilize. In this respect, LAN maintenance deals are quite similar to employee health insurance plans. *See also* BUS NETWORK, COAXIAL CABLE, DUMB TERMINAL, ELECTROMAGNETIC SHIELDING, FILE SERVER, LINK, NETWORK, PEER-TO-PEER NETWORK, RADIO-FREQUENCY INTERFERENCE, RING NETWORK, STAR NETWORK, WIDE AREA NETWORK, *and* WORKSTATION.

Local bus

Inside the main unit of your computer, the large circuit board, called the *motherboard*, has many little boxes soldered to its surface. The little boxes are integrated circuits (ICs). Several of these together form the central processing unit (CPU), or brain, of the machine. Strips of foil on the motherboard provide pathways for data and electrical currents to go to and from the CPU. Such a path is called a *bus*. Some buses consist of wires running from the motherboard to other circuit boards in the computer.

A *local bus* is a high-speed bus that allows devices to be connected to the CPU. It's like a wide freeway along which data can travel in large quantities. This bus is generally used with devices that work with a lot of data per unit of time, such as the display and the hard disk. *See also* BUS, EXPANSION BUS, HOST BUS, INTEGRATED CIRCUIT, *and* PRINTED CIRCUIT.

Logarithmic graph

A *logarithmic graph* is similar to a set of Cartesian coordinates, except that in a logarithmic graph the axis for the dependent variable is logarithmic, rather than linear. The axis or axes for the independent variables are linear.

A two-dimensional logarithmic coordinate system is shown in drawing A. A three-dimensional system is shown at B. Only the positive halves of the axes are shown.

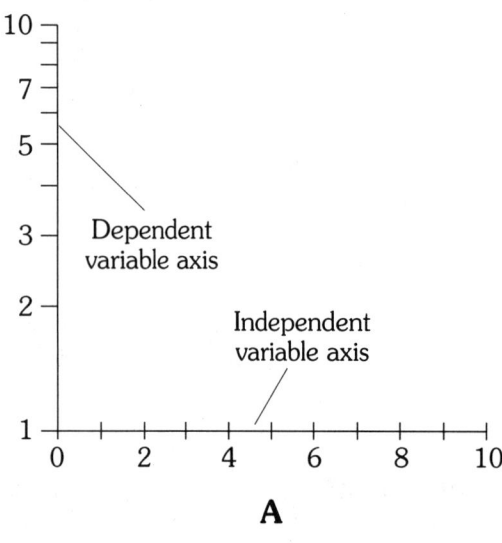

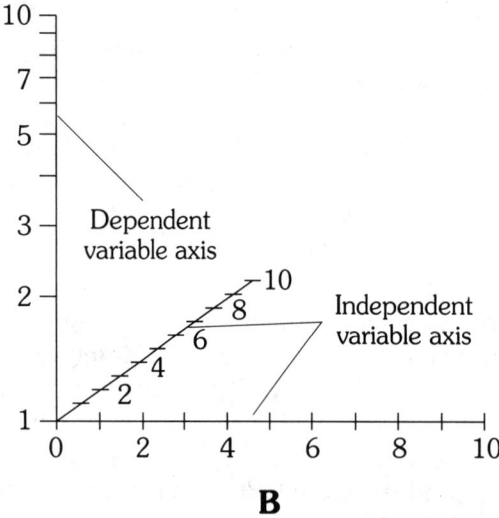

Two-dimensional (A) and three-dimensional (B) logarithmic graphs.

Note that the dependent-variable axis starts at one, not at zero. This is characteristic of logarithmic scales. Such a scale can't go down to zero; that is its chief limitation. This is more than offset, however, by the fact that a logarithmic scale can be repeated over and over, extending the axis through several orders of magnitude (powers of 10). A linear scale that would be miles long can thus be compressed into a few inches, making it possible to show functions in logarithmic graphs that cannot be rendered in conventional Cartesian graphs.

Most good analytical graphics software packages have a provision for generating logarithmic graphs. They are especially useful in scientific work. *See also* ANALYTICAL GRAPHICS, CARTESIAN COORDINATES, DEPENDENT VARIABLE, INDEPENDENT VARIABLE, LOG-LOG GRAPH, *and* SEMILOG GRAPH.

Logic

Logic refers to methods of reasoning used by people and computers. The term is also sometimes used in reference to the digital electronic circuits that comprise most computers.

Boolean algebra. You might be surprised to learn that there are different forms of logic. The most elementary and straightforward type is *Boolean algebra*. This is also known as *symbolic logic, propositional calculus*, or *sentential calculus*. In this context, the term *calculus* doesn't mean mathematical analysis; instead, it refers to a rigorous and simple reasoning scheme. It deduces logical equivalences from facts, using rules.

Boolean algebra uses capital letters, usually from the second half of the alphabet, along with addition, multiplication, and negation, to encode statements. In Boolean algebra, statements always have a truth value, either true (high, or logic 1) or false (low, or logic 0).

Predicate calculus. *Predicate calculus* goes a step further than Boolean algebra, in that it breaks down individual sentences. The structure of a sentence can drastically affect its behavior in a system of reasoning.

In predicate calculus, a sentence is not represented as a single letter like P. Instead, it is represented as a function, such as Px. You probably learned the word *predicate* when breaking down, and diagramming, sentences in high-school English grammar courses.

Predicate logic is not generally used by personal computers, except in an indirect way, by the brute-force application of digital logic.

Reductio ad absurdum. It is possible to prove the truth of some statement, say P, by showing that its denial, −P (not P), leads to a contradiction. The term *reductio ad absurdum* (meaning "to derive an absurdity") is familiar to logicians and mathematicians.

A well-known theorem in propositional and predicate logic can be summed up as, "From a contradiction, anything follows." This means that, if you accept a direct contradiction (P AND –P) as being true, then you must accept every statement in the whole logical system as being true. This reduces the whole system to an absurdity.

Theorem-proving computer programs make use of this technique, which is based on the principle of double negation. The denial of a false statement is a true statement. *Reductio ad absurdum* has been used to prove some of the most famous theorems in all of mathematics.

Mathematical induction. A special form of reasoning, known as *mathematical induction*, allows you, or a computer, to prove an infinite number of facts in a finite number of steps. Usually this is done for a series of countably infinite objects, such as numbers.

Suppose you want to prove that something is true for all the numbers n in the set $N = \{1, 2, 3, \ldots\}$. You must first show that the fact holds for the number 1. Then you must show that if it's true for any number n in the set N, it is true for $n + 1$. In this way, via a sort of logical domino effect, you prove the fact for all the natural numbers 1, 2, 3, and so on, without limit. Imagine knocking over the first domino in an infinitely long row of dominoes, and you can get an idea of the fun mathematicians have when they prove something by induction.

Computers have been used in an attempt to prove things for all the numbers in the set $N = \{1, 2, 3, \ldots\}$, by proving that things hold up to some huge value like 1,000,000,000. However, this is not a valid mathematical proof at all. It resembles inductive logic, a scheme with a similar name, but which, in reality, is vastly different.

Inductive logic. All the logic forms mentioned so far are *deductive*: they are 100% airtight, rigorous methods of reasoning. When you speak, or hear, of having "proven" something mathematically, deductive logic has been used.

Another form of logic, commonly called *inductive logic*, doesn't prove things beyond all doubt. Instead, it derives statements that are true most of the time, or that are reasonable based on the data available. This is the sort of logic that lawyers use in the courtroom when they cannot prove things deductively. "Beyond a reasonable doubt" is the buzz phrase that gives away the fact that inductive reasoning has been used.

Computers are extremely powerful in inductive logic because such reasoning is based on statistical probability, which involves taking huge numbers of samples and combining the data into meaningful form. One of the original intentions of computer engineers was to get a machine to do this kind of work, saving countless hours of bean-counting and paper-shuffling.

Trinary logic. *Trinary logic* allows for a neutral condition, neither true nor false, in addition to the usual true/false (high/low) states of *binary logic*. These three values are representable by logic −1 (false), 0 (neutral) and +1 (true).

You might wonder what use trinary logic could possibly have. Aren't things always either true or false? Perhaps, but in 1930, a mathematician named of Kurt Godel rigorously proved the Incompleteness Theorem which basically says that, in any logical system, there are statements whose truth value can't be determined. That is, certain propositions are undecidable as to truth or falsity. The publication of the Incompleteness Theorem caused an upheaval in the mathematical world.

An undecidable statement might have truth value in an absolute, cosmic sense, but we humans, and our machines too, are somehow barred by fate from unraveling it. The notion of undecidability creates a made-to-order niche for trinary logic, which allows for a "don't know" state.

Fuzzy logic. A more sophisticated and avant-garde concept in reasoning logic, is *fuzzy logic*. This might also be called "analog logic," and harkens back to the days in which analog computer technology was more often used than it is today. In fact, analog technology is far from dead.

In fuzzy logic, the values cover a continuous range from totally false, through neutral, to totally true. Fuzzy logic approximates the sometimes frustrating, bizarre nature of the real world. It allows for, and in fact practically insists upon, some error, which is inevitable in experimental science. Fuzzy logic is well-suited for the control of certain processes. Its use will probably become more widespread as the relationship between computers and robots matures.

For further information. For an in-depth study of logic as it relates to reasoning, there are hundreds of books, ranging from *easy reading* to advanced college texts. Consult a good public library or college library. Engineering textbooks provide treatment of digital logic technology.

See also ALTERNATIVE COMPUTER TECHNOLOGY, ALGORITHM, ANALOG, ANALOG COMPUTER TECHNOLOGY, ANALOGICAL REASONING AND GATE, ARTIFICIAL INTELLIGENCE, BINARY DATA, BONGARD PROBLEMS, BOOLEAN ALGEBRA, COMBINATORIAL EXPLOSION, CONTEXT, DIGITAL, DIGITAL COMPUTER TECHNOLOGY, DON'T CARE STATE, EXCLUSIVE-NOR GATE, EXCLUSIVE-OR GATE, HEURISTIC KNOWLEDGE, HYBRID COMPUTER TECHNOLOGY, IF/THEN/ELSE, INCOMPLETENESS THEOREM, INFINITE

Logic board

REGRESS, INVERTER, KARNAUGH MAP, KNOWLEDGE, KNOWLEDGE-BASED SIMULATION, LOGIC GATES, NAND GATE, NEURAL NETWORK, NOR GATE, PARADOX, PROBLEM REDUCTION, RECURSION, SEQUENTIAL LOGIC, SYNTAX, THEOREM-PROVING MACHINE, *and* WHAT-IF ANALYSIS.

Logic board

See MOTHERBOARD.

Logic gates

All digital electronic devices, including computers, employ thousands, millions, or billions of switches that perform certain functions. These switches, called *logic gates*, have anywhere from one to several inputs, and one output.

Positive and negative logic. Usually, the binary digit 1 stands for true and is represented by about five volts positive (+5 V). The binary digit 0 stands for false and is represented by about zero volts (0 V). This is called *positive logic*. There are other logic forms, the most common of which is *negative logic* (in which the digit 1 is represented by a more negative voltage than the digit 0). The remainder of this discussion deals with positive logic.

Three simple gates. The simplest logic gates are the *NOT gate* or *inverter*, the *OR gate*, and the *AND gate*.

An inverter has one input and one output. It simply changes the state of the input. Thus, if the input is 1, the output is 0; if the input is 0, the output is 1.

An OR gate can have two or more inputs (although it usually has just two). If both, or all, of the inputs are 0, then the output is 0. If any of the inputs are 1, then the output is 1. It only takes one true input to make the output of the OR gate true.

An AND gate can have two or more inputs (although it usually has just two). If both, or all, of the inputs are 1, then the output is 1. Otherwise the output is 0. For the output of an AND gate to be true, all of the inputs must be "true."

Other gates. Sometimes an inverter and an OR gate are combined. This produces a *NOR gate*. If an inverter and an AND gate are combined, the result is a *NAND gate*.

An *exclusive OR gate*, also called an *XOR* gate, is peculiar. It has two inputs and one output. If the two inputs are the same (either both 1 or both 0), then the output is 0. If the two inputs are different, then the output is 1. An XOR gate and an inverter can be combined to get an *exclusive-NOR* gate, also called an *XNOR gate*.

Basic logical operations

Gate type	Number of inputs	Remarks
NOT	1	Changes state of input.
OR	2 or more	Output is high if any inputs are high. Output is low if all inputs are low.
AND	2 or more	Output is low if any inputs are low. Output is high if all inputs are high.
NOR	2 or more	Output is low if any inputs are high. Output is high if all inputs are low.
NAND	2 or more	Output is high if any inputs are low. Output is low if all inputs are high.
XOR	2	Output is high if inputs differ. Output is low if inputs are the same.
XNOR	2	Output is low if inputs differ. Output is high if inputs are the same.

The logic gates mentioned here are summarized in the table. *See also* AND GATE, BOOLEAN ALGEBRA, EXCLUSIVE-NOR GATE, EXCLUSIVE-OR GATE, INVERTER, LOGIC, NAND GATE, NOR GATE, *and* OR GATE.

Log-log graph

A *log-log graph* is similar to a set of Cartesian coordinates, but all of the axes are graduated logarithmically, rather than linearly. This is true for both the independent variable axis or axes, and the dependent variable axis.

A two-dimensional log-log coordinate system is shown in the drawing. Only the positive halves of the axes are shown. Note that both axes start at one, not at zero. This is characteristic of logarithmic scales. Such a scale can't go down to zero; that is its chief limitation. This is

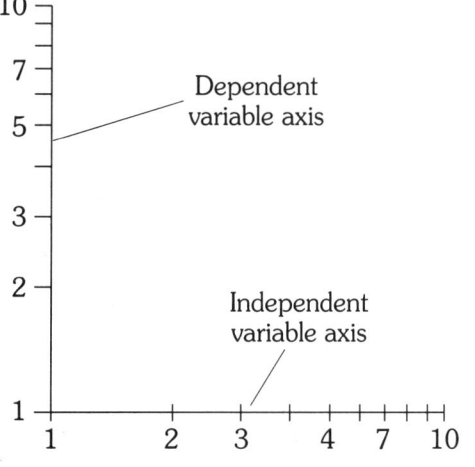

In a log-log graph, all scales are logarithmic.

more than offset, however, by the fact that a logarithmic scale can be repeated over and over, extending the axis through several orders of magnitude (powers of 10). A linear scale that would be miles long can be compressed into a few inches. This makes it possible to show functions in log-log graphs that cannot be rendered in conventional Cartesian graphs.

Most good analytical graphics packages have a provision for generating log-log graphs. Some can generate three-dimensional graphs in which some, or all, of the scales are logarithmic. A three-dimensional coordinate system in which all scales are logarithmic might be called a *log-log-log graph.* All logarithmic-scale graphs are useful in scientific work. *See also* ANALYTICAL GRAPHICS, CARTESIAN COORDINATES, DEPENDENT VARIABLE, INDEPENDENT VARIABLE, LOGARITHMIC GRAPH, *and* SEMILOG GRAPH.

LOGO

LOGO is a programming language especially useful for teaching children to use computers and computerized robots. In LOGO, a child can write programs to design original computer games.

Commands in LOGO take the form of simple motion descriptions. For example, LEFT 45 refers to a 45° turn to the left (counterclockwise). FORWARD 45 would mean "move forward 45 millimeters." By writing the commands in a sequence, the child can make a "turtle" go through these motions on a table or floor. The turtle contains tactile sensors, so that if it comes into contact with something, a signal is sent to the computer. The child might write IF TOUCH THEN RIGHT 90, meaning that if the turtle runs into anything, it should turn 90° to the right (clockwise).

A child can quickly learn to write rather complex programs in LOGO. The result is that the "turtle" acquires a set of behaviors. The child is essentially custom-programming a computerized robot to have a primitive sort of artificial intelligence.

Children like working with LOGO because the system is a toy. While they play, they learn: LOGO teaches concepts ranging from robotics to computer programming, and from AI to coordinate geometry, all at the same time. *See also* PERSONAL ROBOTS *and* PROGRAMMING.

Loop

A *loop* is a repeating sequence of operations in a computer program. The number of repetitions can range from two to billions. Often, the number of repetitions depends on the data input.

In some programs, there are *nested loops,* or loops within loops. It's even possible to have a loop within a loop within a loop.

Lossless and lossy data compression

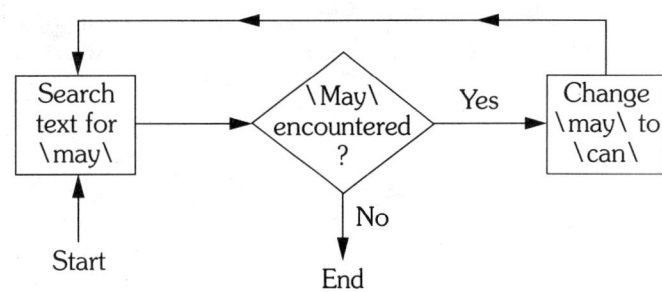

A search-and-replace loop changing all occurrences of may *to* can.

Programming loops are useful in calculations requiring operations that must be done over and over a great number of times. Until computers were developed, many such problems simply could not be solved, not because the problems were all that sophisticated, but because the millions and millions of steps would take a human being centuries to grind out.

Sometimes errors are made in the programming, and a computer ends up having to go through a loop without *ever* reaching a condition in which it can exit the loop. This is called an *infinite loop* or *endless loop*, and results in failure of the program to come to a conclusion.

An example of a loop is shown in the flowchart. In this case, the program is intended to get rid of all the occurrences of the word *may* in a document and replace them with *can*. In word processing, this is called *search and replace*. To indicate where the replaced text begins and ends, separators (backslashes) are used. When all the occurrences of the word have been found and changed, the program exits the loop.

In this kind of search-and-replace loop, you should probably reread the text, since the loop execution might introduce nonsensical words and phrases (such as changing *mayonnaise* to *canonnaise*). These will need to be corrected before the document is sent to the printer! *See also* ENDLESS LOOP, NESTED LOOPS, *and* SEARCH AND REPLACE.

Lossless and lossy data compression

Data compression is a way of maximizing the amount of information that can be stored on disk or transferred from one place to another in a given period of time. Data compression is used in hard disk systems, in communications, and to reduce the amount of storage space taken up by graphic images.

Lossless compression. Ideally, data compression takes place without losing any details. *Lossless data compression* is, in a sense, like getting something for nothing. You might take a file that occupies

200K and compress it to perhaps 150K. If the compression is lossless, the smaller file will contain all the details of the bigger one, even though it is made up of fewer bits.

How is this possible? Consider an example. The word *data* is frequently used in this article. Suppose it were represented by the symbol @, or some other symbol that was not used anywhere else in the article. The word *compression* might be converted to #. The word *the* could be changed to $. The computer could be told to change these symbols into words when you open the file. This compression would be flawless. It's amazing how much data space can be saved this way in plain-text documents.

Lossy compression. Graphic images are harder to compress than text files. Fractal image compression greatly reduces the storage space required by an image while sacrificing almost no detail, but this scheme can be slow if the image is complicated. Other graphic compression methods work faster than fractal image compression, but they are not as effective at retaining the image resolution.

The more detail an image contains, the less it can be compressed before an objectionable loss of resolution takes place. How much loss can be tolerated depends on the application, and also on the temperament of the computer user.

In recent years, image-compression technology has improved, making it possible to get large compression ratios (25:1, 50:1, or more) with loss so minor that a casual observer can't notice it. Although the term *lossy data compression* sounds bad, things really aren't so bad. As far as your eyes can tell, the compression is lossless. *See also* DATA COMPRESSION, IMAGE COMPRESSION, *and* IMAGE RESOLUTION.

Lotus

Lotus is short for *Lotus Development Corporation*, a popular software company. The word *Lotus* became practically generic with the widespread acceptance of their spreadsheet program, Lotus 1-2-3, in the early 1980s. Recently they have introduced a new, vastly improved spreadsheet called Improv.

Lotus 1-2-3. A typical spreadsheet is a large matrix of numbers, like a financial ledger. In fact, finances are the most common application of spreadsheet software. Each space in the matrix is called a *cell*, and is specified by row number (1, 2, 3, and so on) and column letter (A, B, C, and so on). Thus, cells have names like A7, B4, and C5.

Lotus 1-2-3 can work in two or three dimensions, and provides colorful, attractive displays. It can be used with most operating systems.

Lotus Improv. The Improv spreadsheet package offers increased flexibility and power compared with Lotus 1-2-3, yet it's actually easier for beginners to learn and understand. It's like finding out that a jumbo jet is easier to fly than a car is to drive (which some pilots might say is indeed the case).

With Improv, cells are called *items*. Items are named according to what's in them, instead of according to their location. You need not wonder about the contents of, say, cell C5. You address it directly by typing something descriptive of its contents, say, SALES TAX.

Improv is easy to share among PC users, regardless of their relative levels of experience. It is useful to salespeople, accountants, and company presidents, as well as anyone who files their income tax on the long form. *See also* SPREADSHEET.

Low-earth-orbit (LEO) satellite data link

The earliest communications satellites orbited only a few hundred miles above the earth. They were *low-earth-orbit (LEO) satellites*. Because of their low orbits, LEO satellites took only about 90 minutes to complete one revolution. This made communications inconvenient because a satellite was in range of a ground station for only a few minutes during each pass, and there were usually only two good passes every day. Because of this problem, *geostationary satellites* gradually gained dominance.

The LEO satellite concept is being revitalized today. It promises to make computer networks accessible from anyplace, at any time.

Geostationary satellites. The well-known novelist and science writer, Arthur C. Clarke, was among the first people to envision a fleet of satellites orbiting 22,300 miles above the equator. This results in an orbital period of 24 hours, so if the satellite orbits in the same direction as the earth rotates, the satellite stays fixed in the sky relative to all points on the surface. Today there are many satellites in these orbits, and they provide links for telephones, computer systems, television, and other services.

Still, there are some problems with a geostationary-satellite data link. The orbit requires constant adjustment; the slightest change in altitude causes the satellite to get out of sync with the earth's rotation. Geostationary satellites are expensive to launch and maintain. When communicating through them, there is always a delay of at least a quarter-second because of the path length (44,600 miles or more). It takes rather high transmitter power, and a sophisticated, precisely aimed antenna, to communicate reliably.

Of course, geostationary satellites have many advantages, and they will continue to be used in communications systems of all kinds. *See also* GEOSTATIONARY-SATELLITE DATA LINK.

Low-earth-orbit (LEO) satellite data link

The return of the LEOs. The limitations of geostationary satellites have brought about a revival in the LEO concept. Instead of a lone satellite, however, the new concept is to launch a large fleet of them.

Imagine dozens of LEO satellites in orbits such that, for any point on the earth, there is always at least one satellite in range. Suppose also that the satellites can relay messages throughout the fleet. Then any two points on the surface will always be able to make contact through the satellites. This concept is shown in the drawing. It's a cellular communications system, where the repeaters are constantly in motion (on satellites) instead of fixed (on the earth's surface).

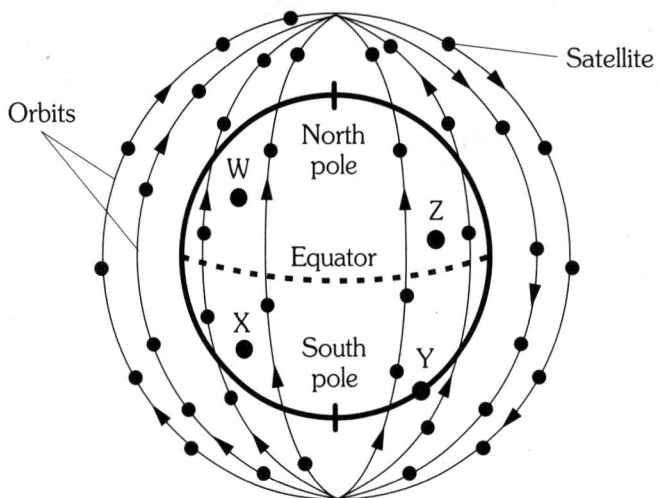

Points W, X, Y, and Z maintain contact because of the large number of satellites, a few of whose orbits are shown by arrowed lines.

Motorola is working on a system of this kind. It uses satellites in polar orbits, strategically spaced around the globe (see the drawing). Because of the large number of satellites, this type of system is called a *big LEO* satellite network. Big LEOs should be of interest to PC users because they will make data communications easier than ever before. Amateur radio operators are especially interested in the systems. If you have a "ham" radio license, you'll be able to conduct non-business packet communications through big LEOs without paying fees for the privilege.

A large, low-earth-orbit (LEO) satellite data link (big LEO) is easier to use than a geostationary satellite. A small, simple antenna will suffice, and it doesn't have to be aimed in any particular direction. The transmitter can reach the network using only a few watts of power. The propagation delay is much shorter than is the case with a geostationary link, generally less than a tenth of a second.

When big LEOs are in place, people will be able to connect PCs to simple transceivers and log onto networks from any point on the planet. It will work in the Himalayas or Antarctica, on a boat or a plane. The universal coverage and the modest cost of equipment make big LEOs appealing to developing countries. They ought to interest many average PC users, too. *See also* AMATEUR RADIO, GEOSTATIONARY-SATELLITE DATA LINK, PACKET COMMUNICATIONS, *and* SATELLITE DATA TRANSMISSION.

Low-level language

In computer programming, the term *low-level language* refers to any programming language with which the computer actually works. These languages are not easy for a person to deal with, for two reasons. First, low-level programming is tedious and time-consuming. Second, low-level format is nothing like plain English, or like any other natural (human) language, for that matter. Examples of low-level languages are assembly language and machine language.

In the interface between a computer and a human operator, the low-level language is almost always converted to a *high-level language*, and vice-versa. This is done via an *interpreter* or *compiler*. You type, click, or speak the instructions, and they are converted to digital signals that the computer can understand. When the computer has something to tell you, its digital signals are converted back into visual and/or audio output that you can understand. *See also* ASSEMBLER AND ASSEMBLY LANGUAGE, COMPILER, HIGH-LEVEL LANGUAGE, INTERPRETER, *and* MACHINE LANGUAGE.

LSI

See LARGE-SCALE INTEGRATION.

Luddites

Whenever there is a major new technological innovation, some people fear that they'll lose their jobs. This fear is not without reason. Machines are more efficient than people at some jobs, reducing the number of people needed for a company to function. Machines are tireless; a computer can work three shifts without a break. Computers are "down" only a small part of the time, and if they do malfunction, they can be quickly repaired and put back into service.

Technophobes. As computers and robots come into the workforce, people become anxious about their job security. Occasionally this is expressed as hostility and paranoia; once in awhile it explodes into violence. People who fear technology, and as a result develop a hatred for computers, robots and other machines, are called *technophobes*. They see only evil in computers. Their opposites are *technophiles*, who see only the good side of new technology. Both points of view are too simplistic.

Luddites

During the Industrial Revolution in England, technophobes went on rampages and destroyed new equipment that they feared would take their jobs from them. Their supposed leader was a man named Ned Ludd. Thus, these people became known as *Luddites*. Progress went ahead, however, regardless of their activities.

Modern reactions. Computers in the workplace have not caused a Luddite reaction in America, Japan, or Europe. Workers today are better informed than they were in Ned Ludd's time. They know that if their employers don't take advantage of new technologies while other companies or nations do, their organization will not be able to compete in the global economy. Employees will lose their jobs if their employer goes bankrupt, just as surely as if they were laid off. People today also know that computers need human programmers, engineers, technicians, and operators, providing new job opportunities.

The general standard of living in many countries improved in the years after computers were invented. Those who prophesy that computers will "take over" have not been taken very seriously because their fears haven't yet materialized on a scale anything like that which they predict. The benefits of computer technology have, thus far, outstripped the problems.

In the case of computers, small businesses have profited so much from them that the reaction to new technology is usually overly optimistic, not paranoid. In America, computers have created many job opportunities in the form of self-employment. For entrepreneurs, PCs have made many dreams come true. Many small companies depend on computers for their very existence.

Concerns remain. Computers make it possible for people to invade other people's privacy. In this respect, there is a real, and growing, danger.

Imagine what it would be like if your medical, tax, credit, and criminal (if any) records were available to anyone who wanted them! With only a PC and a modem, someone could get online and snoop all over the place. Some hackers might even alter your records, creating ruinous and ineradicable lies. To some extent, things are already at this point. As yet, fears about it haven't caused riots like the ones thrown by the original Luddites; the modern recourse is to sue. While government regulation is seen by some as a solution to this growing peril, others warn that the consolidation of the information superhighway will make it easier for bad hackers to conduct their illegitimate activities. Villains speed along freeways faster than law-abiding citizens because they ignore the speed limits.

It is possible to become over-reliant on machines, and computers seem to be especially bad in this respect. Thus, you'll occasionally be frustrated when an entire operation comes to a halt because of a computer problem. Today's equivalents of the old Luddites take a certain perverse delight in events of this kind. Such mishaps serve as a reminder that computers ought to remain the servants, and never become the masters, of humanity. *See also* COMPUTER ADDICTION, COMPUTER OVER-RELIANCE, CYBERPHOBIA, *and* HACKER.

Luggable computer

A *luggable computer* was a quasi-portable machine that is no longer in common use. It was bigger than a modern laptop, but smaller than a desktop computer.

The main difference between a luggable and a laptop was that you had to use 117-volt alternating current (ac) to power the luggable. There were no batteries, so you couldn't use a luggable on a bus or airplane. You could however, use a luggable with a battery and a power inverter if you had access to an electric generator that provided 117 volts ac.

The primary difference between a luggable and a desktop PC was that the monitor was built into the luggable main unit. The luggable was also lighter than the main unit of a desktop computer. Laptop computers have taken the place of luggables. *See also* DESKTOP COMPUTER *and* LAPTOP COMPUTER.

648

Mac Classic

The first Macintosh computer was introduced by IBM's main American competitor, Apple Computer, Inc., in 1984. This machine was new and radical. It even looked different. The monitor was in the same box as the main unit of the computer, and the whole assembly took up very little desk space. This machine became known as the *Mac Classic* or *128K Mac*.

Apple wanted their new line of computers to be as user-friendly as possible, especially for the neophyte. The ultimate goal was to create a computer that was as easy to use as a videocassette recorder, television set, or other home appliance. The Mac Classic came closer to that ideal than any of its predecessors. It needed only the barest minimum of assembly. It was still necessary, of course, to learn how to use the software.

With 128 kilobytes (128K) of RAM (random-access memory), the Classic had more than enough memory to suit the expectations of personal computer users in the early 1980s. The monitor was a monochrome cathode-ray tube (CRT) measuring nine inches from corner to corner. The whole unit, including the circuit boards and monitor, was enclosed in a tamper-resistant cabinet to keep inquisitive hands away from the fragile CRT and the high voltages needed to make it work.

Several variations of the Mac Classic were manufactured after the original 128K Mac. They all had similar design, and the features were much the same as those of the original Mac Classic. Eventually, Apple came out with the Color Classic, a computer with a color monitor. Apple also made the machine somewhat easier to upgrade than its Classic predecessors.

Today, Mac Classics can still be found. They're the "old reliables" of the Mac computer line, especially among users whose demands and requirements are modest. *See also* APPLE COMPUTER INC. *and* MACINTOSH.

Machine knowledge

Computers can store and manipulate information in ways and amounts that people cannot. A good example is the addition of a series of five million numbers. Still, there are many problems that humans can solve and a machine cannot, and perhaps never will. One example is determining how much medication will be needed to anesthetize a hospital patient during surgery. *Machine knowledge* and human knowledge are different. The extent of a machine's knowledge is reflected by the types and variety of problems it can solve.

Artificial intelligence (AI) is the highest form of machine knowledge. A computer with AI can learn from its mistakes and can be said to possess a certain degree of consciousness. Such machines might eventually program themselves. One step beyond this lies a totally automated, robotized computer factory, where the central computer oversees the manufacture of other computers. *See also* ARTIFICIAL INTELLIGENCE, COMPUTER CONSCIOUSNESS, COMPUTER GENERATIONS, COMPUTER POWER, EXPERT SYSTEMS, HEURISTIC KNOWLEDGE, KNOWLEDGE, LOGIC, MACROKNOWLEDGE, *and* MICROKNOWLEDGE.

Machine language

A computer doesn't work with words, or even with the familiar base-10 numbers. Instead, the machine uses combinations of ones and zeros. These are the two *binary states*, also represented by on/off, high/low, or true/false. Data in *machine language*, if written down, might look like a string of numerals such as 111001010001. This can be represented pictorially by black and white blocks, as shown in the drawing, where a black block represents a 1 and a white block represents a 0.

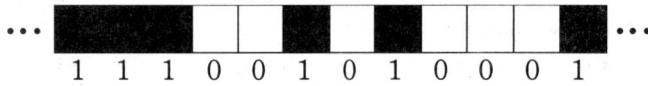

A pictorial representation of 111001010001.

Computer programmers do not write in machine language. It would be incredibly tedious and difficult. A typical program written in machine language would consist of many pages of ones and zeros, seemingly random but in fact in a precise and critical sequence. One wrong digit could cause the program to run poorly or not at all.

When you write a program, or issue a command to a computer, you do it in *high-level language*. This must be converted into machine language, the sequence of ones and zeros, for the computer. The computer output is likewise translated from machine language into whatever high-level language you are using. A *compiler* or *interpreter* takes care of the translation process. *See also* COMPILER, HIGH-LEVEL LANGUAGE, INTERPRETER, *and* PROGRAMMING.

Machine thought

See ARTIFICIAL INTELLIGENCE.

Macintosh

In the early 1980s, Apple Computer, Inc. introduced a line of computers called *Macintosh*. Since then, PCs have evolved along two main lines, the Macintosh series (also known as "Mac") and the IBM-compatible PCs.

Graphical user interface. The Macintosh line caught on fast because of its versatile, innovative features. For example, the graphical user interface (GUI) was first made widely available to consumers in the Macintosh computers. Actually, the idea for using a pointing device and icons, rather than typed commands, was first developed by Xerox Corporation several years before Apple made it well known.

Using a Macintosh system is similar to working with Windows in an IBM-compatible PC. You don't have to memorize a large set of commands; you just "point and click." Macintosh also allows for *multitasking*, or running more than one application at a time. This is especially useful when you must constantly refer to information sources while writing a report, for example. *See also* GRAPHICAL USER INTERFACE, MENU-DRIVEN SOFTWARE, MULTITASKING, SYSTEM 7, *and* WINDOWS.

Desktop publishing. Macintosh PCs entered the business market in the late 1980s by providing a means of desktop publishing at a reasonable price. The laser printer made desktop publishing a reality even for small companies. The main feature of the laser printer is the excellent quality of its printout, comparable to the text and graphics found in glossy magazines.

Macintosh systems continue to be used extensively by publishers and graphic artists. This is in part because of Apple's user-friendly local area network (LAN) concept, the most familiar example being *AppleTalk*. With an AppleTalk LAN at a publishing company, for example, an editor can use one workstation, an illustrator another, and a page designer another; each person gets a complete view of what the final product will look like. This is called *WYSIWYG* (pronounced "WIZZY-wig"), and stands for "what you see is what you

Macro

get." *See also* APPLETALK, DESKTOP PUBLISHING, LASER PRINTER, LOCAL AREA NETWORK, *and* WYSIWYG.

Competition and cooperation. Historically, Apple and IBM have alternately targeted various markets in attempts to gain an advantage. In recent years they have begun to combine forces. For example, Apple, IBM, and Motorola together developed the PowerPC chip. This combination of competition and cooperation keeps up the pace of progress and tends to drive costs down once new technologies gain wide acceptance.

Macintosh PCs have historically used Motorola microprocessors, while IBM-compatible machines have used Intel microprocessors or their clones. As the software gap narrows between Macs and IBM-compatibles, this dichotomy might change in the future. *See also* APPLE COMPUTER INC., IBM-COMPATIBLE PCS, INTEL MICROPROCESSORS, IBM, MAC CLASSIC, MODULAR MAC LINE, MOTOROLA MICROPROCESSORS, PENTIUM, POWERBOOK, POWERPC CHIP, *and* QUADRA.

Macro

A *macro* is a set of commands, functions, or keystrokes that are automatically executed in sequence when you press a key or combination of keys. Macros can save you a lot of button pushing and busywork.

In printers. Many printers have anywhere from one to several built-in macro settings. Suppose a printer has five macros, called MACRO 1, MACRO 2, MACRO 3, MACRO 4, and MACRO 5. You set up the printer so that the macros produce hardcopy as shown in the table. In the table, CPI stands for characters per inch; LPI stands for lines per inch. The form length is the height of a page, measured from top to bottom. Letter-size paper has a form length of 11 inches, and legal size paper has a form length of 14 inches. The typeface indicates the general shape of the letters.

A printer with five macros

Macro	Typeface	CPI	LPI	Form length
1	**Draft**	**12**	**6**	**11 inches**
2	Courier	10	4	12 inches
3	Prestige	17	8	14 inches
4	Sans Serif	12	6	11 inches
5	Sans Serif	20	8	8.5 inches

This hypothetical printer sets itself up in MACRO 1 when it is first switched on. This is indicated by boldface in the table: draft typeface, 12 CPI, 6 LPI, and 11-inch form length. To obtain the other macros, you press the appropriately marked buttons. You can set the printer functions manually, selecting each option independently, but this takes far more time than pressing one macro button.

If you want some font that isn't in any of the five macros, you must set the printer functions manually. This would be the case, for example, if you want to use Courier typeface at 15 CPI, 6 LPI, and a form length of 14 inches. You might reprogram one of the macros if you need this combination frequently. *See also* CHARACTERS PER INCH, FONT, *and* LINES PER INCH.

In software. Macros are useful in all kinds of software. When you must transfer a large number of files between a hard disk and a diskette, for example, macros can instruct the computer to carry out several commands at once. This saves your having to transfer each file individually. Suppose, for example, that you find yourself repeatedly giving the following commands:

```
COPY *.TXT A: <Enter>
COPY *.BAK A: <Enter>
ERASE *.BAK <Enter>
```

This sequence of commands requires that you strike 40 keys. You could encode these commands as a macro assigned to the keys Ctrl-Q, cutting the number of keystrokes down to just two. If you give these commands four times every workday, the macro will save you 160 keystrokes daily. Actually, the savings will probably be somewhat greater because, when typing often-used commands, people rush the process and make mistakes.

Macros can be used to encode often-used pieces of data, not just commands. For example, you might encode someone's address and telephone number as Ctrl-(something). This can save you hundreds of keystrokes daily if you do much correspondence. You can encode phrases, sentences, and even entire pages this way, too.

Macroknowledge

Macroknowledge is a term used in artificial intelligence (AI). It refers to knowledge in an all-encompassing sense; "knowledge about knowledge." It is a synergistic combination of information and logic.

An example of macroknowledge is the classification of living things. Usually, we think of the two main classes as being plants and animals (although some lifeforms share characteristics of both classes). Within the class of animals, we might focus on warm-blooded versus cold-blooded creatures. Ultimately, we might be interested in the class of warm-blooded animals that includes ourselves.

Macroknowledge about living things could be used by a computer-controlled robot to determine whether an approaching two-legged creature is a human being, another robot, or perhaps a gorilla.

Obviously, it's important that the machine get this perception right. You don't want your house guarded by a robot that sees you and thinks you're a gorilla that has escaped from the zoo.

A task like this seems simple enough, but it requires considerable processing speed and power. To make the distinction between you and a gorilla, a machine would need a vision system with a certain minimum resolution. It would have to recognize your height, your voice, and other characteristics about you, such as the way you walk. If the machine were required to single you out from among other people, the computer's macroknowledge would need to be more detailed than for differentiating between you and a gorilla.

In general, the more detailed a digital machine's macroknowledge becomes, the greater must be all the aspects of its computing power. This means a faster microprocessor, more memory, more storage space, and wider data buses. Alternative computer technology might enhance macroknowledge beyond the brute-force digital approach. One example is the *neural network*, which is good at recognizing patterns and relationships. *See also* ALTERNATIVE COMPUTER TECHNOLOGY, ARTIFICIAL INTELLIGENCE, BIN-PICKING PROBLEM, BONGARD PROBLEMS, COMPUTER POWER, EXPERT SYSTEMS, HEURISTIC KNOWLEDGE, KNOWLEDGE, MACHINE KNOWLEDGE, MICROKNOWLEDGE, NEURAL NETWORK, OBJECT RECOGNITION, PATTERN RECOGNITION, RESOLUTION, *and* VISION SYSTEMS.

Magnetic disk

A *magnetic disk* is a circular, flat, magnetic data storage medium. The two most common forms are the *diskette* and the *hard disk*. Diskettes are usually found in either of two diameters: 3.5 or 5.25 inches. Hard disks come in a variety of sizes.

Magnetic disks have all the advantages and limitations of magnetic media in general. Disks enjoy one special advantage over magnetic tape: data can be written onto and read from a disk much faster than to or from a tape. No two bits are ever separated by more than the diameter of the disk, while they might be at opposite ends of a length of tape. There's less mechanical motion in a hard disk or diskette drive as compared with a tape drive, allowing the disk system to work faster.

You'll hear several terms when people talk about magnetic disks. A *platter* is one of the individual rigid disks within a hard disk system. There might be three, four, five, or more platters in the assembly. A *track* is one of many concentric, circular paths on the disk surface, along which data is written. A *sector* is an arc-shaped portion of a track. A *cylinder* in a hard disk system is the set of equal-diameter tracks on all the platters. The *access time* is the length of time it takes to bring up files from the disk. The *disk capacity* is the maximum amount of data, usually measured in megabytes (MB) or gigabytes (GB), that the disk can store. *See also* ACCESS TIME, CYLINDER, DISK CAPACITY, DISKETTE, DISKETTE DRIVE, FLOPTICAL DISKETTE AND DRIVE, HARD DISK, MAGNETIC MEDIA, MAGNETIC TAPE, PLATTER, SECTOR, TAPE DRIVE, *and* TRACK.

Magnetic media

Magnetic media refers to the storage of information in magnetic fields. In personal computing, the most common magnetic medium is the *diskette* or *hard disk*. A *tape drive* is sometimes also used for mass magnetic storage.

How it works. When an object is magnetized, its atoms are all more or less aligned, so that their magnetic fields add together (see A in the drawing). When an object is demagnetized, its atoms are turned at random angles, and their magnetic fields average out to zero (see B in the drawing). A state of magnetization lasts for a fairly long time, but a state of demagnetization lasts forever unless an external magnetic field changes the situation.

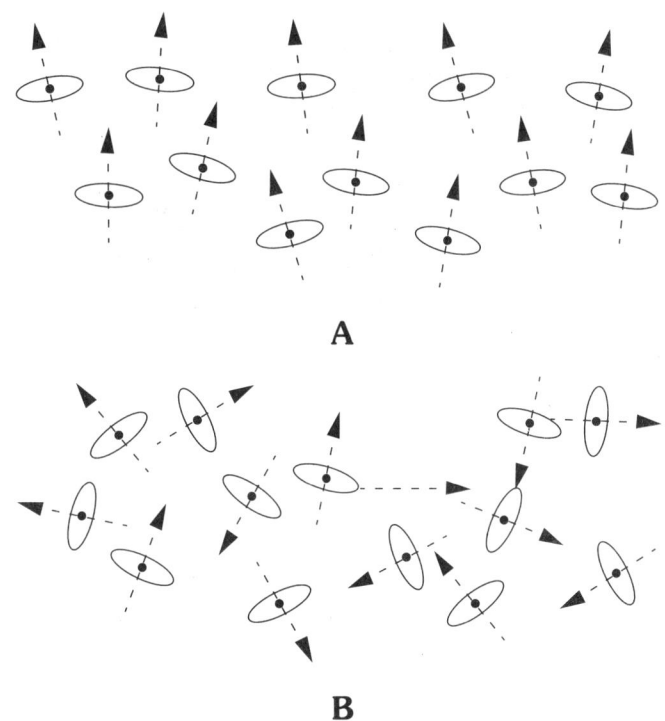

Aligned atoms (A) and nonaligned atoms (B). Arrows indicate north magnetic poles. (This is a greatly simplified rendition.)

In magnetic media, billions of tiny iron-oxide particles are attached to a flat surface, such as a tape or disk. Each particle can be magnetized and demagnetized, again and again. They can maintain magnetization for years. The magnetic polarity can be in either direction (north pole

Magnetic media

facing up, or south pole facing up). Early in the 20th century, audio engineers noticed this property and saw its potential for recording sound. The result was the audiotape recorder. Around the middle of the century, computer engineers adapted audiotapes for use in the first computers. Later, flat disks were used instead because they allow faster data access. *See also* MAGNETIC DISK *and* MAGNETIC TAPE.

Assets. The most important asset of magnetic media is versatility. A wide variety of tapes and disks are available, depending on what kind of data you need to store and how you want to store it. Magnetic data can be erased and overwritten hundreds or even thousands of times. The storage capacity is unlimited, as long as you don't mind having a lot of diskettes or tapes in your archives (data records).

Magnetic media are a form of *nonvolatile memory*; they don't require a source of power to maintain the information content. You can switch your PC off, and the hard disk will keep the files you've stored on it. You can put away a diskette, and then bring it out months later and find all the data unchanged.

Magnetic media have fairly high density. A typical 3.5-inch diskette can hold 1.44MB (megabytes, the equivalent of a long novel). A hard disk can hold upwards of 1000MB. The density of magnetic media keeps increasing with each passing year.

Magnetic media allow rapid reading and writing of data. This is especially important in computing because software programs can be quite long, and you don't want to spend a quarter of an hour waiting for the computer to set itself up after you switch it on.

Limitations. Magnetic media are heat-sensitive. If the temperature is too high, the ferromagnetic atoms move around so fast that they lose their alignment after awhile. Actually, this happens no matter what the temperature, given enough time; heat (over about 100°F) just makes it happen fast enough to cause problems. The solution to this is to store magnetic disks and tapes in a reasonably cool place.

Every so often, you'll want to copy all your archives from the old disks and tapes to new ones. Magnetic media don't last forever, even if you provide ideal storage conditions. Renew everything annually, and it should be all right.

Magnetic media are, not surprisingly, sensitive to magnetic fields. Keep disks and tapes away from magnets, and also from anything that generates magnetic fields. Loudspeakers, headphones, microphones, and the back ends of cathode-ray tube (CRT) monitors are surrounded by magnetic fields. Don't carry your diskettes in a handbag or briefcase along with little refrigerator magnets! Also, don't carry your diskettes and tapes through metal detectors, such as those in airports;

hand them to an attendant instead. *See also* ARCHIVES, DISKETTE, HARD DISK, MASS STORAGE, *and* TAPE DRIVE.

Magnetic tape

Magnetic tape is a data-storage medium commonly used for storing sound, video, and digital information. It is available in several different thicknesses and widths for different applications.

Magnetic tape consists of billions of fine particles of iron oxide, attached to a long strip of plastic or Mylar. A magnetic field, produced by a recording head, causes polarization of the iron-oxide particles. As the field fluctuates in intensity, the polarization of the iron-oxide particles also varies (see the drawing). When the tape is played back, the magnetic fields surrounding the individual iron-oxide particles produce current changes in the playback or pickup head.

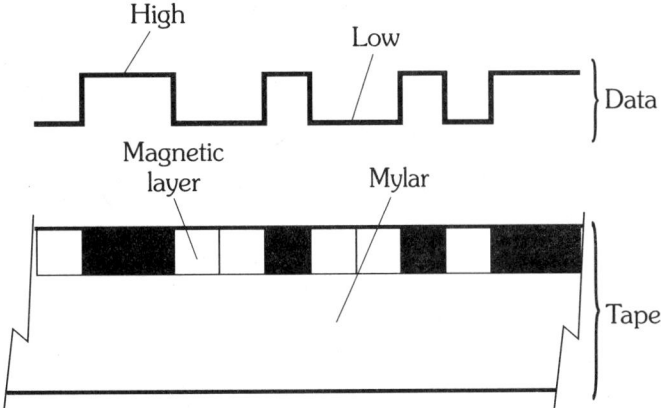

Magnified cross-section of magnetic tape showing effects of data pulses. Shaded regions are magnetized in one direction; unshaded regions are magnetized in the opposite direction.

For sound and computer-data recording, magnetic tape is available either in cassette or reel-to-reel form. In recent years, microcassettes have become popular for recording data on tape. The tape thickness can vary; thicker tapes have better resistance to stretching, but the recording time for a given length of tape is proportionately shorter than with thin tape.

Magnetic tape provides a convenient and compact medium for long-term storage of information. Certain precautions must be observed, however. The tape must be kept clean and free from grease. Magnetic tapes should be kept at a reasonable temperature and humidity, and they should not be subjected to magnetic fields.

Magnetic tape is a *sequential-access* medium, whereas a magnetic disk is a *random-access* medium. The binary digits (bits) on a tape are arranged in a string running lengthwise along the tape. In any given tape track, the distance between two bits can be as great as the length of the tape. Therefore, you can't generally open files from a magnetic tape as fast as from a disk. Nevertheless, tapes are useful for backing up data. The contents of a hard disk can be backed up on a single cassette with a device called a *tape drive*. The same backup might require hundreds of diskettes. *See also* MAGNETIC DISK, MAGNETIC MEDIA, *and* TAPE DRIVE.

Mailbox

In an electronic mail system, a *mailbox* is a sending, receiving, and storage system for personal messages, kept at a single location. Your mailbox is intended specifically for you (see the drawing).

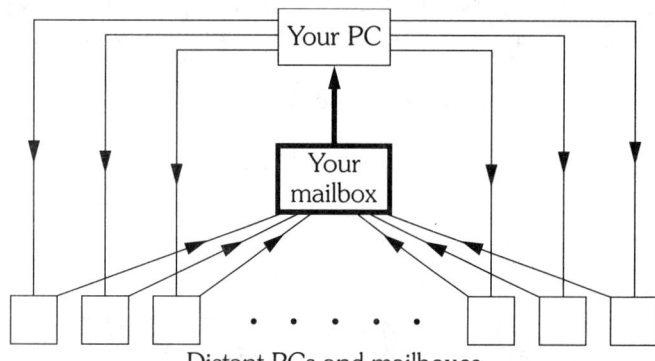

A block diagram of a mailbox system.

People generally do not store messages for each other in their personal mailboxes. That is the function of a bulletin-board system (BBS). Nevertheless, from time to time your mailbox might contain messages for other people. They can retrieve the messages by checking the contents of your mailbox. Because of this lack of privacy, you should use discretion when putting messages into any mailbox. Actually, you should always be careful what you type on your keyboard when you are online, whether or not the system is designed to be private. It's unwise to assume that any computer communications are private—ever.

Mailboxes and BBSs are used in packet communications networks, as well as online. If you have an amateur radio license, you can use packet radio for nonbusiness communications without paying any fees. *See also* AMATEUR RADIO, BULLETIN-BOARD SYSTEM, ELECTRONIC MAIL, MAIL FORWARDING, ONLINE SERVICE, PACKET COMMUNICATIONS, *and* PACKET-RADIO BULLETIN-BOARD SYSTEM.

Mail forwarding

Mail forwarding is a process in which messages are transferred between and among computers in a bulletin-board system (BBS). A mail-forwarding BBS ideally should have an up-to-date list of all the other mail-forwarding BBSs in the United States or in the world.

When you get a message via electronic mail (e-mail), you might see data concerning the path that the message went through to get to you. Your mail was forwarded through the various computers indicated in the list. If you do not use the same online service as the person who sent you the e-mail, the path data might be quite long and complicated. This might happen, for example, if you subscribe to America Online, and someone sends you a message from a local Internet gateway service. If you get a message from another country, the list will be longer still.

In amateur radio, mail forwarding refers to the transfer of messages among stations in a packet-radio bulletin-board system (PBBS). Many packet mail-forwarding routes are on the high-frequency (HF) bands, also known as the "shortwave" radio bands. This allows for the long-distance transfer of messages because signals on these bands can propagate for thousands of miles via the earth's ionosphere. Some packet mail-forwarding routes even employ communications satellites. *See also* AMATEUR RADIO, BULLETIN-BOARD SYSTEM, ELECTRONIC MAIL, INTERNET, MAILBOX, ONLINE SERVICE, PACKET COMMUNICATIONS, *and* SATELLITE DATA TRANSMISSION.

Mail-order business software

Entrepreneurship—breaking away from the corporate mold and going into business for oneself—is becoming ever-more popular in America, partly because PCs can provide assistance to the sole proprietor, making it unnecessary to hire (and pay) employees. *Mail-order business software* is one scheme by which you can increase your one-person-show power.

Juggling act. Mail-order, also called direct-mail, is especially appealing to the would-be entrepreneur. However, when you actually start to set up such a venture, you'll find out that it's a huge juggling act. You must advertise, but where? Which ads are the most effective? How can you get one-time customers to keep coming back? How much of each item do you have in stock right now? How much will you have in 30 days if present trends continue? Do you need to change prices? Have people been requesting things you don't carry? Should you drop some items from your list?

If you had to keep track of all these things on paper, it would be a nightmare of file cabinets, shelves, and time spent shuffling papers. You'd hire someone else to do it all, and in one year this could easily cost you many times the price of a good PC and mail-order business software. With a computer and the right kind of database, you can do it all yourself and recoup your investment in a couple of months.

Taking a new order. Suppose the telephone rings, and someone wants a Whoopie Widget. You key its code in (WW) and get a price: $35.99. The customer wants to charge it to a credit card. You take

Mail-order business software

the data and key it in, and get an online verification that the card status is okay. You key in the customer's name, and discover that this is a first-time order; this person has never ordered from you before. You ask, "Where did you find out about us?" and they reply, "A friend told me." So you let your PC know that the response was via word of mouth (WOM). You get the customer's address, and the PC calculates the shipping charge, adding it to the total.

After the transaction is complete, the computer automatically records the name and address of the person in the "Whoopie Widget" category of your database. It also adds the person to your list of customers, so if they ever call again, that fact will pop up right away.

Of course, you still must pack up the Whoopie Widget and mail it out. There are some things PCs can't do yet. The machine will, however, print the invoice and mailing label for you. A label printer comes in handy here. *See also* LABEL PRINTING.

Repeat customers. The telephone rings again. Someone wants a Junior Widget. You key its code in (JW) and get a price: $9.99. The customer wants to charge it to a credit card—no, wait—they want it sent C.O.D. You type in the name and address, and once again the computer automatically calculates the shipping charge, adding it to the total. The PC also tells you that this person has ordered items from you many times in the past.

"I see that you are a regular customer," you say.

"I've been pleased with everything you've ever sent me," the customer replies.

"Would you like to open an account with us?" you ask.

"I'll think about it and let you know," the customer answers. You note this in the computer. Next time this person calls, you'll see all this data on your screen immediately. Perhaps by then, the customer will be ready to open an account.

"Where did you first hear about us?" you ask.

"Your ad in an issue of *Widget World*," the customer replies. You note this in the database for future reference.

You pack up the Junior Widget and include a copy of an application for setting up an account.

For more information. These examples summarize a few of the things that mail-order business software can do for you. For more details, look at the advertisements in recent issues of the PC magazines. You should also check your local computer store or office-supply store, and pick up brochures for several different packages that interest you. If you're lucky, you might know someone who already runs a mail-order, one-person business, and can recommend a program. *See also* BUSINESS SOFTWARE, DATABASE *and* SPREADSHEET.

Mainframe

A *mainframe* is a large, fast computer with massive memory. Such a system can serve as the "brain" for a large number of peripheral computers and terminals. Mainframes are used by corporations, colleges, and bureaucracies to store information in a central place and supply it to many different users at once.

In recent years, the distinction between mainframes and minicomputers has become less well-defined. According to some experts, the term *mainframe* is almost archaic, the result of the increasing power of personal computers and minicomputers.

The drawing shows the hierarchy of the computer network in a hypothetical small college. The mainframe is the master control center; it serves the administration and all the educational departments. This is by far the most powerful computer on campus. Each of the four educational departments (Mathematics/Science, History, English, and Law) has a minicomputer (shown as large circles in the drawing) connected into the mainframe. Within each department, individual employees have microcomputers (shown as solid dots) and dumb terminals (shown as open small circles) that are connected into the department's minicomputer. *See also* COMPUTER POWER, DUMB TERMINAL, LOCAL AREA NETWORK, *and* MINICOMPUTER.

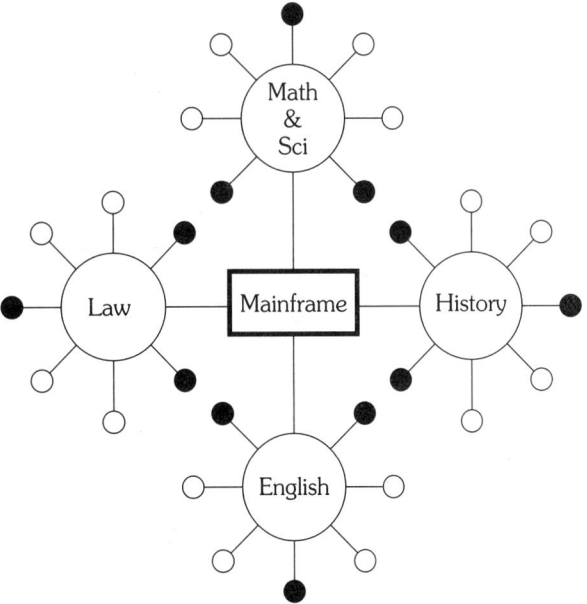

The mainframe serves as the intelligence center for an organization.

Mass storage

In computer systems, there are several different forms of *mass storage* in which data can be kept in large quantities. The kinds of mass storage that are best for you depend on the applications you use the most often, how much data you need to store, and how much money you have to spend on the storage media.

The pyramid. Computer experts categorize mass storage in two ways: access time and cost per megabyte. These factors are directly related. In general, the faster the access time, the greater the cost per megabyte. The actual number of megabytes is a separate concern, being a function of technology and available funds.

The drawing shows a popular method of illustrating mass storage media according to access time and cost per megabyte. The most expensive, fastest form of mass storage is called *flash memory*, and is like a large RAM (random-access memory). Flash memory occupies the top of the pyramid. Moving down, you encounter hard disks, diskettes, tapes, CD-ROMs, and magneto-optical storage.

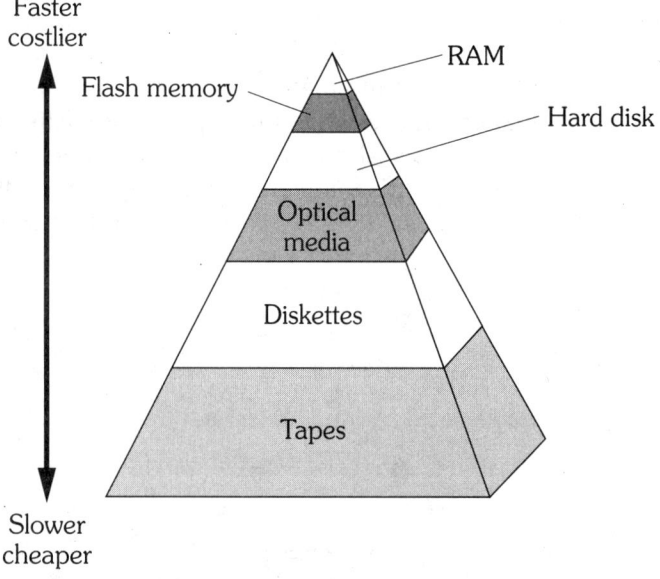

Pyramid paradigm for storage media.

The most expensive, fastest mass storage media usually have the lowest capacity because such schemes are always at the forefront of technology, where speed is a prime consideration. Less expensive forms of mass storage, such as magnetic disks and tapes, have capacity limited only by the amount of shelf space you're willing to devote to them and the amount of money you have to spend. If you have a big warehouse and unlimited resources, you could fill it with high-density diskettes and have millions or even billions of megabytes in your archives.

Memory chips. Binary data, in the form of logic highs and lows, can be almost instantly stored in and retrieved from memory integrated circuits (ICs), also called *memory chips*. Memory takes several forms:

> *Random-access memory (RAM)* stores data in arrays. The data can be addressed (selected) from anywhere in an array. Data is easily changed and stored back in RAM, in whole or in part. A RAM is sometimes called a read/write memory. An example of RAM is the content of a letter that you're writing.

> *Read-only memory (ROM)* can be accessed, in whole or in part, but not written over. ROM is usually programmed at the factory. This permanent programming is known as *firmware*. There are, however, ROMs that you can program and reprogram yourself.

> *Erasable programmable ROM (EPROM)* is an IC with memory of the read-only type, but that can be reprogrammed by a certain procedure.

> *Bubble memory* is a scheme that uses tiny magnetic fields within ICs. It's sometimes used in big computers because a large amount of data can be stored in a small physical volume.

> *Flash memory* is an enlarged sort of RAM, useful especially in high-level graphics, big-business applications, and scientific work. The capacity is comparable to that of a hard disk, except that there are no moving parts. Flash memory is more reliable, and faster, than a hard disk system.

Magnetic media. For permanent data storage, *magnetic media* are commonly used, usually falling into one of these categories:

> *Tape* The earliest computers used tape to store data. This is still possible, but disks are more often used in modern PCs. You might have a tape drive for making a backup of all the data on your hard disk.

> *Hard disk* The hard disk in a typical PC can hold several hundred megabytes of data. The hard-disk capacity of the typical PC doubles every few years, and the trend can be expected to continue indefinitely. Hard disks are usually permanently installed in the computer.

> *Diskette* These can be interchanged in seconds, so there is no limit to how much data you can put on them. A full-wall bookcase of diskettes could hold more work than you'd create in 100 lifetimes.

> *Floptical* This is an enhanced magnetic diskette that uses a laser-operated "guidance system" to increase the number of tracks per inch. As a result, the storage capacity is several times greater than that of a typical magnetic diskette.

Math coprocessor

Other forms. Data can be stored and recovered on compact discs that make use of visible light, infrared, and/or magnetic effects. An increasingly popular mass-storage medium is *CD-ROM* (compact-disc, read-only memory). You generally purchase these ready-made for various applications. You can even get a WORM (write-once/read-many) drive and make your own CD-ROMs, but this technology is expensive as of this writing. The main asset of a CD-ROM is its large capacity. Also, there's no limit to the number of times a CD can be replayed because laser beams are used to recover the data. Light beams do not scratch the CD.

Another alternative form of mass storage is *PCMCIA cards*. These credit-card-sized, removable storage media are becoming quite common in laptop computers. They not only store data, but can play numerous other roles, too, such as acting as a fax/modem.

See also CD-ROM, DISKETTE, FLOPTICAL DISKETTE AND DRIVE, HARD DISK, MAGNETIC DISK, MAGNETIC MEDIA, MAGNETIC TAPE, MEMORY, PCMCIA STANDARD ADAPTER CARDS, RANDOM-ACCESS MEMORY, *and* WRITE-ONCE/READ-MANY.

Math coprocessor

See COPROCESSOR.

Mean time before failure/between failures

The performance of a computer or other machine can be specified in various ways. One of the most common is the *mean time before failure (MTBF)*. The abbreviation MTBF also refers to *mean time between failures*.

Before failure. For a component or system, mean time before failure is the length of time you can expect a new device or machine to work before it fails for the first time. This is found by testing a number of components and averaging how long they keep working.

A simplified example of MTBF, calculated in hours on the basis of the performance of five identical 60-watt lightbulbs, is shown in the drawing. The lifetimes are simply averaged to get the result. It is, of course, possible that five very good bulbs or five exceptionally bad ones might have been chosen for the test. Testing a large number of components eliminates such coincidences.

The MTBF rating depends on the type of device. Some disk drives have MTBFs of more than a million hours. That's an average of 114 years of continuous use before the first failure! Of course, some units will fail much sooner than that, and some will keep working much longer.

Between failures. In the case of a system like a computer or network, mean time between failures is determined according to how

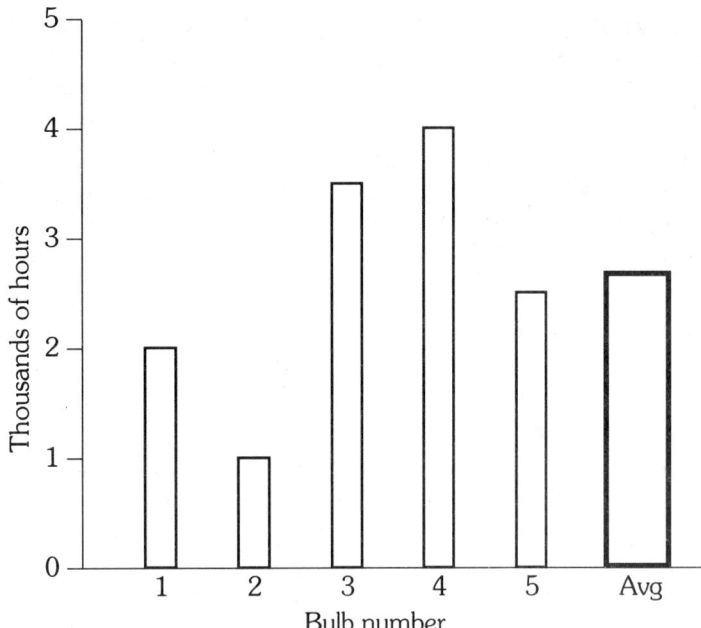

The average life for five hypothetical incandescent bulbs.

often the machine breaks down. As with the component-testing method, it is best to use many identical machines for this test. Conditions of the test should be as much like real life as possible.

With a large network, there are many components, any of which might malfunction. In general, the more complex the system, the shorter the MTBF will be. This does not mean that simple systems are necessarily better than sophisticated ones; it reflects the fact that complex equipment must be responsibly maintained. For computers and networks, therefore, the MTBF rating is not a direct indicator of overall quality. *See also* QUALITY ASSURANCE AND CONTROL.

Mechatronics

Mechatronics is a term originally coined in Japan. A combination of the words *mechanics* and *electronics*, it refers to the technology used in computers and robots. The term has the same literal meaning as *electromechanics*, but *mechatronics* has a more powerful, more industrial sound. In Japan, mechatronics is synonymous with industrial and economic power.

After the Second World War, Japan adopted the motto "Catch and pass the West." They hoped to do this by hard work, innovation, and devotion to quality: the things that have made America prosperous. "Japan, Inc." became a major exporter of mechatronic equipment. The Japanese became especially fond of robots. This was reflected in their large-scale factory automation and also in the kinds of toys they produced. During the 1970s and 1980s, Japan did catch and surpass the rest of the world in some respects. Their products, once regarded as inferior in quality, became standards of excellence.

With the development of artificial intelligence (AI), the relative importance of mechanics compared to electronics will probably dwindle in the field of robotics. In personal computing, however, with the development of personal robots, mechanical technology will have to advance. In America, several small corporations, as well as the large ones, are busy designing the home robots of the future. *See also* ARTIFICIAL INTELLIGENCE *and* PERSONAL ROBOTS.

Medical-office software

Running a doctor's office can be an extremely complicated affair. Patients' appointments must be scheduled. Each patient must have an up-to-date, accurate history. And of course, there is the labyrinth of billing and payment paperwork. *Medical-office software* allows the use of a computer or a local area network (LAN) to smooth the process of medical recordkeeping.

Is computerization necessary? In a private practice with one doctor, a computer might not be needed. Medical-office software isn't cheap, and it might constitute "overtreatment" in a small office. If you're a physician in private practice by yourself, you might not want to spend the money to computerize your office. If you can get along fine without doing so, there's no reason why you should.

In a practice with several doctors, however, computerization can make a big difference, especially if the size of the practice is growing. Joint practices serve more patients, as well as having more doctors. The complexity of schedules and referrals grows geometrically with the number of people involved. Then, too, there are almost as many payment plans as there are patients. Each patient's history changes with each visit to any doctor. The result is a huge, expanding mass of data that must be organized and juggled constantly—exactly the sort of thing that computers are designed to handle.

Features. Medical offices have unique requirements, and medical-office software is designed especially for these situations. The programs combine various functions of database and spreadsheet software. The following are the most common features:

➤ *Scheduling* works like the appointment-scheduling in any office serving a number of clients. A separate record is kept for each doctor in the practice. The date, time, and reason for the visit can be indicated. Each day, the computer can display a schedule of appointments for each doctor. Some programs also post notes to call patients several days in advance to remind them of their upcoming appointments.

➤ *Medical histories* are essential for any doctor who evaluates a patient. This is true whether or not the doctor has seen the patient before. Medical-office software can provide a printout of each patient's history, which the secretary can procure for the doctor on the day of that patient's appointment. Histories can be easily updated on disks, eliminating the need for bulky hardcopies and file cabinets.

➤ *Third-party payment* is a major source of frustration for doctors. The paperwork involved with insurance claims is staggering, and many people believe that this situation will get worse before it gets better. Good software can help ensure that everything gets filled out right and that none of the minutiae peculiar to a given third-party payer (taking the pulse at the ankle for diagnosis of kidney trouble, for example) are overlooked. These details can make the difference between prompt payment and a long delay. Some payers accept electronic submission of claim forms, and this is easily done via computer.

➤ *Statements and billing* can be done before a patient leaves the office, since he or she might want a detailed statement of charges. Statements can be supplied in duplicate or triplicate. Charges can be combined for a family. Past-due accounts are a headache for anyone who serves a large number of customers, and doctors' offices are no exception. The computer can keep track of accounts that run past due for 30, 60 or 90 days. Bills can be modified when partial payments are received. The financial information can be shared online between the doctors' office and the hospital (if any), insurance companies, and other doctors' offices.

➤ *Statistical analysis* can be done for medical data that requires the use of charts, tables, graphs, and mathematics. The more sophisticated medical-office programs combine analytical graphics with database and spreadsheet functions, allowing a physician to keep a record of, say, the number of strep throat cases diagnosed per month for the past several years. It can detect changes in requirements for certain medications, and can be useful in charting the course of a patient's condition.

For further information. Medical-office software is no small investment. There are several different packages available, and, as with any software, the features change constantly to reflect hardware and software advances. The PC magazines sometimes carry articles and advertisements for medical-office software. Medical journals are another source of information. Best of all, perhaps, is a colleague whose office is already computerized, and who can make recommendations. *See also* ANALYTICAL GRAPHICS, DATABASE, *and* SPREADSHEET.

Megabyte

The prefix *mega* means a million or millions. A *megabyte*, abbreviated MB, is a large unit of data, equal to approximately one million bytes.

Computer data is measured in powers of two, rather than powers of 10, because digital information is expressed in base 2, where the only values are 0 (low) and 1 (high). The actual value of one megabyte is therefore not exactly one million bytes, but instead, is 2^{20}, or 1,048,576, bytes. This is exactly 1024 kilobytes (1024K).

The drawing opposite shows the approximate relationship among one bit, one byte (eight bits), one kilobyte (1024 bytes), and one megabyte (1024K). The table shows the capacity, in megabytes, of several different data storage media.

Some PCs have hard disk systems with capacity of well over 1000MB. A typical high-density diskette can hold somewhat more than 1MB of data. A single CD-ROM holds 650MB or more. *See also* BINARY DATA, BYTE, GIGABYTE, KILOBYTE, *and* TERABYTE.

Capacities of several common storage media

Medium	Capacity in MB
640K RAM	0.64
5.25-inch, double-density diskette	0.36
3.5-inch, double-density diskette	0.72
Medium-sized novel	1.0
5.25-inch, high-density diskette	1.2
3.5-inch, high-density diskette	1.44
Hard disk	200 or more
CD-ROM	650

Megahertz

See HERTZ.

Membrane keyboard

A *membrane keyboard* is a lightweight, sealed keyboard whose keys are protected by a flexible piece of plastic. Such a keyboard or keypad looks fake, like a drawing of a keyboard, because the keys, while clearly labeled and outlined, are flush with the surface. The keyswitches are thin and are mounted on a rigid circuit board. The drawing shows a cross-sectional view of one keyswitch on a membrane keyboard.

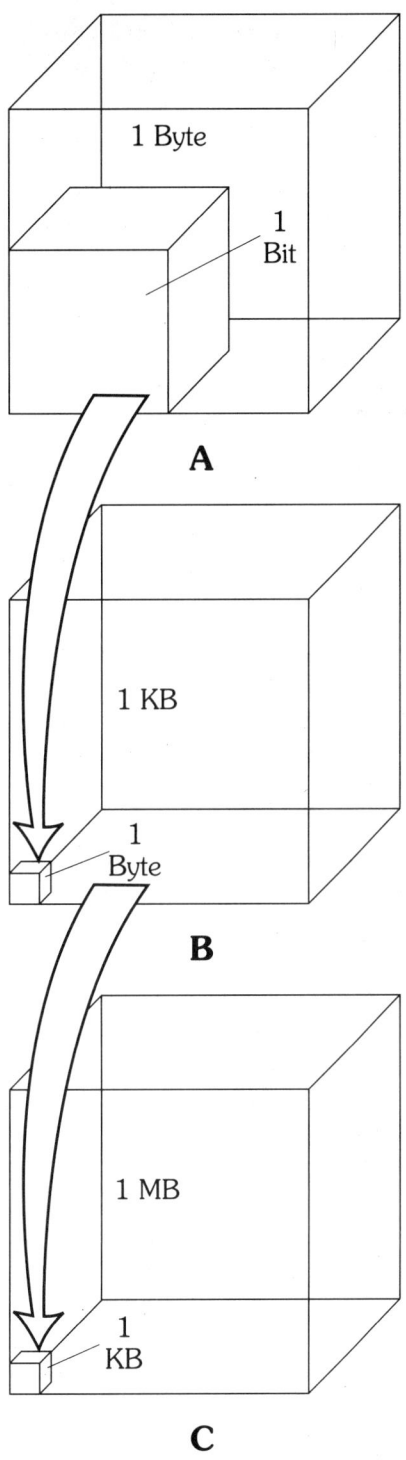

At A, one byte; at B, one byte versus one kilobyte; at C, one kilobyte versus one megabyte.

Membrane keyboards have some assets, including low cost, physical ruggedness, and durability. In a calculator or personal digital assistant (PDA), extensive typing is not done, and a membrane keyboard can suffice in place of a full-size, positive-action keyboard. Membrane keyboards also make water-resistant construction possible (but this

Memory

should not be taken for granted). Membrane keypads are used in some peripherals such as printers, where fast typing is not required.

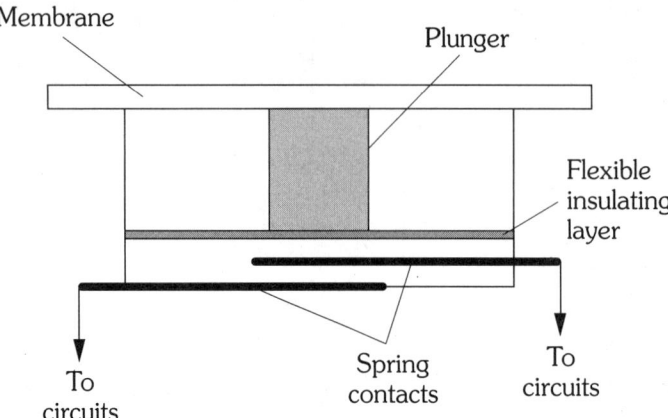

Pressure on the membrane closes the spring contacts.

There are some features of membrane keyboards, however, that make them unsuitable for general computing. First, the keys require considerable pressure for actuation, making touch-typing difficult. The problem is compounded by the fact that the keys lack a positive-action "feel." It's important, especially in applications that require a lot of typing, that the keys be easy to actuate, and that they have a certain amount of up-and-down movement. *See also* KEYBOARD.

Memory

Memory refers to electronic media that allow fast storage and retrieval of computer data. There are several forms of memory. Usually, when you hear someone talking about a computer's memory, they are referring to the *random-access memory (RAM)*, although there are other kinds of memory besides RAM.

Memory capacity is a factor in determining how powerful a computer can be. Memory is generally measured in kilobytes (K or KB), megabytes (MB) or gigabytes (GB). Computer engineers also sometimes talk about terabytes (TB).

RAM. Within RAM, data is stored in *arrays*. An array resembles a grid or matrix. The data can be addressed (selected) from anywhere in the matrix. Data is easily modified and then stored back in RAM, in whole or in part. RAM is sometimes called a *read/write memory.*

An example of RAM is a word processing file as it is being actively worked on. This article, as it was being written, was held in RAM as part of a file of articles starting with *M*. It was periodically saved on the hard disk and also on backup diskettes.

There are two kinds of RAM: *dynamic RAM (DRAM)* and *static RAM (SRAM)*. A DRAM employs integrated circuit (IC) transistors and capacitors; data is stored as charges on the capacitors. The charge must be replenished frequently, or it will dissipate. Replenishing is done several hundred times per second. An SRAM uses a circuit called a *flip-flop* to store data. Flip-flops hold their state indefinitely until they receive a change-of-state pulse; this gets rid of the need to replenish the electric charge. However, SRAM ICs require more elements than DRAM to store a given amount of data. *See also* DYNAMIC RANDOM-ACCESS MEMORY, RANDOM-ACCESS MEMORY *and* STATIC RANDOM-ACCESS MEMORY.

Volatile versus nonvolatile RAM. With any RAM, the data is erased when the appliance is switched off unless some provision is made for memory backup. The most common means of memory backup is the use of a cell or battery. Modern IC memories need so little current to store their data that a backup battery lasts as long in the circuit as it would on the shelf.

Memory from which data disappears when power is removed is called *volatile memory*. If memory is retained when power is removed, it is *nonvolatile memory*. The RAM in a typical PC is volatile. You must save data on a hard disk or diskette, or in some other nonvolatile storage medium, before you switch off the computer, otherwise you will lose everything in RAM. *See also* NONVOLATILE MEMORY *and* VOLATILE MEMORY.

Read-only memory. In contrast to RAM, *read-only memory (ROM)* can be accessed, in whole or in part, but not written over. A standard ROM is programmed at the factory. This permanent programming is known as *firmware*. There are also ROMs that you can program and reprogram yourself. These are called *programmable ROMs (PROMs)*.

An *erasable programmable ROM (EPROM)* is an IC whose memory is of the read-only type, but that can be reprogrammed by a certain procedure. It is much more difficult to rewrite data in an EPROM than in a RAM; the usual process for erasure involves exposure to ultraviolet. An EPROM IC can be recognized by the presence of a transparent window with a removable cover through which the ultraviolet is focused to erase the data. The IC must be taken from the circuit in which it is used, exposed to the ultraviolet for several minutes, and then reprogrammed via a special process.

There are EPROMs that can be erased by electrical means. Such an IC is called an *electrically erasable programmable read-only memory (EEPROM)*. These do not have to be removed from the circuit for reprogramming. *See also* FIRMWARE *and* READ-ONLY MEMORY.

Memory/storage capacity

Bubble memory. A *bubble memory* uses magnetic fields within ICs. This scheme allows a fairly large amount of data to be stored in a small physical volume.

A single bubble is a tiny magnetic field about 0.002 millimeters across. Logic highs and lows correspond to the existence or absence, respectively, of a bubble. The IC contains a ferromagnetic film that acts as a reprogrammable permanent magnet on which bubbles are stored.

While magnetic bubbles do not disappear when power is removed from the IC, they are easily moved by electrical signals. An advantage of bubble memory, then, is that it's a nonvolatile RAM that doesn't need a backup battery. Another asset is that data can be moved from place to place in large chunks. This process is called *block memory transfer*. *See also* BUBBLE MEMORY.

Disks and tapes. Personal and commercial computers almost always use magnetic disks. They come in two forms: the hard disk and the floppy disk or diskette. This is more accurately called "storage," not "memory." Another form of magnetic medium, convenient for mass data storage, is magnetic tape. Hundreds of megabytes can be stored on a small cassette via a tape drive.

Data can also be stored and retrieved optically on CD-ROM (compact disc, read-only memory). This medium offers advantages over magnetic disks in some applications. Optical and magnetic technologies are combined in a Floptical diskette and drive. There are numerous other technologies available for mass storage, such as the Bernoulli box. *See also* BERNOULLI BOX, BYTE, CD-ROM, DISKETTE, FLOPTICAL DISKETTE AND DRIVE, GIGABYTE, HARD DISK, KILOBYTE, MAGNETIC TAPE, MASS STORAGE, MEGABYTE, TAPE DRIVE, *and* TERABYTE.

Memory/storage capacity

In personal computing systems, *memory* usually refers to the *random-access memory (RAM)*, which is the most rapidly accessible. Sometimes a hard disk is called "memory" but this is technically a misuse of the term. The amount of data that can be stored in RAM is measured in kilobytes (K or KB), megabytes (MB), or gigabytes (GB), and is known as the *memory capacity*. For nonvolatile media like disks and tapes, it is called *storage capacity*.

RAM capacity. The size of the RAM in a typical PC has been growing each year. The main factor that affects RAM capacity is the number of transistors that can be fabricated onto a single memory chip. Other factors, such as the speed and overall power of the microprocessor, also have an effect.

The more memory a PC has, the more you can do with it, and the less time it takes. With a memory of 640K, you can store a document of

500 to 600 double-spaced pages, about the size of a novel. You might wonder why anyone would need a fast-access memory larger than that. The answer is that, as computer technology advances, consumer expectations and demands move right along with it. There was a time when people thought 16K was a lot of memory.

Software gobbles up memory; so do graphic images. This is especially true of graphical user interfaces (GUIs) like Windows, Macintosh, and OS/2, and high-resolution photographs and mathematical objects. For a good, detailed rendition of a fractal, for example, several tens, or even hundreds, of megabytes are needed.

It's impossible to quote a standard figure for memory capacity in modern PCs, for two reasons. First, technology is advancing so fast that no figure is valid for more than a few months. Second, PCs vary greatly in memory capacity from low-end to high-end machines.

The actual physics of RAM is changing along with the memory capacity. Most RAM is *volatile memory*; it will "evaporate" (disappear) if there is a power failure. Some new forms of RAM, however, stick around when your PC is shut off. This is *nonvolatile memory*.

Hard disk capacity. Hard-disk drives vary in capacity up to several thousand megabytes. You can store and retrieve information more quickly to and from a hard disk than with diskettes because the hardware works faster. Hard disks are slower than RAM, however.

Hard disk drives keep getting faster and more capacious, just as does RAM. New hard disk technologies are being developed, as are alternatives such as flash memory, magneto-optical storage, and overwriteable CD-ROM.

Hard disk storage has one big advantage over RAM: once data is stored on your hard drive, it is nonvolatile. If there's a power failure, the data on a hard disk will stay there, while the data in most RAMs will vanish. This is why it's important to store files on hard disk at frequent intervals (every few minutes), and whenever you must leave your PC for a short time.

The contents of RAM change with every keystroke you make. To change what's on the hard disk, you must go through the motions (commands or mouse clicks) of storing the data. Some software automatically updates files on the hard disk every few minutes, saving you some work, and also providing insurance in the event of a worst-case scenario. *See also* DATA STORAGE MEDIA, GIGABYTE, HARD DISK, KILOBYTE, MASS STORAGE, MEGABYTE, MEMORY, NONVOLATILE MEMORY, RANDOM-ACCESS MEMORY, TERABYTE, *and* VOLATILE MEMORY.

Memory-management software

All computers have finite RAM (random-access memory), which acts like a "conscious mind" while working in real-time. The larger the amount of RAM available, the more powerful is the PC (all other things being equal), and the more things you can do with it. *Memory-management software* helps a PC use all its RAM, and even some space on the hard disk, to obtain the most efficient possible operation.

Suppose you're managing a baseball team, and you're in the seventh game of the World Series. You're in a tight battle, and you need to squeeze out every last effort from every player on the whole team. You use pinch hitters, pinch runners, and relief pitchers; you might even juggle playing positions from inning to inning. The results you get will depend not only on how skilled the players are, but on the order in which you make the substitutions. Some schemes will result in your having a more powerful team, with respect to a particular opponent, than other schemes. Your job, as manager, is to make optimum use of your team's skill relative to the opponent you're up against.

This isn't a perfect analogy; computers don't envision their jobs as down-to-the-wire struggles, and baseball players are infinitely more sophisticated creatures than kilobytes of memory. Still, for your PC's central processing unit (CPU), managing the memory is something like managing a baseball team in an important game. For complex programs, there's one optimum memory-management scheme that works the best. The job of the memory-management software is to find that scheme and execute it, juggling the various parts of RAM as necessary. *See also* CENTRAL PROCESSING UNIT, EXTENDED/EXPANDED MEMORY, MEMORY, RANDOM-ACCESS MEMORY, *and* VIRTUAL MEMORY.

Memory organization packets

One of the most promising aspects of artificial intelligence (AI) is its use as a tool for predicting future events, based on what has happened in the past. This process is helped by arranging the computer memory into generalizations, called *memory organization packets (MOPs)*.

Some crude examples of MOPs are the following statements:

➤ If the wind shifts to the east and the barometer falls, it will usually rain (or snow in the winter) within 24 hours.

➤ If the wind shifts to the west and the barometer rises, clearing will usually occur within a few hours.

➤ Light winds and a steady, high barometric pressure usually mean little weather change for at least 24 hours.

➤ Foul weather with a steady, low barometric pressure usually means bad weather for at least the next 24 hours.

These are broad generalizations, but they are MOPs based on the experience of meteorologists in temperate climates over the past several centuries.

In AI, the system can be programmed to find the most valid MOPs based on available data. Then, it can apply these MOPs in the most effective possible way to make a forecast in a given situation. *See also* ARTIFICIAL INTELLIGENCE, EXPERT SYSTEMS, *and* FORECASTING.

Memory-resident software

When you think of running a computer program, you usually think of the computer spending all of its effort on that one program. However, it is possible to interrupt a program, pushing it into the "back of your computer's mind." Software that has been put on hold this way is called *memory-resident software*. Sometimes it is called *terminate-and-stay-resident (TSR) software*.

When a memory-resident program is in the background, a little of it stays in the memory. This is how it gets its name. The portion of the program that stays in memory is like a tag that the computer can use for identification, and that the machine can use to "grab" the program when you want to resume running it. If you're using a command-driven interface like DOS, a special key or key sequence, called a *hot key*, loads the memory-resident program and gets it running again. If you're in a graphical interface such as Windows, Macintosh, or OS/2, you can move the pointer to the icon that designates the program, and click or double-click the mouse. *See also* BACKGROUND PROCESSING, FOREGROUND PROCESSING, *and* HOT KEY.

Menu

A *menu* is a set of options from which you choose, in order to get your PC to do something. Menus consist of commands. Each command might be accompanied by an *icon*, a picture that serves as an intuitive reminder of what the command represents. This is the basis for the graphical user interface (GUI).

Menu-driven software is like taking a multiple-choice test. You choose the option you want, rather than "filling in the blank" as you must do in command-driven software. Menu-driven software was developed because many people have trouble remembering the commands in command-driven software such as DOS.

Think of those high-school or college exams in which you had multiple choices, and compare these with the tests where you had to fill in blanks, or worse yet, write out your answers in essay form! In multiple-choice, you can make an educated guess and often get the right answer. It's the same way with a menu. While it's always best to read the instructions, you can learn by just playing around, as long as you don't play with crucial files that you can't afford to lose in case you make a mistake.

Menu-driven software

The drawing shows the two most common forms in which menus appear. The list at A goes across the top of the operating window, and the options are listed one after the other from left to right. This is called a *menu bar*. The list at B goes down, in a small window inside the main window. This is a *menu box*. These examples are from the Macintosh system. In IBM-compatible PCs using Windows, OS/2, or some other graphical user interfaces, the menu configurations are similar.

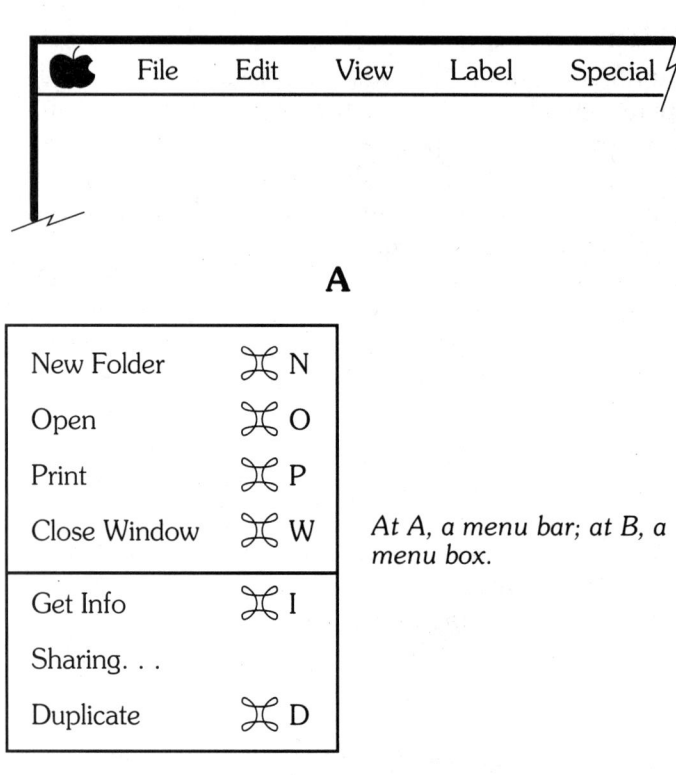

At A, a menu bar; at B, a menu box.

There are two ways you can choose the options from a menu. In the *hot-key* method, you press a keyboard key or key sequence to actuate the option. One of the letters in the option is underlined and/or appears in a different color from the other letters; this is the letter you strike to execute that option. In the *point-and-click* method, you use a mouse, trackball, or other pointing device to guide an on-screen pointer to the option you want. Then you press (click) the button on the mouse once or twice, depending on the system's idiosyncrasies, to execute the option. *See also* GRAPHICAL USER INTERFACE, HOT KEY, ICON, MENU-DRIVEN SOFTWARE, MOUSE, *and* TRACKBALL.

Menu-driven software

Menu-driven software is a PC program in which you choose from among options, rather than giving commands. It's like taking a multiple-choice test.

Assets. The biggest advantage of menu-driven software, compared with the older *command-driven software*, is user-friendliness. Many PC users, especially novices, find it hard to use a command-driven interface. Commands must be memorized, and there are hundreds of them. As if that isn't bad enough, most commands are abbreviated, so it's not intuitive what they do.

Menu-driven software does away with all that memorization, and also minimizes the number of keystrokes you have to make. For hunt-and-peck typists, this helps tremendously. (Of course, for word processing or desktop publishing, you must be a good typist no matter what kind of operating system you use.)

A pointing device, such as a mouse or trackball, is helpful when using menu-driven software. You can work without one, but the device isn't expensive, and it's a sound investment. To choose an option, you slide the mouse or rub the trackball until the on-screen arrow or cursor is in the right spot. Then you click once or twice to actuate the function. *See also* COMMAND, MOUSE, *and* TRACKBALL.

Limitations. Menu-driven software can be slower than command-driven software in some computers. In modern PCs, using advanced microprocessors, this is no longer a problem. Older computers have trouble handling the software, so the advantages are largely offset by sluggishness in operation. Using menu-driven software in an old computer is like puttering around with a 15-horsepower motor on a yacht. The solution to this problem is to upgrade the computer, buy a new PC, switch to command-driven software, or else put up with slow system operation.

Command-driven software still has its place, and it's not likely to become obsolete. As speech recognition and speech synthesis become more commonplace in personal computing, command-driven software will work better than menu-driven software in some applications. This is happening now in some professions, such as medicine. As a doctor examines a patient, the doctor can speak to the computer, giving it information about the patient. Previously, the doctor would have to leave the patient at intervals to enter data into the computer. When talking to a machine, it's easier to give direct commands than to play verbal multiple-guessing games.

Speech-recognition expansion boards are available. Good speech-recognition software allows the computer to "learn" thousands of words, based on the sound of your voice. One problem is that speech-recognition software takes up large amounts of memory—the same problem that once plagued menu-driven software. Memory capacity rapidly grew to overcome the problem in the case of menu-driven software; by all indications, it will do the same with speech recognition. *See also* COMMAND-DRIVEN SOFTWARE, GRAPHICAL USER

INTERFACE, MENU, PERSONAL DICTATION SYSTEM, SPEECH RECOGNITION, *and* SPEECH SYNTHESIS.

Message passing

In a smart computer or in a sophisticated computer network messages are passed from one part of the system to another. A message might be data (information), a command, or a question.

Tell it again. Message handling can be done in various ways. The best method for a particular situation depends on the nature of the message. A good analogy is packet communications. In this type of system, a message is relayed from a source station to a destination station, via intermediate stations called nodes. It's important that each node reproduce the message with perfect (no errors), so it's not corrupted or mutilated when it reaches the destination.

When a message is passed along many times, various things can happen to change the content. This becomes more and more likely as computers get smarter, and the messages become more complicated. The ultimate example is a message that is passed by word of mouth through a long series of human carriers.

Computer embellishment. You have probably experienced altered message content as a result of interpretation by human beings, repeated many times (see the drawing). If you haven't, you ought to try it just for fun. You tell a friend a story, only to hear it later in much different form.

Content and meaning can be completely changed in message passing.

The same thing might eventually become a problem in artificial intelligence (AI) systems. Noise and distortion can alter signals, although this has largely been overcome by modern digital transmission methods. But with ultra-sophisticated computers, another problem crops up. A super-smart machine might misinterpret a message, or even embellish it in ways the programmers did not intend and cannot predict. This is a manifestation of the fact that, when AI systems get sufficiently powerful, they can develop quirks. Small changes, multiplied as a concept is passed from machine to machine, might alter data content beyond recognition. *See also* ARTIFICIAL

INTELLIGENCE, NEUROTIC COMPUTER BEHAVIOR, and PACKET COMMUNICATIONS.

Metal-oxide semiconductor (MOS) technology

The oxides of some metals are electrical insulators, rather than conductors. So-called *metal-oxide-semiconductor (MOS)* devices, which take advantage of this property of certain substances, have been in widespread use for years.

Density and speed. Typical MOS materials are aluminum oxide and silicon dioxide. Metal-oxide semiconductor devices are noted for their low power requirements, making them ideal for use in computers, where it is important that the power consumption be as low as possible. Most MOS integrated circuits, or chips, have high component density, meaning that there are a lot of digital electronic switches, usually in the form of transistors, packed into a small physical volume.

The drawing shows a simplified, and greatly magnified, cross-sectional view of a MOS transistor. The switching signal is applied at the gate. The source is connected to ground, or the minus terminal of the power supply. The drain provides the digital signal output, either high or low (1 or 0). The semiconductor portion provides the signal channel, which is insulated from the gate by a thin layer of metal oxide. Nevertheless, the voltage at the gate has a dramatic effect on what happens in the channel. Depending on the voltage at the gate, the channel either short-circuits the drain to the source (providing logic 0) or insulates the drain from the source (providing logic 1). Switching can occur millions of times per second (megahertz). There can be upwards of a million transistors like this in a single MOS computer chip.

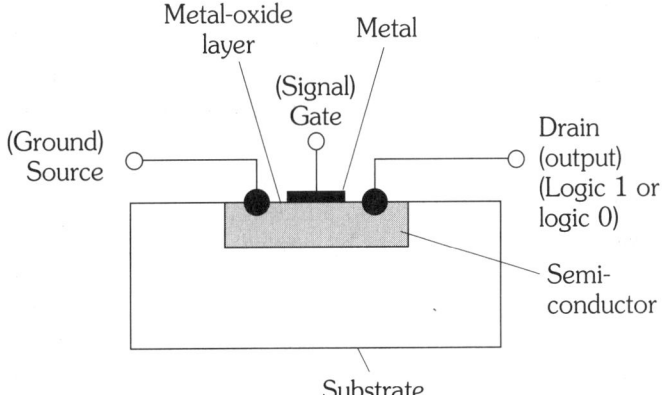

Simplified cross-section of a MOS transistor.

All MOS devices work fast. This is extremely important in computers. The number of instructions per second (IPS) is a direct function of how fast the switches in the computer chips can operate. Overall computer power, in turn, is directly related to the IPS rating.

Micro Channel Architecture

Handling precautions. All MOS devices can be ruined by the discharge of static electricity. Therefore, care must be exercised when working with MOS components. All MOS integrated circuits (ICs) and transistors should be stored with the leads inserted into conducting foam, so that static won't build up. When building, testing, and servicing electronic equipment in which MOS devices are present, your body and all test equipment should be grounded. This means you literally must connect your body to a direct-current electrical ground, so you do not become an electrode capable of "zapping" an IC. It doesn't take much to destroy a MOS device.

Metal-oxide-semiconductor ICs are especially useful in high-density memory applications. Some microcomputer chips also use MOS technology. *See also* COMPLEMENTARY METAL-OXIDE SEMICONDUCTOR (CMOS) TECHNOLOGY *and* INTEGRATED CIRCUIT.

Micro Channel Architecture

Micro Channel Architecture (MCA) is a scheme for data transfer in IBM computers. MCA bus uses 32-bit words.

Older architectures. *Industry Standard Architecture (ISA)* is the set of standards for the hardware in the original IBM PC. That machine used a microprocessor called the Intel 8088. It had an eight-bit external data bus, and a 16-bit internal data bus. In contrast to this, *Enhanced Industry Standard Architecture (EISA)*, common with 80386 and 80486 chips, upgraded to a 32-bit bus.

Changing from an eight-bit bus to a 32-bit bus is like doubling the diameter of a pipe (quadrupling its cross-sectional area). Or, you might think of it as a 400% increase in your vocabulary. This increases the computer power, all other things being equal.

Unique to IBM. The big advantage of MCA is its increased power compared with ISA. In this respect, MCA is like EISA, but MCA was designed especially for IBM computers. It is a custom architecture. There are some advantages to custom design by a manufacturer. Such arrangements offer greater versatility for users who don't mind buying all their parts from one source. In addition, when all your parts come from one manufacturer, you can be confident that the engineers went to considerable trouble to get them to run smoothly together. It's something like the difference between a mass-produced car and a custom-made car. Some people dislike custom designs and components, however, because this approach narrows the range of choices for accessories and replacement parts.

Another advantage of MCA is the fact that it allows you to use more than one microprocessor in a single computer. This produces a *multiprocessor*, which has more power than a single chip alone. It's akin to a popular adage among humans, "Two heads are better than

one." To this the PC user might add, "as long as they interface well."
See also COMPATIBILITY, ENHANCED INDUSTRY STANDARD ARCHITECTURE, *and* MULTIPROCESSOR.

Microchip

See INTEGRATED CIRCUIT.

Microcomputer

A *microcomputer* is a small computer, with the microprocessor enclosed in a single integrated-circuit package. Today, microprocessor chips are available in sizes less than a quarter-inch on a side for specialized control purposes. Larger microprocessors, such as the ones in personal computers (which are technically microcomputers), range up to an inch square or larger.

Types. Microcomputers vary in sophistication and memory storage capacity, depending on the intended use. Simple microcomputers are available for less than $100. They have liquid-crystal displays and small keypads that allow only encoded data entry. A good example of such a microcomputer is a programmable calculator. A somewhat more sophisticated microcomputer is the increasingly popular personal digital assistant (PDA).

Large microcomputers, more often called *personal computers (PCs)*, are the main focus of this encyclopedia. They are used by an increasing proportion of people in many countries, especially in North America, Western Europe, and Japan. Such microcomputers typically cost from several hundred to several thousand dollars. High-end microcomputers, used by medium-sized businesses, increase in sophistication until they are more appropriately called *minicomputers*. The largest computers are *mainframes*. In recent years the distinction between minicomputers and mainframes has become somewhat blurred, to the point where the term *mainframe* appears headed for obsolescence.

Microcomputer control. Microcomputers are often used for the purpose of regulating the operation of electrical and electromechanical devices. This is known as *microcomputer control*. Microcomputer control makes it possible to perform complex tasks with a minimum of difficulty.

Microcomputer control is widely used in such devices as robots, automobiles, and aircraft. For example, a microcomputer can be programmed to switch on an oven, heat the food to a prescribed temperature for a certain length of time, and then switch the oven off again. Microcomputers can be used to control automobile engines to enhance efficiency and gasoline mileage. Microcomputers can navigate and fly airplanes. It has been said that a modern jet aircraft is really a giant robot, because it can (in theory at least) complete a flight all by itself, without a single human being on board.

Microknowledge

One of the most recent, and exciting, applications of microcomputer control is in the field of medical electronics. Microcomputers can be programmed to provide electrical impulses to control erratically functioning body organs, to move the muscles of paralyzed persons, and for various other purposes. *See also* BIOMECHATRONICS, INTEL MICROPROCESSORS, MAINFRAME, MICROPROCESSOR, MINICOMPUTER, MOTOROLA MICROPROCESSORS, *and* PERSONAL DIGITAL ASSISTANT.

Microknowledge

Microknowledge is detailed machine knowledge. In artificial intelligence (AI), microknowledge includes the logic rules, computer programs, and data in memory.

Suppose you have a personal robot, complete with a computer brain, named Hometron X. Hometron X is programmed to do all kinds of tasks around the house. It can clean the bathroom, wash the windows, do the laundry, mow the lawn, and even blow snow off your driveway. All these programs involve an immense number of logical steps. A single error in this microknowledge might result in Hometron X cutting down your hedge, blowing snow off your lawn, washing paper plates, or mopping the carpet in your living room.

Microknowledge can, and often does, change with time. You might change the data stored in Hometron X's computer brain to reflect the fact that you had rearranged the furniture, built a new addition next to the living room, or planted new bushes in the yard.

Some microknowledge does not change with time, or else changes so slowly that it is insignificant for practical purposes. An example of this is a topographical (not a political) map of the earth. If Hometron X knows where Mount McKinley is today, you can be sure it will know where Mount McKinley is 10, 20, or 50 years from now. *See also* ARTIFICIAL INTELLIGENCE, BOOLEAN ALGEBRA, HEURISTIC KNOWLEDGE, LOGIC, MACHINE KNOWLEDGE, MACROKNOWLEDGE, PERSONAL ROBOTS, PROGRAMMING, *and* SOFTWARE.

Microprocessor

The *microprocessor* is the integrated circuit (IC), or chip, that forms the core of your PC's "conscious mind." It coordinates all the action and does all the calculations. It is located on the *motherboard*, or main circuit board, of the computer. This board is also known as the *logic board*.

In American-made PCs, brand-name microprocessors are manufactured by Intel (for IBM-compatible) or Motorola (for Macintosh). There are imitations, or *clones*, of Intel and Motorola devices made by other companies. Intel part numbers include 8088, 8086, 80286 (or 286), 80386 (386), and 80486 (486). After the

486, Intel stopped numbering their chips; the successor to the 486 is known as the Pentium. Motorola uses part numbers such as 68000, 68020, 68030, and 68040. The PowerPC chip is a joint venture between IBM, Motorola, and Apple Computer, Inc. There are several versions of this chip, which represent a radical departure from previous technologies.

The microprocessor, together with peripheral ICs, comprise the *central processing unit (CPU)* of a computer. The peripheral circuits can be integrated onto the same chip as the microprocessor, but they are usually separate. The external chips contain memory and programming instructions.

The CPU forms the complete "brain" of a computer. You might think of the microprocessor as the computer's conscious mind, which directs the behavior of the machine by deliberate control. The CPU, dominated by the microprocessor, represents the PC's entire mind, conscious and subconscious. All the memory and the buses, added to this, create the computer's central nervous system. Peripherals such as printers, disk drives, mice, speech recognition/synthesis apparatus, modems, and monitors are the hands, ears, eyes, and mouth of the machine. In the future, you can expect to see robots, vision systems, various home appliances, surveillance apparatus, medical devices, and other exotic equipment under the control of personal computers. At the helm of every such system will be a microprocessor.

Microprocessors get more powerful every year. Physically, this translates to an increasing number of digital switching transistors per chip. The Intel 486, for example, has more than a million transistors. The number of digital switches that can be fabricated onto a semiconductor chip of a particular size is limited only by the structure of matter itself. It's possible, ultimately, that a single electron could represent one binary digit (bit). Someday, we'll probably see microprocessors with a billion transistors, representing about one thousand times the raw power of the 486. Of course, other factors enter into this picture; alternative computer technology might produce new developments, creating machines with power and speed that we can only dream about today.

See also ALTERNATIVE COMPUTER TECHNOLOGY, ANALOG COMPUTER TECHNOLOGY, CENTRAL PROCESSING UNIT, CLOCK SPEED, COMPUTER ARCHITECTURE, COMPUTER GENERATIONS, COMPUTER POWER, COPROCESSOR, DIGITAL COMPUTER TECHNOLOGY, INSTRUCTIONS PER SECOND, INTEGRATED CIRCUIT, INTEL MICROPROCESSORS, MEMORY, MICROCOMPUTER, MOTHERBOARD, MOTOROLA MICROPROCESSORS, NEURAL NETWORK, PENTIUM, POWERPC CHIP, RANDOM-ACCESS MEMORY, SINGLE-ELECTRON MEMORY, *and* WORD SIZE.

Microsoft Corporation

Microsoft Corporation has become famous for its computer software. It started in the mid-1970s as a small venture run by Paul Allen and Bill Gates. Since then, Microsoft has grown to take over a large share of the software market. Chances are that if you have an IBM-compatible PC, some (perhaps most) of its software was written by Microsoft engineers and programmers.

Some of Microsoft's software has become so common that the names are generic. Examples are DOS and Windows. There are other versions of DOS besides the Microsoft one, and there are other windowing environments besides Microsoft's, but most people, when they hear these generic terms, think of the Microsoft versions.

Microsoft started out by writing software for the IBM PC, the first personal computer sold by IBM. A couple of computer programmers combined intelligence, intuition, ambition, and luck, and created one of the most successful corporations in American history. The exploding computer market will probably spawn more ventures like this in the future, in hardware as well as in software. *See also* DOS *and* WINDOWS.

Microsoft Windows

See WINDOWS.

Microwave data transmission

Microwaves are forms of electromagnetic energy with a wavelength somewhat longer than that of infrared radiation, but shorter than that of conventional radio waves. Microwaves travel in essentially straight lines through the atmosphere and are not affected by the ionized layers.

Microwave frequencies are useful for short-range, high-reliability data links. Satellite communication and control is often done at microwave frequencies. The microwave region contains a vast amount of spectrum space and can hold many wideband signals.

Microwave radiation can cause heating of certain materials. This heating can be dangerous to human beings when the microwave radiation is intense. When working with microwave equipment, care must be exercised to avoid exposure to the rays.

A *microwave repeater* is a receiver/transmitter combination used for relaying signals at microwave frequencies. The signal is intercepted by a horn or dish antenna, amplified, converted to another frequency, and retransmitted (see the drawing). *Microwave data transmission* is used in some computer networks, in control systems, and also to some extent in telephone systems. *See also* COMMUNICATIONS, NETWORK, *and* SATELLITE DATA TRANSMISSION.

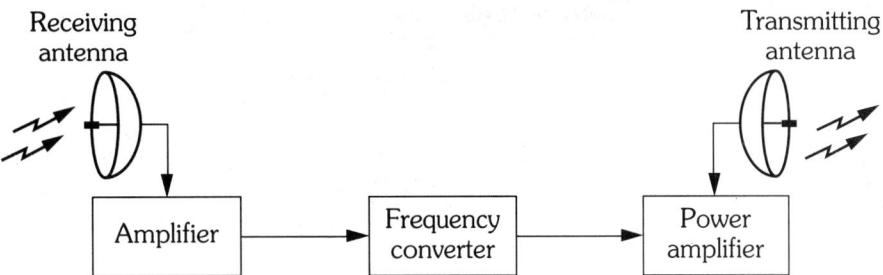

Block diagram of a microwave repeater.

MIDI

See MUSICAL INSTRUMENT DIGITAL INTERFACE.

Military time

Military time is time expressed in a 24-hour system, rather than the more familiar 12-hour system. You've probably heard military time if you've watched war movies, or if you have worked in, or with, any branch of the service. It is used in aviation, by the National Weather Service, and by amateur radio operators, among others. You'll probably encounter it eventually if you spend much time gathering data via online services.

Military time is often standardized to *Coordinated Universal Time (UTC)*, which is the time at zero degrees longitude, the Greenwich Meridian that passes near London, England. Time in UTC is called "zulu," the standard phonetic expression for the letter Z, which is the designator for the time at the Greenwich Meridian.

Table A (on page 686) shows 12-hour time versus 24-hour time. When referring to time in the 24-hour system, people talk in hundreds, so you'll hear expressions like "oh three hundred hours" or "seventeen hundred hours." These are written as *0300* and *1700* and refer to 3:00 a.m. and 5:00 p.m. respectively. When speaking about the time down to the exact minute, people say things like "fifteen forty-three" or "one five four three." This would be written *1543* and means 3:43 p.m. When people are talking about UTC, you might hear something like "one two five zero UTC" or "one two five zero zulu." This is written as *1250 UTC* or *1250Z*. Note that 24-hour time has no colon between the hour and the minute, as does 12-hour time.

Table B (on page 687) shows UTC versus the time in various zones in the United States. Eastern Daylight Time (EDT) is four hours behind UTC. Eastern Standard Time (EST) or Central Daylight Time (CDT) are five hours behind UTC. Central Standard Time (CST) or Mountain Daylight Time (MDT) are six hours behind UTC. Mountain Standard Time (MST) or Pacific Daylight Time (PDT) are seven hours behind UTC. Pacific Standard Time (PST) is eight hours behind UTC.

12-hour versus 24-hour time

12-hour time	24-hour time
12:00 midnight at start of day	0000 hours
1:00 a.m.	0100 hours
2:00 a.m.	0200 hours
3:00 a.m.	0300 hours
4:00 a.m.	0400 hours
5:00 a.m.	0500 hours
6:00 a.m.	0600 hours
7:00 a.m.	0700 hours
8:00 a.m.	0800 hours
9:00 a.m.	0900 hours
10:00 a.m.	1000 hours
11:00 a.m.	1100 hours
12:00 noon	1200 hours
1:00 p.m.	1300 hours
2:00 p.m.	1400 hours
3:00 p.m.	1500 hours
4:00 p.m.	1600 hours
5:00 p.m.	1700 hours
6:00 p.m.	1800 hours
7:00 p.m.	1900 hours
8:00 p.m.	2000 hours
9:00 p.m.	2100 hours
10:00 p.m.	2200 hours
11:00 p.m.	2300 hours
12:00 midnight at end of day	2400 hours

Minicomputer

A *minicomputer* is a machine larger and more powerful than a *microcomputer*, but smaller and less powerful than a *mainframe*. There is no hard-and-fast set of standards by which computers are categorized. A minicomputer is, in general, a machine that can be used by a number of people at once, while a microcomputer is used by one person at a time.

Coordinated universal time (UTC) versus U.S. time zones. Asterisks indicate previous day from UTC.

UTC	EDT	EST/CDT	CST/MDT	MST/PDT	PST
0000	2000*	1900*	1800*	1700*	1600*
0100	2100*	2000*	1900*	1800*	1700*
0200	2200*	2100*	2000*	1900*	1800*
0300	2300*	2200*	2100*	2000*	1900*
0400	0000	2300*	2200*	2100*	2000*
0500	0100	0000	2300*	2200*	2100*
0600	0200	0100	0000	2300*	2200*
0700	0300	0200	0100	0000	2300*
0800	0400	0300	0200	0100	0000
0900	0500	0400	0300	0200	0100
1000	0600	0500	0400	0300	0200
1100	0700	0600	0500	0400	0300
1200	0800	0700	0600	0500	0400
1300	0900	0800	0700	0600	0500
1400	1000	0900	0800	0700	0600
1500	1100	1000	0900	0800	0700
1600	1200	1100	1000	0900	0800
1700	1300	1200	1100	1000	0900
1800	1400	1300	1200	1100	1000
1900	1500	1400	1300	1200	1100
2000	1600	1500	1400	1300	1200
2100	1700	1600	1500	1400	1300
2200	1800	1700	1600	1500	1400
2300	1900	1800	1700	1600	1500
2400	2000	1900	1800	1700	1600

Minicomputers are seen in small and medium-sized businesses. These machines are versatile, and can accommodate the frequent changes such as addition of new workstations that happen in fast-growing companies. Another good place for a minicomputer is in a department of a multidepartmental university, large corporation, or government agency. Minicomputers can be connected into networks, subordinate to the mainframe of the network. Individual workstations are subordinate to the minicomputer. The drawing shows an example of this kind of hierarchy.

Mirror command

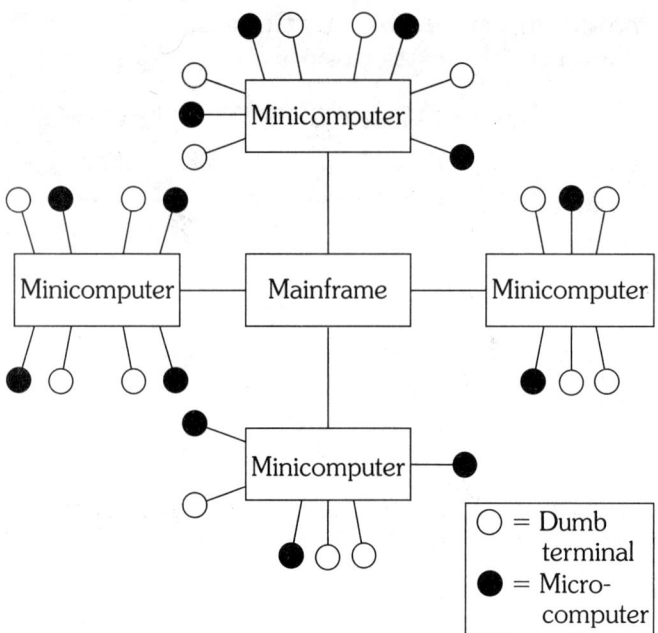

A network with a mainframe, minicomputers, microcomputers, and dumb terminals.

Suppose the history department at XYZ University has a minicomputer serving all of its professors, instructors, and clerical personnel. This minicomputer is connected into a local area network (LAN) serving the whole campus. The LAN is part of a wide area network (WAN) covering several campuses of the university in various towns around the state. The minicomputer can have from two to several dozen terminals. *See also* LOCAL AREA NETWORK, MAINFRAME, MICROCOMPUTER, *and* WIDE AREA NETWORK.

Mirror command

The *MIRROR command* is used in Microsoft's DOS 5.0 and later versions. This command serves as an aid to recovering data in case you accidentally format a diskette or hard disk, or erase files and then decide you want them back.

Formatting. When you use the FORMAT command, the disk or diskette is set up so that it can accept new data. New diskettes and hard disks must be formatted before data can be written onto them. Once a disk has been formatted, it shouldn't be necessary to do so again. The only time you'll normally want to reformat a diskette is when you want to erase all the data it contains, recycling it.

Warning! Never format a hard disk!

Oops! We're all human, and humans make mistakes. Eventually, the day might come when you reformat the wrong diskette and inadvertently lose immediate access to the data it contains. Worse, you might commit a serious blunder and format your hard disk. Even if this happens, all is not necessarily lost. Formatting does not destroy the data on a disk (unless your computer uses single-pass overwrite, a new technology designed to make hard disks work faster). Formatting only tells the computer that it can go ahead and overwrite whatever is there. It leaves your data open to invasion, but the conquest does not begin until you start putting more files on the disk.

Refrain from writing anything on a hard disk or diskette if you have reformatted it by mistake. First, you must restore the disk to its condition before you reformatted it. Then, you can start writing and updating files on it again.

What MIRROR does. When you start up your system and run the MIRROR command, the computer makes two identical files, containing the file allocation table and the main, or root, directory. These files are called MIRORSAV.FIL and MIRROR.FIL. They do not change as you use the system, even if you change the files on your hard disk. They won't change even if you erase all the files on the disk. In fact, they'll remain intact even if you reformat the disk! They are the key to recovering your data if you make the mistake of formatting the hard disk.

If you happen to format your hard disk, or if you erase files and then decide you didn't mean to, you can use *undeletion* or *unformatting* to return the disk to the condition it was in when you first switched your computer on.

Back things up. It's best not to rely on the MIRROR command, undeletion, and unformatting. They are available as a last line of defense, but savvy PC users always keep a current backup of every file they have. It's wise to save files even if you think you'll never need them again; these can be stored on diskettes in your archives. Diskettes are light, small, and cheap. A hard disk can also be backed up using a tape drive. There's no reason to leave anything to chance. *See also* ARCHIVES, BACKUP, DIRECTORY, DOS, FILE ALLOCATION TABLE, MIRRORING, TAPE DRIVE, UNDELETION, *and* UNFORMATTING.

Mirroring

The files on your hard disk are crucial to the operation of your computer. Every PC user fears hard disk failure and the inconvenience it can bring. This fear is justified. If you own a computer long enough, there's a fair chance the hard disk will fail someday.

Back it up! It's extremely important that the contents of your hard disk be backed up, so your data is safe at all times from destruction in the event of a failure of the hard disk. There are several ways to back up files.

Mixed columnar/line graph

Hard disk files can be transferred to diskettes or a tape drive for storage. Tape drives have become increasingly popular in recent years because they're more convenient and more compact than diskettes. Diskettes are somewhat easier to keep current because you can always have one in your computer's diskette drive, accepting file updates at intervals during each work session.

Twin hard disks. Another alternative for hard disk backup that offers absolute up-to-dateness of files is to buy a second hard disk. This is expensive, but it has one big advantage over diskettes or tapes: it makes *mirroring* possible. Mirroring is a process of automatic hard disk backup that writes *every* file on two hard disks at the same time.

When you use mirroring and tell your computer to store a file, you'll hear more whirring and clicking than if you have one hard disk because everything is going onto both media simultaneously. Both hard disks follow each other's movements, creating two sets of platters with identical contents.

Overkill? Some people think mirroring is like shooting a sparrow with a cannon, but if you work with large amounts of data that's constantly changing, and if your time is precious to you, mirroring can be a worthwhile investment. At the least, it can buy you peace of mind. In a mirrored hard disk system, if one hard disk fails, it's not a catastrophe. The system will alert you to the event, and you can order a replacement. You can keep on working uninterrupted until it arrives. It's imperative, however, that you not delay the purchase of the replacement drive. Also, you must back up the contents of the lone hard disk on some other medium, such as tape, until the mirror hard disk is up and running again. *See also* BACKUP, HARD DISK, *and* TAPE DRIVE.

Mixed columnar/line graph

A *mixed columnar/line graph* is a scheme for showing two different functions on the same graph. It can help to illustrate a relationship between effects or variables. The line graph contrasts with the columnar graph, so it's easy to tell which function is which.

The drawing is an example of a mixed columnar/line graph. The columns represent the average maximum high temperature in a hypothetical subtropical town for each month during the year. The line represents the average residential electric bill for the past 10 years in that same town. It should come as no surprise that these two functions are related. Air conditioners consume electricity, and people use air conditioning the most when the weather is hottest.

Mixed columnar/line graphs are especially useful in presentation graphics because they're easy to read. They can also be of use in analytical graphics when researching possible correlations between, or among, different variables. Good presentation graphics packages contain programs that let you create graphs of this kind. *See also* ANALYTICAL GRAPHICS, COLUMNAR GRAPH, LINE GRAPH, MULTIVARIABLE FUNCTION GRAPH, *and* PRESENTATION GRAPHICS.

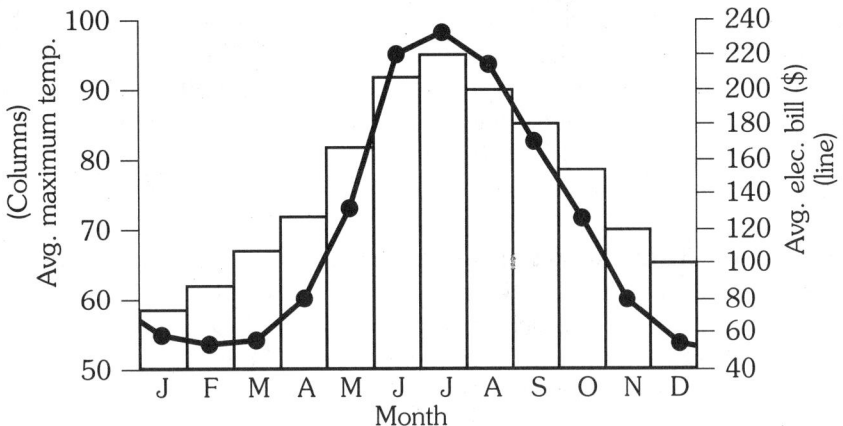

A mixed columnar/line graph shows a relationship between two functions.

Mode command

The *MODE command* is used in DOS to control the way the computer works with its peripherals, such as printers, modems, and monitors. The MODE command is normally in the AUTOEXEC.BAT file, automatically run every time your PC is powered up. It can also be entered manually if desired. The MODE command is an external command. It can be sent over networks.

Printer. The MODE command for the printer allows selection from among several printers connected to the main unit of a PC. For example, you might have a label printer, a dot-matrix printer, and a laser printer, each connected to one of the parallel ports. The command selects the number of characters per line (usually either 80 or 132) and allows control of the spacing between lines (lines per inch).

Suppose that, unless otherwise specified, the computer will send data to printer number 1, and will print out 80 characters per line and six lines per inch. These, then, are the default settings.

Serial ports. The MODE command also allows selection from among the serial ports in the computer. You might have a modem connected to one serial port, a packet-radio terminal node controller (TNC) connected to another serial port, and a serial printer connected to a third serial port. You can set the data speed in bits per second (bps), the parity, the data bits, and the stop bits.

Unless otherwise specified, the defaults are port number 1, even parity, and seven data bits. The data speed can vary over a large range. Standard data speeds keep getting faster as computers and communications systems grow more advanced and complex.

Display. The MODE command for the display lets you select a color monitor or a black-and-white (monochrome) monitor. You can also specify the number of characters in a line (normally 40 or 80) and the number of lines on the screen (usually 25 or 43). The settings that work best depend on the image resolution of the monitor, and also on the shape and size of the screen. A typical monitor shows 80 characters per line and 25 lines per screen. You can also adjust the alignment of the display.

For further information. There are other things you can do with the MODE command that aren't mentioned here. These things are mainly of interest to advanced computer users. If you're using DOS and want to know details concerning the MODE command, refer to your DOS instruction manual and/or help files. *See also* AUTOEXEC.BAT, COMMAND, DEFAULT, *and* DOS.

Modeling

Modeling is the creation of three-dimensional (3-D) objects in graphics programming. You've seen this if you've ever watched someone working with computer-aided design (CAD). The results of modeling are also evident in computer-assisted instruction (CAI) and in many computer games. *See also* COMPUTER-AIDED DESIGN *and* COMPUTER-ASSISTED INSTRUCTION.

Coordinates. To create a computer portrayal of any three-dimensional object, you need to specify its position in 3-D space. There are various coordinate systems you can use for this purpose. The most common is called *Cartesian coordinates*. This system has three axes, each perpendicular to the other two, all meeting at a common point or origin. Another scheme is called *cylindrical coordinates*. Still another is called *spherical coordinates*.

These coordinate systems differ in the way they look, but they achieve the same result: the unambiguous and exact definition of every point's position in 3-D space. This is critical to the successful generation of 3-D graphical models. *See also* CARTESIAN COORDINATES, CYLINDRICAL COORDINATES, *and* SPHERICAL COORDINATES.

Wire mesh versus shading. On a computer display, the two most common ways to render 3-D objects are the *wire-mesh* scheme and the *shading* scheme.

A wire-mesh rendition looks like fishnet or chicken wire. It provides an intuitive picture of the exterior of an object, and also allows you to see through it as if it were transparent. The drawing at A shows a wire-mesh portrayal of a cube. The drawing shows perspective, so you can tell the angle at which you're looking at the cube.

Modeling

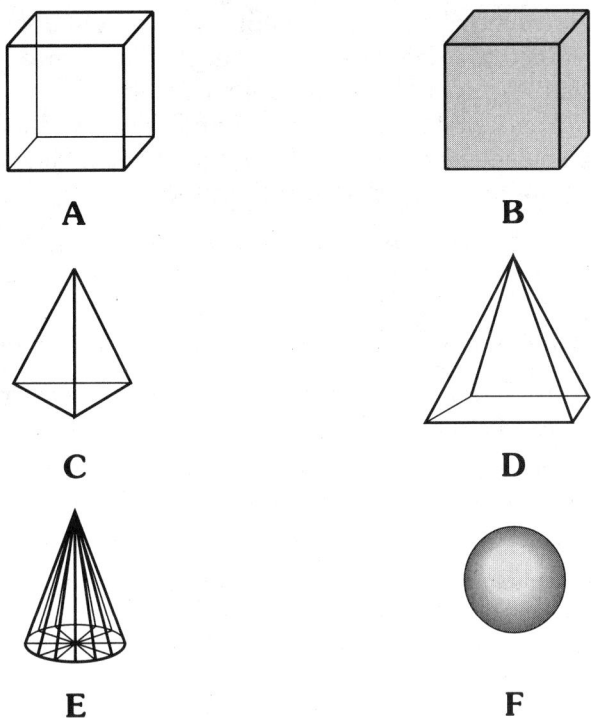

At A, a cube in wire-mesh mode; at B, a cube in shaded mode; at C, a tetrahedron; at D, a pyramid; at E, a cone; at F, a sphere.

Shading makes an object appear solid. It gives you a more easily identifiable picture of what the object would look like if it were made of real matter, such as plaster. However, you can't see details on the far side, because of the opaqueness. The drawing at B shows the same cube, using shading mode rather than wire-mesh mode.

Primitives. All objects are assembled from simpler parts called *primitives*. The following are the most common:

> *Boxes*, also called *parallelepipeds*, include all six-faced objects in which opposite faces are parallel. The cube is the simplest example. Rectangular prisms and "skewed" prisms are more complex examples. The variety of shapes is infinite.

> *Tetrahedra* are triangular pyramids, in which each of the four faces is a triangle. A simple wire-mesh drawing of a tetrahedron is shown in the drawing at C. There exist infinitely many variations on this theme: tall and thin, short and fat, and slanted.

> *Pyramids* have a rectangular base and four triangular slanting faces. As with tetrahedra, there's an infinitude of possible shapes. A wire-mesh example is shown in the drawing at D. Cousins of the pyramids have bases with five, six, or more sides. The slanting faces are always triangles, and they always come to a point, called the *apex*, at the top of the object.

Modeling

➤ *Cones* have a circular base, an apex somewhere above the base, and a curved, slanted face that connects the outer edge of the circle with the apex. In wire-mesh mode, the base is usually rendered as a circle with "spokes," and the curved face is outlined by showing a few of the infinitely many lines that connect the base with the apex (E in the drawing).

The apex of a cone need not be directly above the center of the base. It might be nowhere near the line running perpendicularly through the center of the base. You can probably visualize some of the infinite number of different shapes a cone can have.

➤ *Spheres* have only one possible shape, although their size and location can vary over an infinite range of values. The drawing at F is a shading-mode illustration of a sphere as it would be rendered in a 3-D modeling program.

➤ *Truncated objects* are any primitives that are "cut off." Cones and pyramids are commonly truncated along planes parallel to their bases, as shown in the drawing at G. However, any object can be sliced along a flat plane oriented at any angle.

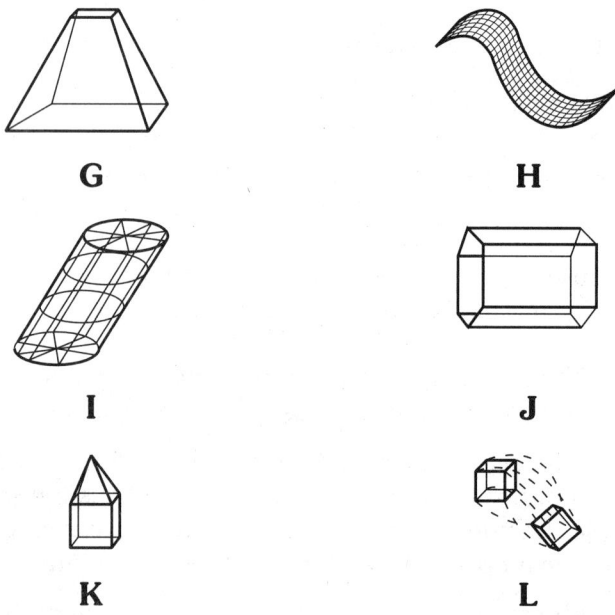

At G, a truncated pyramid; at H, a curved surface; at I, a slanted cylinder; at J, a hexagonal prism; at K, a composite; at L, a simple motion.

➤ *Curved surfaces* can be generated from mathematical functions in three dimensions. Examples include paraboloids, hyperboloids, and an infinite potpourri of strange shapes. You've seen curved surfaces if you've looked closely at advertisements for scientific graphics, or if you've observed someone working with analytical graphics software. The drawing at H shows a wire-mesh rendition of a curved surface.

➤ *Cylinders* are generated by moving a flat disk in some direction not in its own plane. The simplest cylinders have a circular cross-section and some defined height, measured perpendicular to the base or the top. Variations have elliptical bases or are generated by moving the disk through space at a slant. The drawing at I shows a slanted cylinder with a circular base. (The base looks like an ellipse because of the viewing angle.)

➤ *Prisms* are generated in the same way as cylinders, except that triangles, pentagons, hexagons, or other polygons take the place of the circular or elliptical base. The drawing at J shows a wire-mesh rendition of a hexagonal prism.

Hierarchies. Complex shapes are built up from primitives by means of *hierarchical modeling*. The drawing at K shows a wire-mesh rendition of a composite object made by placing a pyramid on top of a cube. The result looks like a little transparent house. This is an extremely simple example of hierarchical modeling.

Composites can themselves be combined, creating supercomposites, which can in turn be combined with primitives, composites, and other supercomposites to get models of anything you can imagine. This is how engineers use CAD to design complex mechanical equipment.

Staging. All the schemes discussed up to this point have involved stationary objects, seen from one angle. Much of the power in modeling software derives from the fact that objects can be moved, rotated, brought nearer, or pushed further away from the viewer. Doing this requires *staging*: the generation of a series of pictures, each of the same set of primitives combined in the same way, but as seen from different points in space.

Creating a sequence of images requires that the computer make a number of coordinate transformations. Although the calculations themselves are enormously complicated, they are all based on the fact that 3-D spaces always have a one-to-one correspondence between their points. (Perhaps you remember this from geometry classes in high school.)

A one-to-one correspondence between the points in two 3-D objects or spaces is called a *homeomorphism*. Basically it means that, however the coordinates might be twisted, stretched, or squashed, they are never ripped apart. In a staged sequence of views of an object, all of its points retain their identity and their uniqueness at all times. Usually, this homeomorphism is of the simplest possible type, known as a *linear transform*. This applies to all rigid objects. A *nonlinear transform* is used either with changing coordinate systems or when the object itself is not rigid. The drawing at L shows a simplified linear transform between two views of a cube. (Imagine this cube as having tumbled to the right and clockwise.)

Modeling

Staging is fun to watch. Portrayals of wire-mesh objects, rotating and gyrating, moving toward or away from you, are like high-tech science-fiction movies. In fact, when staging is taken one step further, the result is computer *animation*, which you have probably seen at the movie theater or on television.

Animation. Animation involves motion of objects, and also of the viewer, in an ongoing sequence. It takes at least 30 scenes per second to produce a realistic animated picture. If you want to create a two-hour, animated computer video, you will therefore need at least

30 images per second × 60 seconds per minute × 60 minutes per hour × 2 hours = 216,000 images!

If that sounds awesome, consider that each image transition will probably involve the independent movement of several complex, modeled objects. Some image transitions will also involve movement of the viewer. This must all be done in a smooth sequence, so that the images don't seem to jerk erratically (unless they are supposed to behave that way). The perspective must be exactly right. All the coordinate transformations must be done with minimum error and maximum speed.

Some of the most exotic and exciting scenes ever generated by computers were shown in the famous *Star Wars* movies. Computers are far more powerful now than they were back then. High-tech computer animation is common in movies and cartoons. Meteors, space ships, strange creatures, and robots all move around as you, the viewer, move among them. Next time you watch one of these videos, keep in mind how much work—by people as well as by digital computers—went into making it! *See also* ANIMATION.

Analogical reasoning. The term *modeling* is also used in reference to *analogical reasoning*, an entirely different application from that of CAD and animation. Analogical reasoning is a scheme whereby computers are used to simulate natural events, social behavior, the spread of disease, and other complex events.

A good example of computer modeling is the prediction of the path a hurricane will take. Although it's impossible to predict very far in advance exactly where, when, or if a hurricane will make landfall, scientists can use computers to generate probable scenarios based on the paths of hurricanes in the past.

Another example of computer modeling is speculation about what will happen to the earth's environment if people keep doing things to increase the amount of carbon dioxide in the atmosphere. Most programs indicate that the average temperature of the earth will increase, and this will cause the oceans to rise and the rainfall/snowfall patterns to change.

Still another example of computer modeling involves predicting the future extent of ozone depletion. The results of such modeling can be made public and might have an influence on what actually happens to our planet in the coming decades. This is not the sort of thing normally done by average PC users; instead, large computers are used in a professional setting such as a government or university lab. *See also* ANALOGICAL REASONING, ARTIFICIAL INTELLIGENCE, EXPERT SYSTEMS, *and* FORECASTING.

Modem

The term *modem* is a contraction of the words *modulator* and *demodulator*. A modem interfaces a PC to the telephone lines or to a radio transceiver. Modems allow you to communicate with other PC users, and also to access the many different online services. You'll need a good modem if you want to get on the information superhighway.

External versus internal. Some modems are self-contained units that you can use with any PC, IBM-compatible or Macintosh. These modems, sometimes called "personal modems" but more often called *external modems*, come in various sizes and shapes. Some fit directly into a utility alternating-current (ac) wall outlet. Others sit on your desk next to your PC or telephone. They all have a cord that runs to the PC's serial port, and another cord that runs to the telephone jack. Most also have a jack into which you can plug your telephone set.

Internal modems are printed-circuit boards, or cards, that fit into one of your PC's expansion slots. You must open your PC to install such a modem. It's inconvenient to switch an internal modem from one computer to another. Still, some PC users prefer an internal modem to an external one because it makes for a neater installation with fewer cords and boxes lying around. Many new computers are sold with internal modems preinstalled.

Drawing A on the following page shows how modems are connected at two different PC workstations, allowing communication over the telephone lines. Drawing B shows modems for communication via radio. A modem that includes some extra features, and which is designed especially for packet communications, is called a *terminal node controller*. *See also* PACKET COMMUNICATIONS *and* TERMINAL NODE CONTROLLER.

How it works. Your computer works with binary digital signals, called high and low, or 1 and 0. These are rapidly fluctuating direct currents. In order for this information to be conveyed over a telephone or radio circuit, the data must be converted to analog form. This is done by changing the digit 1 into an audio tone, and the digit 0 into another tone with a different pitch. The result is an extremely fast back-and-forth alternation between two different tones. This sounds like teletype at slow speeds, but merges into a roar at moderate and high data speeds. If you happen to pick up a telephone

Modem

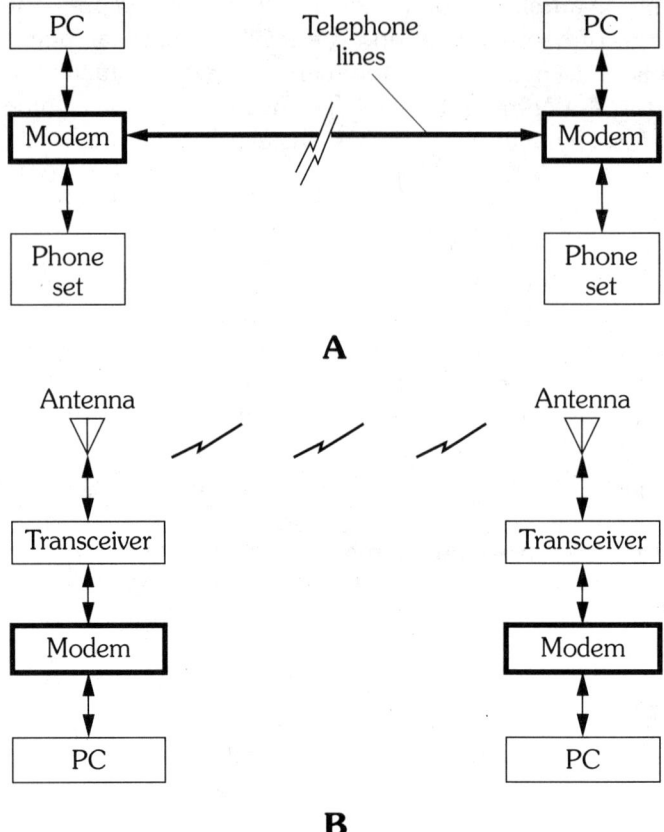

At A, modems connect PCs to telephone lines. At B, modems connect PCs to radio transceivers.

extension while someone is online with the computer from another extension, you'll hear this roar. (Don't make a habit of doing this, though; the PC user will experience interference as a result of your picking up the extension.)

In *modulation*, digital data is changed into analog data. It is a type of digital-to-analog (D/A) conversion. The *demodulation* changes the analog signals back to digital ones; this is analog-to-digital conversion.

Modems work at various speeds, usually measured in *bits per second*, although you'll also hear about a speed unit called the *baud*. Bauds and bits per second are not exactly the same, but they are often confused. The higher the speed, the faster the data is sent and received through the modem.

Drawing C is a block diagram of a modem suitable for interfacing a home or business computer with a telephone line. The modulator converts the digital computer data into audio tones. The demodulator converts the incoming audio tones into digital signals for the computer. The audio tones fall within the frequency range, or band, of approximately 300 Hz to 3 KHz. This is the band needed to clearly transmit a human voice. It's amazing how much computer data can race over a single telephone or radio circuit having such a narrow bandwidth. *See also* ANALOG, ANALOG-TO-DIGITAL CONVERSION, BAUD/BITS PER SECOND, DIGITAL, DIGITAL-TO-ANALOG CONVERSION, *and* MODULATION.

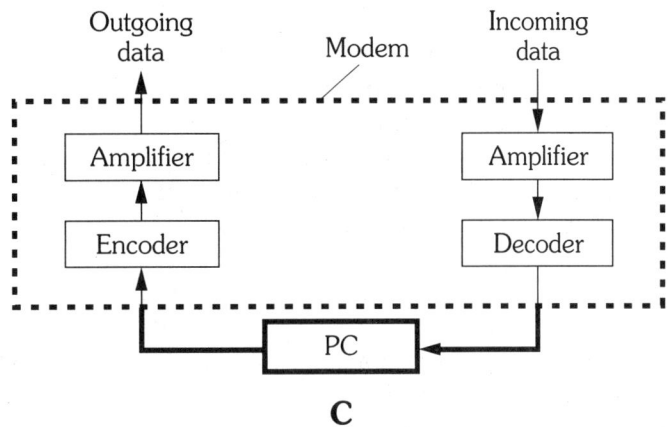

A functional block diagram of a modem.

Software. For your modem to work well, you'll need *terminal emulation software*. Modems are usually supplied with their own software, so you won't have to worry about getting the software somewhere else. If you buy the software separately from the modem, what you need will depend on what you plan to access with your modem. You can download public-domain or freeware modem software from online using a friend's PC, although such software puts your machine at some risk of getting a Trojan horse or virus. You can also obtain shareware versions of modem software online, which is somewhat less likely to contain "germs." These programs come with technical assistance that you can get for a small fee. However, the best programs are usually the ones you buy in the computer store or via a catalog. (Talk to your PC dealer or local "PC guru" for advice concerning the best terminal-emulation software for your needs.)

For amateur packet radio, terminal emulation programs are available from various retail and mail-order dealerships. The amateur radio magazines carry advertisements for these programs. In addition, if you're into "ham" radio, there are many other types of software that can make this hobby an interesting and fun computer application. *See also* FREEWARE, INTERNET, ONLINE SERVICE, SHAREWARE, TERMINAL EMULATION SOFTWARE, TROJAN HORSE, *and* VIRUS.

Modular construction

A few decades ago, electronic equipment was constructed in a much different way than it is today. Components were mounted on tie strips, and wiring was done in point-to-point fashion. This kind of wiring is still used in some high-power radio transmitters, but in recent years, *modular construction* has become the rule.

Modular Mac line

In the modular method of construction, circuit boards, or cards, are used. Each card contains the components for a certain part of the system. The circuit boards are removable, either by hand or with a simple tool resembling a pliers. Edge connectors facilitate easy replacement. The edge connectors are wired together for interconnection between circuit boards.

Modular construction has simplified the maintenance of complicated equipment like computers. In-the-field repair consists of identification, removal, and replacement of the card where the malfunction occurs. The faulty board is then sent to a central repair facility, where it is fixed by technicians. Once the card has been repaired, it can serve as a replacement module when the need arises.

Modular construction has made it possible for almost anyone to modify or upgrade a PC. Suppose, for example, that you want to get more display speed from your machine, but can't afford a new motherboard. You might opt for a video-accelerator board instead. This could be installed in one of the expansion slots on the motherboard. Depending on the make and model, most PCs have from three to a dozen expansion slots for adding memory, enhancing the display, adding a MIDI (musical instrument digital interface), using multiple printers, and even interfacing with robotic devices. *See also* PRINTED CIRCUIT *and* UPGRADING.

Modular Mac line

The *modular Mac line* is a series of Macintosh computers manufactured by Apple Computer, Inc. first introduced in 1987. The modular Macs are somewhat more advanced and more powerful than their predecessor, the Mac Classic.

The most visible difference between the modular Macs and the Classics is that some assembly is needed. The name *modular* derives from the fact that this Macintosh series, like IBM-compatible PCs, uses modular construction. The main unit is separate from the monitor. Inside the main unit, systems are built on individual, easily removable, and interchangeable printed circuit boards.

Another physical difference between the modular Macs and the Classics involves ease of disassembly. Because the monitor is separate from the main unit, it's safe and relatively easy to get inside a modular Mac. This, and the modularization of the design, makes modification and upgrading simpler. Inside the main unit, the components can be easily swapped. Circuit boards can be interchanged for newer, more powerful substitutes. You can add another floppy disk drive or a bigger hard disk system. You can incorporate a larger monitor, a color monitor, or multiple printers.

The modular Macs can be categorized as the *Mac LC series*, the *Mac II series*, and the *Mac Centris series*. The LC and the Mac II are good, solid PCs for serious individual users. The Mac II found its way into many small businesses. The Centris is a good machine for small and medium-sized corporations, and is also favored by individual power users. The Mac II series and the Centris series proved, in large measure, responsible for establishing Apple's reputation as a trailblazer in desktop publishing.

The microprocessors in the Modular Mac line are manufactured by Motorola. The Mac LC started with a chip called the 68020, roughly equivalent to Intel's 80286. The Mac II series also started with the 68020, but later models used a more powerful microprocessor called the 68030, which has about the same power as Intel's 80386. The Mac Centris series introduced the 68040, a versatile, fast chip similar to the Intel 80486. *See also* APPLE COMPUTER INC. MACINTOSH, *and* MODULAR CONSTRUCTION.

Modular programming

When writing very large, complex computer programs, software engineers sometimes use a scheme called *modular programming*. The program is written in blocks, or modules, each of which is responsible for some function or set of functions.

Each module is debugged and perfected, and then the modules are assembled to create the final program. Some debugging might be necessary to get the modules to work well with each other. Some programs can be assembled from "ready-made" modules. It's possible that a collection of modules might, with little or no modification, be put together to get dozens of different programs.

To get an idea of what modular programming is like, suppose you want to write a large textbook about world history. This is a vast subject. In fact, it is so huge that you might have trouble deciding where to start. Programmers sometimes face this same sort of "writer's block" when first starting on a massive software venture.

You could start your book with the formation of the earth in orbit around a star in a galaxy containing 100 billion other stars, and end with a scene in a room in which a humanoid is writing a book about the history of the world, but that would be logistically difficult, and also ridiculous. A more realistic idea is to break world history down into timeframes, as shown in part A of the following drawing. The first section might be called "The Time Before Life"; the second one could be "The Time of Early Life"; the third one might be "The Time of Middle Life"; the fourth one might be called "The Time of Recent Life." Each of the four sections could be roughly the same length in your book, even though they would involve vastly different lengths of time as measured in actual years. You could then work on the four sections independently, assembling them as the final step in the compilation.

Modular programming

The section "The Time of Recent Life" would contain various submodules representing life before civilization, and one final submodule representing the history of civilization (part B). This submodule could itself be modularized, either by time period or by regions of the world. One of the sub-submodules (or sub^2-modules) within this submodule might be called "History of the United States" (part C). This sub^2-module could be broken down into sub^3-modules, perhaps entitled "Before the Revolution," "From Revolution to Civil War," "From Civil War to Cold War," and "After the Cold War" (part D).

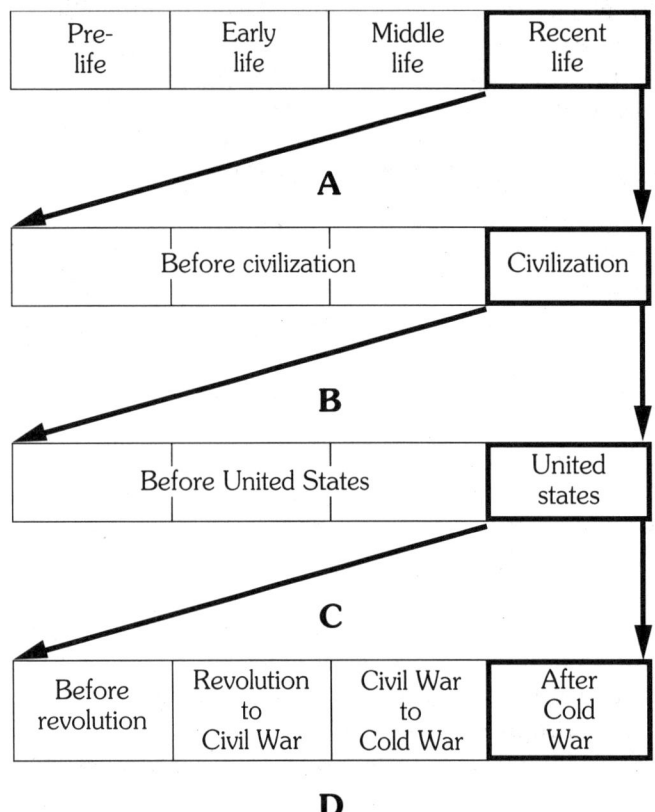

An example of modularization, with parts A, B, C, and D showing progressively smaller submodules.

However you decided to create the modules, submodules, and sub-submodules of your book, you'd want to be sure that the transitions were smooth. You would do this after you were done writing each of the individual modules.

It's the same way with modular programming. Most of the work consists of creating good modules. The finishing touches involve getting the modules to cooperate. Modular programming has become more popular as computer software has become increasingly complex. Modular schemes are especially powerful in graphical operating systems such as Macintosh, Windows, and OS/2. *See also* GRAPHICAL

USER INTERFACE, MACINTOSH, OBJECT-ORIENTED PROGRAMMING, OS/2, *and* WINDOWS.

Modulation

Modulation is the process in which data is sent from one place to another. The data can be in the form of digital signals, sounds, or pictures. The transmitting station is called the *source*, and the receiving station is called the *destination*. When the signals reach the destination, they are usually converted back into their original form. That process is called *demodulation*.

Audio tones. The earliest method of encoding data was the Morse code, a digital scheme. The first Morse signals were sent in the 19th century over wires, as currents that were switched on and off.

Computers talk with each other in a code that works on the same on/off, high/low, digital principle as the Morse code. One such code is *ASCII* (American Standard Code for Information Interchange, pronounced "ask-key"). There are more symbols in ASCII than there are in Morse code, allowing for capital and small letters, numerals, punctuation, and various commands.

Morse was adopted by radio operators when "wireless" was invented. The code was converted by the radio receiver into an audio tone that went on and off. This was an analog signal in the sense that it could be adjusted in pitch and volume over continuous ranges, but it was digital, too, because the information was conveyed by the on/off nature of the signal. The beep-beep-beep of Morse code is a hybrid of analog and digital technologies.

When data is sent by computers over telephone lines, radio waves, or light beams, it travels in a similar hybrid form. One audio tone represents each logic 1, or high, and another tone stands for every logic 0, or low (see the waves in drawing A). These tones alternate so fast that if you listen to them, they sound like a hiss or roar. The tones can have any frequencies, as long as they are sufficiently different in pitch so the modem at the destination can tell them apart. The loudness and pitch of the tones used by a PC modem are set at certain standard values. *See also* ANALOG, ASCII, DIGITAL, *and* MODEM.

Logic 0 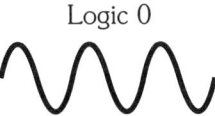   Logic 1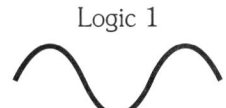

A

Tones for logic 0 and logic 1.

Modulation

Complex data. The scheme used by modems is sometimes called *audio frequency-shift keying (AFSK)*. It is a simple type of frequency modulation (FM). There are just two frequencies, and the signal is always at one frequency or the other.

You might think that the types of data sent via AFSK must be limited to text and software. How, you might ask, can anything complicated, like a scene, human voice, or robot command, be conveyed by using two audio tones? All these things are possible, however. In fact, digital methods work better than older analog schemes for transmitting and receiving analog information because the digits go by incredibly fast. This allows complex encoding and decoding. The processes are called *analog-to-digital conversion* and *digital-to-analog conversion*.

Even an intricate color photograph can be converted into digital highs and lows at a source PC, sent over wire, radio, or light beams, and then converted back into the original picture at the destination PC. If you've done much downloading of data online, you've probably witnessed this for yourself. In the future, you can expect to see control signals, such as the kind used for robots, sent over telephone lines and radio. Actually, farmers are doing some of that now.

Drawing B shows a system for sending a picture via radio. At the source, an optical scanner converts the picture into digital pulses. These pulses are changed into AFSK by a modem. The AFSK is sent to the radio transmitter, which contains a special modulator that impresses the audio onto radio waves. These waves travel through space, perhaps being retransmitted by repeaters along the way. At the destination, the receiver extracts the AFSK from the radio waves. The audio is then fed to a modem, which changes it into digital pulses. These pulses are then sent to the PC, which has software that changes the pulses back into the original picture. *See also* ANALOG-TO-DIGITAL CONVERSION, DIGITAL-TO-ANALOG CONVERSION, FARMING APPLICATIONS, *and* PERSONAL ROBOTS.

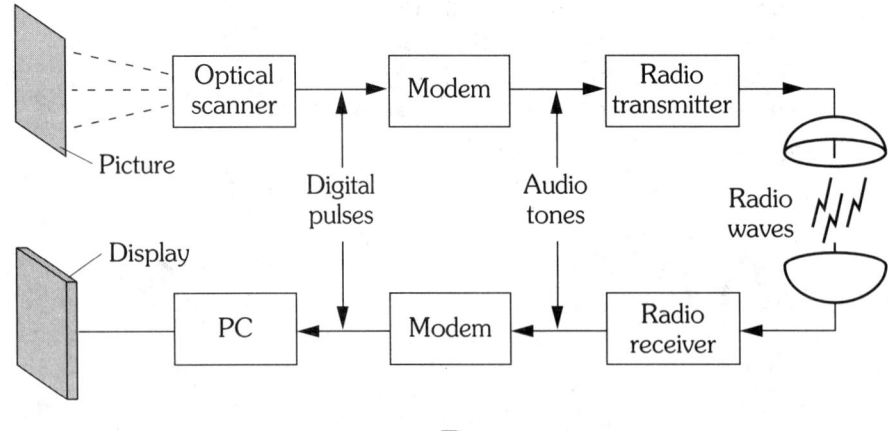

B

A block diagram of digital picture transmission by radio.

Modulation

Getting more for less. Even at fairly high data speeds, it takes a while to send a picture with excellent image resolution. It can also take a long time to send complex software. However, the intended data can be conveyed faster by using fewer logic bits to represent the same information. This is done via a scheme called *data compression*.

Text and software can be compressed to some extent without losing any of the details. Images are a different story. There's always some sacrifice in resolution when a picture's digital representation is squeezed down. Nevertheless, some ingenious methods are available that will let you compress images by factors of 20 or more, and the degradation in image quality is hardly noticeable. To speed up the transmission of the information, the compressed data, rather than the original data, is used to modulate the signals sent over the communications circuit. *See also* DATA COMPRESSION, IMAGE COMPRESSION, IMAGE RESOLUTION, *and* LOSSLESS AND LOSSY DATA COMPRESSION.

Carrier modulation. When AFSK tones are sent by radio or telephone, they are usually impressed onto a *carrier*, which is a signal having a much higher frequency than either of the two audio tones. In amateur radio, for example, the carrier can range from 1.8 megahertz (MHz) to hundreds of gigahertz (GHz).

Modulation in radio and carrier-current transmitters is often done by analog means. In *amplitude modulation (AM)*, the strength of the carrier varies in step with the cycles of the audio tone. In *frequency modulation (FM)*, the carrier frequency goes up and down at a rate corresponding to the frequency of the audio tone. In *phase modulation*, the phase of the carrier shifts back and forth in step with the cycles of the audio tone. In each of these methods, the changes in the carrier are usually smooth and continuous. Such a system is said to be using *analog carrier modulation*.

The amplitude, frequency, or phase of a carrier can change in "jumps," rather than continuously. This is *digital carrier modulation*. The number of levels (specific amplitudes, frequencies, or phases) is always a power of two. This number is the *sampling resolution*. For simple audio tones, a sampling resolution of eight is sufficient (see drawing C); for complicated signals like the music sent by commercial FM broadcast stations, the sampling resolution is normally 16. Another factor that affects the quality of the signal is the *sampling rate*. This is measured in samples per second, or as the time in microseconds between samples. The sampling rate should be at least twice the highest modulating frequency. For an audio signal, a good sampling rate is 8 KHz, or one sample every 125 microseconds.

Another type of digital modulation is *pulse modulation*. The carrier is not sent constantly, but is broken into a series of pulses sent at regular intervals (a tiny fraction of a second). In *pulse amplitude modulation*

Modulation

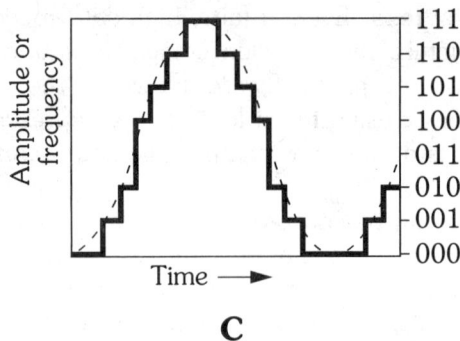

C

The digitization of a wave.

(PAM), the amplitude, or strength, of the pulses changes over a continuous range of values (see drawing D). In *pulse width modulation (PWM)*, the width (duration) of pulses is varied continuously (see E). In *pulse code modulation (PCM)*, either the amplitude or the width can be varied, but not continuously. Instead, there are a number of defined levels that can be reached. Usually this number is eight or 16.

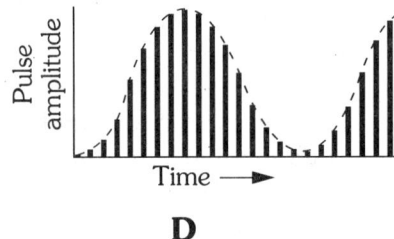

D

The same wave as C, in PAM.

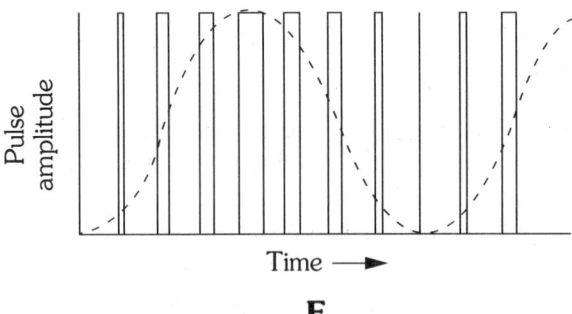

E

The same wave as C, in PWM.

Magnetic media. A different type of modulation is used in the processes of writing and reading data to and from magnetic disk and magnetic tape. In the magnetic writing process, the digital signals are represented by electrical currents. These currents pass through the head, which has a tiny wire coil inside. The coil acts as a miniature electromagnet, producing a magnetic field. This field fluctuates, or alternates, with logical high and low signals. As the magnetically sensitive surface of the disk or tape passes beneath the head, the surface becomes magnetized in different ways for the high and low signals.

When the disk or tape is to be read, the surface passes beneath another head, similar to the writing head. (In fact, reading and writing can be done by the same head.) The magnetized regions on the surface cause currents to flow in the head's wire coil. These currents correspond exactly to the original digital currents that were used in the writing process. *See also* DISKETTE DRIVE, HARD DISK, HEAD, MAGNETIC DISK, MAGNETIC MEDIA, MAGNETIC TAPE, *and* TAPE DRIVE.

CD-ROM and modulated light. The abbreviation *CD-ROM* stands for *compact disc, read-only memory*. The CD-ROMs commonly used in personal computing are intended to be read from, but not overwritten.

The surface of a CD-ROM is etched with millions of microscopic pits. The pits cause scattering of a laser beam that scans over the surface of the disk. Where there are no pits, the surface reflects the light like a mirror. Therefore, as the laser sweeps over the disk, the reflected beam is modulated in a way that depends on the locations of the pits.

The reflected, modulated laser light is picked up by a sensor that works like a solar cell, converting the light into electrical current. The reflected light flashes on and off at a high rate of speed. These on-and-off signals correspond to logic highs and lows. The current from the sensor goes on and off right along with the light that strikes it. The current pulses correspond exactly to the data that was written onto the disk when it was manufactured.

Modulated laser light can also be used to communicate directly. A laser at the source flashes on and off at an extremely high rate, corresponding to logic highs and lows. The destination contains a photovoltaic cell that changes the flashing light into current pulses. Alternatively, a laser can be modulated with AFSK. One laser can carry hundreds, thousands, or even millions of AFSK computer signals. The laser can be sent through clear air or through outer space, or it might be guided along thin strands of glass in a fiberoptic network. *See also* CD-ROM *and* FIBEROPTIC DATA TRANSMISSION.

Modulo

Modulo refers to the number of different values a digit can have in a numerical system. The scheme most often used by people is modulo-10, also called the *decimal number system* or base-10. The digital states in this scheme are 0, 1, 2, 3, 4, 5, 6, 7, 8, and 9. No matter how esoteric or complex a numerical value might be, it is always a combination of these 10 digital values.

Molecular computer technology

The table compares decimal values and those in modulo-2 (also called the *binary number system*), modulo-4, modulo-8 (also called the *octal number system*), modulo-12, and modulo-16 (also called the *hexadecimal number system*). Computers work with binary numbers. There are only two digital states in this system, represented in switching networks as 1 and 0, high/low, on/off, or true/false. Sometimes computers use octal or hexadecimal numbers. Base-4 and base-12 are uncommon. Base-10 is used only when interfacing with humans. *See also* BINARY NUMBER SYSTEM, DECIMAL NUMBER SYSTEM, HEXADECIMAL NUMBER SYSTEM, *and* OCTAL NUMBER SYSTEM.

Decimal numbers in various modulos

Decimal	Binary	Base-4	Octal	Base-12	Hexadecimal
0	0	0	0	0	0
1	1	1	1	1	1
2	10	2	2	2	2
3	11	3	3	3	3
4	100	10	4	4	4
5	101	11	5	5	5
6	110	12	6	6	6
7	111	13	7	7	7
8	1000	20	10	8	8
9	1001	21	11	9	9
10	1010	22	12	A	A
11	1011	23	13	B	B
12	1100	30	14	10	C
13	1101	31	15	11	D
14	1110	32	16	12	E
15	1111	33	17	13	F
16	10000	100	20	14	10
17	10001	101	21	15	11
18	10010	102	22	16	12
19	10011	103	23	17	13
20	10100	110	24	18	14

Molecular computer technology

Every computer is built up from *logic gates*. Each gate is a miniature electronic switch that manipulates digital high and low signals. The power of a microprocessor is a function of the following three characteristics of logic gates:

1 Switching speed

2 Total number of gates

3 Number of gates per unit volume

Of these factors, the third directly affects the first two, and is therefore most significant.

Exponential growth. How much memory does your PC have? How many instructions per second can it carry out? How "smart" is it? It all boils down to one thing: the number of logic gates on each integrated circuit (IC), or chip, in the machine. The more logic gates per chip, the fewer chips are needed for a given amount of computer power, and therefore, the more powerful can be a PC of a given physical size. This is true as long there are no major changes in the way logic gates are manufactured.

Digital electronics technology, particularly in the field of ICs, have advanced exponentially during the late 20th century. There is a limit, however, to how much longer such a pace can continue. More and more logic gates are being crammed into smaller and smaller chips of silicon. Eventually, the structure of matter itself must call a halt to the process. The end is beginning to come in sight. Engineers are actively researching devices called *single-electron memory (SIM)*, in which each digital high or low is represented by the presence or absence of an individual electron.

Carving out a chip. The manufacture of an IC is a fascinating process. It starts with a chip of semiconductor material such as silicon, gallium arsenide, or a metallic oxide. Chips can be "grown" in a lab, in much the same way as you might have seen crystals "grown" in science experiments.

The semiconductor chip is carved in a series of complex layers, something like the way a printed circuit is manufactured. However, the etching process for ICs is thousands of times smaller than that used for circuit boards. The details are initially created on photographic films with extremely fine grain, allowing fantastic image resolution. The images from the film are transferred to the silicon by a special etching process. Layer after layer is etched, creating regions of differing electrical conductivity. The end result is an intricate network of logic gates, all capable of operating together in a coherent fashion that results in your computer's "thoughts."

As the etching process gets finer and finer, there is a point of diminishing returns. In order to carve more logic gates into a chip, an increasing amount of work must be done. The film must have

Molecular computer technology

improved resolution. Ultimately, things reach the point where atoms are being cut away one-by-one.

Imagine a sculptor carving a statue in stone by removing atoms individually! He or she might come to the conclusion that it makes more sense to build the statue up by sticking atoms together, instead of taking atoms away one by one. This is what engineers have begun to say about ICs. Semiconductor chips are grown atom-by-atom in the first place. Why not fabricate an IC as the crystal is growing, and do away with the etching process altogether?

Laying down atoms. It's one thing to talk about putting molecules together like building blocks; it's another thing to actually do it. *Molecular computer technology* involves a sort of biochemical growth process, not manual assembly of atomic matrixes.

Various schemes have been suggested for growing arrays of logic gates. One method involves floating a layer of protein molecules in a container of water. A semiconductor chip is passed through the container, becoming coated with a one-molecule-thick layer of protein (see the drawing). After that, the semiconductor chip is passed through containers with various chemicals, building up layers of molecules on the chip. These interact like amino acids, viruses, and antibodies in an organic mixture. Depending on which chemicals are used, and on the order in which the chip is passed through the containers, different array structures can be grown. These would, it is thought, have a data-storage density similar to that of an animal or human brain.

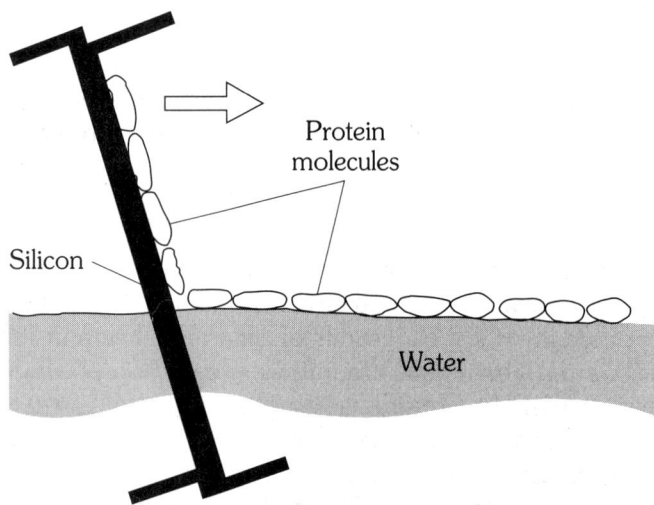

To start the growth process, a silicon chip gets a one-molecule-thick coating of protein.

Molecular computer technology is presently in a stage that might be called "in vitro." It's not fully alive yet, but it has been conceived, and some lab experiments have been done with the idea. *See also*

ALTERNATIVE COMPUTER TECHNOLOGY, BACTERIORHODOPSIN, BIOCHIP, COMPUTER GENERATIONS, COMPUTER POWER, DIGITAL COMPUTER TECHNOLOGY, INTEGRATED CIRCUIT, LOGIC GATES, NANOTECHNOLOGY, OPTICAL COMPUTER TECHNOLOGY, *and* SINGLE-ELECTRON MEMORY.

Monitor

A *monitor* or *display* is a visual interface between a computer and its operator. There are many types of monitors.

The simplest monitors are monochrome. They do not show color. A *cathode-ray tube (CRT)* monochrome monitor is like a black-and-white television set without the tuning or volume controls. A monochrome *liquid-crystal-display (LCD)* is lightweight and thin, and is found in less expensive laptop (notebook) computers. (In laptop and portable computers, the term *display* is generally used instead of *monitor*.)

Color monitors are more versatile than monochrome units, and are a virtual necessity for graphics work. Color adds another dimension to the display. Color displays are available in both CRT and LCD types.

The *image resolution* of a monitor is important. This is the extent to which it can show detail; the better the resolution, the sharper the image. With LCDs, speed of response is also important. The older and cheaper LCD displays are sluggish. This can be an annoyance; it limits the ability of the display to portray motion. Newer LCDs compete favorably with CRTs in terms of speed and image crispness. This is especially true of *active matrix* displays in high-end laptop computers.

A good display is crucial for graphics, with interactive machines, in remote-control robotics, and in action simulators. In addition, a sharp display is more pleasant to work with than a marginal one. For example, if you get used to a high-end SVGA (Super Video Graphics Array) monitor, you'll find that a VGA (Video Graphics Array) seems dull and blurry. You'll notice the difference most in draw or paint programs, and with a graphical user interface (GUI). If you have a VGA and you upgrade to SVGA, you'll become spoiled immediately. *See also* ACTIVE MATRIX, CATHODE-RAY TUBE, COLOR GRAPHICS ADAPTER, ENHANCED GRAPHICS ADAPTER, HIGH-RESOLUTION MONITOR, IMAGE RESOLUTION, LIQUID-CRYSTAL DISPLAY, MONITOR UPGRADING, MONOCHROME DISPLAY ADAPTER, SUPER VIDEO GRAPHICS ARRAY, VIDEO GRAPHICS ARRAY, *and* VISION SYSTEMS.

Monitor upgrading

As you gain experience with your PC, you'll probably be buying more sophisticated software. This might include high-end graphics, spreadsheets, and perhaps desktop publishing. You might consider *monitor upgrading* to ensure that your hardware keeps up with your software.

Monitor upgrading

Do you need a new monitor? Some PC users can get along with one monitor indefinitely, until it wears out. If you do nothing but word processing or simple programming, or if you use your PC only for text-based applications, you might find your original monitor adequate for your needs. In that case, there's no point in buying a better monitor.

If you find yourself scrolling left-and-right because you work with lines longer than 80 characters, however, you might do well with a wider screen. Similarly, if you have to squint to see tiny images on screen, you should think about enlarging the image by getting a bigger monitor. Or, perhaps you're not satisfied with the colors your monitor can display.

If you decide you need a better monitor, shop around. Be sure that what you buy is compatible with your system. A "PC guru" friend, or someone you know and trust at a computer store, can help you out. Take your system manual along to the store and look at all the available monitors and their specifications. There's a good chance that you'll need to purchase a graphics adapter card, too, so the new monitor will work up to its full capability.

If you're buying a whole new PC system, buy the best monitor you can afford. Again, be sure the monitor is compatible with the rest of the system.

Considerations. When shopping for a new monitor, you should keep the following things in mind:

➢ *Screen size* The size of the screen is given as a diagonal measure in inches. Most screens aren't square, but instead have an aspect ratio (width-to-height) of 4:3. A 13-inch monitor is about 10.5 inches wide by 8 inches high, for example. When upgrading, many PC users opt for 17-inch monitors. The increase in monitor screen area is roughly equal to the square of the increase in diagonal measure. Thus, a 17-inch monitor is effectively about 71% larger than a 13-inch unit.

➢ *Image resolution* Perhaps the single most important specification of any monitor is its image resolution. It can be given as a pair of numbers, representing the number of pixels the screen shows horizontally and vertically, or it might be quoted in terms of the *dot pitch*. For a particular screen size, the greater the number of pixels the unit can display, the better the image resolution. In terms of dot pitch, better resolution is indicated by smaller numbers, regardless of the screen size.

➢ *Colors* Some monitors can display more colors than other monitors. The color resolution of a monitor is quoted as a number representing the various hues the unit can display. Color-resolution figures are somewhat oversimplified because color actually has two distinct properties, called the *hue* and the *saturation*. However, in general, the larger the number of colors a monitor can display, the more versatile it will be in practical use.

➢ *Interlacing* A non-interlaced display is better than an interlaced display if you're working with fast-moving graphic images. Interlacing translates into a lower *refresh rate*, and this can cause objectionable "jitter" or jumpiness in a fast-moving image. High-end graphical applications often require that the monitor display fast-changing images. The refresh rate should therefore be as high as possible. A good specification is 70 Hz or more.

➢ *Adapter cards* To get the most out of a new monitor, you'll probably need to install a new graphics adapter card. There are several different types; you'll need to talk with an expert concerning compatibility.

➢ *ELF* If you're concerned about the extremely low-frequency fields produced by monitors, you might consider buying a unit that has been designed to reduce these emissions. You can recognize an ELF-reduced monitor by the mention of the Swedish standard for ELF or magnetic-field emissions.

➢ *Energy consumption* Compare the power requirements of various monitors. How many watts does the unit need when running? Does it have a provision for automatically reducing its output when you leave your PC for a few minutes? An automatic-standby feature saves energy, and it also extends the life of the monitor.

➢ *Gimmicks* If you have unlimited funds, or a taste for the avant-garde, you might consider adapting your monitor to a "big screen" using projection equipment. Imagine coming into the computer room, switching off the lights, reclining in an oversize chair, and playing a computer game on a 10-foot diagonal screen!

Maybe you have other monitor-upgrading gimmicks in mind. Try them at your own risk (to hardware, spirits, and finances). It's important that you not tamper with equipment in such a way as to void its warranty.

➢ *Size and weight* If you buy a monitor with a bigger screen, it will be physically larger than the monitor you're using now. It will also be heavier. That 17-inch monitor you saw in the store was strategically set up with a compatible desk, main unit, and peripherals, so that it looks appealing to potential buyers. It probably won't blend in the same way in your home workstation.

A 17-inch monitor takes up as much space as a 13-inch monitor plus a typical desktop main unit. If you have a 13-inch monitor now, and it is on top of your main unit and behind your keyboard, consider moving the main unit to the side or to the

Monochrome Display Adapter

floor, then set the 17-inch monitor on the desk surface behind the keyboard. This will give you sufficient desk space and will place the screen in a good viewing position.

➢ *Warranty* The length of the warranty is a good indication of the quality of any product. The manufacturers of reliable hardware have more faith in their merchandise than the makers of shoddy stuff. A one-year warranty is good; a two-year warranty is superior. Anything less than six months should make you suspicious.

Brand-name monitors are usually, but not always, the best. If you have "PC guru" friends, ask them which manufacturers or distributors they recommend. If someone has had experience with a company's repair department and can honestly praise the quality of their work and service, that's a huge plus. *See also* DOT PITCH, ELF FIELDS, HIGH-RESOLUTION MONITOR, IMAGE RESOLUTION, MONITOR, PIXEL, *and* UPGRADING.

Monochrome Display Adapter

A monochrome (black-and-white) monitor is a rarity these days, especially in desktop computing. Nevertheless, once in awhile you'll see one in use. A *Monochrome Display Adapter (MDA)* is a driver card made for use with IBM-compatible PCs and monochrome monitors. It allows the display of text without color; it is in shades of gray instead.

For people who use their computers only for text-based applications like word processing, an MDA and monochrome monitor can be adequate. The advantage is low cost. However, the MDA does not generally work well with graphical user interfaces (GUIs) and graphics applications. With the advent of the GUI, it's unlikely that anyone will stay in text-only mode for long. The lure of graphical applications is strong. *See also* GRAPHICAL USER INTERFACE, MONITOR, *and* MONITOR UPGRADING.

Motherboard

The *motherboard* is the main circuit board in a PC. It is located inside the main unit of a desktop computer, and beneath the keyboard in a laptop. It is usually the largest circuit board in the machine. Sometimes the motherboard is called the *logic board*.

The motherboard contains the "guts" of the computer: the central processing unit (CPU), the random-access memory (RAM), and the slots for the expansion boards. If you open up the main unit of a desktop PC, the motherboard is hard to miss. It has dozens of integrated circuits (ICs), or chips. Most modern electronic circuits are fabricated onto these chips, which are made of various semiconducting materials.

How much electronics is on the motherboard of a typical PC? You can get some idea when you realize that each IC on the board has thousands upon thousands of transistors. If a motherboard were constructed from discrete components such as resistors, diodes, capacitors, and transistors, it would occupy a large building. Some of the earliest computers, which were made this way, were so big that they needed their own utility lines and air conditioning plants, and filled several rooms.

The number of expansion slots on a motherboard depends on the computer model. Some motherboards have several slots; others have just one, intended for a *daughterboard*, which contains more expansion slots. *See also* CENTRAL PROCESSING UNIT, EXPANSION BOARD, INTEGRATED CIRCUIT, *and* RANDOM-ACCESS MEMORY.

MOS

See METAL-OXIDE SEMICONDUCTOR TECHNOLOGY.

Motorola microprocessors

Motorola microprocessors are generally used in Apple Macintosh (Mac) computer systems. There are several different types of Motorola chip, the power and versatility of which are comparable to the line of Intel microprocessors common in IBM-compatible PCs.

The early Motorola microprocessors were designated by numbers 68*xxx*. Later, the PowerPC or PowerMac chips, a joint effort among Motorola, Apple, and IBM, began using numbers 6*xx*. (*PowerPC* is a trademark of IBM.) All Mac chips are designed to support a graphical user interface (GUI), the feature that Apple introduced with the original Mac computer line.

The 68000. Also known as the "sixty-eight thousand," the 68000 chip was used in the Mac Classic PCs, the earliest line of the Macintosh. The 68000 employed a 16-bit external data bus and a 32-bit internal data bus. It could address up to 16 megabytes (MB) of memory. The clock speed was eight megahertz (MHz). Even at that speed, which is slow by today's standards, it took four clock cycles to do one instruction.

The 68020. Often called the "sixty-eight twenty," the 68020 chip had a 32-bit data bus, both internally and externally. Its clock speed of 16 MHz doubled that of the 68000. This microprocessor was introduced in the modular Mac line of computers. It could address up to four gigabytes (4GB) of memory if System 7 was added. Otherwise, it was limited to 8MB.

The 68020 can still be found in some older Macs. It is not installed in new computers. The 68020 was a workhorse, powering the Mac II line for serious individual PC users and businesses.

Motorola microprocessors

The 68030. The 68030, sometimes called the "sixty-eight thirty," uses a faster clock than the 68020: up to 50 MHz in some machines. It has a 32-bit bus and can address up to 4GB of memory, although this can be effectively increased with memory management software. This chip is still in widespread use in currently working systems.

The 68030 can work with special memory schemes called *page-mode memory* and *virtual memory*. Page-mode memory compartmentalizes the data in RAM, so that the computer can work with it more quickly. Virtual memory allows disk space to be used as slow-access RAM with practically unlimited capacity.

The 68030 chip makes it possible to fully utilize Apple's revolutionary System 7. This facilitates *multitasking*. For example, print out one document while actively working on another.

The 68040. Also called the "sixty-eight forty," the 68040 improves further on the Motorola line of chips. The advance is of a similar magnitude to the leap from Intel's 80386 to the 486, although the details are somewhat different. The chip became popular in the Mac Centris, and also in the Quadra, both used extensively by businesses.

The 68040 lets the computer carry out an instruction in just a little more than one clock cycle. Compare this with four cycles for the 68000! The reason for this greater efficiency is the introduction of *parallel processing*. The number of instructions per second (IPS) that a 68040-based Mac can perform, per unit of time, is far greater than the IPS rating of a 68030-based Mac in most applications. The practical difference is greatest in applications requiring many instructions.

The 68040 retains the features that make the 68030 so useful, such as page-mode memory and virtual memory. In addition, the 68040 has 16 times as much cache memory as its predecessor. It also includes a coprocessor called a *floating-point unit (FPU)*.

The PowerPC series. Periodically, the architecture (design strategy) of a microprocessor must be significantly changed to keep pace with the demands of the computer market. The PowerPC chips, created by Motorola together with Apple and IBM, represent a radical change over the 68xxx series of microprocessors. New software is needed to take advantage of the capabilities of the new chips, but this should prove to be a small sacrifice in light of the benefits.

Perhaps the biggest difference between the PowerPC series and the 68xxx line is the introduction of *reduced-instruction-set-computing (RISC)* technology. Instructions in RISC are smaller than in the older *complex-instruction-set-computing (CISC)* design, with the result that more instructions can be done per unit of time because the machine finds them easier to do. The PowerPC chips can carry out more than one instruction for every cycle of the clock, which runs at 50 MHz or more. This arises from the chip's superscalar processor architecture.

The table is a summary of the characteristics of Motorola microprocessors. *See also* BUS, CLOCK SPEED, COPROCESSOR, GRAPHICAL USER INTERFACE, INTEL MICROPROCESSORS, MAC CLASSIC, MODULAR MAC LINE, MULTITASKING, PAGE-MODE MEMORY, POWERBOOK, POWERPC CHIP, QUADRA, RANDOM-ACCESS MEMORY, REDUCED INSTRUCTION SET COMPUTING, SYSTEM 7, *and* VIRTUAL MEMORY.

Motorola microprocessors feature summary

Number	Data bus	Memory	Clock speed
68000	16 bits external		
	32 bits internal	16 MB	8 MHz
68020	32 bits	8 MB*	16 MHz
68030	32 bits	8 GB**	>16 MHz
68040	32 bits	**	>16 MHz
PowerPC 601	64 bits	**	>50 MHz

* 4GB with System 7 software.
** Unlimited with virtual memory.

Mouse

A *mouse* is a pointing device commonly used with graphical interfaces such as Windows, OS/2, and the Macintosh system. When you slide the mouse around on a flat surface, a cursor or arrow moves around on the monitor screen, following right along. The process is so intuitive that most people can get the knack of it in a couple of minutes.

A mouse is about the size of a handheld calculator. A cord runs from the mouse to the computer. There are one, two, or three buttons on top of the mouse (see the drawing) used for clicking and double-clicking. When the cursor or arrow is in the spot you want, you click the mouse to make various things happen. For example, you might move an arrow to a box, click the mouse, and then drag the box to some other location on your screen. In this case, the click operation "attaches" the box to the arrow. Clicking the mouse again releases the box, so you can move the arrow around by itself again. You might click the mouse to highlight a certain icon, and then click again to execute the function. Some icons require only one click for execution, others require two.

A mouse needs an area at least eight to 10 inches square for easiest operation. If, for some reason, this space is not available, you might use a *trackball* as the pointing device instead. The operation of a mouse is enhanced by the use of a *mouse pad*. The pad aids in

MultiFinder

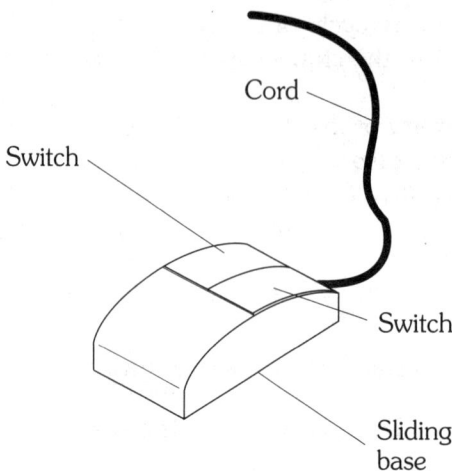

A mouse is a user-friendly computer-control device.

traction for the ball on the bottom of the mouse, minimizing "slippage" of the pointer or cursor. A mouse pad also protects the desk surface from being scratched by the mouse. *See also* GRAPHICAL USER INTERFACE, MENU-DRIVEN SOFTWARE, *and* TRACKBALL.

MultiFinder

In Macintosh computers, *MultiFinder* lets you work, to a limited extent, with more than one application simultaneously. Before the advent of System 7, MultiFinder was a separate, optional utility.

Working in just one application at a time is all right for some PC users. For example, if all you do is word processing, and if you aren't involved in desktop publishing, *Finder* alone might prove good enough for you. Eventually, however, you'll probably want a more powerful system if you graduate to more advanced software and applications.

MultiFinder provides improved operating flexibility over Finder. For example, you can print a document from your word processing files without having to leave whatever else (say, a spreadsheet) you're working on.

MultiFinder creates a distinction between *background processing* and *foreground processing*, but it's not quite as flexible as *multitasking*, in which a computer can actively carry on more than one application at a time. *See also* BACKGROUND PROCESSING, FINDER, FOREGROUND PROCESSING, MULTITASKING, *and* SYSTEM 7.

Multimedia

Multimedia refers to the use of stereo sound, animated video, and online services in conjunction with PCs. Multimedia turns a computer into an interactive gateway to information of all kinds.

Uses. Here are a few applications of multimedia as it exists today:

➤ *Entertainment* Multimedia is just plain fun. You can play sophisticated computer games, complete with animation and sound. You can watch a movie and play the role of one of the characters, taking an active part in the plot. You can use a musical instrument digital interface (MIDI) to compose a symphony and then play it back with a full orchestra.

➤ *Education* Multimedia can make all educational materials interactive. For example, you might put a CD-ROM into the computer and look up the term *hurricane*. You could then watch time-lapse satellite images, get narration explaining how the storms form, and finally watch and listen to the effects of 100-mile-an-hour winds.

➤ *In business* Multimedia is already starting to create work-at-home jobs. No longer is it always necessary to commute and pollute. If you run a business, you can have an online catalog. Your list of names and addresses can include animated audio-visual clips of your associates and friends.

➤ *Shopping* Multimedia is revolutionizing the way people shop for merchandise. Shoppers can select goods from animated catalogs. Online shopping is becoming more and more common. Interactive television sets allow people to order merchandise directly from commercials: the ultimate in impulse buying.

Components. A good multimedia system needs certain hardware and software. The most common items (and a few less common ones) are as follows:

➤ *Computer* To get active in multimedia, you'll need a PC with a powerful microprocessor. The chip should be at least an Intel 80486 or a Motorola 68040. For better results, you should have a PC with a Pentium or PowerPC chip.

➤ *Memory* Your random-access memory (RAM) should have several megabytes (MB) of capacity. While you might get by with 4MB, it's better to have at least 8MB.

➤ *Hard disk* The hard disk should be state-of-the-art, and the bigger, the better. Generally, desktop computers have somewhat larger hard disk systems than laptop (notebook) PCs. A minimal requirement is 30MB of available disk space, but it's best to have 50MB or more available. This will not be a problem with new computers, virtually all of which have total hard disk storage in excess of 200MB.

➤ *Diskette drive* You'll need a 3.5-inch, high-density diskette drive in your computer. (That's the smaller of the two standard diskette sizes. The other is 5.25 inches, and is less widely used.) It's better to have two magnetic diskette drives, one for 3.5-inch

Multimedia

diskettes and the other for 5.25-inch diskettes. A single 3.5-inch high-density diskette holds 1.44MB of data.

➢ *Graphical interface* The computer will require software with a graphical user interface (GUI) such as Windows, OS/2, or the Macintosh system. A mouse is also necessary.

➢ *Monitor* You'll want the best monitor you can get. A 17-inch screen with true color (over a million different colors), and the accompanying video board, will ensure that you get a picture worthy of the images the monitor receives from the computer.

➢ *Sound equipment* You'll need a sound board and speakers. There are many different sound boards available, varying greatly in price. The most important thing is that the board be compatible with the computer. Large speakers can be fun, but they're not essential. If you want big sound, you might need a separate audio amplifier. You should also get headphones for those times when your family or neighbors don't want to listen to your computer.

➢ *CD-ROM* You'll need a CD-ROM drive, so that you can have access to the rapidly growing number of applications, games, and publications available on compact discs. CD-ROMs, which can store upwards of 650MB, are extensively used with graphics, animation, and sound. If you're buying a new computer, consider one with an internal CD-ROM drive.

➢ *Modem* If you want to interact online, you'll need a good, fast modem. You'll also need the software to go with it. Most modems come with the software. Be sure to get the fastest modem your system and telephone line can work with. If you're buying a new computer, consider one with an internal modem.

➢ *Television* If you want to incorporate television, you'll need the requisite receiving equipment, including, if it is your wish, a satellite dish and converter. A color television set is preferable to black-and-white. The larger and more expensive sets will work better than smaller, cheaper ones. With the advent of high-definition television (HDTV), the prospects for TV/PC multimedia are improving. Some people think that TVs and PCs will eventually merge.

For a moment, daydream about the ultimate multimedia system. It would have all of the abovementioned components, with a big-screen projection system for the video, and amplifiers for the four massive speakers. You might recline in an oversize chair, dim the lights, place your keyboard on your lap, and slide your mouse around on a board next to you. If you got tired of looking at the big screen and shaking the walls with audio, you could don a virtual-reality helmet and headphones. The drawing is a block diagram of a typical (but by no means ultimate) multimedia system.

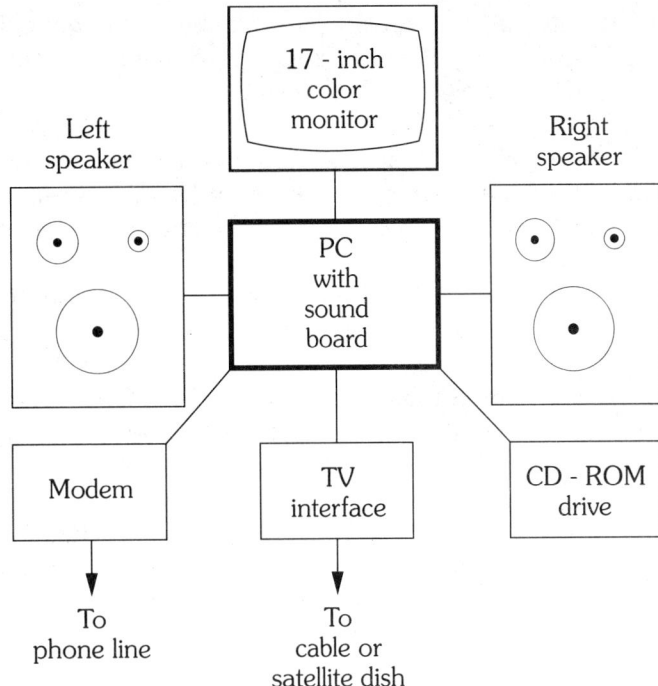

Block diagram of a typical multimedia installation.

Availability and cost. One problem noted with computer technology in general, and multimedia in particular, is its tendency to widen the gap between economic classes. Multimedia equipment, and the attendant software can cost serious money. A system like the "ultimate" one described here is an extreme example; it would cost over $20,000. A more typical price tag for a multimedia setup, such as the one in the block diagram, is $3000 to $6000.

Rich schools can afford numerous multimedia stations to help educate their students, while poorer schools can afford less equipment, or none at all. That's a tragedy, because inherent genius bears no relation to income. If society is to get the most benefit from multimedia, it must be made available to everyone. *See also* CD-ROM, GRAPHICAL USER INTERFACE, HARD DISK, INTERACTIVE TECHNOLOGY, MODEM, MONITOR, RANDOM-ACCESS MEMORY, SATELLITE DATA TRANSMISSION, SOUND TECHNOLOGY, *and* VIRTUAL REALITY.

Multipart forms

Suppose you've written a long manual, and you want to make several copies of it. It's 950 pages long, double-spaced so that you and your boss can edit it. You want to give one copy to your boss, keep another to review yourself, and give a third to your assistant to file.

Options. You might run off one original with your printer, and take this to a print shop, asking for two collated copies. Most good print shops can do this for anywhere from seven to 15 cents per page. This can be a good solution to a problem like this, but it can get expensive. You'd prefer to go a cheaper route. You're also nervous about leaving your document with people you don't know.

Multipart forms might be the answer to your dilemma. These consist of fanfold paper with two, three, four, or even five layers. All the layers except the back layer have pressure-sensitive material on them.

When multipart forms are used with a dot-matrix printer, the pressure from the print head will cause the text to appear on all the copies. You can use them for receipts, invoices, schedules, and whenever you need "carbon" copies. If you buy multipart forms in bulk at an office-supply store, you can expect to pay less than two cents per page (not including the cost of the printer ribbon you use up).

Limitations. Multipart forms represent a convenient, cheap alternative to photocopying, but there are some problems. First, the print quality is not the best. Most multipart forms produce copies in a blue-gray shade that isn't dark or crisp. This might be fine for you and your assistant, but give the original to your boss!

The second problem is that it takes a while to separate the pages and stack them up. If your 950-page manual is broken into 19 chapters of 50 pages each, you'd probably want to print each chapter, tearing off the perforated edges, separating the pages, and collating the copies. This will become tedious long before you're finished.

Another problem is that, when you make several thousand rips in pieces of paper, you'll get paper dust on your desk, fingers, clothes, chair, and floor. You can also expect a few "perf-paper holes" to be scattered around your workstation.

Multipart forms will not work with laser printers or inkjet printers because pressure is necessary to make the copies. Dot-matrix printers are required. This is not normally a problem for plain text, but for high-quality print or graphics, it's better to make individual copies or go to a good print shop.

Some laser printers can do double-duty as photocopy machines so you can make your copies at your desk. They cost more to operate, however, than dot-matrix printers with multipart forms. *See also* DOT-MATRIX PRINTER, FANFOLD PAPER, *and* LASER PRINTER.

Multiplatform environment

Microcomputers fall into two general families: IBM-compatible and Macintosh. There are many different computer models, of varying power, in both families. A *multiplatform environment* allows you to work in both the Mac and the IBM computing environments.

Multiplatform environment

Problems. It used to be common to be inconvenienced by the incompatibility between Mac and IBM. It was as if one system worked in English, and the other in Chinese. In fact, in some ways, the chasm was even wider than the language barrier between Boston and Beijing.

If you took a Mac disk and put it into the drive for an IBM-compatible machine, you might be able to open files, but all you'd see would be "hieroglyphics." Similar problems awaited those who took IBM disks and put them into Mac drives.

Eventually, programs were developed so that Mac data could be converted into IBM format, and vice-versa. Two such systems are the *Apple File Exchange* and the *Macintosh PC Exchange*, both developed by Apple. The translation software makes it possible for Macs to read IBM data, and vice-versa. (All Macs use 3.5-inch diskette drives, so you must have a 3.5-inch drive in the IBM machine to transfer data.) This is not the same, however, as running Windows on a Mac, or System 7 on an IBM clone.

Apple has a reputation for innovation. They captured a portion of the market and have kept their customers. It has been said that IBM users can be persuaded to switch to Mac once in awhile, but devoted Mac users stick with Apple no matter what. Apple and IBM are both starting to see that there's something to be gained from some standardization between their systems. While the two companies compete, they can cooperate also, making things better for both groups of users.

Native versus nonnative. When an application is foreign to the operating system—IBM software in a Mac, or Mac software in an IBM—it is called a *nonnative application.* Increasingly, both Macs and IBM clones are being designed with nonnative application capability as a standard feature. This is not without its difficulties because Intel microprocessors and Motorola microprocessors have different architectures. The contrast runs deeper than mere operating-system language; it's as if the hardware, as well as the software, for the two systems evolved on different continents.

One especially nagging problem is operating speed. Translating between hardware and software platforms involves steps or instructions that would not be necessary if the PC were working in a native application. If you want to run DOS on a Mac, for example, the Mac must be "coached" in command-driven software, the very thing the whole Mac line was designed to do away with! Nor is it any easier for a Mac to run, say, Microsoft Windows. It takes time to adjust.

Because of the extra steps, Macs run more slowly when working in IBM applications than when using the programs they were designed to work with. The same thing happens when you use an IBM to run Macintosh applications. In the future, as microprocessors become faster and software evolves along with them, these speed problems should gradually diminish. *See also* IBM-COMPATIBLE PCS, INTEL MICROPROCESSORS, MACINTOSH, *and* MOTOROLA MICROPROCESSORS.

Multiplexing

Multiplexing is the transmission of two or more messages over the same line or channel at the same time. Multiplex transmission is done in various ways. The most common methods are *frequency-division multiplex* and *time-division multiplex*.

Frequency division. Any channel can be broken down into subchannels. Suppose a channel is 24 kilohertz (KHz) wide. It can theoretically hold eight signals that are 3 KHz wide. The frequencies of the signals must be just right, so they don't overlap. Usually there is a little extra space on either side of each subchannel to ensure that overlapping does not occur. The drawing shows six, 3-KHz signals in a 24-KHz channel.

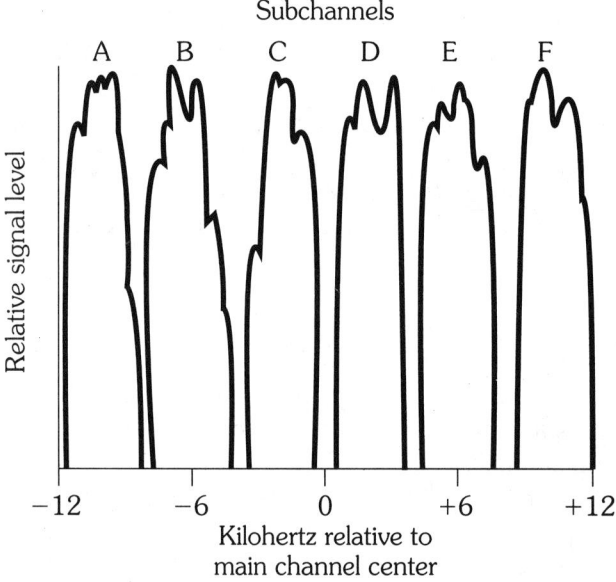

Multiplexing independent subchannels within a main channel.

Time division. Sometimes, data is cumbersome to transmit in parallel form. It can then be converted to serial form using time-division multiplex. In this mode, signals are broken into pieces "timewise," and then the pieces are sent in a rotating sequence. This slows the rate of data transfer by a factor equal to the number of signals. For example, if each of six messages is one second long sent by itself at full speed, the time-division-multiplexed signal will take six seconds. *See also* BANDWIDTH, DEMULTIPLEXING, PARALLEL, *and* SERIAL.

Multiprocessor

In some computing situations, two or more identical microprocessor chips can be combined to get more speed and power than one chip alone can provide. Such an arrangement is called a *multiprocessor*. This is sometimes abbreviated *MP*.

Two halves of a brain. Perhaps you've heard that one half of your brain is good at logic, science, and mathematics, while the other side contains the centers for artistic expression. According to this theory, some people are "left-brain dominant" and others are "right-brain dominant," but both halves are important in every person. You might think of your brain as a microprocessor with two chips. One chip performs the work of balancing your checkbook, working with computer programs, and other tasks that require rational thinking. The other chip comes into play when you paint portraits, listen to music, or make wood carvings. You wouldn't be a complete person without both of these chips.

A PC with two microprocessors works something like a brain with two lobes. With computers, however, it's possible to have three, four, or more chips in tandem. In this way, computers differ from your brain. Also, a computer can get along quite well with just one microprocessor for most applications. Only high-end power users, or groups of people using a single computer simultaneously, really need to think about whether a second processor is necessary.

Four-wheel drive. When microprocessors are combined to get extra computing power, they tend to compete for the available memory. This can be overcome by *memory-management software*, although the problem gets harder to deal with as the number of chips increases. The law of diminishing returns seems to apply here: there is less and less improvement in performance with the addition of each new chip. Most multiprocessors, therefore, employ two chips. The drawing is a simplified block diagram of a PC using two microprocessors.

In tests with multiprocessing, it has been found that two chips won't necessarily double the speed and power of a computer. It depends on the application, on the sophistication of the software, and on the number of people using the computer at the same time. Think of a dual-processor system as being akin to four-wheel drive, while a single-processor system is like two-wheel drive. Four-wheel drive will yield dramatic improvement in some environments, but in other situations it will only burn more gasoline.

Consider the case of someone who is writing a report on a word processor. In a situation like this, there's no use for a second microprocessor. If the user wants more speed and power, the existing system can be more effectively upgraded by increasing the clock speed, adding extra RAM (random-access memory), and installing a larger hard disk.

Multitasking

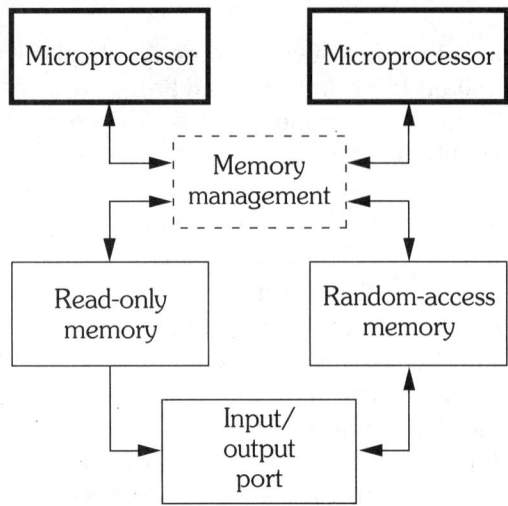

A simplified diagram of a computer with two microprocessors.

In a multiuser system such as an *application server*, in which several people use a computer for different purposes, a multiprocessor can make a big difference over a single chip of the same sophistication. Another scenario where a multiprocessor can be useful is the case of a power user running two or more applications simultaneously, using high-end software for both. *See also* CENTRAL PROCESSING UNIT, MEMORY-MANAGEMENT SOFTWARE, MICROPROCESSOR, MULTIUSER SYSTEM, *and* UPGRADING.

Multitasking

Multitasking is the ability of a computer to do more than one thing at a time. True multitasking can be done in the same or different applications. The execution of one process does not cause the other one to be put on "hold," although there may be brief interruptions.

The drawing illustrates an example of multitasking. The user is working on a database, which appears on the monitor and occupies RAM (random-access memory). The database is in the foreground. At the same time, a document file is being transferred from the diskette drive to the printer. This word processing application is in the background.

In some computers, you might notice periodic hesitations in the foreground process when multitasking because the central processing unit must periodically shift its attention away from the foreground to execute part, or all, of the background process. This hesitation, if it occurs, is most noticeable when the background process is long or involved. For example, if the document being sent to the printer in the background were 100K long, the hesitation would be more noticeable than it would be if the document were just 1K long.

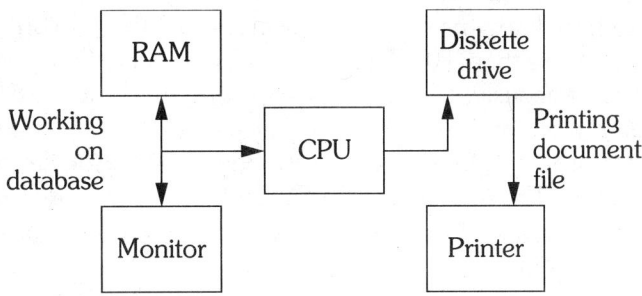

Running two programs at once.

In advanced computers using state-of-the-art microprocessors, multitasking is done without noticeable hesitation, both because the chip works fast and because it can actually "think" about two things at once, without having to alternate back and forth between the processes. It's even possible in some systems to work with three or more files at the same time. For example, a computer might be drawing a diagram via a graphics program (the foreground process), printing a document (first background process), and sending another document over a modem (second background process), all at once. *See also* BACKGROUND PROCESSING *and* FOREGROUND PROCESSING.

Multiuser system

In small businesses and some educational situations, there are times when it's convenient to make one computer available to several people at once. This can be done with PCs having microprocessors at least as advanced as the Intel 80486 or the Motorola 68040.

The drawing shows a block diagram of a *multiuser system* incorporating one PC and three dumb terminals. The primary user, #1, sits at the computer console. The other users, #2, #3, and #4, sit at terminals connected to the PC. The computer's central processing unit (CPU) rotates its attention rapidly around the group of users. Thus, each user gets the feeling of sitting at a computer that's one-fourth as fast, and one-fourth as powerful, as the PC would be with only one user.

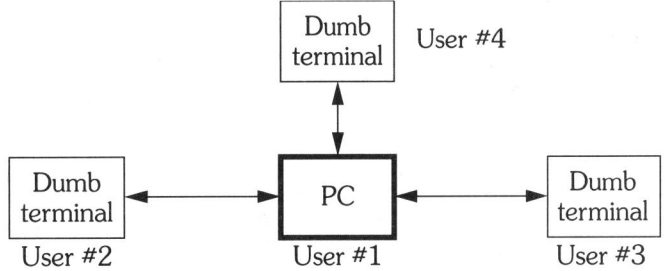

A multiuser system allows several people to use one computer.

Multivariable function graph

The example here happens to show four users, but there might be as few as two, or more than 100. The more people who use a given computer simultaneously, the more powerful the machine must be for good results. If there are more than four or five users in a system, a minicomputer or mainframe is needed for adequate performance at each workstation. The definitions of PC, minicomputer, and mainframe are not etched in stone; the general perception changes as computers become faster and more powerful at all levels. In particular, the distinction between minicomputers and mainframes has begun to blur.

If you have a small, fast-growing business, you might consider installing a local area network (LAN). This is a flexible, expandable multiuser system. Both IBM-compatible and Macintosh LANs are available. *See also* DUMB TERMINAL, LOCAL AREA NETWORK, MAINFRAME, *and* MINICOMPUTER.

Multivariable function graph

A *multivariable function graph* shows a relation in which some quantity depends on two or more factors. Multivariable functions have several independent variables and one dependent variable.

Graphing two-variable functions can be done in two or three dimensions. Usually, two-dimensional (2-D) renditions are less complete than three-dimensional (3-D) versions. The rendering of functions with more than two independent variables is complicated and difficult.

The 2-D method. Drawing A shows an example of a two-variable function, graphed in 2-D rectangular coordinates. The dependent variable is the peak audio power that a hypothetical hi-fi amplifier can produce. It is depicted on the vertical axis. There are two independent variables: duty cycle and temperature. The duty cycle is plotted on the horizontal axis, from zero (always off) upwards through 50 percent (on half the time) to a maximum of 100 percent (on all the time). There are several curves on this graph. Each curve represents the power versus duty cycle for a certain temperature. These curves are labeled according to temperature in degrees Celsius.

You can tell certain things from this graph. The higher the duty cycle, the less peak power the hi-fi amplifier can produce. Also, the higher the temperature, the less power is available at a given duty cycle. This graph does not tell the whole story because it shows curves only for certain temperatures. However, you can use interpolation to get a good idea of the functions for temperatures between those represented by the curves.

The 3-D method. Drawing B shows a coordinate three-space that lets you obtain a complete graph of the power function for the amplifier described above. In this graph, the dependent variable (peak

Multivariable function graph

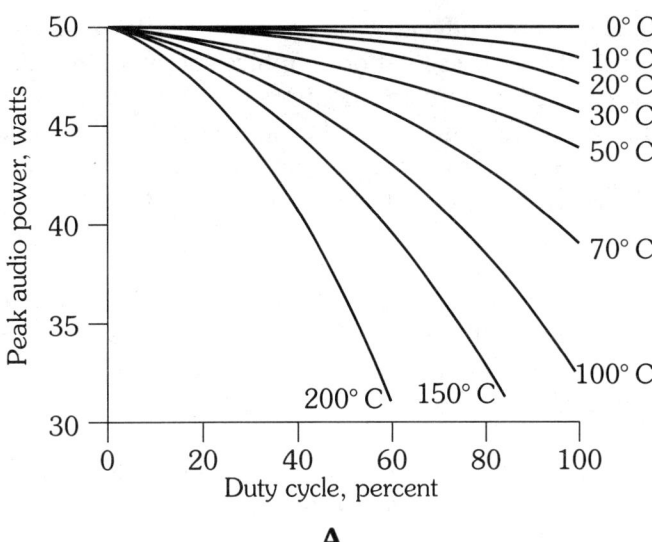

A family of curves.

power output) is plotted on the vertical axis. Duty cycle is on one of the horizontal axes, and temperature is on the other. The temperature axis is meant to recede away from the viewer. In perspective, this makes it seem to go off at an angle. This kind of perspective rendition is common.

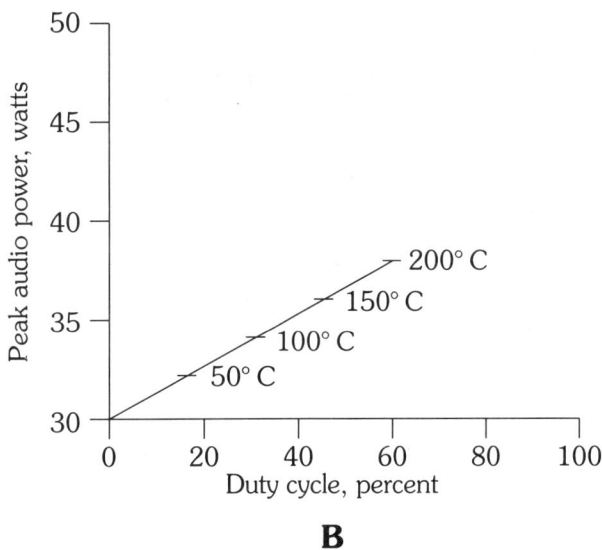

A three-dimensional coordinate space.

The function itself is not shown in the drawing; it is a complex surface. The computer would portray it as a sort of "warped fishnet." You've probably seen such graphs in advertisements for scientific graphics software.

Portraying 3-D graphs effectively is one of the major assets of good analytical graphics or presentation graphics software. You've probably seen surfaces graphed on color monitors or printed with laser printers. While such graphs can have a spectacular appearance, it is usually hard to interpolate values using the graphs alone. For precise data, you must have the computer give you actual coordinate values.

More than 3-D. For functions having more than two independent variables, graphs become increasingly hard to portray in ways that human beings can understand. A function with three independent variables needs four dimensions to be fully rendered; a function with four independent variables needs five dimensions, and so on.

Computers can handle any number of dimensions, but human beings can't directly envision more than three. One of the biggest challenges in graphics is finding ways to make hyperdimensional (4-D or more) graphs that people can comprehend. *See also* ANALYTICAL GRAPHICS *and* PRESENTATION GRAPHICS.

Murphy's Laws

You've probably heard the saying, "If something can go wrong, it will." This epitomizes *Murphy's Laws*, a set of principles that sometimes seem to govern all human affairs. Murphy's Laws are supposed to be jokes, but once in a while, especially with computers, events make it seem as if Murphy's Laws represent some fundamental, sinister truth about the universe.

For hardware. Here are a few examples of Murphy's Laws relative to the electronics and mechanics of computer hardware:

- *Law of Inconvenient Malfunction*: A device will fail at the least opportune possible moment.

- *Law of Cable Compatibility*: If you choose a cable and a connector at random, the probability that they are compatible is equal to zero.

- *Law of Hardware Compatibility*: The probability of a given peripheral being compatible with a PC is inversely proportional to the immediate need for that peripheral.

- *Law of Bad Sectors*: The probability that an untested diskette will have bad sectors is directly proportional to the importance of the data written onto the diskette.

- *First Law of Selective Gravitation*: When an object is dropped, it will fall in such a way as to cause the greatest possible damage to itself and/or other objects on which it lands.

- *Second Law of Selective Gravitation*: The tendency for an object to be dropped is directly proportional to its value.

- *Law of Reality Change*: Unalterable hardware specifications will change as necessary to maximize frustration for personnel affected by said specifications.

- *Law of Noise*: Noise bursts occur so as to cause the most serious errors in data communications, regardless of the actual amount of noise present.

- *Law of Expectation*: Consumer expectations always outpace advances in hardware technology.

- *Law of the Titanic*: If a device cannot malfunction, it will.

For software. Here are a few greatly simplified examples of Murphy's Laws as they relate to PC software:

- *Law of Debugging*: The difficulty of debugging software is directly proportional to the number of people who will ultimately use it.

- *Law of Neurosis*: The chances of software being neurotic (developing bugs spontaneously without apparent reason) is directly proportional to the confusion such neurosis can cause.

- *Law of Available Space*: If there are n bytes in a crucial software program, the available space for its convenient storage or loading is equal to $n-1$ bytes.

- *First Law of Bad Sectors*: The probability of software being mutilated by bad sectors is directly proportional to the value and importance of the programs.

- *Second Law of Bad Sectors*: When a program is mutilated by bad sectors, the damage will occur at the points that result in the most frequent and severe errors when the program is run.

- *Law of Noise*: When a downloaded program is corrupted by noise, the corruption will occur at the points that result in the most frequent and severe errors when the program is run.

- *Law of Software Compatibility*: If two programs are chosen at random, the probability that they are compatible is equal to zero.

- *Law of Option Preferences*: When two people share a computer, their software option preferences will differ in every possible way.

- *Law of Expectation*: Consumer expectations always outpace advances in software technology.

- *Law of the Titanic*: Bug-free software isn't.

As you gain experience in personal computing, you'll discover, and learn to live with, most aspects of Murphy's Laws. It's best that way. If computer novices were fully aware of all the things that could go

Musical Instrument Digital Interface

wrong, they might avoid PCs altogether. Then they'd miss out on all the benefits, and all the fun, of personal computing.

Musical Instrument Digital Interface

Musical Instrument Digital Interface, more commonly called by its acronym, *MIDI*, is a language used in electronic music. A computer can be used with MIDI to compose, edit, store, transmit, or download electronic music. The tunes can be as simple as "do-re-mi" or as complex as Beethoven's Fifth Symphony.

A MIDI tells the computer when to play a note, how long to play it, and how loud to play it. It also sets the tempo of the music, based on how long a quarter-note lasts. A MIDI is something like the roll of paper that runs through an old-fashioned player piano, except that MIDI is electronic rather than mechanical, and MIDI is much more versatile and expanded. MIDI controls the operation of a musical synthesizer, and also allows two or more synthesizers to communicate.

Sound synthesis. Most people hear synthesized music every day; virtually all pop music includes it. Music synthesizers have evolved that can produce all possible sounds. MIDI does not actually generate the sound; it is a protocol that tells the computer what to do with synthesized sound.

If you were to connect a microphone to an oscilloscope, you would see that different sounds have different waveforms. This is particularly noticeable with musical instruments playing a single note. Suppose, for example, that you play middle C on a piano. You note the waveform on the oscilloscope screen. If you play middle C on a clarinet, you'll get a different waveshape. A trombone will produce still another wave. The nature of any sound depends on its waveform.

Now imagine this process in reverse. Instead of playing an instrument and looking at the wave, you draw the wave, perhaps with a mouse and graphics software, then you feed the waveform to a synthesizer. If you draw the waveshape you saw when you played the clarinet, you'll get a clarinet sound from the synthesizer. If you draw the trumpet wave, you'll get a trumpet sound. You can draw waveshapes that do not resemble those of known musical instruments and get notes that don't sound like any instrument you've ever heard, but you can still make them into music.

Next best thing. MIDI programs do not, in general, let you draw any waveshape you want and then play it. That is the job of the synthesizer and its associated software. A typical MIDI gives you control over the sounds produced by a synthesizer. Some synthesizers can produce only a few waveforms, representing the more well-known musical instruments such as the piano, clarinet, and trumpet. Others include such exotic sounds as bongo drums, balalaika, sitar, chirping birds, or baying wolves.

Musical Instrument Digital Interface

Using MIDI with a good synthesizer is like playing a computer game, except that you have more control over the results. Have you ever heard a song in your head, and been convinced that if it were played by a jazz band, rock group, or other combo, it would hit the charts? MIDI can let you hear your tune. You can change the key, the loudness, or the rhythm at will, without having to blow a single horn or twitch even one trumpet valve to do it. It can all be done using a PC and certain peripherals, along with MIDI software.

Even if you're not musically inclined, playing with MIDI can teach you about music. You'll learn the relative pitches (frequencies) of the notes on the treble and bass clefs. You'll also gain an intuitive understanding of which instruments sound best with which types of music. MIDI can become addictive; once you start playing it, you might find it hard to stop.

Computer music system. The drawing is a block diagram of a PC music system. There are, of course, the computer, monitor, modem, printer, and diskette drive. But in addition, there is a MIDI processing unit, a MIDI keyboard (resembling an electronic organ), and at least one MIDI sound module.

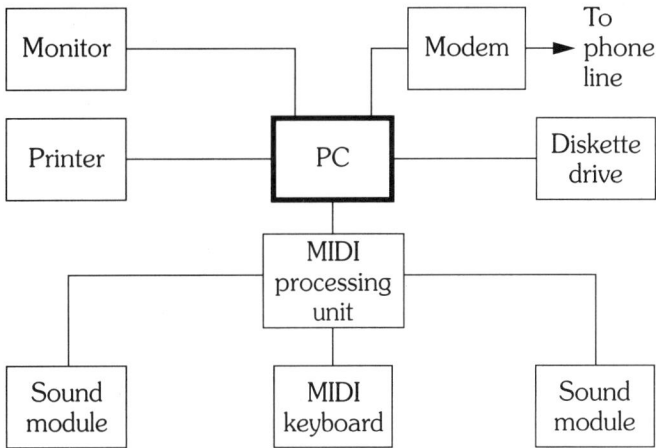

A block diagram of a typical computerized MIDI system.

Composing a piece is as simple as playing each part on the keyboard and programming these parts into the computer. In this way, you can produce the melody and all the harmony, written into your computer's digital memory. The waveforms of music, no matter how complex they might be, are all converted into digital signals (high and low, or logic 1 and 0). That way, they can be held in RAM, on your hard disk, on diskettes, or on any other medium that will accept computer data. They can also be sent and received via modem.

For further information. The best way to get involved in MIDI is to witness it for yourself. Find a "PC guru" friend, or an amicable

Musical Instrument Digital Interface

computer dealer, who will let you play around with his or her MIDI system. After that, you will either be incurably hooked, or you'll decide that other facets of computing are more worthy of your time.

In the event the MIDI bug does bite you, you'll have no trouble getting familiar with it. Self-teaching is a great way to get good at MIDI; your local college or trade school might also offer MIDI courses. *See also* SOUND TECHNOLOGY.

NAND gate

A *NAND gate* is a logical AND gate followed by an inverter. The term *NAND* is a contraction of *not and*.

In a NAND gate, there are two or more inputs and one output. The output is a predictable logical function of the inputs. The drawing shows the schematic symbol for a two-input NAND gate, along with a truth table indicating the output as a function of the inputs.

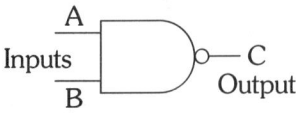

A	B	C
0	0	1
0	1	1
1	0	1
1	1	0

The schematic symbol and truth table of a NAND gate.

The output of a NAND gate is exactly reversed from that of an AND gate. When both or all of the inputs of the NAND gate are one, the output is zero. If one or more of the inputs are zero, the output is one. *See also* AND GATE, EXCLUSIVE-OR GATE, EXCLUSIVE-NOR GATE, INVERTER, LOGIC GATES, NOR GATE, *and* OR GATE.

Nanosecond

A *nanosecond* (ns) is an extremely short length of time, equal to just one-billionth (0.000000001 or 10^{-9}) of a second. In a nanosecond, even the fastest PC's clock can complete only a fraction of a cycle, and a ray of light travels only a foot through clear air or free space. An electric current in a wire goes only a little more than an inch in one nanosecond.

Nanoseconds are important when talking about processes within computer components. When 10 MIPS (ten million instructions per second) are being carried out by your PC's central processing unit, you might say that a single instruction takes 100 ns. The faster and more powerful the microprocessor, the shorter the time per instruction.

A machine working at 100 MIPS takes 10 ns to complete a single instruction. At 1000 MIPS, or 1 GIPS (one billion instruction per second), the time per instruction is down to 1 ns. There are microprocessors available today that can execute well over 1 GIPS. *See also* COMPUTER POWER *and* INSTRUCTIONS PER SECOND.

Nanotechnology

Nanotechnology is the science of superminiature electronic and mechanical devices. In this context, the prefix *nano* means extremely small (it can also mean one billionth, or 10^{-9}).

Nanochips. Computer researchers are always striving to get more "brain" into less space. This means superminiaturization of electronic components. Nanotechnology is important to the development of artificial intelligence, especially if the intelligence is to approach that of a human being.

There is a practical limit to how many logic gates or switches can be etched onto a silicon chip of a given size. This limit depends on the precision of the manufacturing process. As methods have improved, the density of logic gates on a single chip has increased. It has been suggested that, rather than etching the logic gates into silicon to make computer chips, the problem can be tackled from the opposite angle. Is it possible to build nanochips atom by atom? This process might result in the greatest possible number of logic gates or switches in a given volume of space.

Nanorobots. Superminiature, computer-controlled machines called *nanorobots* might find all sorts of exotic applications. An engineer named Eric Drexler has suggested that such machines might serve as programmable antibodies, searching out and destroying harmful bacteria and viruses in the human body. In this way, diseases could be cured; as new strains of malady evolved, the nanorobots could be reprogrammed. Perhaps nanorobotic antibodies could even be controlled by a central computer, implanted within the body, containing programs that would adapt to changes in bacterial and viral characteristics.

There is a dark side to this technology. For one thing, it would be expensive. Critics denounce it, saying it would exacerbate "unnatural selection" that gives wealthy people superior medical care, and therefore improved disease survival rates, compared with everyone else. Proponents of the technology counter by pointing out that this situation is nothing new; it should not deter scientists from future medical research any more than it has prevented progress in the past. A more serious concern is that programmable antibodies could, if they got into the hands of the wrong people, be used as biological weapons. See also ARTIFICIAL INTELLIGENCE, BIOCHIP, and MOLECULAR COMPUTER TECHNOLOGY.

Natural language

A *natural language* is a spoken or written language commonly used by people. Examples are English, Spanish, Russian, and Chinese. Natural languages differ from high-level computer programming languages and machine language.

In the future, it will become increasingly important that computers speak, display, and understand natural languages to the greatest possible extent. This will allow people to use computers regardless of their experience level. Specialized language structure requirements will be eliminated; you will be able to communicate with PCs just as you converse with other people.

Audio natural-language capability is known as *speech recognition* and *speech synthesis*. These features are important to visually handicapped people, and also to people who use computers in environments where it is impossible to work with a keyboard and display.

Natural language will play a major role in the future of robotics. If you want your robot to get a cup of water, for example, you would like to tell it, "Please get me a cup of water." You don't want to have to type a long string of numbers, letters, and punctuation marks on a terminal, or point and click on a dozen icons, or speak in some bizarre "computerese" that is nothing like normal talk. See also HIGH-LEVEL LANGUAGE, MACHINE LANGUAGE, PERSONAL ROBOTS, SPEECH RECOGNITION, and SPEECH SYNTHESIS.

Nested loops

A *loop* is a logical process, or a set of computer program steps, that is repeated twice or more. Sometimes, loops occur inside of other loops. These are known as *nested loops*.

Network

The smaller loop in a nest usually involves fewer steps per repetition than the larger loop, but the number of times the loop is followed has nothing to do with the number of steps it contains. A small, secondary loop might be repeated a million times, while the larger loop surrounding it is repeated only 100 times.

The drawing is a flowchart that shows a simple example of nesting. Squares indicate procedural steps, such as "Multiply by three and then add two." Diamonds are IF/THEN/ELSE steps, which are crucial to any loop. The query symbols inside the diamonds mean that a question is being asked, such as "Is X greater than 587?" The minus sign by a diamond is like a "No" to the question, in which case the process must go back to some earlier point. The plus sign is like a "Yes," telling the process to go on ahead.

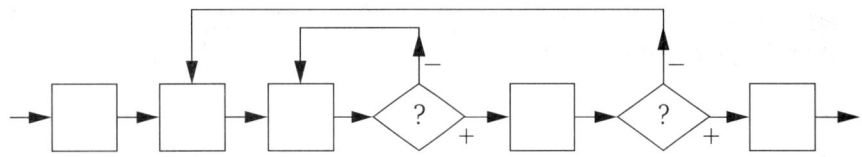

A loop within a loop.

Nested loops are common in computer programs, especially when there are complicated mathematical calculations. Nesting of thought loops probably also occurs in the human mind. This is of interest to researchers in artificial intelligence (AI). The reconstruction of human thought processes could reveal fantastic logical twists, more strange than science fiction—assuming it is *even* possible to break human thought down into purely logical steps. (Some scientists think it can't be done.) Any attempt at computer modeling of human thought will almost certainly require the use of several orders of loop nesting. *See also* ARTIFICIAL INTELLIGENCE, IF/THEN/ELSE, *and* LOOP.

Network

A group of computers and dumb terminals, capable of communicating with each other or with a central mainframe or minicomputer, is called a *network*. There are various ways in which workstations can be interconnected to form a network. The way in which the nodes of a network are arranged is called the *network topology*.

A network that covers a small geographic area, and whose users are limited to a single office, department, or building, is called a *local area network (LAN)*. A large network, spanning cities, countries, or even the world, is called a *wide-area network (WAN)*. See also LOCAL AREA NETWORK *and* WIDE AREA NETWORK.

Uses. Networking is one of the most popular uses of personal computing. A device called a *modem* allows a PC to be hooked into the telephone lines. Sometimes radio communication is used instead of the telephone. By accessing a network, you can get all kinds of information. There are networks devoted to special interests, such as the environment, medicine, robotics, and artificial intelligence. Consumer networks are commonly known as *online services*. Radio amateurs have networks that operate using *packet communications*.

Businesses, educational institutions, and government agencies make extensive use of computer networks. If you want to rent an apartment, for example, the landlord might first check your credit rating through any of several different networks. If you get pulled over for going through a stop sign, the police officer can run your driver's license number through a network to see if you have a criminal record.

Assets. One of the big assets of networking is that it makes a single computer or terminal enormously powerful. For a modest amount of money, anybody can have access to huge reserves of information. Any PC can become artificially intelligent, in the sense that it "knows" whatever data it can access.

Networks make it possible for people, companies, schools, and governments to efficiently communicate more quickly and more cheaply than ever before possible. *Bulletin board systems (BBSs)* allow you to leave and retrieve messages for and from friends and colleagues. *Electronic mail*, also called *e-mail*, is another method of computer communications that offers somewhat more privacy than a BBS. You can communicate with other PC users in real-time via *network conferencing*. A specialized conference group is called a *network forum*. See also BULLETIN-BOARD SYSTEM *and* ELECTRONIC MAIL.

Liabilities. There are problems with networks. Sometimes, data is not updated often enough to keep it accurate. Errors can occur, and the more data you access, the greater the chance for your using an inaccurate piece of information.

If a mistaken piece of information about someone gets into a network, it can be practically impossible to correct. Suppose a "fact" gets circulated stating that John Doe defaulted on a loan from XYZ Bank. This goes into a credit network. It might be downloaded onto hundreds of diskettes, printed in hardcopy form, stashed in manila folders, and placed in file cabinets all over the country. The problem: John Doe has never defaulted on a loan in his life. Lawyers can't always resolve such a situation, but they can try. The lawsuit potential is staggering in cases like this.

Another problem with networks is that data can be used to injure people by accessing supposedly private information, and then giving or selling it to other people. It's not too difficult for people to get, misuse, or change information that is none of their business. As networks grow in the future, legislation will be needed to prevent their misuse, and enforcement will be needed to make sure the laws are complied with. There will be plenty of work for attorneys and government-employed "cybersnoops" (good hackers). *See also* INFORMATION SUPERHIGHWAY, INTERNET, MODEM, ONLINE SERVICE, *and* PACKET COMMUNICATIONS.

Neural network

The term *neural network* refers to any of several forms of *alternative computer technology*. The basic idea behind all neural networks is to mimic the workings of the human brain.

Assets. Compared with digital computers, neural networks are fast. They zip to their conclusions far more rapidly than the most powerful digital machines.

Neural networks are good at things like pattern and speech recognition. They can take small bits of information about an object, sound, or other complex thing, and fill in the gaps to get the whole. This was vividly demonstrated when an early version of a neural network took a 20% complete radar image of a jet plane and, on the basis of that data, produced a complete graphic of the type of aircraft that caused the echoes. If you've ever had your memory "jogged" by some little sight, sound, or taste, bringing back a whole scene to your mind, then you know basically how a neural network fills in missing pieces of information.

Neural networks can also learn from their mistakes, improving their performance with practice. They also exhibit *graceful degradation*, so that if part of the system is destroyed, the rest can keep things going at a slower speed or with less accuracy.

Limitations. Neural networks are imprecise. If you ask one to balance your checkbook, it will come close, but it will not give an exact answer. It wasn't designed to do calculations of the sort a digital computer can carry out. A dime-store calculator will outperform even the most complex neural network at basic arithmetic. In that sense, neural network technology resembles analog computer technology.

Another weakness of neural networks arises from the fact that they must inevitably make mistakes as they zero in on their conclusions. Digital machines break things or problems down into minuscule pieces, meticulously grinding out a solution to a level of exactness limited only by the number of transistors that can be fabricated onto a chip of silicon. Neural networks tackle problems as a whole, modifying their outlook until the results satisfy certain conditions.

One might make the generalization that digital computers are analytical, while neural networks are intuitive.

Fuzzy logic. Digital machines recognize, at the fundamental level, two conditions or states: logic 1 and logic 0. These two logic states can be specified in terms of high/low, true/false, plus/minus, yes/no, red/green, up/down, front/back, or any other clear-cut dichotomy. No matter how sublime your PC might seem to be as it renders music, photographs, programs, or graphics, it all boils down to a complex combination of binary digits (bits) that can attain only two states.

The human brain, on the other hand, is made up of neurons and synapses in a huge network, all of which can communicate with a vast number of others. In a neural network, neurons and synapses are the processing elements and the data paths between them. The earliest neural-network enthusiasts postulated that the human brain works like a huge machine, its neurons and synapses either "firing" or "staying quiet." Eventually, however, it was learned that things are more complicated than that.

In some neural networks, the neurons can send only two different types of signals, and represent the brain as theorized in the 1950s. Still, results can be modified by giving some neurons and/or synapses more importance than others. This creates *fuzzy logic*, in which truth and falsity exist with varying validity.

The drawing shows a small section of a three-level neural network. The circles represent neurons; the lines represent synapses. Signals travel in either direction along the synapses. Note that each neuron at a given level is connected to all the neurons at the adjacent level(s). Because of this, as the number of neurons increases, the number of synapses skyrockets.

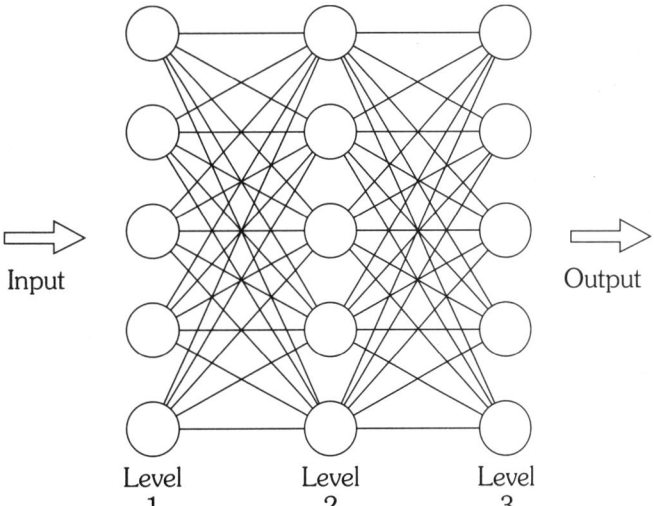

A small section of a three-level neural network. Circles are neurons; lines are synapses.

Neural networks and AI. Some researchers suggest that the ultimate goal of artificial intelligence (AI) might be reached by combining digital and neural-network technologies. Others think

Neurotic computer behavior

neural networks represent a dead end, and that digital technology has clearly proven itself to be the best way to build a computer. Neural-network research has gone through boom-and-bust cycles, partly as a result of differences of opinion.

In the late 1980s, neural-network technology began to pick up momentum again, after about 20 years' dormancy. Psychologists are interested in this technology because it might help them answer questions about the human brain, but no neural network has come close to such complexity. Even the biggest neural networks conceived, with billions of neurons and trillions of synapses, would only be as intelligent as an ant or a wasp. It appears that all roads to true AI, whether mainstream or alternative, will be long and tortuous. *See also* ALTERNATIVE COMPUTER TECHNOLOGY, ANALOG COMPUTER TECHNOLOGY, ARTIFICIAL INTELLIGENCE, GRACEFUL DEGRADATION, LOGIC, OBJECT RECOGNITION, PATTERN RECOGNITION, SPEECH RECOGNITION, *and* SPEECH SYNTHESIS.

Neurotic computer behavior

The strangeness of the malfunctions in a machine are proportional to the complexity of the machine. Computers are extremely complex, and therefore, some bizarre things can go wrong with them.

You're probably familiar with some common neuroses that befall human beings. Sometimes called "hangups," they can interfere with a normal life. Similarly, *neurotic computer behavior* can upset the normal functioning of your PC. When such behavior is severe, it becomes inconvenient or impossible to run programs and applications. Computer neuroses can originate from two causes: hardware bugs and software bugs.

Hardware bugs. Each integrated circuit (IC) in a computer has thousands, or even millions, of transistors fabricated on it. If one of these switches burns out, the result can be persistent PC malfunctioning. Whether this is a major or minor problem depends on where the failure occurs, and on what data goes through that point.

If you live in a place where the humidity is high, of if you're near an ocean where salt spray gets into the air, corrosion is likely to affect keyswitches, disk drives, and other components. A thin film of salt, dust, and oil can gradually build up, so that partial conduction takes place between points that should be totally insulated from each other. With the MOS (metal-oxide-semiconductor) and CMOS (complementary-metal-oxide-semiconductor) components used in PCs, even a tiny current can cause a malfunction. Sometimes these problems are strange and subtle. The cure is to have your machine thoroughly cleaned by a professional.

Neurotic computer behavior

Temperature extremes can also affect your PC's behavior. Although most solid-state circuitry can work over a wide range of temperatures, certain components are more heat-sensitive than others. If you have your air conditioning off on a hot summer day, and if your PC has been on for several hours, one or more of its ICs might get "irritable." The IC will still work, but not within the specifications quoted by the manufacturer. When this happens in two or three places at once, you might be able to use the machine, but it won't work as well as it does under ideal conditions.

Your PC's hard disk and diskette drive contain moving parts. These might eventually fail if you use your PC for several years. Such failure can cause a "neurosis," or it can result in catastrophic failure of the affected drive.

Software bugs. Software errors sometimes exist in commercially marketed packages, but they are a greater risk in programs that you download from an online service. Software bugs are most often found in programs written by amateurs.

In some instances, a software bug can go undetected for a long time, maybe indefinitely, but when the bug is encountered, the results can vary greatly. There might be a miscalculation in an arithmetic problem, or the entire program output might be reduced to nonsense. Sometimes the computer will exhibit a persistent, stubborn misbehavior similar to that of a bad-tempered person—a neurosis in the true sense.

An especially pernicious form of software bug called a *Trojan horse* or *virus* might be placed in a program deliberately by malicious hackers. When such a program is downloaded onto a hard disk, it can cause all kinds of trouble. For this reason, software should not be downloaded directly onto a hard disk; it should be put on a diskette first, and then "treated" with a software *vaccine*.

For example. Consider this example of an interesting neurosis involving overtype mode that developed with a word processing program when the temperature was too high or when the machine was left on for too long.

Overtype mode means that new text goes on top of old text; *insert mode* means that existing text is pushed forward to make room for new text. But when the glitch developed, the overtype mode would only work for one word at a time; if typing continued, it would change into insert mode, even though the cursor still indicated overtype mode. If the cursor were moved to some new location, it would be possible to overtype only up to the end of the new word, and then the PC would revert to insert mode again. Resetting the machine would get rid of the problem for a while.

This behavior was thought, at first, to be caused by a heat-sensitive component in the computer. When the same software was used in another IBM-compatible PC manufactured by a different company, however, the same problem occurred, roughly the same proportion of the time. To this day, the exact cause of this problem remains unknown. Perhaps it is a strange hardware/software "hybrid bug."

Another example. Another, more serious neurosis developed with a diskette drive and directory system. The PC lost its ability to recognize a change in the directory of a diskette. If the diskette in the drive was removed and replaced with a different diskette, the PC would think the old diskette was still there. A request for the directory would show the files on the old diskette, not the new one. To get the PC to recognize a new diskette directory, it was necessary to reset the computer. It could also be done by quitting the word processing program or the printer program, even if neither of those programs had been loaded. Although that would convince the PC that a new diskette had been installed, the machine would still be confused as to how many bytes of data were used or available on the diskette. The best approach was to reset the machine.

If an attempt was made to write a file onto a new diskette without going through these maneuvers, a catastrophe could result. This fact was learned at the expense of all the data on a diskette. When the PC was told to write the file onto the new diskette, it took more than two minutes to do it, splattering fragments of the file all over the new diskette and mutilating most of the data already on it. Fortunately, all the data was backed up.

This neurosis—which was severe enough to border on *psychotic computer behavior*—made it impossible to install any software that didn't fit onto one diskette. It also rendered the PC unable to copy diskettes. The machine could still be used in some situations, but not for really crucial tasks.

If you get very much involved in personal computing, you'll probably witness neurotic computer behavior. It's best not to take it too seriously. Computers do not always work perfectly. *See also* BACKUP, BUG, DISKETTE DRIVE HARD DISK, MURPHY'S LAWS, PSYCHOTIC COMPUTER BEHAVIOR, TROJAN HORSE, VACCINE, *and* VIRUS.

Nickel-cadmium and nickel-metal-hydride batteries

A *nickel-cadmium (NICAD or NiCd) battery* is a rechargeable battery commonly used with laptops and portable computers. It is made of several cells, each of which produce about 1.2 volts. In recent years, the *nickel-metal-hydride (NiMH)* battery, which lasts longer between charges, has largely replaced the NICAD in laptop computers.

Nickel-cadmium and nickel-metal-hydride batteries

Advantages. When properly used and cared for, a NICAD or NiMH battery can be charged and discharged more than 500 times. One of these batteries can pay for itself several times over. Imagine how much it would cost to replace a set of zinc-carbon or alkaline cells 500 times! A NICAD or NiMH packs a lot of energy into a small size and weight; this is important for portable computing.

The voltage of a NICAD or NiMH battery stays almost constant all during the discharge cycle (the time during which you're using the battery). This constancy of voltage is important. If the voltage were to gradually drop as it does with some other types of batteries, your portable PC might start doing strange things, or stop working altogether, long before the battery charge was used up.

Charging. The best way to charge a NICAD or NiMH is to use the charger provided with the machine. It takes several hours to fully charge the battery for a typical laptop computer. The charging unit plugs into an ordinary 117-volt wall outlet.

Some companies advertise quick-charging units. It is unwise to use these unless you're an expert on battery technology and are certain that the battery won't be damaged by the charger. Lots of things can go wrong when you try to take this shortcut. Some quick chargers deliver too much current to the battery during the charge cycle, and this can cause damage to one or more of the cells. Also, the charging voltage might not be right for the battery you're trying to charge.

If you repeatedly discharge a NICAD battery only part of the way, a phenomenon called *memory drain* can occur. Quite a few people will tell you this is common, and that you must never partially discharge any NICAD. However, some researchers have said that they have trouble forcing it to occur so they can study it. The best policy is to use NICADs until they're almost fully discharged, but don't use a NICAD to the point where it is totally discharged. That can cause one or more of the cells to reverse polarity; then, the battery must usually be discarded.

Newer NiMH batteries do not experience memory drain. This is one of the reasons NiMH batteries have practically replaced NICADS for laptop computing in recent years. *See also* LAPTOP COMPUTER.

As a power supply. Large NICAD batteries, called *flooded NICADs*, can be used as direct-current power supplies for heavy-duty applications. This makes them good for stand-alone solar power systems. All the components of a typical desktop PC, except the cathode-ray-tube (CRT) monitor, can be powered directly from such a battery. A power inverter can be used for the CRT and various small appliances.

An uninterruptible power supply can use NICADs to help you save your data if there is a utility blackout or brownout. The batteries charge when the utility power is at 100%. If there is a reduction or interruption in utility power, the batteries go into the discharge cycle, taking over from the utility line to give you time to back up your work on disk before switching off the computer. *See also* INVERTER, POWER SUPPLY, *and* UNINTERRUPTIBLE POWER SUPPLY.

Precautions. Because NICAD/NiMH batteries are made with some dangerous chemicals, you should never break them open for any reason. Never throw these batteries or cells into a fire, and don't throw them out with ordinary trash. They contain cadmium, a highly toxic element. The Environmental Protection Agency classifies discarded NICAD/NiMH batteries as hazardous waste.

If you have NICAD/NiMH batteries that you want to throw away, get in touch with your local trash disposal authorities and obtain instructions on how to safely dispose of the batteries.

Node

A *node* is a focal point for data in a network of computers or terminals. Data can emerge from a node, enter it, or both, as shown in the drawing.

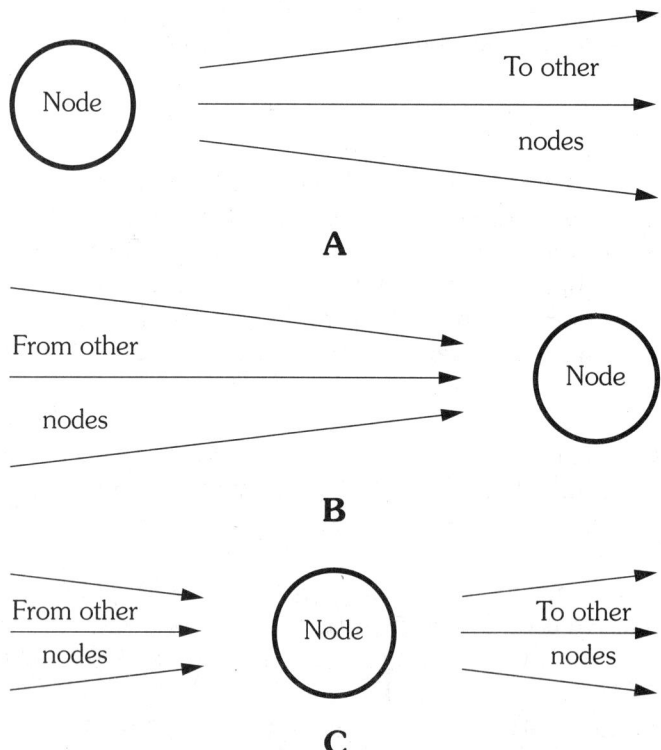

Signals going out of a node (A), signals coming in (B), and signals coming in and going out (C).

In any network, each PC or terminal represents a node. With a dumb terminal, a user can send information to other nodes in the network; it is also possible to receive data. The same holds true for a PC, but in addition to sending and receiving information, the PC can do its own computing. To act as a node in a network, a PC must be equipped with a modem, and also with terminal emulation software that lets it act as a dumb terminal when necessary.

In packet radio communications, a node can not only send and receive data, but repeat it, too. That is, it can intercept a signal from a source station and retransmit the data to some destination station on a different frequency. Because the signals are digital and the station acts as a repeater, this type of node is sometimes called a *digipeater*. *See also* DESTINATION, DIGIPEATER, DUMB TERMINAL, LOCAL AREA NETWORK, MODEM, NETWORK, PACKET COMMUNICATIONS, REPEATER, SOURCE, TERMINAL EMULATION SOFTWARE, *and* WIDE AREA NETWORK.

Node-to-node acknowledgment

In packet or network computer communications, *node-to-node acknowledgment* refers to a message sent back from one node to the previous node. This backward-going signal informs the sending node that the receiving node got the message. The signal only goes back to the node immediately preceding, not to any nodes that might have passed the message before that.

The drawing on page 748 shows a circuit with four nodes between the source and destination. There are five messages sent (MSG 1 through MSG 5): one from the source to the first node, and one from each node to the next node. There are also five acknowledgment signals sent (ACK 5 through ACK 1). The signal ACK 1 goes from node 1 back to the source, and acknowledges MSG 1. The signal ACK 2 is transmitted back from node 2 to node 1, acknowledging MSG 2. The same thing happens, node by node, until ACK 5 is returned from the destination to node 4. Thus, each message is verified independently between adjacent nodes.

In node-to-node acknowledgment, the system doesn't have to pass acknowledgment signals all the way from the destination to the source, so the chance for loss of an acknowledgment signal is much smaller than with end-to-end acknowledgment. *See also* END-TO-END ACKNOWLEDGMENT, NODE, *and* PACKET COMMUNICATIONS.

Noise

Noise is a broadbanded alternating current or electromagnetic field. Its main characteristic is that it does not convey any information. Noise can be natural or human-made.

Noise

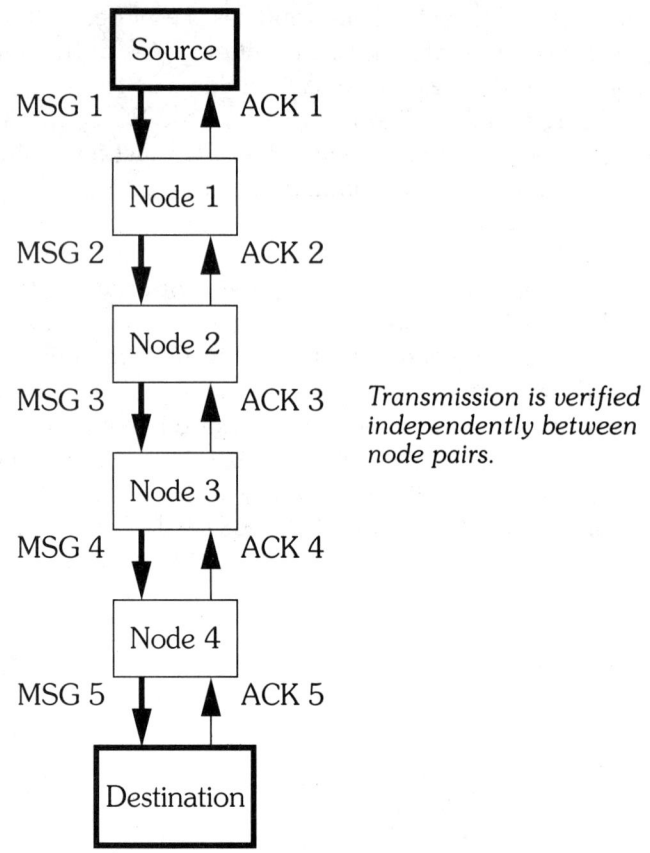

Transmission is verified independently between node pairs.

It's no good! Noise always degrades the performance of a system. It is a major concern in any device or system in which data is sent from one place to another. The higher the noise level, the stronger a signal must be if it is to be received error-free. At a given signal power level, higher noise levels translate into more errors and reduced communications range.

The drawing on the opposite page is a spectral display of signals and noise, with amplitude as a function of frequency. The background noise level is called the *noise floor*. Signals A, B, C, and D are above the noise floor, so they can be received. Signal D is the strongest and will therefore be received with the fewest errors. Signal B is weakest and will be subject to the most errors. Signal E is below the noise floor; its information can't be retrieved unless a more sophisticated destination modem is used or the source power output is increased.

Minimizing noise. The noise level in a communications system can be minimized by using components that draw the least possible current. Noise can also be kept down by lowering the temperature. Some experimentation has been done at extremely cold temperatures; this is called *cryotechnology*.

Nonvolatile memory

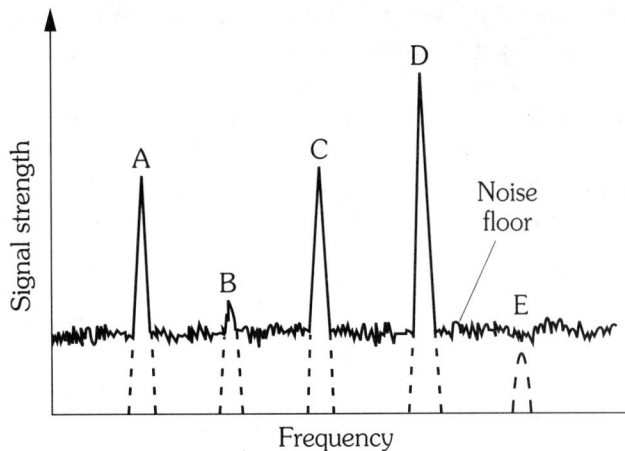

Noise competes with signals in data communications.

The narrower the bandwidth of the signal, in general, the better the signal-to-noise ratio will be. This improvement takes place at the expense of data speed, however. Another way to minimize noise is to user fiberoptics. Fiberoptic data transmission systems are relatively immune to noise effects. Digital transmission methods are superior to analog methods in terms of noise immunity.

It's always there. There is a limit to how much the noise level can be reduced; some noise will exist no matter what technology is used. Noise is the communications engineer's eternal adversary; researchers are constantly trying to find ways to get signals through noise. In that sense, noise is to data communications what friction is to automotive technology. *See also* ANALOG, BANDWIDTH, DIGITAL, *and* FIBEROPTIC DATA TRANSMISSION.

Noninterlaced monitor

See MONITOR *and* RASTER.

Nonvolatile memory

A *nonvolatile memory* is any form of computer memory in which the data stays put when you switch off the power. All magnetic media are nonvolatile. These include diskettes, hard disks, tapes, Floptical disks, and bubble memory. Some optical media, such as CD-ROM, are also nonvolatile. The read-only memory (ROM) chips in a PC have nonvolatile contents.

The advantage of nonvolatile memory is obvious: It's immune to power failures, and it doesn't need a battery backup or refresher circuitry to hold the data. Nonvolatile memory doesn't necessarily last forever, though. Magnetic fields deteriorate over a period of years. Some CDs can lose their data over time, too. Because of this, archives stored in nonvolatile media should be copied periodically. With diskettes and tapes, an annual "renewal" process is a good idea. A

CD-ROM will normally last for as long as you would be likely to use it, so it probably does not need to be backed up.

With the exception of bubble memory, nonvolatile memory has much slower access and storage time than the random-access memory (RAM) in your computer. This is the chief limitation of nonvolatile memory. The contents of RAM change from moment to moment. For example, as this article was typed, each character appeared in RAM the instant the key was struck. However, because RAM is volatile memory, If there had been a power failure during the composition of this article, the data would have vanished.

Data loss in RAM can be minimized by storing the contents of RAM on the hard disk every few minutes, but this takes time and conscious effort on the part of the computer operator. Some software has a feature that automatically backs up the RAM on hard disk at frequent intervals, so the RAM becomes "semi-volatile." It's a bad idea, however, to take this feature for granted. *See also* ACCESS TIME, BACKUP, BACKUP UTILITY, BUBBLE MEMORY, MAGNETIC MEDIA, RANDOM-ACCESS MEMORY, READ-ONLY MEMORY, STORAGE TIME, *and* VOLATILE MEMORY.

NOR gate

A *NOR gate* is an inclusive-OR gate followed by an inverter. The expression *NOR* derives from *not-or*. There are two or more inputs, and one output. The output is a predictable logical function of the inputs.

The NOR gate output is exactly reversed from those of an OR gate. When both or all inputs are zero, the output is one. If one or more of the inputs are one, then the output is zero. The illustration shows the schematic symbol for the NOR gate, along with a truth table showing the logical NOR function for two inputs. *See also* AND GATE, EXCLUSIVE-OR GATE, EXCLUSIVE-NOR GATE, INVERTER, LOGIC GATES, NAND GATE, *and* OR GATE.

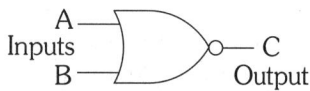

A	B	C
0	0	1
0	1	0
1	0	0
1	1	0

The schematic symbol and truth table of a NOR gate.

Norton Utilities

Norton Utilities is a popular software package for IBM-compatible PCs. It can test overall speed, recover some erased data, and help a PC organize its directories. Norton Utilities includes diagnostic modules to help pinpoint and solve hardware and software problems. Some people have expressed the opinion that, for serious PC users, Norton Utilities has evolved into a virtual necessity.

Benchmark. The benchmark program in Norton Utilities will tell you, quantitatively, how fast your machine works. It's not easy to figure this out by yourself, for two reasons. First, different computers do different tasks differently. Second, most PCs work too fast for you to accurately measure the time.

The benchmark is a set of "dummy" programs that run repeatedly. The total elapsed time is measured, and then the PC outputs a "score" that tells you the speed of your machine compared with an original IBM PC. *See also* BENCHMARK *and* THROUGHPUT.

Undeletion. You should always have a backup of all the data on your hard disk. One good way to do this is to use a tape drive. Another method is to keep all new and updated files on diskettes. Still another is to employ mirroring (use two hard disks at the same time). Different PC users prefer different backup schemes, depending on the volume of work they do, the frequency with which files are updated, the importance of their work, and the amount of money they have to spend on backup hardware/software.

If you haven't backed up the contents of your hard disk recently, and you inadvertently erase a file, you might still be able to retrieve it via *undeletion*. Norton Utilities includes a program that can help you get your machine running again, even if so much data has been erased that the PC can't even boot itself. If you inadvertently erase a file on hard disk, don't do any further work with the PC until you have run the undelete utility. In the case of a diskette, avoid writing any files on the diskette until you have run the utility on it. *See also* BACKUP, FILE ERASURE, *and* UNDELETION.

Defragmentation. Another feature of Norton Utilities is *defragmentation* of the data on disk. Your PC works faster, and catastrophic data loss is less likely, when the data on the hard disk is written on contiguous sectors (each file is in one chunk, instead of in fragments). If you update files on your hard disk often, and especially if the files are large and the hard disk is nearly full, files will get broken up because the machine writes data where it finds room.

A defragmentation program periodically rearranges the data on a hard disk, so that the files are each written on contiguous disk sectors. This

Notebook computer

minimizes the amount of work your PC must do when reading and writing the files. You can use the program on diskettes, too. *See also* DEFRAGMENTATION.

When to buy? The best time to purchase a package like Norton Utilities is immediately when you buy a computer. Some computers are sold with a package like this included as part of the standard software. You can think of Norton Utilities, or its equivalent, as health insurance for your computer. You might never need it, but you can't foretell in advance when something will go wrong. Computer malfunctions seem to be most likely when they will cause the greatest amount of inconvenience.

If you buy a package like Norton Utilities and install it on the hard drive right away, you can have it run critical system tests automatically every time you power up, so you can monitor any potential problems. Having the programs on the hard disk will also reduce the amount of time needed to run them when you need them. *See also* UTILITY SOFTWARE.

Notebook computer

See LAPTOP COMPUTER.

Note-taking software

We all write notes to ourselves. They can be reminders such as, "Get party food," or they can be information such as, "John Doe's phone number is 555-1111." You're probably familiar with date-keeper books, stick-on notes, and other hardcopy methods of note-taking.

Free-form notes. Perhaps you've used your PC to keep some notes. This is usually done using a database, which provides special ways to store and categorize information. Databases are convenient because you can look things up according to a variety of criteria, but they are limited in the amount of information you can store in each "slot." Also, in a conventional database you must adhere to a rather confining format. "Free-form" notes, of the kind you might take during a lecture or on a trip somewhere, don't fit into common databases.

Suppose you have an idea for a novel. Thoughts come to you concerning the plot. You also have several different characters in mind, and gradually, over a period of days, you begin to "know" them. Various scenes pop into your mind. Aspiring and experienced novelists know how sporadic this process can be. Sometimes even dreams bring insights. Wouldn't it be great if you could just run to your computer, call up the file for the character "Sally," and write down that she has shoulder-length brown hair, green eyes, and freckles that never fade, even in winter? Or maybe you thought of a scene where the police are chasing George in a blizzard. There's special *note-taking software* that will let you do this sort of thing.

Search engine. Free-form notes might be a couple of sentences, or 20 pages long. The important thing is that you be able to enter as much or as little information as you want (within reason), and that you have an easy time recalling the data when you want it. Note-taking software always incorporates a *search engine*, a means of zeroing in on data when you can only remember a few fragments of it. Perhaps you forget how long Sally's hair is. You'd search under "Sally" and find something like "Hair is shoulder-length."

To facilitate the search, data must be entered according to some rules, so it's not really completely free-form. Still, these rules give you far more latitude than those in an ordinary database. One popular program for Windows, called "A Place for my Stuff" (Quadrangle Software, Inc.), requires that your sentences conform to a subject/linking-verb/complement (SLVC) structure. An example of an SLVC sentence is "Sally's hair is shoulder-length." Another is "Chase scene is in blizzard." Once you get used to this simple requirement, entering data is no problem.

Notecards. Another popular note-taking program, written for DOS, is called "Random Write" (Custom Businessware). This software allows more freedom in input format. In the case of the novel, this program would let you create several "stacks" of "notecards." One stack might be called Plot, another might be called Characters, and another might be called Scenes.

In the Plot stack, there would be a brief outline of each chapter, with one chapter per notecard. In the Characters stack, one card would be devoted to Sally, and would contain all her vital physical and personality traits. Other cards would describe other characters. In the Scenes stack, you might just create cards as scenes come into your mind, not worrying about the order in which they're arranged. As you wrote the novel, you could periodically "flip" through the stack and pick out scenes as you needed them. Or you could arrange the scenes in order after you'd created a few dozen, inserting new scenes in their proper sequence after that.

For further information. Note-taking programs are occasionally described in PC-related magazines. New versions are constantly coming out. The two packages mentioned here are only to give you an idea of the basic things such programs can do. Some note-taking software has many extra features; this is, of course, reflected in the price you'll have to pay.

Your local PC store will probably carry several different note-taking software packages. It's best to pick up brochures for as many programs as you can, and compare their features to see which ones best meet your needs. *See also* DATABASE.

NOT gate

See INVERTER.

NuBus

NuBus is a system for adding expansion cards to Macintosh computers. Starting with the Mac II in the late 1980s, all Macintosh machines (Macs) have included NuBus.

Technically, NuBus allows for as many as 16 expansion boards. Usually, Macs allow up to six of them, which is still more than enough for most personal applications. Expansion boards are useful when you want to add special peripherals to your system, such as multiple printers, fax modems, oversize monitors, speech recognition systems, or speech synthesizers.

There are two big assets to NuBus. First, it doesn't matter which expansion board goes in which slot. You can just plug a NuBus card in any available slot, and the machine will adjust itself accordingly. Second, the expansion boards are interchangeable among different Mac machines. If you upgrade from a Mac IIsi to a Quadra, for example, you can move the expansion boards from the old machine to the new one, and they'll still work. *See also* EXPANSION BOARD *and* MACINTOSH.

Number Lock key and light

The *number lock (Num Lock) key* affects the behavior of the numeric keypad found on the right side of most IBM-compatible computer keyboards. A light located just above the key and labeled *Num* or *Num Lock* indicates the number-lock function status.

Activated. When the number-lock function is activated (the Num Lock light is on), pressing the number keys will result in the entry of numbers into the computer. Thus, the keypad can serve as an alternative to the number keys in the main part of the keyboard. Some PC users, such as engineers and accountants, find this convenient because the numeric keypad resembles an adding machine or calculator.

Disabled. When you toggle the Num Lock key so the indicator light goes off, the keys in the numeric keypad perform the cursor-movement functions printed on them, rather than entering numbers. For example, pressing the 8 key, which also has an arrow pointing up, will move the cursor up one line on the screen. Pressing 1, which also has End printed on it, will move the cursor either to the end of the line or to the end of the text on the screen, depending on the software you are using. *See also* NUMERIC KEYPAD.

Numeric coprocessor

See COPROCESSOR.

Numeric format

Numbers can be expressed in various ways, depending on the application. If you're balancing a checkbook, you'll use numbers that have two digits to the right of the decimal point. If you're a scientist talking about the number of atoms in a galaxy, you'll use exponential (scientific) notation. Maybe you need to use three numbers to the right of the decimal point at all times; perhaps you need to express something as a percentage. The *numeric format* is the way in which a numerical value is expressed.

Some of the more common numeric formats that you are likely to see in personal computing are depicted in the table for the number 12345.6. There are other numeric formats besides those shown in the table. For example, you might write a date such as April 12, 1999 in various ways, such as *041299*, *04/12/99*, or *04.12.99*.

Methods of expressing numbers

Format description	Example
General	12345.6
Scientific	1.23456E+4
Comma	12,345.6
Percentage	1234560%
Fixed, three decimal places	12345.600
Currency	$12345.60

Sometimes you'll see operations such as rounding of numbers, truncation of numbers, and various graphical methods of showing numerical values. These aren't really numeric formats; they are better termed *numeric modifications*. In spreadsheet work, you'll usually have to specify a certain numeric format for the data you enter in the cells. Most spreadsheet programs give you the option of several different numeric formats and modifications. *See also* SPREADSHEET.

Numeric keypad

The *numeric keypad* is a calculator-like set of keys with numbers and simple arithmetic functions. This keypad is separate from the main, typewriter-like set of keys.

Some of the keys in the numeric keypad are dual-purpose, with cursor-control functions in addition to the arithmetic functions. The Number Lock key controls the behavior of these keys.

Numeric keypad

The drawing shows the numeric keypad on a typical IBM-compatible computer keyboard. The Number Lock key is at the top left. The Number Lock light, which indicates whether or not the number lock function is activated, is in a row of light-emitting diodes (LEDs) just above the numeric keypad. *See also* NUMBER LOCK KEY AND LIGHT.

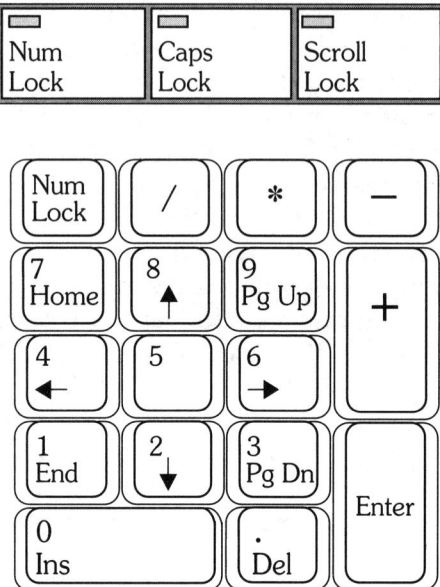

A dual-function numeric keypad.

Object

In computing, the term *object* can have any of several different meanings. For common examples, *see* OBJECT LINKING AND EMBEDDING, OBJECT-ORIENTED GRAPHICS, OBJECT-ORIENTED PROGRAMMING, OBJECT PACKAGER, *and* OBJECT RECOGNITION.

Object linking & embedding

Object linking and embedding (*OLE*, pronounced "oh-LAY") is a method of working with more than one file at the same time. It differs from *multitasking* in that there's one main document, called the *client* document. Other data is brought in from one or more *server* files.

What's an object? The term *object* might cause a little confusion. Usually, people think of an object as something concrete, like a diskette, or else an identifiable picture, such as an icon. In OLE, however, the term refers to part or all of a file.

An object can be as small as a single character in a word-processed document, or it can be as large as a novel. An object can consist of a sound, such as a few bars of popular music, or perhaps even a whole tune. An object can be a chart from a scientific document, some cells from a spreadsheet, or a set of names from a database. It can consist of bitmapped or vector graphics. In fact, anything that can be stored in memory or on disk can be an object. To make data into an object, you must define precisely what is to be included. This process can be simple or complicated, depending on the type of data and what you want to include in the object.

Object linking & embedding

Embedding. When you take an object and place it in some other file, the process is called *embedding*. The document from which the data comes is the server. This has roughly the same meaning as the term *source* in communications. It provides, or serves, as the source of information to be embedded. The document into which the data is embedded is the client; this means essentially the same thing as *destination* in a communications link.

The drawing shows four different servers, each with some data that is embedded in a word-processed client. Suppose the client is a graduate-level thesis and the servers are reference documents. From server 1, a photograph is taken and embedded in the thesis. From server 2, a graph is taken. From server 3, a brief audio passage is taken. From server 4, a set of three tables is taken and combined into one figure. (Permission to reproduce must, of course, be obtained from the authors of all the servers.) These objects each appear as icons within the thesis. The professors who read the thesis can click on these icons and look at, or hear, the objects.

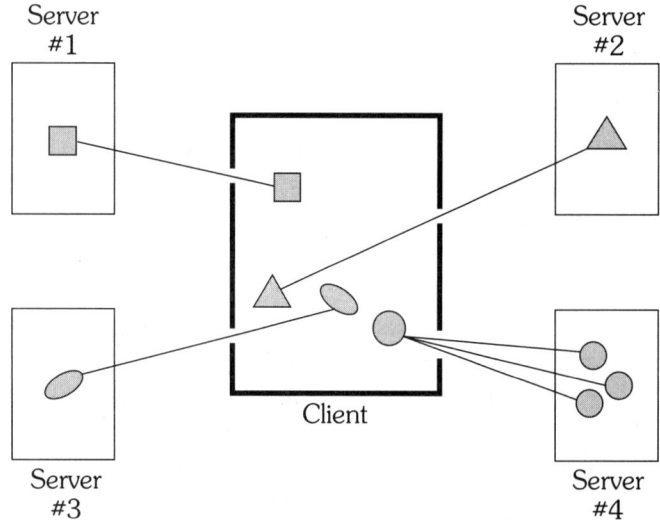

Data exchange between a client and one or more servers.

Now suppose that the grad student is proofreading his or her thesis, with the client and all the servers on the PC. Imagine that he or she wants to edit one of the embedded objects, say the photograph from server 1. The student decides that it includes too much, so he or she crops (trims) it as it appears in the thesis. The client document will therefore shrink in size because the cropped photograph consumes fewer bytes than the original, uncropped photograph. However, cropping the object in the client will not alter the content of server 1 in any way. It only affects the data from server 1 that has been embedded in the thesis. Embedding is a form of *static data exchange*. If an embedded object is changed in one place, it is not affected anywhere else it might appear. *See also* DESTINATION *and* SOURCE.

Linking. Now, imagine the same situation, except that the four servers are the work of the author of the thesis. Perhaps these four servers are presentations currently in progress. This gets rid of any concern over copyright and allows the author to amend the work in any way deemed necessary.

The grad student, seeing that the photograph from server 1 includes too much information, crops it in the thesis. If the photograph also needs to be cropped in the original document, he or she will have to go back to that document and do the operation again there, unless *linking* is used. Linking, sometimes called by the somewhat outmoded name *dynamic data exchange (DDE)*, will save the grad student some work, because when the photograph is edited in the client document, it will change in the server as well.

Suppose a mistake is found in the graph from server 2. The grad student corrects this error in the thesis; with linking, it will be corrected in the original document, too, without the necessity for opening that file and working on it.

The real power of linking becomes evident when an object appears in several files. Perhaps a scientist is working on seven different papers, all of which use one graph in which an error is found. With linking, he or she can make an object out of that graph, and then correct the error in any one of the papers, with the result that the error will be made right in all of the papers. This saves six error-correction sessions. It can also ensure that the scientist doesn't overlook any occurrences of that object, and therefore, improves the accuracy and consistency of his or her work. *See also* DYNAMIC DATA EXCHANGE.

Compatibility. To make full use of OLE, the server and client programs must both be OLE-compatible. Otherwise, you can usually embed objects, but you might not be able to link them.

Full OLE compatibility necessitates that both programs be capable of acting in both the client role and the server role. If just one program has this dual ability, it's not good enough. The concept is similar to full-duplex data communications; if you want to talk and speak at the same time (to interrupt someone or to let someone interrupt you), then both stations must have the ability to talk and hear simultaneously. If you have full duplex but the other person doesn't, then you can be interrupted, but cannot interrupt. If the other person has full duplex but you don't, then you can interrupt, but can't be interrupted.

Partial OLE compatibility means that a program can be either a client or a server, but not both. Unfortunately, there is some confusion about this when programs are marketed. It's important, therefore, to remember that if you want all the features of OLE, all the programs involved must be able to work as a client and as a server. *See also* MULTITASKING.

Object-oriented graphics

One method by which a computer can define things is called *object-oriented graphics*, sometimes called *vector graphics*. It is a powerful technique and uses analog representations, rather than the digital ones used with bitmapped graphics.

An example of an object-oriented graphic is a circle in the Cartesian coordinate plane, defined according to its algebraic equation. Consider the circle represented by

$$x^2 + y^2 = 1$$

This is called a *unit circle* because it has a radius of one unit, as shown in drawing A. The equation is easy for a computer to store in memory, and it is a precise representation.

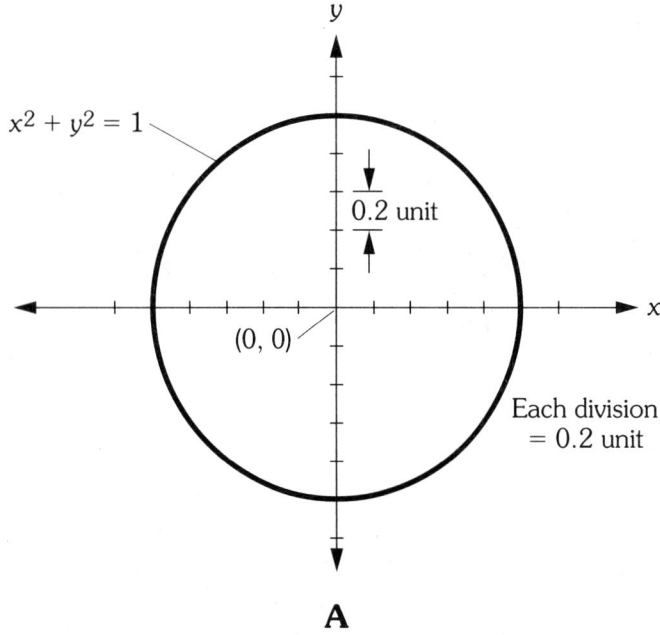

A

Analog representation of the unit circle. Each axis division is 0.2 unit.

Assets. There are two main assets to object-oriented graphics. The first is ease of resizing, reorientation, and movement. If you want to double the radius of the unit circle, for example, you can simply change the equation to

$$x^2 + y^2 = 4$$

or, if you want to increase the radius by a factor of n, you rewrite the equation as

$$x^2 + y^2 = n^2$$

Moving the circle around in the coordinate plane, so that its center is at some other point besides the origin (0,0), is also possible, although the algebra gets a little messy.

If you took analytic geometry in high school or college, you might remember that there were standard equations for parabolas, hyperbolas, ellipses, and other geometric figures. Changing the size, orientation, or location of such an object was just a matter of tailoring its equation. Although the algebra was sometimes clumsy, the technique would always work and would always provide an exact answer. Computers are good at manipulating equations of this kind. Even the most horribly complicated transformations (as a human being perceives them) are simple for a computer to perform.

A digital, or bitmapped, rendition of the unit circle or almost any other figure is not precise and is much harder to resize. The attainable precision in a bitmap depends on the image resolution. If the resolution is 0.1 unit, the digital representation of a unit circle will be rather coarse (see drawing B). Closer approximations can be obtained by making the resolution 0.01 unit or even 0.001 unit, but this will also take up a large amount of memory or storage space. Therein lies the second big asset of object-oriented graphics: It reduces the memory and storage needed to depict many types of images with precision.

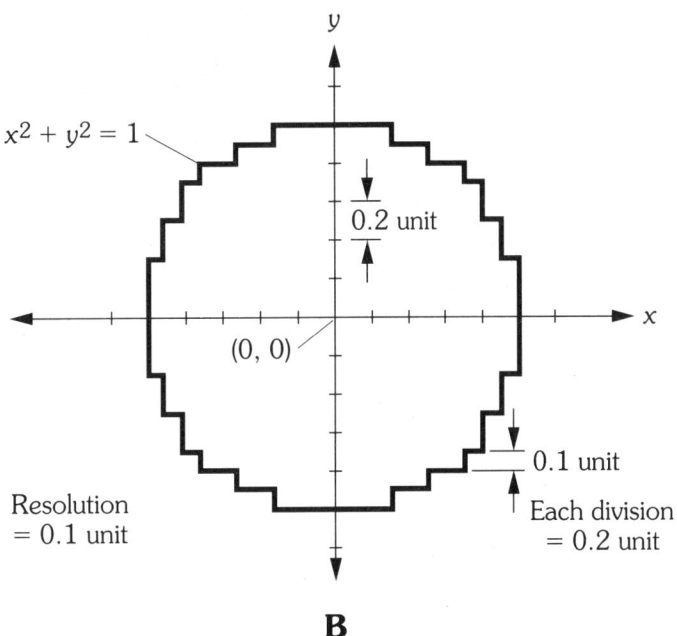

B

Digital representation of the unit circle. Each axis division is 0.2 unit. Image resolution is 0.1 unit.

Limitations. Object-oriented graphics work well in a draw program, when only the outline of an image is to be determined. However, for

Object-oriented programming

filling up the interior of an object, as is done in a paint program, bitmapped graphics usually work better.

When an optical scanner is employed to convert a hardcopy image to computer data, the output is a bitmap. If you want to use object-oriented graphics to change this kind of image, you'll have to convert it from bitmapped form to object-oriented form. This is done by a process called *tracing*.

Object-oriented graphics work differently than bitmapped graphics. If you've been working only with bitmaps, you'll have to spend some time learning how to use object-oriented graphics. If you've had some exposure to analytic geometry, you have a head start. The quality of the software, and of its documentation, has a big effect on the steepness of the learning curve. The highest-level programs are not necessarily the most difficult. For example, CorelDRAW, a powerful program that makes use of object-oriented graphics, is relatively easy to master, largely because it has a user-friendly interface and a concise instruction manual. *See also* ANALYTICAL GRAPHICS, BITMAPPED GRAPHICS, DRAW PROGRAM, IMAGE EDITING, OPTICAL SCANNER, PAINT PROGRAM, *and* PRESENTATION GRAPHICS.

Object-oriented programming

Object-oriented programming (OOP) is an advanced method of computer programming. It has been said that OOP is to computing what the assembly line was to automobile manufacturing. Many experts believe that OOP will revolutionize personal computing, accelerating the pace of software development.

The concept. The old method of programming worked "from the ground up," the way cars were once put together piece by piece. New software was written from scratch. A programmer sat down and started working, writing every step. Collaboration among programmers was difficult. Programming from scratch is a little like writing a long novel; it's hard enough for one person to keep track of the plot, let alone several. Some programs are still produced this way, but in recent years it has become apparent that this method is far from ideal.

When new programs are created or old ones improved, many of the code sequences are identical to those in the older software. It should not, therefore, be necessary to write everything over again. In OOP, reusable portions of programs, called *objects*, are kept in storage for use when needed in new software. When a certain sequence is required, and the programmer knows it has been written in the past, he or she can plug it into the new program.

Consider an example to help illustrate how OOP works. Suppose you're a programmer writing the software for transactions in bank accounts. One function handles deposits, one handles withdrawals, one handles interest, and one handles service charges. Each of these functions is an object. An object can be applied to more than one type of account. For example, the interest object can be applied to a savings account, a certificate of deposit, a checking account, or a loan. It is not necessary to write a separate interest program for each type of account. Although some details about the interest object can change (the rate will vary depending on the prime interest rate and the type of account, for example), the basic interest object, once written, can be used again and again.

Assets. One of the most important features of OOP is user-friendliness. It's easy to transfer parts of an object-oriented program to some other program. Object-oriented programs take up more computer memory, and need more time to run, than conventional programs, but these problems are being overcome as computer memory and speed increase.

The true power of OOP is apparent in applications such as animation, analytical and presentation graphics, personal robotics, remote control, virtual reality, speech recognition, and speech synthesis. The software for these applications is complex, and it makes sense to break it into pieces of smaller size. Software engineers can reuse parts of previously proven programs, saving the trouble of having to rewrite and debug the whole software package each time a new version is developed. It also allows for several people's efforts to be easily coordinated. It is no longer necessary for every engineer to understand all the details of the final product. *See also* PROGRAMMING.

Object packager

If you're using Windows software, and if you also have object linking and embedding (OLE), you can place documents within documents. This can be extremely useful for presentations of all kinds. It is done with a Windows module called *Object Packager*, whose name describes accurately what the feature does: It puts something in a neat little "package" and places it in a larger document.

Consider an example to help illustrate how Object Packager works. Suppose you're a grad student, and you're writing a thesis on some scientific subject. Such a thesis will probably have tables, graphs, charts, drawings, and photographs. Suppose that your professors are computer literate, and that they encourage their students to submit their work on disk. You prepare your thesis using Windows and OLE, so that each figure or table shows up as a small icon within the text.

As your professors read your thesis on their computers, they'll see text on the screen. When they get to a figure or table reference (which should be clearly annotated in the text), they'll see an icon for that illustration. They can then move the mouse so that the pointer is on the icon, and click or double-click. This will bring the illustration on screen, in its own window. Clicking again will cause the figure or table to disappear, and the professors can go on reading the text.

Object Packager is excellent for educational software and for presentation software. This is especially true if the PC is equipped with multimedia. Computer-assisted instruction that employs features such as Object Packager is not limited to teaching children; adults can also find it informative and entertaining. It can be used to create innovative quizzes and examinations. *See also* COMPUTER-AIDED INSTRUCTION, MULTIMEDIA, OBJECT LINKING AND EMBEDDING, *and* WINDOWS.

Object recognition

Object recognition refers to any method that a machine uses to pick something out from among other things. An example is recognizing your face, or getting a tumbler from a cupboard.

A robot example. Suppose you ask a robot to go to the kitchen and get you a tumbler full of orange juice. This involves a great deal of "thought" on the part of the robot's computer "brain." The first thing the robot must do is find the kitchen. Then it must locate the cupboard containing the tumblers. How will the robot pick a tumbler, and not a plate or a bowl, from the cupboard? This is a form of *bin-picking problem*.

One way for the robot to find a tumbler is to identify it by shape, but this presents problems if done by vision alone. A cylindrical tumbler might look like a rectangle as seen from the side as in the drawing at A, a rounded-off rectangle as seen from an angle (B in the drawing), and a circle as seen from the end (C in the drawing).

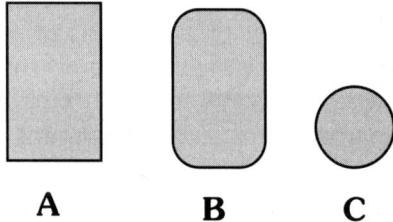

A tumbler as a machine would see it from the side (A), an angle (B), and the end (C).

Another method of object recognition uses tactile sensing. The robot could double-check, after grabbing an object it thinks is a tumbler, whether it is cylindrical. If all the tumblers in your cupboard weigh the same, and if this weight is different from that of the plates or bowls, the robot can use weight to determine that it has the right object.

If a particular tumbler is required, it will be necessary to have all the tumblers marked in some way, such as with bar codes. This is a simple, precise object-recognition scheme, but it involves tagging everything with rather unsightly labels.

Hurdles to surmount. If a machine is to recognize a complex object, such as your face or your fingerprint, a high degree of resolution is required of the vision system. The most common method of depicting complex, irregular objects is with a bitmap. The larger the number of pixels in the image, the higher the resolution will be, and the greater the certainty with which the machine will recognize the image.

The actual recognition process is done by comparing the image as received by the vision system with a stored set of images. Because high-resolution, bitmapped images consume a lot of storage space, a sophisticated object-recognition system needs massive memory and storage media. The other hurdle to be overcome, which is directly related to memory and storage, is processing speed. It takes time for a digital machine to process huge quantities of data.

Suppose there are 10,000 portraits, each taking up 10MB (megabytes), in a program intended to identify a person by his or her face. The entire set of portraits will need 100GB (gigabytes) of storage, and the machine will have to scan many (perhaps all) of them, pixel by pixel, to arrive at its conclusion. Unless the microprocessor is extremely fast, this will take a long time—but identification must be done quickly. For example, if the computer in a surveillance or security system is to check people's identities as they enter a building, the task must be done in a second or two for each person.

Another way. It's possible that some form of alternative computer technology will prove better-suited than traditional digital computers for complex object recognition. A neural network, for example, can work with associations and is good at recognizing patterns in huge quantities of input data. Neural networks also work much faster than digital machines, although this speed comes at the expense of precision. *See also* BAR CODE, BIN-PICKING PROBLEM, BITMAP, IMAGE RESOLUTION, NEURAL NETWORK, PIXEL, SECURITY SYSTEMS, *and* VISION SYSTEMS.

OCR

See OPTICAL CHARACTER RECOGNITION.

Octal number system

The number scheme that people most commonly use, the decimal system, has 10 symbols, or digits, representing powers of the number 10. In computer work, however, other numbering systems are preferred over the decimal scheme. The binary number system, for example, uses only zeros and ones, and is the way most digital computers "think" of numerical quantities. Another scheme,

Octet

sometimes used in programming, is called the *octal number system* because it has eight symbols, or 2^3. These digits are 0 through 7.

The table shows some octal numbers, along with their decimal and binary equivalents. Octal digits are sometimes used by software engineers to represent three-digit groups of binary numbers. Octal numbers can also be used like decimal numbers.

Octal (eight-digit) number system

Decimal	Binary	Octal
0	0000	0
1	0001	1
2	0010	2
3	0011	3
4	0100	4
5	0101	5
6	0110	6
7	0111	7
8	1000	10
9	1001	11
10	1010	12
11	1011	13
12	1100	14
13	1101	15
14	1110	16
15	1111	17

Octal numbers have some interesting properties. For example, in the octal system, if a number is a power of "10" (that is, the digit 1 with any number of zeros after it), you can divide it in half repeatedly until you get the number 1. Octal numbers are also "musical." In ¾ time, there are four measures to the octal number 10; in ¼ time, there are two measures to the octal number 10. *See also* BINARY-CODED DECIMAL, BINARY NUMBER SYSTEM, DECIMAL NUMBER SYSTEM, *and* HEXADECIMAL NUMBER SYSTEM.

Octet

See BYTE.

Office automation

Office automation is the use of machines to assist, and sometimes to replace, human workers in an office environment. The personal computer is perhaps the most important single business machine ever developed.

Assets. Office automation can save work, time, and money if properly implemented in a well-organized office. In a small business, and especially for the self-employed person, a PC can do the work of one or more full-time assistants. This can make the difference between solvency and bankruptcy. Personal computing has helped thousands of people start businesses and keep them afloat.

In a large company, institution, or government agency, computers allow rapid transfer of data from office to office by means of a local area network (LAN) or wide-area network (WAN). This speeds up operations and saves postage. When everyone has access to company files via a computer, there is less confusion and more efficiency. In fact, as technology progresses and people's fear of computers diminishes, the ideal of a paperless office will be approached in many companies.

Liabilities. Machines don't always do better work than people. Automation is desirable in some office environments, but not all. One of the biggest potential problems with office automation is the fact that people are resistant to change. Even if workers don't perceive machines as a threat to their job security, they might be less than eager to radically change their routines and work skills.

At the other extreme, some workers embrace automation with excessive zeal. They'll use the machines to create work that is "too good," wasting time getting rid of flaws that don't cause any real problems.

Whether or not workers are happy about automation, they must be trained to use the new equipment. This takes time and costs money, in addition to the actual cost of hardware and software installation. There will be a learning period during which work efficiency is low.

Computers and terminals cause some worker to have stress problems. People who spend hours every day at workstations are at some risk of developing mental fatigue and cumulative trauma disorders. The situation worsens if supervisors yield to the temptation to monitor keystrokes or otherwise dehumanize their workers.

For further information. If you have an office and are interested in automation, you can contact professional consultants who will objectively assess your situation and make recommendations. Office automation is not an all-or-nothing affair; perhaps all you need is a fax machine or a small PC with a laser printer.

See also APPLETALK, BUSINESS SOFTWARE, CUMULATIVE TRAUMA DISORDERS, DAILY PLANNER SOFTWARE, ERGONOMICS, EXPORT BUSINESS

Off-site data storage

SOFTWARE, LOCAL AREA NETWORK, LUDDITES, MAIL-ORDER BUSINESS SOFTWARE, MEDICAL-OFFICE SOFTWARE, PAPERLESS OFFICE, POINT-OF-SALE SYSTEM, REENGINEERING, SECURITY SYSTEMS, TELECOMMUTING, TELECONFERENCING, *and* WIDE-AREA NETWORK.

Off-site data storage

Almost everyone has some vital personal or business data, such as an income-tax return, business plan, or client list, that you can ill-afford to lose. Much of what's on your PC's hard disk is crucial to your everyday computing life. The loss of even a small part of that information would cause untold inconvenience. If you have only one copy of any vital data, it is vulnerable to destruction in the event of a fire, theft, tornado, flood, or other disaster.

Peace of mind. For peace of mind, it's wise to back up computer data on a daily basis. Long-term backup data records are called *archives*. The best policy is to create two sets of archives, updating them regularly, and to keep one set at a remote location. Special facilities are available, specifically designed for *off-site data storage*.

The advantage of off-site data storage can be shown by simple arithmetic. Suppose that the chance, on any given day, of archive loss is one in 10,000. That's 0.01%. If you have the same data in two places located far away from each other, then the chance for archive loss becomes one in $10,000 \times 10,000$, or one in 100,000,000. That is 0.000001 (one millionth) of a percent.

Commercial data centers. Data-storage facilities are available in all big cities. Most medium-sized towns also have at least one of these commercial data centers, the sole purpose of which is to keep backups and archives safe. The best commercial data centers offer the following features:

➢ *Certified record manager (CRM)* This is a person specially trained in organizing, maintaining, and updating data files.

➢ *Fire protection* Inert-gas systems suffocate fires without damaging paper, diskettes, tapes, or CD-ROMs.

➢ *Climate control* Constant temperature and humidity maximize the life of data, whether it be on paper, magnetic media, optical disks, or microfilm.

➢ *Disaster resistance* The building should be able to withstand catastrophes such as hurricanes, earthquakes, and floods without allowing damage to the data inside.

➢ *Security* This includes guard personnel and electronic surveillance. Armored and unmarked delivery trucks are another good security feature.

➤ *Pick-up and delivery* This is essential if you need to get at your records very often. It can save you incalculable time and mileage.

➤ *Convenient location* The importance of this feature is obvious. You don't want to have to wait days for data when you need it.

➤ *Electronic data transfer* This optional, and rather expensive, feature lets you enter and retrieve your information directly from your computer, using a modem. It will probably go down in cost, however, and become increasingly popular. As modem speeds continue to increase, it might well become the preferred method of accessing off-site data.

For further information. You can get a list of data storage centers in your area by writing to the following address:

Association of Commercial Records Centers (ACRC)
P.O. Box 20518
Raleigh, NC 27619

All the centers in their list are ACRC members and have met certain service standards. Nevertheless, you'll want to visit and inspect any facility before entrusting your data to it. *See also* ARCHIVES *and* BACKUP.

Online service

The term *online service* refers to various networks that you can access with a PC and a modem connected to a telephone line.

The information superhighway. All online services are part of a vast information stream, into which anyone can tap. There are certain hardware and software requirements for access to this information superhighway. Also, fees must be paid in most cases.

The information superhighway, also sometimes called the "infobahn," is constantly changing in structure and content. Its role in society is a subject for ongoing debate. Critics and advocates alike rank it with the telegraph, telephone, radio, and television as a milestone in communications technology. It is quite probable that every household in the developed world will eventually have, or at least want, equipment for accessing the information superhighway.

At one extreme, advocates of this technology see all media merging into one form, with one mode of access—a hybrid of television, radio, telephone, and PC—that will greatly enhance everyone's quality of life. At the other extreme, pessimists see the information superhighway as the ultimate weapon of a "Big Brother" bent on depriving the individual of rights to privacy and self-determination, and a means of widening the gap between economic classes.

Online service

Three things are certain at the time of writing: online services need to be coordinated and governed somehow, people haven't figured out exactly how this regulation will be done, and online services can be of value to most PC users.

What you need. Several components are needed to get online. Interconnection is no more difficult than putting together a television and videocassette recorder, or setting up a hi-fi home entertainment system. You'll need at least the following:

➢ *Computer* Most PCs are adequate for online services. You'll find the going easier if you have a machine with at least an Intel 80286 or Motorola 68020 microprocessor, 30MB (megabytes) or more of available hard drive space, and a color monitor. A graphical user interface (GUI), such as Windows, the Macintosh OS, or OS/2, is advantageous.

➢ *Terminal emulation software* This program allows your computer to work as a dumb terminal for communications purposes while using the PC's computing power for everything else. There are many different programs available. Often, a modem comes with its own terminal emulation program. Some online services have special software that you must install to use their networks.

➢ *Modem* A modem is a piece of hardware that enables your computer to send and receive data through the telephone lines. A modem is actually a digital-to-analog (D/A) and analog-to-digital (A/D) converter combined. Modems operate at various data speeds. These speeds, measured in units called *bauds* or *bits per second (bps)*, keep increasing. Data speed requirements for online services vary somewhat. The best policy is to buy the best modem you can afford.

➢ *Telephone line* You can use the same line to which your regular telephones are connected, or you can have a separate line installed. If there are several people in your household, you'll probably want a separate line for the PC; otherwise, it will tie up the line, blocking incoming as well as outgoing calls. There should be a telephone jack within a few feet of your computer.

➢ *Connection telephone number* If you live in or near a city of at least moderate size, you'll probably find local nodes (local telephone connection numbers) via which you can gain access to online services. If you're in a remote area, you might have to call a long-distance number, which will increase the cost of using the network. A few networks have 800 numbers for toll-free access from locations that are not served by local nodes.

If you have an amateur radio license and equipment, you can also use *packet radio*, a wireless form of packet communications, to gain access to some online services. Check with your local amateur radio club for details.

Online service

Online options. There are many ways you can use a computer online. You can send information, receive it, or converse with people. You can upload and download text files, programs, pictures, and music. You can shop, do your banking, and even work from home in some cases. You can play computer games, meet new people, and generally have a good time. Here are some ways people use online services:

➢ *Real-time communication* Also called "talking," "chatting," or "conferencing," it's actually done in written form closely resembling old-fashioned teletype, except that there's no clunking teleprinter. You can send graphics, music, and software to other computer users.

Abbreviations and symbols are often used in computer communication. The table below lists some common abbreviations. The table on page 772 shows some ways that symbols called *smileys* or *emoticons* can be combined for special effects. Most emoticons are meant to be viewed sideways.

Some popular online abbreviations

Statement/action	Abbreviation
Away from keyboard	AFK
Back at keyboard	BAK
Be right back	BRB
By the way	BTW
Good afternoon	GA
Goodbye	GB
Good evening	GE
Good morning	GM
Laughing	HEE
Laughing out loud	LOL
Oh by the way	OBTW
On the other hand	OTOH
Pardon me for jumping in	PMFJI
Rolling on the floor (laughing)	ROTF
Ta-ta for now	TTFN
Way to go	WTG
Weather	WX
Welcome back	WB

➢ *Teleconferencing* Two or more PC users can get together and have a conference. In some networks, people check in and out, and there can be dozens of different users online at the same time. People can "jump in" at random or go in rotation. People

Some popular symbol combinations

Concept/action	Symbols
Angelic smiling	0:)
Crying	:'(
Devilish grinning	}:>
Frowning	:(
Hug	{}
Laughter	:D
Laughter with tears	:'D
Kiss	:*
Open-mouthed astonishment	:0
Sealed lips	:X
Smiling	:)
Smirking	:>
Sticking out tongue	:P
Winking	;>

who eavesdrop on conferences, but never enter the discussions, are sometimes called "lurkers."

In business, teleconferencing has obvious value. You might need to meet with your home office and a client at the same time. Two business partners might want to discuss a proposal with a prospective client, several scientists might want to share the results of their experiments, or coauthors of a book might want to show an editor examples of new illustrations to be added.

➤ *Bulletin-board system (BBS)* A BBS is like a slow teleconference. It gets its name from the fact that you can "tack up" notes and messages for everyone to see. When you browse through a BBS, you'll see dozens or even hundreds of notes. You can search to see who has left notes recently and who has notes waiting.

➤ *Electronic mail* Also called *e-mail*, this is a more personal form of computer communications. You have a mailbox in which people can leave messages for you; you can also send messages to other mailboxes. E-mail offers more privacy than a BBS, but there is no such thing as 100% privacy when you are online.

In theory, no one else should be able to read your e-mail; also, the e-mail you send to other people should be seen only by them. Unfortunately, however, whenever you put data into a public medium, hackers can get at it without your knowledge or consent. Such people are not dissuaded by the fact that their activities are against the law.

- *Getting news* Most major online networks allow you to browse through up-to-the-minute international, national, and local news. You can zero-in on some part of the world, or you can browse through a list of headlines and buzzwords that is updated every few hours.

  You can also get detailed news about specialized topics. What's the latest news on that new microprocessor Intel has been developing? How is research going into single-electron memory devices? You can often find information like this through online news networks. If what you want is not available in the form of a news story, you can leave a BBS message asking if anyone knows about it.

- *Online consulting* For small business and serious PC power users, engineering and technical consultants are available online. They can help with all kinds of business and personal decisions.

  If you're thinking about installing a local area network (LAN), for example, you might get help to find out what hardware is best for your needs. If something has gone wrong with your system, a consultant can help you troubleshoot it. These services aren't free, but they can often save you time. In business, time equals money.

- *Transferring software* You can get all kinds of programs from various sources online. This is called *downloading*. Such software should generally be downloaded directly to diskettes and not transferred to a hard disk until it has been run through a vaccine to be sure it does not contain a Trojan horse or virus.

  If you've written a program and you want to share it with other PC users, you can send it to them. This is called *uploading*.

- *Shopping* Online catalogs let you shop from your PC. You can read product descriptions, look at pictures, and order merchandise. At first this seems exotic and almost too convenient, but it's really not much different than ordering things over the telephone. The big difference is that no bulky bound catalog gets sent through the Postal Service.

- *Banking and paying bills* Increasingly, people are taking care of their finances via online services. This prevents much of the bother involved with making deposits, writing and cashing checks, licking stamps, and all the other footwork and paperwork that has traditionally gone with financial management.

  There is some risk in doing financial transactions online, as there is with any electronic transfer of funds. Still, many people consider the convenience more than worth the risk. Always inquire about security measures when setting up to do any financial business online.

Online service

> *Working* If you have a desk job, it might be possible for you to do much, if not most, of your work from the comfort of home. Freelance writers, for example, can "modem in" their work to publishers. The same can be done with illustrations, tabular matter, and multimedia presentations.
>
> This kind of *telecommuting* can save thousands of hours of physical commuting every day in a big city. This translates into huge energy savings, a reduction in air pollution, and a reduced number of traffic injuries and fatalities. Perhaps someday, people will do most of their work by telecommuting. They'll look back at the 20th century and wonder how people could stand to drive cars to and from work every day.
>
> The main problem with online work is motivational. Some people seem to lack the discipline to work from home; they need to be physically present in an office setting to get anything done.

Some people find online services rather addicting. Keep tabs on the number of hours you're using the service each month, if there is a per-hour charge. Otherwise, you might get a rude shock when the bill arrives.

Major players. There are several online services from which you can choose. These change often, as is the norm in the computing world. Most online services have toll-free telephone numbers through which you can ask questions or get help. The table shows the addresses and 800 numbers of some popular online networks.

Some popular networks

America Online 8619 Westwood Center Drive Vienna, VA 22182 1-800-827-6364	GEnie 401 North Washington Street, VB2 Rockville, MD 20850 1-800-638-9636
CompuServe 5000 Arlington Centre Boulevard P.O. Box 20212 Columbus, OH 43220 1-800-848-8199	ImagiNation Network 41486 Old Barn Way P.O. Box 1550 Oakhurst, CA 93644 1-800-462-4461
Delphi Internet Services 1030 Massachusetts Avenue Cambridge, MA 02138 1-800-695-4005	Prodigy 445 Hamilton Avenue White Plains, NY 10601 1-800-776-3449

Here are brief descriptions of some online services (for the latest details, and for information about other networks, consult one of the PC-oriented consumer magazines):

> *America Online*, or *AOL*, is intended mainly for graphical user interfaces (GUIs). You don't need to memorize commands; you use a mouse to point and click on icons. The instructions are easy to follow. There are several departments on AOL, including Lifestyles/Interests, News/Finance, People

Online service

Connection, Games/Entertainment, Learning/Reference, Travel/Shopping, Computing/Software, What's New, and Online Support.

America Online provides an extensive network of support, so you can get help when you need it. Assistance is also available for the hearing impaired.

➤ *CompuServe* is the oldest and best-known online services. It gives up-to-the-minute news on several subjects, just as you'd find in a big-city Sunday newspaper. CompuServe lets you shop via computer, talk (type, actually) with other PC users in real-time, have conferences in which several people share views and information, and get data concerning investments, the stock market, interest rates, and other economic matters. The network has an enormous encyclopedia. CompuServe has both a GUI and a command-line interface.

➤ *Delphi* is known for its comprehensive Internet access. It's wise to avoid normal office working hours when working on Delphi. These are peak hours on the Internet, and Delphi has a surcharge for using the service during these hours.

➤ *GEnie* is known for the variety and friendliness of its users. There are games, as well as group "chatting" (for adults and young people). Various business data is available. Special activities are provided for children and novice computer users.

The first two letters (*GE*) stand for General Electric, the owner of the network. GEnie, like most major online services, employs a graphical interface.

➤ *ImagiNation Network (INN)* is devoted mainly to entertainment. It also includes roundtable discussions; these are good for making new friends. You can create your own "look" or style on this service; the character might resemble your real self, or the person you'd like to become, or even a fictitious character. People make up pseudonyms (fictitious names) for use on the network. The INN is known for its dramatic graphics.

The INN was originally called the Sierra Network. It is operated by Sierra Online, Inc., in conjunction with AT&T and General Atlantic Partners.

➤ *The Internet* is the biggest online data service in the world. With it, you can do library research or get data from all kinds of institutions and organizations directly at your PC. Using a feature called Archie, you can search for data by using words likely to be filenames or parts of file descriptions. Another special feature, Gopher, uses a menu system to help you find information you need. Other features fill other needs, like providing a GUI or downloading files.

If you want to get access to the Internet, start by calling the computer science department of the nearest trade school,

Open systems interconnection reference model

college, or university. If you aren't near a school that can provide you with service, you can get connected through a commercial provider.

> *Prodigy* is designed for a graphical interface. The hallmark of Prodigy is user-friendliness; it has a reputation for being easy to work with. General news and sports information is available, as well as contests, shopping/travel services, and family entertainment.
>
> Prodigy is known for its excellent educational information service, which young people especially like. The network occasionally brings in famous people for bulletin-board question-and-answer sessions.

For further information. The PC magazines regularly feature articles about online services and are a good way to keep up-to-date with the latest developments. *See also* AMERICA ONLINE, BULLETIN-BOARD SYSTEM, CABLE DATA TRANSMISSION, CELLULAR TELECOMMUNICATIONS, COMPUSERVE, CONNECT TIME, DELPHI, DOWNLOADING, DUMB TERMINAL, ECOLINKING, ELECTRONIC MAIL, FAX, FIBEROPTIC DATA TRANSMISSION, GEOSTATIONARY-SATELLITE DATA LINK, HACKER, INTERNET, LOW-EARTH-ORBIT (LEO) SATELLITE DATA LINK, MAILBOX, MAIL FORWARDING, MICROWAVE DATA TRANSMISSION, MODEM, PACKET COMMUNICATIONS, PRODIGY, SATELLITE DATA TRANSMISSION, SENIORNET, SHAREWARE, TELECOMMUTING, TELECONFERENCING, TERMINAL EMULATION SOFTWARE, TIME-SHIFTING COMMUNICATIONS, TROJAN HORSE, VACCINE, VIRUS, VOICE MAIL SYSTEMS, *and* WIDE-AREA NETWORK.

Open systems interconnection reference model

In a network, it is important that the computers be able to communicate effectively. To ensure this, the computers' modems must all have certain characteristics in common. The details of modem operation are called the *protocol*. A standard set of protocols is the *open systems interconnection reference model (OSI-RM)*. It is sometimes also called the *ISO/OSI model* because it was developed by the International Standards Organization (ISO).

There are seven levels, called *layers*, in OSI-RM. These are as follows, in order from lowest to highest:

1 The *physical layer* moves the messages from place to place.

2 The *link layer* puts bits of data into units called frames, and transmits the data in this form.

3 The *network layer* finds the best routes, or paths, for the messages through the network. The first packet, or message unit, establishes the ideal route; the following packets follow the same route.

4 The *transport layer* makes sure that the source (sending station) stays in touch with the destination (receiving) station.

5 The *session layer* synchronizes the data between the source and destination stations.

6 The *presentation layer* translates between different forms of data.

7 The *application layer* interfaces messages with the application software that the system computers use. This makes it possible to program computers by remote control, and for computers to program each other.

With all seven OSI-RM layers working right, it is possible to link PCs together to get a "megacomputer" that is much smarter and has much more memory than any of the computers alone. This is a crude form of artificial intelligence. It is slow, however, because it takes time for the signals to get from place to place, especially if the computers are far from each other. *See also* LOCAL AREA NETWORK, MODEM, ONLINE SERVICE, PACKET COMMUNICATIONS, REMOTE CONTROL SYSTEMS, *and* WIDE AREA NETWORK.

Operating system

Every PC must have an *operating system*. A computer without an operating system is like a car without a steering wheel, gas pedal, or brake. A PC might have power, and its operator might be an expert, but for it to be of any use, it must have controls with which the operator can make it work.

The operating system works in conjunction with the basic input/output system (BIOS) to manage the operation of all the hardware in your computer.

User interface. The drawing shows, in greatly simplified form, how a user interface oversees the operating system and mediates between the user and the PC. There are two major types of user interfaces in PCs today. The first type is something like a multiple-choice test, and the second type resembles a fill-in-the-blank exam.

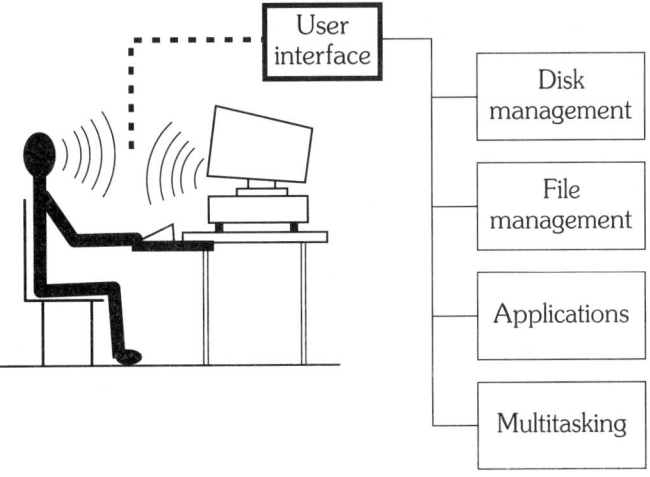

An operating system oversees the computer and provides an interface with the user.

Operating system

The "multiple-choice" user interface uses lists of choices, often with symbols called *icons*, to help the user along and to provide an easy-to-learn environment. This is called *menu-driven software*. If icons are included, it is a *graphical user interface (GUI)*. Examples of menu-driven, graphical interfaces are Windows, Macintosh, and OS/2.

A "fill-in-the-blank" user interface requires that the operator memorize commands and type them in when needed. This is called *command-driven software*. It is somewhat more difficult to learn than the graphical or menu-driven programs, but some people prefer it. The most common command-driven interface is *DOS*.

The popular Windows program is not an operating system all by itself; it's sometimes called an *operating environment*. Windows changes DOS into a GUI. Sometimes you'll hear people say, "Windows sits on top of DOS," meaning you need to have DOS installed if you want to use Windows (at least, as of this writing).

There are other operating systems besides those listed here. Some are designed for IBM-compatible PCs only; others are for Macintosh computers only; still others can work with either IBM-compatibles or Macs. All operating systems act as overseers of the computer's functions, as well as providing an interface with the human operator.

See also BASIC INPUT/OUTPUT SYSTEM, COMMAND-DRIVEN SOFTWARE, DOS, GRAPHICAL USER INTERFACE, MACINTOSH, MENU-DRIVEN SOFTWARE, OS/2, SYSTEM 7, *and* WINDOWS.

Disk and file management. For your computer to make use of the hard disk and diskette(s) in the various drives, the operating system must provide disk and file management. Data on a disk can't just be written anyplace; the disk must be prepared first by formatting so the data will go down neatly.

Each disk, CD-ROM, or tape must have one or more directories telling the computer what files are on it, and where to look for these files. Otherwise, finding data would be like looking for someone's house in a town with no street names, maps, or numbers.

The file management features of an operating system facilitate the moving of files to and from RAM, diskettes, the hard disk, a tape drive, and other storage media. Files can also be renamed, deleted, or moved from one directory to another. *See also* DIRECTORY *and* FORMATTING.

Application software. Your computer can do all kinds of things. You can write books, keep appointment records, draw pictures, communicate with other people, compose music, and play games on your PC. All these activities require specialized *application software*. The operating system provides a sort of "universal translator" that lets hardware communicate with various kinds of application software.

You might compare applications with written languages. It's possible to translate any written human language into any other, at least enough to get the general meaning across. (As a matter of fact, there is software that can do this for you.) Similarly, because of the "translation" features of the operating system, you can use many applications with one user interface. That saves you a lot of trouble. Imagine having to learn Macintosh in order to do spreadsheet programs, command-driven DOS for word processing, Windows for database management, and OS/2 for graphics!

When you buy application software, you must be sure it's the version intended for your operating system and user interface. Software is advertised as being "for Windows," "for Macintosh," or "for OS/2." A single software package is often available in several different forms, each intended for a specific operating system.

Multitasking. With an operating system that provides multitasking, you can run more than one application at a time. For example, you can work on a database and a word processing file simultaneously, or you can work on one file while printing out another and sending still another to someone via modem.

Multitasking is greatly enhanced by a GUI such as Macintosh or Windows. That way, you can have each application in a different place on screen, and you can arrange them to suit your needs. You might want to overlay windows (stack them up) or tile them (spread them all out). *See also* MULTITASKING, OVERLAID WINDOWS, *and* TILED WINDOWS.

Operator

The term *operator* can refer to several different things in personal computing. The most obvious (and often overlooked) example of an operator is the person who operates a computer. The term is also used in mathematics and logic.

In mathematics. A mathematical operator is a symbol that denotes something specific to be done with a quantity. A common example is the "unit imaginary" number i, which means the positive square root of -1. Electrical and electronics engineers use the lowercase letter j to denote this. Numbers such as $3i$, $-5i$, $j8$, and $-j6$ involve the i or j operator (they're exactly the same thing) applied to the numbers 3, -5, 8, and -6 respectively.

Sometimes, symbols like $+$, $-$, $\times$, and $/$, representing addition, subtraction, multiplication and division respectively, are called mathematical operators.

In logic. A logical operator is a symbol that denotes logical negation (NOT), conjunction (AND), or disjunction (OR). Negation is commonly denoted by means of a line over the letter representing a statement or

Optical character recognition

variable. It might also be represented by a minus sign, such as $-X$, or by a prime sign or apostrophe (X'). Inclusive OR is almost always denoted as addition ($X + Y$) in Boolean algebra. The logical AND is denoted by multiplication; this can be indicated by a times sign ($X \times Y$), a star ($X * Y$) or by writing the statements or variables one after the other (XY). *See also* BOOLEAN ALGEBRA, LOGIC, *and* LOGIC GATES.

Optical character recognition

Computers can translate printed matter, such as the text on this page, into digital data. The data can then be used in the same way as if you had typed it on a keyboard. This is done by means of *optical character recognition (OCR)*.

Reading text. In OCR of printed matter, such as the text on this page, a thin laser beam moves across the page. The laser beam scans in the same fashion as the electron beam in a television camera or picture tube. It follows the lines of text, just as your eyes do when you read. White paper reflects light; black ink does not. The reflected beam is therefore modulated; its intensity changes. This modulation is translated by software into digital code for use by the computer.

Optical character recognition is used by writers, editors, and publishers to transfer printed data to computer disks. Advanced OCR software can recognize mathematical symbols and other exotic notation, as well as capital and small letters, numbers, and punctuation marks. Whenever OCR is used, however, the results should always be checked. The system isn't perfect, and errors can creep into places, and occur in ways, that can cause embarrassment if you're not careful.

Vision systems. Computers and smart robots can incorporate OCR technology into their *vision systems*, enabling them to read labels and signs. The technology exists, for example, to build a robot with artificial intelligence (AI), along with OCR, that could get in your car and drive it anywhere. Perhaps someday, this will be commonly done. You might hand your personal robot a grocery list and say, "Please go get these things at the supermarket," and the robot will come back an hour later with just what you ordered: three bags full of various victuals. It might also mysteriously have picked up a couple of T shirts and a half dozen pairs of socks. (No machine is perfect.)

For a machine to read something at a distance, such as a road sign, the image is observed with a television camera, rather than by reflecting a scanned laser beam off the surface. This video image is then translated by OCR software into digital data. *See also* OPTICAL SCANNER *and* VISION SYSTEMS.

Optical computer technology

One of the most promising forms of alternative computer technology makes use of laser beams rather than electric currents to perform digital computations. This is called *optical computer technology*, and is generating interest in the United States and Japan.

Light versus electricity. An electric current flows as charge carriers pass from atom to atom in a conductor or semiconductor. In a wire, these charge carriers are electrons. In some materials, they are electron shortages called *holes*. An electrical current consisting of electrons flows about 18,000 miles per second in a wire, approximately one-tenth the speed of light. A current consisting of holes is usually quite a bit slower than that, but light beams travel at 186,282 miles per second in free space, and only a little slower in optical fibers. This means that, all other things being equal, an optical computer might perform operations 10 or more times faster than an electronic one.

The use of light beams has another advantage over electronic currents: light beams can pass through each other without interacting. Two, three, or a million laser beams can be shone so that they intersect, but there will be no interference between them. Electric currents don't work that way. Because of this, optical computers might be able to perform millions of operations in parallel, something unheard-of with electronic devices. The drawing illustrates the basic principle. There are eight inputs and eight outputs (represented by the binary numbers 000 through 111) in this example, but there could be 16, 32, 64, or any power of two, defining binary numbers having any number of bits. The only limit would be imposed by the number of lasers and sensors that could be packed into a given amount of physical space.

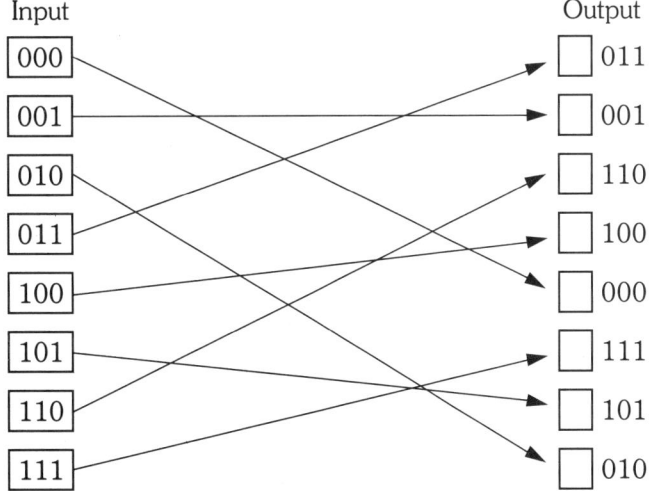

Light beams (arrowed lines) don't interfere with each other when their paths cross. This allows unlimited parallelism.

Highs and lows. In an optical computer, logic 1 (or "high") is usually represented by the presence of a light beam or pulse, while logic 0 ("low") is the absence of a light beam or pulse. However, there are other ways to encode logic into light. The color can be changed; for example, red could equal 1 and green could equal 0. Or the polarization might be altered; vertical might be 1 and horizontal might be 0. It is possible to modulate laser beams via a modem, putting electronic data into beams of light. Thousands of such signals can be carried by one laser.

A gradual changeover? Will optical computers eventually take over, making electronic computers obsolete? Perhaps, in time, that will happen. IBM's AS-400 computer was one of the first midrange systems to incorporate fiberoptic cables in its bus architecture. This resulted in extremely high data transfer rates between the main system and peripherals such as the disk drives.

The changeover to optical computing will probably be gradual, not abrupt; it will most likely be partial, not total. Some optical integrated circuits have already been put into use. One such device takes a video picture and encodes it directly into light beams sent along optical fibers. Another example of the changeover is in communications, where fiberoptic data transmission has become commonplace. In mass storage, the CD-ROM uses optics to read and write data.

Instead of silicon, the semiconductor material most commonly used to make conventional integrated circuits (chips), optical devices have been fabricated from lithium niobate (a compound of lithium and niobium). This allows control of optical pulses by means of electrical currents.

Despite the many advantages of optical technology, it is not a panacea for all the shortcomings of electronics. There are some things that optical technology cannot do, such as maintain a reliable satellite data link. (Clouds get in the way of light beams.) There are some devices and processes that will always work best with old-fashioned electronic technology. *See also* ALTERNATIVE COMPUTER TECHNOLOGY, BACTERIORHODOPSIN, CD-ROM, FIBEROPTIC CABLE, FIBEROPTIC DATA TRANSMISSION, FLOPTICAL DISKETTE AND DRIVE, LASER PRINTER, OPTICAL SCANNER, *and* VISION SYSTEMS.

Optical scanner

An *optical scanner* is a machine that converts hardcopy text and graphics into digital form, suitable for processing and storage in a computer. Text scanners work in conjunction with optical character recognition (OCR) software. A text scanner and OCR system is an "unprinter"; a printer converts binary data into text, a scanner does the opposite.

Convenience. Optical scanners can save untold hours of tedious manual retyping. Perhaps you wrote a manuscript several years ago, before you owned a computer. The hardcopy of that manuscript sits in your basement, awaiting the massive editing that can turn it into a great novel. It needs the power of your computer's word processor, but you can't deal with the prospect of retyping its hundreds of pages! An optical scanner can do away with most of the hard labor involved in getting hardcopy onto disk.

A good scanner, of the type you'd probably want for your novel, might cost $1000 to $2000. For a 1000-page novel, that comes to a dollar or two per page, which is the lowest price you're likely to find for any manuscript typing service. And, after you're done scanning your novel, you'll still have the scanner, which you can use for your poetry collection, important records, or whatever else.

For many entrepreneurs, optical scanning can make the difference between staying afloat and going bankrupt. It can do the work of one or two full-time typists for a tiny fraction of the long-term cost. Big companies can save money, too. Lawyers and doctors find scanners invaluable for backing up files of all kinds.

Range of features. The simplest optical scanners can convert text, but not pictures, into binary data. These scanners only recognize light and dark regions on a page. Each character is analyzed and converted into binary code.

More complex scanners can detect shades of gray. These scanners are suitable for converting black-and-white drawings and photographs into their digital equivalents for storage on disk. They cost somewhat more than text-only types.

The most sophisticated optical scanners can render color images, text, photographs, and everything else needed to make a complete, accurate digital record of any document. Color scanners use three different light beams (red, blue, and green) to get three different images, which are processed and combined in much the same way as a color television camera works.

The image resolution of an optical scanner is measured in *dots per inch (DPI)*. The higher the DPI, the more detail the scanner can "see." For reliable scanning of text, an image resolution of at least 300 DPI is recommended. Many scanners meet this requirement. For photographs, you can often get by with something less. For images, greater detail translates into more memory consumed. Color increases the amount of memory or storage that an image takes up, if the image resolution remains constant.

One convenient scanning feature is known as *TWAIN*. With TWAIN, you can use a scanner to import hardcopy directly into word-

Optical scanner

processed documents, spreadsheets, databases, or presentation packages. You don't have to scan things into a separate file first, and then import that file to your other applications.

For example, you might take an excerpt from a magazine article (after having secured permission to reprint) and put it into a piece you're writing. You can directly insert mailing lists, drawings, or anything else into any application. If you're thinking about purchasing a scanner, be sure to inquire about TWAIN; it can save you a lot of time converting and copying files.

Three forms. Scanners come in three basic configurations. The scanner that's best for you will depend on what you want to do with it, and on how much money you're willing to spend for it.

➤ *Handheld scanner* The cheapest type of scanner is a handheld scanner. It looks something like one of the barcode readers seen in retail stores. You roll the unit over the paper containing the text or graphics you want to scan (see the drawing). Because the unit is not as wide as most pages, you'll have to make two or three passes over the page and "stitch" the results together.

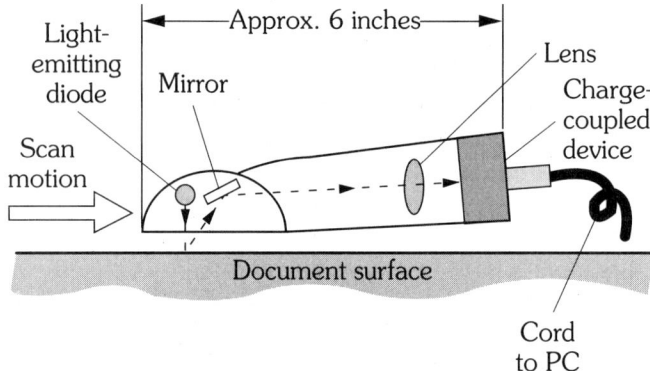

Light beams (arrowed lines) don't interfere with each other when their paths cross. This allows unlimited parallelism.

Handheld scanners are preferred by people who scan small images, such as snapshots. They are lightweight and need almost no desk space. In fact, when you're not using a handheld scanner, you can put it in a drawer. One problem with handheld scanners, however, is that you might try to scan too fast. Some handheld scanners have speed indicators that tell you if you're going too fast. Another potential difficulty is not getting a straight-line scan. Most handheld units have built-in guides (like miniature rolling pins) that minimize this problem.

➤ *Flatbed scanner* If you want to scan a book or magazine, a flatbed scanner is much easier to use than a handheld scanner. The unit looks something like a photocopier. Using a flatbed scanner is similar to working a small photocopy machine. You lay the page or photograph on a clear glass, and the scanning head moves past it, picking up the image.

A flatbed scanner costs two or three times as much as a handheld scanner, but if you do a lot of full-page scanning, the added convenience can prove worth the expense. On the other hand, flatbed scanners consume desk space, which, if you have a couple of printers and a fax machine, might already be at a premium. One solution is to get a separate table for those peripherals you use the least often. Ingenuity is the key here.

➤ *Sheet scanner* A *sheet scanner* is a variation of the flatbed unit, with two main differences. First, in the sheet scanner, you can only scan standard size sheets, one at a time. You can't scan bound books or magazines. Second, the sheet moves through the machine, rather than sitting still during the scanning process.

A sheet scanner would be fine for that manuscript you wrote, assuming it was typed on standard 8.5-by-11-inch paper. If you want to scan a book or magazine, however, you'd either have to rip the page out or photocopy the page and then scan the photocopied sheet.

Precautions. Scanning technology has lagged behind printing technology. "Unprinting" is more difficult than printing for a computer to do. The situation is similar to that for speech recognition versus speech synthesis; recognition is tougher.

Even the best scanners make some mistakes, especially if the text contains nonstandard symbols. Highly technical material presents the worst problems. Some mathematical symbols are so esoteric that the average person is befuddled by them, let alone a machine. Ink spots, stray markings, and smudges on a page can cause scanning errors, in much the same way as background noise confuses a speech recognition system.

A human reader can often tell what a printed letter should be, even when it is severely mutilated. Computers don't have human intuition. To some extent, this can be corrected by a built-in spell checker. Some OCR programs have spell checking, but this introduces its own set of problems because it, too, is imperfect.

If a scanner doesn't recognize a character, it will usually print a *tag*—a blank space, underline, or default symbol such as @ or #. Scanned text must always be carefully proofread, and corrections made with word processing software, after the data has been stored on disk. *See also* DOTS PER INCH, IMAGE RESOLUTION, OPTICAL CHARACTER RECOGNITION, SPELL CHECKING, *and* VISION SYSTEMS.

Ordinate

A graph with two axes is sometimes called the *xy-plane*, because the axes are labeled *x* and *y*. Two-dimensional graphs in Cartesian coordinates are extremely common, and are easily plotted with analytical graphics programs.

Dependent coordinate. In an *xy*-plane graph, every point has two coordinates, represented by ordered pairs (*x,y*). One of the axes represents the independent variable, and the other axis represents the dependent variable. Usually, the independent variable is *x*, and the dependent variable is *y*. Then *y* depends on, or is a *function* of, *x*. The dependent variable almost always has the vertical axis.

The *ordinate* of a point in the *xy*-plane is the dependent-variable coordinate. If (*x,y*) = (3,–4), the ordinate is –4. If (*x, y*) = (–4,2), the ordinate is 2. These examples are shown in drawing A. Sometimes the entire dependent-variable axis is called the ordinate.

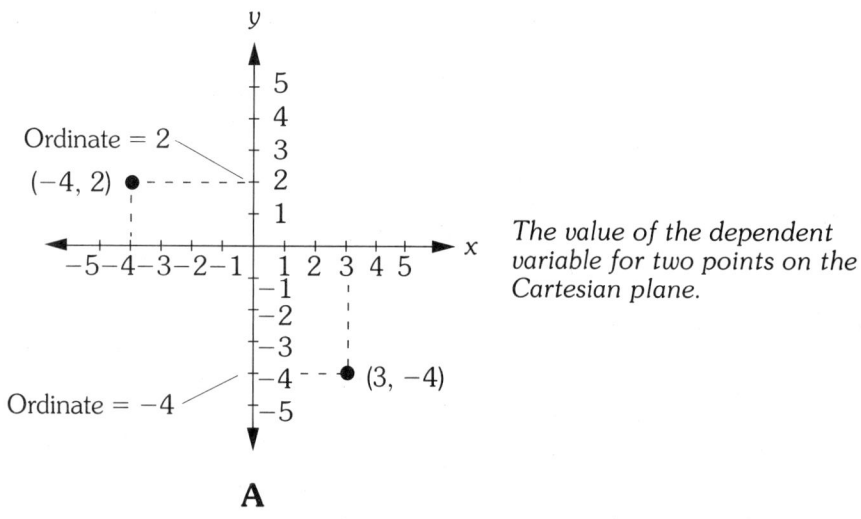

The value of the dependent variable for two points on the Cartesian plane.

A

Parameter. What makes a variable dependent? In science and mathematics, you'll find relationships where one thing depends on another. For example, the temperature at a given outdoor location almost always varies with the time of day. If you graph temperature as a function of the time of day, then temperature is the dependent variable, or parameter; it depends on the time (among other things like location and altitude). If it is 72°F in a given place at 3:00 p.m., then the ordinate for that point is 72°. Drawing B shows an example of a temperature-versus-time graph in which this is the case.

Although you could call time the dependent variable, saying that the ordinate is 3:00 p.m., this would suggest that time depends on other factors. There are situations where that can happen. For example, if the independent variable were longitude, you could move among time zones, and thus time would vary with your location on the earth.

Ordinate

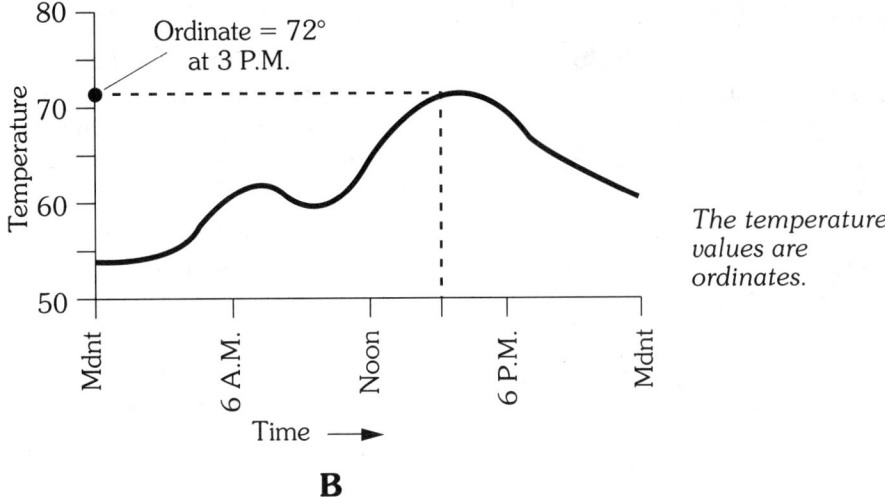

The temperature values are ordinates.

B

Making sense. When graphing things on a PC, you should keep in mind which value should be the ordinate, and which axis should be vertical. This will ensure that your graphs make sense. In a normal temperature-versus-time graph, the temperature would be plotted on the vertical axis; each point on this axis is an ordinate.

If you plot time on the vertical axis, then each time value appears to be an ordinate, as shown in drawing C. This will look strange to a mathematician. If time is, in fact, the dependent variable here, then this curve is not a function. It also suggests that time depends on temperature, a notion that will raise physicists' eyebrows. *See also* ABSCISSA, DEPENDENT VARIABLE, *and* INDEPENDENT VARIABLE.

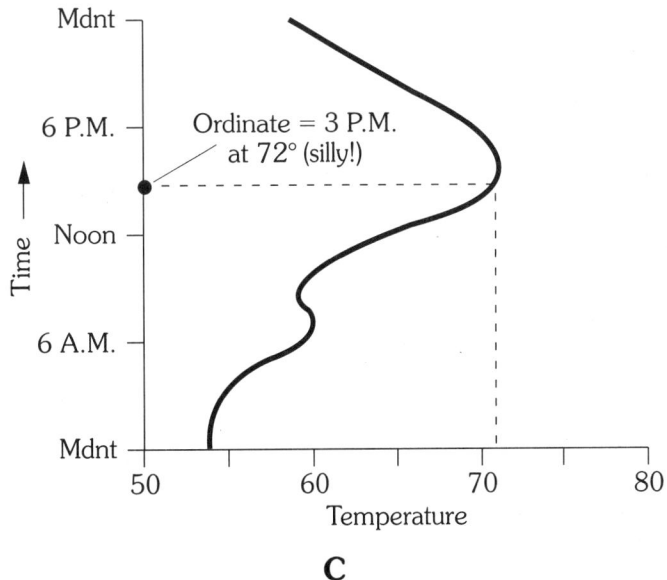

C

Time values are rarely defined as ordinates.

OR gate

An *OR gate* is a digital logic gate with two or more inputs and a single output. The OR gate performs the Boolean inclusive-OR function. If all inputs are zero (false), then the output is zero. If any of the inputs is one (true), then the output is one.

The illustration shows the schematic symbol for an OR gate, along with a truth table for a two-input device. *See also* AND GATE, BOOLEAN ALGEBRA, EXCLUSIVE-OR GATE, INVERTER, NAND GATE, *and* NOR GATE.

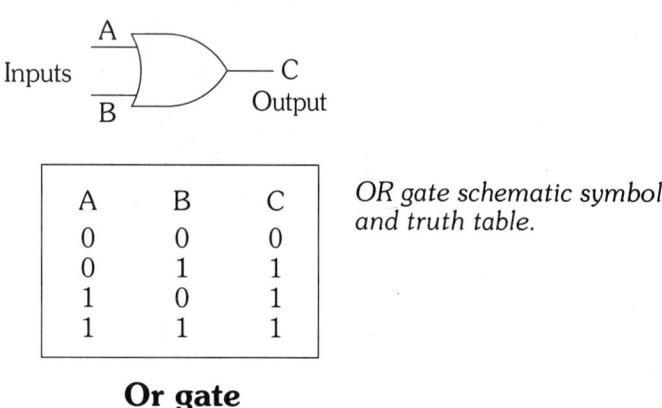

OR gate schematic symbol and truth table.

Or gate

Original PC keyboard

The very first home computer made by IBM was called the PC, for "personal computer." The term *PC* has become generic, and is now used in reference to all desktop and laptop computers manufactured by hundreds of different companies.

The *original PC keyboard* had fewer keys and was less user-friendly than keyboards in today's computers. There were only 10 function keys (instead of 12), located in two vertical rows at the left side of the keyboard. Arrow keys (also called cursor-movement keys) were contained within a dual-function numeric keypad; there was no separate set of arrow keys.

The Enter key was much smaller than is the case today; many PC users complained about this, pointing out that even electronic typewriters had a large key for the carriage return (which is one function of the Enter key). Perhaps most significant, the Caps Lock, Number Lock, and Scroll Lock functions did not have indicator lights. Thus, to tell whether or not these functions were activated, the user had to find out by actually observing the way the computer responded to the keyboard. The drawing shows the general layout of the original PC keyboard. Engineers at IBM acted on consumer suggestions, and improved their PC keyboard design, producing the enhanced PC keyboard. *See also* ENHANCED PC KEYBOARD.

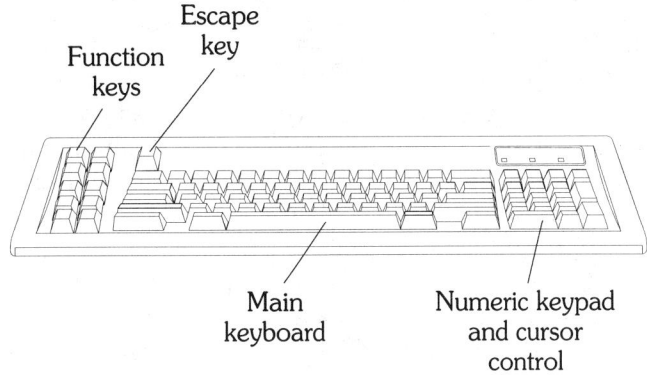

The original PC keyboard had several shortcomings, and has been expanded and improved.

OSI-RM

See OPEN SYSTEMS INTERCONNECTION REFERENCE MODEL.

OS/2

A major contribution of IBM to the software market, *OS/2* (short for *Operating System/2*) combines some of the best features of other available operating systems and environments, especially DOS, Windows, Macintosh, and UNIX.

OS/2 has a graphical user interface (GUI) that closely imitates a traditional office arrangement. The background, called the *desktop*, is organized in a manner similar to the way you would arrange your desk, with folders, a typewriter, and a wastebasket. "Sticky notes" can be used for reminders of important events and things to do. Alarms remind you of appointments. You can have more than one folder open simultaneously. You can do multitasking—for example, work on a database while editing a document in the word processor.

With OS/2 for Windows, you can make use of most of the software you already have if you are now using Windows. However, for optimal performance, you should use the OS/2 native applications, that is, the software designed especially to go with OS/2. For DOS-based applications, OS/2 can function as a virtual DOS machine (VDM). A *boot manager* allows you to start up your computer in the operating system of your choice. The boot manager keeps the different operating systems from conflicting with each other.

OS/2 uses a *High Performance File System (HPFS)* that allows you to have filenames up to 32 characters long. You are not limited to the "eight-and-three" format (eight characters maximum, then a period, then three characters maximum) of traditional DOS. You must be

Outline font

careful, however, if you create a long filename and plan to store it in a DOS system or diskette. If you make a filename that's too long for DOS, OS/2 will cut it off at eight characters for storage in the DOS medium.

A unique feature of OS/2 is that it lets you create your own applications. This is especially good for experienced computer users. If you have special needs that aren't met by any of the commercially available software packages, and if you have the know-how, you can make up your own software and OS/2 will run it.

The GUI in OS/2 differs somewhat from the traditional Windows scheme. For this reason, there is a learning curve involved when switching from Windows to OS/2. The interface bears some resemblance to a graphical UNIX shell; in other ways it is more like the Macintosh system than like traditional IBM-compatible operating systems.

Some people think that OS/2 is the operating system of the future because it can run programs from most other operating systems, including DOS/Windows, Macintosh, UNIX and its variants, and other less well-known systems. *See also* DOS, MACINTOSH, MULTIPLATFORM ENVIRONMENT, MULTITASKING, SYSTEM 7, UNIX, *and* WINDOWS.

Outline font

An *outline font* is a method by which a computer generates letters, numbers, punctuation marks, and other symbols for printing. It is a scalable font because it is easy to resize. An outline font has certain assets and shortcomings compared to the alternative, a *bitmapped font*.

It's all graphics. When a printer receives instructions for an outline font, it's told to make a picture of the characters. That is, the printer regards everything as a graphic, whether it's a drawing, table, chart, or plain text.

All printers make hardcopies by laying dots down on paper. The more dots per inch (DPI) the printer can put on the paper, the better the image resolution. A rating of at least 300 DPI qualifies a printer as a high-resolution, or letter-quality, printer. These days, all types of printers—dot-matrix, inkjet, and laser—can work at 300 DPI or more.

For the printer to change an image into hardcopy, *firmware* is used. An example is a program in Printer Command Language (PCL). When an outline font is used, the computer sends the printer mathematical instructions detailing a complex graphic image that happens to be made up of letters, numbers, and other symbols. The firmware converts this into instructions that tell the printer exactly where to lay down the dots on the paper.

Outline font

Because an outline font requires a printer to treat text just like illustrations, outline fonts print out more slowly than bitmapped fonts. The quality of an outline font is superior to a bitmap font, however, and the type size can be changed without introducing "jaggies" into the characters.

Resizing. The big advantage of outline fonts arises from the fact that the shape of a character for any given typeface does not depend on its size. This is not true for bitmapped fonts, in which smaller characters turn out "coarser" than big ones.

The drawing shows three sizes of an uppercase letter *T* in a hypothetical, simple outline typeface. Although the actual dimensions vary, the proportions are identical in each case. To enlarge or reduce the size of this character, or any other in a given typeface, the computer multiplies all the dimensions by some constant number. For size reduction, this constant is smaller than one; for enlargement it is greater than one. With a high-resolution printer, characters in an outline font look continuous even at very small type sizes. *See also* BITMAPPED FONT, DOTS PER INCH, FONT, HIGH-RESOLUTION PRINTER, IMAGE RESOLUTION, *and* SCALABLE FONT.

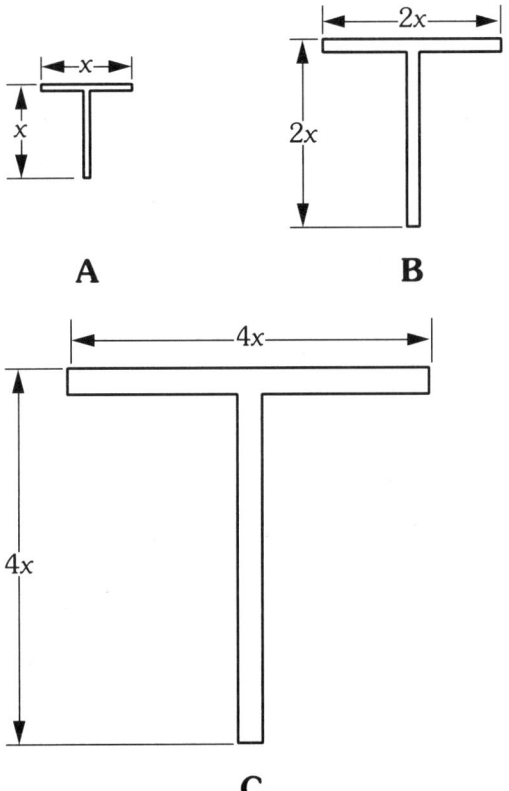

The letter T in three sizes. At A, height and width are x units. At B, they are 2x; at C, they are 4x.

Outline utility

There are many different software packages available for word processing. Each package has features that make it appealing to writers in various specialties. An *outline utility* enhances a writer's ability to organize structured writing.

Outline form. When writing an instruction manual, technical report, or formal magazine article, most writers make an outline before actually starting to write. An outline consists of a main title (the title of the whole work), with two or more major, or level 1, subtitles. Beneath each major subtitle, there can be minor, or level 2, subtitles. (Subtitles are sometimes called subheads.) The hierarchy can continue down to level 3, 4, or even 5. Table A shows an outline for a hypothetical paper, "The History of Electromagnetic Communication."

Table A Original outline

The history of electromagnetic communication

    Wireless Communication
        Continuous waves
        Modulation
    Early Experiments with Electricity
        Lightning
        Batteries
        Generators
        Spark transmitters
    Sending Pictures
        Early experiments
        Black-and-white television
        Color television
    The Digital Revolution
        Digital logic
        Data conversion
        Satellite links
        The information highway

There are rules for outline organization. These can be found in a writing style guide such as *The Chicago Manual of Style*, published by the University of Chicago Press.

Writing. Once you've decided, at least tentatively, how you're going to organize your piece, you'll find that the writing comes easier if you follow the outline as closely as possible. Some writers prefer to write from the lowest, or most minor, subtitles upward, filling in parts of the document as the information becomes available. Once all the "dirty work" is done, the transitions can be written, and the writer can think about reorganizing the work if necessary.

Once you get used to writing with a good word processor, you'll appreciate the power of the PC in helping you to write. If you've been using a word processor for a few months and then go back to a typewriter, you'll really discover this! With the computer, you can fill in the parts of your work without having to work straight through from beginning to end. You can skip around any way you want. There'll be no more correction fluid, scissors and glue, or photocopying sessions. You must be sure, however, that you don't leave any part of the work unfinished. That would be indicated by a subtitle at some level with no text following it.

Outline mode. If you have an outline utility, you need not think, while writing the work, about whether or not it's optimally organized. At any point during the writing process, you can switch to *outline mode* and all the text will vanish, leaving only the subheads. This will show you the outline only. If you do this after all the writing is done, you'll see a lot more in that outline than you did when you first started writing the piece. Think of what you see when you look at a city's street map for the first time; now think of looking at the same map after having ridden a bicycle along every street, avenue, boulevard, and dead-end dirt road in town.

Suppose you decide, after having written the text, to change the organization of the article outlined in Table A (page 792) to that of Table B (page 794). You go to outline mode, and edit the outline as if it were a document. All the text after each subhead, at any level, is a block that moves right along with the subhead. When you expand the manuscript back to text mode, it will be written according to the new outline.

A word of caution: Always proofread a work thoroughly after editing it in outline mode! Some transitional sentences might need rewriting to reflect the organizational changes you have made. *See also* BLOCK *and* WORD PROCESSING.

Overlaid windows

In Windows or any similar graphical user interface (GUI), it's possible to have two or more different files or menus on the screen at the same time. The term *overlaid windows* refers to a "stack" of files or menus, with one fully visible and the others partially obscured (see the drawing). The windows seem to be lying one on top of another.

One of the most effective ways to stack windows is to have them in an orderly pile, with the menu bar of each window visible. This is called *cascading*. Because you can see each menu bar, you know which window is which, even though you can only see the contents of the

Overlaid windows

top window. You can "pull" any window out and place it on top, just as if the windows were file folders. In fact, in Macintosh computers, the term *folder* is used instead of *window*.

Table B Edited outline

The history of electromagnetic communication
    Early Experiments with Electricity
        Lightning
        Batteries
        Generators
    Wireless Communication
        Spark transmitters
        Continuous waves
        Modulation
    Sending Pictures
        Early experiments
        Black-and-white television
        Color television
    The Digital Revolution
        Digital logic
        Data conversion
        Satellite links
        The information highway

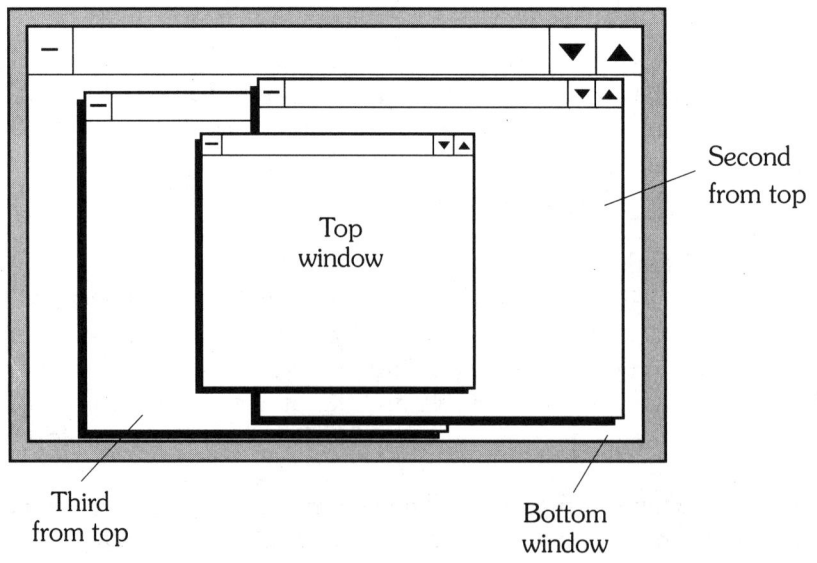

Overlaid windows let you see several files at the same time.

In overlaid windows, the topmost window is the one in which you're working. The file in this window is said to be in the foreground; the others are in the background. When you pull a window from a stack and place it on top, you move its contents from the background to the foreground.

It's possible to place two or more windows on the screen so that all of them are fully visible. This arrangement is called *tiled windows*. *See also* CASCADE, GRAPHICAL USER INTERFACE, TILED WINDOWS, *and* WINDOWS.

Overtype mode

In word processing, *overtype mode* refers to the behavior of text onscreen as you type. In overtype mode, if you place the cursor somewhere within the text and begin typing on the keyboard, the characters you type will go "over" the ones that are already there, replacing them.

For example, suppose you have text that reads as follows:

The Summer Solstice in the Northern Hemisphere occurs at, or near, December 22. At this time, the days are shortest and the nights are longest.

If you've studied any astronomy, you know that this is wrong, and it must be changed. The quickest way to fix it is to change the second word in the passage from *Summer* to *Winter*. Because these two words have the same number of letters, this is a good candidate for overtype mode. You change to overtype mode if necessary (usually by pressing the Insert key) and put the cursor on the *S*. Then, as you type *Winter*, it goes right over the word *Summer*—a perfect fit. In fact, you really only need to type *Wint*, since *er* is in the same place in both words.

When you are finished using overtype mode, be sure to change your word processor back to insert mode. Otherwise, you'll end up replacing text you meant to keep. *See also* INSERT KEY *and* WORD PROCESSING.

Overwriting

Overwriting is the process of replacing data on a hard disk or diskette. When you overwrite a file, the PC partially or completely erases the old data.

When you are about to overwrite a file, the computer will ask you if you're sure you want to do it. This gives you a last-minute "out." If you're using a graphical interface such as Windows, you'll have buttons marked OK and Cancel, or Yes and No. You simply move the pointer to the appropriate button and click the mouse. If you're using DOS, you'll get a question such as "File exists, overwrite it?" If you

Overwriting

want to overwrite, type Y for Yes and press Enter; if not, type N for No and press Enter.

It's always a good idea to keep a backup copy of all your data. That way, even if you accidentally overwrite a file, thereby destroying the old data, you'll still have it in your archives for retrieval.

Some programs automatically back up overwritten files; they appear in the directory with the filename extension .BAK. If you overwrite a file repeatedly, the .BAK file will keep up with the most recent file revision; you'll lose earlier versions of the file unless you have saved them in some other place. *See also* ARCHIVES, BACKUP, DIRECTORY, FILE ERASURE, *and* UNDELETION.

Packaged software

Packaged software refers to a set of programs combined and sold as a unit on diskettes or CD-ROM. You buy them at the computer store, office supply house, or via mail-order.

Commercial software packages, also known as *off-the-shelf software*, are generally the best-quality programs you can find because the programs have been thoroughly tested and debugged. Flaws occasionally crop up in programs that haven't been on the market for long, but customers bring them to the manufacturers' attention right away, and they are corrected in subsequent shipments.

A commercial package is not likely to contain a *Trojan horse* or *virus*. These are programs written deliberately by malicious hackers for the purpose of sabotaging computer systems. Manufacturers are well aware of how hackers can get into software; they subject their programs to rigorous quality control, just as pharmaceutical companies employ safeguards to prevent poisons from getting into their products.

When you get software from an unknown, obscure source, or when you download it from online, there is some risk of "adulteration" by a Trojan horse or of "infection" by a virus. Your safeguard against this is to download software onto diskettes, never onto your hard disk. Then, run the diskette through a *vaccine* before using it. *See also* ALPHA TEST, BETA TEST, SOFTWARE, TROJAN HORSE, VACCINE, *and* VIRUS.

Packet communications

Anybody who has a PC can connect it to the telephone lines using a modem, or to a radio transceiver using a terminal node controller. Then, the PC can communicate with other machines. *Packet communications* (often called simply *packet*) is one way in which computers can communicate.

Packet networks. A *packet* is a message sent from a computer at a *source* station to another computer at a *destination* station. Anyone who has a PC can interface it to the telephone line or a radio transceiver. It is not necessary for the operator at the destination station to be physically present for a message to be received; the computer can store it. For this reason, packet is a form of *time-shifting communications*. Packet provides rapid, error-free transmission and reception of messages.

Packet networks are getting larger, easier to access, and more sophisticated all the time. If you tap in at one point, you can take advantage of a network. Amateur radio operators communicate via a special form of this mode, called *packet radio*.

Fast mail. Packet is like a fast mail service. It's similar to a facsimile network of the type you can access via the telephone. The data speed is high, allowing long messages to be sent in short signal bursts. Packet is also self-correcting.

Reliability and ease of use are important features of packet networks. The day is fast approaching when you will be able to sit down at your PC and address a message to any packet station, anywhere in the world, and be confident that the network will automatically get it there within minutes or, at most, a few hours. As the so-called "information superhighway" evolves, coordinating satellite, microwave, and fiberoptic data links, speed and reliability of packet communications will improve.

Protocol. In order to make a packet network function, all the computers must use *protocols* that adhere to a standard model. The universal standard is called the *open systems interconnection reference model*, abbreviated *OSI-RM*.

OSI-RM is arranged into seven layers, ranging from the physical level to the application level. Amateur packet-radio networks have not yet made use of the full capabilities of OSI-RM. Advanced government systems, and those proposed by well-known figures in the computer world, do employ OSI-RM to its full extent. This allows for the exchange of software via telephone or radio links and for remote control of computers and peripheral equipment.

When you send a packet, the computers do all of the routing work, once the source station operator knows the local node of the desired

Packet-radio bulletin-board system

destination station. The user only needs to type in the destination-station information in order to establish the route. The protocol keeps the connection intact by means of rerouting, in case there is some disruption along a given route. *See also* AMATEUR RADIO, GEOSTATIONARY-SATELLITE DATA LINK, LOCAL AREA NETWORK, LOW-EARTH-ORBIT (LEO) SATELLITE DATA LINK, MODEM, NETWORK, OPEN SYSTEMS INTERCONNECTION REFERENCE MODEL, PACKET-RADIO BULLETIN-BOARD SYSTEM, PROTOCOL, TERMINAL NODE CONTROLLER, *and* WIDE AREA NETWORK.

Packet-radio bulletin-board system

A bulletin-board system (BBS) is a set of stored messages accessible by means of a computer. Many PC users are familiar with BBSs. You access them using a modem to connect the computer to telephone lines. There might be a telephone toll charge associated with the use of a BBS.

Amateur radio makes it possible to communicate over long distances without telephone lines, and therefore without tolls. This is a *packet-radio bulletin-board system (PBBS)*.

With a *terminal node controller (TNC)* connecting a PC to a radio transceiver, you can access PBBSs. Messages can be left for other computer users, or retrieved, in a very short time. It's like a fast mail service.

The PBBS is a form of *time-shifting communications*. It is a way for radio amateurs to send and receive messages, even when the destination operators are not physically at their stations. Because of this, there is often some delay in transferring the message because the operator of the destination station must check the PBBS before he or she can get the message (hence the term *time shifting*, which sounds better than *time delayed*). The PBBS is a public storage system; messages for a large number of people are left on the bulletin board.

As packet radio gets more sophisticated, PBBSs can be expected to become more versatile. It is already possible for different PBBSs to exchange messages. Eventually, there might be a single huge world PBBS (WPBBS?), with individual sub-PBBSs for countries, states, and provinces.

If you want to leave a message for someone who has a packet radio station, but not do it on the general PBBS, you can opt for a quasi-private way know as *electronic mail*. If you must have an absolute guarantee of privacy, no form of electronic media should be used. This includes ordinary telephone conversations. It is one of the less pleasant aspects of modern data communications. The Postal Service ("snail mail") still provides optimal privacy for the average citizen when face-to-face visits are impractical or impossible. *See also*

Page breaks

AMATEUR RADIO, BULLETIN-BOARD SYSTEM, ELECTRONIC MAIL, MAILBOX, *and* PACKET COMMUNICATIONS.

Page breaks

See HARD PAGE BREAKS, PAGINATION, *and* SOFT PAGE BREAKS.

Page-Description Language

When computer data is printed, it must be transformed from the image on the monitor to a set of signals that tells the printer exactly what movements it must make. This transformation function varies depending on the type, make, and model of the printer.

The printer program. When you purchase a new PC, software package, or printer, you'll generally have to install special software, intended specifically for the printer's make and model. There will be dozens of different printers listed, and you'll have to be sure to choose the correct one. This software, once installed, resides on your hard disk. When you tell the computer to print something, this program goes into action, changing the data into the right form, so your printer can deal with it. The transcription process is done within the computer, not within the printer, as shown in the drawing at A.

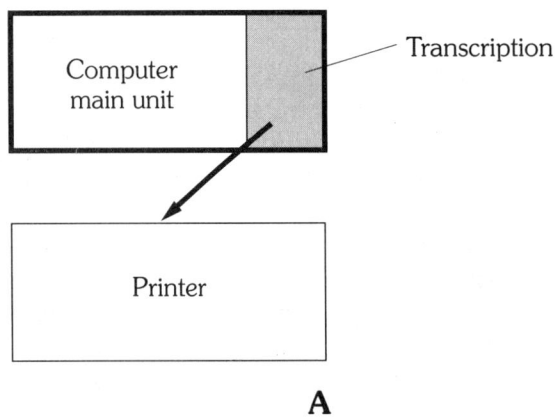

At A, transcription to PDL in the main unit of PC.

If you have two different printers, chances are that you'll need two different printer programs. If you use the wrong printer program, a printer might work to an extent, but ignore or misinterpret the codes for special type styles and other effects. For example, the computer might think it's telling the printer to print italic type, but the printer will interpret this as an order to print oversized characters. In the worst case, the printer won't function at all.

Device independence. Suppose that printers were all equipped to work from the same computer data, so that you wouldn't have to worry about the printer software when changing printers. Of course, the transcription process would still be necessary to change computer data into mechanical movements, but instead of having the computer be responsible for the process, it would be done in the printer instead, as shown in the drawing at B. Such a scheme is, in fact, used with some printers. It's called *Page-Description Language (PDL)*.

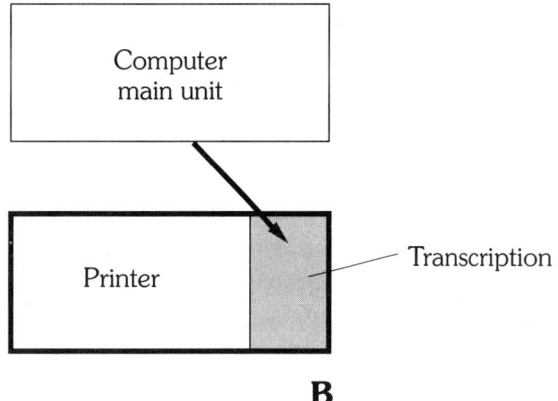

At B, transcription within printer.

For a printer to make use of PDL, it must have its own microprocessor, memory, and translation program (often called an *interpreter*). Because of the additional hardware and software needed for the interpreter, PDL-equipped printers cost more than equivalent printers without PDL. Some computer users find, however, that the benefits outweigh the increased cost.

When your computer outputs in PDL, the data is said to have *device independence* relative to all printers equipped with PDL, meaning you can switch printers without loading different programs. PDL offers hardware convenience without sacrificing precision in the transcribed image. Every detail that the computer "knows" can be rendered in the printed product. All the responsibility for good image resolution is thus placed on the printer, where, arguably, it belongs. This makes a big difference in print and image quality, especially with laser printers working with outline fonts and object-oriented graphics.

In desktop publishing, PDL offers clear advantages over the older printing methods. One especially popular PDL, called *PostScript*, is known to almost everyone who has had any experience in desktop publishing. *See also* DESKTOP PUBLISHING, HIGH-RESOLUTION PRINTER, OBJECT-ORIENTED GRAPHICS, OUTLINE FONT, *and* POSTSCRIPT.

Page Down key

The *Page Down key*, found on most computer keyboards, moves the cursor forward (down) in word-processed text by the equivalent of one full screen on the monitor. On the enhanced PC keyboard, the Page Down key is located in a group of six keys to the right of the main section, as shown in the drawing on the next page.

Page layout program

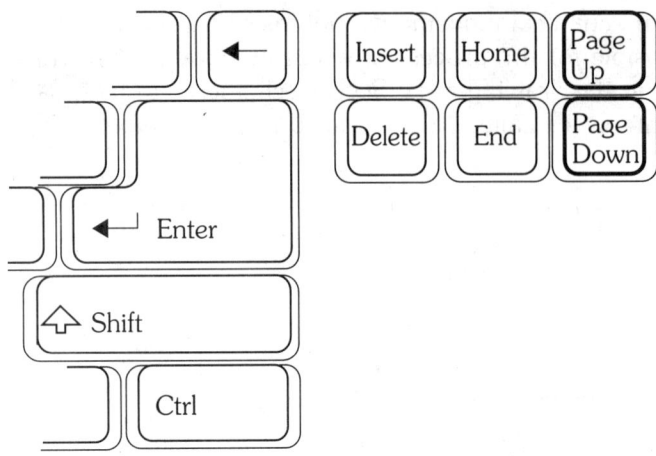

The Page Down key is just to the right of the main section in the enhanced PC keyboard.

When you press Page Down in a long text document, the actual position of the cursor does not change with respect to the screen. Instead, the text appears to scroll upward, so the cursor moves downward relative to the text. *See also* PAGE UP KEY.

Page layout program

A *page layout program* is a combination of word processing and graphics software commonly used in desktop publishing. It gives you a view of each page of your manuscript or publication as it will appear in final, printed form.

A typical page layout, in simplified form, is shown in the drawing. (An actual page-layout display, as seen on a computer monitor, would show more detail than this.) Such a layout is typical of formal reports, brochures, and magazine articles. Illustrations and tables fit into blank rectangles; text is represented by sets of parallel, horizontal lines. Drawing and table captions are represented as dotted lines. Text, drawings, and tables can be imported into the document from other documents.

The user can change the sizes, shapes, and locations of the boxes. The format can be set up as single-column, typical of many books and some magazines; double-column, common in reference books and magazines; or as three or more columns, in the case of, for example, a newspaper. Everything can be tailored for the best overall appearance and the optimum ratio of text to illustrations on the page.

Once the page layout has been finalized on the computer, a hardcopy can be made with the printer. It's always a good idea to do this because errors and formatting problems often stand out in hardcopy, in a way that defies the best page-layout programs. *See also* DESKTOP PUBLISHING *and* WYSIWYG.

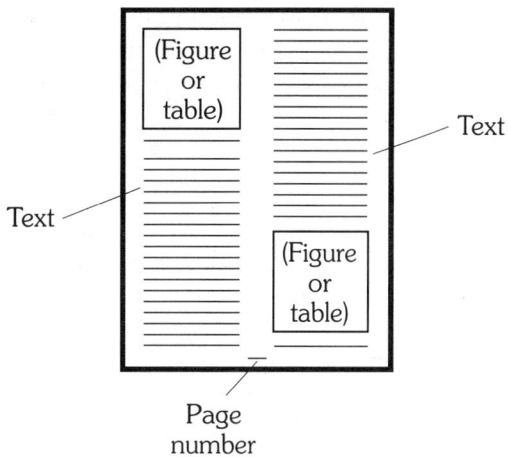

A page layout program shows how text and art are arranged.

Page-mode memory

Page-mode memory is a form of RAM (random-access memory) designed to have short access time. This helps speed up the operation of computers with advanced microprocessors.

The clock speed of a microprocessor sets the pace at which the chip operates, but the actual speed of the computer is determined by other factors too. A slow hard disk, for example, impairs the performance in applications where data must frequently be read from and written onto the disk. Slow RAM is a much more serious constraint because RAM is heavily used in virtually all applications. A computer with a fast microprocessor but slow RAM is like a Ferrari stuck in first gear.

In page mode, the RAM is broken down into compartments called *pages*. When data is stored in RAM, it goes into a certain page, whose location the CPU (central processing unit) "remembers." When that piece of information must be found, the CPU knows exactly where in RAM to find it.

You might think of memory pages as analogous to the articles or page numbers in this book. Imagine how long it would take you to find information about some term in here, if the articles weren't arranged in any particular order and none of them had titles! *See also* ACCESS TIME *and* RANDOM-ACCESS MEMORY.

Page Up key

The *Page Up key*, found on most computer keyboards, moves the cursor backward (up) in word-processed text by the equivalent of one full screen on the monitor. On the enhanced PC keyboard, this key is located in a group of six keys to the right of the main section.

When you press Page Up in a long document, the actual position of the cursor does not change with respect to the screen. Instead, the text appears to scroll downward, so the cursor moves upward relative to the text. *See also* PAGE DOWN KEY.

Pagination

Pagination refers to the process by which text data is automatically divided into pages as it is printed. Pagination consists of the insertion of page breaks into text documents.

Different programs provide varying amounts of control over the pagination. For example, you can usually set the number of lines per page, and insert running headers, page numbers, and other data. You can adjust the software to accommodate nonstandard paper lengths, such as 14 inches (legal size) or 5.5 inches (half size). Some of this pagination data exists within the word processing software, and some is within the printer software. Once you get used to the pagination nuances of your hardware and software, you'll be able to tell where the page breaks will occur in a printed document without actually having to print it. You'll also be able to tailor your document so that the page breaks come out where you want them.

Most printers will divide a printed document into pages, even in the absence of pagination data from the computer. This is done by firmware in the printer. You might select, for example, positions for the left and right margins, as well as the paper length and the number of lines per inch. However, special instructions, such as commands to print italics, boldface, and superscripts, must come from the printer software or page-description language within the computer. A printer can't guess at codes within a word-processed file; such codes must be specifically transmitted from the computer to the printer.

When the page-division process is done by the word processing or printer software in the computer, it is called *background pagination*. When page division is done by the printer firmware alone, it's called *foreground pagination*. A printer will sometimes work faster with foreground pagination than with background pagination, but you have less control over the locations of the page breaks. The speed difference is greatest on old computers with slow microprocessor chips. *See also* HARD PAGE BREAKS *and* SOFT PAGE BREAKS.

Paging memory

Paging memory is a special way to store and organize computer memory. In paging memory, the address is independent of the physical place where the data is situated. Paging is more flexible than other methods of specifying memory addresses. For example, some of the space on the hard disk can serve as an extension of the RAM (random-access memory) for the computer. This is called *virtual memory*.

In the conventional method of memory storage, the data is addressed according to its actual place in the available storage medium. In paging memory, on the other hand, it is addressed according to a mathematical row-and-column scheme. The available memory is mapped onto points in a grid, something like a spreadsheet or a Cartesian coordinate plane. The whole grid or plane represents one page of the memory.

The graph is a simplified illustration of a paging scheme. Memory addresses correspond to points (x,y) in the plane. The points are labeled in binary numbers; there are 64 memory addresses in this example. (In a real computer, there are generally more.) Each block of memory has unique coordinates, such as (110,010) or (011,101). It doesn't matter which points are assigned to what data. Information goes wherever there are available points in the plane. *See also* VIRTUAL MEMORY.

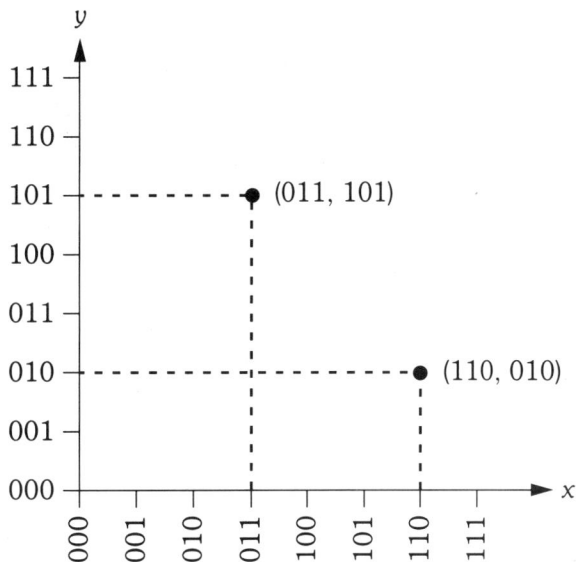

Addresses correspond to points in a coordinate grid.

Paint program

A *paint program* facilitates the creation of graphic art. You can store the work on hard disk or diskette, view it on the monitor, send it to the printer, or send it to another computer via modem.

Bitmapped graphics. Paint programs use *bitmapped graphics*, in which images are built up from tiny pieces on your screen called *pixels* (a contraction of *picture elements*). A paint program differs from a *draw program*, which employs *object-oriented graphics* (*vector graphics*). If you've ever seen a large mosaic, painstakingly assembled tile-by-tile, you have a good idea of how a computer creates an image using a paint program.

Paint program

Suppose you're assembling an 8-by-12-foot (96-by-144-inch) mosaic using one-inch tiles, and have a huge supply of various colored tiles. You have to glue down 96 × 144, or 13,824, tiles, regardless of how complex the image might be. If an artist provides the color codes on the wall, your job is simple, although time-consuming. If you see a spot marked *R*, you put down a red tile; *O* means orange, etc. Even the most elaborate mosaic presents a trivial (and tedious) process for you, the laborer, while the artist takes the credit.

In a paint program, the computer does the job of the laborer and executes your orders. You hardly have to do any work, and you get to take the credit. No matter what a bitmapped image might look like, it's comprised of the same number of pixels as any other image using the same PC and the same program. There are thousands of pixels in a single bitmapped image, but the computer can "glue them down" in just a fraction of a second. Repetitive, trivial processes of this type are exactly the sorts of things computers are designed to do.

Common features. Here are some of the things you can do with paint programs. As you read this list, keep in mind that these programs come with various sophistication levels; low-end programs meant for casual users don't have as many features as high-end programs for professional graphic artists:

> *Filling in* A paint program works by "filling in" outlines you provide. A simple example is shown in the drawing. This is a very small object, only a few pixels in diameter. The pixels are small squares that are either blank or filled in with some color. Most paint programs allow you to choose from many different colors.

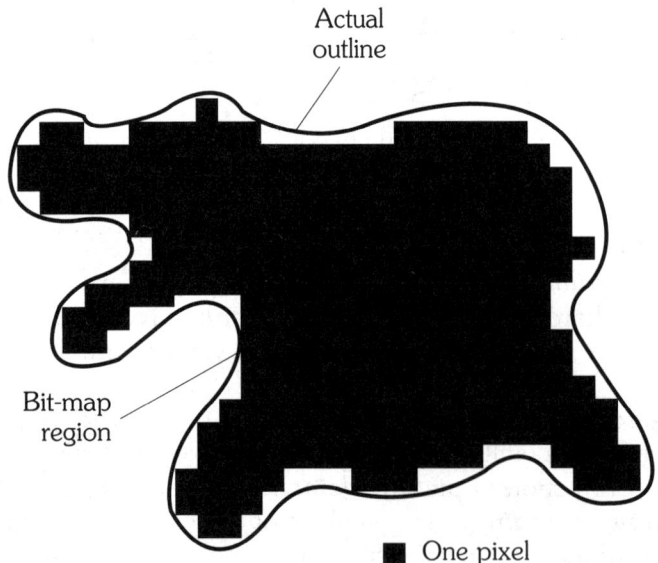

A bitmap fills in a region pixel-by-pixel.

➤ *Lines* You can make lines of varying width. This doesn't work the same way as a draw program, however. When you make a line in a paint program, you're actually filling in pixels to paint a thin stripe. The narrowest stripe you can make is one pixel wide.

➤ *Shapes* You can create basic shapes such as boxes, triangles, other polygons, circles, and ellipses. Outlines can be varied in width. The interiors can be empty (white), or they can be filled with some color.

➤ *Paint tools* Tools such as a spraycan, roller, and brush are typically included, although the names of these items vary from program to program. Rollers and brushes fill in strips of varying width. The spraycan fills in entire regions.

➤ *Erasing* If you decide you want to change something you've created, you can erase part or all of it, and then start over. Erasers work in basically the opposite way from the spraycan, roller, and brush. With an eraser, you "unpaint" a strip or region. Erasers can also be used to change a region from one color to another.

➤ *Text tool* This tool lets you put letters, numbers, and other symbols in your art. The typeface and typesize can vary. You might use text to label items in diagrams or make signs with special visual impact.

➤ *Scanning* With a device called an *optical scanner*, you can take part or all of some hardcopy image and import it into a piece of computer art. Then, using the tools in the paint program, you can edit the scanned image. (Note that you must be careful not to infringe on copyrights when scanning images for inclusion in your own work.)

➤ *Cut and paste* You can take parts of images and import them into, or combine them with, other images. This is especially easy to do when you have a good graphical user interface (GUI) such as Windows, OS/2, or the Macintosh OS. *See also* BITMAPPED GRAPHICS, DRAW PROGRAM, OBJECT-ORIENTED GRAPHICS, OPTICAL SCANNER, *and* PIXEL.

Paired-bar graph

A *paired-bar graph* is a set of two bar graphs placed back-to-back. There are two axes with a common origin at the center, running off horizontally in opposite directions. The two axes can be graduated in units of the same size, but this is not necessary.

Paired-bar graphs are created in presentation graphics software to show a correlation between two phenomena, trends, or sets of events. The drawing is a paired-bar graph for a hypothetical town depicting how the rate of violent crime has gone up as population density has increased. In this graph, population density is charted in thousands of people per square mile along the axis running out to the right of the center. Violent crime per year per 100,000 people is charted along the axis going to the left of the center. Most multipurpose graphics software packages, even beginner-level ones, can help you create charts like this.

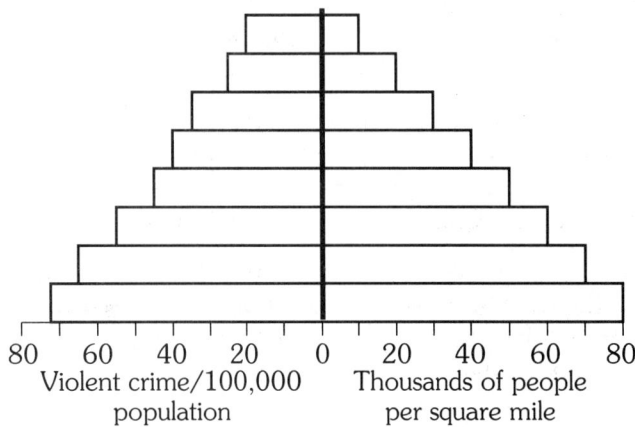

A paired-bar graph shows a correlation between two variables.

The main advantage of paired-bar graphs is that they're simple, and they show correlations (or the lack thereof) clearly. The main disadvantage is the fact that a continuous function can't be rendered; only a limited number of discrete values can be shown.

Paired-bar graphs are not used in analytical graphics as often as they are in presentation graphics. A scientist, for example, would probably use Cartesian coordinates, plotting population density on the horizontal axis and violent crime on the vertical axis. The result would be a set of points that the scientist would connect with a curve or set of straight lines. *See also* ANALYTICAL GRAPHICS, BAR GRAPH, CARTESIAN COORDINATES, *and* PRESENTATION GRAPHICS.

Palette

The *palette* is the range or number of different colors that a computer can display. Usually, this term is applied to displays, but it can also describe the hardcopies produced by color printers.

Primary colors. In a color monitor, the image is made up of tiny red, green, and blue dots. These three colors are known as *primary colors* because, when viewed from a distance, they can combine to get any color you can imagine. Equal brightnesses of the three primary colors will produce gray or white. Zero brightness of all three primary colors will yield black. This red/green/blue scheme is called the *RGB color model*.

When the primary color intensities are not equal (the usual case), some *hue* and *saturation* result. In theory, there are infinitely many possibilities, but in real life, a computer can only reproduce a certain number of them. Most monitors these days can display so many colors that the palette is infinitely varied for practical purposes.

Primary pigments. In a document printed on a color printer, there are three ink shades, called *primary pigments*. They are familiarly known as red, yellow, and blue; more precisely they are magenta (pinkish red), cyan (greenish blue), and yellow. Sometimes black is also included. Equal amounts of the three primary pigments will produce gray or black. A complete absence of pigment results in white copy, assuming the paper is white.

When the amounts of primary pigments aren't equal (the usual case), some hue and saturation result, just as is the case with primary colors. However, primary pigments don't combine the same way as primary colors. There are infinitely many possibilities, but as with the monitor, the computer can only tell the printer to combine the pigments in a finite (although large) number of ways. Good-quality color printers, used with high-end adapter cards, have palettes of infinite variety as far as the eye can tell.

Hue versus saturation. When defining a color, there are two qualities involved: hue and saturation.

The human eye is sensitive to the wavelength of light. The longest waves look red. As the wavelength shortens, the hue changes through orange, yellow, green, blue, indigo, and violet. Hue is a function of the wavelength(s) of light reaching your eyes (see A in the drawing on page 810). There are infinitely many possible hues, just as there are infinitely many positions in a rainbow spectrum.

Saturation can also be called *color vividness*. The greatest saturation results from light of just one wavelength. The least saturation is gray or white. There are infinitely many possible saturations.

Lasers produce light with extreme saturation. If you were to graph the output of a laser with wavelength on the horizontal axis and brightness on the vertical axis, you'd get a "spike." Light of the same hue as the laser, but with much less saturation, appears as a bell-shaped curve on the graph. Part B of the drawing shows graphical examples of the saturation levels of a green laser, a green lightbulb, and washed-out green paint.

When defining the color palette for a computer system, both hue and saturation must be taken into account. If a certain monitor can show, say, 1024 hues and 1024 saturations, then its palette has 1024 × 1024, or 1,048,576 colors. *See also* COLOR GRAPHICS ADAPTER, COLOR PRINTER, ENHANCED GRAPHICS ADAPTER, EXTENDED GRAPHICS ARRAY, MONITOR, PAINT PROGRAM, RGB COLOR MODEL, SUPER VIDEO GRAPHICS ARRAY, *and* VIDEO GRAPHICS ARRAY.

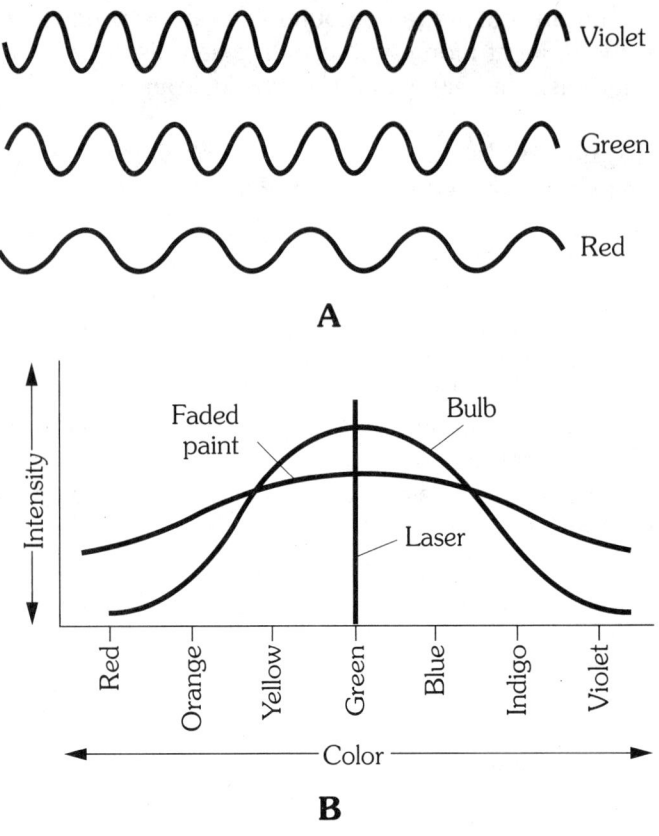

At A, hue is a function of light wavelength. At B, three levels of saturation form a green hue.

Paperless office

As computers get cheaper and easier to use, the ideal of the *paperless office* is coming within reach. This term is not to be used literally; there'll always be some paper in any office. Nevertheless, many of the paper documents in use today can be replaced by data on electronic, magnetic, and optical media.

Assets. Imagine an establishment in which the volume of paper is reduced to the minimum. Here are some advantages it would enjoy over its paper-bound counterparts:

> *Less clutter* The most visible advantage of a paperless office is that less paper means less clutter. Have you ever gotten nervous, or even nearly panic-stricken, by the increasing disorganization caused by too much paper lying around? Things get easier to misplace, and harder to find. Ultimately, a massive cleaning effort must be undertaken, but the gradual process of "office entropy" begins all over again. In a paperless office, this problem does not arise.

> *Less mess* Along with the reduction in the amount of paper, there is a corresponding decline in the prevalence of rubber eraser fragments, correction fluid, and paper cuts. The volume

of trash in the dumpster will dwindle. There will be less chance for fires to get started.

> *Speed* Computer data can be transmitted almost instantly from one place to another. This is called electronic mail or e-mail. It saves time, bulk, and postage. There is also less chance of correspondence getting misplaced.

> *Ease of access* Computer data is easier to access than paper data, as long as the clerical personnel know how the computer filing system works. Such systems are easy to learn; they involve no more expertise than finding documents in ordinary paper file cabinets.

> *Ease of duplication* All computerized data, whether text, audio, or graphic, consists of binary digits (bits) that are either 1 and 0, also known as high and low. Duplication of this information is easy, precise, and can be done in huge quantities. Multiple backup copies can be easily made, effectively reducing to zero the danger of catastrophic information loss. Besides that, it's convenient.

> *Less foot mileage* In a large company, institution, or government agency, computerization can save people having to walk around looking for documents. In a local area network (LAN) or wide area network (WAN), all the data can be accessed from a single terminal. A worker need not move from his or her desk to get any document in the establishment.

> *Simultaneous access* Two or more people can examine or work with the same document at the same time. This saves untold photocopying, running from place to place, and frustration at finding a document missing. It's possible for two or more employees to communicate with each other while they examine a document together. The two people might be in adjacent rooms, in different buildings, or on different continents.

Liabilities. A paperless office is not utopia. There are potential pitfalls, of which managers and employees must be aware:

> *Cyberphobia* Some people cannot seem to adapt to computers. They have a built-in fear of these machines. A person with cyberphobia will "freeze up" when placed in front of a computer or terminal. Most people can get over this unreasonable fear, given time.

> Another form of cyberphobia, quite justified unless the proper precautions are taken, is the fear that data might be lost or that errors might be perpetuated. At worst, these fears can blow up into visions of endless lawsuits, computers going up in smoke, and reputations being ruined by accidental or deliberate libel.

> *Legality* There is controversy over how legal a computerized document can be. When you sign a piece of paper, the marks

Paperless office

you make are unique to you. A signature can be transmitted electronically, but this is the equivalent of duplication (such as photocopying). With computerization, signatures are easy to forge. At the time of writing, this remains one of the biggest areas of uncertainty in technology-related law. For the latest details, you should consult a knowledgeable attorney.

- *Data erasure* Unless computerized information is backed up thoroughly and regularly, data loss can occur, sometimes in large amounts. When computerization of data is properly carried out, however, the likelihood of loss is less than with paper documentation, because file and diskette copies can be made cheaply, easily, and fast. Computer-data insecurity is therefore an illusion.

- *Persistence of error* The flip side of the data-loss illusion is a much more real problem: the possibility that obsolete or inaccurate data, when backed up in several locations, might not be erased when it should be. The result can range from a simple, occasional misstatement to loss of corporate profits. To some extent this problem can be minimized by the use of object linking and embedding (OLE).

- *Sabotage* It's bad enough when errors occur accidentally. As computer systems grow more complex, however, the opportunities increase for hackers to create problems and generate errors on purpose. In a sophisticated computer system, it can be very difficult to pinpoint exactly where such sabotage originates. Two of the most devastating forms of computer sabotage are the *Trojan horse* and the *virus*. These are programs designed specifically for the purpose of altering or destroying computer data.

- *Logistic problems* When several people need to work with the same document at the same time, problems can occur if they try to change the data in different ways. Obviously, a document can retain its identity only as long as it stays in one form.

   Suppose that a document has become obsolete, and that two people decide to update it simultaneously. It's not only likely, but virtually certain, that the two operators won't make the exact same changes. Which document, then, should be the valid one? A well-programmed computer system will alert all parties when a situation like this arises. The operators can then agree on what to do.

- *More paper?* Although the use of computers can, and ideally should, save paper and reduce paper clutter, the opposite often happens. It's easy and tempting to make hardcopies of documents even when it isn't necessary. Before computers, there might have been just one master copy of a document, stored in a big file cabinet. Now, every employee of a company can, in theory, have a copy of every file in the archives.

Computer printers are notorious for wasting paper. Have you seen a letter-size or legal-size sheet that was almost blank, but had some small amount of "vital" data printed somewhere on its expanse?

The future. A completely paper-free office, company, or institution will probably never exist, but it is a goal toward which workers and executives can strive. You can probably think of possible solutions to the above problems. You might also think of new ways in which computers can help save time and generally improve the quality of office life. The historical motivation for automation has been the prospect that it can make people's jobs easier, improve efficiency in the workplace, and thereby enhance profits. Any other use of computers is wasteful and counterproductive.

Perhaps the biggest challenge in office computerization is knowing how computers ought not to be used, as well as how they should be used—and then acting in accordance with this knowledge. *See also* ARCHIVES, BACKUP, CYBERPHOBIA, ELECTRONIC MAIL, HACKER, LOCAL AREA NETWORK, OBJECT LINKING AND EMBEDDING, TROJAN HORSE, VIRUS, *and* WIDE AREA NETWORK.

Parallel

Information can be transmitted bit by bit along one line, or it can be transmitted simultaneously along two or more lines. The latter method is called *parallel* data transfer.

In computer practice, parallel data transfer refers to the transmission of all bits in a word at the same time, over individual parallel lines, as shown in the drawing. Words are generally sent one after the other.

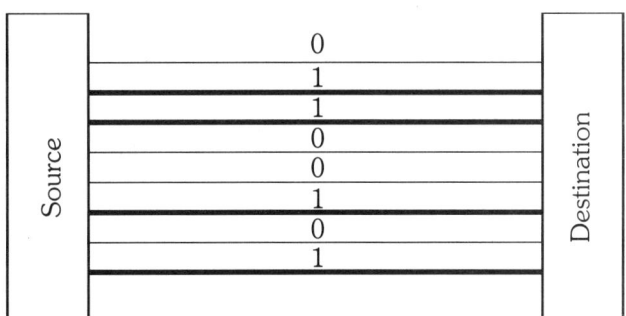

An eight-bit word sent along parallel lines.

Parallel data transfer has the advantage of being more rapid than serial transfer. On the other hand, more lines are required in proportion to the factor by which the speed is increased. It takes eight lines, for example, to cut the data transmission time from a serial value of 80 seconds to a parallel value of 10 seconds. *See also* DATA CONVERSION, PARALLEL PORT, *and* SERIAL.

Parallel port

A *parallel port* is a connector found on the back of a computer's main unit. Data passes through this connector along several lines at once. Because printers almost always work with parallel data, a parallel port is sometimes called a *printer port.*

A parallel port has one big advantage over a serial port: the information moves much faster. If a parallel port has eight lines, it can pass data eight times as fast as a one-line serial port. You might think of this as the difference between a two-lane road and a 16-lane freeway.

Parallel data transmission is a great convenience when printing complex data, such as graphics, or when printing long text documents. Serial transmission is excruciatingly slow in such cases. Perhaps you already know this, having downloaded things like color photographs, complex software, long documents, or long musical compositions from an online service.

The main problem with parallel ports is the fact that there is always some interaction among the lines. The wires in the cable run next to each other, and they carry different electrical signals. The currents conflict if the cable is more than a few feet long because electromagnetic coupling occurs among the wires. An example is shown in the drawing. The center wire carries the actual signal; the top and bottom wires pick up induced signals via electromagnetic coupling. The result is called *crosstalk*.

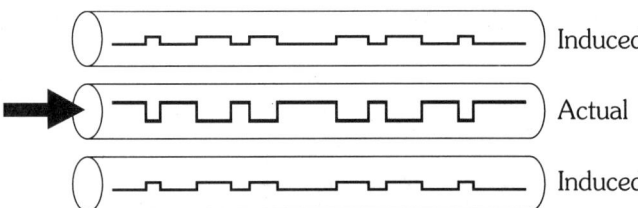

The actual signal (center wire) produces induced signals (top and bottom wires).

Crosstalk in long parallel data lines can be overcome by the use of optical fibers rather than electrical cables. This adds hardware and costs some money; electrical-to-optical and optical-to-electrical conversion must be done at each end of such a link. Nevertheless, fiberoptic data transmission is used in some computer systems and networks. As this technology becomes cheaper, it is replacing cable data transmission. *See also* FIBEROPTIC DATA TRANSMISSION, PARALLEL, PORT, *and* SERIAL.

Parity

The *parity* of an asynchronous data signal is an expression of the number of bits per word. Parity is usually specified as being either *even* or *odd*. If a word has seven bits, for example, the parity is odd; if a word has eight bits, the parity is even.

It is sometimes necessary to have the parity always be even, or always be odd. A *parity bit* is an extra bit added to the binary word in order to ensure that the parity is correct. The parity bit might be either a logic 0 or a logic 1, depending on the situation.

Parity is sometimes used as a means of checking the accuracy of a signal arriving at a destination workstation. If a word comes along that is supposed to have an even number of bits, but actually contains an odd number, the destination computer detects the discrepancy and outputs an error signal. This error signal can be sent back to the source computer, instructing it to send the word again. This is a form of *handshaking*. See also BIT, DESTINATION, HANDSHAKING, *and* SOURCE.

Partition

A *partition* is a portion of a hard disk that is set aside for storage of data. Hard disks are partitioned before they are formatted.

Think of a large kitchen with several cupboards. Suppose the cupboards each have double doors, and are all separated from one another. You might store your best china in one cupboard, your everyday plates in another, the glassware in another, and the cups and bowls in another. The barriers (partitions) prevent the contents of one cupboard from getting mixed up with the contents of other cupboards.

In a partitioned hard disk, each partition can work as an entirely separate disk. You might have DOS installed on one partition, and IBM OS/2 on another. One partition might be called drive C, and the other one called drive D. Each section is called a *logical drive*. Data is separated between logical drives, just as if it were on different disks. *See also* HARD DISK.

Pascal

Pascal (pronounced "pass-CAL") is a high-level programming language similar to BASIC and Fortran in the way it is written. Pascal is used in some schools to teach computer programming. The language gets its name from the French physicist Blaise Pascal. (A unit of physical pressure is named after him, too.)

Pascal makes use of a technique called *modular programming*. In this scheme, parts of the program are written independently, and each part has a specific function. These modules can then be assembled to create the final program. This makes it easier to get a program to run correctly than if the program were written as a whole. If an error exists in a modular program, its location can be narrowed down, and the problem can be fixed more easily than in a single, massive program.

Another big asset of Pascal is its versatility. It can work with either a compiler or an interpreter. Interpreted programs are easier to debug than compiled programs, but compiled programs run faster. Thus, if you're programming in Pascal, you can write and perfect the program as an interpreted language, and then run it with a compiler when actually putting it to work.

In recent years, Pascal has lost some favor because it doesn't run fast enough for many modern business applications. Although Pascal is still used in some schools, the languages C and C++ are more popular in the professional arena. *See also* BASIC, C, C++, COMPILER, FORTRAN, INTERPRETER, *and* MODULAR PROGRAMMING.

Passive transponder

A *passive transponder* is a device that allows a computer or robot to identify an object. Magnetic labels, such as those on credit cards, bank cards, and store merchandise are common examples.

All passive transponders require the use of a sensor of some kind. The sensor detects the presence of the transponder and decodes the information contained in it. The data can be quite detailed. The transponder can be tiny, and can be sensed and decoded from several feet away.

Passive transponders might be extremely useful for personal robots. Suppose a robot needs to choose a tumbler from a cupboard. There might be 85 objects in the cupboard, each with a magnetic label that identifies it precisely. The robot would have no trouble picking out the correct tumbler, as long as it was given data matching the label on the tumbler. *See also* BARCODE, MAGNETIC MEDIA, *and* PERSONAL ROBOTS.

Password

A *password* is a form of security that is used to restrict access to a computer, system, or network. A password need not (and should not) be a word; it can consist of any string of characters up to a certain maximum length.

Making it up. The best way to choose a password is to make something up at random or look through a dictionary and find a strange word. Once you've done this, change one or more of the letters to numbers; for example, *logical* might be changed to *l0g1cal* (with the letter *o* changed to the numeral zero, and the letter *i* to the numeral one). It's a bad idea to use things like your birth date, phone number, or name, or codes like *password*, or *computer*. Passwords made up of only letters or only numerals are not very good, either. Never use the same password on more than one computer; if you do, and a hacker gets the password, it leaves multiple machines open to unauthorized use.

Password

Once you've decided on your password, write it down someplace obscure but permanent. Don't enter it anywhere in your computer system. Don't indicate, next to the password, what it represents. One good scheme is to make the password part of a bogus piece of information. For example, you might write in your address book

John P.
17274 NW 344 Street
Rochester, MN 55901

Jane W.
22020 Lee Boulevard
Vero Beach, FL 47633

Both of these are nonexistent addresses. The security code might be *17274nw* or the word *22020lee* from the street addresses, but you, and only you, know this. Other people might see your data and think, "Gee, I didn't know Rochester was so big," or, "Don't zipcodes in Florida start with three?" You can even make up other dummy addresses that do not contain the password, further confusing would-be hackers (and perhaps yourself eventually).

It's important to have a record of your password someplace. Don't rely on your memory alone. If you forget your password and don't have it written anywhere, you'll lose access to the data secured by the password.

Hierarchical passwords. Some systems allow limited access to data based on partial entry of a password.

Suppose you have personal data, some of which you are willing to let other people see. A few of your friends might have the privilege of entering new data into your files, for example, to write down a reminder to call them on the telephone, but only you have the ability to delete or change information that's already there.

You might choose a long password that consists of several independent parts. If you want someone to be able to look at your data but not modify it in any way, you give them part, but not all, of the password. To let someone look at your data and also enter new information, you might give them a larger partial password. It should be impossible to guess, from either of the partial passwords, anything further within the password. This is important! Partial passwords like *wash* and *washing* can be easily extrapolated into the complete code *washington*.

Many systems have a retry-limitation security feature. This allows the user a certain number, such as three, attempts to get the password right. After that, the system will lock the user out even if he or she

inputs the correct password. This prevents people from breaking in by repeated guessing.

Warning! *Do not* use any of the passwords or combinations suggested in this article. Think up your own. Hackers read computer encyclopedias, too! *See also* PERSONAL INFORMATION MANAGER *and* SECURITY.

Path

The term *path* refers to the process a computer must go through, when working in an operating system such as DOS, in order to find and run a program. It is also the name of a special command that can be written into the AUTOEXEC.BAT file in a PC working with DOS.

Bad commands. If you've used DOS, you've almost certainly had your PC admonish you with the following:

BAD COMMAND OR FILE NAME

Whenever you tell your computer to execute a program that it can't find, this is how it will respond. If you make a mistake when you type in the command, or if the command does not exist in DOS, you'll usually get a somewhat more severe-sounding reprimand:

ILLEGAL COMMAND

Even when the command is valid, you'll run into a "wall" when the file is not in the current directory. There are three possible ways to get around this problem:

➢ Put all DOS programs in every DOS directory.

➢ Type the whole path name whenever you issue a command.

➢ Add a PATH command to the AUTOEXEC.BAT file.

The first of these solutions is a waste of hard disk space because it is redundant. The second solution is an improvement, but it can become a bother if you type commands often. The third, and most efficient, solution is to use the PATH command.

The PATH command. If you can get your computer to recognize certain filenames from the start, it will be able to access those files no matter what directory you might be in at the time. For example, consider the path shown on the next page. The *root directory* is indicated by the backslash (\). In this case, there are nine subdirectories in the root, one of which is called MOUSE. Within this subdirectory, there are several files; one of these is called HIDEDRVR.EXE.

Suppose you haven't put a PATH command in the AUTOEXEC.BAT file, and that you happen to be in the XY directory. Suppose further

Path

Root directory and subdirectories

```
ROOT
\
├── BATCH
├── DOS
├── EIGHT
├── MOUSE ─────┬── ANSWER.COM
├── PRODIGY    ├── CHOOSEDR.SCR
├── TS         ├── COMCHECK.EXE
├── UTILS      ├── DIRERROR.SCR
├── WINDOWS    ├── DIREXIST.SCR
└── XY         ├── DONE.SCR
               ├── HIDEDRVR.EXE
               ├── INSTALL.BAT
               ├── MKCD.COM
               ├── MKCD2.COM
               ├── MKDIR.SCR
               ├── MOUSE.COM
               ├── MOUSE.SYS
               ├── MTRACK40.EXE
               ├── READ.ME
               └── S1.SCR
```

that HIDEDRVR.EXE is only in the MOUSE subdirectory. Then, you must completely spell out the path to the file HIDEDRVR.EXE if you want to utilize it:

`C:\MOUSE\HIDEDRVR.EXE`

To avoid having to specify the path every time you want the computer to execute HIDEDRVR.EXE, you can place a PATH command in the AUTOEXEC.BAT file. In this PATH command, the PC is instructed to be prepared to access HIDEDRVR.EXE from any directory, not just MOUSE. You can also instruct the PC to be prepared to access other files in other directories. It's even possible to tell the machine it should be ready to access files in other drives (such as a diskette drive).

The PATH command only works with command files and program files. You can't use it to access, say, a word processing text file, a spreadsheet, a database, graphic files, or any other plain data. When composing a PATH command, you should not include every directory and executable file in your whole computer, just the ones you use the most often. A "shotgun" approach, encompassing everything, might at first seem like a good idea because it will (in theory) keep you from getting hit with that irritating "Bad command or file name" message, but blanket use of the PATH command makes the computer do a lot of unnecessary searching for files. This slows things down all around.

For details on how to put a PATH command in your AUTOEXEC.BAT file, consult your DOS instruction manual. *See also* AUTOEXEC.BAT, DIRECTORY, *and* DIRECTORY TREE.

Pattern recognition

In a computer vision system, one way to identify an object or decode data is by shape. The machine recognizes combinations of shapes, and deduces their meanings based on information stored in its memory. In artificial intelligence (AI), the technology of *pattern recognition* is important, especially in the evolution of computerized robots. Researchers sometimes use game-like simulations, known as *Bongard problems*, to test and develop pattern-recognition systems.

Imagine a robot that you keep around the house. It might identify you because of combinations of features, such as your height, hair color, eye color, the shape of your nose, the curve of your shoulders, and the motions you make as you walk. Perhaps, with sophisticated-enough technology, your robot could instantly recognize your face, just as your friends do. This would take up a huge amount of memory, however, and would require a microprocessor with extreme speed. For a digital machine, this translates into high cost. Fortunately, there are simpler means of identifying people.

Suppose your robot is programmed to shake hands with anyone who enters the house. It greets everyone with, "Shake hands for identification, please." In this way, the robot might get the fingerprints of the person. It can have a set of authorized fingerprints stored in its "brain." These patterns are complicated, but would probably be easier to store than facial features. If anyone refuses to shake hands, or if their prints fail to match anything in the memory, the robot can actuate a silent alarm to summon police.

Pattern recognition is a major strength of an alternative computer technology called a *neural network*. This type of system was originally designed to imitate the workings of the human brain. Neural networks can find correlations in huge quantities of data with much greater speed than is possible with digital computers.

However, neural networks are less precise than digital machines.
See also BARCODING, BONGARD PROBLEMS, NEURAL NETWORK, OBJECT RECOGNITION, OPTICAL CHARACTER RECOGNITION, *and* OPTICAL SCANNER.

PCMCIA standard adapter cards

PCMCIA standard adapter cards are becoming popular with PCs, especially laptop (notebook) computers. The abbreviation PCMCIA stands for *Personal Computer Memory Card International Association*, a group of companies formed in 1989 with the intention of coming up with a set of standard specifications for adapter cards.

Features. A PCMCIA card works something like an expansion board, except that it's physically smaller and far easier to install and remove. Some features and uses of these cards are as follows:

- *Convenience* You can insert and remove a PCMCIA card as easily as you would a diskette. Contrast this with expansion boards in a desktop PC, where you must take the cover off the main unit to install or remove a board!

- *Memory enhancement* You can add memory, either volatile or nonvolatile, in various sizes, for different purposes.

- *Communications* PCMCIA cards can act as modems, interfacing a computer with a network, online service, or other communications system.

- *Wireless LAN interface* You can connect an antenna to your computer, and have access to a local area network (LAN) without wire interconnections.

- *Disk replacements* A PCMCIA card can work as an extra diskette drive or hard disk system. This allows you to store large quantities of data on a long-term basis.

- *Software* Some PCMCIA cards contain specialized programs, like diskettes and CD-ROMs do.

- *Upgrading* Adding PCMCIA cards can provide a computer with more advanced features. In particular, you can increase your memory space or add an extra effective diskette drive or hard disk.

Three types. A PCMCIA card, also called a *PC card*, is smaller than expansion boards with which you are probably familiar. While the expansion cards, common in desktop computers, are several inches high and wide, PCMCIA cards are similar in size to a bank automatic-teller card. The drawing compares the relative sizes of an expansion board, a 3.5-inch diskette, and a PCMCIA card.

PCMCIA standard adapter cards

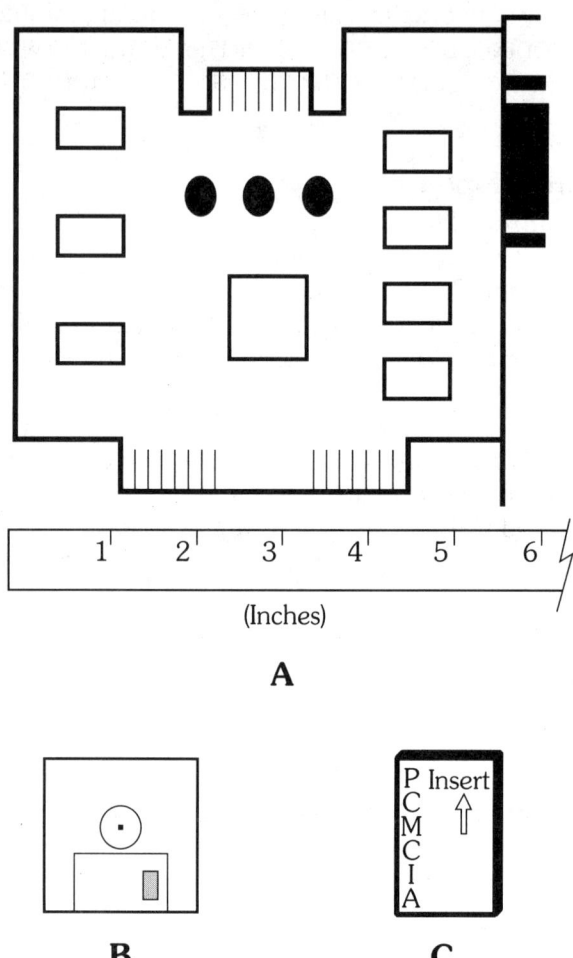

Size comparison of a typical expansion board (A), a 3.5-inch diskette (B), and a PC card (C).

There are three types of PCMCIA cards, each of different thickness, and each with different capabilities:

➢ *Type I* These cards are 3.3 millimeters, or about ⅛ of an inch, thick. Type I cards are used for memory enhancement. This might be RAM (random-access memory), flash memory (similar to RAM, but nonvolatile), or a special form called electrically erasable programmable read-only memory (EEPROM).

➢ *Type II* These are about 5 millimeters, or ⅕ of an inch, thick. They are also used for RAM, flash memory, and EEPROM; they allow for storage of more data than Type I cards. In addition, Type II cards can interface a computer with a LAN, online service, packet communications system, or other communications circuit.

➢ *Type III* These cards are 10.5 millimeters, or a little less than a half-inch, thick. They can do everything that Type I and II cards can do, but on a grander scale. In addition, Type III cards can function like diskette drives or hard disks. Thus, they can contain software.

All three types have 68-pin connectors. All PCMCIA cards are *downwardly compatible*, which means you can use any card up to, and including, the level that your computer can accept. If you're buying a laptop computer, it's wise to consider one with a Type-III PCMCIA card interface. Then, you can use all three types of cards.

Future promise. Many industry experts think that PCMCIA cards will advance along with memory chips, diskettes, and hard disk systems. This means there's no limit to the extent to which you might upgrade a system, within the computing-power constraints imposed by the microprocessor chip. This holds true for desktop computers as well as laptops and other portable machines.

As this technology advances, exotic features such as speech recognition, speech synthesis, companionship software, low-earth-orbit (LEO) satellite linking, multimedia, robot system coordination, and remote control will likely become available as PCMCIA card software. You'll insert the card for the function you want, and your computer will adapt itself instantly. This will be ideal when there are several users (say, a family or a group of students) and a single computer. *See also* EXPANSION BOARD, HARD DISK, MEMORY, NONVOLATILE MEMORY, *and* RANDOM-ACCESS MEMORY.

Peer-to-peer network

A *peer-to-peer network* is a special form of local area network (LAN), in which every workstation is a computer, and each workstation can contain data that is available to all the users in the network. The machines might all have the same processing power, but this is not necessary. Some of the nodes can be minicomputers, some can be mainframes, and others can be PCs. The term *peer-to-peer* means that the machines all have equal importance in the network; it is not a master-slave relationship.

In a peer-to-peer network, each user decides which files he or she wants to designate as *public files*. The public files become available to all users. Thus, each user has access to all the files in his or her own computer, plus those that have been made public by the other users.

There are several different arrangements, known as *topologies*, that can be used in a peer-to-peer network. In the *bus network*, all the PCs are connected to a common line or bus. In a *ring network*, the PCs are arranged at the vertices of a polygon. In a *star network*, one computer is directly linked to all the others. *See also* BUS NETWORK, LOCAL AREA NETWORK, RING NETWORK, *and* STAR NETWORK.

Pel

See PIXEL.

Pen-based computer

A *pen-based computer* is a handheld, portable computer that differs from laptop (notebook) PCs in that it's smaller and lighter, and uses a pen-like stylus to enter data. Pen-based computers generally do not have keyboards, mice, or trackballs. They are lightweight, compact, and battery-powered.

Graphical interface. Pen-based computers let you write data "by hand." More important, they let you operate with a graphical user interface (GUI), similar to Windows, OS/2, or Macintosh software. The pen can be used as a pointing device as well as a writing instrument. The pen is easy to manipulate. Pen-based computers can be hooked up to your desktop or laptop PC for transfer of data. Some desktop and laptop units can also be used directly with a pen-based interface.

Pen-based computers are tailor-made for form-filling applications. A good example is the taking of orders at a restaurant. You've probably seen touch-screen computers in eating establishments; pen-based machines work in much the same way. The order-taker can jot things down by pointing at boxes and icons, and by making simple marks on the screen. This gets rid of clumsy pencil/pad order taking. When you're done eating and are ready to leave, your check will be delivered, neatly printed out, because the pen-based computer can interface with the restaurant's main computer.

You might also use a pen-based computer to take quick notes at lectures. Although this can be done with a laptop PC, the clacking of keys might irritate other lecturegoers. Ideally, you'll know shorthand for note-taking with a pen-based computer; this will greatly reduce the amount of scribbling you must do.

Pen and screen. The stylus in a pen-based PC generates a weak electromagnetic field, the power for which is supplied either by batteries or through a cord. This field is detected by elements in the screen assembly when the pen touches, or is brought near, the screen. In addition to picking up the motions of the pen, the screen serves as a display. There are two screen technologies in common use.

Drawing A shows *underlay technology*. It gets its name from the fact that the input-sensing apparatus is underneath the graphic display. The pen input is detected by a grid of wires below a liquid-crystal display (LCD). A clear glass covers the assembly. When the pen is brought to within a millimeter or two of the glass, the electromagnetic fields are picked up by various intersection points in the wire grid. This data is then fed to the electronic circuits of the computer.

Pen-based computer

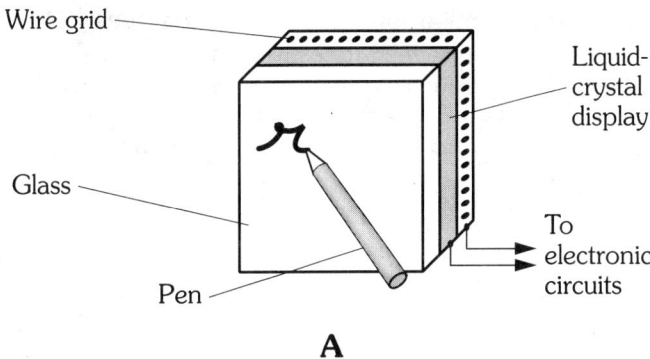

Underlay screen design.

Drawing B shows *overlay technology*. It gets its name from the fact that the input sensor is on top of the display. In this scheme, the sensor is a metallic/glass mixture that is transparent and conducts electricity. The position of the pen is determined according to the relative intensity of currents along the edges of the screen. The LCD is visible through the conducting glass.

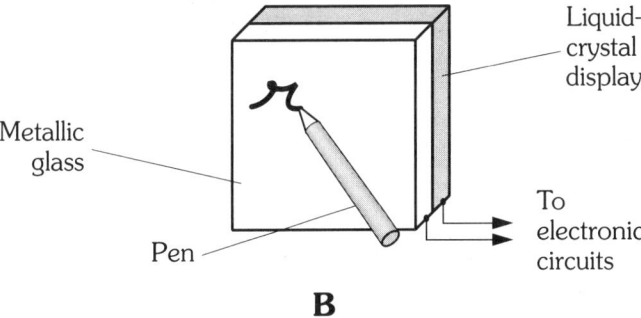

Overlay screen design.

Digital ink. Drawing C shows the path of a pen in making a lowercase, cursive letter *r*. The position of the pen varies in two dimensions; this makes it possible to duplicate the letter in a Cartesian (x,y) plane. The machine memorizes a large number of points along the curve of the letter, creating a bitmap.

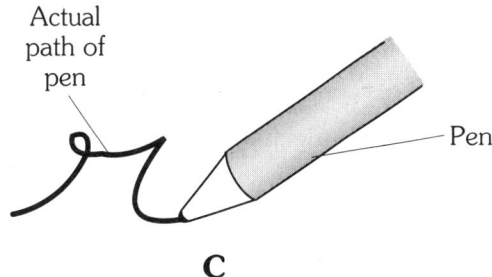

The actual path of the pen to create a cursive letter.

Pen-based computer

When writing this particular lowercase letter, the speed of the pen is not constant. Most people hesitate at the tiny loop at the top left. The pen stops for a moment at the upper right before turning downward. Finally, the pen accelerates on the upswing following the letter. This pen-speed variation can be detected and memorized by the computer.

With a pen-based PC, the *r* might be transcribed as shown in drawing D. Each square represents one pixel. (Here, the pixels are greatly enlarged.) The timing of the pixels' input to the machine varies, depending on the speed of the pen across the screen. The timing, as well as the actual positions of the pixels, is input to the computer memory. This lets pen-based computers quantify pen motion in a way that humans cannot.

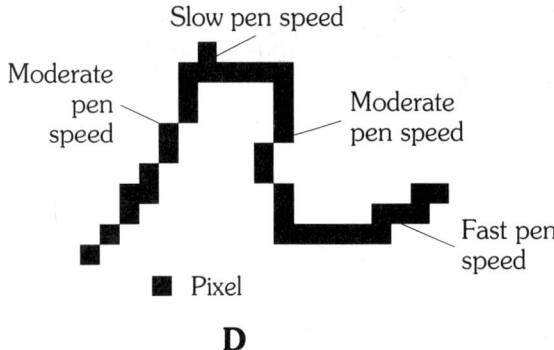

D

A digital-ink rendition of the same letter as in C.

One powerful application for pen-based computers is the duplication and transmission of human signatures. With sufficient image resolution, a pen-based computer might capture enough of a signature to make a positive, unique identification of the signer. But that's not all. *Digital ink*, the transcription of pen movements into data, records the pen's velocity-versus-time function precisely. This gives an added dimension to signature identification, over that of simple pen and paper.

The potential of digital ink for use in civil and criminal court, and the extent to which it will be allowed as evidence, remains to be seen. As pen-based computers become more powerful, this issue will become increasingly significant. Eventually, these machines will be able to use handwriting to uniquely identify a person, just as fingerprints have long been used. There's an ominous flip side, however: signature data, when transmitted to a mechanical writing device, will facilitate perfect forgeries.

Character recognition. Handwriting-recognition technology has been the biggest problem for engineers developing pen-based computing systems. A machine has a hard time deciphering handwritten characters. It's tougher than the optical character recognition that a scanner employs to digitize printed text, since human handwriting varies from person to person. The process is similar to speech recognition, another major challenge for engineers.

There are two ways in which handwritten characters can be deciphered by a pen-based machine. These are *untrainable character recognition (UCR)* and *trainable character recognition (TCR)*.

In UCR, the machine captures the bitmapped image of a character from the screen and compares it with a table of standard characters. There's plenty of room for error. One person's uppercase cursive S might look like another person's uppercase cursive G. Hardly anyone writes the way they were taught in grade school. With UCR, the machine never improves its ability to recognize characters. It will make the same errors over and over, unless the operator compensates by changing his or her handwriting.

In TCR, the machine uses basically the same procedure to recognize characters as is the case in UCR, but TCR gets better as it's used more. The machine becomes familiar with the nuances of the operator's handwriting. Developers of TCR are secretive about the technological details, but two things can be said. First, TCR takes more computer power than UCR because the processes are more complex. Second, TCR is no better than UCR when the operator changes. The machine might get used to you, but this will be useless when your sister scrawls on its screen. The machine will have to relearn the new written "dialect," and that will take time.

It might be possible for a TCR computer to store the idiosyncrasies of several people's handwriting once it has learned each style, but that multiplies the memory required. In any case, no pen-based computer yet devised comes near the average human's ability to recognize and compensate for variations in handwriting style. *See also* CARTESIAN COORDINATES, GRAPHICAL USER INTERFACE, LIQUID-CRYSTAL DISPLAY, *and* OPTICAL CHARACTER RECOGNITION.

Pentium

The *Pentium* is Intel's successor to the 80486 (486) microprocessor. The Pentium improves on previous microprocessors in practically all respects. This chip contains over 3,000,000 transistors.

Software compatibility. The Pentium can run all the software that Intel's earlier chips, the 8088, 286, 386, and 486, can run. This is an extremely significant feature; it can represent a great money savings if you have a lot of software. You can install all your old software on a Pentium-based PC (provided the older software is Intel-compatible), and the software will still work, probably faster than it did with the earlier chip.

Peripherals

Of course, software advances along with hardware. The Pentium runs more powerful programs than the earlier chips can handle effectively. Complex graphics and animation, along with multimedia, enjoy significantly better performance with the Pentium than with previous chips. This continues with each new microprocessor that becomes available; you notice the greatest improvement with the most sophisticated applications. When you're planning to upgrade your system, it always pays to examine the latest hardware and software concurrently.

Computing power. The Pentium can execute hundreds of megainstructions per second (MIPS). This is several times faster than the 486, and many times faster than the 386 or 286.

The clock speed of the Pentium is 66 MHz or more. Although some 486 chips can run up to 100 MHz, the Pentium can execute more than one instruction for each cycle of the clock, a feat unknown with previous chips. The reason for this is *superscalar processor architecture*, wherein the instructions proceed along more than one *pipeline* at a time.

Another advantage of the Pentium is that its external data bus has 64 bits, compared with a maximum of 32 bits for previous chips; the result is like the difference between a two-lane highway and a four-lane turnpike. The data from memory can be accessed at a higher rate of speed. This works synergistically with the high clock speed and the superscalar design.

The Pentium also has a powerful, built-in coprocessor. This saves the microprocessor time in its overall management of the computer's operating system. The calculating "busywork" does not have to be done at the expense of other processes. *See also* COPROCESSOR, INTEL MICROPROCESSORS, *and* P6 MICROPROCESSOR.

Peripherals

In a computer system, *peripherals* are devices other than the main unit. The most common peripherals, which you'll find in almost any PC system, are a printer and a mouse. (The monitor, keyboard, and drives are usually considered part of the main unit.) System peripherals can also include such things as a modem, an extra diskette drive, a CD-ROM drive, a Bernoulli box, a tape drive, musical instrument digital interface (MIDI) equipment, sound equipment, speech recognition and synthesis hardware, a joystick, a fax machine, an amateur radio transceiver, robots, video cameras, video recorders, and television sets.

All peripherals must be properly interfaced with the main unit of a computer if the system is to work right. For example, when you buy a printer, you'll need to be sure you have the software necessary for it to communicate with your main unit. Ultra-high-resolution or large-screen monitors often require expansion boards. Sound equipment, speech recognition and synthesis devices, robots, and other more complex apparatus have highly specialized software.

When shopping for peripherals, you must always be sure that they are compatible with your system. Your PC superstore dealer or a local "PC guru" friend can be of help here.

See also AMATEUR RADIO, BERNOULLI BOX, CD-ROM, COMPATIBILITY, COMPUTERIZED HOME, DISKETTE DRIVE, DOT-MATRIX PRINTER, EXPANSION BOARD, FAX, FAX BOARD, FLOPTICAL DISKETTE AND DRIVE, FULL-MOTION VIDEO INTERFACE, INKJET PRINTER, INPUT/OUTPUT MODULE, INTERACTIVE TECHNOLOGY, JOYSTICK, LABEL PRINTING, LASER PRINTER, MODEM, MONITOR UPGRADING, MULTIMEDIA, MUSICAL INSTRUMENT DIGITAL INTERFACE, OPTICAL SCANNER, PACKET COMMUNICATIONS, PERSONAL ROBOTS, REMOVABLE DATA STORAGE MEDIA, SOUND TECHNOLOGY, SPEECH RECOGNITION, SPEECH SYNTHESIS, TAPE DRIVE, VIRTUAL REALITY, *and* VISION SYSTEMS.

Personal Dictation System

Personal Dictation System (PDS) is the name of a software package marketed by IBM. As its name implies, the PDS can turn a computer into a stenographer.

Requirements. To make use of PDS, a computer should have at least as much processing power as an Intel 80486 (486). In addition, an adapter is needed for sound pickup and transmission. The computer should also have at least 16MB of RAM. This might require the installation of memory expansion boards.

The original PDS operates on top of IBM's OS/2 operating system. Other versions for other operating systems might also be available. The necessary amount of hard disk space varies; as a rule, there should be at least 65MB. Some of this is used only temporarily, while the PDS is learning how to understand your speech patterns.

Features. Science-fiction writers have portrayed speech recognition technology for decades. A person would talk to a computer, and the machine would obey commands or record text, even to the extent of understanding the context and syntax in which words were used. That technology exists to a certain extent today, and is employed in the PDS.

If you say something like, "That's too much food for two people," a human listener knows the difference between *too* and *two*, although the words sound identical. If you speak this sentence into the microphone of a computer with speech recognition, the machine cannot know which word is which, unless it can somehow evaluate

Personal Dictation System

context and syntax. The PDS can be taught to do this; it has the ability to learn speech patterns, improving its vocabulary and understanding with experience. This is a primitive form of artificial intelligence (AI), and it can exist on a 486-based PC!

As supplied, the PDS has a vocabulary of words commonly used in an office setting. It starts out with about 20,000 words and increases as you train the system. Other vocabularies are available, such as a medical word set for doctors and hospitals.

The PDS can let you give commands to the computer, as well as dictate words for it to record. Thus, you can bring up the system, telling it, in effect, "Take dictation now." This gives you a hands-off user interface; there's no keyboard or mouse to bother with, nor need you look at any part of your system as you talk to it. A dentist might use the system while working on a patient's teeth; a pharmacist could use it while putting pills in a bottle.

As the PDS vocabulary expands with improving technology, it will become a boon to physically challenged people. Children will also find it entertaining; they will become comfortable with computers at earlier and earlier ages. Eventually, computers might become a factor in the development of speech patterns in young people.

Limitations. Much of the troubles that plague speech-based computer systems, including the PDS, can be summarized in one word: noise. One problem is a loud working environment. The software is written to ignore steady background noises, but sudden bangs and crashes can cause problems. If you're in a room full of people who talk loudly and constantly, the PDS (as well as your mind) can be distracted by stray words. It's also possible, if you use the system extensively, that your dictation will bother your coworkers.

While the system can be trained to develop familiarity with the nuances of your speech, there will always be some errors. These problems are similar to those encountered by an optical scanner. When the machine is confused, it will let you know in the text it has stored. You can correct most errors when you go back to proofread your dictation. It's even possible to have the machine repeat words aloud for you. Sometimes the PDS will list several alternative words to fill in a blank spot.

There can be translational problems when someone else dictates into the system after it has become used to your speech patterns. Because no two people string words together in exactly the same way, there will usually be more frequent errors in transcribing the speech of a stranger than the speech of a regular user. With time, the machine can adapt itself to a new user, but when a PDS is shared among several people, the error rate will still be higher than when all the dictation is done by the same person.

The future. As the technology of PDS advances, the limitations become less significant. As it exists now, the PDS can pay for itself in a couple of months, compared with the salary a human stenographer requires. Some people say that this reflects an increasingly dehumanizing society, but that is a narrow view. Computers help people go into business for themselves, gaining more control over their professional lives. Computers equipped with good software can help entrepreneurs stay in business, so they can lead the sorts of lives they want.

Information about the IBM PDS can be obtained by writing to

International Business Machines
Mail Stop 2236
Route 100
Somers, NY 10589

For information about other speech-recognition systems, check at your computer store, and keep in touch with technology by reading business-oriented PC magazines. *See also* SPEECH RECOGNITION.

Personal digital assistant

A *personal digital assistant (PDA)* is a small, portable computer that weighs less than four pounds, has a display screen with a diagonal measure of five to nine inches, and uses battery power. Some units have rechargeable nickel-cadmium (NICAD), nickel-metal-hydride (NiMH), or lithium batteries; some use disposable alkaline batteries.

Configurations. Within these constraints, a PDA can come in just about any shape. Some have full keyboards, although they're smaller than standard size. Some look like oversized calculators. Some are taller than they are wide, and resemble large books with screens and buttons. Others are wider, and have flip-up displays; they resemble miniature laptop or notebook PCs. A special form of PDA is the *pen-based computer*. It makes use of a stylus to receive commands and accept handwritten input.

Experts have had mixed reactions to PDAs. While technophiles, also called "techies," have trumpeted the PDA as a landmark in computer evolution, consumers in general have reacted moderately at best. People are tight-fisted these days. They don't often regard fancy gadgets as status symbols anymore. When someone sees a PDA, they'll ask, "How will this improve my life?" and "How much will it cost?"

Personal digital assistant

What it can do. If you're a gadget lover, PDAs can be great fun. Here are some benefits and uses:

➤ *Intuitive operation* A PDA can carry out a task with a minimum of instructions. For example, you might want to send the message, "Please buy some fruit for dessert tonight" to your home. You can tell the PDA, "Send e-mail home" or, "Fax home." The PDA will automatically send the message if you have it connected online.

➤ *Cellular communications* The above e-mail transaction doesn't need a wire connection if you have a cellular telephone. You can plug the PDA into a cellular telephone unit and send the message. Some PDAs have built-in cellular telephones.

➤ *PCMCIA standard adapter cards* PCMCIA cards resemble bank automatic-teller cards. You can insert them into a PDA to get functions like a hard disk, extra memory, or specialized software. They can even program a PDA to recognize human speech, so you might enter data by talking to the machine.

➤ *File transfer* It's easy to move files from a PDA to a laptop or desktop PC. This is done via a serial interface cable, in much the same way that data is transferred via modem. Files can also be transferred from the computer to the PDA, if you need access to certain data while on the move. This can be done with a modem or a cellular link.

➤ *Remote control* Via cellular link or modem, you can control machines at a remote location. For example, you can switch on the oven to cook a meal, so it will be hot and done when you arrive from work. Farmers can use a PDA to control an automatic sprinkling system. Someday, PDAs might be employed as remote-control units for personal robots.

➤ *Wireless LANs* You can connect several PDAs to a group of computers in a wireless local-area network (LAN). This can be useful, say, in a large laboratory where frequent observations must be made by several scientists in different parts of the building. It might also prove useful in hospitals, where nurses could send data on patients back to a central computer.

➤ *Information superhighway access* News reporters and research people will appreciate the fact that PDAs can tap into online services. This makes it possible to gain access to all the data being circulated by the Internet, America Online, CompuServe, and other networks. PDAs might play the role of "motorcycles" on the "infobahn."

➤ *Computer games* The potential for pure fun should never be overlooked, or underestimated, as a major asset in any computer. The compactness and portability of PDAs make them ideal for use as toys. On a long trip with children, a PDA, equipped with game software, can take much of the boredom out of the journey.

➤ *Battery life* PDAs require much less power than laptop PCs. As a result, the batteries last longer. Typical battery life is 50 to 100 hours. With a recharging system or an extra battery pack, you never need to worry about unwanted powering-down.

Growing pains. Before people figure out what to do with a new device, its effect can be exactly opposite to what is intended. Sometimes this continues even after the device has gained acceptance. Machines, including computers, are supposed to streamline the work process, but some gadgets create work and make it more complicated, instead of reducing it and making it simpler. This problem is not limited to PDA, or to computers. Some people have called it the bane of the technological revolution.

The "make-work effect" can occur for two reasons. First, it can result from operating systems with tough learning curves, or that are not user-friendly. This diminishes with human engineering. Second, when new technology increases productivity, it accelerates competition. The treadmill goes faster, and everyone works harder and harder to keep from falling behind.

When the PDA first became available, some people spent upwards of $2000 per unit, expecting it to revolutionize their recordkeeping, note-taking, and business correspondence. When reality turned out less sweet than the dream, PDAs got some less- than-complimentary reviews, putting a damper on sales of PDAs. Such events can prove blessings in disguise, however; great innovations need time to find their niche.

Meeting the need. Some engineers and developers are confident that there's a true public need for PDAs. If the industry can figure out exactly what features (including affordability) PDAs must acquire to satisfy the needs of consumers and businesses, PDAs might become as common as cellular telephones and beepers.

It's likely that the greatest initial demand for PDAs will be in fast-track professional fields. The abbreviation *PDA* might better stand for *professional digital assistant*. The PDA has already proven valuable to traveling salespeople. News reporting, market research, and scientific research are possible take-off points. Once PDAs find their place in the high-energy business arena, more conservative establishments like hospitals, doctors' offices, and law offices might pick them up. Consumers will follow to an extent that depends on general lifestyle changes in the coming years. *See also* LAPTOP COMPUTER, PCMCIA STANDARD ADAPTER CARDS, PEN-BASED COMPUTER, *and* PERSONAL DICTATION SYSTEM.

Personal finance software

If you have trouble keeping track of where your money goes, *personal finance software* can help. There are several programs available, with a variety of features.

Budgeting. Some people have a natural sense of thrift; they never have trouble keeping cash income ahead of outflow. However, many of us, driven by media forces and natural desires, get into trouble unless we watch what we're doing with our money. A computer can greatly enhance the ability to control cash-flow.

Most personal finance programs have an electronic ledger, or balance sheet, on which you can log all income and expenditures, actual and projected. Are you letting the balance on your credit card build up to unmanageable levels? The interest on credit cards can cost you hundreds, if not thousands, of dollars annually. How much money are you spending on food each month? How much does it cost per month to operate your car(s)? To heat your home in winter? To air condition it in summer?

Computerized budgeting has several advantages over the old pencil-and-paper method. For one thing, it's less messy. It's easy to change things; you can just type one number in over another. Many financial programs incorporate a linking feature, so updating or changing one number will automatically correct all the affected figures. A computerized budget can tell you where you can best make adjustments, if needed, to bring your cash outflow under control. With the aid of graphs and charts, you can look at trends and see immediately where things are out of balance.

Of course, no computer program can infuse you with the discipline you need to control your spending. It can only tell you what you should do, and where your willpower might best be applied.

Taxes. Another big asset of personal finance software involves figuring out your income taxes. This is especially important if you are self-employed or run a small business. Self-employed people must make estimated tax payments quarterly. If the payments aren't made on time, if they're greatly different from each other, or if they're not sufficient to meet the year's tax bill, it can raise eyebrows at the Internal Revenue Service. No one wants that! On the other hand, there's no point in making payments that are far too large.

The tax features in personal finance programs can help you predict what your tax bill will be, so that your payments will be as close as possible to the exact amounts due. Some tax programs also help you figure out your deductions. However, be aware that the tax laws change almost every year. Software that relies on last year's rules might not be valid this year. You'll have to check on this before figuring your deductions with software. Some programs let you link into tax information online; this data is updated as tax laws change.

Electronic banking. Some personal finance programs allow you to do your banking electronically, from the convenience of your computer. You can make deposits and write checks, and your bank balance will be updated, both in your records and the bank's records.

Most personal finance software packages have a provision whereby you can print your own checks. This helps with recordkeeping and allows you to customize checks however you want.

Certain payments come due at regular intervals, or on certain dates. Examples include the electric bill, the telephone bill, the mortgage payment or rent, the car payment, insurance premiums, and various tax bills. You can log in reminders for each payment, and the program will automatically inform you when the day for payment arrives. This can be especially helpful if you have many different bills that come at scattered times throughout each month.

With some packages, you can have your computer pay bills electronically, via online services. Of course, for this to be possible, the computer must know how much to pay. Some payments, like your mortgage or rent, remain constant throughout the year. Others, such as the utility bill, change.

As the information superhighway evolves, it's likely that most bill payment will eventually be done online. The institution will contact your computer, informing it of the amount due. The computer will then let you know that the bill has been received and ask you if it's all right to go ahead and pay. Assuming no error has been made, you'll press a key or click on an icon, and the machines will take care of the rest. If an error has occurred, you'll be able to withhold the electronic check and correct the mistake before payment is made.

Financial counsel. Some programs offer tips and tutorials on various aspects of money management. These can be on the diskette itself, but online help is also available. The advice runs much deeper than mere motivational psychology; for example, you might get stock quotes from an online service.

Software can help you decide when it's time to buy a new car, or whether you should refinance your home. A program can tell you how much (if anything) you'll save by consolidating your debts. It can help you plan for retirement or put money away for your child's college education. Some programs can even help you figure out how to get the most out of your vacation fund.

Managing a complex investment portfolio is no job for neophytes. Most individuals do not have the store of facts that a good financial software package can provide. Nevertheless, human intuition works better than any computer in some situations. For at least many years to come, there will be no such thing as an electronic "hunch."

For further information. One person's ideal financial manager might be inadequate or inappropriate for someone else. If you know someone who is using a personal finance software package, and who swears by it, you at least have a starting point for your search. It's even better if that person has finances that are similar to yours.

A computer store is a good place to shop for personal finance software. The PC magazines regularly carry advertisements and articles about these packages; you can write or call the different companies and request brochures. Compare features and find the package that best meets your needs. *See also* DATABASE, PERSONAL INFORMATION MANAGER, *and* SPREADSHEET.

Personal information manager

A *personal information manager (PIM)* is a software package that helps an individual or a small group of people organize everyday affairs. Many different PIMs are available, each with unique attributes.

Instant access. When you're in some application such as a word processor, database manager, or spreadsheet, and you need to access your PIM, you can enter it directly from the other application. You don't need to leave the other application first. When you're done with the PIM, you can leave it, and you'll immediately be back in the original application. The changes you made to the PIM will be retained just as if you had done things the slower, more old-fashioned way.

If you have a graphical interface such as Windows or Macintosh, a PIM can appear in a small window when you access it, while the main application stays put on your screen. You can even jump back and forth between the PIM and the other application, making sure all the facts agree in both programs. An example of such a situation is a book in progress, containing several names and addresses that have recently changed. You can update the book concurrently with your address list, ensuring that there are no discrepancies, without having to open and close files a dozen times. This not only saves time, but helps reduce clerical errors.

Scheduling. Everyone makes appointments, even if they're only reminders to pay bills. To keep complex schedules in order, a computer can be invaluable.

The old-fashioned way to make, keep track of, and fulfill time obligations is the date-keeper booklet. These are available in day-per-page, week-per-page, and month-per-page-spread formats. So are their computer counterparts, but there are some big differences.

Computerized data is free of erasures, correction fluid, crossouts, and ink smudges. Also, a computerized schedule has all the blank space you need. You won't run out, having to use stick-on tags or other space-enhancement schemes. As you add appointments to a day, week, or month, the available space expands to accommodate the new data. There's no limit (within reason) to the amount of information you can include for a given time slot.

Some programs let you jot general notes on a "scratch pad," and store each one in the schedule. When you bring up the schedule and see an icon next to a name or time slot, you can click on the icon, and you'll get the general notes.

Special features. Some PIMs have powerful features that you might not think you need—yet. When shopping for a PIM, you can look for these special capabilities and decide if you need them, or might someday need them:

➢ *Group information manager (GIM)* The higher-end PIMs allow scheduling for groups of people. The old pencil-and-paper method, as you might know from embarrassing experience, allows for conflicts. It's very hard for a single human being to keep track of appointments for a group, especially over a long period of time, without the help of a computer. With a GIM, you can keep track of the affairs for each member of your club, your staff, your volleyball team, or whatever.

➢ *Alarm* The alarm automatically issues an emphatic reminder when an important obligation is coming up. It works like an alarm clock, except that its timeframe is not limited to 24 hours. You can program alarms for events days, weeks, or months in advance.

➢ *Multiple variables* If you think it's tough keeping track of a group's time schedule, try juggling supplies, available space, and other resources simultaneously! For example, you might be organizing a small convention. How many tables do you need? Where will you get them? What about rooms? Food and refreshments? Chairs? You must procure each of these items from some source, at some time. A computer is not only an asset in such a situation, it becomes a necessity. Higher-end PIMs can help with complex organizational affairs.

➢ *Time-slot searching* Suppose you need to coordinate a meeting among a dozen people. The meeting is to last 30 minutes. The problem: each of the members has a different schedule, and each schedule is complicated. With a good PIM, you can have the PC do a time-based search for everyone at once. You can then locate, easily and quickly, 30-minute time slots during which all 12 members are free.

Personal robots

➤ *Automatic dialing* Once you've found several time slots for the meeting, you'll have to telephone each of the people, letting them know some available times. This can be done manually, but you can also have your PIM do it. Electronic mail is especially useful here. Each member will get a message online. They can return your messages, and, after a little electronic "telephone tag," the meeting time can be agreed upon. You can even have the computers for each member of the group update their PIMs, so they're all consistent.

➤ *Security* There are some aspects of your personal information portfolio that you'll need to share with other people to coordinate group affairs, but there are plenty of things you won't want other people to see or change. To protect your data, a good PIM should have a security provision. This usually takes the form of a password.

Some PIMs have hierarchical password security. For example, if someone types the first three characters of your password, they can view your data but not change it. With six characters, they can enter new data. Complete control, including deletion of old data, is possible only when the entire password is entered.

See also CONTACT MANAGER, ELECTRONIC MAIL, MEMORY-RESIDENT SOFTWARE, MULTITASKING, PASSWORD, *and* SECURITY.

Personal robots

For centuries, people have imagined having *personal robots*. Until the explosion of electronic technology, attempts at robot-building resulted in clumsy and often dangerous masses of metal that did little or nothing of practical use. To be effective, personal robots will need speech recognition, speech synthesis, vision systems, and a great deal of processing power with a minimum of physical space and weight.

The big trick. Today, we can buy a computer with a notebook-sized case for a reasonable price. This is largely because of integrated-circuit (IC) technology. Most scientists agree that we haven't yet come near the limit of electronic miniaturization. We can expect that useful personal robots will someday be available. The big trick will be getting people to buy them.

Personal robots could do all kinds of mundane chores around your house. Such robots are sometimes called *household robots*. Personal robots might also be used in the office; these are *service robots*. The following are some examples of duties that household robots might perform:

➤ Bodyguarding

➤ Car washing

- Cleaning
- Companionship
- Fire protection
- Grocery shopping
- Groundskeeping
- Intrusion detection
- Maintenance
- Meal preparation and serving

Around the office, a service robot might do things like these:

- Bookkeeping
- Cleaning
- Coffee preparation and serving
- Dictation
- Equipment maintenance
- Filing
- Fire protection
- Intrusion detection
- Photocopying
- Telephone answering
- Typing

Practical machines versus toys. Some personal robots have been designed and sold, but they haven't been sophisticated enough to be of any practical benefit. They were actually hobby robots, or adult toys. A good household robot, capable of doing even a few of the above chores efficiently and reliably, would cost more than $100,000. In the future, as technology improves and gets less expensive, the cost (in terms of a person's real earning power) will go down.

Simpler robots make good toys for children. Interestingly, if a robot is designed and intended as a toy, it sells better than if it is advertised as a practical machine.

Concerns. Some researchers think that personal robots might be abused, as people direct their hostility at machines rather than at other people. Robots will never be very cheap, however. If you break a $100,000 machine, you'll have to get it repaired or get along without it. Also, robots must be safe to be around, and not pose any hazard to their owners, especially children. This can be ensured with good design.

Suppose a practical personal robot were available for $30,000. Would many people buy it? It's hard to say. As boring as some of the above-mentioned tasks might seem, plenty of people enjoy doing them. Groundskeeping and cleaning can be great exercise. Lots of people love to cook. Some people will never entrust a robot to do things right, no matter how efficient and sophisticated the machines get. And while $30,000 might not seem like a lot of money to some people, others might prefer to save it or spend it on other things. *See also* ANIMISM, ANTHROPOMORPHISM, ARTIFICIAL INTELLIGENCE, ASIMOV'S THREE LAWS, AUTONOMOUS ROBOTS, INSECT ROBOTS, SECURITY SYSTEMS, SPEECH RECOGNITION, SPEECH SYNTHESIS, TELEOPERATION, *and* VISION SYSTEMS.

Petabyte

The term *petabyte* refers to an extremely large unit of computer data. The prefix *peta* means 10^{15}, sometimes called a "quadrillion" and written out 1,000,000,000,000,000. In binary terms, it means 2^{50}. Thus a petabyte is 2^{50} bytes, which equals 1,073,741,824 megabytes (MB), or 1,048,576 gigabytes (GB), or 1024 terabytes (TB). That's about as much data as can fit on a million large hard disks.

The drawing gives an idea of the size of a petabyte relative to other commonly used memory units. At A, the little cube represents 1MB of data, roughly the amount contained in one high-density diskette. The large cube represents 1GB, about twice the data on a CD-ROM. Imagine this compressed into the small cube at B. Then the large cube at B is 1TB. That's almost as much storage as there is in a million high-density diskettes. Now imagine this compressed into the small cube at C. The large cube at C represents 1PB.

To show these relationships, linear or area graphs are not adequate. Volume increases much faster than area or unit length. For example, a doubling of a cube's edge increases its volume by a factor of eight; when the edge becomes 10 times as long, the volume goes up by a factor of 1000. If you doubt that computer disk capacity will ever get this large, you might extrapolate the graph in the article COMPUTER GENERATIONS.

Picosecond

A *picosecond* (abbreviated *ps*) is an extremely short length of time, equal to just one-trillionth (0.000 000 000 001 or 10^{-12}) of a second. In a picosecond, even the fastest PC's clock can complete only a minuscule part of a cycle, and a ray of light travels only about 0.012 of an inch, or 0.3 millimeter, through clear air or free space. In a picosecond, an electric current in a wire travels approximately 0.001 of an inch, or 0.025 millimeter. Picoseconds are not used much yet, even when talking about processes within computer components, but watch for increasing use of the expression in the coming years.

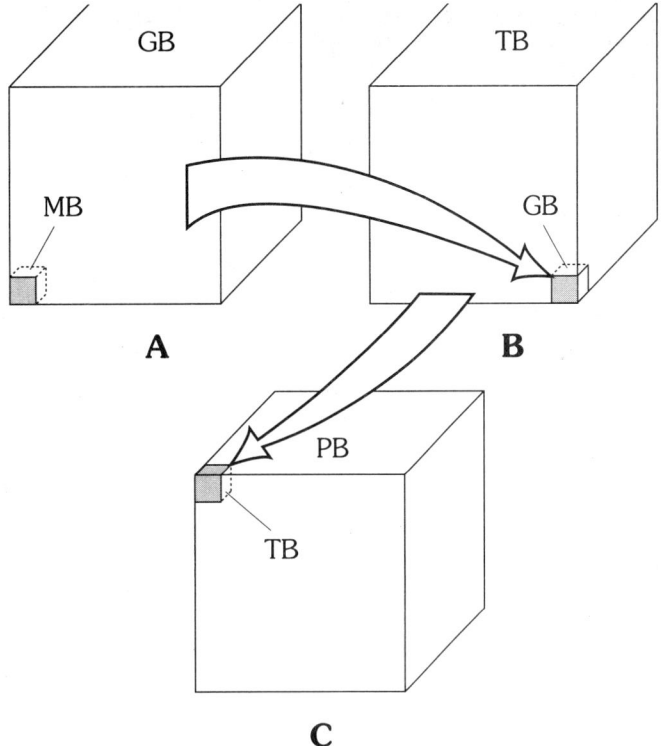

At A, the ratio of megabyte (MB) to gigabyte (GB). At B, GB to terabyte (TB). At C, TB to petabyte (PB).

When 10 GIPS (10 gigainstructions per second, or 10^9 instructions per second) are done by a PC's central processing unit (CPU), you might say that a single instruction takes 100 ps. A machine working at 100 GIPS will take 10 ps to complete a single instruction. When a computer becomes able to do 1000 GIPS or 1 TIPS (one terainstruction per second, or 10^{12} instructions per second), the time per instruction will be down to 1 ps. *See also* COMPUTER POWER *and* INSTRUCTIONS PER SECOND.

PICT

PICT is a graphics program designed for use with Macintosh computers and application software. It is an object-oriented (vector) graphics scheme, although it can work with some bitmapped images too.

In PICT, there are several elementary objects, including circles, polygons, and straight line segments. These can be modified independently and then put together to make more complex objects. This is typical of a draw program.

With PICT, as with most object-oriented graphics programs, you can adjust all the variables of any object, skewing an equilateral triangle to an isoceles or irregular triangle, for example, (see the drawing). Once you've tailored each object so it is just the way you want it, you can put them all together and create complex graphic figures. *See also* DRAW PROGRAM *and* OBJECT-ORIENTED GRAPHICS.

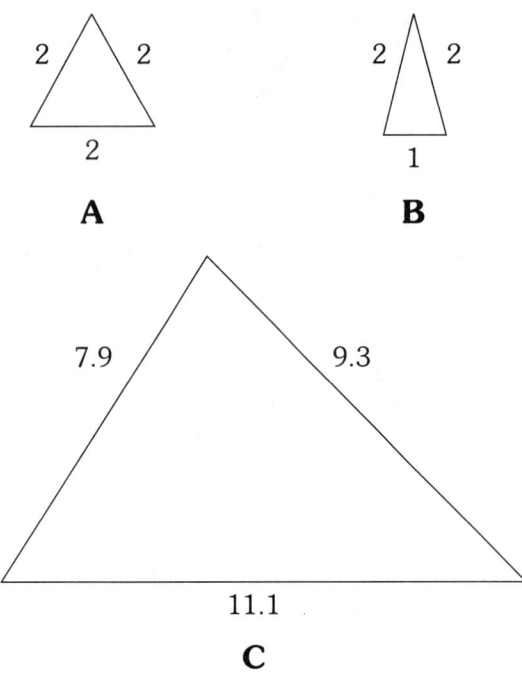

Equilateral triangle (A); isosceles triangle (B); irregular triangle (C).

Pie graph

A *pie graph*, also called a *pie chart*, is a method of displaying the relative proportions of items in a group. The basic graph consists of a circle or short cylinder broken up into wedge-shaped sections like the slices of a pie. The size of each wedge depends on the percentage of the total that it represents. Pie graphs are extremely common in presentation graphics software. Virtually all presentation-graphics packages have a provision for generating pie graphs.

The drawing illustrates a simple pie graph, showing the distribution of age groups in a hypothetical town. One section (age 46–60) has been shaded for emphasis, perhaps because this group is being discussed in accompanying text. As an alternative to shading, coloring can be used; the section might also be pulled away from the main part of the pie.

Usually, the size of one slice of the pie represents its portion of the 360 degrees that make up the total. Thus, for example, the slice for age 46–60 covers 61 degrees, which is about 17% of a full circle. When an item represents only a tiny fraction of the whole, say 0.1%, the width of the slice might be exaggerated somewhat for clarity. *See also* PRESENTATION GRAPHICS.

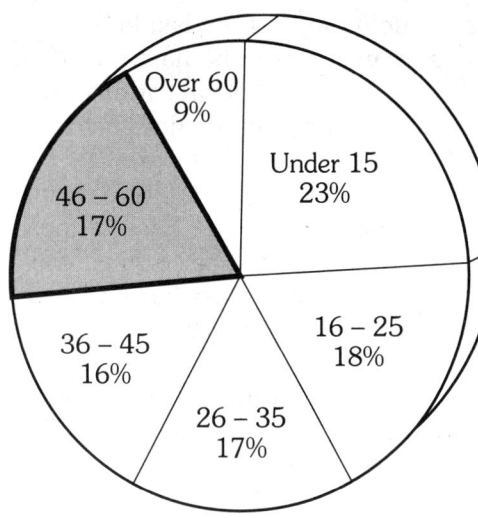

A pie graph is a simple method of showing proportion.

Pitch

The fineness of characters in lines of type, or of dots in a computer-generated image, is indicated by their *pitch*. For example, most printers have adjustable pitch, given in *characters per inch (CPI)*. The most commonly used pitches in text are 10 CPI (also known as standard or pica type) and 12 CPI (sometimes called elite type). Headers, subheads, and titles are often printed with lower pitch, such as 6 CPI. "Fine print" can be printed in 15, 17, or even 20 CPI. The higher the pitch number, the smaller the type.

In a printed graphic, the term *pitch* refers to the number of *dots per inch (DPI)* in the image. The term is also occasionally used in reference to the fineness, or image resolution, of graphics on a monitor or display screen. *See also* DOT PITCH, DOTS PER INCH, *and* IMAGE RESOLUTION.

Pixel

The term *pixel* is a contraction of the words *picture element*. Sometimes this is further shortened to *pel*. A pixel is the smallest unit of visible information in a bitmapped image.

In a typical bitmap, each pixel can have any of numerous hues, saturation levels, and brightness levels, independently of all the other pixels. The larger the number of pixels in an image, the greater the *image resolution*, or amount of detail that can be rendered. A typical monitor can display an image consisting of several hundred thousand pixels.

Pixels are usually square, with the edges oriented horizontally and vertically. A bitmapped image is therefore a fine grid of squares, each with its own characteristics. Because of this grid-like structure, a bitmapped image is almost always a little grainy. There is a limit to the fineness with which a line can be drawn; it can't be narrower than one pixel. Lines and edges that run exactly up-and-down, or exactly left-to-right, look smooth, but curved or diagonal lines/edges have "jaggies."

The drawings show four examples of bitmapped images. Each of these is greatly magnified; if displayed on a monitor, they'd be so small you'd need a magnifying glass to resolve them. At A, the cross has lines one pixel wide; they come out straight. At B, the letter *X* has thin diagonal lines one pixel wide; they appear jagged or beaded. At C, a square with a triangle cut out from the middle has a smooth outer boundary, but an irregular inner edge. At D, an amoeba-shaped, solid blob turns into a many-sided, irregular polygon and its interior.

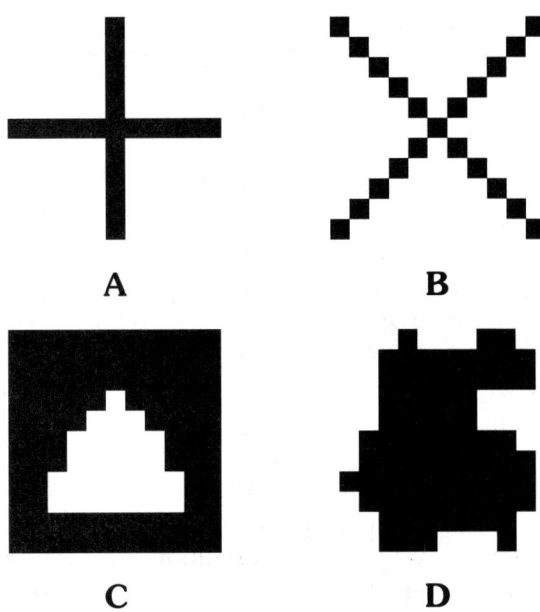

At A, the pixels form smooth lines; at B, jagged lines; at C, smooth and jagged edges; at D, an irregular figure.

As computer graphics and monitor technology have advanced, image pixels have been getting smaller. Monitors have become capable of showing more and more pixels on a screen of fixed size. Today, bitmapped images render enough detail to meet most graphics requirements for the beginning and intermediate computer user. *See also* BITMAP, BITMAPPED GRAPHICS, HIGH-RESOLUTION MONITOR, IMAGE RESOLUTION, *and* PAINT PROGRAM.

PLANNER

PLANNER is a high-level computer language sometimes used in artificial intelligence (AI). The language is goal-oriented in that it seeks a solution to a problem using various different schemes, if necessary.

If a computer is using PLANNER and it fails to solve a problem on the first try, it will backtrack and try again using some other strategy. In this way, PLANNER mimics human intelligence: "If at first you don't succeed, try again."

Some AI researchers see backtracking as a big disadvantage. They ask how you can reach a goal by moving away from it. However, you've probably had setbacks on the way to some goal you sought. If a strategy is wrong, it's better to acknowledge the mistake and go back, rather than waste time at a dead end. Some problems seem to require a trial-and-error approach. Mathematical proofs are often that way, as are some engineering design problems.

Ultimately, all programming languages prove effective at some types of problems and not so good at others. For a computer to have true AI, it will have to incorporate various programs, selecting the most effective program for each problem it encounters. The selection process will itself consist of a program or group of programs. *See also* ARTIFICIAL INTELLIGENCE *and* PROBLEM REDUCTION.

Platform independence

Most personal computers fall into either of two broad categories: IBM-compatible and Macintosh. A network with *platform independence* can accommodate any computer, regardless of its type or operating system. The term also refers to software that can be used with any common operating system.

Flexibility is the main asset of platform independence. Owners of IBM clones and Macs have equal access to a platform-independent network, maximizing the number of users that the network can serve. Platform-independent software practically eliminates concerns over whether or not the package will be compatible with a given computer system.

One possible limitation of platform independence is that data must be transcribed between different operating systems. This slows down the operation of a local area network (LAN) somewhat. However, LANs are usually carefully planned, being assembled within a company, department, or agency. All the computers can thus be supplied with appropriate operating systems and software by the people responsible for making network purchases. *See also* LOCAL AREA NETWORK, MULTIPLATFORM ENVIRONMENT, NETWORK, *and* OPERATING SYSTEM.

Platter

A *platter* is a rigid disk about two to six inches across used in a *hard disk* assembly. Platters are made out of nonmagnetizable material such as aluminum, coated with ferromagnetic particles that store data in the form of microscopic magnetic fields. A typical hard drive contains several platters, each with two read-write heads.

The drawing shows a top view of a stack of six platters. They rotate together on a common axis; the read-write heads are lined up parallel to the rotational axis. Each platter has one head on the top side (facing the viewer) and the other on the bottom side. Thus, in the set of platters shown, there are 12 heads.

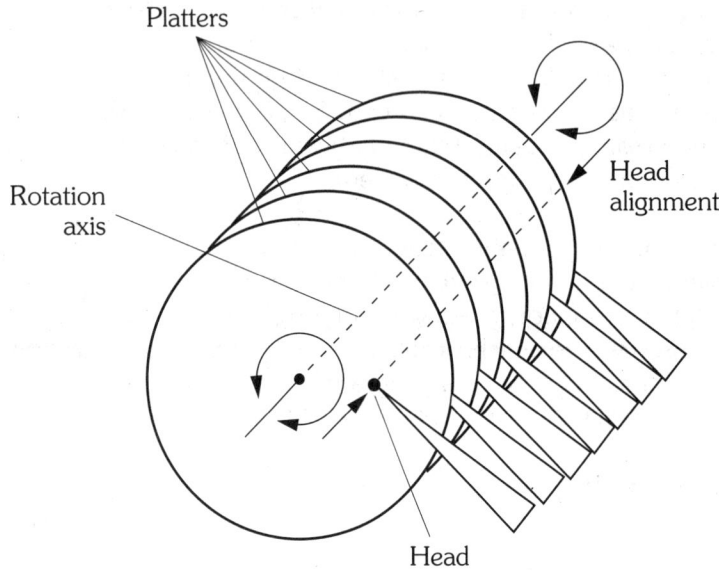

A platter is any of several rigid disks in a hard drive.

The platters in a hard drive rotate at 3600 revolutions-per-minute (RPM) or more. The read-write heads move rapidly back and forth as the platters turn. This takes place at blinding speed. If you ever get an opportunity to see a hard disk system working with the cover removed, don't pass it up. *See also* HARD DISK *and* MAGNETIC MEDIA.

Plotter

A *plotter* is an electromechanical device that can draw graphs, charts, diagrams, and blueprints. A plotter differs from a conventional printer in several respects.

Robotic drafting. The distinction between a plotter and regular printer is vividly apparent when you watch a plotter in operation. While a printer resembles a specialized typewriter or photocopier, a plotter is actually a robot that does drafting.

Plotters generate their output according to a system of Cartesian coordinates. There are two motors that move a marker or pen over the paper, which is treated as an (x,y) plane. One motor moves the pen horizontally, in effect varying the x-coordinate. The other motor moves the paper up and down, or moves the pen vertically, providing the y-coordinate.

Plotters can create multicolored images by using several different colored pens. Some plotters have a provision for eight colors. For example, a machine might render a complex diagram on white paper, using black, red, orange, yellow, green, blue, indigo, and violet pens.

Variety. Plotters are available in many sizes and levels of complexity, depending on the intended application. The price range is similar to that for conventional printers: several hundred dollars for small, desktop units to $12,000 or more for big, floor-standing models used by professional architectural firms and engineering labs. In general, the more expensive plotters can create more detailed images and can accept larger sizes of paper than cheaper plotters. Some plotters can draw on film and transparencies, as well as on paper.

Plotters are less flexible than printers in that the applications are quite specialized. You wouldn't find a plotter any good for printing a term paper, for example. However, a plotter is more versatile than a conventional printer in other respects. Plotters can work with gigantic sheets of paper, and can create extremely precise, fine lines. They create their output in object-oriented (vector) graphics, not as a collection of dots. When a plotter draws a curve, it plots the graph of the equation directly, like a robotic professor of analytic geometry.

Meeting needs. If you create scientific or mathematical documents, or if you're an architect or engineer, you might find a plotter useful. You can use a conventional printer to produce text and some illustrations for your papers and reports, while the plotter renders the charts and diagrams for which it is best-suited.

When considering the purchase of a plotter, be sure that it's compatible with the rest of your computer system. The biggest potential problem is the software. Your PC will need to have a program called a *plotter driver* to translate the digital signals into data the plotter can understand. The situation here is similar to that with printers: consult a knowledgeable, reputable dealer and read carefully through brochures before making a final decision. *See also* PRINTER.

Plug-and-play

When you want to add peripherals to a PC system, *plug-and-play* lets you do it without juggling and experimenting. Plug-and-play, abbreviated *PNP* (not to be confused with a PNP transistor), is becoming common in personal computing, the result of a collaboration between several big computer companies.

Reconfiguring. For a computer to work with peripherals, it must know which peripherals are connected to which ports. When you tell the computer to print a document, you want the data to go to the printer, not to the modem, mouse, or monitor. This doesn't just happen. The system has to be set up that way. If you change

Plug-and-play

peripherals, you'll probably have to reconfigure the system—unless you have PNP.

The more peripherals there are, the more chance there is for something to go wrong with the configuration when the system lacks PNP. If you have a CD-ROM drive, a tape drive, a fax/modem, a sound system, MIDI equipment, and video equipment connected to your PC, the situation can become overwhelming unless the system is designed so that reconfiguring is done automatically.

Imagine what would happen if your body's central nervous system got your arms, hands, legs, and feet confused. You might try to start running, only to find that you were clapping your hands. You might reach to turn on a water faucet, and find yourself kicking the wall. Your nerves would be out of configuration. When the equivalent situation occurs in a computer, the system will usually freeze up. A modem can't print anything, nor can a CD-ROM drive generate music. If your PC tells a peripheral to do something it can't do, it usually does nothing.

For this reason, the process of adding peripherals to a system without plug-and-play is sometimes called *plug-and-pray*. Even today, some new computer systems are sold without the PNP feature.

Requirements. For PNP to function, the computer must be programmed for it. The software must be compatible with peripherals that meet the PNP standard. The peripherals themselves must be designed with PNP in mind. The BIOS (basic input/output system) must be designed for PNP hardware and software.

If a computer system does not have PNP capability, it can usually be upgraded. You'll need to install an operating system that is PNP-compatible, and you'll need to be sure that when you buy new expansion boards, they're designed to the PNP standard. (Your existing boards don't have to be thrown away; the PNP system will adjust to them.)

If you're buying a new computer and you want it to take full advantage of PNP, be sure that the BIOS meets the standard. Then you'll actually be able to plug and unplug peripherals while the computer remains powered-up. This opens up all kinds of money-saving, efficiency-enhancing options, such as sharing a printer among several PCs. In an office, for example, one top-of-the-line printer can be purchased, rather than three or four lower-quality printers.

For a computer to take advantage of PNP, it should have at least an 80386 (386) microprocessor or equivalent, and preferably a 486. You'll need at least four megabytes (4MB) of RAM (random-access memory). *See also* BASIC INPUT/OUTPUT SYSTEM, OPERATING SYSTEM, *and* PERIPHERALS.

Pointer

A *pointer* is an on-screen position indicator employed in a graphical user interface (GUI). It looks like an arrow, a pencil point, an hourglass, or some other easy-to-identify object. Often, the shape of a pointer will change when it moves from one part of the screen to another. In text, the position indicator is called the *cursor* or *insertion point*.

The pointer can be moved with a mouse, trackball, keyboard, or other device. In a true graphical interface, the mouse is the easiest vehicle by which to move the pointer; a trackball is a little touchier. Other devices, such as a *J-mouse* (a pressure-sensitive button on the J key of the keyboard) are occasionally employed. The keyboard should be used only in the absence of other pointer-movement devices.

Once the pointer has been moved to the desired location, you might click the mouse or press a key to actuate a function, indicated by a box, button, or icon that the pointer is touching. *See also* CURSOR, GRAPHICAL USER INTERFACE, MOUSE, *and* TRACKBALL.

Point-of-sale system

The term *point-of-sale system*, abbreviated *POS*, refers to a computer that monitors and controls aspects of a retail business. Such a system speeds up the sales process and increases efficiency in several ways.

A POS can be operated by an employee at the checkout counter of a retail store, grocery store, or restaurant. All the checkout computers are tied into the main PC in the back office. The drawing on the following page is a simplified block diagram of a POS. At A, a checkout terminal is shown. (The store might have several of these terminals.) At B, components of the central computer system are shown.

Inventory and cash flow. Whenever a store makes a sale, the inventory of some item decreases by one unit. (That's obvious, but the fact is all too often overlooked.) With time, inventories decline, faster for some items than for others. When a store has 500 different items, maintaining a reasonable inventory becomes complicated. You don't want to run out of anything because that will make customers unhappy. However, keeping an oversupply ties up your money.

With a POS, you can see, on a daily, weekly, or monthly basis, dollars in versus dollars out. You can see where your money is working for you, and where it isn't. You'll know which items to order more of in the future, and which items are required in lesser quantities.

When dealing with large cash-flow volume, the slightest imbalance can turn a profit into a loss, while a similarly small adjustment can change a loss into a profit. The POS can help you figure out exactly where your inefficiencies lie, thus helping you make profitable decisions in the future.

Point-of-sale system

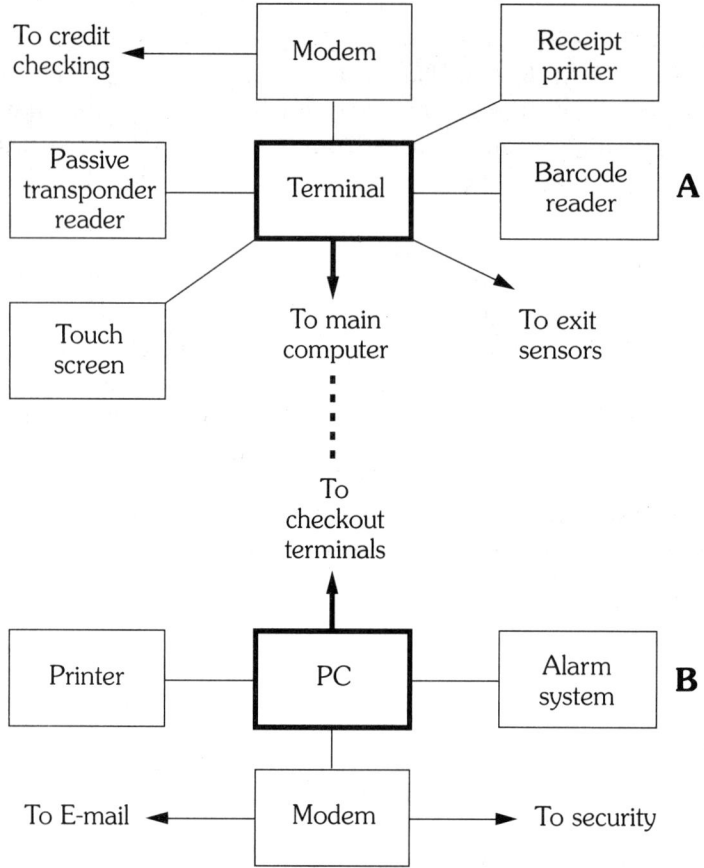

Point-of-sale system: checkout terminal (A) and central computer (B).

Transaction aids. Everyone has heard the "beep, beep, beep" of checkout-counter computers. There are several kinds of devices that hasten the checkout or sales process:

> A *barcode reader* uses an optical scanner to ring up items by "looking at" stripes on a label. It records the price, of course, but it also tells the computer which item is sold. When the scanner recognizes the data on the label, it beeps.

> A *passive transponder* reads a pattern of data from a magnetized strip attached to the item being sold. When the item is rung up, the transponder is encoded with the equivalent of a "sold" label. Passive transponders can be used with electromagnetic theft detection alarms, placed at the exits to the store. If an item passes between the detectors with a transponder that says "not sold yet," the alarm will go off.

> *Touch screens* are common in restaurants. The person at the counter keys in the orders by touching a monitor in various places, as if it were a keypad. Touch screens never wear out as keypads do. The data on the screen can be changed in an

infinite variety of ways to reflect changes in the menu of the restaurant. In addition, touch screens are user-friendly, so even cyberphobic employees can use them. *See also* BARCODE, PASSIVE TRANSPONDER, *and* TOUCH SCREEN.

Charging errors. In certain businesses, such as auto repair or restaurants, it's fairly common for employees to make charging errors. They might forget to charge for some item, such as coffee, or they might charge for the wrong item. Once in a while, an employee will overcharge and pocket the change. All these things become much less frequent when a POS keeps watch over every penny and every transaction.

Charging errors, in the long term, always cost money. In the case of undercharging or omission, the loss is obvious and immediate. The "profit" from overcharging, whether accidental or deliberate, is more than nullified by repercussions that eventually result. Computers make mistakes less likely and pilferage more difficult.

Data linking. A POS keeps track of each sale and every item ordered. The system can thus keep a constant, updated inventory of every item in your store. Tied into every cash register, and also into the back office, the data can be linked between spreadsheets, databases, and even word processing programs.

You'll see immediately, by looking at the database, when you're running low on some items. You can use the spreadsheet to find out which items are selling well and which are not. You can use the word processor to compose and send (via electronic mail, of course!) orders for new items. The system can even be programmed to electronically pay your suppliers.

With a POS, you can keep track of repeat customers. This works similarly to mail-order business software, except, of course, the customers are there in person, rather than miles away via telephone. Suppose Mr. Doe comes in and pays with a credit card. The checkout person enters his credit card number. The POS flashes that Mr. Doe bought a Wizard Widget Mark VII last May. He will probably be surprised when the checkout person cheerfully asks, "Are you enjoying the widget, Mr. Doe?" Even if the widget broke, or has been forgotten in the clutter of toys in his child's bedroom, Mr. Doe will think your personnel are competent. In the long term, little things like that can make a huge difference in the profitability of a business. *See also* DATABASE, MAIL-ORDER BUSINESS SOFTWARE, OBJECT LINKING AND EMBEDDING, *and* SPREADSHEET.

Polar coordinates

There are several coordinate systems used to locate points in two-dimensional (2-D) space. One of these is called *polar coordinates*.

Polar coordinates

Most graphics programs can render 2-D plots in polar coordinates as well as in Cartesian coordinates.

The drawings show the two most common types of polar coordinates, and a method for locating a point, *P*, in such a system.

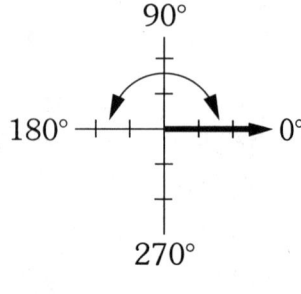

A

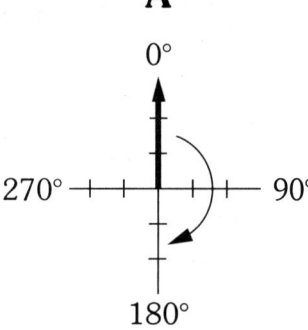

Mathematical scheme (at A), navigational scheme (at B), and location of a point P (at C) using polar coordinates.

B

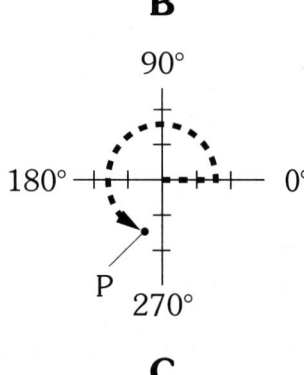

C

First, you decide on an *origin* point. Then, you decide on a *reference ray*, whose end point is at the origin. The reference ray represents zero degrees and is graduated in units. In mathematical graphics, the reference ray runs off to the right ("due east"), and the angle is measured counterclockwise from 0 up to 360 degrees (drawing A). In navigation and geographical applications, the reference ray usually points toward the top of the page ("due north"), and the angle is measured clockwise from 0 to 360 degrees (drawing B).

To define a point *P*, start at the origin and move out the required number of units along the reference ray. This is the radius; it is generally a nonnegative real number. Then go counterclockwise or clockwise, as the case might be, by the necessary number of degrees. That's the angle; it is generally a nonnegative real number less than 360 degrees. Thus, you arrive at the point, as shown in drawing C. In this example, the point is at a radius of 1.7 units, and an angle of 250 degrees. *See also* CARTESIAN COORDINATES.

Polling

In a network, it is useless to access a workstation if the node has nothing to transmit. In fact, it is worse than useless, because it slows down the operation of the whole network. This can be avoided by a scheme called *polling*.

In a polling environment, the network controller checks all the nodes at intervals, in a rotating sequence or according to a predefined list, to see if the stations have any data to send. If a station has information, it is sent, and the controller moves to the next station on the list. If a station is polled and has nothing to send, the controller moves immediately to the next station on the list. The flowchart shows the procedure followed by the controller when polling protocol is in use.

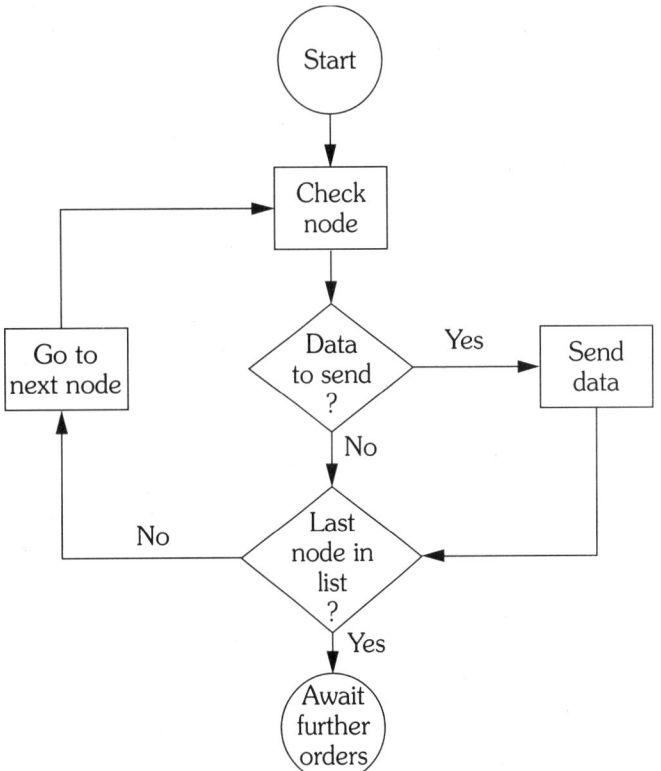

A flowchart showing how polling protocol works.

A polling protocol optimizes network efficiency by minimizing the proportion of time during which no data is being transferred. Polling can be used in a local area network (LAN), a wide-area network (WAN), or a packet communications network. *See also* LOCAL AREA NETWORK, NODE, PACKET COMMUNICATIONS, PROTOCOL, *and* WIDE-AREA NETWORK.

Polyline graphic

A *polyline graphic* is a nonstandard, multisided figure in object-oriented graphics. Broadly speaking, it is a polygon that is custom-made, rather than being supplied as one of the basic primitives in the program.

To create a polyline graphic, you start at some point on the monitor screen and draw a straight line segment. After the line segment has been drawn with the length and direction you want, you stop and change direction, starting a new line segment. You repeat this process as many times as necessary to complete the figure you want.

The drawing shows a 10-sided, irregular polygon and the process by which it is generated as a polyline graphic. The starting point is as shown. Movement is in the direction of the arrows. (The arrows aren't part of the figure.) Stopping points are numbered 1 through 10.

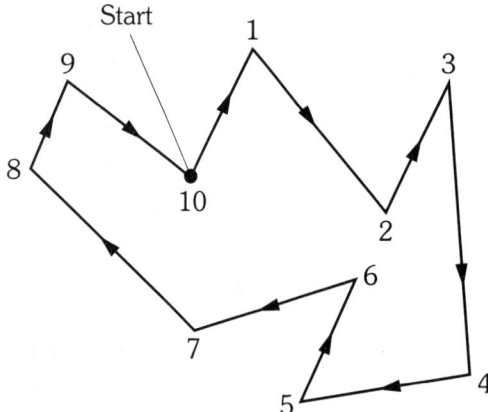

An irregular polygon created with polyline graphics.

Once you've created a polyline graphic, you can use it in a modeling program just as you use other primitives. You can rotate it, flip it inside out, make it larger, make it smaller, or move it around on the screen. You can add it to other primitives to create complex figures. *See also* MODELING *and* OBJECT-ORIENTED GRAPHICS.

Pop-up menu

In menu-driven software, you give the computer commands by choosing from lists of options (menus). Most PC users find this easier than memorizing the commands and typing them in.

Sometimes, when you select an option from a menu, you'll get another menu. This new menu is called a *pop-up menu* because it "pops" onto the screen, seeming to appear out of nowhere when the option is selected. When you select one of the commands or icons on the pop-up menu, the computer executes the instruction and the pop-up menu disappears from the screen. *See also* MENU, MENU-DRIVEN SOFTWARE, *and* PULL-DOWN MENU.

Port

A *port* is a point where data goes into or comes out of a computer. Your PC has one port for the monitor, another for the printer, another for the modem, and so on. There are several different types of ports, named according to how the information passes through.

A port that is used only for data input is called an *input port*. A port that is used only for data output is called an *output port*. A port that is used both for data input and data output is called an *input/output (I/O) port*.

Ports are sometimes also categorized as *parallel* or *serial*. These terms refer to the nature of the data transfer. The binary digits (bits) of data pass through a parallel port in bunches of eight, 16, 32 or some higher power of two. Data bits go through a serial port one by one. *See also* PARALLEL, PARALLEL PORT, SERIAL, *and* SERIAL PORT.

Portable computer

A *portable computer* is a PC that you can carry around easily, and that you can operate while you're away from your usual workstation. Portable PCs come in many sizes and shapes. Characteristics vary greatly. Some portable PCs are little more than calculators; others have as much computational power as a typical desktop PC.

Power source. Most portable computers can work from battery. There are two types of batteries: rechargeable and disposable. The most common rechargeable power sources are nickel-cadmium (NICAD), nickel-metal-hydride (NiMH), and lithium-ion batteries. Nonrechargeable types include zinc-carbon and alkaline batteries.

Battery life depends on the size of the machine and the type of work you do on it. A laptop or notebook PC with a hard disk and diskette drive can run for up to several hours on a single battery charge. A personal digital assistant (PDA) might work for as long as 100 hours before it needs a battery recharge or replacement.

Most portable PCs can work from the 117-volt commercial mains while the battery is recharging. A wall adapter, similar to those used for other small, low-voltage appliances, provides the charging current, at the same time as it supplies the necessary voltage for the operation of the computer.

Portable computer accessories

Display. All portable computers employ power-saving displays. The most common type is the liquid-crystal display (LCD). There are several different kinds of LCD. Some can portray color, and others cannot. Most have backlighting that can be disabled when it is not needed.

The larger laptop computers have displays that measure 9 to 12 inches diagonally. Pen-based computers and PDAs have smaller displays. Some units have displays that flip up when you are operating the computer and fold back down again when you are finished. Others have a screen that is always exposed, like a small television set.

More sophisticated displays include the active-matrix and the plasma display. These are brighter and clearer than conventional LCDs, and are better at portraying motion, but they consume more current.

Data entry. Laptop PCs have keyboards about the size of those found in portable typewriters. A certain minimum key size and spacing is necessary for effective typing and command entry. A full keyboard is a big asset because it lets you conveniently do word processing.

Pen-based computers and PDAs usually have keypads similar to those in electronic calculators. These are not full keyboards, so they do not allow you to do as many things as you can with a laptop or desktop computer. However, with pointing devices, you can use graphical interfaces. Also, some units allow you to enter data in your own handwriting. *See also* LAPTOP COMPUTER, LIQUID-CRYSTAL DISPLAY, NICKEL-CADMIUM AND NICKEL-METAL-HYDRIDE BATTERIES, PEN-BASED COMPUTER, PERSONAL DIGITAL ASSISTANT, *and* PORTABLE COMPUTER ACCESSORIES.

Portable computer accessories

When considering the purchase of a portable PC, especially a laptop (notebook) computer, many people worry that the machine won't have the features or flexibility of a desktop unit. This was a valid concern several years ago, but now there are many accessories available that can make a laptop computer just about as good as a desktop unit.

Trackball/mouse. If you want to enjoy the advantages of a graphical user interface (GUI) such as Windows, Macintosh, or OS/2, you'll need some kind of pointing device. A desktop computer is generally supplied with a mouse as a standard accessory. This is not necessarily true for laptop computers. Pen-based computers and personal digital assistants (PDAs) use a special form of pointer called a pen or stylus, rather than a mouse or trackball.

Many laptop computers have a provision for a trackball or similar pointing devices built-in. The ball, which resembles a ball bearing and can rotate on any axis, is housed in a package usually about half the size of a mouse. You maneuver the pointer/cursor by rubbing the ball around. It's an intuitive process, and requires only a little getting used to. The advantage of a trackball in portable computing environments is that it needs no desk space.

Alternatively, you can connect a mouse to a laptop computer. However, you'll need about one square foot of horizontal space in which to move the mouse. This space isn't always available in transit, although when you get to your hotel, you can use the desk in your room to set up your workstation, including a mouse.

PCMCIA standard adapter cards. PCMCIA cards greatly expand the versatility of all portable PCs. They are small circuit cards, roughly the height and width of credit cards, but thicker and heavier. You insert them into the main unit of the computer, just as you would a bank card in an automatic-teller machine.

A set of PCMCIA cards can endow a laptop PC, pen-based computer, or PDA with several special functions. For example, a PCMCIA card can provide your computer with extra RAM (random-access memory). These cards can also serve as a high-speed, high-volume data storage medium called *flash memory*. Some PCMCIA cards contain special software, such as draw or paint programs, word processors, database managers, and spreadsheets. A PCMCIA card can emulate a hard disk or diskette drive. It's even possible to get your computer to take spoken data input (speech recognition) with the help of such a card.

An often overlooked feature of PCMCIA cards is that they can turn a computer into a game-playing machine. If you're on a long trip and you get tired of sales charts, and you have a spare battery pack, there's fun to be had with game software. Who says computing has to be serious all the time?

Optical scanner. An optical scanner lets you import data from printed matter, such as magazines, books, or brochures. You can also convert photographs to digital data suitable for storage on diskettes or a hard disk. Some optical scanners are small enough to be packed along with a portable computer. Handheld scanners can be plugged into a port in a laptop computer.

Although you don't need much table space (if any) to use a handheld scanner, it helps. You'll find it difficult to scan text or photographs effectively while riding in a bus or plane, for example—although it can be done if you have steady hands and the ride isn't too bumpy. Be prepared, however, for inquisitive glances and questions from other passengers, especially children.

Printer. When you're in transit, a printer isn't something you'll normally take out and start using. Printers consume a lot of current, and must usually operate from a 117-volt utility outlet. Besides, you'd

Portable computer accessories

probably get more than few astonished stares if you started a printing session while riding in an airplane, even if you had a whole set of three seats all to yourself.

Once you reach your destination, however, a portable printer can be a lifesaver. You probably won't need to do large volumes of work on it, so it need not be built like a tank. Several manufacturers sell small, lightweight inkjet printer devices that you can use to make quick hardcopies. Just be sure you've kept up the maintenance routine before you leave on your trip, and take along some paper.

Fax and modem. A modem provides the interface between a computer and a telephone line, allowing you to access the many online services, send and receive messages (electronic mail), or get into a bulletin-board system (BBS). Some laptop/notebook computers have a provision for an internal modem; others require an "outboard" modem.

Some modems also provide facsimile (fax) capability. Using such a fax/modem, you can send faxes either from hardcopies, such as magazines and books, or directly from your computer.

A special form of modem, called a *terminal node controller (TNC)*, interfaces a computer with a radio transceiver. This is done by amateur radio operators ("hams"), and is also used in business computing.

Battery and charger. One of the biggest limitations in portable computer operation is the fact that the batteries only last a few hours. You're quite lucky if you can get six hours' operating time with a laptop computer before the battery pack needs to be recharged.

If you get an extra battery pack, you can rotate the two batteries; one of the batteries can be charging while you're using the other one. You might even get two extra battery packs and one extra charger, if you think you'll need to use your PC that much when there's no source of utility power available.

It's always wise to use a portable PC with the 117-volt power adapter whenever possible. Many laptop and notebook computers will let you operate the computer and charge the battery at the same time, from the same adapter.

Checklist. One of the most infuriating, yet chronic problems that plagues the users of portable electronic equipment is the tendency for cables, connectors, and other little items to "turn up missing." It's easy to forget one cable or connector, resulting in inconvenience or even the inability to use the system.

Make a checklist of everything you'll need for your portable workstation. Do this several days in advance of the trip. Rack your brain for every last detail. Set up your portable workstation in another room, noting every item. Put the list in a file, and give it a filename you can easily remember, such as TRIPLIST.TXT. Print a copy of the checklist before you leave, going through it religiously as you pack. Include the list in your suitcase, and go through it again when you pack for the return trip.

The table is a sample list for a modest portable workstation. Your needs will differ from those shown here, so don't rely on this list alone, but you might use it as a starting point. *See also* COMPUTER GAMES, FAX, INKJET PRINTER, LAPTOP COMPUTER, MODEM, MOUSE, NICKEL-CADMIUM AND NICKEL-METAL-HYDRIDE BATTERIES, OPTICAL SCANNER, PACKET COMMUNICATIONS, PCMCIA STANDARD ADAPTER CARDS, PEN-BASED COMPUTER, PERIPHERALS, PERSONAL DIGITAL ASSISTANT, POWER SUPPLY, TERMINAL NODE CONTROLLER, *and* TRACKBALL.

Sample packing list

On way out	On way back	Item
☐	☐	Computer (DUH!)
☐	☐	All cords, connectors
☐	☐	Extra battery pack
☐	☐	Battery charger/117-volt adapter
☐	☐	Trackball
☐	☐	Printer
☐	☐	Printer paper (100 sheets)
☐	☐	Fax modem with all cords
☐	☐	Handheld scanner
☐	☐	Desk lamp
☐	☐	3-plug wall outlet extension cord
☐	☐	Diskettes, blank
☐	☐	Diskettes with current work files
☐	☐	Game software
☐	☐	PCMCIA cards

PostScript

PostScript, developed by Adobe Systems, is a commonly used *page description language (PDL)* that can be used with many kinds of printers. It transcribes data sent from the computer, so the printer can create the best image on the paper. A PostScript printer has several assets.

First, PostScript allows a printer to take full advantage of its image-resolution capability. All printed documents come out with maximum crispness and clarity; the better the printer, the better the results. This is not always true with printers that don't use PostScript.

Another asset of PostScript is that it allows for resizing of text. Printers that do not use a PDL such as PostScript can produce text in a few sizes, such as 10, 12, 15, 17, and 20 characters per inch (CPI). With PostScript or another PDL, unusual sizes can be used, such as 11 or 13 CPI. It's possible to include more typefaces, too, because PostScript uses an outline font to generate the characters.

PostScript facilitates *device independence*, meaning that any printer can be used with any computer. Suppose you are preparing a thesis for your Ph.D. You want your professors to read a higher-quality copy than your dot-matrix printer can generate. You can take the diskette containing the document to a print shop, where an expensive laser printer, equipped with PostScript, can produce a top-notch printed manuscript. You need not buy a new laser printer yourself (unless, of course, you planned to do that anyway).

PostScript was developed with the future in mind. Printers keep getting better, in terms of the number of dots per inch (DPI) they can render. New PC operating systems are being developed, and new microprocessors are constantly entering the scene. As this evolution takes place, PostScript follows along. PostScript works with DOS as well as all the common graphical user interfaces (GUIs), including Windows, OS/2, and Macintosh.

When you're ready to buy a new printer, it's a good idea to get one that can work with PostScript. That way, you can be sure you're getting the most out of the printer, even when the time comes to upgrade the rest of your system. *See also* FONT, HIGH-RESOLUTION PRINTER, OUTLINE FONT, *and* PAGE DESCRIPTION LANGUAGE.

PowerBook

PowerBook is a series of laptop computers manufactured by Apple Computer, Inc., known for the Macintosh line of PCs. The PowerBook, like most other laptops and notebook computers, has a flip-up, backlit display. You can get either a passive-matrix display or the more sophisticated active-matrix type. The active-matrix is better for high-resolution graphics work, but it costs more. PowerBooks have hard disks, diskette drives, and trackballs or other pointing devices built-in. The RAM (random-access memory) can be enlarged by adding extra circuit boards. There is an option for an internal modem.

The more advanced PowerBooks have special features, including *NuBus*, the Macintosh expansion scheme; a docking station, allowing the computer to be used as a desktop machine; a port for an external diskette drive; provision for a second hard disk; a port for a cathode-ray tube (CRT) monitor; and several other ports for various peripherals. The top-of-the-line PowerBooks compare favorably with desktop PCs in terms of flexibility and computing power.

A nickel-cadmium (NICAD) battery, along with a wall charger, serves as the power supply for earlier PowerBooks, while nickel-metal-hydride (NiMH) batteries are used in the later versions. The NiMH technology provides longer battery life, although it costs more than the NICAD. The wall adapter can be plugged into a 117-volt outlet, and the computer can be used while the battery is charging. Battery life is extended by a special standby feature called "sleep" mode. When the computer is in this mode, it reduces power consumption after a certain period without input. The hard disk is shut off, and the clock is slowed down, but things return to normal the instant the user hits a key. *See also* DOCKING STATION, LAPTOP COMPUTER, MACINTOSH, NUBUS, *and* TRACKBALL.

PowerPC chip

The *PowerPC chip* is a microprocessor developed jointly by IBM, Apple, and Motorola that uses *reduced-instruction-set computing (RISC)* technology. (*PowerPC* is an IBM trademark.) There are several different versions of the PowerPC chip; they are designated by three-digit numbers that start with the numeral 6. The first PowerPC was called the 601; the 603, 604, and 620 followed.

The PowerMac series of computers from Apple is designed around the PowerPC chip. For owners of older Macs, the method of upgrading to a PowerPC depends on the particular Mac. In some cases, the logic board (also called the motherboard) can be exchanged. Other machines use upgrade circuit cards. If you're a Mac user ready to buy a new machine, you might want to consider the PowerMac.

A PowerPC-equipped Mac, whether an upgrade of an old machine or a new PowerMac, behaves just like earlier Macs when first powered-up. System 7 is standard. You can use the same applications as was the case with earlier Macs, although operating details occasionally differ.

Several IBM computers use the PowerPC chip. These are called Power Personal Systems. A major feature of these machines is called *human-centered computing*, a philosophy built around the idea that computers should conform to their users, rather than vice versa.

In PowerPC-based systems, a technique called *emulation* is used to run DOS and Windows. The most exciting developments in native PowerPC software are in high-powered applications, such as videoconferencing and virtual reality.

PowerPC chip

Features. The designers of the PowerPC chips had big goals in mind. The basic objective was to revolutionize personal computing. Here are some of the major features of the PowerPC microprocessor line:

➢ *Cool speed* PowerPC chips are fast, and they generate relatively little heat, considering their computing power. The slowest clock speed is 50 MHz, roughly comparable to the Intel 486. Some PowerPC chips can run at speeds well over 100 MHz.

➢ *Fewer instructions* The RISC architecture makes use of fewer instructions than conventional, *complex-instruction-set computing (CISC)* systems. Because the instructions are easier for the machine to handle, an RISC can do more instructions per second (IPS) than a CISC. The IPS specification is an important aspect of computing power.

➢ *Superscalar design* Another means for increasing the IPS rate of the chip is its *superscalar processor architecture*, which means it can do more than one instruction at a time. The data highway of a PowerPC has, in a sense, more lanes. The PowerPC 601, for example, can do three instructions for every cycle of the clock.

➢ *Energy efficiency* The PowerPC chips give you more computing power for a given amount of electrical energy supplied. Thus, it takes less electricity to do its work. The PowerPC chips are energy efficient in other ways, as well. They run cool, and some of them can run for quite a while from a battery. The 603 is well-suited for laptop (notebook) computers because of its minimal electrical energy needs.

➢ *Versatility* The sheer computing power of these chips makes it possible for them to handle applications that previously required complicated add-ons. For example, IBM's Personal Dictation System (PDS), which makes use of speech recognition technology, runs smoothly on PowerPC chips. The developers of the PowerPC are cooperating with software companies in an effort to maximize the appeal of the chips.

➢ *Multiple operating systems* The PowerPC chips can run DOS, with or without Windows. They can also use IBM's OS/2 or the Macintosh OS. In fact, you can actually run two operating systems, such as Windows and the Macintosh OS, at the same time. This allows for an entirely new dimension in multitasking. Other RISC chips generally offer this operating-system versatility, too.

Hangups. The PowerPC is not just more powerful than its ancestors, the 80x86 and 680x0 chips; a whole new approach is used. It's like the leap from propeller-driven to jet aircraft that shook aviation during the mid-1900s. There were some problems involved in getting jet aircraft to fly and in teaching pilots how to handle them. Those who had confidence in the new design persisted and prevailed.

The main adjustment problem with RISC technology is the fact that not all CISC software works directly with RISC chips. While this means money for software engineers, it can be frustrating to the everyday PC user.

Braking effect. When RISC systems first came out, some technophiles eagerly embraced it, but many held back. They had found machines that satisfied their needs, and did not wish to upgrade simply because another "techno-coup" was underway. While the difference between RISC and CISC is significant to the engineer, it's less important to the everyday PC user on a limited budget. CISC systems have not become obsolete overnight, nor will that fate befall the RISC when the next breakthrough occurs. People can't afford total upgrades very often. Marketplace reality has a braking effect on runaway technomania.

There's no law that says "old" computers are bad or that everyone must have the latest system. Plenty of PC users are content with machines several years behind the forefront. There does come a time, however, when upgrading becomes desirable, even for the most conservative PC users. If you wait too long to upgrade, you run the risk of compatibility problems. *See also* CLOCK SPEED, DOS, INSTRUCTIONS PER SECOND, MULTITASKING, OS/2, REDUCED-INSTRUCTION-SET COMPUTER, SYSTEM 7, *and* WINDOWS.

Power supply

A *power supply* is a circuit that provides a computer or other electronic device with the voltage and current it needs for proper operation. This article is devoted mainly to power supplies for desktop computers, monitors, and printers, but the same principles apply to all power supplies that operate from the utility mains. The discussion concerns power supplies for use with desktop computers. If you have a laptop (notebook) PC, it uses a battery for its power supply, in conjunction with a low-voltage, plug-in recharger.

The power from a typical wall outlet consists of alternating current (ac) at about 117 volts. However, most electronic circuits, including computers, require direct current (dc) at a much lower voltage.

General design. An ac power supply (so named because it supplies an ac output) has only a transformer, as shown in drawing A on page 864. This changes the voltage from 117 to some other value, either higher or lower. Computers do not generally use ac power supplies.

In a dc power supply, the 117-volt utility ac is first stepped down with a transformer to some lower voltage. Then, this low-voltage ac is

Power supply

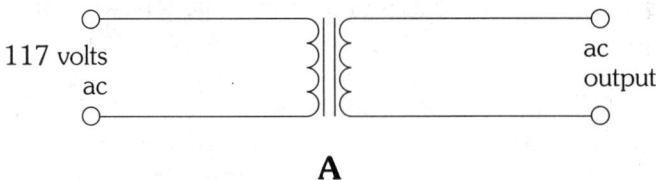

A

An ac supply.

rectified. Rectification is the process of converting ac to pulsating dc through the use of one or more diodes. Then the pulsating dc is filtered, or smoothed out, so that it becomes continuous (like the current from a battery), with positive or negative polarity. Finally, the dc is regulated, so that its voltage does not change when the utility line voltage fluctuates. Computers are rather finicky, insisting on the right voltage all the time. Drawing B is a block diagram showing the stages in a dc power supply.

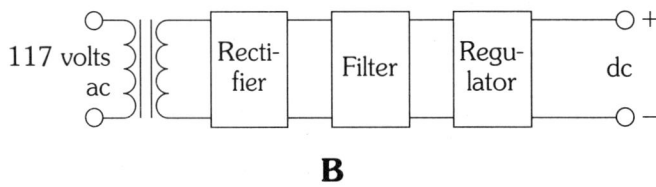

B

A block diagram of a dc supply.

Power supplies that provide more than a few volts must have features that protect the user from electrical shock. All power supplies need fuses or circuit breakers to minimize the fire hazard in case the equipment shorts out.

Half-wave rectifier. The simplest rectifier circuit, called a *half-wave rectifier*, uses one diode to "chop off" half of the ac input cycle. A half-wave rectifier circuit diagram is shown in drawing C.

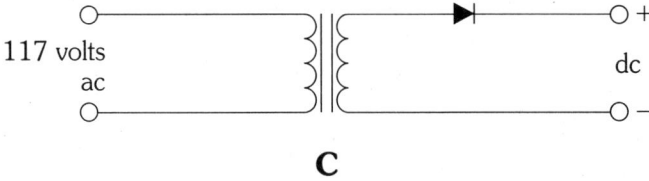

C

A half-wave rectifier.

Half-wave rectification is useful in supplies that don't have to deliver much current, or that don't need to be especially well-regulated. For high-current equipment, a *full-wave rectifier* works better. The full-wave scheme is also better when good voltage regulation is needed.

Full-wave rectifier. A full-wave circuit uses both halves of the ac cycle. Suppose you want to convert an ac wave to dc with positive polarity. You can allow the positive half of the ac cycle to pass unchanged, and flip the negative portion of the wave upside-down, making it positive instead. Drawing D shows the principle behind full-wave rectification. The dotted curves represent the part of the ac input wave that is "flipped over" to get the output, shown by the heavy, solid curve.

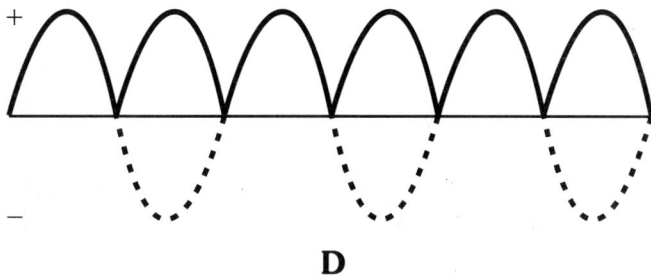

A full-wave rectification.

There are two basic circuits for the full-wave supply. One version, shown in drawing E, uses a center tap in the transformer, and needs two diodes. The other circuit, shown in drawing F, uses four diodes, and is known as a *bridge rectifier*.

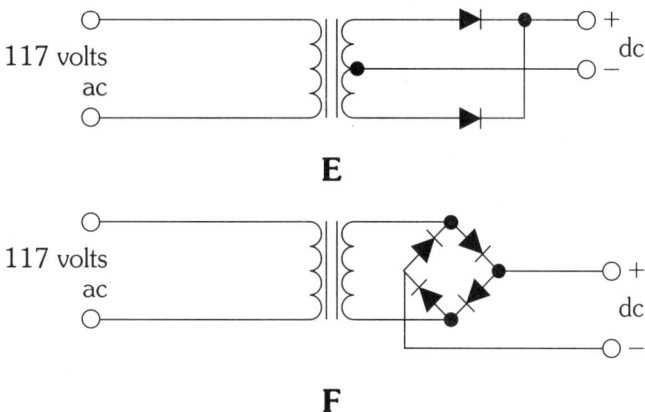

A full-wave, center-tap rectifier circuit; at F, a full-wave bridge rectifier

Filtering. Electronic equipment doesn't like the pulsating dc that comes straight from a rectifier. The ripple in the waveform must be smoothed out, so that pure, battery-like dc is supplied. The filter does this.

The simplest filter is one or more large-value capacitors connected in parallel with the rectifier output. Electrolytic capacitors are almost always used. They must be hooked up in the right direction because they are polarized components. An example of a simple capacitor type filter is shown in drawing G.

Sometimes a large-value coil, called a *filter choke*, is connected in series, in addition to the capacitor in parallel. This provides a

Power supply

smoother dc output than the capacitor by itself. An example is shown in drawing H.

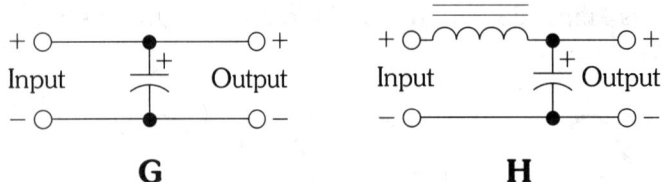

A capacitor filter; at H, a capacitor/choke filter.

Voltage regulation. If a special kind of diode, called a *Zener diode*, is connected in parallel with the output of a power supply, the diode will limit the output voltage of the supply by "brute force" as long as it has a high enough power rating. The limiting voltage depends on the particular Zener diode used. There are Zener diodes to fit any reasonable power-supply voltage. Drawing I is a diagram of a full-wave, center-tap supply including a Zener diode for voltage regulation.

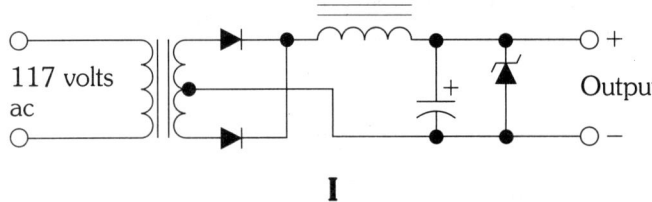

A complete power supply with Zener diode regulator.

A Zener-diode voltage regulator is inefficient when the supply is used with equipment that draws high current. When a supply must deliver a high level of current, a power transistor is used along with the Zener diode to obtain regulation. A circuit diagram of such a scheme is shown in drawing J.

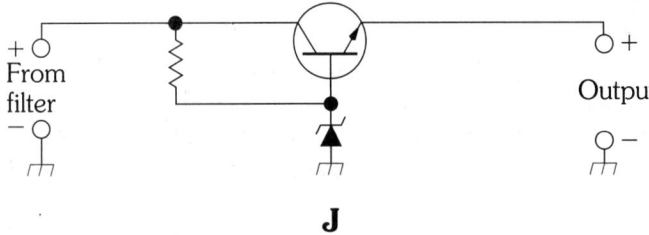

A Zener regulator with transistor.

In recent years, voltage regulators have become available in integrated-circuit (IC) form. You connect the IC, perhaps along with some external components, at the output of the filter. This method provides the best possible regulation at low and moderate voltages.

Transient suppression. The ac on the utility line does not have a clean, perfect, constant wave shape, as you might think. The voltage at a typical utility outlet can range from 100 to 125 volts, even though the nominal figure is 117 volts. Voltage regulators can take care of that; but there are often "spikes," known as *transients*, that can reach hundreds of volts. Without some protection against the effects of transients, sensitive electronic equipment such as a PC can malfunction.

Transients are caused by sudden changes in the load in a utility circuit, such as might occur when power is briefly interrupted. Lightning can also produce them. They are most likely to occur during storms and during times of peak power usage. They can happen at any time, however; they are impossible to predict.

The simplest way to get rid of most transients is to use a commercially made transient suppressor, sometimes also called surge suppressors or surge protectors (both of which are technical misnomers). You install a transient suppressor between the wall outlet and the input to the power supply, then you plug the power supply into one of the several outlets in the suppressor box.

In the event of a local thunderstorm, the best way to protect equipment is to unplug it. A nearby lightning strike can cause voltages high enough to spark across a transient suppressor, damaging the power supply and possibly the computer itself. Perhaps you already know, from bitter experience, how devastating lightning can be.

Fuses and breakers. If a fuse blows, it must be replaced with another of the same rating. If the replacement fuse is rated too low in current, it will probably blow out right away, or soon after it has been installed. If the replacement fuse is rated too high in current, it might not protect the equipment.

Circuit breakers do the same thing as fuses, except that a breaker can be reset by turning off the power supply, waiting a moment, and then pressing a button or flipping a switch. Some breakers reset automatically when the equipment has been shut off for a certain length of time.

Personal safety. Power supplies can be dangerous. This is especially true of high-voltage circuits, but anything over 12 volts should be treated as potentially lethal. In a computer, high voltage exists at the input to the supply (where the 117-volt ac appears). A cathode-ray-tube (CRT) monitor has even higher voltages that operate its deflecting coils.

A power supply is not necessarily safe after it has been switched off. Filter capacitors hold a charge for a long time. In high-voltage supplies of good design, *bleeder resistors* are connected across each filter

Power-up and power-down

capacitor, so that the capacitors will discharge in a few minutes after the supply is turned off. Nevertheless, don't bet your life on components that might not be there, and that can and do sometimes fail.

Although most manufacturers supply safety instructions and warnings with equipment that uses high voltages, never assume something is harmless just because dangers aren't mentioned in the instructions. If you have any doubt about your ability to repair a power supply, leave it to a professional.

Power-up and power-down

Power-up and *power-down* refer to the processes that you and your computer go through to begin, or to terminate, an operating session.

Powering up. When you power-up a computer, you just flip some switches to turn it on, but a lot of things must happen inside the machine when power is applied, for the power-up process to be carried out successfully.

First, the operating system must be installed. Some common operating systems include DOS, Macintosh System 7, and IBM's OS/2. (Windows is a graphical user interface, or GUI, that translates DOS into menus and icons.) The operating system files are usually on the hard disk, but occasionally they're found on diskettes, in which case you must have the proper diskette inserted before applying power.

Most PCs give precedence to diskette drives when looking for the operating system. If there's nothing in any of the diskette drives, the machine will look at the hard disk. Therefore, if your operating system is on the hard disk, you should switch the computer on with the diskette drives empty. Diskettes can be installed after power-up is complete.

Once the operating system is running, you might want to have the computer load the software you use most often. For example, if most of your work is done with a word processing program, you can have the PC load it automatically as part of the power-up process.

Powering down. The power-down process consists of more than just pulling the plug or throwing a power switch. It is a bad idea to disconnect power abruptly with software loaded and data in RAM; that can adversely affect your data. The only time you should cut power that way is when the computer has "crashed" (frozen up), and you've tried every other possible way to get it going again, without success.

When you're done working on your computer, and you plan to take more than a few minutes off, you should power-down. This saves energy. You might have heard of people who leave their PCs running all the time, claiming that it puts a strain on the machine every time it's switched on and off. Actually, PCs are quite rugged, electrically as well as mechanically. You'll probably trade in your computer long before it breaks down as a result of having power applied and removed. Quit the program you're using before you switch the machine off.

The best way to remove power from a computer system is to have everything plugged into a transient suppression box (also called a surge suppressor) with multiple outlets. These boxes have switches that control the power to all the outlets. After you switch the suppressor box off, it's a good idea to pull its plug from the wall outlet, minimizing the chances of it being "zapped" during a thundershower. A nearby lightning strike can induce thousands of volts into house wiring, damaging electronic devices even when they're not in use. You should also unplug the modem from the telephone wall jack because telephone lines can pick up high-voltage transients during thundershowers.

If you've just powered down and you suddenly remember something, necessitating a power-up again right away, wait at least two minutes. This gives the hard disk platters time to come to a complete stop.

The table summarizes power-up and power-down processes for a typical desktop PC workstation. *See also* COLD BOOT, LIGHTNING PROTECTION, OPERATING SYSTEM, *and* TRANSIENT SUPPRESSION.

Power-up and power-down: Basic steps

Power-up process:

1. If operating system is on diskette, install diskette in the proper drive.
2. If operating system is on hard disk, be sure diskette drives are empty.
3. Apply power to system.
4. Plug modem into telephone wall jack if planning to be online.
5. Wait for power-up self-tests to be completed.
6. Load software, or wait for it to be loaded automatically.
7. Begin work session.

Power-down process:

1. Save all data to hard disk and diskette backup.
2. Close all files.
3. Quit software.
4. Remove power from system.
5. Unplug all units from wall outlet. (Ideally, this is done by unplugging transient suppressor, to which all units are connected.)
6. Unplug modem from telephone jack.
7. Wait at least two minutes before powering-up again.

Power user

A *power user* is a person who is extremely proficient at operating a PC. You probably know at least one such person. Power users often work in computer-related fields. They are fond of computers, and they like to talk about them. Power users often provide assistance and guidance to less experienced users.

Some people develop proficiency at one or two applications, such as word processing and desktop publishing, while remaining relatively ignorant in other applications. These people might be power users in their chosen applications, but neophytes in the others. Usually, they have the temperament to become power users in new applications when the need arises.

Computer engineers can be categorized in two groups: hardware experts and software experts. These days, it's rare to find a person who has in-depth knowledge in all aspects of both hardware and software. Computing is such a vast science, and the technology changes so fast, that it's impossible for any one person to maintain a total working knowledge of everything. However, one can be a generalist with a broad knowledge of basic concepts in personal computing.

The ultimate power user, perhaps existing only in fiction, has been nicknamed the *Grand Synthesizer*. At a PC, this virtuoso would be like Mozart at a piano. *See also* COMPUTER ADDICTION, GRAND SYNTHESIZER, *and* HACKER.

Precedence

Some application programs require that the computer do arithmetic operations. The most common are addition, subtraction, multiplication, and division, although exponentiation (raising to a power or taking a root) is sometimes used also.

Without parentheses. When you give mathematical commands to a PC, it's important that you keep in mind the correct precedence for the operations. If you're using a program written by someone else (such as a spreadsheet), you should be aware of the order in which the operations will be done by the machine.

Suppose you have an expression like this:

$$x^2y^3 + 3xy - 1/x^4y^5$$

How do you know the order in which the operations are to be done? Or, assuming your PC has been programmed to figure out expressions like this, how will the machine deal with this case?

There are three levels of precedence in calculations:

Precedence

1 Exponentiation (powers and roots)

2 Multiplication and division (products and quotients)

3 Addition and subtraction (sums and differences)

Level 1 operations are always done first; level 2 operations are done after that; level 3 operations are done last. According to these rules, a calculating program (or mathematician) would deal with the above expression this way:

1 Find x^2, y^3, x^4, and y^5, and store them in memory.

2 Find the products x^2y^3, $3xy$, and x^4y^5, and store these.

3 Divide 1 by x^4y^5, and store.

4 Add x^2y^3 to $3xy$, and store.

5 Subtract the quantity in step 3 from the quantity in step 4.

With parentheses. Parentheses are often used to clarify expressions, especially in complicated calculations, such as trigonometric functions. Often, parentheses are used when they aren't technically necessary, but they must always be used if a calculation is to be carried out in some order different from the standard precedence.

When you see parentheses, it means that the operations within sets of parentheses are to be done first. You start with the innermost sets of parentheses, and work toward the outermost set. For example, if you see

$w + (x(y + z))$

you should add y to z, multiply the result by x, and finally add w.

Suppose you see this expression:

$x^2y^3 + (3xy - (1/x^4)y^5)$

This is written in the same order as the two-variable expression discussed earlier in this article, but the parentheses drastically change its meaning. If you plug numbers into the two formulas, the results will almost certainly differ. A calculating program (or a mathematician) would proceed as follows:

1 Find x^2, y^3, x^4, and y^5, and store them in memory.

2 Find the products x^2y^3 and $3xy$, and store.

3 Find the value of 1 divided by x^4, and store.

4 Multiply $1/x^4$ by y^5 and store.

5 Subtract the quantity in step 4 from $3xy$ and store.

6 Add x^2y^3 to the quantity in step 5.

This kind of arithmetic can be confusing to those who aren't mathematically inclined. Keep three things in mind: first, you'll get better with practice; second, you'll rarely encounter an equation this messy in PC spreadsheet work; third, the computer does all the work in cases like this anyway. *See also* SPREADSHEET.

Prefix multipliers

When dealing with numbers that are extremely large or small, *prefix multipliers* are often used. These are word prefixes indicating that the unit or quantity should be multiplied by a certain power of 10, or sometimes a power of two.

Powers of 10. A good example of a prefix multiplier, commonly used when talking about microprocessor clock speeds, is *mega*. This is abbreviated M, and means millions. When you hear people talk about a clock speed of 100 megahertz (100 MHz), they're referring to a computer whose clock runs at a rate of 100 million pulses per second.

As another example, consider extremely short periods of time. You might hear of a unit called the *nanosecond* (ns), which is one billionth (0.000 000 001 or 10^{-9}) of a second. If you hear someone say that an instruction takes about 10 nanoseconds, you know they mean ten billionths of a second. The table shows the powers of 10 from 10^{-18} to 10^{18}, and the common terms and abbreviations of their prefix multipliers.

Factors, prefixes and abbreviations

Power of 10	Common term	Prefix	Abbreviation
10^{-18}	quintillionths	atto-	a
10^{-15}	quadrillionths	femto-	f
10^{-12}	trillionths	pico-	p
10^{-9}	billionths	nano-	n
10^{-6}	millionths	micro-	u
10^{-3}	thousandths	milli-	m
10^{3}	thousands	kilo-	K
10^{6}	millions	mega-	M
10^{9}	billions	giga-	G
10^{12}	trillions	tera-	T
10^{15}	quadrillions	peta-	P
10^{18}	quintillions	exa-	E

Powers of two. When referring to memory or storage, you'll often hear about *kilobytes* (K or KB), *megabytes* (MB), and *gigabytes* (GB). These are roughly equivalent to thousands, millions, billions, and trillions of bytes, respectively.

In the context of memory or storage, the prefix *kilo* means units of 2^{10}, or 1024; *mega* means units of 2^{20}, or 1,048,576; *giga* means units of 2^{30}, or 1,073,741,824. Beyond this, a *terabyte (TB)* is 1024 gigabytes, a *petabyte (PB)* is 1024 terabytes, and an *exabyte (EB)* is 1024 petabytes. *See also* BYTE, CLOCK SPEED, EXABYTE, GIGABYTE, HERTZ, KILOBYTE, MEGABYTE, PETABYTE, *and* TERABYTE.

Presentation graphics

Presentation graphics is a form of computer software. As its name implies, it can help you compose visual presentations, ranging from lectures to product announcements to history lessons. Sound effects can be used, too, if desired.

How they see it. Presentation graphics can be shown "live," in so-called *slide shows*, or they can be reproduced in printed matter such as brochures and magazine ads. Presentation graphics can also be given to members of your audience on diskette or CD-ROM, allowing them to view files on their own computers. Some presentation graphics programs are interactive, so viewers can become participants in the presentation.

In any visual presentation, contrast and vividness are important. You want to catch your viewers' eyes, without using grotesque colors or resorting to other extremes. Subtle backdrops, such as hills, ocean waves, clouds, or trees, give a professional effect without calling undue attention to themselves. You can change the backdrop from image to image as the presentation proceeds, rotating among different scenes.

There are several ways to get the image from a computer display into the eyes of your viewers. If there are only a few people looking at your presentation, they might watch over your shoulder. If there are many viewers, you'll have to use several computers or project the image somehow.

An overhead projector can be used with a special transparent liquid-crystal display (LCD). You place the LCD on the projector surface where a transparency would normally go. The light shines up through the LCD, then through the lens/prism of the projector, and finally onto a movie screen. There are other big screen techniques; check with a good office-supply store or computer superstore. Some of these devices are quite expensive. One relatively inexpensive projection method is to use a scan converter and a large-screen television set. This sacrifices some image resolution, but it will often suffice.

Presentation graphics

When changing from one image to another in a video presentation, there are various ways to liven things up. One popular scheme is to "flip" images off the screen as transitions are made, as if each image were on a page in a book. Another method is to fade, or dissolve, from image to image.

Sound and animation. For sales presentations, corporate board meetings, and other professional events, there are advantages to having a competent human narrator. A knowledgeable salesperson can answer questions and show genuine enthusiasm. Machines lack these qualities. Recorded sound and music can make a presentation seem insincere and contrived and can make an audience feel as if they are being manipulated for your convenience. If you're trying to sell things, you do not want to alienate your potential buyers.

On the other hand, recorded sound can be useful in presentations intended for children or when sound is an integral part of a product you're trying to sell. You might use sound effectively, for example, in a sales pitch for a musical instrument digital interface (MIDI).

If you decide to use recorded sound, be sure that the speakers are large enough and that the amplification is great enough so everyone can hear the narration and music. Otherwise, even the best sound becomes a liability rather than an asset.

Similarly, adding animation to a presentation can be a good thing, too, if it is used correctly. If you're trying to hold the attention of a group of children, image movement, along with variations in shape and color, can help. Another use for animation is when you want to demonstrate how an animation software package works! Used incorrectly, animation can hamper your personal delivery. Graphs, charts, diagrams, and photographs usually don't have to move to be understood. Too much motion can call attention to itself, distracting your audience from the subject matter of the presentation. Animation also gobbles up huge quantities of computer memory and storage, and requires enormous processing power. This translates into high cost.

As a rule, use sound and animation in presentation graphics only when doing so will benefit your audience and increase your chances of actually selling what you want to sell. This rule seems obvious when stated, but it is often overlooked.

What you need. There are several presentation-graphics software packages available. You can find one that best suits your needs, both now and in the near future, if you shop around.

Virtually all presentation-graphics software is designed for a graphical user interface (GUI), such as Windows, Macintosh, or OS/2. When buying the package, be sure it is compatible with your operating system. In some packages, you don't have to "draw" or "paint" anything at all; templates and outlines guide you along each step of the way. All you need to do is fill in some words to make the presentation applicable to your situation. Other packages include draw, paint, and modeling programs so you can compose your own artwork.

When buying presentation software, be sure your system has enough memory and hard-disk storage to handle the features. Also, be sure the microprocessor is advanced enough. The brochures will tell you how much memory, storage, and computing power you need. You'll want a high-resolution color monitor, ideally with a 17-inch screen. If you want to print your graphics, you'll need a laser printer or inkjet printer. Of course, a color printer is necessary if you want to print documents in color. Considerations like these can affect your final purchasing decision, especially if your funds are limited.

The best way to evaluate presentation graphics packages is to witness some well-organized presentations. If you see brochures, advertisements, or live events that you especially like, ask the people what hardware and software they used. Perhaps you know a "PC guru" who has experience with presentation software. Another good way to get acquainted with presentation graphics is to take a course on the subject at a local college or trade school. *See also* ANALYTICAL GRAPHICS, ANIMATION, DRAW PROGRAM, INTERACTIVE TECHNOLOGY, MODELING, MULTIMEDIA, PAINT PROGRAM, SOUND TECHNOLOGY, *and* VIRTUAL REALITY.

Primary storage

Primary storage is fast-access computer memory. In most computers, this consists of the random-access memory (RAM) and the read-only memory (ROM). Primary storage varies in size depending on the particular PC; the capacity is at least several hundred kilobytes, but can be many megabytes.

One major difference between RAM and ROM is that you can (and will) change the contents of RAM from moment to moment, but you can't change ROM without replacing or reprogramming certain chips inside the computer. The data in RAM is electronic, represented by the presence and absence of voltages or magnetic fields. The data in ROM, on the other hand, is physical, determined by the actual arrangement of the atoms inside integrated circuits (ICs).

RAM is usually a *volatile memory*; that is, it requires a source of power to be maintained. The moment you power-down a computer, everything in RAM disappears. This is also true if there is a power failure or if you must reset the machine because of a crash. It is possible to employ short-term memory backup, via a battery, to keep RAM from "evaporating" in case of an unanticipated mishap. Some RAM devices, such as bubble memory, do not need an external source of power to be maintained.

ROM is always a *nonvolatile memory*. It stays put, having been programmed into semiconductor chips at the factory. The ROM contains *firmware*, which is like software but more permanently installed in the computer.

Data stored on diskettes, hard disks, CD-ROMs, tapes, and other permanent media is called *secondary storage*. Access to this data is slower than for primary storage, but the capacity is theoretically unlimited.

As technology changes, new kinds of primary storage are evolving. Some of these are instantly accessible and changeable like RAM, but nonvolatile like ROM. Also, memory capacity increases with each passing year. There was a time when 640K (kilobytes) of RAM seemed like an inexhaustible supply; these days, even a novice PC user regards 640K of RAM as a small amount. *See also* RANDOM-ACCESS MEMORY, READ-ONLY MEMORY, *and* SECONDARY STORAGE.

Printed circuit

A *printed circuit* is a wiring arrangement made of foil on a circuit board. Printed circuits can be mass-produced inexpensively and efficiently. They are compact and reliable. Most electronic devices today are built using printed-circuit technology.

Printed circuits are fabricated by first drawing an etching pattern, as shown in the drawing. This is photographed and reproduced on clear plastic. The plastic is placed over a copper-coated glass-epoxy or phenolic board, and the assembly undergoes a photochemical process.

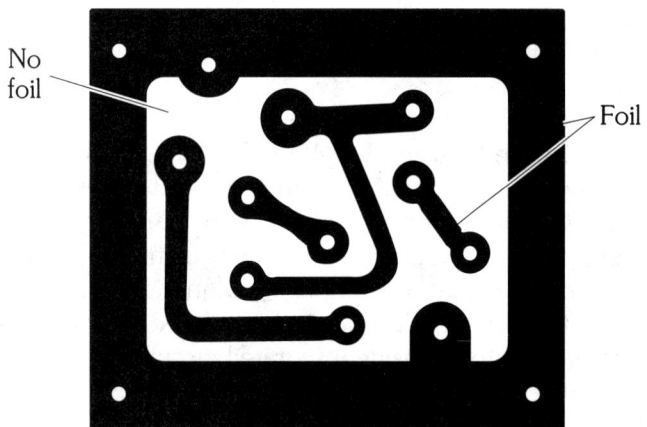

A simple etching pattern for a circuit board.

The use of printed circuits has greatly enhanced the ease with which electronic equipment can be serviced. Printed circuits allow modular construction, so that an entire board can be replaced in the field and repaired in a fully equipped laboratory. *See also* MODULAR CONSTRUCTION.

Printer

A *printer* is any device that produces a hardcopy (paper copy) of data. Printers are used with computers, terminal units, word processors, and many other electronic systems.

In personal computing, printers fall into three major groups, in increasing order of cost: dot-matrix, inkjet, and laser/LCD/LED. The following is a brief summary of these printer types.

Dot-matrix printer. A dot-matrix is the least expensive type of printer both in terms of the initial cash outlay and the cost per page. Dot-matrix printers produce acceptable print quality for most manuscripts, reports, term papers, and theses. The mechanical parts are rugged and maintenance is minimal. Dot-matrix printers are the only common type of printers that allow the use of multipart forms to make several copies in one printing session. Fanfold paper allows printing of long documents, without the need for constant manual paper feeding. Some dot-matrix printers can produce color hardcopy using a multicolored ribbon.

Older dot-matrix printers are quite noisy in operation; newer machines are quieter. They don't have the typeset-grade image resolution of more expensive printers. Dot-matrix printers can produce some graphic images, but the quality is not the best. *See also* DOT-MATRIX PRINTER, FANFOLD PAPER, *and* MULTIPART FORMS.

Inkjet printer. In an inkjet printer, tiny nozzles spray ink onto the paper, in contrast to the dot-matrix printer, which is an impact device. The result is that the machine is quieter in operation. However, multipart forms can't be used because they require mechanical pressure to create the copies.

Inkjet printers require periodic replacement of the ink "well" or container. They also need the right kind of paper; some papers have fibers that carry the ink along via capillary action, causing characters and images to blur.

Inkjet printers are available in single-color and multicolor designs. A high-end inkjet printer costs roughly twice as much as a high-end dot-matrix machine, although some monochrome inkjets are as inexpensive as dot-matrix printers. When properly used and maintained, an inkjet printer can create hardcopies of exceptional quality, comparable to that of a typeset publication. *See also* COLOR PRINTER *and* INKJET PRINTER.

Laser, LCD, and LED printers. Laser printers produce hardcopies of excellent image resolution. These fast, versatile printers have become the standard for professional computer users. The LCD

Print Manager

(liquid-crystal-display) and LED (light-emitting-diode) printers are variations of the laser printer.

A laser printer works according to the same principles as a photocopying machine. In fact, a laser printout has the appearance of a good first-generation photocopy, and the machine itself looks very much like a photocopier. You can get laser printers in single-color and multicolor styles, although color laser printers are quite expensive. Laser printers are nonimpact devices; therefore, they can make only one copy at a time.

Laser printers cost somewhat more than inkjet printers and substantially more than dot-matrix machines. For top-grade hardcopies, however, the laser printer and its variations are the best. *See also* LASER PRINTER *and* LCD/LED PRINTER.

Print Manager

Print Manager is an application program used in Windows software, a common graphical user interface (GUI). This program, as its name implies, is involved with the process of printing documents. It's especially useful when you have a lot of material to print.

When your system is in a long printing session, whether the data comes from one huge file or several smaller ones, there are other things you might be doing on the PC while the printer is carrying on. With Print Manager, you can work on one file while the PC prints others, even if the files are in different applications. For example, you might print a chapter from your novel while you're working out your annual budget. The novel would be in a word processing file, and the budget would probably be in a spreadsheet.

Print Manager takes advantage of a function called *print spooling.* When the printer is working and you decide to use the computer for something else at the same time, the print file goes to temporary space in RAM (random-access memory) if there's room. Otherwise, it goes to a temporary space on the hard disk. The term *spooling* comes from the fact that this process is like winding up the data on a spool, and then unrolling it at the rate the printer needs it. Print spooling frees up RAM for the other application on which you want to work.

With Print Manager, you can create a list of documents to be printed. This *print queue* can be examined at any time, so you can see what's happening. It shows the document filenames, their order within the list, which file is currently being printed, and how much of the current file has been printed so far. It also displays the number of bytes in each file, and when each file was put into the list. The printer prints the files in the order listed, one after the other. All you need to do, while working on other things, is make sure the printer is doing what it should with the paper. You can add or delete files from the print queue at any time. The printout will reflect the changes if the material has not yet actually gone onto the paper.

Print Manager gives you a choice as to the relative priority of the printing process, compared with whatever else you're doing. When you assign a print job "top priority," the documents print at maximum speed, but this comes at the expense of speed in the other tasks. Top-priority printing is normally done when you don't use the computer for anything else at the time. Medium priority causes the printing process to run more slowly, giving more computing attention to other matters. Low priority gives primary attention to matters besides the printing process; this results in the slowest printing. *See also* BACKGROUND PROCESSING *and* FOREGROUND PROCESSING.

Print Screen key

On the enhanced PC keyboard, the *Print Screen key* is located just to the left of the Scroll Lock key and to the right of the F12 key (see the drawing). The function of the Print Screen key depends on the software you're using.

The Print Screen key is located to the right of F12 on the enhanced PC keyboard.

In DOS. When you press Print Screen in "pure DOS," the printer will generally print whatever is displayed on your screen. The Print Screen key is meant to be used for getting a quick copy of the data on the computer display. It's not intended for making hardcopies of documents.

There are some cases when the Print Screen key won't work as you expect. You must be sure that the printer gets the right signals from the computer; this does not always happen when you hit Print Screen. For example, there might be extra spaces between the characters in the printout. Varying type styles (such as bold, italic, and superscript) might not be reflected in the printed copy.

If you press Print Screen in DOS and the printer doesn't correctly reproduce the data on the monitor screen, you can do either of two things: check your system manual and software manuals to correct what's being done wrong, or use commands as you would normally to print a hardcopy of a document. The latter method is the standard way of printing documents in DOS.

In Windows. When using Windows, you can get a screen capture by pressing Print Screen, no matter what the screen shows. This will put

Problem reduction

the image in the Windows clipboard. It will probably consume several hundred kilobytes. To look at the image, click or double-click on the clipboard viewer icon.

Using Print Screen in Windows is an extremely inefficient way to capture text because it takes a bitmap "photograph" of the screen contents. This is like copying a business letter or a page from a book by photographing it with a 35-mm camera. A single screenful of data thus "photographed" will take up hundreds of times as much memory and storage as the same data in a normal text file. The Print Screen key can be effective, however, for occasional storage of complex images such as detailed color drawings and photographs. The main limitation of this scheme is that the clipboard can hold only one screen capture at a time. You can't save a whole series of images conveniently in this way. *See also* SCREEN CAPTURE.

Problem reduction

Complex problems are often made much easier by breaking them down into small steps. This process, called *problem reduction*, is an important part of research in artificial intelligence (AI).

Two common forms. You've used problem reduction in everyday life without being aware of it. You've probably used it consciously, too, especially if you've ever taken a geometry class. Proving mathematical theorems is a good exercise in problem reduction. Another way to develop this skill is to write computer programs in a high-level language.

When breaking a big, difficult problem down into small, easy steps, one can lose sight of the "big picture." Keeping a mental image of the goal, the progress being made, and the obstacles to come is a skill that gets better with practice. You can't sit down and prove profound theorems in mathematics until you've learned to prove simple facts first.

Theorem-proving machine (TPM). Suppose you build a theorem-proving machine (TPM) and assign it an especially tough proof. The drawing is a rendition of this hypothetical problem. In this case, a proof exists. The theorem is true, and it can be demonstrated in a finite number of steps. Often, scientists and mathematicians don't know, when setting out to prove something, if what they want to prove is true. That is, they don't know if they can ever solve the problem. If the problem turns out to be unsolvable, they might spend years striving to do something impossible.

In the example shown here, there are four starting paths: A, B, C, and D. Two of these, B and C, can lead to the desired result; the other two cannot. Even if TPM starts out along B or C, there are many possible dead ends. In this example, there is a crossover

Problem reduction

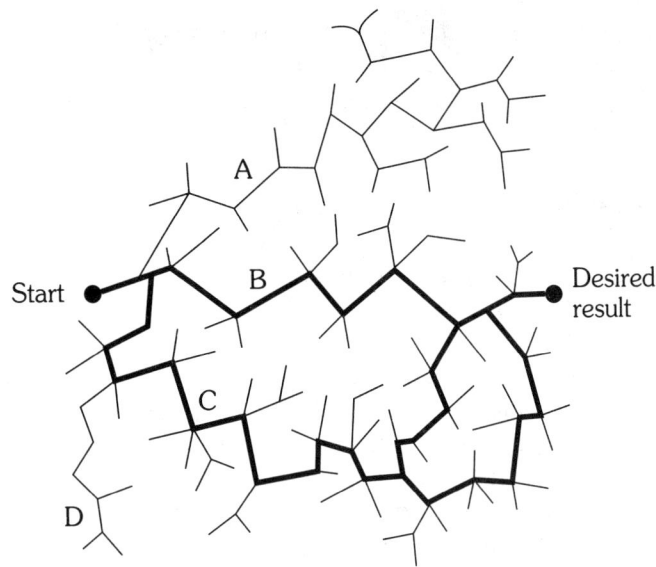

Breaking a big problem into little steps.

between paths B and C: one of the sidetracks from path B can indirectly lead to the desired result via path C. Also, a sidetrack from path C can take TPM to the proof by moving over to path B. However, these crossings-over can also lead TPM back toward the starting point, and possibly even to dead ends on the way back there!

Of course, TPM will never get tired. The greater the memory and processor speed, the sooner TPM is likely to arrive at a conclusion, provided there is a solution. However, TPM must be programmed for the possibility that it has come to a dead end. After a certain length of time, TPM must backtrack and try some other approach to the problem.

Dead ends. As you know from experience, persistence can yield results, but this is not always true. If you try unsuccessfully to resolve a difficult step in a problem for a long enough time, you'll decide you have reached a dead end, and then backtrack. At what point should TPM give up and decide that it has reached a dead end? How many clock pulses, microseconds, or logical steps should TPM take? The answer to this question lies in the ability of TPM to learn from experience. This is one of the most advanced concepts in AI. Practice makes perfect (almost) for humans, and the same holds for truly smart machines. Neural network technology holds some promise for those who hope to develop computers like TPM.

Regardless of how far research might progress, a perfectly reliable TPM will never be built because there are statements in any logical system that can't be proven true or false in a finite number of steps. There are some things that no person or machine can ever know for sure. This was proven by the logician Kurt Godel in 1930, and is known as the *Incompleteness Theorem*. *See also* ARTIFICIAL INTELLIGENCE, INCOMPLETENESS THEOREM, NEURAL NETWORK, PLANNER, *and* PROGRAMMING.

Procedural language

A *procedural language* is a form of software, or computer programming. Such a program tells the machine what to do, in a step-by-step format (procedure).

A program written in procedural language can be portrayed in the form of a drawing, called a *flowchart*. For simple programs, flowcharts can fit onto a single sheet of paper, but for more complicated procedures, flowcharts become too large to draw manually. A person who is good at procedural programming doesn't need to draw a flowchart. Instead, the process is mentally envisioned and can be followed by reading the program itself.

The flowchart shown depicts the steps a computer might take to add two numbers. The numbers are supplied by the programmer as the program is run. This program stores the addends, as well as the sum, in memory for future reference. Imagine you are the computer in this situation. Regardless of the programming language (BASIC, Fortran, etc.), you would have to do the following steps, in more or less this order:

1 Ask for the first number.

2 Obtain the first number from the operator.

3 Store the first number in memory space X.

4 Ask for the second number.

5 Obtain the second number from the operator.

6 Store the second number in memory space Y.

7 Perform the plus operation on the contents of memory spaces X and Y.

8 Store the result in memory space Z.

9 Display the contents of memory spaces X, Y, and Z on the monitor screen in a form the operator can comprehend.

Not all computer languages are intended for solving arithmetic problems, of course. Some programs are designed for other specialties such as databases, graphics, or communications.

Procedural languages work well in some applications, but another approach does better in other situations. It uses facts and relationships, rather than steps to be executed, and is called *declarative language*. *See also* DECLARATIVE LANGUAGE *and* PROGRAMMING.

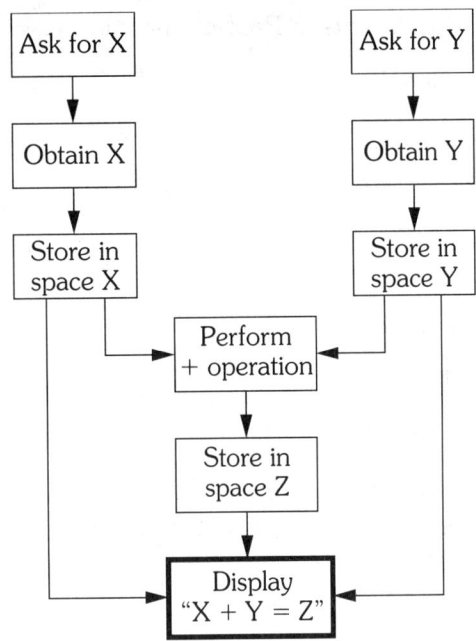

A flowchart for the addition of two numbers X and Y.

Prodigy

Prodigy is a popular online service. You connect a computer to the telephone line, and you have an instant link to thousands of PCs and information sources. With Prodigy, you can obtain software, communicate with other members, get assistance and news from computer experts, and keep yourself informed about current events. Prodigy is also known for its child-friendliness.

Components. All online services require similar components. To use Prodigy, you need at least the following:

- A hard drive with 700K of available space
- Installation diskettes
- A telephone line
- A modem
- Registration codes (supplied when you buy the package)
- Some blank diskettes (for downloading)
- A mouse (optional)

User-friendliness. Prodigy employs a graphical user interface (GUI), making it easy to use. You don't need to memorize commands; the software helps you as you go along. It gives you instructions that are easy to follow. Prodigy also provides an extensive network of technical support, so you can get help when you need it. The instructions are clear, complete, and easy to follow.

Departments. Departments in Prodigy include these:

- Finance and investments
- Sports
- Entertainment
- Travel
- Home and family
- Computers and technology
- Communications
- Kids, fun, and learning

There are several subcategories within each of these departments. Prodigy has a system of code words that help you move around easily among departments and subcategories. For further information about this online service, write or call

Prodigy Services Company
P.O. Box 791
White Plains, NY 10601
1-800-PRODIGY

See also GRAPHICAL USER INTERFACE, NETWORK, *and* ONLINE SERVICE.

Programmable read-only memory

Programmable read-only memory (PROM) is a special form of read-only memory (ROM). It is available in the form of integrated-circuit (IC) chips. Like a ROM IC, a PROM IC is a nonvolatile memory; it will not vanish when power is removed.

You can't change the data in PROM, the way you can with random-access memory (RAM). Therefore, PROM is not used for files you work on actively, such as word processing, databases, graphics, or spreadsheets. A PROM is supplied "blank," and is programmed by the user or manufacturer with special equipment. The process of programming is sometimes called *burning in*. Once the data has been burned into the chip, the PROM is unalterable, and becomes ROM. Software or data burned into a PROM is known as *firmware*.

An *erasable programmable ROM (EPROM)* can be programmed, just like a PROM, but it can also be reprogrammed. Ultraviolet light is used to erase the data on the chip. A window in the case of the IC lets the ultraviolet shine on the semiconductor material. For reprogramming, the chip must usually be removed from the computer, exposed to ultraviolet, and then reprogrammed with new firmware. The EPROM is, in effect, a reusable PROM.

Some reusable PROMs can be erased using electric currents rather than ultraviolet light. These are known by the lengthy name of *electrically erasable programmable read-only memory (EEPROM)*. Electrical erasing and reprogramming is easier and more convenient than the ultraviolet method. An EEPROM can be erased and reprogrammed while it is in the computer circuit.

No PROM is as versatile as a RAM, a diskette drive, or a hard disk. Still, PROM has its place in computer technology. Unlike diskette and hard drives, a PROM chip has no moving parts. Therefore, PROM is not subject to mechanical failure. It will not "evaporate" when power is removed. All PROM chips are extremely reliable. They last for years and hardly ever fail. Were it not for the fact that computer technology changes, most PROM chips would probably be viable for centuries. *See also* FIRMWARE, MEMORY, NONVOLATILE MEMORY, RANDOM-ACCESS MEMORY, *and* READ-ONLY MEMORY.

Program Manager

Program Manager is the central application that helps you organize programs in Windows software. Program Manager is always running when you're running Windows, although you might not see it, since it can be covered up (overlaid) by other windows.

Electronic file cabinet. Imagine a huge file cabinet with a dozen drawers full of manila folders, each with dozens of pages. Imagine all the ways you could change how your programs are organized, as well as create new programs and erase old ones. Program Manager is like that big cabinet, but without the bulk, paper, and general messiness. Program Manager lets you sort, rename, create, delete, and copy programs in your computer.

The details of Program Manager operation are beyond the scope of this book. Windows software is constantly being improved, and new functions are being added. Consult your Windows manual and online help for a thorough discussion of the things you can do with the Program Manager.

Menu bar. As soon as you go into Windows, you're in the Program Manager. The screen is arranged similar to the way it is shown in the drawing.

At the top of the screen is a *menu bar* containing the words *File*, *Options*, *Windows*, and *Help*. You can move the pointer to any of these words using the mouse and click the mouse to activate the function. Alternatively, you can press hot keys: Alt-F for File, Alt-O for Options, and so on.

Choose File from the Program Manager menu to do things like create new programs, erase programs, move programs from one place to another, run programs, or exit Windows altogether. Programs are, after all, files. When you're in the File menu, you can think of them

Programming

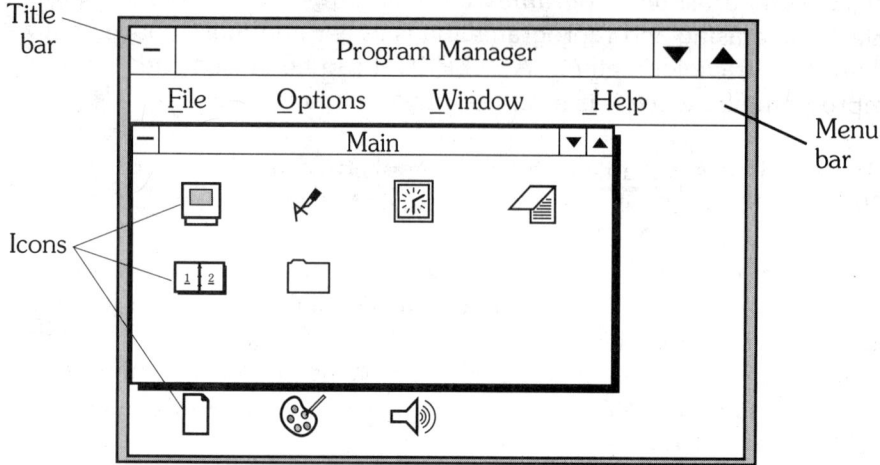

The general appearance of a screen in Windows Program Manager.

just as you would think of databases, spreadsheets, graphics files, or word-processed documents.

If you select Options from the Program Manager menu bar, you become a secretary for your Windows programs. If your screen gets too messy, you can reduce windows to little symbols, or *icons*, so they take up almost no screen space. Then, when you want to expand the window back to full size, you can click on the icon. There are various other tricks you can use to get the different windows set up the way you like them.

When you select Window from the Program Manager menu bar, you can arrange windows in various different ways. Two common methods of showing multiple windows on a screen are called *overlaid* or *cascaded* windows and *tiled windows*. When you overlay windows, they are stacked up with only the menu bars showing. When you tile them, they are laid out side-by-side, but reduced in size.

If you need help figuring out how to work in Windows, you can select from the Help menu. One of the choices here activates a tutorial session that can usually get you out of a jam. It can also ease the learning curve if you're new to Windows. *See also* ICON, MENU, OVERLAID WINDOWS, TILED WINDOWS, *and* WINDOWS.

Programming

Computers do what they're told—nothing more and nothing less. *Programming* is the process of creating instructions for a computer and getting the machine to carry out those instructions efficiently. No matter how powerful a computer is, it won't be of much use if it's badly programmed. A well-programmed PC, on the other hand, is a joy to work with.

High-level programming. As a PC user, most of your programming (if you do any) will be in a *high-level language*. This type of language is much more like human language than the digital codes used by the computer, even though some high-level programs look like hieroglyphics to the uninitiated.

There are several high-level languages in use today. Novice programmers start out with languages such as BASIC, Fortran, or Pascal. After a while, they can graduate to a more sophisticated high-level language like C. Specialized high-level languages exist for practically any application you can imagine. Some of them are educational and entertaining; an example is LOGO, which most children can learn easily.

Generally, programs are written by typing on a computer keyboard, But voice-driven programming is possible with speech recognition systems. Some programs are generated by exotic means, such as via a *teach box*, used with certain robotic devices. *See also* HIGH-LEVEL LANGUAGE, SPEECH RECOGNITION, *and* TEACH BOX.

Low-level programming. Low-level languages include *machine language* and *assembly language*. Machine language is the sequence of digital signals (high and low, or 1 and 0) that the computer actually works with. Programming is never done in machine language; it would be tedious to an extreme, and there's no need for humans to do it when translation can be done electronically between it and other languages.

Advanced PC users might want to delve into the world of *assembly language*. One step up from machine language, it's fast and efficient. When you program in assembly language, you save the computer the work of translating between machine language and the high-level language. A program in assembly language often needs more steps than a similar program in a high-level language, but it takes up less memory.

An assembly language that works with one CPU will not generally work with other CPUs. The programmer must learn a new assembly language for each new CPU that comes along, and this knowledge takes some time and effort to acquire. This is one of the main drawbacks of assembly language. *See also* ASSEMBLER AND ASSEMBLY LANGUAGE *and* MACHINE LANGUAGE.

Declarative versus procedural. High-level languages can be categorized as either declarative or procedural. In *declarative language*, the computer is given a set of facts and relationships. The relationships tie all the facts together.

Declarative languages are used in expert systems, application programs that provide a computer with highly specialized knowledge.

Programming

The machine works with the facts, and uses the relationships to derive conclusions. A few examples include a theorem-proving program, a program for diagnosing illnesses, and software that makes forecasts about such things as population trends, the stock market, or the path of a hurricane.

A program in *procedural language* gives the machine a set of steps to follow in a certain order. That is, it specifies the procedure for solving a problem. A program written in procedural language can be rendered as a flowchart, although when a procedure is complicated, a flowchart becomes impractical because of its sheer physical size.

Procedural languages work well in certain applications, such as arithmetic. They are also used in the programming of robots. Procedural languages are especially good at solving problems by "brute force," such as calculating the square root of 13 to a million decimal places. *See also* DECLARATIVE LANGUAGE, EXPERT SYSTEMS, *and* PROCEDURAL LANGUAGE.

Steps. The programming process is more or less the same, no matter what sort of language you use. The steps are basically as follows:

1 *Concept* You need to decide exactly what you want the program to do. This will help you pick the optimum language and will also give you some idea of how the program will be organized. Problems can often be broken down into parts or modules, which in turn can be broken down into smaller parts. Some people have a natural ability to think in modular terms, working with complex problems. Others have more trouble, but anyone can get fairly good at it with practice.

2 *Writing* This is the process of actually keying or speaking in the instructions that tell the computer what to do. It's important that you not make any errors during this stage. A single misplaced character can cause a whole program to run badly or to fail completely. One printer program for a desktop PC didn't work because of a stray semicolon. When that character was removed, the program ran perfectly. (Finding it was pure luck.) That semicolon probably got there because the programmer had jittery fingers—or perhaps it was a glitch that occurred when the program was copied.

3 *Debugging* Programs usually don't work quite right the first time they are run. The more complex the program, the more likely there will be at least one bug in it. Bugs can result from typos, as with the stray semicolon, but sometimes bugs are more subtle. Perhaps, for example, you didn't quite get the relationship right among the modules in a program. Some bugs can even cause a computer to go into an endless loop, effectively stopping the computer dead in its tracks. Often a program will run, but not as efficiently as it could. Good programmers always strive for the best possible

efficiency; this translates into maximum computer speed. It also gets the most out of the available computer power. Debugging can take several times as long as the original program-writing procedure, but it must be done. *See also* BUG, COMPILER, COMPUTER POWER, ENDLESS LOOP, INTERPRETER, MODULAR PROGRAMMING, *and* SOFTWARE.

PROLOG

PROLOG is a high-level computer language that is of value to researchers in artificial intelligence (AI). The word *PROLOG* stands for *programming in logic*.

PROLOG is somewhat like LISP, another language often used with AI. In PROLOG, the programmer inputs knowledge, along with a set of rules for the computer to follow in working with that knowledge. The program, in a sense, derives theorems from its knowledge base, by means of the rules.

One of the drawbacks of PROLOG is that it takes time to write complex programs. The number of facts in the knowledge base can become staggering. *See also* ARTIFICIAL INTELLIGENCE, EXPERT SYSTEMS, HEURISTIC KNOWLEDGE, KNOWLEDGE, LISP, *and* MACHINE KNOWLEDGE.

PROM

See PROGRAMMABLE READ-ONLY MEMORY.

Prompt

A *prompt* is a computer statement that informs the operator of certain things. It is the machine's way of "talking" to you. When you first boot up a PC using DOS, for example, you'll usually get a symbol something like this:

```
C:\>
```

This is called a *C prompt* or *DOS prompt*. It means the machine is ready to accept input, and when you store it, it will go on the hard disk (drive C). If you type *A:* and press Enter at the C prompt, the following symbol will appear:

```
A:\>
```

That is, as you can guess, an *A prompt*. It means the computer is ready for input, and it will go on the diskette in drive A when you store it.

A prompt can sometimes occur as a question. For example, when you want to store a file using a filename that is already assigned on a particular disk, you'll get a message something like this:

```
FILE EXISTS, OVERWRITE IT?
```

If you press Y for Yes, the file will be overwritten. If you press N for No, nothing will happen.

In a graphical user interface (GUI), prompts take the form of multiple options. The menu at the top of a window is one example, an icon group is another. The OK and Cancel buttons are the Windows versions of DOS's Y and N.

When you want to respond to a prompt, you can click on items or icons in a GUI, or give the machine a command in DOS. There are advantages and disadvantages to either method. Some operators prefer command-driven interfaces such as DOS because this method can sometimes be faster than selecting options. Most neophytes, and quite a few seasoned PC users, prefer graphical interfaces like Windows, OS/2, or the Macintosh OS. These are more user-friendly than DOS; there's no need to memorize commands. *See also* CLICK, COMMAND, COMMAND-DRIVEN SOFTWARE, DOS, DOS PROMPT, GRAPHICAL USER INTERFACE, ICON, MENU, *and* MENU-DRIVEN SOFTWARE.

Proportional font

Alphanumeric characters have various widths. For example, a period is much narrower than the uppercase letter *M*. When you print a document using a *proportional font*, the widths of the characters are taken into account. A standard typewriter, on the other hand, doesn't take the size of the letters into account; it gives *every* character exactly the same amount of space. Nonproportional (or monospaced) fonts work the same way.

The most common nonproportional type sizes are called *pica* and *elite*. These are 10 and 12 characters per inch (CPI), respectively. Each character gets exactly $\frac{1}{10}$ of an inch in a pica document. In an elite document, all the characters are allocated exactly $\frac{1}{12}$ of an inch. Thus, some characters fill up their allowed space, while others leave it practically empty.

In a proportional font such as Helvetica or Times New Roman, the space between the characters is kept constant (see the illustration), instead of forcing *every* letter, numeral, and punctuation mark into rectangular "molds" of identical size. This produces better-looking copy. Most people find it easier to read than nonproportional spacing. New printers almost always have a proportional-font mode.

Proportional fonts are widely used in desktop publishing. With a good laser printer and a large selection of typefaces, you can create top-quality brochures, flyers, magazines, and books. When printing large type sizes or for certain special effects, a process called *kerning* can be used to further fine-tune the character spacing. *See also* DESKTOP PUBLISHING, FONT, *and* KERNING.

> Constant-width printout:
>
> ..... MMMMM ..... MMMMM ..... MMMMM ..... MMMMM .....
>
> Proportional printout:
>
> ..... MMMMM..... MMMMM..... MMMMM..... MMMMM.....

A proportional font optimizes the spacing between printed characters.

Protocol

In communications, a *protocol* is an established set of procedures and standards used by the machines. When computers "talk" with each other, a protocol must be followed by each machine so that there is an efficient flow of data. The data speed (either in bauds or bits per second), the pulses that represent each character, the number of bits per word, full or half duplex, and other variables must all agree if two computers are to communicate, or transfer their files, with optimum effectiveness.

Protocols are not necessarily "either/or" affairs. Two computers can sometimes transfer data to a limited extent even when their protocols are not identical. For greatest communications efficiency, however, the source and destination protocols should be the same.

Think of speaking with another person. To understand each other completely, you must speak the same language with the same accent and the same dialect. If you speak only English, and you're in a room with someone else who speaks only Russian, you won't get any communicating done. The situation would be almost as bad if the other person spoke English, but with the dialect of Chaucer. If you're from Vermont and the other person is from Mississippi, you'll be able to communicate fairly well, although some confusion might still occur from time to time. If both people are lifelong natives of Sioux Falls, South Dakota, the situation is optimum. Your spoken protocols will agree completely.

Protocols are important when you use an online service. If you're checking into a network, you must be sure that your terminal emulation software is set for the same protocol as the network uses. Otherwise, communications will be inefficient at best, and impossible at worst.

In packet communications, the standard protocol is called the *Open Systems Interconnection Reference Model (OSI-RM)*. There are also other, more specific protocols in some packet systems. *See also* COMMUNICATIONS PROTOCOL, FILE TRANSFER PROTOCOL, ONLINE

SERVICE, OPEN SYSTEMS INTERCONNECTION REFERENCE MODEL, PACKET COMMUNICATIONS, *and* TERMINAL EMULATION SOFTWARE.

Prototype

In the design and manufacture of electronic devices of all kinds, a test unit is built before production begins. The test unit is designed according to theory, but it is made to work by trial and error. This process is always necessary. It is extremely rare for an engineer to sit down, draw a plan for a complex device, put the parts together, and have it work perfectly on the first run.

In manufacturing, two or more test units, known as *prototypes*, are built before production is even begun. Each prototype is debugged a little more than the previous one. The final prototype, when perfected, is the basis for the production units.

In computer engineering, the prototype method of design is used with system parts, as well as whole systems. *See also* MODULAR CONSTRUCTION.

P6 microprocessor

The *P6* is the next chip after the Pentium in the line of Intel microprocessors. Intel's line has been called the 80x86 series, where x represents the number 2, 3, or 4. Intel stopped numbering their chips after the 486. The Pentium would have been the 586; the P6 would have been the 686. The P6 chip can run several times as fast as a Pentium chip, and much faster than a 486.

All of Intel's chips are based on a traditional CISC (complex instruction set computing) design. Intel chips, including the P6, are downwardly compatible. That is, they can work with hundreds of existing operating systems and programs, such as the familiar DOS and Windows software. *See also* COMPLEX INSTRUCTION SET COMPUTING, INTEL MICROPROCESSORS, PENTIUM, *and* REDUCED INSTRUCTION SET COMPUTING.

Psychotic computer behavior

Science fiction authors have dreamed about what might happen if a super-smart, insane computer got out of its programmers' control. Is this possible? What forms might *psychotic computer behavior* actually take? Should people be concerned about it as technology advances?

Cyber-psychoses defined. As of this writing, the term *psychosis* has not been seriously applied to computers. Therefore, this article is, for the time being, mostly speculative. Although no formal definition of the term *cyber-psychosis* yet exists, one might call it a system malfunction in which the following three things happen concurrently:

Psychotic computer behavior

1 The computer or network keeps operating.

2 The computer or network loses contact with reality because of altered or misinterpreted data.

3 The computer or network becomes a potential danger to human beings.

Malfunctions. Computer malfunctions are not uncommon. They occur as a result of bad software, faulty hardware, accidents, various physical catastrophes, improper operation, or the activities of malicious hackers. Sometimes the cause is never determined. A mere malfunction is not a cyber-psychosis, however. In a cyber-psychosis, the problem would manifest itself in an organized way, maybe ridiculous, but with the potential for causing real disaster.

A typical computer malfunction results in reduced efficiency or complete shutdown, but a cyber-psychosis would not necessarily reduce the efficiency of the system. In fact, in some ways, the machine would become ruthlessly and uncontrollably efficient. The operators might not notice any problem until the consequences were discovered. The more sophisticated the system, the greater the chance for something like this taking place.

What might happen? A computer *virus*, written and unleashed by a brilliant hacker with a hatred for society or some particular group of people, could create an epidemic of cyber-psychoses. Usually these bugs alter or destroy data, creating inconveniences but not dangers. As microprocessors and computer networks get more powerful, however, the odds increase that a virus will someday cause a great deal of human suffering.

What might happen? One possibility is that certain classes of people would be repeatedly and systematically plagued by bogus police records, damaged credit reports, altered income tax returns, and other problems leading to arrest, detention, and occasional false criminal convictions.

A psychotic human loses contact with reality and can be dangerous to him- or herself or others. The same criteria can be applied to computer psychoses, in the event such behavior is ever actually observed. A computer might "hallucinate" by sensing data that does not exist, or it could develop "delusions," misinterpreting or skewing data to produce false output.

If given control over robots, aircraft, missiles, or other high-powered hardware, a psychotic computer would present an immediate peril. Imagine a virus that renders defensive anti-ballistic missiles inoperative, or causes a navigation error in a spacecraft carrying humans to Mars!

Pull-down menu

Pulling the plug. Computer systems have failed in the past, with potentially devastating consequences had people taken them seriously or been unable to abort their functions. False alarms have been issued for fictitious catastrophes ranging from fire to intrusion to nuclear attack. Such systems are always overseen by human beings, who have power to shut the system down or override it.

Computer psychoses need never present a peril to PC operators. If we keep computers in perspective and don't expect them to do everything for us, PC malfunctions will never be anything more serious than strange, occasionally costly, and sometimes hilarious phenomena. The best defense for viruses is to use a *vaccine* on all downloaded data before inputting it to the computer. *See also* COMPUTER CONSCIOUSNESS, COMPUTER OVER-RELIANCE, NEUROTIC COMPUTER BEHAVIOR, TROJAN HORSE, VACCINE, *and* VIRUS.

Pull-down menu

When working with a graphical interface such as Microsoft Windows, IBM OS/2, or any Macintosh system, you give the computer instructions by choosing from a list of options called a *menu*. The commands are words or symbols (icons) that are more or less self-explanatory.

A menu bar is a list of commands, usually going across the top of the screen. Sometimes when you select one of these commands, you'll get a list of several options in a box that seems to unroll as if it were a window shade you pulled down from the menu bar. This is called a *pull-down menu*. Its general appearance is shown in the drawing.

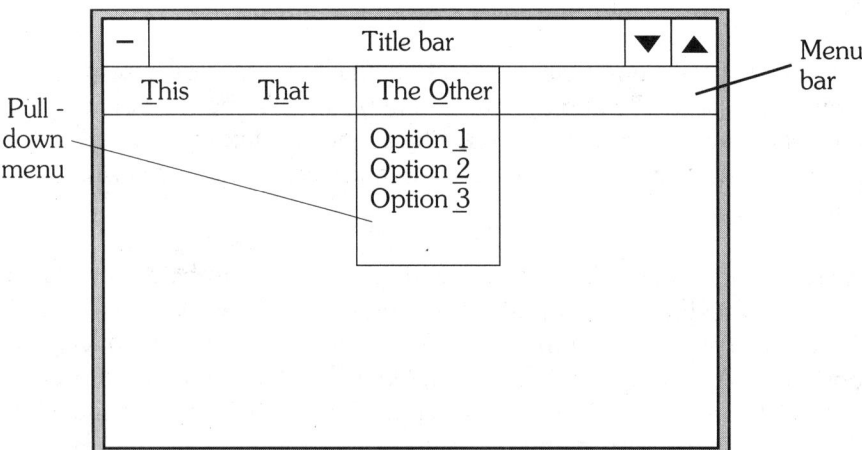

A list of sub-options that drops down from a menu bar.

When you choose one of the commands in the pull-down menu, the computer executes the instruction, and the menu disappears like a windowshade rolling back up after you tug on its cord. *See also* MENU, MENU-DRIVEN SOFTWARE, *and* POP-UP MENU.

Pushdown stack

In some memory circuits, the first data in is the last to come out, and vice versa. Such a circuit is called a *pushdown stack* or *first-in/last-out* (*FIFO*). It is a read-write memory because data can be both stored and accessed.

The drawing shows the principle of a pushdown stack. It is as if the bits are stacked up, so that you must take them off the top first. Bits come out reversed from the way they are put in. *See also* FIRST-IN/FIRST-OUT.

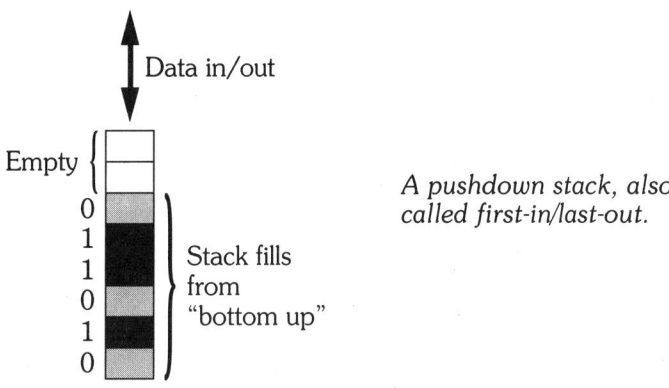

A pushdown stack, also called first-in/last-out.

896

Quadra

Quadra is the name of a series of Macintosh computers manufactured by Apple Computer, Inc. These computers are powerful, intended for businesses and serious individual PC users. Some of the units are housed in floor-standing tower cases, rather than the more familiar desktop cabinets. The Quadra computers are based on Motorola's 680x0 line of microprocessors.

Quadras, like all Macs that followed the original Mac Classic, use modular construction. In this sense, Quadras are not much different from high-end IBM-compatible PCs. The main unit is separate from the monitor. Inside the main unit, systems are built on individual, easily removable, interchangeable printed circuit boards.

Another physical difference between the Quadra and the Mac Classic involves ease of disassembly. Because the monitor is separate from the main unit, it's safe to take the cover off the main unit of a Quadra. This, along with the modular design, makes modification and upgrading relatively simple. Inside the main unit, the components can be easily swapped. Circuit boards can be interchanged for newer, more powerful substitutes. You can add another diskette drive or a bigger hard disk system. You can incorporate a larger monitor, a color monitor, or multiple printers. The video has better image resolution, the hard drives are more capacious, the input/output circuitry works faster. In fact, a Quadra can work quite effectively as a file server in a local area network (LAN).

Quality assurance & control

The Quadra uses an architecture called *complex-instruction-set computing (CISC)*. In recent years, computer evolution has taken off in a new direction that uses instructions that are easier for the machines to process. This architecture is known as *reduced-instruction-set computing (RISC)* technology. The RISC scheme has many assets, although there are some problems with compatibility. One common microprocessor in RISC machines is called the *PowerPC chip*.

The most dedicated RISC enthusiasts might dismiss all CISC technology (including that in the Quadra) as obsolete. Keep in mind, however, that CISC PCs such as the Quadra can fully meet the needs of many businesses. *See also* APPLE COMPUTER INC., FILE SERVER, LOCAL AREA NETWORK, MACINTOSH, MOTOROLA MICROPROCESSORS, MODULAR CONSTRUCTION, POWERPC CHIP, *and* REDUCED-INSTRUCTION-SET COMPUTER.

Quality assurance & control

Quality assurance and control, abbreviated *QA/QC*, refers to the inspection of manufactured products. In the personal computing industry, QA/QC is done for both hardware and software.

Perfect manufacturing. An important, but often overlooked, aspect of QA/QC lies in the production process itself. One way to ensure perfect quality is to do a perfect job of hardware manufacturing or of writing software programs. Of course, this ideal cannot be achieved in the real world, but it is something to strive for.

Robots can do much of the work involved in hardware assembly. Not all robots work faster than humans, but robots are almost always more precise. Creating software, on the other hand, requires a well-trained, alert staff of human beings; no machine yet devised can create innovative, efficient new programs.

Some QA/QC engineers say their jobs shouldn't be necessary. Flawed materials should be thrown away before they are put into products. Assembly robots should do perfect work. Programmers should find and correct their errors before consumers have to call in and complain. This philosophy has been stated by Japanese QA/QC engineer Hajime Karatsu, "Let's do such good work that QA/QC checkers aren't needed." In reality, some quality checking is always needed; it's a question of where and how it is most effectively done.

Hardware QA/QC. Manufacturing will never be perfect. There are always errors in assembly or defective components that get into a factory assembly line. There'll always be a need for at least one QA/QC person to keep bad units from getting to the buyers. Robots can sometimes work as QA/QC engineers, but they can do only simple tasks. Good QA/QC work generally requires that the inspector

Quality assurance & control

have a keen sense of judgment, which even the most sophisticated robots lack.

In modular construction, the assembly method used with computer hardware, a system is comprised of several units (main unit, monitor, printer, expansion boards, etc.). Each unit consists of at least one printed circuit board or card. On each card, there are integrated circuits, or "chips." All chips are checked before installation on a printed circuit card, and each card is tested before it is placed into a unit. Each unit must work if the system is to function correctly. The QA/QC routine is most effective when done at all these levels. When QA/QC processes are followed rigorously at all levels—component, board, unit, and system—failures of "new-out-of-the-box" hardware hardly ever occur (see the drawing at A). Still, damage might be done to a computer when it is transported from the factory to the store, or from the mail-order house to your house. These things are beyond the control of QA/QC engineers.

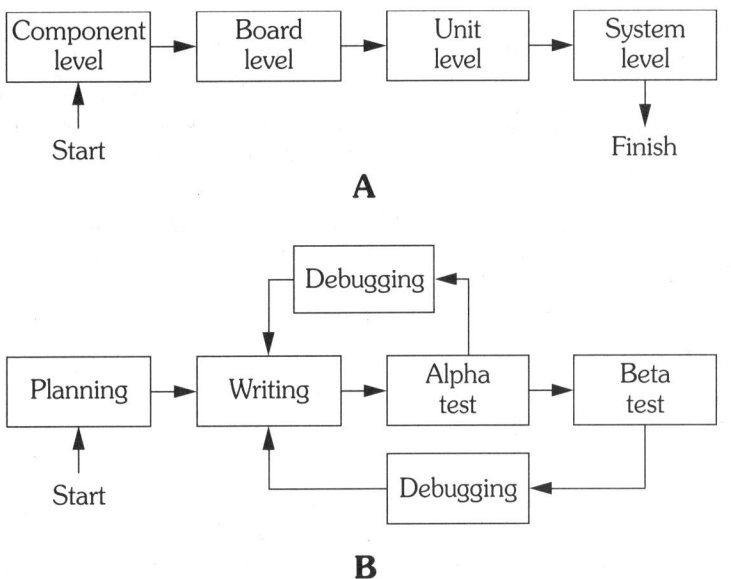

QA/QC levels in hardware manufacturing (A) and a software evolution flowchart (B).

Other hardware items, such as diskettes, drive system motors, cathode-ray tubes (CRTs), cables, and power-supply equipment must also be checked before installation or use in a computer system. In the case of diskettes, you can be your own QA/QC engineer. You should always check a diskette for bad sectors before you entrust data to it. You'll get bad-sector information when you format a diskette; it can also be found by following certain procedures or commands outlined in the instructions for your computer's operating system. *See also* BAD SECTORS, DISKETTE, HARD DISK, INTEGRATED CIRCUIT, MODULAR CONSTRUCTION, *and* PRINTED CIRCUIT.

Software QA/QC. The creation of a computer program involves several steps. The actual writing is only a small part of the whole process. A "game plan" must first be devised. After the program is written, it must be debugged, and then it must be thoroughly tested.

Testing consists of two phases, the *alpha test* and the *beta test*. The alpha test is an "in-house" test. It gets this name from the first letter in the Greek alphabet. Beta testing is done in the field. The program is run in real situations, like a road test for a car. Subtle bugs usually turn up in the beta testing stage. After beta testing, the software company rewrites the programs based on the reports it receives from the beta sites.

The drawing at B (previous page) shows the basic process for software development, from conception through QA/QC. Note that there is no finish point in this diagram. Software is never really finished; it can always be improved upon. Good software developers are aware of this, inviting and heeding customer feedback.

In general, the best software is sold by commercial software publishers. These programs are the least likely to contain *Trojan horses* or *viruses*, bugs deliberately composed by malicious hackers. When you can't determine the origin of a software program, and especially if it is offered free for downloading, you should run it through a *vaccine* before using it. A vaccine is a program that identifies Trojan horses and viruses, and "cleans" the system to eliminate any that are found. Downloaded software should always be put on diskettes, and thoroughly checked for Trojan horses and viruses, before it is installed on a hard disk. *See also* DEBUGGING, PROGRAMMING, SOFTWARE, TROJAN HORSE, VACCINE, *and* VIRUS.

Quantum computer technology

Computers are constantly getting smaller and more powerful. Physicists at the Center for Nonlinear Studies in Los Alamos, New Mexico, are at work on a scheme in which data is represented by certain behaviors, called quantum states, of electrons within atoms. This might be called *quantum computer technology*.

"Digital" atoms. For decades, scientists have known that every atom of matter has a positively charged nucleus, with negatively charged electrons in "shells" around the nucleus. The electrons can "orbit" the nucleus only at certain "altitudes." The bigger an electron's orbital shell, the more energy the electron contains. Because the orbits can have only certain sizes, the electrons can only have specific energy levels. This gives electrons a sort of "digital personality" when they are part of an atom.

Electrons often change energy levels within atoms. If radiant energy having just the right wavelength shines on the atom, a photon, or particle of energy, will strike an electron and make it jump into a bigger, higher-energy shell. An electron can also fall into a smaller, lower-energy shell and give off a photon having a certain wavelength. Different substances have different properties in this respect. For any substance, scientists can cause electrons to jump to higher energy levels by subjecting the atoms to radiant energy of certain wavelengths.

Logic states. The drawings show, in greatly simplified form, an electron in two different orbital shells within an atom. At A, the electron is in a low-energy shell, which can be chosen to represent a logic 0 (low) condition. If a ray of energy having the correct wavelength shines on the atom, a photon will strike the electron and cause it to jump to some higher-energy shell. This shell can be chosen to represent logic 1 (high), as shown at B. A data bit can thus be changed from 0 to 1 simply by shining a pulse of light at the atom. Changing the state back from 1 to 0 is a little trickier, but it can be done, too.

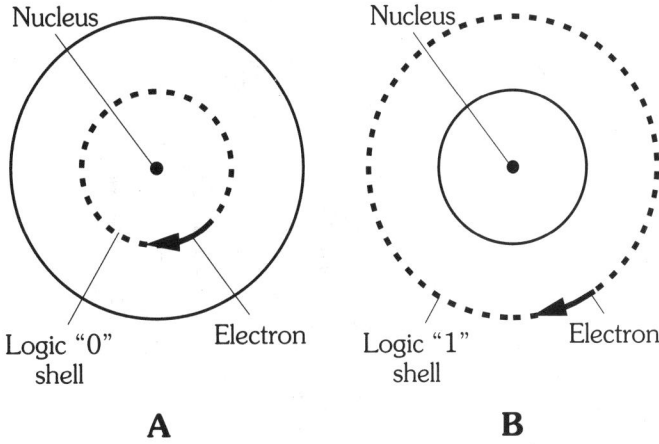

Greatly simplified views of an atom. At A, low electron energy state (logic 0). At B, high electron energy state (logic 1).

In an ideal quantum computer, only one atom would be required for each bit of data. However, at the subatomic level, particles are somewhat unruly. The energy states of electrons can't be completely controlled; they sometimes change as if they have a will of their own. One possible solution to this problem is to have each data bit represented by a majority of the atoms in a "jury." For example, nine electrons in nine different atoms might represent one data bit. If five or more of the electrons are in high-energy shells, then the computer would interpret the bit as a logic 1, otherwise it would show up as a logic 0. *See also* BIT, MOLECULAR COMPUTER TECHNOLOGY, NANOTECHNOLOGY, *and* SINGLE-ELECTRON MEMORY.

Quattro Pro

Quattro Pro is a spreadsheet program originally developed by Borland International. It has high-level features but is easy for a beginner to learn. It is available for use with DOS or graphical user interfaces (GUIs) such as Windows.

3-D format. One significant asset of Quattro Pro is the fact that it works in three dimensions (3-D). Some other spreadsheets, such as recent versions of Excel and Lotus 1-2-3, also have the 3-D feature. Most older, low-end spreadsheets only work in two dimensions (2-D).

Each "sheet" in Quattro Pro is actually a 256-page composite. If you have a calendar for a 30-day month, for example, you get 256 × 30, or 7680 pages, for your data. The drawing shows the difference between a conventional 2-D calendar and a Quattro-Pro-type 3-D calendar. It's as if you have a file drawer with 256 cards for every day of the month. In Quattro Pro, these files are represented by little spiral-notebook symbols.

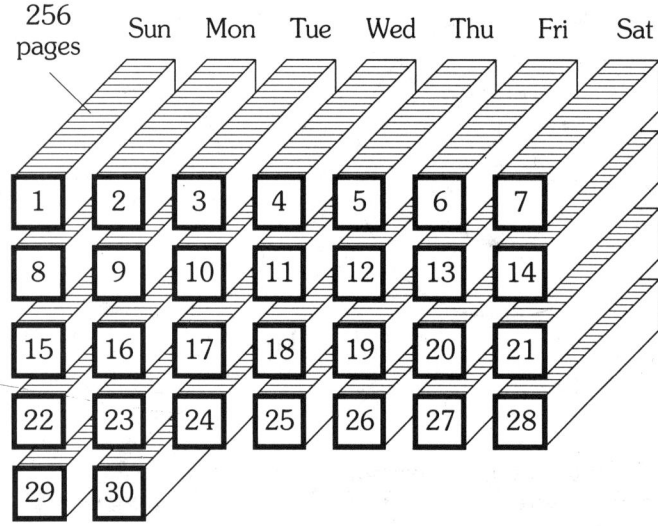

A spreadsheet rendered in 3-D.

When spreadsheets get huge, the 3-D feature becomes extremely powerful. Two-dimensional spreadsheets get messy almost beyond comprehension when they fill up with data, but the Quattro Pro system keeps things neat. Data accessibility is further enhanced by organizational options.

Other features. Here are a few other ways that Quattro Pro can help a spreadsheet user:

➤ *Tab* lets you name each page of every notebook in your spreadsheet, or name groups of pages. This is an immense help when you need to navigate your way through a maze of data.

- *Object inspector* lets you change the way the screen looks. It also tells you the ways in which you can change particular items, such as charts. If you get tired of one format or routine, you can switch things around.

- *SpeedFormat* is a button you can click on that lets you choose text and graphics options to get the spreadsheet to look the way you want. You can pick and combine fonts, colors, shading, and other particulars.

- *SpeedFill* is a button that helps you fill in cells, or ranges of cells, saving work. For example, you can have the computer fill in all the dates (day of the month and day of the week) for a whole year, just by giving it one day to start from, such as "Fri, 01/01/99."

- *Drag-and-drop* lets you move blocks of data from place to place. It's the same drag-and-drop feature you've used if you've worked much with a mouse.

- *Macros* enable you to encode various commands in the form of buttons on the screen. When you click on a button, the computer will execute the command you've assigned to that button. This saves repetitive keystrokes.

- *Graphs* that you can create include line graphs, bar graphs, columnar graphs, and pie graphs. You can make 3-D graphs for multivariable functions.

- *Slide show* lets you create a professional presentation when you need to show your data to other people. Special effects, such as interactivity, are available. You can make slides fade smoothly from one image into the next.

- *Screen preview* lets you see on the monitor exactly how a document will look when it is printed. This is known as *WYSIWYG* (pronounced "WIZZY-wig" and meaning "what you see is what you get").

For further information. The foregoing is only a brief glimpse into Quattro Pro. You can learn more by getting brochures or by seeing the software in action. *See also* SPREADSHEET.

Query

A *query* is a way of asking a computer to search for information. Queries are commonly used in database software. Usually, a query is made by filling in certain blanks supplied by the program. The computer acts on the basis of the input you supply.

Search criteria. When you use a computerized card catalog at a library, you query the computer by requesting certain information. You can search by subject, title, author, publisher, or year of publication. The computer gives you a list of search options, and you choose one

Query by example

by pressing a sequence of keys. Then you fill in a blank by typing at least the first few letters of the field you want the machine to search within.

Suppose you're at a university library and are looking for a book on cosmology. You tell the computer card catalog to search by subject, choosing that option from a menu (list) on the screen. Then, when the computer prompts you to query for subject, you type *cosmology*. Alternatively, just the first few letters might suffice, such as *cosmo*. If nothing shows up via this query, you might try *astrophysics*. If you still get nothing, you'd type in the more general subject, *astronomy*. This would almost surely produce a list of books. (If not, you'd want to go to the librarian and ask for help.)

Digging deeper. Queries can be done in various degrees of depth. In the library example, the list of books would probably give the title, publisher's name, copyright date, and perhaps the number of pages and illustrations. You would have to dig deeper, however, to get more information about the book.

Most computerized card catalogs contain a brief description of each book, along with a code number that tells you which shelf it's on. You might also be able to determine whether or not the book is checked out, so you won't waste time looking for it if it's not available. To get information about a specific book, you type its line number (order in the list).

Hot keys versus mouse. At most public libraries, the computer card catalog uses a text-based interface, not a graphical user interface (GUI). No mouse is supplied.

When purchasing your own database software, on the other hand, you can almost always choose between a GUI version (written for Macintosh, OS/2, Windows, etc.), and a DOS version. Most people find the GUI more user-friendly. With older, less powerful computers, however, the GUI version might run slowly or not at all. That can make the DOS package more attractive for owners of old machines. *See also* DATABASE, DOS, GRAPHICAL USER INTERFACE, MENU, *and* QUERY BY EXAMPLE.

Query by example

Query by example (QBE) is a query scheme used in database software. You specify one or more criteria in which the computer is to search for information.

Mission plan. Suppose you're doing a research project. Your ultimate goal is to figure out how fast the ozone layer is being depleted in the earth's upper atmosphere and to formulate predictions concerning what will happen to life on this planet in 10, 20, 50, 100,

200, and 500 years if present trends continue. You need to get as many different opinions from as many different knowledgeable people as possible.

You obtain a database with the names of all the colleges and universities in the world, and all the faculty members in every one of these institutions. This database also contains the names of all people with degrees in any field of engineering, statistics, physics, biology, or chemistry. This database gives information concerning the work done by these people, the companies employing them, and in particular, the titles of all papers, articles, and books published by each of these people.

As you can imagine, such a database would be gigantic. How might you go about seeking, say, 30 people from this database, with a wide variety of experiences and a high a level of expertise? The database gives you several options for searching; your screen might initially contain a list such as that in the table below. Your mission plan is now laid out. The search begins.

Search criteria

Worldwide scientific professionals database
LAST NAME:
FIRST NAME:
COLLEGE OR UNIVERSITY:
COMPANY:
DEPARTMENT:
PROFESSIONAL DEGREE:
PROFESSIONAL TITLE:
SPECIALTY:
COUNTRY:
STATE OR PROVINCE:
CITY:
BOOK TITLE:
ARTICLE TITLE:
THESIS OR PAPER TITLE:

Narrowing down. Most QBE databases treat a blank entry as a *wildcard*, meaning that the search is conducted for any and all possible items that can go into the blank space. The next table shows an example of a query-by-example list with a little data filled in. Because this database encompasses the whole world, there will undoubtedly still be hundreds, if not thousands, of people found on the basis of this search. There must be a great number of physics specialists in the world who have done research in environmental

Minimal data known

Worldwide scientific professionals database
LAST NAME:
FIRST NAME:
COLLEGE OR UNIVERSITY:
COMPANY:
DEPARTMENT: Physics
PROFESSIONAL DEGREE:
PROFESSIONAL TITLE:
SPECIALTY: Environment
COUNTRY:
STATE OR PROVINCE:
CITY:
BOOK TITLE:
ARTICLE TITLE:
THESIS OR PAPER TITLE:

science. You'll need to narrow things down, or you'll get a list so long that it's hardly any better than guesswork.

The table opposite shows an example of an entry that might produce some useful data for you. You've narrowed things down enough so that your printer won't take all day to generate a hardcopy of the list. In fact, there are probably only a handful of people who meet the criteria specified in this example. You might conduct the same search for several other well-known and well-respected universities, and get a list of people in whose opinions you can place confidence. *See also* DATABASE *and* QUERY.

Queue

A *queue* is a list, or sequence, of things for a computer to do in a specific order. Files might be sent over a modem or to a printer; commands might be executed. In any queue, the computer completes each task and then moves on to the next. The term *queue* is also used in reference to the list of items in a *first-in/first-out* buffer.

A common example of a queue is a set of files to be printed. If you have several short files that you want to print, you can set up a *print queue*. You can start the computer working on the print queue, and go do something else in another room after making sure the printer is working properly. When you return, the files in the print queue will all have been printed in the order you have specified.

There are two basic types of queues. In a *live queue*, each file, task, or item is treated individually within the queue. Items can be modified

QuickDraw

More data known

Worldwide scientific professionals database
LAST NAME:
FIRST NAME:
COLLEGE OR UNIVERSITY: University of Minnesota
COMPANY:
DEPARTMENT: Physics
PROFESSIONAL DEGREE: Ph.D.
PROFESSIONAL TITLE: Professor
SPECIALTY: Environment
COUNTRY: U.S.A.
STATE OR PROVINCE: Minnesota
CITY: Minneapolis
BOOK TITLE:
ARTICLE TITLE:
THESIS OR PAPER TITLE:

after the computer has begun working; as long as the task has not been completed yet, the updates will be heeded by the computer when it gets to them. A *fixed queue* is less flexible, and is treated by the computer as a single file, task, or item. Once the machine starts on such a queue, no changes will be heeded. If changes must be made, the queue must be started all over again afterwards.

The drawing at the top of page 908 shows examples of these two kinds of queues. Tasks are labeled W, X, Y, and Z, and are executed in that order. A relative scale of time (T) is included for reference. The queue in part A is live; the one in part B is fixed. A change is made to task Y at a time when the computer is at work on task X. The change is heeded in the live queue, but not in the other queue. *See also* FIRST-IN/FIRST-OUT *and* PRINT MANAGER.

QuickDraw

QuickDraw is a supervisory software system used in Macintosh computers. It oversees both the monitor displays and the printed matter. QuickDraw is responsible for the *WYSIWYG* feature for which Macintosh is well known. This acronym, pronounced "WIZZY-wig," stands for "what you see is what you get." With WYSIWYG, the image on the monitor is essentially the same as the copy you get when you make a printout.

QuickDraw determines the location of each pixel (picture element) by defining a huge coordinate grid for the desktop, or image workspace you see on the monitor. This grid is a set of Cartesian coordinates with ordered pairs ranging from the binary (00000000,00000000) to

QuickDraw

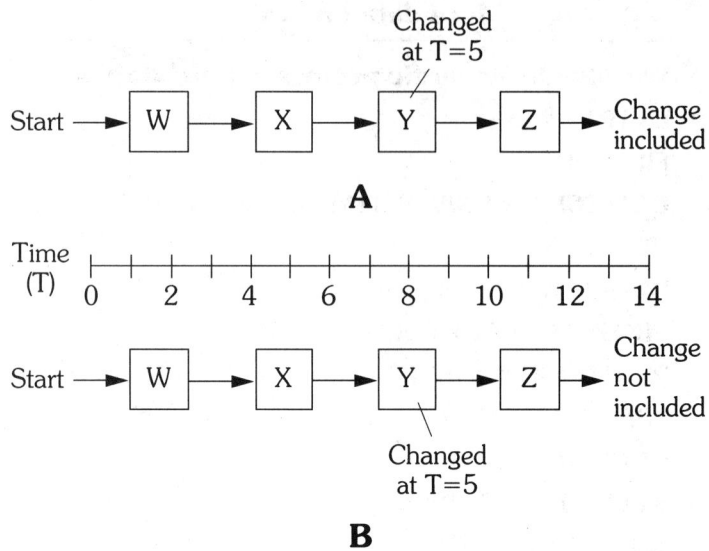

A live task sequence (A) and a fixed sequence (B).

(11111111,11111111). The equivalent decimal values are (0,0) through (65535,65535). There are over four billion possible combinations of values in this system.

The drawing shows a small section of the QuickDraw coordinate grid. Points correspond to intersection points of horizontal and vertical lines. Pixels are the square regions thus generated.

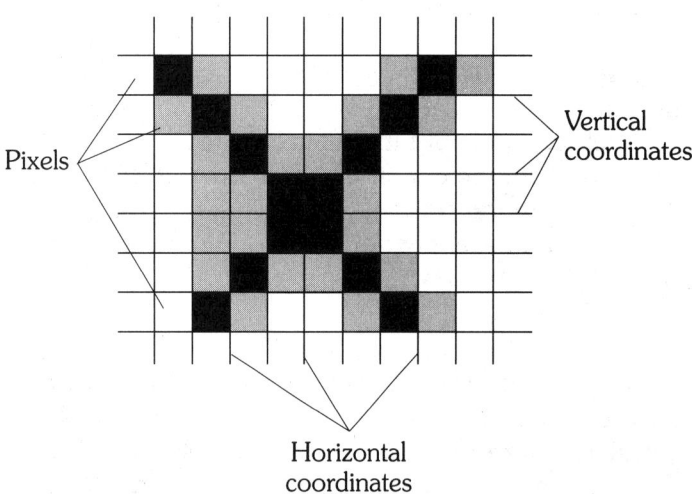

Pixels are defined by squares in a Cartesian coordinate grid.

QuickDraw can display up to 16 million different colors, encoded as 24 bits in a video signal for each pixel. Colors are created by combining red, green, and blue (RGB) in various brightnesses. For complex graphics applications, especially those that involve animation, an enhanced graphics scheme called *QuickDraw GX* is used. *See also* ANIMATION, CARTESIAN COORDINATES, DESKTOP, PIXEL, RGB COLOR MODEL, *and* WYSIWYG.

Quicken

Quicken is personal finance software originally developed by Intuit, Inc. to serve as a computerized checkbook. It has evolved to the point that it can serve as an all-around financial manager for small businesses as well as for individuals.

Features. Quicken is available for graphical user interfaces (GUIs) such as Windows; it is also sold for use with DOS. Here are some of Quicken's features:

➤ *Plenty of room* A single Quicken file can contain up to 255 accounts. It's not likely that you'll ever run out of room, unless you become so wealthy that you can set up a whole corporation solely for the purpose of looking after your financial affairs.

➤ *Bank account* This helps you balance your checkbook, keep track of your savings account, and oversee other accounts you might have, such as money-market or savings-and-loan accounts. You can find out where money in these accounts comes from (deposits), and where it goes (payments).

➤ *Cash account* Many people still prefer the old-fashioned method of buying everyday items: cash. Little cash purchases can add up mysteriously. Most people buy snacks, magazines, newspapers, and other small items with cash, often unconsciously. Then they wonder why they're always going to automatic teller machines (ATMs). Quicken will show you the truth about this "mystery."

➤ *Asset and liability accounts* Tangible things that usually increase in value, such as your home, your lake cottage, the Rembrandt in your dining room, and your gold soup spoons can be overseen by the asset account. Things that decrease in value can also be logged and watched in this account. Cars, boats, and computers are usually "negative assets" that diminish in value with time. These accounts can also help you with your taxes.

➤ *Credit card account* This is a running record of all the transactions and other activity in credit card account(s). It can help you figure out what you tend to buy with credit. It can also tell you how much interest you're paying per year. It's astonishing (and often horrifying) to discover how fast credit-card interest can drain away money you could otherwise save or spend.

➤ *Investment account* This is a boon to Wall Street habitués. It's also good for mutual funds, bonds, precious metals in all their various forms, and other things that you hope will make money for you in the long term. That Rembrandt in the dining room might be recorded here, too.

Quit/Exit

> *Quicken Companion* This program, available in the Windows version of Quicken, helps you manage more complicated financial matters such as estimating your income tax, predicting the future value of your assets, and overseeing the operation of a small business, especially if you are self-employed.

> *Help* If you are having trouble figuring out how to use Quicken, or if you are simply curious about some aspect of its operation, you can get help online as you work with the software. There are also buttons called "QCards" that will give you advice when you activate them.

For further information. Quicken has become immensely popular in recent years, with several million copies in use. You shouldn't have much trouble finding a "PC guru" who has experience with Quicken. A computer superstore is also a good place to witness the program in operation. *See also* PERSONAL FINANCE SOFTWARE.

Quit/Exit

Quit is a command in DOS. Its Windows counterpart is *Exit*. Giving this command tells the computer to leave the application(s) it is currently running. The terms *quit* or *exit* also refer to the act (by the PC operator) of leaving a program, either in preparation for entering another application or prior to powering-down (switching off) the computer.

Suppose you want to print some documents using a word processing program. You switch the computer on, and it automatically goes into DOS. You load the word processing program; then you load the printer software. You make a hardcopy of the document. You are done, for now, with the word processing application, so you want to exit that program. You would issue the Quit or Exit command to leave the word processing and printer programs. The computer is then ready for another application.

If your computer uses DOS, it's wise to quit all software (including Windows) so your computer gives you the DOS prompt before powering-down. This ensures that you won't lose any data you have been working on. It also gets rid of temporary files created while the program was run. In some applications, these temporary files consume significant space on the hard disk. *See also* POWER-UP AND POWER-DOWN.

QWERTY keyboard layout

On the traditional typewriter and computer keyboard, the letters are in a sequence that seems random. The first six letters in the top row are Q, W, E, R, T, and Y. Because of this, the common keyboard is sometimes called the *QWERTY keyboard*. Virtually all English-language typewriters and computers use this arrangement.

QWERTY keyboard layout

QWERTY is not the most efficient keyboard scheme. Ideally, the most-often-used keys (such as E, A, S, and C) would be the easiest to strike. That would place them near the center of the keyboard. If you look at a QWERTY keyboard, you will see that all four of these keys are near the extreme left. To hit them, you must use the small fingers on your left hand. Most people find these fingers the hardest, not the easiest, to move accurately and fast.

Other keyboard arrangements have been suggested; the most well-known is called the *Dvorak keyboard*. None of these schemes have caught on, however. People don't want to make the switch, let alone learn to work on two completely different keyboards. *See also* CHARACTER, DVORAK KEYBOARD LAYOUT, *and* KEYBOARD.

Radio-frequency interference

Radio-frequency interference (RFI) is a phenomenon in which electronic devices upset each other's operation. In recent years, this problem has been getting worse because consumer electronic devices are proliferating, and they have become more susceptible to RFI. Computers sometimes malfunction in the presence of strong radio signals. Computers can also generate RFI, interfering with radio reception.

Causes. Much RFI results from inferior equipment design. To some extent, faulty installation also contributes to the problem. Computers produce wideband radio-frequency (RF) energy in the form of an *electromagnetic field*. Most of this energy comes from cathode-ray tube (CRT) monitors and from the high-speed digital pulses in the main unit. The clock, which sets the pace for the microprocessor, can sometimes cause interference to radio or television receivers. The energy gets out of the computer via the interconnecting cables and power cords because they act as miniature transmitting antennas (part A of the drawing) unless *electromagnetic shielding* is employed.

Computers can malfunction because of strong RF fields such as those from a nearby radio or television transmitter. This can, and often does, happen when the transmitter is working perfectly. In these cases, and also in cases involving cellular telephones, citizens' band (CB) radios, and amateur ("ham") radios, the transmitting equipment is almost never at fault; the problem is almost always improper or ineffective shielding in some part of the computer system. Cables and

Radio-frequency interference

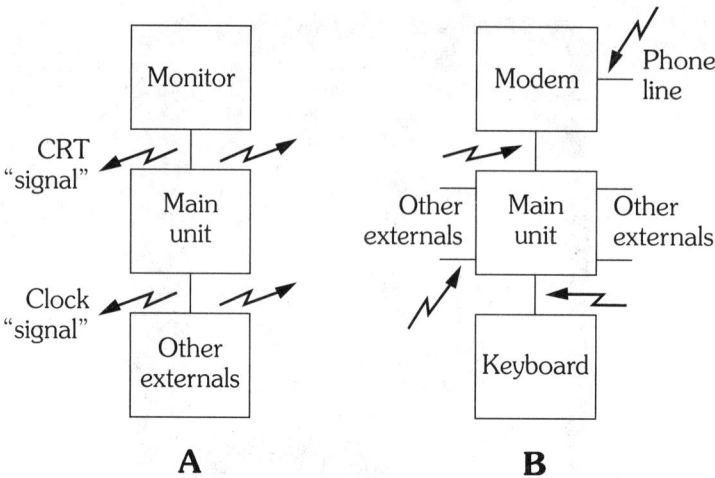

RF "signals" (heavy zigzags) emanating from a computer system (A) and entering through cables and the telephone line (B).

cords can act as receiving antennas (part B of the drawing), thereby letting RF energy into the computer.

Power lines can also radiate electromagnetic energy, causing RFI to sensitive equipment. Fortunately, these fields aren't usually strong enough to interfere with computers directly, although they can cause trouble if you are receiving data via radio. This type of interference is caused by electric sparks. A malfunctioning transformer, a bad street light, or a salt-encrusted insulator can all be responsible. Often, help can be obtained by calling the utility company.

Electric- or gasoline-powered motors and engines occasionally cause RFI. Certain home appliances can sometimes wreak havoc with radio receivers; light dimmers, heating pads, electric blankets, hair dryers, and vacuum cleaners are the most frequent culprits.

Cures. There are methods of keeping RF from getting out of, or into, a computer and peripherals. A *choke* is a coil that blocks RF currents; a *bypass* is a capacitor that shorts RF currents to ground. They are installed in the cables and/or cable connectors. You must be sure these devices don't interfere with the transmission of data through cables, however. For advice, consult the dealer or manufacturer of the computer, a competent computer engineer, or an electronics engineer. If you try to install choke or bypass devices yourself, they might not work properly. You will also run the risk of voiding the warranty on the computer equipment.

Transient suppression, also called *surge suppression*, in the power cord is essential for reliable operation of a computer. A *line filter*, consisting of capacitors between each side of the power line and ground, can help prevent RF from getting into a computer via the utility lines. Some transient suppressors act as line filters; some do not.

As personal computers become more portable and more common, RFI problems will probably continue to worsen, unless manufacturers pay strict attention to electromagnetic shielding. When computers are used as controllers for mechanical devices, the potential consequences can be serious, even dangerous. The hazard is greatest with computer-controlled medical and life-support devices. *See also* ELECTROMAGNETIC FIELD, ELECTROMAGNETIC SHIELDING, *and* TRANSIENT SUPPRESSION.

RAM

See RANDOM-ACCESS MEMORY.

RAM cache

See CACHE MEMORY.

RAM disk

The "working memory" of a PC is the *random-access memory (RAM)*. The data in RAM changes from moment to moment as you manipulate the keyboard, mouse, or other data input devices. RAM isn't the only part of the computer that can store data, however. The information on a hard disk or diskettes is a form of "memory," too, technically called *storage*. It changes when you instruct the computer to write on the disk. The RAM is much faster, in terms of read/write time, than the hard disk or diskettes.

Drives A/B/C/D. If your PC has one diskette drive, it's probably called drive A. If there are two diskette drives, they're most likely called drive A and drive B. The hard disk is usually called drive C. When you want to write data onto, or read data from, a disk, you must indicate which drive the disk is in. The computer will then whirr and click, and the information will go either from disk to RAM or from RAM to disk, depending on whether you're reading or writing the data. This always takes a certain amount of time. For a small file and a hard disk, it's only a fraction of a second. For a large file and a diskette drive, it might be several seconds.

In certain situations, you can make your computer work much faster by designating part of the RAM to function as if it were a disk drive. When you do this, you create a *RAM disk*. This type of "disk," also called a *virtual disk* or *virtual drive*, isn't mechanical like drives A, B, and C. There are no moving parts in a RAM disk. The computer doesn't know that, however; it thinks the RAM disk is another drive, and this virtual drive gets a name, such as drive D.

Assets. The procedure for setting up a RAM disk depends on your operating system. Before you commit any serious data to a RAM disk, read your instruction manual, follow the onscreen directions, and set one up just to practice with.

Random-access memory

The most obvious asset of a RAM disk is the fact that it's so much faster than any mechanical drive. You'll notice this right away. Create some file that you can afford to lose if you make a mistake or if there's a power failure. Then write it onto and read it from the RAM disk. It's practically instantaneous, regardless of the file size.

At this point you might wonder why computers have hard disks and diskette drives at all. Why not just create a huge RAM, and store all the data on it? Sophisticated programs could be loaded instantly, and even an old, slow microprocessor would work with lightning speed. There are several reasons why this scheme is not yet workable, but things are in fact gradually evolving in that direction.

Liabilities. The main problem with a RAM disk is that, in most computers, RAM is volatile memory. Its contents will vanish when you power-down the computer, when a power failure occurs, or if you give the computer the wrong instructions. If you put anything on a RAM disk that you can't afford to lose, you'd better back it up at frequent intervals during your work session, by storing it on the hard disk.

Another problem with a RAM disk is that there's a limited amount of space in your computer's RAM. If you put a lot of data on RAM disks, you'll have less room for things like application programs. Whatever you add in one place, you must take away from someplace else. While this problem can be overcome to some extent by adding memory expansion boards, extra RAM isn't cheap. Building RAM up to the capacity of a typical hard disk would be very costly.

The future. Nonvolatile, high-capacity memory is being developed, and prices are falling. Eventually, the RAM disk (or something like it) will become a preferred operating technique for most computer users. *Flash memory* is one technology that is rapidly advancing, and that holds promise. *PCMCIA standard adapter cards* are another. These cards are already being used as "fast hard disks" in laptop (notebook) computers. In addition to offering the advantages of RAM disks, these cards are removable, like diskettes. *See also* MASS STORAGE, MEMORY, NONVOLATILE MEMORY, PCMCIA STANDARD ADAPTER CARDS, RANDOM-ACCESS MEMORY, REMOVABLE DATA STORAGE MEDIA, *and* VOLATILE MEMORY.

Random-access memory

Random-access memory (RAM) refers to integrated circuits (ICs, also called "chips") that store a computer's working data. RAM is often called simply *memory*. It gets its name from the fact that data can be read from and written into any part of it. RAM is fast and versatile. Its capacity is a crucial factor in determining what a computer can and cannot do.

Binary blackboard. The drawing shows how data moves between a hard disk or diskette and the RAM, and between the RAM and the central processing unit (CPU). When you open a file that's on your hard disk or on a diskette, the data goes immediately into the RAM. The CPU, under the control of the microprocessor, manipulates the data in the RAM as you work on the file. Thus, the data in RAM changes from moment to moment.

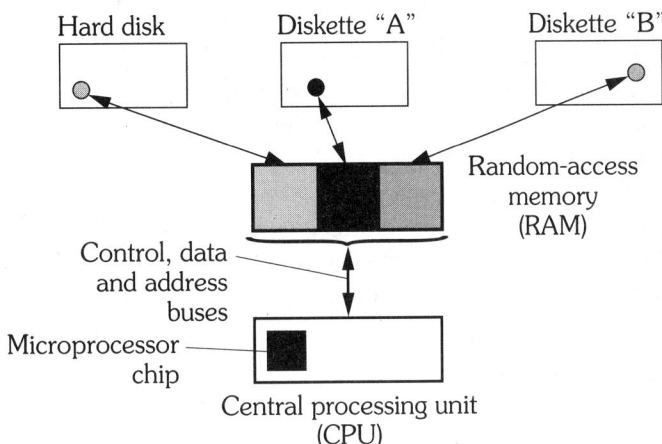

Data moves between disks and the RAM, and between the RAM and the CPU.

It's as if you're composing on a blackboard with chalk and eraser. When you press a key and add a character, or drag the mouse and draw a line that shows up on your monitor screen, that character or line goes into RAM at the same time. If you press the Backspace key and delete a character, or drag the mouse and erase a line on the screen, it disappears from the RAM too. All this while, the original file on the disk stays as it was before you accessed it. No change is made to the disk data until you specifically instruct the computer to overwrite the data on the disk.

When you're done working on a file, you tell the microprocessor to close it. The data then leaves RAM and goes back to the hard disk or diskette from which it came, or to some other place that you might direct. If you tell the computer to overwrite the file on the disk from which it came, most programs send the new data (containing the changes you have made) to unused space on the disk; the old data (as it was before you opened the file) stays in its old location. This is a safeguard, in case you decide to undo the changes you made.

All the data passing between the disks and the RAM, and between the RAM and the CPU, is in machine language. This consists of off and on states, usually called binary digits (bits) 0 and 1. If you could listen to machine language, you'd hear a meaningless hiss. If you could see it on the monitor, it would pass by as a blur of ones and zeros as the digital signals race around in the computer. The data passing between you and the CPU, on the other hand, is in plain English (or whatever other language you prefer), or in some high-level programming

Random-access memory

language, having been translated by the machine into a form you can understand.

Capacity. The amount of data that can be stored in RAM is measured in kilobytes (KB or K), megabytes (MB), or gigabytes (GB), and is known as the *RAM capacity* or *memory capacity.* The size of RAM in a typical computer has been growing each year. It's impossible to quote a standard figure for the RAM capacity of a computer because so many different kinds of machines are in use. Also, operators' needs vary tremendously. For casual operation, several megabytes are typical.

High-end application software needs large amounts of RAM. The same is true of the more advanced user interfaces such as Windows, OS/2, and the Macintosh OS. Several megabytes represent a bare minimum these days. The most esoteric applications, such as artificial intelligence (AI), speech recognition, and virtual reality, can require dozens of megabytes of RAM to properly function. In fact, RAM technology is as significant as, if not more significant than, microprocessor speed when it comes to working in animated, multimedia applications.

The main factor that determines a computer's maximum potential RAM capacity is the number of transistors that can be fabricated onto a single memory chip. Other factors, such as microprocessor power, have a practical effect on the usable RAM capacity. A gigantic RAM will not be of much use if the microprocessor is slow, just as a fast microprocessor will be of little practical value if the RAM capacity is too small for applications that demand high speed.

The actual physics of RAM is changing along with the memory capacity. The amount of RAM you need depends on the applications you intend to run on your computer. Most software packages will tell you how much RAM you need. If you plan to use a RAM disk, you'll need extra RAM, over and above what you'd need otherwise. If your PC doesn't have enough RAM, you can usually add more by installing expansion boards, also called adapter boards or cards.

Volatility. In most computers, RAM is *volatile memory*; it requires a source of power to be maintained. If you switch the computer off or if there's a power failure, you lose all the data in the RAM.

In contrast to RAM, the data on magnetic disks or optical media stay put when the power is removed. When you're working on a file, it's wise to store it every few minutes on the hard disk and/or diskette. That way, in the rare event a power failure does occur, you won't lose much of your work.

You might wonder why RAM must be volatile. Why can't it be designed so that it will be retained when power is switched off? There are in fact forms of RAM that are *nonvolatile memory*. One example, called *flash memory*, shares the assets of a hard disk (nonvolatility and large capacity) and conventional RAM (high read/write speed). It is like a super-fast hard disk without moving parts. Flash memory is expensive, which limits its appeal in the consumer market, but as memory technology advances, this situation is bound to change. It's also likely that new nonvolatile memory schemes will be developed.

DRAM and SRAM. *Dynamic random-access memory*, abbreviated *DRAM*, is RAM in which the binary digits are stored electrically in a metal-oxide-semiconductor (MOS) material. The DRAM chip contains, in effect, thousands upon thousands of tiny capacitors.

The electric charges in DRAM dissipate quickly unless they are automatically replenished at regular intervals because no capacitor is perfect; the thin oxide layer inside the IC is not a complete insulator. Also, because of their microscopic size, the capacitors in a DRAM IC have small values and can't hold much electric charge. The *refresh rate* is the number of times per second that the data is replenished.

The time required to get data from RAM is known as the *access time*. For DRAM, it is less than 0.05 microsecond (millionths of a second), or 50 nanoseconds (billionths of a second). A ray of light travels about 50 feet in 50 nanoseconds; a current in a wire goes about four feet.

A *static random-access memory (SRAM)* does not need to be refreshed. Because of this, SRAM can work faster than DRAM, with an access time on the order of two nanoseconds or less. SRAM is volatile, like DRAM, because it will lose its contents if power is removed. Instead of storing data as charges in tiny capacitors, however, SRAM uses transistors. Each transistor acts as a switch called a *flip-flop*.

The main problem with SRAM is that it costs more per unit of memory capacity than DRAM. In addition, SRAM is physically bulkier than DRAM. As technology advances, however, this situation might change. It's also possible that entirely new forms of RAM will be developed. *See also* ACCESS TIME, CACHE MEMORY, COMPUTER POWER, DYNAMIC RANDOM-ACCESS MEMORY, MAGNETIC MEDIA, MEMORY, NONVOLATILE MEMORY, RAM DISK, READ-ONLY MEMORY, STATIC RANDOM-ACCESS MEMORY, *and* VOLATILE MEMORY.

Range

A *range* is a group of cells in a spreadsheet. A range can be as small as one cell, or as big as the whole spreadsheet. Usually, a range consists of portions of adjacent rows and columns.

Defining a range. A range is always rectangular in shape. It is defined according to two cells: the one at the top left, and the one at the bottom right. You indicate the top-left cell first, by typing or

Range

clicking it, then some dividing expression such as two periods, and finally the bottom-right cell. This is the *range expression*. In a spreadsheet, each range has exactly one expression, and each expression corresponds to exactly one range.

The drawing shows three ranges, X, Y, and Z. Respectively, the range expressions are B6..B13, B18..G18, and F13..G15. The drawing also shows two regions that are not rectangular, and are therefore not ranges in the spreadsheet.

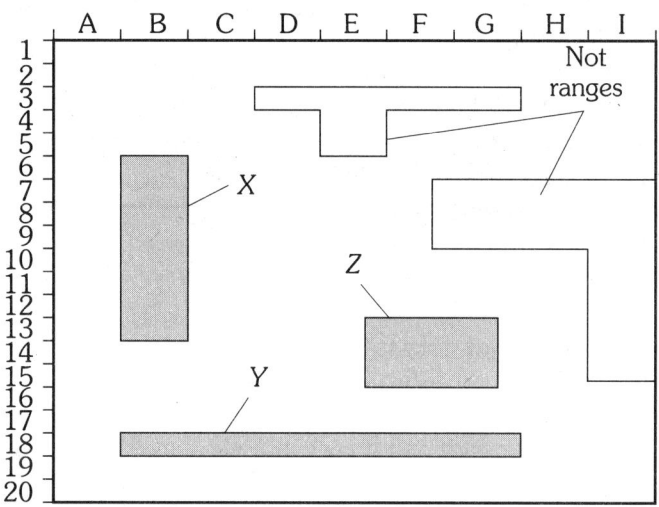

Shaded blocks X, Y, and Z are ranges; unshaded blocks are not.

It's often difficult to remember what a range represents based only on an alphanumeric expression. It can also be hard to recall the alphanumeric range expression based on what data the range contains. Many spreadsheet programs make this association automatically when you use *range names*. In the drawing, the range names are X, Y, and Z, but you'd probably use more imaginative range names. For example, if you're setting up accounts in a single spreadsheet for your three children, you could name the appropriate ranges with your children's names, such as *Jim*, *Sue*, and *Ann*.

Formatting. Consider a spreadsheet that you're using to keep financial records. Most of the cells will contain sums of money. The standard format for money allows for up to several digits, then a decimal point, and then two more digits. You would most likely want to specify a *global format* for sums of money, so that the format applies to all the cells in the spreadsheet.

In a financial spreadsheet, there might be some ranges in which you want to enter nonfinancial data, such as dates. You could specify a *range format* to override the global format for those ranges. For other types of data, the range format would depend on the type of information you wanted to enter. *See also* GLOBAL FORMAT, NUMERIC FORMAT, *and* SPREADSHEET.

Range of function

The *range* of a mathematical function is the set of things (usually numbers) onto which objects in the domain are mapped. Every x in the domain of a function f is mapped onto exactly one value y. There might be, and often are, y values that don't have anything mapped onto them by function f. These points are outside the range of f.

Suppose you are given the function $f(x) = x^2$. The graph of this function is shown in the drawing. This function never maps anything onto a negative number. No matter what the x value in the domain, x^2 is never negative. When you square a real number, the result is always zero or greater. Therefore, the range of $f(x) = x^2$ is the set of non-negative real numbers.

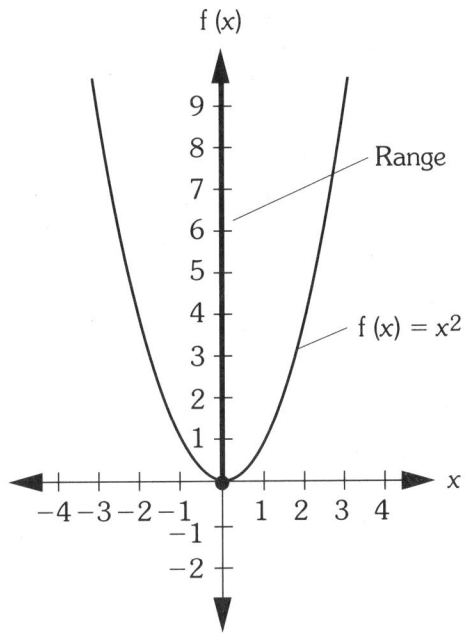

Here, the range of function is the non-negative f(x) axis.

Computers work extensively with functions, both analog and digital. Functions are also important in navigation, location, and measurement systems for computerized machines. *See also* ANALYTICAL GRAPHICS, DEPENDENT VARIABLE, DOMAIN OF FUNCTION, FUNCTION, *and* INDEPENDENT VARIABLE.

Raster

A computer monitor works something like a color television set. The image is comprised of thousands of tiny dots. In a cathode-ray-tube (CRT) monitor, the dots are illuminated by an electron beam that scans rapidly across the screen. The pattern that the beam follows in order to complete one full screen image is called the *raster*.

Raster scan. The *raster scan* takes place at a rate much too fast for the eye to follow. The whole screen is scanned in a tiny fraction of a second; thus, the electron beam creates many full-screen images every second.

Raster scanning goes from left to right and from top to bottom along parallel, horizontal lines, in the same way as your eyes follow the text on a single-column printed page. When the electron beam reaches the right end of a line on the screen, it moves down slightly, and starts at the left end of the next line. One line of the image is created during the left-to-right movement of the beam; this is a *trace*. During the right-to-left *retrace*, the electron beam is switched off so it will not interfere with the image being produced by the traces. This is called *retrace blanking*.

The drawing at A shows a small part of a raster as it appears from a viewpoint in front of the screen. Solid lines are left-to-right traces; dotted lines are right-to-left retraces. This image has been greatly magnified vertically, and somewhat squashed horizontally, to show the nature of the pattern. The number of lines on a monitor screen varies depending on the *image resolution* the monitor is capable of providing. A typical monitor has several hundred lines per screen.

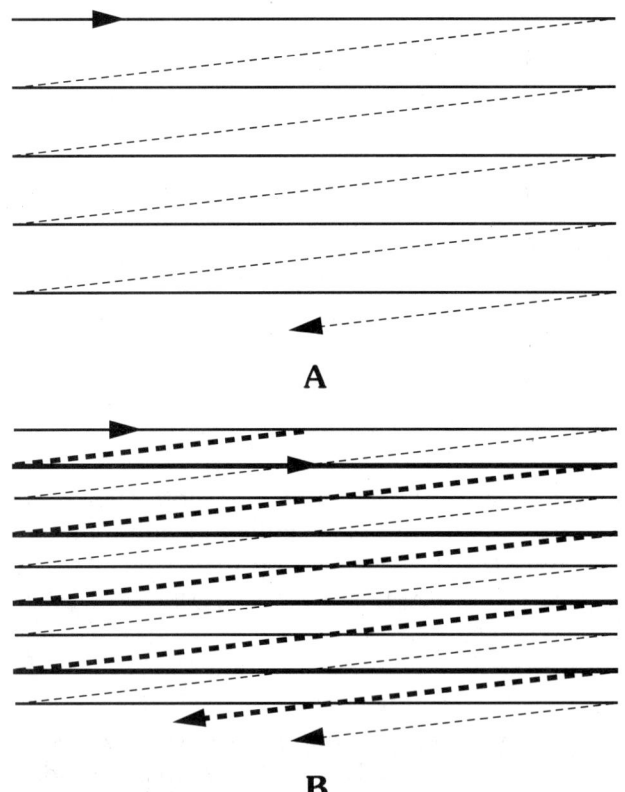

Noninterlaced (A) and interlaced (B) raster.

Interlacing. Some monitors scan the screen twice for each complete video image, so there are actually two rasters instead of one. The two rasters are displaced vertically by a distance equal to half the spacing between lines in either raster. This scheme is called *interlacing*, and is shown in the drawing at B. One raster is shown by thick lines; the other is shown by thin lines. Traces are depicted as solid lines; retraces are depicted as dotted lines.

The advantage of interlacing is that it effectively doubles the image resolution of a monitor without doubling the cost of manufacture. However, interlacing also doubles the time required to produce a complete image. This can cause problems with animated graphics, especially when fast motion must be portrayed.

An interlaced monitor can be useful for fixed-image graphics and text, but some PC users notice a screen flicker that can be annoying. A noninterlaced monitor has only one raster scan per image, keeping flicker to a minimum. For a given image resolution, noninterlaced monitors cost more than interlaced ones, but if you're interested in high-end graphical applications, you'll probably consider the money well spent. *See also* CATHODE-RAY TUBE, IMAGE RESOLUTION, *and* MONITOR.

Raster graphics

See BITMAPPED GRAPHICS.

Ratio analysis software

Ratio analysis software is a special form of business software. It helps executives analyze how well a company is doing, how well it could be doing, and what might be changed to improve profitability.

Financial ratios. Ratio analysis is the process of comparing numbers. Such comparisons tell much more than a bank statement alone. Here are a few examples of ratios via which a computer can tell you what's happening with your personal or corporate finances:

- *Cash flow* You've done ratio analysis with your checkbook, whether or not you've thought of it that way. Your monthly statement tells how much you deposited and how much you spent. You can ascertain the ratio of dollars in to dollars out (call it "in/out"). If in/out is greater than one, you gained during the month. If in/out is less than one, you lost ground. If in/out is less than one for a certain number of months in a row, you will be in financial trouble. This is a simplistic viewpoint, but it is quite valid. The same thing applies to a company. If you spend more than you make for a long time, you will eventually run out of money. A computer can pick up such trends and warn you long before the situation becomes critical. This can help you avert disaster.

- *Solvency* Is your business overextending itself in debt? If so, the interest payments alone can cut deeply into your profit. One

Ratio analysis software

type of solvency ratio divides the total company debts by the total equity. Another divides the profit by the interest the business pays.

Taking another example from personal finance, do you pay only the minimum (or a little more) each month on your credit cards? Do you have a large, ongoing, outstanding balance in one or more of those accounts? You can use your PC to figure out how much interest you're paying in a year, five years, or 10 years. What percentage is this of your total income? How does it compare with your state income tax or your medical insurance premiums? The results might shock you.

➢ *Margin* There are at least three types of margin ratio. One ratio divides the company profit margin by total sales, another is the quotient of the gross margin and total sales, and still another is the quotient of the operating margin and total sales. When computing these ratios (and most others), it's often helpful to chart trends over the years. Also, you might want to compare your ratios with those of other companies in businesses similar to yours.

➢ *Liquidity* A liquidity ratio is a measure of how much of your company's assets can be converted quickly to cash if the need arises. In your personal affairs, you know which assets are the most liquid. Bank accounts are the most common example. While it's good to have some business assets in a form that can be easily liquidated, you don't want the proportion to be too high. Again, consider personal finance: a savings account is convenient, but it pays low interest compared with other, less liquid investments. The current liquidity ratio is based on your situation right now; an average liquidity ratio averages things over a period of time.

➢ *Efficiency* Most companies have certain "assets" that don't normally pay interest and don't exactly represent an investment. The two most common examples are inventory and accounts receivable. How much of your assets are tied up in merchandise sitting on the shelf? How much, as a percentage of your total assets, is in the hands of other people or companies, from whom you are awaiting payment? While it's necessary to maintain a certain inventory, and it's almost universal to extend credit to favored customers, you don't want these things to get out of control. Merchandise does not make money collecting dust in a warehouse. Most companies cannot afford to give out large, long-term, interest-free "loans."

Some common features. Here are some of the features you should look for when shopping for a ratio-analysis software package:

➢ *Versatility* The ratios mentioned are just a few of the many different ways you can analyze your company's performance.

High-level ratio analysis packages can provide a dozen or more ratios, simply on the basis of a few numbers that you type in.

➤ *Comparative data* It can be a big help to compare your company's financial ratios with those of other successful businesses in your field. It's quite possible you'll find at least one way in which you can make major improvements; inconsistencies between your profile and others will stand out vividly. It's also helpful to see the ratios of companies that haven't done well, so that you might avoid their mistakes.

➤ *Graphics* Ratios, comparisons, and events that change with time all lend themselves to graphical analysis. A good ratio analysis package will generate graphs in various forms, helping you spot trends and see ways in which things can be improved. When you need to scrutinize things in detail, analytical graphics can bring out all the subtleties and provide maximum accuracy. For reports, presentation graphics can lend a high-quality appearance for the benefit of clients, investors, etc.

➤ *Report composition* Some packages provide templates and simple word processing software, so you can generate professional-looking reports. There might also be some helpful tips on organization and how best to get your point across.

➤ *Help* A good ratio analysis package will contain on-disk help and online help (preferably via a toll-free number) that can clear up confusion you might have while learning how to use the package. Such help often includes tutorials, so you'll know what all those ratios mean when your computer lists and graphs them. Of course, you might want to hire a knowledgeable outside consultant to make recommendations and help you interpret data.

See also ANALYTICAL GRAPHICS, BUSINESS SOFTWARE, PERSONAL FINANCE SOFTWARE, *and* PRESENTATION GRAPHICS.

README

README refers to text files that contain special instructions on the use of software. README files have updates or special information not included in the manuals provided with application programs. You can easily locate such files by viewing the directory on a diskette. The filename is usually something like README, READ.ME, READ-ME, README.DOC, or README.TXT.

When you first set up a new software package, look for README files, and then carefully go through them. It's a good idea to print them out and insert the hardcopy in the instruction manual(s) because README files frequently have addenda and errata that can save you trouble when using the software. The files might also save you a call to the online help service, by providing answers to frequently asked questions.

Read-only memory

Read-only memory (ROM) is a form of semiconductor memory that is programmed more or less permanently into an integrated circuit (IC, also called a "chip"). While random-access memory (RAM) constantly varies, requiring only a keystroke or a mouse click to change, ROM stays put.

Nonvolatile memory. ROM is a form of *nonvolatile memory*, meaning that it is retained when power is removed from the circuit. Nonvolatile memory has some big assets, the main one being that you never have to worry about losing the data in ROM, even if your computer sits idle for years. The data in ROM is not easy to change. It can be accessed, in whole or in part, but not written over without going to some trouble.

A standard ROM chip is programmed at the factory. This permanent programming is called *firmware*. Most computer users never think about the ROM in their machines. The firmware programs run automatically, without any need for you to worry about them. When you switch your PC on, it comes to life by itself, requiring only a few seconds for the ROM to oversee the routines.

Programmable ROM. Some ROM chips can be reprogrammed. These are called *programmable ROMs (PROMs)*. In an *erasable programmable ROM (EPROM)*, the old data is erased by exposing the semiconductor material to ultraviolet (UV) radiation (the same radiation that burns you if you stay out in the sun too long). A window in the chip case lets the UV in. The IC must be taken from the circuit board when it is exposed to the UV. After the data has been erased, the new programs are written onto the chip via a special process. The new data, like the old, is nonvolatile.

Some EPROMs can be erased electrically, rather than with UV. These go by the lengthy name of *electrically erasable programmable read-only memory (EEPROM)*. An EEPROM chip need not be removed from the circuit for reprogramming; because of this, it's more convenient than a standard ROM or EPROM. However, even an EEPROM is not as flexible as a hard disk or diskette.

What's in ROM? The ROM in a computer is contained in a few ICs that are directly linked to the CPU (central processing unit). The data in ROM usually consists of a *BIOS (basic input/output system)*. The BIOS ensures that everything is in working order, and then it runs a *bootstrap program* to set up the operating system. Common operating systems are DOS with or without Windows, IBM OS/2, and Macintosh System 7. The operating system data itself is usually on the hard disk.

In some computers, the operating-system programs are written in ROM, rather than on the hard disk. The main advantage of ROM-based operating-system software is that it speeds up the bootstrap process. ROM chips aren't cheap, however. Moreover, if the operating system is in firmware, it's much harder to change than if it's written on the hard disk. If your computer had its operating system in ROM and you wanted to upgrade, you'd either have to reprogram the ROM chips (if that were possible) or buy new ones. *See also* BASIC INPUT/OUTPUT SYSTEM, BOOTSTRAP PROGRAM, FIRMWARE, NONVOLATILE MEMORY, OPERATING SYSTEM, *and* VOLATILE MEMORY.

Read-write head

See HEAD.

Real-time

Real-time refers to processing that must meet strict deadlines, or else risk failure. The term applies especially to computers.

Real-time operation is convenient for storing and verifying data quickly. This is the case, for example, when making airline reservations, checking a credit card, or making a bank transaction. Real-time operation is not always necessary. For example, in a big system, it's a waste of expensive computer time to write a long program at an active terminal. Long programs are best written offline, tested in real-time, and then debugged offline.

When using an online service, real-time communication is possible. This requires some getting used to, because you aren't talking and listening; you're typing and reading instead. It's live communications, and there is practically zero delay. With some systems you can even type and read at the same time, just as some people can talk and listen at the same time.

In contrast, when you leave messages for other people via electronic mail, look at your mailbox, look at a bulletin board, or access a database online, you're not using real-time communications. Instead, it is *time-shifting communications* because there is a delay between the sending and the receipt of the information. This delay can be minutes, or it might be months.

In real-time communication, there is always a direct path between the source workstation and the destination workstation. Although the link might contain several intermediate nodes, the data goes from source to destination without having to be stored anyplace. When communication is not real-time, there is always some data storage medium involved between the source and the destination.

In a large computer system, many users can work in real-time simultaneously from different terminals. The most common method of achieving this is called *time sharing*. The computer pays attention to each terminal for a small increment of time, constantly rotating among

Rear-loading printer

the terminals at a high rate of speed. In a powerful system, time sharing provides convenience for a large number of operators. *See also* ONLINE SERVICE, TIME SHARING, *and* TIME-SHIFTING COMMUNICATIONS.

Rear-loading printer

Most dot-matrix printers use fanfold paper for continuous feed. There are various ways to guide this type of paper through a printer. One method, preferred by some PC users, is to feed the paper in from the rear.

Assets. A *rear-loading printer* can be convenient. You don't need a special shelf for paper. You can place your printer on your desk next to your PC, and put a stack of blank paper behind the printer if the desk is deep enough. Alternatively, if there's room, you can put the paper on the floor under or behind your desk. With the printer adjacent to the main unit, it's easy to adjust the printer without moving from your operating position or straining to reach a separate printer stand.

A rear-loading printer pulls fanfold paper through, sheet after sheet, even if you're not at the workstation. While the first few pages are printing, you should make sure the paper stacks up neatly on the floor in front of the operating desk (see the drawing). Once it has been set up and is running smoothly, the printer will type out hundreds of pages with a minimum of supervision.

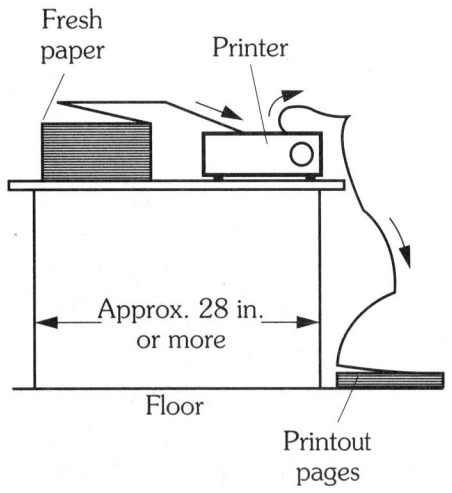

Fresh paper can be set behind the printer; paper emerging from the printer can stack up on the floor.

Drawbacks. Don't stray too far from a rear-loading printer while it's running. If you start a long printing session and then go to the grocery store, the fanfold paper might "hang up" at a fold (some brands are worse about this than others). Then, instead of stacking nicely on the floor, the paper will curl and twist all over the room.

You might not like the appearance of a big box of paper on your operating table. You can get around this by taking about 400 sheets out of the paper box, separating it at one fold, and setting the stack, rather than the whole box, of paper behind the printer. *See also* BOTTOM-LOADING PRINTER, FANFOLD PAPER, FRONT-LOADING PRINTER, *and* TRACTOR FEED.

Recalculation

In a spreadsheet, mathematical operations (such as sum and average) are performed on rows and columns of numbers. *Recalculation* is the process by which the spreadsheet is updated when any of the numbers change.

Cells, rows, and columns. Basically, a spreadsheet is arranged like a ledger into a grid of rectangles, some or all of which are filled in with numbers. Each individual space in a spreadsheet is called a *cell*. The cells are arranged in columns and rows. The columns are usually designated by letters (A, B, C, D, etc.), and the rows by numbers (1, 2, 3, 4, etc.). Thus, each cell is uniquely identified by its column letter and its row number, such as A1, B3, and H12.

Perhaps you've worked with financial ledgers. If so, you know that there are two ways you can add up the numbers: by column and by row. When you add up all the numbers in every column of a ledger, you get a row of numbers at the bottom, which you can then add to get a grand total. When you add all the numbers in each row, you get a column of numbers on the right side of the ledger; the numbers in this column can be added together to obtain a grand total. These grand totals should always be the same. If they disagree, you've made an error. Such an error can be a blatant addition or subtraction mistake, or it might be the result of something more subtle.

Old ways. One of the biggest assets of computers is that they can do huge quantities of arithmetic work without making any errors. This takes a tremendous workload off accountants, small-business bookkeepers, tax professionals, and anyone else who works with numbers. However, the results a computer provides are only as good as the program and its operation. Tables A and B, appearing on the next page, provide two examples of how spreadsheet recalculation, incompletely done, can result in confusion.

These tables show two simple spreadsheets filled in with sums of money. The upper spreadsheets in tables A and B are identical. The column totals are shown along the bottom in row 5; the row totals are shown at the right in column E. The grand total, $460.00, is shown in the lower-right corner, in cell E5.

Now suppose that 50 cents is added to the amounts in each of the cells A1, B2, C3, and D4. This will obviously increase the grand total

Recalculation

Table A Column-wise recalculation

	A	B	C	D	E
1	10.00	20.00	30.00	40.00	**100.00**
2	11.00	22.00	33.00	44.00	**110.00**
3	12.00	24.00	36.00	48.00	**120.00**
4	13.00	26.00	39.00	52.00	**130.00**
5	**46.00**	**92.00**	**138.00**	**184.00**	**460.00**

	A	B	C	D	E
1	10.50	20.00	30.00	40.00	**100.00**
2	11.00	22.50	33.00	44.00	**110.00**
3	12.00	24.00	36.50	48.00	**120.00**
4	13.00	26.00	39.00	52.50	**130.00**
5	**46.50**	**92.50**	**138.50**	**184.50**	**???.??**

Table B Row-wise recalculation

	A	B	C	D	E
1	10.00	20.00	30.00	40.00	**100.00**
2	11.00	22.00	33.00	44.00	**110.00**
3	12.00	24.00	36.00	48.00	**120.00**
4	13.00	26.00	39.00	52.00	**130.00**
5	**46.00**	**92.00**	**138.00**	**184.00**	**460.00**

	A	B	C	D	E
1	10.50	20.00	30.00	40.00	**100.50**
2	11.00	22.50	33.00	44.00	**110.50**
3	12.00	24.00	36.50	48.00	**120.50**
4	13.00	26.00	39.00	52.50	**130.50**
5	**46.00**	**92.00**	**138.00**	**184.00**	**???.??**

by two dollars, because 50 cents has been added to the overall total four times. It will increase each column subtotal by 50 cents, and each row subtotal by 50 cents. In older spreadsheet programs, there were two methods by which spreadsheets could be updated: *column-wise recalculation* and *row-wise recalculation*. Both of these were subject to error.

In the lower spreadsheet of table A, column-wise recalculation has been done, but row-wise recalculation has not. Each of the column subtotals has increased by 50 cents. The row subtotals have not changed because no recalculation has been done for the rows. What, then, is the grand total in cell E5? If the subtotals in column E are added, as would seem to be consistent with the philosophy of column-wise recalculation, the result will be $460.00 for the grand total. That's wrong. To get the right result, the subtotals in row 5 must be added up.

In the lower spreadsheet of Table B, row-wise recalculation has been done, but column-wise recalculation hasn't. Each of the row subtotals has increased by 50 cents; the column subtotals haven't changed. Again, there's confusion about the grand total. If the row-5 subtotals are added, the result is $460.00 for the grand total, which is wrong. In this case the subtotals for column E must be summed.

Clearly, both the row and the column totals must be updated if the recalculation of this spreadsheet is to be accurate. Unfortunately, in some older spreadsheets, inexperienced users sometimes failed to take this sort of thing into account. Errors resulted. Newer spreadsheet programs do *automatic recalculation* for you.

New ways. Whenever you change any number in the spreadsheets shown in the tables, three other numbers will also change. For example, increasing the amount in cell B1 from $20.00 to $21.00 will cause the amounts in cells E1, B5, and E5 all to go up by one dollar. None of the other values will be affected. A good spreadsheet program will make the necessary changes, but no others.

Spreadsheets are usually larger than the ones shown in the tables, and the functions are more complicated. However, the same basic principles apply, no matter what the size or complexity of a spreadsheet. First, a logical order must be established in which calculations are to be carried out. This is similar to the principle of precedence in algebra. Second, the algorithm must be such that errors of the sort depicted by the tables do not occur.

The main advantage of automatic calculation is that the spreadsheet is constantly updated; it's always consistent with itself. When working with a very large spreadsheet, however, automatic recalculation proceeds rather slowly because numerous computations are required every time you change the value in any cell. Things can be speeded up in such cases by *manual recalculation*. In this mode, you can change numbers in various cells, and the machine will wait until you issue a command (by pressing a key or clicking on an icon) to recalculate. Then the recalculation is done all at once, saving time. The trouble with this scheme is that, if you get distracted and forget to give the recalculate command before storing your work, errors will be introduced into the spreadsheet. See also PRECEDENCE and SPREADSHEET.

Record

In a database, a *record* is a collection of anywhere from one to hundreds of pieces of information, all of which are related in some way. The individual pieces of data that comprise a record are known as *fields*.

Suppose you have information about 100 people stored in a database. This information is contained in 100 data records. Each record might contain the following fields:

- Last name
- First name
- Address
- City
- State
- Country
- Zipcode
- Telephone number
- Occupation
- Miscellaneous data

If you were to organize this in a manila file folder, you'd probably have one sheet of paper listing the data for each person. So in all, you'd have 100 sheets of paper, and each page would represent one data record. *See also* DATABASE *and* FIELD.

Recto page

See BINDING OFFSET.

Recursion

Recursion is a self-referential logical process. It is useful in proving mathematical theorems, and is also employed in some legal arguments. On the way to the final goal, or solution to a problem, it is often necessary to take detours.

The objective. Recursion can be intricate; it is one of the most advanced forms of reasoning. For recursion to work, however, the overall direction of progress must always be toward the final goal. Sidetracking might sometimes seem to have nothing to do with the intended result, but in recursion, there is always a reason for it. All the sub-arguments must eventually be brought out and put to some use in the main argument.

Computers are ideally suited for recursive arguments. The sub-arguments can be done and the results put into memory. Humans tend to get confused when there are too many sidetracks, but this does not happen with computers. Computers do precisely what they are programmed to do; they don't get distracted, no matter how many sidetracks there are.

In a complicated recursive argument, the sidetracks can be backed up one on top of another, like airplanes in a holding pattern waiting to land at a large airport. The sub-arguments are held in *pushdown stacks*, or *first-in/last-out* memory registers. The sidetracked results are pulled out of the stacks when needed.

Hangups. If you use recursive logic and get sidetracked too much, you might lose sight of your final objective or go around and around in your mind. This is *unbounded recursion*, sometimes called a *death spiral*. It is not true reasoning because it does nothing toward completing a proof or solving a problem. In a computer, unbounded recursion leads to stack overflows, with consequences similar to those that occur in an endless loop. Another logical trap into which you can fall when making a recursive argument is to "prove" something by inherently assuming that it is already true.

Improper use of recursion can result in a meaningless conclusion or a contradiction. Logicians say, "From a contradiction, anything follows." Suppose a lawyer-computer proves "beyond all reasonable doubt" that Joe is both guilty and not guilty of a crime of which he has been accused. Then logically, the law is invalid, and everyone can legally break it from that day forward. This would be refuted by reasonable human beings, but a malfunctioning or misprogrammed computer could regard it as a valid conclusion. This example has been used to argue against the suggestion that computers can effectively serve as lawyers and judges.

A wise machine? One of the most ambitious dreams of computer engineers is to build recursion into a machine with artificial intelligence (AI). This might result in a computer with the reasoning power of the best lawyers and the most famous mathematicians.

Imagine a supercomputer that could outwit any private eye and could solve problems that would take even a brilliant scientist centuries to unravel! Such a machine would be more than smart—it would actually be wise. Researchers are unsure whether computers can evolve to such a level of AI, but the only way to find out if a goal is attainable is to work towards it. If "machine wisdom" is ever developed, it might take forms alien to human thought, thereby giving us new insights into reasoning processes. *See also* ARTIFICIAL INTELLIGENCE, ENDLESS LOOP, NESTED LOOPS, PROBLEM REDUCTION, *and* PUSHDOWN STACK.

Recycling

Computer users can save money and minimize waste by modifying their computing habits. Three things you can do are recycle spent or

Recycling

used materials when possible, buy recycled materials or used hardware, and strive to get maximum life from hardware.

PC hardware. Here are some earth-friendly suggestions concerning the use and disposal of computer hardware:

➢ *Your old PC* If you're ready to buy a new computer, what do you plan to do with your old one? Certainly, if it still works, you shouldn't just throw it away. You might be able to use it as a second PC, or put it to secondary use at your main workstation. Even if it isn't a fast machine, you might use it for printing while you do more sophisticated work on the new machine. Perhaps someone else in your family can use your old PC.

➢ *Your new PC* You can save money by shopping around for a slightly used machine. If you're not interested in all the very latest gadgets, you probably don't need the cutting-edge microprocessor that everyone is talking about. In fact, a certain amount of skepticism is a good thing when it comes to fresh-from-the-lab technology. A "techie" who upgrades every six months can probably give you a great deal on a very good, slightly used, well-cared-for computer, and might even offer inside tips concerning its operation.

➢ *Packing materials* Foamed plastic, in its myriad forms, is almost universally employed in shipping computers and peripherals. When you receive a piece of hardware in a package, always save the box and the packing material. Then, when it's necessary to ship or transport the hardware, you can pack it up again, and be sure it's properly protected. If you must throw out foamed plastic, recycle it according to whatever procedure is standard in your area. Don't dispose of foamed plastic by burning; this produces dangerous fumes.

➢ *Batteries* Some computer manufacturers accept dead batteries for recycling. There are several types of batteries used in computers. Laptop PCs usually have nickel-cadmium (NICAD) or nickel-metal-hydride (NiMH) batteries. Most computers have clocks that run from lithium batteries. Some laptops have lead-acid batteries. NICAD batteries present an environmental hazard because they contain cadmium, which is toxic. Never dispose of NICAD batteries by tossing them in with the regular garbage. Contact your local waste-disposal authority for instructions.

➢ *Diskettes* Diskettes have a way of accumulating in workstations over the years. While diskettes can be reused many times, they're often employed for file backup, and then stored away and forgotten. Periodically, you should check to see how many of these old diskettes can have their files moved to some other medium, and then reformatted so they can be used again. You might be astonished at how many "new" diskettes you can obtain in this way. Diskettes with bad sectors ought to be discarded, however; there's no point in running the risk of losing valuable data. Even after a bad diskette is resectored, it is suspect. Bad sectors tend to keep developing once the process has started. Check with your local waste-disposal authorities concerning how to recycle diskettes.

➤ *Diskette alternatives* In recent years, methods of mass storage have become available that are far more space-efficient than diskettes. A single tape, for example, can store as much data as 200 or more diskettes. Tapes are widely used for backing up hard disk data. It's also possible to put archives on CD-ROM using a write-once/read-many (WORM) drive. New technologies are rapidly developing in this area, so keep an eye out for them. If you own a business that creates huge amounts of archival data, a tape drive can pay for itself in a short time; it frees up hundreds of diskettes for recycling. In addition to all this, data compression can multiply the effective space of any storage medium.

Printers. Printers are notorious for the volume of waste they create. Here are some suggestions for the use of printers and their supplies:

➤ *Minimize use* While computers have the potential for reducing the amount of printed matter in the world, the reality has been quite the opposite. The so-called paperless office has been, so far, only a figment of idealists' imaginations.

People seem to have an addiction to generating paper documents, whether necessary or not. Try to break that habit. Don't use the printer unless you must. Use the monitor or display for proofreading and general work as much as possible. When you must use the printer, try to get as much data on each page as possible. Use draft printing mode whenever you can get away with it; it will put less wear and tear on the printer, and save ink or toner.

➤ *Paper* Computer paper can be recycled. You can also buy recycled paper for use in your printer. If you work in an office, you can set an example for other workers to follow. You'll need to find a company that buys used paper for recycling. You'll also have to figure out how to get the paper to them; preferably they'll come by periodically and pick it up from you. The paper buyer will probably want you to remove nonpaper items like staples, tape, and paper clips from the paper. They might want you to sort the paper, too. While all this might seem like a lot of work, it can ultimately result in a bigger profit margin for your company or more money in your own bank account.

➤ *Toner* Laser printers and photocopying machines use cartridges containing a compound called *toner*. This is the stuff that makes the printout crisp and dark. Several companies

Reduced-instruction-set computing

collect spent toner cartridges, refill them, and sell the refilled cartridges at a lower price than you can get them new. Toner cartridges can be refilled several times in this way. You benefit twice: once by selling or giving empty cartridges to the refilling company, and again by buying used cartridges rather than new ones. In a medium-sized corporation over the course of a year, this can save thousands of dollars and spare local landfills dozens or hundreds of dumped (but still good) toner cartridges.

➢ *Ink and ribbons* The ink containers in inkjet printers can be refilled and reused in a manner similar to the way toner cartridges are recycled for laser printers. You can have this done by a company that specializes in it. The ribbons used with dot-matrix printers can be re-inked; there are companies that do that, too. Most dot-matrix printer ribbons have a provision for re-inking themselves once. When the type gets light, just use a sharp object and push back the metal tab through the little hole provided for this purpose. (Instructions can be found on the ribbon or on the shipping carton.)

For further information. An excellent book called *The Green PC* by Steven Anzovin (Windcrest/McGraw-Hill, 1993) describes many ways you can improve the overall earth-friendliness of your computing habits. Chapter 5 contains extensive information about recycling, including a long list of companies and organizations that can help you get your own program going. *See also* DATA COMPRESSION, ENVIRONMENTAL RESOURCES, FILE COMPRESSION UTILITY, GREEN COMPUTING, LAPTOP COMPUTER, NICKEL-CADMIUM AND NICKEL-METAL-HYDRIDE BATTERIES, *and* REMOVABLE DATA STORAGE MEDIA.

Reduced-instruction-set computing

One of the most important aspects of computer power is the raw speed at which the machine works. Even if a computer can store massive amounts of data, its level of intelligence is limited by how fast it can process the data. Overall computer speed can be measured in several ways; one common method is to specify the number of instructions per second (IPS).

Instructions versus speed. When a computer processes information, it must carry out *every* single instruction. It is always best to keep the number of instructions as small as possible. The fewer instructions needed to accomplish some task, the faster the task can be done, all other things being equal. Computers are getting faster in general, capable of moving more data from place to place, but sheer processing speed isn't the only way to make data move faster. The data might itself be simplified. This requires a substantial change in the way a computer works.

Reduced-instruction-set computing (RISC) involves data that is organized somewhat differently than the traditional complex-

Reduced-instruction-set computing

instruction-set computing (CISC). One microprocessor that can take advantage of RISC architecture is the PowerPC chip, the product of a joint effort among IBM, Apple and Motorola. The drawing is a simplified block diagram of a computer using a PowerPC microprocessor.

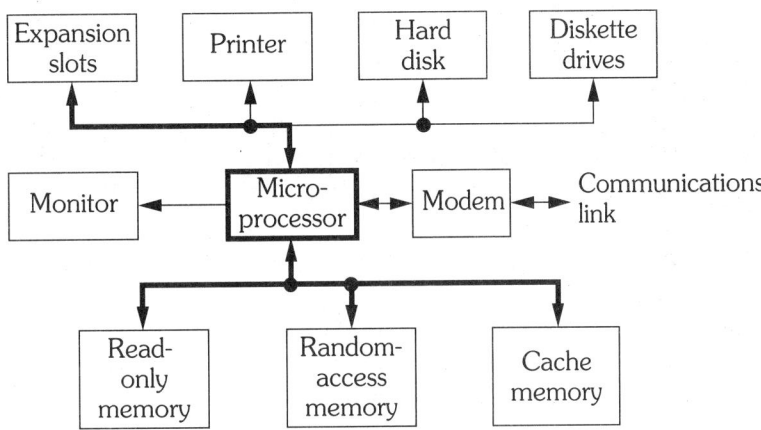

Simplified block diagram of RISC system. Heavy lines show 64-bit buses; others are 32-bit, 16-bit, or 8-bit.

An analogy. Consider the files in which this book was written. The text file PC.A contains all the article titles starting with A, PC.B has all the article titles starting with B, and so on. This article was written in file PC.R. To find this article, you would first access PC.R, and then scroll down until you got to this title. That wouldn't take long. The same would be true for any other title. If a title wasn't in this book, it wouldn't require much effort to find that out.

Suppose the articles had each been given a separate file, say a number from 0001.PC (for the first article) to xxxx.PC (for the last one). To find an article, you would have to guess its number. Suppose you were looking for the article "Robot." You might guess 0423.PC, and get "Microprocessor." You'd figure that "Robot" was in a file with a larger number than 0423.PC; your next guess might be 0999.PC. Suppose this came up as "Virus"; then you'd know that "Robot" must have a number greater than 0423.PC and less than 0999.PC. You'd call up something like 0733.PC, which should be closer to "Robot." However, there's a problem here: "Robot" is not an article title in this book. You'd have to keep checking files until you finally deduced that "Robot" is not an article title. You'd have done a lot of work for nothing.

Clearly, it is far better to have one computer file for each letter of the alphabet, rather than one file for each individual article, because it saves work when you want to find something. Organizing the data by letter of the alphabet is something like RISC architecture, while having each article occupy its own file is more like the CISC scheme. With

Reductionism

fewer files, data can be accessed faster, as long as the organization is clear and logical.

Applications. The RISC scheme is not always better than CISC. Programs must be more detailed with RISC than with CISC. Software isn't always compatible between the two architectures.

Sometimes, the high speed of RISC is not important enough to warrant the revised, more sophisticated programs that are needed. Simple word processing is one such application. Most people find an inexpensive PC, based on a CISC chip such as the 486, more than adequate for writing letters, memos, papers, or books.

In advanced applications such as artificial intelligence (AI), robotics, and virtual reality, high computer speed is necessary. Such applications require the processing of huge quantities of data. Every possible means of speed enhancement becomes worth considering. To support the increased processing power, larger memory capacity is needed. Memory technology has been steadily advancing. New schemes for data storage are constantly being tested and developed.

In some high-level applications, RISC technology holds promise. In complex graphics, multimedia and animation, it works well. The RISC architecture is also good in mathematical and scientific applications that require massive calculating power. *See also* COMPLEX-INSTRUCTION-SET COMPUTING, COMPUTER POWER, INSTRUCTIONS PER SECOND, *and* POWERPC CHIP.

Reductionism

Reductionism is the belief or theory that all human thought can be duplicated by machines. Can everything you think and feel be reduced to logical digits, or to some other form of machine reasoning, such as that of a neural network? A reductionist would say yes.

Although the human brain is far more sophisticated than any computer yet devised, a brain is made of a finite number of cells. For any finite number, no matter how large, there exists a larger number. The reductionist will say that your thoughts and feelings are the result of biological switches working in a huge number of ways, and that there is absolutely nothing more to it. If your brain has a zillion little switches, then it is theoretically possible to manufacture a computer with two zillion little switches. In theory, such a computer could be smarter than you are.

If the reductionists are right, computers might someday acquire life. Some researchers are enthusiastic about this; others fear what might happen. One of those who fears reductionism is Joseph Weizenbaum. He sees a dark side to the idea: reductionistic arguments might be used to justify the treatment of people as automatons. This argument is countered by those who point out that, throughout history, whole classes of people have been treated like machines, whether or not there was any supporting rationale. They assert that the way people treat each other has nothing to do with the sorts of computers they aspire to manufacture.

A more likely scenario is that humans might reduce themselves to servants of the machines they have made. This could happen insidiously, as people and societies gradually and unwittingly become over-reliant on computers. Some people think this has already begun to happen. *See also* ARTIFICIAL LIFE, COMPUTER OVER-RELIANCE, *and* WEIZENBAUM, JOSEPH.

Reengineering

When a business switches from a paper-based, "manual" system of recordkeeping to a computerized system, it's often necessary to change the organization of the business. This might be a minor adjustment or a big restructuring. The process is called *reengineering*.

Considerations. If you decide you want to automate a corporation, you don't just purchase a computer or a local area network (LAN), and then expect everything to work at increased efficiency. Major decisions and changes must be made in several areas, including the following:

- *Hardware* How many computers do you need: just one computer for your whole organization; several computers, one for each department; hundreds of computers so every employee has one; or some combination? How much hard disk capacity will be necessary? How many printers will you need? How about modems, diskette drives, and other peripherals? Who needs what? To help you make these decisions, you might want to hire a consultant. The money you save in the first year alone can amount to several times the consultant's fee.

- *Software* You'll have to decide what software you'll need and what level of sophistication is best for your business. You'll probably want a word processor for writing letters, a database for keeping track of inventory, and a spreadsheet for bookkeeping. You might also want some kind of graphics package. As with the hardware decisions, a consultant can be helpful here. There are hundreds of different software packages that will compete for your money.

- *Training* Each person who uses the computer system will have to learn how to work with the machines. Some employees will have cyberphobia (a fear of computers) and will have a big problem just getting over prejudices against the machines. Others might find the computers too much fun and will use them to make a lot of unnecessary work for themselves. All of them will need to spend hours getting proficient at the software you've chosen.

➤ *Task shifting* The way departments are organized in a noncomputerized company isn't necessarily the best scheme for an automated business. For example, before you installed the computer system, you might have had two secretaries typing all letters, but when each employee, or at least each department head, has a computer terminal, they might do at least some of their own correspondence.

➤ *Morale* Automation can give rise to fears among employees that they'll become obsolete and will consequently be laid off. For example, what will happen to the two secretaries when the department heads type some correspondence themselves? Computers can and do replace people, but there are some things, such as taking orders by telephone, that computers can't do well. While no business manager likes to lay people off, it's sometimes an economic necessity. Alternatively, reassignment can be done; this, too, can have an adverse effect on morale. The negatives must be balanced against whatever advantage automation is expected to have.

➤ *True need* Some businesses operate just fine without automation. Perhaps your company has a low-end PC, purchased years ago for reasons now forgotten, which is collecting dust from lack of use. If you don't need to automate your business, and if the employees in general don't want to do it, you shouldn't do it. A small-town grocery, for example, might never need a computer. A wise businessperson knows when improvements aren't necessary or desirable and does not make changes that will do no good.

An example. Suppose you're the manager of the service department in a small wholesale distributing company that imports two-way radios, camcorders, and videocassette recorders from overseas. Your job involves several duties: overseeing the work of three repair technicians, handling customer complaints and special requests by letter and by telephone, working with the retail dealer network, ordering repair parts from the manufacturer, and over-the-counter sales for those rare occasions when people come in off the street wanting to buy your products.

You begin to think that perhaps a computer could help you manage your work more efficiently. You have several reasons for this. First, you've had a few embarrassing experiences with customers who have had to send equipment in several times for repair. Second, you'd like to know how many of each item that each dealer buys every month, quarter, or year. Third, there are a few dealers who seem to complain often, and you'd like to keep better track of their problems. Finally, you'd like to see which technicians do the best work, in terms of equipment returned again after having been previously repaired.

You decide you can use a 486-based PC with a hard disk of at least 200 megabytes. You also decide you need a low-end word processing program, a good graphical database program, and software that will do analytical graphics. You convince the company president to make the purchases. This request is expedited when you point out that the entire reengineering burden will fall on you, and that the results will be evident in improved customer and dealer relations, better quality of work by the technicians, and clearer reports as to what's going on in the service department.

Downtime. No matter how helpful a computer system might be, it's of no use if it goes down. If there's no backup plan in case of computer failure, the consequences of a breakdown might be more than mere inconvenience. Overconfidence in a computer system can easily lead to computer over-reliance, with the potential for major embarrassment at best, and disaster at worst.

A well-designed computer system, especially when used in a large corporation, should not be subject to catastrophic failure. Instead, if one part of the system goes down, other parts should take up the slack until the problem is fixed. This scheme, known as *graceful degradation*, should be part of any reengineering plan.

See also BUSINESS SOFTWARE, CATASTROPHIC FAILURE, COMPUTER OVER-RELIANCE, CYBERPHOBIA, DATABASE, GRACEFUL DEGRADATION, GRAPHICS, SPREADSHEET, *and* WORD PROCESSING.

Relation

A *relation* is a mapping between sets of numbers, quantities, or objects. Relations are important in science, economics, and mathematics.

The drawing at A (page 942) shows a simple relation between two point sets X and Y. Not every element x in set X necessarily has a counterpart in set Y. Also, not all the y's in set Y necessarily have counterparts in X. It's possible for more than one element of set X to be mapped onto a single element in set Y; also, more than one element of set Y might have a mate in set X. As you can see, there aren't many restrictions concerning what can and can't be a relation.

Relations can exist between continuous sets, such as the real numbers. These relations are generally portrayed as graphs. The drawing at B shows a familiar relation between real-number variables x and y in the Cartesian coordinate system. This is the so-called unit circle, centered at the origin $(x,y) = (0,0)$ and having a radius of 1. The formula for this relation is

$$x^2 + y^2 = 1$$

If a relation has certain specific properties, it is called a *function*. Functions are the basis for much of mathematical analysis. Computers

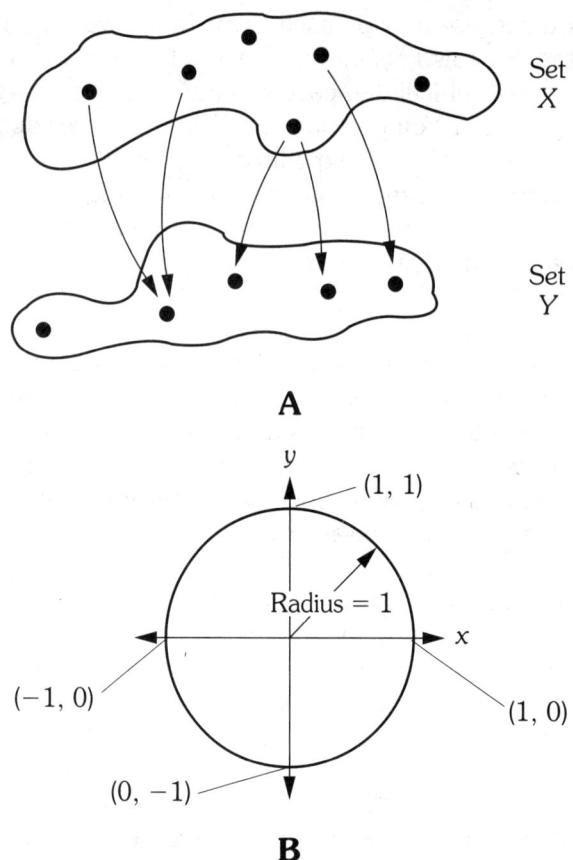

At A, a simple mapping between point sets. At B, the unit circle.

are useful for illustrating all kinds of functions and relations, whether they are discrete (as in the example in drawing A) or continuous (as in the example in drawing B). The most common method of using a PC to render relations is *analytical graphics. See also* ANALYTICAL GRAPHICS, DEPENDENT VARIABLE, DOMAIN OF FUNCTION, FUNCTION, INDEPENDENT VARIABLE, *and* RANGE OF FUNCTION.

Release number

Computer software is constantly being improved. You've probably seen numbers advertised for software, like DOS 5.0, 5.1, and 6.0. In general, the higher the number, the more recently the software was developed.

The *release number* of a software program is the number after the decimal point. If you read about version 6.0 of some program, and then somewhere else you read about version 6.1 of the program, you know that version 6.1 was developed after version 6.0.

Release numbers represent relatively minor upgrades in software. Thus, while version 6.1 of a given program might in theory be more powerful than version 6.0, the difference is not major. There's even a possibility that the program with the later release number has a few bugs that the earlier program did not have.

When a big, or fundamental, change is made to a computer software program, the number in front of the decimal point is increased. If you hear about version 7.0 of some program, it probably represents a radical leap from version 6.1. Again, however, it's possible that there are some new bugs in version 7.0 that did not exist in version 6.1. *See also* BUG *and* VERSION NUMBER.

Reliability

Reliability is a measure of how well, and for how long, machines keep working. It can be expressed in many different ways. Two common specifications for reliability are *mean time before failure* and *mean time between failures*, both abbreviated *MTBF*.

Reliability can be expressed as the proportion of units that still work after they have been used for a certain length of time. Suppose a million units are placed in operation on January 1, 2010. If 920,000 units are operating properly on January 1, 2011, then the reliability is 0.92, or 92% per year. On January 1, 2012, you can expect that 920,000 × 0.92, or 846,400, units will be working. The number of working units declines according to the reliability factor, year after year.

The better the reliability, the flatter the decay curve in a graph of working units versus time. This is shown in the drawing. The terms *excellent*, *good*, *fair*, and *poor* are relative, and depend on many different factors. A perfect reliability curve (100%) is always a horizontal line on such a graph.

Reliability is a function of design, as well as of the quality of manufacture and parts. Even if a machine is ruggedly constructed and

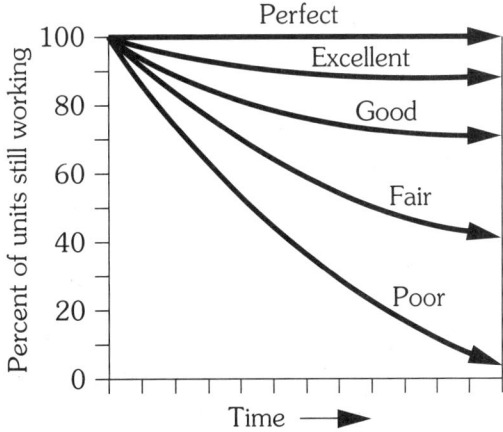

The better the reliability, the greater the proportion of units still working after a given time.

the components are of good quality, failure is more likely with poor design than with good design. Reliability can be optimized by a quality-assurance-and-control (QA/QC) procedure.

In an indirect sense, reliability depends on how well users treat the equipment. Improper installation, inept operation, or the subjection of a computer to extreme conditions (such as heat, cold, salt spray, vibration, or electromagnetic fields) will make it less reliable. Generally, any specification for reliability is based on the assumption that the equipment will be properly set up and cared for. *See also* MEAN TIME BEFORE FAILURE/BETWEEN FAILURES *and* QUALITY ASSURANCE AND CONTROL.

Remote control systems

Imagine that you're on an airplane flight, and you have your laptop PC in front of you, working on a project. You encounter a problem: you need some data that's stored in your home PC, not on the hard disk in your laptop. You pick up the telephone on the seat-back in front of you, connect your laptop to the telephone via the internal modem, and call your home PC. You get the data you need, and in fact, you have access to most other features of your home computer. *Remote control systems* like this, consisting of hardware and software that allows a computer to be operated from a long distance away, have been available for some time.

What you need. The drawing is a simplified block diagram showing the main components of the remote control system needed for this situation. When you remotely operate a computer, the machine you're sitting at is the *remote computer*, while the one you're controlling or accessing is the *host computer*. In the airplane scenario, the laptop on the airplane is the remote unit and the home PC is the host. Obviously, for remote control to be possible, there must be at least one remote unit and at least one host unit.

You'll need a modem to connect the remote unit to the telephone line. There must also be a modem at the host computer site. The modems should have the highest operating speed possible. The speed with which you can carry out remote-control functions will be limited by the slower modem.

You'll also need remote-control software at both sites, so you can look at directories, access data files, and run applications such as word processing, database, spreadsheet, and graphics from the host. You'll be able to store your work on the host machine or the remote machine, or both.

Features. There are various remote-control software programs available, some with basic features only, and others with esoteric capabilities. Here are a few of the features you can look for:

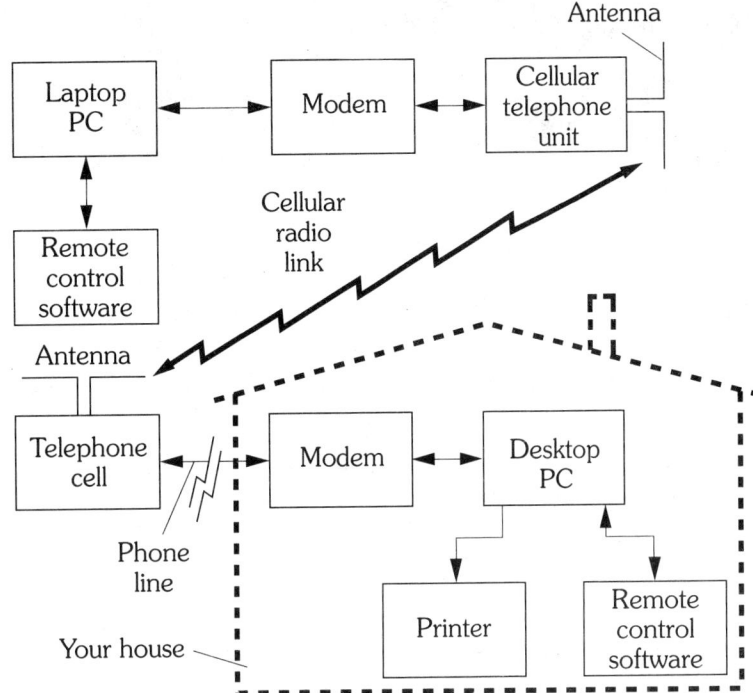

A home computer can be run remotely via a laptop PC on an airplane.

➢ *Operating system flexibility*   Remote-control programs are available for DOS, Windows, Macintosh System 7, IBM OS/2, and other operating systems. You'll want to be sure the software you buy is compatible with your operating systems.

➢ *Networking*   Remote control is a big asset when running on networks. In fact, you can set up a wide-area network (WAN) with one large host computer and numerous remote machines. You might want to have several remote units in operation at once with a single host.

➢ *Multiple hosts*   If you need to access more than one host computer, the software must be compatible among all the machines being used. High-end remote-control programs can let you see and work with several screens, in rotating sequence, switching with a keystroke.

➢ *Modem specifications*   You'll need to determine the range of modem speeds and the types of modems with which your system will work. Ideally, the software should support speeds of 115,200 bits per second (bps) or more.

➢ *Unattended host*   You'll want to power-up, operate, and power-down a host computer even when there is no one attending it. This will be the case, for example, if you're on a trip and need to work with your home PC. In a network situation, there might be a person at the host computer, making this feature unnecessary.

Remote control systems

> *"Chat" mode* This allows you to use online services or communicate with someone attending the host computer. It can also allow the users of remote PCs to communicate with each other through the host PC. This capability has the potential for abuse, however; thus, there might be a time limitation to keep telephone tolls from soaring.

> *Time limitation* Some remote-control systems, especially those with multiple remotes, allow for a time limitation. This can be useful in networks when telephone tolls are involved. The time limit can be programmed in advance. In a network, this can help ensure that the remote users make efficient use of host computer time.

> *Printing* You might want to have the host computer print data. For this to be possible, a printer with automatic paper feed is necessary. Most modern printers have this feature.

> *Call logging* With call logging, every time the host computer is accessed from a remote unit, the call is noted, including the date, time, and duration of the call. If there is more than one remote unit in the system, the identity of each unit is also logged.

> *Hierarchical passwords* Also called *multilevel password protection*, this is a security feature that prevents unauthorized use of the host computer. The password levels allow users various degrees of control over the host machine. A retry limitation prevents hackers from making repeated guesses at passwords in an attempt to break into the system.

> *Online help* Most sophisticated software packages have a provision for calling a toll-free number and getting assistance online. If you are having trouble from a remote computer, you can have the host call the online help number, and then you can communicate with technicians in real-time.

Some software packages have features not mentioned here. Some might not have all of these capabilities. You'll want to see several programs in action before choosing one for your system. The usual shopping advice applies here: Don't hurry, get brochures, and visit a reputable dealer (or two or three). Perhaps you have a "PC guru" friend who has a remote-control system already in place, and who is willing to let you try it out.

In personal robotics. Mechanical devices such as personal robots can be operated from a distance by human beings or by computers. A simple example of such a remote-control system is the control box for a television (TV) set. Another example is a transmitter you might have used to fly a model airplane. The TV control employs infrared to carry the data, while the model airplane gets its commands via radio signals. In this sense, both the TV set and the model airplane are robots.

Remote control can be done by wire or by optical fiber links. Undersea robots have been operated in this way. A person sits at a terminal in the comfort of a boat or submarine bubble, and operates a robot, watching a screen that shows what the robot "sees." The range is limited when wires or optical fibers are used. It's impractical to have a cable longer than a few miles.

Propagation delays. When the remote and host machines are very far away from each other, even radio signals take a long time to cover the distance. A remotely controlled machine on the moon is about 1.3 light seconds away. It would be 2.6 seconds from the time a command was sent to a computer or robot on the moon, before the operator would see the results of the command.

The propagation delay is greater in interplanetary space. The fringes of the Solar System are light hours away; the separation distance is on the order of millions or billions of miles. As Voyager passed Neptune and a command was sent to the probe, the results were not observed for hours.

It might seem unlikely today that personal computing will ever involve the remote control of space probes, but in 100 years, consumers might be routinely communicating with computers and machines in deep space. The possibilities are especially intriguing in education. Grade-school children might get a chance to manipulate probes roaming around on Mars or on the moons of Jupiter.

Ultimate range limit. There is an absolute limit to the practical distance that can exist between any remotely controlled device and its operator. There is (as yet) no known way to transmit data faster than the speed of radio waves or visible light. The nearest stars are several light years away; remote control over these distances would require humans to acquire a form of patience that we do not now possess.

Over distances greater than about 50 light years, it would be impossible for anyone to remotely control anything, because the results would not be observable within his or her lifetime. However, computers, with lifespans on the order of millenia, might control robotic star fleets. There's an idea for aspiring science-fiction writers! *See also* FIBEROPTIC DATA TRANSMISSION, LASER COMMUNICATIONS, MICROWAVE DATA TRANSMISSION, MODEM, NETWORK, ONLINE SERVICE, PASSWORD, PERSONAL ROBOTS, SATELLITE DATA TRANSMISSION, TELECOMMUTING, TELEOPERATION, TELEPRESENCE, *and* WIDE-AREA NETWORK.

Removable data storage media

Removable data storage media are any means by which information can be kept outside of a computer, but used with the machine when needed.

Removable data storage media

Diskettes. Magnetic diskettes have traditionally been the most common form of removable storage for casual PC users. Diskettes are cheap, convenient, and reasonably compact. When properly stored, they hold data for years. A single diskette has room for over a megabyte of data, the equivalent of a good-sized novel. There's practically no limit to how many diskettes you can store; some people have hundreds. Even a thousand 5.25-inch "floppies" take up only a few feet of shelf space.

There are some shortcomings to the diskette method of data storage, however. Diskette drives are not fast. They take more time than a hard disk to read and write data. This might not matter when you access a few small files, but when you work with many big files, you'll notice it. High-end software, as well as graphics, require storage in quantities that diskettes aren't suited to handle. One software package can fill dozens of diskettes; a single high-resolution graphic image might occupy a whole high-density floppy. Diskette data is subject to damage by magnetic fields. The contents of a hard disk can be backed up on diskettes, but it is a tedious process. Tapes are preferred for this. *See also* DISKETTE *and* DISKETTE DRIVE.

Removable disk systems. At first glance, a *removable disk system* looks a little like an external diskette drive, but there are some big differences. For one thing, the cartridges don't look exactly like floppies. The drive is bigger, too. More important, a single removable disk cartridge can hold hundreds of megabytes. Thus, per megabyte, the cartridges are far more compact than conventional diskettes.

A special type of removable disk system is the *Bernoulli box*. Similar to a diskette drive, it uses disks that physically resemble floppies, but with the capacity and speed of a hard disk system. The disks spin fast, and are supported partly by air pressure. Some Bernoulli boxes can work with more than one disk at a time. These devices are rugged because of the method by which the head is supported above the disk surface.

A *Floptical diskette and drive* is a removable disk storage system that employs optical devices to aid in the tracking of the read/write head over the surface of the disk. This is also sometimes called *magneto-optical* technology. A Floptical drive will accept most 3.5-inch diskettes. The capacity depends on the diskette density; high-density diskettes are best. Some magneto-optical devices use smaller diskettes and are compact enough to be convenient for use with laptop computers.

Another removable medium can be provided by *PCMCIA standard adapter cards*. These cards, which are the height and width of credit cards (but thicker), can do many other things besides store data. Because the cards are so small, they are ideal for use with portable computers of all types. They have large capacity. Unlike disk systems, they lack moving parts, and are therefore fast and nearly indestructible. Some experts predict that they are destined to become the preferred method of removable data storage among personal computer users, especially those who travel often. They are already in use in many laptop computers, where they function as "removable hard disks."

An optical compact computer disk, more often known as a *CD-ROM*, can store large quantities of data in a read-only form. Once data is written onto a CD-ROM, it is not normally alterable. A write-once/read-many (WORM) drive allows you to make your own CD-ROMs, with a capacity of about 650MB. If your data becomes obsolete or changes, you can make a new CD-ROM from a blank disk. There are machines that erase CD-ROMs for reuse, but they are expensive. The cost is hard to justify because magnetic media has caught up with CD-ROM in terms of capacity. This is not to say that CD-ROM is anywhere near obsolete; one breakthrough could change everything. *See also* BERNOULLI BOX, CD-ROM, FLOPTICAL DISKETTE AND DRIVE, PCMCIA STANDARD ADAPTER CARDS, *and* WRITE-ONCE/READ-MANY.

Tapes. An increasingly popular method of storing computer data is magnetic tape in various forms. This was the preferred storage scheme in early computers, a few of which can still be found in some institutions. Today's tapes are far smaller than the reel-to-reel monstrosities that whirled atop the refrigerator-sized computers of the 1960s, however. For its physical size, a magnetic tape cassette has far greater capacity than a conventional floppy diskette. One cassette can hold enough data to back up a hard disk. Tape systems are economical and reliable, too.

For computer use, the most common tape is the *quarter-inch cartridge (QIC)* available in various sizes, including standard 3.5-inch cassettes. These are much like ordinary cassette tapes, but they work at a higher level of precision. *Digital audio tape (DAT)* can hold data at increased density because of the helical-scan technology employed. Instead of recording the data in straight tracks, DAT records the data in angled "slices," after the fashion of videotape. This makes more effective use of the tape's surface area.

Tape is not good for direct computing. You can't plug in a tape drive and use it as if it were a hard disk or a diskette drive; the access time is too slow. A file might be anywhere along the length of the tape, and the only way to get to it is to fast-forward or rewind. On a hard disk or diskette, no two items are ever separated by more than a few inches. Normally, if you want to use the data on a tape, you must transfer it to your hard disk first. *See also* ARCHIVES, BACKUP, MAGNETIC MEDIA, MAGNETIC TAPE, *and* TAPE DRIVE.

Repagination

When you use a computer to create a report, manuscript, thesis, or other long word-processed document, editing is usually required. Most experienced writers create a "first draft," and then wait several days (or even weeks) before revising it. That way, major errors and problems are easy to see, and the editing process goes smoothly.

Perhaps the biggest asset of word processing software is the fact that it lets you insert, delete, and move words, sentences, and paragraphs with only a few keystrokes or mouse clicks. The days of literal cutting, pasting, and correction fluid are history. It doesn't matter how massive the revision; the word processor takes care of it with no mess.

When you create a manuscript more than a page long, you'll want to number the pages. Most word processing programs do this automatically. Some show page numbers only in printed hardcopy via *running headers/footers*, others indicate page numbers on the screen, as well as in the printout.

After editing a manuscript, the page breaks are almost certain to occur in different places than they did in the first draft. *Repagination* is a feature found in most word processing programs that automatically inserts new page breaks and new page numbers in their proper places. That way, you'll always get a neat printout. *See also* HARD PAGE BREAKS, RUNNING HEADERS/FOOTERS, *and* SOFT PAGE BREAKS.

Repeater

A *repeater* is a device that extends the range of a network or communications circuit. There are several kinds of repeaters, but all work according to the same principle: they receive data, then process it, and finally retransmit it. The output signal is usually sent simultaneously with the input, although some repeaters can store data for time-delayed retransmission.

In a LAN. In a local area network (LAN), there is a limit to the practical length for interconnecting cables. No cable or wire is a perfect electrical conductor. All cables have signal loss that occurs because of the resistance in the wires or because of dielectric leakage through the insulation between the wires. Because of the loss, the signals get weaker as they travel along the cable, eventually fading to the point where they disappear into the background noise.

By intercepting the signal before it gets too weak, and amplifying it so it is strong again, the length of the cable between two workstations can be greatly increased. The amplifier is called a repeater because the output data is an exact replica of the input data, except that it has been amplified. It is possible to have more than one repeater in a long cable. However, repeaters amplify noise as well as signals. This places a practical limit on the number of repeaters that can be used.

The drawing at A shows a cable connecting two workstations, with a repeater in the middle. The signal strength at points along the cable is plotted graphically, as heavy dashed curves, against the relative vertical scale at left. The signals decrease logarithmically in strength as they get farther from the source workstation and the repeater, respectively.

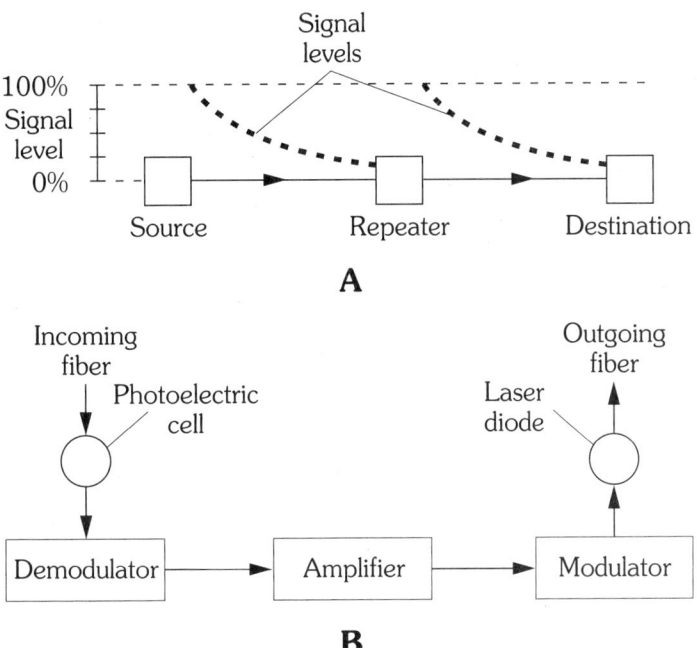

A repeater in network cable (A) and a block diagram of a fiberoptic system repeater (B).

In fiberoptic data transmission, a repeater is a device that extends the range of the fiberoptic link. Fiberoptic repeaters work like LAN repeaters, except that they receive and transmit visible light that is modulated with computer data. Thus, a demodulator and modulator are necessary, along with a photoelectric cell and a laser diode or other visible-light source (see part B of the drawing). A single beam of light can carry many computer signals.

In radio data communications. In radio, a repeater is a special kind of receiver/transmitter. Repeaters are common for packet communications in government and commercial, as well as in amateur, radio. A packet repeater is called a *digipeater*. A repeater on a satellite is called a *transponder*.

The drawing at C (page 952) shows the principle of a repeater in radio communication. Ideally, the repeater is located at a high place, such as on a mountain or tall building. The radius of coverage can be over 100 miles, so two workstations might connect over 200 miles or more. Without the repeater, the range would be about 30 to 50 miles.

A radio repeater has a receiver, a transmitter, an antenna, and a duplexer (part D of the drawing). The output of the receiver goes into the audio input of the transmitter. The transmitter retransmits the signal using the same antenna as the receiver. The transmitter signal differs in frequency from the received signal by a fixed amount, called the *offset* or *split*. The duplexer keeps the transmitted signal from "blocking" reception.

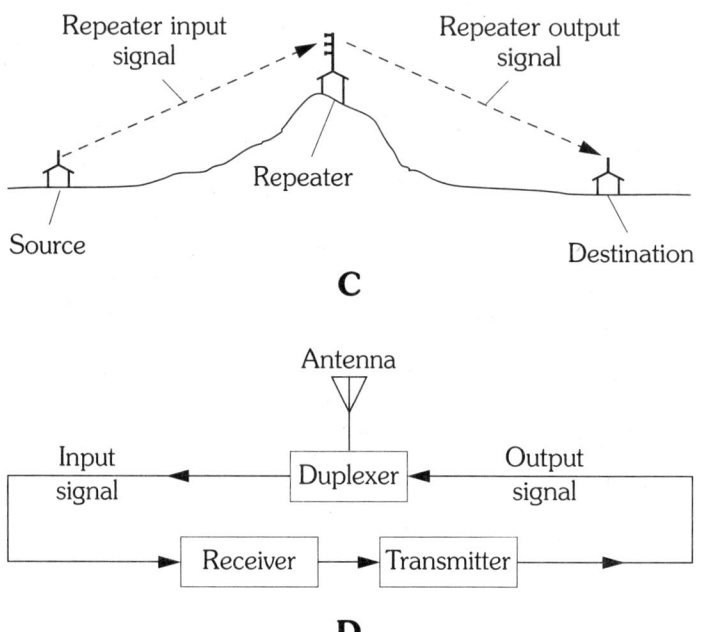

The principle of radio repeater operation (C) and a block diagram of a radio repeater (D).

Radio repeater operation is governed by Federal Communications Commission (FCC) rules. Emergency communication always has priority on a radio repeater. Some repeaters are equipped with telephone interconnects known as *autopatch*, allowing a person with a radio transceiver and a computer to use online services from a remote location such as a car or boat. Access to some repeaters requires that a subaudible tone of a certain frequency be sent along with the other data. This is called *tone squelch* or *private line*.

See also AMATEUR RADIO, CELLULAR TELECOMMUNICATIONS, DIGIPEATER, FIBEROPTIC DATA TRANSMISSION, LOCAL AREA NETWORK, PACKET COMMUNICATIONS, *and* SATELLITE DATA TRANSMISSION.

Reset button

The *reset button* is a momentary-contact pushbutton switch found in some PCs. It is usually located on the front of the main unit or on the keyboard. Pressing this button performs a *warm boot*. Everything in the RAM (random-access memory) disappears, and the entire system starts up again from scratch.

In DOS, if a computer freezes up so it does not respond to any commands or input, the best thing to do is press the key sequence

Ctrl-Alt-Del. If that doesn't work, remove any diskettes from the diskette drives, and press the reset button if the computer has one. The last resort, a brute-force reset technique generally used only when nothing else works, is a *cold boot*. To perform a cold boot, power-down the computer, wait two minutes or more for the hard disk to come to a complete stop, and then power-up again. *See also* COLD BOOT *and* WARM BOOT.

Resident font
See BUILT-IN FONT.

Resident software
See MEMORY-RESIDENT SOFTWARE.

Resolution
The term *resolution* has several meanings in computers and electronics. In general, it refers to the "fineness" of some variable quantity. High resolution implies an optimum level of precision with minimum error. Low resolution suggests coarseness, lower precision, and a larger margin of error.

Monitors and printers. In computer systems, the quality of the image on the monitor or display, and the crispness of the printout, is called the *image resolution*. Image resolution can be specified in several different ways; the most common are dots per inch and dot pitch.

For a printer, the greater the number of dots per inch (DPI), the better the image resolution. Sometimes the number of dots per centimeter (dots/cm) is given instead. For a monitor/display, the dot pitch can be given in dots per inch, dots per centimeter, or as the diameter of one dot on the screen as a decimal fraction of an inch or millimeter. *See also* DOTS PER INCH, DOT PITCH, HIGH-RESOLUTION MONITOR, HIGH-RESOLUTION PRINTER, *and* IMAGE RESOLUTION.

Machine vision. In machine vision systems, resolution is the ability to distinguish between things that are close together. Within objects, resolution is the extent to which the system can bring out details about the object. It is a precise measure of image quality sometimes called *resolving power* or *definition*.

Good resolution requires a wide signal bandwidth. It is also important that the camera tube be properly focused, that the level of illumination be within acceptable limits, and that the signal not contain an excessive level of noise. Poor resolution can be the result of improper focusing, too few pixels in the image, or a signal bandwidth that is not wide enough. Noise in a video system degrades the image quality in general, including the resolution. *See also* BANDWIDTH, IMAGE ORTHICON, VIDICON, *and* VISION SYSTEMS.

Reverse engineering

Position sensing. In computerized position sensing, you might hear about *direction resolution* or *distance resolution*. These terms refer to the ability of sensing apparatus to tell the difference between objects separated by a small angle, or those that are almost the same distance away.

Direction resolution is measured in degrees, minutes, or seconds of arc. Distance resolution can be expressed in feet, meters, or centimeters, or as a percentage of the distance to the object farthest away.

Data conversion. When an analog signal is converted into digital form, the resolution is the number of different digital levels. An analog signal has infinitely many different levels; it can vary over a continuous range. The greater the digital resolution, the more accurate the digital representation of the signal.

A computer signal has a resolution of two levels: high/low, or the logic states 1 and 0 (graph A). In digital broadcasting, voice signals have a resolution of eight levels (graph B); music has 16 levels (graph C); motion video signals might have more levels. All types of data can be converted to computer-compatible digital signals having only two logic states. This is how music, pictures, and other complex information is sent via modem. *See also* ANALOG, DATA CONVERSION, DIGITAL, *and* MODEM.

Reverse engineering

It is often possible to build a machine that does the same things as some other machine, using a different design. When this is done with computers, it is called *cloning*. The more complex a device, the more equivalent designs there are. *Reverse engineering* is a process by which a given machine is copied functionally, but not literally.

If you can duplicate the things a patented machine will do, but use a new and different approach that you thought of independently, you haven't infringed on the patent. Similarly, if you invent something like a smart robot and then get it patented, this doesn't give you a patent for what the device does.

Suppose, however, that someone reverse-engineered your robot by dismantling it and then rebuilding it almost, but not quite, the same way. That person wouldn't have invented a new design. He or she would have used your work in slightly altered form to make a "new" product. If you could prove that this person used your design and did not make substantial changes, you could sue him or her for patent infringement, but proving that sort of thing can be difficult, time-consuming, and expensive. *See also* CLONE.

Reverse video

Reverse video, also called *reverse screen mode*, interchanges the light and dark pixels (picture elements) on a screen of text. Depending

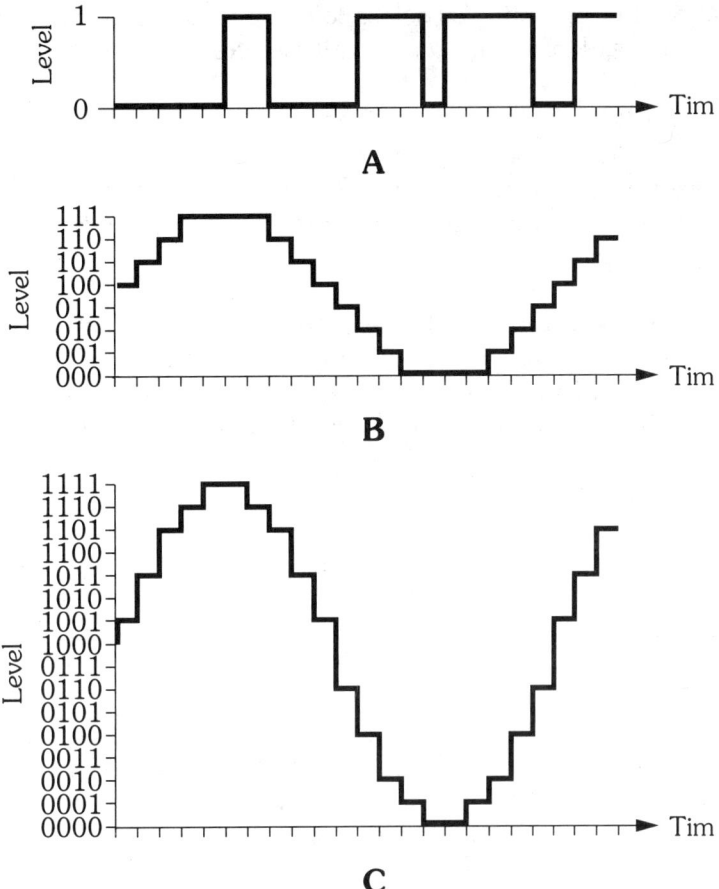

Two-level resolution (A); eight-level resolution (B); 16-level resolution (C).

on what software you use for text-based applications such as word processing, databases, or spreadsheets, your screen normally shows either light characters on a dark background or vice versa.

Highlighting a section of text will reverse the video so it stands out from the rest of the text. This is commonly done with menu-driven user interfaces, in which the user can highlight options prior to making a final choice. Highlighting is also done with blocks of text that are to be given special treatment. For example, you might want to move a sentence from one part of a document to some other part. You would highlight the sentence, either with keyboard keys or using the mouse; this would reverse the video for the sentence. Then you would move the cursor to the spot where you wanted the sentence to go, press a key or click the mouse, and the sentence would be inserted in the new place and removed from its old place.

Sometimes you might want to reverse the video of your whole screen, simply because you're tired of looking at white letters on a black background, or black letters on a white background. Many programs will let you do this, and even select color options like black on green or yellow on dark blue. *See also* HIGHLIGHTING.

RGB color model

All visible colors can be obtained by combining red, green, and blue light in varying proportions. The *RGB color model* is a scheme for computer monitors that takes advantage of this fact; *RGB* stands for "red-green-blue."

Hue, saturation, and brightness. Visible light consists of electromagnetic waves. The color you see is a function of the wavelength, or often many wavelengths combined. When light energy is concentrated mostly at one wavelength, you see a vivid *hue*. A rainbow has some energy at all visible wavelengths, so you see a continuum of all possible hues.

When light energy is confined to a single wavelength (as is the case with a laser), the hue is intense. More often, the hue is less concentrated; sometimes it is diffuse and hard to ascertain. The relative vividness of a hue is called the *saturation*.

The *brightness* of a color is a function of how much total energy the light contains. A ruby laser has high brightness; a small light-emitting diode (LED) has low brightness. On a computer monitor, there is a control for adjusting the brightness, also called *brilliance*.

3-D color. You can get an excellent full-color palette by combining three pure colors in various degrees of brightness. For radiant light, these colors are red, green, and blue. For pigments in printing, they are red, yellow, and blue, or more precisely, magenta (pinkish red), yellow, and cyan (greenish blue).

Color computer monitors and color television sets have thousands of tiny dots arranged in an interlaced pattern. One-third of the dots are red, one-third are green, and one-third are blue. When you look at the screen from a distance, the dots blend together to form a continuous color image.

Imagine each of the three primary hues in its purest possible form, that is, with maximum saturation. The brightness of each can be varied independently, from zero to some arbitrary maximum. Assign each hue an axis in Cartesian three-space, as shown in the drawing. Call the axes *R* (for red), *G* (for green) and *B* (for blue). The values of *R*, *G*, and *B* can range from 0% to 100% of full brilliance. Thus, you could logically graduate each axis in units from 0 to 100. The result is a cube, within which there are $101 \times 101 \times 101 = 1{,}030{,}301$ points. Any point, say $(R,G,B) = (45, 20, 75)$, represents a certain color. There are 1,030,301 possible colors that can be represented in this cube. This is a geometric representation of the RGB color model. In the drawing, points are labeled for black, white, red, green, and blue, and also for $(R,G,B) = (45,20,75)$.

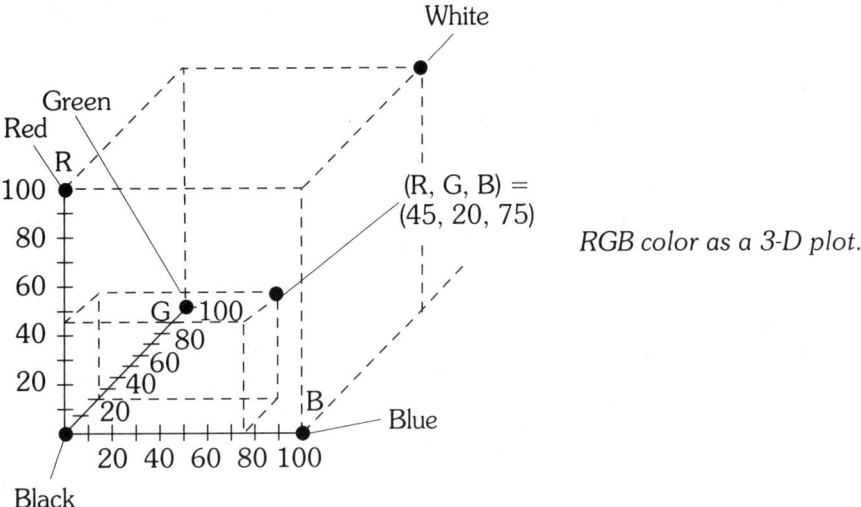

RGB color as a 3-D plot.

In a real computer monitor, there are far more than 101 possible brightness levels for each of the three primary colors. A typical number is 65,535, equal to 2^{16} or the binary 1111111111111111. Thus, the color cube contains a tremendously large number of points. For all practical purposes, the result is infinite color variety, and a perfect representation of the real world. *See also* MONITOR *and* PALETTE.

Ring network

There are several different methods of connecting the workstations in a local area network (LAN). These schemes are called *topologies*. In one type of topology, all the workstations are connected at points around a continuous loop or ring. This is known as a *ring network* or *token-ring network*.

Nodes. An example of a ring network is shown in the drawing on the next page. Each PC represents one workstation, also called a *node*. Some nodes might consist of peripherals like printers. Others might be dumb terminals, consisting of a keyboard and monitor, but no computer.

Every node in the ring network has an *address*, a code that uniquely identifies it. That way, any PC in the LAN can connect to any node. In the drawing, you can see that all the PCs are effectively connected together. For any two nodes in the network, there is a path connecting them. If the ring is large, containing many nodes, this path might be long, but it always exists.

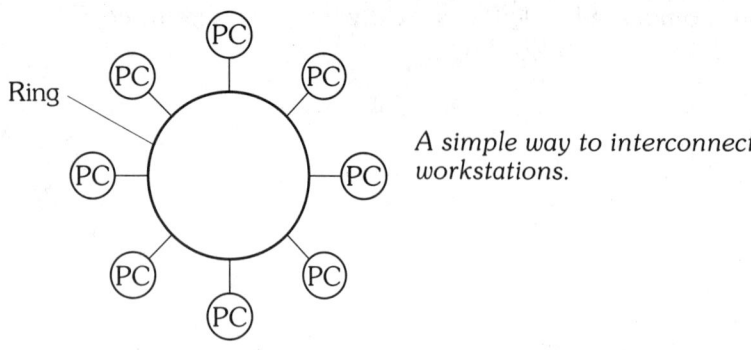

A simple way to interconnect workstations.

Assets. A ring network is simple. Ring networks are easy to enlarge: all you need to do is add more nodes, at convenient points around the ring. A token-ring network has a high *saturation point*, which means that it's difficult to overload the network because of the nature of its design.

The data goes around the ring in an endless loop, but because it is replenished via a repeater at each node, it never dies down to nothing. Repeaters receive, amplify, and retransmit the data. If there are many workstations, the ring can have a large circumference.

Limitations. The separation between nodes in a ring network cannot normally be more than about 1000 feet unless extra repeaters are used between nodes. This is not necessarily a serious constraint, however. In the network shown in the drawing, for example, the ring could be as large as 8000 feet in circumference because there are eight nodes.

If one node malfunctions, all the rest can still communicate with each other unless the node's repeater breaks down. Then, depending on the distance between workstations, the loop might be effectively broken.

Ring networks work quite well when nodes are located at scattered points. The ring need not be a perfect circle. Ring networks are not so well-suited to situations where the nodes are all along a single line of great length. In that case, a bus network is preferable. *See also* BUS NETWORK, LOCAL AREA NETWORK, REPEATER, *and* STAR NETWORK.

RISC

See REDUCED-INSTRUCTION-SET COMPUTING.

Robot controller

A *robot controller* is a computer with specialized peripherals that oversees the functioning of one or more robots. In *autonomous robots*, the controller might be physically within the robot. Alternatively, the controller might be external to the robot, conveying its instructions by some form of remote control. In a fleet of *insect robots*, for example, a single controller is responsible for several (perhaps many) robots; operation is always via remote control.

A functional block diagram of a robot controller is shown in the drawing. The computer is central to the system. Movement instructions are stored in memory.

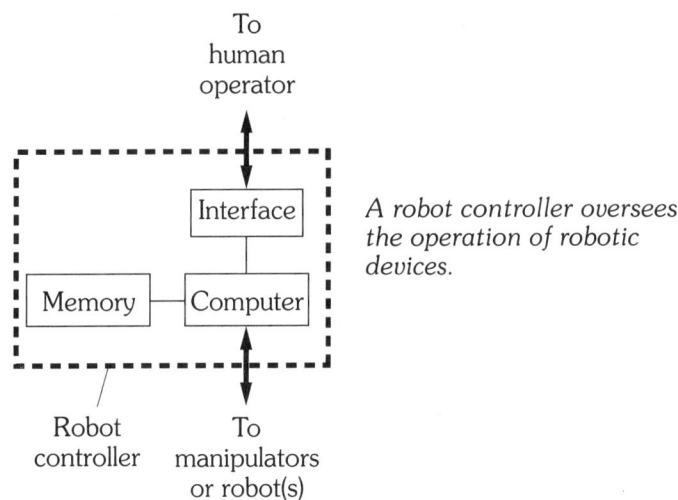

A robot controller oversees the operation of robotic devices.

The robot controller does several things. Primarily, it allows the computer to communicate with a human operator or supervisor. Through the interface, the memory might be reprogrammed to change the robot's movement instructions. The action or functioning of the robot can be displayed on a monitor screen. There can also be various malfunction indicators. Some interfaces have a teach box, which lets the human operator reprogram the motions and path of the robot.

High-end PCs can easily accommodate software that will let them serve as personal robot controllers. A home PC might be operated by remote control, so a household robot can be manipulated from someplace miles away. You might be on a boat in the Caribbean, for example, and have your yard-maintenance robot mow your lawn and trim your bushes in Boston. *See also* AUTONOMOUS ROBOTS, INSECT ROBOTS, PERSONAL ROBOTS, REMOTE CONTROL SYSTEMS, *and* TEACH BOX.

Robot generations

The future is likely to bring an increase in the significance of robotics as an application in personal computing. Some researchers have analyzed the evolution of robots, marking progress according to *robot generations*. This has been done with computers and integrated circuits, so it seems natural to do it with robots, too. The drawing shows a general scheme leading to refinements in computerized robot development.

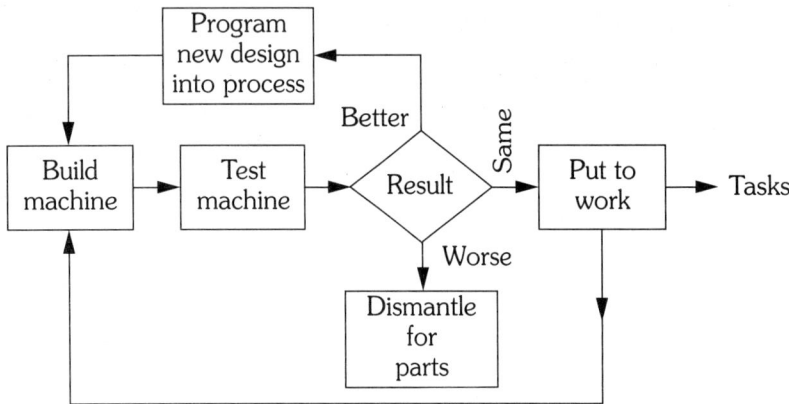

Algorithm for robot design evolution.

First generation. According to Nakano, first-generation robots were simple mechanical arms, lacking even a hint of artificial intelligence (AI). These machines had the ability to make precise motions at high speed, many times, for a long time. Such robots are still used in industry today.

First-generation robots can work in groups, such as in an automated integrated manufacturing system (AIMS), if their actions are synchronized. The operation of these machines must be constantly watched because if they get out of alignment and are allowed to keep working, the result can be a series of bad production units.

Second generation. A second-generation robot has some AI. Such a machine is equipped with sensors that tell it things about the outside world. Such devices include pressure sensors, proximity sensors, tactile sensors, and vision systems. A controller processes the data from these sensors and adjusts the operation of the robot accordingly. These devices came into common use around 1980.

Second-generation robots can stay synchronized with each other without having to be overseen constantly by a human operator. Of course, periodic checking is needed with any machine because things can always go wrong. The more complex a system, the more ways it can malfunction.

Third generation. Third-generation robots were mentioned by Nakano, but after the publication of his paper, some things changed. Two major avenues are developing for "smart" robot technology: *autonomous robots* and *insect robots*. Both of these schemes hold promise.

An autonomous robot can work on its own. It contains a controller and can do things largely without supervision, either by an outside computer or by a human being. A good example of this type of third-generation robot is the personal robot about which some people dream.

There are some situations in which autonomous robots don't do very well. In these cases, many simple robots, all under the control of one central computer, are used. They work like ants in an anthill or bees in a hive. While the individual machines are "stupid," the group is intelligent and efficient.

Fourth generation and beyond. In his original paper, Nakano did not write about anything past the third generation of robots, but you could speculate about a fourth generation of robots yet to be seriously worked on. An example is a fleet of robots that reproduce and evolve, or that have the ability to reason, or that can replace human beings in many capacities. Science-fiction authors have written extensively about fourth-generation robots. The "androids" you see in movies and on television are in this category.

Beyond this, we might say that a fifth-generation robot is something about which nothing has been said, written, or filmed. This includes concepts and schemes that have yet to be imagined. This category is constantly retreating as researchers come up with new ideas.

The table is a summary of robot generations, their general capabilities, and the time periods during which they were developed. *See also* ARTIFICIAL INTELLIGENCE, ARTIFICIAL LIFE, AUTONOMOUS ROBOTS, INSECT ROBOTS, *and* PERSONAL ROBOTS.

Robots are getting smarter and more nimble

Generation	Time first used	Capabilities
First	Before 1980	Mainly mechanical Stationary Good precision High speed Physical ruggedness Use of servomechanisms No external sensors No artificial intelligence
Second	1980–1990	Tactile sensors Vision systems Position sensors Pressure sensors Microcomputer control Programmable
Third	Mid-1990s and after	Mobile Autonomous Insect-like Artificial intelligence Speech recognition Speech synthesis Navigation systems Teleoperated
Fourth	Future	Design not yet begun Able to reproduce? Able to evolve? Artificially alive? As smart as a human? True sense of humor?
Fifth	?	Not yet discussed Capabilities unknown

Root directory

See DIRECTORY.

Running headers/footers

When you're working on a word-processed document, you can have the program automatically number the pages. You can also add information along with the page numbers, such as the date, the document name, and your name. When this information appears at the top of each page in the printout, it's called a *header.* When it appears at the bottom of each page, it's a *footer. Running headers/footers* are automatically inserted or removed along with the pages of text.

Suppose your name is John Doe, and you're writing a magazine article entitled, "How to Live in England on $100 a Week." A good manuscript header or footer to add to the page number might be *England on $100 a Week, J. Doe.*

While you're composing the piece on the computer, you can set the number of lines per page, up to a maximum that depends on the line spacing and form length. (For a double-spaced manuscript on 8.5-by-11-inch paper, there are usually 20 to 24 lines.) When you print out the document, the printer will insert some space to allow for the top and bottom margins. The headers or footers will also appear if you want them printed, along with the appropriate page numbers. Some programs put the headers or footers inside the margins, others put them outside. *See also* PAGINATION, REPAGINATION, *and* SOFT PAGE BREAKS.

964

Satellite data transmission

A computer network can use any medium of communications. *Satellite data transmission* is one of the most interesting. It uses ultra-high frequencies (UHF) and microwaves. Signals are sent up to the satellite, received, and retransmitted on another frequency at the same time by a repeater-like device called a *transponder* (see the drawing). The ground-to-satellite data is called the *uplink;* the satellite-to-ground data is the *downlink*.

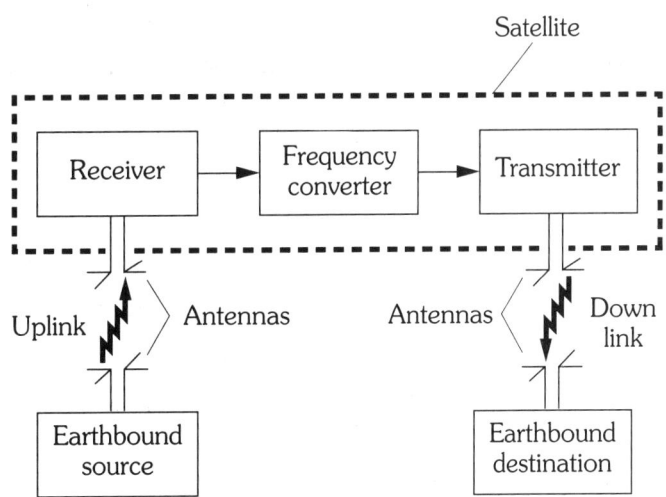

Simplified block diagram of a satellite transponder.

Satellite data transmission

Schemes. Satellite communications links generally fall into either of two categories: the *geostationary-satellite data link* and the *low-earth-orbit (LEO) satellite data link*.

A geostationary link uses a small number of satellites, each strategically placed so that it stays over the same spot on the earth all the time. Such a satellite must be directly over the equator and at just the right altitude, so it goes around the earth once every time the earth makes a complete turn on its axis. Continuous contact can be maintained between any two stations that are both within range of a satellite.

A LEO satellite link employs a "swarm" of satellites, each in a circular orbit that takes it over the geographic poles. The number of satellites can vary. In general, the more satellites there are, the more reliable the communications link will be. The system works like a cellular telephone network, except that the repeaters are moving, rather than fixed, and they are in space, not on the ground.

Uses. Satellite data links do not require long-distance cables. It's as easy to access a satellite system from a remote island, mountain, boat, or aircraft as it is to make the connection from a large city. To access a satellite network, you need a computer, a modem, a radio transmitter/receiver (transceiver), and a suitable antenna. A basic system works in half duplex, allowing the workstation to operate as a source and a destination, but not at the same time. A more sophisticated satellite data link allows full duplex, of the sort you're familiar with if you've had much experience with online services.

A set of satellites called the *global positioning system (GPS)* allows your computer to figure out, to within a few feet, your location on the surface of the earth. This is an invaluable navigational aid for large boats or private aircraft. Even some cars are equipped with GPS links, so you can always determine exactly where you are when driving in unfamiliar territory. A computer display shows you your location on a detailed road map. You can "zoom" to see your position within a country, state, or city.

Amateur radio operators have been exchanging computer data by radio for decades. This is a special form of packet communications known as *packet radio*. Radio amateurs, also called "hams," have pooled their resources and placed several communications transponders on satellites. If you are technically inclined, you might want to study electronics and take the test to get a ham radio license. This can broaden your personal computing horizon and get you in touch with other "techies."

Challenges. The biggest problem with any wide-area network (WAN), including those that employ satellite transmission, is that it takes time for signals to get between computers. This is true no matter how the data is sent. Nothing can go faster than the speed of light (186,282 miles, or 299,792 kilometers, per second).

A satellite might hover in a geostationary orbit, at some fixed spot 22,300 miles above the earth's equator. When such a satellite is used, the total path length is always at least 44,600 miles (up and back), and usually a little more. The smallest possible delay is therefore 44,600/186,282 = 0.24 second. High-speed, two-way processing is impossible with a path delay that long. This problem can be overcome by placing satellites in lower orbit, but for a link to be continuously maintained, a "swarm" of satellites must be used. Then, at least one satellite will always be within range of a workstation on the ground.

One of the biggest challenges facing computer scientists is figuring out how to provide high-speed links between computers that are far away from each other. There is no way to overcome the fact that the speed of light is, in computer terms, slow. This is not a problem for simple data transfer and communications, but it hinders the linkage of computers worldwide to form a multiprocessing supercomputer. The speed of the system as a whole is slowed by signal propagation delays, no matter how fast the individual computers. *See also* AMATEUR RADIO, FULL DUPLEX, GEOSTATIONARY-SATELLITE DATA LINK, HALF DUPLEX, LOW-EARTH-ORBIT (LEO) SATELLITE DATA LINK, PACKET COMMUNICATIONS, *and* WIDE-AREA NETWORK.

Scalable font

In desktop publishing, it's important that you be able to tailor the size of the font. A published document must usually occupy a precise number of pages. By enlarging or reducing the type size and illustration size, you can make a document come out to just the right length and have it look attractive.

It's often necessary to experiment with several different font sizes, illustration sizes, and formats to arrive at a printed document of the proper length. However, all this effort is of no use if the characters themselves are distorted in the resizing process. Printed characters should be crisp and dark, so they're easy to read, and so readers will be impressed with the quality of the work.

Some fonts can be enlarged or reduced without causing distortion, or *jaggies*, along the edges of the characters. Such a font is called a *scalable font*. You've seen jaggies; they look like little saw teeth and give printed matter a low-budget, amateurish appearance. In general, an outline font is scalable within certain limits. A bitmapped font, on the other hand, is not scalable; it usually can't be resized without introducing jaggies.

One popular scalable font technology used extensively in desktop publishing is called *PostScript*. Another is known as *TrueType*. These

Scaling

fonts are available for use with graphical interfaces such as the Macintosh OS, IBM OS/2, and Microsoft Windows. *See also* BITMAPPED FONT, DESKTOP PUBLISHING, FONT, JAGGIES, OUTLINE FONT, POSTSCRIPT, *and* TRUETYPE.

Scaling

When working with analytical graphics software, it's important that the graph axes be labeled so the display is clear and meaningful. The axes should cover ranges appropriate for the data being graphed. *Scaling* is the process of choosing and optimizing the range of values in a graph. In general, the vertical scale, which represents the dependent variable, tends to be more critical than the horizontal scale, which reflects the independent variable.

Suppose you want to graph temperature as a function of time for a 24-hour period. The drawings show two renditions of such a graph, based on a typical summer day in the American Midwest. In graphs A and B, the horizontal axis shows time, starting at midnight, running through 6 a.m., noon, 6 p.m., and midnight again. The temperature is plotted on the vertical scale in both examples.

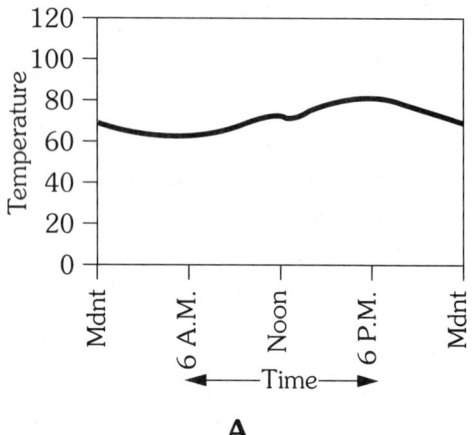

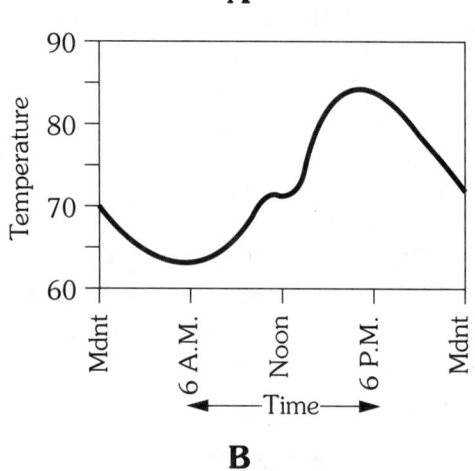

Example of poor scaling (A) and good scaling (B).

Scatter plot

In graph A, the vertical axis allows for a range of temperatures far greater than the variation that actually takes place. This makes it hard to read the temperatures. It looks as if the temperature were nearly constant throughout the day. In fact, relative to the range shown (0 to 120 degrees Fahrenheit), the day's temperature doesn't fluctuate very much. This is an example of poor scaling. It does not make good use of the vertical scale of the graph.

Graph B shows the same data, but the vertical scale has been stretched out so the day's variation in temperature shows up clearly. Here, you can tell that the day's minimum temperature was about 63°F and occurred just before 6 a.m., while the maximum temperature of about 87°F took place around 5 p.m. The scaling in this graph is optimal for this temperature range. The curve fits neatly into the available space, without going outside it.

If the values on the vertical axis were stretched out still further—say, from 70 to 80 degrees—the curve would go off the graph both above and below. This would be a poor choice of scaling, since it would obliterate some of the data. A range of 70 to 100 degrees would not render the day's coolest temperatures, and would also be a poor choice of scaling. A range of 50 to 80 degrees, similarly, would be inadequate because it would cut off the day's hottest temperatures. *See also* ANALYTICAL GRAPHICS, CARTESIAN COORDINATES, DEPENDENT VARIABLE, *and* INDEPENDENT VARIABLE.

Scanner

See OPTICAL CHARACTER RECOGNITION *and* OPTICAL SCANNER.

Scatter plot

A *scatter plot* is a specialized graph consisting of points rather than a curve. Scatter plots are used in analytical graphics programs, and also occasionally in presentation graphics software. These graphs tell you if there is a correlation between two variables, and if so, whether the correlation is weak or strong, or positive or negative.

Scatter plots are especially useful in scientific work. They can reveal correlations that might be overlooked by examining tables or charts. They are usually plotted in Cartesian coordinates.

The drawing on page 970 shows an example of a scatter plot, showing the height and weight of several people. The variables, *Height* and *Weight*, are graphed on perpendicular axes. The value of *Height* increases as you move to the right; the value of *Weight* increases as you move up. Each point in a scatter plot corresponds to a unique ordered pair (*Height*, *Weight*).

In this graph, there is a correlation between height and weight. In general, tall people are heavier than short people. Of course, the correlation is not 100%; this is reflected by the fact that the points

Scheduling software

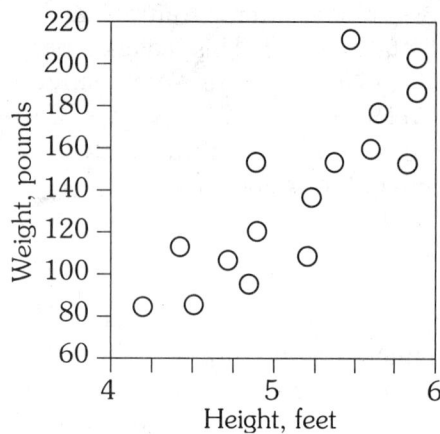

A scatter plot shows correlation between two variables.

aren't all exactly along a line or curve. They're scattered; hence the name for this type of graph.

It's important to realize that the existence of a correlation does not say anything about cause and effect. In this example, one might argue that height affects weight. (Children grow heavier as they grow taller.) However, there are instances in which correlated variables are both affected by some third, perhaps unknown, variable. One must be careful not to hastily conclude a causal relationship solely on the basis of a correlation shown by a scatter plot. *See also* ANALYTICAL GRAPHICS, CARTESIAN COORDINATES, CORRELATION, *and* PRESENTATION GRAPHICS.

Scheduling software

See DAILY PLANNER SOFTWARE *and* PERSONAL INFORMATION MANAGER.

Scientific notation

Scientific notation is a shorthand way of expressing very large or small numbers. It saves space, reduces confusion, and allows a computer or calculator to handle a far greater range of numerical values than would otherwise be possible.

This article contains some messy arithmetic. You need never work out problems of this nature yourself. A computer can do such calculations easily. In fact, that is the purpose for which computers were originally invented.

In science. The general form for scientific notation is:

$a \times 10^b$

where a is a number whose value is at least 1 but less than 10, or greater than -10 and less than or equal to -1. The number b is an integer, that is, some whole number from the set

Scientific notation

{. . ., −3, −2, −1, 0, 1, 2, 3, . . .}

Examples of numbers written in scientific notation are

2.90×10^{15}
8.00×10^{-23}
7.6689×10^{0}
-4.559×10^{-3}

Because the values are always multiplied by powers of 10, this scheme is sometimes called *power-of-10 notation*. If you've taken any physics, chemistry, or other science-related courses at the college level, you have undoubtedly seen this notation.

The table shows powers of 10 and their equivalent values as written out in "long hand," for values from 10^{-8} through 10^{8}. When the value of the exponent changes by one, the value of the equivalent expression changes by a factor of 10. Such a difference is called an *order of magnitude*. When some quantity has increased or decreased by several orders of magnitude, it means that it has changed by a factor of several powers of 10, such as 1000 or 0.000001.

Power-of-10 and exponential forms

Power-of-10	Exponential	Longhand expression
10^{-8}	E−8	0.00000001
10^{-7}	E−7	0.0000001
10^{-6}	E−6	0.000001
10^{-5}	E−5	0.00001
10^{-4}	E−4	0.0001
10^{-3}	E−3	0.001
10^{-2}	E−2	0.01
10^{-1}	E−1	0.1
10^{0}	E+0	1
10^{1}	E+1	10
10^{2}	E+2	100
10^{3}	E+3	1000
10^{4}	E+4	10,000
10^{5}	E+5	100,000
10^{6}	E+6	1,000,000
10^{7}	E+7	10,000,000
10^{8}	E+8	100,000,000

The number a in scientific notation always has one digit to the left of the decimal point. This digit can be anything except zero. There can

Scientific notation

be any number of digits to the right of the decimal point. (Look again at the examples.) The total number of digits in *a* is called the number of *significant figures* in the expression. The more significant figures there are, the more precise the expression.

In computing. Computers and calculators employ a different method of expressing powers of 10. The number is just the same as in the power-of-10 scheme, but, instead of writing 10 with an exponent, the capital letter *E* is written, followed by the exponent number with either a plus or minus sign. Also, no multiplication sign is used.

The table shows computer-style notation for exponents ranging from −8 to +8. The four examples shown in power-of-ten notation are, in this notation, written as follows:

2.90E+15
8.00E−23
7.6689E+0
−4.559E−3

The numbers written out in full would look like this:

2,900,000,000,000,000
0.00000000000000000000008
7.6689
−0.004559

Now you can see how much neater scientific notation can be, compared with writing numbers out in full. When the exponents become extreme, such as 10^{345} (E+345) or 10^{-7855} (E−7855), this notation is the only sensible way to denote numbers.

Products and quotients. When a computer multiplies or divides numbers in scientific notation, the values of *a* are multiplied or divided. The exponents are added in the case of multiplication, and subtracted in the case of division. For example, suppose you want to multiply the first two numbers in the set of four example expressions. In power-of-10 notation, you would do it like this:

$2.90 \times 10^{15} \times 8.00 \times 10^{-23}$
$= (2.90 \times 8.00) \times 10^{(15 + (-23))}$
$= 23.2 \times 10^{-8}$
$= 2.32 \times 10^{-7}$

The last expression is changed to get the number *a* between 1 and 10 (23.2 is too big). Because the decimal point is moved one digit place to the left, the exponent (the number *b*) decreases by 1. In exponential notation, the calculation goes like this:

2.90E+15 × 8.00E−23
= (2.90 × 8.00)E(15 + (−23))
= 23.2E−8
= 2.32E−7

Now imagine dividing the third expression by the fourth one. In power-of-10 notation, you'd do it this way:

$7.6689 \times 10^0 / -4.559 \times 10^{-3}$
$= (7.6689/-4.559) \times 10^{(0-(-3))}$
$= -1.682 \times 10^3$

In exponential notation, it would work this way:

7.6689E+0/−4.559E−3
= (7.6689/−4.559)E(0 − (−3))
= −1.682E+3

Never fear. The foregoing examples are messy. If it weren't for computers, there would be a high risk of making mistakes, with all the plus and minus signs, decimal numbers, and arithmetic operations. Manipulating signs, and keeping track of precedence (the order in which to multiply, divide, add, and subtract the numbers), can befuddle any person who tries to do such calculations, but a computer can perform these sorts of numerical gymnastics without getting confused. Your only responsibility is learning to read expressions in scientific or exponential notation. It takes a little getting used to, but it's no more complicated than spreadsheet or database notation.

For further information about scientific notation, refer to a good high-school or college introductory physics textbook. *See also* PRECEDENCE, PREFIX MULTIPLIERS, *and* SIGNIFICANT FIGURES.

Screen capture

A *screen capture* is a "snapshot" of the image on a computer screen. A screen capture can be printed, stored in memory, or merged into data files.

In DOS. If you're using DOS, the simplest way to get a screen capture is to use the Print Screen key. However, this doesn't always produce an exact copy of the image on the monitor. For example, shading will not generally be rendered. If your text is white on a black background, the printout will probably be black on white paper.

The biggest limitation of the Print Screen key used in DOS is that it only allows for printing out what's on the screen. Pressing this key will not store the screen contents in the form of a data file, unless you have installed a program specifically intended for this purpose, or unless you have Windows installed on top of your DOS.

Screen capture

In Windows. If you have Microsoft Windows version 3.1 or later, you can take screen captures and save them on hard disk or diskette, in addition to creating hardcopies. To do this, press the Print Screen key. (With some computers, you'll have to press Alt-Print Screen or Shift-Print Screen, holding down Alt or Shift while you press Print Screen.) This will put an exact replica of the screen contents into the clipboard, no matter what is on the screen: text, images, File Manager, or anything else.

The data in the clipboard can be changed if you want. You might decide, for example, to alter the shading, add new lines, add text, or do various other things. This is facilitated by using the Paintbrush paint program supplied as part of Windows software. (For details on the use of Paintbrush, refer to your Windows instruction manual.)

To save a screen capture, click on the Clipboard Viewer icon. Choose Save As, and give the screen capture a filename of up to eight characters, followed by a period, and three more characters for the filename extension. Usually, you'll use the extension .BMP to indicate that the file is a bitmap, or .CLP to indicate a clipboard file. The file will be saved on your hard disk in any directory you want. You can also save it on a diskette by choosing a diskette drive icon (say, drive B) and placing a diskette in the drive.

When you save a screenful of text this way, you might be astonished to discover how much disk space it requires. For example, if you're on the Internet and you decide you want to save a screenful of text, you can do so by pressing the Print Screen key. This might at first seem like an excellent way to save data from online. Later, when you click on Clipboard Viewer, you'll see exactly what you saved. If you then transfer this to a permanent file, say ONLINE-1.CLP, and look at the directory where the file is, you'll discover how grossly inefficient this file transfer method actually is. One screenful of text (about 200 words) takes up about 308K of storage instead of the normal 1K or so. Saving a 10-page document would require 10 separate screen captures, with 10 different files, for a total of 3.08MB of disk space!

Screen capture software. While Windows can let you save screen captures, there are some limitations. If you're a casual PC user, these limitations might never be a problem for you, but if you intend to get into serious graphics work, or if you plan to do desktop publishing, you'll want to consider buying screen capture software. Here are some of the features of a good screen-capture program:

> ➢ *DOS/Windows/Mac* Packages are available for DOS, Windows, Macintosh, and other operating systems. Be sure you get the version that is compatible with your operating system. If you are currently using plain DOS, consider changing over to a windowing environment. Windows is not only more user-friendly than DOS, it allows you to do much more in terms of graphics.

➤ *Importing* Screen-capture software lets you import images into text files. This is essential in desktop publishing. You can also import screen captures into other graphic images. This will prove invaluable in serious graphics work. Some programs offer WYSIWYG (what-you-see-is-what-you-get) capability, so you don't have to make a printout to see what your document will ultimately look like.

➤ *File conversion* There are several different graphics file formats in common use. The two broad categories are bitmapped graphics and object-oriented graphics (also known as vector graphics). When importing screen captures into other files, you'll need to ensure that the formats are compatible. Screen-capture software allows you to do this.

➤ *Color/black-and-white/gray-scale* Suppose you want to convert a color screen capture to gray-scale, or a gray-scale image to pure black-and-white. You might need to do this sort of conversion if, for example, your printer can't portray color. You might then print red as crosshatching, blue as a fine grid of dots, green as vertical lines, etc. The software will give you a variety of choices.

➤ *Cropping* You can crop your screen captures just like you would crop photographs. With cropping, you can take any rectangular portion of the screen image, and store it alone. You can capture all of the screen, or a specific part, as you choose. When you recall the stored data, the region you have chosen will comprise the entire image.

➤ *Editing* There are many things you can do to alter or enhance an image. You might want to resize, rotate, mirror, dither, or compress files. Some programs offer more than others in this respect.

If you have high-level graphics aspirations, you should consider getting an image editing utility in addition to the screen capture software. *See also* BITMAP, BITMAPPED GRAPHICS, CLIPBOARD, DITHERING, FILENAME, IMAGE EDITING, OBJECT-ORIENTED GRAPHICS, PAINT PROGRAM, PRINT SCREEN KEY, *and* WYSIWYG.

Screen saver

A cathode-ray tube (CRT) monitor should never be allowed to display a bright, stationary image for a long time because the phosphor is gradually damaged by electron bombardment. This is especially true of older CRTs. If certain regions get hit by more electrons than others over an extended period, the screen will develop blotches that never go away. The phosphor in these areas will be less sensitive than the phosphor in other parts of the screen.

There are two ways in which you can minimize damage to the phosphor on a CRT, and thereby prolong a monitor's useful life. The

Scrolling

simplest scheme is to dim the monitor whenever you are not actually using your PC. If you must get up to do anything, even if you think it will be for only a minute, turn the brightness control all the way down. (You never know when you'll be distracted and end up spending an hour away from your computer.) The trick is remembering to do this *every* time you leave your PC.

The second method involves buying and installing a *screen saver*, a program that prevents your monitor from receiving a stationary image for more than a few minutes. The simplest screen savers automatically darken the monitor. More complex (and fun) screen savers put animated graphics on your screen.

Have you ever walked into an office or friend's house and seen a CRT monitor that looked like the view screen on a starship moving at "warp" speed? That's a screen saver in action. You can get screen savers with all sorts of animation. Some programs let you make up your own moving graphics. You can even add sound, so your PC acts like an electronic arcade game waiting to be played.

When you want to resume your work, the screen saver will stop, and the monitor will display exactly what was on it before you were interrupted. Simply move the mouse or hit a key, and the computer will be ready for you to start working where you left off. Some screen savers have the option of password protection, so only you and people you authorize can return to data files from the screen-saver mode.

Eventually, any monitor will wear out, no matter how well you care for it, but a screen saver can extend the life of a monitor severalfold. *See also* ANIMATION, CATHODE-RAY TUBE, *and* PASSWORD.

Scrolling

Scrolling refers to the movement of a cursor, window, or pointer within a document as displayed on a monitor screen. The simplest example of scrolling is movement of the cursor in a text file, using the Up or Down Arrow keys. In most word processing programs, pressing the Up Arrow will move, or scroll, the cursor up by one line; pressing the Down Arrow will scroll the cursor downward by one line. Holding down these keys will cause the cursor to scroll upward or downward at a rate of several lines per second.

If you want to scroll fast, you can use the Page Up or Page Down keys. Pressing these keys once will move the cursor upward or downward by one full screen. Holding the keys down will cause the cursor to scroll upward or downward at a rate of several screens per second.

In a graphical user interface (GUI), scrolling can be done via the mouse as well as by means of keyboard keys. The methods vary somewhat from program to program. One common method requires you to move the pointer to an up arrow or down arrow in a corner of the active window, and hold down the left mouse button. *See also* ARROW KEYS, CURSOR, PAGE DOWN KEY, PAGE UP KEY, POINTER, *and* SCROLL LOCK KEY AND LIGHT.

Scroll Lock key and light

The *Scroll Lock* key is found on the keyboards of IBM-compatible PCs. It is usually located in the upper right part of the keyboard, just to the right of the function keys, and to the left of the Num, Caps, and Scroll lights (see the drawing).

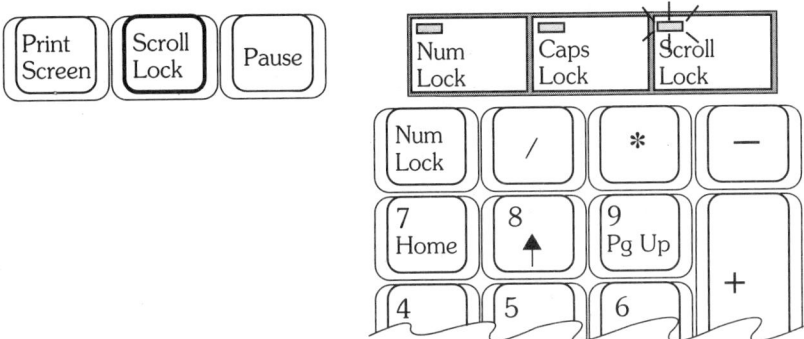

The Scroll Lock key and light on an IBM-compatible PC keyboard.

The Scroll Lock key toggles on and off. That is, when you press it once, the Scroll Lock function is activated, and when you press it again, the function is deactivated. The status of Scroll Lock is indicated by the Scroll light.

The function of Scroll Lock depends on the program you're using. For details, read the instructions for your software. Alternatively, you can play around with this key and learn what it does by trial and error. If it has any effect at all, it will usually be on the behavior of the arrow keys. Always do this experiment with a file that has been backed up on diskette, so you don't irreparably corrupt your data if something unexpected happens. *See also* ARROW KEYS.

SCSI technology

The abbreviation *SCSI*, pronounced "scuzzy," stands for *Small Computer System Interface*. It refers to a method of connecting peripherals in a PC system.

Conventional versus SCSI. The conventional scheme for hooking up peripherals requires the use of a separate expansion board for each unit. You'll need one expansion board for a CD-ROM drive, another for a fax/modem, another for sound equipment, and another for a high-resolution monitor. Most desktop PCs have provision for several expansion boards, but if you become a real power user, it's possible that you'll run out of expansion slots.

SCSI technology

The drawing at A is a simple block diagram showing a PC main unit with four peripherals connected. The peripherals are labeled P1, P2, P3, and P4. Each external item has its own expansion board.

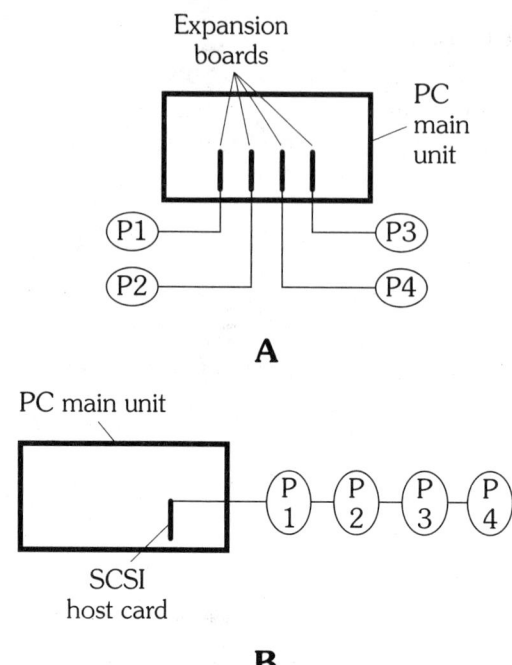

A conventional peripheral interconnection (A) and a SCSI interconnection (B).

The engineers at Apple Computer, Inc. who designed the Macintosh line of computers came up with an alternative idea for connecting peripherals to the main unit of a PC. Why not use a single expansion board or adapter, capable of handling all the peripherals? That way, things would be less messy and less bulky, and there would be less hassle involved when adding peripherals to a system. The peripherals, rather than being connected to the main unit via independent lines, would be hooked up along a single line in *daisy-chain network* fashion, as in the drawing at B. This train of thought led to the SCSI.

Today there are several variations of SCSI. You might hear about *SCSI-2 technology*, a refinement of SCSI, and about *SCSI-3 technology*, a further advance along the same lines. The SCSI-3 scheme is more often called *FireWire*, a name coined by Apple Computer, Inc. Other computer manufacturers have designed their own variations of SCSI technology.

Operation. In a SCSI chain, each peripheral is assigned an address, like items in a computer memory. The main unit also gets an address. The addresses are numbers, or *IDs* (identifications), from binary 000 to 111 (decimal 0 to 7). The peripherals can have ID 000 to ID 110 (decimal 0 to 6); the main unit always has ID 111 (decimal 7). In drawing B, there are four peripherals, labeled P1 through P4. They might have ID 001, ID 010, ID 011, and ID 100 (decimal 1 through 4). The main unit has ID 111 (decimal 7).

When the main unit needs to communicate with a given peripheral, it must know the ID of the peripheral. Then, the message from the main unit proceeds along the chain until it gets to the peripheral having the correct ID. Only one "conversation" can take place along the chain at any given time. If two peripherals try to communicate with the main unit simultaneously, the peripheral with the higher ID number will be heeded first, and then the peripheral with the lower ID will be accommodated. If the main unit wants to communicate with any peripheral, it must ensure that the chain is clear before sending out a command.

A SCSI system uses a tactic called *handshaking* to verify the accuracy of signals sent along the chain. Commands are always acknowledged. That way, there is minimum chance of confusion, such as a fax/modem receiving and trying to act upon instructions intended for a CD-ROM drive.

Assets and limitations. The biggest advantage of SCSI technology is that it's a *plug-and-play* scheme, at least in theory. You need only one adapter card, called a *SCSI host card*, rather than several different expansion boards. This saves money and minimizes the headaches you'll have when installing peripherals—provided that the peripherals are SCSI-compatible. Therein lies the main problem with SCSI: compatibility, or more accurately, incompatibility.

The industry has not yet devised universal standards for SCSI technology. Thus, there is a potpourri of software around, some of which will work with some systems, and some of which will work with others. This sort of situation is nothing new to anyone with experience in personal computing.

If you're having trouble getting a SCSI-equipped system to work, you can enlist the help of a "PC guru" friend or call the toll-free technical support number for the equipment in question. Always read brochures and specifications before purchasing peripherals for a SCSI system, and be sure that the device is compatible with your system. Don't be afraid to ask questions. If the dealer can't help you, take the brochures home and call the manufacturers yourself until you're satisfied that you'll be spending your money on something that will work properly with your system.

SCSI is fast. The daisy chain is like a multilane turnpike, compared with the cables in a conventional system, which are more like two-lane roads. All of the connections in a SCSI chain are *parallel* interfaces, transmitting and receiving bits of data in bunches; in conventional

Search and replace

systems, some of the interfaces are *serial*, transferring data one bit at a time.

The SCSI scheme is well-suited to use with laptop computers because it saves physical space. SCSI host circuitry can be fabricated onto PCMCIA standard adapter cards, which are now standard with most portable computers. This eliminates the need for expansion slots. *See also* DAISY-CHAIN NETWORK, EXPANSION BOARD, HANDSHAKING, PARALLEL, PCMCIA STANDARD ADAPTER CARDS, PLUG-AND-PLAY, *and* SERIAL.

Search and replace

Search and replace is a feature found in most word processing programs and some other applications. It allows you to replace a character string (such as a word or phrase) with some other character string throughout a text file.

An example. Suppose you're writing a magazine article. You are aware of the fact that you use the word *may* too often, and in places where it really shouldn't be used. This is a common mistake that writers make. An example is found in this sentence, "If you leave your PC on all the time, data may be lost in the event of a power failure."

Using the search and replace function, you can have the computer go through the whole article, changing every instance of *may* to *might*. Then the aforementioned sentence would become, "If you leave your PC on all the time, data might be lost in the event of a power failure."

There is a potential problem with this, as you might guess. There are instances where *may* is a proper word to use. An example is the imperative:

"You may not switch the computer off until you have quit the application program." You would not want to change this to *might*—the resulting sentence would hardly make sense. Nor would you want to use *can*. (Of course you can switch a computer off any time you feel like it!)

If you use search and replace, you'll want to check every instance where a change is made, to ensure that the changes don't result in absurdity. Consider the sentence, "Keep liquids away from your computer keyboard. This includes sandwiches containing condiments such as ketchup or mayonnaise." This sentence is strange enough as it is. Indiscriminate use of a *may*-to-*might* search and replace would make it nonsensical.

Search only. These examples might scare some people entirely away from search and replace. That's an overreaction. An alternative is to use a simple *search*, in which the computer locates occurrences of a character string one by one.

Searching for *may* from the beginning of a document will cause the cursor to jump to the first instance of that string. You can then decide if you want to change it. If you want to make a change, you can choose to do so. Searching from that point, the cursor will jump to the second occurrence of the string, where you can again decide what to do. The search function can be repeated until you reach the end of the document. This scheme requires more time than search and replace, but it reduces the likelihood that embarrassing errors will get into print.

Obviously, it's important to proofread documents before they are sent to their recipients. A slow, thorough proofreading will help you catch subtle mistakes, typos, and other problems. If you set a piece of work aside and then proofread it a few days later, mistakes will be obvious, and you'll be able to correct them easily. *See also* WORD PROCESSING.

Secondary storage

Secondary storage is a form of data storage with large capacity. It can vary in size from a few hundred kilobytes (KB) to more than 1000 megabytes (MB). It differs from primary storage in several respects. First, it's usually bigger. Second, the access time and storage time are generally longer. Third, it's nonvolatile, meaning that it keeps its contents even when electric power is removed. (Primary storage is usually volatile, which vanishes the instant the power is switched off.) Fourth, it is not part of the computer's main memory.

Types. The most common secondary storage media are disks of various kinds. Tapes are also used, as well as other, nonmagnetic forms of storage. Here are the most common types of secondary storage used with a PC:

- *Diskette* Conventional magnetic diskettes can only hold somewhat more than 1MB of data. However, there's practically no limit to the number of diskettes you can have in your archives. One problem with conventional diskettes is that high-level programs can take up dozens of them. This makes installation tedious.

- *Hard disk* Most PCs have a hard disk with a capacity of at least several hundred megabytes. Some hard disks can hold more than 1000MB, or a gigabyte (GB). These are the fastest mechanical secondary storage media. Depending on processor speed, a 1MB file might need less than one second, or up to several seconds to access or store.

- *CD-ROMs* These are optical media. CD-ROMs have high capacity, more than 600MB per 5-inch disk, but they are considerably slower than diskettes or hard disks. Also, it's not generally possible to overwrite data on a CD-ROM; to do that, you need an erasable optical drive, which is rather expensive.

Secondary storage

- *Tape* Magnetic tape is an economical, compact way to store large volumes of data. A tape drive is not expensive; a small hard disk can be backed up on one cartridge. Tape drives are slow because the data is written and accessed sequentially. Thus, they aren't well-suited to everyday computing, but tapes are ideal for archives.

- *Flash memory* This is an extremely fast storage medium, rivaling RAM (random-access memory) in access time. The capacity is upwards of 40MB. Flash memory has no moving parts, as do disk and tape drives. However, flash memory is comparatively expensive.

- *PCMCIA cards* Some of these cards, which resemble bank automatic-teller cards, can work as flash memory. They're as easy to exchange as diskettes.

- *Bernoulli box* This is a specialized drive that combines the assets of a hard disk and a diskette drive system. Bernoulli cartridges can hold as much data as a small hard disk, but can be interchanged as easily as diskettes.

- *Floptical diskettes* These are diskettes with enhanced capacity. They work by compressing the data tracks. The read/write head of the drive is guided along by an optical system that increases its precision severalfold over a conventional diskette drive.

Hardcopy is a form of secondary storage, too, although it is the oldest, slowest, and bulkiest way to store data. It's also uneconomical. There's no good reason to make hardcopies for use as archives or backups, but many people stubbornly cling to the belief that hardcopy is better than magnetic, electronic, or optical media.

Assets and limitations. Secondary storage is vital to any computer system. One of its biggest advantages is that it's nonvolatile. It won't "evaporate" in the event of a power failure. When you put away a diskette, tape, or CD-ROM, you can be confident that the data will stay intact for months, if not years.

Another advantage of secondary storage is its unlimited capacity. A 5.25-inch, high-density diskette can hold 1.2MB of data. You can put 10 such diskettes into a storage box just a little more than an inch thick; 10 of these boxes, side by side, occupy a foot of shelf space and can store 120MB. If you're willing to sacrifice access speed, you can easily store that much data on one cassette tape.

Still another asset of secondary storage (with the exception of hardcopy) is that it's easy and cheap to duplicate. You can keep one copy of your archives near your PC at home and another copy at work. You might have a third copy at the house of a good friend or relative. That way, even a catastrophe such as a fire, hurricane, or burglary will not destroy your data.

The main limitation of secondary storage (with the exception of flash memory) is that you can't work directly with it. That is, it does not change from instant to instant, as RAM does. This is not a serious constraint for most computer users. For power users who need a super-fast secondary storage medium, and who are willing to pay the price, flash memory will usually suffice.

See also ACCESS TIME, ARCHIVES, BACKUP, BERNOULLI BOX, CD-ROM, DISKETTE, FLOPTICAL DISKETTE AND DRIVE, HARD DISK, MAGNETIC DISK, MAGNETIC MEDIA, MAGNETIC TAPE, MASS STORAGE, MEMORY, NONVOLATILE MEMORY, PAPERLESS OFFICE, PCMCIA STANDARD ADAPTER CARDS, PRIMARY STORAGE, RANDOM-ACCESS MEMORY, READ-ONLY MEMORY, STORAGE TIME, TAPE DRIVE, VOLATILE MEMORY, *and* WRITE-ONCE/READ-MANY.

Sector

A *sector* is a small portion of a magnetic disk usually containing 512 bytes of data. A disk can have from several hundred to several thousand sectors, depending on the configuration.

Circles and arcs. On a magnetic disk, data is arranged in circles called *tracks*. Magnetic-disk tracks differ from those in a CD-ROM. A CD-ROM track is a long, tightly wound spiral, but magnetic disk tracks are separate, concentric circles.

Each track in a magnetic disk is divided into several equal-size arcs. These arcs are the sectors. The number of sectors per track varies depending on the type of disk. In general, the higher the disk density, the more sectors per track. The drawing shows how sectors compare with tracks. Sectors have constant angular measure. The physical length of a sector therefore depends on where the track is located. Sectors on inner tracks are shorter than sectors on outer tracks.

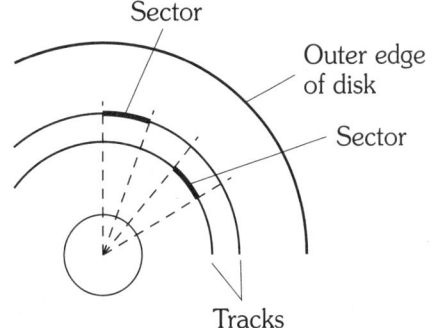

An arc within a track on a magnetic disk.

Particle "responsibility." All magnetic media, including disks, contain millions of tiny particles, each of which is a magnet. The particles are magnetized and demagnetized by the read/write head as it moves over the surface of the medium. The more particles in a given region of the medium, the greater the data storage capacity of that region.

The particle density is constant everywhere on a magnetic disk. However, because sectors always have 512 bytes, and because inner sectors are shorter than outer ones, data is more dense near the center than near the outside of the disk. This, in effect, gives the innermost particles more "responsibility" than the outermost ones. (This harkens back to the days of phonograph disks, in which the groove bumps were more closely bunched near the center than near the outside.) Disk systems take this into account when writing onto new disks. The outer sectors are used up first; as the disk is filled, data is written onto sectors closer and closer to the center.

Bad sectors. When you format a diskette, be sure to check the byte count that your computer displays upon completion of the process. If there are *bad sectors*, throw the diskette away. Otherwise, data might be corrupted when stored on the diskette. Many computer users have paid a steep price for inadvertently using diskettes with bad sectors to store vital data.

On a hard disk, bad sectors are not normally a problem. Most new hard disks have a few bad sectors; the computer simply works around them. *See also* BAD SECTORS, CD-ROM, CYLINDER, DISKETTE, HARD DISK, MAGNETIC DISK, MAGNETIC MEDIA, PLATTER, *and* TRACK.

Security

Security refers to the protection of data against unauthorized snooping and tampering. Security programs are available for PCs. Some utility packages contain security software. This article describes some common features of security programs.

Passwords. The most obvious way to limit access to secured data is to use a password system. The best passwords combine letters and numbers in a form that is *easy* for authorized users to recall, but difficult for hackers to guess at or generate via a random attack. An example is *ll0ness* where the second and third characters are the numerals one and zero, respectively.

Suppose you want 100 people to be able to read a file, but not change any of its contents. Of these people, perhaps 25 might be allowed to add material to the file, as well as read it; however, they can't change data already in the file. A subgroup of this group, say five people, might have full access to the file, including authorization to change existing information. In this situation, you would need a *multilevel password*, also known as a *hierarchical password*.

If you have a set of files to which everyone has equal access, you can have just one password. Then, anyone who uses that password (whether single-level or multilevel) will be able to get into all of the files. However, you might want some people to have access to some of the files, while other people are allowed into other files. In that sort of situation, you'd need different passwords for different files. Some of these passwords might be single-level, while others might be multilevel.

The most complex password system assigns a separate password or set of passwords to each person authorized to access a set of files. In this way, you can tailor each person's extent of access in exactly the way you want. In the extreme, each individual will have a separate password for each authorized file. If there are 15 people and 20 files, then, there could be as many as 300 different passwords, some single-level and others multilevel.

If someone tries to break into the system by making repeated guesses at a password or part of a password, the computer can deny access after a certain number of attempts. Usually, three attempts is enough for an authorized person to get the password right. When access is denied because of too many attempts, the date, time, and identity (if available) of the user can be logged.

Other features. Further safeguards against tampering and snooping can be added to a security scheme. Sometimes, even authorized personnel must be kept from installing, copying, or sabotaging data and software. Here are some typical security features, in addition to password-protection:

> ➤ *Encryption* is the conversion of data into a nonstandard form. It adds an additional security step, after use of a password, to keep data from getting into the wrong eyes. If a password is broken or stolen, a decryption program must be used to make sense of encrypted information. Each user must have, in addition to a password or set of passwords, a decryption package.

> ➤ *Hard disk lockout* keeps people from storing anything on a PC's hard disk. The main reason for having this feature is to keep a Trojan horse or virus from getting into the computer. A Trojan horse or virus can derail the machine's operating system. In the worst case, the result can be a catastrophic loss or leakage of secured information. With lockout, it's still possible to read the data on the hard disk, provided the user has gotten through the password and decryption barriers.

Security systems

> *Copy protection* keeps people from putting secured data on diskettes, and thereby helps to ensure that the information doesn't leak. Even people with the passwords and decryption codes—that is, supposedly authorized personnel—can't always be trusted. Copy protection can also keep people from transmitting the data out of the system via modem.

> *Access attempt logging* notes the date and time whenever anyone tries to gain access to secured data. This can be useful in case secured information does happen to leak out. Irregularities in the use pattern often show up in an access attempt log.

High-level security. For the protection of especially sensitive archives and classified information, a complete, high-level, computerized security system can be installed. It works in the same way as a property-protection security system, except that data, not material, is the object of the security effort.

With a high-level security system, you can not only restrict people's ability to access data from a computer, but also keep unauthorized people from physically getting near the machine. In addition, every person who logs onto the system can be positively identified, along with the date, time, and filenames accessed. *See also* CRYPTANALYSIS/CRYPTOGRAPHY/CRYPTOLOGY, ENCRYPTION, HARD DISK, PASSWORD, SECURITY SYSTEMS, TROJAN HORSE, *and* VIRUS.

Security systems

Computerized *security systems* are "smart" intrusion-prevention devices. They range from simple machines such as card readers or pushbutton-code mechanisms to sophisticated electromechanical networks under the control of a computer.

Less complex security systems are usually adequate for homeowners and small businesses. Large corporations, government agencies, and businesses with high-value inventory are more likely to be interested in advanced security systems.

Knowledge-based. The *knowledge-based security system* is the simplest type. Authorized people are issued numerical codes. The entrances to the property are equipped with locks that disengage when the proper sequence of numbers is punched into a keypad. It works like a bank automatic-teller ID code. There might be just one access code given to all the personnel, or there might be a different one issued to each authorized person. The term *knowledge-based* arises from the fact that, in order to gain entry, a person must know a specific piece of information (in this case the access code).

One of the main advantages of this type of system is that the codes can't easily be guessed. The authorized people should memorize their access numbers. The numbers should never be written down in any form that will give away their meaning or purpose. Another asset of knowledge-based security systems is their relatively low cost.

A disadvantage of this scheme is that access codes occasionally leak out. People tend to give secrets away when situations come up that make it expedient to do so. Also, codes are sometimes forcibly stolen. Once a code is stolen, anyone who has it can get into the property until that code is invalidated.

Possession-based. A more sophisticated scheme is the *possession-based security system*. This gets its name from the fact that authorized people must possess some object that unlocks the entry to a property.

Magnetic cards are a popular form of possession-based security device. You insert the card into a slot, and a microcomputer reads data encoded on a magnetic strip. This data can be as simple as an access code of the sort you punch on a keypad, or it might contain many details about the card-bearer. A smart card can be used for security purposes. So can bank ATM cards, credit cards, and PCMCIA standard adapter cards.

The *passive transponder* provides another form of possession-based security system. These are magnetic or barcode tags that can be carried or worn by authorized personnel. They're the same little things that department stores use to deter petty thieves. The transponder need not be inserted in a slot; it can be read from several feet away. If you've ever been leaving a store and been detained because an electronic detector beeped at you, you've experienced a passive transponder at work.

The main advantage of possession-based security systems is convenience. You need not worry about forgetting a code number. However, this is more or less nullified by the fact that little plastic cards can easily get misplaced. They're also easy to steal.

Biometric. A highly advanced intrusion-prevention scheme, the *biometric security system*, gets its name from the fact that it ascertains, or measures, biological characteristics of the people who are authorized to enter a property. Such a machine can employ vision systems and object recognition to check a person's face. It might use speech recognition to identify people by the waveforms of their voices. It might record a handprint or fingerprint. It could employ a combination of all these things. A powerful computer analyzes the data obtained by the sensors and determines whether or not the person is authorized to enter the premises.

Biometric systems are essentially foolproof. However, they must be backed up by threat of force if they are to be of real use. Wherever security requirements are so strict that a biometric security system is needed, there will probably be a few brilliant and daring people intent upon defeating it and getting into the premises. A government embassy in a hostile country is a prime example of such a property. While the system can be almost impossible to fool, it must also be set up so that it can't be overcome by a brute-force surprise attack. History shows that it is difficult to do this, and at the same time ensure that no authorized personnel can be injured because of a system error.

For homeowners and small businesses, biometric systems are generally too expensive. But, of course, this depends on what's on the property. Top-secret archives, priceless works of art, and some scientific experiments (and research personnel) justify the most sophisticated security systems available, no matter what the cost.

Robotic. A multipurpose personal robot might be deployed as a security device or as a backup to a biometric security system. A large, armed robot might deter some intruders by intimidation. If an unauthorized person succeeds in entering a property, a security robot could drive the offender away or detain the offender until police arrive.

Robots of this sort have been depicted in movies. Some people think such machines will eventually become commonplace. However, there are numerous bugs and a few potential dangers (conveniently ignored by movie producers).

Here are some examples of the challenges facing designers of the ultimate security robot. They're stated as questions, to which the engineers will have to provide satisfactory answers and solutions:

- Can a robot be made quick enough, and with good enough vision, to chase down an intruder or win a fight with a human being who is in good physical condition?
- Can such robots be designed to detect any intruder, any time? Or will it be easy for a burglar to sneak by undetected?
- Can such robots be tamper-proof?
- Can such a machine be designed to withstand an assault with practically any weapon?
- Will property owners ever be able to trust their security robots to work all the time?
- What if the robot malfunctions and thinks an authorized person is an intruder?
- Can a machine lawfully use deadly force, although it is not alive and thus cannot have its life endangered?

> If a robot can't legally use deadly force, of what real use is it?
> What if a security robot injures or kills an intruder?

The block diagram illustrates a hypothetical computerized security system, with advanced technologies including autonomous robots and insect robots (labeled AR and IR, respectively). This is the sort of system you might encounter if you ever find yourself working for a corporation involved in 21st-century top-secret government contracts.

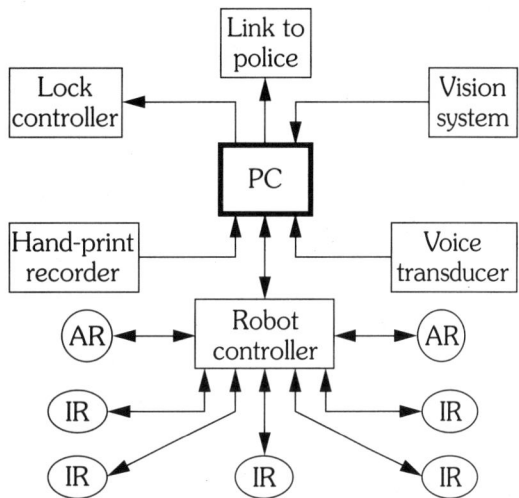

A plausible 21st-century computerized security installation using autonomous robots (AR) and insect robots (IR).

See also ARTIFICIAL INTELLIGENCE, ASIMOV'S THREE LAWS, AUTONOMOUS ROBOTS, BARCODE, CARETAKERS, COMPUTERIZED HOME, INSECT ROBOTS, OBJECT RECOGNITION, PASSIVE TRANSPONDER, PASSWORD, PATTERN RECOGNITION, PCMCIA STANDARD ADAPTER CARDS, PERSONAL ROBOTS, REMOTE CONTROL SYSTEMS, SMART CARD, SPEECH RECOGNITION, SPEECH SYNTHESIS, SPY SOFTWARE, TELEOPERATION, TELEPRESENCE, *and* VISION SYSTEMS.

Semilog graph

A *semilog graph* is a specialized form of Cartesian coordinates. In conventional Cartesian graphs, all the axes have linear scales; that is, the units are all the same size. In a semilog graph, some (but not all) of the axes are graduated logarithmically.

An example of a two-dimensional semilog coordinate system is shown in the graph. The y axis is linear, and extends from zero in both the positive and negative directions. The x axis is logarithmic and starts at 0.1, going only in the positive direction.

Logarithmic scales can't go down to zero, but they can be repeated over and over, extending the axis through several orders of magnitude

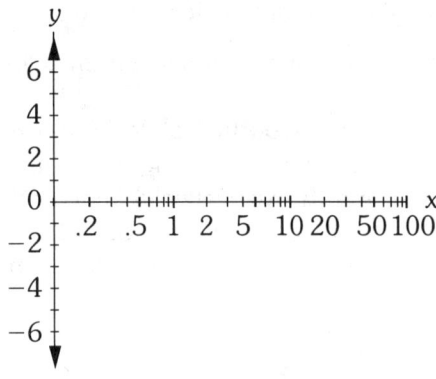

In this example, the x axis is logarithmic and the y axis is linear.

(powers of 10). In the drawing, the x axis range is from 0.1 to 100, covering three orders of magnitude. This in effect compresses the scale. Imagine how long the x axis would have to be if it were marked off in increments of 0.1, all the way from 0.1 to 100! To be readable, it would have to be at least several feet long. A computer display would be nowhere near big enough to accommodate it. This is the chief advantage of semilog graphs. With them, you can get extremely elongated or large graphs down to a manageable size.

When the independent variable axis or axes of a semilog graph are graduated linearly, and only the dependent variable axis has a logarithmic scale, the system is called a *logarithmic graph*. When all the axes are logarithmic, the system is known as a *log-log* graph.

Analytical graphics software packages usually have a provision for making semilog graphs. Most can generate two- and three-dimensional coordinate systems in which some, or all, of the scales are logarithmic. These are especially useful in mathematical, engineering, and scientific work. *See also* ANALYTICAL GRAPHICS, CARTESIAN COORDINATES, DEPENDENT VARIABLE, INDEPENDENT VARIABLE, LOGARITHMIC GRAPH, *and* LOG-LOG GRAPH.

SeniorNet

In the 1980s, Mary Furlong, an education professor at the University of San Francisco, conducted research into the benefits that online services might provide for older people. The eventual result was *SeniorNet*, now a popular PC communications network. Most users of SeniorNet say that it has enriched their lives. In some cases, it has helped to make "techies" out of former cyberphobics.

SeniorNet is a nonprofit organization based in San Francisco. It is intended for people aged 55 and over, and is accessible throughout the U.S. and in some foreign countries. There is a modest annual fee for membership. The network operates through America Online, a major online service.

Components. All online services require similar hardware. To use SeniorNet, you will need the following:

- A PC with a hard disk
- Communications software
- A telephone line
- A modem
- Access to America Online

Features. SeniorNet offers a wide variety of activities to hold the interest of its users. Some of these are as follows:

- *Online activities* Members can "chat" with other members, leave messages on bulletin-board systems (BBSs), send and receive electronic mail (e-mail), download software and data, and join special-interest discussion groups. It's even possible to develop online romances.

- *Learning centers* There are dozens of SeniorNet learning centers around the U.S. They offer classes in application software, as well as general technical assistance. After you've made friends online, you can meet some of them at these centers.

- *Newsletter* A magazine called *Newsline* keeps members informed about new software, technological advances, the Internet (sometimes called the information superhighway), and special projects. There's a calendar of online activities, and a "Corner Store" catalog of books and workstation accessories.

- *Books* SeniorNet publishes books on various subjects of special interest to older computer users. Much of the material for these publications comes from the members' experiences.

- *Discounts* Members can get special bargains on certain publications and software packages. Sometimes there are free giveaways, as well.

- *National conferences* A large convention is held periodically, where SeniorNet members can meet with computer experts and industry executives. Workshops are given in various subjects, at all experience levels. At these conferences, you can meet online friends not only from your locale, but from all over the world.

For more information. SeniorNet, like other online services, is evolving and expanding. Seniors are becoming an increasingly large part of the population, and PCs are becoming more affordable and more powerful. For complete information on SeniorNet, write to

SeniorNet
399 Arguello Boulevard
San Francisco, CA 94118

See also AMERICA ONLINE, INTERNET, *and* ONLINE SERVICE.

Sequential access memory

In *sequential-access memory (SAM)*, data can be recalled (accessed) only in a certain order. Any form of memory can be designed to work this way. The most common forms of sequential-access memory are the *first-in/first-out* (FIFO) and the *pushdown stack*.

SAM differs from random-access memory (RAM). One way to think of the difference between SAM and RAM is to compare audiotapes and CDs. In this sense, SAM is analogous to an audiocassette tape, while RAM works like a compact disc.

If the addresses in a memory are numbered, such as 1, 2, 3, . . . n, then a common sequence for recall is upward from 1 to n. A downward sequence, from n to 1, is also fairly common. Sometimes there are sequences in which the addresses "jump around." However, even if the order seems random or nonsensical, it is programmed that way for some good reason.

The data from a SAM might be addressed in two or more different sequences. This is typical of read-only memory (ROM). If data can be written in and recalled in any order, the memory is RAM, sometimes called a *read/write memory*. *See also* FIRST-IN/FIRST-OUT, MEMORY, PUSHDOWN STACK, RANDOM-ACCESS MEMORY, *and* READ-ONLY MEMORY.

Sequential logic

In digital electronics, the term *sequential logic* refers to any circuit or circuit element whose output depends both on present and past conditions.

A sequential-logic circuit has one or more inputs, and one output. The present state of the output depends on the present states of the inputs, and also on the immediately previous state of the output. An example of a sequential-logic circuit is a *flip-flop*, also called a *bistable multivibrator* or *latch*. *See also* FLIP-FLOP *and* LOGIC GATES.

Serial

Information can be transmitted simultaneously along two or more lines, or it can be sent bit by bit along a single line. The first method is known as *parallel data transfer*. The latter method is called *serial* data transfer. The term *serial* is used because data is sent in a predetermined sequence or series of bits, one after another.

In computers, serial data transfer requires that a word be split up into its bits, then sent over the line, and reassembled at the other end of the line in the same order as originally (see the drawing).

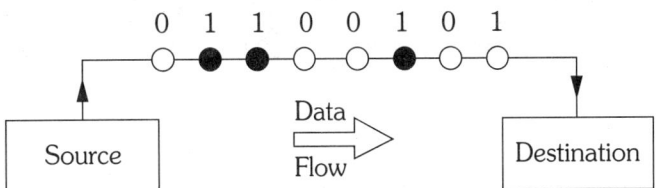

An eight-bit word sent along a single line.

Serial data needs only one transmission line, while parallel data requires several lines running side-by-side. This is the main asset of serial data transfer. Another advantage is that serial data can be sent over longer distances than parallel data because there is no crosstalk, or interaction among signal lines. The main limitation of serial transmission is that, all other things being equal, it can be done at only a fraction of the speed of parallel data transfer. *See also* PARALLEL.

Serial port

A *serial port* is a connector found on the back of a PC's main unit. Data passes through this connector one bit at a time. Serial ports are used with peripherals that work at comparatively slow data speeds. Such peripherals include modems, mice, tape drives, and some printers.

A serial port has one big advantage over a parallel port: simplicity. Only one line is needed for data transfer. This makes it possible to send data over long distances without crosstalk. This feature is also the serial port's most significant limitation, however. A serial port can transfer data only a fraction as fast as a typical parallel port. Consider this analogy:

SERIAL PORT : SINGLE-LANE ROAD
::
PARALLEL PORT : MULTI-LANE FREEWAY

That is, a serial port is to a single-land road as a parallel port is to a multilane freeway. Both routes can get you where you want to go, but there's a huge difference in transit time.

Serial data transmission is convenient and efficient when simple files of small size must be sent a long distance. The limitations of serial data transfer become apparent when you want to send or receive very long files or programs online, or when you want to print large volumes of data.

Serial data transmission is being done at faster and faster speeds as technology advances, making it practical to transfer fairly large files and programs via serial ports. This situation should continue to improve as applications like remote-control systems, telecommuting, teleconferencing, and teleoperation evolve. These demand high-speed serial data transfer capability. *See also* MODEM, ONLINE SERVICE, PARALLEL, PARALLEL PORT, PERIPHERALS, REMOTE-CONTROL SYSTEMS, SERIAL, TELECOMMUTING, TELECONFERENCING, *and* TELEOPERATION.

Server

In a local area network (LAN), there are several nodes, also called workstations. These are all interconnected so they can share data. There are various arrangements, called *topologies*, for LANs.

When all LAN workstations derive their data from a central machine, the LAN is called a *client-server network*. Each workstation is a *client*, and the central computer is the *server*. While some high-end PCs can operate as servers, a mainframe or minicomputer is often needed, especially if the LAN has very many workstations.

Imagine a LAN with 10 workstations. Four of the nodes might be dumb terminals, and the other six PCs. Each node is connected to the server. There are no intervening nodes between any workstation and the central computer. When diagrammed, the network resembles a Ferris wheel (see the drawing). The server is the "hub"; the nodes are the "cars," and the data links are the "spokes" of the wheel.

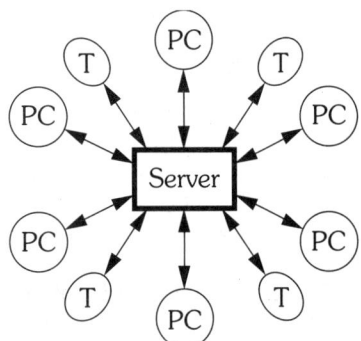

A server provides data for computerized nodes (labeled PC) and dumb terminals (labeled T) in some kinds of networks.

Suppose you own a small, rapidly expanding business that's starting to make a lot of money. You decide you need a LAN with 10 workstations and one server. You might buy 10 PCs for the workstations, and a minicomputer to act as the server. The network can be expanded later, simply by adding more workstations (clients). *See also* CLIENT, DUMB TERMINAL, FILE SERVER, LOCAL AREA NETWORK, MAINFRAME, MINICOMPUTER, NODE, *and* STAR NETWORK.

Shareware

Computer software can be obtained in a variety of ways. You can purchase it in a store, packed in neat boxes. You can order it over the telephone, through the mail, or online, and have it sent to you. In some cases, it can be downloaded from online, via modem.

Direct-purchase software is the most expensive way to obtain computer programs. Some direct-purchase packages cost in excess of $1000. You can be reasonably sure that the programs will work, however, because part of the price you pay has gone into extensive testing of the package prior to marketing.

Some software is free. It's in the public domain, and can be exchanged online, or on diskettes, without restriction. You might have obtained such *freeware* from friends, government agencies, or benevolent organizations. This is generally the least reliable software. It often works just fine, but it has not been tested as thoroughly as direct-purchase software.

Still other software can be obtained on a trial basis, and paid for only if you like it enough that you want to keep it. This is called *shareware*. It's just about as good as direct-purchase software, but it's been created with lower overhead. The advantage of shareware is that it's generally cheaper than direct-purchase software (if you choose to buy it). Another asset is that you get to check the programs out at your leisure, on your own computer, in your own space. You won't feel rushed or pressured, as you might feel in a store.

Shareware is commonly distributed on CD-ROM (compact-disc, read-only memory), as well as on conventional magnetic diskettes. It's possible to put several dozen programs on a single CD-ROM. Encryption is used to prevent would-be buyers from downloading the software onto their hard disk or onto diskettes before they pay for it. If you have obtained shareware, and you like a program enough to buy it, you can call a toll-free number and use a credit card to pay. The vendor will supply you with the code to decrypt the software and install it in your system. *See also* FREEWARE *and* SOFTWARE.

Shift key

The *Shift key* is found on all computer keyboards. Its function is similar to that of the Shift key on an electronic typewriter. There are usually two of these keys, one at the lower left on the keyboard, and the other at the lower right (see the drawing). Both keys have identical functions.

Without Caps Lock. When you're typing characters on a computer keyboard, they are either uppercase or lowercase. This depends on whether or not you are holding down the Shift key. It also depends on the status of the Caps Lock key.

Shift key

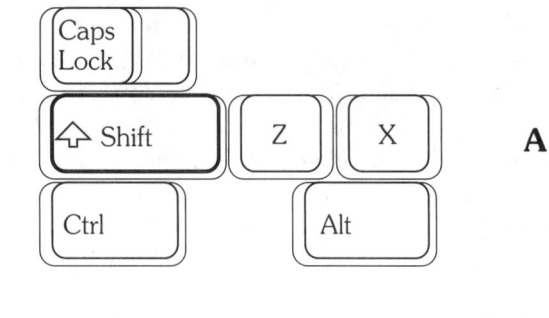

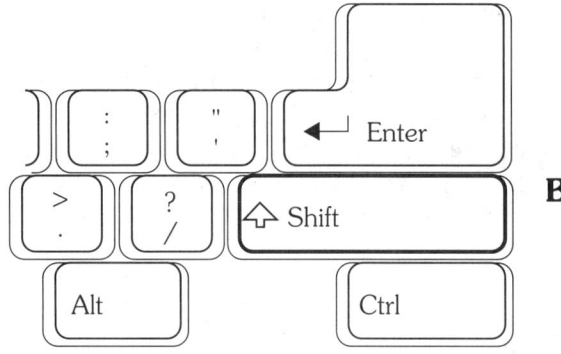

Shift keys are found at lower left (A) and lower right (B) of the keyboard.

Suppose you strike a certain sequence of keys, getting this result:

123 abc xyz ,./

In this case, the Shift key is not being held down, and the Caps Lock function is not actuated. The letters are lowercase. If a key has two symbols on it (top and bottom), the bottom symbol will appear on the screen.

If you press the same sequence of keys while holding down the Shift key, the result will be

!@# ABC XYZ <>?

The letters become uppercase. For keys with top and bottom symbols, the top symbols appear on the screen.

With Caps Lock. Now suppose you press Caps Lock, so the Caps light comes on. Then, if you hit the same sequence of keys again without holding down the Shift key, you'll get

123 ABC XYZ ,./

The letters become uppercase. For keys with top and bottom symbols, the bottom symbols appear on the screen.

Finally, leave the Caps Lock key actuated and hold down the Shift key. The result, when you strike the same 12 keys, will be

```
!@# abc xyz <>?
```

The letters become lowercase again. For keys with top and bottom symbols, the top symbols appear.

Some keyboards work in ways other than that described here. The key functions on most keyboards can be changed by software. The best way to get acquainted with the idiosyncrasies of the Shift key is to play with it on a "test file" whose contents are not important. *See also* CAPS LOCK KEY AND LIGHT.

Side-by-side column format

Side-by-side column format, also called *parallel column format*, is a special method of arranging an onscreen or printed document. In one sense, it's like plain text, because it can include complete sentences and paragraphs. In another sense, it's like a table, because blocks of text are aligned with each other.

Side-by-side column format is not the same as the two-column format you've seen in books and magazines. In two-column format (also called newspaper format), you read down the left column until you get to the bottom of the page, and then you start at the top of the right column. In side-by-side column format, you read a block of text on the left, and then a corresponding block on the right. Instead of staying in the same column as you read, you constantly alternate columns.

The table shows an example of a side-by-side column document. The left column holds terms and the right column has the definitions for the terms. The definitions are, of course, longer than the terms themselves, so the right column is wider than the left one. Nevertheless, the top lines of all the text blocks are aligned horizontally, so the terms and definitions visually match up.

Side-by-side column format

Backspace	A key that moves the cursor backward one space in a text document.
Caps Lock	A key or function that changes characters from uppercase to lowercase, or vice versa, as it is toggled.
End	A key that moves the cursor to the end of the screen or block of text.
Page Down	A key that moves the cursor down one full screen in a text document.
Shift	A key that changes the case of characters only when held down.
Tab	A key that advances the cursor from one tabular marker to the next.

Side-by-side column format is used in scientific and technical writing. It's also seen in instruction manuals, textbooks, and business reports. Most word processing programs can format text in side-by-side column format. You can adjust the widths of the columns to suit your needs. *See also* SINGLE-COLUMN FORMAT *and* TWO-COLUMN FORMAT.

Significant figures

Significant figures refers to the number of meaningful digits in a numerical expression. The greater the number of significant figures, the more precise the expression.

Definition. In scientific notation, quantities are written as decimal numbers followed by powers of 10. The "computerese" variant of scientific notation is exponential notation. The decimal part of the expression can have anywhere from one to several digits. This number of digits is the number of significant figures.

Consider the following four numbers written in exponential form:

2.90E+15
8.00E−23
7.6689E+0
−4.559E−3

The number of significant figures in these expressions is three, three, five and four, respectively.

Written out in full, the above quantities are:

2,900,000,000,000,000
0.00000000000000000000008
7.6689
−0.004559

These expressions contain 16, 24, five, and seven digits, respectively. It might seem that these are also the numbers of significant figures. In "long-hand" expressions like these, however, the number of significant figures isn't always clear. This is one reason why experts prefer scientific and exponential notation.

Importance. The precision with which a number is expressed is crucial in scientific work, especially true in experimental science and in statistics. When two numbers are combined arithmetically, there is a limit to how many digits can be taken seriously. Consider the numbers 3.45 and 1.00000001. If you multiply these on a calculator having a 10-digit display, you'll get:

$3.45 \times 1.00000001 = 3.450000035$

There's a problem with this. The number 3.45 has three significant figures, while the number 1.00000001 has nine significant figures. Scientists have coined this rule: when combining expressions of differing precision, the precision of the result can never be greater than that of the least precise component. Thus, the above product has only three significant figures. A scientist would therefore write:

3.45 × 1.00000001 = 3.45

Scientists don't want to claim any more accuracy than that to which they're entitled. Doing so can yield misleading or false results.

Suppose you have several instruments that you must read while doing an experiment. If the results depend on all the instrument readings, then the accuracy of your data is limited by the least precise instrument. An old cliché illustrates this principle very well: A chain can only be as strong as its weakest link.

Computers can be programmed to work out problems taking significant digits into account. That way, you don't have to worry about them. You can rest assured that you aren't overestimating the accuracy of your data. For further information about significant figures, refer to a good introductory physics textbook. *See also* SCIENTIFIC NOTATION.

Simulation

Simulation is the use of computers to mimic real-life situations. There are various kinds of simulators; some simulators involve teaching skills for the operation of machinery, others are programs that predict (or try to predict) events in the real world.

Interactive simulators. An *interactive simulator* is like a video game. In fact, computerized video games today are more sophisticated than some simulations. There is a video monitor, a set of controls, and a set of indicators. There might also be audio devices and crude motion-imitation machines. The controls depend on the scenario.

Suppose you get into a simulator intended to mimic the experience of a racecar driver in the Indianapolis 500. The controls include an accelerator, brakes, and a steering wheel. There is a speedometer and a tachometer, as well as speakers that emit noises similar to those a real driver would hear. Perhaps the seat vibrates or rocks back and forth as the "car" goes around "curves." A screen that shows a realistic, animated, perspective-enhanced view of the road, other cars, and the surroundings.

Interactive simulation can be used as a training aid for complex skills, such as flying an aircraft. This technique is especially useful in the military, for training in a wide variety of skills.

Event simulators. An *event simulator* is a computer program that imitates, or models, the behavior of a system. For example, you might want to start a business. How well will it operate? Will you go bankrupt? Will you make a million dollars in your first year? The event simulator, if it is sophisticated enough and if it is given enough data, can help provide answers to questions like these.

An especially interesting event simulator is the forecasting model used by the National Hurricane Center in Miami, Florida. As a hurricane approaches, computers predict the most likely place for landfall. The computers compare the current situation with past storm tracks. This gives an indication of where the storm will be in 12, 24, or 36 hours. The model can also provide an idea of whether the storm's intensity will increase, decrease, or stay the same during the next few hours. The farther into the future the forecasters try to predict things, the wider the margin for error. The model can't predict where, or how strong, the hurricane will be in a week.

As event simulators get more advanced, they might incorporate artificial intelligence (AI) to draw their conclusions, but there will always be an element of uncertainty that will limit the effectiveness of event simulators. *See also* ARTIFICIAL INTELLIGENCE, COMPUTER-AIDED DESIGN, *and* COMPUTER-ASSISTED INSTRUCTION.

Single-column format

In word processing and desktop publishing, *single-column format* refers to text lines that extend all the way across the page within the allotted margins. Single-column format is used in business correspondence, novels, many nonfiction books and textbooks, theses, reports, and manuscripts.

Single-column format is "reader-friendly," while *two-column format* suggests formality. Thus, by your choice of columnar format, you can tailor the attitude with which readers approach your work. The mood adjustment is subconscious, but it occurs in the minds of your audience the moment they look at the page.

There are two ways in which single-column format is commonly printed: ragged-right and full-justified. In ragged-right text, the left margin is straight and well-defined, but the right-hand margin is irregular. In full-justified text, both the left and right margins are neat. Ragged-right text adds informality to single-column format.

A typewriter produces ragged-right print. To obtain full-justified print, you need a word processing program that adjusts word spacing so all the lines are exactly the same length (except perhaps the last lines of each paragraph).

For pleasing appearance, a single-column document must be printed in a bigger type size than a two-column document. Therefore, single-column format allows fewer words per page than two-column format.

The placement of illustrations and photographs is also affected by the choice of single-column or two-column format. *See also* FLUSH LEFT/RIGHT/CENTER, JUSTIFICATION, *and* TWO-COLUMN FORMAT.

Single-electron memory

A digital computer "thinks" in bits that can have two states, logic 0 (low) and logic 1 (high). This is known as *machine language*. All the data in a digital PC, no matter what it represents or how complicated it might be, is comprised of logic bits. This is true whether the data is in motion, as in a communications line, or whether it is fixed, as in memory.

Charge carriers. In a semiconductor memory chip, the presence or absence of electrical charge carriers determines whether a stored bit is a logic 0 or a logic 1. An *electron* is a particle with negative electric charge. It is the most common type of charge carrier. (There's another type, called a *hole*, which is an electron absence. It has a positive electric charge.) In a semiconductor chip, a single bit of data is represented by thousands of charge carriers. If this number could be reduced to just a few charge carriers per bit, the memory capacity of a chip would be greatly increased.

Computers are growing more powerful every year. The trend seems to show no sign of slowing, but there is a limit to how much data can be contained in a given physical volume. A single data bit requires, in theory, at least one charge carrier if it is to be stored in a material medium like a chip. Engineers would like to see this limit attained. It would represent a huge memory-density increase over current technology.

The electrical charge in an atom varies in steps. An electron contains a unit charge, which is always the same. This is equal, but opposite, to the positive charge in a *proton*, a heavy particle found in the nucleus of an atom. You might remember, from chemistry or physics courses, the simplified model of an atom. Electrons are wispy and light, and move among atoms. Protons are dense; it takes a big event (a nuclear reaction) to move them from one atom to another.

Suppose it were possible to have one electron make the difference between a logic 0 bit and a logic 1 bit? If this data could be stored, it would be a *single-electron memory (SEM)*. Engineers are currently working on the development of a SEM.

Ionic SEM. Some atoms have exactly the same number of electrons and protons. The positive and negative charges balance, and the atoms are electrically neutral. Suppose such an atom represents a digital logic 0 condition.

By adding one electron to an electrically neutral atom, a negative ion is created. The atoms of some substances readily accept extra

Single inline package

electrons. If a chip were made of atoms that would easily accept extra electrons, then a negative ion could represent a logic 1 bit. The movement of one electron could change the logic state of an atom. This might be called *negative-ionic SEM*.

When an electron is taken away from an electrically neutral atom, a positive ion results. The atoms of some materials readily give up electrons. If a chip were made of atoms that would easily give up electrons, a positive ion could represent logic 1 bit. This, again, would be a memory in which the movement of a single electron would make a difference. It could be called a *positive-ionic SEM*.

If a chip were composed of both these types of atoms—some "electron acceptors" and some "electron donors"—it would be possible to have three logic states: –1, 0, and +1. A negative ion could represent a logic –1 bit; a neutral atom could be a logic 0 bit; a positive ion could be a logic +1 bit. This is called *trinary logic*, in contrast to conventional *binary logic*.

Quantum SEM. Every atom of matter has electrons in shells around the nucleus. The electrons orbit the nucleus at defined altitudes. The bigger the shell, the more energy an electron has. Thus, the electrons in an atom have defined energy levels. Electrons can, and frequently do, change energy levels within atoms.

If a ray having just the right amount of energy hits an electron within an atom, the electron will move to a higher-energy shell (one with a larger diameter). An electron might also fall to a lower-energy shell and give off energy. These so-called *quantum states* make it possible for single electrons to indirectly carry digital information.

In a *quantum SEM*, a given orbital shell might represent a logic 0; a higher-energy shell could represent a logic 1. In this way, the movement of a single electron within one atom of matter could change a logic 0 to a logic 1. The challenge is to make the electrons behave themselves, so it is possible to control the logic states that they represent. *See also* BINARY DATA, BIT, INTEGRATED CIRCUIT, LOGIC, MACHINE LANGUAGE, MEMORY, *and* QUANTUM COMPUTER TECHNOLOGY.

Single inline package

A *single inline package (SIP)* is a housing for integrated circuits (ICs, also called "chips"). A flat, rectangular box containing the IC is fitted with pins along one side, as shown in the drawing. There might be just a few pins, or more than a dozen. The pins are electrical contacts that conduct signals into and out of the device. The SIP is easy to install in, and to remove from, a circuit board. It can be soldered in, or sockets can be used to allow easy component removal and replacement.

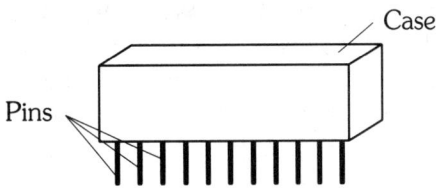

In a SIP, all the pins are along one edge of the case.

A circuit board with chips for extra RAM (random-access memory) having connectors all along one edge is called a *single inline memory module (SIMM)*. When you read the specifications for a new computer, you'll want to know how much the RAM can be expanded. Usually, extra RAM is added by purchasing and installing one or more SIMMs. *See also* DUAL INLINE PACKAGE, INTEGRATED CIRCUIT, *and* RANDOM-ACCESS MEMORY.

Small Computer System Interface

See SCSI TECHNOLOGY.

SmallTalk

SmallTalk is a high-level computer-programming language. It differs in structure from simpler languages like BASIC and Fortran. While programs in those languages are written as sequences of statements or commands, SmallTalk is an object-oriented language. The difference is like that between command-driven and graphical-user-interface (GUI) operating systems. SmallTalk was originally developed at the Xerox Corporation.

The SmallTalk GUI helps in complex design and research problems, such as those encountered by scientists and engineers. Pictures can be worth many words in programming environments, as well as in operating systems. One potential problem with SmallTalk is that it requires a large amount of memory in order to be effective. This is partly because of the GUI; graphics are known for their big memory appetites. It also results from the fact that SmallTalk is a powerful programming language. *See also* GRAPHICAL USER INTERFACE *and* OBJECT-ORIENTED PROGRAMMING.

Smart card

A *smart card* is a combination credit card, bank card, debit card, telephone calling card, and identification card. All the data is in one piece of plastic that's physically the same size as a conventional credit card. In addition to the magnetic data usually encoded on credit cards, a smart card contains a microprocessor chip along with one or more nonvolatile memory chips.

Smart cards, originally developed as a joint venture by AT&T and Chemical Bank, make use of a technology similar to that of PCMCIA standard adapter cards. In fact, it's possible that smart cards and PCMCIA cards will evolve toward a common product. Eventually, most personal computer data, programs, and functions might be contained in cards of this type. Many of your everyday affairs will then be expedited by one little rectangular piece of plastic.

A smart card can store all kinds of information about the cardholder. Bank account numbers, credit card numbers, telephone authorization numbers, insurance numbers, medical information, and other data can be included. While this offers convenience, it is risky unless you have at least one backup of the card data stored in a safe place.

The data on smart cards is encoded with the intention of preventing unauthorized people from reading it. However, hackers are always striving to find ways to break security codes. When using a smart card, it's wise to follow the same commonsense rules that you follow when using bank cards, credit cards, and other "electronic money." No matter what the data-reliability percentage claimed by system vendors, always check your bank statements, credit card statements, and other financial data when you get them, whether it be by mail, online, or by other means. In addition, be sure you know exactly what to do if your smart card is lost or stolen. *See also* NONVOLATILE MEMORY *and* PCMCIA STANDARD ADAPTER CARDS.

Smart paper

Smart paper is a method of obtaining, acknowledging, and processing data with a computer and a fax machine. It employs neural-network and optical-character-recognition (OCR) technology, along with communications software and a database. Such a system can take the place of two or three human clerical workers.

Smart paper, also called *image-based character recognition (ICR)*, can take orders for merchandise, process insurance claims, conduct polls, and take surveys. This technology might someday replace the traditional ballot box for election of government officials, if systems can be adequately protected from the activities of malicious hackers.

In action. Suppose you want to order some office supplies. You call a toll-free number, press some buttons in response to a computerized order-taking system, and receive a form on your fax machine. This form contains multiple-choice options, similar to those you've seen on standardized tests. There are also blanks for you to fill in. You darken the appropriate circles or boxes, and print data in the blank spaces, just as you would do when ordering merchandise with a catalog order form. You sign the form, and then fax it back to the vendor.

Let's switch points of view, and see what happens at the vendor site. The incoming fax (your completed order form) is received and read, not by a human being, but by a PC. The computer is equipped with software that picks up the fax electronically. There need not be an operator attending the computer while this happens, although there might be someone using it for another application at the same time. The computer sends a fax back to the customer site (your home or office), verifying receipt of the order.

The filled-out order form is read via OCR, with pattern recognition enhanced by neural-network technology. That's a fancy way of saying that the machine reads the handwriting or typing that you put in the blank spaces. Neural networks are especially good at interpreting complex and subtle patterns such as those in human handwriting. The information then proceeds to a database, where the order is filled by shipping department personnel. The merchandise will be sent to you that business day or the next (depending on the time of day your order arrived).

Assets. There are several ways in which smart paper can help a small business. Here are three of the most significant assets this technology offers:

> ➤ *Speed* Machines can process data many times faster than people. This is one of the functions for which computers are designed. Computers don't get eye fatigue, nor do they get distracted by the sorts of things that cause people's minds to stray. They don't misplace data or get things confused as often as human beings do.

> ➤ *Accuracy* No matter how complex an order might be, it's ultimately all the same to a computer: digital high and low states (ones and zeros). Humans make errors more often when information is complicated, compared to when it's simple. Not so with machines. If you've ever taken large numbers of orders, you are well aware of what mental fatigue can do. Computers don't have that problem. Errors do occur, however, with OCR technology.

> ➤ *Cost savings* A computer costs less to operate and maintain than a human being needs in the form of wages and benefits. A single PC equipped with ICR software can not only take the place of two or three human workers, but it can be used for other applications at the same time as it's processing smart paper.

Limitations. Smart paper has some shortcomings. Here are three significant limitations of this technology:

> ➤ *Imperfect OCR* Optical character recognition is not completely accurate. Errors inevitably occur. Mistakes tend to be more frequent with alphabetic characters than with numeric characters. A single error can have disastrous consequences if it occurs in a critical place. Computers have no sense of priority in this regard. When an error occurs in the worst possible place,

a machine "cares" no more than it does if the mistake is inconsequential.

➤ *Strange handwriting* Some people's handwriting is hard for people, let alone machines, to read. Anyone who has seen a doctor's prescription knows this. Some people put lines through the numeral 7 and the letter Z; some write a numeral 1 so that it looks like a 7. Idiosyncrasies like these confuse OCR. It's trained to read handwriting of the sort people are taught in grade school, not the scribbling that many people actually do.

➤ *Overconfidence* It's possible to rely too heavily on computers and their ability to process data. If the system goes down, it can bring a company's order-taking processes to a halt. Meanwhile, customers will call other vendors. Errors in orders can irritate customers, resulting in inconvenience, delayed payments, and possible damage to a company's reputation.

Requirements. If you're interested in smart paper for your business, here is what you will need:

➤ *Computer* It's best to have a machine with at least a 486 or 68040 microprocessor. This will ensure that the computer can handle the graphical applications, and will also allow multitasking should you want to use the PC for something else while it's working with smart paper. You'll want at least 8MB of RAM and 50MB to 75MB of free hard disk space.

➤ *Software* There are several software packages available for ICR applications. They vary in complexity and capability. Be sure that the version you get is compatible with your operating system, and that you have enough RAM and hard disk space to accommodate it. If possible, you should test several packages before committing yourself to the purchase.

➤ *Human overseer* As previously mentioned, OCR makes mistakes. A smart-paper-equipped PC generally makes errors less often, per thousand orders, than a human clerical worker, but that's no comfort to a disillusioned customer. For your peace of mind, a human being should keep an eye on the smart-paper system, looking out for improbable or ridiculous data that gives away the fact that a computer error has been made.

➤ *Maintenance and backup system* If the system goes down, you'll need to get it fixed in the minimum possible time. This is true whenever cash flow is dependent on a computer. You'll need to set up a servicing scheme ahead of time, so a technician can come out immediately when something goes wrong. If you have more than one computer, you should make arrangements to switch the ICR to a backup machine in case the main PC fails.

See also ARTIFICIAL INTELLIGENCE, COMPUTER OVER-RELIANCE, FAX, MULTITASKING, NEURAL NETWORK, OPTICAL CHARACTER RECOGNITION, OFFICE AUTOMATION, *and* PATTERN RECOGNITION.

Soft page breaks

In word processing, a page break is the space that the program inserts in text, so that the printer will produce attractive margins at the tops and bottoms of the pages. There are two main ways in which you can put page breaks into text.

Soft page breaks are inserted automatically by the software, at regular intervals in a text document. With standard 8.5-by-11-inch paper forms, you can set the page length as a number of lines ranging from one to about 50. You might wish to use running headers/footers with the soft page breaks so your pages will be neatly numbered, and your document identified, when you make the hardcopy.

When you edit a document containing soft page breaks, the breaks will move as necessary to ensure that the printout always has the correct margins and the specified number of lines per page. For example, if you must add or delete a significant amount of text on page 23, all the page breaks following page 23 will be readjusted to compensate. This will occur no matter how much text you add or delete.

Hard page breaks, in contrast to soft breaks, always stay fixed relative to the surrounding words of text. You can create a hard page break in various ways, depending on the program. If you edit the document, however, you'll have to manually change all the hard page breaks. *See also* HARD PAGE BREAKS, HARD RETURNS, RUNNING HEADERS/FOOTERS, *and* SOFT RETURNS.

Soft returns

In word processing, a return ends one line of text and begins another. There are two ways you can insert returns into text: *soft returns* and *hard returns*. Most people with experience in word processing prefer soft returns within paragraphs because they are automatically added and removed as necessary during manuscript edits.

In most programs, text will automatically go to the next line when it spills beyond the right margin so you can keep on typing without having to press the Enter key. All the returns will occur in the correct places. With a function called *wordwrap*, a word that's too long to fit at the end of a line will be entirely moved down to the next line.

When a text document has soft returns within paragraphs (as most do), you can add or take away a word, phrase, or sentence, and all the returns will be automatically readjusted so the paragraph maintains a neat appearance.

When you get to the end of a paragraph, you'll usually need to insert a hard return. This ends the paragraph even if the line has not reached the right margin. A hard return is made by pressing the Enter key. If you like, you can press Enter again, adding an extra line before starting the next paragraph. Hard returns are also useful when you want to cut a single line short, even though it does not occur at the end of a paragraph, such as for a title. *See also* HARD PAGE BREAKS, HARD RETURNS, *and* SOFT PAGE BREAKS.

Software

In a computer system, the programs are called *software*. Software can exist as magnetic impulses on tapes or disks, as pits in a CD-ROM (compact disc, read-only memory), as impulses on a communications line, or as electrical or magnetic bits in a computer memory.

Things versus happenings. Think, for a moment, of your body and mind. The brain is a part of the body, made of neurons and chemicals; it is a chunk of matter. It has weight and volume, and occupies a defined physical space. The brain and body are analogous to computer *hardware*: chips, circuit boards, wires, disks, peripherals, and other physical objects.

Your mind, in contrast to your brain, has neither weight nor volume. The mind consists of thoughts, which are abstract. You can't hold a thought in your hand or look at it under a microscope. Some people say that thoughts are simply the result of interactions among atoms in your brain and nervous system. Others argue that there's something more, something nonphysical, to the mind, of which science remains ignorant. Thoughts are analogous to computer software. Brains and hardware are things; minds and software are happenings.

Your thoughts govern the actions of your body, while software is responsible for the functioning of a computer and its peripherals. Your mind is a link between you and others, and software provides the interface between a computer and the world.

Thought universe. Software needs an operating system to work, just as it needs hardware. The operating system is the environment in which all the programs run. Think of the operating system as your PC's "thought universe," and the programs as smaller, more specific thought processes within the operating system (see the drawing). Some people say software "sits on top of" the operating system. Others say the programs "work within" the operating system.

There are several operating systems available for use with computers. They each have assets and limitations. When buying a new computer system, try to get familiar with the major features of all the available operating systems, so you can choose one that will best meet your

Software

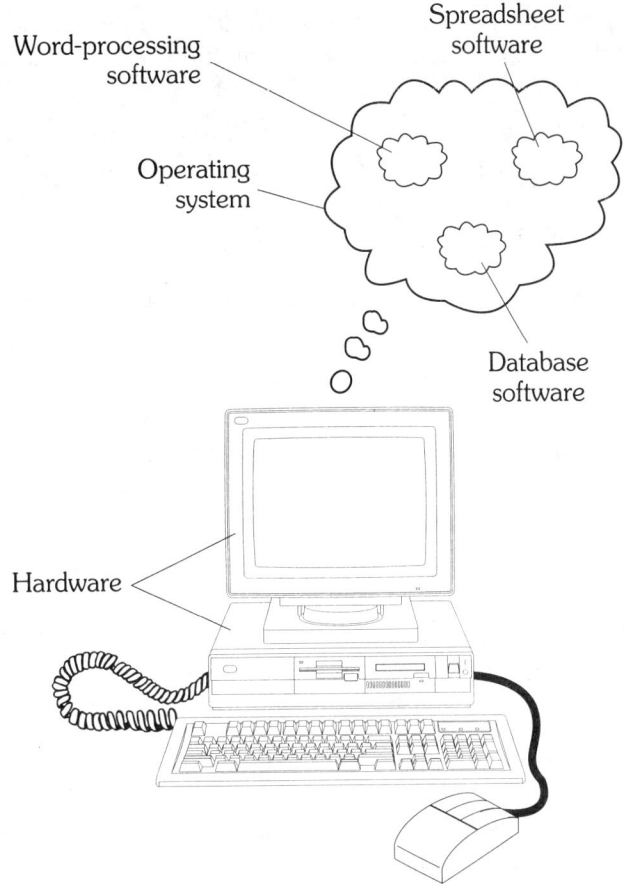

Software, the "thoughts" of a computer.

present and future needs. Operating systems fall into three major categories:

➢ *Command-driven* One method of communication between a PC and its operator is through the use of commands and prompts. You issue commands to the computer by typing instructions on the keyboard. For example, if you wanted to see the directory of the diskette in drive A, you might type *DIR A:* and press Enter. The most common command-driven user interface is DOS.

The one big problem with the command-driven operating environment is that the operator must memorize dozens, or even hundreds, of commands. This makes the learning curve slow and steep. In addition, the operator must be a fairly good typist.

The main advantage of a command-driven environment is that it doesn't require a very powerful computer. The disk space requirement is modest, and even a low-end microprocessor will run DOS reasonably fast.

➢ *Menu-driven* Using a command-driven interface is like taking a "fill-in-the-blank" exam, while a menu-driven interface is a

Software

multiple-choice" format. The menu-driven interface is easier for computer users to learn, just as "multiple-choice" exams are easier to take.

A menu is a list of options (actually commands) from which you can choose. There are two ways to choose commands in a menu-driven environment. One way is to use a mouse or trackball to move a pointer around the screen until it touches the option you want; you click the mouse to actuate the command. Another way is to press a hot key, indicated by a highlighted or underlined letter in the menu option.

➤ *GUI* An advanced form of menu-driven system is the graphical user interface (GUI), which makes use of special symbols called *icons*. These are intuitive, and reinforce the items in the menu. When you use a GUI, you must usually have a mouse or trackball to move the pointer around on the screen.

To open a file in a GUI, you move the pointer until it touches an icon that might look like a folder or a file cabinet. Then you click the mouse (press a button on it) or press a certain keyboard key. To close a file, you move the pointer to a box with a certain symbol in it and click the mouse or press a key again.

The big advantage of menu-driven and graphical interfaces is that they are user-friendly. They're easy to learn, and they provide a sort of intuitive map of what you are doing with your computer. A GUI, however, needs considerable memory and processing power because it takes a large number of logical digits to represent the windows and icons you see on the screen of a computer using a GUI.

When you purchase software, be sure it's compatible with the operating system in your PC. Most programs are available in several forms, one for each common operating system. If your machine uses DOS, you'll want the version written specifically for DOS. If you have the Macintosh OS, you'll want the Mac version.

System versus application. Perhaps you've heard psychologists talk about the subconscious mind and the conscious mind. In the subconscious, things go on without you having much awareness of them. In the conscious mind, you are alert to everything all the time. Perhaps this dichotomy is an oversimplification, but it illustrates the difference between the two main types of computer software.

The "mind" of your PC has some *system software* and some *application software*. The system software is analogous to the goings-on in your subconscious mind. Application software is like conscious thought. Both types of software are essential to the effective operation of a computer, just as both forms of thought are necessary to the healthy functioning of your mind.

Software

System programs keep your PC running efficiently. Every time you power up, the machine automatically runs and loads certain programs. Once the computer is ready to go, you can (and often will) load application programs yourself, but the system programs are executed without your having to intervene in any way.

When you switch on a typical IBM-compatible machine, you'll see words and numbers flashing on the screen for a few seconds; you might also hear some beeps coming from inside the main unit. If your machine is set up to begin in DOS, you'll eventually see the DOS prompt:

```
C:\>
```

This means the machine is ready for you to load application programs.

There are many kinds of application programs. You can probably think of a few right away: communications, database, graphics, spreadsheet, word processing. If you're into advanced computer work, you might have been exposed to analytical graphics, presentation graphics, musical instrument digital interface (MIDI), personal finance software, personal information manager software (PIM), and others. If you're a real power user, you might be familiar with some esoteric forms of application software, such as speech recognition and synthesis, personal robotics, and virtual reality.

Application software works "in the now," like conscious thoughts. The computer reacts directly to the input of the user. The user receives, and responds to, prompts and queries from the machine.

Software distribution. There are several ways to obtain software. The price you pay depends on how you get the programs, how complicated they are, the purpose for which they are intended, and who wrote them. Prices vary from nothing (free) to thousands of dollars for a single software package.

You buy *direct purchase* software in office supply stores, electronics stores, and computer stores. It's advertised in the computer magazines, too. You can buy it over the counter or order it through the mail. You pay a one-time price, and then the software is yours.

In general, direct-purchase software is the most reliable because it has been thoroughly tested. On the other hand, direct purchase is the most expensive way to get software. Common word processing, database, and spreadsheet packages are priced from about $150 to $500; more powerful packages cost more. Software intended for professional use, especially if the targeted consumers fall into a high-income bracket, can run upwards of $2000 for a package. An example is medical-office software.

Software

You can get *shareware* software for use on a trial basis. You use the programs as much as you want, sometimes up to a certain maximum number of test runs. If you decide you want to keep the software, you pay for it. Shareware is available on CD-ROM (compact-disc, read-only memory), diskettes, and from online services.

Shareware is just about as good as direct-purchase software. Its big advantage is that it's relatively inexpensive compared with direct-purchase programs. You also get an opportunity to run the programs before you buy them. However, shareware has not usually been tested as thoroughly as direct-purchase software. Thus, it's more likely to contain bugs. It might not turn out to work the way you expect. Also, software that is freely shared is more subject to tampering by malicious hackers. There is a possibility that such a program will contain a hidden "disease" called a *Trojan horse* or *virus*. These subprograms, cleverly written into software, can sabotage your operating system. A program called a *vaccine* can help you search for and eradicate Trojan horses and viruses.

Freeware is software that has been copyrighted, but that can be used to a limited extent without cost. You can use freeware personally all you want, but you may not sell it to someone else with the intent of making a profit from it. At first, freeware seems like a great deal; you get something for nothing. However, because its developers aren't concerned with the profit motive, the quality of freeware is generally somewhat lower than that of direct-purchase software or shareware.

Freeware, like shareware, is commonly available online, as well as on diskettes. Because of this, it is also somewhat prone to contamination by Trojan horses and viruses. If you plan to use freeware, always download it onto diskettes, or use the diskettes directly. Don't put it onto your hard disk. Run each program through a vaccine before using it.

See also ALPHA TEST, ARTIFICIAL INTELLIGENCE, ASSEMBLER AND ASSEMBLY LANGUAGE, BETA TEST, BOOTSTRAP PROGRAM, BUG, COMMAND-DRIVEN SOFTWARE, COMPUTER GAMES, DATABASE, DESKTOP PUBLISHING, DOS, ELECTRONIC CIRCUIT DESIGN SOFTWARE, EXPERT SYSTEMS, FIRMWARE, FREEWARE, GRAPHICAL USER INTERFACE, GRAPHICS, GROUPWARE, HARDWARE, HIGH-LEVEL LANGUAGE, INTEGRATED SOFTWARE PACKAGE, LOW-LEVEL LANGUAGE, MACHINE LANGUAGE, MEMORY-MANAGEMENT SOFTWARE, MEMORY-RESIDENT SOFTWARE, MENU-DRIVEN SOFTWARE, MODULAR PROGRAMMING, MUSICAL INSTRUMENT DIGITAL INTERFACE, OPERATING SYSTEM, OS/2, PACKAGED SOFTWARE, PERSONAL DICTATION SYSTEM, PRESENTATION GRAPHICS, PROCEDURAL LANGUAGE, PROGRAMMING, REDUCTIONISM, RELEASE NUMBER, SHAREWARE, SOFTWARE INSTALLATION AND UNINSTALLATION, SOFTWARE PIRACY, SPEECH RECOGNITION, SPEECH SYNTHESIS, SPREADSHEET, SPY SOFTWARE, SUITE, SYSTEM 7, TERMINAL EMULATION SOFTWARE, TROJAN HORSE, UNIX,

UTILITY SOFTWARE, VACCINE, VERSION NUMBER, VIRUS, WETWARE, WINDOWS, *and* WORD PROCESSING.

Software installation and uninstallation

If you like to keep a PC as long as possible, trading up only when necessary, you'll install and uninstall many programs during your computer's lifetime. Software installation is easy; the vendors want things that way. Removing software is more complicated.

Putting it in. Whether you're working in "pure DOS," Windows, the Macintosh OS, OS/2, or any other operating system, the process of installing software is routine. The package comes as a set of diskettes or CD-ROM. An instruction book is almost always provided with software. Read the installation directions completely before inserting the first diskette into your PC. When you know what you'll have to do, then you can go through the motions of installation without much risk of running into trouble.

If you have problems while installing software, files with the words *help* or *readme* in their names can be of assistance. Failing that, most software vendors provide toll-free telephone numbers where you can get assistance directly from trained computer operators and technicians.

Of course, you can't install software if you don't have enough room for it on your hard disk. If your PC has been unfortunate enough to become infected with a virus or invaded by a Trojan Horse, you might find software installation to be impossible. You'll have to run a vaccine to locate, and hopefully eradicate, the gremlins. You will also have trouble if your computer is not advanced enough to handle the software, or if you don't have the right version of the package. Windows programs don't run well on a 286 machine, for example, nor can you expect a Macintosh program to work with an IBM-compatible PC.

If you have almost, but not quite, enough room for a software package on your hard disk, you can install the program if you're willing to remove other files or programs to make space. If you've kept a lot of old files on your hard disk that really don't have to be there, you can transfer them to diskettes and remove them from the hard disk. Perhaps there is old software that you don't use anymore. You can remove these programs to free up additional hard disk space.

Taking it out. Before trying to uninstall any software, you should back up your hard disk. A tape drive is ideal for this purpose. (A hard disk can be backed up on diskettes, but it is very time-consuming.) The reason for backing up is that you don't want a little mistake in the uninstallation process to have disastrous consequences. If you've ever lost vital data because of failure to back things up, you have learned this lesson the hard way.

DOS-based software isn't difficult to remove. It's usually just a matter of erasing the files in the program directory or directories. You must be careful, however, not to erase files having to do with other software. It's amazing how easily that can happen. Don't hurry the process. Be sure you're wide awake. Make a list beforehand of precisely which files are to be deleted. Be careful when you press those keys.

In a graphical user interface (GUI) such as Windows, OS/2, or the Macintosh OS, getting rid of old software is best facilitated by a utility designed for that purpose. For Windows, a utility called Uninstaller, by MicroHelp, will do the job cleanly and quickly. It will also let you "un-uninstall" files in case you change your mind and decide you want to keep certain things. You can find out, before actually uninstalling a set of programs, exactly how much disk space you'll free up. Uninstaller will also find duplicate files and get rid of the redundancy, giving you a little more disk space.

Software-uninstallation utilities aren't completely perfect, but they're improving all the time. If you have the Macintosh OS, OS/2, or some other high-level, non-Windows operating system, ask a "PC guru" friend about uninstallation programs. These utilities are also advertised in the PC magazines.

If, after having uninstalled software, you get strange or inexplicable error messages, you probably left some parts of the old software behind. These fragments can try to run by themselves, but they are not complete programs, and thus they cannot do anything useful. The solution is to carefully glean them out and get rid of them, making sure to back up the hard disk first. *See also* BACKUP, BACKUP UTILITY, FILE ERASURE, SOFTWARE, TAPE DRIVE, TROJAN HORSE, UNDELETION, VACCINE, *and* VIRUS.

Software piracy

Computer data is easy to copy. A high-density, double-sided diskette can hold over a million characters, but a PC can copy it in seconds. The contents of diskettes, CD-ROM, and other electronic media is often copyrighted. This includes software. Anyone who uses copyrighted software without having paid the fee (if any) is committing *software piracy* and runs the risk of being sued for copyright infringement.

Stool pigeons. Software is like music. Songwriters and performing artists are supposed to get royalties every time their work is broadcast over radio or television, or sold on tape or compact disc. However, people can and do record performances off the air, copy tapes, or convert CDs to tape. As a result, the musicians get cheated, according to copyright laws that work in the creators' and publishers' favor. There are also copyright laws that work for the originators and publishers of computerized text, graphics, and software.

Software piracy

Isolated, one-time cases of copyright infringement are rather difficult to detect, but the stakes are high. Settlements can run into millions of dollars. The chances of getting caught are highest for those who copy something—music, software, graphics, printed text, or whatever—and then try to resell it for a profit. Every black-market buyer is a potential stool pigeon. The more money a pirate makes illegally, the better the chance of being sued, and the larger the settlement is likely to be.

Why be honest? There are at least three good reasons to keep yourself, and your company, "clean" when it comes to copyright infringement of any kind:

> *Avoidance of lawsuits* The legal fees and damages arising from an infringement settlement can be more than enough to bankrupt a person or entity who is found guilty. Besides that, lawsuits can take years to grind out, and they cause untold emotional turmoil.

> *Peace of mind* The best way to stay out of trouble is not to commit the offense. The burden of proof then falls on the plaintiff if a case actually goes to court.

> *Two-edged blade* You can't expect other people to be more righteous than you are yourself. If you ever decide you want to create and sell computer programs, you have a right to expect a profit. When you deny that right to other vendors, you in effect deny it to yourself.

The Software Publishers Association (telephone 800-388-7478) publishes a videotape about the legal aspects of software copyright infringement. The U.S. Copyright Office (202-707-3000) publishes information about copyright laws and provides kits for registration of copyrighted material.

Things you can do. Here are several suggestions to follow when obtaining and using copyrighted software:

> *Pay what you owe* If you are supposed to pay a certain price for the use of software, then pay it. Whether you use a credit card, pay cash, or write a check, keep the receipt so you'll have an irrefutable record of the purchase. (It's wise to keep the receipt when you buy any software or hardware.)

> *Read the fine print* Read everything in a software licensing agreement, then rigorously adhere to the guidelines. Not all agreements are alike. Be sure everyone who uses the software is aware of the details of the agreement. If you are in a managerial position within a company, be sure all your employees adhere to the terms of the agreement.

> *Register* Fill out software registration cards and send them back to the seller immediately after purchase. In the case of

shareware, you need do this only if you decide to buy the programs.

➢ *Keep it secure* Keep the original software media (such as diskettes) in a safe, secure place. This will minimize the chance of theft and will deter would-be unauthorized users.

➢ *Get legal advice* If you're in doubt about the legality of something you plan to do with software, consult a copyright attorney. Because of the complex and evolving state of technology, laws concerning electronic publication change often and are not always clear-cut.

See also FREEWARE, GROUPWARE, SHAREWARE, *and* SOFTWARE.

Sound technology

The user-friendliness and versatility of computers is enhanced by audio, as well as visual, interfaces. *Sound technology* refers to hardware and software that works with voices, music, and other sound.

Applications. Sound technology has dozens of applications, from electronic music processing to security systems. Here are some things for which sound is used in computer systems:

➢ *Hands-off computing:* With speech recognition, a computer can accept verbal commands, rather than keystrokes and mouse clicks. Speech synthesis makes it possible for the machine to respond verbally to a human operator. In some applications, these technologies are of little or no value, but in other applications, sound makes the difference between usability and nonusability. With sound, you can use a PC without looking at it or touching it.

➢ *Nonvisual interface* Sound technology opens up the universe of personal computing to visually handicapped people, especially in word processing and database management. Some applications, such as graphics, don't lend themselves as obviously to sound technology. Certain emerging applications, such as virtual reality, become available to the blind through speech recognition, speech synthesis, music, and sound effects.

➢ *Telephony* With speech recognition and synthesis, a computer can interface with a human being via sound alone. Thus, it becomes possible to give commands to, and get responses from, a computer by calling it up and literally conversing with it. This technology, called *telephony*, makes every telephone set in the world effectively a node in a network. This is true even if there is no computer at the telephone set. Of course, a PC or dumb terminal enhances any telephony node.

➢ *Medical* When a doctor is examining a patient, it's not easy for the doctor to write things down on a notepad or type data into a computer. With speech recognition, a computer becomes an audio notebook. The doctor can literally dictate data from across the room. This is only the beginning. Although it seems farfetched now, a surgeon might say to a robot, "Scalpel," and the robot computer will heed the request, locate, pick up, and give the surgeon a scalpel.

➤ *Presentations* Audio can be used with presentation graphics. Sound is especially appreciated by children. In professional settings, sound can be a blessing or a curse. There's some risk that an audience will dislike computerized audio; a live narrator makes clients feel that they matter enough to warrant human attention. In any presentation sound system, the speakers must be big enough, and the amplification must be sufficiently powerful, to allow easy listening for everyone.

➤ *Tutorial software* For learning purposes, audio-visual methods work far better than video alone. Perhaps you remember silent home movies. How much more interesting home video is today! The same thing happens when sound is added to computer-assisted instruction (CAI). Sound also multiplies the effectiveness of animation. Speech recognition and synthesis is especially useful in tutorials for children; a well-engineered program with excellent sound and video can hold a child's attention for hours.

➤ *Music processing* Popular music bands use computers to process the sounds they generate with their instruments. This is true both in live concerts and in recordings. The Musical Instrument Digital Interface (MIDI) has practically revolutionized this industry. With MIDI, you can connect a synthesizer to your PC, compose your own tunes, create harmony, and determine the rhythm. The computer will combine all the elements, play the finished composition, and even display or print out a musical score.

Although computer programs can compose music, there is debate about whether such songs constitute true art. Computers can generate, process, and combine musical notes, but the resulting tunes usually sound emotionless. Music's main purpose is to communicate emotionally with listeners. Perhaps computer-generated tunes might serve as springboards for human works. At least, computer-generated music can be intriguing. With the evolution of artificial intelligence, computers might develop the capacity for emotion, although this too is debatable. An emotional computer might become a true musical composer.

➤ *Games* Computer games have used sound for many years. Audio cues, such as beeps and crashes, make these games interesting. This is especially true in simulations. Suppose you're using a computer game in which you "drive" a race car in the Daytona 500. The video shows you speeding along with other cars. The sound imitates the rush of the wind, the roar of the engine, and the squeal of the tires. This effect is greatly enhanced by the use of headphones.

Sound technology

- *Virtual reality* Sound plays an even more important role in virtual reality than in computer games. Headphones are a necessity; they are part of the head-mounted display (HMD) that you wear. Stereo sound and stereo vision combine to produce hyperreal sensations. Speech recognition and synthesis might be used to give you the impression of conversing with aliens on a strange planet. Or you might watch, and be watched by, dolphins as you swim with them along a coral reef.

- *Security systems* In a high-level intrusion-detection system, sound equipment can pick up unusual noises that might be caused by an unauthorized person. A speech synthesizer can issue a command to a person at the gate to a property, "State your name and password." Then, speech-recognition and waveform-analysis software can interpret and analyze the voice, letting the computer know whether or not the person is legitimate.

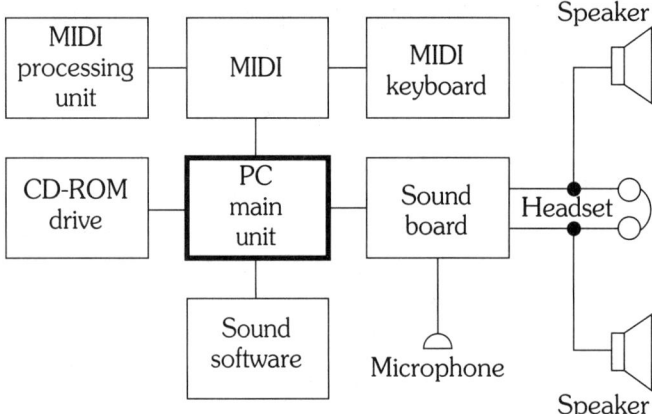

A computer sound system, showing some common components.

Hardware. If your PC doesn't have a sound system, it's not difficult to install one. You need several components, as shown in the block diagram. The following hardware is basic:

- *Sound board* This is an expansion board that fits into one of the expansion slots inside the main unit of the computer. You must switch off and unplug the machine and all peripherals, remove the cover, and place the board into the slot according to the instructions. Sound boards vary in price, depending on their sophistication. Generally, they are quite affordable.

- *Microphone* There are several different kinds of microphones. Some are unidirectional, responding to sound mainly in one direction. Others are omnidirectional, picking up sound from all directions. A communications microphone responds to a restricted range of frequencies, and works for voice but not for music. A hi-fi microphone responds to all audio frequencies, and is necessary for inputting music and most sound effects. The microphone plugs directly into the sound board.

➤ *Speakers* Although most PCs have internal speakers, they are not adequate for sound applications. A pair of external speakers, similar to hi-fi speakers but smaller, must be plugged into the sound board. An audio amplifier might also be required. The size of the speakers you need depends on how large an area you want the sound to cover. You'll also have to consider the application; headphones will suffice if the system is intended for use by only one person at a time.

➤ *Headphones* These are identical to stereo hi-fi headphones. There are many styles. Some cover the ears completely, shutting out most external noise. Others fit into the external ear; these will not keep you from hearing outside noises. All headphones offer privacy and keep your coworkers (or cohabitants) from hearing your computer-generated sounds. Headphones can enhance some sound effects because they offer the best possible channel separation, or isolation between the left and right sound circuits.

➤ *CD-ROM* Sound systems let you play music CDs on a CD-ROM (compact-disc, read-only memory) drive. Of course, you can still use the drive for all its other applications. A computer sound system won't render stereo hi-fi as well as a top-of-the- line home-entertainment system, but you can plug a sound board directly into such a system to get the audio equivalent of a big-screen video monitor.

➤ *Electromagnetic shielding* Sound systems can develop into "spiderwebs" with many interconnecting wires and cables. The circuits can be susceptible to radio-frequency interference (RFI). Nearby radio or TV broadcast stations, amateur or citizen's band (CB) radio transmitters, automatic pagers, and other devices can wreak havoc with a sound system that does not employ adequate electromagnetic shielding. Be sure to use coaxial cable whenever possible between the computer and the other elements of the sound system. If this fails, other remedies can be tried, although problems of this sort are sometimes hard to eliminate. If you find your sound system plagued by RFI, you might need to consult a professional electronics engineer.

Software. In addition to the hardware in a sound system, there are software features. Here are some common programs and devices.

➤ *Sound board programs* unique to that particular board come with all sound boards. Installing the programs is a matter of following the instructions and proceeding according to the onscreen menus. Files are copied from the sound system diskettes to the PC's hard disk. Be sure you have enough space on your hard disk for all the programs supplied with the sound

Sound technology

board. Low-end sound boards have only basic programs and don't require much hard disk space. High-end sound systems have numerous programs, some exotic, and need considerable room on the hard disk.

➤ *Object linking and embedding* enables sound bites, such as a bar of music or a synthesized word, to be placed (embedded) in another file. For example, you can embed words into music or vice versa; you can also embed parts of one musical tune into another. *Linking* connects specific objects in different files, so that if the object changes in one file, it changes in all the others.

➤ *Musical Instrument Digital Interface*, or *MIDI*, as it's commonly called, refers to an interface protocol used to send information between computers and music synthesizers. A computer can be used with MIDI and a synthesizer to compose, edit, store, transmit, or download electronic music. Even if you're not musically inclined, playing with MIDI can teach you about music. You might think of MIDI as a modern analog of the piano rolls used with old-fashioned player pianos.

➤ *Speech recognition* allows you to give basic commands to a computer by talking to it. The program converts spoken words into digital impulses via analog-to-digital (A/D) conversion. The machine has a vocabulary of words and a means of comparing this with the incoming audio signals. The size of the vocabulary is proportional to the memory needed. A good system requires a lot of memory. Interpretation errors always occur, although the better the program, the less frequent the errors. Loud external noises can sometimes be mistaken for speech.

➤ *Speech synthesis* technology is somewhat more advanced than speech recognition. A computer's responses or output, which normally appear as screen prompts, are translated into speech by a digital-to-analog (D/A) conversion process. Text files can be "read" by a machine and converted into a synthesized voice. With optical character recognition (OCR) in addition to the sound system, text can be picked up from a printed page and read by the machine out loud. Speech synthesis does not convey emotion in a piece of writing; the machine can only "mouth" the words. If you give a speech synthesizer a classic short story to read, the results will almost certainly sound strange.

See also ANALOG, ANALOG-TO-DIGITAL CONVERSION, ANIMATION, BANDWIDTH, BASEBAND, CD-ROM, COMPUTER-ASSISTED INSTRUCTION, COMPUTER GAMES, COMPUTER MUSIC, DIGITAL, DIGITAL SIGNAL PROCESSING, DIGITAL-TO-ANALOG CONVERSION, ELECTROMAGNETIC SHIELDING, EXPANSION BOARD, MULTIMEDIA, MUSICAL INSTRUMENT DIGITAL INTERFACE, OBJECT LINKING AND EMBEDDING, PERSONAL DICTATION SYSTEM, PERSONAL ROBOTS, PRESENTATION GRAPHICS, RADIO-FREQUENCY INTERFERENCE, SECURITY SYSTEMS, SPEAKERS, SPEECH

RECOGNITION, SPEECH SYNTHESIS, TELEPHONY, VIRTUAL REALITY, *and* VOICE MAIL SYSTEMS.

Source

In computer communications, any PC or terminal that sends data is called a *source*. A workstation that receives data is a *destination*. In a complete communications circuit, there is always at least one source and at least one destination.

When you send someone a message via electronic mail (e-mail), your computer is the source and the recipient's computer is the destination. If you leave data on a bulletin-board system (BBS) where anyone can read it, there can be an unlimited number of destinations. This situation is shown in the drawing at A. When you read the contents of a BBS where many people have posted messages, your PC is the destination of data coming from many different sources, as shown at B.

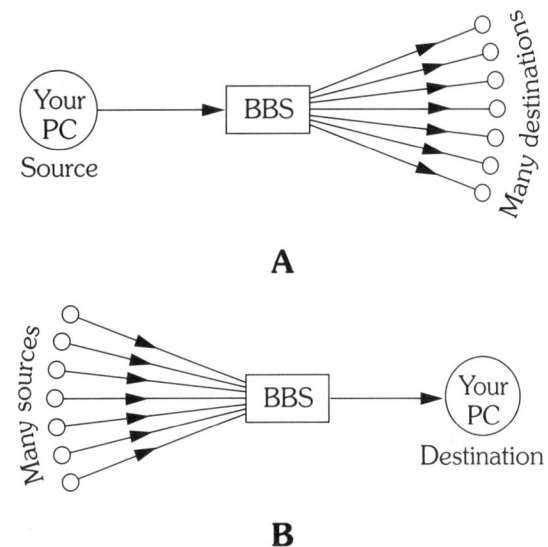

One source with many destinations (A) and many sources with one destination (B).

When two PCs are in real-time communication, they can both act as a source and a destination simultaneously. You might be typing data to someone, and reading his or her incoming messages on your screen at the same time. This is called *full duplex* because data is going in both directions at once. The destination can interrupt the source at any time.

If simultaneous transmission and reception is not possible, a communications circuit is working in *half duplex*. One PC acts as a source while the other acts as a destination; the roles constantly switch. In this environment, the destination cannot interrupt the source. *See also* BULLETIN-BOARD SYSTEM, DESTINATION, ELECTRONIC MAIL, FULL DUPLEX, *and* HALF DUPLEX.

Speakers

Most computers come with small internal *speakers*. They beep or tweet to get your attention. Internal speakers are fine for many applications, but if you're serious about sound technology, you'll need a set of external speakers.

Features. There are dozens, if not hundreds, of speaker sets that will work with PCs. They resemble stereo hi-fi loudspeakers. The main difference is that PC speakers are smaller than most hi-fi speakers. Here are some of the features and assets of external PC speakers:

- *Size/shape* Computer speakers come in pairs and range in size from that of cigarette packs to shoeboxes. They can handle from about two to 10 watts per channel. Small speakers can fill a bedroom with sound; big ones are enough for classroom use. Some speakers are simple, with one transducer for all audio frequencies. Others have separate woofers, midrange units, and tweeters. Most speakers are in rectangular boxes, but a few have exotic shapes such as cylinders, spheres, or saucers.

- *Amplification* Many small speaker sets have built-in audio amplifiers powered by batteries that you install inside the speaker enclosure. Alternatively, a small ac power adapter can be employed if you don't want to use batteries. The amplifiers aren't powerful, but they boost the sound considerably, so it can be heard in a medium-sized room or when there is some ambient noise.

- *Sound board* If you have an older computer, you might have to install a sound board and its attendant software to make external speakers work. You'll usually need an amplifier, too. The amplifier power rating will depend on how large an area you want to cover. It's not too hard to install a sound board, amplifier, and software. Simply read and follow the instructions. Some sound packages come with installation programs.

- *Coverage area* External speakers are a necessity for demonstrations, games, multimedia, tutorials, and presentations. Small speakers are adequate if you're working in a bedroom, den, or small office. In a classroom or conference room, you'll need larger speakers with a suitable amplifier. If you intend to give presentations in an auditorium, you might consider connecting the PC audio into the public-address system or into a stereo hi-fi amplifier with large speakers.

- *Shielding* Good external speakers have electromagnetic shielding. As the audio signals travel from the PC to the speakers, the currents generate electromagnetic fields, like low-frequency radio waves. The same thing occurs when the audio gets to the coils in the speakers. These fields can cause "static" on a computer monitor unless they are kept within the cables and coils. Unshielded speakers and cables can also pick up external radio signals, resulting in radio-frequency interference to the PC. Therefore, you must be certain that the cables and speaker enclosures are shielded.

➤ *Audio mixing* Some speakers have a provision for combining more than one audio signal. This is useful when you want to create special sound effects, such as a voice on top of music. You can adjust the proportion (ratio) of the two input levels, and in some cases their relative phase, too.

➤ *Volume/tone* Some speakers have only a volume control; others have separate adjustments for loudness and tone. You might even find speakers with separate volume controls for the woofer, midrange unit, and tweeter (bass, midrange, and treble, respectively). As you might expect, the bigger and costlier the speakers are, in general, the more sophisticated the volume and tone controls.

➤ *DSP/ARS* Some speaker systems have digital signal processing (DSP). This technology enhances sound quality and expands the stereo effect. Usually, PC speakers are located close to each other, so you don't get much channel separation. With DSP, the speakers sound like they're on opposite sides of the room and can seem much bigger and more powerful than they really are. A similar scheme, ambient recovery circuitry (ARS), gives the impression of audio in full space. You hear "three-dimensional" rather than "two-dimensional" sound. It seems to come from above, below, and all around you.

Shop around. Getting a set of external speakers is like buying a pair of new shoes. No matter how attractive they look in the advertisements, and regardless of what the specifications say, you should get a chance to try them before you buy them.

A computer store or music store is a good place to check out several different speaker sets. They should be connected to a PC so you can play with the system. Try out the volume and tone controls; see what DSP and ARS actually do. Perform these experiments when the store isn't busy, so there isn't a lot of background noise.

Once you've heard a few sets of speakers, get the brochures, go home, and imagine how the speakers will look in your workstation. Think about your future needs as well as what you require right now. Read the brochures, compare prices, return to the store, and make your decision. *See also* DIGITAL SIGNAL PROCESSING, ELECTROMAGNETIC SHIELDING, MULTIMEDIA, MUSICAL INSTRUMENT DIGITAL INTERFACE, RADIO-FREQUENCY INTERFERENCE, *and* SOUND TECHNOLOGY.

Speech recognition

Your voice consists of audio-frequency energy, with components ranging from about 100 hertz (Hz, or cycles per second) to several kilohertz (kHz, or thousands of hertz). This was known even before Alexander Graham Bell sent the first voice signals over electric wires.

As computers and computer-controlled machines evolve, people want to give them commands, input data, and control them by talking to them. A *speech-recognition* system makes this possible.

Components of speech. Perhaps you've spoken into a microphone that was connected to an oscilloscope, and seen the jumble of waves. How can any computer be programmed to make sense out of that? The answer lies in the fact that, whatever you say, it is comprised of only a few dozen sounds, called *phonemes*.

In communications, engineers have found that a voice can be transmitted quite well if the bandwidth is restricted to the range of 300 Hz to 3000 Hz (3 kHz). Certain phonemes, like "ssss," contain energy at frequencies of several kilohertz, but all the information in a voice, including the emotional content, can be conveyed if the audio passband is cut off at 3 kHz. This is the typical voice frequency response in a two-way radio.

Drawing A is a frequency-versus-time voice print of a spoken word with five syllables. Most of the energy is in three frequency ranges, called *formants*. The first formant is at less than 1000 Hz. The second formant ranges from 1600 Hz to 2000 Hz. The third formant is at 2600 Hz to 3000 Hz. These ranges are approximate, and vary somewhat from person to person. Between the formants there are gaps, or ranges of frequencies at which little or no sound occurs.

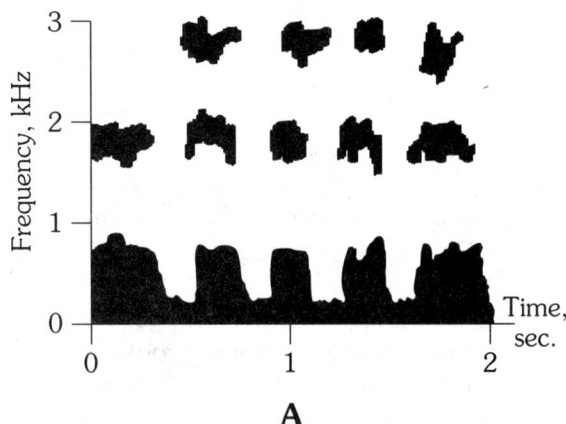

A typical voice print.

The formants and the gaps between them stay in the same frequency ranges for each person's voice, no matter what is said.

The fine details of the voice print determine not only the words, but the emotional content of speech. The slightest change in tone of voice will show up in a voice print. Therefore, in theory, it is possible to build a machine that can recognize and analyze speech as well as any human being. The challenge is to put this theory into practice.

A/D conversion. The passband can be reduced greatly if you are willing to give up some of the emotional content of the voice in favor of efficient information transfer. In recent years, a technology called *analog-to-digital (A/D) conversion* has been developed and refined that does this very well.

An A/D converter changes the continuously variable, or analog, voice signal into a series of digital pulses. This is the audio equivalent of optical scanning, in which a drawing or photograph is converted into digital signals for storage in a computer. Several different characteristics of a digital pulse signal can be varied, including the pulse amplitude, the pulse duration, and the pulse frequency.

A digital signal can carry a human voice within a passband less than 200 Hz wide. That is less than $\frac{1}{10}$ the passband of the analog signal. The narrower the bandwidth, in general, the more of the emotional content is sacrificed. Emotional content is conveyed by inflection, or variation in voice tone. When tone is lost, the signal resembles written data, but it can still carry some of the subtle meanings and feelings, as you know from reading good books or magazine articles.

Word analysis. For a computer to decipher the digital voice signal, it must have a vocabulary of words or syllables and some means of comparing this knowledge base with the incoming audio signals. This system has two parts: a memory, in which various speech patterns are stored, and a *comparator* that checks these stored patterns against the data coming in. For each syllable or word, the circuit checks through its vocabulary until a match is found. This is done very fast, so the delay is not noticeable.

The size of the computer's vocabulary is directly related to its memory capacity. An advanced speech-recognition system requires a large amount of memory. In this sense, speech recognition is the audio equivalent of visual object recognition.

Context and syntax. The output of the comparator must be processed in some way, so that the machine knows the difference between words or syllables that sound alike, such as *two* and *too*, or *not* and *knot*. For this to be possible, the context and syntax must be examined. This analysis places extreme demands on the computer.

Speech recognition

Consider the following three sentences:

- I have one, too.
- I have won two.
- I have won, too.

Each of these can make sense in a certain situation or context. To some extent, a computer might figure out which of the three sentences is being spoken in a given situation by analyzing surrounding words and sentences. However, the amount of data to be analyzed and the speed with which it must be done puts many scenarios beyond the interpretation abilities of computers in existence today.

There must also be some way for the computer to tell whether a group of syllables constitutes one, two, three, or four words. The more complicated the words coming in, the greater the chance for confusion. The word *radioisotope*, for example, might be confused in several different ways. The word *antidisestablishmentarianism* would befuddle almost any speech-recognition system.

Any speech-recognition system will sometimes make mistakes, just as people sometimes misinterpret what you say. Such errors will become less frequent as computer memory capacity and operating speed increase, but there might never be a computer that can transcribe speech with perfect accuracy in every possible situation. Drawing B is a simplified block diagram of a speech-recognition system.

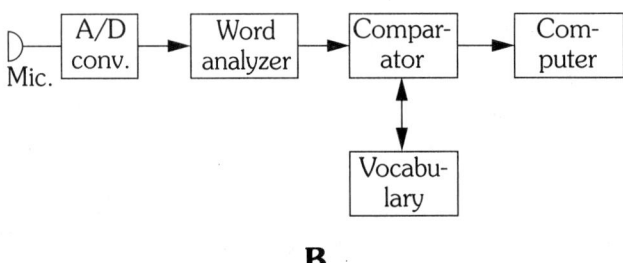

B

A simplified diagram of a speech-recognition system.

Emotional content. The A/D converter in a speech-recognition system removes some of the inflections from a voice. In the extreme, all of the tonal changes are lost, and the voice is reduced to the equivalent of written language. For computers, this is adequate. If a system were 100% reliable in simply transcribing the words it received, speech-recognition engineers would be very happy.

When accuracy does approach 100% (as it will in time), there will be increasing interest in getting some of the subtler meanings across, too. Take the sentence, "You will go to the store after midnight," and say it with the emphasis on each word in turn. The meaning changes dramatically depending on the *prosodic features* of your voice: which word or words you emphasize.

Tone is also very important for another reason: a sentence might be either a statement or a question. Thus, "You will go to the store *after* midnight?" represents something completely different from, "You *will* go to the store after midnight!"

Even if all the tones are the same, the meaning can vary depending on how fast something is said. The timing of breaths can make a difference, too.

For further information. Speech recognition is a rapidly advancing technology. Some engineers consider it to be one of the most important aspects of artificial intelligence. The best source of up-to-date information on speech recognition is a good college library. *See also* ANALOG, ANALOG-TO-DIGITAL CONVERSION, ARTIFICIAL INTELLIGENCE, BANDWIDTH, CONTEXT, DATA CONVERSION, DIGITAL, DIGITAL SIGNAL PROCESSING, GRAMMAR CHECKING, SOUND TECHNOLOGY, SPEECH SYNTHESIS, *and* SYNTAX.

Speech synthesis

Speech synthesis is the generation of sounds that mimic the human voice. This technology is somewhat ahead of *speech recognition*. It's easier for a machine to talk than to listen.

What is a voice? All sounds, including music, barking dogs, roaring jet engines, ticking clocks, and human speech, are combinations of alternating-current (ac) waves, having frequencies between about 20 hertz (Hz, or cycles per second) and 20 kilohertz (kHz, a thousand Hz). These take the form of vibrations in air molecules. The patterns of vibration can be duplicated as electric currents.

Drawing A on page 1028 shows a simple compression wave of the kind that travels through the air when there is a sound. Also shown is the electrical current that produces this wave when the current passes through the coils of a loudspeaker or headset. The maximum positive current in this example corresponds to the greatest compression of air molecules. The maximum negative current corresponds to the lowest compression of air molecules. The speaker or headset is an *acoustic transducer* because it changes electrical current into audible sound.

In speech, a frequency range (band) of 300 to 3000 Hz is wide enough to convey all the information and emotional content in anybody's voice. Therefore, speech synthesizers only need to make sounds within this range. The challenge is to produce waves at exactly the right frequencies, at the correct times, and in the correct phase combinations. The modulation must also be just right.

Speech synthesis

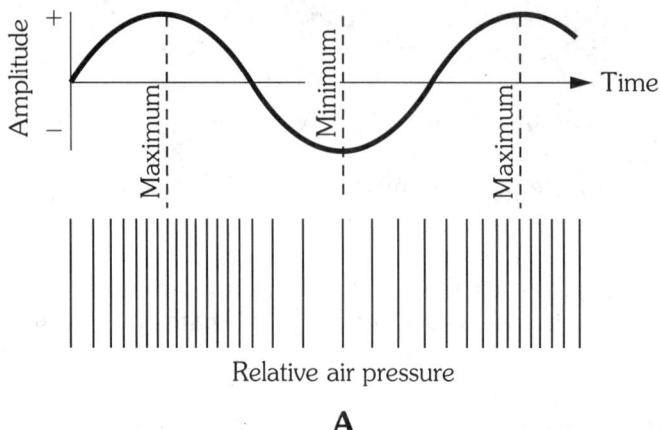

A

Audio currents and the corresponding air compression.

In the human voice, the volume and frequency rise and fall in subtle and precise ways. The slightest change in modulation can make a big difference in the meaning of what is said. You can tell, even over the telephone, whether a person is anxious, angry, or relaxed. A request sounds nothing like a command, and a question differs from a statement, even when the words themselves are identical.

Tone of voice. In the English language there are 40 elementary sounds, known as *phonemes*. In some languages there are more phonemes than in English; other languages have fewer phonemes.

The exact sound of a phoneme can vary depending on what comes before and after it. These variations are called *allophones*. There are 128 allophones in English. These can be strung together in millions of different ways.

The tone of a voice can depend on whether the person speaking is angry, sad, scared, happy, or indifferent. These subtle inflections are the *prosodic features* of the voice. They depend not only on the actual feelings of the speaker, but on age, gender, upbringing, and other factors.

Besides this, a voice can have an *accent*. You can tell when a person is angry or happy, regardless of whether that person is from Texas, Indiana, Idaho, or Maine. Some accents sound more authoritative than others; some sound funny if you haven't been exposed to them before. Along with accent, the actual words can be a little different in different regions. This is *dialect*.

You don't want a talking machine to sound angry all the time, or constantly unhappy, or endlessly blissful. You don't want the machine to convey the wrong mood for a situation. Imagine your computerized personal robot rolling up to you and drawling, "Y'all gonna dah if you don't skedaddle outa this house raht nah-yow." You'd probably laugh, until you realized that the robot was telling you your house was on fire. For engineers, producing a speech synthesizer with a credible tone of voice is a great challenge.

Record/playback. The simplest "speech synthesizer" is a set of tape recordings of individual words. You have probably heard these in telephone answering machines and services. Some cities have a telephone number you can call to get local time; this also uses word recordings. They all have a characteristic choppy sound.

There are several drawbacks to these systems. Perhaps the biggest problem is the fact that each word requires a separate recording on a separate length of tape. These tapes must be mechanically accessed, and this takes time. It is impossible to have a large speech vocabulary using this method. Perhaps the greatest objection is that this really isn't speech synthesis; it is speech reproduction.

Reading text. A written text can be "read" by a machine and converted into a digital code called ASCII (pronounced "ASK-key"). The method used for this is known as *optical character recognition*. ASCII can be translated by integrated circuits (ICs) into voice sounds. In this way, a machine can read text out loud. Although they are rather expensive at the time of this writing, these machines are being used to help blind people read written text.

Because there are only 128 allophones in the English language, a machine can be designed to read almost any text. However, a machine doesn't have any sense of which inflections are best for various "scenes." With technical or scientific text, this isn't too important, but when reading a story to a child, mental imagery is crucial. A good story is an imaginary movie, helped along by the emotions of the reader. If these emotions are wrong, or if they do not exist, the listener can't relive the thoughts and feelings of the author.

No machine can paint pictures or elicit moods in a listener's mind as well as a human being can. The appropriate inflections in a sentence might depend on what happened in the previous sentence, paragraph, or chapter. Technology is a long way from giving a machine the ability to understand and appreciate a good story, but nothing short of that level of artificial intelligence will really work if a machine's voice is to create the essential daydream in a listener's mind.

The process. There are several different ways in which a machine can be programmed to produce speech. A simplified block diagram of one process is shown in drawing B on the next page. Whatever the method used for speech synthesis, certain steps are necessary:

1 The machine must access the data and arrange it in the right order.

2 The allophones must be assigned in the right sequence.

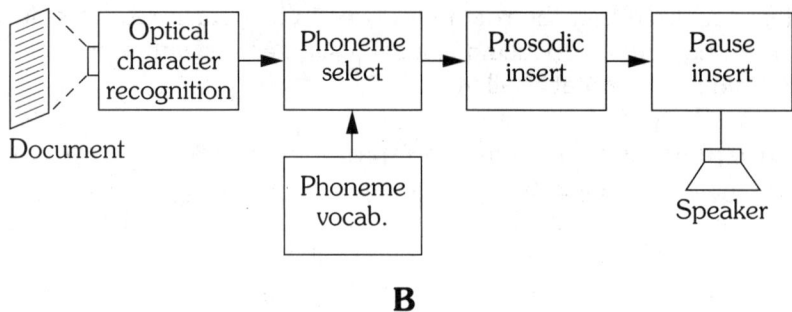

B

A text-reading speech synthesizer.

3 The proper inflections (prosodic features) must be put in.

4 Pauses must be inserted in the proper places.

In addition to these, for enhanced performance, additional features might be included, as follows:

5 The right mood can be conveyed (joy, sadness, urgency, etc.) at various moments.

6 Overall knowledge of the content can be programmed in. For example, the machine can know the significance of a story and the importance of each part within the story.

7 The machine can have an "interrupt feature" to allow conversation with a human being. If the human says something, the machine will stop and begin "listening" with a speech-recognition system.

This last feature could prove extremely interesting if two highly advanced machines got into an argument with each other. Some engineers can hardly wait for the day they get to try this. One machine might be a Republican and the other a Democrat; the engineer could bring up the subject of taxes, and let the two machines carry on a debate. The result might be an endless loop, as has been the case between human politicians for decades.

For further information. Speech synthesis is a challenging and fast-changing technology. A detailed discussion is beyond the scope of this book. The best source of up-to-date information is a university library. *See also* ANALOG, ARTIFICIAL INTELLIGENCE, BANDWIDTH, CONTEXT, DATA CONVERSION, DIGITAL, DIGITAL SIGNAL PROCESSING, GRAMMAR CHECKING, MESSAGE PASSING, OPTICAL CHARACTER RECOGNITION, SOUND TECHNOLOGY, SPEECH RECOGNITION, *and* SYNTAX.

Spell checking

Many word processing programs have a feature called *spell checking* to help writers and editors locate misspelled words and typographical errors. Some authors like spell checking, others prefer not to use it.

Spell checking

How it works. Spell checking compares the words in a text document with a vocabulary of words stored in memory. The program scans through the document, isolating words on the basis of the spaces and punctuation marks that separate them. When the program comes to a word that isn't in its vocabulary, it stops so the user can then determine whether or not the word is correct. If the word is correct, the user instructs the program to continue scanning the document. If the word is wrong, the user corrects it, and then tells the software to resume the scan.

Spell checkers often stop at words that are spelled correctly because of the limited size of the vocabulary. Many spell checkers allow you to add to the vocabulary, reducing the frequency of "false stops." Some words repeatedly confuse spell-checking programs. People's names (such as *Gibilisco*) and place names (such as *Okeechobee*) aren't generally included in spell-checking vocabularies. If a writer uses certain names often, they can be added to the vocabulary.

Assets. Spell checking can catch typographical errors (typos) that might otherwise be missed. If you've done much writing or editing, you know that errors can defy all human attempts to keep them from getting into print. Perhaps you've written a piece and proofread it a dozen times, until you were certain there were no errors. Then, when you saw it in print, three or four embarrassing typos jumped out at you. You looked at your original copy, and sure enough, there were the errors. It was as if goblins inserted the typos while you weren't looking.

Even the best writers sometimes make spelling errors. Spell checkers can catch them before others see them. If you're trying to impress someone who is not familiar with your work, this can be a big help; it keeps you from inadvertently damaging your credibility.

Limitations. Spell checking can't sense improper word usage when the word in question is correctly spelled. To find errors of that sort, a program must be able to interpret context and syntax. These subtle and complex characteristics of writing are far more difficult for a computer to evaluate than mere spelling. Here's an example of an error that a spell checker won't pick up:

Your radio is turned up to loud.

The intended sentence is, "Your radio is turned up too loud." Because *to* and *too* are both legitimate words, the spell checker will "pass" both of the above sentences, even though the first one, taken literally, doesn't make sense. Spell checkers can find some mistakes, but they can't necessarily tell you how to correct those mistakes. You must figure that out yourself.

Your choice. Some writers never use spell checking. They say that writers should know how to spell. They argue, "If you're not sure how to spell a word, look it up in the dictionary." Other writers and editors counter, "Yes, but even the best writers make typos, and a spell checker can weed out typos that human proofreaders miss."

The use (or nonuse) of spell checking is a personal decision. One suggestion: When buying word processing software, get a program with a large, expandable spell-checking vocabulary, whether or not you think you'll ever want to use it. *See also* CONTEXT, SYNTAX, *and* WORD PROCESSING.

Spherical coordinates

Several coordinate systems can be used to locate points in three-dimensional (3-D) space. One of these schemes is *spherical coordinates*. Most analytical graphics software can render 3-D plots in spherical coordinates, as well as in Cartesian coordinates, cylindrical coordinates, and other forms.

Scheme. The drawing shows the method for locating a point, *P*, using spherical coordinates. To set up the system, you must decide on an origin point. Then, you decide on a reference plane containing the origin. In that plane, you choose a coplanar reference ray. To locate *P*, you first measure the distance to *P* from the origin, on a straight line through space. This distance is the radius.

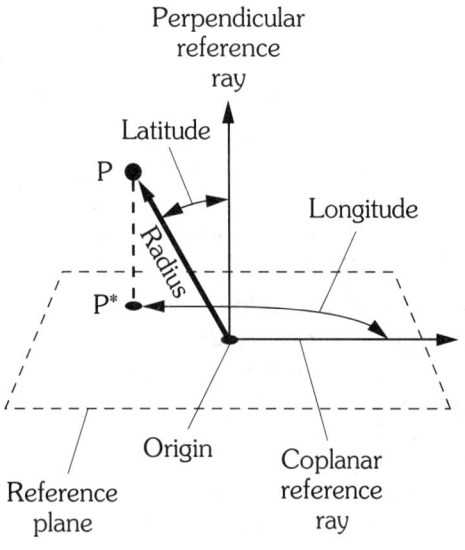

Spherical coordinates locate a point P, *according to radius, longitude, and latitude.*

Next, you measure a longitude angle in the reference plane, counterclockwise from the coplanar reference ray to *P*'s "shadow," *P**. The line connecting *P* and *P** is perpendicular to the reference plane, as if the "shadow" were cast by a distant light source directly above or below the reference plane. The longitude can be any angle from 0 to 360 degrees.

Finally, you measure the angle between the radius line (connecting *P* with the origin) and a perpendicular reference ray, starting at the origin and shooting straight up out of the reference plane. This angle is the latitude, and can vary from 0 degrees to 180 degrees.

Friend with a balloon. Here's an example of how you might use spherical coordinates to locate a point in space. Imagine that you're standing in an open field, and a friend is nearby, holding a helium balloon attached to a long string.

The balloon is 60 feet from you, as measured in a straight line through space. That's the radius. You choose north as the reference direction (toward the right in the drawing). The balloon is southwest of you; that's an angle of 135°, measured counterclockwise from due north. Therefore, the longitude is 135°. The balloon is 30° from the zenith. The latitude is therefore 30°. The coordinates of the balloon are:

(radius,longitude,latitude) = (60,135,30)

in units of (feet,degrees,degrees).

Spherical coordinates are commonly used in analytical graphics. Scientists and mathematicians use Greek letters to represent the angles and the lowercase letter *r* to represent the radius. *See also* ANALYTICAL GRAPHICS, CARTESIAN COORDINATES, *and* CYLINDRICAL COORDINATES.

Spreadsheet

A *spreadsheet* is a computerized ledger. It can be of assistance in personal and business financial management. Along with database management, word processing, graphics, and communications, a spreadsheet is one of the most common applications in personal computing. There are dozens of spreadsheet software packages available.

Basic layout. The drawing shows how an almost-empty spreadsheet looks on a computer display. Each little rectangle is called a *cell*. Cells are arranged in columns (designated by letters of the alphabet) and in rows (designated by numbers). Every cell thus has a unique identification code, or *address*. In the drawing, cells E4, E5, E6, E7, and E20 have numbers in them; the rest are blank. This particular spreadsheet has 10 columns and 20 rows, for a total of 200 cells. Some spreadsheets are smaller than this, some are bigger, some are shorter and fatter, and some are taller and thinner. Many spreadsheet programs allow you to tailor the size and shape to suit your needs.

Any cell in a spreadsheet can contain a numerical value with a certain *numeric format*, or method of expression. Text can also be inserted in cells. In the drawing, all the filled cells are numerically formatted to

Spreadsheet

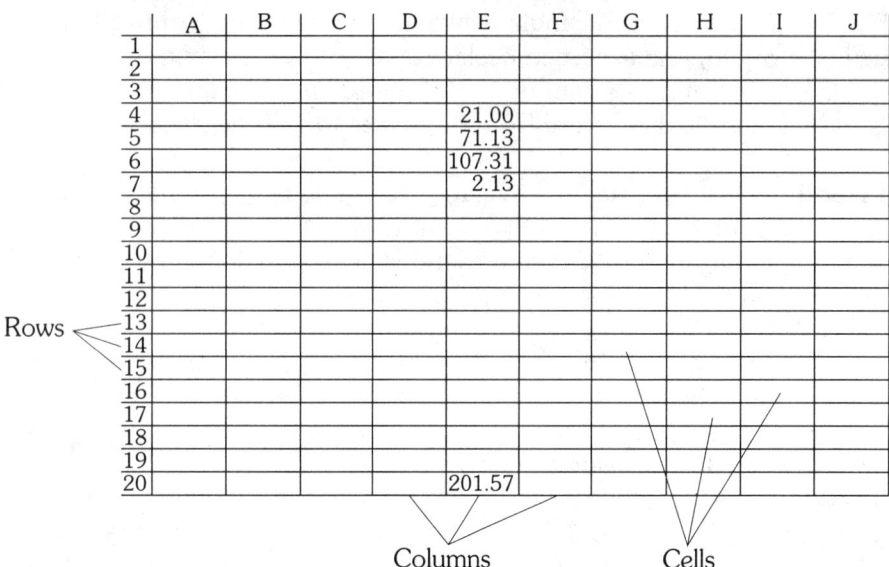

A spreadsheet with numbers are in cells E4, E5, E6, and E7; their sum is in cell E20.

indicate sums of money (dollars and cents). Cells can also contain formulas for purposes of calculation.

All the cells in the spreadsheet can be linked to facilitate the sort of calculations that you want the program to carry out. There are literally trillions of different ways in which the cells and formulas can be arranged. In fact, there are so many possible formulas that it can become hard to remember where they are and how they're linked. Therein lies one of the potential pitfalls of spreadsheet software: you can make mistakes if you lose track of what's happening in which places.

Cells can be grouped together in rectangular blocks called *ranges*, with the upper-left and lower-right cells determining the location and shape of the rectangle. Ranges are used to set off parts of a spreadsheet for different purposes. Sometimes a numeric format is specified for a range of cells, rather than for just one cell; this is called a *range format*. A numeric format for the whole spreadsheet is called a *global format*.

Recalculation. Numbers are entered into a spreadsheet using either the number keys above the main part of the keyboard or via the numeric keypad. Numeric-keypad entry is preferred by accountants because this pad resembles a calculator or adding machine.

The powerful features of a computer spreadsheet become apparent when you want to do arithmetic operations on groups of numbers. A simple example is shown in the drawing. The four numbers in cells E4, E5, E6, and E7 have been summed (added up); the total is displayed in cell E20. The spreadsheet could average, multiply, or

combine these numbers for you in almost any way you can imagine. Different groups of numbers, operated on differently, could occupy other groups of cells in the spreadsheet. The operations might be done row-wise or column-wise. In the drawing, the sum has been done column-wise.

Suppose you have nearly filled a spreadsheet with numbers and functions. Often, changing one number affects the values in many cells. The computer can do a *recalculation* when you change the value in a cell. If the recalculation is done instantly with every numerical change, it is *automatic recalculation*. If the recalculation is done only in response to a command from you, it is *manual recalculation*.

Other features. Spreadsheet programs do more than add, subtract, multiply, and divide numbers. Here are three features you'll find in more advanced spreadsheet packages:

- *Forecasting* By changing the numbers in certain cells of a spreadsheet, you can get an idea of what might happen in various situations. Suppose your income will increase 10% next year, with overall inflation of 4% but a medical-insurance increase of 35%. Your tax bracket will change, so will your deductions. If you have a well-arranged spreadsheet set up, you can change a few numbers to see whether you'll be better off or worse off next year, at least on the basis of these factors. This is called *what-if analysis*, and is a special kind of forecasting.

- *Graphs and charts* Many types of graphs and charts can be used in conjunction with the spreadsheet. Graphs let you do things like compare prices, observe trends, note similarities and differences, pinpoint possible trouble spots, see how you might improve a company's profit margin, and forecast future events. Graphs are excellent tools for investors in stocks, mutual funds, real estate, or anything else whose values fluctuate. You can work with analytical graphics if you need to scrutinize data closely, or you can set things up to produce presentation graphics for corporate reports, sales meetings, and publications.

- *Three dimensions* Although the drawing here shows a two-dimensional spreadsheet, some spreadsheet programs can create a three-dimensional *spreadcube* or *spreadspace* in addition to the conventional spreadsheet.

  You might think it would be impossible to work with spreadcubes. As if it's not complicated enough dealing with rows, columns, and the combinations of functions possible with them, you'd have to fuss over *stacks*, too! Fortunately, three-dimensional spreadsheets aren't hard to master, especially when the software is well-written and user-friendly, as is the case with such programs as Lotus 1-2-3 and Quattro Pro.

Spy software

What do you need? If you purchase an integrated software package, a basic spreadsheet will almost certainly be included, along with database, graphics, and word processing functions. This spreadsheet might be powerful enough for you. Spreadsheets are general-purpose application programs. They haven't been tailored for specialized, individual needs, which vary tremendously from person to person. Although a spreadsheet is useful for keeping simple financial records, you might find it inadequate if your estate is complex and needs expert long-range planning.

If you are into serious money matters, you should look into personal finance software, tax preparation software, and other high-level programs. If you know any accountants, you might ask them which programs they would recommend (in addition to their personal services, perhaps) for your unique financial portfolio. *See also* ANALYTICAL GRAPHICS, AREA GRAPH, BAR GRAPH, BUSINESS SOFTWARE, COLUMNAR GRAPH, EXTRAPOLATION, FORECASTING, GLOBAL FORMAT, HIGH/LOW/OPEN/CLOSE GRAPH, HISTOGRAM, INTEGRATED SOFTWARE PACKAGE, INTERPOLATION, LINE GRAPH, LINKED GRAPH, LOTUS, MIXED COLUMNAR/LINE GRAPH, MULTIVARIABLE FUNCTION GRAPH, NUMERIC FORMAT, PAIRED-BAR GRAPH, PERSONAL FINANCE SOFTWARE, PIE GRAPH, PRESENTATION GRAPHICS, QUATTRO PRO, QUICKEN, RANGE, RATIO ANALYSIS SOFTWARE, RECALCULATION, STACKED-COLUMN GRAPH, SUITE, *and* TAX PREPARATION SOFTWARE.

Spy software

When employees use computers on the job, especially if the machines are connected into a network, supervisors can monitor what's happening at each workstation. *Spy software* refers to programs that facilitate this.

How it works. Spy software is installed in conjunction with a local area network (LAN). The supervisor has a workstation through which he or she can monitor what is being done at any of the employees' workstations. The supervisor can view each employee's screen in real-time, clicking the mouse or pressing a hot key to go from one workstation to another in a rotating sequence. The program can keep track of each employee's keystrokes so the supervisor can tell, without leaving his or her office, which employees' workstations are active and which ones are idle. Active versus idle time can be tallied on an hourly or daily basis for each employee. A record can be kept of all files and software used, copied, or deleted. Electronic mail messages, both incoming and outgoing, can be stored. Information can be logged for each workday.

The good. From a management point of view, spy software has a legitimate purpose. Some employees make extensive personal use of company equipment during company time. Some employees simply do not feel compelled to put in an honest day's work. When employees know they are being monitored, they are unlikely to misuse company time and hardware, and they tend to work harder and more efficiently. This translates into higher productivity, at least in theory, which in turn increases profits over the situation when employees are not monitored.

Spy software can also be useful from a security standpoint. It can keep confidential or classified data from leaking out. It can help to pinpoint instances of software piracy. This creates a "trust but verify" atmosphere. People are unlikely to break the law or breach security when they believe they'll be caught if they do.

The bad. From an employee point of view, monitoring is an intrusion. It's as if the supervisor were constantly looking over every employee's shoulder. Responsible employees are sometimes insulted by monitoring. Resentments can arise, and tensions can mount. Employee turnover might increase. Some studies have shown that employee monitoring causes workers to suffer more stress-related ailments, both physical and mental, compared with a work situation in which employees are not monitored.

If monitoring is done, it's best if employees are told about it when they are hired. There are three reasons for this. First, employees must know they're being monitored if it is to have the desired effect. It's like a "Speed Zone Ahead" sign on a highway. People behave better when they know the rules are being enforced. Second, morale can be shattered when spy software is used without the knowledge of the employees. Sooner or later, someone will probably find out about it and tell everyone. Once trust has been destroyed in a company or department, it can't easily be restored. Third, lawsuits can occur as a result of clandestine employee monitoring. This is especially true if the employee is fired—no matter what the reason—and later discovers that he or she was being secretly monitored. *See also* ELECTRONIC MAIL, KEYSTROKES, LOCAL AREA NETWORK, *and* SOFTWARE PIRACY.

Stacked-column graph

A *stacked-column graph* is a set of two or more columnar graphs in one. There is one horizontal axis and one or two vertical axes. The horizontal axis represents the independent variable. The vertical axes represent dependent variables. Several functions can be represented by a stacked-column graph. They must all have the same independent variable, which is usually time, but the functions can have different dependent variables.

Stacked-column graphs are used in presentation graphics to show a relationship or correlation between two phenomena, trends, or sets of events. The drawing is a stacked-column graph showing the high and low temperatures for a week in a hypothetical town. In this case, there is only one dependent-variable axis, calibrated from 50°F to 90°F. The horizontal axis has seven discrete points, one for each day of the week (Sunday through Saturday, June 7 through June 13). The low temperature for each day is indicated by the top of a shaded column. The high temperatures are shown by unshaded extensions of the columns. This makes it easy to see how the high and low temperatures vary throughout the week. It's also easy to see the difference between the high and low temperatures, and to read the actual highs and lows, for each day.

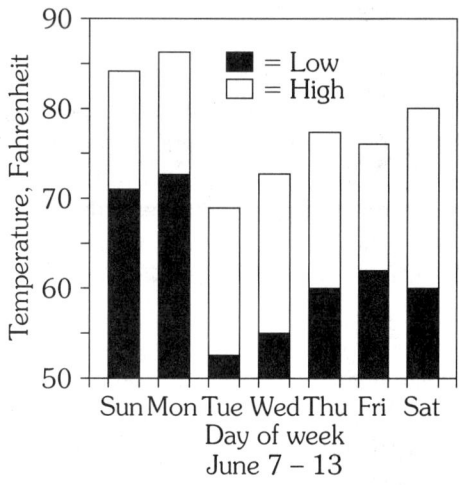

A stacked-column graph compares two or more discrete functions.

The main advantage of stacked-column graphs is that they're simple, and they show relative values and differences clearly. The main disadvantage is that a continuous function can't be rendered; only a limited number of discrete values can be shown.

Stacked-column graphs are not used in analytical graphics as often as they are in presentation graphics. A meteorologist might want to see the temperature for the week plotted at intervals of an hour or less. Then, the result would be a set of points connected by a curve.

Most graphics software packages can help you create stacked-column graphs with two, three, four, or more levels. When there are more than four levels, stacked-column graphs can be hard to read. *See also* ANALYTICAL GRAPHICS, CARTESIAN COORDINATES, COLUMNAR GRAPH, *and* PRESENTATION GRAPHICS.

Star network

There are several different methods, or *topologies*, for connecting PCs and terminals in a local area network (LAN). In one type of topology, all the workstations are connected to a central processor. This is called a *star network* because, when diagrammed, the data lines emanate outward from the "hub" like rays of light from a star.

Star network

Coordinating the nodes. An example of a star network is shown in the drawing. Each computer (labeled *PC*) or dumb terminal (*T*) represents one workstation, called a *node*. Every node has an *address*, a code that uniquely identifies it. That way, any node in the LAN can connect to any other. In the drawing, all the nodes are effectively connected together. For any two nodes in the network, there is a path between them. This path always runs through the central PC; it's never a direct connection. The "hub" PC coordinates communications among the workstations.

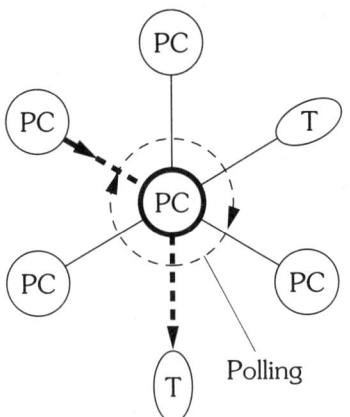

In a star network, all nodes are connected to a central PC.

The central computer ensures that, if two or more nodes send data at the same time, the signals don't conflict. To do this, the central PC checks each node in a rapid, rotating sequence. If a workstation has something to send, then the central PC takes some of the data and stores it, along with the address of the intended destination. When the rotation reaches the destination address, the data is delivered. This *polling* scheme also ensures that no workstation consumes more than its proper share of network time.

Advantages. A star network is versatile. It allows for several network "conversations" to proceed simultaneously. It's even possible for two or more sources to send data to a single destination at the same time because of the polling scheme, which divides the central processor's attention among all the nodes.

If one node malfunctions, all the rest can still communicate with each other. For a major disruption to take place in the star network, something must go wrong with the central processor. This is both a blessing and a curse. It prevents disaster in the event of node failure, but it leaves the system open to catastrophic failure if the central PC goes down.

Star networks are easy to enlarge; all you need to do is add more nodes. The limit is determined by the power of the central processor.

Static random-access memory

Star networks are well-suited to situations where nodes are located at scattered points.

Limitations. The radius of a star network cannot normally be more than about 1000 feet because signals die off rapidly along the cable. If the distance between the central PC and any node must be more than 1000 feet, a *repeater* is needed between that node and the hub of the star. Repeaters are circuits that receive, amplify, and retransmit the data.

Star networks need more interconnecting cable, for a given number of nodes, than other types of networks. This makes star networks comparatively expensive and difficult to install. Also, the powerful central processor adds to the cost of a star network, compared to a simpler ring network which does not have this extra hardware. When nodes are located more or less on a long, straight line, a star network is not the ideal LAN topology. In that situation, a bus network will work better. *See also* BUS NETWORK, LOCAL AREA NETWORK, NETWORK, POLLING, REPEATER, *and* RING NETWORK.

Static random-access memory

Static random-access memory, abbreviated *SRAM*, is a form of random-access memory in which data is stored in tiny transistors that are etched in a wafer of semiconductor material.

Switches. In SRAM, the digit 1 (high) is represented by a closed (turned-on) electronic switch. The digit 0 (low) is represented when the switch is opened (turned-off). This can be reversed; that is, a closed switch can be the digit 0 while the open switch is the digit 1. It doesn't make any difference from an operating standpoint, as long as things are consistent within the circuit.

Unlike the situation with its cousin, dynamic random-access memory (DRAM), there are no electric charges in SRAM to leak away. Thus, there's no need to replenish the charge every few milliseconds (thousandths of a second) in an SRAM chip, as is the case with a DRAM device. Because the computer need not spend any time making sure that the SRAM data is replenished, the machine can devote more attention to computing. The result is that the PC works faster.

Flip-flops. The switches in SRAM are actually sets of transistors. Each set is interconnected to form a circuit called a *flip-flop*. These maintain their state indefinitely as long as they're supplied with electricity, until they receive a pulse that tells them to change from logic 0 to 1 or vice versa.

The drawing is a schematic diagram of four metal-oxide-semiconductor (MOS) transistors connected as a flip-flop. In an actual integrated circuit (IC), each of these flip-flops is microscopic; the drawing is enlarged

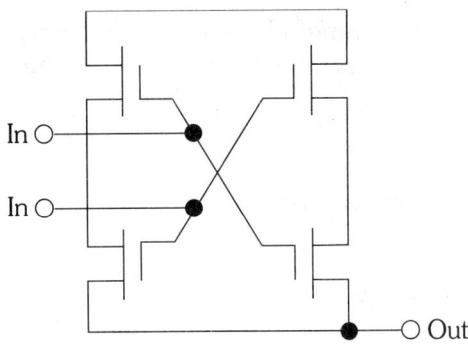

A schematic diagram of an SRAM switch using four MOS transistors.

many thousands of times compared with the real thing. Shrink the drawing down, change it from a schematic into a literal representation, multiply it by a few million, and you have an SRAM IC.

Because SRAMs need more transistors than DRAM to get the same amount of memory, an SRAM chip of a given physical size can hold only a fraction as much data as a DRAM chip of the same size. Engineers would say that the *memory density* of SRAM is lower than that of DRAM. This is one disadvantage of SRAM technology.

Microprocessors and SRAM. As microprocessor chips become faster, the necessary access time and storage time for SRAM will get shorter. It's possible to use a very fast SRAM chip with a slow microprocessor, but this is not ideal because it requires the use of wait states. A fast microprocessor with a slow memory is no better; a slow memory limits the clock speed at which the microprocessor can work.

Some microprocessors have SRAM cache memory built-in; some computers have SRAM caches on their motherboards. This speeds up some applications considerably. *See also* DYNAMIC RANDOM-ACCESS MEMORY, FLIP-FLOP, INTEGRATED CIRCUIT, *and* RANDOM-ACCESS MEMORY.

Storage time

When you save data to a medium, it takes time to get written in. Sometimes it goes in almost instantly; in the newest PCs you can save a file onto the hard disk so fast you might not even notice any delay. However, if the file is very long, if the processor speed is rather slow, or if you're saving the file to a diskette or other external medium, it can take awhile.

Within a computer. The delay between the save or store command and the storage of a file is called the *storage time*. The shortest storage times are for small files (a few kilobytes) going to a hard disk. Getting data onto a diskette takes longer. For tape drives, it's longer still.

The bigger the file, the longer the storage time, all other factors being equal. With files of several hundred kilobytes on a floppy diskette, the storage time might be a quarter of a minute.

When you want to retrieve data from a hard disk or diskette, there is also a delay. This is called the *access time* or *transfer rate*.

In communications. When you send data into a bulletin-board system (BBS) or via electronic mail (e-mail), it usually goes in almost right away. Bulletin-board and e-mail messages are short, and they don't take long to send, even via modem. The storage time might be a couple of minutes at most. The only potential problem is if a BBS is full, so there isn't room for any more messages in it, or if there are too many people trying to use it at once.

If you intend to save a large file on the hard disk or diskette drive of a remote computer, the storage time can be several minutes. This is because, when you send data via modem, it is sent bit-by-bit in *serial* fashion. Data takes much longer to be sent serially, compared with *parallel* data transfer, which is the rule within a single workstation. All things considered, however, even this serial process is pretty fast. You can usually send a long report to a colleague or client via modem in a few minutes. *See also* ACCESS TIME, BULLETIN-BOARD SYSTEM, ELECTRONIC MAIL, MODEM, NETWORK, *and* SERIAL.

Suite

A *suite* is a high-powered software package designed especially for business and institutional use. Suites generally have a word processor, a database, a spreadsheet, an information manager, presentation graphics, and communications software. There might also be analytical graphics, calendars, and other specialized items. Suites are sometimes called *bundles*.

Assets. Perhaps the greatest asset of a suite is that all the programs share the same user interface. The icons or commands all behave the same way, and have the same meanings, in the various programs.

Another advantage of a suite, compared with the purchase of separate programs, is lower up-front cost. You buy all the programs at once, and there's nothing more for you to worry about, at least until your needs outgrow the features provided by the suite. Also, when you install a bundle, you save memory compared with installing separate programs because there is less redundancy among the applications; some features are shared.

Suites commonly employ *object linking and embedding (OLE)* to provide a "connection" among all the different programs in the suite. For example, you can click on an icon while you're working in a spreadsheet, and call a file from the database, word processor, or graphics modules. It's even possible to embed sound bites in business files.

Suppose you have a list of clients' names and addresses in the suite's database manager. You write letters and keep them in the word processing portion of the package. People move frequently, so you'll have to update your database at regular intervals. With the linking feature, if you change the address of a person or company in the course of writing them a letter, the address will change in all the other applications, including the database, at that very moment. With the embedding feature, you can add photos and sound bites to the database files for each person or company, and click on icons to get animated, up-to-date, audio-visual presentations.

Limitations. Suites aren't for all businesses. It's largely a matter of preference whether you buy a suite for all your applications, or separate programs for each application.

Although you can save money in the short term by buying a suite instead of separate programs, the long-term scenario is harder to predict. Companies evolve just as people do. Your company's needs, and its relative demand for various applications, will probably change during the next few years. If you're willing to be flexible and buy separate programs, each tailored to your anticipated needs as well as your current needs, the long-term payoff might exceed the higher short-term capital outlay.

With modern OLE, separate programs can work together just about as well as they can in a suite. If you have enough money and a large enough hard disk, you can install separate programs, each of the highest caliber available, for each major application. The OLE will coordinate them. This gives you optimum power in each application. There might be variation in behavior from program to program, but if you and your employees spend a bit of extra time learning the system, this won't be a problem.

If you have a small business that's rapidly growing, and especially if you're hiring people to do specialized jobs, you might want to buy separate software packages, one for each workstation. You can link the workstations in a local area network (LAN). You can then add OLE to the system, getting the advantages of integrated software along with versatility in each application.

If you decide you want to purchase a suite, shop around. Look for one that provides the most power in those applications for which your needs are greatest. Think about what you'll need in the near future, as well as what you need right now. *See also* BUSINESS SOFTWARE, DYNAMIC DATA EXCHANGE, INTEGRATED SOFTWARE PACKAGE, LOCAL AREA NETWORK, *and* OBJECT LINKING AND EMBEDDING.

Super Video Graphics Array

Super Video Graphics Array (SVGA) is a monitor display standard for IBM-compatible PCs. SVGA is an upgrade of the older Video Graphics Array (VGA) monitor standard. An SVGA monitor is a high-resolution monitor.

An SVGA can show a huge number of colors. The image resolution is superior to that of a VGA. The quality of the image is good enough for virtually all personal computing applications, including high-level graphics programs. A noninterlaced SVGA will work for sophisticated computer games, high-speed animation, simulation, and interactive technology.

If you are using an older computer with a VGA and don't need the high resolution and true color of SVGA, there is no need to upgrade your monitor. For simple word processing, database, spreadsheet, and paint programs, a VGA is generally sufficient. If you expect to become much more seriously involved in computing in the next couple of years, you might consider purchasing an SVGA monitor and video board if your system does not currently have SVGA.

In new computers, SVGA has become standard. If you're purchasing a new system, you will probably want an SVGA monitor to go with it. The *dot pitch* is the most direct indicator of monitor resolution; 0.28 dot pitch is considered good for SVGA monitors. Some SVGA monitors have dot pitch even finer than this; the lower the number, the better the image resolution. *See also* DOT PITCH, HIGH-RESOLUTION MONITOR, MONITOR UPGRADING, *and* VIDEO GRAPHICS ARRAY.

Surge suppression

See TRANSIENT SUPPRESSION.

Swap file

A *swap file* is a means of increasing the effective size of a computer's RAM (random-access memory). Swap files get their name from the fact that portions of the RAM are exchanged, or swapped, between the actual memory chips and the hard disk. A swap file makes use of a scheme called *virtual memory*.

For a swap file to work well, it must have a section of hard disk space that is continuous, or unfragmented. This will ensure that data is written onto and read from the hard disk at the fastest possible speed. It's a good idea to run a defragmentation program before setting up a swap file. The program should be run at frequent intervals if you plan to keep using swap files regularly.

The main advantage of a swap file is that it can let you run bigger programs than you could using the RAM alone. There are shortcomings and potential pitfalls, however. Swap files are slow compared with RAM because they bring the mechanical components of the hard disk into play. The RAM, in contrast, is completely electronic, and has no moving parts; therefore, it's practically instantaneous. A swap file shouldn't be used when it's not really needed, because the access and storage times are much slower than they are with real RAM. If your hard disk space is at a premium, a swap file might cut into the space you need for other data or software.

A swap file shouldn't be placed in a RAM disk. That's easy to do inadvertently, but it's like taking from your right hand to give to your left, after you took from your left hand to give to your right. A RAM disk is the opposite of a swap file. Putting a swap file in a RAM disk takes away from both your RAM space and your hard disk space, giving you nothing in return. See also ACCESS TIME, DEFRAGMENTATION, RAM DISK, RANDOM-ACCESS MEMORY, STORAGE TIME, and VIRTUAL MEMORY.

Synchronous data

Computers communicate via digital signals called *machine language*. This language is made up of discrete units, each of which is either high (logic 1) or low (logic 0). Each unit is called a *bit*. Each character (letter, number, or punctuation mark) consists of several bits.

Data bits. A data signal can be displayed on an oscilloscope. If you adjust the oscilloscope correctly, you can see the data bits. A digital signal has a squared-off appearance; the highs and lows are quite obvious.

There is only one correct way to interpret a series of digital bits. If the destination PC is running in sync with the source computer, then the received data will make sense. If the destination PC is ahead of or behind the source PC, the destination might misinterpret the entire message. It will be as if the source computer were talking in a foreign language. This can occur even when the time difference is only a tiny fraction of a second.

Bit by bit. One way to ensure that the destination and source machines are in sync is to have them both follow an independent signal that "keeps the beat." It's like a dancing couple who have their steps coordinated perfectly. The device that sets the beat, keeping the machines in sync, is called a *clock*. This scheme is called *synchronous data* transmission. Such a system is simple in theory, as the block diagram shows. In practice, however, it is a little tricky.

Clock signals, like any data impulses, take time to get from place to place. Ideally, the signal distance from the clock to the source should be the same as the distance from the clock to the destination. In the drawing, the clock signals should take the same time to travel over line X as over line Y. If this is not the case, then the source will "hear a different drummer" than the destination, and the synchronization will

Syntax

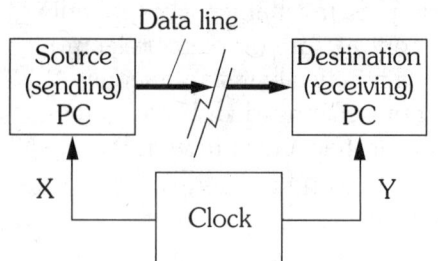

The source and destination are paced by a clock via lines X and Y.

be upset. At the extreme data speeds typical of synchronous systems, even a small difference in the lengths of lines X and Y can cause problems. Another disadvantage of synchronous systems is that they tend to be expensive because the clock must be extremely accurate, and the system alignment is critical.

The biggest advantage of a synchronous data link is that it can work at high speed. This can be important when complex programs or large volumes of data must be transferred among computers.

Start/stop instructions. Another way to keep PCs in sync is to have the source tell the destination when each character begins and ends. This is called *asynchronous data* transmission.

In this type of system, when the source is ready to send a character, it transmits a *start bit.* When it's done with the character, it sends a *stop bit.* The destination PC then displays the character. Start bits and stop bits break up the data so there is no confusion among characters, but these extra bits take time to be sent. Because of this, it takes longer to send a given amount of information in an asynchronous system than with a synchronous data system.

Personal computers generally use asynchronous data. It's fast enough for most PC users' needs. An asynchronous system is cheaper than a synchronous system. Because there is no clock and associated transmission lines, an asynchronous system is also easier to install and maintain than a synchronous system. *See also* ASYNCHRONOUS DATA, BIT, CHARACTER, *and* MODEM.

Syntax

Syntax refers to the way a written or spoken sentence is put together. Syntax is important in speech recognition and speech synthesis. It is also important in computer programming. Each spoken and written human language has its own unique syntax. The same is true for high-level computer programming languages.

Sentence structure. Perhaps you remember studying sentence structure in English classes. Most students find it boring, but it can be fascinating if you have a good teacher. Diagramming sentences is like working with mathematical logic. Computers are good at this sort of thing.

There are several basic sentence forms; all sentences can be classified into one of these forms. The sentence "John lifts the tray," for example, might be called *SVO* for subject-verb-object. In this case, *John* is the subject, *lifts* is the verb, and *tray* is the object. A computer can take any sentence and analyze it, and then generate new sentences with the same structure. Given a large enough vocabulary and enough sentence-structure information, a machine can be made to understand and generate millions of different sentences.

Syntax rules. Different languages have different syntax rules. In the Russian language, "I like you" is said as, "I you like." That is, an SVO sentence is really SOV. The meaning is clear, as long as the syntax rules are known, and as long as they remain consistent in the language. A computer designed to speak and understand Russian would need a somewhat different set of syntax rules than a computer for the English language, although the basic nature of the processes would be the same.

If syntax rules are not clearly defined, or if they aren't consistent within a language, the meaning can be confused or lost. If you say, "I you like" to a friend, he or she will probably respond, "What?" Keeping a machine's syntax clear and consistent becomes more difficult as the conversational level increases. It takes more computing power to generate and understand a language at the college level, for example, than at a middle-school level, even if the vocabularies are the same. College students know more syntax rules (even if they aren't consciously aware of it) than middle-school students.

Memory and speed. When designing a computer that can converse with people, engineers must program syntax rules into the computer's memory. Otherwise, the machine will make nonsensical statements and will not be able to correctly interpret everything people say to it. The machine must also access and store data to and from memory at a high enough speed so it can keep up with human conversational companions.

For a given amount of computer power, speed is forced down as the syntax rule set is made larger. Conversely, as the speed of a given machine is made faster, its syntax finesse decreases. This effect is shown in the graph. A particular PC will work more slowly at the college language level than at the middle-school level. An increase in computing power translates into greater conversational capability, as reflected by the relative positions of the curves in the graph. *See also* COMPUTER POWER, SPEECH RECOGNITION, *and* SPEECH SYNTHESIS.

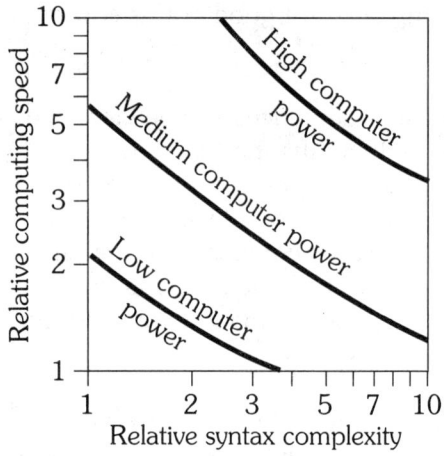

Processing speed versus syntax complexity for various amounts of overall computer power.

System 7

System 7 is an operating system designed for use with Macintosh computers, which are manufactured by Apple Computer, Inc. System 7 has advanced features, some of which can accommodate inventions that haven't yet come off the drawing boards.

What you need. To run System 7, you need a Macintosh computer, preferably with a Motorola 68030 or later microprocessor. System 7's graphical user interface (GUI) and other high-level features work best if you have at least 4MB of RAM (random-access memory).

Because System 7 can work with more than one program at a time, and because it can handle sophisticated software, you should have as much hard disk space as you can manage. It's impossible to quote an exact minimum specification because hard disks keep getting bigger and software keeps being published with features that gobble up hard disk space.

What it can do. System 7 has had a big influence on the way people and businesses do their computing. Here are some features System 7 offers:

➢ *Multitasking* You can run more than one program at a time. True multitasking can be done within a single application or between different applications. The system can "think" about more than one task at once.

➢ *Virtual memory* Part of the hard disk can be used as RAM, thereby expanding the effective size of the RAM for applications in which extra memory is needed.

➢ *Menu-launched software* You can start a program simply by selecting its name or designator from a menu (list of programs and files). The selection can be carried out instantly by pressing a key or clicking the mouse.

➢ *Network file sharing* In a local area network (LAN), computers can directly access files on the hard disks of other computers. This, in effect, creates a multiterminal minicomputer or mainframe. There is no need for a file server.

➢ *Dynamic data exchange* If you change data in one file, it will change in all the others instantly. There's no need to search for all occurrences of an item and change them all (nor need you worry that you might miss one).

➢ *Scalable fonts* On the screen and in printouts, System 7 uses outline fonts, which can be resized or scaled without the jaggies (distortion) that occur when some fonts are resized.

➢ *Extension architecture* Perhaps the most significant feature of System 7 is its open design. When you buy a Mac equipped with System 7, you can be confident that you'll be able to add applications in the future, even if you have no idea at the moment what they might be.

See also DYNAMIC DATA EXCHANGE, FONT, GRAPHICAL USER INTERFACE, LOCAL AREA NETWORK, MACINTOSH, MENU, MENU-DRIVEN SOFTWARE, MULTITASKING, OBJECT LINKING AND EMBEDDING, OPERATING SYSTEM, OUTLINE FONT, *and* VIRTUAL MEMORY.

1050

Tab key

The *Tab key* is a key found on all PC and typewriter keyboards. Its function in a computer is similar to that in a typewriter. The Tab key is usually located on the left side of the keyboard (see the drawing), and sometimes also on the right side. It is most commonly used in word processing.

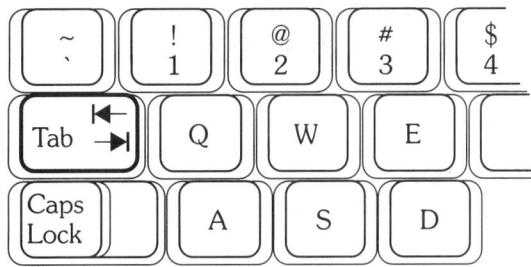

The Tab key is on the left side of the keyboard.

In a text file, you can set tab stops at various points between the left and right margins. You can also set the margins themselves. The left-to-right position of the cursor on the screen is represented in inches, or by a number between 0 and some maximum, usually 200 or more.

Suppose your document has one-inch left and right margins, and you set tab stops at one-inch intervals between the margins. When you press the Tab key with the cursor at the left margin, it will jump to the first tab marker, at 2 inches. If you press the Tab key repeatedly, it will stop at 3, 4, and so on, until it reaches the right margin. If you press

Tape drive

the Tab key with the cursor at the right margin, the behavior of the cursor will depend on the word processing software you have. In most cases, it will move through the tab stops on the next line. *See also* CURSOR *and* WORD PROCESSING.

Tape drive

A *tape drive* is a high-precision tape recorder that is useful for backing up a hard disk. As its name implies, the device writes data onto and reads it from magnetic tape. A typical tape can hold several gigabytes of data.

The medium. Computer tape is similar to the tape used in audio and video recording. It is a plastic strip coated with ferromagnetic particles. These particles can be individually magnetized and demagnetized.

For computer-data recording, magnetic tape is available either in cassette form or reel-to-reel form. In recent years, microcassettes have become popular. The tape thickness can vary. The thicker tapes have better resistance to stretching, but the recording time for a given length of tape is shorter than with thin tape. Thinner tapes let you put more data into a smaller physical volume, but there is a greater risk of the tape stretching or jamming in the drive mechanism.

On the tape, data is recorded in *tracks*. These tracks can be parallel to the edges of the tape, as shown in drawing A, or slantwise, as shown at B. Angled tracks require a more complex drive mechanism for reading and writing data, but they make better use of the tape's surface area, resulting in greater data density.

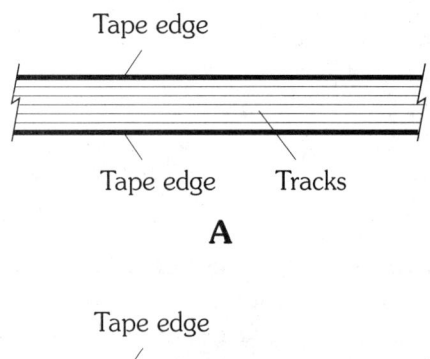

Tracks in QIC tape (A) and DAT (B). Track spacing is exaggerated for clarity.

Drive types. There are two major kinds of tape drives in use today: *quarter-inch-cartridge (QIC)* drives and *digital-audio-tape (DAT)* drives. Parallel tracks are the norm in QIC drives. There are between 8 and 32 tracks on the tape. Recording is done from end-to-end along one track, and then the tape reverses, and the recording starts on an adjacent track. This process continues, with the tape going back and forth from end to end, until all the tracks are full or until the hard disk has been completely backed up.

Angled tracks are employed in DAT drives. The read and write heads are skewed, so they put data on the tape at an angle of a few degrees. An error-correction scheme ensures that the data is recorded properly on the tape from the computer's memory. Specialized recording techniques maximize the data density on the tape, making the best possible use of the available surface area.

A tape drive can automatically locate files when you request them. It works like a hi-fi stereo system where you can select the songs you want via codes on the tape. However, it takes much longer for a tape drive to locate a file than it does for a hard disk or diskette drive because of the way the data is written along the length of the tape.

Assets. Tape drives are reasonably priced. They pay for themselves not by acting or looking spectacular, but by preventing disaster. They're like an insurance policy.

In your PC, there are probably many programs that have been tailored to meet your needs. In addition, there are dozens or hundreds of files arranged in a system of directories that has evolved according to your taste. The contents of the hard disk is important not only in terms of the actual data written on it, but also because of the way the data has been arranged and edited. If your data were suddenly lost because of hard-disk failure, you might never get things back exactly as they were.

The contents of a hard disk can usually be backed up on a single cassette in a few minutes with minimum supervision by the operator. The same backup requires dozens, even hundreds, of diskettes, and requires constant attention in the form of diskette swapping.

Limitations and precautions. Tapes must be stored in a clean, dust-free, grease-free place where the temperature and humidity are within reason. Salty beach air is not good for them. Tapes must never be subjected to magnetic fields. Avoid storing them near speakers, headphones, or other devices containing permanent magnets or electromagnets. Also, keep them away from "live" electrical wiring.

The most noticeable limitation of a tape drive is that it's slow. Magnetic tape is a sequential-access medium, whereas a magnetic disk is a random-access medium. The binary digits (bits) run lengthwise

Tax-preparation software

along the tape. The distance between two bits can be anything between a fraction of a millimeter and the entire length of the tape (hundreds of meters). You can't access files from a tape as easily as from a disk. People don't buy tape drives for speed, however, they buy them for peace of mind. *See also* ARCHIVES, BACKUP, DISKETTE, HARD DISK, MAGNETIC DISK, MAGNETIC MEDIA, MAGNETIC TAPE, *and* MASS STORAGE.

Tax-preparation software

Depending on the complexity of your finances, income-tax preparation and filing can be a simple annual chore or a major undertaking that needs constant updating and planning. *Tax-preparation software* won't do all your tax work, but it can make preparation and filing easier and more accurate. It can also save you money, perhaps paying for itself several times over the first year of use.

Who needs it? If you have a professional accountant who prepares your tax returns, you can probably benefit from tax-preparation software. It's possible that your PC can take the place of your accountant, saving you the annual expense of paying a human expert. At least, the software can help you keep accurate records.

If you file short forms, you can probably do your taxes all by yourself, without the help of a computer or a human accountant. There are few or no deductions involved, except for personal exemptions. Young people, new to the workforce, often fall into this category.

As your financial picture begins to include things like a home, a small business, stocks, and other responsibilities, the complexity of your tax return seems to blow up exponentially. Every year you read about "paperwork reduction" acts being worked out in the legislature; every year your paperwork load increases. Ultimately, you might decide that a computer, with some form of personal finance software or business software, has become a necessity. At this point, tax-preparation software is no longer a luxury of the rich, but a real means of helping the average taxpayer.

Tax-preparation software is available in versions to match practically any operating system and user interface, including DOS, Windows, OS/2, and the Macintosh OS. Prices are quite low, in some cases less than $30, and rarely more than $100.

What can it do? The main purposes of tax-preparation software are to make your work easier, ensure accuracy, give you every break to which you're legally entitled, and minimize the probability that your return will be audited. There are many "extras" in the fancier packages. Here are some of the features you'll commonly find:

➤ *Annual updates* Tax laws and forms change every year. For this reason, most tax-preparation software vendors supply new

Tax-preparation software

packages annually. A preliminary package comes out in the autumn, and the final package comes out just after the first of the year. Only the final package can be used for actual filing purposes; the preliminary version is for those who need or want extra time to get things in order.

➤ *Tax forms* You can print out dozens of different tax forms, each of which is updated to reflect changes in the tax laws. This saves you the tedium of photocopying them at the public library or ordering them from the Internal Revenue Service. The forms can be printed out and then filled in by hand, or you can fill them out on your PC and have the printer produce a neat, finished document for each form.

➤ *Interview feature* The program will ask you a series of questions about your finances. You need only answer the questions, as if the computer were interviewing you. The software will then choose the forms you need and supply you with specific instructions on how to complete them. It will also partially fill in the forms, based on numerical data you have given in the interview.

➤ *Information transfer* In most states of the U.S., you must pay income tax to the state as well as to the federal government. Much of the data from your federal return is used in the state return. (The details vary from state to state.) When you get a tax-preparation package, you can order a supplement for your particular state. The appropriate data from your federal return will be automatically inserted into the state return, so you don't have to enter the information twice.

➤ *Electronic filing* For a number of years, it has been possible to file tax returns via modem. A good tax-preparation package contains the software you need to do this. You should always be sure to keep at least two backup copies of the return on diskettes in separate locations. If you prefer to file your tax the old-fashioned way (by mail), you can do that, too. Don't forget to sign the return and include your Social Security number!

➤ *Accuracy check* Humans are prone to making arithmetic errors. The IRS won't normally penalize you for a simple error in adding, subtracting, multiplying, or dividing, but frequent errors probably increase the chance that you will be audited, and errors are as likely to be in the IRS's favor as in yours, causing you to overpay your tax. The tax-preparation program will go through your whole return in a few seconds, checking to be sure all the arithmetic has been done correctly.

➤ *Deduction search* Most people don't take all the deductions to which they're entitled, or they try to itemize when in fact they would be better off taking the standard deduction. A good tax program will alert you to every possible deduction you can get based on the information you give it in the interview. This

Tax-preparation software

feature alone can save you enough money to buy tax-preparation packages for the next several years, the cost of which, ironically, might qualify for deduction.

➤ *Audit flags* Certain items raise eyebrows in the IRS. Theories abound as to what, exactly, the IRS people look for. A tax-preparation program includes data about things that have been known to trigger audits. The program will search your return for "audit flags," and alert you to them so you can, if possible, eliminate them.

➤ *Estimated tax* Businesses and self-employed people must make quarterly tax payments. The IRS requires that these come out to at least a certain percentage of the total tax owed for the year; otherwise, they assess a penalty. However, there's no point in making estimated payments that are far too high. It's hard to make four equal payments that are just right, especially when you don't know exactly what your income will be for the year. Tax-preparation software can't guarantee that you'll be accurate to the dollar, but it can get you closer to the ideal (paying exactly what you owe) than you're likely to be if you rely on guesswork.

➤ *Shoebox* This feature gets its name from the fact that many people actually keep receipts in shoeboxes. If you have a small business or are self-employed, you probably accumulate hundreds of receipts every year. You should always keep these receipts, but you can enter the amounts in your tax program, saving yourself the work of dumping the receipts on a table and frantically adding them up every April. A good shoebox feature has several categories for deductible expenses, corresponding to the categories found on tax forms, such as Schedule C or Schedule E, for the year.

➤ *Supplemental graphics* Has your tax liability been increasing or decreasing with the years? An increase is not always a bad thing; it could mean you're getting rich. A sudden jump or drop might alert you to an error you have made, however, the nature of which could trigger an IRS audit. Some tax-preparation packages have supplemental charts and graphs that you can use to figure out where your money is going.

➤ *Help* If you get confused with any aspect of a tax-preparation software package, most vendors have toll-free telephone numbers that you can dial to reach a technician or advisor. Online help is also available. Special information concerning revisions in the tax laws can be found here. Some programs even outline strategies that you can use to make sure you pay exactly the amount of tax that you legally owe (no more, no less), not only for this year, but for years to come.

For more information. Tax-preparation software is regularly advertised in the PC magazines. A tax accountant (preferably not the one who is at risk of losing your business to a PC!) might also be willing to make recommendations. If you are self-employed, you might talk with a few of your colleagues and see which programs they're using. Go to a computer store and collect as many brochures as possible.

Keep in mind that, no matter which tax-preparation package you decide to buy, your tax return is ultimately your responsibility. One of the big limitations of this software is that your PC will not pay any interest or penalty that results from its misuse.

See also BUSINESS SOFTWARE, DAILY PLANNER SOFTWARE, DATABASE, EXPORT BUSINESS SOFTWARE, INTEGRATED SOFTWARE PACKAGE, MAIL-ORDER BUSINESS SOFTWARE, MEDICAL-OFFICE SOFTWARE, PERSONAL FINANCE SOFTWARE, PERSONAL INFORMATION MANAGER, RATIO ANALYSIS SOFTWARE, SPREADSHEET, *and* SUITE.

Teach box

When a computer-controlled machine must perform repetitive, precise, complex motions, the movements can be entered into memory. Then, when the memory is accessed, the machine will go through the movements. A *teach box* is a device that memorizes motions or processes for later recall. Machine control can be broken down into four levels, from the most primitive to the most sophisticated.

Levels 1 and 2. An example of a level-1 teach box is an automatic garage-door opener. When the receiver gets the signal from the remote unit, it opens or closes the door. Another example of a level-1 teach box is the remote control that you use to change the channel and adjust the volume on a television set. These need not involve computers at all.

An example of a level-2 teach box is the integrated circuit (IC) that controls a telephone answering machine. When a call comes in, the sequence of operations is recalled from the firmware in the IC. The machine answers the telephone, makes an announcement, takes the message, and resets itself for the next incoming call. This uses a programmable microchip, but it's still not as advanced as a PC.

Levels 3 and 4. Reprogrammable teach boxes, which are rudimentary computers, are used in industrial robots. They also lend themselves to use in personal robots. Movements are entered by pressing buttons. It's possible to guide, or teach, the robot manually, and have the movements memorized precisely. The machine's path, as well as variations in speed, rotations, and gripping/grasping movements, are all programmed and memorized. When the memory is recalled, the robot will behave just as it was taught. This is known as *task-level programming*, and is an example of a level-3 teach box.

Level 4 in the machine programming hierarchy supersedes the teach box, and makes use of artificial intelligence. A machine thus equipped is a "smart robot," the kind that most people imagine, and the kind that you've seen in the movies. These robots are taught according to complex software, similar to that used in virtual reality, animation, and other high-level applications. Such machines can be categorized either as *autonomous robots* or as *insect robots*, depending on whether or not each machine has its own computer. *See also* ARTIFICIAL INTELLIGENCE, AUTONOMOUS ROBOTS, INSECT ROBOTS, *and* PERSONAL ROBOTS.

Telecommunications

See CELLULAR TELECOMMUNICATIONS, MODEM, ONLINE SERVICE, REMOTE CONTROL SYSTEMS, TELECOMMUTING, TELECONFERENCING, *and* TELEPHONY.

Telecommuting

Telecommuting refers to the use of computers and communications links, usually telephone lines, to minimize the need for people to physically commute between homes and offices. Using a PC, a modem, and software, employees can work from the privacy and comfort of home.

Assets. There are numerous advantages to telecommuting, making it an attractive idea to people in management and labor alike. Here are some significant benefits:

➤ *Eliminate "commuting tax"* If you spend 30 minutes each way driving to and from work every day, you take five hours a week in transport. For a 40-hour-a-week job, that effectively cuts your pay by 12.5%. Few politicians would even think of suggesting an income-tax surcharge that big, but this "commuting tax" is actually worse because you're paying to be robbed of free time. If you could salvage some of that time, you'd get an effective pay increase (same salary, fewer hours), entirely tax-free. You'd spend less on gasoline, car maintenance, car insurance, and perhaps medical bills, too.

➤ *Save time* Five hours a week adds up to 250 hours a year for the average worker; in a 40-year career, that's 416 round-the-clock days. This time could be spent with your family, exercising for health or for sport, or otherwise enjoying life. Your car would rack up fewer miles each year. Perhaps you'd opt to use that mileage driving to and from a lake cottage (where you might do some work by telecommuting). You might play more with your children after school, or ride a bike in the evening.

➢ *Lower stress* Many people enjoy driving, but few people care much for rush-hour driving. It can make you tired even though it doesn't burn any calories. It can be irritating; in large cities, traffic jams are an everyday rush-hour occurrence. You might imagine you're nothing but a corpuscle in a collective social monster with clogged arteries. Besides all that, you must get dressed up and made up for work. Many offices are plagued with controversies unrelated to the job; these stresses have been increasing in recent years. Many people would prefer to work at home, closing the door on worldly madness. (There are some exceptions to this, however. These are discussed later in this article.)

➢ *Reduce pollution* In some cities, air pollution has become so severe that pollution alerts are issued on some days of the year. Maybe you've heard these reports on the morning news as you were commuting to work: "Don't breathe hard today." Virtually all of the air-pollution problems in modern cities are caused by automobile exhaust, especially ozone (an eye and lung irritant) and carbon monoxide (a gas that disrupts the body's ability to absorb oxygen). Pollution levels tend to peak during rush hours. These peaks would be less hazardous to everyone's health if there were fewer cars belching out exhaust.

➢ *Reduce accidents* In large cities, serious traffic wrecks occur almost every day, and minor accidents are frequent. Many of these take place during rush hours. You notice them when they delay your arrival at your office or home. Perhaps, during your daily commute, you keep the car radio tuned to a station whose traffic reports you trust. If you telecommute, you need not listen to these reports, nor put up with the delays caused by accidents along your route. If you drive less as a result of telecommuting, you reduce the probability that you'll be involved in one of these mishaps.

Limitations. Telecommuting is not without drawbacks. It's not a universal solution to all commuting woes. Here are some potential problems associated with it:

➢ *Nonapplicability* Not all jobs lend themselves easily to telecommuting, and some work simply can't be done that way. If you're a plumber, you can't fix someone's toilet by remote control. Doctors must be at their offices and make hospital rounds on a regular basis. Salespeople, while able to give some presentations via teleconferencing, must still travel often, and this can involve far more driving mileage than the average commuter puts in.

➢ *Lack of benefits* Many telecommuting jobs are part-time or temporary affairs. These generally do not carry benefits such as health insurance. You'll have to buy the insurance yourself; individual policies tend to be more expensive than group

Teleconferencing

policies. It is possible, however, that you might qualify for a home-office tax deduction, along with a partial deduction for the cost of the health insurance. (Tax laws change annually, so check to see what deductions you can take.)

> *Reduced motivation* Some people can't work effectively unless a supervisor is right there, watching. Counting keystrokes, or otherwise monitoring employees via spy software, is possible even when employees telecommute, but this raises the specter of electronic eavesdropping in employees' homes. Many workers regard spy software as an intrusion in a traditional office; monitoring home behavior might stir even deeper resentments. From the management viewpoint, employee motivational difficulties (or the fear thereof) can breed a lack of trust, and thus an unwillingness to implement telecommuting.

> *Isolation* For some people, going to the office is an integral part of life. These people might not enjoy the commute itself, but they need the face-to-face companionship of their coworkers. When you work at a computer in your home, you work alone except for an electronic link with the world. This can cause loneliness, boredom, anxiety, and depression in some people. Unmarried, fast-track professionals often prefer an active working environment. For them, telecommuting might be an option for the future, but an untenable scenario for the present.

For further information. Several books are available on the subject of telecommuting, such as *The Telecommuter's Handbook* by Brad Schepp (Pharos Books, World Almanac Education). You might also look for *The Green PC* by Steven Anzovin (Windcrest/McGraw-Hill), especially chapter 6. *See also* BUSINESS SOFTWARE, CELLULAR TELECOMMUNICATIONS, ENERGY-EFFICIENT COMPUTING, ERGONOMICS, GREEN COMPUTING, KEYSTROKES, LAPTOP COMPUTER, OFFICE AUTOMATION, ONLINE SERVICE, PAPERLESS OFFICE, REMOTE-CONTROL SYSTEMS, SATELLITE DATA TRANSMISSION, SECURITY, SPY SOFTWARE, TELECONFERENCING, TELEPHONE-DIALING SOFTWARE, TELEPHONY, TERMINAL EMULATION SOFTWARE, TOT-PROOF WORKSTATION, *and* WIDE-AREA NETWORK.

Teleconferencing

An increasing number of companies are using PCs equipped with communications software and modems to hold conferences online. *Teleconferencing*, as it's called, can save thousands of dollars every year in travel and commuting expenses. It's convenient and efficient; the software and hardware are not too expensive.

Types. There are basically two kinds of teleconferencing: *videoconferencing* (visual only) and *multimedia* (audio-visual). Both types work best with a graphical user interface (GUI), such as Windows, the Macintosh OS, or IBM OS/2. Multimedia requires that the computers be equipped with sound boards, sound software, speakers, and microphones.

Videoconferencing involves only the kind of data that can be displayed or printed out, such as text, graphics, databases, and spreadsheets. The data can be in black-and-white, gray-scale, or full color. It's possible to work in full duplex with high-level teleconferencing systems, so that all workstations, or nodes, can act both as a source and a destination at the same time. This allows rapid and efficient exchange of information.

Multimedia teleconferencing includes audio information, usually voice communication, along with the digital data. Multimedia signals need a larger bandwidth than videoconferencing signals, but telephone lines have a limited ability to carry broad-banded signals. Because of this, it's necessary to sacrifice some data speed in multimedia, compared with videoconferencing. Most multimedia networks use digital signal processing (DSP) to get the most information into the smallest possible bandwidth. Data compression can also be used. Drawing A shows a multimedia teleconference in which DSP combines the video and audio data for transmission along a single telephone line. An alternative is to use two separate lines, one for the video data and the other for the audio, as in drawing B.

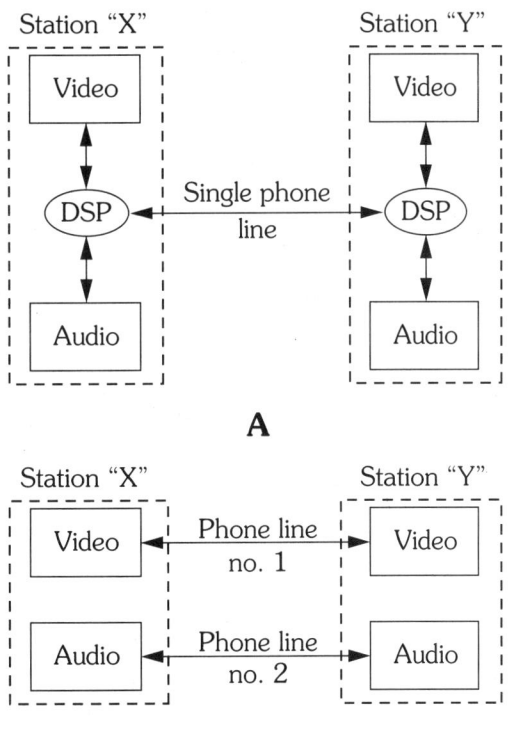

Multimedia on a single telephone line via DSP (A), and on two separate lines (B).

Teleconferencing

What it can do. Here are some applications to which teleconferencing is especially well-suited:

> *Business meetings* Imagine you're a company president, sitting at the computer in your den at home, having a videoconference with several other company presidents. One of them is on his houseboat, another is at her lake cottage, another is at his home, and one is at her office. This sort of thing is not the exclusive privilege of rich eccentrics. With moderately-priced teleconferencing software, it's realistic for many executives.

> *Telecommuting* Note that of the five executives (including yourself) having the meeting, only one is at the office. The other four are telecommuting, working via computer from places other than the office. Teleconferencing and telecommuting go naturally together. They make it possible to "be at work" from practically any location. Taken together, they can save huge sums of money because of the millions of travel miles they render unnecessary. For some businesses, the money thus saved in the first year can pay for two or three new PC systems, complete with teleconferencing software.

> *Sales* Sales presentations can be given via teleconferencing. This can be done "one-way" (in half duplex), so high-speed data exchange is not important and multimedia becomes practical. Certain kinds of products, such as computer software, can be demonstrated in real-time via teleconferencing. The basic "pitch" can be given in multimedia, and then the interactive session can be done via full-duplex videoconferencing. Other merchandise, such as medical equipment, might require that the salesperson be physically present at the clients' location, but teleconferencing can still be used to set up appointments and give preliminary presentations.

> *Technical support* If you've ever used an online help service for new software or a new peripheral, you've already done teleconferencing of a sort. With a full teleconferencing program, the technician can demonstrate exactly how a process should be done. You can watch onscreen while the technician literally operates your computer for you. It's like a real-time correspondence course.

> *Education and training* You've probably heard advertisements from colleges, telling you that you can get a degree by taking courses at home. This used to be done on television; you'd watch the show and take notes, sending in your papers when you were ready. With teleconferencing, you can, in effect, be in the classroom. You can ask the professor

Telephony

questions and get answers in real-time. Some fantastic things have been done in this vein. For example, students worldwide can interact with a professor at a university, while everyone watches, and communicates with, a SCUBA diver on a coral reef in the Florida Keys—all in real-time.

See also BANDWIDTH, BUSINESS SOFTWARE, CELLULAR TELECOMMUNICATIONS, DATA COMPRESSION, DESTINATION, DIGITAL SIGNAL PROCESSING, FULL DUPLEX, HALF DUPLEX, LAPTOP COMPUTER, MULTIMEDIA, NETWORK, ONLINE SERVICE, PERSONAL DIGITAL ASSISTANT, REMOTE-CONTROL SYSTEMS, SATELLITE DATA TRANSMISSION, SOUND TECHNOLOGY, SOURCE, TELECOMMUTING, TELEPHONY, TERMINAL EMULATION SOFTWARE, *and* WIDE-AREA NETWORK.

Teleoperation

Teleoperation is the technical term for the remote control of autonomous robots. A remotely controlled robot is sometimes called a *telechir*.

In a teleoperation system, the human operator can control the speed, direction, and other movements of a robot from some distance away. Signals are sent to the robot to control it; other signals come back, telling the operator that the robot has followed the instructions. These signals are called *telemetry*.

Some teleoperated robots have a limited range of functions. A good example is the Voyager space probe, hurtling past some remote planet. Earthbound scientists sent telemetry to Voyager, aiming its cameras and sometimes even fixing minor problems. Voyager was, in this sense, a teleoperated robot.

Teleoperation can be used in personal robots that can look after their own affairs most of the time, but occasionally need the help of a human operator. When the human operator has complete control of the robot at all times, the system is said to employ *telepresence*. *See also* AUTONOMOUS ROBOTS, PERSONAL ROBOTS, REMOTE CONTROL SYSTEMS, *and* TELEPRESENCE.

Telephony

If you've placed telephone orders for merchandise or received automated sales calls, you've almost certainly been exposed to computer *telephony*. You have interacted directly with a computer. Computer telephony has been around for some time. Apple Computer, Inc. began development in the mid-1980s. In recent years, telephony has progressed rapidly.

Telephony

What it can do. Telephony turns any telephone jack into a potential node in a wide-area network (WAN). Here are a few common features of telephony systems:

➤ *Data entry*   Telephone sets with tone dialers (keypads) allow you to make selections from an audible menu. For example, you might hear a voice say, "For world news, press 1. For national news, press 2. For local news, press 3. For weather information, press 4. For stock market information, press 5. For sports scores, press 6 . . ." You can make your selection at anytime.

➤ *Voice commands and responses*   Some telephony networks can function even without tone-dialing keypad entry. You simply say a word, such as "Now," when the item you want is announced by the computer, and speech recognition circuitry acts on your command. The most sophisticated systems work with command-driven software, in which the commands are spoken by the user. Computer responses can be made via speech synthesis.

➤ *Computer connections*   Each node can be converted into a fully functional terminal by plugging a modem into the telephone jack and hooking a computer to the modem. The computer might be a desktop unit, a laptop, or a personal digital assistant (PDA). Some people think that telephony might be the killer application for PDAs, and PDAs the killer hardware for telephony systems.

➤ *Cellular systems*   All cellular telephone sets can function as nodes in a telephony WAN. Laptop computers and PDAs, equipped with cellular telephones and built-in modems, thus become take-anywhere links to the entire network. You might log onto a network while hiking in the mountains, carrying only a handheld cellular telephone set.

➤ *High-volume order processing*   You can place orders for merchandise via telephone, just as you do with human operators, but computers process orders in far greater volume than human order-takers ever could. Most large mail-order companies' order departments are partially or fully computerized.

➤ *Debt collection*   Computers can call people who have outstanding debts. The machine places the call, and then ascertains if it is "talking" to an answering machine. If it's talking to a machine, the computer hangs up and tries again later. If a real person answers the call, the computer starts its message.

➤ *Caller ID*   With a telephone/computer set, you can get the telephone number, name, and even the address of the person calling you. This is based on the assumption that the caller is using his or her own telephone line, and not a telephone booth or the line of a friend or relative.

➤ *Call screening* This works in conjunction with caller ID. You can store a set of telephone numbers from which you will accept incoming calls. If a call is made to your telephone set, your set will ring only if the call originates from one of the numbers stored in memory.

➤ *Teleconferencing* Telephony can improve the efficiency of the multimedia form of teleconferencing. Voice, fax, data, and video can be exchanged over parallel telephone circuits. The voice or fax can be handled by one circuit, the data by a second circuit, and the video by a third circuit. This can be costly because it ties up multiple lines, but it allows for higher data speed than is possible via a single connection.

For further information. Telephony is a complex field. The best place to get up-to-the-minute information is to chat with experts via an online service. Information can also be obtained through business-oriented and technical PC publications.

See also CELLULAR TELECOMMUNICATIONS, COMMAND-DRIVEN SOFTWARE, DIGITAL SIGNAL PROCESSING, FAX, KILLER, LAPTOP COMPUTER, MODEM, MULTIMEDIA, NETWORK, NODE, ONLINE SERVICE, PERSONAL DIGITAL ASSISTANT, REMOTE CONTROL SYSTEMS, SATELLITE DATA TRANSMISSION, SOUND TECHNOLOGY, SPEECH RECOGNITION, SPEECH SYNTHESIS, TELECOMMUTING, TELECONFERENCING, TELEPHONE DIALING SOFTWARE, *and* WIDE-AREA NETWORK.

Telephone-dialing software

If you've used an online service, you've probably used *telephone-dialing software (TDS)*. TDS turns your computer into an automatic telephone dialer, saving you from picking up the telephone receiver and doing it yourself. The software for most online services has built-in TDS.

You can obtain TDS for everyday use and have your PC take over all the dialing jobs you do from your workstation, whether or not you plan to use the PC online. These dialing programs are extremely simple. You can obtain one by downloading it from online in the form of freeware.

The most obvious advantage of TDS is that it's fast and saves you some work, especially if you make a lot of telephone calls from your workstation. This can be important, for example, if you're a salesperson telecommuting (working at home). You can store the numbers of all your contacts in contact manager or personal information manager (PIM) software, along with other pertinent data. If TDS isn't already in your contact manager or PIM, you can add it. Another asset of TDS is that it's error-free. Once you have the number typed correctly into the computer, the TDS will always dial the right digits.

Telepresence

Most telephone-dialing software can't pick up and dial telephone numbers from any file in your computer. For example, if a text document contains a telephone number, you can't normally move the cursor to it and use a stand-alone TDS program to dial it. However, there are "extended TDS" programs you can buy and install, some of which will allow you to do this.

A note of caution about downloading: Never download anything directly onto a hard disk. If you want to obtain TDS by downloading, put it onto a diskette and then run it through a vaccine (antivirus program) to find and eliminate possible Trojan horses or viruses. When you're sure the program is "clean," you can install it on your hard disk. *See also* CONTACT MANAGER, FREEWARE, ONLINE SERVICE, PERSONAL INFORMATION MANAGER, TELECOMMUTING, TELECONFERENCING, TELEPHONY, TROJAN HORSE, *and* VIRUS.

Telepresence

Telepresence is a refined, advanced form of machine remote-control. The operator of the machine gets a sense of being "on location," even if the machine, or *telechir*, and the operator are miles apart. Control and feedback are done via *telemetry* sent over wires, optical fibers, or radio.

What it's like. In a telepresence system, the machine is usually an autonomous robot with a humanoid form. The more humanoid the robot, the more realistic the telepresence. This technology is nowhere near fully developed. There are many problems to overcome, but eventually, most of these troubles should be resolved. What will it be like to operate a robot using advanced telepresence?

The control station will consist of a suit that you wear or a chair in which you sit with various manipulators and displays. Sensors will give you feelings of pressure, vision, and sound.

You'll wear a helmet with a viewing screen that shows whatever the robot camera sees. When your head turns, the robot head, with its vision system, will follow. Thus, you will see a scene that changes as you turn your head, just as if you were at the location of the robot. Binocular vision will give you a sense of depth. Binaural hearing will let you perceive sounds as your ears would hear them if you were on-site.

Propulsion might be via a track drive, a wheel drive, or robot legs. If the propulsion uses legs, you'll propel the robot by walking around a room or on a treadmill. Otherwise, you will sit in a chair and "drive" the robot like a car.

The robot will have two arms, each with grippers resembling human hands. When you want to pick something up, you'll go through the motions. Back pressure sensors and position sensors will let you feel what's going on. If an object weighs 10 pounds, it will feel as if it weighs 10 pounds, but it will be as if you're wearing thick gloves. You won't be able to feel texture.

You might throw a switch, and something that weighs 10 pounds will feel as if it only weighs one pound. Maybe this will be called "strength x10" mode. If you switch to "strength x100" mode, a 100-pound object will seem to weigh one pound. This would, of course, require a robot with great mechanical power and structural soundness. The drawing is a simple diagram of a telepresence system.

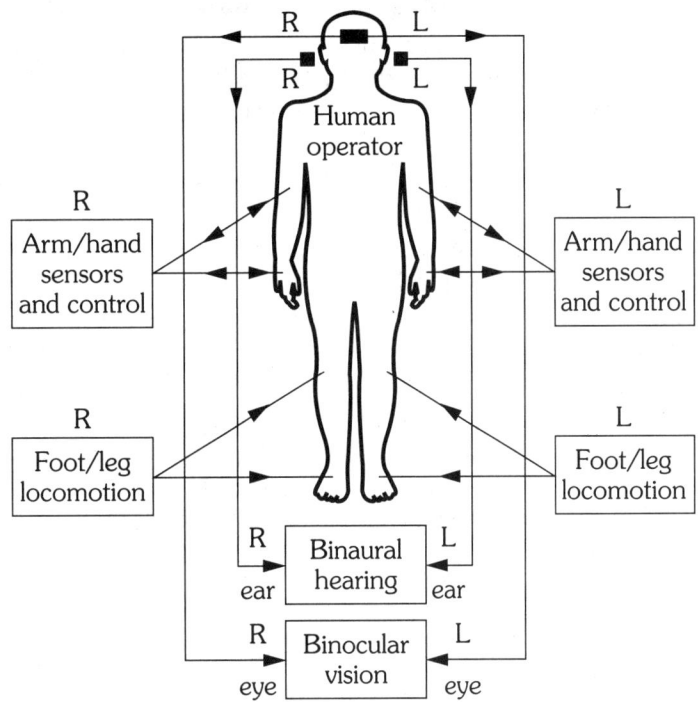

A sophisticated remote-control system.

Applications. You can probably think of many uses for a telepresence system. Some might include the following:

- Working in extreme heat or cold
- Working under high pressure, such as on the sea floor
- Working in a vacuum, such as in space
- Working where there is dangerous radiation
- Disarming bombs
- Handling toxic substances
- Performing police robotics
- Acting as a robot soldier
- Performing neurosurgery

Terabyte

Of course, the robot must be able to survive conditions at its location. Also, it must have some way to recover if it falls over.

Challenges. In theory, the technology for telepresence exists right now. There are some problems, however. The most serious limitation is that telemetry cannot, and never will, travel faster than the speed of light in free space. This might seem fast at first (186,282 miles, or 299,792 kilometers, per second), but it is slow on an interplanetary scale. The moon is more than a light second away from the earth; the sun is eight light minutes away. The nearest stars are at distances of several light years. The delay between sending a command and getting the return signal must be less than 0.1 second if telepresence is to be realistic. This means that the robot cannot be more than about 9300 miles (15,000 kilometers) away from the control operator.

Another problem is the resolution of the robot's vision. A human being with good eyesight can see things with several times the detail of the best fast-scan television sets. To send that much detail at realistic speed would take up a huge signal bandwidth. There are engineering problems (and cost problems) that go along with this.

Still another limitation is best put as a question: How will a robot be able to "feel" something and transmit these impulses to the human brain? For example, an apple feels smooth, a peach feels fuzzy, and an orange feels bumpy. How can this sense of texture be realistically transmitted to the human brain? Will people allow electrodes to be implanted in their brains to facilitate long-distance teleperception?

For further information. Telepresence is a vast and fascinating subject. For details about the latest progress in this field, look in a good college or university library for books and articles on robotics, teleoperation, and telepresence. *See also* AUTONOMOUS ROBOTS, REMOTE CONTROL SYSTEMS, TELEOPERATION, *and* VISION SYSTEMS.

Terabyte

The prefix *tera* means a trillion (1,000,000,000,000 or 10^{12}). It can also mean trillions. A *terabyte*, abbreviated *TB*, is a massive unit of digital information, equal to a little more than one trillion bytes.

Computer data is measured in powers of two, rather than powers of 10, because digital information is expressed in base 2, where the only values are 0 (low) and 1 (high). The actual value of 1TB is not exactly 10^{12} bytes, but instead, is 2^{40} bytes. This is 1024 gigabytes (GB), or 1,048,576 megabytes (MB), or 1,073,741,824 kilobytes (KB or K). The drawing shows the approximate relationship among 1K, 1MB, 1GB, and 1TB of data. The table on page 1070 shows the capacity, in terabytes, of several different data storage media.

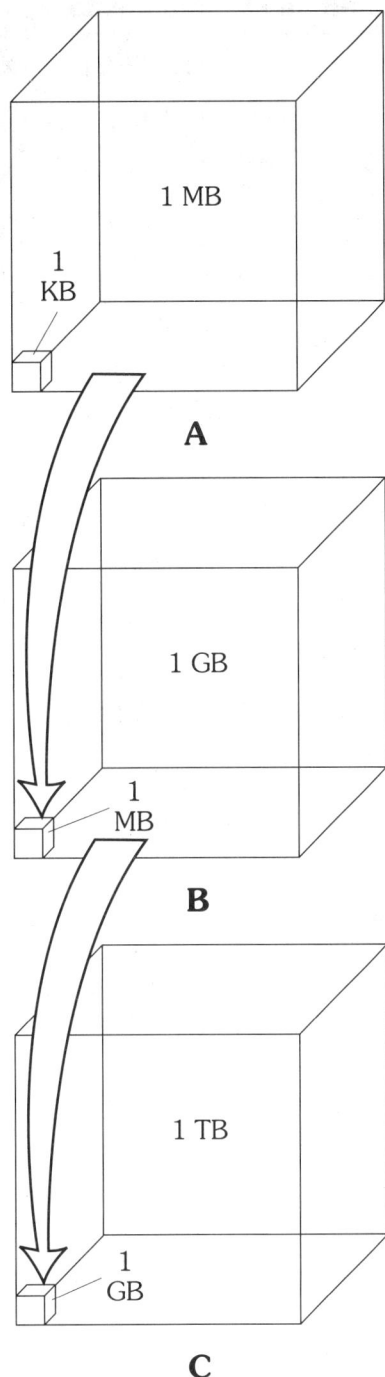

One kilobyte versus one megabyte (A); one megabyte versus one gigabyte (C); one gigabyte versus one terabyte (C).

Many PCs have hard-disk capacities of upwards of 1GB, which is 1/1000 of a terabyte. A typical high-density diskette can hold somewhat more than 1MB of data; therefore, 1TB would occupy almost a million diskettes. A stack of a million 5.25-inch diskettes would be about 1.5 miles high. *See also* BINARY DATA, BYTE, EXABYTE, GIGABYTE, KILOBYTE, MEGABYTE, *and* PETABYTE.

Terminal

Capacities of several common storage media

Medium	Capacity in TB
640K RAM	0.00000064
5.25-inch, double-density diskette	0.00000036
3.5-inch, double-density diskette	0.00000072
Medium-sized novel	0.000001
5.25-inch, high-density diskette	0.0000012
3.5-inch, high-density diskette	0.00000144
Hard disk	0.0002
CD-ROM	0.00065

Terminal

See DUMB TERMINAL *and* NODE.

Terminal emulation software

In digital communications, PCs are used as terminals. A PC can send and receive data in many forms. For a PC to work as a communications terminal, specialized software is needed. Such programs are widely available, and are known as *terminal emulation software*.

Features. Computer communications is not new. Terminal emulation software was originally developed to allow small computers to work with large mainframes. Engineers have had a long time to work out user-friendly programs. Here are a few of the features of a modern terminal emulation package:

- *Several media* You can send and receive text, graphics, databases, spreadsheets, all kinds of software, sound, and other data. In general, if a computer can work with data, the communications software should be able to handle it, too. The future holds exciting things in the communications field, such as telepresence, virtual reality exchange, and remote control.

- *Contact database* The software can store a list of names, addresses (both for regular mail and electronic mail), and telephone numbers of personal and business contacts. To send something to one of these people or companies, you press a hot key or click the mouse, and the software sends whatever messages you have ready for them.

- *Automatic dialing* You can select a person from your contact database, and the computer will dial the number and set up the link without your having to give it any further thought. You can store hundreds of different telephone numbers and electronic-mail addresses.

> *Chat mode* You can "talk" with other PC users in real-time. Some systems provide for full duplex (sending and receiving simultaneously), while others will only work in half duplex (sending and receiving alternately).

> *File compression and decompression* Large files take time to send over a modem because online communications is a serial mode, in which data goes one bit at a time. Using data compression at the sending station or source, the number of bits is reduced while essential information is retained. This shortens the time needed to send the file. At the destination, the data is decompressed back to normal.

> *Modest PC requirements* It's not difficult for a computer to behave as a terminal. In fact, it's a step down in many respects. A typical communications program needs less than 640K of RAM (random-access memory) and can work in DOS, Windows, OS/2, or the Macintosh OS. A high-powered microprocessor chip is not needed.

Your needs. Most new computers have terminal emulation software already installed. If you find the existing program adequate for your needs, you won't need to buy a separate terminal emulation program. If you decide you need a separate program, there are plenty of choices, most of which are moderately priced.

You might consider buying your terminal-emulation software as part of an integrated software package or suite. If possible, check out several programs in real-time. Perhaps you have friends who swear by their communications programs and will let you try their software. Of course, you'll need to get the version that matches your operating system. *See also* DATA COMPRESSION, DESTINATION, DUMB TERMINAL, ELECTRONIC MAIL, FILE COMPRESSION UTILITY, FULL DUPLEX, HALF DUPLEX, INTEGRATED SOFTWARE PACKAGE, ONLINE SERVICE, PACKET COMMUNICATIONS, REMOTE CONTROL SYSTEMS, SERIAL, SOURCE, SUITE, TELEPHONE-DIALING SOFTWARE, TELEPRESENCE, *and* VIRTUAL REALITY.

Terminal node controller

A *terminal node controller (TNC)* is a special-purpose modem, often with its own built-in memory. It interfaces a PC or dumb terminal to a transmitter/receiver (transceiver) in a packet radio station. Packet radio is computer communications done via radio, rather than over the telephone lines.

The TNC assembles messages, called *packets*, that are composed on and stored by the computer. The TNC converts these packets into a form suitable for transmission by radio. This is done by *digital-to-analog (D/A) conversion*. The TNC also takes packets from the radio receiver and puts them in the right form to be displayed and/or stored by the computer. This process is called *analog-to-digital (A/D) conversion*.

If a TNC has its own memory, it can store an incoming message indefinitely, and send it out again at any time. If a PC is used with the TNC, the PC can store the message, allowing any packet radio station to function as a communications repeater. Because the packets are in digital form, such a repeater is called a *digipeater*. Each digipeater is a node in a gigantic wide-area network (WAN).

Packet-radio networks can either work in real-time, or they can employ time-shifting communications. The drawing is a block diagram showing how the TNC is connected in a simple packet-radio station. The heavy dotted lines enclose the components of the transceiver and the TNC. *See also* ANALOG-TO-DIGITAL CONVERSION, DIGIPEATER, DIGITAL-TO-ANALOG CONVERSION, MODEM, NODE, PACKET COMMUNICATIONS, REAL-TIME, TIME-SHIFTING COMMUNICATIONS, TERMINAL EMULATION SOFTWARE, *and* WIDE-AREA NETWORK.

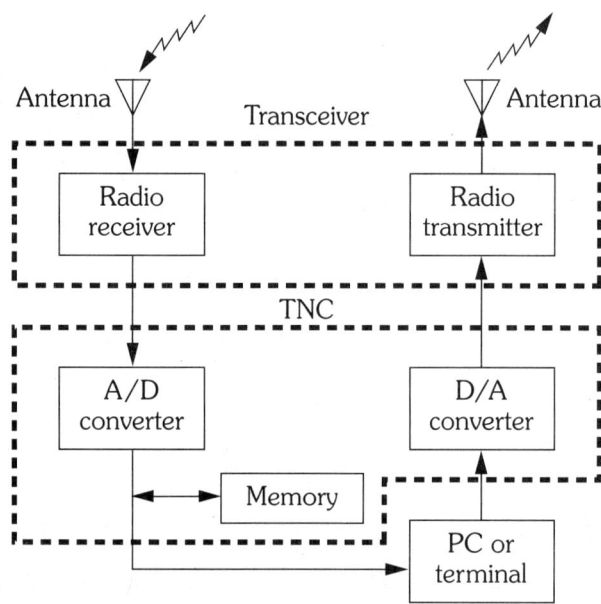

A TNC serves as a modem in a packet radio station.

Terminate-and-stay-resident software

See MEMORY-RESIDENT SOFTWARE.

Text editor

See EDITOR.

Theorem-proving machine

If you've taken geometry or calculus, you have had to prove *theorems* (logically true statements) derived from *axioms* (statements assumed to be true). Some of these logical proofs have many steps, but the step-to-step transition is easy. Some proofs have only a few steps, but require deep insight.

Logical processes. A computer, given axioms and logical rules, can crank out theorems by the thousands, creating a so-called *mathematical universe*. Digital computers use a simple form of logic, known as *Boolean algebra*, to carry out all their operations. Boolean algebra works on a true/false basis. Truth is assigned the number one, and falsity is assigned zero. These logic states are called high and low, respectively. Combinations of ones and zeros, no matter how complex, can always be represented as machine language in a computer. The two-state digital computer is, in theory, perfect for true/false logical theorem-proving.

In Boolean algebra, variables such as X, Y, and Z represent sentences. Addition and multiplication represent disjunction (OR) and conjunction (AND). An arrow pointing to the right means IF/THEN. The equals sign represents logical equivalence. The result is a crude logic called *sentential calculus* or *propositional calculus*.

Computers prove theorems in propositional calculus by testing all possible combinations of truth and falsity. If there are only a few variables in the equation, the resulting truth table is not too big, and a human can work it out. If there are many variables, however, the truth table becomes enormous. It would take a person hours or days to check each formula, but a computer can go through the array in a fraction of a second. Computers prove theorems by brute force.

David versus Goliath. A computer proving a theorem per second can generate 3600 theorems in an hour, 86,400 theorems in a day, and 31,536,000 theorems in a year. However, a machine has no sense of which theorems are significant and which are not. That distinction is made by human beings, based on curiosity or scientific need. The computer must be told not only to prove things, but which things to prove.

Most mathematical systems employ reasoning much deeper than propositional calculus. While these processes can be put into machine language, the transcription is far trickier than with Boolean algebra. This makes the computer's job more difficult. Similarly, a musclebound brute can throw a football 99 yards, but it takes more than sheer force to complete a touchdown pass.

Starting with a proposition, human mathematicians try either to prove that it's true or that it's false. Often, the truth value is not suspected beforehand. A free-running *theorem-proving machine (TPM)* will decide the matter eventually if the problem has a solution that can be found in a finite number of steps. (Some theorems cannot be proven in a finite number of steps.) But will it take a minute or a thousand years? The TPM user can only wait.

No computer yet built has the power of intuition. Humans have always had this power. Some of the greatest theorems in mathematics were proved not by prolonged mental effort, but as a result of a sudden hunch. A computer makes a good mathematical Goliath, but a human being makes a better David. Computer TPMs can assist, but not yet replace, human mathematicians and scientists. *See also* ARTIFICIAL INTELLIGENCE, ARTIFICIAL LIFE, COMPUTER CONSCIOUSNESS, BOOLEAN ALGEBRA, INCOMPLETENESS THEOREM, LOGIC, *and* MACHINE LANGUAGE.

Thermal printer

A *thermal printer* uses temperature-sensitive dye and/or paper to create hardcopy text and images. Some thermal printers produce only black-and-white images, while others can render full color.

Inkless printing. The simplest thermal printers employ a special paper that darkens when it gets hot. The print mechanism works something like that of a dot-matrix printer, but instead of the print head pressing ink onto the page, the pins in the print mechanism are heated, causing the paper to darken. There is no ink, and the pins don't have to strike the page with much force.

The main assets of a basic black-and-white thermal printer are that it needs no ink, and it's quiet, compact, and portable. It's convenient for use with a laptop (notebook) PC. The main shortcomings involve the paper. The surface can darken in sunlight or if you place the printed copy too close to a high-wattage lamp. It has a sheen that makes it unsuitable for professional correspondence or desktop publishing. The paper comes in rolls, so finished printouts tend to curl up.

If you are traveling and you need a few pages of good printout, you can use your laptop's black-and-white thermal printer and take the pages to a photocopying center. (Be sure the photocopy machine isn't hot from use.) The resulting hardcopy won't be as crisp as that from a laser or inkjet printer, but at least the pages will be flat, the paper will look normal, and the copy will be insensitive to heat.

Color printing. The demand for color printers has been increasing in recent years. A reliable, simple color printer with a modest price tag is a desirable item indeed. Thermal printing techniques have been adapted to this end.

A color thermal printer uses thick, heat-sensitive dyes of the primary pigments: magenta (pinkish red), yellow, and cyan (bluish green). Sometimes black dye is also used, although it can be obtained by combining large, equal amounts of the primary pigments.

The print head uses heat to liquefy the dye, so it bleeds onto the paper. This is done for each color of pigment separately. It takes place in patterns determined by the hot print head. There are three separate, overlapping images produced, one for each primary pigment.

A color thermal printer must always be kept in proper alignment to ensure that the three pigment images are properly positioned with respect to each other. If the images don't coincide perfectly, the resulting hardcopy will be blurred and laced with multicolored borders, like you sometimes see in newspaper supplements. *See also* COLOR PRINTER, DOT-MATRIX PRINTER, INKJET PRINTER, LASER PRINTER, *and* PRINTER.

Throughput

There are several ways in which computer power can be evaluated. Factors that affect the power of a computer include the clock speed, the amount of memory, and the word size. These all determine the number of instructions per second (IPS) the machine can carry out under ideal conditions. *Throughput*, on the other hand, is the most meaningful quantitative indicator of how much power a computer actually has for performing real-world tasks.

The benchmark. Specifications such as clock speed and word size are determined by running the computer through specialized *benchmark* tests. These tests are done under controlled conditions, so that precise numerical results are obtained.

Think of your body's measurable signs when you get a physical exam. The computer's clock speed might correspond to your heart rate, or pulse. The size of the computer memory can be compared to your lung capacity. The PC's word size might correspond to the amount of weight you can lift. All these body measurements can be combined by a fitness evaluator, who will come up with a figure that supposedly indicates your overall physical condition.

The composite fitness figure will tell you more about your physical condition than any one of the factors by itself, but even the composite figure, which might be compared to a computer's IPS rating, won't tell you everything because the composite fitness figure, like the IPS rating, is obtained under artificial conditions. The fitness composite doesn't indicate how well you will do in a sport like soccer, just as computer benchmark tests do not always portray the machine's power when it is used in applications like desktop publishing.

The real world. The only true way to evaluate the power of a computer is to conduct as many tests, in as many true-to-life applications, as possible. This is the equivalent of going through, say, the Mayo Clinic physical exam routine, compared with getting a quick checkup from one doctor.

If you really want to know all about your physical health, you'll need to have blood tests, urine tests, and all sorts of other things done. Similarly, to determine the throughput of a computer, the machine must be put through a routine carefully designed to cover all the different ways people are likely to use it.

Throughput, while meaningful, is only a number. The type of computer you buy, and especially the characteristics of your system and peripherals, is more a matter of personal taste than a decision based on scientific data. You might want a certain PC because your "power user" friend has one and likes it. You might purchase a monitor because you like the shape and color of its case. If you plan to do desktop publishing, you can learn more at a party of publishing professionals than by reading brochures and talking with salespeople. Computer conventions are especially informative if you plan to do serious work of any kind on a PC system. And of course, the price is a consideration for most people.

Suppose, before the Super Bowl, all the players on both teams get the most exhaustive physical exams ever given to human beings. The results can't predict which team will win. A good computer system depends not only on its hardware, but on its software—and on its users. *See also* BENCHMARK, CLOCK SPEED, COMPUTER POWER, HARDWARE, INSTRUCTIONS PER SECOND, MEMORY, RANDOM-ACCESS MEMORY, SOFTWARE, *and* WORD SIZE.

Tiled windows

In Windows or any similar graphical user interface (GUI), it's possible to have two or more different files or menus on the screen at the same time. *Tiled windows* are laid out so that all are fully visible, as shown in the drawing. Each window is smaller than it would be if it were the only window on the screen. (In Macintosh computers, the term *folder* is used instead of *window*.)

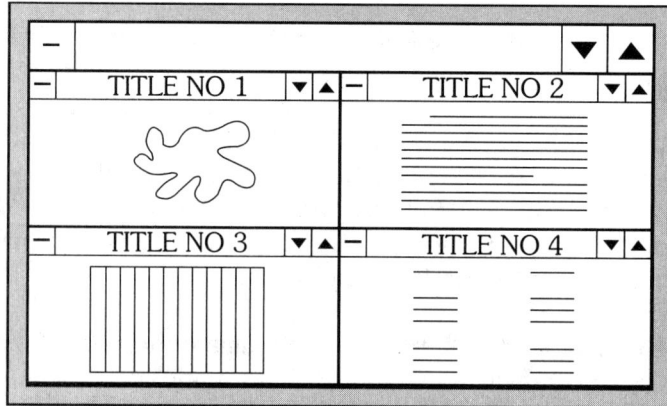

Tiled windows let you work in several files at once.

Tiled windows become difficult to read if there are more than four on the screen because they get so small that their contents are likely to be blurred by the limitations on the monitor's image resolution. Even with a high-resolution monitor, when the images are too small, you can get eye strain from looking at them.

When windows are tiled, one of them represents the application in which you're working. This window is said to be in the *foreground;* the others are in the *background.* You can select any window and enlarge it so it fills the screen. When you enlarge a window, you move its contents to the foreground.

It's also possible to place two or more windows on the screen without reducing their size very much. This requires that the windows be laid one on top of another, so that only the top window is fully visible. This scheme is called *overlaid* or *cascaded* windows. *See also* CASCADED WINDOWS, GRAPHICAL USER INTERFACE, OVERLAID WINDOWS, *and* WINDOWS.

Time-division multiplexing

See MULTIPLEXING.

Timekeeper

The *timekeeper* is the device inside a computer that keeps track of the date and time. The timekeeper is generally backed up by a small battery, so it keeps running whether or not the PC is powered-up.

Most PC timekeepers are little, if any, more precise than a wind-up wristwatch. For casual computing, most people don't need a timekeeper that records events down to the fraction of a second. If it's within a quarter of an hour, it's usually good enough for purposes such as directory listings, an example of which is shown. You can set your PC's timekeeper once a month, and it will stay within a couple of minutes.

Directory entries show date, hour, and minute

BATCH	<DIR>		7-20-02	10:59a
DOS	<DIR>		6-12-02	1:58p
FINDDEMO	<DIR>		5-17-02	5:12a
MOUSE	<DIR>		6-12-02	2:02p
PRODIGY	<DIR>		2-20-02	5:14p
UTILS	<DIR>		6-12-02	2:02p
WINDOWS	<DIR>		6-12-02	1:59p
XY	<DIR>		7-20-02	10:59a
AUTOEXEC	400	145	7-30-02	12:08p
BIBLIO		10902	4-22-02	6:20a

Time sharing

If you're running a business, you'll be more concerned about the time than the casual PC user, especially if more than one employee has access to the machine. Telephone-call logging, computerized security systems, data that has been downloaded or uploaded, and accounting details can require time that is accurate down to a few seconds. For this purpose, you can set your machine online through the Automated Computer Time Service (ACTS) by dialing 1-303-494-4774 (from locations within the United States). If you do this once a week, your machine should stay within one minute of the actual time as determined by the National Bureau of Standards. Software is available for this purpose.

Accurate timekeeping becomes extremely important when a computer is involved in navigation, synchronous data communications, high-security applications, and certain kinds of scientific experiments. In these situations, you might want to have your computer timekeeper automatically synchronized with an official time standard. A special scanner radio connected to your PC through an expansion board can pace the timekeeper and keep it within a small fraction of one second at all times. Automatic synchronization is also possible via the Global Positioning System (GPS) satellites. Automatic timekeeping systems cost anywhere from about $1000 to $5000. They are advertised in magazines aimed at serious PC users and professionals. *See also* MILITARY TIME, SECURITY SYSTEMS, *and* SYNCHRONOUS DATA.

Time sharing

In large corporations, schools, government agencies, and online services, multiuser computers are often employed. A minicomputer or mainframe can handle many workstations. Each workstation, or subscriber, in such a system can be either a PC or a dumb terminal.

Actually, the computer does not function simultaneously for all subscribers in a multiuser system. Instead, the central computer shifts it attention from station to station in rapid rotation. This is called *time sharing*. The principle is similar to that of time-division multiplexing on a communications line. The rotation is done so fast that each subscriber gets the illusion of being alone with the computer.

When you're at a workstation in a time-sharing system not overburdened with active subscribers, the computer responds to your commands almost instantly. A dumb terminal becomes a link to a machine far more powerful than the average home computer. As the number of active subscribers increases, each station's share of time goes down in proportion to the overall power of the central computer. The effects of this are not usually noticed, however, until the number of active subscribers reaches a critical level.

When a time-sharing system is working near its capacity, a small increase in the number of users will cause a significant degradation in performance at each workstation, as shown by the graph. It will take a while to log on, and processes will be carried out more slowly than when the system is working considerably below its capacity. This is similar to what happens in a PC when the size of a file challenges its RAM (random-access memory) or when a program is too sophisticated for the microprocessor.

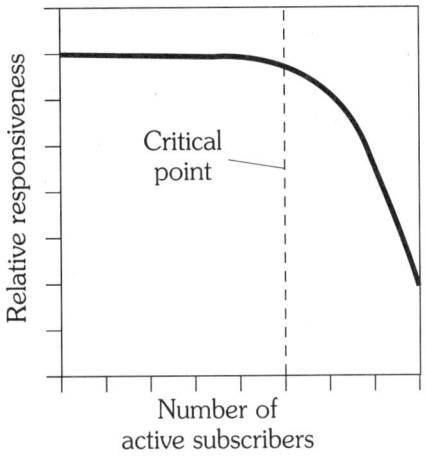

Workstation responsiveness is a function of the number of users.

If you have access to a time-sharing system, try to use it during off-peak hours. If you are in charge of such a system, you should conduct periodic use-versus-time tests. Although the heaviest usage will probably be during local business hours, this rule does not always apply. In some systems, certain days of the week, or certain times of the day, show dramatic usage peaks that you might not notice without conducting such tests. *See also* DUMB TERMINAL, LOCAL AREA NETWORK, MINICOMPUTER, MAINFRAME, NETWORK, ONLINE SERVICE, *and* WIDE-AREA NETWORK.

Time-shifting communications

When you engage in real-time online communication, you sit at your computer and type what you want to say. You can read the other person's remarks by looking at your monitor screen. In half duplex, your conversational companion's signals are displayed only when you aren't typing. In full duplex, it's possible to type and read at the same time.

When you use a bulletin-board system (BBS) or electronic mail (e-mail), you can leave messages for people even when they aren't at their computers. This is called *time-shifting communications* because the recipient does not get the message at the same time as it is sent from the source computer.

When a series of messages is sent via time-shifting communications, they need not be received in the same order they were sent. Suppose you leave 12 messages for 12 different people in a BBS. They will almost certainly be picked up in a different order from that in which you sent them. Even when you leave several messages in one mailbox, the recipient doesn't have to read the messages in the same order you wrote them. *See also* BULLETIN-BOARD SYSTEM, ELECTRONIC MAIL, FULL DUPLEX, HALF DUPLEX, PACKET COMMUNICATIONS, *and* REAL-TIME.

Tot-proof workstation

Children, especially very young ones, can get into places they don't belong. If you have tots in the house, there are times when you'll want to keep them away from your computer workstation. There are several things you can do to protect computers and small children from each other.

Lock the room. If possible, it's always best to have a computer room that you use for your workstation only. That way, you can close the whole room off to keep it out of the reach of unauthorized people.

Having a separate computer room also ensures that you have privacy when you need it. Are you a serious power user? Are you writing a novel or doing some important work with your PC? It's nice to be able to lock yourself in sometimes, as well as locking tots and pets out. If you have a home office, a separate room makes it easier to calculate how much (if any) of the rent or mortgage you can deduct from your income tax. Check the income-tax rules for information on possible home-office deductions.

Desk. Of course, there are times when you'll want to keep the computer room open so family members can communicate with you. Maybe you have chosen (or been forced) to put your workstation in a corner of a large room. In these situations, inquisitive creatures are likely to snoop around your equipment when you're not there.

A sturdy work desk with plenty of room on top is a good idea for any PC workstation. It's especially important if there are children or pets in the house. A table with folding legs is *not* adequate. If a child happens to get under such a table and one of the legs buckles, serious injury could result. Computers and monitors, especially, are heavy. Also, the monitor's cathode-ray tube (CRT) might break if the unit falls.

File cabinet. Keep valuable items, such as diskettes, software, instruction manuals, and files, in a cabinet that has a lock. That way, children can't get at those things.

Suppose you put a few magnets, some irreplaceable diskettes, and a little child into a room together, and leave them for a few minutes. Naturally, the child will rub the magnets on the diskettes, thereby mutilating the data. And of course, the more important the data, the less time will elapse before the catastrophe occurs, and the more complete the data destruction will be. The moral: Keep your data away from children! (In addition, you might avoid purchasing magnets of any kind.)

File cabinets can be placed underneath a door to make a solid, large work table. Two-drawer cabinets come in heights of about 28 inches, which is ideal for a desktop. You can get a door that's 28 to 36 inches wide, preferably made of solid wood (not a hollow door). You should paint and/or varnish it so that it has a glossy finish, and then set it on top of the file cabinets. Such a table is sturdy, and it will survive the assaults of small children.

Equipment placement. Naturally, you'll want to place all your hardware so it can't topple off your desk if it gets a hard knock. A PC main unit with a monitor on top of it weighs 60 to 120 pounds; such a mass isn't likely to go anywhere via the power of anyone not old enough to respect it. The printer is a different story, as are small items like paper trays and lamps. You might want to consider gluing these things down to the desk. The problem with this, of course, becomes evident when you want to move them.

Items like pencils, pens, markers, rulers, and drawing apparatus should be kept in the locked file cabinets when not in use. This will prevent children from putting these things into their mouths. Some drawing devices, such as compasses, have sharp points that can cause puncture wounds.

The monitor. The CRT in a computer monitor is a form of vacuum tube, and it will implode if it is struck with very much force. This can be a violent event, scattering shards of glass and spooking the wits out of a toddler. It can cause serious injury, too.

For your peace of mind, consider disconnecting your monitor and placing it out of children's reach when you're gone and the room is open. Alternatively, you can build a solid wooden box that will fit over the monitor, and strap this box down so that a child can't lift it off.

Wiring. All computers have a certain number of cables running from unit to unit. Only the power cords carry significant voltage (117 volts), and they are well insulated so they normally don't present a danger. It is possible that a cat might chew through one of them, however, or that a child might try to cut one with scissors. The solution to that problem is to use a transient suppressor (also called a surge suppressor or surge protector) with several outlets in one box; when the PC is not in use, unplug the whole unit from the wall outlet. This also protects your equipment from damage if lightning strikes the power lines nearby.

The other interconnecting cables (main unit to monitor, keyboard, printer, and external drives) can be tucked away out of sight. They

Touch screen

should never be out in the open where inquiring hands might give them a tug. If you wish, you can tape the cables down to the desktop in various places.

Noise reduction. In this context, the term *noise* refers to the acoustic, not the electrical, variety. Examples include crying, screaming, singing, foot stomping, meowing, and barking.

The best way to avoid noise distractions when you're working at your PC is to close the door and keep everyone else out of the room. If this isn't possible, consider installing a carpet on the floor and acoustical tile on the ceiling. If you are fortunate enough to have a choice of where you might locate your computer room, the upstairs (even a refinished attic) is usually quieter than the downstairs part of a house.

If all else fails, you try adjusting your hours of computer operation to correspond to the least noisy times in your household. This might be while the kids are at school or preschool, during their naps, or before anyone else has awakened in the morning.

Food and drink. The best policy concerning food and drink is to keep it all away from the computer workstation. This applies to adults and children alike. You don't want to scold your child for having soda at the computer, and then spill your own coffee into your keyboard!

Keyboards can be protected against liquids by covering them with a clear, flexible skin designed so that you can see and actuate the keys even while the cover is in place. This cover also prevents dust from accumulating on the keyboard. Nevertheless, when children are around, the policy should be, "Absolutely no food and drink is allowed near the computer."

Archives and backups. Backing up your data is a good idea whether or not you have children or pets. Hard disk failure, fire, theft, and other unforeseen disasters can befall you. If you work with computers long enough, a catastrophe will almost certainly happen someday. For your peace of mind, you should be prepared.

Keep all your data archives relatively up-to-date. They should be stored in at least two different places that are far enough apart so that they can't both be destroyed simultaneously. The same is true for software; backup copies of all software should be kept at the same locations as your archives. *See also* ARCHIVES, BACKUP, ERGONOMICS, *and* YOUTH-FRIENDLY COMPUTING.

Touch screen

A *touch screen* is a simple device for inputting data to a computer. Touch screens are especially popular in restaurants and retail stores.

Some bank automatic-teller systems also use them. You might find one at your public library if it has a computerized card catalog.

A touch screen consists of a monitor equipped with proximity sensors. The sensors are underneath the glass on the screen, and are transparent so the image can shine through them. The screen display affects the data that is sent by the sensors to the computer. Input is made by simply touching the correct spot on the glass with your finger. As the display changes, the function of each sensor changes to adapt to the image on the screen.

Touch screens provide a user-friendly graphical user interface that people can learn to operate quickly. No special pointing device is needed. There are no moving parts to wear out or make noise. One screen can provide an unlimited number of input functions; a new "keyboard" appears every time the display changes.

While touch screens work well in some applications, they cannot be used in others. For example, a touch screen is ideal for many kinds of computer games, but it is impractical for use as a keyboard in word processing or desktop publishing. Another problem with touch screens is that they get smudged and must be cleaned often. *See also* GRAPHICAL USER INTERFACE *and* MONITOR.

Tower case

In some computer systems, the main unit is housed in a case that sits upright on the floor. Such a case is called a *tower case* because it's taller than it is wide. Tower cases are generally somewhat larger than desktop units. The drawing shows a PC workstation with a tower case, 17-inch monitor, keyboard drawer, and printer, as seen from directly in front at desktop level.

Advantages. A tower case gives you plenty of room on the desk surface. This is especially useful if you have a large monitor or several peripherals. If you have an external CD-ROM drive, a fax machine, two printers, and a high-resolution monitor, a tower case is worth considering.

The main unit of any full-size PC is heavy. If you have a large monitor, the main unit, and several peripherals all on one desk, you'd better be sure the desk can withstand their combined weight. When a tower case is used, the stress on the desk is reduced. Noise levels are lower, too, because the fan and drives are farther from your ears.

Tower cases have more room inside than desktop cases. Because of this, you can install extra hard disks, diskette drives, CD-ROM drives, and tape drives in the main unit, further reducing clutter on the workstation. A tower case also has room for more expansion boards than a desktop case.

Track

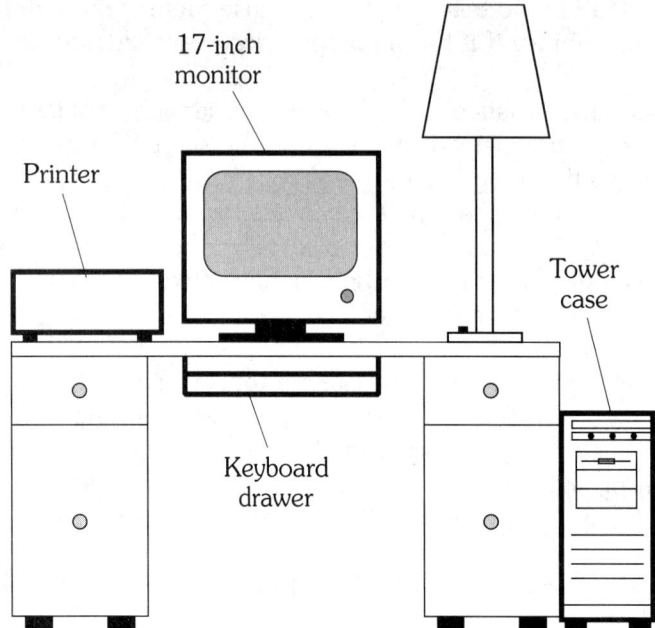

A tower case stands upright on the floor, making room on the desktop.

A desktop case can be stood on end to function as a tower case, but this is not always convenient because the diskette drives, power switch, and reset button might not all be easy to reach from where you sit. Still, some PC users prefer this arrangement because they like to have as much room as possible on their desks.

Disadvantages. The drive bays and controls are harder to reach on a tower case than on a desktop case when the tower case is on the floor. This is true even though most tower cases are ergonomically designed. Reaching down to get at things is less natural than reaching straight out. Some PC users dislike tower cases for this reason. Others adapt, exchanging diskettes less often and making use of the extra desk space that the tower case frees up.

It's hard to see the indicator lights on the main unit of a tower unit because it's down below you, rather than in front of you. Some PC users never look at these lights, so this is of no consequence. Still, the disk light, which indicates that the hard disk is working, can be useful; it sometimes gives away hardware or software problems by flashing incessantly. You won't be likely to notice this if the light is under your desk. *See also* DESKTOP COMPUTER.

Track

On a magnetic disk, magnetic tape, or CD-ROM (compact disc, read-only memory), a *track* is a path along which data is written and read. A track can be a circle, a line, or a spiral.

Disk tracks. Each track on a hard disk or diskette is a perfect circle whose center corresponds to the geometric center of the disk.

A track is always a complete 360° circle. The circumference of a track depends on its radius, that is, on its distance from the center of the disk. Inner tracks are shorter than outer tracks (see A in the drawing). This affects the way the data is written onto and read from the disk.

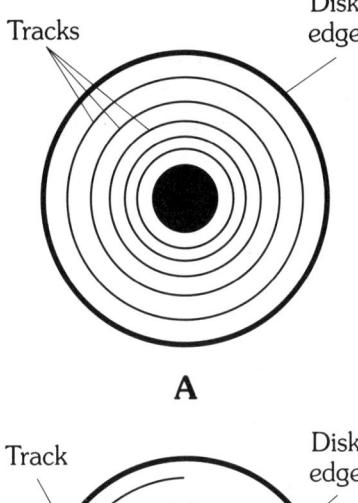

Tracks on a magnetic disk (A) and on a CD-ROM (B). Radial scale is exaggerated for clarity.

A disk rotates at constant speed, so the read/write head moves faster along outer tracks than along inner tracks. Because of this, the outer tracks offer better read/write precision than the inner ones. The same thing was true of vinyl hi-fi disks. They revolved at constant speed (33⅓ revolutions per minute) regardless of whether the needle was near the edge or the center. The needle moved fastest over the disk when it was near the edge, so the outside bands gave the best sound.

Tape tracks. There are two ways the tracks can be arranged on a magnetic tape. In either case, the tracks are always straight. In a *quarter-inch cartridge (QIC)*, the tracks are parallel with the edges of the tape. In *digital audio tape (DAT)*, the tracks are at an angle with respect to the edges.

A magnetic tape moves at constant speed through the drive mechanism. Because the tracks are straight, the data always moves past the read and write heads at the same speed. This is true for both QIC tapes and DAT. No part of the tape is better than any other part, as far as read/write precision is concerned.

CD-ROM tracks. The track on a CD-ROM is a long spiral, similar to the groove in an old-fashioned vinyl hi-fi disk. Data is written on the disc surface in the form of microscopic pits. The pits scatter the light from a laser beam shining on the disc. Where there are no pits, the surface is smooth and reflective, and the laser bounces off as if it had struck a mirror.

The track on a CD-ROM spirals inward, with each complete trip around the disk getting shorter as the laser gets closer to the center (see B in the drawing). But relative to the pits, the laser moves just as fast when it's near the center of the CD-ROM as it does when it's near the edge. Therefore, all parts of the CD-ROM are equally easy for the drive mechanism to read; the outside is no better than the inside. *See also* CD-ROM, CYLINDER, DISKETTE, HARD DISK, MAGNETIC DISK, MAGNETIC MEDIA, MAGNETIC TAPE, PLATTER, SECTOR, *and* TAPE DRIVE.

Trackball

A *trackball* is a device for guiding the pointer on a computer display or monitor. A trackball can take the place of a mouse. In fact, it's essentially an inverted mouse. Trackballs, like mice, are intuitive and user-friendly.

When you move a mouse, a ball bearing on the bottom of the device rolls around on the surface, and motion detectors translate the bearing's movements into instructions for the pointer. With a trackball, you push directly against the ball itself.

Trackballs are popular with laptop computers because they do not need a flat surface on which to work. This is the chief advantage of a trackball over a mouse. If space is limited, a trackball lets you take full advantage of a graphical user interface (GUI).

Trackballs vary from marble to golf-ball size. A trackball can be set in the keyboard, or it can be an external device that you clip to the side of the keyboard. The bearing can be rolled in any direction (see the drawing).

Some trackballs cause the pointer to move in a nonlinear way with respect to the force you apply. If you push such a trackball hard, the pointer moves fast; if you push the trackball gently, the pointer slows

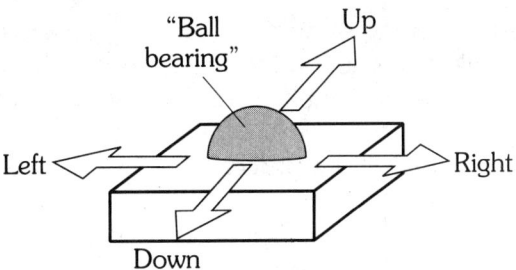

A trackball moves the pointer on a computer display.

down. This can help you accurately position the pointer on the screen. Some people like this feature because it provides enhanced precision, but other computer users find it unnatural. *See also* GRAPHICAL USER INTERFACE *and* MOUSE.

Tractor feed

Tractor feed, sometimes called *sprocket feed*, is a means of keeping paper moving straight and smoothly through a dot-matrix printer. Tractor feed is convenient because you can use it with fanfold paper to print out long documents without constantly attending to the printer.

A tractor-feed mechanism has "spikes" that fit into holes on either edge of the paper (see the drawing). As paper moves along, the tractor keeps the paper straight and ensures that there is no slippage. If the paper moves past the print head and then encounters the tractor, the printer is working in *pull-tractor* mode. If the paper goes through the tractor and then past the print head, the machine is in *push-tractor* mode.

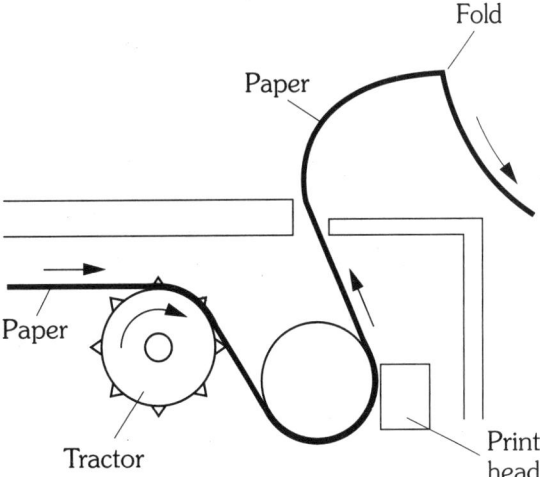

A tractor feed pulls or pushes fanfold paper through a printer.

Before you start a printing session, be sure the paper is in the printer so the tractor "spikes" line up in the holes along either edge of the paper. Start the session and make sure the first few pages stack up how and where you want. Once this is underway, the PC and printer will take care of the rest of the process.

While a tractor-feed printer is in operation, you can do other things, but it's a bad idea to wander too far away. For example, don't start printing a 300-page document and then go to the dentist. Fanfold paper is designed to stack up neatly after coming through a printer, but if the paper gets hung up at a fold, it will curl, tangle, and possibly jam the printer. If the document is long and you've let the paper go awry, you'll have a mess when you return to your workstation. *See also* DOT-MATRIX PRINTER *and* FANFOLD PAPER.

Transfer rate

See ACCESS TIME *and* STORAGE TIME.

Transient suppression

Home computers are designed to work with alternating-current (ac) electricity at 60 hertz (cycles per second) and about 117 volts. The figure of 117 volts is the "root-mean-square (RMS)" value, the engineer's way of stating average or effective ac voltage. The peaks of the cycles actually reach about +165 and −165 volts.

If the ac voltage fluctuates very much, the operation of a PC can be upset. The most common irregularity is a sudden "spike" or *transient*. A transient lasts for only a few millionths of a second, but it can rise to several hundred volts, either positively or negatively (see the drawing at A). Transients are caused by nearby thundershowers, transformer arcing (sparking), and certain large appliances. Transients can't be detected without special equipment connected to the power line to monitor the ac waveforms.

Somewhat less common is a voltage *surge*. This is a drop or rise in voltage that lasts for several cycles (B in the drawing). You notice surges because they cause a visible, momentary dimming or brightening of the lights in your house. Surges affect the operation of a computer in much the same way as do transients.

Although some transients and surges have no effect on computers, others can occasionally cause a PC to *crash*, or "freeze up." If that happens, the machine will have to be rebooted, and you'll lose the data in RAM (random-access memory). It's impossible to predict when a severe transient or surge will occur. Therefore, it makes sense to protect your equipment as much as possible at all times.

Most transients and surges can be kept from reaching your computer by means of a *transient suppression* device, sometimes called a *surge*

Transient suppression

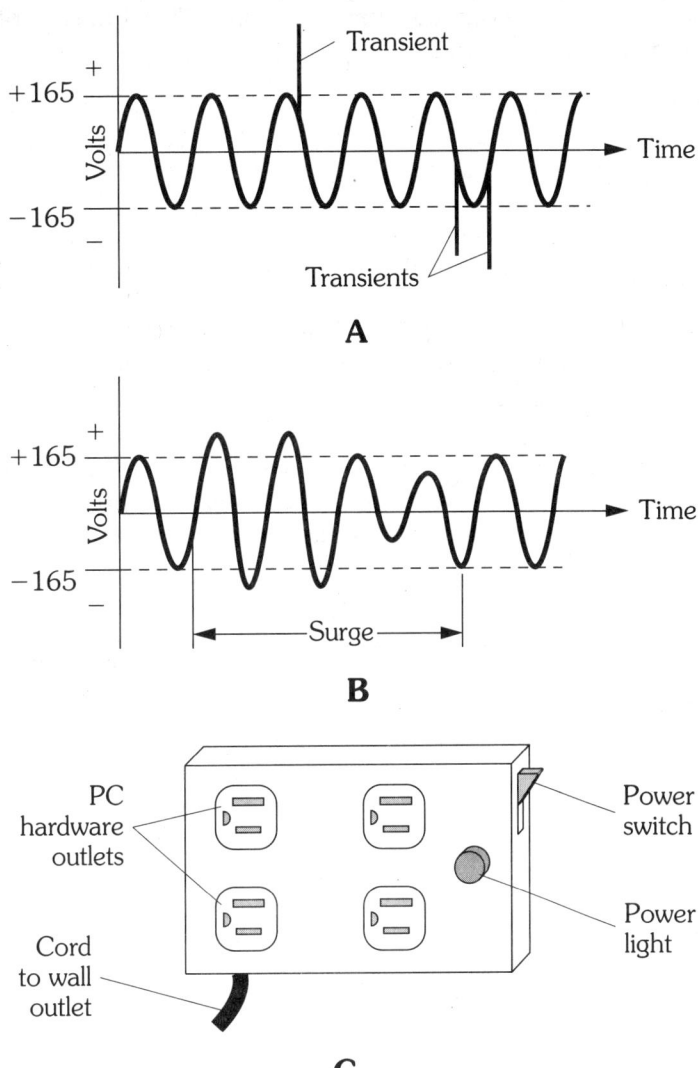

Transients on an ac wave (A); a surge (B); a typical transient suppressor box (C).

suppressor. (The term *surge protector* is used occasionally, but this is a technical misnomer.) A typical transient-protection device is a box with several three-prong outlets and a power switch (C in the drawing). It plugs into the wall outlet. You plug your PC and all your peripherals into the outlets in the box. You can use the suppressor-box power switch to control power to the entire workstation. Transient suppressors come in a variety of designs, ranging in price from a few dollars to several hundred dollars.

It's a good idea to unplug all your equipment from the wall socket when your workstation is idle. Doing this ensures that your equipment is not damaged in the event of a heavy thunderstorm. If lightning strikes near your home, the resulting transient can reach more than 10,000 volts at the wall outlets. Such a transient can cause serious, permanent damage to computer hardware, including the suppressor box itself. *See also* CRASH.

Trinary logic

See LOGIC.

Trojan horse

A *Trojan horse* is a program that is written into software with the intent of disrupting a PC's operating system. It is something like a virus, but while a virus can replicate itself, spreading through networks and affecting vast numbers of machines, a Trojan horse usually does its damage only within one computer.

The name "Trojan horse" comes from a legend about the city of Troy, known for its seemingly impenetrable wall. Anyone who climbed the walls was thrown back down by defenders. Because brute force did not work, the invaders resorted to trickery.

The people of Troy worshipped statues of animals. Enemy troops built a huge, hollow wooden horse on a wheeled platform. A number of soldiers crawled inside. The idol was left at the gate of the city, supposedly as a gift from anonymous benefactors. The people of Troy opened the gate, wheeled in the wooden horse, and put it in the center of town. That night the soldiers came out of the statue and took over Troy.

This legend is an excellent depiction of the way a Trojan horse gets into a computer and incites chaos. A diskette, advertised as having some unique and fabulous contents, is sold or given away. The data might also be available online, so PC users can download it onto their hard disks. People fall for the gimmick in large numbers. Within the software, there is a program that can mutilate or erase data on a computer's hard disk, sabotaging the operating system.

Why do some people, with knowledge of computers, deliberately mass-distribute software that harms PCs? There are several reasons. Some people distribute Trojan horses because they hate society. Some do it for revenge against an employer who fired them. Many are mentally ill. Some are "cyber vandals" who enjoy damaging other people's property. It is, of course, a crime to distribute Trojan horses with the intent of disrupting computer systems. Unfortunately, it is not always easy to find the culprits so they can be prosecuted.

The best way to protect your PC against Trojan horses is to avoid downloading online software directly onto your hard disk. Put it on diskettes first. A program called a *vaccine* can test diskettes, often finding and erasing Trojan horses before they reach the hard disk. You should also be skeptical of "too-good-to-be-true" software sold cheaply or given away online or on diskettes. *See also* VACCINE *and* VIRUS.

TrueType

TrueType is a method of printing and displaying scalable fonts. It's an inexpensive, simple alternative to PostScript. The technology was developed by Microsoft Corporation and Apple Computer, Inc. TrueType works with graphical user interfaces (GUIs) such as Windows and System 7.

Printers and monitors without TrueType (or its cousin, PostScript) can print or show text in a few standard sizes and fonts only. TrueType, in contrast, allows for a wide choice of font and type size because TrueType employs *outline font* technology rather than bitmapped fonts.

TrueType, like PostScript, lets a printer take advantage of its maximum image resolution. All printed documents come out with the best possible clarity. The font and type size you see on the monitor correspond closely to what you get when you print out the document. In that sense, TrueType is a WYSIWYG ("what you see is what you get") scheme.

Also like PostScript, TrueType allows for *device independence*, meaning that any printer can be used with any computer. In fact, TrueType can do this with less software than PostScript. Suppose you are preparing a thesis for your Ph.D. degree. If your professors want higher-quality copy than your dot-matrix printer can generate, you can submit it to them on diskette only, with the text in TrueType or PostScript fonts, and they can print it on their own printers. (Be sure they'll accept submissions on diskette before you hand in your thesis that way.) Alternatively, you can take your document diskette to a printing shop, where the personnel will use a laser printer to produce a clear hardcopy. *See also* FONT, OUTLINE FONT, POSTSCRIPT, *and* WYSIWYG.

Turing, Alan

Alan Turing was a genius who became known for his work in pioneering artificial intelligence (AI). He was an Englishman, born in 1912, who lived to be 41 years old.

Turing was interested in mathematics and mechanical engineering. He grew up during the advent of radio, television, and other electronic devices. It's not surprising, given his background and temperament, that Turing got interested in the concept of smart machines.

In his twenties, Turing played with the ideas involved in computing. In his thirties, he started trying to build a computer. This was just around the time of World War II, when the earliest computers were being conceived.

Turing was especially interested in machine knowledge. Can machines really know things, in the sense that people do? Can a machine have a

Turing test

mind, and not just an electronic brain? Turing tried to think up all possible arguments that people might formulate in an attempt to prove that machines can't think. Then he tried to argue the case for machine thought.

Three major arguments that are commonly put forth against machine thought are as follows:

> ➤ A machine can only process data. It can't come up with ideas of its own.
>
> ➤ A machine has no mind unless it can dramatically affect other minds, for example, write a profound novel all by itself.
>
> ➤ Souls are necessary for true thought. Humans have souls. Machines don't and can't.

None of these arguments, however, takes into account the possibility that machine thought might prove completely different from human thought. Turing was aware of this so-called tunnel-vision syndrome, in which people refuse to believe in anything that is not familiar to them. In addition, these three arguments, however compellingly they might be stated, are assumptions. None of them have been scientifically proven true. Not everyone believes them all; some people don't believe any of them.

Turing invented tests to use on computers, to find out whether they were really "thinking." It's tempting to speculate about what he would think of PCs if he were alive today. *See also* ARTIFICIAL INTELLIGENCE, ARTIFICIAL LIFE, ANIMISM, COMPUTER CONSCIOUSNESS, KNOWLEDGE, MACHINE KNOWLEDGE, *and* TURING TEST.

Turing test

The *Turing test* is a way to find out if a machine can think. It was invented by Alan Turing. The test is conducted by placing a man (M), a woman (F), and a questioner (Q) in three separate rooms (see the drawing). None of the people can see the others. The rooms are soundproof, but each person has a video display terminal so the people can communicate.

The object: Q must find out which person is male and which is female, on the basis of questioning However, M and F aren't required to tell the truth; both are told in advance that they may lie to any extent they want. It is the man's job to mislead the questioner into a wrong conclusion. Obviously, this makes Q's job difficult, but the test is not complete until Q decides which room contains the man and which contains the woman.

Suppose this test is done 1000 times, and Q is right 479 times and wrong 521 times. What will happen if the man is replaced by a smart computer that's programmed to act like a man? Will Q be right more

A measure of a computer's worldly wits.

often, less often, or the same number of times as with the real man in the room?

If the machine is "stupid," then Q will be correct more often than when a man was at the terminal. That is to say, Q will be less easily fooled by a machine than by a man. Maybe Q would be right 890 times out of 1000 with the machine in place of the man.

If the machine is as "smart" as the man, Q should be right about the same number of times as when the man was at the terminal—say, right 490 times and wrong 510 times. The man and the machine would be equally adept liars.

If the machine is "smarter" than the man, then Q ought to be wrong most of the time—say, correct 150 times and mistaken 850 times. The machine would be a better liar than the man.

There are other ways to test the intelligence of a machine, such as its ability to play chess and checkers, but these aren't good indicators of worldly "smarts." (Turing must have believed that smart people are always good liars.) Besides that, the two games are vastly different. Machines have proven extremely adept at checkers, and somewhat less expert at chess. Maybe you know a brilliant doctor, lawyer, or teacher who is a poor chess player, or someone who plays a great game of checkers, but can't balance a checkbook.

The Turing test was designed to measure machine intelligence in real-world terms, against an arguably appropriate standard of dishonesty.

No computer has yet come near passing by proving itself to be as devious as, or more devious than, a human being.

One important limitation of the Turing test, often overlooked, is that it is designed only to measure the extent to which a machine has human-like intelligence. According to some researchers, computer intelligence might evolve in forms alien to humans. Then, a machine might be quantitatively as smart as a person, but in a fundamentally different way, which the Turing test cannot accurately measure. Porpoises, for example, flunk Turing tests miserably, but some scientists believe they are extremely intelligent in their own way. *See also* ARTIFICIAL INTELLIGENCE, CHECKERS-PLAYING COMPUTER, CHESS-PLAYING COMPUTER, KNOWLEDGE, MACHINE KNOWLEDGE, *and* TURING, ALAN.

Two-column format

In word processing and desktop publishing, *two-column format* (also called *newspaper format*) refers to text lines that extend a little less than halfway across the page. The text is arranged in two columns, side-by-side. Both columns are usually the same width. You read down the left column, then move to the top of the right column and go to the end of the page (see the drawing). Two-column format is found in some textbooks, some reference books, and many magazines and newspapers. You'll almost never see it in novels. It should not be used in manuscripts, theses, or most business correspondence.

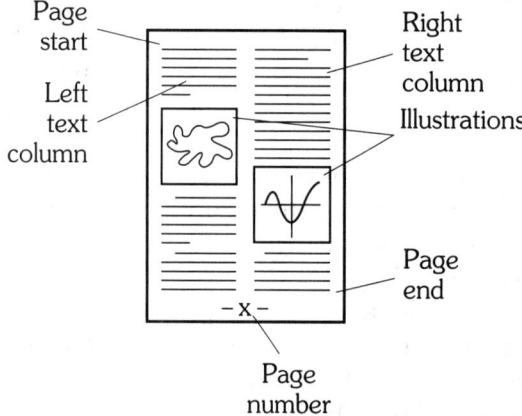

Columns are written and read from top to bottom, left to right.

Two-column format looks severe compared with *single-column format*, which lends a more relaxed tone to written work. The format you choose has an immediate effect on your readers' moods. If you're publishing something, ask yourself how you want your readers to feel, based solely on the physical appearance of the printed pages. A technical dictionary for nuclear physicists would look good in two-column format, but rather strange in single-column format. The opposite holds true for a young children's storybook.

Two-column format can be printed ragged-right or full-justified. In ragged-right text, the left margins of each column are straight and well-defined, but the right margins are irregular. In full-justified text, both the left and right margins of each column are straight and neat. Full-justified text is preferred for two-column format, as long as the column width is not too narrow. Some magazines use ragged-right text with two-column format.

To get full-justified or two-column format, you need a word processing program that adjusts word spacing and column placement. Two-column format allows for more words on a page than single-column format. The type size is also usually smaller in two-column format. The locations and relative sizes of illustrations are affected by choice of format. When you do this sort of word processing, it helps to have a WYSIWYG ("what you see is what you get") display. *See also* FLUSH LEFT/RIGHT/CENTER, JUSTIFICATION, SIDE-BY-SIDE COLUMN FORMAT, SINGLE-COLUMN FORMAT, WORD PROCESSING, *and* WYSIWYG.

Typeface
See FONT.

Ultimate Teacher program

The *Ultimate Teacher program* was originally written by engineer Charles Lecht. The software taught a computer user about astronomy, and in particular, about the way gravity affects things on different planets. The term *Ultimate Teacher* might now be applied to any computer-assisted instruction (CAI) software that teaches people by creating fantasy worlds.

Lecht's program took the computer user on an imaginary round of golf. Each hole was on a different planet in the Solar System. Because of differences in gravitation, the game would vary from planet to planet.

The drawings on page 1098 show hypothetical par-4 golf holes as they might be laid out on Earth (A), on Mars (B), and on Jupiter (C). Jupiter is thought to have no solid surface, but for the moment, imagine that it does. The shaded areas are sand traps. On Mars and Jupiter, artificial turf is used for the tees, fairways, and greens, since grass does not grow on those planets.

Although CAI is in its infancy, it is already revolutionizing the way people learn. It can help students at all levels confront life in ways new and old, real and fantastic. As any futurist knows, today's fantasies are tomorrow's realities. *See also* CHOREOGRAPHER PROGRAM, COMPUTER-ASSISTED INSTRUCTION, *and* VIRTUAL REALITY.

Uncanny valley

A Japanese roboticist and computer scientist, Masahiro Mori, has suggested that animism (the belief that everything has the essence of

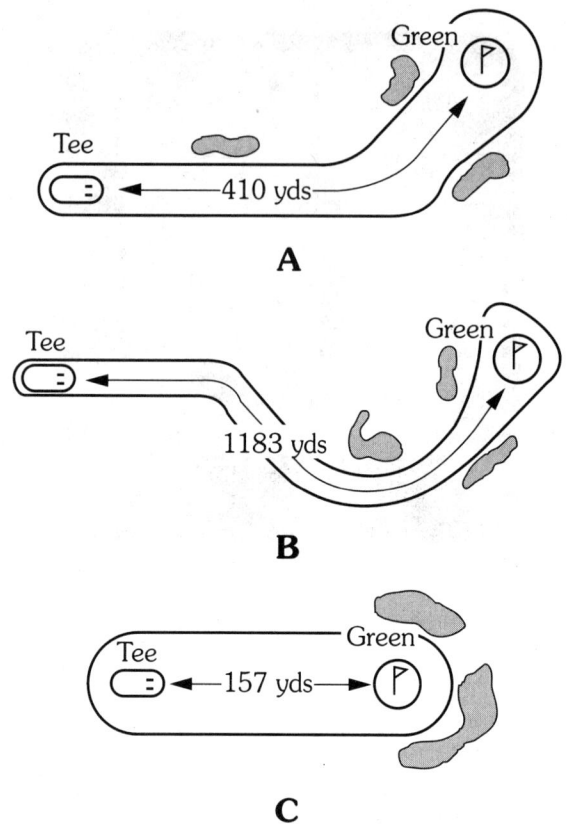

The Ultimate Teacher program simulates par-4 golf holes on Earth (A), Mars (B), and Jupiter (C).

life in some degree) and anthropomorphism (the belief that all intelligence must operate as human intelligence does) might cause people to behave erratically around intelligent machines. According to Mori's notion, the more a machine resembles a human being, the more comfortable people are with it, up to a certain point. When the machine gets too much like a human being, however, users become intimidated. As the machine becomes still more human-like, Mori speculates, people might get over their apprehension and start to develop trust in the machine.

Mori drew a graph to depict his theory (see the drawing). The curve has a dip at the point where people get nervous around computers or robots. Mori calls this the *uncanny valley*. How human-like must a machine become to trigger an uncanny-valley reaction in its users? It probably varies depending on the culture and personality of the user.

No one has tested Mori's theory to see if people's behavior around machines really follows a curve like this, but there is no doubt that some people are afraid of powerful computers. Most anyone can work with pocket calculators, adding machines, cash registers, TV remote controls, and the like. When certain people get in front of a PC,

Undeletion

however, they freeze up. This is called *cyberphobia*, an irrational fear of computers.

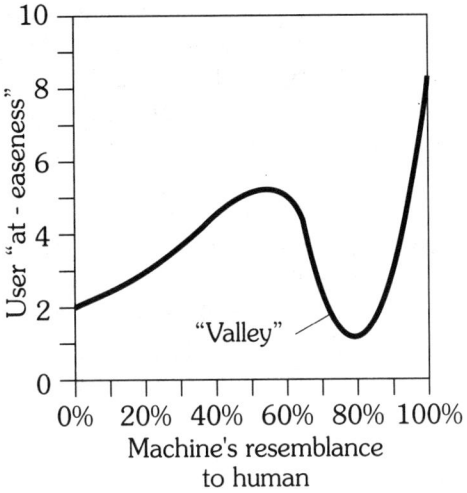

If machines become too smart too fast, people might get uncomfortable around them.

Some cyberphobics are so overwhelmed by PCs that they develop a mental block immediately, and can never get rid of it. Others get comfortable with PCs after awhile, and only have problems when they try something new or attempt to install complex features such as multimedia, robot controllers, or virtual-reality hardware. Still other people never let computers bother them at all.

Some researchers think the uncanny valley problem can be avoided by introducing new technologies gradually. But, as you know, things happen fast in personal computing. The best approach can be summed up by the adage, "Take what you can use, and leave the rest." *See also* ANIMISM, ANTHROPOMORPHISM, ARTIFICIAL INTELLIGENCE, *and* CYBERPHOBIA.

Undeletion

If you accidentally delete a crucial file from a hard disk or diskette, you can get it back by a process called *undeletion*. The undelete feature is standard with all advanced operating systems. If your operating system doesn't have undeletion capability built-in, it can be added by purchasing and installing an undelete utility.

Purpose. Undelete functions and utilities exist for one reason: to prevent disaster as a consequence of a single errant mouse click or keystroke. Without the undelete feature and the software structure that lets it work, your PC might not forgive you for an accidental file erasure. Most people, if they've worked much with computers, have erased a file (or even a whole disk or directory) and then, to their

Unformatting

horror, discovered that some of the data was irreplaceable and crucial. This is an *effective*, but not a *recommended*, way to learn that precautions must be taken to protect data against human error.

If you erase a file and then suddenly realize you made a mistake, stop work immediately. Undelete the file before you write anything else on the disk. When a file is erased, its name is removed from the file allocation table (FAT), like taking the street number off the door of a house. The contents of the file aren't destroyed until the file is overwritten by new data.

Simple, better, best. A simple undelete process lets you get data back if, but only if, it hasn't yet been overwritten. If you discover your error too late, this undelete function won't work; some or all of the file will be gone. A better scheme stores each erased file in a *delete sentry* complete with a *sentry directory*. Then, even if the original data is overwritten, a duplicate copy remains in the sentry, which is off-limits to normal file erasure. The delete sentry can be kept from consuming too much disk space by periodically purging it of files whose originals are elsewhere on the disk.

If you want the best possible protection against data loss, you should keep backup copies of all important files on diskettes. Back up *every* new file, and update *every* changed file, on a diskette at the end of each work session. Make this a law that you obey without fail. It's also a good idea to frequently back up your entire hard disk using a tape drive. If, in addition to these measures, you keep two complete, up-to-date sets of archives at two separate sites, and also make sure your computer has undeletion capability, your data will be essentially 100% accident-proof. *See also* ARCHIVES, BACKUP, DIRECTORY, FILE ALLOCATION TABLE, FILE ERASURE, FORMAT COMMAND, FORMATTING, TAPE DRIVE, *and* UNFORMATTING.

Unformatting

There are several ways of formatting a diskette or hard disk. The most powerful method, called *unconditional formatting*, obliterates every last byte of data on the disk. Usually, however, formatting erases only the file allocation table (FAT) and the directories. The data remains undisturbed, but "hidden," until you write other data onto the disk.

Data recovery. Many PC users are surprised to learn that file erasure and formatting don't always physically destroy computer data. There's a good reason for *safe formatting* and *quick formatting*, as the less-powerful schemes are called. If you accidentally format a disk on which you have stored crucial data, you can get the data back via *unformatting*. If you format a disk and then realize you didn't intend to, don't write any new files onto that disk. Use the unformat command immediately.

When you use the safe or quick methods of formatting diskettes, it's like emptying a file cabinet, putting all the old papers in a box, and then placing the box in your attic. You'll have to scrounge around if you need to get at one of the items, but the data is safe, although hidden, unless or until you actually discard it.

Hard disks. Under normal circumstances, a hard disk should never be formatted. This is sufficiently important to warrant a notice:

Warning! Never format your hard disk!

If, for some reason, you accidentally perform an unconditional format of your hard disk, you can still get the data back if you've duplicated its contents on a tape drive. If you inadvertently perform a safe or quick format on a hard disk, you can use the unformat command to restore access to the data. You must unformat right away; data might be overwritten if you save any new files on the disk.

The existence of the unformat command should not be taken as a license to format a hard disk as a method of cleaning it up when it gets cluttered. There are utilities designed to get rid of hard-disk clutter without placing essential data at risk.

Backups and archives. It's a good habit to make at least one backup of every file that's important to you. Most PC users have backup files on diskettes. Whenever you update one of these important files on a hard disk, update the diskette file too. If you want to be as safe as possible, keep two sets of archives in two separate locations, in addition to the backup diskettes. These archives should both be updated at reasonable intervals. The hard disk can be backed up via a tape drive.

The details of unformatting and file retrieval vary depending on your computer's operating system. For more information about unformatting disks and retrieving erased files, refer to your operating-system instructions. *See also* ARCHIVES, BACKUP, DIRECTORY, FILE ALLOCATION TABLE, FILE ERASURE, FORMAT COMMAND, FORMATTING, TAPE DRIVE, *and* UNDELETION.

Uninterruptible power supply

When a computer is operated from 117-volt, alternating-current (ac) power, there's always a possibility of a power failure. If the power to a PC main unit fails, even for a moment, all data in RAM (random-access memory) will be lost. This is inconvenient at best, and catastrophic at worst. To prevent the data in RAM from being lost in case of a short-term power outage, an *uninterruptible power supply (UPS)* can be used.

The drawing is a block diagram of a UPS. It serves only the main unit. The monitor and peripherals will fail if the 117-volt power goes out;

Uninterruptible power supply

only the PC main unit will continue to receive power. This will cause a suspension in normal operation (mainly because the monitor will go dark), but will preserve the information contained in RAM. It will also let you take quick action to save the contents of RAM on hard disk or diskette in case the power outage is prolonged.

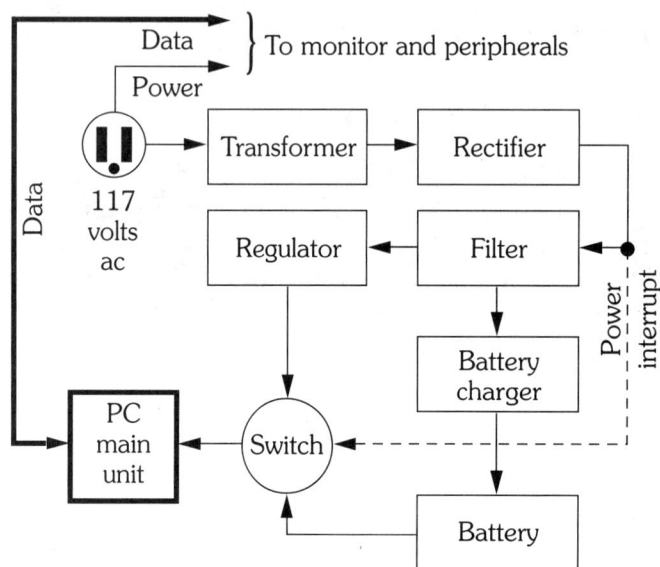

A UPS provides emergency battery power to the PC.

Data (heavy line in the drawing) passes between peripherals and the main unit independently of the electrical power. The peripherals each have their own built-in power supplies. Under normal conditions, the main unit gets its power via the transformer, rectifier, filter, and voltage regulator (thin, solid lines). A rechargeable battery, such as a lead-acid or nickel-cadmium (NICAD) type, is kept charged by a small current from the filter. If the power goes out, a power-interrupt signal (dotted line) causes the switch to disconnect the PC main unit from the regulator and connect it to the battery. When utility power returns, the switch disconnects the main unit from the battery and reconnects it to the regulator.

If you leave your PC powered-up most of the time, as is often the case in a business, a UPS can give you peace of mind. Still, it's a good idea to save data in a nonvolatile memory such as the hard disk or diskette whenever you leave the PC, even if it's only for a few seconds. While working, get into the habit of saving data on disk every five to ten minutes. This should become an automatic reflex on your part, whether or not you have a UPS.

If power does fail and you have a UPS, save all RAM data immediately on the hard disk, and also on a diskette if possible. Then switch the main unit, and all peripherals, off until normal power returns. If the outage has occurred because of an electrical storm, it's wise to unplug all equipment by physically removing the power cord of the transient suppression box from the wall outlet until the storm has passed. *See also* NICKEL-CADMIUM BATTERY, NONVOLATILE MEMORY, POWER SUPPLY, RANDOM-ACCESS MEMORY, TRANSIENT SUPPRESSION, *and* VOLATILE MEMORY.

UNIX

UNIX (pronounced "YOU-nicks") is an operating system originally designed for computer games in the 1960s. It has evolved into a complex, powerful, and enduring operating system, variants of which are still in use today. The original UNIX employs commands similar to those used in DOS.

Features. There is debate over the suitability of UNIX for personal computing. Some people call it overkill because it has features designed for larger computers. Others think that UNIX, or one of its variants, might become a "killer" operating system, particularly in business PC applications.

One of the most important features of UNIX is its expandable command set; the user can tailor the commands to suit specific needs. This requires that the user be willing to learn a large number of commands. In recent years, UNIX shells have been developed that bring the operating system within the grasp of less serious computer users.

Another major feature of UNIX is *multitasking*, which enables you to run more than one application at a time. For example, you can run a spreadsheet, a database, a word processing program, and an analytical graphics program simultaneously, if your computer has enough processing power to handle the workload.

UNIX is good for use in a large local area network (LAN). It lets one PC serve multiple users. This feature is not important to the PC user working on family finances, a musical composition, or the great American novel, but it is ideal for businesses. RISC (reduced-instruction-set computing) technology, and the newest, most powerful processor chips make it possible for a PC running UNIX to serve as the server in a business LAN. A UNIX system also offers password protection so that only authorized people can access the data. This minimizes the chance for such mishaps as classified-data leakage, intrusion of viruses, unwanted file alteration, or unauthorized file erasure.

In some operating systems, notably DOS, you can't give a file a name longer than eight characters, followed by a period, followed by three more characters. Also, other systems don't generally distinguish between uppercase and lowercase characters within filenames. In UNIX, there's no limit (within reason) to the length that a filename can have. You can mix uppercase and lowercase letters. In UNIX, you can give files names like "The Presidency of Gerald Ford," "Miami Beach in the 1990s," or "The File with No Name."

Problems. Despite its power and sophistication, UNIX has characteristics that some computer users do not especially like. One drawback is that the commands in UNIX are greatly abbreviated. Because there are so many of them (more than 200), a user faces the daunting task of mass memorization. This takes time and makes the system less user-friendly than other operating environments.

Also, because the UNIX system is so flexible, programmers have invented all kinds of "mutants" with names like Ultrix, XENIX, and UNIXWARE. The XENIX operating system, for example, was developed by Microsoft Corporation especially for use with IBM computers and clones. There is a UNIX-based form of Windows software, also from Microsoft, known as X Windows. Compatibility is a major issue with UNIX. If you think you "know" UNIX because you've used one variant, you might have problems when you try to use another PC equipped with a different variant.

A related problem is that UNIX is not very good about letting the user know when something is wrong. This arises because error messages depend on the contents of the command set, which differs among variants in the system. Also, programmers who write new commands are more interested in what they can get the machine to do than in having the machine let them know about their mistakes.

Finally, full-featured versions of UNIX are bulky. They need lots of hard disk space. This is not necessarily a problem on PCs with hard disks of 250MB or more, but it can cause trouble on older computers, especially laptops, with smaller hard disks. Pared-down variants of UNIX can be used on these computers.

The future. During the early years of personal computing, especially in the 1980s, UNIX was overwhelmed by DOS, Windows, and Macintosh systems, which are simple, straightforward, and user-friendly. UNIX probably has a future, given its remarkable tenacity. Computer users should keep watch for new and possibly revolutionary variants of this operating system. *See also* DOS, GRAPHICAL USER INTERFACE, LOCAL AREA NETWORK, MAINFRAME, MINICOMPUTER, MULTITASKING, MULTIUSER SYSTEM, OPERATING SYSTEM, PASSWORD, REDUCED-INSTRUCTION-SET COMPUTING, *and* SECURITY.

Upgrading

When you want to improve your PC system, you can buy a new computer, monitor, printer, sound board, and other peripherals all at once, but it's not necessary to *upgrade* a system that way, even if you have the money to do it. You can upgrade a PC by changing the microprocessor or installing accelerator boards. You can purchase improved peripherals for the applications you use most. You can also get new software.

What to do? Upgrading a system is a personal decision for individual PC users. In a business, the needs of the company, both current and anticipated, must be determined before any purchases are made.

Each PC user has unique preferences, both in hardware and in applications. Rarely does anyone's needs stay unchanged for very long. There are too many exciting things happening in the field of personal computing. Expectations grow as technology advances.

Suppose you bought a PC several years ago, intending to use it only for word processing. You wrote magazine articles, and had some of them published. Gradually you added features. You got a more powerful word processing package. You decided to get into desktop publishing, so you needed a good graphics program. You also needed more RAM (random-access memory). The graphics files consumed hard disk space. Then you got online, where you became interested in exchanging musical compositions with other PC users.

You are not the same PC user that you were several years ago. Your original machine is no longer adequate for your present needs. You must have something bigger and faster. You might speed up the microprocessor, get a bigger hard disk, and expand the RAM. Will that be enough? Or will a fascination with virtual reality, artificial intelligence, or speech recognition and synthesis get the better of you, suggesting the purchase of a machine with the newest, most revolutionary processing scheme? Only you can decide exactly what to do. If you plan to buy something at the forefront of technology, get the opinions of several experts before spending a lot of money.

Main unit. Some of the most significant upgrades involve changes to the main unit of a desktop computer. Some of the following upgrades are also possible with laptops:

> - *CPU* You can increase the clock speed of the existing microprocessor, or you can upgrade to a more powerful chip. Upgrade kits are available through advertisements in the PC magazines.
>
> - *Motherboard* Some upgrades require that the whole motherboard be replaced. This is still much less costly, in general, than buying a new PC.
>
> - *BIOS* The BIOS (basic input/output system) in your computer can be improved. This might require replacing only a few integrated circuits (ICs), or it might entail replacing the motherboard.

Upgrading

- *Memory* Expanding the RAM usually involves adding new ICs and/or an expansion board.

- *Diskette drives* If your PC happens to have an old double-density diskette drive, you will probably want to change to a high-density diskette drive. You might also add extra drives. There are specialized drives with extra-large capacity that you can consider.

- *Hard disk* You can replace your old hard disk with a new one several times the capacity. The capacity of the largest hard disks roughly doubles every year. In five years, that's more than a 30-fold increase.

- *Software* New software comes out so often that you could easily bankrupt yourself buying everything that comes along. It pays to choose your software wisely. Downward compatibility and upward compatibility are major issues with all software, especially in computers more than a couple of years old.

- *Utilities* The operation of your system can be streamlined, and the security of your data ensured, by means of utility software. Programs are available for specific applications, and also as part of integrated packages.

Peripherals and accessories. You can improve the performance of a system by getting better peripherals. Here are a few possibilities:

- *Display* You can get a bigger monitor with better image resolution and color. The monitor you need depends on your applications. Animated graphics requires the most advanced monitors; straight word processing can be done with a simple monitor.

- *Printer* While a dot-matrix printer is adequate for general word processing use, you'll want an inkjet or laser printer for desktop publishing. A color printer might also be worth considering.

- *CD-ROM* Books, fonts, software, and most other kinds of data can be stored permanently on compact discs. A CD-ROM drive can be a worthwhile addition to any PC system, especially if it's used for instructional or educational purposes.

- *External mass storage* There are several ways to store data in large quantities. You can add such items as a Bernoulli box, a tape drive, PCMCIA standard adapter cards, a Floptical diskette and drive, and a WORM (write-once/read-many) drive.

- *Fax* Adding a fax board to your machine will let you look at faxes on the monitor and usually print them, too. You can send certain computer files to anyone who has a fax machine. You can store faxes on disk.

- *Pointing devices* The most common pointing mechanisms are the mouse and the trackball. You might add a joystick for use with computer games. A touch screen can also be used as a pointing device.

➤ *Scanners* You can convert printed matter to digital form, suitable for storing and editing in a computer, using an optical scanner. These come as handheld units, or you can get more sophisticated flatbed units.

➤ *Voice input/output* With speech recognition, you can give verbal commands to your machine. Speech synthesis lets the computer talk back to you. You can thus dictate letters, operate a machine over the telephone, or enter data when you aren't in a position to handle a keyboard.

Applications. Here are a few of the more exotic applications/extensions that can be added to a basic computer system. These all require sophisticated software:

➤ *Remote control* You can control your home PC from a remote location such as your car, a boat, an aircraft, or a desert island. This usually requires two PCs (the host and the remote), both equipped with remote-control software.

➤ *Robot control* Robotics offers, at the very least, some great opportunities for having fun. It's possible that personal robots will become household items in many families within the next generation, as PCs themselves became common in the last quarter of the 20th century.

➤ *Smart computing* The highest level of software, artificial intelligence (AI), can help you solve some of life's most difficult problems. Or, if you prefer, AI can make your problems harder to solve. At least, AI can be a lot of fun, especially if you enjoy programming and computer games.

➤ *Amateur radio* If you're interested in communications technology, perhaps amateur radio will interest you. Radio "hams," as they are called, communicate using PCs and radio transceivers, sending signals all over the world by such exotic means as meteor scatter, ionospheric propagation, satellite data transmission, and even "moonbounce."

➤ *Hypersensation* In conjunction with AI, virtual reality can let you explore strange places and dimensions. You might swim with sharks, walk on the moon, or travel through time.

For more information. Upgrading often involves some trial-and-error, especially for hardware that requires you to get into the "guts" of your equipment. If you're afraid to open up a computer box, enlist the help of an expert. You can have upgrades done by professionals at computer centers, although the labor can get quite expensive.

New upgrade opportunities come out as fast as the technology changes. In personal computing, that's every day. Check the

Uplink

consumer PC magazines for the latest information and advertisements. You also can chat with "PC gurus" online about this subject. The supply of opinions is virtually infinite.

See also ACCELERATOR BOARD, ADAPTER, AMATEUR RADIO, ARTIFICIAL INTELLIGENCE, BASIC INPUT/OUTPUT SYSTEM, CD-ROM, CENTRAL PROCESSING UNIT, CLOCK SPEED, COMPUTER POWER, DOUBLE-DENSITY DISKETTE, DOWNWARD COMPATIBILITY, EXPANSION BOARD, FAX, HARD DISK, HIGH-DENSITY DISKETTE, HIGH-RESOLUTION MONITOR, HIGH-RESOLUTION PRINTER, IMAGE RESOLUTION, INTEL MICROPROCESSORS, JOYSTICK, MASS STORAGE, MEMORY, MICROPROCESSOR, MODEM, MONITOR, MONITOR UPGRADING, MOTHERBOARD, MOTOROLA MICROPROCESSORS, MOUSE, MUSICAL INSTRUMENT DIGITAL INTERFACE, ONLINE SERVICE, OPTICAL SCANNER, PACKET COMMUNICATIONS, PERSONAL ROBOTS, PRINTER, RANDOM-ACCESS MEMORY, REMOTE CONTROL SYSTEMS, SOFTWARE, SPEECH RECOGNITION, SPEECH SYNTHESIS, TAPE DRIVE, TOUCH SCREEN, TRACKBALL, UPWARD COMPATIBILITY, UTILITY SOFTWARE, *and* VIRTUAL REALITY.

Uplink

The term *uplink* refers to the signals that a communications satellite receives from earth-based stations. These signals are usually sent on radio frequencies of 100 megahertz (MHz) or more. Communications satellites are used in some telephone systems. It's possible, therefore, that you've sent or received computer data through a satellite.

All communications satellites work in basically the same way: they receive signals in one range (or band) of frequencies, the *uplink*, and retransmit them in another band, the *downlink*. The device that does this is called a *transponder*. The uplink and downlink frequency bands must be different enough so the downlink transmitter doesn't interfere with the uplink signals.

Communications satellites are used by amateur radio operators. If you have a "ham radio" license, or are interested in getting one, you probably know this already. Hams communicate with their PCs over the radio in much the same way as you use your PC to communicate with other people via the telephone. This is called *packet radio*. Some of it is done through amateur radio satellites. *See also* AMATEUR RADIO, DOWNLINK, PACKET COMMUNICATIONS, *and* SATELLITE DATA TRANSMISSION.

Uploading

Uploading is the process of sending data into a network so other PC users can access it. You can upload programs, files, graphics, or any other digital data onto an online service from your RAM (random-access memory), diskette, or hard disk. A common way of doing this is to leave messages on a bulletin-board system (BBS).

Uploading

You can also upload data from one part of your PC system to another. Generally, the term refers to the transfer of data from a less substantial place to a more substantial place.

Whenever you save a file on diskette, hard disk, or tape, the file is uploaded from RAM. Magnetic media are more permanent than RAM; data disappears from the RAM when you switch your PC off, but it stays on diskette, hard disk, or tape. If you access a file from a diskette, hard disk, or tape, storing it temporarily in RAM so you can edit it, you are *downloading* data.

You can upload all kinds of information, programs, and even photographs through a modem to an online service. You can give a friend a program, or a photograph, or even a musical tune by uploading it. Computer hobbyists often exchange data in this way.

The drawing illustrates uploading to an online service. Files or programs from the diskette drive or hard disk (the large ellipse labeled *D*) pass through the computer (the large circle labeled *PC*) to the online service. The service, or network, distributes the data to distant PCs (small circles), which download the data onto diskettes (the small ellipses labeled *D*). The distant computer users should run all downloaded data through a vaccine (antivirus program) before allowing the data onto their hard disks or into their RAMs. Vaccines should always be used with downloaded data. The drawing shows five distant computers to which data is uploaded from the local computer, but this is just an example; there might be as few as one, or as many as a thousand or more.

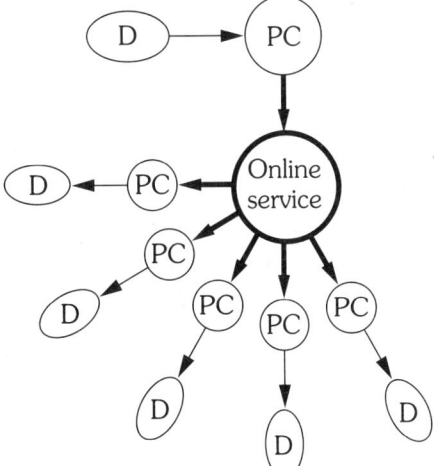

Data goes from a local disk through a local PC to an online service. From there, it is sent to distant computers.

You must be cautious when you upload data into a network. It's important that you not upload copyrighted material without first obtaining permission, in writing, from the owners of the copyright. You might have to pay a fee in addition to getting the written permission. Some copyright owners will not allow you to upload their

Upper memory area

data under any circumstances. The reason for this is *easy to understand* if you put yourself in their place. When you upload anything to an online service, you are in effect giving it freely away. *See also* BULLETIN-BOARD SYSTEM, DOWNLOADING, MODEM, ONLINE SERVICE, TROJAN HORSE, VACCINE, *and* VIRUS.

Upper memory area

See HIGH MEMORY AREA.

Upward compatibility

Upward compatibility is the extent to which old products, especially software, will work with newer products. Sometimes old software will work directly with new hardware or operating systems. This is *100% upward compatibility*. Often, however, you'll need to alter your old software to use it with a new system. This is *partial upward compatibility*. Occasionally, you must buy completely new software for a new PC or operating system. The old software is then *upwardly incompatible* with the new system. This sort of thing is quite common because of the fast pace of technological change in the personal computing world.

Compatibility problems were not much of an issue with Intel microprocessors in the 80x86 series. There were a few minor difficulties with the introduction of the Pentium microprocessor. The Pentium represented a radical improvement over previous designs; to achieve such an improvement, it was necessary to change certain basic processing schemes. A similar, and more dramatic, situation has arisen with the advent of RISC (reduced-instruction-set computing) microprocessors, which represent a whole new way of doing things compared with the older CISC (complex-instruction-set computing).

The more serious you are about personal computing, the more often upward compatibility will be an issue for you. You'll want to upgrade your system periodically. There's no absolute rule concerning how often you should do this. Some people purchase new PCs whenever a more powerful microprocessor comes out, while less serious users upgrade at intervals of about five years. A few people wait until their old system breaks down or until compatibility problems become overwhelming.

When compatibility becomes a big issue, it's time to consider a major upgrade. If you use your computer in your business, then income taxes become a factor in addition to your overall working efficiency. (You can deduct part of all of the cost of the new system.) You might have to buy new software at the same time as you buy a new system, but if you do it all at once, you can get a substantial tax deduction. *See also* COMPATIBILITY, COMPLEX-INSTRUCTION-SET COMPUTING, DOWNWARD COMPATIBILITY, HARDWARE, REDUCED-INSTRUCTION-SET COMPUTING, SOFTWARE, *and* UPGRADING.

User friendliness

See ERGONOMICS *and* HUMAN ENGINEERING.

Utility software

Utility software, also called *utilities*, are programs that help keep a computer running smoothly. Utilities can minimize the chances for inconvenience in case something goes wrong with your system or if you make an error that could result in the loss of data. Some utilities help protect data, computers, and systems against people with malicious intent.

Utilities are available for specific purposes. They are also available in multipurpose packages. The table shows some common types of utilities, along with brief descriptions of what they do.

Common utilities

Term	Definition
Backup	Copies files to protect against loss.
Defragmentation	Consolidates data on disks.
Encryption	"Scrambles" and "unscrambles" data.
File compression	Makes files consume less memory.
File conversion	Translates files among different formats.
File transfer	Moves files among computers.
Formatting	Prepares disks for storing data.
Integrated	Provides many utilities in one package.
Memory management	Optimizes the use of computer memory.
Mirroring	Backs up hard disk data on another hard disk.
Object linking and embedding	Keeps data consistent among files; places files within other files.
Outline	Helps writers organize and edit work.
Security	Restricts access to, and use of, data.
Software uninstallation	Removes unwanted programs from hard disk.
Undeletion	Restores data after unintentional file erasure (sometimes).
Unformatting	Restores data after unintentional disk formatting (sometimes).
Vaccine	Erases Trojan horses and viruses (usually).

It's an excellent idea to purchase a good all-around utility package when you buy a new PC. If you don't have a utility package now, it would be wise to buy one immediately. They're available at computer stores, office-supply stores, and through PC-oriented magazines and catalogs.

Utility software

See also BACKUP UTILITY, DEFRAGMENTATION, ENCRYPTION, FILE COMPRESSION UTILITY, FILE CONVERSION, FILE TRANSFER UTILITY, FORMATTING, MEMORY-MANAGEMENT SOFTWARE, MIRRORING, NORTON UTILITIES, OBJECT LINKING AND EMBEDDING, OUTLINE UTILITY, PASSWORD, SECURITY, SOFTWARE, SOFTWARE INSTALLATION AND UNINSTALLATION, TROJAN HORSE, UNDELETION, UNFORMATTING, VACCINE, *and* VIRUS.

Vaccine

A *vaccine* (also called an *anti-virus program* or *anti-virus utility*) is a program or utility that searches for, and usually eliminates, a Trojan horse or virus from a diskette or hard disk.

Using a vaccine. You can buy vaccines all by themselves, but advanced operating systems have them already included. For example, in Microsoft DOS 6.0, a vaccine called Microsoft Anti-Virus is a standard feature of the package.

When downloading files or software from online, always put them on a diskette. Don't download anything directly onto your hard disk. If there's a virus or Trojan horse in downloaded data, it will be less likely to devastate your computer's operating system if it is kept away from the hard disk.

After you've downloaded the data onto a diskette, run the diskette through a vaccine. The vaccine will notify you if it has found any "germs." If the vaccine finds something suspicious, it will let you know. Some vaccines give you the option of leaving the diskette as it is (and taking your chances with it), or cleaning it up. Other vaccines automatically erase anything suspicious. Once the vaccine has cleaned up the diskette, and has indicated to you that there's nothing apparently wrong with the data, you can transfer the data to your hard disk if you want. There is still some risk involved with this; vaccines aren't perfect.

Vaccine

Some vaccines can be added to the AUTOEXEC.BAT file (or equivalent) so that they are automatically run every time you power up. You must still be sure to check downloaded data that comes in during a work session, however.

How it works. The flowchart shows a typical data vaccination process. Circles represent steps taken by you, the PC operator. Rectangles are steps taken by the vaccine program or utility. Diamonds are branch points, at which the procedure can take either of two different paths. The steps proceed in the following fashion:

1 *Download* You transfer a file or program from online to a diskette. This data can be anything: a text file, a musical tune, a photograph, a drawing, a game, a program. If the data won't fit onto a single diskette, it must be broken up into pieces, each of which will fit onto a diskette. Each diskette must then be vaccinated individually.

2 *Start vaccine* You give a command or make a menu selection telling the computer to begin running the vaccine program or utility.

3 *V/TH scan* The vaccine searches the diskette for a virus (V) or Trojan horse (TH).

4 *Anything unusual? (Y/N)* If something out of the ordinary is detected on the diskette, the vaccine gives you a warning to that effect. If nothing strange is found, the vaccine tells you that, too.

5 *Notify op* You are told that something is out of the ordinary with the data on the diskette.

6 *Eradicate? (Y/N)* You can choose whether you want to erase the strange data or leave it intact. You might do any of these things:
 • Reformat the diskette
 • Erase the newly downloaded data from the diskette
 • Take the risk of using the data from the diskette
 • Take the greater risk of transferring the data to your hard disk
 The flowchart stops with a question mark at this step because you have so many choices, and because the fate of your operating system might depend on which option you choose.

 Caution! It is strongly recommended that you let the vaccine try to erase suspect data, and never allow anything suspicious onto your hard disk.

7 *Remove suspicious data* The vaccine erases the suspect item from the diskette, and then goes back to the V/TH scan to look for more suspicious data.

8 *Give "All clear"* You are told that nothing appears out of the ordinary with the data on the diskette.

9 *Install on HD* You can, if you wish, transfer some or all of the diskette data to your computer's hard disk. It's a better idea, however, to leave it on the diskette and use it from there if possible.

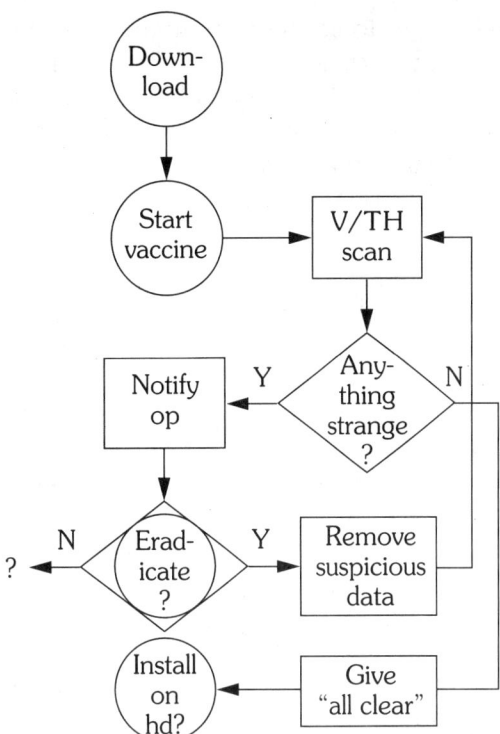

Typical vaccination process for a diskette.

No guarantee. The creators of viruses and Trojan horses are clever. They're always developing new strains that escape detection and eradication by vaccines. It's quite possible that a vaccine will fail to find a virus or Trojan horse, even though one is present. It's also possible that the program will find one and then fail to get rid of it, even though the vaccine tells you it's gone.

Viruses can sometimes be extremely difficult to eliminate. There have been cases in which users have gone so far as to reformat an infected hard disk, only to discover a virus still there afterwards. This is like burning down a house to get rid of a rat, and then finding the rat alive and well in the ashes. Formatting a hard disk is an unwise and dangerous thing for a computer novice to do; it can obliterate all the data on the disk, doing more damage than the virus itself. If you encounter a virus that a vaccine can't eliminate, you should get expert assistance.

Caution! Hard disks should never be reformatted, except by computer experts.

Viruses and Trojan horses will probably always be with us. Some of the people who create and distribute them might decide to use their talent in more constructive ways. Meanwhile, computer users must be aware that such things exist, and act accordingly.

Vector graphics

Vaccines are updated periodically in an attempt to keep pace with the evolution of viruses and Trojan horses. If you plan to use your PC online very often, and especially if you plan to download files and programs, you should consider buying a vaccine that is updated regularly. One example is the Norton Anti-Virus utility. *See also* DOWNLOADING, HACKER, TROJAN HORSE, *and* VIRUS.

Vector graphics

See OBJECT-ORIENTED GRAPHICS.

Version number

Software and operating systems are always changing, usually for the better. They're advertised with numbers. You'll see things like DOS 6.0, or Windows 3.1, in ads and specification sheets. Usually, the number is correlated with the time of development. The higher the number, the more up-to-date you can expect the product to be. This number is the *version number.*

For example, if you read about version 3.2 of some program, and then somewhere else you read about version 4.0 of the same program, you can be reasonably sure that version 4.0 was developed after version 3.2. You can also surmise that version 4.0 is probably more powerful than version 3.2.

Version numbers make sense only for a single program or operating system. Comparisons between different applications or environments are meaningless. It's not necessarily true that DOS 6.0 is better than Windows 3.1, for example. Some (but not all) PC users think Windows is an improvement over DOS, no matter what the version numbers. On the other hand, everyone would probably agree that DOS 6.2 is vastly superior to DOS 4.1, and that CorelDRAW 5 is much more powerful than CorelDRAW 3.

A change in the whole-number part of a version number (the digit to the left of the decimal point) represents a substantial upgrade. A change in the decimal part of the version number (the digit or digits, if any, to the right of the decimal point), known as the *release number*, reflects a minor improvement. Chances are good that version 4.0 of a program is more powerful than version 3.2, but that doesn't always mean that it will work better for you. A program or operating system with a new version number will sometimes contain bugs that earlier versions did not have. These flaws can offset the improvements until the vendor perfects the software or operating system. Such improvements are usually reflected by a change in the release number. *See also* BUG *and* RELEASE NUMBER.

Verso page

See BINDING OFFSET.

Videoconferencing

See TELECONFERENCING.

Video Graphics Array

The term *Video Graphics Array (VGA)* refers to a display standard for IBM-compatible PCs. When it was introduced, it offered improved image resolution and color-display capability compared with a Color Graphics Adapter (CGA) or Enhanced Graphics Adapter (EGA). Today, typical monitors employ the more advanced Super Video Graphics Array (SVGA) technology, although VGA monitors can be found in older computer systems.

A VGA can show a large number of colors; for most applications it can be considered almost a continuous color palette. The image resolution varies depending on the number of colors displayed and on whether the application is text-only or includes graphics. VGA's image resolution is adequate for most casual PC use, such as working with word processing, databases, spreadsheets, draw programs, and paint programs. If you demand better image resolution and color rendition, you will need an SVGA monitor.

There are several variants in the VGA standard. They were marketed along with IBM-compatible PCs when VGA was the most common type of monitor. Some of these VGA variants have slightly improved image resolution compared with the original VGA. *See also* COLOR GRAPHICS ADAPTER, ENHANCED GRAPHICS ADAPTER, HIGH-RESOLUTION MONITOR, IMAGE RESOLUTION, *and* SUPER VIDEO GRAPHICS ARRAY.

Vidicon

Video cameras use a form of electron tube that converts visible light into varying electric currents. One common type of camera tube is called the *vidicon*.

A camcorder in a common videocassette recorder uses a vidicon. Closed-circuit TV systems, like those in stores and banks, also employ the vidicon. The main advantage of the vidicon is its small physical bulk; it's easy to carry around, making it perfect for vision systems in advanced computer communications.

In the vidicon, a lens focuses the incoming image onto a photoconductive screen. An electron beam scans across the screen in a pattern of horizontal, parallel lines called the *raster*. The scanning in the vidicon is exactly synchronized with the scanning in the picture tube that displays the image "seen" by the camera tube.

As the electron beam scans the photoconductive surface, the screen becomes charged. The rate of discharge in a region on the screen depends on the intensity of the visible light falling on that region. A simplified cutaway view of a vidicon tube is shown in the drawing on the next page.

Virtual disk

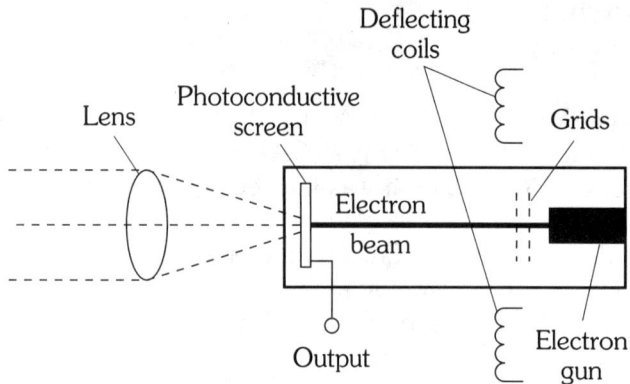

Simplified cutaway view of a vidicon camera tube.

A vidicon is sensitive, so it can see things in dim light. The dimmer the light gets, however, the slower the vidicon responds to changes in the image. You've probably noticed this sluggish response when using a camcorder indoors at night. Rapid motion of the camera or of objects in the field of vision causes the images to blur. *See also* IMAGE ORTHICON *and* VISION SYSTEMS.

Virtual disk

See RAM DISK.

Virtual memory

Virtual memory (VM) refers to an extension of a PC's RAM (random-access memory) by using space on the hard disk instead of the memory chips themselves. In most computers, the hard disk has many times the data-storage capacity of the RAM.

How it works. Suppose you have some file folders (the old cardboard sort) in the drawers of your workstation desk. You've accumulated papers until the drawers are packed full. You need more space, but you don't want to buy another desk. So you buy a file cabinet, one of those massive metal monsters that stands as tall as a person. You put it in a walk-in closet to get it out of the way (and because it's ugly). Now you have a dozen times the filing space you previously had, although it takes longer to get at the files in the cabinet, compared with the ones in your desk. This is the pre-computer equivalent of VM.

Virtual memory works best when it's automatically used, as necessary, by the operating system. The data "spills over" from RAM onto the hard disk, as shown in the drawing. That way, you don't have to think about it. This is called *virtual-memory management (VMM)*. Most microprocessor chips are able to do this.

The main asset of virtual memory is that it multiplies the effective size of RAM. This is especially useful in high-resolution graphics, or in any

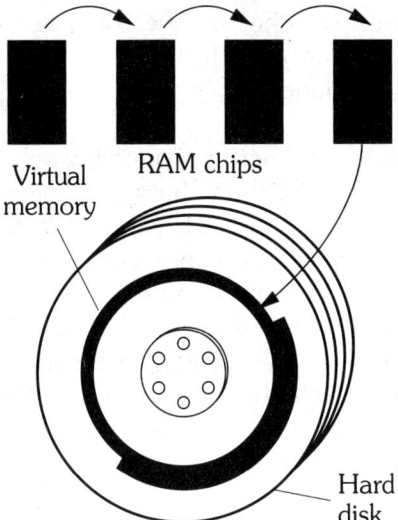

Data (shaded regions) is written on the hard disk when the RAM capacity is exceeded.

other application where files become very large. The downside of VM is that it slows down access time and storage time. The hard disk, with its moving parts, is sluggish compared with purely electronic memory. The speed of VM can be maximized by ensuring that the hard disk has plenty of contiguous sectors available, so the VM data can be written in unfragmented form.

Swap files. When virtual memory is needed within a given application, a *swap file* can be used. Part or all of a file is exchanged between RAM and the hard disk, as a result of a command from the computer operator.

Swap files, like VM in general, work best when they can be written onto contiguous hard-disk sectors. If you're not sure whether your hard disk has enough contiguous sectors to allow a swap file to be written "in one piece," you can run a defragmentation utility to consolidate the data on the hard disk.

A swap file should only be used when the extra space is required because, like all VM, it will slow down the operation of the PC. Also, a swap file should not be put in a RAM disk. *See also* ACCESS TIME, DEFRAGMENTATION, HARD DISK, RAM DISK, RANDOM-ACCESS MEMORY, STORAGE TIME, *and* SWAP FILE.

Virtual reality

Virtual reality (VR) is the ultimate simulator. The user sees, hears, and perhaps even feels sensations in an artificial realm called a *VR universe.* Hardware and software developers in several countries, particularly the United States and Japan, are actively involved in VR technology.

Virtual reality

Forms of VR. There are three degrees, or types, of VR. They are categorized according to the extent to which you, the operator/witness, participate in the experience.

The first type, *passive VR*, is a "hypermovie" with enhanced graphics and sound. You can watch, listen, and feel the show, but you have no control over what happens. An example of passive VR is a ride in a virtual submarine, a small room with windows through which you can look at a rendition of the undersea world. In the *second type*, *exploratory VR*, you have some control of the contents. You can choose scenes to see, hear, and feel, but you can't fully participate in the experience. An example of exploratory VR is a ride in a tour bus on an alien planet, in which you get to choose the planet. These first two forms are sometimes called *virtual virtual reality (VVR)*.

The third type is *interactive VR*. Interactive VR is what most people imagine when they think of true VR. You have as much control over the virtual environment as you would if you were really there. Your surroundings react directly to your actions. If you reach out and push a virtual object, it moves. If you speak to virtual people, they respond (if they're in the virtual mood).

Software. As you can probably imagine, the program that contains all the particulars for each VR session is complicated and sophisticated. It's called the *simulation manager*. The complexity of the simulation manager depends on the form of VR.

In passive VR, the simulation manager consists of a large number of frames, one representing each moment in time. The frames blend together into a space-time *experience path*. You might think of this, in greatly simplified form, as a set of points strung out along a straight line in one geometric dimension (drawing A). Each point represents data for one instant of time in the VR session. This is similar to the way frames exist in a movie or a videotape.

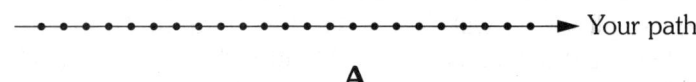

A

The experience path in passive VR.

In exploratory VR, there are several different sets of frames from which you can construct the experience path. Imagine each set of frames as lying along its own individual line, creating the two dimensions shown in drawing B. You choose the line along which you want to "travel." Again, this is a highly simplified rendition; there are far more points in an actual exploratory VR session than are shown here. This is similar to having a selection of movies or videotapes from which to choose.

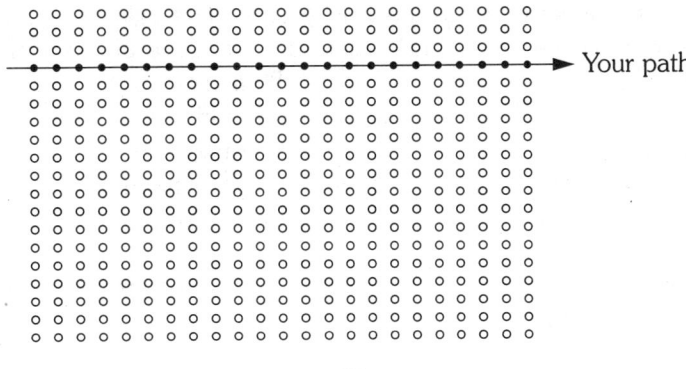

An experience path in exploratory VR.

Interactive VR is "three-dimensional"; the sequence of frames depends on your input from moment to moment, adding another dimension to the programming. Such a three-dimensional space is shown in drawing C. The drawing shows only a few points along one path. Actually, there are billions, trillions, or even quadrillions of points in the interactive *experience space*. The number of possible experience paths is vastly larger than the number of points themselves. It's impossible to make an analogy with movies or videotapes in this case. The software for interactive VR is far more powerful than that in the passive or exploratory types.

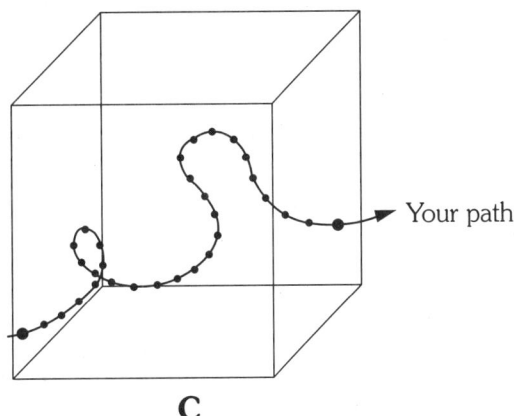

An experience path in interactive VR.

Hardware. Several hardware items, in addition to the programming, are required for VR. For VR to be possible, even in the simplest form, a computer is necessary. The amount of computer power depends on the VR type. Passive VR requires the least computer power, exploratory VR needs more, and interactive VR takes even more. A high-end PC can provide passive and exploratory VR with moderate image resolution and speed, but large minicomputers are necessary for high-resolution, high-speed, vivid interactive VR. The best interactive VR equipment is too expensive for most PC users.

Virtual reality

Video and sound systems are also necessary. The video system can be a simple monitor screen, a big screen, a set of several monitors, or a *head-mounted display (HMD)*. The HMD gives a spectacular show, with binocular vision and sharp colors. Some HMDs completely shut out your view of the real world; others let you see the virtual universe superimposed on the real one. The HMD uses small liquid-crystal display (LCD) screens, whose images are magnified by lenses or reflected by mirrors to obtain the desired effects. Color and high image resolution enhance the effects, but require tremendous memory and processing power.

Stereo, high-fidelity sound is the norm in all VR universes. Loudspeakers can be used for group VR experiences. In an individual system, a set of headphones is included in the HMD. The sound programming is synchronized with the visual programming. In a fully interactive system, this multiplies the complexity of the software, further increasing the required memory and processing power, compared with a visual VR universe alone. Speech synthesis can be used so that virtual people, virtual robots, or virtual space aliens can communicate their virtual thoughts and feelings to the user.

Passive and exploratory systems need only these elements, while interactive systems can also make use of a variety of mechanical input devices. The nature of the device depends on the VR universe. For example, driving a car requires a steering wheel, gas pedal, and brake (at least). Games need a joystick or mouse. Devices called *bats* and *birds* resemble mice, but are movable in three dimensions rather than only two. Levers, handles, treadmills, stationary bicycles, pulley weights, and other devices allow for very real physical activities. For complete hand control, *VR gloves* can be used. These have air bladders built in, providing a sense of touch and physical resistance, so grasped objects seem to have substance and weight. The computer might be equipped with speech recognition so that the user can talk to virtual creatures.

Drawing D is a block diagram showing the hardware for a typical interactive VR system, in which the user gets the impression of riding a bicycle down a street. This can be used for exercise as well as for entertainment. The system provides sights, sounds, and variable pedal resistance as the user negotiates hills and encounters wind.

Applications. Virtual reality has been used as an entertainment and excitement medium. Passive and exploratory VR equipment for large groups of people have already been installed in several theme parks in the United States and Japan. People sit in chairs while they watch and listen to the portrayal of an intergalactic journey, a submarine ride, or a trip through time. The main limitation is that everyone has the same virtual experience.

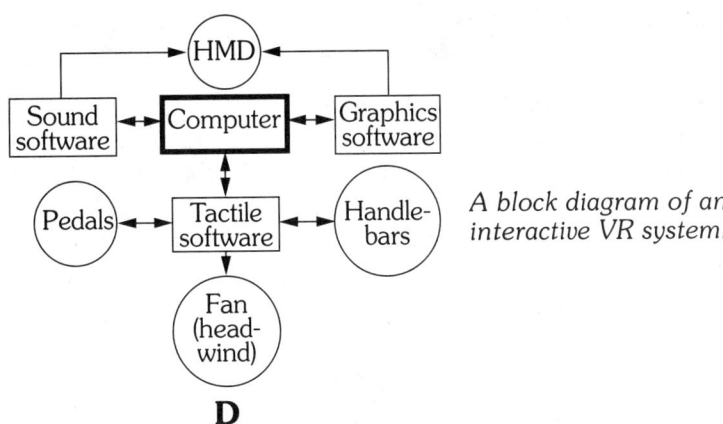

A block diagram of an interactive VR system.

D

Interactive VR intended for individual users is also found in theme parks. Because of the extreme complexity of the equipment, the cost of a single 10-minute VR session is upwards of $10. You might walk on an alien planet inhabited by robots, ride in a moon buggy, or swim with porpoises. The environment reacts to your input from moment to moment. Thus, you might go through the same 10-minute "show" 100 times, and have 100 different VR experiences.

Virtual reality also has practical applications:

➤ *Education* Virtual reality can be used in computer-assisted instruction (CAI). A person might be trained to fly an aircraft, pilot a small submarine, or operate complex and dangerous machinery, without any danger of being injured or killed in training. This form of CAI has been used by the military for some time. It has also been used for training medical personnel, particularly surgeons, who can operate on "virtual patients" while they perfect their skills.

➤ *Hostile environments* In conjunction with robotics, VR facilitates remote control using *teleoperation* and *telepresence*. This allows a human operator to safely operate machines located in dangerous places such as the deep sea, a collapsing mine, or the core of an atomic power-generating plant. People using such a system get illusions similar to those in theme parks, except that a robot, at some distance, is actually following the operator's movements. Teleoperated robots have been used for rescue operations, for disarming bombs, and for maintaining nuclear reactors.

➤ *Warfare* Remotely controlled robot soldiers, tanks, planes, and boats could be used in combat and operated via telepresence. One person could operate a super android with the strength of 100 soldiers and the endurance of a well-engineered machine. Such robots would be immune to deadly radiation and chemicals. They would have no mortal fear, which sometimes

Virtual reality

causes human soldiers to freeze up at critical moments in combat.

> *Exercise* Walking, jogging, riding a bike, skiing, playing golf, and playing handball are examples of virtual activities that can provide most of the benefits of the real experience. The user might not be doing the real thing, but calories will be burned, and aerobic benefits will be realized. There'll be no danger of getting maimed by a car while cycling on a virtual street or breaking a leg while skiing down a virtual mountain. Still, outdoor people will doubtless prefer the real activity to the virtual one, no matter how realistic VR becomes.

> *Escape* Another possible, but not yet widely tested, use for virtual reality is as an escape from boredom and stress in the real world. You might put on an HMD and romp in a jungle with dinosaurs. If the monsters tried to eat you, you could take the helmet off. You could walk on some unknown planet, or under the sea. You might fly high above clouds or tunnel through the center of the earth. You could choose from a great variety of worlds, each available on a medium such as CD-ROM, PCMCIA card, or super-high-density magnetic diskette.

VR and space exploration. The 20th-century American space program climaxed when Apollo 11 landed on the moon and, for the first time, a creature from Earth walked on another world. Some people think the visitor from Earth could have been, and should have been, a robot.

Spacecraft have been remotely controlled for decades. Communications satellites use radio commands to adjust their circuits, and sometimes even to change their orbits. Space probes such as Voyager, which photographed Uranus and Neptune in the late 1980s, are controlled by radio. Satellites and space probes are crude robots. The displays seen by the personnel at NASA were virtual in the sense that they were computer-enhanced, but they were representations of real objects. This is an example of how VR can be used to heighten the senses and extend their range.

Some people say that robots might be used to explore outer space, while people stay safely back on Earth and work the robots via telepresence. Humans could wear control suits and have robots mimic all their movements. Stereoscopic vision, binaural hearing, and a crude sense of touch could be duplicated. Imagine stepping into a gossamer-thin suit, walking into a chamber, and existing, in effect, on the moon or Mars, free of the danger from extreme temperatures or deadly radiation!

One drawback to this is that the distance between any VR-controlled robot and its operator cannot be very great. The control signals can't go faster than the speed of light (186,282 miles per second, or

299,792 kilometers per second). A distance of 186,282 miles (299,792 kilometers) is called a *light second*. The moon, for example, is 1.3 light seconds from the earth. If a robot, rather than Neil Armstrong, had stepped onto the moon on that summer day in 1969, its operator would have had to contend with a delay of 2.6 seconds between command and response. True telepresence is impossible with such a delay. Experts say that the maximum allowable delay is 0.1 second, so the distance between a machine and its controller can't be more than 0.05 light second. That's 9314 miles, a bit more than the diameter of the earth.

Suppose astronauts are in orbit around a planet whose environment is too hostile to allow an in-person visit. An example of such a planet is Venus, whose crushing surface pressures would kill an astronaut clad in even the most advanced pressure suit. A "shuttle robot" might be sent down instead. It would be relatively easy to sustain an orbit of less than 9300 miles above Venus, so telepresence would be feasible. The main problem would be to keep the severe surface conditions from destroying the robot or its telemetry hardware.

Will robots equipped with VR devices make good astronauts? In some situations, maybe. But virtual reality will always lack one quality that's essential for great space missions: a romantic sense of adventure. For some people, "virtual adventure" is simply not good enough.

Problems and limitations. The field of VR is complex, challenging, and difficult from an engineering standpoint. Dreaming up uses and scenarios for VR is one thing; putting them into action at reasonable cost is quite another.

A top-notch, interactive VR system can cost as much as $250,000. While a PC and peripherals, costing about $5000 total, can be used for interactive VR, the image resolution is low and the experience paths are limited. The response is rather sluggish because of the formidable memory-capacity and processing-speed requirements. PCs are becoming more powerful and less expensive all the time, however. RISC (reduced-instruction-set computing) technology holds promise for personal VR. Further refinements in computer architecture can be expected. Various forms of alternative computer technology also offer possibilities in the quest for ever-more-powerful PCs.

PC's memory capacity has also been increasing, roughly doubling every year. The latest efforts towards development of single-electron memory chips raise hopes of PCs rivaling the human brain in terms of data density. Processing speed, too, keeps increasing as clock speeds get faster and data buses get wider. Unfortunately, expectations in VR seem to run ahead of technology, probably because VR has been over-hyped. People expect VR to be "more real than reality itself," with the PC acting as some harmless, virtual drug. Even if that were possible, and even if there were no mental-health risks involved, it would require artificial intelligence (AI) of a near-human level. Most researchers think that won't happen for a long time.

If interactive VR were perfected, people subject to computer addiction might find it so compelling that they would use it as an escape from reality, rather than as an entertainment device. They'll not only want VR; they'll need it. The proponents of VR argue that this does not reflect a problem with VR, any more than PC addiction represents a problem with PCs. The trouble, they say, is in people who are maladjusted to begin with.

On the other hand, some people are downright scared of VR. This is not entirely unreasonable, especially with interactive systems that make use of HMDs. People with cyberphobia might be reluctant to wear an HMD. Some VR illusions are as intense as the hallucinations caused by certain drugs. Another problem results from the *uncanny valley* phenomenon, in which people get apprehensive around smart machines. You can always pull an HMD off if you don't like the show, however. Also, VR doesn't subject the body to chemical changes that cause flashbacks, psychoses, and other problems that have historically plagued users of illicit drugs.

Still, with any advanced technology, there is always a potential for misuse and abuse. Some people fear that VR could be employed to brainwash people, or to otherwise alter their behavior, by subjecting them to illusions over an extended period of time. Those who saw the movie *A Clockwork Orange* can appreciate the horrors that might attend such abuse of VR. Proponents of VR counter such arguments by asking a rhetorical question: Does the fact that technology can be abused mean that we should put a stop to all technological development?

For more information. Virtual reality is frequently discussed in popular PC-oriented magazines. Scientific journals have articles dealing with specifics at the forefront of the technology. A good university engineering library is recommended for in-depth study on this subject.

See also ALTERNATIVE COMPUTER TECHNOLOGY, ARTIFICIAL INTELLIGENCE, COMPANIONSHIP SOFTWARE, COMPUTER ADDICTION, COMPUTER-AIDED DESIGN, COMPUTER-ASSISTED INSTRUCTION, COMPUTER POWER, CYBERPHOBIA, FULL-MOTION VIDEO INTERFACE, IMAGE RESOLUTION, INTERACTIVE TECHNOLOGY, JOYSTICK, LIQUID-CRYSTAL DISPLAY, MOUSE, REDUCED-INSTRUCTION-SET COMPUTING, SIMULATION, SOUND TECHNOLOGY, SPEECH RECOGNITION, SPEECH SYNTHESIS, TELEOPERATION, TELEPRESENCE, ULTIMATE TEACHER PROGRAM, UNCANNY VALLEY, *and* WETWARE.

Virus

A *virus* is a malicious computer program, or a fragment of mischievous programming code, that causes a computer to do strange and unexpected things. A virus can alter or erase the data on a hard disk making the computer less efficient or even inoperative.

How it works. A virus gets into a computer when infected software is downloaded from some other system. A virus is more destructive than a Trojan horse because a virus can reproduce (make copies of itself). It can attach to all kinds of different programs within a computer system. Then, if any of these programs is downloaded into some other computer system, that system will also become infected. It's like a disease epidemic, and this is where the term *virus* comes from.

A computer virus might remain latent for some time before it springs into action, similar to the way a disease virus behaves in the human body. Some command, date, or the execution of some program or part of a program will activate the virus. Even during the latency period, however, the virus can make copies of itself, some or all of which end up on diskettes that have been used with the infected computer.

Virus makers. Virus creators are almost always computer experts. They give various explanations for why they do what they do. Here are four categories into which these people might be grouped:

➤ *Graffiti writers* Some people create viruses simply because they aren't supposed to. They are naughty children who never grew up. These people's viruses don't necessarily harm a computer. They might cause the colors on your screen to change suddenly, or make the machine play a musical tune, or display a message on the screen for a second.

➤ *Mentally ill* These people are bitter and cynical. They suffer from serious mental or emotional disorders. They often appear in cyberspace (online) with usernames taken from science fiction or horror stories. Many come from eastern Europe and underprivileged countries. Their viruses are intended to wreak the greatest possible havoc on the largest possible number of computers. As worldwide computer networks grow, the dangers posed by these people will probably increase.

➤ *Revenge takers* These people often hold good jobs. A "revenge taker" might produce a virus and keep it stored on a diskette at home. In subtle ways, such a person might let the boss know that he or she is not the sort of person it would be wise to lay off or fire. In the event he or she is actually laid off or fired, the virus can be uploaded or otherwise installed in the company computer, resulting in costly loss of data.

➤ *Whiz kids* Computer "whiz kids" might decide to write viruses just to see if it can be done and to witness the results. This is a more or less innocent motive, but the consequences can be demoralizing. Because most new computers now have modems and software for online services installed, there is some danger

Virus

that viruses written by curious kids might get into cyberspace and cause widespread problems.

Protecting against infection. You can buy programs called *antivirus programs* or *vaccines* that search for viruses. If one is found, the program will erase the virus. To completely get rid of the virus, the vaccine must be run through the data on every diskette that you use with the system. You must avoid using any of the infected diskettes, and make new ones to replace them. But this is hard because you might not know which diskettes are infected! Obviously, a vaccine must be used before the damage is so severe that a computer won't work anymore.

The best protection against viruses is to avoid "infections" in the first place. Here are some precautions you can take:

- Be wary of mail-order software; the seller must guarantee that the software is free of viruses.

- Don't download software unless you have acquaintances who have used it recently and are having no symptoms of infection in their computers.

- Never use software that has been, or that you suspect might have been, transferred illegally. (This is called *pirate software*.)

- Never download software onto a hard disk. Put it on diskettes instead, and keep it off the hard disk.

- Buy a vaccine, and use it without fail to check all new software before the first use.

The National Computer Security Association (NCSA) and 3M Corporation publish a booklet called "How to Avoid Computer Viruses." It is available from NCSA at the following address:

National Computer Security Association
10 Courthouse Avenue
Carlisle, PA 17013

Cyber wars and plagues. In artificial intelligence (AI), a virus would have the effect of doing "progressive brain damage": the machine would get stupider and stupider until it was a complete idiot compared to its former self. Or a lunatic. The possibilities are as bizarre, funny, and horrible as you care to imagine.

As computers become more important in societies, the potential danger posed by viruses gets greater and greater. Imagine a virus that could slowly infect an AI system in charge of Wall Street! There might be a strange bull market, during which everyone would be happy (except the doomsayers, who are always miserable). Then, one morning, we would awaken to the Big Crash. It might be months before the cause was determined. Maybe nobody would ever know what set the catastrophe in motion. Conceivably, it could be brought about by some 13-year-old precocious hacker, sitting in a basement with a computer—a lonely, frustrated genius just looking for some way to have fun.

Viruses have the potential to alter credit reports. A virus might create criminal records for people who have never had so much as a traffic ticket. Then, when such a person ran a red light, he or she could end up in jail. Companies might engage in vicious games of computer sabotage. Election returns could be falsified. At its worst, a virus could cause a computerized defense system to think its parent nation was under attack by nuclear missiles.

Perhaps someday, if humanity gets too dependent on computers and AI, a virus will cause a great tragedy. If this happens, however, it will have at least one good result: It will make people see that they have given machines too much power. People might decide it is time to put human intelligence first again, and to demote machine intelligence to a subordinate role. *See also* ARTIFICIAL INTELLIGENCE, COLOSSUS, HACKER, NEUROTIC COMPUTER BEHAVIOR, PSYCHOTIC COMPUTER BEHAVIOR, TROJAN HORSE, *and* VACCINE.

Vision systems

One of the most advanced specialties in computer science and artificial intelligence (AI) is the field of *vision systems*, also called *machine vision*. There are several different types. The best method of machine vision depends on the application.

Components. A visible-light vision system must have a device for receiving incoming images. This is usually a vidicon camera tube or a charge-coupled device. In bright light, an image orthicon can be used.

The camera produces an analog video signal. For best machine vision, this must be processed into digital form by analog-to-digital conversion. The digital signal is then clarified by digital signal processing. The resulting data goes to the computer or robot controller. The drawing is a block diagram of this scheme.

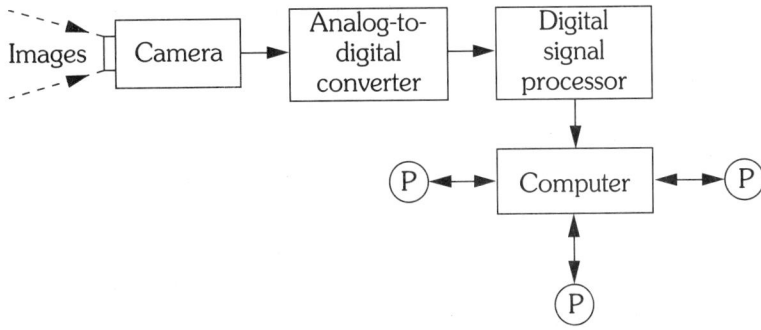

Components of a visible-light vision system. (Circles labeled P are peripherals.)

Vision systems

The moving image received from the camera and processed by the circuitry contains an enormous amount of information. It's easy to present a PC with a detailed moving image. Getting the machine to "know" what's happening is a more complex affair. Processing an image, and extracting meaning from it, is the great challenge for vision-system engineers of the future.

Vision and AI. There are subtle things about an image that a machine will not notice unless it has an extremely advanced level of AI. How, for example, is a robot to know whether an object presents a threat? Is that four-legged thing a dog or a tiger? How is a machine to know the intentions of an object, if it has any? Is that biped object a human being or a mannequin? Why is it carrying a stick? You know right away if a person is carrying a jack to help you fix a flat tire, or if the person is clutching a tire iron with which to smash your windshield. It would be important for a police robot or a security robot to know what constitutes a threat, and what does not.

The variables in an image are much like those in a human voice. A vision system, to get the full meaning of an image, must be at least as sophisticated as a speech recognition system. Technology has not even begun to reach the level of AI needed for human-like machine vision and image processing.

Sensitivity and resolution. Two important specifications in any vision system are the *sensitivity* and the *resolution*.

Sensitivity is the ability of a machine to see in dim light, or to detect weak impulses at invisible wavelengths. In some environments, high sensitivity is necessary. In others, it is not needed and might not be wanted. A machine that works in bright sunlight doesn't need to be able to see well in a dark cave. A robot designed for working in mines, pipes, or caverns must be able to see in dim light, using a system that might be blinded by ordinary daylight.

Resolution is the extent to which a machine can differentiate between objects. The better the resolution, the keener the vision. Human eyes have excellent resolution, but machines can be designed with greater resolution. In general, the better the resolution, the more confined the field of vision must be. To understand why this is true, think of a telescope. The higher the magnification, the better the resolution (up to a certain point). However, increasing the magnification reduces the angle, or field, of vision. Zeroing in on one object or area is done at the expense of other objects or areas.

Sensitivity and resolution depend somewhat on each other. Usually, better sensitivity means a sacrifice in resolution. Also, the better the resolution, the less well the vision system will function in dim light.

"Invisible" and passive systems. Machines have a big advantage over people when it comes to vision. Machines can see at wavelengths to which humans are blind.

Human eyes are sensitive to electromagnetic energy whose wavelength ranges from about 390 to 750 nanometers (nm). The nanometer is a billionth (10^{-9}) of a meter. The longest visible wavelengths look red; as the wavelength gets shorter, the color changes through orange, yellow, green, blue, and indigo. The shortest waves look violet. Energy at wavelengths somewhat longer than 750 nm is called *infrared* (*IR*); energy at wavelengths somewhat shorter than 390 nm is *ultraviolet* (*UV*).

Machines need not, and often don't, see in the range of wavelengths to which human eyes respond. Insects can see UV that we can't, while being blind to red and orange light that we can see. A robot might be designed to see IR and UV, as well as, or instead of, visible light. Video cameras can be sensitive to a range of wavelengths much wider than the range we see.

Machines can be made to see in an environment that is dark and cold, and that radiates too little energy to be detected at any electromagnetic wavelength. In such a case, the machine provides its own illumination. This can be a simple lamp, a laser, an IR device, or a UV device. Alternatively, the machine might emanate radio waves and detect the echoes; this is *radar*. Some robots can navigate via acoustic (sound) echoes, like bats; this is *sonar*.

For further information. The technology of machine vision is rapidly advancing. Comprehensive information can be found in a good college or university library. The best libraries are in the engineering departments at large universities. Ask the librarian for recent articles in professional engineering journals, particularly in the subject area of robotics.

See also ANALOG, ANALOG-TO-DIGITAL CONVERSION, BIN-PICKING PROBLEM, BLACKBOARD SYSTEM, CHARGE-COUPLED DEVICE, COMMONSENSE SUMMER PROJECT, COMPOSITE VIDEO SIGNAL, COMPUTER MAP, DIGITAL, DIGITAL SIGNAL PROCESSING, DIGITAL-TO-ANALOG CONVERSION, IMAGE ORTHICON, IMAGE RESOLUTION, OBJECT RECOGNITION, OPTICAL CHARACTER RECOGNITION, PERSONAL ROBOTS, REMOTE CONTROL SYSTEMS, RESOLUTION, TELEOPERATION, TELEPRESENCE, VIDICON, *and* VIRTUAL REALITY.

Voice recognition

See SPEECH RECOGNITION.

Voice synthesis

See SPEECH SYNTHESIS.

Voice-mail system

Almost everyone has dealt with a *voice-mail system (VMS)*. The simplest VMSs are common telephone answering machines. You prerecord a greeting, and callers leave messages on cassette tapes. Computerized VMSs are much more sophisticated.

Features. When a VMS is used with a computer, the machine can take the place of one or more human operators. This makes computerized VMSs ideal for large businesses. Here are a few things a computerized VMS can do:

➤ *Tone actuation* Suppose you call the toll-free ordering number for TAB/McGraw-Hill. You'll hear a voice recording that instructs you to press various telephone keypad buttons to make choices. This is one way in which a computerized VMS can route incoming calls. A tone-dial telephone set is necessary to make the selections.

➤ *Digitization* A computerized VMS can take voice messages, just as a conventional answering machine does, but instead of recording the analog voice directly onto a tape cassette, the message undergoes analog-to-digital conversion and is stored on a hard disk as digital ones and zeros. This consumes considerable hard-disk space.

➤ *Fax and data* Facsimile messages and computer data can be left at a computerized VMS. The only constraint is imposed by the capacity of the PC's hard disk. Complex graphic images use up disk storage in a hurry, as do voice messages that have been converted into digital data. A picture is indeed equivalent to thousands of words.

➤ *Message/fax forwarding* It's easy to retrieve messages and faxes that have been left for you, no matter where you are. You simply call the VMS and follow its instructions for retrieving voice mail or data. You'll need a modem and a PC at your remote location if you want to look at faxes or text messages. These can then be stored on the remote PC's hard disk.

➤ *Electronic mail* You can send and receive e-mail messages with a computerized VMS. In effect, this makes the PC into a network node, bulletin board, and mailbox combined. E-mail text takes up far less space on a hard disk than voices or graphics; this is its chief advantage.

➤ *Exotic features* Some VMSs have speech recognition and synthesis, allowing callers to talk with the computer. Some systems allow the transfer of animated data. These features consume huge amounts of storage space, and they require high processing power. VMSs of this caliber are used only in big corporations and government agencies.

Requirements. The following components are needed for a complete VMS. The block diagram shows how the hardware items are interconnected in a typical merchandise-ordering VMS:

➤ *Computer* The PC must have at least the equivalent of an Intel 80286 microprocessor; some VMSs require a 386 or 486. The hard disk should have at least 40MB (megabytes) of free space; 200MB is better. The most advanced VMSs need a minicomputer or mainframe with thousands of megabytes of disk space.

➤ *Telephone* You'll need at least one telephone set so you can handle real-time calls. There should be a modular jack installed at the point where the sets and the PC go into the telephone line. Most VMSs work in the background, so you can use the PC for other applications while it handles messages.

➤ *Software* Several VMS packages are available, ranging in price from less than $100 to upwards of $1000, depending on the complexity of the system. Always read the brochures before purchasing VMS software, so you know if the program is compatible with your PC.

➤ *VMS board* An expansion board, which fits in a slot inside the PC main unit, is needed to provide the interface between the telephone line, the computer, and the software. Be sure your PC has an expansion slot available for this purpose.

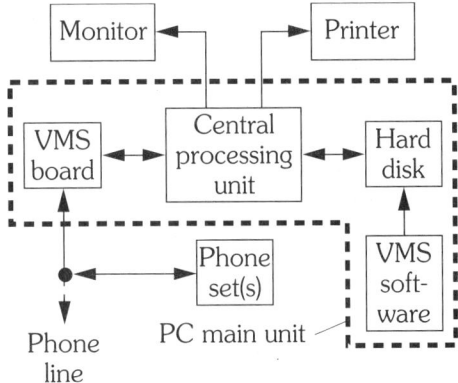

A block diagram of a typical VMS for taking orders via telephone.

Do you need a VMS? Individuals rarely need the enhanced features of a computerized VMS; simple answering machines are sufficient for the average household. The same is true for many small companies. The benefits of a VMS are realized in medium-sized and large businesses that have many employees, or that receive many incoming calls.

Volatile memory

Here's a brief test that you can use to decide whether or not a computerized VMS is worth considering for your business:

1 Are there 10 or more employees?

2 Do employees often leave memos for each other?

3 Do you need two or more order lines to handle the customer demand load?

4 Do you take orders for more than eight hours a day?

5 Will your customers tolerate a machine?

This is by no means an absolute standard, but if your company meets most of these criteria, you might want to start shopping around. (You can also check the options with your local telephone company.) The last question is perhaps the most important. Some customers deal with machines better than others. Young people will put up with more automation than will older people. If your business caters mainly to senior citizens, you might want to use human order-takers, no matter how large your business gets.

Human operators should always be available to help customers, regardless of their age, with special questions and problems. Callers should be able to easily manipulate the VMS to get in touch with a human being, especially in the service or warranty department. *See also* BULLETIN-BOARD SYSTEM, ELECTRONIC MAIL, FAX, MODEM, ONLINE SERVICE, REMOTE-CONTROL SYSTEMS, SPEECH RECOGNITION, *and* SPEECH SYNTHESIS.

Volatile memory

The contents of a computer's RAM (random-access memory) change almost constantly and immediately. For example, as you type a report or use a mouse to draw things on your monitor, the characters or lines appear as soon as the key is struck or the mouse is moved. The big asset of RAM is its immediacy. It's fast, and it's right there with you as you work. But there's a downside: If the computer loses power, even for a moment, all the data in RAM will disappear.

If you've written a novel entirely in RAM and haven't saved it elsewhere (such as on your hard disk), you can lose weeks of work in a heartbeat. RAM is called *volatile memory* because it can easily "evaporate."

You can minimize the danger of massive data loss by frequently saving the RAM contents on disk. This take some conscious effort, but it's an essential habit. You can also get a utility to automatically back up the data in RAM every few minutes, so you don't have to remember to do it. If you're the type of person who always learns things the hard way, perhaps you should consider buying such a utility.

In contrast to volatile memory, *nonvolatile memory* is immune to power interruptions. All magnetic disks and tapes are nonvolatile. ROM (read-only memory) is also nonvolatile. Disks are slow, however, and the contents of ROM can only be changed by going through a rather complex process. With data, you must pay a price for permanence.

There are alternatives to periodically saving RAM data on disk. Fast-access, nonvolatile memory can be facilitated by PCMCIA standard adapter cards. These "best-of-all-worlds" devices offer most of the advantages of RAM, diskettes, and hard disks, while doing away with most of their drawbacks. An increasing number of new PCs, especially laptop models, are being manufactured with PCMCIA card capability as a standard feature. Another option is to obtain an uninterruptible power supply (UPS). Even if you use a UPS, however, it's a good idea to back up data on the hard disk fairly often. *See also* ACCESS TIME, BACKUP, BACKUP UTILITY, MAGNETIC MEDIA, NONVOLATILE MEMORY, PCMCIA STANDARD ADAPTER CARDS, RANDOM-ACCESS MEMORY, READ-ONLY MEMORY, *and* UNINTERRUPTIBLE POWER SUPPLY.

Volume graph

A *volume graph* is a pictorial method of depicting large ratios or fractions. Such graphs are sometimes created with analytical graphics or presentation graphics software.

Three dimensions. A volume graph requires the computer to display an illusion of three dimensions (3-D). This can be done via perspective effects, shading, and other techniques familiar to artists and draftspeople. Most volume graphs show cubes that appear to sit inside one another, each with a common corner, as shown in the drawing. Some volume graphs use spheres, rectangular prisms, or other 3-D objects.

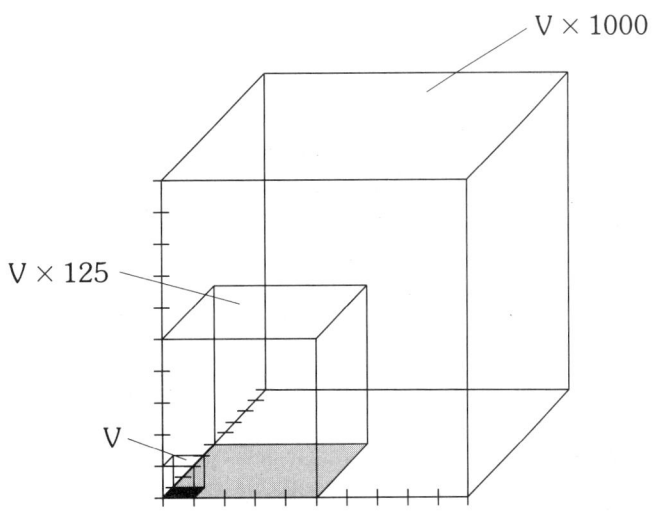

A volume graph is a method of illustrating large ratios.

Volume label

In 3-D, the *volume* is the displacement or space that an object takes up. The volume of a cube increases according to the third power of the length of any edge. (This is why the third power of a number or variable is often called the cube.) If the length of an edge doubles, the volume of the cube increases by a factor of 2^3 (eight). If the length of an edge goes up by a factor of five, the volume becomes 5^3, or 125 times as great; if the edge becomes 10 times as long, the volume increases by a factor of 10^3, or 1000.

In the drawing, cubes are shown with volumes of one, 125, and 1000 units. This depicts the ratios 1:125 and 1:1000 clearly within a linear range of 10 units. The cube edges measure one, five, and 10 units, respectively.

Assets and limitations. The main asset of volume graphs is their ability to show large ratios in a reasonable display area. When computers are used to create volume graphs, the software can let you rotate and tumble the whole display, so you can get the clearest possible impression of the relative volumes.

The biggest problem with volume graphs is that they aren't precise. It's hard to gauge an exact ratio just by looking at the display. Volume graphs are deceptive because the volume of a 3-D object "blows up" much faster than length or diameter. Viewers must be told, numerically, the displayed ratios; the ratios are not intuitively apparent from the graph alone.

In this encyclopedia, volume graphs are used in several articles to illustrate large ratios. *See* GIGABYTE, PETABYTE, *and* TERABYTE. *See also* ANALYTICAL GRAPHICS *and* PRESENTATION GRAPHICS.

Volume label

When you format a diskette, you'll probably want to give it a name. This name is called a *volume label*. It's the equivalent of a filename, except that a volume label refers to the whole diskette, rather than to only one file on it.

To give a diskette a volume label while formatting, wait for the computer to ask for it. In DOS and Windows, you can enter up to eight characters. You can also include a volume-label extension by typing a period, and then up to three more characters. Extensions are optional. If you don't want to give the diskette a name, press the Enter key when the computer requests the volume label.

Some PC users never assign volume labels to diskettes, while others always do it. A volume label can help you keep track of things when backing up data in a directory or subdirectory whose size does not exceed the capacity of a diskette. Suppose, for example, that you have data in directories called HOUSE, CAR, JOB, and TRAVEL. You can give the backup diskettes volume labels that correspond. If the data in a directory exceeds the capacity of a diskette, you can use multiple diskettes, giving them volume labels such as HOUSE.1, HOUSE.2, CAR.1, CAR.2, and CAR.3. *See also* DIRECTORY, DISKETTE, FILENAME, *and* FILENAME EXTENSION.

Von Neumann bottleneck

The *von Neumann bottleneck* is a fundamental limitation of computers that process data one bit at a time. Such computers are said to be built according to the *von Neumann architecture*, named after the scientist who first described, in detail, how a digital computer could work. When data passes through a machine one bit at a time, the computer is said to use *serial* processing.

There are several ways to measure computer power. One of the best indicators is the number of instructions per second (IPS). Modern computers can work in millions of IPS, called *megainstructions per second (MIPS)*, or billions of IPS, called *gigainstructions per second (GIPS)*. It's no longer very far-fetched to imagine machines functioning in trillions of IPS, or *terainstructions per second (TIPS)*. But no matter how many instructions a computer can do in one second, that number can be doubled simply by doubling the number of bits that the machine processes at a time.

When data passes through a machine more than one bit at a time, the computer uses *parallel* processing. This is one way to get around the von Neumann bottleneck. The larger the word size, the faster the computer can work, and the more powerful it can be.

Another way to beat the von Neumann bottleneck is to overcome it via brute force. This is done by increasing the clock speed of the microprocessor chip. The clock sets the tempo at which the whole computer works. *See also* CLOCK SPEED, COMPUTER POWER, INSTRUCTIONS PER SECOND, PARALLEL, SERIAL, *and* WORD SIZE.

1138

Warm boot

A *warm boot* is a method of resetting a computer without switching it off. It's sometimes called a *reboot*. (The expression *boot* is short for *bootstrap program*, a set-up routine that computers run to prepare themselves for work.)

A warm boot is usually necessary in the event of a crash, or freeze-up. When a PC crashes, it becomes unresponsive to input. Whatever you type on the keyboard, and whatever you do with the mouse, the machine simply ignores you.

For PC users who aren't aware that crashes can and do happen, the first experience with this phenomenon is horrifying. It seems as if the computer has broken down. Some people call toll-free technical help numbers. Others look through instruction manuals and/or computer reference books such as this encyclopedia, hoping to learn that the problem is minor, and that it can be easily solved (which is true of most crashes). A few PC users pack their machines up and send them back to the manufacturer for repair, unnecessarily losing days or weeks of PC use.

The easiest way to reboot an IBM-compatible PC is to press the keyboard keys Ctrl-Alt-Del simultaneously. The machine might ask some questions during the reboot process. You'll lose the contents of RAM (random-access memory), but in a system crash you have no choice. A more forceful rebooting tactic is to press the Reset button (if your machine has one).

Usually, a warm boot is sufficient to reset a computer. If this doesn't do it, you can shut the machine off, wait a couple of minutes, and then switch it back on again. This is called a *cold boot*, and should be used only if a warm boot does not work.

If there's a power failure during a work session, shut the PC off immediately. Then, if the power returns after only a few seconds, it won't kick your hard drive back into action before it has had time to wind down. *See also* BOOTSTRAP PROGRAM *and* COLD BOOT.

Weizenbaum, Joseph

Joseph Weizenbaum is a futurist and computer scientist. He has expressed a belief that artificial intelligence (AI), no matter how advanced it gets, will probably never include true human-like emotion. He is not alone in this philosophy.

Technocentrism. Weizenbaum has warned that society might become so dependent on computers that the collective mindset will change, not necessarily for the better. Since the publication of his book, *Computer Power and Human Reason*, our society has evolved in some of the ways Weizenbaum described.

Are we letting computers control us, instead of vice versa? Who hasn't been in a store, bank, post office, or other place where computers are used, and been told to wait or come back later because the computer was down? Are computers making people less human? This effect, which has been well documented, is called *technocentrism*.

Some people get so technocentric that they lead unbalanced lives. Perhaps the same thing can happen to a whole society. Some experts suggest this is now taking place in so-called advanced nations.

Who, or what, is in charge? A computer takes data, processes it, and returns it to the operators in altered form. Does the computer introduce anything new? This is a subject for debate. Some scientists say no because you never get something for nothing. Others say that maybe, if a machine gets smart enough, it might have original thoughts.

Joseph Weizenbaum wrote that if machines ever come up with original ideas, these ideas will probably be alien to human minds. He argued that the differences between machines and humans run deeper than the material. Humans were created by processes extending billions of years into the past, but computers have existed for only a few decades. Computers also differ from humans in a more subtle, but perhaps more significant, way. Humans, and all other life forms on this planet, are direct products of nature. But computers are built by human beings, and in this sense they are indirect products of nature. Because of these differences between humans and computers, we should not be surprised if AI evolves in strange and unanticipated ways.

Computers can be fun, and people can get fond of them. Sometimes computers seem to have their own living minds. When you work with PCs and related devices, no matter how powerful or fascinating they are, remember that you're in charge of them, not vice versa. *See also* ANIMISM, ANTHROPOMORPHISM, ARTIFICIAL INTELLIGENCE, COMPUTER CONSCIOUSNESS, KNOWLEDGE, MACHINE KNOWLEDGE, TURING TEST, *and* UNCANNY VALLEY.

Well-structured language

A *well-structured language* is an advanced form of high-level computer language. These languages are used in object-oriented programming, artificial intelligence (AI), and robot controllers.

Assets. The main advantage of a well-structured language is that it helps a person write efficient, logical programs. Well-structured software can be changed easily. It often uses *modules*, or programs within programs. Modules are rearranged and substituted for one another as necessary for various applications. Well-structured programs also lend themselves to easy debugging because flaws tend to stand out clearly.

In most high-level languages, a computer program can be written in many different ways. Some schemes are more efficient than others. The relative efficiency of different versions of a program can be determined according to two criteria: the size of the program (in kilobytes or megabytes) and the amount of computer time needed to run the program. These factors are closely correlated. An efficient program almost always needs less memory and runs faster than an inefficient one. If you can reduce the amount of memory that a program consumes, the computer can access the data in less time, so it can solve more problems in a given length of time.

Two forms. Program structuring can take either of two forms, which might be called "top-down" and "bottom-up."

In the top-down approach, the computer user looks at the whole scenario, and zeros in on various parts, depending on the nature of the problem to be solved. A good example of this is the use of a network to find information about building codes in Dade County, Florida. You might start with a topic such as "state laws." There would almost certainly be a directory for that topic that would guide you to something more specific, and maybe even to the exact department you want. The programmer who wrote the software would have used a well-structured language to ensure that users would have an easy time finding data.

In the bottom-up approach, you start with little pieces and build up to the whole. A good analogy is a course in mathematical analysis. The first thing to do is learn the basics of algebra, analytical geometry, coordinate systems, and functions. Then, you learn to use these things together to differentiate, integrate, and solve other complex problems. In a computerized math course, the software would be written in a well-structured language so you (the student) wouldn't waste time running into dead ends.

See also ARTIFICIAL INTELLIGENCE, HIGH-LEVEL LANGUAGE, OBJECT-ORIENTED PROGRAMMING, PROGRAMMING, SMALLTALK, *and* SOFTWARE.

Wetware

Wetware is an expression for the linking of computers with the human brain. The term was originally coined by science-fiction writers, but wetware is on its way to becoming a reality.

Brain waves. The concept behind wetware is simple: connect a computer to an electroencephalograph (EEG), which picks up, amplifies, and displays brain waves. Then, try to get the computer to respond in a controlled manner to variations in these waves. The challenge is putting this idea into action. Despite several major obstacles, researchers have managed to achieve some success.

Medical people have known for decades that certain mental and physical states are accompanied by brain waves having various frequencies and shapes. The table lists some of the commonly recognized brain wave types, their usual frequency ranges in hertz (cycles per second), and the mind and body conditions they accompany. The signals from the brain of a sleeping person are vastly different from those in a wide-awake person. Muscular movement is attended by unique frequencies and waveforms. Anger, fright, and contentment each have their own characteristic "signatures." Even if the frequency remains constant, the wave shapes and the attendant mental states or functions can differ.

Even if a computer can't infer the operator's intentions directly, it can be programmed to recognize waveforms and frequencies.

Types of brain waves

Term	Frequency range	Functions or indications
Alpha waves	8 to 13 Hz	Awake, alert, relaxed
Mu waves	8 to 13 Hz	Nerve and muscle activity (Feeling and movement)
Beta waves	13 to 30 Hz	Intense mental concentration
Delta waves	0.5 to 5 Hz	Deep sleep
Theta waves	4 to 7 Hz	Light sleep with dreams

Suppose a PC were programmed to act on beta waves, which take place when you are putting forth a lot of mental effort. Then, by focusing your thoughts on some difficult problem, you could cause the PC to carry out some function, such as switching on a lamp. This has been done under controlled conditions.

The block diagram shows the components of a mind-actuated computer system, complete with peripherals. By adjusting your mood, you might send the contents of a file via modem to a bulletin-board system. By changing your train of thought, you could cause the PC to print a document or get a robot to mow your lawn.

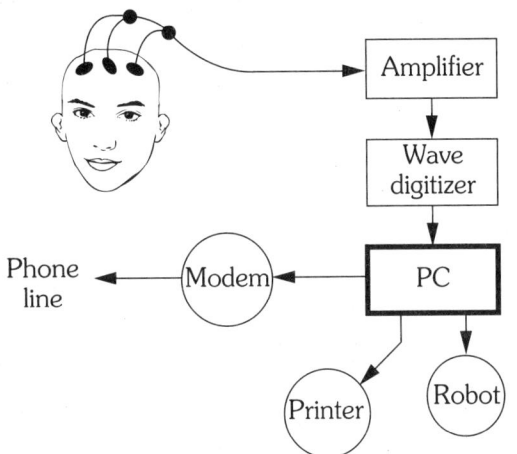

A simplified diagram of a thought-controlled PC and peripherals.

Some researchers have suggested that wetware systems might learn to adapt to human users' brain-wave patterns. The neural network is one form of alternative computer technology that holds promise in this field.

Applications. Of what use is mental control of computers and peripheral hardware? Here are some ideas that have been suggested. Some of them seem bizarre by today's standards, but technology can turn the ridiculous into the routine:

➢ *Prosthesis control* The most promising, and arguably the most compelling, use for wetware is in the control of prostheses, or artificial limbs. Imagine being able to walk with artificial legs, simply by thinking about it in the back of the mind, as is the case with biological legs! It would be necessary to learn a new way of giving mental commands, but the human mind is astonishingly good at adapting itself to challenges of this sort. It might also be possible to use wetware to control electronic nerve and muscle stimulators, so that people with paralyzed limbs could use them again.

➢ *Machine control* Imagine what could be done if complex mechanical equipment could be operated by "cyber telepathy."

An army general could sit in a quiet, dark room, eyes fixed on a monitor screen, watching the movements of robot soldiers, tanks, ships, or planes in distant combat zones. The enemy would be another general, in some distant darkened chamber, watching a different screen portraying the same theaters of battle. The winner would be the general with the better hardware, wetware, and software. Such a "virtual war" would be an improvement over the way wars have historically been waged. Eventually, the generals might decide to eliminate the military hardware (robots, tanks, ships, and planes) altogether.

➢ *Sensation*   Instead of having one's thoughts control the movements of muscles, artificial limbs and machines, suppose that signals could be processed and sent into the brain? A pair of camera tubes might become a set of eyes; a pair of microphones could become a set of ears. Tactile sensors could allow a person to feel heat, cold, texture, and pressure. The data would be sent to electrodes on the scalp or implanted in the brain or spinal cord. Such technology could not only be of use to handicapped people, but might be employed for enhanced *telepresence*, in which robots take the place of human beings in dangerous or inaccessible places.

➢ *Artistic expression*   Some musicians have expressed interest in the idea of converting brain waves into sound. This has been tried using computers and electronic music synthesizers, with mixed results. Mind-controlled paint and draw programs could be employed to generate "brain-wave art." It has been suggested that a mind-reading computer could help authors put their thoughts into words. This level of wetware appears unlikely to be reached for at least several decades.

➢ *Games*   This is probably the most interesting application for wetware at the present time. There's no risk, and the technology already exists. You might compete with friends to see who can achieve the finest degree of control over an animated display, such as an aircraft landing or a cartoon character's movements. The "virtual war" example could be adapted to personal computer games, changing the scenario from combat to baseball, football, basketball, or almost any other competitive sport.

Problems. Wetware has aroused ethical questions and concerns. There are also some logistic hurdles to be overcome if the technology is to realize its potential.

Imagine having a PC that could interpret your moods. If you were angry, it could have your home intercom pipe relaxing music all over the house. If you were depressed, it could tune to a comedy show on television. Many mundane chores could be done by computer-controlled machines and robots, without your having to move a muscle. But is all this really necessary? Is it that difficult to manually tune a radio to a relaxing music station or a television to a sitcom? It's easy enough to click a mouse and get a PC to send a file via modem or print it out. It seems silly to go to the trouble of hooking one's body to electrodes, and then to strain one's brain, when the touch of a finger will do the job as well or better.

If wetware actually reaches the level of near-perfect precision, it will be necessary for the operator to maintain rigorous control over his or her thoughts. The idea might flash into the operator's mind, "Robot, go over to the window and kick the glass out." Human beings often have passing thoughts like that, and they can be nearly impossible to control. Wetware-operated machines would place a tremendous burden of mental discipline upon people. This challenge might prove too great; many PC users would probably forgo wetware rather than cope with it.

Wetware in its present state cannot read a person's mind; it can only identify certain brain wave frequencies and shapes. However, given time, the technology might evolve to the point that mind-reading becomes a reality. This would make wetware a formidable tool for both good and evil purposes. A "cyber psychic" could be invaluable in a court of law, but it could just as easily be used for coercion, brainwashing, and perhaps even mass thought policing. What would happen if a Trojan horse or virus were to get into such a computer?

For further information. Good information on wetware is not easy to find. There's plenty of hype, but hard factual data is sparse. The best place to research this subject is a university library. Consult professional journals. There are some people online who are interested in this subject, but one must beware of "false prophets." *See also* ALTERNATIVE COMPUTER TECHNOLOGY, ARTIFICIAL INTELLIGENCE, NEURAL NETWORK, PERSONAL ROBOTS, TELEOPERATION, TELEPRESENCE, *and* VIRTUAL REALITY.

What-if analysis

What-if analysis is a method of using spreadsheet software to predict or extrapolate events. It helps people and businesses work out financial strategies. It can tell you how your financial landscape will be affected if there are changes in your income, expenses, or taxes.

For individuals, what-if analysis is useful for budgeting, especially when it comes to paying off mortgages, credit card balances, and other loans in which interest is charged. In long-term loans, the total interest can amount to more than the principal (the cost if you were to pay all at once). The longer the loan payments are stretched out, the greater is the total interest payment compared with the principal.

Determining the amount of interest on a loan is a complicated and tedious process if done without the help of a computer because of the complex way in which interest adds up over time, and also because of the schemes used by lending institutions to extract every penny from you that the law allows. With a spreadsheet, you can simply plug in numbers, and the computer does all the work.

Suppose you're buying a new home for $200,000. You can save an astonishing amount of money if you get a 15-year mortgage rather than a 30-year mortgage, but you can only save that money if you can afford somewhat higher monthly payments. Can you afford them? What-if analysis can help you decide, based on all the factors that might come into play, including the possibility that if you take the 15-year mortgage, you might talk the seller into lowering the price to $185,000.

A mortgage might be available for 9.5% from one bank and 9.3% from another, with down payments of $15,000 and $20,000, respectively. The mortgage you choose will affect how much money you have left in the bank, and therefore how much interest it will earn. It will also affect your income tax. It might even influence your ability to pay off other loans, each with its own rate of interest. Before there were PCs and spreadsheet software, finding the optimum scheme in such situations involved either sheer guesswork or the hiring of an accountant. Some spreadsheets even offer financial tips or advice. *See also* SPREADSHEET.

What you see is what you get

See WYSIWYG.

Wide area information system

See INTERNET.

Wide area network

A *wide area network (WAN)* is a group of computers that are all linked together, but are separated by long distances. The interconnections are made via the telephone lines or radio, or both. Because the individual workstations (nodes) can be thousands of miles apart, the link delays are significant in terms of computer speed.

When radio is used for a WAN, satellites are the preferred mode, although conventional radio or microwave links can be employed. Amateur radio operators have set up specialized WANs that use packet communications for long-distance computer communication via radio. This is known as *packet radio*.

The biggest advantage of a WAN over a single PC is that it gives each workstation access to the data in all the computers in the network. A WAN can encompass hundreds, or even thousands, of individual computers. In effect, the files and programs of all the computers join forces, resulting in a system with enormous data storage capacity.

Suppose a WAN has 1000 computers, with an average of 1GB (gigabyte) of available space on each hard disk. Then in theory, the WAN has one terabyte (1000 gigabytes) of available storage. In practice, however, the power of the WAN is not equivalent to that of a single, gigantic supercomputer with a 1TB hard disk because there are delays in data transfer among the nodes of the WAN. The delays occur because the data takes time to propagate through space, cables, or optical fibers from node to node, and also because the computers each take some time to process data. This limits the speed at which the computers can function together. While storage capacity adds up arithmetically among the computers in a WAN, processing power does not.

A common type of WAN in personal computing is an *online service* such as America Online, Delphi, CompuServe, and Prodigy. The largest WAN for personal computing today is the Internet. It can be accessed through commercial online services, and also through local business, government, and educational network servers.

In businesses, teleconferencing is a useful and popular way of connecting computers together in a WAN. The drawing depicts a simple WAN that makes use of telephone lines and satellite radio links to bring six PCs together, even though the machines are located on three different continents. *See also* INFORMATION SUPERHIGHWAY, INTERNET, LOCAL AREA NETWORK, ONLINE SERVICE, PACKET COMMUNICATIONS, *and* TELECONFERENCING.

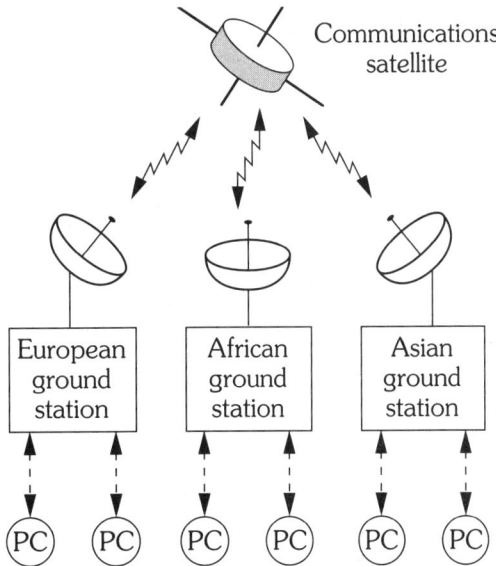

Zigzag lines represent radio signals; dotted lines represent telephone links.

Wildcard

A *wildcard* is a symbol that can stand for an arbitrary character or string of characters. Generally, the question mark (?) is used to represent a single character. An asterisk (*) can stand for a string of one or more characters.

Text searching. Suppose you want to search a document file for words having the suffix *ism*. You could tell the computer to look for the following character string containing an asterisk wildcard:

*ism

The cursor would then stop at any word containing the letters *ism*, such as *capitalism* or *socialism*. The cursor would also stop at the word *prism* if it appeared. It would stop at *charismatic*, too. These, of course, are not instances of the suffix *ism*. You could either tolerate these distractions, or conduct individual searches for strings such as these:

*ism,
*ism.
*ism;
*ism:
*ism!
*ism_

The underline symbol (_) represents a space here; in the actual search you would press the space bar.

Filenames. Wildcards can be used in filenames. This is especially useful when you want to copy a set of files, say from your hard disk onto a diskette.

The asterisk wildcard came in handy when backing up files for this encyclopedia. The original text filenames for this book were PC.A, PC.B, PC.C, and so on, organized in three directories covering the letters A through F, G through P, and Q through Z. The files were divided in such a way that the total number of bytes in each directory was no greater than the capacity of a single diskette. This article, for example, was written in file PC.W within the directory PCPART3. All the text files for letters Q through Z in this encyclopedia were backed up on a diskette with a single DOS command:

```
COPY \PCPART3\PC.* A:
```

The table (opposite page) shows some examples of wildcards using the asterisk and the question mark. In some programs, a set of three periods (...) is used instead of the asterisk wildcard. *See also* FILENAME *and* WORD PROCESSING.

Windows

Windows refers to a group of graphical user interface (GUI) schemes for PC operation. When people talk about "Windows," they are

Windows

Wildcards stand in for characters or strings

Example	Can represent	Can't represent
*ism	mannerism prism capitalism	radio anthropology peculiarity
??ism	prism	mannerism capitalism
PC.*	PC.A PC.W PC.XYZ	PCA P.CW PCXYZ
PC.?	PC.A PC.B	PC.XYZ P.CB

almost always referring to Microsoft versions, such as *Windows 3.11* or *Windows 95*. Microsoft originally developed Windows to make it easier to use IBM-compatible PCs.

User-friendliness. In Windows, you give commands to the computer by choosing from option, in the form of menus or icons on the screen. Windows makes use of a mouse, trackball, J-mouse, or similar pointing device. The selection process is called *point-and-click*. When you've chosen an option, part or all of the screen changes, giving you new options.

One or more rectangular portions of the screen can be set aside, in which you can see what's happening in different files. This is especially convenient for multitasking, when you have one file in the foreground while others are in the background.

Windows operation has been compared to pointing and grunting like a baby, rather than using words like an adult. Another way to think of the difference between Windows and DOS is to imagine Windows as a multiple-choice test, and DOS as a fill-in-the-blank test. Windows is easier to learn, and generally easier to use, than DOS. As computers continue to become more complex, user-friendliness becomes more important.

Limitations. Windows graphics require a certain minimum amount of processing power. A computer with an Intel 80386 (386) microprocessor is needed to run Windows at moderate speed. A 486 or faster microprocessor speeds things up appreciably. All other factors being equal, the speed of the graphical interface is proportional to the microprocessor's clock speed. Thus, a 486DX4 at 100 MHz will run Windows faster than a 486SX at 33 MHz. Processors have come far enough so that Windows is not normally difficult to run, except on very old computers.

There are some applications for which Windows is not well-suited. For example, it's of little use if you want to converse, in spoken words,

Word processing

with a computer or a smart robot having speech recognition and speech synthesis abilities. Such conversations would consist of specific verbal commands and responses, not multiple-choice oral quizzes.

For visually handicapped PC operators, a GUI is essentially useless. Command-driven systems are a requirement. "Straight DOS," along with speech recognition and synthesis, will work well for these operators. This does not mean that old-fashioned DOS will suffice, but rather, that DOS has future potential. Voice-interactive, command-based computing requires at least as much processing power as a GUI.

As robots become common, users will want to be able to use keyboard entry, spoken words, and GUIs like Windows to control the machines. You'll switch modes whenever you want, depending on which mode is easiest to use at the moment. *See also* BACKGROUND PROCESSING, COMMAND-DRIVEN SOFTWARE, DOS, FOREGROUND PROCESSING, GRAPHICAL USER INTERFACE, ICON, MENU, MENU-DRIVEN SOFTWARE, MOUSE, MULTITASKING, OPERATING SYSTEM, OVERLAID WINDOWS, SPEECH RECOGNITION, SPEECH SYNTHESIS, TILED WINDOWS, *and* TRACKBALL.

Word processing

Word processing is the use of a computer as an aid in writing and editing. In many offices, it has taken the place of the typewriter. Some people claim that it has doubled or tripled their productivity and improved the quality of their work. Word processing has been called a *killer* application: it alone served as the motivation to buy a PC.

The basics. Word-processing programs range in complexity from the simple editor that comes with an operating system or environment to advanced packages with features most people never even imagine. Here are a few features and functions common to most word processing software:

➢ *Margins and tab stops*   You can set the left and right margins anywhere you want. The same is true of the tab stops. You can change these settings at various points within documents. All settings are embedded electronically.

➢ *Justification*   You can specify flush-left/ragged-right, flush-left/flush-right, ragged-left/flush-right, or centered text. These can be changed an unlimited number of times within documents, and all the settings will be embedded as part of the file.

➢ *Page length and line spacing*   You can select any number of lines per page up to a certain maximum, and the program will automatically insert page breaks after the specified number of lines. You can also tell the printer to use double, triple, or multiple spacing between lines. These settings can be changed within a file.

- *Running headers/footers* Your hardcopy can have page numbers and headers or footers to help readers keep track of your documents. This is ideal for large projects such as reference books and novels, in which chapter names can appear on each page, and pages can be numbered within chapters.

- *Typeface* You can select normal type, boldface, underlined text, italics, superscript, subscript, and combinations of these. You can also change the font and size of type. These things can be changed at will within a document, and they will be reflected in the hardcopy.

- *Insertion and deletion* You can add or remove characters, symbols, words, phrases, lines, sentences, paragraphs, and defined blocks of text, at any point or points you want. All the surrounding text automatically moves to compensate. If you've used running headers and footers, or paginated your document for printing, repagination occurs automatically, so the document still prints out neatly.

- *Cut and paste* You can take a block of text from one part of a document and move it to another place, or add it to a different document altogether. This is done by defining the beginning and end of the block, scrolling to the new spot, and inserting the block there. You can also duplicate blocks of text, moving them to new locations in addition to the old ones.

- *File merging* You can insert an entire file into a word-processed document, at any point you want. The imported material might be a text file, or it might be in some other form, such as clip art. You can merge file X into file Y more than once; you can merge X into Y at the beginning or ending, or both. You can even merge X into itself.

- *Sorting* This function lets you arrange text according to various criteria. You might put items in alphabetical or chronological order, or arrange them by zipcode or telephone area code. This function is especially useful when your documents contain tables, lists, or other database-like information.

- *Search and replace* You can search for certain strings of characters. The cursor will stop at each occurrence of the string, and you can then (if you wish) change the string. You can also instruct the machine to automatically change character strings throughout a document. For example, you might want to change the word *however* to *but*, or *may* to *can*, throughout a file. Always proofread the work after this kind of search-and-replace operation, to be sure that the text still makes sense.

Word processing

- *Wordwrap* You do not need to press the Enter key to move from line to line as you type. You can type continuously, as if everything were in one long line. The program will automatically ensure that words stay whole, and that the lines don't stray outside the specified margins.

- *Spell checking* The computer can be told to search for words that it does not recognize, based on a large internal dictionary or vocabulary. The cursor will stop at unfamiliar letter sequences. You can then check to see if it's a legitimate word, a typo, or a misspelled word. If the word is legitimate and you use it often, you can add it to the spell-check vocabulary.

More powerful features. If you do much word processing, you'll begin to find a need for some of the more sophisticated functions that these programs can perform. Here are some examples:

- *Exotic page layouts* You can arrange text in unusual ways to achieve certain effects. For example, some poets scatter the words around to influence the way in which a reader will react to the work. You can arrange text to make graphics, or graphics to make text. Color printing multiplies the possibilities.

- *Grammar checking* This feature actually points out grammatical errors and makes suggestions for improvement. The program will check for improper word usage, poor sentence structure, and sometimes even unclear statements. You must be careful with this feature, because grammar can be subtle, and there are cases in which the program will be wrong. Sometimes, writers deliberately construct bizarre sentences for effect. This will drive a grammar-checking program crazy.

- *Thesaurus* Have you ever known there was a perfect word for making your point, but you could not recall it? You stopped and racked your brain for the word, but it would not come, so you settled for a second-best synonym. With a thesaurus, you can pick something close to that elusive word; chances are that one of the synonyms will trigger your memory. A thesaurus can also help you avoid the excessive use of favorite words.

- *Outline utility* This lets you make an outline for your work with subtitles, sub-subtitles, and so on down to four or more levels. As you write, the utility keeps track of what's under each subtitle. You can change the outline, and the whole manuscript will be restructured to reflect the new organization. In this way, you can create several versions of a piece and pick the one that presents your subject in the best way.

- *Mathematics* Some programs are designed to handle symbols unique to mathematics. Some of the more exotic symbols are the integral sign, the summation sign, and letters of some non-

English alphabets such as Greek and Hebrew. The best programs can help you arrange symbols correctly. This is called *mathematical grammar*, and it is crucial to the accuracy and conciseness of technical writing.

- *Foreign languages* Word-processing programs are available for languages other than English. While some languages use the same alphabet as English, others, such as Russian and Japanese, do not. Even those languages with mostly English characters, such as Spanish and French, must have specialized spell checkers and grammar checkers.

- *WYSIWYG* This stands for "what you see is what you get." It gives you a good idea, on the monitor screen, of what the hardcopy will look like, including art, tabular matter, and even photographs. WYSIWYG is especially useful for small publishing efforts. It can also be used in electronic publishing, circumventing the need for paper.

- *Desktop publishing* This is the ultimate in word processing and production. With it, you can publish a magazine or book from your own home or office. A one-person publishing house becomes a realistic ideal. Self-published books can be found on the shelves of libraries. You can even publish your work online, although this invites copyright infringement.

The table on page 1154 briefly defines some common features and functions in word processing programs.

Exotic features. The most intense word processing programs can convert speech into text, compose quasi-original work, and perhaps even react to brain waves. With high-level speech recognition technology, you can have a PC write down what you say. Errors always occur because the translation process isn't perfect, but you can edit the work later. Some people find that they do their best work when they dictate into a tape recorder and then have someone type what they have said; a voice-operated word processor eliminates most of the typing in this process. IBM's Personal Dictation System is an example of an advanced speech-recognition software package.

Computer brain power, in the form of artificial intelligence (AI) and expert systems, might someday even enable computers to write original documents. Some people have developed software that can do this, but the work tends to be shallow, and the style is rather drab. While a computer-written article or book might be informative, however, there is doubt as to whether a machine will ever write an epic story. Some researchers say machines can't make art because art is human by definition. Other people suggest that machines might open up new dimensions of thinking and feeling. At least, a computer might give an author ideas.

Word processing

Common word processing features and functions

Term	Definition
Arrow keys	Move cursor without affecting text.
Backspace	Backs cursor up, erasing text.
Chain printing	Prints documents in predetermined sequence.
Clip art	Simple graphics embedded in text.
Clipboard	A temporary place for storing text.
Compound document	Several text files combined into one.
Document comparison	Finds differences in text files.
Downloadable font	A font provided as software.
End key	Moves cursor to end of screen page.
Full-page display	Shows what printed page will look like.
Grammar checking	Helps writers improve grammar.
Hard page breaks	Gaps that stay fixed in text.
Hard returns	Returns that stay fixed in text.
Home key	Moves cursor to beginning of screen page.
Justification	Aligns text.
Kerning	Adjusts letters to save space.
Optical scanner	Converts hardcopy to digital data.
Overtype mode	Writes new characters on top of old ones.
Page Down key	Moves cursor down one full screen.
Page Up key	Moves cursor up one full screen.
Pagination	Breaks up text for page printing.
Proportional font	Optimization of letter spacing.
Running headers/footers	Information at top or bottom of pages.
Scalable font	A font that can be changed in size.
Scrolling	Movement of cursor up or down.
Search and replace	Changes selected words in text.
Soft page breaks	Gaps that move in text.
Soft returns	Returns that move in text.
Spell checking	Improves spelling and corrects typos.
Tab key	Moves cursor horizontally to defined points.
Wordwrap	Keeps words in one piece.
WYSIWYG	Displays what printout will look like.

Even the best writers have trouble expressing feelings as words. It's a difficult thing to do, and it takes practice and patience to get it right. This is why the art of writing, especially fiction, can seem a little like witchcraft to the average person. People speak of the muse, or the writer's trance, or the contagious dream state that a good story creates. Is it possible that a PC, connected via electrodes to your brain, might write your thoughts better than you can via conscious effort? Some people think so, although brain-actuated computer technology, called *wetware*, is a long way from that level of sophistication.

For further information. The features and functions described here are by no means a complete overview of word processing. New schemes are constantly being devised. Personal-computing magazines often have articles describing the latest innovations. You can also look at advertisements, brochures, and instruction manuals.

See also ADOBE TYPE MANAGER, AUTOMATIC FONT DOWNLOADING, BITMAPPED FONT, BUILT-IN FONT, BUSINESS LETTERS, CHAIN PRINTING, CHARACTER, CLIP ART, CLIPBOARD, COMPOUND DOCUMENT, CURSOR, DESKTOP PUBLISHING, DOCUMENT, DOCUMENT COMPARISON, DOWNLOADABLE FONT, EXPERT SYSTEMS, FONT, FULL-PAGE DISPLAY, GRAMMAR CHECKING, GRAPHICAL USER INTERFACE, HANGING INDENT, HARDCOPY, HARD PAGE BREAKS, HARD RETURN, HYPHENATION, INDEXING SOFTWARE, JUSTIFICATION, KERNING, LABEL PRINTING, LETTER WRITING, MULTIPART FORMS, NOTE-TAKING SOFTWARE, OPTICAL SCANNER, OUTLINE FONT, OUTLINE UTILITY, PAGE LAYOUT PROGRAM, PAGINATION, PAPERLESS OFFICE, PERSONAL DICTATION SYSTEM, POSTSCRIPT, PROPORTIONAL FONT, REPAGINATION, RUNNING HEADERS/FOOTERS, SCALABLE FONT, SCROLLING, SEARCH AND REPLACE, SIDE-BY-SIDE COLUMN FORMAT, SINGLE-COLUMN FORMAT, SOFT PAGE BREAKS, SOFT RETURNS, SPEECH RECOGNITION, SPEECH SYNTHESIS, SPELL CHECKING, TRUETYPE, TWO-COLUMN FORMAT, WETWARE, *and* WYSIWYG.

Word size

In computing, a *word* is a unit of digital data. The *word size* varies depending on the sophistication of the computer. Word size is one of several specifications that define PC processing power.

The earliest computers had words that were eight bits, or one byte, in size. As the technology advanced, words expanded to two bytes (16 bits), then four bytes (32 bits), then eight bytes (64 bits).

In a computer with a given amount of memory and a certain clock speed, the overall power increases as the words are made larger. This principle is illustrated by the drawings on page 1156. Data buses are shown as transparent "pipes"; each byte appears as a ball. The computer at A in the drawing has words that are two bytes long. The machine at B has four-byte words, and the one at C has eight-byte words. The amount of data moving through the bus is proportional to the word size, as long as the transit speed remains constant. *See also* BYTE, CLOCK SPEED, COMPUTER GENERATIONS, COMPUTER POWER, DATA BUS, MEMORY, *and* RANDOM-ACCESS MEMORY.

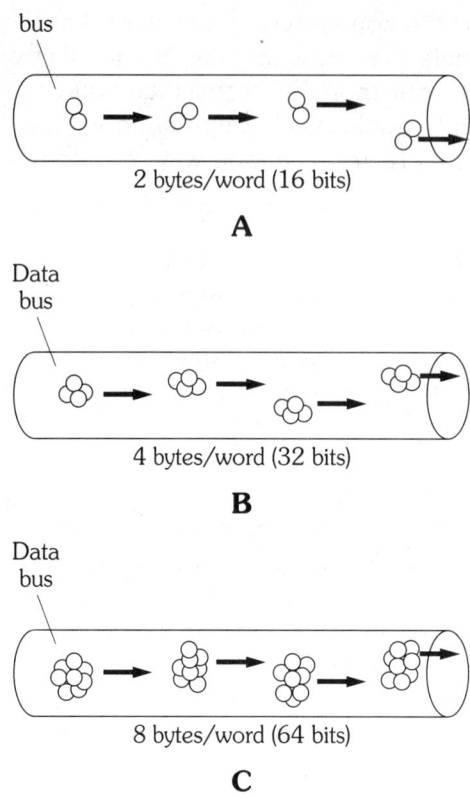

Data buses carrying various word sizes.

Words per minute

Data speed is sometimes given in *words per minute (WPM)*. In this context, a word consists of five characters plus one space, for a total of six characters. Generally, then, the number of words per minute is about ⅙ the number of characters per minute.

Units of WPM aren't often used nowadays. You might see printers advertised as able to print so many WPM, but lines per minute and pages per minute are more often quoted. The standard specification for data speed in communications is the number of bits per second (bps). A unit called the *baud* is sometimes used instead. Bauds and bps are not generally equivalent, but many people speak of them as if they were. *See also* BAUD/BITS PER SECOND.

Working directory

See DIRECTORY.

Workstation

A *workstation* is a complete computer setup, including the main unit, monitor, keyboard, printer, modem, and other peripherals. In networks, the term is synonymous with *node*.

In the 1960s and early 1970s, a typical workstation was a dumb terminal resembling an old-fashioned teleprinter. Such workstations could be found in schools and businesses. The computer itself might be located miles away, perhaps in another town or another state. A single mainframe computer served hundreds of workstations via telephone-line interconnection. The central mainframe used time sharing to accommodate the workstations, so that each user got the impression of being in constant communication with the computer. By today's standards, computing was excruciatingly slow. The earliest computer workstations printed on continuous-feed paper at 60 words per minute, about six characters per second. Monitors, graphics, and most of today's familiar PC applications were known only to scientists and engineers in large universities and government institutions.

In recent years, home offices have become common. People are telecommuting part-time or full-time. Computers help people to become self-employed and work from home. The PC and peripherals in a home office are often referred to as the workstation, even when they're used for recreational purposes. *See also* DUMB TERMINAL, ERGONOMICS, LOCAL AREA NETWORK, NODE, ONLINE SERVICE, TELECOMMUTING, TELECONFERENCING, TIME SHARING, *and* WIDE AREA NETWORK.

World Wide Web

See INTERNET.

Write-once/read-many

Write-once/read-many (WORM) refers to a special type of optical diskette and drive. A WORM drive can record new CD-ROM (compact disc read-only memory) diskettes, as well as read existing ones. As its name implies, a WORM system can write the data onto an optical disk only once. Overwriting, familiar to users of magnetic disks, is not possible.

The WORM drive writes data onto an optical diskette by using a laser to melt the plastic on the disk surface. The blank disk, treated with special dye, absorbs the laser light, heats up, and melts in microscopic craters or pits, each of which represents one bit of data. A laser reads the data by scanning the disk surface at high speed. The pits scatter the light, while the smooth surface reflects it.

A WORM system can be useful for creating archives. It can also be used to make copies of large software programs and graphic images. A single compact disc can store over 650 megabytes (650MB) of digital information, the equivalent of more than 500 high-density magnetic diskettes. The optical medium is immune to damage from magnetic fields and lasts several years.

Write protection

The main problem with WORM technology is that it's comparatively expensive. The price of a typical WORM drive is dropping, but it's still more than most PC users are willing to spend. A tape drive can serve as a mass storage medium just as well as a WORM system, and costs far less. *See also* ARCHIVES, CD-ROM, MASS STORAGE, *and* TAPE DRIVE.

Write protection

Write protection is a means of preventing erasure or overwriting of data with magnetic diskettes. If you try to put anything onto, or erase anything from, a write-protected diskette, the PC will say something like

WRITE PROTECT

and will refuse to carry out the command.

For 5.25-inch diskettes. When you buy a box of 5.25-inch floppy diskettes, you'll usually get a set of stick-on labels, and also a set of small black stick-on tabs. The small tabs are for write protection. If you look at a 5.25-inch diskette, you'll find a notch near one corner (see the drawing at A). To write protect the diskette, peel off one of the little black tabs from its backing, and wrap it around the edge of the diskette so it covers the notch.

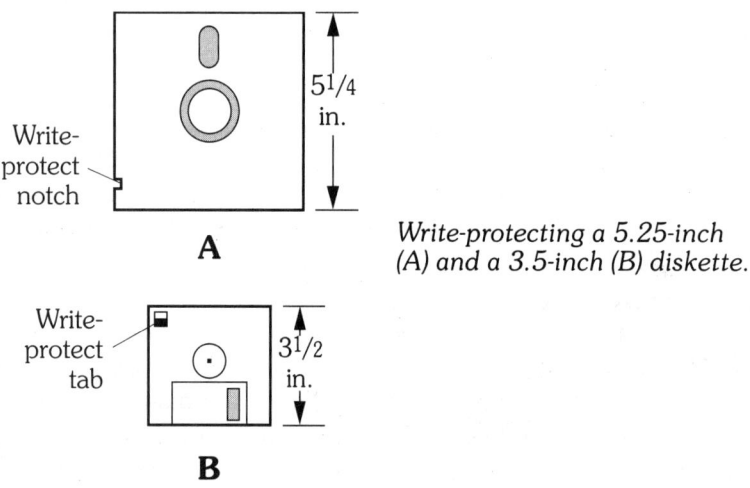

Write-protecting a 5.25-inch (A) and a 3.5-inch (B) diskette.

You must use the black tab, not transparent tape, to write protect a 5.25-inch diskette. The drive mechanism employs an electric eye to check for write protection. The light beam will shine through transparent tape, telling the computer that it's okay to alter the contents of the diskette.

For 3.5-inch diskettes. With 3.5-inch diskettes, there's a switch-like device near one corner, as shown in the drawing at B. To write protect the diskette, slide the switch so there's a little square hole in the diskette case through which you can see. Move the switch with the point of a pencil to be sure that it snaps into place. (If it doesn't snap into place, it might move when you insert the diskette into the drive, allowing data to be written onto the diskette.) If you want the diskette to be alterable (not write-protected), slide the switch so the hole is blocked off, and again, be certain that it clicks into place.

With 3.5-inch diskettes, double-check the position of the write-protect switch if you want to ensure the safety of your data. It's easy to forget about this switch, possibly leaving data vulnerable when you think it's write-protected.

Back it up! Don't rely on write protection alone to safeguard your most valuable data. Back everything up on duplicate diskettes. You might want to make two write-protected sets of backup diskettes for your irreplaceable archives, storing one set near your workstation and another set in a remote place, such as a safe-deposit box. If your files consume a lot of storage space, you might want to keep your archives on tape instead, using a tape drive to update them at regular intervals. Other archiving methods also exist. *See also* ARCHIVES, BACKUP, DISKETTE, MASS STORAGE, *and* TAPE DRIVE.

WYSIWYG

WYSIWYG (pronounced "WIZZY-wig") is an acronym that stands for *what you see is what you get*. With WYSIWYG, the display looks very much like the hard copy will appear when you print it out. WYSIWYG is especially useful In desktop publishing because it saves printer time and paper.

Consider the example of a small magazine publishing house. The editor, graphic artist, proofreader, and production specialist each sit at a workstation in a local area network (LAN), looking at the page layout for next month's issue. If the editor makes changes that result in a longer or shorter article, the graphic artist can see the effects of these changes on the page layout, and can alter the size of one or more illustrations to compensate. The production person might see what the editor and graphic artist have done, and decide that an illustration should be moved from page 25 to page 26. The editor and graphic artist can then examine what the production specialist has done, and decide whether further changes are needed at their ends. All this while, the proofreader can be checking to be sure no typographical errors have been introduced, no illustration captions have been dropped, and so on.

A WYSIWYG system cannot show you all the subtle aspects of the printed copy, but it will provide you with a good preview. The screen font might not agree exactly with the printer font. Colors on the

WYSIWYG

monitor might not appear to have quite the same hue or saturation as they come off the printer. And of course, a screen view is only a picture of whatever it portrays, unless you are publishing the work online, on diskette, or on CD-ROM. *See also* DESKTOP PUBLISHING *and* LOCAL AREA NETWORK.

XENIX

See UNIX.

X-height

In printed or displayed text, the *x-height* is the vertical size of the lowercase letter *x*. It can be given in millimeters, inches, or points. The x-height can be used to specify the type size. The other common measure of type size is the number of characters per inch (CPI) horizontally.

Depending on the font, characters of a given x-height can look considerably different in size. The drawing (next page) shows the word *faxing*, as in, "I am faxing a document to someone," in three different fonts. At A, the top of the *f* and the tail of the *g* extend somewhat above and below the x-height limits. At B, the top of the *f* and the tail of the *g* extend further beyond the x-height limits. At C, the top of the *f* goes only a little bit above the upper x-height limit, and nothing goes below the base line. Although these three fonts look quite different from one another, their x-heights are identical.

When the x-height and the CPI specification are both the same for two different fonts, the fonts are equivalent in size for practical purposes. However, they might still look much different from each other. Personal preference and ease of reading are the main factors that influence the choice of screen and printer fonts.

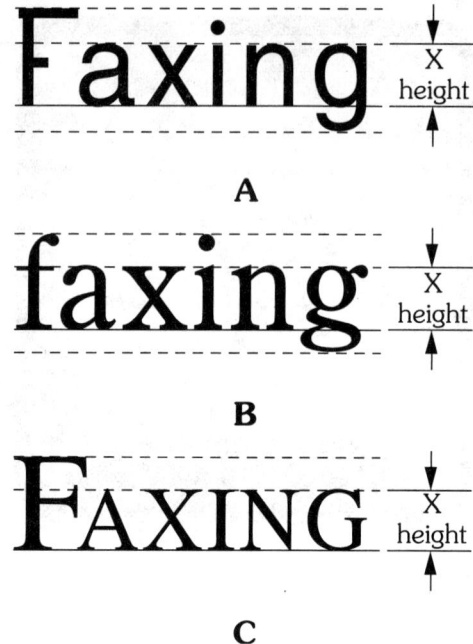

Three different fonts (A, B, and C) with identical x-heights.

XMS memory

See EXTENDED/EXPANDED MEMORY.

XR robots

The *XR robots* are a series of PC-controlled educational devices that were conceived, designed, and built by a company called Rhino Robots. The XR robots are actually just robot arms. There are several purposes, or motivations, behind the XR robots:

➢ To demonstrate how robots work

➢ To show how PCs and personal robots naturally go together

➢ To prove that computer-controlled robots are practical

The XR robots were introduced during the 1980s, selling for a little under $3000 apiece. They are able to do numerous tasks with high precision. For simple jobs, the robots use a programming device similar to a teach box. For tasks involving many steps to be carried out in specific order, a PC can serve as the robot controller.

The XR robots have proven most useful as teaching aids in corporations and schools. Many people get uneasy around robots, especially the programmable type. Machines like XR robots help alleviate these people's fear of smart computers and robots. *See also* EDUCATIONAL ROBOTS, PERSONAL ROBOTS, TEACH BOX, *and* UNCANNY VALLEY.

X Windows

See UNIX and WINDOWS.

X/Y/Z axes

The *x/y/z axes* are the lines in a Cartesian coordinate system representing different variables. They are always straight lines in true Cartesian systems. The increments might differ in size from axis to axis, but graduations are uniform throughout the span of any single axis. Cartesian coordinates, in two and three dimensions, are commonly used in analytical graphics programs.

The x axis. In a Cartesian plane, the x axis is horizontal (A in the drawing). The independent variable is represented by this axis; it is sometimes called the *abscissa*. In Cartesian three-space, the x axis is one of the two independent variables, the other being represented by y (B in the drawing). The x axis runs left and right, and can be thought of as width. Typical variables that the x axis depicts include time, position, distance, and category (in business graphs).

The y axis. In the Cartesian plane, the y axis is the vertical axis, as shown in drawing A. The dependent variable is represented by this axis; it is sometimes called the *ordinate*. In a mathematical function f of an independent variable x, you write $y = f(x)$. This means that the function maps x values into y values.

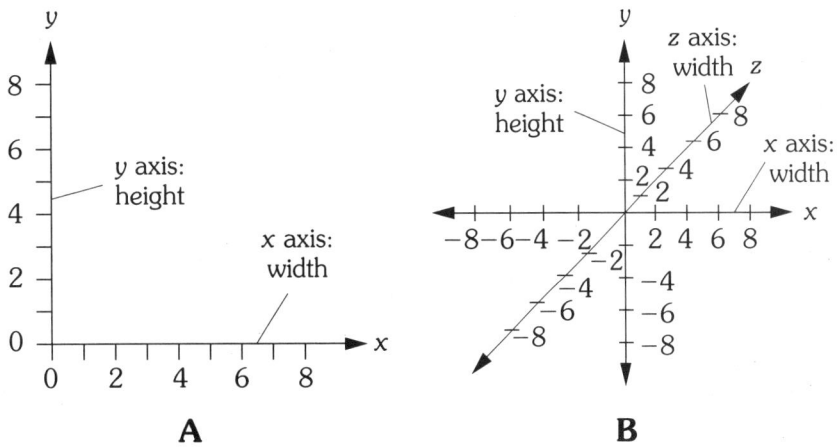

A Cartesian plane (A) and Cartesian three-space (B).

In Cartesian three-space, also called *xyz-space*, the y axis is one of the two independent variables, the other being represented by x (see drawing B). The y axis usually runs up and down, and can therefore be thought of as height. Typical variables shown on the y axis in a Cartesian plane include temperature, intensity, or anything else that depends on the value of x. In xyz-space, the y axis represents the same kinds of things as the x axis.

X/Y/Zmodem

The z axis. In *xyz*-space, the z axis is always the dependent variable. Its values depend on *x* and *y*, the two independent variables. The z axis runs perpendicular to both the *x* and *y* axes, as shown in drawing B. A function f maps values *x* and *y* into values *z*, such that $z = f(x,y)$. The actual orientation of the z axis can't be shown on a flat surface such as a sheet of paper or a computer display, so it's usually drawn in perspective, representing depth. Typical variables graphed on the z axis include temperature, intensity, cost, or anything else that might depend on the values of *x* and/or *y*.

The xy, xz, and yz planes. In Cartesian *xyz*-space, you will sometimes read or hear about specific two-dimensional subsets of the system:

➤ The *xy plane* is the flat surface containing both the *x* axis and the *y* axis. In drawing B, it corresponds to the surface of the paper.

➤ The *xz plane* is the flat surface defined by the *x* and *z* axes. If you hold a sheet of paper so its edge is along the *x* axis in drawing B, and so it stands straight up perpendicular to the page, you can get a good idea of the orientation of the *xz* plane.

➤ The *yz plane* is the flat surface containing the *y* and *z* axes in Cartesian three-space. If you hold a sheet of paper so its edge is along the *y* axis in drawing B, and so it is perpendicular to the page, you can see how the *yz* plane is oriented relative to the system.

Variations. Sometimes you'll see Cartesian *xyz*-space with the *y* and *z* axes transposed, compared with the way they are shown here. That is, the *y* axis will be depth, and the *z* axis will be height. It doesn't make any difference, as long as usage is consistent throughout a document or presentation. *See also* ABSCISSA, ANALYTICAL GRAPHICS, CARTESIAN COORDINATES, DEPENDENT VARIABLE, INDEPENDENT VARIABLE, *and* ORDINATE.

X/Y/Zmodem

In data communications, the terms *Xmodem, Ymodem*, and *Zmodem* refer to error-correcting modes. They use a data-checking protocol, in which the destination (receiving) PC and source (transmitting) PC exchange information via a scheme called *handshaking*.

Xmodem. In Xmodem, data is sent 128K, or 131,072 bytes, at a time. As the first block is sent, both the source PC and the destination PC tally up the bytes. When the source PC has sent 131,072 bytes, it pauses and awaits the "verdict" from the destination. If the destination has received exactly 131,072 bytes, it tells the source to go ahead and send the next block of data. If the destination has received more or fewer than 131,072 bytes, it tells the source to retransmit the block it just sent.

X/Y/Zmodem

The Xmodem protocol operates according to the fact that, if any error occurs in data transmission, it will usually affect the received number of bytes. This does not always happen, however. It is possible for a character to be misread, but counted as one character nevertheless. Therefore, Xmodem does not provide a 100% guarantee that data will be received error-free.

Ymodem. In Ymodem, the protocol is similar to Xmodem except that, rather than sending data in blocks of 128K, it sends them in blocks of 1MB, which is equal to 1024 kilobytes or 1,048,576 bytes.

The Ymodem scheme allows for the transmission of bigger packets of data. Files often exceed 128K in size; it's not as common for them to be bigger than 1MB. With Ymodem, you can sometimes even send the contents of a directory or a high-density diskette in a single block.

Zmodem. The Zmodem protocol improves on both Xmodem and Ymodem. Basically, it works like Xmodem, with one important exception. If an error is found during transmission, the source retransmits only that portion of the data following the error. This saves time because the source does not have to retransmit the whole 128K every time a single byte gets misplaced. The Zmodem scheme requires somewhat more sophisticated handshaking between the source and the destination, so that the location of the error can be found.

The flowchart illustrates the basic principle of the Xmodem, Ymodem and Zmodem protocols. *See also* DESTINATION, HANDSHAKING, MODEM, *and* SOURCE.

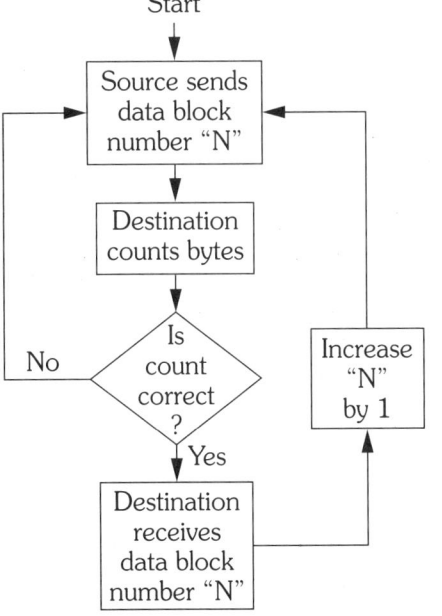

X/Y/Zmodem protocols verify accuracy in data communications.

Yoke

See JOYSTICK.

Youth-friendly computing

Personal computing is destined to become a part of every person's life in the developed nations of the world. There was a time when one might get around this, but today computer literacy is almost as important as the ability to read and write. It's never too early to get children comfortable with PCs.

The computer. There's no such thing, in any computing scenario, as a PC that's too powerful. You can let your child work on the same computer that you use. The difference is only in the software (presumably yours will be more advanced than your child's), and in the peripherals, particularly the input devices.

The machine should be well-built, because small children often hit keys and buttons with unnecessary force. You might want to get a "keyboard skin" to protect the keyboard from possible liquid spills. If the child hasn't learned how to read and type yet, you can disconnect the keyboard altogether, possibly substituting a special keyboard designed for use by tots.

Graphical interface. A very young child can't read, much less type. Therefore, if a tot is to make any use of software, the program must have a graphical user interface (GUI). Of course, this doesn't mean you should go out and buy the latest Macintosh, Windows, or OS/2 package for your two-year-old, but a young child can do a lot more things than you might expect, when a machine makes noises and shows pictures. Interactive software is a must.

Perhaps you have friends or relatives who have children and PCs, and have successfully "interfaced" them. If not, you can inquire at your local computer store or toy store. Tot-friendly software is available for both Macintosh and IBM-compatible systems. *See also* GRAPHICAL USER INTERFACE.

Monitor. The bigger and more colorful the picture, the better a child will like it. Tots are exposed to television from the day they get into the house. They are apt to be unimpressed with a computer screen that's any less spectacular than home video.

A 17-inch monitor with true color capability (over a million possible hues/saturations of color) doesn't come cheap, but it will maximize the fun factor of computing for a young child. That's the most important thing in getting a tot to work with computers. (Arguably, adults could stand to give the fun factor a little more weight, too.) You should get a high-resolution monitor.

Be sure to place the monitor where the child can't damage it, or hurt him- or herself by knocking it over. It can be set on top of the computer's main unit, or on the desktop, well away from the edge of the desk. A big monitor weighs more than 40 pounds, but children are stronger than you might suspect. *See also* HIGH-RESOLUTION MONITOR, MONITOR, *and* TOT-PROOF WORKSTATION.

Printer. Another important piece of hardware is a printer that can produce hardcopies of the things your child creates on screen. The printer must be compatible with the rest of the system. Usually this is a matter of software.

A color printer will, naturally, appeal more to a child than a black-and-white printer. While a laser printer will create the best-quality graphic images, you might not want to spend the money for one. You can obtain a good color inkjet printer for a reasonable price.

You'll have to protect the printer from damage by the child, and also prevent the child from being injured by the printer. The best way to ensure the mutual safety of the two is to keep them away from each other, except when you are directly supervising the child's every move. *See also* COLOR PRINTER, INKJET PRINTER, *and* LASER PRINTER.

Special input devices. The typical keyboard is no tool for a tot. Pointing devices are a necessity. A four- or five-year-old might learn to use a mouse. Younger children will need more straightforward things like a light pen or a touch screen.

You'll be amazed at the variety of manipulators invented specifically for use by children. There are, for example, several variations on the joystick theme. Increasingly, too, you'll find speech recognition in computers for children as this technology advances in power and comes down in price. *See also* JOYSTICK *and* SPEECH RECOGNITION.

Sound. The more bells and whistles (literally!) in a computer, the more it will appeal to a young child. Tots love noise. The louder and more varied, the better. Of course, this axiom must be tempered by reason. Window-shattering monster growls will frighten a child and annoy you.

Sound technology makes it possible to play all kinds of interactive games with a computer, bringing to life the thrill of racecar driving, speedboating, or any other noisy adventure.

This is a good place to mention computer games and software that cannot, in good conscience, be recommended for children. These include anything with fighting and especially with killing—of people or animals. Children learn by example. They should learn that computers enrich life, and should not get the idea that computers are in any way associated with the destruction of life. If you hear gunfire coming from the computer room, check it out right away. (Once children get PC-savvy, they'll start trading software.)

Computers can be a great way to introduce your child to music. While many children rebel when forced to practice the piano or any other musical instrument, they'll often become little Mozarts when exposed to a MIDI (musical instrument digital interface). This is especially true when children reach grade-school age. *See also* MULTIMEDIA, MUSICAL-INSTRUMENT DIGITAL INTERFACE, *and* SOUND TECHNOLOGY.

Robots. Computers and robots go well together. Primitive examples of robot toys include radio-controlled model cars, boats, and airplanes. In the future, children might be able to connect these devices to computers, programming a scaled-down Grand Prix, regatta, or air show. These devices, naturally, appeal to older children, of ages 10 to 15.

Simple educational robots, connected to a PC, can be great learning tools for young children. Robots of this kind have become popular among tots in Japan, and increasingly in America as well. Robots are intimidating to some children, but once a child gets used to working or playing with machines, robots can become companions or even friends. Of course, robot "pals" should never take the place of human friends. *See also* PERSONAL ROBOTS.

Virtual reality. The ultimate computer experience for children is virtual reality. This brings animation into the realm of 3-D (three dimensions), and also allows for panoramic vision and sound.

Virtual reality is for older children, not for tots. There's a fright factor with this technology. Many adults are hesitant to put on virtual-reality goggles or helmets for fear that their senses will be overwhelmed. While children might be more brave, some will like the experience, and others will not.

Virtual reality offers exciting possibilities in education. No one has ever gone on an interstellar journey, or been down to the bottom of the Marianas Trench, seven miles under the sea. What would it be like to ride in a starship or a super submarine? Scientists have a good idea of what such experiences would entail, and they can program this knowledge into computer software. The PC, equipped with virtual reality, can then take a child to such places with most of the true-to-life effects and none of the risk. *See also* VIRTUAL REALITY.

Zero-slot network

A *zero-slot network* is an interconnection of PCs directly through data ports. The term *zero-slot* refers to the fact that no interface cards are used; network access requires zero expansion slots. Instead, the data passes through each PC's serial port. The serial port must be used because a parallel port won't work directly for data transfer over distances of more than a few feet.

The main asset of a zero-slot LAN is simplicity. Because no expansion boards are needed, the cost is minimal. Access is easy, requiring only the interconnecting cables for a local area network (LAN), and a modem for a wide-area network (WAN) or online service.

The big limitation of a zero-slot network is that serial data transfer is slower than parallel data transfer. Serial data goes bit-by-bit along a single communications line. This works all right for small files and simple data, but it is not adequate for large or complex masses of information. Detailed graphic-image transmission, for example, becomes frustrating. You know this if you've downloaded a high-resolution color photograph from an online service. Applications such as telepresence, in which huge amounts of data must be exchanged with minimal delay, are impractical with serial data transfer.

In LANs that require constant transmission of data at high speeds, each computer must have a network interface card (NIC). This expansion board allows the computer to send and receive data via its internal data bus, to and from which information can proceed much faster than is possible through the serial port. *See also* DATA BUS, EXPANSION BOARD, LOCAL AREA NETWORK, MODEM, ONLINE SERVICE, PARALLEL, PARALLEL PORT, SERIAL, SERIAL PORT, *and* WIDE-AREA NETWORK.

Zero wait state

Computer power is a function of several things. The most important specifications are the microprocessor clock speed, the capacity of the RAM (random-access memory), the RAM access time and storage time, and the data word size. These factors are interdependent. A fast microprocessor is of little use if the memory cannot hold much data, or if the data is forced to move in small chunks, or if data takes a long time to be accessed and stored.

All the criteria for computer power advance with the evolution of technology. Memory capacity grows; clock speeds increase; access and storage times become shorter. These factors don't all improve at the same pace; for example, the increase in microprocessor speed can outstrip the decrease in memory access and storage time. When this happens, the overall computer power does not go up nearly as much as it would if the factors improved in sync with each other. A fast microprocessor with a slow memory is like a Porsche stuck in first gear. The power is there, but it can't be effectively used.

When a computer's clock speed is far out of proportion to the RAM access and storage time, there are some clock cycles during which nothing happens. The microprocessor must wait until the RAM catches up to it. Each idle clock cycle is called a *wait state.* These idle cycles are, as far as the microprocessor is concerned, a waste of time. If you've ever ridden a bicycle alongside someone who was walking, you can get an idea of the situation faced by a powerful microprocessor when the RAM isn't fast enough for it.

As RAM technology advances and access and storage time improves, a point is reached where a given microprocessor no longer must waste clock cycles waiting for RAM to keep up. A computer in which clock speed and RAM speed are matched is called a *zero wait state* machine. *See also* ACCESS TIME, CACHE MEMORY, CLOCK SPEED, COMPUTER GENERATIONS, COMPUTER POWER, PAGE-MODE MEMORY, RANDOM-ACCESS MEMORY, STATIC RANDOM-ACCESS MEMORY, *and* STORAGE TIME.

Zone

A *zone* is a set of network computers or terminals that are treated as a unit. In an institutional local area network (LAN), for example, the PCs within each department can be, and often are, combined into zones. In a wide-area network (WAN), zones are usually based on geographic location, according to the postal zipcode, the telephone area code, the state, the county, or the city.

The drawing shows a hypothetical system of 12 PCs comprising the LAN for a small magazine publishing house. There are four zones: editorial (three computers), graphics (three computers), production (four computers), and proofreading (two computers). One employee sits at each PC. Communication is possible among all the workstations, or nodes, in this LAN. This particular LAN is a ring network, but it could have any configuration.

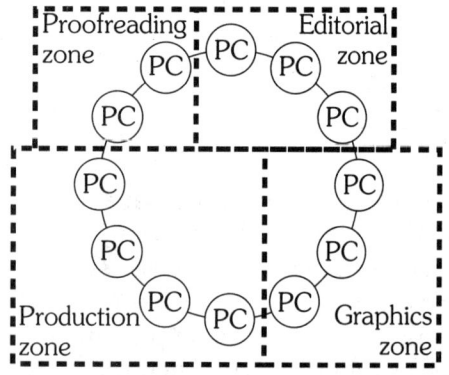

Defined zones, or portions, of network subscribers.

The advantage of LAN zoning is that it helps make information transfer efficient. In the LAN shown by the drawing, there is no need for editorial people to be burdened with data that is only of use to illustrators. Proofreaders need to see the combined efforts of all department personnel; they can't do anything with illustrations alone (of interest mainly to the people in the graphics zone) or text alone (the business of people in the editorial zone). The person in charge of the LAN must see to it that the PCs in each zone get exactly what they need—no more and no less.

In a WAN, such as an online news service, headline information can be sent selectively to various geographic zones. The path of a hurricane might be of primary importance to subscribers in Houston, and of minor interest to subscribers in Chicago. If scientists predict an imminent earthquake on the West Coast, people in Los Angeles ought to pay close attention, but people in Orlando need not give it immediate consideration. *See also* LOCAL AREA NETWORK *and* WIDE-AREA NETWORK.

Zooming

In a graphical user interface (GUI), the term *zooming* refers to magnification of the image. If you want to look at a certain part of the screen in more detail, you can zoom in on it.

In Windows and Macintosh environments, zooming can be used to enlarge part of the contents of a window. This can be useful in text-based as well as graphical applications. It's often done, for example, in spreadsheet programs when the user wants to see only part of the data. This not only brings the desired portion of the spreadsheet into clearer view, it also gets rid of distractions.

Graphics software can turn any PC into a viewscreen with infinite possibilities. It's fun to imagine that the cosmos might be reducible to an equation you can type on the keyboard of a PC. Then you could see, via zooming, every galaxy, every star system, every world, continent, town, and house in the universe. Of course, the more detail you wanted to see, the more RAM (random-access memory) your computer needs, the more powerful its microprocessor needs to be, and the more capacity is required of the hard disk. *See also* ARTIFICIAL INTELLIGENCE, FRACTAL, FRACTAL-GENERATION SOFTWARE, GRAPHICAL USER INTERFACE, *and* WINDOWS.

Appendix
Comprehensive list of abbreviations & acronyms

Term	Meaning
ABS	absolute value
AC, ac	alternating current
ACI	asynchronous communications interface
ACIA	asynchronous communications interface adapter
ACK	acknowledge signal
ACRC	Association of Commercial Records Centers
A/D	analog-to-digital
ADB	Apple Desktop Bus
ADC	analog-to-digital converter
ADI	Apple Desktop Interface
ADPCM	adaptive differential pulse code modulation
AF	audio frequency
AFE	Apple File Exchange
AFP	Appletalk Filing Protocol
AI	artificial intelligence
AIX	Advanced Interactive Executive

Appendix

Term	Meaning
ALT	alternate
	alternative
	Alt key
ALU	arithmetic-logic unit
AM	amplitude modulation
ANSI	American National Standards Institute
AOCE	Apple Open Collaboration Environment
AOL	America Online
APA	all points addressable
API	application program interface
APL	A Programming Language
APPC	advanced program-to-program communications
ARCnet	Attached Resource Computer Network
ARPAnet	Advanced Research Projects Agency Network
ASCII	American Standard Code for Information Interchange
ARLL	advanced run-length limited
AT	Advanced Technology (IBM computers)
ATM	Adobe Type Manager
	automatic teller machine
AT&T	American Telephone and Telegraph
A/UX	Apple UNIX
AUX	auxiliary port
AVI	audio-video interleaved
BASIC	Beginner's All-Purpose Symbolic Instruction Code
BBS	bulletin-board system
BCD	binary coded decimal
BCO	binary coded octal
BIOS	basic input/output system
BIP	binary image processor
B-ISDN	broadband integrated services digital networks
bit	binary digit
BITBLT	bit block transfer
BITNET	Because It's Time Network
B-REP	boundary representation
BPS, bps	bits per second
B/W, B&W	black and white
bw	bandwidth
CAD	computer-aided design
CADD	computer-aided design and drafting

1174

Comprehensive list of abbreviations & acronyms

Term	Meaning
CAI	computer-assisted instruction
CAM	computer-aided manufacturing
	content-addressable memory
CASE	computer-aided software engineering
CAT	computerized axial tomography
CATA	computer-assisted traditional animation
CAV	constant angular velocity
CBT	computer-based training
CCD	charge-coupled device
CCI	common-channel interface
CCIS	common-channel interface signaling
CCITT	*Comite Consultatif International Telephonique et Telegraphique* (International Consultative Committee for Telephony and Telegraphy)
CD	compact disc
	carrier detect
CDEV	control-panel device
CD-I	compact disc, interactive
CDMA	code division multiple access
CD-ROM	compact disc, read-only memory
CD-ROM-XA	compact disc, read-only memory extended architecture
CE	computer engineering
CGA	Color Graphics Adapter
CGI	computer-generated image
CGM	color graphics metafile
CICS	customer information control system
CIM	computer-integrated manufacturing
CISC	complex-instruction-set computing
CLV	constant linear velocity
CMOS	complementary metal-oxide semiconductor
COBOL	Common Business-Oriented Language
CODEC	coder/decoder
COM	computer output on microfilm
COMDEX	Computer Dealers' Exposition
CPI	characters per inch
CPI-C	common programming interface for communications
CPM	critical path method
CPS	characters per second
CPU	central processing unit
CRC	cyclic redundancy check

Appendix

Term	Meaning
CRM	certified record manager
CRT	cathode-ray tube
CS	computer science
CSG	constructive solid geometry
CSMA/CD	carrier-sense multiple-access with collision detection
CTD	cumulative trauma disorder
CTRL	Control key
CTS	clear to send
D/A	digital-to-analog
DA	desk accessory
DAC	digital-to-analog converter
DAM	data-addressed memory
DART	data-analysis recording tape
DAS	direct-access storage
	data acquisition system
DASD	direct-access storage device
DAT	digital audiotape
DBM	database management
DBMS	database management software
DC, dc	direct current
DD	double-density
DDE	dynamic data exchange
DEL	delete
	Delete key
DES	Data Encryption Standard
DIF	data interchange format
DIP	document image processing
	dual inline package
DLL	dynamic link library
DMA	direct memory access
DMAI	direct memory access interface
DOS	disk operating system
DP	data processing
DPI	dots per inch
DPMI	DOS Protected Mode Interface
DQDB	Distributed Queue Dual Bus
DRAM	dynamic random-access memory
DRDA	Distributed Relational Database Architecture
DS	double-sided

Comprehensive list of abbreviations & acronyms

Term	Meaning
DSR	data set ready
DT	data transmission
DTE	data terminal equipment
DTP	desktop publishing
DTR	data terminal ready
DVI	digital video interactive
EARN	European Academic Research Network
EATA	enhanced AT attachment
EBCDIC	extended binary-coded-decimal interchange code
EC	error correction
EDI	electronic data interchange
EDP	electronic data processing
EEMS	enhanced expanded memory specification
EEPROM	electrically erasable programmable read-only memory
EGA	Enhanced Graphics Adapter
EISA	extended industry-standard architecture
ELF	extremely low frequency
e-mail	electronic mail
EMB	extended memory block
EMI	electromagnetic interference
EMS	expanded memory specification
ENIAC	Electronic Numerical Integrator and Calculator
EOF	end of file
EOL	end of line
EOP	end of page
EPROM	erasable programmable read-only memory
EPS	encapsulated PostScript
ESC	Escape key
ESD	electrostatic discharge
ESDI	enhanced storage device interface
F	function key
FAT	file allocation table
FCC	Federal Communications Commission
FDC	floppy drive controller
FDDI	fiber distributed data interface
FDM	frequency-division multiplex
FDSP	fixed disk setup program
FEC	forward error correction
FEPI	front-end programming interface

Appendix

Term	Meaning
FIFO	first-in/first-out
FILO	first-in/last-out
FM	frequency modulation
FORTH	Fourth-generation Programming Language
FORTRAN	Formula Translator
FOSDIC	film optical scanning device for input to computer
FPS	frames per second
FPU	floating-point unit
FRUGAL	Fortran rules used as general applications language
FTP	file transfer protocol
FUBAR	fouled up beyond all recognition
G	giga-
	gigabyte (1,073,741,824 bytes)
GB	gigabyte
GDI	Graphics Device Interface
GFF	graphics file format
GHz	gigahertz
giga-	1,000,000,000 (10^9)
	1,073,741,824 (2^{30})
GIGO	garbage in, garbage out
GIPS	gigainstructions per second
GM	General Musical Instrument Digital Interface standard
GPS	Global Positioning System
GUI	graphical user interface
HC	hardcopy
HCD	hardcopy device
HD	hard disk
	high-density
HFS	Hierarchical Filing System
HGA	Hercules Graphics Adapter
hi-fi	high fidelity
HLL	high-level language
HLOC	high/low/open/close
HLS	hue/luminance/saturation
HMA	high memory area
HMD	head-mounted display
HP	Hewlett-Packard
HPFS	high-performance file system
HPGL	Hewlett-Packard graphics language

Comprehensive list of abbreviations & acronyms

Term	Meaning
HPPCL	Hewlett-Packard printer control language
HSM	high-speed memory
HSV	hue/saturation/value
HTL	high-threshold logic
HVC	hue/value/chroma
Hz	hertz
IAC	interapplication communications
IBM	International Business Machines
IBM PC	IBM Personal Computer
IC	integrated circuit
	internal connection
ICBS	interconnected business system
ICR	image-based character recognition
ID	identification
IDE	Integrated Drive Electronics
IDP	industrial data processing
	integrated data processing
I/O	input/output
INIT	initialization program
INS	Insert key
IP	Internet protocol
IPC	interprocess communications
IPS	instructions per second
IPX	internetwork packet exchange
IRET	interrupt return
IRQ	interrupt request
ISA	industry standard architecture
ISDN	integrated services digital network
ISO	International Standards Organization
ITT	International Telephone and Telegraph
JCL	Job Control Language
JPEG	Joint Photographic Experts Group
k, K	kilo-
K, KB	kilobyte (1024 bytes)
KBPS	kilobits per second
kHz	kilohertz
kilo-	1000 (10^3)
	1024 (2^{10})
KIPS	kiloinstructions per second

Appendix

Term	Meaning
LAN	local area network
LCC	leadless chip carrier
LCD	liquid-crystal display
LED	light-emitting diode
LEO	low earth orbit
LERP	linear interpolation
LIM	Lotus-Intel-Microsoft
LIM EMS	Lotus-Intel-Microsoft expanded memory specification
LISP	List Processing
LIX	liquid crystal
LOG	logarithm
	logarithmic
	logic
LPM	lines per minute
LQ	letter quality
LSB	least significant bit
LSD	least significant digit
LSI	large-scale integration
LTROM	linear transformer read-only memory
LUN	logical unit number
LUT	lookup table
M	mega-
	megabyte (1,048,576 bytes)
m	milli-
MA	memory address
Mac	Macintosh
MAR	memory-address register
MB	megabyte
MBPS	megabits per second
MBM	magnetic bubble memory
MCA	Micro Channel Architecture
MCB	Micro Channel Bus
MCC	master control center
MCCI	master control center interface
MCGA	Multicolor Graphics Array
MCI	Media Control Interface
MCM	multichip module
MDA	Monochrome Display Adapter
MDK	multimedia development kit

Comprehensive list of abbreviations & acronyms

Term	Meaning
meg	megabyte
mega-	1,000,000 (10^6)
	1,048,576 (2^{20})
MFM	modified frequency modulation
MHz	megahertz
MICR	magnetic ink character recognition
micro-	0.000 001 (10^{-6})
	highly miniaturized
	a very small fraction of
MIDI	Musical Instrument Digital Interface
milli-	0.001 (10^{-3})
MINIDOS	miniature disk operating system
MIPS	megainstructions per second
MIR	memory information register
MIS	management information system
MMU	memory management unit
modem	modulator/demodulator
MOS	metal-oxide semiconductor
MOSROM	metal-oxide-semiconductor read-only memory
MPC	multimedia personal computer
MPEG	Motion Picture Experts Group
MPX	multiplex
MS-DOS	Microsoft disk operating system
ms	millisecond
MSI	medium-scale integration
MTBF	mean time between failures
	mean time before failure
MUI	multimedia user interface
MUX	multiplexing
MVS/ESA	Multiple Virtual Storage/Enterprise System Architecture
μ	micro- (Greek lowercase letter *mu*)
μP	microprocessor
μs	microsecond
n	nano-
nano-	0.000 000 001 (10^{-9})
	extremely miniaturized
	an extremely small fraction of
NBP	name binding protocol
NEAT	New Enhanced Advanced Technology

Appendix

Term	Meaning
NESC	National Electrical Safety Code
NET	network
NETBIOS	network basic input/output system
NFF	native file format
NLQ	near letter-quality
NOR	NOT-OR logic operation
NOS	network operating system
ns	nanosecond
NTSC	National Television Standards Committee
NUM LOCK	Number Lock key
OC	object code
OCE	Open Collaboration Environment
OCF	object code file
OCR	optical character recognition
ODBC	open database connectivity
OEM	original equipment manufacturer
OLE	object linking and embedding
OOP	object-oriented programming
OOPS	object-oriented programming system
OPC	organic photoconductive cartridge
OS	operating system
OS/2	IBM Operating System/2
OSFDCE	Open Software Foundation Distributed Computing Environment
OSI	Open Systems Interconnection
OSI-RM	Open Systems Interconnection Reference Model
PACM	pulse-amplitude code modulation
PAD	packet assembler/disassembler
PAM	pulse-amplitude modulation
PARC	Palo Alto Research Center
PAX	private automatic exchange
PBX	private branch exchange
PC	personal computer (generic)
	Personal Computer (IBM)
	personal computing
	printed circuit
PCB	printed circuit board
PC-DOS	IBM personal computer disk operating system
PCL	printer control language
PCM	pulse code modulation

Term	Meaning
PCMCIA	Personal Computer Memory Card International Association
PCN	personal communications network
PCS	personal communications service
PDA	personal digital assistant
PDAS	programmable data acquisition system
PDL	page description language
PDM	pulse duration modulation
PDS	Personal Dictation System (IBM)
	processor direct slot
pel	picture element
PFF	proprietary file format
PFM	pulse frequency modulation
PGA	pin grid array
PG DN	Page Down key
PG UP	Page Up key
PIA	peripheral interface adapter
pico-	$0.000\,000\,000\,001\ (10^{-12})$
PIF	program information file
PILOT	Programmed Inquiry Learning Or Teaching
PIM	personal information manager
	pulse interval modulation
PI/O	parallel input/output
pixel	picture element
PLCC	plastic leaded chip carrier
PM	pulse modulation
PMM	paged-memory management
PMMU	paged-memory management unit
PN	Polish notation
PNP	plug and play
POS	point of sale
	programmed option select
POST	power-on self test
	point-of-sale terminal
POV	point of view
PP	peripheral processor
PPM	pages per minute
PRAM	parameter random-access memory
PRF	pulse repetition frequency
PROLOG	Programming in Logic

Appendix

Term	Meaning
PROM	programmable read-only memory
PRTSC	Print Screen key
ps	picosecond
PS	personal system (generic)
	Personal System (IBM)
	power supply
PSM	pulse-spacing modulation
PS/2	IBM Personal System/2
PTM	pulse time modulation
PWM	pulse width modulation
	plated-wire memory
QA	quality assurance
QBE	query by example
QC	quality control
QIC	quarter-inch cartridge
QWERTY	standard typewriter keyboard layout
RA	random access
RAD	rapid applications development
RAID	redundant array of inexpensive drives
RAM	random-access memory
RCL	recall
R&D	research and development
RDB	relational database
RDBMS	relational database management system
res	resolution
REXX	Restructured Extended Executor
RF	radio frequency
RFI	radio-frequency interference
RFID	radio-frequency identification
RGB	red/green/blue
RISC	reduced-instruction-set computing
RLL	run length limited
RMM	read-mainly memory
RO	read-only
ROM	read-only memory
RPG	Report Program Generator
RPM	revolutions per minute
RPS	revolutions per second
RSI	repetitive strain injury

Comprehensive list of abbreviations & acronyms

Term	Meaning
RTF	rich text format
RTS	request to send
RTTY	radioteletype
RTZ	return to zero
RW, R/W	read/write
RWF	read/write file
RWM	read/write memory
RX	receive
	receiver
SAA	Systems Application Architecture
SAM	sequential-access memory
SASI	Shugart Associates' Standard Interface
SBC	single-board computer
SCAI	switch-computer applications interface
SCC	serial communications controller
SCSI	Small Computer System Interface
SCM	software configuration management
SEM	single-electron memory
sfx	sound effects
SI	standard international system of units
SIG	special-interest group
SIMM	single inline memory module
SI/O	serial input/output
SIP	single inline package
SLIP	serial line interface protocol
SMD	surface-mount device
SMDS	switched multimegabit data service
SMT	surface-mount technology
S/N	signal-to-noise ratio
SNAFU	situation normal—all fouled up
SNOBOL	String-Oriented Symbolic Language
SNR	signal-to-noise ratio
SONET	synchronous optical network
SOP	standard operating procedure
SPARC	Scalable Processor Architecture
specs	specifications
SPX	sequenced packet exchange
SQL	Structured Query Language
SRAM	static random-access memory

Appendix

Term	Meaning
SS	single-sided
SSI	small-scale integration
SU	segmentation unit
SVGA	Super Video Graphics Array
SVID	System 5 Interface Definition
sync	synchronization
SYSINIT	system initialization
sysop	system operator
T	tera-
	terabyte (2^{40} bytes)
TB	terabyte
TCP	transmission control protocol
TCP/IP	transmission control protocol/Internet protocol
TCR	trainable character recognition
TDM	time-division multiplex
TDMA	time-division multiple access
tera-	1,000,000,000,000 (10^{12})
	2^{40} or $1,048,576^2$
TIFF	tagged image file format
TI	Texas Instruments
TIGA	Texas Instruments Graphics Architecture
TIPS	terainstructions per second
TM	technical manual
TP	transaction processing
TPI	tracks per inch
TQM	total quality management
T/R	transmit/receive
TR	terminal ready
TS	time sharing
TSOP	thin small outline package
TSR	terminate and stay resident
TSS	time-sharing system
TTY	teletype
TU	terminal unit
TX	transmit
	transmitter
UAE	unrecoverable application error
UART	universal asynchronous receiver/transmitter
UCR	untrainable character recognition

Comprehensive list of abbreviations & acronyms

Term	Meaning
ULSI	ultra-large-scale integration
UMA	upper memory area
UMB	upper memory blocks
UNIPOL	Universal Problem-Oriented Language
UNIVAC	Universal Automatic Computer
UPC	universal product code
UPS	uninterruptible power supply
USART	universal synchronous/asynchronous receiver/transmitter
USRT	universal synchronous receiver/transmitter
UUID	universal unique identifier
VAC	vector analog computer
VAR	value-added reseller
VCR	video cassette recorder
VCSR	voltage-controlled shift register
VDM	virtual DOS machine
VDR	video disk recorder
VDT	video display terminal
VDU	video display unit
VE	value engineering
VGA	Video Graphics Array
VLSI	very-large-scale integration
VM	virtual memory
	voice mail
VMM	virtual memory management
VMS	voice mail system
VR	virtual reality
VRAM	video random-access memory
VSA	voice stress analysis
VSAT	very-small-aperture terminal
VTAM/NCP	Virtual Telecommunications Access Method/Network Control Program
VTL	variable threshold logic
VTR	videotape recorder
VU	volume unit
VVR	virtual virtual reality
WAN	wide area network
WATS	wide area telephone service
WMF	Windows metafile format
WORM	write-once/read-many

Appendix

Term	Meaning
WP	word processing
WPM	words per minute
WYSIWYG	what you see is what you get
x	variable quantity
XCFN	external function
XCMD	external command
XCVR	transceiver
XGA	Extended Graphics Adapter
XMS	extended memory specification
XNOR	exclusive NOT-OR logic operation
XOR	exclusive OR logic operation
XT	Extended Technology (IBM computers)
xtalk	crosstalk
y	variable quantity
YMC	yellow/magenta/cyan
YMCK	yellow/magenta/cyan/black
z	variable quantity
ZIF	zero insertion force

Suggested reading

There are dozens of magazines and hundreds of books devoted to personal computing. If you're a beginning or intermediate PC user interested in supplementing your general knowledge, the following publications are among the best. If you're an advanced PC user, you can get up-to-the-minute, specialized information online.

Books

Steven Anzovin, *The Green PC* (Windcrest/McGraw-Hill, 1993)

D. P. Dern, *The Internet Guide for New Users* (McGraw-Hill, 1994)

Dan Gookin, Wally Wang and Chris Van Buren, *Illustrated Computer Dictionary for Dummies* (IDG Books Worldwide, 1993)

Dan Gookin and Andy Rathbone, *PCs for Dummies, 2nd Edition* (IDG Books Worldwide, 1994)

Joe Kraynak, *Plain English Computer Dictionary* (Alpha Books, 1992)

Aubrey Pilgrim, *Upgrade or Repair Your PC* (Windcrest/McGraw-Hill, 1993)

John Rizzo and K. Daniel Clark, *How Macs Work* (Ziff-Davis Press, 1993)

James L. Turley, *PCs Made Easy* (Osborne/McGraw-Hill, 1993)

Ron White, *How PCs Work* (Ziff-Davis Press, 1993)

Bibliography

Magazines

Byte
P.O. Box 558
Hightstown, NJ 08520

Computer Buyer's Guide and Handbook
Bedford Communications
150 Fifth Avenue
New York, NY 10011

HomePC
P.O. Box 420212
Palm Coast, FL 32142

Laptop Buyer's Guide and Handbook
Bedford Communications
150 Fifth Avenue
New York, NY 10011

MacWorld
501 Second Street
San Francisco, CA 94107

PC Computing
Ziff-Davis Publishing Company
P.O. Box 58229
Boulder, CO 80322

PC Kids
The Falsoft Building
P.O. Box 385
Prospect, KY 40059

PCNovice
P.O. Box 85380
Lincoln, NE 68501

PCToday
P.O. Box 85380
Lincoln, NE 68501

PC World
P.O. Box 51833
Boulder, CO 80321

Index

A

abbreviations, 771, 1173-1188
ABS function, 2-4
abscissa, 1-2, **2**
absolute values, 2-4
ac supplies, 863, **864**
accelerator keys, 524
accelerator boards, 4-5
accelerators, graphics accelerators, 481-483
accents, speech, 1028
access, 5-6
access numbers, bulletin board systems (BBS), 141
access time, 6-7, 503, 654, 1042
accounting software (*see* personal finance software)
aches and pains from computer use, 251
acoustic couplers, 7-9, **8**
acoustic transducers, 1027
acronyms, 9-10, 1173-1188
active files (*see* file management)
active matrix, LCDs, 11-12, 545, 711
active memory, 12
active window, 12-13, **13**
activity tracking software, 13-14
adapters/adapter cards, 14-16, **15**, 713, 821-823, **822**
  ANSI specifications/standards, 16, 34-35
  color graphics adapter (CGA), 187
  enhanced graphics adapter (EGA), 368-369
  expansion boards/slots, 386-389, **388**, **389**, 406, 715, 754
  PCMCIA standard adapter cards, 314, 607, 664, 821-823, **822**, 857, 916, 948, 982, 1003-1104, 1106
  plug adapters, 14-15
  super video graphics array (SVGA), 317, 369, 711, 1044, 1117
  telephone cord adapters, 15-16
  video graphics array (VGA), 369, 711, 1044, 1117
addiction, computer addiction, 215-216, 228-229, 257, 473-474, 870
addresses, 16-17, 263, 356, 395, 570-571, 957, 1033
Adobe Illustrator, 17-18, **18**
Adobe Type Manager, 18-20, **19**
aggregates, 20-21
alarms, 239
alert messages, 21-22, **21**

algorithms, 22-23
aliasing, 123, 579, **580**
alignment of heads, 508-509, **509**
alignment of text (*see also* justification), 23-24, 434-435, **435**, 499-500, **500**, 584
Allen, Paul, 684
allocation, 24, 25, 411-412
allophones, 1028
alpha testing, 27, 111-112, 138
alphanumeric sequence, 25-27
ALT key, 31, **31**
alternative computer technology (*see also* anticipatory sciences; artificial intelligence; artificial life; futuriural networks; optical computer technology; wetware), 27-30, 55-56, 118, 119, 156-157, 184, 189, 190, 209, 218-220, 223-227, **223**, **226**, 254-255, 452-453, 461-462, 547, 567-568, 581-582, 736-737, 740-742, **741**, 781-782, **781**, 900-901, **901**, 1142-1145, **1143**
amateur radio (*see also* packet communications), 31-33, 107-108, 153, 206, 237, 295-296, **296**, 487-488, 616-617, 643-645, **644** 699, 1107
ambient recovery systems (ARS), 1023
America Online, 33-34, 574, 774-775
American National Standards Institute (ANSI), 16, 34-35
American Radio Relay League (ARRL), 33
American Standard Code for Information Interchange (*see* ASCII)
amplitude modulation (AM), 705
amusement robots, 35-36, **36**
analog baseband (*see* baseband)
analog processes, 28, 36-42
  analog-to-digital (A/D) converters, 37, 45-46, **46**, 273-274, **274**, 299, 300, 704, 770, 954, 1025, 1072
  computer technology using analog processes, 38-42
  digital-to-analog (D/A) conversion, 37-38, 274, 299, 300, 301, 704, 770, 1071
  error accumulation, 379-380
  future of analog computing, 42
  hybrid computers, 30, 42, 526-528
  logic states, 40-41, **40**
  pros and cons of analog computers, 41-42
  sampling/sampling rates, 45, 46, 273-274, 705

Illustrations are in **boldface**

Index

analog processes *continued*
  sampling resolutions, 46, 273, 705
  signals, analog signals, 36-37, **37**
  slide rules, 39-40
  variable voltages, 41
  waveforms, 36-37, **37**
analog-to-digital (A/D) converters, 37, 45-46, **46**, 273-274, **274**, 299, 300, 704, 770, 954, 1025, 1072
analogical reasoning, 43-45, 696
analytical engines, 47, 53
analytical graphics, 17, 48-49, **48**, 245-247, **246**, 942, 968-969, **968**
anchoring, 49-50, **50**
AND logic gate, 50, **50**, 128, 585, 638, 779, 780
androids (*see also* artificial intelligence; artificial life; robotics/robots; 36, 53-54, 67, 69, 119, 218-220
animation (*see also* graphics; virtual reality), 51-52, 999-1000
  choreographer programs, 177-178
  computer/hardware requirements, 52
  eye lag in animation, 51, **51**
  full motion video interface (FMVI), 458-459
  holographic animation, 52
  modeling, 692-697, **693**
  multimedia, 351, 530, 718-721, **721**, 1060-1063, **1061**
  presentation graphics, 49, 873-875
  scanning, 51, **51**
  software programs for animation, 52
  virtual reality (*see* virtual reality)
animism, 52-53
anthropomorphism, 53-54
anti-aliasing, 54-55, **54**, 123
anti-viral (*see* vaccines; Trojan horses; viruses)
anticipatory sciences, 27-30, 5-56, 118, 119, 156-157, 184, 189, 190, 209, 218-220, 223-227, **223**, **226**, 254-255, 461-462, 547, 567-568, 581-582, 708-711, 736-737, 740-742, **741**, 900-901, **901**, 1142-1145, **1143**
Anzovin, Steven, 347
APPEND command, 193
Apple Computer, Inc. (*see* Macintosh computers)
Apple File Exchange, 723
AppleTalk, 57-58, 381, 651
application layer, 777
application servers, 726
application window, 321
applications, 58-59, 145, 778-779, 1010-1011
Archie searches, 133, 572
archiving (*see also* backups), 59-60, 75-76, 95, 100, 101, 500-501, 1101
area graphs, 60-62, **61**
arithmetic mean, 20
arithmetic operators, 62-63, 73-74, 779-780, 870-872
arithmetic/logic unit (ALU), 169
ARPAnet, 570
arrow keys, 63-64, **63**
artificial intelligence (*see also* androids; artificial life; learning; neural networks; robotics/robots), 42, 55-56, 64-69, 69-70, 118, 119, 184, 189-190, 209, 218-220, 222, 248, 254-255, 324, 90-391, **390**, 461-462, 468-469, 473-474, 492-494, **493**, 526, 581-582, 614, 889, 960-961, 1091-1126, **1120**, **1121**, **1123**, 1140-1141
  algorithms, 23
  animism, 52-53
  anthropomorphism, 53-54
  backward chaining, 93
  blackboard systems, 123-124, **124**
  Bongard problems, 127-128, **127**, 820
  branching, 131-133, **132**
  caretakers, 156-157, 189-190
  checkers-playing computers, 174
  chess-playing computers, 176-177
  combinatorial explosion, 191-192, **191**
  Commonsense Summer Project, 203-204
  ELIZA, 359-360
  focus specialists, 124
  forward chaining, 445-446, **446**
  frames, 451-452, **451**, **452**
  heuristic knowledge, 511-512, 594, 595
  hybrid computers, 30, 42, 526-528
  immortal knowledge, 547-548, 595
  incompleteness theorem, 549-550, **550**, 598
  infinite regress, 553-555, **554**
  insect robots, 83, 224, 558-559, 959, 961, 1058
  Jungian-world theory, 583-584
  k-line programming, 594, **595**
  knowledge (*see* knowledge, learning, and reasoning)
  knowledge-based simulation, 597-599, **598**
  learning (*see* knowledge, learning, and reasoning)
  logic (*see* logic)
  macroknowledge, 653-654
  mechatronics, 665-666
  memory organization packets (MOPs), 674-675
  message passing, 678-679, **678**
  microknowledge, 682
  molecular computer technology, 29, 708-711, **710**
  nested loops, 640, 737-738, **738**
  neural networks (*see* neural networks)
  optical character recognition (OCR), 172-173, **173** 780, 1029
  pattern recognition, 127-128, **127**, 820-821
  PLANNER language, 844-845
  problem reduction, 880-882, **881**
  recursion, 553-555, **554**, 932-933
  simulations, 597-599, **598**, 999-1000, 1119-1126, **1120**, **1121**, **1123**
  specialty circuits, 124
  teach boxes, 216, 1057-1058
  theorem-proving machines (TPMs), 880-882, **881**, 1072-1074
  Turing test, 1092-1094, **1093**
  uncanny valleys, 568, 1097-1099, **1099**, 1126
  viruses, 112, 138, 141, 161, 228, 229, 265, 455, 492, 699, 743, 797, 892-894, 900, 1012, 1090, 1109, 1113-1116, **1115**, 1126-1129
  vision systems, 1129-1131, **1130**
  well-structured languages, 1141-1142
artificial life (*see also* artificial intelligence; androids; biochips; molecular computer technology; nanotey; robotics/robots), 118, 119, 218-220, 461-462, 938-939, 960-961
ascension, celestial coordinates, 243
ASCII, 70, 71, 363, 392-393, **393**, 415-416, 703, 1029
Asimov's Three Laws, 70-71, 453
aspect ratio, 71-72, **72**
assemblers, 72-73, 515
assembly language, 72-73, 887
ASSIGN command, 193
Association of Commercial Records Centers (ACRC), 769
asterisk, 73-74
asynchronous data, 74-75, 1046
atomic computers, 900-901, **901**
ATTRIB command, 193
attributes, 75-76, 514
audio frequency shift keying (AFSK), 107, 704
audit trail, 76-77
auto dial, 239
AUTOEXEC.BAT files, 77-78, **78**, 235, 818-820
automated computer time service (ACTS), 1078
automated integrated manufacturing systems (AIMS), 216

Index

Automatic Sequence Controlled Calculator, 80-81
automation (*see also* robotics/robots), 81-82, 216-217, 217-218, 223-227, **223**, **226**, 292, 402-403, **403**, 581-582, 960-961, 1058-1060
  office automation, 766-768, 810-813
  personal robots, 117-118, 119, 223-227, **223**, **226**, 254-255, 526, 614, 682, 838-840
  quality assurance and control, 898-900, **899**, 944
  smart paper, 1004-1007
autonomous robots, 82-83, 224, 961, 1058
autopatch, 952
autorepeat, 83, 90, 588-589
auxiliary storage (*see also* memory), 83-85
averages, 20
axioms, 549-550, **550**, 1072

B

Babbage, Charles, 47, 53, 87
background processing, 87-89, **88**, 580, 718, 726-727, **727**
backlighting, 89-90
backspace key, 90, **90**
BACKUP command, 193
backups, 91-93, 276, 424-425, 688-690, 751, 768-769, 1101
  archiving, 59-60, 75-76, 95, 100, 101, 500-501, 1101
  automatic backups, 79-80
  auxiliary storage, 83-85
  battery backup, 104-105
  brownouts, 135-136
  catastrophic failures, 161, 247-248, 471-473, **472**, 509-510, 892-894
  CD-ROM, 60, 166
  compression, 60, 270-272, **273**, 537-539, 641-642, 705
  full backups, 457
  hardcopy, 500-501
  off-site data storage, 768-769
  overwriting, 424, 795-796
  tape drives, 100, 457, 655, 657-658, **657**, 663, 828, 949, 982, 1052-1054, **1052**, 1085-1086
  utilities for backup, 92-93
  write once read many (WORM) disks, 60, 166, 374, 504, 664, 935, 1106, 1157-1158
  write protection, 60, 1158-1159, **1158**
backward chaining, 93
bacteriorhodopsin (BR), 93-94, **94**
bad sectors, 91-92, 94-95, 984
band-gap semiconductors, LEDs, 615
bandwidth, 95-96, **96**, 106, 134
bar graphs, 97-98, **98**, 342-343, **343**, 807-808, **808**
barcodes, 96-97, **97**, 849-851, **850**
base fonts, 99
base memory, 100-101
baseband communications, 98-99
BASIC, 73, 102-103, 210, 515, 603, 815, 887, 1003
basic input/output system (BIOS), 100, 103, **103**, 926, 1105
batch files, 77-78, 103-104
batch processing, 103-104
batteries, 89-90, 104-105, 628-629, **629**, 744-746, 605-606, 628-629, **629**, 858, 934
baud rate, 70, 95, 105-107, **107**, 140, 698, 770
beam deflection, CRTs, 162
Beginner's All Purpose Symbolic Instruction Code (*see* BASIC)
Bell 103 and 202, 107-108, **108**
Bell, Alexander G., 1024
benchmarks, 108-109, 751, 1075
Bernoulli boxes, 109-110, 314, 504, 828, 948, 982

beta testing, 27, 111-112, 138
beta-particle CD-ROM, 110-111, 309
Bezier curves, 18, **18**, 48, 112-113, **113**, 453, 454
bin-picking problems, 117-118, **118**, 764
binary codes, 362-363
binary data, 113-114
binary logic, 598, **598**, 637
binary number systems, 114-115, 296, 512, 708, **708**
binary search, 115-116
binary states, 650
binding offset, 116-117, **117**
biochips (*see also* artificial life; molecular computer technology; nanotechnology), 29, 118, 708-711, **710**, 1001-1002, 1142-1145, **1143**
biomechatronics, 119
biometric security systems 987-988
BIOS (*see* basic input output system)
bistable multivibrators, 992
bit count, 208
bitmapped fonts, 18-19, **19**, 122-123
bitmapped graphics, 17, 123, 337, 453, 478-479, **480**, 495-496, **496**, 540, 579, **580**, 805
bitmapping process, 120-122, **121**
bits (*see also* bytes), 38-39, 119-120, **120**, 363, 1045
bits per second (BPS), 70, 95, 105-107, **107**, 140, 698, 770
blackboard systems, 123-124, **124**
bleeder resistors, 867-868
block (text) operations, 125, **125**
block file transfers, 125-126, 137, 672
block memory transfers, 672
boilerplates, 126, 144, 614-615
Bolles, Robert, 485
Bongard problems, 127-128, **127**, 820
books on disk (*see also* CD-ROM), 165-166, 294, 350-352, **352**
Boolean algebra, 128, 585-587, **586**, 597, 635, 1073
boot, 128-129, 186-187, 247-248, 250, 506, 868-869, 952-953, 1139-1140
bootstrap programs, 100, 130, 186-187, 926, 1139
Borland International, 902
bottlenecks, Von Neumann bottleneck, 1137
boxes, 693
brain-to-computer links, wetware, 1142-1145, **1143**
branch control structures, 131
branching, 131-133, **132**
BREAK command, 197
breakers, 867
bridge rectifiers, 865, **865**
bridges, 133, **134**
brightness of color, 956
brilliance of color, 956
broadband data, 134-135
Brooks, Robert, 558-559
brownouts, 135-136
bubble memory, 136-137, **136** 663, 672
buffers, 137, **137**, 275
bugs (*see also* debugging; viruses; Trojan horses), 138, 228-229, 277, 362, 455, 456, 468, 742-744, 1126-1129, 1126
built-in fonts, 138-139
bulletin board systems (BBS), 139-142, **139**, 215, 570-571, 739, 772, 1042, 1079-1080
  downloading, 80, 333-334, 1109
  mail forwarding, 658-659
  mailboxes, 658, **658**
  packet radio bulletin board systems (PBBS), 799-800
  uploading, 1108-1110, **1109**
bundled software (*see* suites)
burn-in, 142, 884

Index

bus networks, 146-147, **147**, 263, **630**, 631, 823
buses, 142-143, 230
  benchmarks, 109
  data bus, 268-269, **269**
  enhanced industry standard architecture (EISA), 369-370, **369**, 393-394, 553
  ground buses, 488
  host bus, 523-524, **524**
  industry standard architecture (ISA), 369, 394, 553, 565, 680
  Micro Channel Architecture (MCA), 394, 680-681
  local buses, 633-634
  NuBus, 754, 860-861
business letters, 144
business software, 145-146
buttons, 478
bytes, 147-148, 230, 382-383, **383**, 468, **470**, 594, 668, **669**, 840, 841, 873, 1068-1069, **1068**,

C

C language, 149, 210, 515, 603, 887
C++, 149-150, 515, 603
cable data transmissions, 152-153
cabling, 150-153, **150**, 407-408, **407**, 632
cache memory, 153-154, **154**, 268, 269, 306-307, **307**
calculators, 87, 352-353, **353**, 590
call-waiting, 141
cameras
  digital cameras, 475
  vidicons, 1117-1118, **1118**
capacity, disk capacity, 307-309, **309**, **310**, 502-503, 520-521, **521**, 654-655
Caps Lock key, 154-156, **155**, 995-997, **996**
capture screen, 156, 879-880, 973-975
caretakers, 156-157, 189-190
carpal tunnel syndrome (CTS), 251, 589, 592
carrier modulation, 705
carrier-sense multiple access with collision detection (CSMA/CD), 157
carriers, 158
Cartesian coordinates, 1, 158-159, **159**, 242, 619, 692, 786
cascaded windows, 886
cascading, 160-161, **161**
case sensitivity, 27
catastrophic failures, 161, 247-248, 471-473, **472**, 509-510, 892-894
cathode ray tubes (CRTs) (*see also* image resolution; monitors), 161-162, **162**, 289, 544-547, **546**, 604, 711, 921-923, **922**
CCITT standards, 163
CD command, 197, 305
CD-ROM, 28, 60, 101, 156, 163-167, **164**, 291, 312, 314, 350, 351, 352, 504, 664, 672, 673, 707, 828, 949, 981-983, 1019, 1106
  beta-particle CD-ROM, 110-111, 309
  de Broglie wavelengths, 111
  disk capacity, 308, **310**
  document image processing (DIP), 320-321
  erasable optical disk, 374-375
  holographic data storage, 520-521, **521**
  importing files, 549
  multimedia, 351, 530, 718-721, **721**, 1060-1063, **1061**
  presentation graphics, 49, 873-875
  tracks, 1084-1086, **1085**
  wavelengths, 111
celestial coordinates, 243
cellular telecommunications, 167-168, **167**, **168**
cells, spreadsheets, 1033
Center for Nonlinear Studies, Los Alamos, NM, 900
center pivot irrigators, automated, 402-403, **403**
central processing unit (CPU) (*see also* buses; integrated circuits; motherboards), 143, 168-170, **169**, 524, **524**, 558, **558**, 633-634, 683, 714-715, 1105
certified record managers (CRMs), 768
chain printing, 170-172, **171**
chaining, backward and forward, 93, 445-446, **446**
chairs and seating, 376-377
chaos theory, 45, 439-440, **440**
character attributes, 76
character recognition, trainable and untrainable, 826-827, 826
characters, 172, **172**
characters per inch (CPI), 436, 620, 843
charge-coupled devices (CCDs), 172-173, **173**, 475
CHCP command, 197
CHDIR command, 197
check boxes, 477
checkers-playing computers, 174
checksum, 174-176, **175**
chess-playing computers, 176-177
child data, 399
child-proof workstations, 1080-1082
CHKDSK command, 194
choke coils, 914
choreographer programs, 177-178
ciphers, 248, **249**, 364
circular references, 178-179, **178**
Clarke, Arthur C., 643
click/double-click, 179, 477
client-server networks, 422, 630, **630**, 631, 994
clients, 180, 994
clip art, 180-182, 540-541
clipboards, 182
clocks/clock speed (*see also* integrated circuits; instructions per second; microprocessors), 105, 108-109, 182-183, 230-231, **231**, 510-511, **510**, 560-561, 1045-1046, **1046**, 1077-1078, 1169-1170
clones, 183-184, 682, 954
CLS command, 197
clusters, 282
coaxial cables, 151, 184-186, **185**, 632
COBOL, 73, 186, 210, 515, 603
cold boots, 129, 186-187, 248, 506, 868-869, 953
cold links, 525
collision detection, 158
collisions, 158
color, 956-957
  palettes, 808-809, **810**
  RGB color model, 162, 316, 808, 956-957, **957**
color graphics adapter (CGA), 187
color monitors, 712-713
color printers, 121, 187-189, **188**
Colossus: The Forbin Project, 157, 189-190
column formatting, 24
  newspaper column format, 1094-1095, **1094**
  parallel column format, 997
  side-by-side column format, 997-998
  single-column formats, 1000-1001, 1094
  two-column format, 1094-1095, **1094**
columnar graphs, 190, **190**, 342-343, **343**, 690-691, **691**, 1037-1038, **1038**
combinatorial explosion, 191-192, **191**
command buttons, 478
COMMAND command, 193, 194-203, **203**
command processors, 198
command-driven environments (*see also* DOS), 12, 201-202, 324, 325, 569, 677, 778, 1009
COMMAND.COM, 193, 194, 569
commands, 192-202, 396, 569-570, 818, 910, 1046-1047, **1048**
Commonsense Summer Project, 203-204

Index

communications, 204-207, **205**, 593, 1164-1165
  abbreviations used in online communications, 771
  amateur radio, 31-33, 107-108, 153, 206, 237, 295-296, **296**, 487-488, 616-617, 643-645, **644**, 699, 1107
  AppleTalk, 57-58, 381, 651
  asynchronous data, 74-75, 1046
  audio frequency shift keying (AFSK), 107, 704
  bandwidth, 95-96, **96**, 106
  baseband, 98-99
  baud rate, 70, 95, 105-107, **107**, 140, 698, 770
  Bell 103 and 202, 107-108, **108**
  bit count, 208, 363
  bridges, 133, **134**
  broadband data, 134-135
  bulletin board systems (BBS), 139-142, **139**, 215, 570-571, 739, 772, 1042, 1079-1080
  carrier-sense multiple access collision detection (CSMA/CD), 157
  cellular telecommunications, 167-168, **167**, **168**
  checksum, 174-176, **175**
  connect time, 237
  connection protocols, 235-237, **236**
  data communications, 269-270
  demodulation, 108, 140, 698, 703
  demultiplexing, 135, 286-287, **286**, 724
  destination, 205, 294-295, 758, 1021
  digipeaters, 237, 295-296, **296**, 747, 951-952, **952**, 1072
  downlinks, 332, 965, 1108
  duplexing (see full-duplex; half-duplex)
  electronic mail, 139, 205-206, 356, 488, 570-571, 658-659, **658**, 658, 739, 772, 799
  end-to-end acknowledgment, 366, **367**
  error detection, 208
  Ethernet, 380-381, **381**
  fax, 404-406, **405**, 858, 1106
  file transfer protocol (FTP), 423, 571-572
  frequency shift keying (FSK), 107
  full duplex, 207, 295, 457-458, **458**, 494-495, 558, 1021
  future of communications technology, 206-207
  geostationary-satellite data links, 466-468, **467**, 643, 966
  half-duplex, 207, 295, 458, 494-495, **495**, 1021
  handshaking, 175-176, 208, 270, 498-499, **499**, 815, 979, 1164-1165
  Hayes compatibility, 507-508
  heterogeneous networks, 511, **512**
  laser communications, 608-609, **608**
  links, 621, **621**, 759, 966
  low-earth-orbit (LEO) data links, 643-645, **644**, 966
  message passing, 678-679, **678**
  microwave data transmissions, 684, **685**
  modems (see modems)
  modulation, 95, 108, 140, 152, 162, 698, 703-707, **703**, **704**, **706**
  multiplexing, 135, 286, 724, **724**
  node-to-node acknowledgment, 366, **367**, 747, **748**
  noise, 747-749, **749**
  online services (see online services)
  open systems interconnection reference model (OSI-RM), 776-777, 798, 891
  packet communications, 107, 206, 237, 265, 332, 798-799, 1071, 1108
  packet radio bulletin board systems (PBBS), 799-800
  parameters, 207, **208**
  parity, 208, 814-815
  PCMCIA standard adapter cards, 314, 607, 664, 821-823, **822**, 857, 916, 948, 982, 1003-1104, 1106
  propagation delay, 947
  protocols, 163, 207, 235-237, **236**, 423, 570, 798-799, 853-854, **854**, 891-892
  radio, 206
  real-time communications, 771
  remote control systems, 944-947
  repeaters, 147, 684, **685**, 950-952, **951**, **952**
  satellite communications (see satellite communications)
  source, 205, 758, 1021-1022, **1021**
  start bits, 1046
  stop bits, 208, 1046
  synchronous data, 75, 1045-1046, **1046**
  telecommunications software, 140
  teleconferencing, 771-772, 1060-1063, **1061**, 1065
  telephone, 205-206, **205**, 1063-1065
  terminal emulation software, 139, 140-141, 344, 699, 770, 1070-1071
  terminal node controllers, 206, 292, 295, 697, 799, 858, 1071-1072, **1072**
  time-shifting communications, 206, 798, 799, 927, 1079-1080
  transponders, 332, 816, 951-952, 965, 1108
  uplinks, 332
  voice-mail systems, 1132-1134, **1133**
COMP command, 194
companionship software, 209
comparators, 1025
comparison of documents, 319-320
compatibility, 145, 183-184, 210, 334-336, 384, 506, 511, 607, 1110
compilers, 210-211, 385, 515, 576, 603, 651
complementary metal oxide semiconductor (CMOS), 211-212, **211**, 221
complex instruction set computing (CISC), 212-213, 726-727, 892, 898, 936-938
complex numbers, absolute value (ABS), 3, **4**
compound documents, 213-214
compression, 60, 270-272, **273**, 537-539, 641-642, 705
CompuServe, 214-215, 574, 774, 775
computer-aided design (CAD), 75-76, 216, 353, 522
computer-aided engineering (CAE), 217, 353
computer-aided instruction (CAI), 217-218, 530, 1097, 1123
computer-aided manufacturing (CAM), 216-217
computer-aided testing (CAT), 217
computer-integrated manufacturing (CIM), 217
concordance files, 232, 552
concurrency control, 196, 233, **233**
cones, 694
conferencing, 739
CONFIG.SYS files, 234-235
configuration, 77, 234-235
conjunctions (see also AND gate) 50, **50**
connect time, 237
connection protocols, 235-237, **236**
connectors, 340-341, 348, **348**
consciousness, computer consciousness, 218-220
contact manager software, 238-240, 261-262, **262**, 836-838
context, 240
Control key, 202, 240-241, **241**
control menu, 241-242, **242**
control/timing unit (CTU), 169
convection cooling, 625
conventional memory, 100
conversion, data (see also analog-to-digital conversion; digital-to-analog conversion), 37-38, 45-46, 272-275, 275, 299, 300, 301, 415-416
cooling systems for computers, 625-626, **626**
coordinates, 242-243
  0-degree reference ray, 258
  Cartesian, 1, 158-159, **159**, 242, 619, 692, 786

1195

Index

coordinates *continued*
  celestial coordinates, 243
  cylindrical coordinates, 258-259, **258**, 692
  independent, 1-2, **2**
  latitude and longitude, 243
  log-log graphs, 243
  logarithmic graphs, 242
  modeling, 692-697, **693**, **694**
  more than three dimensions, 551
  ordinates, 786-787, **786**, **787**
  polar coordinates, 243, 851-853, **852**
  rectangular coordinates, 158-159, **159**, 242
  semilog graphs, 242
  spherical coordinates, 692, 1032-1033, **1032**
  three-dimensional, 551-552, **552**
  xy coordinates/plane, 1
Coordinated Universal Time (UTC), 685, **686**, **687**
coprocessors, 244-245, **244**
COPY command, 197-198
copy protection, 986
CorelDraw, 762
correlations, 245-247, **246**
corrupted data (*see* error detection; error rates)
count, 20
CPQ-DOS (*see* DOS)
crashes (*see also* catastrophic failures; graceful degradation), 247-248, 250, 471-473, **472**, 509-510, 892-894
creating files, 413
crosstalk, 151
cryptanalysis, 248-250
cryotechnology, 748
cryptography (*see also* encryption), 248-250
cryptology, 248-250
Ctrl key, 202, 240-241, **241**
Ctrl-Alt-Del (warm boot), 250
CTTY command, 198
cumulative trauma disorders (CTDs) (*see also* carpal tunnel), 250-252
cursors/cursor movement, 253-254, **253**, 889-890
  anchoring, 49-50, **50**
  arrow keys, 63-64, **63**
  autorepeat keyboard function, 83, 90
  backspace key, 90, **90**
  direction keys, 63
  drag-and-drop, 337
  dragging, 336-337, **336**
  pointers, 849
curved surfaces, 694
cybercops, 157
cybernetics, 254-255
cyberphilia, 257
cyberphobia, 157, 229, 255-257, 321, 374, 452-453, 456, 500, 632, 645-647, 810
cybersapiens, 68-69
cylinders, disk, 257-258, **257**, 502, 654
cylinders, graphic, 695
cylindrical coordinates, 258-259, **258**, 392

D

D flip-flops, 429
D-shell connectors, 340-341
daily planner software, 261-262, **262**
daisy-chain networks, 262-263, **263**
daisy-wheel printers, 264, **264**, 548
data acquisition systems, 264-265, **265**
data bits, 74-75
data bus, 268-269, **269**
data communications (*see also* communications), 269-270
data compression (*see* compression)
data conversion (*see* conversion)
data highway (*see* Internet)
data redundancy, 276
data terminal equipment (DTE), 277
databases, 146, 265-268, **267**, 409-410, 903-904, 904-906, 932
  geocoding, 465
  geographic information systems (GIS), 465-466
  graphical databases, 474-476
  joins, 581
  linked objects, 623-625, **624**
  thematic shading, 465-466
DATE command, 198
daughterboards, 715
dc supplies, 863, **864**
death spirals, 933
de Broglie wavelengths, 111
debugging (*see also* alpha testing; beta testing; bugs), 138, 228-229, 277, 362, 742-744, 888-889
decimal number system, 114-115, 278, **278**, 707-708, **708**
declarative languages, 278-279, 887-888
declination, celestial coordinates, 243
decoding, 279-280
decryption, 248-250, 280
deductive logic, 636
default fonts, 139
defaults, 280-281
deflection, CRTs, 162
defragmentation, 281-283, **282**, **283**, 413, 450-451, 503, 751-752
DEL command, 198
Delete key, 283-284, **284**
deleting files, 413
Delphi, 284-286, 574, 774, 775
demodulation, 108, 140, 698, 703
demultiplexing, 135, 286-287, **286**, 724
density, diskettes, 310, 311, 314, 331, 515
dependent variables, 1, 287-288, **287**
Descartes, Rene, 158
desk for computer use, 377
desktop, 288
desktop computers, 289-292, **289**
desktop publishing (DTP), 146, 292-294, 651, 1153
  CD-ROM, 165-166
  clip art, 180-182, 540-541
  compound documents, 213-214
  drop cap, 339-340
  duplex printing, 344
  flash tests, 473, **474**
  frames, 451-452, **451**, **452**
  full page display, 459
  grammar checking, 473
  kerning, 587
  page description languages (PDLs), 800-801, **800**, **801**, 859-860
  page layout programs, 802, **803**
  side-by-side column format, 997-998
  single-column formats, 1000-1001
  WYSIWYG, 293, 459, 651, 907, 1091, 1153, 1159-1160
destination, 205, 294-295, 758, 1021
device independence, 801, 860, 1091
dialects, speech, 1028
dialog boxes, 477
dielectrics, 151, 185
digipeaters, 237, 295-296, **296**, 747, 951-952, **952**, 1072
digital audio tape (DAT), 949, 1053, 1086
digital ink, pen-based computers, 824-827, **825**, **826**
digital baseband (*see* baseband)
digital cameras, 475
digital processes, 27-28, 38-39, 42, 296-299, **297**
  asynchronous data, 74-75, 1046
  Babbage's first calculator, 87
  digital signal processing (DSP), 299-301, **300**
  digital-to-analog (D/A) conversion, 37-38, 274, 299, 300, 301, 704, 770, 1071
  error accumulation, 379-380
  hybrid computers, 30, 42, 526-528
  logic states, 40-41, **40**

1196

Index

machine language, 298
motion, digital motion, 296-297
digital signal processing (DSP), 299-301, **300**, 1023
digital-to-analog (D/A) conversion, 37-38, 274, 299, 300, 301, 704, 770, 1071
DIR command, 198
direction keys, 63
direction resolution, 954
directories/subdirectories, 198, **199**, 302-303, 412, 818-820, **819**
  allocation, 24, 25
  auxiliary storage, 83-85, **85**
  branch directories (subdirectories), 304-305
  change directories (CD) command, 305
  default directory, 280-281
  file allocation table (FAT), 412
  hierarchical file systems (HFS), 514
  paths, 818-820
  root directory, 302, 304, 412, 818-820, **819**
  sentry directory, 1100
  subdirectories, 302, 304-305
  tree, directory tree, 302, 303, 514
  window, directory window, 305-306, 305
  working directory, 302-303, 302
directory tree, 302, 303-305, **304**
directory window, 305-306
discrete cosine transform (DCT) compression, 538
disk caching, 306-307, **307**
disk capacity (see capacity of disks)
disk drives (see CD-ROM; floppy disk drives; hard disk drives)
disk icon, 288
disk operating system (see DOS)
DISKCOMP command, 194
DISKCOPY command, 194
diskettes/diskette drives (see floppy disk drives)
displays (see monitors)
distributed processing system, 315-316, **315**
distributions, 519-520
dithering 316-317
divide-and-conquer, 116
DO-WHILE loops, 331-332
docking stations, 317-318, **317**, 423, 607
document comparison, 319-320
document image processing (DIP), 320-321
document window, 321-322, **322**
documents, 318-319
domain of function, 322-323, **322**, 459
domains, domain abbreviations, 571
don't care state, 323
DOS, 12, 130, 192-202, 323-324, 396, 476, 534, 569-570, 684, 688, 691, 778, 789, 861, 910, 1009, 1013, 1014
  alert messages, 21-22, **21**
  AUTOEXEC.BAT files, 77-78, **78**, 235, 818-820
  COMMAND.COM, 193
  commands, 192-201, 396, 569-570
  CONFIG.SYS files, 234-235
  formatting disks, 441, 442-443
  graphics accelerators, 483
  prompt, 324-325, 889-890
  shell, 325-327, **326**, 427
  SMARTDRV.SYS, 307
DOS shell, 324-325, 427
dot pitch, 329-330, **330**, 517, 712
dot-matrix printers, 188, 327-329, **327**, 330, 518, 548, 877
dots per inch (DPI), 330-331, 518, 545, 783, 843, 953
double-click, 477
double-density diskettes, 310, 331, 515
double-sided diskettes, 310, 331
downlinks, 332, 965, 1108
downloadable fonts, 332-333, 437
downloading, 80, 333-334, 1109
downward compatibility, 334-336
DR-DOS (see DOS)

drag-and-drop, 337
dragging, 336-337, **336**
draw programs, 337-338, **338**, 480, 540, 841-842, **842**, 907-909, **908**
Drexler, Eric, 736
drive bays, 338-339, **339**
drives (see floppy disk drives; hard disk drives)
drop cap, 339-340
drop-in/drop-out, 340
dual inline package (DIP) 341, **342**, 561
dual-ordinate graphs, 342-343, **343**
dumb terminals, 264-265, **265**, 277, 315, 343-344, 422
duplexing (see full-duplex; half-duplex)
duplex printing, 116-117, **117**, 344
Dvorak keyboards, 344-345, 911
dynamic data exchange (DDE), 345, 525, 759
dynamic linking, 564
dynamic RAM (DRAM), 153, 346, 671, 919, 1041

E

e-mail (see electronic mail)
eccentricity in shapes, 337
ecolinking, 347, 366-368, 485-486, 933-936, 1058-1060
edge connectors, 348, **348**
Eisenhower, Dwight, 555
electrically erasable programmable ROM (EEPROM), 375, 671, 885, 926
electricity (see power supplies)
electroluminscent diodes (see light-emitting diodes)
electromagnet fields (EM), 151, 252, 348-349, **349**, 357-359, **358**, 377, 409, 913-915, **914**
electromagnetic shielding, 151, 349, 350, **350**, 913-915, 1019
electron beams cathode ray tubes (CRTs), 161-162, **162**
electronic calculators, 352-353, **353**
electronic data interchange (EDI), 355-356
electronic mail, 139, 205-206, 356, 488, 570-571, 658-659, **658**, 658, 739, 772, 799
Electronic Numerical Integrator and Calculator (ENIAC), 357
electronic publishing (see also CD-ROM; desktop publishing), 165-166, 294, 350-352, **352**
electronic-circuit design software, 353-355, **354**
electrostatic discharge (ESD), 388-389, 680
elite type, 436
ELIZA, 359-360
embedded formatting, 360-361
embedded objects (see also object linking and embedding (OLE), 361, **362**, 757-759, **758**
embedding, 758
emoticons, 771
empirical design, 361-362
emulation, 861
encoding, 362-364, **363**
encryption, 248-250, 280, 363-364, 985
End key, 364, **365**
end-to-end acknowledgment, 366, **367**
endless loops, 131, 179, 365-366, 432, 553-555, **554**, 641
energy-efficient computing (see also ecolinking), 366-368, 485-486
enhanced graphics adapter (EGA), 368-369
enhanced industry standard architecture (EISA), 369-370, **369**, 393-394, 553
enhanced PC keyboards, 370-371, **370**, 588
enhanced storage-device interface (ESDI), 371
ENIAC computer, 357
Enigma computer, 248
Enter key, 371-373, **372**
entry-level system, 373-374
environmentally concious computing (see ecolinking)

Index

erasable optical disk, 374-375
erasable programmable ROM (EPROM), 375, 427, 663, 671, 884-885, 926
ERASE command, 416-417
ergonomics (*see also* human engineering), 250-252, 375-379, **376**, 397-398, **398**, 525-526
error accumulation, 379-380
error detection, 174-176, **175**, 208, 269-270, 498-499, **499**
error rates, 269-270
Escape key, 380, **380**
Ethernet, 380-381, **381**
Euclidean plane geometry (*see* geometry)
event-driven environments, 381-382
exabyte, 382-383, **383**, 873
exclusive NOR (XNOR) gates, 383, **384**, 638
exclusive OR (XOR) gates, 383-384, **384**, 638
executable program, 384-385
exercise software, 385-386
EXIT command, 198
expandability, 386
expanded memory, 394-396, **395**
expansion boards/slots, 386-389, **388**, **389**, 406, 715, 754
experience paths, 1120, **1120**, **1121**
experience spaces, 1121
expert systems (*see also* artificial intelligence; automation), 67-68, 93, 278-279, 390-391, 439, 445-446, **446**
exploratory virtual reality, 1120, **1121**
export business software, 391-392
exporting data/files, 392, 549
extended character set, 392-393, **393**
extended graphics array (XGA), 393
extended industry standard architecture (EISA), 393-394, 680
extended memory, 394-396, **395**
extensions, filename, 73, 281, 319, 413, 420-422, **421**
external commands, 192-193, 396
external hard disk drives, 504
extrapolation, 396-397, **397**, 438-439, **439**, 575-576
extremely low frequency (ELF) emissions, 252, 357-359, **358**, **359**, 377, 604, 713
eye lag in animation, 51, **51**
eye strain, 251-252, 378, 397-398, **398**

F

family relationships in computing terminology, 399-400, **400**
fanfold paper, 130, **130**, 401-402, **401**
farming applications, automated, 402-403, **403**
FASTOPEN command, 194
fault-resilient computers, 403-404
fault-tolerant computers, 404
fax, 404-406, **405**, 404, 858, 1106
fax boards, 406
fax modems, 239, 292, 406
FC command, 194
FDISK command, 194
fiberoptics, 28-29, 147, 152, 350, 407-409, **407**
 baud rate, 70, 95, 105-107, **107**, 140, 698, 770
 electromagnetic fields, 409
 interference, 409
 laser communications, 608-609, **608**
field-effect transistor (FET), 410-411, **410**
field-emission display (FED), 411, **412**
fields, 409-410, 932
fifth generation computers, 222
file allocation table (FAT), 412, 1100
file management (*see also* directories/subdirectories), 302-305, 411-414
 active files, 9-11
 allocation of files, 411-412

archiving, 59-60, 75-76, 95, 100, 101, 500-501, 1101
asterisk wildcard, 73
attributes, 75-76
automatic backups, 79-80
auxiliary storage, 83-85
backups, 11, 424-425
block file transfers, 125-126, 137, 672
closing/exiting files, 10-11
compression, 60, 270-272, **273**, 537-539, 641-642, 705
conversion of files, 415-416
creating files, 413
defragmentation, 281-283, **282**, **283**, 413, 450-451, 503, 751-752
deleting files, 413
directories/subdirectories (*see* directories/subdirectories)
downloading, 80, 333-334, 1109
embedded objects, **361**, **362**
erasing files, 416-417
exporting, 392, 549
extensions, filename, 413, 420-422, **421**
file allocation table (FAT), 412, 1100
File Manager, Windows, 305-306, 417-419, **418**, 478
filenames, 17, 73, 281, 319, 413, 419-420, 1147-1148
filtering files, 426-427
folders, 435-436, 514, 794, 1076
fragmentation, 271, 281-283, **282**, **283**, 413, 450-451, 503
hidden attributes, 514
hidden files, 514
hierarchical file systems (HFS), 514
high performance file system (HPFS), 789-790
importing, 392, 549
losing data accidentally, 11
merging, 361, 541, 1151
object linking and embedding (OLE), 214, 262, 425, 624, 757-759, **758**, 763-764, 1020, 1042
opening files, 9-11, 424
overwriting, 424, 795-796
saving changes to files, 10, 11
undeleting, 417, 689, 751, 1099-1100
updating files, 423-425
uploading, 334, 1108-1110, **1109**
write protection, 60, 1158-1159, **1158**
File Manager, Windows, 305-306, 417-419, **418**, 478
file servers, 180, 422, **422**, 630
file transfer protocol (FTP), 423, 571-572
filenames, 17, 73, 281, 319, 413, 419-420, 1147-1148
fill, 425-426, 806, **806**
filter chokes, 865-866, **866**
filters/filtering, 426-427, 865-866, **866**, 914
finances, personal finance software, 834-836
FIND command, 194
Finder, 427, 718
fire protection, automated, 224
FireWire, 978
firmware, 130, 427-428, 876, 884, 926
first generation computers, 221
first in/first out (FIFO), 137, 428, **428**, 992
first in last out (FILO), 428, 895, **895**, 933
fixed point numbers, 431
flash memory, 662, 663, 857, 919, 982
flash tests, 473, **474**
flat cable, 151
flatpack integrated circuits (ICs), 428-429, **429**, 561
flip-flops, 429-430, 671, 919, 992, 1040
floating point numbers, 430-431
floating-point units (FPUs), 716
floppy disk drives and diskettes (*see also* flopticals), 100, 312-314, **313**, 655-657, **655**, 663, 672, 934-935, 948, 981-983, 1106

Index

access time, 1042
alignment, 23-24
bad sectors, 91-92, 94-95, 984
benchmarks, 109
capacity, disk capacity, 307-309, **309**, **310**, 502-503, 520-521, **521**, 654-655
clusters, 282
default drive, 280
defragmentation, 281-283, **282**, **283**, 413, 450-451, 503, 751-752
density of diskettes, 515
diskettes, 310-312, **311**
double-density diskettes, 310, 331
double-sided diskettes, 310, 331
drive bays, 338-339, **339**
file allocation table (FAT), 412, 1100
formatting disks, 441
fragmentation, 271, 281-283, **282**, **283**, 413, 450-451, 503
heads, 508-509, **509**
magnetic disks, 654-655
magnetic media, 655-657, **655**
PCMCIA standard adapter cards, 314, 607, 664, 821-823, **822**, 857, 916, 948, 982, 1003-1004, 1006
sectors, 281, 441-442, **442**, 983-984, **983**
tracks, 983-984, **983**, 1084-1086, **1085**
transfer rate, 1042
very high density (VHD) drives, 314
write protection, 60, 1158-1159, **1158**
flopticals, 308, 314, 431-432, 504, 515, 663, 948, 982
flowcharts, 22, 432-434, **433**, 882, **883**
flush left/right/center, 433-435, **435**, 584
flux, electromagnetic flux, 349, **349**, 357
focus specialists, 124
folders, 435-436, 514, 794, 1076
fonts, 144, 436-438
  adding fonts, 437-438
  Adobe Type Manager, 18-20, **19**
  automatic font downloading, 80
  base fonts, 99
  bitmapped fonts, 18-19, **19**, 122-123
  built-in fonts, 138-139
  characters per inch (CPI), 436, 620, 843
  default fonts, 139, 281
  downloadable fonts, 332-333, 437
  elite type, 436
  hard fonts, 332
  nonproportional fonts, 436
  outline fonts, 18-19, **19**, 122, 790-791, **791**, 1091
  pica type, 436
  points, 436
  printer fonts, 80, 437
  proportional fonts, 436, 890, **891**
  sans serif fonts, 436-437
  scalable fonts, 437, 967-968
  screen fonts, 437
  script fonts, 437
  serif fonts, 437
  soft fonts, 332-333
  TrueType fonts, 967-968, 1091
  type size, 436
  typefaces, 436
  x-height, 1161, **1162**
food preparation, automated, 225
forecasting, 438-440, **438**, **439**, **440**, 1035
foreground processing, 440-441, **441**, 580, 718, 726-727, **727**
foreign languages, 1153
form feed, 444-445, **444**
form length, 445
formants, 1024
FORMAT command, 194-195, 441, 442-443, 688-689, 688
formatting data or text, 360-361, 470-471
formatting disks, 441-444, **442**, 502, 688-689, 1099-1100, 1101

Fortran, 73, 210, 445, 515, 603, 815, 887, 1003
forums, 215, 739
forward chaining, 445-446, **446**
fourth generation computers, 221
fractal image compression, 538, 539
fractal transforms, 539
fractals, 446-449, **447**, **449**, 539
fragmentation, 271, 281-283, **282**, **283**, 413, 450-451, 503
frames, 451-452, **451**, **452**
Frankenstein scenario, 452-453
Freehand, 453-454, **454**
freeware, 995, 1012, 1014-1016
frequency division demultiplexing (FDD), 287
frequency division multiplexing (FDM), 724
frequency modulation (FM), 705
frequency shift keying (FSK), 107
front-loading printers, 455-456, **455**
FUBAR, 456
full backups, 457
full-duplex, 207, 295, 457-458, **458**, 494-495, 558, 1021
full motion video interface (FMVI), 458-459
full page display, 459
full-wave rectification, 864-865, **865**
function keys, 460-461, **461**
functions, 459-460, **460**
  domain of function, 322-323, **322**, 459
  independent variables, 550-552, **551**, **552**
  logical functions, 460
  mapping functions, 459
  multivariable functions, 288, 551, 728-730, **729**
  ordinates, 786-787, **786**, **787**
  range of function, 921, **921**
  relations, 941-942, **942**, 941
  single-variable functions, 550-551, **551**
  software functions, 460
fuses, 867
futurists, 27-30, 55-56, 118, 119, 156-157, 184, 189, 190, 209, 218-220, 223-227, **223**, **226**, 254-255, 461-462, 547, 567-568, 581-582, 614, 645-647, 708-711, 870, 900-901, 1140-1141
fuzzy logic, 598-599, **598**, 637, 740-741

G

games, computer, 220-221, 1017
  checkers-playing computers, 174
  chess-playing computers, 176-177
garbage in/garbage out (GIGO), 468-469, 468
gates (see logic gates)
Gates, Bill, 568, 684
gateways, 463, **464**, 570
genealogy software, 463-465
generations of computers, 221-223, **222**, 229
generations of robots, 960-961, **962**
genetic logic, 599
GEnie, 774, 775
geocoding, 465
geographic information systems (GIS), 465-466
geometric mean, 20
geometry, Pythagorean theorem, 3
geostationary-satellite data links, 466-468, **467**, 643, 966
Gibb's effect, 539
gigabytes, 147, 223, 230, 468, **469**, **470**, 873
glare, 378
glitches, 742-744
global format, spreadsheets, 470-471, 1034
global positioning system (GPS), 966, 1078
glossaries, 471
gloves used in virtual reality, 1122
Godel, Kurt, 68, 549, 598, 637
Gopher menu system, 133, 572
Gore, Al, 555
graceful degradation, 404, 471-473, **472**, 740

Index

graded-index optical fiber, 407
GRAFTABL command, 195
grammar checking, 473, 1152
Grand Synthesizer, 473-474, 870
grandchild/grandparent data, 399
graphical databases, 474-476
graphical user interfaces (GUIs (*see also* DOS; Macintosh computers; operating systems, Windows), 201, 202, 288, 593, 651, 714, 715, 770, 778, 789, 856, 890, 1010, 1014, 1148-1150, 1166, 1171
   active window, 12-13, **13**
   alert messages, 21-22, **21**
   anchoring, 49-50, **50**
   application window, 321
   C and C++ programming, 149
   control menu, 241-242, **242**
   document window, 321-322, **322**
   DOS shell, 325-327, **326**
   drag-and-drop, 337
   dragging, 336-337, **336**
   event-driven environments, 381-382
   graphics accelerators, 481-483
   highlighting, 516
   hypermedia, 528-530
   icons, 534
   integrated software packages, 563-564
   menu bar, 321, **322**
   menu-driven environments, 676-678
   menus, 675-676, **676**
   mice, 717-718, **718**
   pen-based computers, 824-827, **825**, **826**
   point-and-click method, 676
   pointers, 849
   title bar, 321, **322**
   touch screens, 1082-1083
graphics, 145-146, 293, 478-481, **480**
   accelerators, graphics accelerators, 481-483
   adding text to graphics, 543
   Adobe Illustrator, 17-18, **18**
   aliasing, 123, 579, **580**
   analytical graphics, 17, 48-49, **48**, 245-247, **246**, 942, 968-969, **968**
   animation, 51-52
   anti-aliasing, 54-55, **54**, 123
   aspect ratio, 71-72, **72**
   attributes, 75-76
   Bezier curves, 18, **18**, 48, 112-113, **113**, 453, 454
   bitmapped graphics, 17, 123, 337, 453, 478-479, **480**, 495-496, **496**, 540, 579, **580**, 805
   blurring graphic images, 543
   CD-ROM, 165
   choreographer programs, 177-178
   clip art, 180-182, 540-541
   color, 543
   cropping images, 543
   discrete cosine transform (DCT) compression, 538
   dots per inch (DPI), 330-331, 518, 545, 783, 843, 953
   draw programs, 337-338, **338**, 480, 540, 841-842, **842**, 907-909, **908**
   eccentricity in shapes, 337
   environment required for graphics, 541
   families of shapes, 399-400, **400**
   file conversion, 416
   fill, 426, **426**, 806, **806**
   flowcharts, 432-434, **433**
   fractals, 538-539
   Freehand, 453-454, **454**
   geocoding, 465
   geographic information systems (GIS), 465-466
   Gibb's effect, 539
   gray-scale system, 483-485
   halftones, 495-496, **496**
   image compression, 537-539
   image editing, 540-543, **542**
   importing images, 540-541
   jaggies, 17, 54-55, **54**, 123, 331, 479, 540, 579, **580**
   JPEG image compression, 538-539
   lossy and lossless compression, 538, 641-642
   masking, 541
   memory requirements, 541
   merging graphics, 541
   mirroring of graphic images, 542
   modeling, 692-697, **693**
   monitors, 541
   morphing, 543
   multimedia, 351, 530, 718-721, **721**, 1060-1063, **1061**
   object-oriented graphics, 17, 123, 337, 453, 479-480, **480**, 540, 760-762, **760**, **761**, 805
   page description languages (PDLs), 800-801, **800**, **801**, 859-860
   paint programs, 337, 479, 540, 805-807, **806**
   palettes, 808-809, **810**
   pen-based computers, 824-827, **825**, **826**
   PICT graphics, 841-842, **842**
   pixels, 54, 123, 453, 483-484, 495-496, **496**, 517, 579, **580**, 805, 843-844, **844**
   polyline graphics, 854, **854**
   presentation graphics, 49, 873-875
   printers and printing, 541
   QuickDraw, 907-909, **908**
   raster graphics, 479
   repeating graphic images, 542
   resizing graphics, 542
   rotation of graphic images, 542
   scaling, 968-969, **968**
   software for graphics, 481
   special effects, 541-543, **542**
   texturing, 541
   thematic shading, 465-466
   tools in draw programs, 337
   TWAIN interface, 541, 783-784
   vector graphics, 540, 805, 760-762, **760**, **761**
   zooming, 541, 1171
graphics accelerators, 481-483
GRAPHICS command, 195
graphs, 1035
   area graphs, 60-62, **61**
   bar graphs, 97-98, **98**, 342-343, **343**, 807-808, **808**
   Cartesian, 1, 158-159, **159**, 242, 619, 692, 786
   columnar graphs, 190, **190**, 342-343, **343**, 690-691, **691**, 1037-1038, **1038**
   dependent variables, 1, 287-288, **287**
   dual-ordinate graphs, 342-343, **343**
   geocoding, 465
   geographic information systems (GIS), 465-466
   histograms, 519-520, **520**
   independent variables, 1, 287-288, 550-552, **551**, **552**
   interpolation, 575-576, **575**
   line graphs, 619-620, **619**, 622, **622**, 690-691, **691**
   linked graphs, 621-623, **622**, **623**
   log-log graphs, 243, 639-640, **639**
   logarithmic graphs, 242, 634-635, **634**
   mixed columnar/line graphs, 690-691, **691**
   multivariable function graphs, 288, 551, 728-730, **729**
   ordinates, 786-787, **786**, **787**
   paired-bar graphs, 807-808, **808**
   pie graphs, 623, **623**, 842, **843**
   plotters, 846-847
   range of function, 921, **921**
   rectangular coordinates, 158-159, **159**
   scaling, 968-969, **968**
   scatter plots, 969-970, **970**
   semilog graphs, 242, 989-990, **990**
   single-function graph, 287, **287**

Index

single-variable functions, 550-551, **551**
stacked-column graphs, 1037-1038, **1038**
thematic shading, 465-466
two-function graph, **287**, 288
volume graphs, 1135-1136, **1135**
x/y/z axes, 1163-1164, **1163**
gray-scale system, 483-485
"green" computing (*see* ecolinking)
ground buses, 488
ground loops, 488, **488**
grounding, 486-488, **488**
groupware, 488-489, **489**

H

HACKER program, 492-494, **493**
hackers, 250, 473-474, 491-492, 568, 743, 870
half-duplex, 207, 295, 458, 494-495, **495**, 1021
halftones, 495-496, **496**
half-wave rectification, 864, **864**
ham radio (*see* amateur radio; packet communications)
handheld computers, 496-498, **497**
handshaking, 175-176, 208, 270, 498-499, **499**, 815, 979, 1164-1165
hanging indent, 499-500, **500**
hard disk drives, 100, 271, 272, 501-505, **501**, 663, 672, 673, 981-983, 1106
   access time, 6, 503, 654, 1042
   alignment of head, 23-24
   bad sectors, 91-92, 91, 94-95, 984
   benchmarks, 109
   Bernoulli boxes (*see* Bernoulli boxes)
   capacity, disk capacity, 307-309, **309**, **310**, 502-503, 520-521, **521**, 654-655
   catastrophic failures, 161, 247-248, 471-473, **472**, 509-510, 892-894
   CD-ROMs (*see* CD-ROMs)
   clusters, 282
   crashes (*see also* catastrophic failures; graceful degradation), 247-248, 250, 471-473, **472**, 509-510, 892-894
   cylinders, 257-258, **257**, 502, 654
   default drive, 280
   defragmentation, 281-283, **282**, **283**, 413, 450-451, 503, 751-752
   disk caching, 306-307, **307**
   drive bays, 338-339, **339**
   external hard disk drives, 504
   file allocation table (FAT), 412, 1100
   flopticals (*see* flopticals)
   formatting a hard disk, 441, 502
   fragmentation, 271, 281-283, **282**, **283**, 413, 450-451, 503
   heads, 501, 508-509, **509**
   integrated drive electronics (IDE) drives, 504, 536
   internal hard disk drives, 503-504
   laptops, 607
   logical drives, 815
   magnetic disks, 654-655
   magnetic media, 655-657, **655**
   Norton Utilities, 751-752
   parking heads, 509
   partitions, 815
   platters, 257-258, **257**, 308, 501, **501**, 845-846, **846**
   power-up and power-down, 868-869
   RAM disks, 915-916
   removable hard drives, 948
   sectors, 281, 441-442, **442**, 502, 983-984, **983**
   small computer system interface (SCSI), 504, 536, 977-980, **978**
   storage units, 271
   tracks, 502, 654, 983-984, **983**, 1084-1086, **1085**
   transfer rate, 1042
   unformatting, 1100-1101
   virtual drives, 306-307, 915
   WORM drives (*see* write once/read many (WORM))
hard fonts, 332
hard hyphenation, 531
hard line (*see* coaxial cable)
hard page breaks, 505, 1007
hard return, 505-506, 1007
hard wiring, 507
hardcopy, 500-501
hardware, 506
hardware reset button, 506
Hayes compatibility, 507-508
head crash (*see* catastrophic failures; crashes)
heads, 23-24, 501, 508-509, **509**
head-mounted displays (HMD), 1122
headers/footers, 950, 962-963, 1151
Hertz, 510-511, **510**
Hertz, Heinrich, 510
heterogeneous networks, 511, **512**
heuristic knowledge, 511-512, 594, 595
hexadecimal number systems, 512-513, **513**, 708, **708**
hidden attributes, 514
hidden codes, 513-514
hidden files, 514
hierarchical file systems (HFS), 514
hierarchical modeling, 695
high-density diskettes, 515
high-level languages, 72-73, 149-150, 186, 210, 385, 445, 492, 515, 576, 603, 628, 651, 815-816, 844-845, 887
high-level programming, 887
high-level security, 986
high-performance file system (HPFS), 789-790
high-resolution monitors, 516-517, 517-519
high-resolution printers, 557-558
highlighting, 516
histograms, 519-520, **520**
Hofstadter, Douglas, 220
holographic animation, 52
holographic data storage, 520-521, **521**
Home key, 523, **523**
home, computerized home, 223-227, **223**, **226**
home-design software, 522
homeomorphism, 695
host bus, 523-524, **524**
host computers, 571
hot keys, 524, 675
hot links, 525
household robots, 838
hue, 316, 808-809, **810**, 956
human engineering (*see also* ergonomics), 250-252, 375-379, **376**, 397-398, **398**, 525-526
human-centered computing, 861
hybrid computers, 30, 42, 526-528
HyperCard, 529
hypermedia, 528-530
hypersensation, 1107
hypertext, 529
hyphenation, 530-531

I

I-beam cursors, 254
IBM/IBM-compatibility, 145, 183, 210, 270, 384, 533-534, 652, 680, 682, 684, 715, 722-724, 831, 845
icons, 388, 534, 675
ideal circuit or component, 534-536, **535**
idle bits, 75
idle loops, 382
IF-THEN-ELSE, 131, 537, 738
Illustrator, Adobe, 17-18, **18**
image based character recognition (ICR), 1004-1007

Index

image compression, 537-539
image editing, 540-543, **542**
image orthicon, 543-544, **544**
image resolution, 187, 290, 315, 316, 329, 516-517, 544-547, **546**, 711, 712, 843, 922, 953
ImagiNation, 774, 775
immortal knowledge, 547-548, 595
impact printers, 548
importing, 392, 540-541, 549
incompleteness theorem, 549-550, **550**, 598
independent variables, 1-2, **2**, 287, 550-552, **551**, **552**
indexing, 25-27, 232, 552-553
inductive logic, 636-637
inductive reasoning, 598
industry standard architecture (ISA), 369, 394, 553, 565, 680
inference engines, 390, 446
infinite loops, 432, 641
infinite regress, 553-555, **554**
information superhighway (*see* Internet)
initialization files, 556-557
inkjet printers, 188, **188**, 557-558, 877
input/output (I/O) module, 558, **558**
input/output (I/O) ports, 855
insect robots, 83, 224, 558-559, 959, 961, 1058
Insert mode, 592
Insert/Overtype key, 559-560, **560**
insertion point (*see* cursors)
Insite Peripherals Inc., 431
installation/uninstallation, software, 1013-1014
instructions per second (IPS), 222, **222**, 560-561, 566, 1137
integrated circuits (IC), 4, 211, 221, 222, 561-562, 581, 714
   biochips, 118
   dual inline package (DIP) 341, **342**, 561
   erasable programmable ROM (EPROM), 375, 427, 663, 671, 884-885, 926
   field-effect transistor (FET), 410-411, **410**
   flatpack integrated circuits (ICs), 428-429, **429**, 561
   large-scale integration (LSI), 370
   metal oxide semiconductor (MOS) technology, 679-680
   metal-can integrated circuits (ICs), 561
   single inline packages (SIPs), 561, 1002-1003, **1003**
   single electron memory (SEM), 29, 709, 1001-1002
   TO package integrated circuits (ICs), 561
   ultra large-scale integration (ULSI), 370
   very large-scale integration (VLSI), 370
integrated drive electronics (IDE), 504, 536
integrated software packages, 563-564
Intel microprocessors, 564-566, 682-683, 827-828
Interactive Image Technologies Inc., 354-355
interactive technology, 351, 567-568
interactive virtual reality, 1120
interfaces (*see also* graphical user interfaces), 568-569
   enhanced storage-device interface (ESDI), 371
   full motion video interface (FMVI), 458-459
   graphical user interfaces (*see* graphical user interfaces)
   hypermedia, 528-530
   integrated drive electronics (IDE), 504, 536
   musical instrument digital interface (MIDI), 292, 732-734, **733**, 828, 1017, 1020
   peripheral interfaces, 568-569, 828-829
   small computer system interface (SCSI), 504, 536, 977-980, **978**
   TWAIN interface, 541, 783-784
   user interfaces (*see also* graphical user interfaces), 777-778
interference, 151, 409
interlace vs. noninterlace monitors, 317, 713, 923
internal commands, 192-193, 396, 569-570
internal hard disk drives, 503-504
International Standards Organization (ISO), 776
Internet, 133, 201, 284, 555-556, 570-574, 775-776
   addresses, 570-571
   Archie searches, 133, 572
   ARPAnet, 570
   bulletin board systems (BBS), 139-142, **139**, 215, 570-571, 739, 772, 1042, 1079-1080
   domains, domain abbreviations, 571
   electronic mail, 139, 205-206, 356, 488, 570-571, 658-659, **658**, 658, 739, 772, 799
   file transfer protocol (FTP), 423, 571-572
   gateways, 463, **464**, 570
   Gopher menu system, 572
   host computers, 571
   newsgroups, 571
   protocols, 163, 207, 235-237, **236**, 423, 570, 798-799, 853-854, **854**, 891-892
   servers, 572
   Telnet sites, 573
   usernames, 571
   Veronica searches, 572-573
   Wide Area Information System (WAIS), 573
   World Wide Web (WWW), 573
interpolation, 397, 575-576, **575**
interpreters, 385, 515, 576, 603, 651, 801
inversion, 585
inverters, 576-577, **577**, 638
investments, personal finance software, 76-77, 834-836, 909-910

J

J-mouse, 849
J-K flip-flops, 429
jaggies, 17, 54-55, **54**, 123, 331, 479, 540, 579, **580**, 967
Jobs, Steven, 56-57
jobs, 580-581
JOIN command, 195
joins, 581
Joseph, Earl, 581-582
joysticks (*see also* mice; trackballs), 582-583, **583**, 1167
JPEG image compression, 538-539
Jungian-world theory, 583-584
justification (*see also* alignment of text), 24, 434-435, **435**, 584, 1150

K

k-line programming, 594, **595**
Karnaugh maps, 585-587, **586**
Karnaugh, Maurice, 585
kerning, 587
key assignments, 587-588
key-status indicators, 591-592
KEYB command, 195
keyboards, 290, 377, 588-589, 787-789, 828
   accessories for keyboards, 589-591, **590**
   assigning keys, 587-588
   autorepeat, 588-589
   Dvorak keyboards, 344-345, 911
   enhanced PC keyboards, 370-371, **370**, 588
   extended character set, 392-393, **393**
   key-status indicators, 591-592
   keystrokes, keystroke counters, 592-593
   membrane keyboards, 668-670, **670**
   numeric keypad, 755-756, **756**
   QWERTY keyboards, 344, 910-911
   rollover feature, 588
killer applications, 593, 1150
kilobytes (*see also* bytes), 147, 223, 230, 594, 873
knowledge, learning, and reasoning (*see also* logic), 220, 595-597, **596**, 613-614

Index

acquisition of knowledge, 595
analogical reasoning, 43-45, 696
backward chaining, 93
branching, 131-133, **132**
combinatorial explosion, 191-192, **191**
conscious computers, 220
domains of knowledge, 595-596
forward chaining, 445-446, **446**
heuristic knowledge, 511-512, 594, 595
immortal knowledge, 547-548, 595
Jungian-world theory, 583-584
k-line programming, 594, **595**
knowledge-based simulation, 597-599, **598**
learning, 613-614
logic, 635-637
machine knowledge, 595, 650
macroknowledge, 653-654
microknowledge, 682
parallel worlds, 43
problem reduction, 880-882, **881**
recursion, 553-555, **554**, 932-933
rule-based computer reasoning, 390
teach boxes, 216, 1057-1058
theorem-proving machines (TPMs), 880-882, **881**
knowledge-based security systems, 986-987
knowledge bases, 278-279

L

LABEL command, 195
label printing, 601-602
languages (*see also* high-level language; machine language; programming), 278-279, 298, 385, 415-416, 445, 576, 602-603, 628, 640, 645, 650-651, 737, 800-801, **800**, **801**, 815-816, 844-845, 882, **883**, 887-888, 889, 1001, 1003, 1141-1142
laptops, 603-607, **604**, 647, 855-856, 856-859, 944-947
  active matrix, 11-12, 545
  backlighting, 89-90
  batteries, 89-90, 605-606
  compatibility, 607
  docking stations, 317-318, **317**, 607
  field-emission display (FED), 411, **412**
  image resolution, 544-547, **546**
  liquid crystal display (LCD), 11-12, 604, 626-628, **627**
  passive matrix, LCDs, 11-12
  peripherals, 606-607
  plasma displays, 545
  traveling with your computer, 858-859
large-scale integration (LSI), 370
laser communications, 608-609, **608**
laser printers, 188, 609-612, **610**, 877
lasers, 615, 707, 781-782, **781**, 809
latches, 992
latitude and longitude, 243
LCD/LED printers, 610, 612, 877-878
leading, 620
learning (*see* knowledge, learning, and reasoning)
Lecht, Charles, 177, 584, 614
letter writing (*see* word processing)
light modulation, 707
light-emitting diodes (LEDs), 615, **616**
lighting, 378, 591
lightning protection, 487, 616-617, 867
line graphs, 619-620, **619**, 622, **622**, 690-691, **691**
line-of-sight communications, 608-609, **608**
linear and nonlinear transforms, 695
linear programming, 618, **618**
lines per inch (LPI), 620-621
link layer, 776
linked graphs, 621-623, **622**, **623**
linked objects (*see also* object linking and embedding), 623-625, **624**
links, 621, **621**, 759, 966

baud rate, 70, 95, 105-107, **107**, 140, 698, 770
cold links, 525
dynamic linking, 564
hot links, 525
low-earth-orbit (LEO) data links, 643-645, **644**, 966
object linking and embedding (OLE), 214, 262, 425, 624, 757-759, **758**, 763-764, 1020, 1042
liquid cooling, 625-626, **626**
liquid crystal display (LCD), 11-12, 315, 545, 604, 626-628, **627**, 711, 1122
LISP, 492, 515, 603, 628, 889
list boxes, 477
lithium batteries, 105, 606, 628-629, **629**
local area networks (LANs), 82, 630-633, **630**, 651, 727-728, **727**, 738, 767
  AppleTalk, 57-58, 381, 651
  baseband, 98-99
  bridges, 133, **134**
  bus networks, 146-147, **147**, 263, **630**, 631, 823
  cable data transmission, 153
  cabling, 632
  carrier-sense mult acs coll detect (CSMA/CD), 157
  carriers, 158
  client/server networks, 422, 630, **630**, 631, 994
  clients, 180, 994
  coaxial cables, 151, 184-186, **185**, 632
  collision detection, 158
  collisions, 158
  concurrency control, 196, 233, **233**
  connection protocols, 235-237, **236**
  data acquisition systems, 264-265, **265**
  distributed processing system, 315-316, **315**
  dumb terminals, 264-265, **265**, 277, 315, 343-344, 422
  file servers, 180, 422, **422**, 630
  gateways, 463, **464**, 570
  groupware, 488-489, **489**
  heterogeneous networks, 511, **512**
  mainframes, 661, **661**
  minicomputers, 686-688, **688**
  multiuser systems, 316
  network interface cards (NICs), 1169
  nodes, 146, 180, 262, 316, 746-747, **746**, 957, 1039
  peer-to-peer networks, 157-158, 316, 630, **630**, 631, 823
  platform independence, 845
  polling, 853-854, **854**, 1039
  radio frequency interference (RFI), 632
  repeaters, 147, 684, **685**, 950-952, **951**, **952**
  ring networks, **630**, 631
  servers, 994, **994**
  spy software, 1036-1037
  star networks, **630**, 631, 1038-1040, **1039**, 1038
  time sharing, 1078-1079, 1078
  topologies, 146, 630, **630**
  zero-slot networks, 1168-1169
  zones, 1170-1171
local buses, 633-634
local feature focus, vision systems, 485
lockout, 985
log-log graphs, 243, 639-640, **639**
logarithmic graphs, 242, 634-635, **634**
logic (*see also* knowledge, learning, and reasoning), 597-599, **598**, 645-647
  analogical reasoning, 696
  AND logic gate, 50, **50**, 128, 585, 779, 780, 638
  artificial intelligence (*see* artificial intelligence)
  backward chaining, 93
  binary logic, 598, **598**, 637

Index

logic *continued*
  Boolean algebra, 128, 597, 635
  combinatorial explosion, 191-192, **191**
  deductive logic, 636
  don't care state, 323
  exclusive NOR (XNOR) gates, 383, **384**, 638
  exclusive OR (XOR) gates, 383-384, **384**, 638
  flip-flops, 429-430, 671, 919, 992, 1040
  frames, 451-452, **451**, **452**
  fuzzy logic, 598-599, **598**, 637, 740-741
  gates (*see* logic gates)
  genetic logic, 599
  incompleteness theorem, 549-550, **550**, 598
  inductive logic, 598, 636-637
  infinite regress, 553-555, **554**
  inversion, 585
  inverters, 576-577, **577**
  Karnaugh maps, 585-587, **586**
  knowledge-based simulation, 597-599, **598**
  learning (*see* knowledge, learning, and reasoning)
  machine knowledge, 650
  mathematical induction, 636
  microknowledge, 682
  mutation, 554-555
  negative logic, 120, 638
  NOT, 585
  operators, 779-780
  OR, 585
  positive logic, 119-120, 638
  predicate calculus, 635
  problem reduction, 880-882, **881**
  propositional calculus, 597, 635
  recursion, 553-555, **554**, 932-933
  reductio ad absurdum arguments, 554, 635-636
  sentential calculus, 597, 635, 992
  symbolic logic, 635
  theorem-proving machines (TPMs), 880-882, **881**, 1072-1074
  trinary logic, 598, **598**, 637
  truth tables, 585
logic board (*see* motherboards)
logic gates, 638-639
  AND logic gate, 50, **50**, 128, 585, 638, 779, 780
  exclusive NOR (XNOR) gates, 383, **384**, 638
  exclusive OR (XOR) gates, 383-384, **384**, 638
  inverters, 638
  NAND gates, 638, 735-736, **735**
  negative logic, 120, 638
  NOR gates, 638, 750, **750**
  NOT gates, 638
  OR gates, 638, 787, **788**
  positive logic, 120, 638
logic states, 40-41, **40**
logical drives, 815
logical functions, 460
login security, 986
LOGO language, 640, 887
loops, 22, 179, 640-641, **641**
  branch control structures, 131
  circular references, 178-179, **178**
  DO-WHILE loops, 331-332
  endless loops, 131, 179, 365-366, 432, 553-555, **554**, 641
  idle loops, 382
  IF-THEN-ELSE, 131, 537, 738
  infinite loops, 432, 641
  infinite regress, 553-555, **554**
  nested loops, 640, 737-738, **738**
  search-and-replace loops, 641
lossy and lossless compression, 538, 641-642
Lotus, 642-643, 1035
Lovelace, Countess of (*see* analytical engines)
low-earth-orbit (LEO) data links, 643-645, **644**, 966
low-level languages (*see also* machine language) 515, 603, 645, 887
low-level programming, 887

Ludd, Ned, 646
Luddites, 645-647
luggable computers, 647

M

machine knowledge, 650
machine language, 27, 210, 298, 385, 515, 576, 603, 650-651, 887, 1001, 1045
machine vision (*see* vision systems)
Macintosh computers, 57, 130, 145, 202-203, 288, 384, 525, 533, 534, 569, 649-650, 651-652, 682, 700-701, 702, 717, 722-724, 770, 778, 789, 845, 856, 860-861, 897-898, 1013, 1014, 1048-1049, 1048
  application window, 321
  document window, 321-322, **322**
  event-driven environments, 381-382
  Finder utility, 427
  folders, 435-436, 514, 794, 1076
  integrated software packages, 563-564
  Motorola chips, 715-717, **717**
  MultiFinder, 718
  NuBus, 754, 860-861
  QuickDraw, 907-909, **908**
Macintosh PC Exchange, 723
macroknowledge, 653-654
macros, 652-653
magnetic bubble memory (*see* bubble memory)
magnetic disks, 654-655
magnetic media, 655-657, **655**, 706-707
magnetic tape (*see also* tape drives), 657-658, **657**
magnitude, 3
mail forwarding, 658-659
mail-order business software, 659-661
mailboxes, e-mail, 658, **658**
mainframes, 661, **661**, 681, 686
Mandelbrot sets, 448, 449
Mandelbrot, Benoit, 45, 449
map, computer map, 227, **227**
mapping, 459, 465-466
margins, 144
Mark I computer, 80-81
masking graphics, 541
mass storage (*see also* memory), 662-664, **662**
math coprocessors, 244-245, **244**
mathematical induction, 636
mathematical universes, 1073
mathematics, 66-67, 1152
matrices, LCD, 11-12, 545
maximum values, 20
MBAware, 390
McCarthy, John, 628
mean time before/between failures (MTBF), 664-665, **665**, 943
mechatronics, 665-666
median, 20
medical-office software, 666-667
megabytes (*see also* bytes), 147, 223, 230, 668, **669**, 873
MEM command, 195
membrane keyboards, 668-670, **670**
memory, 169, 222-223, 714, 1106
  active memory, 12
  addresses, 395
  allocation, 24, 25
  archiving, 59-60, 75-76, 95, 100, 101, 500-501, 1101
  auxiliary storage, 83-85
  base memory, 100-101
  basic input/output system (BIOS), 100, 103, **103**, 926, 1105
  battery backup supplies, 628-629
  benchmarks, 109
  blackboard systems, 123-124, **124**
  block file transfers, 125-126, 137, 672
  bootstrap programs, 100, 130, 186-187, 926, 1139

Index

bubble memory, 136-137, **136**, 663, 672
buffers, 137, **137**, 275
burn in, 884
bytes, kilobytes, megabytes, gigabytes, 230
cache memory, 153-154, **154**, 268, 269, 306-307, **307**
capacity of memory, 672, 918
CD-ROM, 165, 664, 672, 673
conventional memory, 100
disk caching, 306-307, **307**
drop-in/drop-out, 340
dynamic RAM (DRAM), 153, 346, 671, 919, 1041
electrically erasable programmable ROŌ (EEPROM), 375, 671, 885, 926
erasable programmable ROM (EPROM), 375, 427, 663, 671, 884-885, 926
expanded memory, 394-396, **395**
extended memory, 394-396, **395**
firmware, 926
first in/first out (FIFO), 137, 428, **428**, 992
first in last out (FILO), 428, 895, **895**, 933
flash memory, 662, 663, 857, 919, 982
flip-flops, 429-430, 671, 919, 992, 1040
floppy disk drives, 663, 672
flopticals, 308, 314, 431-432, 504, 515, 663, 948, 982
graphics, 541
hard disk drives, 663, 672, 673
host bus, 523-524, **524**
input/output (I/O) module, 558, **558**
magnetic media, 655-657, **655**
mass storage, 662-664, **662**
memory organization packets (MOPs), 674-675
memory-management software, 674, 725
memory-resident software, 675
nonvolatile memory, 136, 307, 656, 671, 673, 749-750, 876, 919
pages/page-mode memory, 395-396, 716, 803, 804-805, **805**
PCMCIA standard adapter cards, 314, 607, 664, 821-823, **822**, 857, 916, 948, 982, 1003-1104, 1106
primary storage, 875-876
programmable read only memory (PROM), 671, 884-885, 926
pushdown stack, 895, **895**, 992
RAM disks, 915-916
random access memory (RAM) (*see* random access memory)
read only memory (ROM) (*see* read only memory)
read/write memory, 992
registers, 170
secondary storage, 981-983
sequential access memory (SAM), 992
single-electron memory (SEM), 29, 709, 1001-1002
static RAM (SRAM), 153, 671, 919, 1040-1041, **1041**
swap files, 1044-1045, 1119
terminate-and-stay resident (TSR) software, 675
upper memory, 394
virtual drives/memory, 306-307, 716, 804-805, 1044-1045, 1118-1119, **1119**
volatile memory, 104-105, 671, 673, 749-750, 875, 918-919, 1134-1135
write once read many (WORM) disks, 60, 166, 374, 504, 664, 935, 1106, 1157-1158
memory organization packets (MOPs), 674-675
memory-management software, 674, 725
memory-resident software, 675
menu bars, 288, 321, **322**, 477
menu-driven environments, 569, 676-678, 778, 1009-1010
menu-driven software, hot keys, 524
menus, 675-676, **676**
  cascading, 160-161, **161**
  commands vs. menus, 192
  control menu, 241-242, **242**
  menu-driven environments, 676-678
  pop-up menus, 854-855
  pull-down menus, 894, **894**
merging, 361, 541, 1151
message passing, 678-679, **678**
metal oxide semiconductor (MOS) technology, 679-680, **679**
metal-can integrated circuits (ICs), 561
mice, 64, 291, 379, 477, 717-718, 828, 849, 856-857, 1106, 1107
  click/double-click, 179
  drag-and-drop, 337
  dragging, 336-337, **336**
  laptops, 606-607
Micro Channel Architecture (MCA), 394, 680-681
microcomputers, 681-682, 686
microknowledge, 682
microphones, 1018-1019
microprocessors, 4, 170, 682-683
  80286 and 80386 chips, 565
  80486 chips, 565-566
  8088 and 8086 chips, 565
  benchmarks, 1075
  clock speed, 182-183
  complex instruction set computing (CISC), 212-213, 716-717, 892, 898, 936-938
  coprocessors, 244-245, **244**
  digital signal processing (DSP), 299-301, **300**
  dynamic RAM (DRAM), 153, 346, 671, 919, 1041
  enhanced industry standard architecture (EISA), 369-370, **369**, 393-394, 553
  extended industry standard architecture (EISA), 393-394, 680
  floating-point units (FPUs), 716
  generations, computer, 221-223, **222**
  Hertz, 510-511, **510**
  host bus, 523-524, **524**
  ideal circuit or component, 534-536, **535**
  industry standard architecture (ISA), 369, 394, 553, 565, 680
  instructions per second (IPS), 560-561, **560**, 566
  integrated circuits (ICs), 561-562
  Intel, 564-566
  local buses, 633-634
  metal oxide semiconductor (MOS) technology, 679-680, **679**
  Micro Channel Architecture (MCA), 394, 680-681
  molecular computer technology, 29, 708-711, **710**
  Motorola, 715-717, **717**
  multiprocessors, 725-726, **726**
  P6 microprocessors, 566, 892
  parallel processing, 716
  Pentium processors, 566, 827-828
  pipelines, 828
  power, computer power, 229-231, **231**
  PowerPC chip, 716-717, 861-863, 898
  reduced instruction set computing (RISC), 213, 716-717, 861, 898, 936-938, **937**
  static RAM (SRAM), 1040-1041, **1041**
  storage time, 1041-1042
  superscalar processor architectures, 828
  SX and DX chips, 565-566
  throughput, 1075-1076
  Von Neumann bottleneck, 1137
  zero wait states, 1169-1170
Microsoft Corp., 534, 568, 684
microwave data transmissions, 684, **685**
military time, 685, **686**, 687
miniaturization, 496-497, **497**
minicomputers, 681, 686-688, **688**
minimum values, 20
MIRROR command/mirroring, 688-690
mirroring of graphic images, 542

1205

Index

mixed columnar/line graphs, 690-691, **691**
MKDIR command, 198
MODE command, 195, 691-692
modeling, 439, 692-697, **693**, **694**
  analogical reasoning, 696
  boxes, 693
  computer modeling of systems, 696-697
  cones, 694
  curved surfaces, 694
  cylinders, 695
  hierarchical modeling, 695
  homeomorphism, 695
  linear and nonlinear transforms, 695
  parallelepipeds, 693
  primitives, 693
  prisms, 695
  pyramids, 693
  shading schemes modeling, 692-693, **693**
  spheres, 694
  staging in modeling, 695-696
  tetrahedra, 693
  transforms, 695
  truncated objects, 694
  wire-mesh modeling, 692-693, **693**
modems, 134, 140, 205, 239, 291-292, 378, 406, 697-699, **698**, **699**, 738-739, 770, 828, 858, 1164-1165
  acoustic couplers, 7-9, **8**
  bandwidth, 95-96, **96**
  baud rate, 70, 95, 105-107, **107**, 140, 698, 770
  bits per second (BPS), 70, 95, 105-107, **107**, 140, 698, 770
  broadband data, 134-135
  Hayes compatibility, 507-508
  internal vs. external modems, 697
  laptops, 607
  MODE command, 691-692, 691
  modulation and demodulation, 108, 698, 703-707, **703**, **704**, **706**
  telephone cord adapters, 15-16
  telephone line connection, 141
  terminal emulation software, 139, 140-141, 344, 699, 770, 1070-1071
  V.22 modems, 163
modular construction, 699-700
modular Mac line, 700-701
modular programming, 701-703, **702**, 815-816, 1141
modulation, 95, 108, 140, 152, 162, 698, 703-707, **703**, **704**, **706**
  amplitude modulation (AM), 705
  analog-to-digital (A/D) conversion, 704
  audio frequency shift keying (AFSK), 107, 704
  carrier modulation, 705
  CD-ROM, 707
  compression, 60, 270-272, **273**, 537-539, 641-642, 705
  digital-to-analog (D/A) conversion, 704
  frequency modulation (FM), 705
  light modulation, 707
  magnetic media, 706-707
  phase modulation (PM), 705
  pulse amplitude modulation (PAM), 705-706
  pulse code modulation (PCM), 706
  pulse modulation (PM), 705
  pulse width modulation (PWM), 706
  sampling/sampling rates, 45, 46, 273-274, 705
  sampling resolutions, 46, 273, 705
modules (see integrated software packages)
modulo arithmetic, 3, 707-708, **708**
molecular computer technology (see also biochips; nanotechnology), 29, 708-711, **710**
monitors, 290, 314-315, 377-378, 541, 711-714, 828, 1106, 1166-1167
  accelerators, graphics accelerators, 481-482
  active matrix display, 11-12, 545, 711

adapter cards, 713
aspect ratio, 71-72, **72**
backlighting, 89-90
bacteriorhodopsin (BR), 93-94, **94**
bitmapping, 120-122, **121**
cathode ray tubes (CRTs), 161-162, **162**, 289, 544-547, **546**, 604, 711, 921-923, **922**
color graphics adapter (CGA), 187
colors, 712-713
dithering, 316-317
dot pitch, 329-330, **330**, 517, 712
enhanced graphics adapter (EGA), 368-369
extended graphics array (XGA), 393
extremely low frequency (ELF) fields, 252, 357-359, **358**, **359**, 377, 604, 713
eye strain, 251-252, 378, 397-398, **398**
field-emission display (FED), 411, **412**
full motion video interface (FMVI), 458-459
full page display, 459
glare, 378
gray-scale system, 483-485
high-resolution, 516-517
highlighting, 516
hue, 316
image orthicon, 543-544, **544**
image resolution, 187, 290, 315, 316, 329, 516-517, 544-547, **546**, 711, 712, 843, 922, 953
interlacing, 317, 713, 923
liquid crystal displays (LCDs), 11-12, 315, 604, 626-628, **627**, 711
MODE command, 691-692
monochrome display adapters (MDAs), 714
palettes, 808-809, **810**
pixels, 54, 123, 453, 483-484, 495-496, **496**, 517, 579, **580**, 805, 843-844, **844**
plasma displays, 545
radiation exposure, 358-359, 604
rasters, 921-923, **922**
retrace blanking, 922
reverse video, 954-956
RGB color model, 162, 316, 808, 956-957, **957**
saturation, 316
scan rate, 922
screen savers, 975-976
scrolling, 976-977, **977**
size of screen, 517, 712
super video graphics array (SVGA), 317, 369, 711, 1044, 1117
Swedish ELF radiation standard, 359
touch screens, 1082-1083
upgrading monitors, 711-714
video graphics array (VGA), 369, 711, 1044, 1117
vidicons, 1117-1118, **1118**
WYSIWYG, 293, 459, 651, 907, 1091, 1153, 1159-1160
monochrome display adapters (MDAs), 714
MORE command, 195
Mori, Masahiro, 1097-1098
Morse code, 703
MOSFETs, 211
motherboards (see also buses; integrated circuits; microprocessors), 142-143, 633, 682, 714-715, 1105
  buses (see buses)
  enhanced industry standard architecture (EISA), 369-370, **369**, 393-394, 553
  extended industry standard architecture (EISA), 393-394
  Micro Channel Architecture (MCA), 394, 680-681
  modular construction, 699-700
  printed circuits, 876, **876**
motion, digital motion, 296-297
Motorola (see also Macintosh computers; microprocessors), 682-683, 715-717, **717**
MS-DOS (see DOS)

multidimensional quantities, ABS function, 3-4
MultiFinder, 718
multimedia, 351, 530, 718-721, **721**, 1060-1063, **1061**
multipart forms, 721-722
multiplatform environments, 722-724
multiplexing, 135, 286, 724, **724**
multiprocessors, 725-726, **726**
multitasking, 87, 240, 395, 440. 651, 716, 718, 757, 779, 726-727, **727**
multiuser systems, 316, 727-728, **727**
multivariable function graphs, 288, 551, 728-730, **729**
Murphy's Laws, 730-732
music (see sound and music)
musical instrument digital interface (MIDI), 292, 732-734, **733**, 828, 1017, 1020
mutation, 554-555

N

n-tuples, ordered, 3-4
Nakano, Eiji, 960-961
NAND gates, 638, 735
nanoseconds, 736
nanotechnology (see also anticipatory science; alternative computer science; biochips; molecular computer technol
  9-30, 353, 736-737, 900-901, **901**, 1142-1145, **1143**
National Bureau of Standards, 1078
National Computer Security Association, 1128
National Fire Protection Association, 617
native applications, 723
natural languages, 602, 737
negation, 576
negative logic, 120, 638
nested loops, 640, 737-738, **738**
network interface cards (NICs), 1169
network layer, 776
networks, 269, 651, 727-728, **727**, 738-740, 767, 883-884
  access time, 7
  addresses, 263, 570-571, 957
  AppleTalk, 57-58, 381, 651
  application layer, 777
  ARPAnet, 570
  baud rate, 70, 95, 105-107, **107**, 140, 698, 770
  bridges, 133, **134**
  bulletin board systems (BBS), 139-142, **139**, 215, 570-571, 739, 772, 1042, 1079-1080
  bus networks, 146-147, **147**, 263, **630**, 631, 823
  cable data transmission, 153
  cabling, 632
  carrier-sense multiple access with collision detection (CSMA/CD), 157
  carriers, 158
  client/server networks, 422, 630, **630**, 631, 994
  clients, 180, 994
  coaxial cables, 151, 184-186, **185**, 632
  collision detection, 158
  collisions, 158
  concurrency control, 196, 233, **233**
  conferencing, 739
  connect time, 237
  connection protocols, 235-237, **236**
  daisy-chain networks, 262-263, **263**
  data acquisition systems, 264-265, **265**
  digipeaters, 237, 295-296, **296**, 747, 951-952, **952**, 1072
  distributed processing system, 315-316, **315**
  domains, domain abbreviations, 571
  downloading, 80, 333-334, 1109
  dumb terminals, 264-265, **265**, 277, 315, 343-344, 422
  electronic mail, 139, 205-206, 356, 488, 570-571, 658-659, **658**, 658, 739, 772, 799

  end-to-end acknowledgment, 366, **367**
  Ethernet, 380-381, **381**
  fiberoptics, 147
  file servers, 180, 422, **422**, 630
  file transfer protocols, 423, 571-572
  forums, 739
  gateways, 463, **464**, 570
  groupware, 488-489, **489**
  handshaking, 175-176, 208, 270, 498-499, **499**, 815, 979, 1164-1165
  heterogeneous networks, 511, **512**
  host computers, 571
  link layer, 776
  links, 621, **621**, 759, 966
  local area networks (see local area networks)
  mainframes, 661, **661**
  message passing, 678-679, **678**
  minicomputers, 686-688, **688**
  modems (see modems)
  multiuser systems, 316
  network interface cards (NICs), 1169
  network layer, 776
  neural networks (see neural networks)
  newsgroups, 571
  node-to-node acknowledgment, 366, **367**, 747, **748**
  nodes, 146, 180, 262, 316, 746-747, **746**, 957, 1039
  online services, 739, 769-776
  open systems interconnection reference model (OSI-RM), 776-777, 798, 891
  packet radio networks, 206, 237, 739, 798-799, 1071, 1146
  packet radio bulletin board systems (PBBS), 799-800
  parity, 208, 814-815
  PCMCIA standard adapter cards, 314, 607, 664, 821-823, **822**, 857, 916, 948, 982, 1003-1104, 1106
  peer-to-peer networks, 157-158, 316, 630, **630**, 631, 823
  physical layer, 776
  polling, 853-854, **854**, 853, 1039
  presentation layer, 777
  propagation delay, 947
  protocols, 163, 207, 235-237, **236**, 423, 570, 798-799, 853-854, **854**, 891-892
  public files, 823
  radio frequency interference (RFI), 632
  radio networks (see packet communications)
  remote control systems, 944-947
  repeaters, 147, 684, **685**, 950-952, **951**, **952**
  ring networks, 263, **630**, 631, 823, 957-958, **958**
  saturation points, 958
  SeniorNet, 990-992
  servers, 572, 994, **994**
  session layer, 777
  spy software, 1036-1037
  star networks, 263, **630**, 631, 823, 1038-1040, **1039**
  Systems Network Architecture (SNA), 270
  teleconferencing, 771-772, 1060-1063, **1061**, 1065
  telephones, 1063-1065
  terminal emulation software, 139, 140-141, 344, 699, 770, 1070-1071
  terminal node controllers, 206, 292, 295, 697, 799, 858, 1071-1072, **1072**
  time sharing, 1078-1079
  time-shifting communications, 206, 798, 799, 927, 1079-1080
  topologies, 146, 262-263, **263**, 511, 630-631, **630**, 738, 823, 957-958, **958**, 1038-1040, **1039**
  transport layer, 776
  uploading, 1108-1110, **1109**
  usernames, 571

Index

networks *continued*
  wide area networks (*see* wide area networks)
  workstations, 262
  zero-slot networks, 1168-1169
  zones, 1170-1171
neural networks (*see also* artificial intelligence; hybrid computers), 30, 42, 67-68, 118, 526-528, 740-742, **741**, 820-821, 1145, **1143**
neurotic computer behavior, 742-744
newsgroups, 571
newspaper column format, 1094-1095, **1094**
nickel-cadmium (NiCad) batteries (*see also* batteries), 105, 605-606, 629, 744-746
nickel metal hydride (NiMH) batteries (*see also* batteries), 606, 744-746
NLSFUNC command, 196
node-to-node acknowledgment, 366, **367**, 747, **748**
nodes, 146, 180, 262, 316, 746-747, **746**, 957, 1039
noise, 747-749, **749**
noise floor, 748
nonnative applications, 723
nonproportional fonts, 436
nonvolatile memory, 136, 307, 656, 671, 673, 749-750, 876, 919, 926
NOR gates, 638, 750, **750**
Norton Utilities, 751-752
NOT gates, 585, 638, 779
notebook computers (*see* laptops)
notepads, 239
note-taking software, 752-754
NuBus, 754, 860-861
Number Lock key, 754
number systems, 707-708, **708**
  binary number system, 114-115, 296
  decimal number system, 114-115, 278, **278**
  hexadecimal numbers, 512-513, **513**
  octal number system, 765-766, **766**
  one-to-one correspondence, 115
  scientific notation, 970-973
numeric coprocessors, 244-245, **244**
numeric format, 755, 1033
numeric keypad, 755-756, **756**
numerical addresses, 16-17

O

object linking and embedding (OLE), 214, 262, 425, 624, 757-759, **758**, 763-764, 1020, 1042
object oriented graphics, 17, 123, 337, 453, 479-480, **480**, 540, 760-762, **760**, **761**, 805, 841-842, **842**
object oriented programming (OOP), 762-763
Object Packager, 763-764
object recognition, 117, 124, 127-128, **127**, 764-765
objectivity in learning, 613-614
objects, 757
octal number systems, 708, **708**, 765-766, **766**
off-site data storage, 768-769
off-the-shelf software, 797
office automation (*see also* paperless office), 766-768, 810-813
offset, 952
one-to-one correspondence, 115
online services, 256, 555-556, 739, 769-776, 883-884, 990-992
  abbreviations used in online communications, 771
  America Online, 33-34, 574, 774-775
  bulletin board systems (BBS), 139-142, **139**, 215, 570-571, 739, 772, 1042, 1079-1080
  CCITT standards, 163
  CompuServe, 214-215, 574, 774, 775
  connect time, 237
  Delphi, 284-286, 574, 774, 775
  electronic mail, 139, 205-206, 356, 488, 570-571, 658-659, **658**, 658, 739, 772, 799

file transfer protocol (FTP), 423, 571-572
GEnie, 774, 775
hardware requirements, 770
ImagiNation, 774, 775
Internet, 775-776
modems, 770
Prodigy, 574, 774, 776
real-time communications, 771
services offered online, 773-774
Sierra Network, 775
telecommuting, 774
teleconferencing, 771-772, 1060-1063, **1061**, 1065
telephones, 770
terminal emulation software, 139, 140-141, 344, 699, 770, 1070-1071
open systems interconnection reference model (OSI-RM), 776-777, 798, 891
opening files, 424
operating systems (*see also* DOS; graphical user interfaces; Macintosh computers; OS/2; Unix; Windows), 12, 201-202, 323-324, 723, 777-779, 789-790, 847-848, 861-863, 868-869, 926-927, 1008-1010, 1103-1104
operators, 62-63, 779-780, 870-872
optical character recognition (OCR), 172-173, **173**, 780, 1029
  pen-based computers, 824-827, **825**, **826**
  smart paper, 1004-1007
  trainable character recognition (TCR), 827
  untrainable character recognition (UCR), 827
optical computers (*see also* CD-ROM; flopticals), 28-29, 93-94, **94**, 374-375, 431-432, 781-782, **781**
optical scanners (*see* scanners)
option buttons, 478
OR, 585, 638, 779, 780, 787, **788**
order of magnitude, 971
ordered n-tuples, 3-4
ordinates, 786-787, **786**, **787**
orthicon, image orthicon, 543-544, **544**
OS/2, 77, 130, 525, 534, 569, 702, 770, 778, 789-790, 856, 1013, 1014
outline fonts, 18-19, **19**, 122, 790-791, **791**, 1091
outline utilities, 792-793, **794**, 1152
over-reliance on computers, 229, 257, 645-647
overlaid windows, 793-795, **794**, 886
Overtype mode, 592, 795
overwriting, 424, 795-796

P

P6 microprocessors, 566, 892
packaged software, 797
packet communications, 31-33, **32**, 107-108, 206, 235-237, **236**, 265, 295-296, **296**, 332, 739, 746-747, **746**, 966, 1071, 1108, 1146
packet radio bulletin board systems (PBBS), 140, 770, 799-800
page breaks, 293, 1007
page description languages (PDLs), 800-801, **800**, **801**, 859-860
Page Down key, 801-802, **802**
page layout, 193, 802, **803**, 1152
Page Up key, 803-804
page-mode memory, 395-396, 716, 803, 804-805, **805**
pagination, 804
pain from prolonged computer use, 251
paint programs, 337, 479, 540, 805-807, **806**
paired-bar graphs, 807-808, **808**
palettes, 808-809, **810**
paperless offices, 810-813, 1004-1007
parallel, 813, **813**, 1042
parallel cable, 151

Index

parallel column format, 997
parallel ports, 814, **814**, 855
parallel processing, 716, 1137
parallel worlds, 43
parallel-to-serial conversion, 275, **275**
parallelepipeds, 693
parameters, 1
parent data, 399
parity, 208, 814-815
parking heads, 509
partitions, 815
Pascal, 150, 515, 815-816, 815, 887
passive matrix, LCDs, 11-12
passive transponders, 816, 987
passive virtual reality, 1120
passwords, 816-818, 984-985
PATH command, 198
paths, 818-820
pattern recognition, 127-128, **127**, 820-821
PC-DOS (see DOS)
PCMCIA standard adapter cards, 314, 607, 664, 821-823, **822**, 857, 916, 948, 982, 1003-1104, 1106
peer-to-peer networks, 57, 82, 157-158, 316, 630-631, **630**, 823
pels, 483
pen-based computers, 824-827, **825**, 831, 856
Pentium microprocessors, 566, 827-828
peripherals, 568-569, 828-829
personal computers (PCs), 681
Personal Dictation System (PDS), 829-832, 1153
personal digital assistants (PDA), 593, 831-833, 856
personal finance software, 76-77, 834-836, 909-910
personal information managers (PIMs), 238-240, 261-262, **262**, 836-838
personal robots, 117-118, 119, 223-227, **223**, **226**, 254-255, 526, 614, 682, 838-840
petabytes, 148, 230, 840, **841**, 873
phase modulation (PM), 705
phonemes, 1024, 1028
photographs, 495-496, **496**
physical layer, 776
pica type, 436
picoseconds, 840-841
PICT graphics, 841-842, **842**
pie graphs, 623, **623**, 842, **843**
pipelines, 828
piracy of software, 1014-1016, 1128
pitch, 843
pixels, 54, 123, 453, 483-484, 495-496, **496**, 517, 579, **580**, 805, 843-844, **844**
PLANNER language, 844-845
plasma displays, 545
platform independence, 845
platters, 257-258, **257**, 308, 501, **501**, 845-846, **846**
plotters, 846-847
plug-and-play, 847-848, 979
point-and-click method, 676
point-of-sale (POS) systems, 849-851, **850**
pointers, 288, 849, 1106, 1107, 1167
points, 436
polar coordinates, 243, 851-853, **852**
polling, 853-854, **854**, 1039
polyline graphics, 854, **854**
pop-up menus, 854-855
portable computer accessories, 856-859
portable computers (see also laptops), 855-856
ports, 855
  input/output ports (I/O), 855
  parallel ports, 814, **814**, 855
  serial ports, 855, 993-994
positive logic, 119-120, 638
possession-based security systems, 987
PostScript, 801, 859-560, 967-968, 1091
power supplies, 863-868, **864**, **865**, **866**
  ac supplies, 863, **864**

batteries, 104-105, 605-606, 628-629, **629**, 744-746
bleeder resistors, 867-868
breakers, 867
bridge rectifiers, 865, **865**
brownouts, 135-136
choke coils, 914
consumption of power, typical PC, 367
dc supplies, 863, **864**
energy-efficient computing, 366-368
filters/filtering, 426-427, 865-866, **866**, 914
full-wave rectification, 864-865, **865**
fuses, 867
ground buses, 488
ground loops, 488, **488**
grounding, 486-488, **488**
half-wave rectification, 864, **864**
Hertz, 510-511, **510**
ideal circuit or component, 534-536, **535**
inverters, 576-577
lightning protection, 487, 616-617, 867
nickel metal hydride (NiMH) batteries, 744-746
nickel-cadmium (NiCad) batteries, 744-746
power-up and power-down, 868-869
radio-frequency interference (RFI), 487-488, 913-915, **914**
rectification, 864-865, **864**, **865**
safety around power supplies, 867-868
spikes (see transients)
surge suppressors, 914, 1089
transients/transient suppression devices, 15, 135-136, 187, 247-248, 487, 867, 914, 1088-1090, **1089**
uninterruptible power supply (UPS), 136, 746, 1101-1103, **1102**
voltage regulation, 866, **866**
zener diodes, 866, **866**
power, computer power (see also clocks/clock speed; instructions per second), 221-223, **222**, 229-231, **231**
power users, 870
power-of-10 notation, 971
power-up and power-down, 868-869
PowerBook computers, 860-861
PowerPC chip, 715, 716-717, 861-863, 898
precedence in arithmetic operations, 62-63, 870-872
predicate calculus, 635
prefix multipliers, 872-873
presentation graphics, 49, 873-875
presentation layer, 777
primary color/pigments, 809
primary storage (see also memory), 875-876
primitives, 693
PRINT command, 196
Print Manager, 878-879
Print Screen key, 879-880, **879**, 973-975
printed circuits (see also integrated circuits; motherboards), 876, **876**
printer fonts, 80, 139, 437
printers and printing, 291, 378, 517-519, 541, 828, 857-858, 877-878, 935-936, 1106, 1167
  background printing process, 88
  binding offset, 116-117, **117**
  bitmapping, 121
  bottom-loading printers, 130-131, **130**
  built-in fonts, 138-139
  capture screen, 156, 879-880, 973-975
  chain printing, 170-172, **171**
  characters per inch (CPI), 436, 620, 843
  color printers, 121, 187-189, **188**
  daisy-wheel printers, 264, **264**, 548
  default fonts, 80, 139, 437
  dot pitch, 329-330, **330**
  dot-matrix printers, 188, 327-329, **327**, 330, 518, 548, 877
  dots per inch (DPI), 330-331, 518, 545, 783, 843, 953

Index

printers and printing *continued*
  downloadable fonts, 332-333
  duplex printing, 116-117, **117**, 344
  fanfold paper, 130, **130**, 401-402, **401**
  form feed, 444-445, **444**
  form length, 445
  front-loading printers, 455-456, **455**
  hardcopy, 500-501
  high-resolution printers, 517-519, 557-558
  image resolution, 187, 290, 315, 316, 329, 516-517, 544-547, **546**, 711, 712, 843, 922, 953
  impact printers, 548
  inkjet printers, 188, **188**, 518, 557-558, 877
  kerning, 587
  label printing, 601-602
  laptops, 606
  laser printers, 188, 518-519, 609-612, **610**, 877
  LCD/LED printers, 610, 612, 877-878
  leading, 620
  lines per inch (LPI), 620-621
  MODE command, 691-692
  multipart forms, 721-722
  page description languages (PDLs), 800-801, **800**, **801**, 859-860
  page layout programs, 802, **803**
  pagination, 804
  parallel ports, 814, **814**
  pitch, 843
  plotters, 846-847
  PostScript, 859-860
  Print Manager, 878-879
  Print Screen key, 879-880, **879**, 973-975
  queues, print queues, 878, 906-907
  rear-loading printers, 928-929, **928**
  soft fonts, 332-333
  spooling, print spooling, 878
  thermal printers, 1074-1075
  tractor feeds, 1087-1088, **1087**
  x-height, 1161, **1162**
prisms, 695
private lines, 952
problem reduction, 880-882, **881**
procedural languages, 882, **883**, 887-888
Prodigy, 574, 774, 776, 883-884
product, 20
Program Manager, 478, 885-886, **886**
programmable read only memory (PROM), 671, 884-885, 926
programming, 468-469, 618, **618**, 701-703, **702**, 762-763, 815-816, 882, **883**, 886-889, 1058, 1137
PROLOG, 889
PROMP command, 199
prompts, 160-161, **161**, 324-325, 889-890
proofs, 22
propagation delay, 947
proportional fonts, 436, 890, **891**
propositional calculus, 597, 635, 1073
prosodic features, speech, 1027, 1028
protocols, 163, 207, 235-237, **236**, 423, 570, 798-799, 853-854, **854**, 891-892
prototypes, 362, 892
psychotic computer behavior, 744, 892-894
public files, 823
pull-down menus, 894, **894**
pulse amplitude modulation (PAM), 705-706
pulse code modulation (PCM), 706
pulse generation, clock speed, 182-183
pulse modulation (PM), 705
pulse width modulation (PWM), 706
pushdown stack, 895, **895**, 933, 992
pyramids, 693
Pythagorean theorem, 3

Q

Quadra computers, 897-898
quality assurance and control (*see also* automation), 898-900, **899**, 944
quantum computer technology, 900-901, **901**, 1001-1002
quarter inch cartridges (QIC), 949, 1053, 1085-1086
Quattro Pro, 902-903, 1035
queries, 903-904
query by example (QBE), 904-906
queues, print queues, 428, 878, 906-907
QuickDraw, 907-909, **908**
Quicken, 909-910
Quit/Exit command, 910
QWERTY keyboards, 344, 910-911

R

R-S flip-flops, 429
R-S-T flip-flops, 429
radiation exposure from computers, 252, 357-359, **358**, **359**, 377, 604
radio analysis software, 923-925
radio communications (*see* amateur radio; packet communications)
radio frequency interference (RFI), 487-488, 632, 913-915, **914**, 1019
ragged right text justification, 584
RAM disks, 915-916
Rand Corp., 176
random access memory (RAM), 100, 230, 268, 269, 663, 670-671, 672-673, 915-916, 916-919, **917**, 992
  active memory, 12
  allocation, 24, 25
  block file transfers, 125-126, 137, 672
  bubble memory, 136-137, **136**, 663, 672
  cache memory, 153-154, **154**, 268, 269, 306-307, **307**
  capacity of memory, 918
  disk caching, 306-307, **307**
  dynamic RAM (DRAM), 153, 346, 671, 919, 1041
  expanded memory, 394-396, **395**
  extended memory, 394-396, **395**
  flash memory, 662, 663, 857, 919, 982
  flip-flops, 429-430, 671, 919, 992, 1040
  nonvolatile memory, 307, 671, 673, 749-750, 876, 919
  page-mode memory, 395-396, 716, 803, 804-805, **805**
  static RAM (SRAM), 153, 671, 919, 1040-1041, **1041**
  swap files, 1044-1045, 1119
  upper memory, 394
  virtual memory, 804-805, 1044-1045, 1118-1119, **1119**
  volatile memory, 307, 671, 673, 749-750, 875, 918-919, 1134-1135
random-access media, 657
range of function, 921, **921**
ranges, 919-921, **920**, 1034
raster graphics, 479
rasters, 921-923, **922**
RD command, 200
read only memory (ROM), 103, 230, 268, 269, 663, 671, 875, 926-927, 992
  basic input/output system (BIOS), 100, 103, **103**, 926, 1105
  bootstrap programs, 100, 130, 186-187, 926, 1139
  electrically erasable programmable ROMs (EEPROMs), 375, 671, 885, 926
  erasable programmable ROMs (EPROMs), 375, 427, 663, 671, 884-885, 926

Index

firmware, 926
  nonvolatile memory, 926
  programmable ROMs (PROMs), 926
read/write memory, 992
README files, 925, 1013
real numbers, 3
real-time communications, 771
real-time events, 927-928
rear-loading printers, 928-929, **928**
recalculation, 929-931, **930**, 1034-1035
records, databases, 409-410, 932
RECOVER command, 196
recovery (*see also* backups; security; undeleting), 443-444
rectangular coordinates, 158-159, **159**, 242
rectification, 864-865, **864**, **865**
recto pages, 344
recursion, 553-555, **554**, 932-933
recycling, 933-936
reduced instruction set computing (RISC), 213, 528, 716-717, 861, 898, 936-938, **937**
reductio ad absurdum, 554, 635-636, 635
reductionism, 938-939
redundancy of data, 276
reengineering, 939-940
refractive index, fiberoptics, 407
registers, 170
regression, infinite regress, 553-555, **554**
relational databases, 268
relations, 941-942, **942**
release numbers, software, 942-943
reliability, 943-944, **944**
remote control systems, 944-947, 1066-1068, 1107
removable data storage media, 947-949
REN command, 199-200
repagination, 949-950
repeaters, 147, 684, **685**, 950-952, **951**, **952**
REPLACE command, 196
reset buttons, 506, 952-953
resolution (*see also* image resolution), 187, 273, 484, 516-517, 518-519, 544-547, 953-954, **955**, 1130
retrace blanking, 922
Return key, 371-373, **372**
returns, hard and soft, 505-506, 1007-1008
reverse engineering, 954
reverse video, 954-956
RGB color model, 162, 316, 808, 956-957, **957**
ribbon cable, 151
ring networks, 263, **630**, 631, 823, 957-958, **958**
Rittner, Don, 347
RMDIR command, 200
robots (*see also* androids; artificial intelligence; artificial life; automation), 35-36, **36**, 53-54, 55-56, 81-82, 184, 189-190, 209, 216-217, 218-220, 223-227, **223**, **226**, 254-255, 292, 452-453, 485, 492-494, **493**, 526, 537, 581-582, 614, 988-989, **989**, 1107, 1140-1141, 1168
  artificial intelligence, 67
  Asimov's Three Laws, 70-71
  autonomous robots, 82-83, 224, 961, 1058
  bin-picking problems, 117-118, **118**, 764
  biomechatronics, 119
  Bongard problems, 820
  branching, 131-133, **132**
  caretakers, 156-157
  Colossus: The Forbin Project, 157, 189-190
  controllers, 959, **959**
  cybercops, 157
  cyberphobia, 157
  generations of robots, 960-961, **962**
  household robots, 838
  insect robots, 83, 224, 558-559, 959, 961, 1058
  k-line programming, 594, **595**
  linear programming, 618, **618**
  map, computer map, 227, **227**
  mechatronics, 665-666
  microknowledge, 682
  nanotechnology, 736-737
  object recognition, 117, 764-765
  passive transponders, 816
  pattern recognition, 127-128, **127**, 820-821
  Personal Dictation System (PDS), 829-832
  personal robots, 117-118, 119, 223-227, **223**, **226**, 254-255, 526, 614, 682, 838-840
  remote control systems, 944-947
  service robots, 838
  speech recognition, 1024-1027, **1024**, **1026**
  speech synthesis, 1027-1030, **1028**, **1030**
  task-level programming, 1058
  teach boxes, 216, 1057-1058
  telemetry, 1063, 1066
  teleoperations, 1063
  telepresence, 1063, 1066-1068, **1067**
  uncanny valleys, 568, 1097-1099, **1099**, 1126
  well-structured languages, 1141-1142
  XR robots, 1162
rollover feature, 588
root directory, 302, 304, 412, 818-820, **819**
rotation of graphic images, 542
routing, 295
rule-based computer reasoning, 390
running headers/footers (*see* headers/footers)

S

safety, 867-868, 1080-1082
sampling/sampling rates, 45, 46, 273-274, 705
sampling resolutions, 46, 273, 705
Samuel, Arthur, 220, 553-555
satellite communications, 332, 466-468, **467**, 965-967, **965**, 1108
  downlinks, 332, 965, 1108
  geostationary-satellite data links, 466-468, **467**, 643, 966
  global positioning system (GPS), 966, 1078
  links, 621, **621**, 759, 966
  low-earth-orbit (LEO) data links, 643-645, **644**, 966
  microwave data transmissions, 684, **685**
  packet radio, 966, 1108
  transponders, 332, 816, 951-952, 965, 1108
  uplinks, 965, 1108
  wide area networks (WANs), 966-967
saturation, 316, 808-809, **810**, 956
saturation points, 958
scalable fonts, 437, 967-968
scaling, 968-969, **968**
SCANDISK command, 196
scan rates, 922
scanners (*see also* optical character recognition), 51, **51**, 475, 495-496, **496**, 780, 781-782, **781**, 782-785, **784**, 857, 1107
scatter plots, 969-970, **970**
scientific notation, 430, 970-973, 998-999
scrambling, 364
screen capture, 156, 879-880, 973-975
screen fonts, 437
screen savers, 975-976
script fonts, 437
Scroll Lock key, 977, **977**
scrolling, 976-977, **977**

Index

search-and-replace loops, 641, 980-981, 1151
search techniques, 115-116, 133, 239, 427, 572, 904-906
second generation computers, 221
secondary station identifiers (SSID), 295
secondary storage (*see also* memory), 981-983
sectors, 91-92, 94-95, 281, 441-442, **442**, 502, 983-984, **983**
security (*see also* access; passwords), 224-225, 768-769, 984-989, **989**, 989-990, 1018, 1126-1129
SELECT command, 196
semilog graphs, 242, 989-990, **990**
SeniorNet, 209, 990-992
sentential calculus, 597, 635, 1073
sentry directory, 1100
sequential access memory (SAM), 992
sequential logic, 992
sequential-access media, 657
serial, 992-993, **993**, 1042
serial cable, 151
serial ports, 855, 993-994
serial-to-parallel conversion, 274-275, **275**
serif fonts, 437
servers, 572, 994, **994**
service robots, 838
SET command, 200
session layer, 777
shading schemes modeling, 692-693, **693**
SHARE command, 196
shareware, 140-141, 995, 1012, 1014-1016
shell, DOS, 325-327, **326**
shielded vs. unshielded cable, 151, 185, 349
Shift key, 995-997, **996**
side-by-side column format, 997-998
Sierra Network, 775
significant figures, 430, 972, 998-999
simulation managers, 1120
simulations, 597-599, **598**, 999-1000, 1119-1126, **1120**, **1121**, **1123**
single-column format, 1000-1001, 1094
single electron memory (SEM), 29, 709, 1001-1002
single function graph, 287, **287**
single inline package (SIP), 561, 1002-1003, **1003**
single-variable functions, 550-551, **551**
slide rules, 39-40
slide shows, 873-875
small computer system interface (SCSI), 504, 536, 977-980, **978**
SmallTalk, 1003
smart cards, 1003-1004
smart homes, 223-227, **223**, **226**
smart paper, 1004-1007
SMARTDRV.SYS, 307
smileys, 771
snooze function, 239
soft fonts, 332-333
soft hyphenation, 531
soft page breaks, 505, 1007
soft returns, 505-506, 1007-1008
software, 506, 797, 1008-1016, 1106
 alpha testing, 27, 111-112, 138
 applications software, 1010-1011
 beta testing, 27, 111-112, 138
 distribution of software, 1011-1012
 freeware, 1012, 1014-1016
 installation/uninstallation, 1013-1014
 operating systems, 1008-1010
 piracy of software, 1014-1016
 shareware, 1012, 1014-1016
 suites, 1042-1043
 system software, 1010-1011
 Trojan horses, 1012
 utilities, 1111-1112
 viruses, 112, 138, 141, 161, 228, 229, 265, 455, 492, 699, 743, 797, 892-894, 900, 1012, 1090, 1109, 1113-1116, **1115**, 1126-1129

software functions, 460
SORT command, 196
sorting, 25-27, 239, 1151
sound and music, 292, 1016-1021, **1018**, 1167-1168
 ambient recovery systems (ARS), 1023
 artificial intelligence, 66-67
 CD-ROM, 165, 1019
 digital signal processing (DSP), 1023
 electromagnetic shielding, 1019
 games, 1017
 microphones, 1018-1019
 multimedia, 351, 530, 718-721, **721**, 1060-1063, **1061**
 musical instrument digital interface (MIDI), 292, 732-734, **733**, 828, 1017, 1020
 object linking and embedding (OLE), 214, 262, 425, 624, 757-759, **758**, 763-764, 1020, 1042
 radio frequency interference (RFI), 1019
 security systems, 1018
 sound boards, 1018, 1019-1020
 speakers, 1018, 1022-1023
 speech recognition, 124, 201, 478, 526, 737, 829-832, 1020, 1024-1027, **1024**, **1026**, 1024, 1107
 speech recognition, 1020, 1024-1027, **1024**, **1026**
 speech synthesis, 478, 526, 737, 829-832, 1020, 1027-1030, **1028**, **1030**
 virtual reality, 1018
sound boards, 1018, 1019-1020
source, 205, 758, 1021-1022, **1021**
space exploration and virtual reality, 1124-1125
speakers, 1018, 1022-1023
specialty circuits, 124
spectrum analyzers, 95
speech recognition, 124, 201, 478, 526, 737, 829-832, 1020, 1024-1027, **1024**, **1026**, 1107
speech synthesis, 478, 526, 737, 829-832, 1020, 1027-1030, **1028**, **1030**
spell checking, 1030-1032, 1152
spheres, 694
spherical coordinates, 692, 1032-1033, **1032**
spikes (*see* transients)
split, 952
spooling, print spooling, 878
spreadcubes/spreadspace, 1035
spreadsheets, 146, 178-179, **178**, 425, 642-643, 902-903, 919-921, **920**, 929-931, **930**, 1033-1036, **1034**
spy software, 1036-1037
squelch, 952
stacked-column graphs, 1037-1038, **1038**
stacks, 1035
staging in modeling, 695-696
standards, 34-35, 163, 680-681, 776-777, 798
star networks, 263, **630**, **631**, 823, 1038-1040, **1039**
start bits, 75, 1046
static data exchange, 758
static electricity, 680
STARTUP files, 77
states, 45
static RAM (SRAM), 153, 671, 919, 1040-1041, **1041**
step-index optical fiber, 407
stop bits, 75, 208, 1046
storage (*see* memory)
storage units, 271
storage time, 1041-1042
stranded wire, 150, **150**
Stroustrup, B., 149
subdirectories (*see also* directories/subdirectories), 302, 304-305
subjective variables, 192
subjectivity in learning, 613-614
SUBST command, 197

Index

suites (see also integrated software packages), 1042-1043
sum, 20
super video graphics array (SVGA), 317, 369, 711, 1044, 1117
superscalar processor architectures, 828
surge suppressors, 914, 1089
Sussman, Gerry, 492
swap files, 1044-1045, 1119
Swedish ELF radiation stanard, 359
symbolic logic, 635
symbols, 62
synchronous data, 75, 1045-1046, **1046**
syntax, 1046-1047, **1048**
synthesized sound (see also musical instrument digital interface; sound and music; speech synthesis) 732-734, **733**
SYS command, 197
System 7 computers, 1048-1049
system killer apps (see killer applications)
system software, 1010-1011
system unit, 290
Systems Network Architecture (SNA), 270.

T

T flip-flops, 429
Tab key, 1051-1052, **1051**, 1150
Tamarack Storage Devices, 521
tape drives, 100, 457, 655, 657-658, **657**, 663, 828, 949, 982, 1052-1054, **1052**, 1085-1086
task-level programming, 1058
tax preparation software, 834-836, 1054-1057
teach boxes, 216, 1057-1058
technocentrism, 1140
technophobes/technophiles, 215, 218, 645
telecommunications software, 140
telecommuting, 486, 774, 1058-1060, 1062
teleconferencing, 771-772, 1060-1063, **1061**, 1065
telemetry, 1063, 1066
teleoperations, 1063
telephone-dialing software (TDS), 1065-1066
telephones, 205-206, **205**, 379, 770, 1063-1065
  adapters for telephone cords, 15-16
  call-waiting, 141
  cellular telecommunications, 167-168, **167**, **168**
  modem connections, 141
  telephone-dialing software (TDS), 1065-1066
telepresence, 1063, 1066-1068, **1067**
television
  full motion video interface (FMVI), 458-459
  interactive technology, 567-568
Telnet sites, 573
templates, keyboards, 589
terabytes (see also bytes), 148, 230, 309, 873, 1068-1069, **1068**, **1069**
terminal emulation software, 139, 140-141, 344, 699, 770, 1070-1071
terminal node controllers, 206, 292, 295, 697, 799, 858, 1071-1072, **1072**
terminate-and-stay resident (TSR) software, 675
tetrahedra, 693
text boxes, 477
texturing graphics, 541
thematic shading, 465-466
theorem-proving machines (TPMs), 880-882, **881**, 1072-1074
theorems, Boolean algebra, 128-129
thermal printers, 1074-1075
thesaurus, 1152
third generation computers, 221
three-dimensional coordinates, 551-552, **552**
throughput, 109, 231, 1075-1076
tiled windows, 795, 886, 1076-1077, **1076**
TIME command, 200

time division multiplexing (TDM), 287, 724
time management, 239-240
time sharing, 927-928, 1078-1079
time-shifting communications, 206, 798, 799, 927, 1079-1080
timekeepers, 105, 1077-1078
title bar, 321, **322**
TO package integrated circuits (ICs), 561
toggle keys, 154, 477
tokens, 272
tone squelch, 952
tools in draw programs, 337
topologies, 146, 262-263, **263**, 511, 630-631, **630**, 738, 823, 957-958, **958**, 1038-1040, **1039**
tot-proof workstations, 1080-1082
touch screens, 849-851, **850**, 1082-1083, 1167
tower cases, 290, 1083-1084, **1084**
trackballs, 64, 291, 477, 606-607, 717, 849, 856-857, 1086-1087, **1087**, 1106, 1107
tracks, 502, 654, 983-984, **983**, 1084-1086, **1085**
tractor feeds, 1087-1088, **1087**
trainable character recognition (TCR), 827
transducers, 8, 1027
transfer rate, 6-7, 1042
transforms, 695
transients/transient suppression devices, 15, 135-136, 187, 247-248, 487, 867, 914, 1088-1090, **1089**
transistors, FET, 410-411, **410**
transponders, 332, 816, 951-952, 965, 1108
transport layer, 776
trash icon, 288
traveling with your computer, 858-859
TREE command, 197
tree, directory tree, 302, 303, 514
trinary logic, 598, **598**, 637
Trojan horses (see also hackers; vaccines; viruses), 112, 138, 228-229, 265, 455, 492, 699, 743, 797, 900, 1012, 1090, 1126-1129
troubleshooting algorithms, 22
TrueType fonts, 967-968, 1091
truncated objects, 694
truth tables, 50, **50**, 383, **384** 128, 585
tuples, 3-4
Turing test, 1092-1094, **1093**
Turing, Alan, 68, 248, 613, 1091-1092
TWAIN interface, 541, 783-784
two-column format, 1094-1095, **1094**
two-function graph, **287**, 288
TYPE command, 200
Type Manager, Adobe, 18-20, **19**
type size, 436
typefaces, 436, 1151

U

Ultimate Teacher, 1097, **1098**
ultra large-scale integration (ULSI), 370
unbounded recursion, 933
uncanny valleys, 568, 1097-1099, **1099**, 1126
unconditional formatting, 1100
undeleting, 417, 689, 751, 1099-1100
underlay technology, 824
UNERASE command, 417
unformatting, 1100-1101
uninterruptible power supplies (UPS), 136, 746, 1101-1103, **1102**
UNIX, 130, 789, 1103-1104
untrainable character recognition (UCR), 827
updating files, 423-425
upgrades, 942-943, 1104-1108
  accelerator boards, 4-5
  accelerators, graphics accelerators, 481-483
  coprocessors, 244-245, **244**

Index

upgrades *continued*
 downward compatibility, 334-336
 expandability, 386
 expansion boards/slots, 386-389, **388**, **389**, 406, 715, 754
 modular construction, 699-700
 monitors, 711-714
 NuBus, 754, 860-861
 PCMCIA standard adapter cards, 314, 607, 664, 821-823, **822**, 857, 916, 948, 982, 1003-1104, 1106
 version numbers, 1116
uplinks, 332, 965, 1108
uploading, 334, 1108-1110, **1109**
upper memory, 394
upward compatibility, 1110
user interfaces (*see* graphical user interfaces)
user-friendliness, 525-526
usernames, 571
utilities, 1106, 1111-1112

V

V.22 modems, 163
vaccines (*see also* Trojan horses; viruses), 1113-1116, **1115**, 1128
variables
 dependent, 1, 287-288, **287**
 independent, 1-2, **2**, 287, 550-552, **551**, **552**
 multivariable functions, 288, 551, 728-730, **729**
 subjective variables, 192
vector graphics, 540, 760-762, **760**, **761**, 805
Venn diagram, 399, **400**
VER command, 200
VERIFY command, 200
Veronica search, 133, 572-573
version numbers, 1116
verso pages, 344
very high density (VHD) drives, 314
very large-scale integration (VLSI), 370
video accelerator, 5
video graphics array (VGA), 369, 711, 1044, 1117
videoconferencing, 1060-1063
vidicons, 1117-1118, **1118**
virtual DOS machines (VDMs), 789
virtual drives, 306-307, 915
virtual memory, 804-805, 716, 1044-1045, 1118-1119, **1119**
virtual memory management (VMM), 1118
virtual reality (*see also* artificial intelligence; simulations), 52, 65, 386, 522, 567-568, 593-594, 999-1000, 1018, 1107, 1119-1126, **1120**, **1121**, **1123**, 1168
 applications for virtual reality, 1122-1125
 computer-aided instruction (CAI), 217-218, 530, 1097, 1123
 experience paths, 1120, **1120**, **1121**
 experience spaces, 1121
 exploratory virtual reality, 1120, **1121**
 gloves, 1122
 hardware requirements, 1121-1122
 head-mounted displays (HMD), 1122
 interactive virtual reality, 1120
 knowledge-based simulation, 597-599, **598**
 liquid crystal displays (LCDs), 1122
 passive virtual reality, 1120
 simulation managers, 1120
 virtual virtual reality (VVR), 1120
virtual virtual reality (VVR), 1120
viruses (*see also* hackers; Trojan horses; vaccines), 112, 138, 141, 161, 228, 229, 265, 455, 492, 699, 743, 797, 892-894, 900, 1012, 1090, 1109, 1113-1116, **1115**, 1126-1129
vision systems, 1129-1131, **1130**
 angular or azimuth resolution, 546
 Bongard problems, 127-128, **127**, 820

charge coupled devices, 172-173, **173**
direction resolution, 546
distance resolution, 547
image orthicon, 543-544, **544**
image resolution, 187, 290, 315, 316, 329, 516-517, 544-547, **546**, 711, 712, 843, 922, 953
local feature focus, 485
object recognition, 764-765
optical character recognition (OCR), 172-173, **173**, 780, 1029
optical computer technology, 781-782, **781**
pattern recognition, 127-128, **127**, 820-821
pen-based computers, 824-827, **825**, **826**
ranging, 546
resolution, 953-954
vidicons, 1117-1118, **1118**
visual purple, 93
vividness of color, 809
voice-mail systems, 1132-1134, **1133**
VOL command, 200
volatile memory, 104-105, 307, 671, 673, 749-750, 875, 918-919, 1134-1135
voltage, 41
voltage regulation, 866, **866**
volume graphs, 1135-1136, **1135**
volume labels, 1136-1137
Von Neumann bottleneck, 1137

W

wait states, 382, 1169-1170
warm boots, 129, 187, 247, 250, 506, 952-953, 1139-1140
Wasubot, 36
waveforms, 36-37, **37**
wavelengths, 111
Welzenbaum, Joseph, 360, 1140-1141
well-structured languages, 1141-1142
wetware (*see also* biochips), 1142-1145, **1143**
what-if analysis, 1145-1146
Wide Area Information System (WAIS), 133, 573
wide area networks (WANs), 738, 767, 966-967, 1146-1147, **1147**
 bridges, 133, **134**
 cable data transmission, 153
 data acquisition systems, 264-265, **265**
 Ethernet, 380-381, **381**
 gateways, 463, **464**, 570
 minicomputers, 686-688, **688**
 network interface cards (NICs), 1169
 polling, 853-854, **854**
 terminal node controllers, 206, 292, 295, 697, 799, 858, 1071-1072, **1072**
 zero-slot networks, 1168-1169
 zones, 1170-1171
wildcards, 73, 272, 427, 905, 1147-1148
Windows, 192, 288, 477, 478, 525, 534, 569, 684, 702, 717, 770, 778, 789, 856, 861, 1013, 1014, 1148-1150
 accelerator boards, 5
 active window, 12-13, **13**
 application window, 321
 background processing, 87-89, **88**, 580, 718, 726-727, **727**
 cascading, 160-161, **161**, 886
 control menu, 241-242, **242**
 directory window, 305-306
 document window, 321-322, **322**
 DOS shell, 325-327, **326**
 drag-and-drop, 337
 event-driven environments, 381-382
 File Manager, 305-306, 417-419, **418**, 478
 formatting disks, 443
 initialization files, 556-557
 integrated software packages, 563-564
 menu bar, 321, **322**
 Object Packager, 763-764
 overlaid windows, 793-795, **794**, 886

Index

Print Manager, 878-879
Program Manager, 478, 885-886, **886**
tiled windows, 795, 886, 1076-1077, **1076**
title bar, 321, **322**
wire-mesh modeling, 692-693, **693**
word processing (*see also* desktop publishing), 145, 239, 256, 593, 1150-1155
   alignment of text, 584
   anchoring, 49-50, **50**
   arrow keys, 63-64, **63**
   attributes, 75-76
   block (text) operations, 125, **125**
   boilerplates, 126, 144, 614-615
   business letters, 144
   compound documents, 213-214
   concordance files, 232
   desktop publishing (DTP) (*see* desktop publishing)
   document comparison, 319-320
   documents, 318-319
   drop cap, 339-340
   embedded formatting, 360-361
   file conversion, 415-416
   flash tests, 473, **474**
   flush text: left/right/center, 434-435, **435**, 584
   font selection, 144
   foreground processing, 440-441, **441**
   foreign languages, 1153
   formatting text, 360-361
   frames, 451-452, **451**, **452**
   full page display, 459
   grammar checking, 473
   hanging indent, 499-500, **500**
   hard and soft returns, 505-506
   headers/footers, 950, 962-963, 1151
   hidden codes, 513-514
   highlighting, 516
   hyphenation, 530-531
   Insert mode, 592, 559-560, **560**
   justification, 584, 1150
   kerning, 587
   letter writing, 614-615
   margins, 144
   merging files, 1151
   newspaper column format, 1094-1095, **1094**
   office automation (*see also* paperless office), 766-768, 810-813
   outline utilities, 792-793, **794**, 1152
   Overtype mode, 592, 559-560, **560**, 795
   page breaks, 505, 1007
page layout programs, 802, **803**
   pagination, 804
   ragged right justification, 584
   repagination, 949-950
   returns, hard and soft, 1007-1008
   scrolling, 976-977, **977**
   search and replace, 980-981, 1151
   side-by-side column format, 997-998
   single-column formats, 1000-1001, 1094
   sorting, 1151
   spell checking, 1030-1032, 1152
   tabs, 1150
   two-column format, 1094-1095, **1094**
   typefaces, 1151
   undeleting, 1099-1100
   wildcards, 1147-1148
   wordwrap, 1007, 1152
   WYSIWYG, 293, 459, 651, 907, 1091, 1153, 1159-1160
word size, (*see also* buses), 230, 1155, **1156**
words per minute (WPM), 1156
wordwrap, 1007, 1152
working directory, 302-303
workstations, 262, 315, 1156-1157
World Wide Web (WWW), 133, 573
wrist rests, 589
write once read many (WORM) disks, 60, 166, 374, 504, 664, 935, 1106, 1157-1158
write protection, 60, 1158-1159, **1158**
Writers in the Sand compound document, 213-214
WYSIWYG, 293, 459, 651, 907, 1091, 1153, 1159-1160

X

XCOPY command, 197
x-height, 1161, **1162**
x/y/z axes, 1163-1164, **1163**
Xerox Corp., 57, 1003
Xmodem, 1164-1165
XR robots, 1162
xy-plane, 1, 786

Y

yard work, automated 225-226, **226**
Ymodem, 1164-1165
youth-friendly computing, 1166

Z

zener diodes, 866, **866**
zero wait states, 1169-1170
zero-slot networks, 1168-1169
Zmodem, 1164-1165
zones, 1170-1171
zooming, 541, 1171

About the author

Stan Gibilisco was born in 1953, the son of Dr. and Mrs. Joseph A. Gibilisco. His father served for over 30 years as a physician at the Mayo Clinic in Rochester, Minnesota. A mathematician educated at the University of Minnesota, Stan has authored or coauthored more than two dozen nonfiction books.

In 1978 and 1979, Stan served on the technical staff for *QST* Magazine of the American Radio Relay League in Newington, Connecticut. From 1979 to 1982, he was Vice President of Engineering for International Electronic Systems in Miami, Florida. In 1982, he became a full-time writer.

Stan first attracted attention with *Understanding Einstein's Theories of Relativity* (TAB Books, 1983) and *Encyclopedia of Electronics* (TAB Professional and Reference Books, 1985). The encyclopedia was annotated by the American Library Association as a Best Reference of the 1980s. Stan's work has also gained a reading audience in Japan.

Stan's "Virtual Images," paintings of nature as seen by computers, have been exhibited by the Rado Gallery of Miami Beach, Florida and earned him a listing in the 1994 edition of *Art in America*.

Stan plans to keep writing about electronics and computers. He also aspires to write fiction stories and children's science books.